Oracles of Celestine Light

Complete Trilogy of Light
GENESIS, NEXUS & VIVUS

Revealed by
Embrosewyn Tazkuvel

SOME OF THE TREASURES WITHIN...

"Thus it is that amidst the vexing trials and tribulations of mortal life that in humility all can fulfill their potential to become a Child of Light; called from the gentle promptings of their heart to believe in a divinity their eyes cannot see, and a wonder their mind does not know; to feel coursing through every fiber of their being a sure knowledge that they are a cherished Child of God." *Genesis 2:6*

"For faith and love are the greatest of all powers, the very dynamic by which all things were, and are created and exist." *Genesis 2:8*

"Every plant in endless variety has been given unto you for food, and shelter, and comfort, and to heal your wounds and illnesses with prudence and faith. And behold, I have given you every herb bearing seed which is upon the face of all the earth, and every tree whose seed bears fruit of sweetness or meat; and the milk of the animals, and the non-fertile eggs of the fowls, and the honey of the bees, and these shall be your food." *Genesis 3:16-17*

"Mortality is merely the brief, fierce wind that blows away the chaff of facade and falsehood, that the wheat of truth and light may grow in grandeur in eternity." *Genesis 8:61*

"In mortality or immortality it is upon this foundation of harmony that the eternal progression of man goes forward; that man may say, '*Here I am today, but with greater desire and efforts, there I will be tomorrow because that is the tomorrow that calls to me.*' Thus man is rewarded in mortality and immortality with the harmony of his choice, be it light or darkness, and is always afforded the opportunity to seek a new harmony and a greater light if he is willing to make the effort." *Genesis 11:35-36*

"As to the purpose of life: there are many. But the greatest is to reach a state of consciousness in which you have an inner peace which transcends mortality, making you one in spirit, thought and action with the boundless light of the Celestine realms." *Genesis 11:44*

"Never forget amidst the travails of mortality that you are sons and daughters of the divine Father and Mother and are connected in spirit to all living things both on earth and beyond. You are radiant rays of light that can illuminate the deepest darkness." *Genesis 11:49*

"Love and nurture the temple of your body, for in that you honor Elohim the creator. But do not forget it is but a temporary shell given to many imperfections, vagrancies, infirmities, disease and death. Do not forget that this very temporary shell is not you, it is only the physical covering of your soul for a breath of eternity. Therefore, do not separate yourselves by the colors of your skins, or hair or eyes, or the beauty of your face, or the youth or suppleness of your body, for these things are not you, merely an artists covering to hold the brilliant sun of your soul." *Genesis 11:52-54*

"The masterpiece is not outside of you, it is inside of you." *Genesis 11:55*

"Return to eternal oneness and there is no place for strife, sickness or sorrow; for man only wars with that which is not in harmony with his eternal soul." *Genesis 11:60*

"Now in mortality, a veil of forgetfulness has come upon you that you may develop faith, that you might find your bosom welling up with feelings of overwhelming love as you connect again with your spirit to our divine Mother and Father, not from things that you see, which may be an illusion, but from that which you feel in your soul as it becomes one with all that is and rises to a new resonance as it recognizes the true harmony of its existence." *Genesis 11:67*

"Seek to be one with the divine in your heart, soul, mind and spirit, and no challenge of the world will be able to overcome you." *Genesis 11:71*

"Therefore, ever seek to fulfill the divinity of your creation, ever doing good, ever welcoming the resonance of the spirit of Elohim into the bosom of your soul, ever seeking the perfection of your being in every way. This is your destiny." *Genesis 11:125*

"From the beginning of creation, all who humbly sought the truth, and lived in ways pleasing to God, and had faith in the greater power and majesty of God, received a portion of his light to guide and uplift them according to their faith and goodness." *Nexus 3:4*

"Life is given by God and it is most precious, for it is in life that you fulfill your purpose on earth and create your eternity to come. If you would love God, love everything God has created with a pure love that sings in your soul; for all life has a grand purpose that connects to all other life." *Nexus 11:15-16*

"And I say unto you that faith is the foundation of all truths, for it is the power by which all things are and can be. To know faith abiding in every fiber of your essence is to fulfill one of the great purposes of your life and to unlatch the door to your glory in eternity." *Nexus 1:-17*

"Hate merely continues upon an endless circling path that takes away the years of your life and gives nothing in return; only reciprocated love and respect can break the cycle of destruction and build a bridge of light to tomorrow. And by this may your enemies become your friends." *Nexus 11:20-21*

"Love and faith can prevail against all obstacles, even death, if it is the will of our Father and Mother in Heaven." *Nexus 11:23*

"The true light of God is to do unto others as you would have them do unto you. In this is the fullness of the spirit of truth and any teaching of a different spirit cannot be of Elohim when it concerns someone who has done you no grievous wrong." *Nexus 16:30*

"And I say unto you that the Almighty Elohim, the creator of Heaven and earth, is not a God who does nothing, but the God to which nothing is impossible..." *Nexus 23:35*

"Even among the honest of heart, it is the nature of man to see and hear that which he wishes to see and hear; and to the contrary, he is blind and deaf. How many times have you held the answer to your question in your hand, but have not seen the truth because you were not seeking it?" *Nexus 24:14*

"Every life is a stewardship given by God to prove the valiant, and only the good steward will see the face of God and the light that is eternal." *Nexus 29:41*

"And I say unto you, life should be a circle of unity, where each person contributes the excess of their gift for the benefit of all; be it the creation of wealth or the creation of the arts, or the wisdom of the spirit, or whatsoever God has given unto them; and thus the family of man becomes like unto the spokes of a wheel, where each supports the others and benefits the others, and in unity rolls forward." *Nexus 30:8*

"Embrace your trials with thankfulness, for because of them men turn to God and find faith; which is the greatest of all powers, with which the world and all the stars in Heaven were made. For the faith you gain carries with you beyond this short life, and serves you well in the eternity to come." *Nexus 30:46*

"But I will share with you now a great secret: if you desire peace that never ends, then among those who desire such, I say unto you, kill no creatures whatsoever. Eat only of the plants God has put onto the earth to sustain you, and foods made from the milk and eggs of the animals loved as friends and not caged, and of the honey of the bees. Then a spirit of peace shall prevail over you always." *Nexus 39:8*

"When great blessings are given, great responsibilities follow; for God gives us blessings that they may be magnified and returned with love to our brothers and sisters of the world, with the purity of our faith and by the deeds of our life; for thus do we grow and expand our lights and prove our faithfulness to the Father and Mother, and show that we desire to be like them." *Nexus 41:10*

"And I know you, for you are a Child of Light, my brothers and sisters of spirit. It matters not the color of your skin, whether you are male or female, young or old, rich or poor, or the religion you profess. By the good actions of your life you have been numbered among the Children of Light, and I now call you to come and embrace your true family and the path of greater glory and fulfillment." *Vivus 99:12*

"You were endowed with gifts of Celestine Light before you were born into this life- the power to hear when others have not spoken, the power to travel from one place to another without traveling, the power to levitate objects and yourself, the power to make fire by calling the aeon and focusing it in your hands. And many, many other powers of Celestine Light have you been gifted with." *Vivus 99:84*

"You are the Children of Light. You are the guardians of the world. You are the bulwark that stands between the sanctity of the earth and all living things upon it and the darkness that would overcome it if unchallenged." *Vivus 81:47*

"You are the master of the Celestine Light that dwells within you. If you choose to embrace the light, there is no darkness deep enough to overcome you." *Vivus 27:10*

"For when the power of the light unites as one, the darkness has no place to be. Darkness of itself is nothing, but the absence of the light. When the light asserts its place in brilliance, the darkness is no more." *Vivus 99:128*

"Therefore, remember these things, and never fear the darkness or the evil intentions of men upon you, for you are the light, and the light shall always have the power to overcome the darkness." *Vivus 92:160*

"Your actions are the gold of your life... In the world to come, it will not be asked of you what you believed in life, but what did you do?" *Vivus 27:55*

"Laugh and play and listen and watch and wonder; be a child each day, for it is one of the secrets of perpetual joy and communion with God, and for this cause have you been created and given this world; that you might have joy in abundance." *Vivus 27:59*

"Seek knowledge everyday; for ignorance is slavery, and knowledge is freedom; and these enliven your soul." *Vivus 27:62*

"Therefore, do not live today for tomorrow, but live today for today. The days to come will have their own challenges. For a life of peace, joy and true fulfillment, sufficient is the day for the challenges therein. *Vivus 45:141*

"Do not condemn others for their lifestyles and choices that are different from yours, and do not despise those who do not believe as you do, or hold the same things of value. The more you judge others, the more they will reciprocate and judge you. And with the disdain that you show, so shall you be disdained." *Vivus 45:142-143*

"...There are many mysteries of heaven, and the world shall know them not; but none shall be kept secret from the Children of Light once they are prepared to receive them." *Vivus 47:22*

"The people of the world understand that they are affected by mysterious aeons, but to them the cause is unknown. Among the Children of Light let those mysterious aeons be known and understood that they may be called upon as needed." *Vivus 51:6*

"You are in the world, but you are not of it. The world looks at you, but they do not see you for who or what you are." *Vivus 36:36*

"If you did not have challenges in life of all kinds: physical, mental, spiritual and emotional; you would leave mortality no greater than you came into it. You would be like the tree standing alone on the plain, always receiving water and sun but never growing tall and mighty among its kind for lack of the challenge of competing in the grove. In trees and man it is not good nourishment alone that builds greatness, but also learning to deal with adversity and growing stronger and taller because of it." *Vivus 54:16-17*

"Unto you it has been revealed the secrets of youth and vitality, and if you follow all that you have been given, you will be young in body, heart, mind and spirit until the very last breath of your mortality." *Vivus 54:41*

"...It is in times of greatest challenge that the true person of light and power can emerge from within the shell in which they are usually held by everyday life..." *Vivus 68:22*

"Where much is given much is required, and where the tests are greatest there stand the mightiest." *Vivus 81:40*

"...You are the lights of the world. Go forth and shine in your glory. Fear not, for always I am with you. Always I will love you." *Vivus 100:120*

Published by Kaleidoscope Productions
1467 Siskiyou Boulevard, #9; Ashland, OR 97520
www.kaleidoscope-publications.com
ISBN 978-0-938001-50-8

Book design and layout by Sumara Elan Love
www.3wizardz.com

Table of Contents

GENESIS: THE FIRST BOOK OF LIGHT

Introduction....15
Chapter 1: Xeon, the Land of Pre-existence....19
Chapter 2: The Creation of the Worlds....21
Chapter 3: Garden of Eden....23
Chapter 4: Fate of the Edenites....29
Chapter 5: The City of Enoch....41
Chapter 6: The Coming of the Ark....51
Chapter 7: The Great Flood....57
Chapter 8: The Descent into Darkness....65
Chapter 9: The Lands That Time Forgot....73
Chapter 10: The Seed Bearers....83
Chapter 11: The Destiny of Man....87

NEXUS: THE SECOND BOOK OF LIGHT

Chapter 1: Light of Yeshua the Messiah....97
Chapter 2: Preamble of the Apostles....101
Chapter 3: Nature of God....105
Chapter 4: Visits of the Angel Gabriel....107
Chapter 5: Births of the Savior and the Herald....111
Chapter 6: Coming of the Magi....115
Chapter 7: Rebellion of Yochanan....119
Chapter 8: Yeshua Confounds the Temple Priests....123
Chapter 9: Healing a Broken Heart....127
Chapter 10: Discovery in the Wilderness....129
Chapter 11: Miracle at Gimron....131
Chapter 12: A Life Renewed....133
Chapter 13: Among the Sparrows and the Lion....135
Chapter 14: A Stranger From Afar....137

Chapter 15: Breath of Life....141
Chapter 16: Sage of Jerusalem....147
Chapter 17: Celebrate the Life....151
Chapter 18: Marriage of Yeshua and Miriam....153
Chapter 19: Wedding Feast at Cana....155
Chapter 20: Family Joys in Nazareth....157
Chapter 21: Sermon in Nazareth....159
Chapter 22: Enduring Blessings....165
Chapter 23: Truth of a Prophet....167
Chapter 24: Sermon in Bethany....171
Chapter 25: Caravan to Egypt....177
Chapter 26: Robbers of Zin....179
Chapter 27: Conversation at the Wadi....183
Chapter 28: Yeshua and Miriam Speak on Women....187
Chapter 29: Yeshua Speaks of Wealth....189
Chapter 30: The Purpose of Life....193
Chapter 31: Communities of Light....197
Chapter 32: Conversion of Kudar Iluna....201
Chapter 33: Travels in Egypt....205
Chapter 34: Miracle of the Blind Girl....209
Chapter 35: Yochanan's Treasure....211
Chapter 36: The Twelve Commandments....213
Chapter 37: Mystery of Moses....217
Chapter 38: Sojourn with the Nubians....223
Chapter 39: Sanctity of Life....227
Chapter 40: A Worthy Husband....229
Chapter 41: Miriam's Query....237
Chapter 42: Path of Three....239
Chapter 43: Path to Enlightenment....243
Chapter 44: Revelations on the Road to Palestine....251

VIVUS: THE THIRD BOOK OF LIGHT

Chapter 1: Second Sermon in Bethany....257
Chapter 2: Sojourn in the Wilderness....263
Chapter 3: Announcement to the Family....269
Chapter 4: Confrontation in Capharsalama....273
Chapter 5: Commitment of the Light....281
Chapter 6: Covenant of Light....285
Chapter 7: Yochanan the Baptizer....289
Chapter 8: Oneness by the Lake....293
Chapter 9: Equality of Women....295
Chapter 10: Temptations of Yeshua....301
Chapter 11: Baptisms of Yeshua and Miriam....303
Chapter 12: Disciples of Yochanan....307
Chapter 13: Kingdom of God....309
Chapter 14: Disciples from Bethsaida....313
Chapter 15: The Samaritan at Jacob's Well....317
Chapter 16: Wrath in the Temple....321
Chapter 17: Enlightenment of Nicodemas....323
Chapter 18: Baptisms in Bethany....327
Chapter 19: Testimony of Yochanan....331
Chapter 20: Imprisonment of Yochanan....335
Chapter 21: Challenges in Nazareth....341
Chapter 22: Healing the Nobleman's Son....345
Chapter 23: First Sermon at Gennesaret....347
Chapter 24: Sermon on Unorthodox Marriages....351
Chapter 25: Sermon at Syncthopolis....357
Chapter 26: First Sermon at Ptolemais....361
Chapter 27: Second Sermon at Ptolemais....367
Chapter 28: By Their Fruits You Shall Know Them....373
Chapter 29: A Prophet Rises to His Glory....377
Chapter 30: The Nature of Eternity....383

Chapter 31: Second Marriage of Martha of Bethany....387
Chapter 32: Challenges of the Children of Light....391
Chapter 33: Sermon in Capharsalama....399
Chapter 34: From This Day the Light Goes Forth....405
Chapter 35: Many Miracles at Gennasaret....411
Chapter 36: Callings of the Children of Light....417
Chapter 37: The Gifts of Elohim....425
Chapter 38: The Calling of Mattayah....429
Chapter 39: Standing For the Truth....431
Chapter 40: The Old and the New....437
Chapter 41: Passover at Jerusalem....439
Chapter 42: By Their Love You Will Know Them....443
Chapter 43: Calling of the Twelve Apostles....447
Chapter 44: Salome....453
Chapter 45: Sermon on the Mount....457
Chapter 46: Miracles and Suffering....469
Chapter 47: Setting Apart the Apostles....475
Chapter 48: Builder of Eternity....479
Chapter 49: Destiny Fulfilled....483
Chapter 50: Eternal Love....489
Chapter 51: The Powers of Lanaka....493
Chapter 52: In the World but Not of It....501
Chapter 53: The Destiny of Miriam....509
Chapter 54: The Youthfulness of Age....513
Chapter 55: Miracles of Body and Mind....517
Chapter 56: He Who Shall Be Last Shall Be First....521
Chapter 57: Sins Forgiven....523
Chapter 58: Confrontation Upon the River Qishon....527
Chapter 59: Belief and Faith....533
Chapter 60: Miracles of Knowledge....543
Chapter 61: Miracle at the Ladder of Tyre....547

Chapter 62: Lessons at the Beach....553
Chapter 63: Gifts of the Earth....561
Chapter 64: The Healing of Tyre....565
Chapter 65: Escape From Tyre....575
Chapter 66: Bringing the Light....581
Chapter 67: Greater Gifts Come Forth....585
Chapter 68: A Peculiar People....587
Chapter 69: Secrets of Magic Revealed....593
Chapter 70: Conversion of Adronicus and Yunia....599
Chapter 71: Astonishing Powers of Heaven Revealed....607
Chapter 72: Yeshua Explains the Celestine Powers....615
Chapter 73: Question of Nudity....619
Chapter 74: The Importance of Dreams....623
Chapter 75: Unrighteous Taxation....627
Chapter 76: Circles of Power....635
Chapter 77: The Power of Sound....641
Chapter 78: The Power of Colors....643
Chapter 79: The Power of Stones....649
Chapter 80: The Power of Herbs....653
Chapter 81: The Power of the Aura....655
Chapter 82: Preparations for a New Beginning....659
Chapter 83: Yeshua Walks on the Sea....667
Chapter 84: Last Tour of the Holy Land....671
Chapter 85: Resurrection of Lazarus....687
Chapter 86: Conspiracy of the Sanhedrin....699
Chapter 87: Eternal Principles of Truth and Light....701
Chapter 88: The Last Supper....707
Chapter 89: The Garden of Gethsemane....717
Chapter 90: The Trials of Yeshua....721
Chapter 91: Crucifixion and Resurrection....733
Chapter 92: Illumination by the Jordan....745

Chapter 93: Harmony and Resonance..755
Chapter 94: Portal Between Worlds..761
Chapter 95: Explanation of Entities..765
Chapter 96: Rebellion and Fall of Lucifer..771
Chapter 97: The Sixth Kingdom..775
Chapter 98: The Fifth Kingdom..787
Chapter 99: Pathway to Exaltation..803
Chapter 100: The End of the Beginning..813

Introduction

by
Embrosewyn Tazkuvel

The Oracles of Celestine Light Trilogy of Genesis, Nexus and Vivus, is a portal in time for positive, sincere seekers of greater light and enlightenment. It contains the lost account of the life and teachings of Yeshua of Nazareth and the ancient knowledge of the earth. It includes 155 chapters of wisdom, secrets, mysteries and miracles found no place else, revealing hidden knowledge of health, longevity and happiness. Though a very spiritual book, it belongs to no religion, and is a blessed gift to all.

Many people have wondered about the source of the *Oracles of Celestine Light* and have asked, "Who is Embrosewyn that such a book should come through him?" It would seem appropriate that I take a few moments to answer those questions. But let this put to rest the inquiries about Embrosewyn because this book is not about me. It is not even really by me, I was just the scribe recording the events. I was merely fulfilling a sacred task given to me as any of you would have done.

I am humbled to have been called by the light of God to do this work. In many ways my life changed from that moment. In other ways it continued on in the mundane routine of the world. It has taken me some time to finally accept my calling to bring forth the fullness of the teachings of Yeshua of Nazareth as revealed in the *Oracles of Celestine Light* for the perfecting and joy of the Children of Light.

Before I began recording the events of the *Oracles of Celestine Light* I held back for quite a time simply because I felt unworthy and incapable of fulfilling all that has been asked of me. Nor would anyone claim that I was qualified by any criteria to bring forth a work of this magnitude, save by the all-knowing wisdom of God. I am not a theologian, nor do I have a collection of academic degrees. My life has been one of challenge, both in succeeding as the world counts success, and in overcoming my own inadequacies. Though I still felt there were many better qualified and worthy messengers of God than me, the moment came when I could no longer procrastinate one of my important purposes on earth; and I began to revelate, to see the visions and hear the spoken words that were the substance of the *Oracles of Celestine Light*, to walk in the footsteps of Yeshua of Nazareth and his original twelve Apostles, and become the scribe of sacred history.

Please do not assume that this is a Christian book or in any way an adjunct to the Christian Bible because of my reference to Yeshua and the Twelve Apostles. The Yeshua and Apostles that I have come to know as dear friends are far different in thought, action and deed than those commonly depicted, and the teachings of Yeshua herein are not confined to the adherents of any one religion or faith, but are a beacon set on a hill to give additional illumination to Children of Light wherever they may be, within any faith, within any religion.

With few exceptions, this is not a word for word transcription but a revealed manuscript, quoting the speakers exactly, but recounting and writing the narrative as seems most appropriate, and using a somewhat poetic and archaic style to frame the time period and uniqueness of the document, especially in Nexus. It should be noted that in many instances, especially when he was teaching, this was the way Yeshua spoke.

Most of the *Oracles of Celestine Light* was shown to me by the Apostles in vivid, life-like visions of the events that occurred, with the opportunity to see and hear all that transpired as if I were physically present. It was an amazing experience and it oftentimes felt as if I was literally walking side by side with them. After receiving a small portion of each story or event, I put it in writing to the best of my ability and recollection, and then continued on and received more.

I used my own method of writing that by the request of Yeshua, was simplified and without undue embellishment, while scrupulously endeavoring to faithfully record all that I saw and heard. If in my recounting, I did not adequately communicate an event or the exact words that were said, or omitted something considered essential, I was corrected by one of the Apostles. Frequently, I was asked to use specific wording.

Only a small portion of the life of Yeshua during the time of Nexus and Vivus was included in the *Oracles of Celestine Light*. There were many other important and insightful events that occurred during this time period, but I only recorded the ones I was told to write. Yeshua's life was so full. Most Christians refer to Yeshua as Jesus, and as it notes in John 21:25 of the Christian Bible, *"There are many things which Jesus did, which if they should be written, every one, I suppose that even the world itself could not hold all the books."*

Though I know the *Oracles of Celestine Light* will be pilloried by many well-meaning people, I also know that for anyone with an open mind and a humble heart, there are great treasures to be found, and the opportunity to discover Yeshua of Nazareth and his teachings of light and life in ways that transcends all that has been previously known.

This is the life and teachings of Yeshua of Nazareth with a completeness that will fill your soul and uplift your life. It is given to you that you may discover the glory within yourself, and your immutable connection to the divine. Truly, there is a greatness within you waiting to come out, more magnificent than you can imagine. The *Oracles of Celestine Light* will help you discover the majesty of who you really are, the divine reason you are here upon the earth, and unlock the resplendent magic that is your birthright. Your life will never be the same...

~ Embrosewyn Tazkuvel

October 2009

THE FIRST BOOK OF CELESTINE LIGHT
CALLED
GENESIS

CHAPTER 1

Xeon, The Land of Pre-existence

Describes the creation and ancestry of mankind, including pre-earth existence in Xeon. Recounts who created us and how creation was accomplished, not just for mankind, but for every living thing that has ever existed or will exist.

n the beginning before the earth was, or the stars in the heavens above, there was the Father, and the Mother, and the Son abiding in everlasting majesty beyond the horizon of infinity.

2 They are the Elohim: the one God of all that is, three divine and perfected personages, separate in body and spirit, but united as one in purpose, knowledge, vision, power, and faith. They are Elohim: the One.

3 By the joint desire of the Father and the Mother and the agreement of the Son, the spirits and eternal essence of all things that live in a physical form, that have ever lived, and that will ever live, were first created and existed in a spiritual state.

4 Nor has the spiritual essence of any living thing ever come into physical existence with the breath of life, except by their divine intention embraced by their endless love and faith.

5 And it came to pass that in the beginning by the union of love of our Heavenly Father and Heavenly Mother, all the spirits of men and women were created; in the likeness of their celestial parents they were created, every one.

6 Into their spirit was placed an eternal soul, a sliver of the very essence of the Father and the Mother, to never know death and to always speak in a still, small voice calling upon their spirit to manifest in their lives the greatness they could become as true sons and daughters of God.

7 Know then that all living things have spirits and existed spiritually before they existed physically. But only the children of men and women have been blessed with eternal souls, a piece of Elohim, a light inside that ever beckons them to a higher path of virtue and righteousness.

8 The souls of men and women are as innumerable as the sands of the seas; each and every one is gloriously unique, with special gifts and blessings given unto them by their Heavenly Father and Mother that they might manifest the majesty of their celestial heritage and fulfill the full measure of their divine creation.

9 In the realm called Koropean, in the land of Xeon, abide all things spiritual before they pass into the physical.

10 Nothing that lives, that has lived, or that will ever live throughout the worlds of the heavens exists physically except it is first created spiritually and dwells in the land of Xeon, in the realm of the Koropean.

11 And it came to pass that each of the Elohim came often to visit the spirits in Xeon, to

teach them many things so they could grow and expand, and to embrace their souls with their boundless love that love would ever be their guiding light.

12 And it came to pass that the spirits of men and women lived in Xeon in joy and happiness, even for a great time beyond time.

13 They began as children and grew into men and women of spirit, detailed in form and substance, each with a unique personality, cherished hopes and dreams, grand opportunities to learn and grow, and soaring joy from knowledge gained, and cultivation of eternal relationships with other spirits, bonded through shared experiences beyond time and space.

14 And it came to pass that many of the spirit children of the Father and the Mother expanded their knowledge and progressed from their varied experiences and relationships to the limit of their possibilities as beings of spiritual substance and form.

CHAPTER 2

The Creation of the Worlds

An explanation of the creation of the worlds through the organization of time and space and the reason behind it.

And it came to pass that the Father and the Mother looked into the chaos of darkness they had not yet organized and desired to coalesce a part of it into a physical realm of order and light; that their spirit children might have worlds of physical substance to go to and inhabit; and that they might continue to grow and expand from their experiences and relationships and acts of faith, in ways that were impossible for beings of spiritual form alone, living in the presence of the Elohim.

2 And it came to pass that Heavenly Father and Heavenly Mother decreed that balance and order should come from the chaos of darkness and from balance and order that time and space would exist.

3 And it came to pass that Heavenly Father and Heavenly Mother decreed that all of their children of spirit should take upon themselves a mortal tabernacle of flesh and blood, after they had advanced as far as they could in knowledge, ability, faith, and relationships in Xeon, as beings of spiritual substance alone.

4 And it came to pass that Heavenly Father and Heavenly Mother decreed that forgetfulness would come upon the minds of every child of spirit when they passed into the physical realm of their choice and that they would not remember their life as spiritual beings in the presence of their Heavenly Father and Heavenly Mother and the firstborn Heavenly Son.

5 Unto each child was given the loving promise that their souls would ever be a part of the Elohim and that the light of celestial truth would abide forever in their hearts and whisper in their higher minds, ever stirring them with a longing for a divine eternity, and a subtle but sure knowledge that within them was something great calling for something much greater.

6 Thus, it is that amidst the vexing trials and tribulations of mortal life and that in humility, all can fulfill their potential to become a Child of Light; called from the gentle promptings of their heart to believe in a divinity their eyes cannot see and a wonder their mind does not know; to feel coursing through every fiber of their being a sure knowledge that they are a cherished Child of God.

7 And all this that they might come to know great faith; that it might resound with every beat of their heart and resonate from their mind to their toes; and that it might be a shield of protection in life, the power to make miracles, and the ever-burning lamp to guide the way home to Celestine glory.

8 Verily, faith and love are the greatest of all powers, the very dynamic by which all things

were and are created and exist.
9 Love comes easy to the willing and compassionate heart, but faith is a struggle of virtue and
humility, and the means to obtain it only comes to those who conquer themselves and are totally
open to the flow of light from God. But be of good cheer, for these are among the preeminent
gifts of Elohim unto the children of men.
10 For this cause and to learn and grow further by their experiences in the flesh are the
children of men born into the world; that they might be tested by the challenges of mortality
and learn to see without seeing, to hear without hearing, and to do without doing; such is the
power of faith, and only by acquiring this power may they progress into a greater state of being.
11 And it came to pass that the earths were without form or substance; where there would be
worlds, there was only chaos; and darkness permeated all of space.
12 And the Father and the Mother spoke to their firstborn Son and bade him to go into
the chaos and to organize it; that their children of spirit might take upon themselves physical
tabernacles and have the opportunity to gain faith and further light and knowledge.
13 And they decreed that all things which they had created spiritually, the animals and the
birds, the fishes and the insects, and all manner of plants and all manner of life, should be created
physically to abide with their children in physical worlds of paradise.
14 The Son obeyed his parents and by his faith he spoke, and by the power of his word his
light issued into the darkness and chaos; and the darkness was rent, and the chaos was put into
intricate balance and order. And so it came to pass that the physical worlds and all the heavens
began to come into existence.
15 And it came to pass that all living physical things that were made manifest at the beginning
of the physical worlds were organized and made to reproduce after their kind and given freewill
and the ability to learn and grow and evolve in every way.
16 By him and through him, by the manifesting power of his love and faith, were all things
made. And without him, there was not anything made that was made during the days of first
light.
17 And into all creatures that the Son made, the Father and the Mother breathed the breath
of life, and they awakened to their world.

CHAPTER 3

Garden of Eden

The true story of the creation and destruction of the Garden of Eden, as well as the creation of the first twelve men and twelve women who were made upon the earth in the image of our Father and Mother in Heaven.

pon the earth of our home, the Son created a most perfect garden upon a large island encircled by two mighty rivers.

2 Upon this garden island abided all the energies of life, and all things in the garden flourished with joyous vitality. And the Son called this land the Garden of Eden.

3 Into the garden and upon the world at large, he put a great diversity of creatures: from those so tiny they could not be seen to those so immense that to them man was insignificant; from those who moved only by instinct to those who gathered into tribes and took actions with forethought and reason.

4 And into these, Heavenly Father and Mother breathed the breath of life, and they awakened to their world.

5 Upon the garden isle of Eden, the Son formed twelve diverse tabernacles of flesh for men in many hues, in the image of God the Father, and twelve diverse tabernacles of flesh for women in many hues, in the image of God the Mother.

6 And the Father and the Mother sent forth twelve stalwart brothers of spirit and twelve choice daughters of spirit from the land of Xeon and called for their souls to enter into the tabernacles of flesh the Son had made, and they breathed into them the breath of life and they awakened to their world.

7 These were the first people upon our earth that had been created in the image of our Father and Mother in Heaven.

8 One of the brothers was called Adam and one of the sisters was called Eve, and they fell into a deep and abiding love in the tabernacles of their flesh, even as it had been for them in the tabernacles of their spirits before the world was. But it was a pure and innocent love, filled with attraction and admiration, but absent of lust.

9 And the twelve brothers and twelve sisters lived in paradise in innocence, nakedness, and purity for the days and the nights were warm and comforting; the waters pure, delightful, and delicious; fruits, nuts, and vegetables grew wild and abundant everywhere within their reach, and for them this was food, pure and unspoiled, full of life, not death.

10 From time to time, the Father or the Mother or the Son of the Elohim would speak to them in visions while they slept, to teach them again the Celestial laws of the Elohim they had

known so well in Xeon, including the laws of love and stewardship, and the law of faith by which all things are and will be.

11 And it came to pass that the Elohim gave unto the twelve brothers and twelve sisters a commandment that they should be bonded together as male and female in a sacred union of love and respect, one female to one male, as they were all worthy and of equal number. And by this, each of the twelve brothers and twelve sisters would have a special companion to share and create life with.

12 And the voice of the Father came like thunder from a cloudless sky of sun and, with authority and admonishment, bonded each of the men to their wife in holiness.

13 Elohim the Father commanded them to be fruitful and to multiply, and Elohim the Mother stirred their loins—husband for wife and wife for husband—and revealed unto their understanding the ways in which a man could cleave unto a woman in mutual joy and pleasure and become one in body and desire; and that from this sacred union would come children, that the race of men in the image of God might spread forth across the earth.

14 And the voice of the Father shook the very ground, saying, "Unto the children of Eden dominion is given over all the life of earth, over every creature that flies in the air or walks upon the ground or swims in the sea.

15 "You shall have sacred dominion over the fish of the sea, and over the fowl of the air, and over every living thing that moves or grows upon the earth; that in your stewardship they also might be fruitful and multiply and spread forth over the earth in abundance.

16 Every plant in endless variety has been given unto you for food, shelter, or comfort and to heal your wounds and illnesses with prudence and faith.

17 And behold, I have given you every herb bearing seed which is upon the face of all the earth and every tree whose seed bears fruit of sweetness or meat, and the milk of the animals and the non-fertile eggs of the fowls and the honey of the bees, and these shall be your food.

18 And to every animal of the earth and to every fowl of the air, and to everything that creeps upon the earth, wherein there is life, I have given every green herb from the smallest to the largest, for their meat.

19 Take heed therefore to be good and faithful stewards and cherish all life, for the slothful steward shall be held accountable for every life diminished because of their neglect or disdain.

20 Verily, if you take life or diminish the quality of life of the creations of Elohim without cause, so shall the bounty of your eternal reward be taken from you. But as you add to the quality of the life of all that you are a steward over, your blessings in Heaven shall be magnified.

21 The splendor of your eternity is created by the respect and love of your humble everyday actions. As you do in life, so shall you be rewarded in eternity."

22 The first people of the Garden of Eden did as Elohim commanded and were fruitful and multiplied, and they lived in peace and abundance with each other and as good stewards of all life in the land of Eden.

23 Though they were naked, no man lusted for any but his wife and no woman desired any but her husband; and they saw not their nakedness as anything other than pure beauty created by Elohim to be revered and respected as a temple of God.

24 Despite all that they had been given, it came to pass that some among the Edenites began to forget the God that gave them life and did forget to thank Elohim for all that they had, and it came to pass that many of them heard the voice of God no more.

25 Now among all the people of Eden, Adam was the most diligent in giving thanks for all things unto Elohim and the most truthful and faithful in keeping the teachings he had been given, living his life with honesty and uprightness.

26 Thus, it came to pass that Elohim called Adam to be a prophet unto the people of Eden; that the will and words of God could be communicated unto them, even to those who could hear the voices of the Elohim no more; that they might still prosper in the land and grow and expand from their experiences and choices by following the teachings Elohim gave unto Adam.

27 And there was no murmuring or discontent that Elohim had chosen Adam to be the prophet unto the people, for all agreed he was a just and upright man of humility and sincerity, who loved Elohim with all of his heart and was the most appropriate person to be called as a prophet.

28 And it came to pass that the Edenites prospered and grew in the land, and one day Esiac, one of the twelve brothers, said unto Adam, "What do you suppose is beyond the land of Eden?"

29 Adam answered that he did not know, but that Elohim had commanded that they not pass beyond the borders of the garden, which was a vast land and extended beyond sight in all directions.

30 Now Esiac was not hurtful or disobedient, but he had a great curiosity that yearned to know what lay beyond the edges of the garden. And he said unto Adam, "Let us travel just to the border, and step not over it, but travel along it that we can see with our eyes what wonders might be upon the other side."

31 And Adam said unto him, "There are no wonders, for Elohim has said that beyond Eden is only destruction and desolation."

32 Then Esiac replied, "I desire to see what destruction and desolation looks like, so let us be brave and go to the border. We will not disobey Elohim and pass to the other side."

33 Thus, it came to pass that Adam and Esiac and another brother, named Tomad, parted from their families and traveled for two days until they came to the banks of one of the great rivers that encircled Eden.

34 And the three brothers looked about them in astonishment. Behind them, they could see the lush foliage of Eden, but in front of them only stark desolation and barrenness, and they marveled at the power of Elohim.

35 The realization came upon them that even if they desired, they could not pass beyond the borders of Eden, for so vast and swift were the waters of the river that surely no man could cross them.

36 Then Adam turned to go back to his family, but Esiac and Tomad persuaded him to continue to follow along the river that they might see if a change came upon the land on the other side at any place.

37 Thus, the three brothers continued their travel along the borders of Eden until the Sabbath when they rested and gave thanks and prayers unto Elohim.

38 Upon the sunrise of the next day, they began again to walk along the banks of the great river. Though the land beyond the far bank was bleak and dreary, they did see life in their travels, both plants and animals, and birds flew freely back and forth across the river; thus, they wondered what might be beyond their sight.

39 On three occasions, they saw what appeared to be bands of animals moving through the rocks and once a small group that had somewhat the appearance of men, but they were in the distance and indistinct.

40 On the second day after the Sabbath, they came upon four such creatures standing on the other side of the river, and they stared at them secretly from behind the fronds of bushes, in great curiosity.

41 They stood on two feet like men, but in a hunched manner, and they were covered in dark hair like animals. The brothers looked at one another in amazement and could not fathom what the creatures were, for no such animals that looked almost like men existed in Eden.

42 Tomad commented with astonishment to his brothers, "They are men like unto us."

43 Esiac scoffed in reply, "No, Tomad, for they are exceedingly hairy and walk in a most peculiar manner."

44 Then Adam said unto his brethren, "Be they men or beasts they are not made in the image of God as we have been, and they dwell beyond the land of Eden, which land is forbidden to us. Therefore, let us continue our journey, and suffice it that we know there is some life in the barrenness beyond the boundary of Eden, even if it is not life as we know it."

45 Tomad shook his head questioningly, "But why has Elohim not told us of life beyond Eden, and why are there creatures there that do not dwell upon our isle?"

46 Then Adam said unto him, "We are but babes upon this land, and Elohim teaches us only those things which give us a necessary foundation to spring up to new knowledge from which we can further grow and expand.

47 As we firmly gain one step, we are prepared with faith to take the next; and are then given more light and knowledge from Elohim.

48 Thus, we grow step by step, kept in the warm embrace and counsel of our heavenly parents while encouraged to reach further and higher and become more than we are without risking all that we have.

49 For it would be foolish and reckless to reach for a higher step without the foundation of a lower; sometimes we would be lucky and not fail, but as the sun rises, so there would soon come a day when we would not be lucky and would fall into an emptiness that knows no solace.

50 Let us always remember that on our own, man is nothing, but with Elohim, all things are possible."

51 Now there was another brother of spirit who had not been chosen to be among the first to go and dwell in a physical tabernacle upon the earth or to be one of the progenitors of the children of men.

52 He had rebelled mightily against Elohim and was forever cast out of the realm of Celestine Light and condemned to never obtain a physical body, for only by the union of the energy of Heavenly Father and Mother could a soul become one with a body of flesh and blood; thus was his eternal progression forever damned.

53 His name was Lucifer, and he vowed to make man break his covenants to Elohim that man would fall into darkness, even as he was, and suffer the wrath of Elohim, even as he had.

54 For Lucifer was jealous of those who had been given honor before him and wroth that they could have a physical body and eternal progression such as he was forever denied.

55 And his spirit went forth among his former brothers and sisters who now dwelt upon the earth in the land of Eden, whispered into their minds, irritated their hearts, and sowed dissension among the twelve brothers and twelve sisters so much so that they disobeyed Elohim, who had made them and given them life.

56 Elohim had told the twelve brothers and the twelve sisters to eat freely of any fruit of the garden, but of the Tree of the Knowledge of Good and Evil to not eat, save when a fruit of the tree was given to them by the Elohim.

57 They were warned with great seriousness that on the day in which they ate a fruit of the tree not given to them by the Elohim, the life they knew and cherished would perish and that evil would forever find a place in their hearts, creating a war within between good and evil that would never end.

58 And other commandments were given to them that they might gain faith by following the admonitions of Elohim, who loved them with a love beyond the light of the sun; for with obedience they would see that as they followed the word of Elohim, they prospered on the land. And by this their faith would grow.

59 But Lucifer misled them in their minds insomuch that they thought they understood something greater than Elohim had told them.

60 And the voice of Lucifer whispered in their minds, "You cannot progress if you know not more of good and evil. You will always be as little children if you do not gorge yourself upon the forbidden tree.

61 The Father and the Mother know everything of good and evil and they have become the Gods of all that is. The Elohim made the tree, so surely they have eaten all of its fruit.

62 How can you become like unto them if you do not know what they know? They have only forbidden you to eat freely of the fruit to see if you have the initiative to seek out the things, which can help you grow despite the obstacles that may be in your path. You will see that the

fruits you have been denied are the most delicious of all fruits, and tasting of them will open many new delights unto you."

63 Thus, they were all persuaded, every one, even Adam, and they ate the other fruits of the tree that the Elohim had not given to them.

64 The fruits were delicious as Lucifer had said and they looked around and saw the garden remained in beauty even as it always had been, and they began to doubt and disbelieve the word of the Elohim, who had told them that the life they knew would perish if they ate of the forbidden fruit.

65 Then all the men looked at all the women and the women at the men, and they lusted in their loins such as they never had before; and they fell upon one another in their lust even as the animals, and no longer cherished each other in sacredness.

66 At that moment, the Elohim became distant to all of them, even unto Adam; for Elohim called out to them in their hearts to forsake their evil, but they heeded not the promptings of their hearts.

67 When their lust was satiated, they were overwhelmed by a sudden understanding of good and evil. And they now had desires for both, whereas before they had known only a little of evil and desired only good.

68 As the men now lusted without love for women other than their wives and the women for the men, they covered the glory of their bodies, for it now shamed and frightened them, and they hid themselves in guilt, feeling unworthy to be.

69 With a suddenness of thought, they understood that for emptiness they had abandoned fullness.

70 As the light of comprehension dawned in their minds, they knew that they had been misled by Lucifer, and they cried out in anguish for their innocence, which they could never again regain.

71 In their bitterness, they heaped scorn upon themselves, for they now understood that Heavenly Father and Mother would have given all knowledge to them as they were ready to receive it.

72 But in disobeying the commandment of Elohim, they gained knowledge before they understood how to use it wisely and learned of evil before they were prepared to defend against it.

73 That night, a great and dreadful earthquake shook the land, and scalding fiery hot air with sickening fumes blasted forth from the ground insomuch that all the Garden of Eden began to burn.

74 In the morning, the skies remained dark from the smoke of the enormous fires and from great flocks of birds that filled the sky as they fled from the island.

75 And it came to pass that a line of molten stone rent the great river and hardened into a bridge and Elohim called all the creatures of Eden unto it, and in a line one behind the other, both the great and the small, they departed from the doomed land of Eden.

76 And the twelve brothers and their wives, children, and grandchildren fled from the fires of the garden and tried to cross the bridge of stone, but Elohim surrounded them with a high wall of flame through which they could not cross.

77 And it came to pass that only after all of the animals and creatures that could neither swim the river nor fly into the sky had crossed over the stone bridge did Elohim open a path in the circle of fire whereby the Edenites could reach the bridge of stone and cross the river into the Land of Barrenness beyond.

78 The Edenites looked back in anguish as their garden isle of peace and plenty burned and disappeared in a great cloud of smoke. And the bridge across the river, their last connection to the beauty and wonder that had been their life, collapsed behind them as they stood in forlorn turmoil upon the rocky ground of the Land of Barrenness.

CHAPTER 4

Fate of the Edenites

After being cast out of Eden, the Edenites journey into the Land of Barrenness where they undergo many trials and tribulations, but make their new home in the Land of Nodkash on the shores of Lake Kamoya. Three new brothers of light, Jared, Micah, and Enoch, come to earth from the Celestine Light of Elohim to teach the people of Nodkash things that will help them to better survive the harshness of the land. The true story of Cain and Abel is revealed in great detail. Elohim the Father speaks twice from the heavens above, which is the last time he speaks to the people at large and thereafter only speaks to the people through a prophet.

And it came to pass that a great fear came upon the Edenites in the Land of Barrenness, for they knew it not at all and knew not what was to become of them. Their fears caused many to shake with uncontrollable tremors, and they could not speak, but only wail in grief and anxiety.

2 While the daylight was still upon them, they looked across the river in agony as the land of Eden burned and they wept and sobbed in sorrow until they could weep no more, and most just curled up tightly upon the ground, exhausted in the depth of their sadness.

3 As night fell upon them, the fires on the Isle of Eden still burned and the sky glowed red with an eerie light, and dark shadows seemed to move upon them from all directions.

4 Suddenly, Ninichur, son of Kasher, gave a loud and forsaken scream, and ripping his clothes and pulling on his hair, he jumped up and ran quickly to the river, and before anyone could move to stop him, he leaped in and was immediately carried away by the swift current, never to be seen again.

5 Many of the Edenites gathered to the riverbank and looked downstream by the pale red glow of the burning fires to see what had become of Ninichur. But barely had they gathered upon the bank than Calliya, the wife of Ninichur, rushed passed them and flung herself into the roiling waters to join her husband in oblivion.

6 Then it was that the demented thought to dive into the river of no return came upon several of the Edenites, and in an instant, many sprang forward to fulfill their pitiful desires. And three, standing upon the bank, jumped into the river before the other Edenites could react, and others rushed from further back to reach the river before anyone could stop them.

7 And it came to pass that Adam stood upon the riverbank with his back to the river, and holding up his arms, he commanded in a loud voice, "Stop! Let none approach the river! Move back from the river!"

8 Many stopped upon hearing his words, but still three more Edenites, overcome in their

sorrow and grief, ran and leaped into the river even as Adam was speaking.

9 Then it was that Adam looked to his brethren among the twelve who still seemed to have their wits about them, and he called out to them saying, "Brothers! Come quickly to me! Stand beside me and form a barrier that no more of our children will depart in madness!"

10 Heeding his call, the eleven other original brothers of Eden quickly came to Adam and spread out with their backs to the river, facing their children and grandchildren, and prevented any more from leaping into the river of no return.

11 So stood the twelve brothers of Eden, all through the night until the dawn of the next day. And seeing their fathers and grandfathers standing as one united in their love and purpose, the children of Eden lost their madness and fell upon the ground, both sitting and lying, in stupors of disbelief at all that had transpired.

12 The following day, the Isle of Eden was naught but a smoldering ruin, and even the Land of Barrenness seemed desirable in comparison. So it was the Edenites that remained, began to lift their heads and wonder what lay beyond the cleavage of the ridge of the small canyon near the river upon which they had come across the stone bridge from Eden.

13 There was no food among them, and other than occasional clumps of an unknown short grass, there was no food to be found within sight. Thus, it was that Adam and his brothers and sisters conferred, and it was decided by the Elders that the Edenites should venture away from the river through the cleft in the ridge, where the animals from Eden had passed, and seek out food and discover what lay beyond.

14 Before they left, Adam gathered them all into a circle of prayer and spoke unto Elohim for all of them, saying, "Dear Father and Mother of Light, forgive us; oh forgive us, for the errors of our ways. We have learned the painful lesson of the consequences of not following and heeding your words, given to us in love for our happiness.

15 "We venture forth now into a new and frightening world. Nevertheless, like unto Eden, we know it was created by you. Therefore, help us to remember that truth that we will not be afraid of the unknown.

16 Please look upon your children with mercy. We have injured among us and mothers who nurse and many young children. We beseech you to ease our suffering and guide us to food and shelter that we might survive, to prove to you that we are worthy children and can become greater than we have been.

17 These things we humbly ask in the name of your son, even he who has called us brother, who comforts us, and abides in our hearts."

18 And it came to pass that the Edenites journeyed out of the canyon by the river and passed through the cleft in the ridge.

19 As each of the Edenites stood upon the crest of the ridge, they took a moment to look out into the Land of Barrenness. To their surprise, they discovered that it was not barren after all, for they could see trees near some hills not far off and many unusual plants within sight, and the occasional sounds of animals and the songs of birds could be heard.

20 It was decided by the Elders, the twelve brothers and twelve sisters who were the original Edenites; that they should seek to reach the hills in the distance where they could see trees growing on the hillsides and imagined water would run downhill and gather into streams.

21 Though the hills seemed not that distant from the ridge, as the sun set, after a long walk in the hot sun through the day, the Edenites failed to reach the hills and dejectedly lay upon the ground uncovered, with empty stomachs and parched of thirst from their journey of the day, for they had no containers among them to carry water from the river and had left the canyon with only the water they could carry in their stomachs.

22 Shortly after sunrise the next day, they began again to travel toward the hills, spurred onward by their ever-growing thirst.

23 Hunger was also gnawing at their stomachs. In their innocence and ignorance, everyone ate freely of the red berries they encountered on short bushes while they walked toward the hills.

24 But shortly thereafter, those who had eaten earliest began to get dizzy and their mouths began to burn, and their stomachs brought forth that which they had eaten.

25 Those who had eaten the most passed out, and Miliya, daughter of Yaconi, did not awaken. And Yaconi shook his daughter and pleaded with her to awaken, but her breathing stopped and she awoke not.

26 Yaconi looked to Adam and implored him, "Has Elohim forsaken us? How can my daughter sleep and not be able to be awakened? Why would berries Elohim has put upon the earth cause her to sleep so deeply? I do not understand anything at all that has happened to us. Help me, Brother Adam, for I am lost."

27 Adam put his hand upon Yaconi's shoulder and spoke aloud to Elohim, saying, "Dear Father and Mother of Light, hear the words of my mouth and feel the pain of our hearts. We do not understand all that has befallen us. We beseech you in utter humility to give us the light of knowledge."

28 And it came to pass that the voice of Elohim the Father rumbled across the sky and was heard by each of the Edenites. And the voice of the Father said unto them, "My children learn now the Law of Consequence; that each action you do begets another action; the good to good, and the bad to bad.

29 "And learn the Law of Knowledge and Ignorance; that knowledge brings reward and ignorance brings penalty. And the knowledge you must possess, you must gain from your efforts and experiences and desire and focus, for never again will it be given to you freely as it was in Eden.

30 So you have now learned that beyond Eden there are things that look to be desirable that instead will hurt you if you partake of them. And that the action ripples like a stone upon water, with like actions, be they good or bad.

31 In Eden, you had never seen death, but in the world it shall be your regular companion, even now, as the girl does not sleep, but has returned to us, and will be among you upon the earth no more.

32 In Eden, there was nothing you could not eat, save the fruit of the Tree of Knowledge of Good and Evil, but upon the world into which you are now cast there are more plants to bring pain, suffering, and death than to bring health and life.

33 In Eden, all animals were your friends, but in the Land of Bareness, many will be your enemies, and many will seek you to be their food, so beware.

34 In Eden, sickness and suffering were unknown, but in the Land of Bareness, you will only be as healthy and free from sickness as you are faithful to the commandments and guidance we have given you.

35 Among women, their travails will be many, and in pain they will now bring forth children, unless they abide strictly by the teachings of the Elohim.

36 Among men, never again will the earth bring forth fruits unto you in unbidden abundance, but you must work with sweat and perseverance, fighting the thorns and the thistles and praying for rain and sun, to bring forth the food that in Eden came freely unto you.

37 In Eden, there was a balance between the male and the female inside each of you, thereby the men never angered and the women never wavered.

38 But now in the world that is yours, the men will need to strive to remember the female within them lest they are overcome by the male and become even as the animals.

40 And the women must ever strive to hold onto the male within them, lest they become without a voice and mere chattel to the men.

41 Nor will the Elohim ever again speak openly to the children of men, save once more in great condemnation. Hereafter, only to the prophet or prophetess we have called will we speak words for all people to heed, but only the worthy will hear their voice and take to their hearts the words we have spoken unto them.

42 This is the world you have called unto you by your actions; and so the ripples shall go forth

throughout time, generations upon generations, until the end of times.

43 You will experience great sadness in your travails, but so too will you find great joys, even greater than those of Eden in your accomplishments of eternal significance.

44 Therefore, fear not, for we are still with you. If you seek us out and live as we have given you, you shall always have our spirit to be upon you, and guide you, and bring you toward the Celestine Light."

45 And it came to pass that in sadness the Edenites continued on their journey toward the hills and took turns carrying the body of Miliya, for they did not know what they should do with it. None of the others perished from eating the red berries but most were sick, some more than others.

46 Shortly before dusk, they reached the hills and under Adam's direction, two parties of three men each quickly set out in opposite directions along the base of the hills to seek out water. As evening fell, both parties returned, their missions unfulfilled, and another day passed for the Edenites without water or food.

47 The following day, Adam sent out three parties of three men each. Two were told to explore further along the base of the hills and the third to climb to the top of the hills and ascertain what lay beyond. All were instructed not to return until they had found water or were unsuccessful after two days.

48 While the main exploration parties were gone, the Edenites set up a rudimentary camp making shelters from what tree branches and brush they could gather.

49 Additional exploration parties ventured out short distances from camp and brought back several kinds of berries, plus some fruits that were the same as fruits that had grown in Eden.

50 The Edenites were hesitant to eat the unknown berries but were overjoyed to see fruits they recognized. The entire camp quickly returned to the spot where the largest fruit tree had been found and gorged themselves on the ripe fruit, except for saving a couple of dozen of the least ripe fruits to give to the men of the main exploration parties when they returned.

51 While eating at the fruit tree, Ezias, one of the twelve brothers, spoke to Adam, saying, "This tree requires water to live and it is thriving on this spot. Though we see no water nearby there must be some beneath the ground to feed the tree. Therefore, let us dig beneath it that we might come upon the source of its water and be able to partake of it."

52 Adam agreed that Ezias had an excellent thought, and after explaining it to the others, the men began to dig enthusiastically.

53 By mid-afternoon, they had dug a hole of the height of three men, which was no small feat considering the compact hardness of the ground, and that they lacked tools other than their hands and sticks.

54 But still they had not found water or any trace of it, and all were now greatly fatigued from their efforts and their initial enthusiasm had been replaced with disappointment.

55 Dejectedly, everyone returned to their camp to await the hoped-for arrival of the three exploration parties with better news of success.

56 Back at camp, Eve came to Adam and spoke unto him, saying, "Adam, why is it that you and your brethren are only doing what seems to you best in search of water and food, instead of inquiring of the Elohim?"

57 Adam answered Eve, saying, "The Father has said he will speak to us no more and that we must discover and learn for ourselves from our experiences."

58 "No," Eve replied. "That is not what he said. The Father said that the Elohim would still speak to their prophet, for how else might their children be guided in light and truth? And it is you, Adam, who is the prophet of Elohim. And so it has been long before we were cast out of Eden."

59 Adam looked down at his feet for a moment and then looked up at his wife and said unto her, "You are true in your words, Eve. I will go and inquire of our Father and Mother and Brother."

60 But before Adam could leave the camp and seek out a place of privacy to speak with Elohim, there was a sudden scream from one of the women and they looked to see Hamaqila, daughter of Sesh, writhing upon the ground.

61 Rushing over to her, Adam and Eve saw two puncture wounds on her wrist and a snake, such as they had never seen before, slithering off into the brush.

62 Adam looked at the friends of Hamaqila and asked, "Did the snake bite her?" And they nodded affirmatively, and one said, "It was such a pretty little snake, she just picked it up to hold it, even as she had done with snakes many times in Eden, but it bit her with viciousness and immediately she fell to the ground in pain."

63 Adam looked closely at the two wounds, saying to himself, but loud enough for others to hear as well, "But this is a most strange bite. What snake has only two teeth?"

64 His question was answered by Gorag, son of Kilith, who spoke to all, saying, "Like everything in this miserable place, what was harmless in Eden, even a small, pretty-colored snake, can be the source of pain and bitterness here in the Land of Barrenness."

65 "You speak true, Gorag," Adam replied. "Until we know that something is harmless or beneficial we must assume the opposite."

66 They moved Hamaqila to the place of greatest comfort that they could make and prayed over her that Elohim would help her to live.

67 That night, most slept fitfully, anxious in their hearts for the exploration parties that remained away and because of the many unknown and disquieting sounds they heard moving about in the darkness beyond their camp.

68 After the passage of two days, none of the exploration parties had returned and most of the Edenites lay upon the ground too fatigued and parched to move. But on the morning of the third day, the party that had gone into the hills and the one that had gone into the rising sun returned. Both had found small quantities of water to sustain them, and each had found some plants such as those that grew in Eden for food. To the delight of everyone, they brought back as much of the food as they could carry and some water in hollow gourds.

69 But there was more to their reports. Obetas of the hill party spoke first, saying, "We did not find a place ascending the mountain that would be good for our people to reside, for nowhere did we find upon the mountain a large body of standing water or a running stream of substance. But there are great trees and much material for building up on the slopes.

70 "We saw many kinds of animals and some birds, but we recognized only a few from the Isle of Eden.

71 When we topped the hill we looked down into a vast valley which we could not see the end of. It is bound by hills on three sides and we were at the end of it upon the place where we stood. In the valley there is a large lake, so there is a constant water source and probably a good place to make our permanent camp."

72 Everyone's mood was buoyed by this news, for it gave them hope of which they had begun to sorely lack.

73 Then the team that had gone into the sun along the base of the hills gave their report, and Yammigon spoke unto the Edenites, saying, "We also saw many beasts, some in the hills above us and some upon the plains. Not as many as in Eden but some very terrifying in size, equal to three or four Zarumps from Eden."[a]

74 At this proclamation, many stared at Yammigon in amazement, for the Zarump was the biggest animal of Eden.

75 "There cannot be an animal so large," scoffed Cain, a son of Adam.

76 "Yammigon speaks true," defended Haglad, who was one of the two that had accompanied him on the exploration. "And more than this, we saw tracks of a creature that is likely twice the size of that beast.

77 We also found some plants to eat that were the same as those from Eden, but there were not many and we found only small catch basins of water."

78 "You have done well, my brothers," Adam commended. "It would seem that we should make our way over the hills and down into the valley, unless the third party returns with better news."

79 Night was falling when two of the men from the third party that had traveled along the hills with the sun at their backs returned. They were greatly fatigued and collapsed into the arms of their brethren.

80 "Where is Dolash?" asked his father with apprehension.

81 "He is as Miliya," answered one of the two men. "On our second day, shortly after the sun had risen, we came upon a group of five or six very strange creatures. They looked somewhat like men, but they wore no clothes and were covered with hair, and walked with a stoop. They are also very broad of body, but short of stature.

82 We approached seeking to befriend them, but they immediately fell upon us and commenced to beat us with heavy sticks. Dolash was felled by a blow to the head and then hit again until his head was no more."

83 Hearing this, the parents of Dolash wailed in grief as did many of his friends. But Adam grabbed the hand of the man speaking and asked, "How is it that you escaped?"

84 "We ran," answered the man. "We ran very fast and very long. But in truth we did not need to run much, for these manlike creatures cannot run fast at all. Nevertheless, we ran until we could run no more to put as much distance between us and them as possible."

85 Considering the news brought by the three exploration parties, the Elders met in the early evening beneath the light of a full moon and decided to make their way over the hills and down into the valley beyond shortly after first light and to eat and drink as they traveled whenever a source for either was found.

86 In the morning before leaving, after a short prayer by Adam remembering her goodness, they buried the body of Miliya in the hole they had dug at the base of the fruit tree, for it had begun to stink and they knew not what else to do with it.

87 Hamaqila was still very sick and weak from her snakebite, so her father and brothers made a litter to carry her upon.

88 Remembering the admonishment of Eve, before they departed, Adam beckoned everyone into a circle of prayer and called upon the Elohim to watch over them, to help them be cautious of the unknown, and to lead them to a new home where they could thrive and prosper upon the land and to sufficient food and water in their travels to sustain them.

89 Their journey over the hills and down into the valley was uneventful. Along the way, they were able to forage water from small catch basins hidden in the shade and food from plants that they recognized from Eden, so by the time they reached the valley floor, they were greatly invigorated.

90 The Edenites that came into the valley were just over five hundred in number, with skin hues of many shades and physical appearances of great diversity.

91 And the years passed one after another and the Edenites grew upon the land, and the women bore many children, and the Edenites multiplied in numbers greatly.

92 The Edenites came to call the Land of Barrenness Nodkash, meaning bitter salvation, for though they were able to till the ground for food, catch fish in the lake, and harvest some fruits in the wilderness, life was very difficult and challenging, and they worked from dawn until dusk every day except the Day of Elohim, simply to survive.

93 And the community that they built upon the lake, they called Kamoya and the lake they named after the community, calling it Lake Kamoya.

94 Even as the Edenites welcomed new life with the birth of many children, so too did they come to experience much of death of which they had never known on the Isle of Eden.

95 During the first hundred years of the cycles of the sun in the Land of Nodkash, the old ways of eating were followed by everyone, and they had no sickness among them.

96 But death and injury and infection still came to them, for many were the dangers upon

the land.
97 There were large and fearsome creatures hidden in the lake that from time to time leaped above the surface, swamping the logs upon which they fished, grabbing even the most alert of fishermen, and pulling them beneath the surface never to be seen again.
98 So too had many a wild forager gone into the wilderness to gather fruits only to be attacked by terrifying wild beasts and pulled from the arms of their valiant friends and dragged away into the forest.
99 In the early days in Kamoya, many men were lost, leaving behind grieving widows and children and parents.
100 And the face and voice of Elohim the Mother came unto Adam while he slept and told him it was not good that any woman should be without a husband or child without a father. And he was commanded that the men of Kamoya should take unto them the wives and children of the men that had fallen, if the widow would choose them for a husband and their wife should agree, and they should be their wives and their children too.[b]
101 And it came to pass that Adam spoke unto the people of Kamoya and told them the words Elohim the Mother had spoken unto him.
102 Some of the men heeded his dream and when they were chosen by a widow and their wives agreed, they took unto them the wives and children of men who had fallen and joined them to the wife and children that were already theirs, and they became one family.
103 But others heeded him not and ridiculed him, scoffing that he would presume that God would speak to him and command him concerning their private affairs.
104 Therefore, there remained some widows without husbands and children without fathers, and these were taken in by the parents or brothers of the widow until such time as they could be joined in a union with another family.
105 And it came to pass that for all the joy that children brought, so too was their sadness, as from time to time a mother would perish while giving birth to her newborn son or daughter.
106 Seeing all the calamities continuing to befall his people, Adam prayed mightily to Elohim, asking for wisdom that the Edenites might know how to better be protected from harm and prosper on the land.
107 And the Elohim heard the pleas of Adam and gave unto the Edenites greater wisdom, which came into their minds like a sudden wind that was not expected.
108 From this new knowledge, they came to build stout homes of stone that kept out the strongest winds and rain.
109 And they began to make greater observations of the animals that roamed about the Land of Nodkash and learned that they could fish in the early morning safely, for the creatures of the lake slept until the midday. And they learned that they could forage for fruits in the wilderness when the sun was high in the sky, for this was when the beasts of the land were most likely to rest and digest their morning meals.
110 Nevertheless, the people of Kamoya continued to lose men to the creatures that consumed them and women to the pains of childbirth. So too were parties of men sometimes attacked by hordes of the manlike creatures that flitted mostly unseen in the shadows of the forest. And though these were easily outrun, broken bones from the crushing blows of clubs were often the penalty before they could escape.
111 Once again Adam prayed mightily unto the Elohim seeking greater wisdom, but they answered him not.
112 And it came to pass that Adam desired greatly to hear the words of the Elohim, therefore he fasted for twelve days, drinking water only, that he might be free from the concerns of the world and able to hear the voice of God.
113 And it came to pass that Elohim the Mother came to him again in a dream and told him they would send down more of their sons, even as Adam and his brothers and sisters had first come to Eden, and they would bring more knowledge that the people of Kamoya could have

greater safety and more prosperity.

114 And it came to pass that three more sons of Elohim came down upon the earth, and they appeared the next day before the house of Adam.

115 Though the Mother had told him of their coming, Adam was astonished when he saw them before him, for though they seemed familiar, they were men he had never before encountered since he had been placed in the garden, and they were dressed in colorful and astounding ways, not like the people of Kamoya.

116 Seeing Adam speechless before them, one spoke unto him, saying, "Adam, we have come from the presence of our Father and Mother in the great Celestine Light. I am Jared, and these are my brothers, Micah and Enoch. We are now to be numbered among you and have come to bring you greater knowledge."

117 And it came to pass that Adam embraced his new brothers who had come from the light of Elohim, and he called all the people of Kamoya to come to him that they might meet the sons of Elohim who had come in answer to his fast and prayers.

118 The people came, everyone, to see for themselves. And most were even more astounded than Adam, for other than within their own community, they had never before seen men who resembled sons of Elohim.

119 Nor could they remember their lives in the great light, before the world was, for a veil had been put over their memories by the Elohim that they could grow in faith.

120 And it came to pass that Jared, Micah, and Enoch taught many things to the people living in the Land of Nodkash that greatly improved their lives and safety.

121 So it was that the people of Kamoya became learned in the ways of extracting metals from the rocks of the earth and melding them one with another, and from this, they made sharp-pointed spears and daggers to protect the wild foragers and fishermen from the beasts that would consume them.

122 And they fashioned axes from the metal and honed their edges and used them to fell trees and built a great palisade of thick, vertical poles with sharpened points completely encircling Kamoya to keep out the predators of the day and the night.

123 They were instructed in the creation of large canoes linked three abreast by beams; from these, they were able to travel safely far out into the lake and catch many more fish than they had ever previously been able, and the monsters of the lake could no longer breach their vessels before they could fend them off with long spears.

124 So too did they teach them the way of writing in great detail and of engineering that they could build a tall and magnificent temple to honor Elohim from whom all blessings flowed.

125 But there were some among the people of Kamoya, including Cain, a son of Adam and Eve, who did not accept the coming of Jared, Micah, and Enoch and wished to cast them out from amongst them.

126 Yet most people marveled at their coming and accepted them to be numbered among them.

127 And it came to pass that the three brothers from the Celestine Light took unto them as wives the widows of men who had died and who had not yet found new husbands among the people of Kamoya.

128 Seeing that the three brothers took unto them wives whom others had rejected, many of the other men and their wives were shamed, and many of the wives having husbands went to the widows whom they had previously rejected and asked them to come with their children and be one with their family.

129 And it came to pass that there were no more widows among the women of Kamoya, for all were welcomed into the homes of others and many new families were thus created, and there was joy among most in the land.

130 Nevertheless, there began also to be schisms among some of the people, even among Cain and Abel, the two eldest sons of Adam and Eve.

131 For Cain was opposed to the marriages of widows or that one man should have more than one wife.

132 And he had anger toward the three newcomers and resented the immediate authority and respect that they were given, whereas he had labored faithfully for the people of Eden all of his life and was not so esteemed.

133 And it came to pass that Cain began to kill animals with his spear, not for defense but to drink their blood and eat their flesh.

134 Seeing that Cain did not die from eating the flesh of the animals, others of the Land of Nodkash began to kill animals so that they too could drink their blood and eat their flesh, for that was a much easier way to get a full belly than tilling the fields for endless days.

135 Upon seeing this, Adam and Eve had great sorrow as did the three brothers who had come from the light, and many of the other people of Kamoya, especially those who had lived the longest in Eden.

136 Adam came to his son and pleaded with him to cease killing animals to drink their blood and consume their flesh, but Cain said unto him, "I will not cease, for I have found a great treasure that the Elohim have kept hidden from you. I watched the great beasts of the world kill and eat the smaller beasts and I thought that I too could be great upon this land if I killed and ate the beasts, instead of waiting for them to try and kill and eat me.

137 "Now I have strength such as I have never known, and my time is freed from toiling for many hours each day in the fields. It is you who should begin to eat the animals and you will discover a life more fulfilling than the simple one the Elohim gave us to live."

138 Thereafter, Adam was greatly saddened because of Cain, for he would heed not any of the commandments of Elohim and thought that he knew better than God.

139 A significant number of others agreed with Cain and aligned themselves with him in opposition to the newcomers and many of the new ways that had been adopted by the people of Kamoya and also began to take joy in the slaying of animals and the consuming of their flesh and blood.

140 Thus was the last innocence of Eden destroyed, and a lust for blood and callousness for the sanctity of life did come upon the world.

141 Abel came to his brother Cain upon a hillside where he was hunting and tried to persuade him to return to the ways of Elohim, saying, "We are only doing as Elohim has commanded, and you can see that by obeying the loving commandments of our parents of light, our people are happier and prosper on the land."

142 But Cain was very wroth with his brother Abel, and he shouted at him, saying, "Do not instruct me! I am your elder brother, and it is you who must listen to me! Truly, I am happier with one wife, and a belly full of animal flesh than you can ever possibly be!"

143 Abel was surprised by the vehemence of his brother Cain. But he did not back down and said unto him, "I will listen to you when you are speaking wisdom and heed you not when you speak foolishness, even as you should do with me."

144 "You are younger and are always more foolish," sneered Cain. "You have never said anything in all of your life worth listening to, and you have never given me the respect that is my due."

145 Abel was saddened by the words of his brother and held his head down contemplating how he should answer, and thus he did not see Cain withdraw his dagger. But sensing his movement, he looked up into his brother's eyes, even as Cain drove the dagger into his heart, saying, "Respect me now with your last breath." And then Abel fell to the ground dead with Cain's dagger protruding from his heart.

146 Realizing what he had done, Cain pulled the dagger from his brother's body and dragged his body to a nearby gully and collapsed the rocky hillside upon him. He then returned to Kamoya and spoke nothing of what had happened to anyone.

147 As evening fell, Adam and Eve and the wives of Abel began to ask if anyone knew where

he was or where he had last been seen, for he was not within the walls of the community, and it was unsafe to be beyond the palisade at night because of the beasts that roamed about in the dark.

148 When Adam asked Cain if he knew the whereabouts of his brother, he answered with some fear, saying, "Why do you ask me? Am I my brother's keeper?"

149 But the night came and went, and the new day dawned without Abel appearing, and the worst began to be feared.

150 During the day, search parties were sent out to look for Abel, and on the second day, a party led by Enoch noticed the freshly collapsed gully where Cain had buried his brother; being led by the spirit of Elohim, he asked the men with him to dig into the rocks, and in only minutes, they discovered the dead body of Abel. One of the men stripped, and they used his garment to cradle Abel's body and returned with him to Kamoya.

151 As the searchers passed through the palisade, the people of Kamoya quickly saw that Abel whom they carried was dead, and many women began to weep and wail and many men too had tears in their eyes for he had been much loved in the community.

152 Though there were many wounds from the rocks Cain had collapsed upon him, the single wound in Abel's heart was still evident, and the Elders and searchers and people of Kamoya knew not what to make of it.

153 "What manner of beast kills with a single tooth through the heart?" wondered many.

154 "It is like a spear or dagger wound," ventured another.

155 Then Cain rose up among them and feeling somewhat contrite for having slain his brother, he said unto them, "It is a dagger wound, which I know, for I am the one who stabbed him in the heart when he spoke to me with condescension."

156 Upon his confession, there was an audible and collective gasp from everyone near enough to have heard his words, and whispers passed quickly back to those further away of the foul deed just confessed.

157 Cain continued saying, "We fought with words, and in my anger I slew him that he would not speak as he had to me ever again. I am sorry now for what I have done, but I cannot bring back my brother."

158 Adam looked at Cain as if he had never known him and asked, "Yesterday you said you knew not of your brother's whereabouts and that you were not his keeper. Yet today you admit this terrible deed. How could you say nothing yesterday, extending the anxiety of everyone, and speak openly today?"

159 Cain answered him, saying, "Yesterday I was ashamed for what I had done and sought to hide what occurred. Today I am sorry, but feel justified because of the way in which Abel has treated me, his elder brother for many years, as if he were better than me."

160 Adam stood before his son, and though he was smaller in stature, he seemed to tower over him in his wrath, saying unto him, "You have done the greatest sin. You have killed another. You have stopped the eternal progression of your brother by taking him from this mortal life before his time.

161 "Such a thing has never occurred in the history of man and now you have begun the chain that will have no end while man reigns upon the earth.

162 "For this great horror there can be no justification; no, not one; save the defense of your own life. Yet by your own admission, it is you that attacked Abel. How can you possibly seek to justify the unjustifiable?"

163 Cain bristled at his father's words and his contriteness vanished, replaced instead with anger. And he said unto his father, "What do you know? Your head is always in the clouds speaking to a God of your imagination whom nobody else can hear!

164 "Though Abel attacked me not with a weapon, his words cut me just as deep and caused pain to wounds he had inflicted upon me all my life. Therefore it was in self-defense, to stop his endless attacks of words upon me, that I at last could take no more and silenced him forever. He

brought his own death upon him, so do not think to cast it upon me."

165 Then there was a great shaking and rumbling of the ground, and dark clouds gathered quickly, hiding the sun, echoing with thunder, and flashing lightning out and all around the people of Kamoya.

166 And the voice of Elohim the Father rumbled from the clouds and everyone heard, and with every word he spoke, the earth shook. And the Father said, "Cain, your life shall be desolation and your eternity shall be darkness. You sought to stop the eternal progression of Abel, but you have only succeeded in damning your own.

167 "Abel shall be reborn into mortality once more to resume his journey, but you have dropped yourself into a deep abyss, and only through time unmeasured will you be able to come again even to the place you were the day you did this great sin.

168 Therefore, leave Kamoya and journey to another land. Take with you all who drink the blood and eat the flesh of animals, save they repent this very moment and sin no more. And know that it is from the killing of the innocent animals and the eating of their flesh, that callousness for death has been nurtured and made manifest in the evil you have done."

169 And it came to pass that Cain left Kamoya, and all of his family went with him. And many of the people of Kamoya also departed with Cain, even all those that desired to still kill animals and eat their flesh and repented not. And these numbered over three hundred people, including children.

170 The meat-eaters journeyed far away from Kamoya and the Land of Nodkash, and after some years, it was only with the infrequent visits from traders of goods were they still known by the people of Kamoya that had seen them depart.

171 Thereafter, the meat-eaters were called Caininites, after Cain whom they had followed rather than obey the voice of God that had spoken to them.

172 And those that remained were no longer remembered as Edenites, but thereafter were called Kamoyans.

* * * * * * * * * * *

73 a: A Zarump is about a third larger than the size of a modern day African bull Elephant

100 b: This involved men who were already married as the people of Kamoya married very young and there were no single men of a mature age available.

CHAPTER 5

The City of Enoch

Adam dies at 830 years old and Enoch is called by Elohim to be the next prophet of the Children of Light. Eleven generations have been born since the time of the Isle of Eden, and the people have multiplied greatly and spread out upon the earth. Many have become very wicked in their ways, with numerous wars between the clans, and many people are slaughtered. Only the Children of Light who remained at Kamoya remain true to the teachings of Elohim. Enoch prays for guidance so the Children of Light may be spared from the attacks of other clans. Elohim creates a new island for them to live on and sends twelve special brothers of spirit to inhabit physical bodies upon the earth to help the Children of Light. The people of Enoch build a most beautiful city made of marble with spires of gold. Because of their righteousness they are rewarded by Elohim and taught to use the secrets of Heaven that are their birthright. They never taste death as the earth can no longer contain their goodness, and the entire city of Enoch, including all of the people, except twelve families chosen to bring their light into the world, ascends into the sky.

And it came to pass that the days of Adam were 830 years upon the land and then he died,
and Eve soon followed him to their eternal reward.
2 Upon the passing of Adam, Enoch was called by Elohim the Father to be the next
prophet to the Children of Light, and from that day forth, Elohim the Mother began to come
to him in his dreams to show him the days to come and give him wise counsel that the Children
of Light might be forewarned of the coming calamities and tribulations.
3 And it came to pass that eleven generations had been born since the time of the destruction
of the Isle of Eden and the people made in the image of the Elohim multiplied on the face of
the earth, and many sons and daughters were born unto them and they spread out upon the earth
far beyond the land of Kamoya.
4 But many of the descendants of the Edenites became wicked in their ways, forgetting the
Elohim who had formed them in their image and given their forefathers life. And many began
to revel in all manner of wickedness, defiling the temples of their bodies in many and diverse
manners.
5 And it came to pass that clans formed after the desires of their hearts and the gods of their
imaginations, and each chose a place upon the earth to call their own, and this became their land.
6 And it came to pass that the clans began to war against those in the other lands, and great
was the slaughter of men, women, and children across all of the earth.
7 So great was the killing of men that in many places there came to be many widows without

men to take them again as wives and many virgins without a man to find as a husband.

8 The Elohim were greatly saddened by the descent into darkness by the children of men, how they had turned to false gods, and how they had taken to killing and eating the flesh of animals and from this, murdering one another all across the land.

9 Only the Children of Light who remained at Kamoya stayed true to the teachings of the Elohim and they alone prospered on the land.

10 Many were the clans and descendants of the Edenites from afar who regularly came upon the Kamoyans seeking to kill the men and enslave the women and children.

11 It grieved the hearts of the Kamoyans that in their defense they needed to slay those who attacked them to whom they still felt a kinship, but they knew they must slay or be slain to protect themselves and their land and their wives and children.

12 But the Kamoyans grew increasingly wary of maintaining their ever-vigilant defense and slaying their attackers, which was repugnant to their souls. Therefore, at a meeting of the Elders, it was asked of Enoch to inquire of the Elohim how they might better protect themselves from the wickedness and dangers of the world, for even in their stout defense, fifteen Kamoyans had been slain by the clans in the last solar cycle.

13 Enoch prayed mightily to the Elohim, seeking knowledge and wisdom, and the Mother came to him in a dream as a most beautiful woman and spoke unto him, saying, "This night, while the people of Kamoya sleep, an island as large as Eden shall come forth from the waters of the great lake.

14 On the morrow, begin to remove your people to this new land, and there you shall be safe from the attacks of all those from the lands afar.

15 We shall send seeds of all kinds that are right for this place to grow in abundance upon your island, and within a cycle of the sun, it shall be a bountiful land.

16 And we shall send down twelve more of our sons and they shall venture out into the lands with few men, because of all the clansmen that have been killed, and find virgins of greatness, and they shall return to the island sanctuary to be married and create lineages of renown.

17 Following the calamities to come, these lineages and others from Kamoya shall spread forth over the land that Children of Light might walk upon all parts of the earth."

18 And it came to pass that the next day the people of Kamoya awoke to not only see a vast island in the middle of the great lake, but also an island mountain that towered high up into the sky above all other things.

19 As the people of Kamoya stared in incredulity at the island, Enoch came and explained all that Elohim the Mother had told to him in his dream the last night.

20 As he finished speaking, twelve men of great height appeared among them and their appearance was startling, for though Enoch had just spoken of their coming, none had seen how they had come to be among them.

21 And the Kamoyans marveled at the twelve sons of Elohim that had just come, for the smallest one was more than a head taller than the tallest Kamoyan.

22 And it came to pass that one of the twelve came up to Enoch and falling to one knee, he bowed his head, saying, "Enoch, blessed prophet of Elohim, I am Brontiis, and these are my brothers, sons of glory, of the Father and Mother, even as you are, and the twelve sons and daughters of Eden were.

23 We have been sent down by the Elohim to bring more Celestine Light unto the world, lest it should vanish before its time."

24 Enoch smiled at Brontiis and embraced him in welcome. Now Enoch was not a small man, but was large in stature. Nevertheless, in his embrace his arms but encircled the waist of Brontiis and his head came but to his chest.

25 And it came to pass that after remaining with them for a short time, the twelve sons of Elohim departed to the lands afar that they might find virgins of greatness for wives as they had been commanded by the Elohim.

26 During the current and following moon, teams of workers traveled to the island and began to construct new homes for the Kamoyans.

27 Enoch and the Elders decided to not abandon their village on the shore of Lake Kamoya, but to remain living there for at least a solar cycle while the vegetation grew upon the island, which they named Latani, meaning Abundant Fortress.

28 One solar cycle had nearly gone by, and the attacks by clans upon the Kamoyans had increased and intensified with every passing moon so much so that all of the women and children had been ferried to the island for permanent resettlement by the seventh moon.

29 By the eleventh moon, another eight men had been killed by raiding parties, and Enoch was in Kamoya directing thirty Kamoyans in the final disassembly and burning of the village so it could not be occupied and used by one of the clans.

30 As the Kamoyans were completing their final task in the abandoned village, they were attacked by over one hundred warriors of the Scasdon clan.

31 Having burned their buildings, toppled their stones, and removed and floated the logs of the palisade to Latani, the Kamoyans had no place of cover to take refuge in, and ten men were felled by the rocks of slings before the Kamoyans even had time to react to the attack.

32 Gamiel, a mighty warrior chief of the Kamoyans, quickly took charge commanding, "Retreat quickly to the tri-canoes, six encircle and protect the prophet, all others begin such an onslaught of stones from your slings that the enemy dare not lift his head. Leave none behind, be they dead or wounded."

33 As Gamiel commanded, so it was, and under the cover of a hail of stones from their slings, the Kamoyans succeeded in reaching their tri-canoes, but the Scasdons charged them as they boarded; as they could not both board and fight, several others were felled by stones even as they pushed their canoes out into the safety of the great lake.

34 Then a mighty roar was heard from behind the Scasdons and all eyes, both the Scasdons' and the Kamoyans', turned to see the source of the enormous sound, and there running down the hillside toward the battle was a gigantic man, one of the twelve sons of Elohim.

35 The Kamoyans knew him immediately, for he was the largest of all of the twelve sons, easily twice the size of an ordinary man, and he had flaming red hair such as was not commonly seen. His name was Tanonza.

36 For both the Kamoyans and the Scasdons, it seemed for a few moments as if time had stopped as everyone stared at the living mountain that was rapidly descending upon them in a rage.

37 As he neared, the chief of the Scasdons roused his warriors to begin slinging rocks at the man creature. Most were still too petrified by the raging giant running toward them to react, but some did begin to load their slings.

38 But before they could launch their missiles, each was struck dead by a rock to the head, hurled by Tanonza, not with a sling, but with his bare hand and the mighty strength of his arm, which flung his missiles with such rapid speed that it seemed that he killed two Scasdons with every stride.

39 Spying the chief commanding the others, Tanonza reached into the sack of rocks that hung about his neck to waist level and, aiming with sure accuracy, felled the chief with such power that he was lifted off his feet by the impact and thrown far backward.

40 Seeing their chief felled by a man such as they had never before seen or imagined, the remaining Scasdons panicked and quickly fled in chaos in several directions.

41 Tanonza came to the empty beach and fell to his knees, and bowing his head with his face into the sand, he began to weep in great sobs.

42 The Kamoyans on the lake quickly returned to shore, and Enoch came to Tanonza and comforted him, saying, "You have saved us, Tanonza. I know why it is that you weep, for to kill any living thing is a sorrow and our own kin, a tragedy. But in defense of our lives, Elohim looks with understanding and forgiveness upon your actions."

43 But the words of Enoch did not soothe him, and Tanonza remained as he was weeping loudly with his face in the sand and his hands to the sides of his head so that none could see him and he could see nothing.

44 Then a most beautiful woman appeared among them. She came down from the hill that Tanonza had descended. She came up to him and put her hand upon his neck and said unto him, "Tanonza of the sun, weep not, for on this day you have protected not just the life of me and these men, but have insured the future of an entire people.

45 "Deeply sad was the deed you had to do, but by doing it, you have put a great fear into those who would harm the people of the light that you have spoken to me so much about, and in that, I think you have preserved many more than are here upon the beach this day."

46 At her words, Tanonza looked up into her eyes. Despite the sand upon him, his face was handsome, and she held his large head between her two hands and kissed him lightly upon his sand-covered forehead.

47 Tanonza looked from her to Enoch and said unto them, "I have been upon this world for such a short time, barely one solar cycle. I came from a most beautiful place where all people were good and no man thought to injure another.

48 Though most cannot remember their life before this life, it has been given to the twelve sons of Elohim to remember all things.

49 I was shown this world before I came. I saw the evil that men do to one another, but in my naivety, I thought that it would not be a part of my life.

50 I have traveled far now in this world of men and save for this people and those of the goddess standing beside me, I have seen little worth saving, for men fall upon beasts and other men with a lust for killing, and when they are not killing, they are living in all manner of debauchery, without thought for Elohim, the living God of this world.

51 Now I have killed and though I understand that I am forgiven, for it was in defense of those I love, nevertheless, I feel so far now from my Father and Mother in Heaven. The sadness of this feeling is what overwhelms me with grief."

52 Then Tanonza stood and wiped the sand and tears off his face and clothes, and holding the hand of the woman beside him, who was also uncommonly tall for a woman, even as tall as Enoch, he said unto Enoch, "This is Eden, she whom I have found to be my wife. Her father is Yocahtan Ku of the clan of Amorites. He is a good man and named his daughter after the garden of his ancestors.

53 In my travels, I came upon her people, all whom are taller than the people of other clans I encountered.

54 Elsewhere, I was attacked at every turn, and only among the Amorites was I welcomed, as were three of my brothers who traveled with me.

55 I am the first to return here as we were commanded by the Elohim, but my brothers among the Amorites shall soon follow with the women who would be their wives."

56 Enoch beamed with happiness upon hearing the words of Tanonza and welcomed Eden, saying, "Most gracious lady, it is our honor to have you among us. You are obviously the mate of the soul for Tanonza, and you are most welcome to become one with the Children of Light upon the island of Latani."

57 "Thank you," Eden said, bowing her head toward Enoch in acknowledgment.

58 And it came to pass that the Children of Light upon Latani prospered on their island sanctuary and never again lost men to the clans upon the mainland, for seldom did they venture off their island except to catch fish upon the lake or to mine metals in the mountains to the south.

59 And Enoch and all the people prayed mightily to the Elohim for many a day that their island would be protected from all harm, and so it was.

60 During the generation that followed, from the mountain upon the island, vast quantities of fine white marble were quarried and the most beautiful city that had ever been built upon the

earth was raised, with tall circular towers with spires gilded in gold reaching up to the heavens.

61 They named the city Enoch after the prophet to whom the Elohim had spoken and who had guided them to a new land of Eden.

62 Of the twelve sons of Elohim, eight returned after some time to the island with a virgin from the lands afar to be their wife. And of the four, which did not return, Enoch inquired of the Elohim and was shown that one had been killed and three had been asked by Elohim to travel to lands far and away and that these would never return.

63 And the people of Enoch became exceedingly righteous in every way, and the spirit of Elohim filled them so much so that they were able to discover the gifts that had been given to them by Elohim, even the power to move objects with their thoughts and to speak silently with one another in their minds when they desired, and many other gifts of power.

64 Empowered by their gifts, the people of Latani were no longer fearful to travel away from their island sanctuary, for they were always aware of any danger before it fell upon them and could either avoid it or counter it with their Celestine gifts of power.

65 And Elohim the Mother came to Enoch in a dream, and she said unto him, "Enoch, it is given to men to have strength of body and to women to have strength of the gifts of Heaven and to each a little of the other, but only to a rare man or woman to have both, even one such as you, Enoch the Prophet.

66 Therefore, encourage now the women to discover and claim their special gifts of Heaven that they might know the power that is the birthright of all women of virtue.

67 Show unto them the gifts of light we have given unto you, for there is naught that you can do that they cannot also do, save speak with the Elohim for all of the people.

68 Let them gather together to learn of their gifts and how to use them for great good that the people of the city of Enoch may be lifted closer to the Celestine Light of Heaven."

69 And it came to pass that Enoch did as Elohim the Mother commanded, and the women of Latani gathered together and Enoch showed unto them all the special gifts the Elohim had shown unto him that he had never before shown unto any other.

70 And the women of Latani began to practice that which Enoch had shown unto them, and they called upon their Celestine gifts and their gifts came to them, and great were the wonders which they wrought, even the moving of immense stones without the hand of man touching them, great knowledge of herbs and healing, and the ability to affect many things by coming together in unison and intent.

71 And the women of Latani joined hands and came together in one great circle, then separated into three, with a smaller circle within the larger and a still smaller circle within it.

72 As the men of Latani watched, the women sang a prayer of rhyme; louder and louder they sang it, with each circle moving opposite of the circles surrounding it at an ever-increasing speed.

73 Then in unison, they suddenly stopped, and lifting their hands together toward the heavens, they let out a final shout of joy and triumph.

74 From that day forth, it was as if a great spell had been cast over the mainland about Lake Kamoya, and never again did any member of another clan come within the boundaries of the land of Kamoya except they came in peace, and the people of Latani walked freely once more upon the mainland, without fear.

75 And it came to pass that Elohim the Mother appeared again to Enoch in a dream and said unto him, "The people of the city of Enoch have become more virtuous and righteous than any people who have ever lived upon the earth so much so that the earth shall soon no longer be able to hold them, and they shall be lifted to a higher glory without tasting death.

76 But the world beyond the city of Enoch has descended far into darkness, and even as the city of Enoch is being pulled to a greater glory. Sadly, the cities of the earth are being pulled toward a great destruction by the perversities of the people.

77 But this is not solely because of their own wantonness, and because of that, the day of destruction is held in abeyance that they might still repent and turn to the light.

78 For they have been led astray and their own dark propensities encouraged by their leaders who once served the Elohim.

79 Therefore, despite their wickedness, the people of the world shall be given one more opportunity to turn from darkness and seek the light. Yet most will not, for the pleasure of their moments of depravity blinds them to the eons of darkness they are creating for their inheritance and the emptiness they create in their daily life.

80 But if those who are great lights of virtue stand before them and speak to them and show them a better way, there are a few who will repent and seek the greater light and be saved.

81 Therefore, consider prayerfully who among the people of Latani might go into the world to seek out these few to save, knowing they will never again be able to return to this place of paradise while they still live upon the earth.

82 For this place and all of its people shall soon rise to a greater glory, but those walking in the world will be left behind when the city of Enoch rises to its glory."

83 Enoch was startled by all that the Mother told unto him and asked, "How can a man leave all that is light to be in the darkness, knowing he can never return again to the light and his family and friends?"

84 Elohim the Mother answered him, saying, "Remember time, Enoch. It is not what men suppose. Despite the darkness that surrounds them and stains them, the pure in heart will always be drawn back into the Celestine Light and be with their family and friends in eternal glory. Though it may not be upon the day of your ascension, it shall be upon another day, and the time between will be as nothing.

85 And great is the reward for the valiant, for the Elohim are the Celestine Light, and when light is given in service upon the earth by the pure in heart, greater light flows to them from the Elohim and they shall be lifted even higher in their eternal reward."

86 The Mother prepared to leave and walk out of Enoch's dream, but Enoch pleaded with her to stay one moment more, and he asked her, "Most high Mother of all that is, you spoke of those who once served the Elohim, who have led the people into sin. I would know more of this if you will, for never did I suppose that those who served Elohim could lead men into sin."

87 The Mother replied, "I will answer you, but reveal not my words, save to those who have a great faith and understanding of the Celestine Light, lest they fall away not being able to comprehend the immensity of life beyond the world they know.

88 In the Celestine Realm, where the Elohim dwell, there are many forms of man in many states of exaltation.

89 None are there who have not been drawn to that great light, by the worthiness of their lives.

90 Nevertheless, there is not one who is bound by any power, force, or coercion, to continue to be good, to be sons and daughters of the light, and the choice to do evil is still present, for it is only in having to fight the darkness that ever abides within that the light of the soul is empowered in its brightness.

91 There are some spirit children in the Celestine Realm who have existed for a great time among us and have yet to come down onto an earth to abide their spirit within a physical tabernacle of flesh and bone, for they have so great a love for where they are they cannot bear to depart.

92 The eldest of these, we call to fill duties as angels, and they are given glorified bodies of flesh and bone that they can fulfill their missions whether it is on Heaven or earth.

93 This is not the fullness of the glory given to those who have been resurrected, but sufficient that they can exist in both Heaven and on earth, which is a gift given only to angels.

94 In time, as the angels who were male looked down upon the mortals of earth, some began to lust after the comely and beautiful daughters of man, and they did not fight the darkness that rose within them.

95 They came to us and asked the Elohim to be sent down onto the earth as full grown men

and not as babes, even as had the twelve sons of Elohim, that they might take daughters of men as wives.

96 But this we forbid, for they were not as advanced as the twelve sons, and it was needful for them to complete their full progression, beginning as babes that they might grow into the fullness of the Celestine Light.

97 Our decision angered many of the male angels, and they did not abide by our words. Two hundred cast off their callings as angels and departed from the Celestine Realm and came upon the earth that they could take unto them the daughters of men and fulfill their unrighteous lusts.

98 These fallen angels have sowed great evil in the hearts of men. They have revealed some of the secrets of Heaven to men and taught them of war and led them into even greater unrighteousness of lust.

99 Therefore, because of them, the Day of Judgment upon man does not yet fall, and there is time for some from Latani to go into the world and bring back the Celestine Light to those who still seek it."

100 Now Enoch was incredulous at the words of the Mother, for he had a memory of the Celestine Realms and never imagined that those so high would fall so greatly. And he asked of her, "I remember many of my brothers and sisters who served as angels. Who are those who have fallen?"

101 And the Mother answered him, saying, "Semyaza was their leader, and he persuaded the others, showing them the fairness and beauty of the women of your earth and telling them he was going down to take a mortal for a wife, even if they all were too afraid.

102 But the others said they were not afraid and they too would go down and take mortal women as wives.

103 Then Semyaza said unto them, 'I fear you will not agree to do this deed, and I alone shall have to pay the penalty of a great sin.' But they answered him, saying, 'Let us all swear an oath, and all bind ourselves by mutual vows not to abandon this plan but to do this thing.' Then they all swore together and bound themselves with mutual vows upon it.

104 And they descended upon the earth shortly after you and Jared and Micah came down, and they have been a plague upon it since that day.

105 "Semyaza is their leader and Araklba, Rameel, Kokablel, Tamlel, Ramlel, Danel, Ezeqeel, Baraqiyal, Asael, Armaros, Batarel, Azazel, Ananel, Zaqiel, Samsapeel, Satarel, Turel, Yomyael, Sariel are each chiefs of ten.

106 Each group went into a different land upon the earth that they might spread the secrets of the Celestine Realms far and wide and pervert the light of men with knowledge beyond their understanding.

107 And all took unto themselves women, some as wives and some not, and some chose one and others more, not with love and righteousness, but with lust and perversion.

108 And they began to go unto them and to defile them, and they taught them charms and evil enchantments and curses. Their wives and women became pregnant, and they bore children who were taught in the evil ways of their fathers, and many of these have fostered a blood lust upon the land and they lay waste to everything before them.

109 They taught men to make swords and knives and shields and breastplates and made known to them the metals of the earth and the art of working them into intricate bracelets and ornaments, as well as the use of antimony and the workings of all types of costly stones, and the creation of all coloring tinctures and the coloring of the eyelids.

110 These things brought out much darkness in the people of the world and there arose great vanity, greed, jealousy, coveting, sexual depravity, and violence because of the fallen angels, for many people have been corrupted in all their ways."

111 Enoch was astounded by all that the Mother told unto him, and he asked her, "Why have the Elohim allowed this great calamity upon the world and upon the innocents who remain here? Would my own people not have been slain by the marauding clans if these fallen angels

had never come to earth and spewed their poison?"

112 The Mother reached out to him and touched him in his dream and said unto him, "We are the Watchers. We do not intercede, save we must to fulfill the destiny of man or because of prayers of great faith and perseverance from the righteous.

113 Nor need we, for the power has been given to all of our children of spirit, both those that walk in the Celestine Light and those that walk in the darkness, to change their lives and the world to the reality of their desire with faith, love, knowledge, and action.

114 Though it grieves us to see the pain they sometimes suffer and inflict upon one another, we must allow them to learn from their experiences and give them the freedom to grow into their greatness, even when such freedom can cause great misery and even death."

115 Enoch awoke the next day, understanding many things he had not comprehended before because of his dream. But the knowledge of why evil propagated by the fallen angels occurred on the earth did not take away the pain in his heart from the losses inflicted upon the innocent, and he grieved and was quiet and reflective for many days thereafter.

116 Many years passed following Enoch's dream, even unto the birth of three more generations. The city of Enoch and the lands of Latani and Kamoya became like a different world from the rest of the places upon the earth, for the people were exceedingly righteous and good, even unto the perfection of mortality.

117 They were of one heart and one mind in all things of virtue, and upon their lands, there was great peace.

118 Of the darkness upon the face of the earth, they knew little, for few ventured beyond the domains of their homeland, for in it they found everything they desired. And it was only through the stories told by traders who visited from the surrounding clans that they understood how different the world beyond was.

119 When Enoch was an old man, even in his 362nd year, the Mother came to him again in a dream and said unto him, "Enoch, the time for your immortality is at hand and that of all the people who are counted among you.

120 They have found great favor in our eyes because of their exceeding goodness and virtue, even unto the perfection of their mortal tabernacle such as has never been done before on your earth. In their righteousness, they exceed even the very first Edenites from the dawn of man.

121 And we marvel that these glorious lights have done all of this surrounded by a world of darkness, without a memory of the great Celestine Light from which they have come, save for a few such as you.

122 Marvelous is their faith and love and focus and purpose. In this, they have earned a great reward, even to pass from mortality to immortality without tasting death, to go from an imperfect body which they have nourished so lovingly to a body perfected which shall sustain and uplift them for eternity.

123 Every man, woman, and child numbered among you has earned this reward, and it shall come to pass in one moon from this day.

124 Therefore, go to your people and tell them these glad tidings that they might prepare themselves for a greater glory.

125 As they have been together in life, so shall they be together in eternity.

126 But as I have told you before, it is not good that all the light of the people of Enoch should be taken from the earth, for there are still souls upon the world that might see the light and remember who they are, even sons and daughters of God, and turn from the darkness.

127 That even one more soul might be saved, go unto your people now and say that the Elohim ask some of them to stay upon the earth to bring light to those who will receive it, that even one more soul might be saved.

128 Not of all do we ask this, but only of twelve.

129 Let them go with their eyes open and not naively or with false illusions, for the darkness will come upon many with sore trials and tribulations.

130 But this is our promise to the brave and the valiant who would forgo rising to Heaven with their loved ones and instead remain for a time in the world of darkness: They shall never be shaken in their peace or purity, despite the turmoil around them.
131 When they have done all that they can do and the world will hear them no more, they shall not die, but like those that went before, they shall be changed in the twinkling of an eye from mortality to immortality, and they shall rise with the speed of thought to the Celestine Realms to be once more with those that they love and to so remain forever more."
132 And it came to pass that Enoch did as the Mother directed and spoke to his people of all that would come to pass and of the great reward they had earned by their exceeding righteousness, even to never taste death, but to be changed in the twinkling of an eye from mortality to immortality.
133 And great was the joy of the people of Enoch.
134 When Enoch explained that the Elohim desired twelve to stay behind upon the earth and that by their light, they might still guide some in the darkness to the fulfillment of their soul, all the people of Enoch shouted as one that they should be numbered among the twelve and that they would stay upon the earth and do the bidding of the Elohim.
135 Enoch smiled and was thrilled to see all of his people united as one even in this. And he said unto them, "The Mother has said only twelve, but in this I am sure she meant twelve families, for surely families who have lived each day together should not be parted.
136 So it would be fair to all, we will draw lots to choose the twelve families that shall remain."
137 And it came to pass that the following day a large, empty cauldron was filled with stones, one for each family in the city of Enoch and the lands of Latani and Kamoya. All of the stones were green, save twelve that were white.
138 One by one, the heads of each family came forth and drew a stone from the cauldron, until all had drawn.
139 Among the twelve that drew the white stones were the families of Darlonz, the grandson of Tanonza, and Noah, the great-grandson of Enoch.
140 And it came to pass that seven days later, the twelve families that drew white stones said good-bye to the people of Enoch and all of their friends and extended family whom they had known and loved so well.
141 But during the three days before their departure, there was the greatest celebration and feast that had ever been known among the people of Enoch.
142 And there were no tears shed. In everyone's heart was only joy, and even among those who were departing into the world, there was a peace upon their hearts that all would be well and that soon they would be together again with their friends and the community they loved.
143 And it came to pass that the twelve families departed out into the world of darkness, each in a different direction, to fulfill the desire of the Elohim to bring their lights into the world so that even one more soul might be saved from the darkness.
144 The following day, Enoch climbed to the top of the tallest white tower in the gleaming city of Enoch so that he might be seen and heard as he spoke to all of the people.
145 And everyone who was of the people of Enoch and lived a life of virtue and righteousness came into the city of Enoch from all the lands of Latani and Kamoya.
146 Enoch spoke in a loud but melodious voice such that every ear heard him, even those that were far away from the high tower from which he spoke.
147 And after saying a prayer of thanksgiving, he said unto them, "Brothers and sisters of light, my dearest friends, clasp the hand of the person next to you on each side and let every person be holding the hand of the person next to them on both sides so that there are none who are not holding the hand of the person to their right and the person to their left, be they man, woman, or child. Then let us give thanks as a people for the many blessings the Elohim have continuously poured upon us. Let us be of one heart and one mind and one purpose."
148 And it came to pass that the people of Enoch did as he bid and held hands united. And

Enoch came down from the tall tower and came among the people, holding the hand of his two wives, one on each side.

149 And the people raised their hands above their heads and looked up into the heavens and spoke with one voice, and their hearts beat in unison as one and they thought the same thought with one mind and joined together in love in one purpose. And they cried out with joy, "The Celestine Light of Elohim is upon us! We are the light! We are the light! We are the light!"

150 Then with a mighty rumble that was heard and felt far and wide across the land, the entire city of Enoch and a great swath of land beneath it pulled free from the earth and rose up above the ground and, in a blinding light, ascended majestically up into the sky.

151 All across the land of darkness far and away, the denizens of the clans trembled at the great rumbling and shaking of the earth, and looking toward the city of Enoch, they saw it rising into the sky, emanating a brilliant light like unto the sun, and they were struck with a fear such as they had never known.

152 Each of the twelve families of the city of Enoch that had remained upon the earth also heard the great rumbling and felt the earth move as the city of Enoch tore free of its earthly bonds and began ascending to Heaven.

153 And every member of the twelve families looked back upon the city of Enoch as it rose up into the heavens, and they were overcome with love filling every fiber of their being as their hearts beat as one with their brothers and sisters who were rising above the world to their glory. And with tears of happiness in their eyes, they experienced a joy and fulfillment such as they had never known or imagined.

CHAPTER 6

The Coming of the Ark

Elohim the Father speaks to Noah in a dream and tells him that the earth must be cleansed to be rid of the wickedness that now dominates the world. But Noah is given forty years to preach the light, to see if the light can grow and the earth spared. Fallen angels are seen to be the root of the evil upon the world, and Elohim creates the damned class of demons from the former angels and condemns them to a horrible fate. When Noah fails in his forty-year quest to bring light back to the world, Elohim tells him the cleansing must come. All the Children of Light from across the world and thousands of animals converge on Kamoya to await the coming of the Ark. When all are gathered into the great valley, an enormous V-shaped ship appears in the sky and everyone watches in awe as the Ark descends to hover above them. So great is its size that the Children of Light and all the animals easily find space within it, and they vanish like a star into the sky while the earth and all the people remaining upon it await their fate.

And it came to pass that after the days of Enoch, the people of the earth became even
more wicked, and save for some of the descendants of the twelve families that had
remained upon the earth when the city of Enoch ascended into Heaven, there were
precious few people who walked in the light.
2 Elohim the Father came to Noah, the great-grandson of Enoch, in a dream and spoke
with him as one man speaks to another. And he said unto him, "Noah, we are distressed greatly
because of the wickedness that man has become, for most all of our children of spirit are losing
great parts of their eternity to darkness because of their wickedness in mortality, which expands
each day upon the earth because the light that remains is too small and weak to hold back the
darkness.
3 "We are considering now whether man upon the earth should be consumed that the earth
and all life therein might be renewed and man might begin anew unburdened by the great
weight of darkness. What think you, man of light?"
4 Noah looked at Elohim in wonder that he had asked his opinion, and he answered saying,
"Great Father, who am I to know the course that God should take?"
5 Elohim spoke to him again, saying, "You are he whom we have called to be our prophet, to
hear our voices, to see our faces, and to speak to those in the light that they might know our will
and of the things to come.
6 "It is your world of which we speak and your mortality. Because we love you, son of the son
of the son of Enoch, we desire to know your thoughts concerning these things."

7 Emboldened by the words of the Father, Noah spoke now with confidence, saying, "Great Elohim, I think you should stay your hand and not destroy man upon the earth, for there is much other life and animals, many that are innocent and pure that would also see the end of their lives before their time, and they do not deserve an early end to their mortal progression.

8 So too are there many souls of men upon this earth whom I believe would turn to the light if they were not surrounded by so much darkness.

9 Therefore, take not man from the earth and so much of other life therein, but take those fallen angels from the earth that have brought so much of the darkness upon it that they can no longer spew their poison. Then perhaps the light can again begin to overcome the darkness."

10 Elohim considered the words of Noah and he was pleased, and he said unto him, "Well thought, son of the son of the son of Enoch. It shall be done even as you have spoken, but not entirely in the way you have imagined. Sleep now and I will return to you another night."

11 And Noah slept, but the next day, he remembered all that he had dreamed.

12 And it came to pass that Elohim the Father appeared atop the tallest mountain upon the earth, and with a mighty voice, he commanded, "Come!" and the air reverberated with thunder at his word, and the earth shook and great avalanches of snow rushed down the mountainsides, and in the blink of an eye, all of the fallen angels that were upon the earth appeared before him.

13 Shivering in the bitter cold on the high mountain and being suddenly compelled to appear before Elohim the Father, they shook with great fright. And the Father's light was brighter than the sun so much so that they could not see his face, but only the outline of his body, and they cowered into the snow in a futile attempt to hide from his light.

14 And he spoke unto them, saying, "It grieves me to see how low you who were so high have fallen, even to the corruption of the people of an entire world, simply to satisfy your lusts that are here today and gone tomorrow.

15 Great gifts of power and ability were given to you because of your virtue and faithfulness, but you were corrupted by the power and lured into darkness by your vanities and unrighteous lusts.

16 Despite all of the evil you have caused, we have stayed our hand upon you, hoping you would remember who you are and return to the light from whence you came and bring again the light to the world that you were called to bring.

17 But year upon year has passed and one generation has been added to another, and instead of returning to the light, you have darkened the earth almost beyond recognition from the Eden we created.

18 And not even one of you has taken the tiniest step back into the light. Therefore, it is a great sadness to see that you have become unredeemable and your eternal progression must end."

19 At the Father's last words, one of the fallen angels rose to speak, but before the first word could leave his lips, the Father pointed his finger at him and the fallen angel was entirely encased within a thick block of ice.

20 "None of you shall speak!" the Father commanded with thunder. "You are no longer even worthy to exist in the divine bodies made in our image.

21 By your actions, you have changed the destiny of man and forced us, who intended to be Watchers only, to intercede.

22 We gave you life, and we could take all life from you, but that would be a blessing upon you, ending your existence without a taste of the suffering you have caused others.

23 Therefore, this is your fate for eternity: Your progression is damned. You are condemned to never again have a physical or immortal body of flesh and bone, but shall forever more be beings of dark spirit only.

24 You shall continue to have all of the desires of a physical body, but shall never again be able to satisfy or even taste the least of them. You shall be forever tormented because of your unfulfilled passions so much so that you will crave to be even a worm, to feel again the pleasures of the physical. But it will be your eternal torment to forever desire that which you will never

again have.

25 You shall still have the ability to influence the minds of the weak in the most subtle of ways, but the sons and daughters of light shall have the power to destroy you in pain and anguish. But because you can never die, you will suffer a thousand deaths, over and over again.

26 Nor shall you ever see your numbers grow or diminish, and you shall grow to hate one another even more than you have despised the sons and daughters of men.

27 You who once were among the chosen of our children are now lower than the lowest of all life. You are demons, you are cursed forever to be what you have become, and that shall be less than the least of all life.

28 "So be it!" As he spoke, the Father waved his hand, and in the blink of an eye, all of the fallen angels vanished from the physical realm. From that moment on, they became beings without substance except the substance of darkness which they were. So it is even today.

29 The following night, Elohim the Mother appeared to Noah in a dream, and she said unto him, "Noah, the fallen angels have been condemned to never again be able to taste any of the pleasures they desire. They are still upon the earth, but without physical form or substance and now can only subtly influence the weakest of men.

30 "Nevertheless, the greater threat remains, which is not the adversaries outside of man, but the adversary inside of man, even his own dark side.

31 No being that exists is without both light and darkness, even the Elohim, for it is necessary to have opposition, even within yourself, that the light may grow stronger as it holds back and overcomes the darkness.

32 The people of the earth have given up their light and completely embraced their darkness. By their great fall, they have made all the world around them a dreary and forlorn place, even so much that the world must be washed clean and begin anew unless you can reverse the tide and show that the light returns and the darkness abates.

33 Now that the fallen angels are no more upon the earth, you shall have forty years to preach the light and help others to turn back the tide of darkness within them and that the light may again flow with great strength. Enlist all within your family and all that you meet who are still guided by the light in this cause.

34 When forty years have passed, we shall weigh the light and darkness of the world again on the scales. If light has gained even the smallest amount over darkness, the world shall be spared.

35 But if darkness has continued to gain over light, then we must intercede, for this is not the destiny of our children of spirit, and the world shall be washed clean to begin anew."

36 Noah heard the words of Elohim and immediately went forth and did as they had commanded. From that day, he went unto the world as a prophet of Elohim, proclaiming, "Repent, repent, for the terrible day of God comes unless you repent."

37 Noah also sent his three sons, Shem, Ham, and Yapeth, out into the world to preach repentance, and for forty years, they also labored.

38 The brothers took turns traveling away for six months and then returning and remaining home. When one arrived, another would leave, while the brother that returned would remain home with his family for one year to tend to their needs.

39 But Noah traveled into lands far away, and sometimes his family did not see him for as many as three or four years at a time.

40 And the women feared not while the men were away, for great was the power of the spells of protection they wove and no harm ever came upon them or any of their children from beasts or men.

41 And great was their joy whenever Noah or his sons would find someone still living in the light.

42 To each of these, they gave encouragement to labor among their brethren that they might still find others to turn from the darkness into the light.

43 Each was given instructions that on the day forty years after Noah had spoken to Elohim,

they must all be at Kamoya to hear the words of the Elohim and discover the fate of man.

44 Thus, it came to pass that forty years after Noah and his sons had begun to preach repentance, the land of Kamoya was swelled by the Children of Light who came from near and far to be upon that spot on that day, as Noah had directed.

45 Counting only the adults, there were 144 Children of Light who were in Kamoya that day. Among them were people of many hues and sizes, including Darlonz the giant and his family. And everywhere there were children.

46 Seven days earlier, Noah had gone atop a high hill to fast and pray and communicate with the Elohim. When he came down into Kamoya, his hair had turned all white, and he gathered the people to him and spoke with great solemness.

47 And he said unto them, "The Elohim have weighed the light and darkness of the people of the world in the balance and found them destitute, and the great and terrible day of God is upon us.

48 The world shall be cleansed, and God, who has given all men life, shall take it away now from many who had received such a great gift.

49 From this day forth and continuing for forty years, the earth shall be convulsed in great agony. Some mountains shall spit up liquid fire, which shall cover much land. Other mountains shall sink into the sea and disappear, while some places that are plains shall rise up into mountains.

50 Rain shall fall such as it has never fallen in ferocious storms with terrifying winds such as you cannot imagine in your worst nightmares, and great shall be the floods in various and sundry places.

51 Even more calamitous, immense storms shall come upon the seas, and they shall spurt as fountains and shall assault the lands upon the shores with terrible fury.

52 In some places, crops shall fail for lack of water; in others, because of too much, and all the people of the earth shall fear and tremble knowing not what shall become of them and a great many shall perish.

53 But because of the convulsions of the earth, those that remain shall remember the power of the God, who made them, and comprehend how small they are compared to the immensity and greatness of God. Perhaps after all of this, they will turn again to the light and be spared an endless time of darkness in the life to come."

54 The people in Kamoya showed many emotions as they heard the words of Noah; some feared, and others excited and wondered. And many voices cried out at once, seeking answers for the questions that had come into their minds.

55 "What of the innocent animals?" cried one.

56 "What of our families who are not with us?" shouted another.

57 "What will become of us?" asked another in earnestness, and many others repeated his words crying unto Noah, "What will become of us?"

58 Noah raised his hands and answered them, saying, "The animals shall be spared as much as is possible. They shall have time to flee to higher ground and escape the floods and shall be warned by Elohim to move away from the places that shall be consumed by liquid fire.

59 "As for your families who are not among us, if they return to the light, they might yet be spared, but that is beyond our power to know, for their fate is in their hands not ours, for they are the ones who have created it and they are the only ones who have the power to change it.

60 As for us, I have something to tell you which will seem the most strange thing you have ever heard, but I tell you this in all seriousness as the prophet of Elohim, so do not make light of that which I shall reveal to you, even though it will be beyond your understanding.

61 Our Heavenly Mother came to me and spoke to me several times concerning this, for even I could not at first comprehend the fullness of her words.

62 Tomorrow upon this spot, a ship shall come for us, but it is not a ship of this world. Nor is it a ship of the sea. Verily, it is a ship of the sky.

63 I have seen this ship in my dreams and surely it is real, for it is something I never could

have imagined, and it is unlike anything I have ever known.

64 The ship is black as night with lights like little suns upon its edge. And it shimmers like waves of heat upon the desert. It is shaped like the wings of a giant bird, and it is more immense than anything you can use to compare.

65 Days before this day, Elohim called many of the animals of the world to come to this place, those that would be in danger of not surviving the catastrophes, and they shall converge here when the sun rises tomorrow and shall go into the ship with us.

66 Ask me not where we shall go, for I know not. Nor ask me how a ship can be in the sky without falling to the earth, for that too I know not, save to say that with Elohim, all things are possible."

67 When Noah stopped speaking, many others began speaking at once, and many questions again flew toward Noah.

68 And though they were Children of Light, one and all, many spoke with doubts, not only that there could be such a thing as an enormous ship of the sky, but even if it were true, how would the animals survive the gauntlet of hungry clans to reach the land of Kamoya? And how would they who had gathered survive on a ship when they had only a few days of food among them?

69 Hearing all these things, Noah spoke again unto the people, saying, "Doubt not the Elohim, and have a true faith in your hearts. You have trusted the teachings of Elohim all of your lives for things small and great, and they have not failed you.

70 Do not waver now in your faith simply because you are asked to trust in something beyond your understanding, for surely all things shall be made known to those who hold fast to their faith."

71 And it came to pass that the people of Noah did as he exhorted and held strong to their faith.

72 The following day, as the sun rose, a loud clamor was heard coming toward Kamoya. And expecting the arrival of the animals, the people went to the top of the nearest rise that they could see for themselves the source. And great was their wonder at what they saw.

73 Coming from every direction were animals of all descriptions, birds of many colors in the air and beasts of every type upon the ground. There were snakes and elephants, mice and lions, and many creatures that no one had ever before seen.

74 People of the clans could be seen in the distance staring at the animals as they passed, but they looked at them confounded and attacked them not.

75 In only a few hours time, the small valley of Kamoya was filled with animals and the air overhead and the trees all around with multicolored birds of great variety.

76 Noah called all the people to gather together in a group, and they came to him, standing near the lake upon the original site of the first Kamoya that had been torn down and burned when the people of Enoch had moved to the island of Latani on the lake.

77 Then Noah raised his staff and pointed to the eastern sky. All eyes turned to see a large immensely bright light approaching with the speed of a shooting star.

78 As it drew close, its light dimmed until it was gone altogether, and hovering over their heads, low above the nearby hills, was a great black V, like the wings of some monstrous bird, with lights like suns upon its edges.

79 So great was its size that though the point of the V was centered over their heads, the expanse of the wings covered the entire valley of Kamoya, and the tips could not be seen before they were lost from view beyond the rising hills.

80 Then before the amazed eyes of all upon the ground, an opening appeared in the bottom of the ship on the right wing and a vast ramp unfolded, extending downward toward the ground and doubling back upon itself several times.

81 As the ramp descended, three small figures, appearing like men, walked down upon it, even to the point that it touched the ground, and two men and a woman wearing strange clothing

stepped off the ramp and onto the earth.

82 The people of Noah parted in awe that the strange visitors from the sky could pass, and the three walked directly toward Noah and stood before him.

83 And the woman, who stood between the two men, held her hands near her chest in the prayer position and said unto Noah, "Greetings, good prophet of Elohim. I am Jelatana." And pointing to her right and then left, she continued, "And these are my counselors, Rabak and Gensai."

84 Then she pointed to the vast ship that hovered soundlessly in the sky above them, and she said unto him, "This is our home. It is called Ark. We have come at the command of Elohim to take you and your people and all the animals of your world that have gathered here, upon the Ark. Will you come with us now?"

85 Noah was speechless for a moment, overwhelmed by the strangeness of all that he was seeing. But soon he nodded his head slowly and said unto her with awe in his voice, "We too have heard the call of Elohim, and we are ready. We will come."

CHAPTER 7

The Great Flood

The Children of Light depart with Noah on the Ark as the earth sinks into forty years of convulsions, cataclysms, and great storms. Aboard the Ark, a ship from another world, Noah and his people learn many wondrous things. As they return to earth after forty years, they begin to create the civilization that would come to be known as the mythical Atlantis.

And it came to pass that Noah and all the Children of Light, gathered at Kamoya, walked up the ramp and into the ship of the sky, their eyes filled with wonder at every step.

2 They were followed by great hoards of animals that entered the ship in various ways. Birds flew up into the portal with ease, while most of the animals took much longer, walking up the long switchback ramp.

3 Over one hundred people came down from the sky ship and shepherded the animals who were small or crawled or moved slowly, leading some and carrying others and taking care to keep all the animals in the center away from the precipitous edge of the ramp.

4 And the animals, though wild, were all as docile as domestic pets and resisted not at all to be touched by the people of the sky ship.

5 Once all the animals had boarded and the people of the sky ship had returned, the ramp was drawn up inside the ship, and it silently lifted high into the sky.

6 Though it appeared black from the outside, from the inside the entire outer hull of the ship was transparent and the Children of Light looked in awe and incredulity, touched somewhat with fear, as the ship rose higher and higher into the sky and they saw the land below recede until the details could no longer be seen.

7 The Children of Light were led into a large room and once assembled, Jelatana entered, and standing on a dais, she addressed them, saying, "Good people of light, it is an honor to be among you. I am Jelatana, the leader, for a time, of the people of this ship.

8 I know you have many questions, for we have heard as you have asked them among yourselves. I will answer them now that you may know we aspire to be your trusted friends.

9 Some of you have wondered if we are Elohim. We are not. We are Alamars created in the image of the Elohim, even as you are. But our people were created and have existed long before your first ancestors were born upon this world you call earth.

10 We come from one of the tiny stars you see in the sky. I know you cannot comprehend that at this time, but you each will be assigned a personal teacher and in time your knowledge and understanding will grow, such as it can.

11 We are from a planet like your earth called Oolar. Like you, we honor and follow the light of our Heavenly Father and Mother. Like you, we are led by a prophet called by Elohim.

12 Elohim spoke to our prophet who lives on our home world, whose name is Deltarni, and told him that your world was soon to suffer great calamities because of the wickedness of the people, and that a ship, even our ship, the Ark, was to be sent to bring to safety the Children of Light and male and females in multitudes of all the animals of earth, before the great and dreadful day when your earth would begin to shake and convulse.

13 There is so much more to tell you, but much of it will be difficult for you to comprehend without first having a wider foundation of understanding.

14 "Therefore, I invite you to turn and greet the person who shall now come to you, males to males and females to females. These are your mentors, and they will teach you step by step that your minds may be opened and your understanding filled.

15 We shall be together for forty of your years. Very quickly I hope we can become as one family, that you will be able to cherish your time among us, and that all of us may grow from our shared experiences."

16 Jelatana then stepped down from the dais, and the Oolarians who had been assigned as mentors came forth from where they had been standing, along the outer walls of the room, and came to greet those to whom they had been partnered.

17 During the next weeks, the Ark came down to hover over several other spots on earth and lowered its ramp to take up many more animals that had lived too far away to travel to Kamoya, but had gathered at the call of Elohim.

18 They also came for forty-four more adults and their children, who were Children of Light. Though they lived far from Kamoya and knew not the people of Noah, Elohim the Mother had come to them in dreams, and they were prepared when the ship of the sky came for them.

19 On the day that the last Child of Light was aboard the Ark and the last animal had been taken into it, earth began to convulse, the ground began to erupt liquid fire, the sky darkened, great torrents of rain began to fall, and day became as night.

20 While one solar year passed with fury upon earth, aboard the Ark, despite the best intentions of both the people of earth and the people of Oolar, they had not become as one family, and among most, the gulf between their understandings of almost everything was very great.

21 And it came to pass that Noah and Jelatana sat down together, along with her two counselors and the sons of Noah, to try to understand why the chasm between their two peoples remained so wide.

22 Noah answered Jelatana's query, saying, "Your people are aloof. They speak to us in ways we do not comprehend, of things we know not. And there are but 188 of us, but of your people there is no end, for you are many thousands and we often feel very isolated because of our small numbers and ignorance of almost everything you know and understand."

23 "We have tried with great patience to teach our brothers and sisters of earth," Rabak interjected, speaking directly to Jelatana, "but honestly and truthfully, they are a very primitive people. We are so far advanced from the reality they have known that even after a year, many of them seem to still think we are Elohim and seem to make little effort to understand the things we try to explain."

24 "It is true," added Gensai, also speaking only to Jelatana. "You try to explain the simplest of things to them, such as how to grow a plant hydroponically, and they simply stare at you as if their brain is asleep. They seem unable to comprehend that plants can grow without soil. Even though they can see it happening, they seem to think it is some miracle of Elohim and not something that they can do."

25 "We try to understand your ways," interrupted Yapeth, the son of Noah, "but it is difficult, for it seems that all we thought we knew is wrong, and though we can see a new reality, such as plants that grow without soil, the experience of our lives still tells us that we must have soil to grow plants."

26 "Nor are we accustomed to seeing people walk about with so few garments, especially women," added Ham, the son of Noah; "or to see women commanding men. Our women have

always wielded great power, more than most men, but they do it in support of our community, in circles of women, not as women in positions of power over men."

27 All three of the Oolarians laughed at the words of Ham, and Gensai said unto him, "We are more modest than the people of most worlds in the coverings of our bodies, and if you have trouble with our attire, we best not take you to Feyranth or Yobnog or any of the many worlds where they wear no clothes at all, but adorn themselves only in jewelry and thin harnesses embedded with jewels."

28 "The Elohim permit such things even while our world is to be up heaved for far less!" exclaimed Shem.

29 "Why would the Elohim be concerned with nakedness?" asked Gensai in honest confusion. "It is how they created us. It is not nakedness that is a sin, but immoral acts that are committed, whether naked or clothed.

30 We observed your world as we approached, and it is the most immoral we have ever seen. The fact that most of the people wear a great deal of clothing to cover their nakedness has not prevented their descent into wickedness."

31 "As for women commanding men," interjected Jelatana. "I suppose you put me at the top of that list, but aboard the Ark, there are none that command, neither men nor women. Each of us only serves the others in the ways we are most capable and at their discretion.

32 I did not seek out my position. Even as our prophet is called by the Elohim, so I was called by my people aboard the Ark to lead them because of my experience. On any day, I may step down by my own choice, or they may call another to take my place. It is an honor to be called to serve our brothers and sisters however we can."

33 Shem was about to reply, but Noah held up his hand so that he would refrain. And Noah spoke unto them all, saying, "We are speaking much of our differences, and surely there is a great gulf. But I failed to discern how we are attempting to walk a common path that leads to a greater good for both our people and the feeling of one family that we both have claimed to desire.

34 "And there is more to consider here than simply learning to understand the ways of one another or for us to comprehend even a small part of your greater knowledge.

35 For through all of this journey, my people are grieving. They are hurting terribly in their hearts as they look through the walls of your ship each day and watch their world, their home, the place where they left many loved ones behind, wracked by the most awful storms, with mountains falling, the seas rising, and many other terrible calamities that strike dread into their hearts, even though they are here safely aboard the Ark."

36 The Oolarians nodded their heads in understanding with the words of Noah, and after consulting among themselves for a couple of minutes in their own language, Jelatana said unto him, "We have not sufficiently considered your pain at what you see transpire each day upon your world, nor done enough to help you comprehend our world, which is the Ark. You are the prophet among us, Noah, what would Elohim have us do?"

37 Noah considered her question for a moment and closed his eyes and reached out to the Elohim in his mind. And they answered him as quick as he thought his question, and Noah opened his eyes and spoke unto those in the room, saying, "It is not enough that you teach one-to-one with personal mentors, for it is too much like a parent and a child, even a babe.

38 If we are to be with you for thirty-nine more years we have more than enough time to learn all that you know, if you will teach us in a serious manner.

39 Therefore, set up schools for us that we may all gather, as we are prepared to understand that which is taught, both children and adults, and teach us line upon line, knowledge upon knowledge that we may come to a fullness of understanding."

40 Hearing his words, Noah's sons nodded in agreement, but Jelatana and her counselors conferred quietly among themselves and seemed far less enthusiastic. And Jelatana spoke unto Noah and his sons, saying, "For you and the other Alamars that will survive on earth, it is important that you evolve in your knowledge and society on a path of self-discovery, otherwise

both as individuals and as a people, you will develop weaknesses of judgment.

41 If we were to teach you all that we know and then put you back upon the earth among people who are even more primitive than you are, you would be like gods to them and the chance of creating an imbalance of society and civilization, between those with greater knowledge and those without, would be too great.

42 Perhaps not you, but surely your descendants would be tempted to exercise dominion over the other people of the earth, and this is not the way of the Elohim."

43 Noah nodded his head in agreement and said unto her, "You speak the truth in all that you say, Jelatana, and I know not how this will be resolved. But you asked me to inquire of the Elohim as a prophet, and this I did and the answer I gave unto you is the light they gave unto me."

44 And it came to pass that despite the misgivings of the Oolarians, according to the word of the prophet Noah as he said Elohim had spoken, schools were set up on the Ark that the people of earth might learn all that the Oolarians had to teach.

45 The Oolarians taught them as they would their own children from their earliest days in school. Thus, they learned the Oolarian alphabet and language as well as their history and the history of the entire universe that was known to the Oolarians.

46 Some progressed more than others because of their greater desire and perseverance, and these were sent to schools of specialized learning beyond the basic education. Thus, some of the people of earth became knowledgeable in many of the advanced sciences of the Oolarians involving healing and engineering and manufacturing and other fields of endeavor.

47 And the people of Noah reciprocated, passing on their knowledge of earth plants and herbs and of sewing and weaving and many other skills to the Oolarians.

48 As all aboard the Ark were devoted to the Elohim, Noah gained a special place among them, for he was a prophet of Elohim, and the Oolarian Prophet lived far away on their home world, a place none on the Ark had ever been.

49 Among the higher priesthood of both the Oolarians and his own people, Noah taught the greater paths and powers of spirit, and the kinship of spirit that formed between all of them was very strong indeed.

50 A special bond also formed between many of the women, as the Oolarian women knew of the Celestine powers given by Elohim only in theory and none had actually ever attempted to manifest their inherent gifts.

51 Thus, it became the great delight of the women of earth to teach their Oolarian sisters how to use the Celestine gifts of power the Elohim had given to all Children of Light, but that were most easily manifested by women.

52 And it came to pass that thirty-nine years passed swiftly away, and even as earth below was convulsed in the throes of rebirth, the people aboard the Ark experienced a time of peaceful bliss and had become as one family.

53 Thus, when the day quickly approached for the return of the people of earth to their home world, there was a great sadness among everyone aboard the Ark.

54 At this time, difficult decisions that had been avoided also needed to be faced and resolved, and for this, Noah and the Council of Elders met with Jelatana, her two counselors, and a body of twelve other Oolarian advisers.

55 Jelatana spoke to them, saying, "My friends, my family, the time has passed so quickly and now we must say good-bye to our brothers and sisters of earth whom we have come to love and be loved by.

56 When we first began this journey together and began to teach you, the people of earth, the knowledge of Oolar, we postponed deciding how we would deal with the greater knowledge you gained when it came time to return you to your primitive world.

57 We can delay no longer, for the time is upon us, for the fires on the earth have gone out and the waters receded.

58 We meet together now with the Council of Elders from earth and the Council of Advisors from the Ark. Let us discuss among us how to resolve this conflict and make a good decision by the unanimous agreement of everyone."

59 After an opening prayer there followed many hours of discussions with a break for meals twice. Two issues emerged as the thorniest: How to return the people of Noah to earth without disrupting the natural evolutionary balance and how to deal with the seventeen families that had blossomed from marriages between the people of earth and those of Oolar?

60 At first, many of the Oolarians insisted that the memories of all those returning to earth must be taken away for the time they had lived aboard the Ark to insure that the natural evolution of the people of earth would continue.

61 But Noah and the Council of Elders objected strongly to that suggestion for they had gained much knowledge in their time aboard the Ark, which they treasured and were unwilling to lose.

62 "But it is not something you will miss," explained one of the Oolarians. "You will be returned as you came to us, with no memory of your time aboard the Ark or the things you have learned. You cannot miss that which you do not remember."

63 "If you cut off all of our right arms and took away our memory that we ever had right arms, we would still miss them, for we would be able to do less with one than we could with two," interjected a member of the Council of Elders. "Thanks to Oolarian training in engineering I now know how to build structures that will withstand the storms of time. How does giving this up and returning to a state of ignorance help the evolution of man?"

64 And so the discussions continued, back and forth with no resolutions, let alone unanimous decisions.

65 Among the Oolarians who had married people from earth, there was an equal trepidation, for they too were threatened with memory loss as a condition for returning to earth with their families.

66 Nor could their families remain aboard the Ark, for earth had been depleted during the forty-year cataclysm and needed all of the survivors aboard the Ark to return to help the planet renew.

67 And it came to pass that the meeting of the councils ended for the night without resolution.

68 Before he slept, Noah prayed to Elohim, asking for guidance and a solution for the problems that seemed unsolvable.

69 And the Elohim heard the prayers of Noah, and Heavenly Mother came to him in a dream and showed unto him all that must be done to reach unanimity, and for the benefit of the people of Noah and earth, which was their home.

70 The next day, the councils met once again. But before they could renew their disagreements of the previous day, Noah rose and spoke to them, saying, "I speak to you now as a prophet of God, even the voice of the Elohim who guide us in all things of great consequence, even such as the things we speak of today.

71 "Last night, I prayed to be shown a resolution to the questions we have pondered and discussed, and our Heavenly Mother came to me while I slept and showed me the true path.

72 It is not good that knowledge should be taken that has been gained by either experience or dedication to learning, for then the reward for achievement would be a punishment and the memory of this would linger even if the memory of the knowledge was taken, and such lingering would cause a loathing for learning that would harm man for generations unborn.

73 But neither can we who have been given knowledge beyond the comprehension of the survivors of earth be allowed to live among them with this knowledge, for surely we would be raised upon the dais as gods and become perverted by our power and greater knowledge and succumb to evil, even as the fallen angels, which was the beginning of the end of earth.

74 Would we dare to put ourselves in a place where these forty wrenching years of rebirth might be repeated again someday in the future because of our actions?

75 But there is a solution. One that will allow us to return to earth and the Oolarians who are now part of our families as well, without the loss of any memories or any threat to the evolution of man. This the Elohim have shown to me clearly.

76 Therefore, open your ears and hear people of earth and Oolar, for this is the path of light that Elohim has revealed to me.

77 The Ark shall bring us to a blessed island where no man lives, upon a warm sea with a land bathed in sunlight from Elohim, where the weather is almost always ideal, and life in all forms from plant to animal to fish flourishes in great abundance.

78 Tall mountains rise into the mist upon this island, and many crops of different varieties can be grown at the various elevations.

79 Upon this spot, we will live, and our posterity shall build beautiful cities, both on the island and floating upon the sea.

80 We shall live a life of purity and even as on the Ark none shall have disease, and as in the days of father Adam, great shall be the age to which we live.

81 The knowledge and understandings of the devices of the Ark shall come with us, as will all of our knowledge that we might build not just a new Eden, but a better Eden than any of our forefathers could have imagined.

82 We will be far from the remaining people of the world, and they will know of us only vaguely, like people of a mist who come from the sea in strange ships to trade and then vanish again to a place unknown.

83 Some of our posterity will migrate to other remote islands and in a like manner establish outposts of our civilization.

84 So too will we and our posterity go forth upon the earth as it is ready and spread again the Celestine Light of Elohim upon all parts of it that the darkness will never again reign over the light.

85 And we must never forget the cataclysm that has happened upon the earth and all of its people for the last forty years, and this because of the evil that men had become.

86 Let the story of this cataclysm be passed down to all the people of the earth, lest they ever again let darkness reign and the earth need to be cleansed once more.

87 And let us pray every day in humility and thankfulness for the blessings that are ours and strive to live worthily of all the Elohim have given us.

88 And take heed: Where great things have been given, great things are expected, and we are asked to be a light all the moments of our lives.

89 Know with a surety, that if we, or our posterity, ever stray from the path of light, all that we have been given shall be taken away, not in forty years as we have seen, but in a single day and night.

90 Teach that well to our children that such a day will never come. Remember to live worthy of the blessings you have been given and to reflect the light given to you that others may bask in its warmth as well."

91 And it came to pass that as Noah had spoken, so it was accepted in unanimity.

92 The following day, the Ark hovered over an immense island in an archipelago of thousands of smaller islands, and with tearful good-byes for the Oolarians they would never see again, the people of Noah went down the long ramp back onto earth.

93 With them came seventeen Oolarians who had married among the people of Noah while on the Ark. Typical of their race, they were tall and blue-eyed, with either red or blond hair. And their good-byes were even more tearful and heart wrenching as they parted with the families they had known all of their lives to embrace a primitive world just reborn.

94 And these were the Oolarians who came to live among the people of earth, by their age, oldest to youngest, being ten males and seven females: Atalas, Aiainia, Colches, Thrinchea, Barean, Guache, Aquilaz, Olgy, Chramat, Saka, Karad, Hespar, Blest, Naamlin, Gresus, Zeunean, and Nibirum.

95 During the next days, the Ark visited many places upon earth, repopulating the animals upon the reborn lands and seas, prudently putting pairs of like animals in several locations to maintain the strength of the bloodlines.

96 As they passed closely over earth, the Oolarians were surprised to look down upon many survivors of the cataclysms of the last forty years.

97 Seeing them, Gensai commented to Rabak that it seemed that more survived than perished. And Rabak answered saying, "Hopefully with more respect for the power of Elohim and a greater willingness to live the light when it is shown to them."

98 And so came the Children of Light back onto earth and so began the Second Dispensation of Elohim upon earth.

* * * * * * * * * * * *

Notes: *This chapter was the briefest overview of what occurred during the forty years Noah and his people were aboard the Ark. A several-hundred-page book could be written just to cover that amazing period in detail. A couple of things worthy of mention that are not detailed in the chapter include the fact that the return of Noah, his people, and the seventeen Oolarians and the advanced civilization they established was the basis for the later stories of Atlantis. However, contrary to modern theories that place Atlantis either in the Mediterranean or in the Atlantic Ocean, the actual location of the return of Noah was a large island in the eastern Indian Ocean.*

This is a somewhat-incongruous chapter with all the others in the Oracles of Celestine Light as it takes place in what would seem to be a science fiction setting and deals more with practical matters than spiritual ones. However, this chapter is literally true, and as astounding a premise as it sets—pointed now in the right direction—it can all be proved by modern science and archeology if anyone cares to follow the leads.

In the interest of modern science, we would also note that the Ark was both levitated and propelled by a gravity drive that interacted and utilized the gravity field of earth or any other celestial body, even those a great distance away, when traveling through space.

One other note that may be of interest to some is that during the forty years on the Ark, they had friendly contact on three different occasions with other space-traveling races of non-Alamar origin.

CHAPTER 8

The Descent Into Darkness

Noah and his people disembark from the Ark and settle upon an island they name Salatis (known to us today as the fabled island of Atlantis). There they build a magnificent city named Kamari, employing many of the advanced technologies they learned from the Oolarians. They spread out upon the land, populating areas beyond the island of Salatis. Building technologically advanced communities far away from more-primitive populations, they prosper greatly, living many generations in peace and tranquility. However, there begins to be contentions between the different cities, and over time, an angry schism is created, leading many down a path of darkness and the conversion of peaceful technologies into those of war.

And it came to pass that the Children of Light descended from the Ark and came down upon the great island which, in honor of their benefactors of the last forty years and the hope they had for the new earth, they named Salatis, meaning promise in Oolarian.

2 And the people of Noah and the Oolarians who had come to earth with them lived and prospered on the island of Salatis, and many generations were born and passed away in peace and prosperity.

3 They built a magnificent city named Kamari, meaning "one with God" in the ancient language of Noah and Adam, and it was here that Noah was buried when he died at 636 years.

4 Noah was succeeded as prophet by Valanjara, who was called by the Elohim at the young age of 170, and became the new prophetess, after confirmation by revelation to the Council of Twelve Elders. Her selection was acclaimed by the citizens, for she was loved deeply by many because of the numerous good works she had done to benefit the people.

5 During the time of Valanjara, the people of Salatis went forth to many places around the world; for being directed by God, she was determined that the light of Elohim should be brought to the barbarians who were the descendants of the survivors of the Great Flood.

6 Now the Children of Light of Salatis and Kamari had brought with them from the Ark much of the knowledge of the Oolarians, and from the time of their landing upon Salatis, they began to build their civilization according to the engineering and expertise of the advanced Oolarian knowledge.

7 So it was that Kamari rose to become the most beautiful city, with walls made of stones of various types and colors that were liquefied and poured into wonderful curving shapes and then solidified in place as natural stone. And many smaller communities were built upon the island and adjacent islands and even floating upon the sea.

8 When the Kamarians were called by Valanjara to go forth into the world to bring the light

of Elohim to the barbarians, they did so in marvelous airships patterned after the technology of the Oolarians.

9 There were four basic types of ships from the large double-decked domed saucer that held over one hundred people, which was called Vimi and appeared as a bright, luminous cloud when it flew, to the small, pointed cylindrical craft that carried one to five people, which were called Jatals.

10 All of the sky ships were both lifted and powered by the same gravitational drives that had been used by the Ark, and the engines of the Vimi were large enough to lift it into earth's upper atmosphere.

11 To not frighten the barbarians they encountered, each craft employed some form of invisibility. The Vimi simply looked like a brilliantly glowing cloud, while the Jatals actually were cloaked in such a way that they could not be seen by the human eye, and others appeared merely as small bright lights in the sky.

12 In contrast to the choices made when Salatis and earlier outlying communities were begun, it was decided that the new enclaves would be established near large concentrations of the barbarians so they could be used for the manual labor that the people of Salatis had come to disdain. The largest group of barbarians was located in the valleys of the high mountains of Tibra, which were the highest on earth, and had been the final refuge of many of the survivors of the Great Flood.

13 Seven towns were founded in the valleys of the Tibran Mountains and each was initially settled by one hundred families from Kamari and the communities of Salatis, and in the generations that followed, these seven communities each grew into beautiful cities known collectively as the "Seven Cities of Tibra" and the people known as Tibrians. And the capital city of the Tibrians became Retiashi.

14 Four other communities, also founded by one hundred families, were placed at other high-mountain locations around the world where many barbarians had escaped the flood, and a fifth was located on an isolated island in the western ocean that it might become a remote and protected repository of all knowledge.

15 Many of the Kamarians and Salatisians had reservations when the new communities had been built with the intent to have daily interaction with the barbarians. But the barbarians who lived near the new Cities of Light were blessed to be there, for the Children of Light came among them and uplifted them with the teachings of Elohim; many of the barbarians became one with the Children of Light, and they were barbarians no more and the cities grew and prospered.

16 But beyond the trading area of the Cities of Light, where the barbarians still had little contact with the Children of Light, the life of the people was still very primitive.

17 And many more generations passed away, and earth continued to blossom with new life in many and varied forms springing up by the design of the Elohim.

18 Every thousand years, there was a great millennial celebration among all the Children of Light upon earth. At this time, a ship of the Oolarians, similar to the Ark, would come to earth to renew the bonds of the Oolarians with the Children of Light upon earth, and this was the only direct contact the Oolarians maintained with the descendants of the Noahites.

19 For one week upon the island of Salatis, there was a great feast and celebration, and the Children of Light from all over earth traveled by every airship available to attend the festivities and greet the Oolarians, the Children of Light from the stars.

20 And so did time pass upon earth, and among many generations, there was bliss.

21 But beginning at the time of the prophet Gartan Kul, the bliss began to vanish and was replaced by strife and descent into darkness among many of the Children of Light.

22 The Seven Cities rose in power so much so that they outshone the grandeur and majesty of Kamari. And the people of the Seven Cities began to think and act differently than their forefathers, and they disavowed the supremacy of the prophet at Kamari and the Council of

Twelve Elders and named their own prophet and Council of Twelve.

23 But having been called by man and not by God, when the prophet and Council of Elders of the Seven Cities inquired of the Elohim, they heard only their own imaginations in return.

24 In the land of Salatis, the people were most disturbed by the schism with the Seven Cities, and there arose a great anger among many that the Seven Cities would dare break away.

25 The prophet Gartan Kul and the Council of Elders tried to reason with their people, to convince them that they were overreacting, but their words only further angered the populace.

26 In their unrighteous anger, Dlamraka, self-styled "the Great," arose to power. He was a man of glib tongue, and he incited the people in their anger toward the citizens of the Seven Cities so much so that he convinced them that only by force could justice be rendered and the traitors be punished.

27 And Dlamraka, who was a very wealthy man, raised an army to mount an offense against the Seven Cities and capture their leaders. He marshaled the knowledge and abilities of many of the great minds of Salatis and Kamari to turn the peaceful technology of their cities into engines and vessels of war and violence that retribution might be rained upon the Seven Cities.

28 Seeing this, the prophet Gartan Kul spoke as a prophet in the name of Elohim to the people of Salatis and Kamari and plainly told them that they were straying from the path of Elohim and must not make war upon their brothers or upon anyone except in self-defense of their lives.

29 Dlamraka argued that they were defending their lives and way of life, which by the very act of succession, the people of the Seven Cities were threatening.

30 Back and forth went the conflicting words of Gartan Kul and Dlamraka for many months. And the Council of Twelve also went out among the people each day to counter the persuasions of Dlamraka and remind them what it meant to be a Child of Light.

31 But each day, the people listened with boisterous agreement more to the words of Dlamraka and hissed in rejection at the words of the prophet.

32 Feeling their unwavering disdain, Gartan Kul prayed often to the Elohim that he might be shown a way to bring his people and the people of the Seven Cities back into the light.

33 One night while he slept, Elohim the Mother came to him in a dream in answer to his faithful prayers, and seeing her, he kissed the hand that she offered and asked, "Dearest Mother of Light, a great schism grows between the Children of Light, and many are turning to ways of darkness, not in depravity, as in the days of Noah, but in their machinations and thoughts of violence against their brothers afar. What can I say or do to avert the tides of war and reconcile and heal the rifts?"

34 The Mother answered him, saying, "You have said well and with truth, all the words that must be said, as have the Council of Twelve. If the Children of Light will not hearken unto your words, they have by their choice thrown off the halo of light that was upon them and chosen by their freewill to walk a path that will lead to their destruction."

35 Hearing this, Gartan Kul was distraught, and he pleaded with the Mother of Light, saying, "Surely I can do something, exhibit some great power to show the majesty and truth of Elohim, or even I pray that you would do something, such as send a great wave or darken the sky or show some mighty sign of displeasure that the people will see the error of their ways before it is too late."

36 The Mother shook her head and said unto him, "When we created the earth, we put all things upon it that men and women could show by their actions the extent of their light or the depth of their darkness.

37 We gave a mortal life to the immortal soul that men and women could have a time of weakness and temptation, but also a time of great learning and expansion, to allow them to become one with the energies of eternity in which they found the greatest resonance that they could determine by their own choices the world of their eternity.

38 We understood that sometimes they would give into their weaknesses and partake of their

temptations and be pulled further into darkness.

39 Therefore, we left inside all men and women the spark of divinity that is our light, that they might always know right from wrong, that even when they chose the darkness their soul would still be calling them to the Celestine Light.

40 That the errors of their mortality might be redeemed and men and women become greater than their weaknesses, we offered the path of repentance, whereby the sins of their past can be forgiven and forgotten, and they can live once again fully in the light, drawn to an eternity of fulfillment in resonance with their illuminated, immortal soul.

41 All this we have created that men and women might fulfill the destiny they make for themselves, that on the day of judgment, when they will be pulled to the world of their eternity, be it light or darkness, that all of the actions and choices of their lives will be upon their shoulders, and they will not be able to say, 'It is because of this circumstance or this person that I gave into temptation and walked a path of darkness.'

42 Beyond this, we are Watchers only, Watchers with sadness whenever we see our children make the wrong choices. But also Watchers with love, confident we have given our children the best path and sufficient opportunities to create an eternity for themselves worthy of the greatness they each have within them."

43 Hearing the words of the Holy Mother, Gartan Kul nodded in understanding, but still he pleaded for her help, saying, "Good Mother, I understand all of the words you have spoken, and I ask you not to compel my people to the light, but merely give them such a great sign of your majesty that they will remember who they are ~Children of Light~ and return again to the path of light.

44 If I may be so bold, in the days of Noah, you acted not as Watchers only, but intervened in the lives of all men and animals and plants upon the earth, and a very great event the cataclysm was. Do I ask too much to beg you to intervene in a much smaller way with my people that they may be awakened to the errors of their choices and return again to the light?"

45 The Mother answered him again, saying, "In the days of Noah, we intervened only because the earth had become perverted from our design by the fallen angels of Heaven and not solely by the actions of man.

46 Such is not the case in your time, when men descend into darkness by their own choice.

47 You fear, my son, for the tribulations your people may bring upon themselves, and you are wise to fear, for the very earth itself shall become their enemy if they become wells of darkness.

48 This would not be a punishment from us, but the energy of destruction man calls upon himself by his own choices of needless violence."

49 And the Holy Mother opened the eyes of Gartan Kul in a vision, and he saw the future destruction of the entire island of Salatis as it sank into the sea in a great eruption of fire and explosion of the land into many pieces that sank into oblivion deep in the ocean.

50 The Mother said unto him, "This is the fate of Salatis and Kamari and all the people of this land if they turn to violence as a way to force their will upon their brothers of the Seven Cities. And this is not by our hand, for we are Watchers only, but the doom they call upon themselves by their actions of destruction.

51 Nor shall the fate of the Seven Cities or the other cities established by your people fare better if they too walk the path of senseless violence. Each in their own way shall call destruction upon them and only the Library of Guache will survive, for only upon their small, isolated isle do they have nothing to do with the foolishness of the rest of your people."

52 Gartan Kul was shaken by the visions the Holy Mother had shown to him, and in a faltering voice, he asked her, "Is what I have seen a vision of destiny or possibility?"

53 The Mother answered him, saying, "You know that all men and women are called to greatness. That is the destiny we have prepared for all of our children. But each is given their freewill and a portion of darkness to tempt them, but also with a greater portion of light to ever draw them to the ways of truth and light.

54 Whether their destiny of greatness is fulfilled depends upon the choices they make by their own free will; for only they are the masters of their destiny.

55 When many people unite in a common cause, be it good or evil, they call the forces of light or darkness upon them with great power by their choices, and their destiny is written by their actions, be it blessings or destruction.

56 The visions you saw are only that which shall occur if your people pursue a path of senseless violence, even to the killing of their brothers and sisters of the Seven Cities. If they turn from that path, you need only look to the days of glory of this land, to see the greater destiny of peace and prosperity they shall inherit."

57 Again Gartan Kul nodded his head in agreement, but once again, he questioned the Mother of Celestine Light, asking, "Holy Mother, clearly I understand the words you have spoken, but still I return to my original questions. Is it too much to ask that you imbue me with some marvelous ability to manifest your power that I might turn the hearts of my people back to you or that you or the Father would manifest mighty deeds yourself that my people would remember and return to the pure ways of the Elohim which you have taught us?

58 In this quick way, how great a multitude of lives might be saved? For if the words of war escalate into action, many shall perish, including many innocent women and children, even to the destruction of our entire island and all the life upon it, much of it innocent, especially the animals and plants who are completely without a part in the befuddled actions of my people."

59 Elohim the Mother answered him, saying, "Do not lose your perspective of eternity, my son. Your life and the lives of all the animals and plants upon the earth are but a single breath in eternity, a single blink of your eyes.

60 A most important breath and blink it is, but the sadness of death, even the most horrible, must be tempered with the unfailing conviction and understanding that life is eternal, as are the relationships of the innocent and the virtuous, be they man or beast.

61 Mortality is merely the brief, fierce wind that blows away the chaff of facade and falsehood that the wheat of truth and light may grow in grandeur in eternity. And every living thing is promised the fullness of mortality, be it in one life or more."

62 With those words, the Holy Mother disappeared from the vision of the prophet. When he awoke, he was greatly disturbed by what he had seen and called a meeting of the Council of Twelve to share with them all that he had seen and heard.

63 After hearing his words, the council made haste to redouble their efforts to turn back the rising calls for war. But despite all of their actions and words, the people heeded them not at all; nor did they listen to the prophet. Instead, falling further into the darkness, they turned their backs upon all things having to do with God and church and religion and became very worldly in all that they did.

64 And save for a handful, they no longer gathered together on the holy day of Elohim each week to celebrate all of their blessings and be edified and uplifted.

65 In the Seven Cities, the people walked down the same dark path, turning their backs upon all things of Elohim and living in the ways of the world, gluttons of gold and all the things gold could buy, for their cites were exceedingly wealthy.

66 And the schism between the people of Kamari and the people of the Seven Cites grew into such a great gulf that even trade was greatly curtailed between them, and threats of war flew back and forth with greater stridence and frequency.

67 In the twenty-ninth year after the vision of the prophet, the great millennial celebration occurred. And it was with wistful and expectant hearts that the prophet and the Council of Twelve and the few others who kept the faith with them hoped for a reconciliation with their brethren in the Seven Cities, as all of the descendants of Noah would be coming to Kamari to celebrate and greet the Oolarian ship that came every thousand years for the occasion.

68 And so they came, from all parts of earth where the descendants of Noah had settled. Most came by airships, but many also by ships of the sea.

69 But there was a tension between the people of the different cities, and it was not mollified by the many feasts or sporting games or celebrations. And there were numerous fights and brawls among the men of the various nations over trivial arguments and puffed-up vanities.

70 By the last day, as all the people gathered on the great lawn of the Holy Temple to await the coming of the Oolarian ship, it was all most could do to restrain themselves from yelling and fighting with the people from other lands, for great did they each perceive their grievances.

71 But the day turned to night, and the Oolarian ship did not appear. And that night, there were many fights among the people of the various nations and cities as they released their pent-up anger toward one another, and 123 people were slain that evening in many incidents of anger and violence around the city.

72 On the morning of the next day, word was sent out that the prophet would address all the people at noon at the Holy Temple concerning the Oolarians. People no longer cared to listen to the words of the prophet, but they did wish to know about why the Oolarians had not appeared, so when noon arrived, the great lawn was once again teeming with people from many lands.

73 And the prophet stood upon a high balcony atop a minaret that he could be seen by all the people, and his voice and image were cast mechanically throughout the entire city. And he said unto them, "Oh, you who should be Children of Light, you who are loved so greatly by Elohim, our Holy Father and Mother, and elder brother. How have you strayed so far from what you know to be true?

74 Why have you turned away from love for one another and embraced violence? What can violence bring you but more violence? What have you gained by turning away from the light of Elohim? What is your reward for giving your brothers and sisters of other lands a painful blow instead of a brotherly kiss?

75 Verily, the Elohim have given you freewill and have not compelled you to walk their path. But your choices have consequences, greater and more deleterious than you have realized.

76 When you tend a fire, it grows or shrinks depending upon how much wood you feed it. And the fire can do good or evil depending upon how you are applying it.

77 You could use it for evil and burn down your neighbor's house, or you could use it for good to melt and fashion gold and silver and create beautiful jewelry and art.

78 If you use it for evil and burn down your neighbor's house, you can continue to add fuel to the fire and burn down many houses or even an entire city. But what is gained by such foolishness? Smug pride, that you put your insulting neighbors in their place?

79 Perhaps, seeing the destruction you have wrought, you will have a feeling of satisfaction, but will that feeling last once you realize that you no longer will be able to obtain that exquisite wine you so savor because you have burnt the vineyards? Or that special fish you like for the Jartera celebration because you have sunk the fishing fleet?

80 Do not think to yourself that you can bring forth violence and not have it snap back and strike you an even greater blow. Violence begets violence, even as love begets love.

81 If you burn your neighbor's house, do you think that those that survive will leave your house unscathed? If you destroy your neighbor's vineyard, do you think that yours will somehow be spared? If you sink your neighbor's fishing fleet, do you think that yours will somehow survive?

82 If you beat or kill your neighbor, do you not think that your neighbor's friends and family will not now look to ways that they might beat or kill you and your family?

83 Violence only begets more violence, and if you continue to travel upon the road you have embarked upon, painfully evidenced by the deaths that came to some last night, then you may consider what I have just spoken of, not mere stories, but prophecies from Elohim of what shall come to pass in your lives in the days to come.

84 And more than this, my brothers and sisters, much more than this, so hear my words well. Verily, I speak to you as the prophet of Elohim, and my words are the visions the Elohim have shown to me.

85 With words of soberness, I say unto you that if you persist in talk of war instead of words

of peace, that you shall find that which you seek. But in it, you will lose more than your houses and your vineyards and your fishing fleets. You will lose your very lives, all of you. And the great cities you have built will be no more.

86 The world will survive. The barbarians will still be upon it, but you will not. The violence you beget will come back to hurt you hundredfold, even thousand fold, even unto your deaths. Your land shall be laid waste, and your cities shall be completely annihilated.

87 You who are great upon the earth, you who have built majestic cities that rival the mansions of Heaven, shall be as if you never were. Your cities shall be utterly destroyed so much so that the generations of the barbarians to come will have no memory of the Children of Light that came from Noah or that the magnificent and wonderful cities they built ever even existed.

88 You consider yourselves enlightened men and women, people of intelligence and knowledge. Yet you speak with hatred toward those who are different than you and initiate violence against those who do not agree with you, simply because they do not.

89 Are you using violence as a tool to achieve that which you cannot gain by reason or a worthy and just pursuit?

90 I beseech you! Remember who you are and the light of Elohim that has guided our people for generations upon generations.

91 It is not in violence or war that you will find peace or justice, but only in love and agreement, with a gentle eye and a forgiving heart for differences.

92 Violence only brings destruction. Your passions become inflamed, your sorrows increased, and your hatred multiplied.

93 Today, we gaze upon the sad sight of over one hundred of our people from all parts of the world, murdered in a night of senseless violence. What comes next, a retaliation and escalation of what was brought in the night? Do not give into that temptation.

94 More killing will not bring back the dead. It will only deepen the darkness. If you create more darkness, it will not take away the night that has occurred; only greater light can accomplish that miracle.

95 If you are motivated by revenge to increasing your hatred, it will not do away with the hatred that also motivates your opponents. Only love can bring that new dawn.

96 And I love you still, as do the Elohim, and I implore you to remember who you are and how greatly you have been blessed and live up to your highest potential, not descend down to your lowest.

97 You are not Kamarians or Tibrians or Celians. You are all brothers and sisters. You are not black or white, or yellow or red, you are simply the children of the most high, each given a beauty of your own.

98 The more you separate yourselves by the country you live in, the differences of your customs, or the color of your skins, the more you are inviting violence into your lives.

99 It is for this cause, because of your separation instead of unification, because of your desires for war instead of peace, for violence instead of reason, that the Oolarians have not come, nor will they ever again, save you become once again Children of Light, who live by the light.

100 But I perceive that I speak to the air. You see my lips move, but your ears hear not my words.

101 I will have no more to say to you, for you have hardened your hearts toward me and the words I speak, which come from Elohim.

102 You are in the last minute of the last hour before your destruction. But even now it is not too late to turn from hate and embrace love, to refute violence and propagate peace.

103 Your fate is in your hands, as are the fates of your children and your animals and your homes and your cities.

104 Hear well my words. When you stand before Elohim, as you one day will, you will not be able to say you were ignorant, for I tell you plainly that on the road you travel to violence and war, there are no winners, nor will there be victors, for your mutual destructions shall be total

and final.

105 Knowing that, can you be so blinded by foolishness that you would give up everything for nothing?"

CHAPTER 9

The Lands that Time Forgot

Contentions between the lands of the Seven Cities and the lands of Salatis lead to war, which results in the nuclear destruction of the Seven Cities of Tibar and the subsequent earthquakes and volcanoes that swallowed the great city of Kamari and all of the surrounding islands, giving birth to the legend of Atlantis. Before the great destruction, the remaining Children of Light who had remained faithful are forewarned of the imminent devastation and instructed by Elohim the Mother in their dreams to leave their homes, undetected by airship, and go to the islands of Guache, where the Great Library of Knowledge resides. For many generations, they expand in peace and prosperity, living fully in the light of Elohim. However, due to their advanced knowledge in the sciences, they begin to meddle in areas they should not, so Elohim intervenes in a most surprising manner.

And it came to pass that the people derided the words of the prophet and hearkened not unto them. Instead, they departed in anger, each to their own land.

2 During the months that followed, the tides of war rose, both in the lands of Salatis and in the lands of the Seven Cities.

3 In the cities of Celine, Patona, Iironth, and Ubarzaz, which had been created in the high mountains across the world at the time of the great migration from Salatis and the establishment of the Seven Cities, the people were restless and anxious because of the talk of war between the Kamarians—the homeland of Salatis—and the Seven Cities of the Tibarians.

4 For years, they had tried to remain neutral as the tensions between the Kamarians and the Tibarians escalated, but now they were being threatened by both sides and pressured to align with one or the other or suffer the consequences.

5 As violence and intimidation increased, in equal proportion did the people fall away from the teachings of Elohim, and the ways of the Elohim were no longer in their hearts or minds, save for a few in each city who remained true to the light.

6 In Kamari and the land of Salatis, Dlamraka was chosen by the people to be the supreme leader, and with their backing, he intensified his efforts to convert the Oolarian technology, which they had inherited, into vessels and means for war.

7 The Seven Cities of Tibar were not idle while Dlamraka was busy marshaling his lands for war. They too turned their technology into engines of destruction, and it was inevitable that once created, these mutual engines of war would be used.

8 And it came to pass that each side began to make probing incursions against the other and to attack and destroy each other's airships and outposts when it could be done subtly, without evidence left behind of the source or likelihood.

9 But each side knew it was not by happenstance that their airships and crews began to disappear. Nor did they imagine it was barbarians that raided and destroyed their outposts.

10 Soon, open warfare commenced, and it was the lands of Salatis that began to suffer defeat upon defeat, for their population was dispersed upon hundreds of islands, which, due to their isolation and relatively small populations, were not easily defended against the airships of the Seven Cities.

11 Many tens of thousands were killed, and hundreds of thousands of refugees from the outer islands began to stream into Kamari and to the main island of Salatis.

12 The people clamored for Dlamraka to protect them, but a few called upon Elohim to guide them in the light and the right.

13 It seemed for a time that the Kamarians would go down to certain defeat, for the Tibarians had moved rapidly once they committed to war and had destroyed much of the Kamarian air fleet before they were fully aware that they were under full-scale attack.

14 But Dlamraka was not worried, for his scientists were on the verge of creating a new super-weapon that would annihilate the Seven Cites, and he rallied his people to be valiant in their defense of the homeland, for though destruction rained all around them, he promised victory was almost theirs. And they believed him.

15 And despite their horrific loss of life and property on the outer islands, they did mount a more stubborn defense on Salatis and held the Tibarians at bay insomuch that the beautiful city of Kamari remained relatively untouched by destruction.

16 However the military leaders of the Kamarians were angry and frustrated at their inability to wreck equal havoc upon the Tibarians. Because the Seven Cities were high in the mountains, they were much more impregnable and unassailable than the dispersed low islands of the Kamarians.

17 But then Dlamraka went to them and showed them the weapon of the sun that his scientists had almost completed, and then they understood his calm in the storm of destruction around them. And they too smiled with evil smirks of glee at the destruction they imagined would soon befall the Seven Cities of Tibar.

18 The Prophet and the Council of the Twelve continued each day to go into the city and preach the light of Elohim to try to turn their people back to the light, but it was of no avail. Those few families who hearkened unto their words had already sought sanctuary inside the Holy Temple and upon its grounds. But the rest of the Kamarians closed their ears to their words and turned their backs upon them.

19 And it came to pass that the Holy Mother came to the prophet in a dream as he slept. And she came also in a like manner to the leader of those who still followed the light in the Seven Cities and the cities of Celine, Patona, Iironth, and Ubarzaz.

20 And Elohim the Mother spoke, saying, "The time has come for you who are still Children of Light to leave your homes and flee with haste, for the destruction of your cities and your lands is imminent.

21 Take only what you can carry upon your back and leave by the evening of the morrow. Embark upon your speediest ships of the air. Lock your compass upon the isles of Guache, for it is only there that you shall survive and prosper as guardians of the light and the Great Library of Knowledge.

22 Save for this group of islands and the people upon them and the library within its womb, all else of your people in all other places shall be destroyed by their own hands and a consequence of their actions.

23 You must travel in a most circuitous route, even if you must circle the entire globe, and this that you will neither be destroyed by those at war or followed to your destination.

24 And upon the isles of Guache, the Children of Light shall be blessed with peace and prosperity until the time of their fulfillment upon the earth. So be it."

25 The words of the Holy Mother were shocking to all who had heard them in their dreams,

but they doubted them not, and with steadfast voice and sincerity that none could doubt, they related all that they had been told to their brothers and sisters of the light.

26 And each of those who were told the revelation of the Holy Mother prayed on their own to Elohim and received confirmation of the truth of the revelation.

27 Therefore, all did as they had been forewarned to do, and that evening from Kamari and each of the Seven Cities and also the cities of Celine, Patona, Iironth, and Ubarzaz, airships took to the skies and shot off into the night in many different directions. None were captured or destroyed.

28 And in a single day, all of the Children of Light that had remained at any of the former cities of light upon earth vanished.

29 And it came to pass that so much had the people of the cities forgotten Elohim and the teachings of Elohim that it was not even noticed that a few followers of Elohim had disappeared.

30 In Kamari, seven days passed before one of the officers of Dlamraka commented casually to him and fellow officers that neither the prophet nor any of the Council of the Twelve had been preaching in the streets for some days.

31 Rather than be concerned about this, everyone laughed, made jokes, and generally agreed that having the religious people keep out of sight and quiet was the most helpful thing they could do.

33 Thirteen days after the Children of Light had departed, Dlamraka called a meeting of his highest military officers and revealed that the sun weapon was completed and had already been mounted to his personal airship.

34 "Let us see a demonstration," implored one of his officers.

35 "No, no, that is not possible," cautioned Dlamraka. "It is too powerful of a weapon to demonstrate on anything other than an actual target and that can be no less than a city, for the destruction it will unleash will obliterate everything as far as your eye can see."

36 His words were incomprehensible to almost everyone present, for until that moment, the most powerful weapon they had ever seen was the Takka Beam, which could do little more than destroying a ship or blasting large holes in buildings.

37 Then Dlamraka outlined his plan to annihilate the Seven Cities. "But they are still our brothers," protested some of his officers. "We cannot use a weapon such as this upon them that will completely obliterate them and the great cities they have built from the face of the earth."

38 "And what of the spoils of victory?" asked another. "True victory would not be to completely destroy our former brothers, who are now our enemies, but to humiliate them and take their lands and their wives, and their cities and their wealth."

39 "Is that what they are doing to you?" screamed Dlamraka. "We have innumerable refugees in our city. Many of our outlying towns have been completely destroyed. There has been no mercy shown. Can there be any doubt that if given the opportunity the Tibarians would exterminate us all and our cites as well?

40 No, your sentiments are noble, my friends, but they cannot be given into with such an implacable enemy as the Tibarians have become."

41 With such words, Dlamraka swayed those who counseled restraint, until even with misgivings, all were in agreement that they would attack and destroy the Tibarians until there were none remaining.

42 And it came to pass that five days later, Dlamraka boarded his airship, and accompanied by the six fastest ships remaining in the fleet, cloaked in invisibility and piloted by his most loyal officers, they sped into the night sky on their deadly mission of doom.

43 Each of the seven ships carried a Death Arrow, as they called it, one for each of the Seven Cities.

44 It was not many hours before they were approaching the cities high in the Tibar Mountains. Their ships had been detected once they were over the lands of the Seven Cities, but due to their rapid speed, they were unable to be pinpointed or intercepted.

45 Dlamraka's eyes were wide with an almost crazed anticipation, and it seemed to be with great joy that he gave the order to "shoot the arrows."

46 At his command, a Death Arrow was shot out from beneath his ship and from beneath each of the six ships that accompanied him. Silently, they shot forth with blinding speed, making no sound other than the wind whistling mournfully through the tail fins and leaving no trail, each flying with unerring accuracy toward the heart of one of the Seven Cities.

47 Immediately after releasing their arrows, all seven ships banked sharply and headed away from the Seven Cites as rapidly as possible.

48 But looking back out their rear portals, the Kamarians saw seven brilliant flashes, followed by immense columns of fire that mushroomed into enormous clouds.

49 Seeing this, they knew they had succeeded and that the Seven Cities and all the people in them were no more. With that poignant understanding, several of the officers became overwhelmed with grief and hung their heads, and many wept as they realized for the first time the enormity and irreversibility of the horrific action they had just taken.

50 Even Dlamraka was quiet and reflective as he realized that in an instant, they had killed untold numbers of people and destroyed magnificent cities that had taken many generations to build.

51 As their airships landed in Kamari, the men disembarked without enthusiasm, and none spoke of the terrible deed they had just accomplished. In truth, most were greatly ashamed and sorrowful, for they knew they could never right the wrong they had done.

52 But they did not have long to contemplate their sorrows or evil deeds. The immense explosions they had unleashed, which had obliterated seven great cities, had also sent waves of shock and tumult through earth, and these resounded within it like a bell.

53 And earth shifted and moved within. And suddenly all across the planet, earthquakes began to rumble and volcanoes began to spew forth hot red lava.

54 Upon the islands of Salatis, death and destruction came suddenly and without end, for all of their mountains were volcanoes with every island composed of one or more peaks that had slept peacefully, even before the days of Noah. But now they awakened in a great anger because of the bell that had rung inside the earth when the arrows had destroyed the Seven Cities.

55 In a single day and a night, the island of Salatis and almost all of the islands of the Kamarians exploded or sank into the sea, wracked by immense earthquakes and buried by boiling hot lava.

56 And like the Tibarians who had lived for generation upon generation in the Seven Cities, the Kamarians, in all of their cities, upon all of their islands, were no more.

57 The distant, independent cities of Celine, Patona, Iironth, and Ubarzaz also experienced great destruction because of the shaking of earth. Though many people were killed, many also lived and the cities survived for a time.

58 But with extensive damage and loss of life and trade extinguished with the great cities of Salatis and the Seven Cities of Tibar, the remaining four independent cities languished, and within one hundred years, all were overrun by barbarian hordes, their cities destroyed, and the survivors taken into slavery.

59 But amidst a world in upheaval, the islands of Gauche were an oasis of calm. The arriving airships carrying Children of Light from all over the earth were greeted by the few Children of Light already inhabiting the islands with joy and welcome.

60 The new immigrants quickly assimilated into one people, for all still followed the teachings of Elohim and they immediately felt the pull of brotherhood and sisterhood as Children of Light.

61 On their one hundredth year upon the islands of Guache, an Oolarian Ark ship descended from the sky, and once again, the millennial celebration between the Children of Light of earth and the Children of Light from the stars was reborn, only now to occur upon every hundredth year.

62 During the next millennia, the islands of Guache remained isolated from the rest of the

world, except for scientific-exploration parties. They were completely self-sufficient, and having been informed by Elohim of the complete destruction of all of their former cities, they sought no trade with the barbarians beyond the shores of their islands, and they lived peacefully and fully in the light and teachings of the Elohim, save for the guilt some felt at not bringing the light of Elohim to the barbarians.

63 The greatest task of the Savasi, or Blessed Ones as they came to call themselves, was the care and expansion of the Great Library of Knowledge, setting to record within crystals and stones all knowledge of every science, the recipes for their longevity and healing elixirs, and diverse secrets of their ancestors and their spiritual powers.

64 During the succeeding generations, Savasi exploration parties went to the far corners of earth, making detailed studies of the plants, animals, cultures, histories, and ways of the various primitive tribes.

65 All knowledge was encoded into either rounded, bi-color elongated stones or sharp-sided, clear crystals. Upon paper of any kind, there was nothing written of consequence or importance.

66 Besides the fact that organic materials would decay with time and eventually turn to dust, the rocks and crystals allowed the Savasi to record a great amount of information in small and compact containers that would seem nothing more than innocuous rocks to anyone unaware of how to unlock the secret information stored within their structure.

67 And amazing knowledge was stored within the rocks and crystals; not only all the knowledge of earth and its true history, but also all the knowledge of the Oolarians and of all of the known worlds inhabited by myriads of civilizations beyond earth.

68 After a thousand years had passed, it was decided that some barbarians would be brought to the islands to help in the menial tasks that the Savasi loathed needing to take the time for. In exchange, the barbarians would be taught the path of light and given greater knowledge to raise themselves above the level of their creation.

69 An expedition was undertaken that went out to several tribes of barbarians. Once contact was made and goods traded, the Savasi tried to convince the barbarians to come with them into their airships and be taken to a new life of plenty and peace, but none were interested in leaving their lands or flying in ships in the sky.

70 For thirty-three years, the Savasi persistently went forth to various tribes of barbarians in many places around the world, but convinced none to come with them to their islands.

71 Finally, at the end of the thirty-third year, when they were about ready to abandon the idea of bringing barbarians to their islands, two tribes agreed to accompany them.

72 Both were tribes they had long had contact with, who had become familiar and trusting of the Savasi.

73 One tribe of ninety-three adults and their children lived on the continent near the sea that had been the location of the islands of Salatis. The other, comprising 110 adults and their children came from the far north of the great continent.

74 Within one generation, the barbarians were as civilized as the Savasi and they came to be known as the Gersan or People of earth.

75 Though their physical appearance was very similar to that of the Savasi, they were in fact a different species, and both the Savasi and the Gersans were forbidden by the word of Elohim, through the prophet, to be married to one another or have physical relations, because it was not possible for them to create children from their union.

76 Nevertheless, there were some Savasi who did not agree with the decree that the two species should not mix, and in secret collaboration with rogue geneticists over several years, they succeeded in changing the genetic template of some of the Gersan women, successfully enabling them to bear children from a Savasi mate.

77 They were gleeful in their success and despite the hesitant misgivings of some, most were anxious to announce their breakthrough and fully expected to be lauded as great scientists and pioneers.

78 Upon announcing that they had succeeded in creating genetic modifications enabling Gersan women to mate with Savasi men, some people did laud their achievement. But the far greater number were shocked that the men had so blatantly disobeyed an edict of Elohim to not have physical relations with the Gersan.

79 And the prophet Dilallon came to them and said unto them, "That you have disobeyed a commandment from Elohim is a serious mistake, especially that in your error, you have chosen to override the template Elohim gave for the Gersan, which is an unthinkable wrong."

80 But Letav, the leader of the geneticists, dismissed the words of the prophet and said unto him, "You speak foolishly, sir. We change the templates of the flowers to make them brighter in color. We change the template of the bees to make them produce more honey and allow them to live longer lives. For this, we are not upbraided but encouraged and lauded. Why then should we be condemned in the case of the Gersan?

81 We were not commanded to refrain from changing the template of the Gersan, but told to not have relations with them because a union of a Gersan with a Savasi could not produce children. We have now made that possible, so the prior edict needs be void. No one has been hurt or taken advantage of in this, so how can you find fault and come upon us with such harsh words?"

82 The prophet shook his head and looked first upon the ground and then up into the heavens. Then he spoke, saying, "How wrong you are, Letav, to think that no one is hurt by your actions. Do you think that given the opportunity to mate with a Savasi, any of the Gersan women so chosen will instead tell you "no," that they would prefer to find a mate among the poorer, more-simple-minded Gersan men?

83 It will not be long before all the Gersan women are the second, third or fourth wives of a Savasi, while the Gersan men will find not even one single female amongst them to fight over for a mate. Would not these wonderful, kind Gersan men be hurt by your altering of their females, even to the dying out of their lineages?

84 And if you find a way to allow Gersan men to mate successfully with Savasi women, do you think that even one Savasi woman will desire to do that? For the Gersan men are not as comely as the women. So again, the Gersan men are left to a fate of solitude, loneliness, and the end of their lineages.

85 We have always been encouraged by the Elohim to modify their simple creations such as plants and insects to better suit them to our needs, whether by hybridization or genetic modification, it is the same.

86 But to fundamentally change the template of a Savasi, made in the image of Elohim, or a Gersan, made near the image of Elohim, is to tell our Holy Father and Mother that you think you can recreate their highest creations in a superior way. In this, you mock God, a very dangerous path to take, for God will not be mocked and remain idle.

87 Therefore, I implore you to repent of this error in your thinking and undo the harm you have done before it creates ramifications that cannot be undone."

88 Hearing the words of the prophet, Letav laughed and then laughed some more, as did his friends who were standing with him. And he answered, saying, "You are stuck in the mud of the past, dear prophet. Maybe God once spoke to you, but if you cannot see the simple logic of what we have done, then I am not sure you still hear God today. Therefore, I will politely have to disagree with your point of view, and we shall carry on as we have."

89 Hearing this, the prophet was greatly saddened, and he said unto them, "I hoped to reason with you and bring you to repentance, but if you insist on persisting on this course, I must go before the Council of Elders and clearly state the position of Elohim that the force of our laws will then compel you to abandon your reckless foolishness, even if your respect for Elohim does not."

90 True to his word, the very next day, Dilallon came accompanied by his Council of Twelve, six men and six women, and spoke to the Council of Elders, also six men and six women, who

ruled the islands of Guache, and requested in the name of Elohim that they pass and enforce a law prohibiting the genetic modification of Savasi or Gersan, except for things that improved their health and did not interfere with the sacred powers of reproduction laid down in a template by Elohim.

91 Each of the Council of Twelve also spoke before the Council of Elders, in support of the words of Dilallon.

92 The Council of Elders then heard testimony from Letav and his fellow geneticists and supporters, and after five days of deliberation, they called all the parties to hear their decision. And though only a few dozen people attended the hearing in person, all the people of the islands of Guache waited in anxious anticipation to hear the outcome.

93 The chief of the Elders spoke, saying, "Upon careful and prayerful deliberation and a review of many scriptures from the records of the prophets, by a 7–5 vote, we support the actions of Letav and do not feel there is sufficient cause, despite the words of the prophet Dilallon, to create a law preventing the actions of the geneticists.

94 If they are in error and acting against the will of Elohim, as has been asserted by the prophet Dilallon, then Elohim shall be their judge, not us.

95 In our eyes, their argument that we were not forbidden as a people to manipulate the template of the Gersan women to make them fertile to the seed of the Savasi men is not refuted by anything we have read in the records of the prophets, and as the current prophet is still living, it has not yet been decided which of his words shall be deemed scripture, therefore at this time, none of his words can carry the weight of Elohim with certainty, though he speaks in their name."

96 Among the vast majority of the population, both Savasi and Gersan, there was incomprehension and shocked disbelief at the decision of the Council of Elders. Nevertheless, their decision became the law of the land, and the geneticists proceeded on with their work.

97 The prophet gathered with the Council of Twelve and, with prayer and thought and earnest discussion, sought to still find a way that they might counter the path the geneticists had chosen and the judges of the land had upheld; for in all things they knew they must support the commandments of Elohim above the decrees of men.

98 The Council of Twelve and the prophet formed a Circle of Power so that they could create a group connection to Elohim, and they called upon the great dormant power stored in the earth to come forth and connect them to Heaven.

99 At their command, a mighty whirlwind arose from the ground and lifted and expanded up high into the sky beyond the sight of men, engulfing those at its base.

100 And Elohim the Father came into each of their minds as they stood, one and all the same, in the Circle of Power within the whirlwind. And the Father spoke unto them, saying, "Precious and righteous Children of Light, our hearts do have great joy in you. You are greater than the world in which you live and greater than many among whom you live.

101 Like unto Enoch, you will be taken in three days and be no more upon the earth, you and all of your families, even to the last of the Savasi.

102 But it is not to the Celestine Realms that you will come at this time as did Enoch, for you still have much to discover and great works to do in mortality, for neither you nor any of your people are perfect, as were Enoch and his people.

103 The earth is no longer a proper home for the Savasi. The gap of knowledge and ability between you and the others upon the earth has become so great that your people have begun to give into the temptations to make themselves creators even as the Elohim.

104 But they create not from love and for the betterment of all, but only to satisfy their own egos and selfish desires. Therefore, they take upon themselves the creation power without vision, love, or devotion to their creations.

105 They take unto themselves the power of the gods, but with irresponsibility like foolish children.

106 Like in the days of Noah, three days hence, an Oolarian Ark ship shall come for you and all of your people. You shall be taken to another earth where the people are more advanced and equal to you in their knowledge and technology. There you shall continue your mortal journey. None shall remain behind.

107 Seal the Library of Knowledge and all of its branches safely beneath the earth that its wisdom may come forth again to another generation of Children of Light; long after all that man has now built upon the earth has passed into forgotten memories.

108 Gather everything you possess that you will not carry with you and place them on the small desolate Isle of Holaq, where they and the island will be consumed by the ocean on the day of your departure. Prepare now, for your time is short. So be it."

109 With those words firmly imprinted upon the minds of all within the whirlwind, it quickly fell back down into the ground and disappeared.

110 The following day, the prophet again appeared before the Council of Elders accompanied by the Council of Twelve and related to them all that Elohim the Father had told unto them.

111 Now it was the judges who were shocked, and the chief of the Council of Elders, Merisherlas, opened her hands in disbelief and said, "It is an impossible thing for all of the Savasi to leave in three days. What about our homes and our lands and our pets? And what of our exploration parties that are in far-off lands? And what type of stewards would we be to leave the Gersan here to fend for themselves and our lands and property to wither without our care?"

112 "I simply will not go," added another Elder. "The Oolarians can come and all of you who wish to leave may do so, but I like it here just fine and I am not going anywhere."

113 "I think our prophet means well, but he is getting old and touched in the head," added another Elder. "Surely Elohim did not tell him such a thing."

114 Frabara, one of the Council of Twelve, stepped forth at the words of the judge and proclaimed, "It is not the prophet alone who heard the commands of Elohim, but all twelve of us as well. And each heard every word spoken the same. What Dilallon has spoken shall come to pass. To remain was not an option given to any of us, so it would be best if you prepared to depart, for surely, at the appointed time, you shall depart."

115 The prophet again stepped forward. He thanked Frabara for his words, and then spoke again to the Council of Elders, saying, "The Savasi are still, by and large, a goodly people, worthy to be called Children of Light. But this world is no longer good for us and neither are we good for it.

116 Other than the few Gersan who live among us, what good have we done upon the earth in the time since our ancestors first came to these shores?

117 Let us not fight the will of Elohim and draw their wrath upon us. The Father has spoken not in anger, but in love, tinged perhaps with a little frustration at our weaknesses, which we give into more than seek to build our strengths.

118 Let us rejoice that we are so loved by the Elohim that they are bringing us to a new earth that we may more perfectly progress in our mortality.

119 I call upon each of you now and upon all the Savasi to go in private prayer to Elohim and ask if the words I have spoken are true.

120 Whether you support me or are against me, whether you believe I am the prophet of Elohim or a crazy old man, I know that Elohim will answer your prayers.

121 Though you may not like the answer, I know there will be no doubt in your mind and heart that the words I have spoken to you are true.

122 Precious time is being wasted squabbling about this now. I assure you that you will leave at the appointed time. Therefore, make haste to find your answer to prayer that you may have time still remaining to put your affairs in order, and prepare for your voyage to a new earth."

123 At his words, everyone moved to make haste: some because they knew he spoke true, others because they feared he might, and still others who doubted he did but wanted to take precautions and be prepared just in case.

124 And their prayers were answered, and all of the Savasi came to know with conviction that the will of Elohim was for them to leave earth forever on the third day.

125 Around noon on the third day after Elohim the Father had spoken, an enormous Oolarian Ark ship descended from the sky and hovered a little above the height of the trees over the temple.

126 As in the days of Noah, a long, wide ramp descended from one wing of the giant ship, turning back and forth upon itself several times before it touched the ground. But unlike in the days of Noah, no Oolarians came down, but they chose instead to remain aboard and await the Savasi.

127 During the remaining hours of the day and into the night, the Savasi walked up the long ramp and into the ship. Many carried their pets in their arms and they were allowed to board, and many were in tears at all they had to leave behind, including many of the Gersan whom they had befriended.

128 The words of the prophet and all that had been told by Elohim the Father had been sent within moments after his last meeting with the Council of Elders to all of the scientific-exploration parties scattered across the earth, and all raced to return to the islands to be with their families and board the Oolarian Ark.

129 All of the airships, every one, were flown up into an even-larger opening in the other wing of the Ark, and many carried equipment and devices of the advanced sciences of the Savasi so that none would be left behind to do harm to the Gersan.

130 The prophet came up in one of the last ships with his family. Pulling a small two-wheeled cart with the help of two of the twelve, he bore a most precious cargo: a complete copy, encoded on crystals and stones, of the entire Library of Knowledge.

131 The momentous task of copying all the knowledge of the library had begun over two years earlier at the direction of Elohim the Father, who knew even then all that would come to pass, as he does even to this day and beyond.

132 So too did he and the Council of Twelve insure that all entrances to the Great Library, and all of its branches were securely sealed in ways that would defy intrusion until the time Elohim called for the knowledge to come forth again upon earth.

133 However, all the Savasi did not willingly go up the ramp and into the Oolarian Ark. Some took elaborate actions to remain undetected until the ship had departed.

134 But it was to no avail, as once together, to fulfill the word of Elohim, the Council of Twelve joined in a Circle of Power and sent forth a spell of desire over all the islands of Guache, and any Savasi not yet aboard the Ark felt an overpowering urge to be there and raced to join the others already on board.

135 Near midnight of the third day, the Oolarian Ark ship silently rose into the starry sky as the Gersan remaining on the islands watched in awestruck wonder.

136 The Savasi crowded to viewing windows and portals as the Ark broke free of the atmosphere; they looked back upon the world that had been their home with much reflection and an outpouring of feelings.

137 But as earth quickly became just another indistinguishable star in the sky, they turned their thoughts in expectant contemplation and quiet conversations with one another to the new earth that would soon be their home and considered all the adventures and wonders that might be before them.

138 And most at some point in the first hours aboard the Ark fell to their knees in most earnest prayer and gave thanks to Elohim for their blessings—so great they were—beyond the expectations of men.

CHAPTER 10

The Seed Bearers

Approximately twelve hundred of the Savasi return to earth from the planet Harbonta in the Seven Sisters star system at the request of Elohim the Mother who comes to the prophet Leolian in a dream. They are the "seed bearers" and from them come the twelve great ancient civilizations of man upon earth.

nd it came to pass that after the departure of the Savasi from earth, the primitive civilization among the tribes of Gersan scattered across the world remained almost unchanged for many millennia that followed.

2 The Savasi that had departed traveled to the planet Harbonta in the star system of the Seven Sisters, as this was the nearest world to earth from which they had come where the inhabitants were their equals in culture, technology, and spiritual understanding.

3 There they lived and prospered for generations upon generations, but not without turmoil, both from within and without.

4 Within the star system of the Seven Sisters on nearby planets and upon Harbonta, there dwelt a few communities of Oolarians: the Savasi, the new settlers from earth; Surtuas, another Alamar race civilization; and three other non-Alamar races. Other than the Savasi, all the others were at similar levels of technological advancement.

5 Amongst these groups, especially between the Alamars and the non-Alamars, there were often frictions and hostilities, but never destruction or warfare. But those accounts are best left for another time.

6 And though the Oolarians were friends with the Savasi, they never shared with them the secrets of their great ships of space, and even after millennia, the Savasi were unable to duplicate the technology of even short off-planet space travel.

7 After several generations had come and gone, many of the descendants of the Savasi fell away from faithfulness to the light of Elohim, and the history of the departure of their ancestors from earth seemed to most Savasi to be only a myth.

8 After a time, the Oolarians abandoned their communities and did not return, and this contributed to the vanishing of the stories of earth from the memories of the Savasi.

9 But upon a fateful day, in the eighty-eighth year of the prophet Leolian, Elohim the Mother came to Leolian in a dream and said unto him, "The earth has matured and its people have evolved. It is good soil, waiting for the planting of good seeds that it might fulfill the fullness of its destiny.

10 "You and your people are the Seed Bearers. It is given to you to do what your ancestors could not: to plant the seeds and cultivate the garden and bring to pass the blossoming of earth

and the people therein.

11 Gather unto you twelve hundred men, women, and children that hold most true to the light and return to the planet of your ancestors.

12 That the darkness will wane and the light will wax, go to the twelve places upon the earth wherein dwells the largest number of people. Divide yourselves into twelve groups and let each settle amongst the people of one of these twelve places.

13 Bring nothing with you of the civilizations of Harbonta, save those of simple workings. Let each adult carry only the clothes on their back, the knowledge in their minds, their personal possessions, and one hundred chavrons of gold with which to begin a new life.

14 Consider yourselves to be Celestine teachers, and the people of earth are your students. This is your sacred duty and calling from us.

15 We have given unto all the children of earth, born for the last seven generations, our light written upon their souls. Because of this, they were born not entirely in the mold of their parents, and they are in our image and ready for the greater light that you can bring.

16 Teach them line upon line, by word and by example, of knowledge both temporal and spiritual greater than they know, that they may become a people as great as has been promised to them from before their world began.

17 But seek not to transform them in a generation or even two or three. Give them greater knowledge only as they are capable of holding it with greater responsibility and stewardship.

18 As I have spoken. So let it be."

19 And it came to pass that the prophet Leolian did as the Mother directed and gathered twelve hundred of the brightest lights from among his people to return to earth, the long-forgotten planet of their ancestors.

20 But in this task, he had many challenges, for at first there were few, even among the most stalwart, who were willing to act upon his words and leave the comforts and security of all their homes and civilization to journey to a more-primitive world so distant it could not be seen even with the most powerful stargazers.

21 It was only after much persuasion, prayer, and fasting that 312 families, comprising just over twelve hundred individuals, agreed to make the journey to earth and leave everyone and all they had known for all of their lives on Harbonta behind forever.

22 Once again, it fell to the Oolarians and an Ark ship to return the new settlers of earth to the planet. But few Oolarians still followed the ways of Elohim and a ship and crew were only procured after payment of three hundred chavrons of gold per passenger.

23 It is fortunate that the divine Mother only directed the settlers to bring one hundred chavrons of gold each, as that was all most had left after selling all of their property and most of their possessions to raise the fee demanded by the Oolarians for passage to earth.

24 Even after divesting themselves of all of their possessions, it was only after some of the wealthier settlers and some with less children paid the passage for those still lacking the fee and some who were remaining on Harbonta contributed, that the entire 369,000 chavrons of gold was paid to the Oolarians.

25 The trip to earth took over three years, but finally the day arrived when the blue planet came into view and few were those who were not awed as the Ark approached ever closer.

26 There was much discussion before their arrival about how best to make their presence known and integrate into the native populations, and the Ark circled the planet for three months after its arrival to give the settler's time to study the languages and customs of the various native groups to which they would be going amongst.

27 A varied approach to first contact, depending upon the inclination for violence or peace by the local people, was agreed upon.

28 The families were divided into twelve groups of approximately one hundred each.

29 Eight of the settler groups were coming among peaceful people, and they were quietly disembarked in secluded locations near local populations with the intention to first establish

their own community and, shortly thereafter, make contact with the local people and integrate into their communities.

30 The four groups of settlers that landed near native groups likely to be hostile, were settled atop high, easily defended pinnacles, with the intention to fortify their positions and make gradual contact with the natives from their protected enclaves.

31 Thus were the descendants of the Savasi returned again to earth in number, and through them and their descendants, over the course of varying times, sprang forth the twelve great ancient civilizations of earth before the coming of Elohim the Son.

CHAPTER 11

The Destiny of Man

Approximately one thousand years before Yeshua comes to earth, the prophet Yasvon is visited in her dreams by Elohim the Son, who answers her many questions about mankind. He explains in exquisite detail why we are here on earth and what our personal destinies and potentials are.

Ever a thousand years before Elohim the Son came to earth, there lived in the city of Eridu, in the land of Kiengir of the two rivers, the descendants of one of the twelve groups of Savasi that had returned to earth to bring back the light and lift the state of man spiritually and temporally.

2 This was the eleventh generation that had been born since the time the Savasi had first returned to earth.

3 Quickly after their arrival, their ancestors had become one with the native people through marriage, and now they were indistinguishable from the Saggiga people who had come from the north generations before the Savasi had returned to inhabit and farm the rich land of the delta of two rivers.

4 Nevertheless, it was not forgotten among the descendants of the Savasi the stories of how their ancestors had returned to earth to bring back the light, and though the Saggiga worshipped a wide variety of false gods, the descendants of the Savasi still remained faithful to the true light of Elohim.

5 Thus, it was that they still kept the ways of Elohim that had been taught to them by their parents and looked, with faith, to a prophet called of God to give them the pure guidance, light, and truth of Elohim.

6 In her forty-fourth year, Yasvon the Wise was called by Elohim and confirmed by unanimous support of the Council of Twelve to be the new prophetess when Hasslamar the Astute died.

7 And it came to pass that the prophetess Yasvon fulfilled her calling, and through her came a wonderful book of scripture concerning the destiny of man.

8 These are the words she spoke to the Council of Twelve and the Children of Light on that day so long ago:

9 "Beloved friends, it is such a humbling honor to be numbered among you, and to speak to you this day of a great dream from Elohim that came upon me seven nights ago.

10 Many times in my dreams, I have spoken with the divine Mother and received her loving guidance that we might all become better than we are and continue to prosper in this land.

11 Occasionally, the divine Father has also come to me in my dreams, and his presence, though equal in love to the Mother, is so very different than hers.

12 It could be no other way, for we are male and female and have been created in their divine

images. Male and female we marry and two become one; that in the two that are one there is a balance of love and light and strength and wisdom; that we and our children may always be blessed by the balance.

13 But seven nights ago, someone came to me in my dream who has never appeared before. Though the divine Mother and Father speak often of him, never had I seen him or heard his voice. But on this holy night, Elohim the Son came unto me.

14 He told me that he had come to answer my question. In truth, I was surprised, though I should not have been, for I had been thinking much of late upon a most vexing question, but I had spoken of it to no one, save to Elohim in my prayers.

15 I had been pondering upon the history of man, from the times of Eden and Noah and our ancestors' travels to another earth, up into this time in which we live.

16 It seemed to me as I reflected upon the history of man that time after time, there was a cycle of coming closer to Elohim and then falling away.

17 This could happen to one person in a lifetime or to a group of Children of Light over the span of many generations.

18 I contemplated how it could be possible for men and even Children of Light, in many times past, to witness marvelous wonders and miracles from Elohim and still walk away from the light and the joy that living in the light brings.

19 As I looked back upon the history of man from the time of Eden until the time we live, try as I might, I could not understand how it is that man never seems to learn from the follies of history and that the errors made by one generation, rather than being remembered as lessons of what not to do, are instead forever repeated by generations that follow, who become doomed by their foolish actions to suffer the same pains in mortality and immortality as their ancestors.

20 Why has this cycle never been broken? Is man so thick-skulled and dim-witted that no matter how many times he hits himself on the head with a mallet, he cannot comprehend what is causing the pain?

21 Why, throughout history, have men from earth continued to war with one another and kill one another and do all manner of atrocities to one another, despite the evidence after every war that victory is hollow and that which is lost by both sides is far greater than anything won by the victor?

22 From our parents and grandparents, we know that in worlds beyond this earth, this lesson has been learned, even by people more primitive than we of earth are today. If it is so elsewhere, then why not here upon this earth, with these men?

23 And how is it possible that Children of Light who have been blessed with knowledge and understanding and Celestine abilities above all others have ever been able to turn their backs upon the light and embrace the misery and loneliness of the darkness, even to participate in a level of war and destruction so great as to not be imagined by the men of earth today, so great that those few Children of Light who survived were our ancestors who fled this planet.

24 But that which vexed me most was truly my incomprehension as to why after millennia of time, after repeated help and intervention from Elohim, after countless wars of pointless destruction, after countless lives of misery led by those walking in darkness, the state of man today upon the earth is less than it was even at the time of our ancestors the Savasi or of Noah or of the Edenites.

25 Upon the return of our people from the stars, we have given the people who were here on earth new technologies that have propelled them to greater heights of civilization, but are there less wars? Is man kinder and more compassionate to his fellow man? Has loving service to one another replaced forced servitude and slavery? Beyond our small circle, do people have greater love for the temple of their bodies?

26 As was promised, our ancestors have been the seeds from which the new civilizations of man have sprouted, but that is simply a level of greater comfort for the shell of man. What seed of light has sprouted within the eternal spirit of man? Why after millennia upon millennia is

man still in so great a darkness, still repeating the errors of every generation that has gone before, instead of learning the lessons and becoming greater in spirit and love than every generation that has gone before?

27 This was the question I have pondered and asked of Elohim. And in a dream, Elohim the Son came to me, and these are the words he spoke unto me:"

28 "Beloved sister of spirit, to understand the answer to your question, you must more fully comprehend where those who dwell upon the earth have come from, why they are here in mortality upon this earth and not another earth, the fullness of the purpose of life, and the promise of life everlasting.

29 Mortality is not the first step nor the last, but a middle step in the eternal progression of man.

30 The earth you live upon is only one of many earths that men live upon, so many in number that they are like the sands of the sea.

31 When children are taught in school, are the boys sent to learn beside the girls or the girls beside the boys? No, they are not, for the ways of the male are not the ways of the female; therefore, they are taught separately, in different manners, each for their greatest benefit.

32 Even within the schools of the boys and the schools of the girls, are there not still greater separations? Some learn quicker than others, and they are placed with their peers. Others need special attention to help them focus, and they are grouped with others like unto themselves.

33 By this, each has the greatest opportunity to learn to the fullest of their potential by being taught in a manner most in harmony with their spirit and studiousness, while the door still remains open to a greater harmony with another school if they desire something more in their life.

34 And so it is even in the hereafter, where each is drawn to that which is most in harmony with their spirit and their proclivities, be it light or darkness, but with the door always open to a greater light if they are willing to walk the path that leads to the door.

35 In mortality or immortality, it is upon this foundation of harmony that the eternal progression of man goes forward, that man may say, 'Here I am today, but with greater desire and efforts, there I will be tomorrow because that is the tomorrow that calls to me.'

36 Thus, man is rewarded in mortality and immortality with the harmony of his choice, be it light or darkness, and is always afforded the opportunity to seek a new harmony and a greater light if he is willing to make the effort.

37 Therefore, think of each earth as a school, and to each school of mortality upon each earth are sent the students who are most in harmony with one another, be that harmony of light or harmony of darkness, that they will have the greatest opportunity to learn and grow and become more than they are.

38 Since the beginning of its creation, upon your earth, some of the greatest lights of Heaven have been sent to be teachers, by precept and example, and you and the Children of Light are among them.

39 And they have been sorely needed, for your earth has ever been filled with the malcontents of Heaven, those who, even in the life before life, were disruptors rather than peacemakers, doubters rather than believers.

40 Your earth is their harmony. And their harmony is often war and destruction and abominations.

41 Unto these have you been sent and many other great lights of Heaven before you that you might teach by precept and example and raise their harmony to a greater height;

42 Not all the world at once, but line upon line, precept upon precept, example upon example, one person at a time.

43 Therefore, be not discouraged by the repetitions of the follies of man. Understand the harmony of the earth upon which you live, even though to you it is disharmony. And know that despite the repetition of foolishness, you can change the world and bring it into greater light,

one person at a time.

44 As to the purpose of life, there are many. But the greatest is to reach a state of consciousness in which you have an inner peace which transcends mortality, making you one in spirit, thought, and action, not only with your earth and all life therein, but also with the boundless light of the Celestine Realms.

45 In this, you are in Heaven even amidst the trials and tribulations of life, and no challenge or vexation of mortal life that comes upon you can sway or topple you from your inner serenity.

46 Before mortality, you lived in greater freedom; no one sought your life, forced you to pay taxes, or compelled you to act against your beliefs. You did not have to squander the hours of your life laboring at that which you despise just to survive and provide food and shelter and clothing for your family.

47 In the life to come, this freedom will be even greater and your spirit will soar upon freedom's wings.

48 In mortality, you may not be confined in a prison of stone, but you are confined within the prison of your physical, mortal body and all of its weaknesses. You can fall sick or be injured physically, emotionally, mentally, or spiritually, and you can die. But so can you live.

49 Never forget amidst the travails of mortality that you are sons and daughters of the divine Father and Mother and are connected in spirit to all living things, both on earth and beyond. You are radiant rays of light that can illuminate the deepest darkness.

50 In the life before life, you were as you are now: sons and daughters of God. But that knowledge was ever present, and because of that, many came to no longer appreciate the great treasure that is their souls source, for the knowledge of it was always with them.

51 Now you are cast with the others into the darkness and forgetfulness of mortality for a lifetime. How can you best fulfill the purpose of this life? By reaching through the darkness and discovering yourself—the divinity from which you have come—and living the greater light which is revealed.

52 Love and nurture the temple of your body, for in that, you honor Elohim the creator. But do not forget it is but a temporary shell given to many imperfections, vagrancies, infirmities, disease, and death.

53 Nor forget that this very temporary shell is not you. It is only the physical covering of your soul for a breath of eternity.

54 Therefore, do not separate yourselves by the colors of your skins or hair or eyes or the beauty of your face or the youth or suppleness of your body, for these things are not you, merely an artist's covering to hold the brilliant sun of your soul.

55 The masterpiece is not outside of you. It is inside of you.

56 But for you to know and love your eternal soul and spirit, you must be one in spirit with the source of all creation, even our divine Father and Mother.

57 For by their command have all things come into existence, and there is not one thing that exists or has existed or will exist that is not from them.

58 You are a part of Elohim, and they are a part of you, even as you are a part of all that lives and all that lives is a part of you.

59 The cause for all of man's problems and sickness and sorrow is that the connection between man and God, and man and all life has been severed. Reconnect man to God and man to all life, in heart and spirit, and the man shall be transformed from darkness to light.

60 Return to eternal oneness and there is no place for strife, sickness, or sorrow, for man only wars with that which is not in harmony with his eternal soul.

61 Cease looking at the differences between men and women on the outside and instead remember and embrace the divine inner harmony that all people can have through the divinity by which they were created.

62 The resonance of this earth has been dim and dark, separated from the harmony of Elohim that is bright and light.

63 Guide those in darkness to the light by precept and example, and many will resonate again with the light that is the source of their creation and eternity.

64 All the sorrow that comes upon the children of men, all the weeping, all the pain, all the sufferings, come only when man is separated in spirit from the healing love of the divine Mother and Father, which is an abiding peace and tranquility that overcomes all sorrow and pain and grief.

65 You were created before this world was as true sons and daughters of God to progress eternally that someday you might even become as our divine Mother and Father now arc.

66 In the life before life, you werc closer to understanding and being one and in harmony with that awareness.

67 Now in mortality, a veil of forgetfulness has come upon you that you may develop faith, that you might find your bosom welling up with feelings of overwhelming love as you connect again with your spirit to our divine Mother and Father, not from things that you see, which may be an illusion, but from that which you feel in your soul as it becomes one with all that is and rises to a new resonance as it recognizes the true harmony of its existence.

68 Remind yourself continually, until it is never forgotten, that your outer shell and the physical world are of little importance. Therefore, why should the challenges of the outer life cause you despair?

69 Be at peace and in harmony with your inner eternal soul and your eternal love and connection to Elohim and all that is, and nothing that assails you on the outside can affect your inner serenity.

70 It is your eternal soul and spirit that are of monumental importance, and all the mortal world has been created simply to help you more clearly find your eternal soul and, once found, to connect in a oneness of love to Elohim and all life; for the divine Mother and Father and all life are eternally a part of you, even as I am.

71 Seek to be one with the divine in your heart, soul, mind, and spirit, and no challenge of the world will be able to overcome you.

72 The men of the world seek to connect to the divine by making gods of kings and following elaborate ceremonies and rituals within a myriad of religions. In this, their spirit remains vacant, for you cannot find the spiritual, which remains forever in time beyond this world, with things of the physical, which are here today and gone tomorrow.

73 Therefore, have no ritual or ceremony of religion save those of simplicity that move your heart and soul to connect in a oneness with all living things, a oneness with Elohim, and a oneness with the divine that is within you.

74 You are in mortality to perfect yourselves, to overcome your weaknesses and make them your strengths, to increase the length and breadth and depth of your good character even so much that your children honor you and hold you as their ideal, that many in need have been helped by your service, and that when you pass from mortality it will be remembered that to have been your child or your friend was a blessing that lives on.

75 As a Child of Light, your destiny in mortality is not to become a great leader or to be revered as a wise sage or a great healer, although you may become all of these things and more if it is your desire and focus.

76 But your destiny is far greater than any of these. It is a destiny given to all, but realized by few. Your destiny is simply to live up to the potential of your divine heritage and become as perfect in your life as is possible, given time and circumstances.

77 Begin with your attitude, for in this, you light the fires of your actions. Be sweet of disposition, praising of others, not critical. Be excited and curious, always looking to grow and expand your knowledge and good experiences.

78 Act with wisdom, ever mindful of the perfection you seek.

79 Remember the laws of health and vitality and live them well that your body might always be well, even into your ancient age.

80 Be moderate and temperate in all things, but also passionate in the joys of your righteous pleasures.

81 Ever seek to develop and maintain a perfect physique for your age, with health and strength and stamina that belies your years.

82 Never be satisfied with where you are, for when you stop reaching, you do not remain where you are, but slide backward to become less than you were.

83 Cultivate the garden of your mind. Nourish the flowers within, that your garden may always remain vibrant, but also plant new flowers of knowledge each day that your garden may ever be growing and expanding, even until it holds flowers from all the world.

84 Be noble and pure in your thoughts. Purge your mind of pettiness, greed, vanity, jealousy, craving, and hurtful ambition.

85 Cultivate divine thoughts and sentiments. See the good in people and situations, and you will bring it out in them and in yourself.

86 Think not so much of what you can do for yourself, but more of what you can do for others.

87 Consider how you can be a light of benefit, happiness and help to others, especially to your family and those you love with a sacred love.

88 Let not your mind think along dark and crooked paths, but seek out the straight and narrow, illuminated by the brilliant light of virtue.

89 It is the weak man who gives up the light of his mind and turns it to darkness, becoming crude in language and actions, cunning, sly, manipulative, secretive, a hidden danger to all who know him.

90 Seek instead examples of greatness and light and emulate them. Be idealistic in your character and ever strive to reach your ideals.

91 Look at other men and women who have achieved at least a part of that which you seek, who have obtained the pinnacle of a mountain of character you desire to embody.

92 Consider how you can be like unto them, for surely as one man has become, so may others be; for in every light that you see, so too can you shine.

93 And if you thus endeavor for perfection in your life, not as a zealot, but in harmony, peace, forbearance, and love, then you shall find the bliss that you seek, the harmony of oneness, and the precious bond to the love of our divine Mother and Father that is the balm to all pains and the river to transcendent joy.

94 Even if you never reach the ideal you seek, be not discouraged, for if you strive faithfully, you will become the embodiment of the character which you sought.

95 Therefore, in your pursuit of sweet perfection, do not be a perfectionist or berate yourself for falling short, for perfection is not for this life but the next, and if you are seeking your goals with honest effort, you are achieving them even while you seek.

96 Verily, if you strive with sincerity and purpose to embody a divine character and never abandon your sweet spirit or idealism, you are a success in your endeavors of eternal significance, every day of your life.

97 Is it little wonder that even in a society of darkness that the man or woman who embodies such an ethical and moral character becomes a priceless jewel, a firm, reliable tower of light from which even those in darkness take comfort?

98 When you are challenged by mortal life, as you always shall be, let this be a time when the true divinity of your character comes forth. Do not allow times of stress and turmoil to shake you from your foundation.

99 And what is your foundation? You are a child of God, a Child of Light, literally a priceless son or daughter of divinity. Even through the fog of mortal upheavals and the tumults and tribulations, always remember you are still a child of God and shall inherit joy and kingdoms beyond measure, as you remain true to your light.

100 Elohim the Father and the Mother are the source of all things that exist, and you are a part of the source and they are a part of you. Even when the agitation and anxieties of life cloud

your memory, it does not change the truth: You are a child of God, a Child of Light, a priceless son or daughter of divinity.

101 You are founded upon Celestine Light. You live, move, and have your soul filled with the divine light, whether you know it or not.

102 Everything that exists, that has existed, or that will exist, both the living and the inanimate, were created through the Celestine Light of Elohim. That divine light remains within them, a part of them, throughout all eternity.

103 Because the divine light of Elohim exists within all things from their creation, so Elohim remains in all things and all people. Elohim is all-pervading. By the word of Elohim countless earths and the stars that surround them were created, and the Celestine Light of Elohim is inseparable from them.

104 Though people and places may become shrouded in darkness, there will always remain at least a sliver of the light. And from that sliver, the light may always grow, even until it overcomes the darkness.

105 Therefore, remember, remember, when you are of weak faith or downtrodden by the torments of mortality, that you are ever a child of God whether you remember it or not, that within you waiting always to see the light is a divine perfection, a divine bliss, a divine love for the sacred and the holy.

106 When men do evil, they cover the light of their divine nature and hide it from themselves and others. The more evil they do, the more the light is hidden.

107 But never forget that no matter how evil a man becomes, he can never eradicate the divine light of Elohim that is inescapably a part of his soul forever.

108 And the same divine light of the soul that calls man to his greatness will also condemn the man who heeds not the calling and instead does evil in his life.

109 For after mortality, there will come a day of judgment, and it will be the divine light of his own soul that judges the man, when he looks into the light and sees his shadow.

110 If his light has been hidden by his evil acts, it will shine but a glimmer of its former glory and great will be his shadow. But if he has fulfilled his destiny, the light of his soul will be brilliant; radiating forth in every direction, even so much that there will be no shadow.

111 Thus, man is judged not by the Elohim, but by his own soul, by his light and his shadow, which shows without prejudice or favor how well he fulfilled his own destiny of divinity in mortality.

112 Now you live upon a tumultuous earth. Disease, famine, pestilence, and war may overcome you at any time. If you live in the light of Elohim, you will be prepared, and through all these challenges, you will more likely stand, even while others fall.

113 Nevertheless, if your sojourn in mortality ends before you have been able to strive in fullness for your perfection, you have no cause to mourn, for your opportunity has not ended, nor can it ever end, for there is no end to your radiant, eternal spirit, and soul.

114 Remember, you are not the frail mortal shell which you see in the mirror, but a radiant, immortal child of divinity, which weapons cannot kill, fire cannot burn, disease cannot wrack, and sadness cannot overwhelm.

115 You were not born, nor can you die. You are eternal, permanent, beyond time, and death has no meaning for you. You are everlasting, immortal, indestructible, deathless, and without birth, save the birth of your spirit and soul through the love of your Heavenly Father and Mother before this world was.

116 Whatever tragedies, afflictions, or sorrows occur in your life, even unto death, happen not to you, but only upon your shell of mortality, the frail covering of flesh and bones housing your soul.

117 This oh-so-temporary shell does not need a pestilence or disease or war to destroy it. When it becomes old, if it survives the wars and pestilences and diseases, it will still wear out and cease to be.

118 Therefore, be not so concerned about the number of years given to your mortal shell, for there are a myriad of ways by which it can come to an end—some sooner, others later—but to an end it shall always come.

119 Be more concerned with your indestructible and immortal soul and what you can do in the years given unto you in mortality to perfect it and help it to radiate its glory. This is your destiny.

120 And if through accident or disease or war or tribulation, your sojourn in mortality ends before its time, you shall be given another, even until you have had ample opportunity to fulfill the full measure of your mortal experience.

121 Like unto the schoolhouse in your town burning down, the destruction of your mortal shell, if premature, does not end the opportunity for your soul to expand in mortality; for even as another school would be built in your town that you could continue your education, so shall another mortal shell be given unto your soul in another mortal life, perhaps even on another earth, that you might have the opportunity to fulfill the full measure of your mortality.

122 I say again, fear not the frailties of mortality, even unto death. Even were all life upon your earth to be destroyed by the follies of man, you remain, you are not touched, you are not destroyed, for you are sons and daughters of God and you are as eternal as the Elohim.

123 Your destiny remains true and clear; you are not the body, but the soul. Your soul is you, and you are eternal.

124 You are light; you are good; you are one with all of creation.

125 Therefore, ever seek to fulfill the divinity of your creation, ever doing good, ever welcoming the resonance of the spirit of Elohim into the bosom of your soul, ever seeking the perfection of your being in every way. This is your destiny."

THE SECOND BOOK OF LIGHT

CALLED

NEXUS

CHAPTER 1

Light of Yeshua the Messiah

This is the only chapter in the Oracles of Celestine Light where Yeshua is speaking directly to you, as the reader. Yeshua speaks about the past and the promises of the future

Thus spoke Yeshua the Messiah: "I am Yeshua of Nazareth. I came upon the earth to bring the fullness of the Celestine Light of God, and I ascended into Heaven with my peace and teachings upon the hearts of the Children of Light.

2 Then came the vicissitudes of the world, and in less than a generation, many of the great truths that I spoke and lived became as dust blowing in the wind, lost and forgotten in the annals of men.

3 But the whirlwind comes, and upon its breath, the fullness of truth shall rise up and the Celestine Light shall shine once again.

4 Unto the Children of Israel, I gave simple laws of life and eternity, promising that unto those who believed in me and lived that which I taught, the Holy Spirit would come to lift their hearts and their lives would be filled with peace and wonder.

5 Unto my Apostles who walked with me in life, I taught the mysteries of God, for they were sent forth unto the tribes of Israel and into a world that would love them not; therefore, I gave unto them a fuller understanding of all things that they might have a shield of greater knowledge and a well of deeper faith to withstand the persecutions to come.

6 Unto the valiant Children of Light, who fully lived the foundations given unto them, my Apostles were directed to endow with a greater knowledge as they were guided by the Holy Spirit, but these gifts were bestowed only to a precious few of the worthy and faithful before my friends were martyred or departed from the earth. And those precious lights became voices from the past, crying in the wilderness to people who heard them not.

7 While I ministered unto the children of men, many of the faithful wrote the words which I spoke and of the things I did. Nevertheless, not until after the fall of the temple at Jerusalem did there begin to be a gathering of that which had been recorded and then by those who had not known me in the flesh; therefore, that which was written again was not always that which had been, and because of persecutions and religious prejudices, more of what I said and did was lost and cast out than was saved.

8 And it came to pass that the full and faithful accounting of my life and many of the plain and precious precepts which I spoke and lived were altered in the oral and written words of men: some to offer appeal to the Children of Israel and others to offer appeal to the Gentiles.

9 And precious understandings and stories of the light were lost because of the intolerance of men, even the righteous, when the words and remembrances of my beloved, Miriam, who knew

me more than all others, were cast out and found no place in the canons of acceptance.
10 And I ask you who seek the truth: where are the writings of the eleven who walked faithfully with me and broke bread with me and were living testaments to my life and teachings?
11 Verily, they were honestly written by their learned disciples, but cast out by both the pious and persecutors, for they gave the fullness of my teachings and not the words and precepts men desired to hear.
12 To some, my life was a storm. For I came not only to uphold the true laws given by God, but also to throw upon the ground and trample under feet the unjust laws of men and the false traditions given in the name of God that lead the innocent astray. Because of this, for many, it was easier to give up their life in my name than to understand and live the fullness of the Celestine Light which I taught.
13 I am the good shepherd, and I have ever called upon the Children of Light of pure heart to be of one fold, with a common understanding and acceptance of the fullness of the truth, to faithfully follow the path that I taught by precept and example, with humility and love. I truly sorrow for the foolishness and weakness of men when it is not so.
14 Nevertheless, all things come to pass as they need to be, and for the honest and open of heart, Elohim shall always give succor to that which they seek that they might be sustained, despite all that men and evil may do.
15 And to those of contrite spirit who seek the truth with openness and a sincere desire to understand, the Holy Spirit of Elohim will testify with warmth in their heart and illumination in their mind.
16 My Father and Mother know all things which shall come to pass and allow adversity to be in the world that the valiant might gain faith and those who search earnestly for truth will find it, by the strength of their faith.
17 And I say unto you that faith is the foundation of all truths, for it is the power by which all things are and can be. To know faith abiding in every fiber of your essence is to fulfill one of the great purposes of your life and to unlatch the door to your glory in eternity.
18 In the days of old, after a time, came one flock into preeminence by grace of the Romans, and they organized unto their persuasion, choosing for their foundation the writings and revisions of the words of my Apostles and disciples that agreed with their desires and burying those which did not. Thus, like many others, they used my name to sway the hearts of men to follow the portions of the truth which were pleasing unto them and served their purposes, demanding obedience to their dictates and not to the fullness of the Celestine Light of Elohim, which I had given by precept and example.
19 Then were many plain and simple truths of Heaven hidden by the persecutions, desires, and craftiness of men, and the Children of Light could only find the truth in their hearts and in their dreams of the night, when the Holy Spirit testified to those who cried out in humility and faith.
20 But that which has been lost is given again in fullness, for my teachings bring joy and that which I ask does not burden but enlightens, for it is the Gospel of love, of life, and of light.
21 Verily, I say unto you: This generation shall not pass away until all that has been hidden is brought again into the light, for it is the epoch for the fulfillment of promise.
22 Unto this generation has my Father and Mother saved the greatest spirits of Heaven to come forth upon the world, and to them will be given the plentitude of truth, both that which was lost and that which is new.
23 And the fullness of the Celestine Light of God shall lift up the righteous, but it shall blind the wicked and in their lack of sight, they shall fight against the restoration of truth and the brightness of the new light, even in the name of God, who knows them not.
24 Woe unto such, for it is better that they had never been born. And he who sows a wicked seed against God shall reap an eternal harvest of misery infinitely greater than the seed he sowed.
25 Now come my brethren, the Apostles who walked with me upon the earth, to speak

with the prophet I have called in this age, in word and vision; unto him have been given keys and authority that the plainness and mysteries of my Gospel shall be made known among the children of men to prepare the world for the glory to come.

26 That which has been hidden is now declared unto the world by my word. As I gave unto my Apostles of old, I say again that in wholeness, upon the foundation of Prophets, Apostles, Bishops, Evangelists, Seekers, and the Adepts among them; with support from Pastors, Seventies, Elders, Priests, Deacons, and Teachers, the fullness of Celestine Light shall stand; that there may be a unity of faith and an edification and perfecting of the Children of Light.

27 Prepare now for the coming of the glory of the kingdom of God on earth; like a whirlwind from the desert, through the stinging sand, the new day dawns, and those who love me no longer need seek me in the mists of confusion, for they will find me in the brightness of the sun."

CHAPTER 2

Preamble of the Apostles

The Apostles share with us the pure foundations of truth as they testify of their first-hand experiences with Yeshua of Nazareth and admonish each of us to seek through prayer with Elohim, our own testimonies of the truth. ~ The special Admonition of the Apostles to all seekers of truth. ~ The Apostles explain the true status of Paul of Tarsus.

Thus spoke the Apostles of Yeshua: "Herein is the true account of the most important
events and teachings in the earthly life of Yeshua of Nazareth, the only begotten son of
God; who though glorified and without sin, came to earth of lowly birth that the path
to God would be made clear for all mankind.
2 He is our friend and salvation, and so much more than you have known.
3 We speak to you of the things which we have seen with our own eyes and heard with our
own ears, and also of the testimonies of other disciples of that which they have seen and heard;
much of which was written and is no more, and some of which was never written except upon
the hearts of those who were witnesses.
4 Verily, the fullness of the truth that has been hidden is now brought into the light that all
righteousness may be given unto you.
5 Know that because of prejudices and false beliefs and partial truths that have prevailed for
millenniums, the words of this book shall turn the world upon its head, and many will be those
who will fight against it, for it will challenge the foundations of their beliefs.
6 Therefore, we would ask that when you read these things, which the spirit of God has led
you to read, that you would not blindly heed the exhortations of men.
7 But go in humility to seek out God, in a quiet place of solitude, in the brightness of the sun.
And upon your knees, with palms together, with an open heart humbly desiring to know the
light of truth, lift up your face to the warmth of the sun, and in the name of Yeshua the Messiah,
ask to know the truthfulness of our words and of our accounting of the life of our elder Brother
of Spirit.
8 And if you shall ask with a humble spirit, with an open heart, and in all sincerity desiring to
know the truth, the spirit of God shall flow into you.
9 And you shall know the truth and the truth will set your spirit free; and with an overflowing
joy in your heart and a clear knowing in your mind, the Holy Spirit of God will testify to you;
whereby you may know the truth of all things.
10 As a child, he was called Yeshua and this was the name by which he was known by his
family and friends, save a few who called him Yeshu.
11 But in Galilee, the land of his holy ministry, Greek prevailed in commerce and among

many of the people since the time of Alexander of Macedonia. Under that influence he came to be known throughout the land as Iesous of Nazareth.

12 In other tongues Yeshua was called still differently and it matters not; for it is enough that a believer calls upon him with the name by which they know him and with a humble spirit, and by that name, he will answer; for though he is called by many names, in many tongues, it is not because of the name, but because of the spirit of the heart that seeks him that he answers; and by no other name except one spoken with a contrite heart and a true desire for truth, will he answer.

13 To you we give his name Yeshua, the simple name by which he asked his closest friends to call him; that you may know that as you believe in him and follow his teachings and the example of his life, you have the never failing love of your truest friend.

14 So too do we call Yochanan, his kin who prepared his way, by his birth name, for he and Yeshua were the bridge between the old ways and the new, between the Children of Israel and the world. And likewise, their parents who were observant of the old ways are called by the common names of their birth.

15 But we wish that you not be burdened with comprehending unfamiliar names, and therefore leave to Embrosewyn, who has been given this work to bring forth, to use names as seems to him best, except where we otherwise direct.

16 Know that we speak with authority from God, to give the pure foundations of truth to all the world; for we were called by Yeshua, ordained and set apart to be special witnesses to teach his Gospel. To our eternal joy, we walked with him during our earthly sojourn and lived with him during his ministry, and had the humbling honor to know him as no other men ever will.

17 Therefore, know that Cephas - "The Rock," the Bonerges - "Sons of Thunder" and sons of Zebedee -- Ya'akov and Yohhanan, Amram, Philip bar Talmai, Yakov of Nazareth, Yuda, Toma, Shim'on "the Zealot," and the Sons of Cleopas -- Mattayah, and Yuda declare unto you that our Lord Yeshua lives!

18 In his love, Yeshua called us out of the world and set us apart to be Apostles of his Gospel; first to the tribe of Judah and the remnants of the twelve tribes in Israel; then to the dispersed tribes of Israel in other lands, and lastly unto the Gentiles.

19 Among many in the world today we are known as Peter, James, John, Andrew, Philip, Thomas, Simon, Matthew-Levi, James, and Jude. But the world truly knows us not. Yet we present you, the seekers of light, also with these names, as they are the ones you may associate with us in your day, though for the most part they are not ours.

20 Like our Lord, it matters not the names by which we are thought of, but matters only the spirit that carries the thought.

21 And know that we speak not at this time of two other Apostles whom you shall come to know, whose cherished works for Yeshua have been erased and perverted in the records of men, but are written forever in glory in the annuals of God. And they are numbered among us and speak as one with us.

22 And there was another; a great Evangelist. He was not an Apostle among us, but his imprint was indelible. After his resurrection, Yeshua called the persecutor, Saul of Tarsus unto repentance; and in humility he repented and took the name Paul to signify the change within his heart; that he had been born anew.

23 He was most learned and eloquent, and much loved for the depth of his faith; truly the inspired seed for a great multiplying of the believers among the Gentiles and of much good in the world.

24 For the Gentiles were roused in their souls by the teachings of Paul and more receptive to many of the new paths of light that had been given by Yeshua than were the Children of Israel.

25 Most of the words of Paul were true and wonderful, given as poetry to the soul. Nevertheless, he had contentions with many Apostles, for there were important foundations of truth which he was reluctant to teach because they differed from what he believed, and he had not heard Yeshua teach them as we had; therefore he continued to cling to a few tired prejudices which Yeshua had

done away with, or taught differently.

26 For this cause he was sent only unto the Gentiles who could more abide his ways than the Children of Israel, among whom the Apostles labored first and foremost.

27 In the millenniums that came to pass, the words and partial understandings of Paul, a convert who knew not Yeshua in life, became the foundation for the faith of many, and the only Gospel known to the Gentiles to whom he preached; while the words of we who spoke the complete truth as we had heard it from the lips of Yeshua, and as we had witnessed by the example of his life, were in great measure lost unto the world.

28 But we do not lament this; verily it was meant to be; for the world was not prepared to receive the fullness of the truth. Even as Yeshua was rejected by men when he was among them, so the fullness of his teachings required an openness of heart and mind that few could find.

29 Despite his missteps, Yeshua loved Paul for the great good that he did among the Children of Men, and forgave him for the truths which he taught not, and for the few doctrines which he taught in error; and he resides now in glory, for he fulfilled the full measure of his creation and was faithful unto Yeshua even unto death.

30 In the days that came to pass after the resurrection of the Lord of Light, other Apostles were called by the authority given to us by Yeshua, both men and women among them, to replace those who had been martyred or sent unto the lost tribes never to return; that there might continue to be twelve special stalwarts of the Messiah, blessed with a personal witness of his divinity, to guide and direct the Children of Light upon the earth.

31 As Yeshua had commanded, we went first to the Children of Israel in the land of Palestine, and then unto the tribes of Israel dispersed in many lands, near and far, who had forgotten the God of their fathers, and lastly unto the Gentiles.

32 Under the direction of the council of the twelve Apostles, others who were strong in the faith were called to be Seventies, charged with a dedication to spreading the good news, and sent forth to every nation, kindred, tongue and peoples that they might find to share the Gospel of Yeshua the Messiah.

33 And it came to pass that with the Holy Spirit in our hearts and the truth of God guiding our paths, the Gospel of the Celestine Light of Yeshua spread forth among the people of the land that the Children of Light might be found.

34 We preached that the old ways had become as dust, and that those who followed Yeshua were born into a new light.

35 A few of the faithful found a place for a fullness of our words, and the Holy Spirit resided fully in their hearts. But many were those who agreed only with a part of our teachings and preferred to cling in some traditions and beliefs to their ways of old.

36 And they changed the purity of the Gospel of Celestine Light to be pleasing unto them; thus the light was withdrawn in its fullness; and it came to pass that Apostles walked the earth no more, and the mysteries were hidden again until a more worthy generation should come forth to receive the plentitude of truth and herald the glory to come.

37 Unto the Children of Light who read these words and seek the truth from God; we say unto you, that you are the chosen generation, for now is the time for the fullness of truth, and it is to you that we speak.

38 We bear witness that Yeshua came from Heaven to walk among men, to preach the wonder of the Celestine Light and open the door to eternal expansion and happiness.

39 In humility and purity, he showed by his life the path that all who would know God must follow, and in his love brought forth the resurrection to exaltation for all who walk the path of truth and light.

40 And he gave a cherished promise of glory, joy and fulfillment, in this life and the next, unto all who repent of their sins, believe in him, obey his teachings and follow his ways.

41 Wherefore, knowing the path to eternal exaltation that Yeshua made open by his love, should it not be your earnest desire to follow his example and live as he has asked in your short

moment upon the earth; that you may inherit the full promise of eternity?

42 Verily, like Paul, we call upon you to put away the ways of the world and fulfill the full measure of your creation, for nothing less is worthy of the radiant light that you are, and the endless love of God given unto you."

CHAPTER 3

Nature of God

A detailed description of the true nature of God as well as the trinity.

❖ ❖ ❖

Our Father in Heaven, would that you should know that all light that permeates the
universe, both the physical and the spiritual, comes from God; that God is our Father
and our Mother in heaven and their only begotten Son in the flesh, Yeshua the Messiah.
And these three are the Elohim, the God of Heaven and earth.
2 And the Celestine Light of Elohim issues forth from the Father and the Mother through
Yeshua, for so they have decreed, and shines into the darkness of the world, and the darkness
cannot overcome it.
3 When thickest lays the oppressing night, the rays of the Celestine Light of Yeshua the
Messiah bridges the dark void between God and man.
4 From the beginning of creation, all who humbly sought the truth and lived in ways pleasing
to God and had faith in the greater power and majesty of God received a portion of their
Celestine Light to guide and uplift them according to their faith and goodness.
5 Near and far across the earth and through all time, God has touched the righteous and
bestowed riches of wisdom and spirit upon the pure in heart who humble themselves before the
majesty of the Almighty and do good works with selflessness and charity.
6 Among the Hebrews, the Christians, the Muslims, the Buddhists, the Taoists, and the
Vedics, verily, among all who sought truth and light that they might draw closer to God, they
have ever been illuminated with a portion of their glory.
7 Now unto all who will receive it, is given the fullness of the Gospel of Celestine Light as
it was taught by the Son of Light when he walked upon the earth; those who would be called
Children of Light will be strangers no more, but one with the source that they may prepare the
world for the glory to come.
8 Therefore, we now impart the fullness of the Gospel of Celestine Light, which has been
hidden from the world, but is now given unto you. If you are humble of spirit and love Yeshua
with gladness and thanksgiving, the truth will resonate in your heart with a sweet melody.
9 In the beginning was the Son, and the Son was with our Heavenly Father and Mother.
10 And the Father and the Mother are God and the Son is God, and these three individuals
are the Elohim, the Trinity of Light, with immortal bodies of flesh and bone as tangible as man's
but glorified and perfected in every way.
11 And the Celestine Light of the Elohim issues forth in spirit and essence from their presence
to fill the immensity of space. It illuminates all the suns in the heavens and gives life to all things,
even as their Holy Spirit fills the hearts of all the Children of Light wherever they may dwell.

12 The power and will of the Father and the Mother focuses through the Son, and the light of Yeshua illuminates and guides the faithful through the whisperings of the Holy Spirit, which is the united spirit of the Trinity of Light, of the Elohim.

13 When the Son speaks, he speaks for the Father and the Mother, and when prayers or words are spoken to the Father, so is the Mother also acknowledged, for they are but one God.

14 Even as a king and a queen are both sovereigns, the Son is also a sovereign, for he but does the will of his Father and Mother and they are not three sovereigns but one, for they speak with one voice concerning the kingdom, even as the Father and the Mother and the Son speak of one accord concerning the Kingdom of Light and Truth; whether on earth or in Heaven, it is the same.

15 Before the Son was born in the flesh, his spirit was birthed in the Celestine Realm of the Elohim that existed before the heavens we see and the earth we know.

16 Like the firstborn Son, before any children of earth were born of women in the flesh, their spirits were firstborn of their heavenly parents in the realm of God.

17 We are all therefore true siblings of Yeshua the Messiah; he is our elder brother, even as we are all brothers and sisters of one another, born in spirit of the same heavenly parents and imbued with the same spiritual essence within our souls.

18 Therefore, it behooves us to love one another, to have remorse when we sin against our brothers and sisters, to forgive those who ask forgiveness with a sincere heart, and to do all we can to be at peace with our kindred across the world.

19 Unto this end might each fulfill their duty to be an elder brother unto all who seek the light, to support them and care for them and help them to grow; even as Yeshua is the elder brother unto us all and has shared with us everything he has, that we might come to know the fullness of our creation and the wonder of our purpose.

CHAPTER 4

Visits of the Angel Gabriel

The priest and prophet, Zekaryah, is visited by the angel Gabriel and told that his wife who is barren and advanced in years shall bear a son and his name shall be Yochanan. Because of his disbelief, Zekaryah is struck mute. The angel Gabriel then appears to Miryam, a virgin engaged to Yosef, in a dream and tells her that she will conceive a son and he shall be named Yeshua. The angel Gabriel appears then to Yosef in a dream telling him the true circumstances of Miryam's pregnancy, and he quickly marries Miryam.

There was a man sent again from God, a faithful stalwart whose name was Yochanan, who came to bear testimony and to bear witness to the Celestine Light of Elohim that all who would hear his words would be prepared to receive the brightness of the light to come.

2 He was not the light, but came to bear witness of the light, for the pure Celestine Light of Elohim, given to enlighten the children of men, was about to be known unto the world.

3 In the days of Herod, king of Judea, there was a priest and a prophet named Zekaryah, a Levite of the division of Abi'jah, and he had a wife, also of the daughters of Aaron, and her name was Elizabet.

4 And they were both righteous before God, walking blameless in all the commandments and ordinances lived by the Children of Israel to obey God.

5 But they had no children because Elizabet was barren, and both were advanced in years.

6 Now while he was serving as priest before God, when his division was on duty, according to the custom of the priesthood, it fell to him by lot to enter the temple of the Lord and burn incense.

7 And the whole multitude of the people were praying outside at the hour of incense.

8 Then the angel Gabriel appeared to Zekaryah, in a vision, standing on the right side of the altar of incense.

9 And Zekaryah was troubled when he saw her, and fear fell upon him.

10 But Gabriel said unto him, "Do not be afraid, Zekaryah, for your prayer is heard and your wife Elizabet will bear a son, and you shall call his name Yochanan.

11 You will have joy and gladness, and many will rejoice at his birth, for he will be great before God.

12 He shall drink no fermented wine or strong drink, nor eat the meat of animals or birds or anything that defiles the body, and he will be filled with the Holy Spirit of the Celestine Light, even from his mother's womb.

13 His words will have the power to grab hold of the hearts of men, and with the spirit of
Eli'jah, he will turn many of the Children of Israel to the Lord their God and the hearts of the
fathers to the children, and the disobedient to the wisdom of the just; that he may make ready
for the Lord to come, a people prepared."
14 Then was Zekaryah troubled, and he said to the angel, "How shall this be? For I am an
old man, and my wife is advanced in years, therefore, how can it be that we would have a child?"
15 With firmness, the angel rebuked him, saying, "I am Gabriel, who comes from the presence
of the Elohim, and I was sent to speak to you and to bring you this good news.
16 Behold, because you doubted my words, you shall now be struck mute and be unable to
speak until the day that these things come to pass, which will be fulfilled in their time as Elohim
desires, and in this, you will learn that nothing is impossible to God."
17 And the people were waiting for Zekaryah, and they wondered at his delay in the temple.
18 And it came to pass that when he came out, he could not speak to them, and they perceived
that he had seen a vision in the temple, and he made signs to them and remained mute to all.
19 Then when his time of service was ended, he went to his home, and his wife was amazed
at his silence and understood that great things of God were transpiring.
20 Shortly thereafter, his wife Elizabet conceived, and for five months, she hid herself, but
each day gave prayers of thanksgiving with abiding joy, saying, "Thus, the Lord has blessed me in
these days when he has looked on me, for he has taken away my shameful reproach among men,
that now I am no more barren, but carry a wonder of God within me."
21 In Elizabet's sixth month, the angel Gabriel was sent from the presence of the Elohim to
a city of Galilee named Nazareth to a virgin betrothed to a man whose name was Yosef, a fine
worker of woods, and of the lineage of the house of King David. The young woman's name was
Miryam, and she was a tender and loving soul.
22 Gabriel appeared to her vividly in a dream while she slept at night and said, "Hail, O
favored one, God is with you!"
23 But she was greatly troubled at the angelic woman's salutation and considered in her mind
what sort of greeting this might be.
24 Seeing her hesitancy, Gabriel said unto her, "Do not be afraid, Miryam, for you have found
favor with God, and behold, you will this night conceive in your womb and nine months hence
bear the only begotten Son of God in the flesh, and you shall call his name Yeshua.
25 He shall be the light of the world, the Son of the most high Father and Mother. He will
show the path in life that leads to eternal redemption and exaltation and open the door to let
man on the path. He will bring the laws of love that the world may have peace when it follows
him, and the laws of Celestine Light that man may be more than he is."
26 And Miryam said to the angel, "I know all things are possible with God, but how shall this
be since I am a virgin and have not yet a husband?"
27 And the angel said unto her, "The Holy Spirit of Elohim will come upon you, and the
power of the most high will overshadow you, and the seed of your Father and Mother in Heaven
shall be planted within your womb to grow and be nurtured; therefore the child to be born will
be holy, the very Son of God.
28 Therefore, from this day henceforth, because you will be the vessel for the divine, eat not
the flesh of any creature of warm blood or any that nurtures its young.
29 Eat only fruits and vegetables that still retain the essence of vitality and grains that have
been soaked in water so that new life springs forth from their seeds before they are made into
bread.
30 Nor shall you take strong drink or drink wine except unfermented of the pure grape or
take anything that is harmful unto your body, for the holy child you carry has been consecrated
unto God from before the days that the world was created, and his body must not be defiled.
31 Behold, your kinswoman Elizabet in her old age has also conceived a son by her husband
Zekaryah and she who had been called barren is now in the sixth month, and the son she carries

is one of the greatest lights of God, even as yours shall be the very Celestine Light of Elohim made manifest among men."

32 Then Miryam bowed her head in humility and said, "Behold, I am the handmaiden of the Lord; let it be to me according to your word."

33 And by the power of the Father and Mother in Heaven, so it was, and the angel departed from her.

34 For three days after the appearance of the angel, Miryam was overwhelmed in her spirit and said nothing to Yosef of the miraculous message from God.

35 On the evening of the third day after the angel Gabriel had visited her, Miryam revealed unto Yosef all that had transpired and he was disbelieving that it could be true, for he esteemed Miryam to be a virtuous woman and in sadness, he imagined that she was with child because of sin and had created the story to hide her transgression.

36 Therefore, he thought to break their engagement, but feared for shame or harm to come upon Miryam, whom he still loved, and decided to ponder the matter until the morrow.

37 As he considered this, behold, the angel Gabriel appeared to him in a dream, saying, "Yosef, son of David, do not fear to take Miryam for your wife, for she has known no man and that which she nurtures in her womb is the seed of God.

38 By her purity and faithfulness, she has been chosen to carry the holy child of the Father and Mother of Heaven, and her name shall be blessed for all the generations to come.

39 Miryam will bear a son, and you shall call his name Yeshua, for he is the Messiah, the Celestine Light who is salvation, and will save his people from their sins."

40 When Yosef awoke from sleep, he did as the angel of the Lord commanded him and straightway married Miryam, but knew her not in the way of the flesh until she had borne the son of God, as foretold by the angel Gabriel.

41 Shortly after her conception and marriage, with the blessing of Yosef, Miryam arose and went with haste into the hill country of Judah, and she entered the house of Zekaryah and greeted Elizabet.

42 And when Elizabet heard the greeting of Miryam, the babe she carried leaped in her womb, and Elizabet was filled with the Holy Spirit and exclaimed with delight, "It is my fortune that the most favored daughter of God should come to me this day; blessed are you among women, Miryam, and blessed is the fruit of your womb, and when the voice of your greeting came to my ears, the babe in my womb leaped for joy!"

43 And Miryam said, "My soul magnifies the Lord, and my spirit rejoices in God, for without regard for the low estate of his handmaiden, he has bestowed blessings beyond measure upon me. He who is mighty has done great things, and holy is his name.

44 He has turned away from the proud and the imagination of their hearts; he has put down the mighty from their thrones and exalted those of low degree; he has filled the hungry with good things, but the rich he has sent away empty.

45 He has blessed Israel with remembrance in his mercy and kept a covenant with our fathers, even Abraham and his posterity forever."

46 And Miryam remained with Elizabet and cared for her during the remainder of her term and the labor of birth and then returned unto her home in Nazareth.

CHAPTER 5

Births of the Savior and the Herald

Elizabet gives birth to Yochanan. On the eighth day, Zekaryah once again is able to speak and he is filled with the Celestine light of Elohim as he prophesizes the calling of his son to be the prophet of the most high, giving knowledge of salvation to his people for the forgiveness of their sins. Miryam gives birth to Yeshua in their humble abode in Nazareth of Galilee. Shepherds witness an awesome symphony of heavenly lights and melodies and hear in their heads a voice proclaiming, "The Messiah is born," and immediately afterward go to Miryam and Yosef to reveal all that they had witnessed. A devout and righteous man name Shim'on and a prophetess named Anna both proclaim Yeshua to be the Light of Salvation.

Now the time came for Elizabet to deliver and she gave birth to the son that had been
foretold by the angel, and her neighbors and kinsfolk heard that the Lord had shown
great mercy to her and they rejoiced with her.
2 On the eighth day, they came to circumcise the child, and they desired to name him
Zekaryah after his father but his mother said, "Not so, for he shall be called Yochanan."
3 And they were baffled and said to her, "None of your kindred is called by this name."
4 Assuming that Zekaryah was also deaf, they made signs to him, inquiring what he would
have him called, and he asked for a writing tablet and wrote, "His name is Yochanan," and they
all marveled.
5 Immediately thereafter, the mouth of Zekaryah was opened and his tongue was loosed, and
he spoke, blessing God, and awe came upon all their kinsfolk and neighbors.
6 And all these things were talked about with amazement through all the hill country of
Judea, and many who heard of it saw the hand of God in his birth and wondered, "Who then
will this child be?"
7 Upon the birth of his son, Zekaryah was filled with the Holy Spirit of the Celestine Light
and prophesied, saying, "Blessed be Elohim, the Lord God of Israel, for he has visited and
redeemed his people and has raised up a horn of salvation for us in the house of his servant
David, as he spoke by the mouth of his holy prophets of old that we should be saved from our
sins and from the hands of all who hate us to perform the mercy promised to our fathers and to
remember his holy covenant, the oath which he swore to our father Abraham, to grant us that
we, being delivered from the hand of our enemies, might serve him without fear, in holiness and
righteousness before him all the days of our lives, as we honor and obey him."
8 Then holding his babe above his head for all to see, Zekaryah said, "You, child, will be called
the prophet of the most high, for you will go before the Lord of Celestine Light to prepare his

way, to give knowledge of salvation to his people for the forgiveness of their sins and through the tender mercy of our God, when the day shall dawn upon us from on high to give light to those who sit in darkness and in the shadow of death, and to guide our feet into the way of peace."

9 Now Miryam and Yosef were very poor, and when the time came for Miryam to bring the babe she carried into the world, she gave birth to her firstborn son in their humble two-room abode in Nazareth of Galilee. And they wrapped the baby in the swaddling cloths of his father and laid him on a fresh bed of straw in a simple cradle made by Yosef of cast-off wood.

10 On that night in the region, there were shepherds out in the field keeping watch over their flock, when suddenly there was a flash of brilliant light in the heavens, and for a moment, it was as bright as midday.

11 And though the night was clear and cloudless, they heard a mighty thunder rolling across the heavens and a soft voice spoke in their head, saying, "Be not afraid, for behold good news of great joy, for this day in the city of Nazareth, wrapped in swaddling clothes and lying in a cradle, the Anointed of Israel and the Messiah of all the world is born!"

12 Suddenly, the very heavens began to resound in a most strange and melodious harmony; stars of brightness fell from the sky and flew over their heads with great tails of light so much so that the shepherds fell to their knees in awe and wonder and praised God.

13 And when the stars that flew had disappeared and the heavenly sounds had faded, there was a great silence in the night and the shepherds whispered one to another, "Let us go into Nazareth and see for ourselves this wonder that has happened, which God has made known to us."

14 They went then with haste and found Miryam and Yosef and the babe lying in a cradle and many of the people of the town gathered round.

15 And when they saw them, they related the events which they had witnessed concerning the child, and all who heard it praised God at what the shepherds told them.

16 And Miryam thought about all these things, pondering them in her heart, remembering everything that had taken place since the day when the angel had first appeared to her. And she was greatly humbled.

17 After each had seen the babe and said a prayer unto God, the shepherds returned to their fields, glorifying and praising God for all they had seen and heard.

18 At the end of eight days, when he was circumcised, the babe was called Yeshua, the name given by the angel before he was placed within the womb.

19 When three and thirty days had passed after the blood of Miryam's purification, according to the law of Moses, they brought Yeshua up to Jerusalem to present him to the Lord, as it is written, "Every male that opens the womb shall be called holy to the Lord."

20 At this time of significance, they made an offer by sacrifice to fulfill the law. It was the custom that the sacrifice should be of a young lamb and a turtledove, but due to their poverty they gave a sacrifice of two young turtledoves instead, as the law allowed.

21 Now there was a man in Jerusalem whose name was Shim'on, and this man was righteous and devout, looking for the consolation of Israel, and the Holy Spirit was upon him.

22 And it had been revealed to him by the Holy Spirit that he should not see death before he had seen the Messiah, and moved by the Spirit, he came into the temple.

23 When Yosef and Miryam brought in Yeshua, to do with him according to the custom of the law, Shim'on asked to take him up in his arms and, giving praise to God, said, "Lord, now you can let your servant depart in peace, according to your word, for my eyes have seen your salvation, which you have prepared in the presence of all peoples, a light for revelation unto the Gentiles and for glory to your people Israel."

24 Yosef and Miryam marveled at what was said about Yeshua, and Shim'on blessed them and said to Miryam, "Behold, this child is the keystone for the fall and rising of many in Israel."

25 And there was also a prophetess, Anna, the daughter of Phan'u-el of the tribe of Asher; she was of a great age, having lived with her husband seven years from her virginity and as a widow

till she was eighty-four.
26 Now in her old age, Anna knew the time of final sleep was soon upon her, and she did not
depart from the temple, worshiping with fasting and prayer night and day that she might be in
harmony with God.
27 When Yosef and Miryam came upon her, she bowed her head to Yeshua and gave thanks
to God and exhorted all who were looking for the redemption of Israel to see the child before
them, and the very Celestine Light of God come into their midst.
28 And some of the people considered that she was enfeebled of the mind in her old age;
others thought she was seeing Heaven as she prepared to pass from life and therefore saw earthly
things in heavenly ways. But Miryam and Yosef praised Elohim unto themselves, for they knew
God had given a witness of the truth unto her.
29 When Yosef and Miryam had performed everything according to the laws of the temple,
they returned to Galilee to their own city, Nazareth.

CHAPTER 6

Coming of the Magi

Noble Magi, having seen the celestial signs of the birth of the "King of Light," come to pay tribute. They inquire of King Herod of Judea as to the location of the infant, but on the council of his advisers, Herod mistakenly sends them to Bethlehem. When the Magi do not find him there, a skipping ball of light appears which they follow to the home of Miryam and Yosef in Nazareth. After paying homage, the Magi open their treasures and offer the infant Yeshua gifts of gold, silver, spices, perfumes, and other tributes. An angel appears to Yosef in a dream and warns him that they must flee to Egypt and remain until the death of Herod. Elizabet also receives a vision that she must flee with her son Yochanan. King Herod demands the death of Yochanan and all children under the age of two with special signs around their births.

Now when Yeshua had passed his first year, behold, noble Magi and their retinue appeared
from lands beyond Judea and came to Jerusalem.
2 And the Magi came before King Herod of Judea and asked, "Where is the King of
Light that has just been born? For we have journeyed far to pay tribute to him."
3 When Herod, the king, heard this, he was troubled, and thinking to mask his motives, he
inquired of the wise men how they, being foreigners, knew of the king that was born.
4 And the Magi said unto King Herod, "We have seen an unusual conjunction of the stars in
the sky foretelling the birth in this land upon the summer solstice, at the time of greatest light,
of a king of light that shall rule all the world.
5 We have therefore journeyed to Jerusalem to see for ourselves the king that the very stars
bear witness of, that we might honor him, but we know not exactly where in this vicinity to find
him, and therefore make inquiry of you."
6 Herod was astounded at what they said, and assembling all the chief priests and scribes,
he inquired of them in private where the Anointed One was to be born. They told him, "In
Bethlehem of Judea, for so it is written by the prophet Micah, 'And you, O Bethlehem, in the
land of Judah, are by no means least among the rulers of Judah, for from you shall come a ruler
who will govern my people Israel.'"
7 Then Herod summoned the Magi secretly, and he sent them to Bethlehem, saying, "Go
and search diligently for the child, and when you have found him bring me word, that I too may
come and worship him."
8 Following the directions of the king, the Magi proceeded forth, but arriving in Bethlehem,
they found no sign of the infant king and thinking Herod had deceived them, they looked again
to the stars for direction.

9 As they were thus engaged, a small ball of shimmering light appeared before them, skipping above the ground in momentary flashes; only to disappear and then reappear again as they traveled in the direction it beckoned them.

10 When they saw this sign, they rejoiced with exceedingly great joy, and they followed it both night and day until it led them to the very door of the humble house of Yosef and Miryam, in the town of Nazareth of Galilee.

11 Entering into the house, they saw the child with Miryam, his mother, and they each touched a knee to the ground and paid homage to him and related to Yosef and Miryam all the miraculous occurrences that had led them to their home.

12 And the Magi opened their treasures and offered Yeshua gifts of gold, silver, spices, perfumes, and other tributes. Then being warned in dreams not to return to Herod, and feeling no obligation because of his deception, they departed by another way to their own country.

13 From that time forth, Yosef and Miryam were barrenly poor no more, but using the treasures of the Magi frugally, they were able to increase their stature.

14 Nevertheless, being told by an angel in a dream, they buried most of the gifts in the ground that they might be brought forth at another time to serve God.

15 Now when the Magi had departed, behold, an angel of the Lord appeared to Yosef in a dream and said, "Rise, and use a part of the gifts of the Magi to take the child and his mother and flee to Egypt. Remain there until I come again to you, for Herod is about to search for the child, to destroy him."

16 Then Yosef rose and took Yeshua and Miryam and departed to Egypt and remained there until the death of Herod. This was the first fulfillment of what the Lord had spoken by the prophet Hosea, "Out of Egypt have I called my son."

17 That same evening, Miryam's relative Elizabet received a vision of an angel at her bedside, warning her to flee with her infant son Yochanan, and without a word to her husband Zekaryah who was in the temple; she went up into the hills and hid him.

18 When Herod realized that he had been tricked by the Magi, he was in a furious rage and jealous that any other should be regarded as a king in the land of Judea or have the audacious honor to be called the king of the world.

19 His priests had told him that the scriptures foretold of the king to be born in Bethlehem, and uncertain as to whether the Magi had spoken of the most recent summer solstice or the previous, he inquired of his priests if there were any children born in Bethlehem or all of Judea, in the last two years, which had been noticed of the people or shown signs of wonder.

20 His priests told him of the son of the priest Zekaryah and of the many signs that had accompanied his birth and of the prophecies of his father. Then Herod gave specific instructions that the son of Zekaryah should be destroyed and that any other children under two years of age in all of Judea, which had great signs about their birth, should also be killed. And because of this evil decree, twelve children returned to God.

21 With grim resolve, the soldiers of Herod went forth upon their mission to destroy the son of Zekaryah, and having searched his house and finding it empty, they appeared at the temple and, standing before Zekaryah, demanded to know the whereabouts of his infant son, whom the people already proclaimed.

22 Zekaryah held forth his empty palms and professed ignorance, noting he was serving the Lord in the temple and knew not the things that were transpiring without.

23 Then Herod's soldiers were wroth with Zekaryah and threatened him with their weapons, saying, "Tell us in truth, where is your son? Know you not that your life is in our hands?"

24 But Zekaryah again disavowed knowledge of the whereabouts of Yochanan and told the soldiers that if they spilled the blood of an innocent man in the service of God, they would have no forgiveness in the world to come.

25 But the guards regarded not his words and slew him at that moment, spilling his blood upon the temple court.

26 As punishment for his evil, the Lord cursed Herod with a sore curse, and from that day
forth until his death, his body was consumed from within by worms, which caused him great
pain and agony.
27 And the evil he did fulfilled that which was spoken by the prophet Jeremiah: "A voice was heard in Ramah, wailing and loud lamentation, Rachel weeping for her children; she refused to be consoled, because they were no more."
28 When Herod died and his son Herod Archelaus reigned over Judea in place of his father, behold, an angel of the Lord appeared in a dream to Yosef in Egypt, saying, "Rise, take the child and his mother and return to the land of Israel, for he who sought the child's life is dead."
29 Then he rose and took the child and his mother and went to the land of Israel to the town of Nazareth of Galilee, which was his family's home, and there raised Yeshua in humble surroundings so that what had been spoken by the prophets might be fulfilled: "He shall be called a Nazarene."

CHAPTER 7

Rebellion of Yochanan

At the tender age of twelve, Yochanan's outspoken words of righteousness and authority on the true path to God do not sit well with the priests and results in his forced exile to the isolated community of Gimron, where he must now live.

Yochanan grew and became strong in the spirit of the Lord.

2 His mother found great happiness with his devotion to God, for she knew he had been called from birth to be a prophet of the most high and she was glad that he endeavored to be worthy of his calling and that it might be fulfilled.

3 Nevertheless, she worried for the activities of youth, which he shunned and had no interest, and for his penchant to speak with authority to adults, which oftentimes incurred their anger.

4 It was seldom possible for Yochanan to sit in silence during lectures given to the youth by the priests and teachers, as was expected of children. Frequently, he would stand and rebut what was being said or even the man who was speaking, and this caused much distress to his mother and among his kinsfolk.

5 Thus, he was frequently reprimanded by his elder kinsfolk, but they could not sway his spirit of defiant righteousness, for he knew he had been called by Elohim for a high and holy purpose and even in his tender years, the spirit of God swelled his heart and spoke to his mind.

6 One day, his uncle Nathanael came to him and said, "Yochanan, you are a mighty youth of Elohim, but you must show more respect for your elders and those in authority, for soon you will be a youth no more but a young man, and such things will not be tolerated and can cause harm to both you and your kinsfolk."

7 Yochanan shrugged his shoulders and answered him, saying, "I speak only the truth. Is it so painful for those in high places to hear?"

8 Nathanael shook his head in disapproval and answered, "It is the truth only as you think in your inexperience of youth. Consider that if you are at odds with the laws and traditions of our people that have been given unto us by God, is it not against God that you are being rebellious?"

9 And Yochanan said unto him, "I do not speak against the law, only against those who use the law or their position to sin and hide their iniquities or twist the law to justify themselves or hold power over others."

10 Then was Nathanael disturbed and said, "It is given only to God to judge the hidden things that men do. Can you not see that it is not your place to speak against upright men whose lives in private, be they sinful or sinless, you know not? Nor is it proper for youths to question the

interpretation of the law by those to whom it has been given to oversee."

11 And Yochanan answered, "I do not speak of things I cannot see, only the hypocrisy that all can see, and I do not speak to condemn a man for I know that only God can judge. But I speak boldly of the sins men do; that all the others who hear my words will know without doubt of the things which are pleasing unto God and those that are not; that in their greater understanding they might not sin."

12 And if God has given a true understanding of the law unto me, I cannot stand idly by while it is perverted, for I am accountable to God, not unto men."

13 Nathanael pulled upon his hair in frustration as he spoke again unto Yochanan, saying, "It matters not whether the words you say are true or false, only that it is not a youths place to say such words to men. You must stop this foolishness, or we will be forced to send you away to a lonely place in the wilderness where you will not be able to speak disrespectfully to those in authority."

14 A great smile came upon Yochanan, and he said, "Perhaps you will then be doing me a favor, Uncle, for away from the stench of men, in the temple of the wilderness built by God, I will find him in ways I have never known."

15 Thus, it was that Yochanan became even bolder because of the admonitions of his uncle, as he looked with expectation for the day when his kinsfolk would exile him into the wilderness.

16 After he had attained the age of twelve years, Yochanan had reached the time of transition into manhood when, as was spoken by Nathanael, his affronts to those in authority would not be tolerated as lightly as they had been when he was a youth.

17 And it came to pass that Yochanan was sitting in a class to educate young men in the history of the Children of Israel and to train them in their adult responsibilities. Upon this day came a priest of great esteem from Jerusalem named Asa to teach the young men in the ways they should go.

18 And Asa taught many things to them, and Yochanan sat in silence nodding his head in agreement for much of what was spoken.

19 Then Asa came to speak on the duties of men according to the laws of God. And the list was very long.

20 And Asa said unto the young men, "Remember every word of these laws that they may be inscribed on your hearts, for only he who keeps the letter of the law and the traditions handed down by our fathers will be granted favor by God."

21 Then it was that Yochanan stood up, which was not allowed, and began to speak unto Asa, as one man of authority speaks to another, which thing was also forbidden.

22 And Yochanan said unto him, "Rabbi, obeying the law is as worthless as dust unless a man has a repentant heart and brings forth fruits worthy of a true repentance, for all men are sinners and no amount of laws obeyed can bring man to God, but only the love of God inscribed on his heart and the light of God reflected in his life."

23 But Asa, having been forewarned of the disruptive character of Yochanan by the local priests, had prepared for such an encounter. And rather than simply put him back in a place of silence as befitted his age, he said unto him, "God Almighty chose the Children of Israel and gave unto them his laws that they might live pleasing unto him and have his favor. If a man fully lives the law, he will be without sin; therefore, you are an impudent youth who speaks out of turn with words without knowledge. Sit down before you embarrass yourself further."

24 Everyone then looked to Yochanan, who did not sit down, expecting him to reply in a fury, but instead he laughed at Asa, which thing was much worse. And he said unto him, "Forgive me, learned rabbi, I thought we were speaking in seriousness and did not realize you would bring humor to our conversation, for surely you were jesting to say that if a man fully lived the law, he

would be without sin, for none but God is without sin."

25 The rabbi Asa was flustered that Yochanan had perceived the error of his words, and he answered haltingly at first, "That is true, only the Almighty is completely without sin . . . for God is a power not a person . . . but you dishonor the righteousness of good men by the things that you say, for there are many who are close to perfection, who give great alms, who pray often and with great devotion, and who follow all the details of the law in their lives as God has asked all of his chosen children to do.

26 Sit down now with attention and learn of the ways of your fathers that you may follow in the footsteps of your father Zekaryah and someday become a priest of the temple."

27 Now Yochanan was building a righteous intensity, and he said unto the rabbi, "I will never be a priest of the temple built by man, but only a priest of the temple built by God, which I am even now as I stand before you.

28 And of what value are great alms to God unless a man is willing in his heart to give all that he has to God and be happy when he is called upon to do so?

29 And I say unto you that God loves the poor more than the rich, for they give more of what they have little of, while the rich man gives little of what he has more of.

30 Only when the rich man gives so much of his wealth that he must miss a meal as the poor do when they give alms will his gift be counted as pure righteousness before God.

31 And of what worth are frequent public prayers? Is a man more righteous because he prays loudly in public that others may notice? I say unto you no! Verily, God is unseen and unknown except to those who seek him in solitude and humility.

32 And it is the evil things that men do in secret that others do not see that condemns them, and then the law they obey in public for others to see does nothing for them except brand them as hypocrites before God, and verily, only a contrite spirit worthy of repentance will help them."

33 Then the rabbi was very wroth at the words of Yochanan and he said unto him, "I cannot tolerate another moment of your blasphemous words. For the sake of your father, I desired to teach you in ways that are good, but I can see you have been corrupted by the nonsense of your imagination, therefore depart and return no more to this school until you have vowed to respect your elders and the laws of God."

34 And Yochanan answered him, saying, "I will go with happiness to a place of greater purity, but I shall return again when I have been filled by the Almighty. Watch therefore for me, and perhaps we can speak once more when you see the whirlwind coming from the desert."

35 Then Yochanan returned to the house of his uncle and related all that had occurred and his uncle was very wroth, and upon calling all the kinsfolk, it was decided that Yochanan would be sent to the isolated community of Gimron to be taught by the sternness of those there so that he might yet be able to fulfill his potential without causing himself harm.

36 The very next day, Yochanan and his uncle began the journey.

CHAPTER 8

Yeshua Confounds the Temple Priests

As a youth, Yeshua is instructed by many wise men, and with an impeccable memory, he retains everything he reads and learns. At the age of twelve, Yeshua travels to Jerusalem for the Passover feast with his family, and after all the days of the feast are concluded, his family leaves, thinking he is with them. When they find he is not, they hurry back to Jerusalem but do not find him for three days. During this time, he is speaking with authority to the priests in the temple who do not take kindly to his knowledge of the scripture in ways they do not, or cannot, fathom. The first night after the families return to Nazareth, an angel appears to Yosef in a dream and tells him that Yeshua must spend two years living in the community of Gimron with Yochanan to gain greater wisdom and stature.

And it came to pass that Yeshua grew and became strong, filled with wisdom, and the favor of God was upon him.

2 His father Yosef taught him in the ways of wood in which he was very adept, and Yeshua became well practiced in the making of wheels, yokes, tables, and chairs.

3 Prudently, using portions of the treasure of the Magi, Yosef and Miryam afforded Yeshua the opportunity to have instructions from wise men, particularly Greeks and others who came from beyond Galilee.

4 And it came to pass that Yeshua was continually gaining wisdom and knowledge from every person he met and from everything he encountered in his life. And from every word of importance that he heard and from every written script his eyes beheld, he remembered all things; nor did he ever forget anything that he learned or ever cease in his desire to acquire knowledge.

5 Each year upon the Passover, Yosef and Miryam went up to Jerusalem with their kinsfolk to take part in the feast.

6 According to the admonitions of the angel Gabriel whom visited Miryam when Yeshua was conceived, they ate not the flesh of any animal of warm blood or that nurtured its young nor drank anything except pure water and wine of the pure grape. And whenever possible, they ate not any creature that had been killed at all or of any plants except those that had just been harvested and still retained the essence of vitality.

7 Thus, it was that when Yeshua was twelve years of age, he went to Jerusalem with them and many of their family, according to the custom of the feast.

8 When Yosef and Miryam and their kinsfolk had fulfilled all the days of the feast, they

departed Jerusalem to return again to Nazareth of Galilee.
9 They supposed that Yeshua had returned with them and was among their kinsfolk, but
unbeknownst to them, he had tarried in Jerusalem.
10 His parents, upon discovering that he was not among them, hurried back to Jerusalem to
search for him and, after three days, found him in the temple, sitting in the midst of the priests
and learned men in earnest discourse, listening to them and asking questions and giving answers.
And a large group of people had gathered, and upon hearing Yeshua speak, they were astonished
at his understanding.
11 As Yosef and Miryam approached, a priest said unto Yeshua, "You say Elohim desires man
to not eat the meat of creatures of warm blood and is more pleased if man eats meat not at all
of any animal or fowl or even fish, but only plants and a little of honey and eggs and milk foods.
12 Yet the sacred scrolls tell us that Elohim said unto Noah, "The fear of you and the dread
of you shall be upon every beast of the earth and upon every bird of the air, upon everything that
creeps on the ground and all the fish of the sea; into your hand they are delivered. Every moving
thing that lives shall be food for you."
13 And Yeshua answered unto him, "Verily, those are the false words of men written into that
which is sacred to justify themselves, for the scrolls also say of that day, and God saw the earth
and behold, it was corrupt; for all flesh had corrupted their way upon the earth."
14 Then were many of the priests angry with him insomuch that they desired to rend their
garments, for he had said that some of that which was sacred to them was of men, not God, but
they were restrained because of his youth.
15 And another priest said, "The sacred scrolls tell us that Elohim has said that man is to have
dominion over the fish of the sea and the fowl of the air and everything that moves upon the
earth. By this, we also know that man can eat the clean creatures of the world if he desires, for
they are under his dominion."
16 Yeshua answered him with authority, saying, "Verily, dominion does not grant permission
for man to kill animals as he desires, merely allows that Elohim has sanctioned man to use them
to help with his labors, and with thanksgiving, take a little of their honey and milk and eggs to
make into food as needed. But to kill them without great cause is to turn upon God, the creator
of all.
17 Had Elohim desired man to eat the flesh of animals, he would have made the bodies of
man into great hunters with large sharp teeth and claws like the bear and the lion, not weak and
frail, with small teeth and thin little nails, less than even the cattle and the chickens."
18 Consider instead that man was made in the very image of God, and do you think that
Elohim would desire to see the reflection of God wantonly killing those creatures which Elohim
has made to also have a life?
19 Then the priests were wroth, and many murmured against him even though he was only a
youth. And Yeshua, knowing their thoughts, said unto them, "Herein is the proof of the words I
speak and the falsehood of the words of man posing as God revealed:
20 Verily, I say unto you the commandments of Elohim are given for the good of man that
man might be abundantly blessed as he honestly lives the commandments given.
21 Therefore, how can it be that the sacred scrolls record Elohim giving a commandment to
eat only the plants and fruits of the earth to Adam, but then after the days of Noah, God would
say that every moving thing that lives shall be food for you?
22 It is not because Elohim suddenly requires less of man, but because in his wickedness,
man no longer desires to live the higher laws and therefore cannot receive the greater blessings
of God.
23 Then to justify himself, man perverted the word of God, writing lesser commandments
upon the sacred scrolls in the name of Elohim to uphold his weakness. So it was in the days
of Noah and so it was in the days of Moses, and so it is even today as weak men uphold their
contrary deeds with words of false scribes shrouded in the sacredness of ancient scrolls.

24 Verily, I say unto you Elohim would not give a good commandment unto the children of men that they might be blessed, then when they are wicked as in the days of Noah, give unto them a lesser commandment because of their weakness, for then he would be becoming as man desired, instead of man becoming as God desired, nor could any blessing come from wickedness.

25 In truth, the sacred scrolls say that after God had made all the earth and all life upon it, he said that it was good. Therefore, it is the sacred trust of man to protect that which God has said is good, not to kill it and destroy it; else, man stands in opposition to the good and will of Elohim.

26 And God said unto Adam, who came before Noah, 'Behold, I have given you every plant yielding seed which is upon the face of all the earth, and every tree with seed in its fruit; to you it shall be for meat.'

27 Now let me ask a question of you, my learned Elders. For what reason did the people in the times before Noah live for many hundreds of years, and Methuselah even for nearly a millennium, yet after the days of Noah, man lived scarcely any time on earth at all?"

28 And none could answer him.

29 Then said Yeshua unto them, "Verily, it is because in the times before Noah, men did as Elohim commanded and killed not the creatures of the earth at all and, for meat, ate only plants and the good things the animals gave unto them in life. Thus did they have the vitality of life and walked upon the earth for hundreds of years in health and vigor.

30 Then because of wickedness came the flood, because the children of men that came after Noah were corrupt and killed the animals and despoiled the world God had made. As they took death into them, so they died before their time.

31 And I say unto you that in the days of Adam, God gave a fullness of the light and man ate only plants and the gifts of the animals; then after the days of Noah, man became exceedingly wicked and lost the knowledge Elohim gave to man for long life upon the land.

32 But the day shall come when the children of men are again worthy of the fullness of light, for as the Prophet Isaiah said, 'The wolf shall dwell with the lamb and the leopard shall lie down with the kid, and the calf and the lion and the fatling together and a little child shall lead them. The cow and the bear shall feed; their young shall lie down together; and the lion shall eat straw like the ox. The sucking child shall play over the hole of the asp, and the weaned child shall put his hand on the adder's den. They shall not hurt or destroy in all my holy mountain, for the earth shall be full of the knowledge of the Lord as the waters cover the sea.'"

33 And the priests desired to answer him but could find no words, and all who listened were amazed at the teachings of Yeshua.

34 Then Yosef and Miryam came over to him and were overjoyed to embrace him, and Miryam said unto him, "Son, why have you remained here without telling us? Behold, your father and I have searched for you for three days and have had much sorrow wondering what had become of you."

35 And Yeshua answered them, "Why did you search for me other than here? Did you not know that I must be in the house dedicated to my parents and about my Father's business?" And they were confused by the words which he spoke to them, but Miryam remembered these things in her heart and knew that she must someday share them with others.

36 The first night as they returned to Nazareth, while Yosef slept, an angel of God appeared to him in a dream and said, "Yosef, your son has been called of God before the world was; you must make straight his path that he may fulfill that which God would have him do.

37 Therefore upon your return to Nazareth, prepare him to journey to the community at Gimron and there to join Yochanan, the son of Zekaryah and Elizabet, and remain for two years that he may further increase in wisdom and stature and find favor with God and man."

38 And being an upright and righteous man, who had seen wonders such as few men had seen, Yosef did not hesitate or doubt that which he dreamed and, straightaway upon their arrival in Nazareth began to make ready for Yeshua to depart.

CHAPTER 9

Healing a Broken Heart

On the way to the community of Gimron, in company with his mother's brother, Abraham, Yeshua encounters a man beating his donkey. After confronting Yeshua in anger and being offered the light in return, the man prostrates himself before God and asks for forgiveness. Two days before the arrival of Yeshua, an angel appears to Yochanan in a vision and instructs him to prepare a place for Yeshua. Then an angel also appears to the three chief priests to testify of the truthfulness of Yochanan's words. Great then is the welcome that Yeshua receives when he arrives, which is highly unusual for someone of such a young age.

Thus, it was that shortly after the families returned to Nazareth, Yeshua journeyed along the river Jordan to the community at Gimron in the company of his mother's brother, Abraham.

2 Along the route, they came upon a man pulling a heavily laden donkey by a rope near a low watery spot next to the edge of the river, amidst a grove of date palms. As they made to pass, the donkey stopped and refused to move further, despite the man's forceful tugging on the rope about his head.

3 Yeshua and Abraham looked back behind them as they traveled by to see what would become of the man and donkey, when to Yeshua's dismay, the man took his staff and began to beat the donkey about the head and body while cursing at him in a most foul way.

4 Before Abraham realized his intent, Yeshua ran back to the man to prevent the evil he would do.

5 Already in his youth, Yeshua was large for his age and strong because of his work in carpentry with his father. Thus, it was that when the man pulled back to take a mighty blow upon the donkey, Yeshua took hold of the staff from behind him and pulled it suddenly from his grasp, leaving him to swing forward in emptiness, whereupon he fell upon his face.

6 The man rose in a rage and went to strike Yeshua a blow, but Yeshua drove one end of the staff into the soft ground and, holding it upright before him, used it as a shield insomuch that the man's intended blow hit the staff, causing him great pain and agony, whereupon he sat upon the ground, holding his injured hand and cursing all around him.

7 Then came Abraham up to him, saying, "What is in your heart this day to attack a youth and recklessly utter such foul curses about?"

8 And the man said, "Tis an insolent boy who has caused me much pain by acting upon me when it was not his right, and I demand recompense for this offense."

9 Now Abraham was of a mind to pay the man a coin and be about their journey and away

from the trouble that was here, but Yeshua stood before the man and said unto him, "We will pay you nothing, for it is you who have sinned this day by striking an innocent beast who serves you without reward. Verily, you are not even worthy to clean its stall."

10 Then the man rose up to contend again with Yeshua and Abraham, but Yeshua took the staff and threw it upon the ground at the feet of the man and said unto him, "There is your weapon, strike me if you will, but you know in your heart whether it is good or evil that you would do, and if it be evil, then I say unto you that it would be better that you had lived in Sodom and Gomorrah at the day of devastation than you live today, for God does not smile upon the wicked, and their end is destruction."

11 The forceful words of Yeshua gave the man pause in his steps, and overcome by his troubles, he began to tremble and weep, and he fell to his knees and, through his tears, told unto them of his life of misery that they might understand the anger that was within him.

12 Then Yeshua came unto the man and put his hand upon his shoulder and said unto him with tenderness, "Many of us are poor and have vexing troubles that come upon us. Thus is life that we may grow and become better than we are. In all of your cares, have you prayed with a contrite heart to God that he might make you greater than your burdens?"

13 And the man answered, "God abandoned me long ago, along with my wife and family and friends."

14 Then Yeshua stood in front of the man, put a hand on each of his shoulders, and looked into his eyes, and said unto him, "Elohim will never abandon the Children of Light. It is because you have abandoned God that there is only darkness in your life.

15 Repent of your sins, forsake the darkness you have been living, and call upon God in humility and passion to bring the Celestine Light unto you.

16 If you turn away from the darkness and seek out the God of light, you will find him. And there is no burden too great to bear when Elohim is with you."

17 The man whose name was Dryhus was mightily moved in his soul by the words and compassion of Yeshua and prostrated himself upon the ground. And with great humility, through tears of remorse and thankfulness, he did as Yeshua bade and called upon God to forgive him for his sins and promised to make amends for his wrongs and to hereafter do only good.

18 Afterward, he arose and kissed Yeshua upon each of his cheeks and went to his donkey and kissed it on each of its cheeks.

19 Thereafter, they parted ways and Abraham and Yeshua continued on their journey to Gimron, and Abraham considered in amazement all that he had witnessed.

20 Now Yochanan had been at Gimron sometime prior to the arrival of Yeshua and had already come into favor with the Elders because of his studious ways, good labor, and quick mind. Two days before Yeshua's arrival, an angel appeared to Yochanan in a vision and said, "Behold, your kin Yeshua does even now journey to Gimron. Prepare a place for him."

21 Yochanan did as the angel directed and arranged a sleeping area for Yeshua next to his and passed a message through the hierarchy to the Elders concerning the arrival of Yeshua, whom he assured them was blessed greatly of Elohim.

22 Then an angel of God appeared in a vision to the three chief priests and testified of the truthfulness of that which Yochanan had spoken.

23 And the spirit of God filled the hearts of the men and women of Gimron such that they knew that an unusual moment was arriving.

24 Thus, it was that when Yeshua arrived at Gimron, there was a crowd of people who greeted him as he entered the village in such a way not accustomed for a youth of his tender age.

25 Before he departed to return alone to Nazareth, Abraham made a small donation of silver and a vessel of resins of pine to the community from the treasures that had been given by the Magi when Yeshua was a babe so that they might care for and teach both Yeshua and Yochanan.

26 From that day forth, Yeshua and Yochanan began to spend every minute of almost every day with each other, continuing to forge the bond that united them in purpose and understanding to fulfill the desires of God.

CHAPTER 10

Discovery in the Wilderness

Yochanan and Yeshua begin to suspect the divine nature of Yeshua's creation when, on one of their outings, plants of all kinds spring up out of the barren ground in abundance wherever Yeshua steps. Yeshua falls out of favor with the Elders and priests of Gimron when he affronts the established order by speaking out as a youth, which strengthens his resolve to fulfill his purpose on earth.

And it came to pass that Yeshua remained for two years at Gimron as the angel had bid Miriam. He grew strong in the wilderness and climbed often upon the steep peaks about the village to meditate and commune with God.

2 Yeshua and Yochanan studied diligently with the priests and people of Gimron, nevertheless they were not part of them, and this was acknowledged in the community insomuch that when their daily spiritual and temporal duties were completed they were given freedom to do as they wished.

3 And it came to pass that they spent much time together wandering in the wilderness about Gimron, praying and fasting and communing with God.

4 Yeshua and Yochanan spoke often of the sacred scrolls and the prophecies of old and of that which had happened in their lives. They knelt many times together in prayer upon the mountains and called upon God for wisdom. Through these efforts, they each began to understand who the other was and Elohim's plan for them insomuch as was revealed to them at that time.

5 It was during one of their wanderings in the wilderness that they discovered with certainty the divine nature of Yeshua, for one day as they walked along a dry creek bed, Yochanan lamented the barrenness and spoke of how green it might appear after the spring rains.

6 And Yeshua said to Yochanan that he could also see its beauty in his mind and as he thus spoke, thick clouds quickly formed like a column over the area, and in moments, they were laughing as rain fell in torrents in the late summer when there should be none.

7 As Yeshua continued to walk with Yochanan behind him, Yochanan beheld that plants of all description began to spring forth out of the ground in abundance, in a circle of green, expanding behind the feet of Yeshua. And they stopped and looked around them in amazement, and Yochanan nodded his head with understanding, saying, "Surely, you are more than my kin Yeshua, for by the son of no man could these things occur."

8 Thus, it was that Yeshua and Yochanan first came to ponder upon the divine origin of Yeshua, and they gave much thought to his purpose in life.

9 But of these things, they spoke to no one and Yeshua said, "Perhaps it is so Yochanan, but let us keep that within our own hearts, for I am still young and have much to learn and would not be presumptuous before God."

10 When they were not in the wilderness about Gimron or working in the fields, they studied long hours with the priests at Gimron and learned from the sacred scrolls of the teachings of the prophets and of the history of the Children of Israel in Egypt and even down into the present day and how God had joined them in days past.

11 And it came to pass that one day as Yeshua and Yochanan sat silently at the rear of the brethren in meeting, as was proper for the youth, and they listened intently as the spiritual leader of the community spoke of the heresy of the current priests of Jerusalem and mourned the loss of the old ways of the Israelites of Egypt.

12 Then Yeshua forgot his place as a youth and a guest and posed a question, saying, "The paths of the Almighty are pure and simple. Therefore, what does it matter, the old ways or the new ways of the priests, when both are more concerned with unnecessary ritual than the foundations of salvation and the perfection of life?"

13 At this proclamation, all the Elders and priests were taken aback, both at the affront to the hierarchical order which the community strictly adhered to and at the very words Yeshua had spoken.

14 Rather than answer him in anger, the leader bade both Yeshua and Yochanan to depart from the room, and thereafter, Yeshua was not so favored, having greatly affronted the established order.

15 But from that simple moment, he was changed, for he had again spoken the truth before the priests and the brethren, despite their disapproval, even as he had at the temple in Jerusalem and felt not cowed by being in disagreement with men in high places, but strengthened because he spoke forthrightly for the Elohim whom he loved.

16 Thus did a fire come alive in his heart, and a restless longing began to stir in his soul, calling him to fulfill his purposes on earth.

CHAPTER 11

Miracle at Gimron

Yeshua performs his first resurrection of the dead by bringing the head priest of Gimron, Tobiah, back to life after he was struck dead by a Roman soldier. Yeshua explains the importance of love and faith.

ne day, when Yeshua's time among the community of Gimron was drawing to a close, a party of eight Roman soldiers came into the village, demanding a tribute to Caesar from all inhabitants.

2 Though the brethren were wroth with the Romans, they dared not show it and incur the wrath of armed soldiers; therefore, the three priests that led the community approached the Romans, and the head priest Tobiah spoke to them, saying, "We are a poor village of humble means dedicated to preserving the strait paths of God. We have little and what we have, we share in common; we therefore have no means to give Caesar individual tribute."

3 In that instant, without a word, but on a signal from the officer, a soldier stuck Tobiah with a deep prick from his pilum. And the community was of great sorrow and desired to rush to the side of Tobiah as he lay dying, but the Romans forbid it until the tribute was brought forth.

4 Everyone then made haste and soon gathered a small pile of valuables including a silver coin that Abraham had left for Yeshua and Yochanan. The leader of the soldiers noticed the coin and made inquiry how it was that an isolated community had possession of a coin from Persia.

5 But the Priests disavowed knowledge of the origin of the coin, and the Romans departed after beating the remaining two priests of the community leadership.

6 When the soldiers were beyond sight, the community rushed to the side of the stricken Tobiah, but they were too late for he had already breathed his last breath.

7 They mourned loudly because of his death, and one of the priests began to issue instructions to prepare their friend for burial when Yeshua quietly walked among them; they noticed him not as he knelt down beside the body of Tobiah and, placing a hand upon his head, was heard by a few who were near to quietly say, "By the will of my Father."

8 At that very moment, the eyes of Tobiah opened brightly and he sat up with a startled expression. And all the community marveled that he lived; and it was noticed by only a few, including Yochanan, that it was Yeshua who had wrought this miracle, and to these, Yeshua held his extended finger to his lips, making a sign that they should remain silent to what they had seen.

9 There was a certain woman in the community named Rachael, the wife of Rubin, who had befriended Yeshua and Yochanan and looked in upon them with motherly concern. Because of her closeness to them, she perceived they were favored of the Lord.

10 She was among those who had witnessed Tobiah, who had been killed, return to life upon

the touch of Yeshua. One day before he departed, she came up to Yeshua and whispered to him in private, "Tell me in truth, did you bring life back to the body of he who had died?"
11 And Yeshua answered, "I do nothing of my own; only by the will of our Father in Heaven did he return from his sleep."
12 But Rachael was of inquisitive mind and perceived there must be a deeper answer hidden still, and she asked, "By what power does God so work miracles in you?"
13 And Yeshua answered, "Upon the strength of love and faith was his life restored."
14 Then Rachael replied, "By the power of whose love and whose faith? For was this not the same Tobiah who was among those who forbid you entrance to the lectures of the Right Leader? Did God so love him to return his life or was his faith so great? Or did you whom he had chastised hold such great love for him?"
15 And Yeshua answered unto her, "Life is given by God and it is most precious, for it is in life that you fulfill your purpose on earth and create your eternity to come.
16 If you would love God, love everything God has created with a pure love that sings in your soul, for all life has a grand purpose that connects to all other life.
17 Love the birds in the air, the beasts upon the ground, and the fish in the sea. Remember, in their demeanor, they only reflect that which they see and can only give back to you that which they receive from you.
18 Love the plants that grow in abundance, for they give great beauty to the world and vital sustenance to man.
19 Even love your enemies and those who have wronged you that the mirror of life will reflect back to you that which you have shown.
20 Verily, hate merely continues upon an endless circling path that takes away the years of your life and gives nothing in return; only reciprocated love and respect can break the cycle of destruction and build a bridge of light to tomorrow.
21 And by this, may your enemies become your friends.
22 And then, if you have love, add to it a faith without doubt and your life will witness miracles and wonders, and that which you ask in love and righteousness, which serves the purposes of God, will ever be given to you by Elohim.
23 Verily, love and faith can prevail against all obstacles, even death, if it is the will of our Father and Mother in Heaven."
24 And Rachael bowed her head in awe and reverence, saying, "How can a young man do and know such things? Surely you are chosen of God."
25 And Yeshua bid her to keep those thoughts within her heart and to tell no one, for it was not yet time for him to be persecuted.

CHAPTER 12

A Life Renewed

Yeshua leaves the community of Gimron with his uncle, Abraham. Staying at an inn for the night on their return, they happen to cross paths with the same man, Dryhus, whom they had encountered on the way to Gimron, but he is now a very different man. Dryhus introduces Yeshua to his son, Teoma, who expresses his gratitude for the change Yeshua wrought in his father's life, which has brought fulfillment and happiness back into his life and the lives of his family.

And it came to pass that Abraham came to Gimron to return Yeshua to his parents in Nazareth, and he again imparted a small portion of the treasure of the Magi to the community that they might maintain Yochanan until such time as he was ready to leave, this despite the fact that Yochanan worked diligently in the fields to produce food and assisted in creating the perfume of Gimron, which the community used in trade.

Now Abraham remained with Yeshua and Yochanan for some days at Gimron that he could have a full account from the Elders of Yeshua's sojourn among them so that he could relate it to Yosef and Miryam and their kinsfolk in Nazareth.

3 The three high priests of Gimron had mixed feelings about Yeshua, and they were quick to add Yochanan as well.

4 And Tobiah, the high priest whom Yeshua had saved, said unto Abraham, "They are most peculiar boys. They both have good heads, and it would seem that Yeshua forgets nothing. But in truth, they have been very trying on us, for they question everything, even the very correct answers to the questions they have asked.

5 They speak when they should be silent, and when given permission to talk, they say a great many more words than are necessary.

6 They are hard workers when we can get them to stay in the village and work, and they have always met the quotas of work and study we have assigned unto them, but not always in a timely manner, for they often disappear to explore the emptiness in the wilderness; we suppose to commune with the lizards, but in truth we know not what draws them to the barrenness."

7 The priest said a great deal more, both favorable and critical of Yeshua and Yochanan, and once they had concluded, Abraham gave them additional coins of silver that they might continue to keep Yochanan and train him in strictness, despite the disruptiveness of his spirit.

8 When the time finally came for Yeshua and Yochanan to part, it was almost more than either could bear, so great was their brotherly love one for another. And among all the people, only Yochanan knew that Yeshua was chosen of God in a way beyond that which any man had ever been chosen. And as he embraced him one last time, he whispered into his ear, "When next we meet, I shall acknowledge you, my Lord."

9 And Yeshua answered, "And I shall acknowledge you, my brother; the prophet of Elohim."

10 After saying good-bye to Yochanan, Yeshua and Abraham began to make their journey back to Nazareth. As they traveled, Abraham told Yeshua all that had occurred in Nazareth while he had been away. And Yeshua related to him many of the wonders he had discovered and learned in Gimron. But of all that had been revealed by God to him and Yochanan, he said nothing.

11 And it came to pass as they journeyed back to Nazareth that they passed through the forest of date palms along the river Jordan and stopped for a night in the town of Shiloh, for Abraham desired to see a merchant there, and for a roof, they retired to a humble inn.

12 As they were taking their evening meal at a crude table, a merchant and his son, who was older than Yeshua, came in and asked to sit beside them, as it was the only available place.

13 Abraham readily agreed, but soon regretted his kindness when he realized the merchant was the very man with whom Yeshua had painfully divisive words about the donkey when they had first traveled to Gimron.

14 Seeing this, Abraham grabbed Yeshua by the front of his tunic that he might pull him up and make quick haste to depart. But before Yeshua could stand, the man named Dryhus leaped to his feet and, pointing at Yeshua, exclaimed in a high voice, "It is you!"

15 Yeshua looked upon him with great calm and Abraham with great apprehension, fearing the worst. But lifting Yeshua to his feet, Dryhus gave him a warm embrace and, pointing to his son, said unto him, "Behold my son, Teoma, who was lost to me for many years because of my wickedness, but now is found because of my light, which blessing you caused me to know."

16 Then turning to his son, he said, "This is the youth I have spoken about in whom the spirit of God flows like the faithful river Jordan."

17 Teoma came over to Yeshua and embraced him and said unto him, "Words can never tell of the gratitude my family has to you. My father never ceases to speak of the day upon the river when his life was worthless and you came and gave it value again. I do not understand how all this can be, but I know that before that day, because of the iniquities of my father, my mother and brothers and sisters were no better off than the rats of the refuse.

18 Our father had abandoned us and left us with nothing and so angered our relatives that we had but crumbs from their tables.

19 When our days seemed numbered upon the land, we prayed as a family, my mother and brothers and sisters and I, to the Almighty God, such as we had never prayed before. We asked with the most contrite hearts for God to deliver us.

20 Three days later, our father returned home. But it was not the man that had left or the man anyone had ever known, but a new man filled with the spirit of God and desiring only to do good with his life.

21 From that day forth, our fortunes changed, and today my father is a respected merchant, and my mother and brothers and sisters have again a good roof over their heads and bellies that are full.

22 I just thought you might like to know the good that came from that day."

23 Yeshua was greatly moved by the words of Teoma and again embraced both him and his father and said unto them, "The path of light is sweet, even as the path of darkness is bitter. Having known the dregs of bitterness and now tasted the cream of sweetness, let us give thanks for the mercies of God, who ever loves the repentant sinner and blesses those who live with virtue."

24 And there in the little inn, in the town of Shiloh, they prayed together until their hearts were touched, one by another, and they were lifted up in their spirits and saw the Celestine Light of God about them and felt the Holy Spirit of Elohim swelling in their hearts.

CHAPTER 13

Among the Sparrows and the Lion

Yeshua admonishes three boys who killed some sparrows for food to look instead to the abundance of plants that they can use so they need not take a life. He then brings the sparrows back to life. On another day, Yeshua encounters a young male lion being chased by some hunters and beckons him to his side. As he is running his hands through his mane, the hunters come upon him and are amazed at what they see and are awed by what he says.

Immediately upon his return to Nazareth, Yeshua began to work again in carpentry with his father Yosef and his brothers, making plows and yokes and many other useful items.

2 Nevertheless, his family knew he had a holy calling from God, though they knew not yet what it was, and he was given much free time to pursue the things he desired.

3 Therefore, Yeshua would wander off for days at a time and was often in solitary reflection and communion with God about the banks of Lake Gennesaret or in the hills around it, and he frequently journeyed to the coast of the great lake west of Nazareth.

4 One day as he was walking across the land approaching Lake Gennesaret, he came across several snares that had been set for sparrows, and he beheld three boys gathered around a pile of dead birds they had captured.

5 Yeshua walked over to the boys and asked, "Why have you killed these gentle wonders of God, who were children, even as you are?"

6 And the boys looked at one another in confusion as to why someone would ask such a silly question. And they replied, "It is for food that we have killed them."

7 Then Yeshua pointed to several plants growing around them and said, "You have no need to take the life of such loving creatures to sustain your own. Look here at this plant and this one and still another over here. Even as your heavenly parents have provided food for the birds, so do they provide it in abundance for you who are worth far more."

8 So saying, he waved his hand over the dead sparrows, and they came again to life and flew off with a great noise.

9 And the boys were frightened by what they had seen, and they ran home and told their parents, but none believed them and thought only that they made up a story to excuse that they had returned without meat.

10 On another day, as Yeshua was journeying to the shore of Lake Gennesaret, he heard much shouting ahead of him, and a young male lion suddenly bounded out of the brush from a steep hillside and stood before him with a great roar.

11 And it came to pass that Yeshua calmly knelt down and held his arms out wide with his palms forward and quietly beckoned to the lion, and it came to him and stood beside him.

12 He was running his fingers gently through its short mane when several men with clubs and slings and javelins burst upon him. But they stopped suddenly in astonishment when they beheld him embracing the head of the lion which they were hunting.

13 Then Yeshua stood beside the lion and said unto them, "Why do you seek to kill this creation of God, which has been given to have its life as much as you have yours? He means you no harm, but is only fierce as he seeks to preserve his life against your attacks.

14 Verily, the lion is greater than you, for it hunts only to sustain its life, while you seek to kill it only to puff up your pride.

15 I say unto you that it is because of the wanton slaughter upon its kindred by men that the lions teach their children to be an enemy to man to whom they would otherwise be friends.

16 The prophet Isaiah has said, the day will come when the lion shall lay down with the lamb, but before that day, the hearts of men must change. Verily, if this be so, then why not begin today to change your hearts and let this creature go its way in peace?"

17 And there was much astonishment among the men, who had never before imagined such a thing as they now saw that a youth could stand in peace with a lion and command the most ferocious beasts of the desert to obey him and then speak to them as a most learned rabbi. And in confusion, they turned and fled.

18 When they returned to their city, they told the priests everything which they had seen, and the priests inquired of the description of the boy and ascertained that it was Yeshua bar Yosef of whom they had already heard several strange reports. Then they determined to look more closely at him to see whether he was a threat or of God.

CHAPTER 14

A Stranger from Afar

In Yeshua's fifteenth year, a man named Anish, who learned of Yeshua from one of the Magi, came to visit him from the land known today as India. He stays at a nearby inn for one year and, during that time, imparts much wisdom to Yeshua, as he is a very learned man. He teaches Yeshua about the greeting, "Namaste," which Yeshua uses for the rest of his life. Yeshua in turn teaches Anish the ways of truth and light so the rest of his days would ever be fruitful.

When Yeshua was in his fifteenth year, there came a traveler from the east to his parents' house and asked for Yeshua by name. Now this man was dark skinned and told them he had journeyed a great distance from the land of Bharat to speak with Yeshua, and he brought gifts of fine spices to give to Miryam.
2 He said, "Many years ago, I spoke with a Magus who had paid tribute to Yeshua when he was a babe. After several years to put my affairs in order, I have at last made the journey to see what had become of the child that was so proclaimed by the Magus. I wish to learn of him and perhaps have some knowledge I can impart unto him."
3 Now Yosef and Miryam and all their children and kinsfolk were amazed at the appearance of this stranger, but Yeshua said, "My Father has told me of your coming; peace be upon you." And after hearing him speak thus for many years, almost everyone in Nazareth knew that he spoke not of Yosef, but of his Father in Heaven.
4 And the visitor from afar, whose name was Anish, was welcomed. He sought lodging at a nearby inn and remained in Nazareth for one year, meeting often with Yeshua and his family.
5 Anish and Yeshua would speak late into the night by the light of the stars and the Moon, and Anish learned more of Yeshua than any man at the time, except Yochanan. Truly, it would fill a great book to write all that Yeshua and Anish said to one another.
6 Anish taught Yeshua many things, for he was a very learned man. Often Yeshua's brothers and parents and kinsfolk would gather in respectful silence to hear the deep discussions on many subjects Yeshua and Anish would share.
7 Whenever they would meet or depart, as was the custom of Anish, they would each place their two palms together with the five fingers of the left hand against the five fingers of the right hand and hold them close to their heart and with a slight bow of the head, looking into the other's eyes, proclaim, "Namaste," which as Anish said means, "The light of God that is in me honors the light of God that is in you."
8 Concerning "Namaste," Anish expounded, saying, "In this word, which is both a greeting and a parting, there are many truths; it speaks of one person and the spirit of God within them, respectfully acknowledging another person and the spirit of God that dwells in them.

9 In so saying this, we accept that everyone who is blessed with "Namaste" has within them light and truth and peace, even if they have lived in darkness and deceit and violence, for the light of God can never be extinguished, only forgotten.

10 Furthermore, "Namaste" reminds us that though we may be of different skin colors and different cultures, we are one, and we are brothers, for we have the same divine light inside of us.

11 To say "Namaste" in humility and love is to realize that there is a magnificent oneness that connects all creation."

12 And Yeshua said unto him, "Verily, Anish, you have greater understanding of the ways of truth than the priests of Israel, for the light of God is a part of the heart and spirit of every person, ever guiding them with a still, small voice that they may know right from wrong, truth from falsehood, and light from darkness."

13 And it came to pass that Yeshua learned the history of Bharat and all the countries to the east. And Anish taught him many of the words of his native tongue and also of Persian.

14 Anish also taught him of the religions of many other cultures and people and said unto him, "I am a student of truth and I seek out truth wherever it may be, and if you so desire, I will impart to you some of the jewels I have discovered on my journey."

15 Yeshua smiled warmly and answered him, saying, "With a glad heart and a willing mind, I will savor the words you have to say and will show unto you the source of all of your jewels, in return."

16 Thus, it was that Yeshua and Anish shared many treasures with one another. And Yeshua taught Anish of the Elohim and of their light and of all their aspects and showed him how many of the teachings of other religions and of all the jewels of truth he treasured were reflections of the pure teachings of the one true God.

17 Anish expounded further on the foundations of religions, saying, "Some noble faiths teach that suffering and misery, birth, disease, old age, and death are inescapable realities of the journey of man."

18 And Yeshua replied unto him, "Believe in Elohim and follow their precepts and the pains of life will be less and death shall have no sting."

19 Anish answered, "It is said by some that all suffering is caused by lust, be it lust for things carnal or lust for riches or fame or any other thing, and by the ignorance of truth that creates such lust. Therefore, it is vital to seek knowledge and gain wisdom that lust will have no power over you."

20 Yeshua replied saying, "There are many men who have fallen to lust despite their great knowledge, for lust overcomes both the wise and the ignorant and knowledge alone gives no protection.

21 Only those who seek out the Elohim and follow the purity of their ways will be able to conquer the fiery arrows of lust that pierce the shields of those who might otherwise do good.

22 Verily, I say unto you only the righteous shield of Elohim never fails; therefore, only when a man turns away from God can lust have power over him, regardless of how great his knowledge is in all other things."

23 Anish replied, "Some say that only if you do away with the ignorance that creates lust can you do away with the lust and the suffering caused by lust and ignorance."

24 Yeshua responded, "Many a great man has fallen to lust in full knowledge of the evil he does, but incapable of stopping himself from doing it. Even as King David sinned in his lust for Bathsheba.

25 And this must always be, for the carnal man is an enemy to God and to himself and to his family; this has ever been so since the beginning of time.

26 Yet verily, lust cannot be done away with, for it is a part of the passion that is the whole of man. If you do away with passion, you destroy the passion for good, as well as the passion for evil.

27 But if your eye is single to the glory of God and to the righteousness they ask of you, then your passion will be for good and for light, and the spirit of Elohim will be with you always and

evil and darkness shall have no power over you.
28 Of his own, man can do nothing, for lust will always prevail. But lust does not always bring
men unto destruction. God has given the ability to lust unto man that they might use it to find
God; and when a man has been broken by the wages of lust, he can choose to abandon hope and
be further degraded, or in all honesty and without excuse, he can turn to the Celestine Light of
Elohim and, in his unworthiness, ask for forgiveness and bring forth fruits worthy of repentance.
29 Elohim so loves the repentant sinner that they will fortify them in the light. As they seek
so shall they find, and never again will they be a slave to the lust that had been their master, as
long as they stay faithful and true to the light of God."
30 Many were the things that Yeshua and Anish discussed, and many were the people that
wondered, saying, "How can this be the carpenter's son, for he speaks in ways that touch our
hearts and draw us to our God."
31 When the priests heard of the meetings of Yeshua and Anish, they were of a mind to go
and hear their words. But Yeshua, knowing the ensnaring and judgmental thoughts of some of
them, warned Anish, and with much spirit and love, he departed from Yeshua and his family and
the kinsfolk of Yosef and Miryam and began the journey back to his country.
32 But he did not leave as he had come, for when he arrived, he was a mere seeker of truth,
finding jewels of light only after much fruitless time searching in the mud. When he departed,
it was with Elohim, the source of all truth, lighting his path that every precious moment of his
life thereafter would be fruitful.
33 Nor was Anish ever forgotten by Yeshua who thereafter greeted his kinsfolk with "Namaste,"
in remembrance of his friend Anish and of the light of truth that shone forth from that greeting;
but among the Children of Israel, he did not, for they would not honor what it meant.

CHAPTER 15

Breath of Life

Yeshua shares some of the wisdom that Anish imparted to him with his family, which are movements very similar to yoga. Below are the detailed instructions for the three exercises that make up the Contemplative Meditation Movements.

A few moons after Anish had departed from Nazareth, the family of Yeshua began to be concerned because of his activities. Usually, it was accepted that his ways were different than others, and it was accustomed to leave him to do as he would without explanation, even though some of his actions were peculiar.

2 But of late, he had been given to rise before daybreak and journey beyond the confines of Nazareth, not to return until about one hour after sunrise. This he had been doing ever since the departure of Anish, and finally one day upon his return, his mother Miryam asked him, "What great things are you doing early in the morning that have kept you away from home every day until after the sun has risen?"

3 And Yeshua said unto her, "There were many secrets Anish gave unto me, which seekers of truth from far-off places have used to commune with God in Heaven and God in our soul. I have been practicing his teachings away from the eyes of others to prove them, be they true or false, and not to be noticed of men and thereby bring ridicule to my family."

4 Then Miryam came and embraced her son and said unto him, "There is nothing that you could do that would cause shame upon our house, and many have been amazed at your life."

5 Yeshua returned the embrace of his mother with deep affection and said unto her, "You are kind, but I know that for every person who hears my words with an open heart and a discerning mind, there are many who laugh at my strangeness of words and actions."

6 But Miryam did not allow such sentiments and said unto him, "Elohim is with you every moment of your life, and when God stands with you, of what significance are those who stand against you? I tell you in truth, you would honor me and your father Yosef and your brothers and sisters, if you would share at least with us, your closest family, some more of the things you have learned from Anish."

7 So it was that upon the following morning, just as the sun was cresting the horizon, the family of Yeshua, his mother and father and sisters and brothers, made their way together to the side of a small hill outside of Nazareth.

8 And Yeshua said unto them, "Just before he departed, Anish shared with me a ritual which he said was one of the most powerful ways for man to come closer to God and to discover the god within himself. It is a set of meditations involving the movement of the body and breath in harmony with the mind and heart. And this he called the Contemplative Meditation

Movements of the Breath of Life.

9 This is not known among the Children of Israel. Therefore, lest I be led astray, I first asked my Father and Mother in Heaven to know whether that which Anish revealed was of light or darkness.

10 The Holy Spirit of Elohim testified within my heart and mind that this teaching was in harmony with God. Then I heard the voice of my Father and felt the promptings of my Mother in my heart, which guided me to change that which Anish had given, that it would be even more pleasing unto them and of greater benefit unto man.

11 I have done these movement meditations taught by Anish, as amplified by God for many days now, and proven their worth, for they have caused me to know myself more.

12 So too have I come to feel my heart beat as one with the earth and all of nature and come closer to my Father and Mother in Heaven and to all men and women and children upon the earth.

13 Therefore, I say unto you that which Anish has given and God has magnified is good, although it may seem strange to the children of men."

14 As they seemed ready to learn, Yeshua asked all of his family to remove their sandals so their feet stood upon the bare ground and to hold their arms outstretched to their side to measure how far to stand apart from one another, then to relax, standing with their arms hanging comfortably at their side.

15 And he said unto them, "Anish asked that whenever possible, to do these movements and contemplations facing the sun as it rises each day, saying the new day's sun gives energy directly from God through the eyes and skin and into the heart of man.

16 Thus have I found it to be, for when the day begins in contemplation with the warmth and light of the sun filling the body, the thoughts and actions of man are of peace and harmony and more called to the light of Elohim throughout the day."

17 Then Yeshua asked each of his family to stand comfortably, facing the rising sun with their palms together and their fingers pointing up, and to position their hands thus joined against their chest, near their heart, then to close their eyes and to slightly bow their head. And this he said was the prayer position.

18 Next, Yeshua said unto them, "Take a deep comfortable breath through your nose and push it out slowly and deeply and thoroughly through your mouth. Throughout the Contemplative Meditations, breathe in through your nose and out through your mouth, as deeply as you can in gentle comfort and as often as you need.

19 Upon the next breaths, contemplate the Father, that is God and the good and responsible energy of the male that is within you.

20 Upon the next breaths, contemplate the Mother, that is God and the good and nurturing energy of the female that is within you.

21 Upon the next breaths, contemplate the Son, that is God and the good and playful energy of the child that is within you.

22 As you continue to thus breathe, consider how Elohim has made the heavens and the earth and you and all the people of the world upon it. Let your spirit feel the connection of the creator running through you and through the earth and through the sun and all the heavens. Reach out with your spirit and feel the spirits of the people beside you.

23 While in this contemplation and expansion of your spirit and while continuing to breathe comfortably and deeply, raise your head to a level position and lift your hands in unison until your arms are outstretched above your head, with your open palms facing the rising sun, your fingers wide open, and your thumbs and forefingers touching, forming the Triangle of the Trinity of Elohim.

24 While in the same contemplation and expansion of your spirit, exhale slowly and deeply. Then with your arms and fingers raised up and outstretched and your open palms facing the sun, separate your hands and smoothly rotate your arms down in opposite directions, until your arms

are outstretched at your waist level, with your palms still facing the sun.

25 As your arms are descending, open your eyes for a long blink and gaze upon the fiery orb of the sun and contemplate the physical light of God, which shines forth upon the earth and gives life to all things.

26 With closed eyes and movements close to the body, return your hands to the prayer position. All of this is called Welcome to Light. Repeat it two more times if you desire."

27 And thus did Yeshua and all of his family.

28 Then Yeshua showed them the second contemplative movement, which he called the "Bridge of Light" in which they should feel the energy of earth and all living things upon it; flowing through them and the power of God coming from the heavens through them, to benefit all the world.

29 At the beginning of the Bridge of Light, Yeshua asked his family to each say aloud the words he would tell them, if they felt them to be true in their hearts. And thus spoke Yeshua, "I covenant to keep the temple of my body pure inside and out and to faithfully live the light of Elohim that I might always be a worthy vessel to be a bridge between Heaven and earth."

30 Then Yeshua said unto them, "Stand now relaxed, with your arms low at your sides, your open palms facing the sun, and spread your feet in a comfortable way, about the distance of your shoulders.

31 Take a deep breath and slowly raise your arms to shoulder height, fully extended to each side, with palms facing the sun and fingers spread apart. Hold this position as you slowly and thoroughly exhale.

32 As you take in another deep breath, bring your outstretched arms in front of you until your extended fingers are again in the Trinity Triangle, with palms facing the sun and the sun framed within the triangle. Then exhale a slow, thorough, and gentle breath.

33 Hold that position and look through slightly parted eyelids at the sun. Breathe several calm and normal breaths through your nose and expand the boundaries of your spirit through earth and connect with all living things; feel the wetness of the oceans and lakes and the coolness of the forests; smell the salt in the air by the sea and fields of wildflowers; feel the cold of the snow upon the mountaintops and the sand moving between your toes on a warm beach; hear children laughing and the music of creeks flowing over rocks; connect your spirit to earth and all that is upon it. Be one with earth and all life that is upon it.

34 Now take a deep breath through your nose and, holding the Trinity Triangle, thrust the triangle up toward the heavens and exhale. Then take a big breath and exhale slowly as you lower the triangle down toward the ground, bending over at the waist and with knees gently bent as far as necessary to touch your hands or at least your fingertips to the ground, holding the Trinity Triangle.

35 As the triangle descends from the apex to the ground, in your mind, call upon all the life force of the earth and all living things upon it to touch your hands and swirl within the Triangle of the Trinity.

36 Continuing to hold the Trinity Triangle, take a deep breath and bring your hands up along your legs with palms facing your body, pulling your connections to all the life forces upon the earth up through your body.

37 Your greatest point of incoming breath is near the area of your heart. At this spot, move your palms forward so they are facing the sun while still holding the Trinity Triangle.

38 Now quickly push your hands upward while forcefully and fully exhaling, ending with your hands in the Trinity Triangle, facing upward toward the sky.

39 Now lower your arms in front of you until you are again looking at the sun framed within the triangle. Hold this position and breathe normal easy breaths. Send your spirit forth to Elohim bringing with it all of the spiritual connections you have made to all the life of the earth and ask Elohim to bless all the earth with goodness and light.

40 Then, with words in your mind and feelings in your heart, ask Elohim to use you as a

worthy vessel; feel the power of God swirling in your hands between the Triangle of the Trinity, coursing up through your arms and swirling through your body, filling your heart and expanding your mind so much so that the light of Elohim is radiating from you.

41 Repeat this contemplative meditation movement two more times if you desire, beginning at this position. As you move your hands back toward the earth with love and humility, send the power of Elohim whose spirit dwells within your heart, back through you, and into the earth and unto all living things upon it that for a moment in time, they might feel the exquisite joy of the Celestine Light of Elohim."

42 After this last contemplation, there was much complaining from many of the family of Yeshua, for the movements were awkward to them and not in the ways they were accustomed to move and hold their bodies.

43 And Yeshua said unto them, "It was also difficult for me in the beginning, for so much was I caught up in the unfamiliar movements and breathing that I was not able to benefit as much in my spirit as I was after several more days of effort, when the movements and the breathing had become easy.

44 Each contemplative meditation movement can be done just once if it is easier for you, and you can still gain many good things. But take heed to not dismiss these things because of their difficulty on your first attempts or because of the strangeness from the teachings and traditions which you know.

45 For I say unto you that they work greatly to balance your spirit and the powers of your body and mind. They help you to begin your day in harmony with God, in rhythm with the earth, and connected in peace and oneness to all life. These contemplations are good for the soul and of benefit to man during all of his day."

46 Then Yeshua showed them the third contemplative movement, which he called, the Wind of Love.

47 And he said unto them, "The ills of the world, wars, plagues, famines, pestilences, disease, and all other things, that haunt man and make his sojourn on earth a trial come to man because of his lack of love.

48 Because a man does not love God, he does not have the spirit of God to inspire him to do good or the Celestine Light of Elohim to guide him and help him in his life. Therefore, he inherits the opposite of the light, which is darkness.

49 Because a man does not love his neighbors, he covets their life and possessions and thinks of ways to deprive them of that which they have, which brings jealousy, adultery, dishonesty, murder, war, and plundering.

50 Because a man does not love himself, he does not keep the temple of his body pure and clean on the inside and the outside or give his best effort at his labors or in relationships with his family and the children of men. And this brings many plagues upon man: diseases, pestilences, famines and other hardships, and an early end to a life that could have been much longer and fuller and given to greater joy.

51 Therefore, it is the purpose of this contemplative meditation movement to reach out your spirit to all living things and to send your love and thanksgiving to them with the essence of your spirit.

52 Whereas before everyone moved in unison, during most of the Wind of Love, each will move as their spirit guides them, which may be different every time you do the contemplation. Because each person's spirit and the way it communes with others is unique to them and to that moment in time.

53 Remaining within the space where you are standing, close your eyes and stand comfortably with your arms held loosely at your side, with your palms facing the sun.

54 Now breathing as you desire, begin to move any part of your body as little or as much as you desire, in ways that your spirit calls upon you to commune with the energy of all living things.

55 Begin by reaching out with your mind and your heart to send the essence of your spirit to

touch the essence of the spirit of the person next to you and then the person beyond them and then beyond them.

56 Touch no one with your body, but touch everyone with your spirit. Nor should you make any sounds other than the quiet sounds of your movements and your breathing.

57 Take all thoughts of worldly things from your mind and think only of the unconditional love that the nobility of your spirit is giving to the nobility of the spirit of the person next to you, with thankfulness for the good things they bring to your life. Then do likewise with the person beyond them and then all of the people in this town and then in this land and then in the lands beyond, even to lands you have never known and people you cannot even imagine.

58 Now think of the animals that are kept by man and known to you, being in or near your home, and send them your spirit of unconditional love and thanksgiving for the good things they bring to your life. Then expand your spirit to touch all of the animals kept by man in this land and then to all those in nearby lands and then to all in the world.

59 Return again to the spot where you move as your spirit directs and think of all of the wild animals that dwell here. Send your love to them for the grace and beauty they bring to man and balance to the earth and for the many lessons they teach. Now send your love beyond this land to all the lands of the earth and to all the wild beasts that roam those lands, even those you know not and cannot imagine.

60 Return again to the spot where you move with a free spirit upon the earth, sending out your essence of love and receiving love from all who send it to you. Now send your spirit of love into the seas and the fishes, many which give their lives to feed the multitudes. Swim with them in your mind and spirit and be one with them

61 Return again to the spot where you move freely. Now send your spirit of love out to the birds in the sky, fly with them and see the world from above through their eyes, and feel the lightness of your spirit as you move effortlessly through the air.

62 Return again to the spot where you move in harmony with your spirit. Now send your essence of love and thanksgiving to all men and women and children upon the earth, for they are your brothers and sisters, though they know it not.

63 Return again to the spot where you move in joy and send love and thanksgiving unto every plant and tree and crop that nourishes both man and beast, gives beauty to the eye, shelter from the storm, and warmth on nights of cold.

64 Now stand as one, facing the sun with arms outstretched from your sides, and hands intertwined in the hands of those beside you. Breathe in and push out deeply for three breaths as you sense and feel and see in your mind the essences of your souls united, radiating out from every part of your body and spreading across this spot, across this town, across this land, and across the world with the marvelous light of love.

65 After three breaths, return to the prayer position, take one more deep breath and push it out, then open your eyes and turn to the people around you and greet them with 'Namaste.'"

66 Yeshua continued to do the Contemplative Meditation Movements most of the days of his life as the sun crested the horizon each morning. But even among his family, most were not inclined to continue that which he taught that day, nor among many who later came to follow him, for he did not teach it as a commandment of God. But in the days to come, there were those who heeded that which he showed, and the secret of the Contemplative Meditation Movements went forth into the world.

CHAPTER 16

Sage of Jerusalem

In Yeshua's sixteenth year, an angel appears in a dream to an elderly, crippled priest by the name of Ezra. He is told that he needs to teach Yeshua the intricacies of the Law of Moses and the ways of Israel. When he arrives at Nazareth, Yeshua heals him of his infirmity. Although Ezra is a very good teacher, there is not much that Yeshua does not already know of the law, so Ezra has fun coming up with precarious situations related to "the law" and moral values to see how Yeshua will resolve them.

In Yeshua's sixteenth year, there was an elderly priest by the name of Ezra, who being widowed and greatly crippled of arthritis had retired to the south of Lake Gennesaret, at Philoteria, to live out his years.
2 One night as he slept, an angel of God appeared to him in a dream and said, "Ezra, Ezra, you have a great work yet to do before you take the last sleep. Journey to Nazareth and there find the house of Yosef, the carpenter whose firstborn son is Yeshua, the Anointed One of Israel and of all the world.

3 Teach him the Law of Moses and the ways of Israel, as taught by all the prophets and traditions, and give him difficult tests that his mind might become quick, and great shall be your reward in the world to come."

4 Upon the sunrise, Ezra made the journey to Nazareth and in three days' time came to the house of Yosef and Miryam and related all that the angel had told him.

5 When Yeshua, who had been away, returned to his parents' home, Ezra marveled at his countenance and said, "Surely this is the Anointed One, for the light of God shines from his very face."

6 And Yosef related all that Ezra had told unto them, and Yeshua said unto Ezra, "You are a chosen priest of God that in your old age and frailness, you would nevertheless heed the call of God."

7 Then Yeshua touched his hand and said, "Verily, I say unto you, Ezra of Amasa, God loves you for the good man that you are, and as you love God, may the ease of your youth be restored to your joints," and immediately Ezra's affliction left him and he stood amazed looking at Yeshua.

8 And Yeshua bade him speak to no one of that which he had done or that which he knew of him, and he said unto him, "It is by your own faith and because of your exceeding love for God that your infirmness has departed. I merely opened the door to the light of your soul that God could touch it with his love."

9 And it came to pass that Ezra remained in Nazareth for long periods to teach Yeshua of the law and traditions, but found there was little he did not already know.

10 From time to time, Ezra would return to his home on Lake Gennesaret, and at times,

Yeshua would visit him there.

11 It became the delight of Ezra to design precarious situations of the law and moral values to see how Yeshua would resolve them. And he told him to speak his heart and not to be constrained by what others might say or think of his words.

12 One of many such challenges was as this: Ezra said unto Yeshua, "King David lusted after Bathsheba, the wife of his faithful soldier Uriah the Hittite, and arranged his death to have her.

13 Then came Nathan, the prophet of God, unto King David with God's condemnation and judgment.

14 And King David abashed himself for his wickedness and came unto a sorrowful repentance. From that day forth, he loved God greatly and brought forth good fruits.

15 Bathsheba later bore him a son named Solomon, who became the king all Israel still praises. What then was the greater sin? That King David lay with Bathsheba or caused Uriah the Hittite to be killed?

16 And lest you say that death is the greater sin, remember that Uriah was a foreigner, and because of his death, David became a better man than he was and a son was born that became a great king for the benefit of all Israel.

17 Yeshua did not hesitate to answer and said unto him, "To take a life unnecessarily is to dam the progression of the soul from the good it came into mortal life to obtain.

18 David is counted as great among the kings of Israel as is Solomon, but verily, I say unto you the deeds he did these days will forever lessen the good he otherwise did, and his throne in eternity shall be taken away and given to another.

19 Think not that Solomon needed to be birthed from Bathsheba, for David had many wives and God could have given Solomon unto any of them.

20 Therefore, David first sinned by lying with Bathsheba. But this was a lesser sin, for with repentance, the consequences would not stop the progression of the soul, though they may still carry the judgments of men.

21 But David then conspired to have a loyal and faithful guardian killed in battle that he might take his wife and then sought to hide the truth, but he could not hide it from God.

22 Therefore, I say unto you some sins are greater than others; when you consider the depths of the evil, ponder upon the eternal consequences of the foul deeds that are done.

23 For every sin, there must be remorse and a sincere repentance if the light of God is to burn once more in the heart of the sinner, for God cannot shine in an unclean tabernacle.

24 And for those sins which hurt or take from another, there must be an open confession and sincere restitution.

25 But for some sins, such as murder, there can never be full restitution, for how can a man restore the experiences and joys that will now never be?

26 Therefore, as much good as David then did all of his life, it could never balance the evil that was done. As much as God loved David for his goodness, mercy could not rob justice, for in this case, David took that which could not be repaid in his life; in so doing, he took from himself some of the eternal reward he would have otherwise earned.

27 There are those among the Children of Israel who would say that it was not murder David did that day because Uriah was a foreigner to whom the laws given by God to the Children of Israel did not apply. And that David did not commit the act, but merely put the man in harm's way and left it to God to spare him or take him.

28 But I say unto you all people are God's children. All stand before him in equality, and that which God has said, he has said unto all the world. An evil against any child of God is a sin against God.

29 Nor think that merely because the account is written in sacred texts that it is from God, for kings and priests have ever inscribed words of their desire to justify their own deeds, and God suffers it to be so that the righteous man might seek out the light of Elohim in prayer to know the truth.

30 Verily, the true light of God is to do unto others as you would have them do unto you. In
this is the fullness of the spirit of truth, and any teaching of a different spirit cannot be of Elohim
when it concerns someone who has done you no grievous wrong."
31 And Ezra was amazed at the depth of understanding Yeshua had, blasphemous though it
would be deemed by most, and therefore posed unto him another question, saying, "What then
is murder? And what of killing to sustain your life against an enemy?"
32 And Yeshua said unto him, "Elohim created all life. Therefore all life is sacred unto God.
Elohim made the earth a garden of abundance for man and gave man dominion over all things
upon the earth to use as he needed to help him in his labors and for sustenance as long as he
honored life.
33 Elohim, who created all, said that it was good and, in so saying, charged man to be a good
steward over that which was given unto him. And a good steward does not take life without
necessity.
34 When man kills man, God can never condone it, save it be in direct defense of family and
friends and then only when there was no other way to preserve the life of the innocent.
35 Therefore, woe unto the man that becomes a soldier whose army journeys to another land
and kills a people that have not attacked his homeland, even as the Romans have done in the
land of Palestine and the Israelites have done before them. A soldier such as this is not justified
in the eyes of God.
36 God does not condemn him as severely as he would a murderer who wantonly kills for his
own desires, for the soldier was compelled because of his duty, but neither does Elohim spare
him from justice; and it would be better for a soldier to lay down his weapons and suffer the
consequences with his commanders than to attack and kill people in another land that have not
first come into his country with murder and mayhem.
37 But if a man kills a man or an animal that has attacked his land or his family and poses
mortal threat to them, he is justified in the eyes of God.
38 Yet the sacred texts are full of the accountings of God commanding the Children of Israel
to conquer and kill the people of the lands they invade, even unto all of the women and children.
39 And I say unto you that you may know with great surety that these are the writings of
men trying to cloak their wickedness in the name of God. For never would my Father in Heaven
command for the innocent to be slain!
40 Again, I give you this test that you may know the truth, do unto others as you would have
them do unto you. This is the foundation of all the laws and the will of God."
41 And Ezra never ceased to marvel that such wisdom and understanding of God could come
from one so young.
42 And Yeshua continued to be tested for two years by Ezra in the evenings after his work
with his father Yosef and brothers and during the times when he was not away on his own
journeys.
43 And because of the good teaching of Ezra, Yeshua became exceedingly learned in reading
and writing Hebrew, Aramaic, and Greek.
44 So quick was his mind that in two such years, he held all of the knowledge that Ezra had
gained in his entire life as a priest.
45 And all the moral sayings of Yeshua given in answer to the challenges of Ezra and from
the time of his youth in Nazareth and many of his conversations with Anish are recorded in the
book of Yakov, his brother, written to the Children of Light in Jerusalem.

CHAPTER 17

Celebrate the Life

In Yeshua's seventeenth year, his father Yosef dies. Yeshua explains that mortal death is merely passing over to another land, and for those you love, there is no separation because they are still with you, for love is eternal, and you will be reunited. Therefore, we should not mourn, but celebrate the lives of those we love when they pass on.

In Yeshua's seventeenth year, his father Yosef died.

2 Many of his family called upon Yeshua to bring his father back from the dead, as it was rumored he had done with a priest at Gimron, but Yeshua said, "My Father in Heaven has called him to his glory, and though I miss him and feel the sorrow of my mother Miryam, it is not for me to call him back, for his time in this world is done.

3 He has been a good and faithful servant and has fulfilled his calling. He goes now to the place of Celestine Light and glory to await his friends and family and prepare a place for them.

4 Therefore, do not feel a deep emptiness, for nothing is lost. He who you love has merely traveled to another land, apart from you only for a time. But his essence is still here with you each day and will remain with you as long as you desire it to be so. For that long will he continue to watch over you, to give you comfort, and to whisper his wisdom to you in your dreams.

5 I say unto you, have not sorrow but joy, for all those who live righteously shall be with him again in a marvelous wonder, from everlasting to everlasting.

6 Verily, mortal death is merely a small step on your eternal journey of life. While you tarry in life, never forget those who have passed beyond the veil, for they are with you still. Remember them in your prayers each day, for they are not dead; they live! And in their prayers, they remember you.

7 Therefore mourn not, for the righteous are only parted in body for a breath of eternity, and in the spirit in your heart, not at all. I say unto you, rejoice, make glad music and dance, celebrate the life of the one we love!"

CHAPTER 18

Marriage of Yeshua and Miriam

Yeshua marries Miriam of Magdala shortly after his eighteenth birthday, in the town of Cana of Galilee, at the house of his father's brother, Ethan, which is witnessed by many respected friends and family.

❖ ❖ ❖

As was the custom, shortly after Yeshua passed his eighteenth birthday he was married to Miriam of Magdala, a virgin of the tribe of Judah to whom he had been engaged for two years, having met her during a visit to Jerusalem for the Passover feast three years previous.

2 She came from a wealthy family of good report from the city of Bethany, but due to one of her father's interests as a procurer of fish, they maintained a villa in Magdala near Lake Gennesaret, just beyond the baths at Tiberias where she spent much of her life with her family. Yeshua had occasion to visit her four times during their engagement, and she visited him in the company of her parents on two occasions in Nazareth.

3 They were engaged in their hearts the very first day they saw each other near the temple, and from the first moments they exhibited a great affection for one another that was not customary among men and women.

4 In the beginning her parents were not in favor of the marriage, considering that Yeshua was only a poor carpenter from the destitute town of Nazareth. Nevertheless, to appease the anger of their eldest daughter, who was very headstrong, they agreed to allow Yeshua to visit at their home and reluctantly traveled to Nazareth with Miriam to visit Yeshua's family.

5 When they visited Nazareth and heard with their ears his teachings and saw with their eyes the reverence in which he was held by his kinsfolk and friends, they understood that God was with him and thereafter they approved of the marriage and willingly betrothed their daughter to Yeshua, a man they knew was called of God to a high and holy calling.

6 Now the marriage of Yeshua and Miriam occurred on the fourth day of the week, in the town of Cana of Galilee, at the house of Ethan, a brother of Yosef who assumed the responsibilities of the groom's father.

7 Miriam's extended family and many friends journeyed up from Bethany and from Magdala and Tiberias, and Yeshua's mother Miryam as well as his brothers and sisters and many kinsfolk and friends of childhood attended from Nazareth.

8 The families of Yeshua and Miriam were both well respected in the region, and upon the evening a large processional of townsfolk and kinsfolk and friends of both families proceeded through the town to escort the bride and groom to the marriage ceremony with many candles and torches, accompanied with much singing, dancing, and joy.

9 Miriam's father and mother walked with her to the groom's tent, and exceeding was the joy which shone from their faces.

10 And Miriam was covered from head to foot in a flowing veil, woven by her with golden threads, and she wore great amounts of flowers in strings about her neck.

11 When Miriam was given to Yeshua and wed to him beneath the canopy, he gave her a gold coin to represent his commitment to her and said unto her, "Miriam, my heart sings and my spirit rejoices, for you are my eternal companion with whom I will create."

12 And Miriam replied to Yeshua, looking steadfastly into his eyes, "I will never leave you, my Lord. Your light will always guide my paths. And with you I will create."

13 As the sacrament was concluded there was a rumble in the heavens and the very earth shook from its power, and many bowed their heads or knelt to the ground in reverence or fear, but Yeshua and Miriam remained standing, holding each other's hands and looking into each other's eyes; and it would seem to be that they were unaware of the commotion about them.

14 As the people rose to their feet, Yeshua and Miriam turned to them, and Yeshua said unto them, "On earth as in the heavens, man is not without woman, nor woman without man in the light of Elohim.

15 "And of this, I bear witness to my friends and family and all the world that upon this day we have fulfilled the desires of Elohim and of our hearts; and upon that fulfillment have the windows of Heaven been opened, for we now see the greater blessings that await the man and woman united in love and in God.

16 Verily, with our eyes now open, we see the wonder before us; so marvelous it is that we had not even imagined."

CHAPTER 19

Wedding Feast at Cana

The wedding feast of Yeshua and Miriam, which lasts for seven days as was customary, is held at the home of Ethan, the brother of Yeshua's father, Yosef, in the town of Cana of Galilee. Because so many people attend, on the third day of the feast, the wine runs out. Lest Ethan be disgraced as a bad host for running out of wine, Yeshua's mother, Miryam, asks Yeshua if he could ask a small favor of God that some more wine may be found. In response, Yeshua turns six stone jars of water, each containing twenty to thirty gallons, into the purest of wines.

Following the wedding, Yeshua's uncle Ethan gave a great feast in honor of the bride and
groom that lasted for seven days and was attended by many friends and relatives from
both families.
Ethan bore the cost of much of the feast, but Yeshua's mother also gave Ethan one gold coin
of the Magi.
3 And unto Yeshua and Miriam, she gave all the remaining gifts of the Magi as a wedding
present. All the years since the visit of the Magi, she and Yosef had hidden most of the treasure
and lived a humble life so that Yeshua might be given the gifts when he wed and have the
freedom to devote his time to God without neglect to his family.
4 On the third day of the feast, because of the great multitude that attended, the wine ran out,
and the servants prepared to go to the wine merchants to obtain more. But Ethan was distressed
at the time it would take to fetch more wine and felt disgraced lest his guests should know that
he had run out of wine. Therefore, Yeshua's mother bid him to assist Ethan that he would not be
disgraced.
5 Yeshua was in happy conversation with his friends and did not understand the depth of his
mother's request and said unto her, "O Mother, what has this to do with you or me, for we are
not the hosts but the guests and what would you have me do that cannot be done by those whose
charge it is, for is not my time due elsewhere?
6 Then Yeshua sensed his mother's sorrow and felt contrite for his words and embraced her
and said, "Whatsoever you would have me do, I will do."
7 And Miryam implored him, "It is now that we must have wine for the cups of the guests
are dry. Can you not ask a small favor of God that some wine may be quickly found until more
can be obtained from the merchants?"
8 Yeshua then clasped his hands by his heart, and after gazing up into Heaven, he looked
upon Miryam and said unto her, "As you wish, Mother Miryam. Please ask the servants to bring
some water."

9 And his mother said to the servants, "Whatever Yeshua bids you, do in haste."
10 Now six stone jars were standing nearby for the rites of purification, each filled with twenty to thirty gallons of water. The servants brought Yeshua to them, and he touched each for but a moment. Then reaching his finger into one, he then brought it to his lips and said to them, "Why go to the wine procurers? This is not water, but wine of the finest grape; draw some out and take it to Ethan." And in bewilderment, they took it.
11 When Ethan tasted it, he was amazed, for it was the purest wine of the grape and delicious to the taste, and he asked his servants from whence it came.
12 The servants too were astounded, and they pointed to Yeshua, saying, "We filled the jugs earlier to the brims with water, but when we drew from the jugs to give you a drink as he directed, behold, the water had become wine."
13 But Ethan knew that with Yeshua, great miracles were possible, and he called to Yeshua and gave him exceeding thanks, saying, "God has saved me disgrace by this wonder and has brought honor to my house, for this is exceedingly fine wine. It is delicious yet pure, without affliction to the mind. Because of this, instead of only serving the best wine first as is the custom, we have the best wine to serve both first and last, and great shall be the memory of your wedding in the hearts of men."
14 And Yeshua bade Ethan and the servants and his friends who were present that they tell no one of the miracle which they had witnessed, for it was not yet his time to be known in the world.

CHAPTER 20

Family Joys in Nazareth

Yeshua and Miriam live four peaceful years in Nazareth. During this time, Miriam gives birth to two children: first to a son they name Uriel and then to a daughter they name Dara. Yeshua becomes very adept working with all manners of wood and Miriam with the spinning of fabrics. Together, they plant a wondrous garden where they grow a great variety and abundance of fruits and vegetables that they sell. Once Yeshua's brother Yakov is engaged to be married, his obligation as the eldest son to provide for the family is fulfilled, and Yeshua and Miriam prepare to leave with their children for Egypt.

◆ ◆ ◆

As he was the eldest son, Yeshua determined to remain in Nazareth, working with his brothers as a carpenter until such time as his brother Yakov had married and could take up the responsibilities of overseeing the affairs of the family with their younger brothers: Yosef, Simon, and Yudas.

2 So it was that Yeshua and Miriam remained in Nazareth for four years, and Miriam gave birth to a son, Uriel, for he was born in the summer sun and the light of God shined on him from the heavens, and to a daughter, Dara, for she showed the wisdom of God, who balanced the spirit of the son with the spirit of a daughter.

3 And Yeshua and Miriam were content. They lived with their children as the other humble families in Nazareth did: playing with them, laughing with them, and delighting in their every new expression and accomplishment.

4 Yeshua became an expert carpenter, adept in all manner of woodwork, from fashioning plows and yokes to carving chairs and boxes. And Miriam visited the elderly master weaver of Nazareth often and became adept in the spinning and weaving of fabrics. Together, they grew a great variety and abundance of fruits and vegetables, which they sold. And the greenness and vitality of their garden was a wonder known beyond the boundaries of Nazareth.

5 Visitors from distant places continued to journey to Nazareth to speak with Yeshua, and friends and kinsfolk in the town continued to gather on starlit evenings to hear Yeshua speak with the visitors.

6 And it came to pass that several learned Greeks visited, prompted by inexplicable urgings, and they marveled at how quickly Yeshua was a master of their language and writing. It was from this time forth that some began to call him by the name which the Greeks did: Iesous of Nazareth.

7 Yeshua continually bade his visitors not to speak of him in Galilee or Judea, and his friends and family knew this already.

8 Now many of the teachings that were spoken by Yeshua after he was married and lived in Nazareth during this time are written in the book of his brother Shimon.

9 Yeshua did not do many miracles during this time, for many in Nazareth had not the faith to manifest a miracle, for they knew Yeshua too casually from his childhood and could not see him in his glory.

10 During their years in Nazareth, Yeshua drew very close to Miriam, his wife, such that they were often together and in ways not accustomed to the people of Nazareth or Israel; she sat in councils with him, and he honored her; she spoke only as men were accustomed to speaking, and she did not wear a veil in public.

11 And for this, some murmured against Yeshua, even some of his friends, saying, "He is breaking the law to allow his wife such privilege as is given only to men and to allow her to go forth without a veil and a cloak."

12 Then some who were upset with him spoke to the priests of the area concerning this matter and the priests were wroth at the privileges Yeshua gave to Miriam and began to plot against him.

13 And it came to pass that at the beginning of the fifth year of Yeshua and Miriam's life in Nazareth, his brother Yakov was wed to Susanna and thus was fulfilled that which Yeshua had waited for.

14 By early spring, Yeshua and Miriam and their children made ready to depart from his family and kinsfolk and friends to journey to the land of Egypt.

CHAPTER 21

Sermon In Nazareth

On the last day before Yeshua and Miriam leave for Egypt with their children, at the request of his family and the people of Nazareth, Yeshua imparts some words of wisdom to help expand and uplift all those who hear him speak.

On Yeshua's last day in Nazareth, before he and Miriam began their journey to Bethany, his family and kinsfolk and the people of Nazareth, realizing that Yeshua was leaving perhaps never to return, asked him to give them some words of wisdom before he departed.

2 Even those that had always looked down upon him as strange and peculiar asked him to speak, for they knew despite their disdain that he held knowledge few men had.

3 Thus, it was that nearly all the people of Nazareth came to the little hill outside of town where Yeshua had taught his family the Contemplative Meditation Movements. And they sat upon the gentle slope and gazed upward at Yeshua standing atop the rise that all might see and hear his voice.

4 And Yeshua said unto them, "Hear the thanks of my heart to you, my family and friends, and neighbors of Nazareth. It is here among you that I have been sheltered and nurtured and learned much of life and truth. Wherever I go in the days to come, you will always be with me in my heart, and God will always look with favor upon you for the kindnesses you have given unto me and my wife and my children.

5 "I know not where to begin, therefore let one of you stand and ask of me the questions of your mind and the troubles of your heart, and from that, I will give unto you a fullness of my knowledge as God has given me the substance for which was asked."

6 Then to the surprise of many, before a man could stand, Shavna, the widow, stood and quickly said to him, "I have been a widow for three years. My only son was crucified by the Romans the year before last and my parents are dead. I still have three children in the tiny hovel of my home and barely exist upon baskets that I make for a merchant and the little that my brother, who is here with me and himself infirmed, can give me.

7 "According to the law, I must be double veiled and cloaked to be outside, so that even now I can scarcely see you or breathe. Why is life so hard and especially why does God allow women to be treated barely above the animals? Even to speak to you as I now am shall bring condemnation upon me."

8 Yeshua was very moved by her words and said unto all the multitude. "Hear me, O Children of Israel. This woman's words cause anguish to my soul."

9 And he asked for Miriam, his wife, to come and stand with him on the hill. And she alone,

among all the women of Nazareth was not cloaked or veiled.
10 And Yeshua said unto the multitude, "This is Miriam, my beloved wife, and you see the
fairness of her face as fully as I do. And it is I that have asked her not to hide the beauty of the face God has given. For what God has given is not for man to take away.
11 She is not a harlot, but a most virtuous and pleasing daughter of God, a delight to Elohim in her every word and deed.
12 Verily, the wicked lusts of men are not her sin but theirs, for she does not look to them or entice them, and any who lusts upon her shall be held accountable for every impure thought on the Judgment Day.
13 And more, she sits beside me at councils and in all things do I consider her opinion, and many have been the wise words she has given unto me.
14 I say unto you that it is man that is too often the abomination unto God and women in their virtue who God favors, for it is man that makes war and man that enslaves and man that rapes and man that despoils and man that murders and man that does all manner of evil in the world.
15 But of all the sins men do, the trampling of women underfoot, even their very wives and daughters, is among the most loathsome sins unto God.
16 "If Miriam was to stand here naked before you and innocent of all offense or outward temptation, whose sin would it be? Verily, it could not be her sin for she was merely being as God had made her, but it would be the sin of every man who lusted upon her and the sin of every man or woman who judged her in her nakedness.
17 Therefore, I say unto you, ask not women to cloak and veil themselves, if it is not their desire; for the crown of their temple is their eyes and their face and their hair, which is beautiful as God has made, and to see this wonder in purity and respect is to honor the maker.
18 Ask instead to have control over the evil inside of you to not imagine perverted thoughts of the temple God has built. For I say unto you that on the Day of Judgment, man shall be weighed in the balance by every impure thought as well as act.
19 And to the men I say again, seek not to be masters over your women, especially not to the point of servitude and degradation, but seek rather to be master of the carnal man within you who lusts after the virtuous and sins against the righteous.
20 And to the women I say, fear not to show your face, for it is a glory of God, but be modest in your dress and look not at men to entice, nor to allure them by sensual speaking, for then the fault is yours for the evil you stir in the hearts of men; and then it is both you and the man that shall be accountable on the Day of Judgment.
21 Let all remember as Solomon has said, 'He that conquers himself is greater than he that takes a city.' Therefore, I say unto you, be masters of yourselves.
22 There once was a hermit who was so afraid to sin that he left his family and built a one-room house without windows outside of the city walls so that he would not see anything that would tempt him to sin. He never came out except once each week, clothed in a robe with a deep cowl, to go to a market on the outskirts of the city to sell the trinkets he made and buy a little food.
23 And so he passed his life until the day when he was an old man, and a great storm came from the desert and knocked down his little house and blew away his possessions and left him standing in the brightness of the sun with only the clothes on his back.
24 The man was forced to go into the city to seek food and shelter, and he passed much devastation, for many had been afflicted by the storm.
25 Then came a well-dressed man through the streets with many people following him. And spying the hermit, he asked him to come with him and told him that he would give him shelter and food. So the hermit went with the man.
26 As they passed through the streets, the well-dressed man called others who had misfortune to him, promising shelter and food. And many people followed the man as he climbed a hill at

warmth and care; that she keeps the commandments of Sinai; that she makes her home a piece of Heaven, no matter how humble it may be; that it is always a refuge of peace and comfort for her husband and her children; that she plays with her children and sees to their education and welfare; that she is of service to her sisters in need as she can be; and that she loves and respects her husband and ever encourages and supports him and helps him to expand his light and have joy.

55 You have been accustomed to think of yourselves as separate families living within the town of Nazareth. May you begin to consider yourselves as the family of Nazareth, living within the Celestine Light of Elohim.

56 As one undivided, the happiness and comfort of all is magnified. As one undivided, the trials and tribulations of life are eased. As one undivided, you will live long upon the land and prosper, despite the Romans and all else the world may do. My brothers and sisters of light, make it so."

57 And Yeshua continued to hear the questions of the people of Nazareth and give answers unto them that lifted their spirits and filled their souls. And all of the other words that Yeshua spoke that day are written in the *Book of Yakov*, given to the Children of Light in Jerusalem.

CHAPTER 22

Enduring Blessings

As Yeshua, Miriam, and their children travel to Bethany, they encounter a destitute family along the way whom they nourish with food for their bellies and food for their souls.

Some of Yeshua's family, including his mother, and some of his kinsfolk asked him to remain in Nazareth and not to journey to Egypt. But Yeshua insisted they must go and said unto them, "I must be about my Father's business and there are in Egypt things of which I must learn and do."

2 Even after all the years his family and kinsfolk in Nazareth had known him, only a few understood that in saying this, he spoke of his Father in Heaven and not of Yosef, who had died.

3 When one of his relatives asked the day in which he should return, Yeshua could not answer and said, "I know only the beginning of my journey into Egypt, not the end, for my Father has not yet revealed it to me."

4 Yeshua noticed that his mother was sad, imagining that she might not see him again, but he said unto her and everyone there, "Fear not, for as you see us depart, so shall you see us return, for it is in Galilee and Judea that I will fulfill that which my Father has called me to do."

5 Thus, it was that Yeshua and Miriam and their two children departed from Nazareth and began their journey to Egypt. They all walked and carried their meager belongings, and only Yeshua's carpentry tools, their food, and water supplies and some of Miriam's weaving materials were carried on the back of the donkey they brought with them.

6 Yeshua was exceedingly strong, and he often carried both children strapped in a long cloth about his back. When he tired, he put them in a little cart he had made that he pulled or harnessed to the donkey.

7 They intended to journey first to Bethany that they might see the family of Miriam before they departed to Egypt. As they were traveling on that route and evening approached, they came upon a family of a man and his wife and four children at a well, and they appeared greatly enfeebled and destitute.

8 Miriam came to the woman and asked, "By what are you afflicted that you can barely stand beside the well?"

9 And the woman answered, "We are journeying from Sychar to the house of my brother in Malatha, south of Jerusalem. We hunger greatly, for we have had but crumbs to eat for weeks since the Romans put us into the street for taxes we cannot pay, for my husband was injured and cannot work."

10 Immediately, Miriam went to the supplies upon their donkey and gave the family most of their bread and cheese and all of their dried fish, leaving her own family only a little bread and

cheese remaining for the evening meal and milk for Dara from her mother. And for this, she did not even speak to Yeshua, knowing he would act the same.

11 Then Yeshua came over to them and asked if they would mind if his family journeyed with them as far as Bethany that they might have safety together in greater numbers. He asked this not for necessity, but to give an opportunity for his family to remain with the family in need for a time, in a way that the man could retain his dignity.

12 The following day, the family of Yeshua gathered leaves and roots of plants for food and showed the family from Sychar the plants that were good to eat so that they might never hunger again upon their journey. And when they came again unto a village, Miriam purchased some more cheese and bread.

13 And it came to pass that the family from Sychar journeyed with them to the outskirts of Bethany, but when they were invited to continue to the house of Miriam's parents, they declined with great thankfulness for that which they had received, but insisted upon their desire to continue south toward their destination as quickly as possible.

14 Before they parted, the man came to Yeshua and said unto him, "I perceive that you are a man of God, but even as that may be, I have never seen such kindness as you and your family have shown to mine. I desire to know from what spring you have drunk that you and your wife and your children are so different from all I have known."

15 And Yeshua said to him, "You are our brother and were in need, and your wife our sister, and your children our children. Verily, we are all children of Elohim; therefore, when we help one another, it is the same as if we were doing it unto God.

16 "If you would have enduring blessings from this day, then remember to do unto your brothers and sisters across the land, even as you would do unto God and even as we have done unto you."

17 Thus, it was that the family of Sychar parted from the family of Yeshua, and never again did their paths cross. But the love they had received from Miriam and Yeshua and their children remained with them always, and heeding the words of Yeshua, it was magnified many times across the land.

CHAPTER 23

Truth of a Prophet

Yeshua travels to the community of Gimron with Miriam's brother Lazarus to visit Yochanan where they spend eight days, during which time Yeshua gives a sermon on how to know a true prophet of God. Yochanan decides to accompany them to Bethany to meet Miriam and then travel on to Egypt with them.

When the family of Yeshua came into Bethany, to the home of the parents of Miriam, there was much rejoicing, and all of her kinsfolk came to see them. And Miriam's sister Martha and her brother Lazarus welcomed them with exceeding happiness; but her brother Zadok and her sister Rebecca did not greet her with enthusiasm, for they supposed she had too many favors of their parents.

2 And it came to pass that Yeshua and Miriam remained together in Bethany for the space of eleven days, and during this interval, Miriam and Martha spent much time in each other's company as did Yeshua and Lazarus.

3 After this time, Yeshua declared his desire to visit his kinsman Yochanan at Gimron before departing to Egypt. And thus, it was that Miriam and their children remained in Bethany at the home of her father while Yeshua journeyed to Gimron, and Lazarus went with him.

4 Now Gimron was in a desolate place where few desired to be, but it was not far from Bethany, and thus it was that Yeshua and Lazarus arrived there shortly and great was Yochanan's joy when he saw his kinsman again. He embraced Yeshua with vigor and greeted him, saying, "My Lord, great is God that he has blessed me to see you again so soon. He has told me that you should arrive and I have prepared a place for you."

5 Yeshua also embraced Yochanan with enthusiasm, saying, "Yochanan, prophet of the most high, I am honored to be again with you. The years apart have been long for me, and I have missed you."

6 Yochanan was humbled by Yeshua's greeting and replied, "No, Yeshua, it is I who am honored to be again with you. I have missed you as well. Time has had little meaning in my life here, but the memory of our discoveries with God seems to me to be just yesterday."

7 Hearing their dialogue, Lazarus was perplexed. He did not understand the manner in which Yeshua and Yochanan greeted each other, nor that in so doing, they were fulfilling the vows they had made to one another when last they parted.

8 Yeshua and Lazarus remained with Yochanan for the space of eight days, and Yeshua related to Yochanan all that had transpired in his life since he had left Gimron and Yochanan did likewise, accounting for his time in Gimron.

9 Lazarus sat in attendance at all their conversations and thus learned somewhat of Yeshua

and Yochanan that few men knew. Of these things, Yeshua asked that he speak to no one, except Miriam to whom he could speak of all things.

10 While Yeshua had been away from Gimron, Yochanan had grown in stature spiritually as well as physically, and many in the community now looked to him for guidance and inspiration because of his fervor and conviction.

11 Thus, it was on the following day, that there were sermons being given by the high priests, and Yochanan and Yeshua and Lazarus were invited to attend and listen. And Yochanan, though still unmarried, was asked to speak at the end of the meeting to rouse their spirits.

12 And it came to pass that the high priests spoke on the calling of a prophet and how the penalty of Moses for a false prophet was death by stoning. And there were lamentations from many in the room about the many false prophets wandering the land of Israel, leading good people astray and away from the purity of the principles of God.

13 One of the men present, named Tomas, exclaimed, "I have heard some called prophets in Jerusalem, and each sounds as good as the other, but they proclaim different teachings. How then are we to know which one to stone and which one to heed? For God will surely condemn us if we put to death a man whom he had called and will not forgive our error or ignorance."

14 After much debate upon this subject, Yochanan was asked to say the final words. And Yochanan rose and said unto them, "My esteemed brethren and Elders, I know that God chooses whom he will to reveal his secrets and desires unto the children of men, and it is not for men or priests or governments to judge the prophets God has called or the truths that they reveal; nevertheless, they do.

15 "And among the Children of Israel, it would seem that to know a true prophet is very simple, for as the priests tell us, either a prophet teaches the Law of Moses or he does not, and by this you may know them.

16 But though I am young, I have learned that blindly following the law does not always lead to the light. I have learned that if we would know pure truth, we must not obey without question the persuasions of men or the authority of the priests, but each of us must ask God to reveal the truth unto us and trust that the spirit of Elohim will let our hearts understand things our minds cannot know.

17 If your own discernment is lacking, which I think all of us would agree is sometimes the case, then I say it is good to consider the discernment of those whom you respect in these matters for their wisdom and fairness; those whom you know accept not the dictates of men, but weigh each matter with God.

18 And in this, I know there are some who look to me, and I am greatly humbled by such an honor, especially in consideration of my young age and inexperience with life.

19 But upon the foundation of such worth that men may esteem me, I would like to give my place to Yeshua bar Yosef of Nazareth whom I testify has been called of God; whom I testify speaks the words of God. This I know to be true. With every breath of my body, this I know to be true."

20 Then Yochanan sat down abruptly and amid an exquisite silence Yeshua rose among them and said unto them, "Men are only led astray by false prophets because of the vanities of their hearts and the delusions of their minds.

21 Of vanity, man must repent and forsake, and of delusions, man must do all he can to reason the truth in his mind and then humble himself before God and ask for the Holy Spirit to give a sure knowing of the truth in his heart.

22 And unto the righteous, the Holy Spirit of Elohim will always speak in a still small voice in his mind and a warm contentedness in his heart that all men of virtue may know truth from falsehood.

23 But the man seduced by the world, in his vanity, in his desire for comfort and ease, in his desire to indulge his sins and wanton ways, in his desire to keep authority over his fellow men, becomes deaf and dulled to the promptings of God.

24 Though he may inquire still of God in his times of need, his ears will hear only the deafening sound of silence, for Elohim does not speak even in the smallest of voices to the man who mocks God by the manner of his life.

25 Thus, man is left standing alone, with a part of him seduced to the ways of the world and a part of him still longing for the sweetness of God, and he is wracked with torment inside, not knowing the way to turn.

26 Verily, I say unto you the ways of God are easy to know and that no man may ever be deceived; take now the lamp that I bring, whereby in its light, you may see and discern truth from error when men say they speak from God.

27 Many have said that the Law of Moses clearly tells how the people may know a true prophet from a false; therefore why do we speak of these things?

28 But I ask, do you worship a dead or a living God? For if all you have for your faith and the actions of your life are the laws of ancient times, then you have only a part of what God has given for the good of man.

29 Some say a true prophet will never speak anything that is contrary to what has been given in the law, saying the law came from God; therefore, anything that is different cannot be of God.

30 Think you that the world never changes? That never is there a need for greater light to illuminate the darkness of a world far different than the one in which the ancient prophets lived?

31 Think you that the children of men never become better than their ancestors and worthy of greater light?

32 And I say unto you that if the words of God to men were meant to never be added upon, then you would not need the writings of many ancient prophets to say these words, but the writings of only one, for God would have spoken just once, unto a single prophet, to reveal all that man would ever need.

33 But God continued to speak from prophet to prophet because man continued to need new light and additional knowledge and guidance for the challenges of his times.

34 Even as the prophet Amos has said, "Surely the Lord God will do nothing, but that he first reveals his secrets unto his servants, the prophets."

35 And I say unto you that the Almighty Elohim, the creator of Heaven and earth, is not a god who does nothing, but the God to which nothing is impossible. And by the mouths of his holy prophets, his will is made known unto men.

36 In the days to come, there will walk upon the earth children of men worthy of a far-greater light than has even been given to you or to Moses or to Abraham. And unto them will Elohim bless with greater and glorious understanding.

37 From my lips, you will hear words you have never heard, for I do not repeat the dusty laws of the past you memorized long ago, but give unto you greater light and knowledge, even as the prophets of old each gave greater light and knowledge to the Children of Israel who walked with them.

38 Many of the ancient laws in the sacred texts were given only for that people, in that time, concerning their lives and their challenges, which were unique to them.

39 Thus, does God always bless those who strive for the light so that as they live worthy, they will always have a prophet in their midst to guide them through the perils of their day.

40 Nevertheless, Elohim has also given sacred laws that are not just for that time, but are eternal and inviolate, meant to be lived by all men, for all time, such as the commandments of Sinai.

41 How then can men know which laws of the prophets of old are meant for all time and which are only meant for a season of time? How can men know if a prophet today utters true words from God or false words to deceive?

42 I say unto you that laws that are meant for all men in all times are laws that have eternal significance, both on earth and in Heaven.

43 The eternal paths of God are scarcely concerned with the temporal ways of man, save that

man keeps the commandments of Sinai and respects the temple of his body, which God has made, both on the inside and the outside, and this that he might live long upon the land and have many years to do good and prove that he honors God by honoring the temple God has given him.

44 Therefore, it matters not to God how many steps one takes on the Sabbath or other such pious dictates from the dusty past, for what has this to do with things of forever?

45 Man is upon the earth to learn to draw near to the light and to flee from the darkness; to prove by his life that he follows Elohim and the goodness thereof, by striving each day to cleave to the light; to be a better husband and father and brother and do good to all men.

46 You have heard it said that man is made in the image of God. Think you that these hallowed words speak only of the way man appears? I say unto you, nay. The image of God means as well all the attributes of Elohim.

47 It is given to man in this life to emulate God and to show by his life how greatly he desires to be like him.

48 You are wise to be wary because of false prophets, for there are many that come to men in the name of God clothed as meek sheep, but inside are ravenous wolves.

49 Therefore, when a man comes forth proclaimed by himself or others to be a prophet of God, see that you test the teachings that he says, not in how they call men to the letter of the law or to some strange doctrine, but whether they cause men to do good to their fellow men and to take righteous and pure actions or entice them into darkness or constrain their spirit with the needless dictates of men, especially those given by man but proclaimed to be of God.

50 And see that you test the man that his life fulfills the good teachings he proclaims, for though Elohim may call a sinner who has repented to be a prophet, he will not give his light to any who remain in darkness by their words or deeds.

51 Look therefore to the simple examples Elohim has given for all men to see. Do men gather grapes of thorns or figs of thistles? Even so, every good tree brings forth good fruit and only good fruit; even as a true prophet of God calls upon man to do good and only good in ways that expand his spirit, not shut it in a box.

52 When men find a tree that brings forth bad fruit, they hew it down and burn it in the fire, for it is worthless unto them, and left in place only is a hindrance to the good that might grow in the soil.

53 Wherefore, I say unto you, of true prophets, by their fruits, you shall know them."

54 And many were amazed at the words of Yeshua, and for some, the impact on their heart was powerful and it changed them from that moment. But others were very wroth at him and considered him a false prophet who ridiculed the law upon which all prophets must stand and blasphemed the true concepts of God.

55 The following day, as Yeshua and Lazarus prepared to return to the home of Lazarus, Yochanan declared that he was going to journey to Bethany with them that he might meet Miriam whom he knew was most favored of God and continue to travel to Egypt with them, for there was something there he had wished to do for many moons.

56 Yochanan was a large man and fiercesome in his countenance with his beard and long hair all askew. When he professed his desire to accompany them, Lazarus immediately saw that his presence would contribute to their safety and heartily encouraged him to come along.

57 Thus, it was that Yeshua and Yochanan and Lazarus returned to Bethany to the house of the father of Lazarus.

58 When they arrived, Miriam met Yochanan for the first time, and she bowed her head before him and said, "Welcome, the prophet of Elohim." Yochanan also bowed his head before her and said, "Blessings to the chosen of the Son of Light." And everyone else present except Lazarus was perplexed by these greetings.

59 On the first night of the return to Bethany, during the evening meal, Yochanan was struck by the beauty of Miriam's sister Martha and she by his effervescent presence. Miriam noticed their frequent glances at one another and smiled to herself, knowing love was already blossoming, even as Yeshua had told her in secret that it would.

CHAPTER 24

Sermon in Bethany

While Yeshua and Miriam are visiting her family and kinsfolk in Bethany, on their last night they all gather to hear Yeshua speak. Yeshua expounds upon the true nature of God: the Father, the Mother, and the Son. He also speaks about eternal marriage and what is meant by "keeping the inside of the cup clean as well as the outside."

Yeshua and Miriam spent two more days in Bethany and after the evening meal on the last night, Miriam's family and kinsfolk gathered to hear Yeshua speak, for many had heard stories of his teachings in Nazareth, and some thought he might be a Prophet.

2 And Yeshua said unto them, "There are those that say the Kingdom of God is outside of you; that it is in the sky and in the sea and in the temple built by man of great stones and precious woods. But I say unto you, that the greater Kingdom is inside of you, for you are the temple of light, built by God.

3 When you come to know yourselves in purity, forgetting the conceptions of the world and the teachings of men, then you will realize that you are true sons and daughters of the living Father and Mother in Heaven and are inheritors of all that your parents have, as you live worthy to receive your inheritance.

4 In ignorance, some will say it is blasphemy to speak of God in the plural, as a male and a female, a husband and a wife co-creating; to them I say, have you not heard of the creation of the world where it is written in the sacred scrolls, let *us* make man in *our* image, after *our* likeness; and of when man was cast out of the garden God said, behold, the man has become as one of *us*; and of when God confounded the languages at Babel and said, let *us* go down and confound their language?

5 The sacred texts teach that man was made in the image of God. How then do men claim that God is only a male, for does not the body of a man differ greatly from the body of a woman? Therefore, I say unto you, man is made in the image of the Father and woman is made in the image of the Mother.

6 In fullness, a man is not without woman, nor husband without wife, neither parents without a child. And the perfection of God is the Father and the Mother and the Son; three lights each to their own, but they are one God, united in perfect spirit, understanding and purpose.

7 Did not Isaiah see the parents speaking of the coming of the Son unto the children of men and of the rejection of the truth thereof? For it is written, I heard the voice of the Lord, saying, whom shall I send and who will go for us?

8 Then said I, here I am, send me.

9 And he said, Go and tell this to the people: hear you indeed, but understand not; and see

you indeed but perceive not.

10 The hearts of this people are fat; they make their ears heavy and shut their eyes; lest they hear with their ears and see with their eyes, and understand with their hearts, and convert, and be healed.

11 Again Isaiah spoke of the Father that is Lord, and of the Mother, the spirit that touches the hearts of men, and of the Son, who redeems the righteous, for it is written, from the beginning, from the time that it was, there am I: and now the Lord God and his spirit has sent me."

12 And Yeshua said unto them, "He who has ears to hear and eyes to see; let him hear and see."

13 Then Levi son of Phinehas, who had studied the law, said, "I have eyes and ears but I have not seen or heard of the God you describe taught in the sacred scrolls. If God is three divine individuals acting as one, and not one divine essence, then why is this not more plain? For there are thousands of places in the sacred scrolls that refer to God as one force, which is personalized in a masculine way, and only these few you have given to the contrary that may merely be errors of transcribing. What more can you say about this vital subject?"

14 Yeshua answered him, saying, "Even among the honest of heart, it is the nature of man to see and hear that which he wishes to see and hear; and to the contrary, he is blind and deaf. How many times have you held the answer to your question in your hand, but have not seen the truth because you were not seeking it? Read again that which you have read, and look for the gems that speak of the plurality of God, and you shall find that which you seek.

15 Verily I say unto you, Elohim is the name for God, and as used in the sacred books it is a word of both male and female nature and reflects the plural, not the individual; and of it, the holy scrolls speak thousands of times. Verily, it is the Father and the Mother, and through the Son they do all things."

16 Then Yeshua took a stick and wrote the letters YHVH on the ground and said unto them, "This is the sacred name of the Father, given unto the children of men; which name should not be spoken, but only written in reverence, and never defaced.

17 Before the world was, the Elohim decided that which each of them should do to bring to pass the eternal progression and exaltation of the spirit children of the Father and the Mother.

18 The Son said he would do whatsoever the Father and the Mother asked of him, and that through him their will would be manifested among the children of men.

19 The Mother said she would be the spirit of Elohim that would reside within the hearts of every child upon the earth, and stay with them for all of their days as they kept their temple worthy to have her, and sincerely lived for truth and righteousness.

20 The Father said he would connect to every particle of existence that he might ever receive the supplications of the children of men that the Elohim could bless the righteous.

21 Therefore, the Children of Light should pray to the Father and the Mother, who are one and over all; and ask in the name of the Son, through whom all good things occur, that they may be touched in wisdom and richly blessed, as they seek righteousness in harmony with the will of Elohim. And the humble shall be comforted with heavenly love by the Mother, who sends forth the Holy Spirit of Elohim to manifest sweet blessings unto the Children of Light.

22 Among the Children of Israel this is not understood, but it is now known unto you.

23 When you have a goodly need, and are humble and not proud, seek out God by calling on Elohim; for even as the word leaves your lips the love and attention of the Father and the Mother and the Son comes upon you in fullness and power."

24 Then said Levi, "How strange a doctrine you teach, but you speak as one with authority, therefore I will study upon the things you have said. But tell me this, for it is a mystery to me; if we are to ask of the Father in the name of the Son, what then is the name of the Son?

25 Yeshua answered unto him, saying, "Look again in the sacred scriptures and you will find it there as it was spoken by your fathers; but verily I say unto you, that in your life, you will live to hear the name of the Son as it is known among the children of men, spoken on the lips of many

people, some with great anger and some with great love."

26 Then Gideon, a cousin of Miriam, asked, "Speak to us of marriage and Heaven, for in our family it is a tangled web; we have marriages that have come after marriages, some with a man and a widow and some with a man married to several wives, some whom are widows. I have heard conflicting things from different Rabbis regarding this matter. What has God said to you of this?"

27 And Yeshua said unto them, "When you marry, you have heard it said that at death the marriage is ended, be it a marriage of one man and one woman or one man and several women; and so it is for the marriages sanctified by man, for they have no force in Heaven.

28 But I say unto you that if it is by God, with the man and the woman having asked together for the blessings of Elohim; and sealed with vows between them for it to be a sacred and eternal covenant, and this before the witness of family and friends; then it is not parted at death, but with the righteous, remains in force for time and all eternity, as long as both the man and the woman live worthy of the blessing.

29 In the hereafter, everyone will have eternal life and come forth to their just and resonate reward, be it joyous or despairing, according to their faith in God and the paths they choose in life. But even among the most righteous, man cannot be without woman or woman without man if they desire to go forward into the greatest exaltation.

30 But if a marriage is by the authority of man, or the rituals of men, or the governments of men, or the priesthoods of men, then it ends with death; for in the eternity God is not bound by the ordinances of man which have no power to bind in Heaven; they become as dust and are trampled under feet in the world to come.

31 Nor can marriage be performed in Heaven, for it is an ordinance given to be fulfilled in the flesh, that it may be proven that the man will faithfully cleave unto the woman and the woman unto the man, despite all that evil may tempt.

32 In fidelity to their marriage they magnify the gift of life God has given, and shall therefore have so much more reward in the world to come.

33 But whosoever is married only by the authority of man, or of governments, or the priesthoods of men, shall not be married in Heaven, until their love is fulfilled by a resonant proxy of two in the flesh.

34 Moreover, know that as a man is not without a woman, nor woman without a man, neither can either stand before Elohim without the other, for alone they are but half of a whole, and only in the wholeness and balance of love and commitment can the Celestine Light of God be fully manifested."

35 Then Gideon said, "But what of those who may love true, but pass from life unknowing of the way to secure their relationship for eternity?"

36 And Yeshua said unto him, "The covenant that binds for eternity is forged in the love that endures and grows stronger through all the trials of life because it is lit by the Celestine Light of Elohim and the unselfish oneness of two. It is a beautiful flower nurtured with exceeding tenderness and consideration that upon life's passing is most brilliant.

37 Every day of life together is a witness to the world of their devotion to God and to each other. Such a love, after many years together to prove its truth, is dedicated to continue in eternity by the holy desire of those that love, and enshrined in the heart of Elohim from everlasting to everlasting."

38 And Gideon replied, "But is there not an exact way in which holy ordinances should be performed?"

39 Yeshua answered him, saying, "With man, the letter of the law is so important, but with God it is the conviction of the heart, the righteousness of the life, and worthy desires of the soul that matters.

40 And Yeshua, perceiving that some were confused by that which he spoke said, "Verily, if you will not listen to your heart, which speaks the truth your customary mind does not know,

then you do not know yourselves, and you will dwell in poverty, and it is you who are that poverty, no matter the riches of the world which you may possess."

41 And the people were amazed for never before had they heard such teachings.

42 Yeshua continued, saying, "Recognize what is in your sight, and the feeling that is in your heart. Pray to your Father and Mother in Heaven for the light of understanding to expand into the testimony of truth, and then that which is hidden from you will become plain to you, and there is nothing hidden which will not become illuminated by the Celestine Light of Elohim."

43 They understood that he spoke of his teachings, but only a few understood that he also spoke of himself; and some people nodded in agreement but others shook their heads in disbelief.

44 And Yeshua spoke again, saying, "If you bring forth the light which is within you, what you bring forth will save you. If you do not bring forth the light within you, if you allow yourself to be blinded by the darkness of the world and the teachings of men, then what you do not bring forth will condemn you at the last day."

45 Perceiving from their mumblings that some among his listeners were concerned with following the dictates of the law and their appearances before men, and desired to not quietly find the light within themselves, he said, "Why do you wash the outside of the temple but the inside leave dirty?

46 If it is pleasing for the outside to be clean, which is only seen by men, how much more pleasing is it for the inside to be clean, wherein resides that which nourishes you and is seen by God? Do you not realize that he who made the inside is the same one who made the outside?

47 If you would find favor with God, then be as concerned for the inside of your temple as for the outside, and let those that are high be like those that are low."

48 Then Nahor, son of Salathiel said, "All of these things you have said are strange doctrines that would seem to ridicule the law, and blasphemy the God of our fathers, and make women the equal of men."

49 Yeshua replied to him, saying, "The Celestine Light of the Kingdom is like a wise fisherman who one day was told by the king that he and all of the other fishermen of the village, could dive for pearls in the king's reserve and keep all that they found; but they must open each one before they gathered another so that none were wasted.

50 The other fishermen made haste to bring to shore and open as many oysters as they could harvest; and finding beds close to shore in shallow water, they soon had discovered a few small pearls; but the wise fisherman dove throughout the day in the deepest water, looking for the one large oyster that would have a pearl of great price; and he was ridiculed by his friends for the efforts he wasted in his faith.

51 As the sun began to set, many of the fishermen had small piles of pearls while the wise fisherman rose from the water again with nothing; and he was laughed at again for his foolishness and faith.

52 But the wise fisherman's faith could not be shaken and with one last great breath he dove again to the deepest depth, and there he found an oyster of such size as men had never seen. And bringing it to the shore and opening it, he found the pearl of great price for his faith, and all the pearls of all of his friends put all together would not be a thousandth of the worth of his pearl.

53 Whoever has ears to hear, let him hear.

54 Verily, I say unto you, only when you look into your heart and find the child of God, only when you make the inside like the outside and the outside like the inside, only when those who are high are like those that are low, and only when you make the male and the female equal, so that they are two halves of one whole; only then will you have the light."

55 Hearing his words some were upset with his teachings and departed in anger, but more were amazed and delighted and held him in awe.

56 The following day, when the time came for them to depart, Lazarus asked his father if he might go with them to Egypt, as he was familiar with the trade routes and the caravan's, having traveled them previously with his father, who was a notable merchant with varied interests.

57 His father agreed that Lazarus should also journey to Egypt, but as a trader not just a visitor. He told him to go in the company of two servants, and entrusted him with two camels carrying fabric with gold thread and jewelry to trade with the Egyptians. And he gave Yeshua and Miriam a second donkey so they would have one to carry the children.

58 Then he asked Lazarus to make a promise that he would return to Bethany by the time of six moons, lest they begin to fret about the fate of those that journeyed to the land of the Pharaohs.

59 Martha was distressed because she also wanted to go to Egypt, but this her father forbade.

CHAPTER 25

Caravan to Egypt

Lazarus seeks to find a caravan for himself, Yochanan, Yeshua, Miriam, and their children to accompany to Egypt, but no caravan master is willing to travel with a woman and children. Elohim sends a powerful dream to a Palestinian caravan master named Ibrahiim, opening his heart to allow the group of Hebrews to travel with one of his caravans led by his son, which is departing for Egypt the very next day.

Some days after departing from Bethany, the travelers came to Gaza to seek out a caravan to accompany to Egypt. Yeshua and Miriam and Yochanan remained encamped outside of the town while Lazarus departed into the market to secure a position for them.

2 As dusk fell upon the desert, Lazarus returned and said, "I spoke with two caravan masters of Judah, and neither will agree to journey across the Red Desert with a woman and children. The trip is always difficult, and since the Romans have conquered Egypt, there are fierce robbers in the desert and only caravans with speed and numbers have safety between the Roman outposts."

3 Then Yeshua invited everyone to pray with him, and they knelt upon the ground, Miriam beside Yeshua and the children on each side of them and Yochanan and Lazarus across from them, and they held hands in a circle of faith.

4 And thus did Yeshua pray, "Almighty Father and Mother in Heaven, we thank you for bringing us together this day, to this place, that we might grow closer to one another and through our shared experiences come into your greater light. We seek safe passage to Egypt that we might bring to pass greater things in your name. If it be your will, we ask you to open the hearts of the masters of the caravans that there will be a place for us, that we might fulfill all that you would have us do."

5 And from time to time, Yeshua and each of his party, including the children, offered more prayers that day that they might have fulfillment of their righteous needs.

6 As evening began to fall and they sat together for the evening meal, Lazarus asked Yeshua if God had given him yet any insights into their problem.

7 And Yeshua said unto him, "Upon the rising sun of the new day, journey again into Gaza and take Yochanan with you. On the water side of town, you will find a large white home with a tile roof, framed by two large date palms. There you will find a man by the name of Ibrahiim. When he sees you, he will know who you are and will help us to obtain passage with a caravan."

8 Lazarus was curious about the words which Yeshua spoke and he asked, "How will this be, for only I among us has been to Gaza. The name Ibrahiim says he is not of the faith of our fathers and I know no such Palestinian, and were I to know one, why would he give account to that which I desired?"

9 Yeshua answered him, saying, "Tonight God shall send Ibrahiim a most powerful dream and in the morning when he arises, you will appear before him, and Yochanan shall be the life of his dream."

10 So it was that at the first break of the sun in the darkness, Lazarus and Yochanan journeyed to the house of Ibrahiim as Yeshua had described. When they arrived, they were surprised by the large size of the home and by the two armed servants who barred entry at the gate.

11 And Lazarus said, "Yeshua was wanting in his description, for he did not warn us that we would be coming to the house of a great merchant or need to contend with guards at the gate."

12 Nevertheless, Lazarus and Yochanan went forward to make entry, but they were barred by the servants at the gate and no amount of persuasion would alter their determination. And seeing the wild appearance of Yochanan, they were even more resolved to keep him from their master.

13 Lazarus and Yochanan were about to leave when an elderly man leaned out and spoke from the window above and commanded his servants to allow them entrance into his home. With some astonishment, they did as he bade.

14 Ibrahiim came down and met them in the entryway, and he was astounded to see Yochanan and said, "You are the very man of whom I have had a fitful night of dreams. Have you come to haunt me now while I am yet awake?"

15 Yochanan politely replied, "No, kind sir, but tell me what is it that you dreamt?"

16 And Ibrahiim said, "I saw you appear before me and a voice echoed all around me, commanding me to do as you bid. All through the night, I saw the crumbling of my wealth and of my home and of my trade, if I did not do as you bid; and more dreadful, I saw the death of my only son who was attacked by thieves while on a caravan to Egypt.

17 Then again, I saw the life of my son and the continued flourishing of my family if I did as you bid. But in my dream, I could never see what it was that you would have me do. I beseech you therefore to tell me, for never have I had such a dream; more powerful than life, it was."

18 Then Yochanan told Ibrahiim the purpose of their visit, and after hearing it, Ibrahiim quickly put the seal from his ring to a piece of papyrus and, handing it to Yochanan, said, "Surely God has a hand in this, for in truth, without such a portent as my dream, I would never allow Hebrews or a woman and children to journey with my caravan. But I know it must be God's will; therefore, go to the departure point and seek out my son whose name is also Ibrahiim and give to him my seal, and he shall allow you to go with the caravan that departs soon to Egypt."

19 And it came to pass that Lazarus and Yochanan quickly made to return to the camp of Yeshua, but were met along the road by Miriam walking beside the donkeys with the children and Yeshua leading the camels, for Yeshua already knew of the success of their meeting at the house of Ibrahiim.

20 Around midday, they met Ibrahiim, the son of Ibrahiim, and without regard to the seal, he disbelieved that his father would allow Hebrews or a woman and children to accompany the caravan; therefore, he sent a messenger back to the house of his father to determine the truth of this unusual circumstance.

21 Shortly thereafter, the messenger returned with a command from his father to take the Hebrews with him and see to it that they were well cared for. Only then did he reluctantly agree.

22 Thus, it was that Yeshua and his family and friends found passage with a small caravan to Egypt in which was counted forty-two camels and drivers, fifteen guards, plus Yeshua and his kin.

23 And from the moment the caravan departed Gaza on the rise of the next sun, Ibrahiim did fret because of the Hebrews who accompanied them and the slowness he imagined they caused to the caravan.

CHAPTER 26

Robbers of Zin

The caravan that Yeshua and company are traveling with is attacked by a band of fearsome robbers from the wilderness of Zin. When they threaten Miriam and his children, Yeshua calls forth a blinding, sizzling light, and the ground shakes, immediately subduing the attackers. Then Yeshua approaches the leader of robbers, and the man asks him for forgiveness. He also asks if he can travel with them that he may learn more of Yeshua and his teachings.

On the journey of the first day, Ibrahiim sought to speak with Yochanan and said unto him, "Tomorrow, we enter into an area where there are vicious robbers, therefore take heed and warn your friends to be watchful and prepared to defend against attack."

2 "What of the Romans?" Yochanan asked. "Do they not patrol these roads? And would robbers be so bold as to attack us so close to Gaza?"

3 Ibrahiim pursed his lips and let forth a loud breath of air, saying, "The Romans remain within their fortified posts and fear these robbers, for whenever they seek to kill them, it is always the robbers who instead slay the Romans."

4 Yochanan looked at Ibrahiim with surprise and asked, "Who are these robbers, and from where do they come? I think you exaggerate for I have never heard of a band of robbers that could defeat Roman soldiers, when all of the Children of Israel and Palestine chaff under their rule."

5 Ibrahiim answered solemnly, "There are many robbers along the trading routes, seeking spoils, and most are of no consequence to a well-armed caravan. But those I speak of are the robbers of Zin. They are a mysterious people. It is rumored that they are remnants of the Amorites and live in the mountains of the wilderness of Zin. They are said to be tall and fearsome warriors who eat only the flesh of animals and no grains, but I know not, for thanks to God I have never seen them. But I fear them on this trip, for we do not have enough men to account for all of our animals, and your women and children slow us."

6 Then Yochanan went and related to Yeshua and Lazarus the strange story that Ibrahiim had told him. And he said unto them, "I think perhaps he is telling a tale to frighten his unwanted Hebrew guests. Robbers we may see, but I doubt they will be tall and ferocious, more likely underfed, undersized, and sneaking in the night to steal what they can when no one is watching."

7 Yeshua shook his head and replied, "Would that it would be so brother, but his fears shall be fulfilled, for on the night of the next day, the robbers he has described shall strike."

8 Lazarus was frightened by these words and Yochanan fretful, but Yeshua and Miriam remained calm, and Yeshua said, "Trust in Elohim and be prepared to peacefully deal with the wicked, save they seek to take your life.

9 Fear not those who can take of your worldly possessions, for they can be replaced and are worth less than you esteem them.

10 Fear only those who desire to take from the treasures which you store up for eternity or to take your life or that of your family. Against such, release your righteous fury, with calm and meted justice. And when the dust has fallen, remember forgiveness for those who offer sincere repentance."

11 After Yeshua's revelation, Yochanan went and spoke again with Ibrahiim and repeated all the words that Yeshua had spoken concerning the robbers and the night to come. And he said unto him, "Though you are not of the faith of our fathers and may give no value to that which I say, you should know that Yeshua is blessed of God. If he foretells that something shall be, then it is certain that it shall occur."

12 Ibrahiim took these words of warning to heart, remembering the letter of his father and the unusual treatment he accorded unto these Hebrews.

13 Therefore on the next day, Ibrahiim was mindful of the words of Yeshua, and while the sun was still three fists in the sky, he ordered the caravan to stop for the night at a small grove of six date palms lying in a depression in the desert.

14 Ibrahiim posted sentries atop the rim of the depression so that they could see a great distance in all directions and warn those below of the approach of any people. He also directed a small wall to be built, completely encircling the encampment from the bulky goods carried by the camels. And inside of the wall, the camels lay down, and at the center, the men encamped.

15 Then while all but the family of Yeshua were sitting about the campfires, cooking their evening meals, there arose a muted cry from one of the sentries, and before it was clear what was happening, they were surrounded by a band of strangely garbed robbers who had appeared like ghosts in the middle of their camp out of the emptiness of the desert. And so sudden was their surprise appearance that it was but a short fight before all the men in the caravan were disarmed, with some wounded and a few killed.

16 Yeshua calmly gathered Miriam and the children about him, and they knelt down together as the short battle raged.

17 And it came to pass that all the men but Yochanan had been subdued by the robbers, but taking the leg bone of a camel, which he had earlier found lying upon the ground, he laid forth with mighty swings and quickly felled three robbers when Yeshua called to him and bade him to fight no more; else, he would lose his life to the thieves.

18 Thus, it was that Yochanan hesitated for a moment to consider the words of Yeshua, and in that time, he too was subdued by the robbers. Due to his stature and ferocity, they bound him tightly that he could do no more harm. And one of them made ready to kill him, but another made a sign to him and he did not.

19 Then the robbers began to plunder the caravan and to gather the camels to take with them.

20 Yeshua, Miriam, Lazarus, and the children remained in a tight group and thus far had not been bothered.

21 Whispering into his ear, Lazarus exclaimed to Yeshua, "Who are these strange tall men, some with pale faces and hair? I have never seen their like, not in all of Palestine or in any of my travels."

22 Upon that moment, three of the robbers approached them. And they spoke in a curious language which none had ever heard.

23 One came forward and roughly pushed Yeshua and Lazarus to the ground, while another sought out their possessions.

24 The last grabbed Miriam and began to pull her away from her children, who huddled on the ground, clinging to her leg and crying.

25 Seeing this, Yeshua stood up quickly, and though his face was as calm as a sea of glass, Lazarus saw a fire in his eyes such as he had never before seen.

26 Miriam saw it too and began to struggle with the man who held her. She commanded him

in a voice of power, "Release me! You know not what you do!"

27 But the robber did not heed her warning. Suddenly, there was a blinding flash of light, a terrifying sizzling sound in the air, and a deep rumbling and shaking of the ground as if a mighty mountain had fallen. All the robbers and the merchants along with Yochanan and Lazarus tumbled to the earth, blinded by the lightning and frightened by shaking earth and the booming thunder that had reverberated from the clear night sky.

28 Miriam fell to one knee but then rose and went calmly to her children and huddled with them at the feet of Yeshua, who knelt quietly and embraced them all. It was some minutes before the sight returned to any of the men, and they all remained upon the ground in a stupor.

29 Then Yeshua walked over to the leader of the robbers and gave him his hand and pulled him to his feet. The man spoke to Yeshua in Aramaic and asked, "Is it you that commands the lightning of the sky and the angry roar of the heavens and the earth?"

30 Yeshua answered him not as he asked, but said unto him, "I have done nothing of my own, but that which you do here tonight is evil, and it is the power of the Almighty God of Heaven that you have seen and felt. He has had mercy on your soul and sent you this warning to repent of your sins and henceforth do only good with your life."

31 And the man was humbled deeply in his heart by Yeshua, and by all he had seen and heard, and was astonished that the man he would have harmed offered his hand and would do him no harm.

32 He fell to one knee before Yeshua and said, "I am Kudar-Iluna. Never before have I seen such things, and by whatever God is, I know there is something more here than the works of men.

33 I cannot speak for the others, but as for me, I ask you to forgive me for the wrong I have done, for I have known in my heart that it was without honor. You are not as other men, this is plain. Henceforth, if you will allow me, I desire to come with you on your journey and learn more of you and the things you would teach."

34 And Yeshua said unto him, "Shed your old skin, be glistening and new, follow me, and I will help you discover the Celestine Light of God that is within you."

35 Upon hearing these words, some of the other bandits shouted in disgust, and then silently all of the rest moved away from the encampment and returned into the darkness from whence they had come.

36 Upon the new day, despite the grumblings of Ibrahiim and the merchants and even Yochanan and Lazarus, Kudar-Iluna still remained in the camp, and he came with Yeshua into Egypt after the caravan had buried their dead and tended to the wounded.

37 Many in the caravan clamored for Kudar-Iluna to be put to death. And it was only because of the command of his father Ibrahiim to be kind to the Hebrews and only because none had seen Kudar-Iluna kill anyone and only because of his sorrow for his evil that Ibrahiim allowed him to travel with them upon their journey; and then only under the promise of Yeshua and Yochanan and Lazarus that they would be responsible for him and never let him leave their sight.

CHAPTER 27

Conversation at the Wadi

Yeshua, Miriam, Yochanan, Lazarus, and Kudar-Iluna gather in a circle beneath the full moon and share an in-depth conversation. Yochanan and Yeshua speak somewhat about the unusual circumstances of their births and some of their experiences together while at the community of Gimron, and Miriam relates some of the unusual occurrences with Yeshua that she has witnessed. Through their prayers and experiences, Yochanan and Yeshua have come to know a great deal about each other and their destinies, but both are still seeking to know the fullness of their callings and themselves.

After another day of difficult travel across the barren Red Desert, they came to a Wadi sitting beside the brook that marked the boundary into the Sinai wilderness of Egypt.

2 When the coolness of the night fell upon them, they gathered together as friends, sitting in a circle on the cooling desert sand beneath the light of a full moon, and began a conversation of great depth.

3 Kudar-Iluna walked over to sit with them, but Lazarus forbade him as he was still rankled that he had been among the thieves that had attacked their caravan. But Yeshua knew the heart of Kudar-Iluna had been changed from darkness to light and said, "This man is not of the Children of Israel, but he is now of the Children of Light. Therefore, give him a place among us as a friend, for it is with us that his heart now resides."

4 Lazarus scowled a bit and was still hesitant, but he did as Yeshua bade. And Kudar-Iluna sat and listened for the entire night, but spoke not a word.

5 There was a bit of an awkward silence after Kudar-Iluna sat down, but then Lazarus inquired of Yeshua and Yochanan if they would speak more about their lives of which he had heard somewhat when he was in Gimron with them.

6 Yochanan nodded in agreement, saying, "Ours is a strange story, for many things have happened to us and to our parents, which are not usual in occurrence. When we were in Gimron, in our youth, we spoke of these things often and prayed mightily to God, trying to understand who we were and why God had put us on the earth. The circumstances of both of our births were very unusual, and therefore, we knew from an early age that Elohim had a great purpose for our lives."

7 Then Yeshua and Yochanan related to Lazarus and Kudar-Iluna some of the events of their births and of their early lives, and Lazarus came to believe that they certainly must be chosen of God for holy purposes.

8 And Lazarus asked, "Who is it then that you are? And why are you here?"

9 Yochanan answered, saying, "I do not yet know in completeness who I am for the purposes

of the Almighty, because I do not fully comprehend all God has shown unto me. But Elohim has given me many dreams to know that Yeshua is the chosen vessel upon the earth, who brings a lamp that will light all the world.

10 In humility, from all I know and feel, I say unto this small circle of family and a special friend that Yeshua is the Son come among men."

11 Lazarus raised one eyebrow and seemed somewhat perplexed by the words Yochanan had spoken, and he asked, "When you say Yeshua is the "son," do you mean the sun in the sky or the prophet of Elohim or something different?"

12 Before Yochanan could answer, Yeshua said, "It is Yochanan who is the prophet of Elohim, for both my Father and Mother in Heaven have shown this unto me many times and have spoken this truth into my ears. Yochanan also knows this is true, but he is too humble to say it until the time of his calling is to be fulfilled. But verily, I say unto you Yochanan shall grow into such a prophet as the world has never seen."

13 Yochanan seemed humbled by Yeshua's words and added, "I will do as Elohim directs. They do speak to me also in visions and in words in my mind, and I continually seek to know and fulfill their will. I know not what shall become of me in the future, but I know that today, they would have me walk with Yeshua and tomorrow. And until the end of my days, I will proclaim him.

14 As to Yeshua, I have seen with my own eyes miracles that he has done that no man or even any prophet of God that has ever lived could do. Though I would be stoned as a blasphemer among the men of Jerusalem, to you I must speak my truth; and my heart says only the living Son of the living God could do such wonders.

15 The priests of Jerusalem, and even of Gimron, say that God has no body, that God is neither male nor female, and therefore, there can be no son of God. This is what I have been taught all of my life.

16 Yet I have also known Yeshua all of my life; he is like us, but then again so unlike us, there is nothing even to compare.

17 And despite all that men say of God, there is a voice that speaks in my mind and a feeling that warms my heart; and in my mind's eye, I see God the Father and God the Mother, standing before me as they speak of Yeshua.

18 Though he also is humble and desires not the recognition, I know he is who I have said he is. Thereby, I know that God is not an emptiness of form but as tangible as you and me, and that by the Father and the Mother has come the Son."

19 Lazarus was fascinated by the words which he heard and bade Yochanan to tell him more. Yochanan looked to Yeshua and an unspoken understanding passed between them, and Yochanan said, "We will tell you many things Lazarus, but you and Kudar-Iluna must speak of them to no one outside of this circle until the time of our purposes on earth have been fulfilled." And to this, Lazarus and Kudar-Iluna readily agreed.

20 Then Yochanan recounted some of the miracles of Yeshua, which he had witnessed; he had seen the living plants of earth come to life as he passed over them, and he had seen Tobiah, who was dead, return to life at his touch.

21 He had spent more time with Yeshua than any man, and he had one great testimony of him.

22 And Yochanan said, "Though his miracles are mighty, beyond the miracles of the greatest of the prophets, there are other things about him, which testify he is unlike any other man.

23 There is a great goodness and kindness in Yeshua and virtue beyond the most righteous. When he is a part of us, we are inspired to do more with our lives."

24 And Lazarus and Kudar-Iluna nodded silently in agreement.

25 Yochanan spoke more unto them, saying, "There is another aspect of Yeshua, which testifies to me that he is of a divine nature greater than all others despite his mortal tabernacle, and that is this: he is like a sponge that remembers all things, and there is not one thing which he has ever

heard, or one thing which he has ever read, or one thing which he has ever seen, which he does not remember with perfect clarity and exactness."

26 Hearing this, Lazarus was astounded. And Kudar-Iluna was so startled he almost broke his vow of silence.

27 Miriam also testified to some of the miracles she had been witness to as the wife of Yeshua, which no other person had ever seen, and she also bore witness that Yeshua remembered all things and that there was not even one thing which he forgot that he wished to remember.

28 Lazarus asked his sister to tell more of the miracles she had seen, but she refused and said unto him, "Perhaps, someday, when it is needed, I shall tell them all, but for now I think the truths Yeshua teaches by his words and his precepts are the most glorious miracle.

29 That Yeshua raised a dead man is good for the previously deceased, but what has it to do with our eternal salvation? Yet if we hear his words and follow them, they change our lives; they are the real treasure of Yeshua, and they have eternal significance upon our souls."

30 Lazarus was unhappy with the words of his sister and said, "Great words are said by many, but miracles are not often seen among men. Therefore, such evidence lends belief that Yeshua might be more than a man."

31 Miriam answered him, "A faith built on seeing or knowing of miracles is like standing on wet sand at the beach, and the waves come in and the ground that seemed so sound washes away beneath your feet.

32 It is easy to believe in Yeshua when you see and know of his miracles, for they are mighty. But what of the day when he leaves this world and his miracles become only stories handed down from generation to generation?

33 If a person's faith has been forged from miracles alone, when the persecutions of the world come, they will wash away the foundations of the faith, for it has no depth. Only when faith is founded upon the everlasting principles of light that have been revealed by Yeshua, can it stand firm against all that the world may bring."

34 Miriam's words deeply affected Lazarus, touching his spirit. As he continued to ponder all he had heard and felt in his heart, he asked, "It would seem that Yeshua could be as Yochanan attests, the Son of Elohim that has come to earth in the flesh, but to what end? And is this not the same teaching as the false beliefs of the Egyptians and the Greeks? How will the Children of Israel ever accept such a thing to be true, even with the miracles you speak of which Yeshua has done?"

35 Yeshua answered Lazarus, saying, "Though the Children of Israel rebuke the beliefs of the Egyptians and the Greeks, verily, parts of the religions and myths of the Egyptians were given to them by inspiration from Elohim to prepare the hearts and minds of the children of men to accept the fullness that God would yet reveal.

36 When you see the Son come to earth, it is not from the Egyptians or the Greeks, but from the Elohim of the Celestine Light; the beliefs of these religions were merely the heralds of the greater truth that was coming, preparing the hearts and minds of the children of men to be ready to receive it.

37 Now, my brothers, I am humbled by the kind words that have been spoken, but I do not wish for you to say to anyone that I am the Son of Elohim, any more than we are all sons of God.

38 Yochanan and Miriam speak highly of me and I am honored, but I am still pondering upon the fullness of who I am and why I am here.

39 I know that Elohim is a Father and a Mother, and that they are two glorified personages, not just one. Nor is God merely a force of the universe, for I have spoken with my Heavenly Father and Mother face-to-face; and the light that radiates from them is as bright as the sun at noonday, burning within reach.

40 That I might see this light, which no mortal eyes could withstand, my body changed for that moment to a body more divine by far, and I caught a glimpse of the magnitude of Elohim.

41 I know that Elohim works mighty miracles through me. I feel a oneness with all life and

feel a part of all things; each day that passes, the feeling grows stronger. I have come to understand that others do not have this feeling, even my beloved Miriam and my brother Yochanan.

42 I speak to my Father and Mother in Heaven every day; and hear their voice with my ears as if they were standing next to me.

43 And I know with a surety that whatsoever I should ask of them, they would do.

44 By them I am called Son, and it resonates deep in my heart.

45 They have told me that I lived with them before the world was, and I remember all the things of which they relate.

46 Yet it is presumptuous to speak as we have spoken: to say that I am the very Son of God. I do not have the desire to speak it, nor do I wish others to, for I am still seeking to fully understand all that I have learned.

47 So too, there is knowledge of the true nature of all things and the full knowledge of what is to be. But my Father waits to reveal these things to me when I am more prepared to receive them.

48 But I say unto you that every day our Father and Mother in Heaven do speak to me, and they bestow marvelous understandings upon me, and through these revelations, I know they desire me to be perfect, which is a hard thing to be, for I am as tempted as is any man by the allures of the world and to squander the precious hours of life.

49 They have commanded me to teach by both precept and example, to show my brothers and sisters of spirit by my life and teachings, how they can become better than they are, eternally progressing until they are without sin, even as our parents in Heaven are perfect.

50 And there is something more, but unknown, which I know I must do, but of that mystery, they will not speak, for they say it is not the time for me to know. When that time comes and I am one with all that I am and understand all that I must do and the world has witnessed it, then Elohim would have you speak the fullness of the truth, whatever that may be.

51 There are many other things of which my Father and Mother in Heaven have spoken to me that I tell only to Miriam. And you must understand that everything I know of my life and purpose and the teachings of our Father and Mother in Heaven, she also knows, and even as Yochanan and I walk paths that intertwine, Miriam and I walk a path of one, and we are one."

CHAPTER 28

Yeshua and Miriam Speak on Women

Yeshua speaks about the importance of the equality of women as it relates to balance and one's eternal progression and wholeness before God. Miriam speaks about the dream she had, beginning at the age of twelve, foretelling her marriage to Yeshua and how their destinies are intertwined.

Lazarus was filled with an understanding of the words Yeshua spoke. Yet still he had questions, and he asked, "You give great deference to my sister. Though I love her too, she is just a woman, and yet you would give her the privileges of a man and add what many would consider sin by allowing her to go forth among men unveiled, even uncloaked. When this becomes known, it will not bode well for you, and in truth, I do not understand why you treat her so."

2 Yeshua answered him, saying, "On earth and in Heaven, man is not without woman or woman without man if they desire to be whole and balanced and eternally progressing.

3 Therefore, those that would make woman less than man, given to serve man, and not be seen by any but he who in fact, if not law, owns her, comprehends not that in the stifling of her spirit, he cuts off his only path to Heaven.

4 There is a man, and the spirit and energy that flows in him is different than the spirit and energy of a woman. But they are two halves of the same whole, and one without the other is like unto half of a wheel, for it cannot take you anywhere.

5 Now if a man has dominion over his wife and excludes her from his conversations of importance and considers not her opinion, then he can only confront his problems and challenges like a man with one eye, for alone, he has no depth of perception and thus is more likely to fall into a pit."

6 Lazarus nodded his head in understanding and then asked, "Miriam how is it that you who have been raised in a patriarchal order have so easily become what many would call a fallen woman who consorts with men and knows not your place?"

7 Miriam laughed and said, "I have not fallen, dear brother, I have risen. Where before I was under the weight of tradition and the rule of men, because of Yeshua I now understand the true wonder that a man and a woman can have together and the marvels that are given for a woman of equality to find, which are things I had never before supposed.

8 You know that our parents have always said of me that I had too strong of a head for a woman. I will tell you how I came to be that way: When I was twelve years of age, an angel of God appeared to me in a dream while I slept. She told me that I would soon meet a young man

who would become my husband, that he would change the world, and that I would help him. As she spoke, I saw Yeshua in great detail as he was on the day when we first met.

9 I had this dream many more times, so it was that when I met Yeshua, it was as if I was meeting someone I had always known; and in truth, the angel said that it was so.

10 The angel told me that I was called of God and that my purpose on earth was ever intertwined with the youth in my dream, and more, that we would walk together through life and eternity and, by our lives, show a greater light.

11 Knowing this, dear brother, has never allowed me to be as other women are. As Yeshua has said if men and women are to grow beyond the confines of their existence, they must do so together as co-inheritors of glory."

12 Then Yeshua asked Lazarus, "Can a man create a babe without a woman?" And Lazarus said he could not.

13 Yeshua said unto him, "Verily, there will never be upon the earth a greater miracle than a child, but this, the most marvelous creation of man and woman, relies upon the woman in a magnitude far greater than the man, for the child is nurtured within her womb. Therefore, how deceived is the man who thinks to himself that he can be without the woman for the lesser things of life and still find God's favor?

14 Verily, I say unto you unless a man puts his wife upon a throne as the co-regent of his kingdom, he will only have a kingdom of one in the world to come, and desolation will be its name.

15 For as man metes out to women in life, be it with esteem or disdain, so shall Elohim mete out to him in the world to come, returning to him the energy he gave in life that he might live imprisoned or freed within the bonds or wings of his own making in the life to come.

16 Unto the man of faith and righteousness who shows by his actions that a virtuous wife is his greatest treasure, God will bless them as one with a kingdom in Heaven that has no end."

CHAPTER 29

Yeshua Speaks of Wealth

Lazarus inquires why Yeshua, with all of the knowledge that he has, is not a wealthy man instead of a poor carpenter. Yeshua explains that Elohim gives each person talents and abilities that they can magnify them and share them freely with others. Unfortunately, most people that have been given the gift of acquiring wealth do not share it as easily as those who have other types of talents. Yeshua explains this in great detail using a very effective parable to make his point.

Lazarus continued to be awakened in his spirit by all that he heard and asked of Yeshua, "Yochanan and Miriam have said how you retain all knowledge and have performed such miracles that it would seem that nothing is impossible for you. How can it then be that you are just a poor carpenter? Surely, even now at your young age, you could be a mighty man."

2 Yeshua smiled and answered him, saying, "Being a carpenter is one of my great joys. I create. I shape and form and make things of beauty and function, even as Elohim has made the world. I provide for the needs of my family by doing something I love, which causes me to have tranquility and serenity, not unhappiness or anxiety, and it brings happiness into the lives of others, not anger or dispute.

3 As you have seen me do, for that which calls to you, do likewise, and you will find a peace that few know.

4 Concerning wealth and power, I have not come into the world to become esteemed of men in the ways of the world. And I would give away any riches, were they offered to me.

5 I desire to speak deeply of this to you as it will be a great decision in your life because you are a rich young man from a wealthy family. You must understand very clearly that a man who gathers unto himself the treasures of the world and shares not generously to lift the world and the people therein also bars his own path to Heaven.

6 Verily, it is impossible for a rich man who hoards his wealth and gives it in great part only to himself to reach glory in Heaven, and unto him is reserved only a place of barrenness like unto that which he gave unto his brothers and sisters of light when in the life.

7 If a rich man loves money so much that he gains it and retains it to himself in abundance, even opulence, then that is what his eye is fixed upon, and therefore, though he may honestly search and sincerely desire, he can never fully find the path of Celestine Light, for his eye never leaves his wealth long enough to see it.

8 Verily, I say unto you the steps to Heaven begin with a steadfast love for God and continue with humility, charity, and selfless service to others, especially those less fortunate than you.

9 It is not found in living grandly, when it would be possible to be comfortable with less.

10 "It is not found in hoarding the wealth of the world, but in giving your excess to the service of God and your brothers and sisters of light in need.

11 Consider this: Why does a man have a house with many rooms of grand size and more than his family needs? Why must it be finished with the finest stone and wood and precious things? Why must a man have many servants that jump to his commands? Is it to please God that he has these things?

12 I say unto you no! It is for his vanity that he may be puffed up in his own mind, that he may have comfort beyond his needs and be esteemed by other men that he has these things.

13 The rich man may pay tribute to God with his pious words and prayers and his hefty offerings of gold equal to ten other men, but his true heart is far from God whom he proclaims, and it will always be so until the day he is a good and faithful servant and returns to God the treasure given in his stewardship.

14 Among the poor, God is content if they return to God a tithe of 10 percent of their increase above their bare needs, in whatever form they can, for they must sacrifice of their simple pleasures to make such a gift and great shall be their blessings for their faithfulness.

15 But the rich can return 50 percent of their increase or more to God, plus pay large taxes to Caesar, and still have greater luxury than the poor can dream of.

16 Therefore, until a rich man loves God more than money and is ready to give to God with a joyous heart in the same humble spirit and happy manner of sacrifice as the poor man, he is buying his earthly pleasures at the price of his heavenly rewards."

17 Now Lazarus was vexed by the things that Yeshua said, for he came from a very rich family. And he asked, "Do you condemn my father for his wealth or even me, his son, who will inherit it? What would you have my father do, give away all the wealth he has worked so hard for?"

18 Yeshua answered him with a question, "Who gave your father his wealth?"

19 Lazarus seemed surprised by the question of Yeshua, and he said, "My father gave it to himself by his awareness of opportunities, his discernment of value, and his keenness of judgment."

20 And Yeshua replied, "And how did he gain these qualities that have been of such benefit to him?"

21 Lazarus thought for a moment in silence, and then answered, "He was taught well by his father who was also a merchant, and he has always had a drive for success that exceeds that of most men."

22 And Yeshua replied, "Verily, I say unto you, all that your father has, was given to him by God. He was born to goodly parents who gave him a foundation for success because Elohim sent his spirit to the womb of his mother, and he came into the world with the qualities you have spoken of because they were given unto him by the Elohim as gifts at his birth.

23 It was the desire of God from before he was born that he would be given the way to acquire wealth; it is the same for all men who gain riches in honesty.

24 But to others, God gives gifts of a sweet spirit, of artistic ability, of harmony, of spiritual insight, of a comforting spirit, of peacemaking, of loyalty, of making home a heaven, and of many other fine qualities that bless all who are touched by those with the gifts, which they give freely in great abundance to everyone whom they meet.

25 Verily, many good gifts, which have eternal significance, may have little value in the marketplace, even though they bring marvelous light to the world and are greatly esteemed by Elohim.

26 Then comes the rich man whom God has blessed in his fortune and often with other gifts as well. Does he freely share with his brothers and sisters of light the gift Elohim has given to him? Does he return his excess to God to fulfill the purpose of his gift?

27 Foolish is the rich man who is seduced by the comfort and power wealth can bring when it is kept, for he gives himself a life of ease that is here today and gone tomorrow, at the price of a glory and abundance that is everlasting.

28 Wise is the rich man who does not puff himself up, but lovingly returns his excess to God in righteousness and thankfulness. He is the good steward whom Elohim cherishes. His life shall be blessed, he will be esteemed by the valiant in life, and his eternity shall be overflowing with joy."

29 Yeshua added, "I tell you these things that you might learn wisdom, that you and your family may yet receive the great blessings that wait for you.

30 Know that Elohim does not condemn the errant who are good of heart and seek to understand the truth, for they are better at forging their own condemnations and creating their own obstacles to eternity and punishments in this life. But because their heart is good, they still have a chance to see the light of truth and receive the eternal promises God gives to the worthy.

31 Consider this: Every moment a man works for wealth beyond his simple needs, he takes away from time with those he loves, and he knows not how many more breaths are left in his life.

32 He will stand naked at the door to eternity without a penny from his earthly treasures, empty of the joy of eternal relationships with those he loves because he was too busy in life, chasing his fortune that is now but dust to invest in his family that could have been forever.

33 Every time a rich man hoards a coin that he does not need, he lets a child of God go hungry.

34 Every time a rich man builds a mansion for himself, he consumes that which could have built houses for many of the needy.

35 Every time a rich man buys another unneeded comfort, he takes away from the money that could be used to build a temple of God that could give comfort to many of the Children of Light.

36 Every time a rich man squanders gold to give his children the best clothes and lavish gifts, he takes the money that could be used to give many children simple necessities.

37 Every time a rich man buys luxury for himself, he takes away from those whose life each day is a struggle to survive.

38 The love of money and power and fame and carnal pleasures are the greatest tools of Satan to seduce men away from the Celestine Light of God.

39 To a rich man come all of these luxuries if he desires, and it is only the purest of heart, who love God, and know from whom it is that all blessings flow that can withstand the great weight of the temptations of the rich.

40 Because of this, it is easier for a rich man to go through the eye of a needle than to be worthy of Heaven.

41 Every life is a stewardship given by God to prove the valiant, and only the good steward will see the face of God and become one with the Celestine Light that is eternal.

42 If God has given you or allowed you to have wealth beyond your needs, it is a test to see if you will be a good steward of that which you have been given and will magnify the purposes of God and be of service to your brothers and sisters of the world. As you do, so it shall be done with you in the hereafter.

43 If you are blessed by wealth and would also serve God, then take only what you need to continue your livelihood, provide simple comfort for your family, reasonable opportunities for your children, and live in a humble way not to be noticed among men.

44 Then give all that remains of your annual accumulation to the purposes of God, that the excess Elohim has blessed you with may be used to further the kingdom of God on earth and to help those less fortunate in a manner that also helps them to gain a measure of self-sufficiency and self-esteem.

45 If you do this not, you are like the foolish young merchant who found favor with the king of the land and, as a gift, was sent into a far city of the kingdom and given a new stall in a big bazaar in which the king paid for all manner of goods that the young merchant might have worthy things to sell and find happiness from his efforts.

46 And the king sent experienced merchants to the young man to teach him in the ways of

commerce, and they gave him the foundation that he might be successful. And for this, the king asked that the young merchant return to him one-half of all that he earned, that he might use his profit to help others in his kingdom.

47 And it came to pass that the young merchant had great success because of all that his benefactor had done for him.

48 But when some time had passed and the king had not heard from the young merchant, he went unto the bazaar in the distant city and, finding him and seeing his thriving business, asked why he had not yet received any of the profits as they had agreed.

49 The young merchant protested, 'This arrangement we have made is not fair, for I do all of the work, which is hard and takes all of my time, and it is a great thing to ask for half of all that I earn. In truth, you are in a far city, and it is only because of my good talents that I have had such great success. Had I been another man with lesser talents, there would be far less expected because far less would have been made.

50 Therefore let me pay you for the goods you gave me to begin and that much again for your kind help in starting me here and then each year a tenth of what I earn as a tribute. But beyond that, it is not reasonable to ask that I give so greatly and that my money for which I have done everything to obtain would then go to people who have done nothing.'

51 Hearing his words the king was wroth, and the young merchant discovered too late his great mistake. And the king said unto him, 'Foolish man, I gave unto you when you were in need because of my love for you and asked only that you continue to help me to help others, even as I had helped you, while letting you still keep to yourself enough for a comfortable life.

52 But now, because you would turn your back on those who are in need, even as you once were, I shall turn my back upon you.

53 Do you not understand that it is not only this one stall that is mine, but all of this bazaar and every stall and every bazaar across the land? And each of these, your fellow merchants are those to whom I have given the same gifts as I have given you, that they might find a life of happiness.

54 But because you have hardened your heart to your fellow man, all that has been given to you shall be taken away, and you shall have nothing from my kingdom. All of your days will be spent begging for coins that you might know how worthy it is, the good you have scorned.'

55 Then was it done, even as the king decreed, and the young merchant forever tasted the life of those to whom he would not comfort.

56 If you have ears to hear, Lazarus, please hear."

57 Lazarus nodded his head in understanding and replied, "I hear your words and a part of them resides in me, but it is a very hard thing you are asking. Would it not be better to retain a greater portion of wealth and with this make a greater fortune from which a greater gift can be given than from the smaller fortune that would have otherwise been?"

58 And Yeshua answered, "This is the same argument given by the young merchant in the parable. But what matters to God are the actions you take every day, not that you would store up for yourself treasures on earth to luxuriate in all of your life and then, only when you are old and soon to no longer be able to hold them, to give a part of your wealth to the poor.

59 Each day, you need to be looking to the gifts you will give to others, not just of money, but of love and understanding, of compassion and comfort, of time and assistance.

60 And when you give of your time or your love or any other good thing, let it be only as a gift, with nothing desired in return, and if it be money, then let it not even to be known among men that it was you that gave the gift; and for that which you do in secret, Elohim shall reward you openly.

61 Neither borrow nor lend money to your friends or family, for by such are the doors of unhappiness and discontent thrown open, but if those you love are in need, bless them with a gift; thereby nothing is expected in return, and only love can bloom from the blossom.

62 Remember, O remember, what you do with the excess you gain, be it selfish or unselfish, righteous or unrighteous, you do it to God, and you shall be accountable for in the hereafter."

63 Lazarus nodded in comprehension but continued to be vexed by the words of Yeshua and had much to ponder upon as they retired unto sleep.

CHAPTER 30

Purpose of Life

Yeshua expounds further upon wealth. He explains that life should be a circle of unity, where each person contributes the excess of their gift for the benefit of all so the family of man becomes like the spokes of a wheel, where each supports and benefits the others and, in unity, rolls forward.

As the new day rose, Lazarus was still troubled by the things Yeshua had said about rich men and inquired of him for further explanation.

2 Sensing his thoughts, Yeshua told him, "Men think to use their wealth and save their wealth for the benefit of their family, and that is righteous within moderation.

3 But remember that all the people of the world are God's children; all are your brothers and sisters of spirit; all are your family. And this understanding is especially important for the faithful Children of Light to fulfill among one another within the body of the Celestine Light.

4 Therefore, when a rich man uses his wealth to benefit many people upon the earth, rather than just a few of his close family in excess abundance, he fulfills the full measure of his creation and walks a path that leads to God.

5 Verily, all people are connected and all serve a vital purpose, one to another. To some, it is given to have wealth; to others, mastery of art or music or invention or to understand higher truths as servants of God. Should not the gifts of one be there to benefit all? I tell you that it is for this cause that God has given the gifts unto them.

6 But if the musician or the artist or the inventor or the servant of God has to spend all of their time working at a task that is not their gift in order to feed their family, they may have no time remaining to develop and exercise the gift God gave them, and a great loss is then upon the world, both upon the rich and the poor; for the greatness of an inspiration that could touch souls and change the world might never be for lack of time to cultivate the genius within the man.

7 Therefore, has God called the rich man, whom he has given to have more than his needs, to be his special steward: that he can generously share his bounty with the many whose gifts bring joy to the world but not riches to the giver, that they might bring forth the fruits of their gifts and thereby benefit all of God's children on earth and give unto them eternal treasures, which moths and rust do not corrupt.

8 And I say unto you life should be a circle of unity, where each person contributes the excess of their gift for the benefit of all, be it the creation of wealth or the creation of the arts or the wisdom of the spirit or whatsoever God has given unto them, and thus the family of man becomes like unto the spokes of a wheel, where each supports the others and benefits the others and in unity rolls forward.

9 And woe unto the man who inherits wealth that came from the efforts of his father or

kinsman and then hoards the wealth unto himself. If it is a sin for a rich man to hoard his wealth unto himself, then it is a sin upon a sin for he who inherits another's wealth to do so, for he has not even earned it by the sweat of his brow or the intellect of his mind.

10 In this, Elohim has given the inheritor a blessing by which he may in humility bless others, and as he does, he proves to be a good steward and God shall store up for him great treasures in Heaven; and as he does not, so shall God take away from his eternal reward.

11 Verily, I say unto you this life is but a breath in eternity, yet it is the most important breath you will ever take, for the day shall come when all will stand before the throne of Elohim and be weighed in the balance and judged according to how they walked in life, after the manner of men or after the manner of God, and be pulled into their place in the kingdoms of eternal life, be into darkness or into light, by the resonance from their life on earth.

12 And if they walked according to the manner of men, then they shall be given a lesser reward for all eternity, equal to the reward they gave to their brothers and sisters of light in their breath of mortal life.

13 But to those that walk after the manner of God, unto them shall be given a reward in Heaven that surpasses their understanding and uplifts their soul into the Celestine Light that shines forever.

14 And to those who receive the generosity of others, let them not accept it as beggars, who receive gladly but return nothing, for in that, sustenance is gained at the price of dignity.

15 But let them accept the help of others as part of the wheel of fellowship: that as they receive a gift from one, they give a gift to another, not in money of which they have none, but in their time and talents. Thereby, upon every turn of the wheel, there are no weak spokes, for with such as they have, in dignity do all give."

16 And Lazarus said unto Yeshua, "Your words are powerful. They enter my heart and rumble inside. But you must forgive me, for I still do not understand. I know that some are born into a life of ease and treat others without respect, and for such, I have no pity; but there are many, like my father, who have earned every coin they have by hard work and ingenuity far beyond the efforts other men make.

17 My father has done this because he loves his family and wished us to have more than he had as he struggled with life. And though I will inherit, I have tried to follow in his footsteps and be a diligent man who succeeds from effort and inspiration so that my family who has supported and comforted me can be in turn supported and have comfort.

18 The other people of the world, not of my family, have not supported me or my father. Why then should we be asked to help them as greatly as you say and not just with a small portion, which to them is a great amount?"

19 Yeshua answered him, saying, "Whether you are rich or you are poor, this life is not easy. It is full of the most painful trials and tribulations.

20 Unto each person is given the opportunity to prove their worthiness and the power of their soul over the adversities with which they are the weakest, that they might grow strong and gain faith in the Celestine Light of Elohim, a power greater than themselves and all the adversity of the world.

21 Life is a crucible that either burns up the children of men or purifies them. And the day will come to every man, when they will either abandon themselves to the evil that tempts and torments them, or humble themselves and call at last in sincere faith upon the higher power of Elohim to fill them with their Celestine Light that they may overcome the darkness.

22 To some, it is given to be tempted by carnal pleasures that they may become the master over their own passions and learn to cherish the sanctity of virtue.

23 Others are challenged by the allure of gambling and the temptation of easy money that they may learn to value diligence and effort.

24 To some, it is given to be beautiful that they may overcome vanity and learn selflessness.

25 To many, it is given to experience great personal loss at times in their life that they might

come to understand the timelessness of eternity and the bonds of forever that seal the faithful.

26 To some, it is given to be poor in material things that they may find a true happiness, which is not based upon having the things of the world.

27 While others are given to be rich that they might learn to be humble and generous and value time with their family greater than time with their work or pleasure.

28 Each of these and many more trials of life are seen as torments, but they are really blessed gifts. For every temptation, weakness or challenge provides the opportunity to become more righteous, virtuous, and full of light. Conquering weaknesses of the flesh turns them into strengths and places you firmly on the path to true fulfillment of spirit- a gift so great that all the treasure of the world cannot buy it.

29 But the sweetest of the gifts that prove the man is the gift of wealth. For some adversities are horrors to bear, and the only consolation is knowing that the greater is the trial, the greater is the reward for those who find the light.

30 But to have wealth as a test is to have a temptation that brings continual pleasure to bear and in that, it is most insidious, for it deceives the rich man who does not see wealth as a vexation to be rid of, but as a blessing to retain.

31 Wealth is therefore one of the most difficult of all trials. Therefore, God gives the gift of wealth only to those who are counted among the most valiant spirits.

32 Lazarus, I love you, my brother. And for this cause, I am going to give you a greater understanding than is known among men, that you may clearly see the light of truth and ever walk the path of righteousness, as you come to know who you are and why you are here.

33 Before you were born into this world by your parents, you were born into a Celestine glory as a spirit child of your heavenly parents. The children of men are literally sons and daughters of God. Therefore, knowing this, it is given to you to fulfill your nobility with honor and righteousness.

34 Your mortal life is but the blink of an eye in the eternity that is yours. But in that blink is determined, in a great measure, your inheritance in the heavens to come, which can be far greater than all the inheritances of men upon the earth.

35 You lived for countless time in the Celestine glory, learning and growing from your experiences and relationships. Before this world was, you were.

36 For most, it follows to have one physical, mortal life after they have gained all there is to gain in the heavenly glory, before they came into the world.

37 Millenniums of existence prepare each soul for the fateful day when they are born with forgetfulness of the realm of Celestine Light and enter into the world of darkness and despair, where the Celestine Light does not abound but must be sought and cherished and claimed.

38 For though some may be born into very trying circumstances, none are born without the spirit of Elohim residing in their heart, waiting to be found; that the world of darkness may also become a world of light unto them; and that in their forgetfulness of the glory that was, they might find an abiding faith, as they live for the glory that can be.

39 And to each are given special gifts, some as trials and some as blessings, but all that they might learn in the furnace of the world to share their good gifts with their brothers and sisters.

40 Remember, when you have a candle in the darkness, you do not hide it under your cloak so that only you can see, but you hold it high that it may give light to everyone. And the good that you thus do gives greater light to you as well.

41 Now there are many gifts that can benefit the children of men and the Children of Light that walk among them. There is music, dance, art, a cheerful disposition, spiritual insight, invention, willing service to others, a respect for all men, fairness, and creativity in many forms.

42 But one of the most powerful gifts is wealth, for with it, many of the gifts of others can be empowered to come forth in abundance and glory. Alas, it can also be the most selfish of the gifts that prove the man, and only they who conquer themselves can free the gift and reap the blessings that are eternal.

43 For the part of man that is allured to darkness is ever seduced to selfishness, and many are the gifts of others that never have the opportunity to give light to the world, when the rich man succumbs to the darkness instead of the light.

44 Verily, without the patronage of the rich, many of the poor are ground down by daily existence and never find the foundation of stability and freedom of time to let their light shine.

45 Because wealth so tempts the righteous into selfishness, our Father and Mother in Heaven chose the most valiant spirits of the premortal glory to be given the stewardship of wealth in life on earth, that they would remember who they are and why they are here and be the candle that lights many more, that darkness would retreat upon the world because they fulfilled their blessing.

46 If the musician thinks that he will only play one day a week, how many less smiles are there?

47 And if the artist thinks that he will only create on Jubilee, how much inspiration is he giving to the world?

48 And if the man with spiritual insight thinks to only share his illumination on the Sabbath, how much poorer are his brothers and sisters all the other days of the week?

49 And if the man who has riches thinks to only share a portion of his wealth and not the excess of all he has been blessed with, how many candles will never be lit because of his selfishness?

50 Why are you here? You are a child of God. You have been given marvelous gifts. You are here for a grand purpose.

51 Embrace your trials with thankfulness, for because of them men turn to God and find faith, which is the greatest of all powers, with which the world and all the stars in Heaven were made. For the faith you gain carries with you beyond this short life and serves you well in the eternity to come.

52 Let your greatest garden be the cultivation of loving and respectful relationships with all whose lives you touch, especially your parents and your wife and your children; for on the day of judgment and sorting, these will be the voices that sing your praises or your shortcomings; and in the world to come, the coin of the realm is the loving time you spent with those of your heart and the good that you helped others to do.

53 Nor ever forget that the gold you hold is that which the Elohim has made possible for you to have, and this was done because of your valiant spirit, trusting that you, who were among the most noble in the glory before the world, would find that place in your spirit while in mortality that reminds you of your greatness, that you might fulfill the full measure of your creation and be the candle that lights the wicks of many, that the world might be filled with a glorious light."

54 Lazarus was humbled, and at last, he understood the fullness of the words Yeshua spoke. There was gladness in his soul and happiness in his heart, and even from that moment, he began to plan the good things he would do.

CHAPTER 31

Communities of Light

Yeshua speaks in great detail describing the growth and principles of the Communities of Light and how they shall be organized.

eshua perceived the change in the heart of Lazarus and was exceedingly glad, and he said unto him, "I feel your heart beat in rhythm with mine, Lazarus; are we now then one in spirit?"

2 And in humility, Lazarus answered, "We are one, Yeshua."

3 Yeshua smiled broadly and said unto him, "It is good, my brother, and my cup overflows with joy for the understanding you have.

4 "I would that you should consider events that shall shortly come to pass, before your children have left your home, that you might be pondering even now the things you must do."

5 And Lazarus was startled, saying, "But I have neither children nor a wife."

6 Yeshua answered with an all-knowing smile, "I speak of things that will soon be, my brother. In the days to come, many shall join unto us, and they shall be Children of Light, united together to manifest the Celestine Light of Elohim and uplift and magnify one another.

7 And the Children of Light shall gather unto the body of the Celestine Light and shall grow mighty among the children of men, despite all that the Romans and the priests of the world may do.

8 Like the fresh breath of spring that turns barrenness into green where the rains fall, so shall the family of the Children of Light turn the darkness of the world to the light of truth and virtue wherever they dwell.

9 It is given unto you to be a pinnacle among them and gather them into Communities of Light within the body of Celestine Light, that they may support and edify each other and have wholeness and wellness in all areas of their lives, as they walk the path of truth amidst the world of darkness.

10 Therefore, whenever one who has been in darkness finds the light, let them not live separated from their brothers and sisters, but let them join into a Community of Light of their choice that also chooses them.

11 And let all who join into a Community of Light be bound by a covenant to live the Twelve Commandments and to follow the laws of health as revealed by God to the Children of Light; and may all visitors who pass through the gates adhere to the same obligations while they are within the boundaries of the community.

12 And let the community be as one extended family: that all Children of Light are brothers and sisters and desire to support and encourage the spiritual and temporal well-being of all

others, according to their ability and as they are called upon by the Elders of the community.

13 And let the Elders be leaders from among those longest in the community, given to be responsible for overseeing all of the temporal needs of the community and the assignments of duties to each member, and may all that is given be fair and just.

14 And may the Elders be eleven in number, with three or four chosen every year by a majority of the adult members of the community who have taken the covenants and lived in the community for at least one year.

15 If a majority of the covenant members desire it, they may ask those whose time of service is finished to serve another term, which the Elder may do, if they are not called by family duties and continue to have an abiding heart for the responsibility.

16 Let the Elders serve without salary or wages but only with recompense for their reasonable expenses.

17 Upon the formation of each community, let all of the founders come together and agree upon the enterprise in which the community will labor. And after one enterprise proves successful, may others come forth as the Members of the Covenant desire and the Elders direct that the Children of Light may prosper and have abundance on the land.

18 And let the enterprises be endeavors that are pleasing unto God and beneficial to other Communities of Light in places near and far, wherein each may give to the others and so provide for many of the temporal needs of the members.

19 Therefore, let there be communities of the bees, and of the orchards, and of the weavers, and of the gardens, and of the fields of grain, and of the mills, and of the dairies, and of the fish, and of the builders, and of the crystals, and of many other common pursuits that will help the community to prosper on the land and give abundance to the members and help them to bond to one another in their labors and goals.

20 Let each member give equally of their time for the benefit of the community according to their skills and abilities.

21 Upon the winter solstice, let the increase gained from the community enterprises beyond what is needed for the coming year to insure continued growth and vigor and security against misfortune, be divided in equal shares by each adult covenant member who labored equally in the enterprises from the beginning of the year. And let each child of those covenant members also receive a portion according to the contribution of their time and abilities of their age.

22 And let not the talents of one be counted as greater than the talents of another, but allow all to contribute whatever their talent may be, as the Elders discern, and in equality and with fairness according to the time that is given.

23 And let none be asked to give so many hours to the community that they do not have sufficient time to earn their livelihood, give bountiful love and nurturing to their family, and have private time for introspection and relaxation.

24 And let the Children of Light gather each day to share the main meal as a community, with each person, both male and female, adult and child, giving of their time in equality and fairness to accomplish the meal.

25 When the community grows beyond the size for all the families to sit at a single meal, divide into neighborhoods that one meal each day may still be shared with those closest to their home.

26 On the winter and summer solstice, let the community gather with a feast meal across all the neighborhoods and a day of uplifting communion among the Members of the Covenant that the hearts of the Family of Light will remain together.

27 Upon the spring and fall equinox, let there be a gathering of the entire community and a Jubilee celebration with three days of feasts and music, with words of wisdom from those whom God has called, that the hearts of the Children of Light will be bound one to another, with eyes single to the glory of God.

28 And let all in the community be good stewards of the earth and of the animals upon it and

value all life and take only what is needed, according to the commandments of Elohim.

29 And let the body of Celestine Light own all of the land and all rights to the water and the resources of the land, but let small parcels for private homes be leased to resident Members of the Covenant, as the Elders of the community deem right, with all other common lands and buildings and equipment within the community held in trust by the body of Celestine Light for all the current community Members of the Covenant to be administered by the community Elders as they deem right.

30 And let the community strive toward self-sufficiency in all areas as reasonable, especially for food, education, health, and labor of livelihood.

31 And let those with expertise in commerce locate their personal enterprise within the community that other members may find a worthy place in which to labor.

32 And let each member of the community and each place of work in the community, which hires laborers, tithe one tenth of their income before all other expenses and more if the Elders deem necessary, and a majority of the covenant members agree, or if a member so desires, to maintain and prosper the community. And let this be done with individual honesty and anonymity and by no other means.

33 And let education be of great importance so much so that every member, both young and old, seeks to often be engaged in formal instruction of a new skill or greater knowledge, and let the community provide places and foundations for the continual education of the members and their children.

34 And let artistic pursuits be encouraged for all members and community craft houses built, wherein each member may learn new talents and expand their abilities as their desires lead them.

35 And let the care of the temple of the body be taught to all, that everyone may have health and vigor for all of their years as they follow the precepts given by Elohim.

36 And suffer not the divisive to be among you, but put them out of the community if they will not quickly repent, ask forgiveness, and be divisive no more.

37 And let there be no weapons of death kept by any in the community or allowed to any visitors, but maintained only in a community vault of security for times of common defense for use only after every method of honorable peace has failed.

38 And suffer not the violent, either by force of voice or body, to remain among you, if they will not quickly repent, ask forgiveness, make restitution, and be violent no more.

39 And teach everyone to cultivate balance in all things with forbearance and compassion.

40 In all that you say and do, remember that you are a peculiar people whom God has called out of darkness into a marvelous light. Show forth the brightness of your soul, the sweetness of your spirit, and the industry of your abilities, that the world may see the harmony and abundance of the men and women and children of the Communities of Celestine Light and wonder what marvel God has wrought."

41 Lazarus soaked in the warm words of Yeshua and affirmed that when the time came to fulfill that which Yeshua had spoken, he would be a rock upon which the foundation of the Communities of Light could be built, even as Yeshua had given.

CHAPTER 32

Conversion of Kudar-Iluna

Kudar-Iluna, the former bandit traveling with Yeshua and company, speaks about his background, where his people are believed to have come from, and why they have been reduced to plundering for a living, which he laments. Yeshua speaks about a better way to live, and his words have a very powerful effect on Kudar-Iluna so much so that in tears of humility, he repents of his sins and vows to henceforth only walk in the light. Lazarus is also profoundly moved and also covenants to live a righteous life.

For seven more days, they contended with the Red Desert, and it was endless and barren. Nor was there comfort in the sea they often walked near, for the water was salty and could not be drunk or bathed in without fresh water to rinse.

2 But in the evenings, sitting in the Circle of Friends, under the light of the Moon and the stars and the fires of the merchants, they learned somewhat of Kudar-Iluna that he was the son of the leader of his people, which were the remnants of the Amorites, but now were very few in number, yet had once been a mighty people upon the land of Palestine.

3 And Yochanan asked, "Where is it that your people came from? For with your pale skin and hair and eyes blue like the sky and great height and sharply pointed beard, you are a most strange-looking man."

4 Kudar-Iluna answered, saying, "The legends of my people say we came from the north during a time of great cold. More than that, I know not. We have married many Hebrews and other races as we have dwindled as a people, and there are few still that remain as our ancestors did in appearance, as I do."

5 Then Yochanan asked him the question that vexed him, "Why do your people rob the caravans and plunder and kill? Although in asking that, I should first thank you for not allowing the one who desired to kill me that day do his evil deed."

6 At that question, Kudar-Iluna held down his head and was very sad and said, "It is what has been left to us. My people were once a proud warrior race with great dominion over the lands the Hebrews now hold. But our ancestors were defeated in battle at diverse places. Almost all perished in battles with the Hebrews many generations ago.

7 We who survive do so only in our mountain wilderness of Zin, a barren place, stealing women to be our wives and plundering to exist. I am ashamed of what I have been, but it is the only life my people know. If there was another way to live, surely we would."

8 Everyone was moved by the story of the people of Kudar-Iluna. And Yeshua said, "There is another way my friend: a way of love and righteousness, a way of peace and happiness, a way

of respect and generosity, a way that leaves the sins of the past trampled upon the ground and henceforth walks only in the Celestine Light of God."

9 Kudar-Iluna shook his head in disbelief, "This cannot be the god of the Hebrews you speak of, for in his name, my ancestors were killed. Nor has he protected the Hebrews from the Romans or given them peace or happiness. As they took it from my people, so it has been taken from them."

10 Yeshua replied gently, saying, "Kudar-Iluna, I do speak of the god of the Hebrews and the god of the Amorites, and the god of the Egyptians, and the god of everyone. The people of the world worship their conception of God in honest devotion in diverse forms, but their sincerity does not change their ignorance. Therefore, the god that the world worships but knows not, I now declare unto you.

11 There is but one God, the creator of all that is: this is Elohim. But Elohim is not one but three, and these three are not three but one, for verily the God of the earth and all the heavens above is our Father and our Mother in Heaven; and they are two, a male and female, that in balance creation may be, but they act as one, and for us, they are one God. And from them came their firstborn Son of spirit and only begotten of flesh, and through him, their will is made manifest in all things.

12 And Elohim the Father laughs that men would think that he alone would create life or that life would spring from an ethereal force, for life comes from life, not from the ethers.

13 Be it a babe coming forth from a mother's womb or a spirit into the heavens, it is only by the power of the male joined to the power of the female that life holding the divine spark of Celestine Light springs forth.

14 From our Celestine Father and Mother, our spirits were born, and because of them, we are all brothers and sisters; and through the common roots of our spirits, we are all connected and receive sustenance from the same spiritual source.

15 Therefore, if a man does injury to his brother or sister, he does injury to himself. And when the spirit of my brother or sister cries out, it wounds my spirit; and when my spirit cries out, it pains the spirits of my brothers and sisters.

16 Likewise, when a man helps his brother or sister, he helps himself. And when a man gives a good gift to his brother or sister, he gives a good gift to God."

17 Yeshua taught many truths of light unto Kudar-Iluna that night. And Kudar-Iluna was humbled by the words of Yeshua, for they were like sweet water unto a parched mouth upon the desert, and he desired to know more. And he said, "Would that it could be true that we are brothers in spirit and that we had parents in the heavens that care about us, but this is contrary to all I have ever known and how could it be that you know things such as this that the priests of many religions know not?"

18 Then Yochanan said unto him, "I have known Yeshua since we were small boys for we are kin, and I tell you, with all my heart, that he knows the heart and mind of God, for he is chosen of God; and I have seen with my eyes and heard with my ears great wonders that only he who is beyond a prophet of God could say and do."

19 But Kudar-Iluna still did not have faith in the things he had heard even though his heart testified of the truth. And he said, "You speak such strange teachings; how can there be a mother in the heavens, and how could we have lived before we lived and remember it not, and if these things are true, then why do even the priests of the Hebrews not speak of any but the Father and then only to give a name to the ethers they know not? Nor do they speak of a life that was, but only of the life to come"

20 Yeshua explained, "It is because of the wickedness of the people and the priests of old that they could not accept the full teachings of the prophets, and now the sparseness of truth, which was taught because of the weakness of men, has become the fullness of traditions that men give the power of the law.

21 And throughout the history of men, the rulers of the land have always used religion to

control the people.

22 Verily, many plain and precious parts of the truth have been hidden from men by the priests and the princes and the kings, that those in power might have greater dominion over those who otherwise would have known a more-glorious light.

23 When Moses came down from the mountain with the commandments of God, it was not ten, but Twelve Commandments that he brought forth. But upon seeing the wickedness and idolatry of the Children of Israel, he broke the tablets of stone upon the ground in anger and they turned into dust.

24 Then Moses returned in sorrow to the mountain of God and lamented upon the wickedness and weakness of the people; and the finger of God came forth from the burning bush and wrote ten new commandments upon another stone, which Moses brought down again unto the Children of Israel; and they are commandments which could be lived by the weakest of the people and did not call them to their greatness.

25 Verily, where less is expected, less is given.

26 But the time is soon coming when all that has been lost shall be restored; and where much is given, much will be expected; and by his life and his words shall a man be justified, and by his life and his words shall he be condemned.

27 Then shall the fullness of truth be lost again, but it will come forth once more before the end of days, that the Children of Light will know their way home."

28 And the mouth of Kudar-Iluna moved as if to speak, but no words came out.

29 And Yeshua said, "Do not marvel at this that you have a father and a mother in Heaven and that we have lived before we lived. Is it not written that God spoke to the prophet Yirmeyahu in the days of old and said unto him, 'Before you were formed in the belly, I knew you, and before you came forth out of the womb, I sanctified you and ordained you to be a prophet unto the world.'

30 Verily, the words of Elohim are plain. Therefore, he who has ears to hear, let him hear."

31 Yeshua stood and he bade Kudar-Iluna to stand with him, and Miriam and Yochanan and Lazarus to stand with them. They stood in a circle, with their right arm upon the near shoulder or waist of the one beside them and their left arm upon the back or waist of the one to the other side. And the deepest feelings of their hearts, they shared with one another.

32 Yeshua looked into the eyes of Kudar-Iluna and into his soul, and Kudar-Iluna wept as he looked into the eyes of Yeshua and saw the brightness of the light within him.

33 And Yeshua admonished, "My brother, believe in Elohim, the one true Almighty God, and in the love of our Father and Mother in Heaven, and that it is a profoundly deep love for you. Know that you are a most precious child of God. If you will repent of your sins and henceforth walk the path of Celestine Light and righteousness, your sins are forgiven, they are no more, and you shall be born again."

34 And Kudar-Iluna fell to his knees and wept mightily, and all in the circle knelt beside him and embraced him with love. And he did covenant from the depth of his soul to henceforth walk in the light.

35 And Lazarus too was overcome by the words of Yeshua and also began to weep mightily and called upon God and Yeshua and Miriam and Yochanan to forgive him his transgressions and promised with great humility that he would henceforth walk only in the Celestine Light of God.

36 And these things did not go unnoticed by the merchants, and some of them murmured against the Hebrews and the bandit, but others were moved by all that they had seen and heard.

CHAPTER 33

Travels in Egypt

After stopping in Pelusium and Qantara for some days, the caravan of Yeshua arrives in Heliopolis, one of the greater Egyptian cities of the time. Yeshua spends considerable time, exploring the city and the markets, asking many questions. It is in the market one day that Yeshua comes across a merchant who is crying in the back of his stall. Having compassion for the man, he proceeds to share an inspiring parable that relates to the man's situation. After two months of successful trading, Lazarus decides to return to Palestine, and Kudar-Iluna decides to depart with him that he may return to his land and people to share all that he has learned from Yeshua.

It came to pass that the caravan arrived at Pelusium and tarried for eighteen days that the merchants could trade.

2 Lazarus bought some fine cedar wood that had just arrived by boat, and Yeshua fashioned this into several small, intricate chests for the keeping of precious things; and they sold them, all save one, which Yeshua gave to Miriam.

3 Happy with the quick sales of Yeshua's chests, Lazarus purchased another supply of fine cedar and other rare woods that Yeshua could carve more chests and other things for the Egyptians and the Romans as they traveled.

4 As he walked through the city, Kudar-Iluna made quite an impression upon the people, for none had ever seen a man who looked as he looked. And he won several pieces of silver from the Romans for none could best him in skills of war.

5 To pass time, Yochanan assisted Yeshua in the working of the woods such as he could, but he waited to trade his treasures in Memphis.

6 Miriam braided fine strings of hair and gold thread, which Lazarus also sold profitably in the market.

7 And it came to pass that they left Pelusium and journeyed to Qantara, where they tarried for seven days, and from thence, they journeyed further into Egypt.

8 Thus, it was that they arrived at Heliopolis, one of the greater cities of the Egyptians, and here Lazarus had much success in his trading and knew that his father would be well pleased.

9 While in Heliopolis, Yeshua spent much time, wandering the markets and the city and observing the Egyptians and their ways and the ways of the many visitors from other lands to be found within Heliopolis. And he asked many questions that he might have greater knowledge.

10 And it came to pass that one day as Yeshua was walking through the market that he saw a merchant crying in the back of his stall, and having compassion he went unto him and said, "Good sir, why do you weep?"

11 The merchant was ashamed to be seen with his emotions so openly, especially by a foreigner, and he replied, "I have not been weeping. I merely had some sand in my eye, which was hurting me, and I was trying to get it out."

12 And Yeshua said unto him, "As there seems to be nobody here for you to speak with at this time, and I am in need of a rest, do you mind if I sit for a moment in the shade and tell a story to you for the privilege?"

13 The merchant, seeing only an empty stall, assented to Yeshua's request. And Yeshua, knowing in his heart that he was despondent for the failure of his trading and in pain for his hungry children at home, whom he loved, said unto him, "There once was a small caravan of three brothers that left Egypt to trade with the tribes in the desert.

14 Now the names of the three brothers were Strength, Righteous, and Perseverance."

15 Word spread quickly from one stall to another that a storyteller was in the marketplace, and as this was a cherished entertainment, people began to gather to hear the words of Yeshua.

16 And Yeshua said unto them, "Two elder brothers, Wisdom and Faithful, were left behind to care for the families, while their younger brothers sought to find success in trading, for all were in distress because of lack of money.

17 They traveled for three days, seeking to find tribes that encountered few traders that they might earn a good reward for their efforts.

18 On the third day, a great sandstorm came upon them, and they suffered under the wind and the stinging sands for a day and a night.

19 Not being familiar with the desert, they had been following the trail of camels that had passed before them. But now the storm had wiped away all traces of previous travelers, and in every direction, there was only barrenness.

20 The three brothers were despondent and could not decide which way to go. Even to return the way they had come was imperceptible to them.

21 And Righteous said unto his brethren, 'I should have remained at home to care for the families and let Wisdom come in my place, for he would know which way to go.'

22 And Strength said unto his brethren, 'A little sandstorm is nothing! We still have seven days of water, and we are younger and better fit than Wisdom for a journey such as this. If we reason together, surely we can come upon the best way to go.'

23 And Perseverance said unto his brethren, 'We are squandering time as we speak. Come, let us choose which way to go and get on with it.'

24 And Righteous replied, 'You speak well, brothers, but let us place a marker here with our names and circumstances upon it, that any who may come upon it after us will know we have been here and were three days out of the city.'

25 Thus, it was that they decided to head into the sun as it was the one constant they thought they could rely upon. But this was not always easy as the terrain was hilly and they sometimes needed to change direction to get around obstacles, which put the sun at their side or at their backs.

26 Being from the city, where they lived among buildings, they had never paid much attention to the sun before. To their dismay, they noticed that it did not remain near the same spots of land as they thought it would, but moved vastly across the sky during the day, which caused great confusion as to the direction they should travel.

27 After seven days of suffering, they were sinking into the sand with exhaustion; their water was almost gone, and they had encountered no villages or any other travelers. They stopped upon a barren patch of sand, in the empty desert of sand, and Strength and Righteous were ready to abandon hope and leave their bones upon that spot.

28 Only Perseverance still had hope and looked for a way of salvation. Then it was that he spied a few small plants that came only to his ankle, growing in a low spot between sand dunes. And he called to his brothers and said, 'Look here, brethren! Here is a plant; surely it must have water to survive. Therefore, let us dig here, and we will find our salvation.'

29 But his brothers were too fatigued to move, so Perseverance began to swiftly dig through the soft sand, first with his bare hands and then with a small pick, which they had brought with them, as the sand began to be packed and hard.

30 Soon he had a deep hole dug, but it was as dry inside of the hole as outside. Perseverance called unto his brothers saying, 'Come, help expand this opening for it makes a spot of shade, and beneath the level of the ground, it is cooler.'

31 Then his brothers came and with great slowness helped him to widen the hole so they all could fit inside. Perseverance pointed to the thread of a root from the plants that still continued deeper into the ground. And he said unto his brothers, 'Let us continue to dig deeper, for surely, this root must be going to water, or the plants would have withered in the sun. We owe it to our families to keep on trying to find life.'

32 Righteous was moved by his brother's words, and he began to help him dig. Resting often, they continued to dig until nightfall, until the hole was as deep as all three brothers standing on top of one another, but still the sand was dry.

33 The next day, neither Righteous nor Strength could be persuaded to help Perseverance dig deeper, so while they lay still, he continued on his own.

34 After he had dug the depth of another man, his pick hit upon solid rock and he could go no further. In frustration, he threw the pick upon the stone and went back to his brothers to tell them.

35 And he said unto them, 'Even me, who never before has given up, must admit defeat. Let us bury ourselves in the hole we have dug, that our end will be quick and the desert can swallow us in our unworthiness, for we have left our families to destitution.'

36 And Strength was in sad agreement and, being the largest, stood to reach up and pull the sand upon them to bury them.

37 But Righteous reached for and held his arm to prevent the thing he would do, and he said unto them, 'Before we dishonor our families and take an action that cannot be undone, let us do the one thing that is yet left to us. We have sought salvation from ourselves alone, and life has rewarded us with misery. Let us now pray to the gods that they might intervene in our lives and save us.'

38 Strength and Perseverance agreed that nothing further could be lost by praying unto the gods, but amongst them they were uncertain as to which gods to pray to, and Righteous said unto them, 'Let us pray to the mightiest God, without a name. Let us just pray to the Almighty God.'

39 And it came to pass that the three brothers called out to the Almighty God and poured forth their hearts to him. In the greatest humility, they confessed their sins and promised to henceforth do only good with their lives. They beseeched him to save them, for the sake of their families.

40 They prayed all through the day to the Almighty God, and they began to feel a oneness with each other, and even with the desert and the grains of sand, such as they had never before felt or imagined. Then together they fell into a deep sleep.

41 Upon the sunrise, they awoke as one, and each had the same thought come alive in their head that the plant must still have water and that it must be beneath the rock.

42 Then Strength descended into the bottom of the hole and began to strike at the rock with mighty swings of the pick. But for all his efforts, there was nothing except a large hole in the rock.

43 But when at last his strength was failing and he thought he could swing no more, he determined to take one more mighty swing and as the pick hit upon the rock, it split asunder, and a geyser of water shot forth in such abundance that the brothers had to move quickly out of the hole to not be drowned.

44 And it came to pass that not only were the brothers saved, but they soon discovered the marker, which they had left only a short distance from the spring; and seeing a city in the

distance, they discerned that in all their wanderings, they were not ten days away from their homes as they had assumed, but had circled almost back to the beginning of their journey and were now close to the city from which they had left and to their wives and children.

45 Shortly thereafter, they moved their families and the families of their brothers, Wisdom and Faithful, to the spring they had discovered, and soon it blossomed into a garden of green and plenty that became a favored resting spot for the trading caravans.

46 And the brothers and their families prospered.

47 And from this story are many gems to enrich your life. Return to it again and again, and you will continue to find new treasures.

48 But the greatest treasure of all is to understand that there is an Almighty God in Heaven, and after all that man can do, there is still more that God will do for those who ask good things of them with a repentant heart and a humble spirit.

49 And I say unto you this day, look into your heart; reflect upon the journey of your soul in this life. Do not wait until you are dying in the desert to call upon the Almighty God; today is the day you are called unto repentance; today is the day you are called to humility; today is the day you are called to give yourself to God.

50 And whosoever hears my words and acts upon them shall know the true and living God, and they shall drink from the spring of everlasting water and never thirst again."

51 Then turning to the crowd that had gathered, Yeshua looked out among them all. And they had been captivated by his story and waited now for his next words. And he said unto them, "He who has ears to hear, let him hear." Then he parted the crowd and walked away and returned to his family.

52 After two moons had passed, Ibrahiim began to make ready for the caravan to travel back into the Sinai. Despite his initial misgivings, he had come to respect Lazarus as a clever and honest trader and invited him to continue the journey with his caravan.

53 Lazarus had prospered and now had five camels of trade goods. He came to council with his companions and said, "I am of a mind to leave in three days hence with Ibrahiim, that I may travel back to Bethany to keep the promise to my father to return within six moons. Ibrahiim is of a mind to join with several other caravans and together travel to Suez and from thence to Aqaba, and from thence to Petra, and from thence back to Judea. It is a long journey that holds good promise for more trading."

54 At the mention of Petra, Kudar-Iluna perked up, "I have learned much of the ways of righteousness and truth in my days with Yeshua, but now I would like to journey with Lazarus, for the caravan will pass near the wilderness of Zin, which borders Petra; from there I desire to return to my people that I might share with them the truths and wonder I have come to know."

55 Thus, it was that Lazarus and Kudar-Iluna departed with the caravan of Ibrahiim, and Yeshua and Miriam and Yochanan and the children remained in Egypt.

56 After the caravans had vanished into the distance, Yeshua turned to Miriam and Yochanan and said unto them, "We must journey now to Memphis, for there are many paths I must walk that begin at Memphis, and there will Yochanan find those who desire his treasure."

CHAPTER 34

Miracle of the Blind Girl

Arriving in the city of Memphis, Yeshua, with his family and Yochanan, goes to the house of a merchant by the name of Babuaten. After an unwelcome meeting, Yeshua beseeches him to look within his heart to know that there is more to God than he has been led to believe. In return, the merchant's love, along with the hand of God, can return the sight of his only daughter's eyes. In a very touching scene, his daughter's sight is restored.

So it was that Yeshua and Miriam and Yochanan, and the children traveled to Memphis. As they journeyed near to the center of the city, they came to a house of a merchant by the name of Babuaten. Yeshua went straight to the gate and bade the servants to tell their master that Yeshua of Aten was at the gate.

2 The master Babuaten soon arrived at the gate in confusion and was angry that poor, unbecoming travelers, even Hebrews, would appear at his gate and give such offense as to use the name of Aten, the God whom he worshipped. And speaking in Greek, he said, "What have you to do with me, rabble of a desolate land? Be gone from my home before I call the pharaoh's guards."

3 And Yeshua said, "Would you chase the spirit of Aten from your home? For verily, if you put us away, so shall the spirit of Aten no more reside with you."

4 Babuaten was very wroth at these words, and he said, "Who are you to say such blasphemous words! You know not Aten and I know not you; therefore, be gone this instant!"

5 Yeshua responded with a voice of authority, saying, "The God of all the earth and all the suns in the heavens has sent me to you, and if you turn me away, so shall the God of all that is turn his face away from you; but if you will repent of your anger and hear my words, and give a place for my family, then verily, as you love, so the God of Heaven and earth shall restore to you that which is most precious and has been lost."

6 Now at these words, Babuaten trembled, for he had a daughter, most precious to his heart, and she had been spitted upon by a cobra when drawing water from a well and had been blind ever since. He knew in his heart that it was of his daughter that Yeshua spoke. And Yeshua had invoked the name of Aten, whom he did venerate, and in humility, he said, "You speak of my greatest treasure, and though I understand not at all, I will give you entry into my home for a time to see if there is weight behind the lightness of your words."

7 Thus, it was that Yeshua and Miriam and Yochanan entered the house of Babuaten, and when they had washed their feet, a young girl entered with a servant bringing water to drink, and she clung to her father, and all could see that she was blind, for where her eyes had been, there were only crusts.

8 And Babuaten said, "This is my only daughter Nanu, whom I love more than life. It is a great miracle that she lives at all, and I am thankful to Aten for every moment I have her. I took her to the priests, and though they can do great magic, they could not give back her eyes which the cobra took."

9 And Yeshua said, "You called us rabble of the desolate land, yet because you worship Aten, you know also of the pharaoh Akhenaten. Verily, I say unto you that Akhenaten and the Children of Israel are ever intertwined, but they and the Egyptians know it not. There is much more here than you know. Therefore, can you, hearing this, give a place for my words in your heart?"

10 Babuaten nodded in silence. And Yeshua said, "The priests of Egypt cannot heal your daughter's eyes because neither their eyes nor their hearts are single to the glory of the true God, but are divided by the many false gods of their beliefs. Nor can magic heal such as this, but only true faith, with nothing wavering.

11 And I say unto you that above all creation, both in the heavens and on the earth, there is one true God, and Aten of the sun, which you worship, is only a reflected glimpse of the light of the glory of the one true God.

12 Verily, when Aten was revealed to the children of Egypt by the pharaoh Akhenaten, it was a great step for them, and all they could hold.

13 But in the belief that you hold are the seeds of the fullness of truth, and I declare unto you that beyond the Aten you worship as the God of the sun is the one true God from whom the sun and all the stars of the heavens have been born; and they are numberless unto man, but they numbered unto the Almighty God, for they are his.

14 Therefore, if you will humble yourself and carry your belief beyond Aten by whom your daughter's eyes have not been healed and believe with greater faith in Elohim, the one true God of all the earth and of the sun, and of the uncountable stars of the heavens, and this with all of your heart, and give love to the Almighty God even as great as you love your daughter, then by the power of your faith and your love, your daughter's eyes will return."

15 Babuaten wept and said, "Your words touch my heart, and I do believe that which you say is true, for always have I known in my deepest places that there is much more to God than Aten. I now have an overflowing of light inside me such as I never could conceive. I pray if it is within your power, if the Almighty God Elohim of all of which you speak loves you, then ask him please to love my daughter too and give back to her that which the serpent took."

16 Yeshua bid the servants to bring some wet, green clay, and they shortly returned with the clay. And the mother of Nanu and her brothers also appeared, and though they were agitated by the visitors within their home and understood not the words Babuaten spoke to them in Greek, they remained silent out of respect.

17 And Yeshua bade Nanu to lie upon a bed, and he bade Babuaten to place some wet clay upon her eyes and to keep his hands upon her eyes and said unto him, "As you place this clay upon the eyes of your daughter, think about how much you love her and how much more your Father and Mother in heaven, which are the one Almighty God, love you.

18 As your own daughter calls to you for help, call out now with great depth of sincerity and desire to Elohim, the Almighty one and true God, and ask the Father and the Mother that are God that if it be their will, that they would send their love, greater than any love that men may know, through your heart and through your hands, and give back to your daughter that which was taken."

19 And Babuaten called upon Elohim, even as Yeshua had bade him. And he called out in Egyptian; therefore, his wife and his sons and his daughter and his servants all heard the words he spoke.

20 And so great was his feeling that great rivers of tears ran from his eyes, and everyone in the room, including Yeshua and Miriam, wept with him.

21 And Yeshua placed his hands on top of the hands of Babuaten, and together they lifted the clay from the eyes of his daughter Nanu. And her eyes that had withered away were restored in beauty, and her sight, which had gone, returned in fullness. Great was the joy and the tears of all who witnessed this miracle.

22 And the servants prepared to go quickly to tell the joyous news to all the people, but Yeshua forbade them and asked that they tell only a few of the close friends of the family, until he had departed because he did not wish to be known in Egypt by the pharaoh or the priests.

Cont →

CHAPTER 35

Yochanan's Treasure

After Yeshua helps restore of the sight of the only daughter of an Egyptian merchant, in appreciation, the man offers him a small house to live in with his family while they are in Memphis. Yochanan seeks out a sect of Egyptian priests that he knows are interested in the use of crystals for their rituals and, with the help of Yeshua's translation skills, is able to sell the crystals that he had gathered in the desert about Gimron for a tidy sum of money. Yeshua explains to Yochanan how he can benefit from the crystal of rainbow light.

❖ ❖ ❖

Babuaten was so overcome with happiness that he could not speak for many minutes and cried greatly with exceeding joy, and his wife did also.

2 At last, he came unto Yeshua and said, "You have given me back my most precious treasure. Therefore, anything I have I would give to you. What do you desire?"

3 And Yeshua said, "I have only shown you the path to the one true God and the miracles that you can accomplish with your own love and faith. As to my family, I must remain in Memphis for some time, and we seek a house wherein we may abide and where I can do my work in carpentry."

4 Babuaten answered joyously, "I have a house upon the far reaches of the southern part of the city that is near a well and has even now just become empty. It has only three rooms, but they are large and you may stay there as my guest for as long as you are in Memphis."

5 Yeshua thanked Babuaten for his kindness and accepted his offer to abide in the house to which he directed. Shortly thereafter, with many heartfelt thanks for Babuaten and his family, Yeshua and his family bid them good-bye, with a promise to return.

6 A short time after they had deposited their belongings in the house at Memphis that Babuaten had offered them, Yochanan desired to journey back into the city to seek out a certain sect of priests who were familiar with the use of rare crystals of the earth and used them in their rituals. And he asked Yeshua to travel with him that he might speak to the Egyptians.

7 Thus, it was that after some inquiry among the people and visits to other temples, they came to a particular temple where they had been told dwelt the priest of the crystals. And they went in and found the priests that Yochanan sought.

8 When Yochanan revealed his treasures, those that he had kept hidden, the priests were delighted to see the clear crystals of rainbow light, which he possessed, especially those with two opposite points, one larger than the other; those with ghosts; and those with spots of blood and silver frozen inside.

9 Though Yochanan had but two small sacks full, they gave him gold of twice the weight of

every crystal that he gave them, and for some, they gave triple their weight in gold. And they pleaded with him to return with more, for to them, the rare natural crystals were more valuable than gold or diamonds or rubies or emeralds.

10 As they returned to their home, Yeshua said, "How is it that you obtained the rainbow crystals or knew that these priests of the Egyptians would desire them when those at other temples did not?"

11 Yochanan chuckled and answered, "When I was a youth living in Gimron, an Egyptian priest came into the community. He stayed with us for three days and showed us some strange crystals, even those such as I delivered today to these priests that he was seeking. He said that if ever we were to find any crystals such as these, that his sect, which was in Memphis, would pay for them in gold.

12 In my wanderings after you had departed, I often journeyed far from the community. One day when I was in the wilderness, I came upon an area with many small holes in the rock ground. When I looked inside the holes, there were crystals all covered with dirt. I took all that I could easily reach.

13 Some days later, when I washed them with water and removed a dirt most difficult to get off, I saw that they were different than others I had seen, and I remembered the words of the Egyptian priest and kept them. When I came upon this journey with you, I knew I must take these crystals at some point to the priests at Memphis."

14 Yochanan had not sold all of his crystals to the Egyptians, and he placed one of the two rainbow crystals that he had retained in the hand of Yeshua and said, "I know not what use the Egyptians have for these stones, but they are pretty. I will keep one and give the other to you. Perhaps, you would like to give it to Miriam as a gift."

15 "Thank you, my brother," Yeshua replied. "You should know that the gift you give has more value than you think or even than the Egyptians understand. Nor is it because it is rare, for it is more common upon the earth than men realize.

16 Look then into the rainbow light when the sun is upon it after you have fasted for a day and hold the pure love of God within your heart with malice toward no man. Then call upon Elohim that you might understand that which is beyond your knowing. And the rainbow light will be about you, and you will be within it; and your spirit shall leave your body upon the earth and commune with God amongst all that is.

17 Verily, the rainbow crystals have no power unto their own, but they can help the Children of Light to find the peace and power of God within their heart, mind, and soul."

18 Yochanan was amazed by Yeshua's explanation of the uses of the rainbow crystals, and he said, "Had I known their worth, I would not have parted with them."

19 And Yeshua replied, "You have all that you need, my brother, and whatsoever you have need of in the days to come, Elohim will provide when you seek for a righteous purpose, with a true love and faith."

20 When they returned to their house, they greeted Miriam, and Yeshua showed her the rainbow crystal, which Yochanan had given to him. Miriam looked at Yochanan and gave a mischievous smile and pulled from her wrappings a golden string that hung about her neck. Upon the string, held in a gold wire, was a clear rainbow crystal just like the crystals of Yochanan.

21 And she said, "This was a present from Yeshua upon the day that we were married. It is most sacred to me and I do not show it to others, but I look upon it often, for it helps move my spirit to commune with the life of all the earth and all the heavens.

22 And in that moment, I am so close to God and at peace with my soul and all the world, and I know with a certainty that I am a daughter of the most high God and far more than this mortal body."

23 Then Yeshua returned to Yochanan the rainbow crystal, which he had given unto him, and said, "Thank you greatly for your generosity, but keep this crystal that you may give it to your wife soon to be, that she may have a portal to leave the world and commune with God. And keep the other that you may also have this portal to open the heavens in your times of need."

24 Yochanan protested weakly, saying, "But what of you, my brother? Shall I and my wife to be and Miriam, all have such a treasure and you have not?"

25 And Yeshua said, "The rainbow light surrounds me in my every breath, and the spirit of God communes with me in my every thought. Therefore, I have no need for that which already is in my soul."

CHAPTER 36

The Twelve Commandments

Lazarus returns to Egypt to do some more trading and announces his engagement; he wishes for Yochanan, Yeshua, Miriam, and their children to return with him. However, Yeshua says that he and Miriam must remain in Egypt, but Yochanan returns with Lazarus. Yeshua journeys frequently into the hills of the eastern desert, south of Memphis, to commune with his Heavenly Father and Mother, and he receives great revelations and understanding. It is on one such journey that he receives the Twelve Commandments of Sinai.

Yochanan decided to remain in Memphis with Yeshua and Miriam until God called him elsewhere. And Yeshua taught Yochanan some more of carpentry, and they created many fine things of wood, which they sold to the Egyptians.

2 Shortly after their arrival, they paid for a message to be carried in a caravan to Jerusalem that Miriam's family might know of their whereabouts, and it came to pass that ten moons after they had come to Memphis, Lazarus arrived at their home, having returned with another caravan. And in this trip, he had twelve camels of trade goods and several servants with him.

3 They had a two-day feast to celebrate the arrival of Lazarus and to hear the news of Bethany, not the least of which was Lazarus's announcement of his betrothal to Hannah, the daughter of Mordecai. And Miriam chided her older brother in a playful way for having waited so long to marry.

4 Lazarus remained with them in Memphis for one moon and had very successful trading while there.

5 At the beginning of the new moon, he told them that he must return again to Bethany and asked them to return with him, for Miriam's mother longed for her and her sister Martha also missed her greatly, and he wished for Yeshua and Yochanan to be at his wedding, which would take place as soon as he returned.

6 Yochanan felt moved by Elohim and agreed to return with Lazarus to Palestine, for he also desired a wife from among the tribe of Judah before he became an old man, and for that cause, he wished to call upon Martha, the sister of Miriam, and to see again his friends in the community of Gimron.

7 But Yeshua and Miriam remained in Memphis, and Yeshua said, "Our hearts and blessings go with you, but we must remain here for some seasons, for there is much still to learn and there are those who hunger for truth and light and we are the torchbearers."

8 And it came to pass that Lazarus and Yochanan departed from Memphis, and Yeshua and Miriam and the children remained for the greater purposes of God.

9 Yeshua journeyed frequently into the wilderness in the hills of the eastern desert, south of Memphis, to commune with his Celestine Father and Mother. Before he had returned to Judea, Yochanan sometimes accompanied him, and other times Miriam went with him, but more often he was alone.

10 On some trips, he would travel to the top of a mountain overlooking the sea. Seeing the world expanding in vastness beyond the horizon in every direction helped him more easily feel one in spirit with all creation.

11 Marvelous revelations and understandings came to Yeshua in great clarity from Elohim the Father and Mother in the emptiness of the wilderness, away from the clutter of people and the creations of man.

12 It was here, atop a mountain of the desert sea that Yeshua asked his Father if he would give again to the choicest children of men the Twelve Commandments which he had given unto Moses, but which Moses had destroyed because of the weakness of men.

13 Yeshua implored his Father, saying, "I know these are sacred laws, which only the righteous can live and receive the blessings thereof. And for lack of righteousness among the people, they have been held in the realms of Celestine Light.

14 But in my sojourn upon earth I have been blessed to be joined by some of the choicest of your spirit children. They are among the greatest of my brothers and sisters, sent here at this time to help bring forth the Celestine Light of truth. They are worthy to receive the higher laws and the greater blessings of heaven from obedience to the laws."

15 Elohim the Father replied to Yeshua, saying, "My beloved son, you know that whatsoever you desire, I will do for you. Therefore, you may give to the choice Children of Light, who are your friends and family, the higher laws of heaven. But let them keep them unto themselves while they first prove capable to live the greater laws and receive the greater blessings.

16 If they prove worthy of this blessing, then the Twelve Commandments shall abide because of them through the time of spiritual gestation in the world, to be revealed again in the latter days unto the royal generation, which I have saved to come forth upon the world in its time of greatest need.

17 So it shall be that when the Children of Light of the royal generation read the words of the Twelve Commandments, the greatness of the higher laws shall resonate in their hearts, and the Holy Spirit will stir their souls, and they will know that it is they who have been called to come forth to the wonder of the world in the last days of the old epoch and the first of the new. The world will see the brilliant Celestine Light of the Elohim made manifest in them, and will know with sureness that the light of the Almighty is among them."

18 Yeshua inscribed the words of the Twelve Commandments upon a scroll that his family and those who would become his Apostles might read them. But they remained unknown to the people of the world in the days of Yeshua and all the days that followed, until the time of the royal generation was upon the world.

19 Behold, rejoice and give thanks, for that time has come and this is the royal generation of which was spoken. This is the day blessed to have the pure Celestine Light of Elohim shine forth. Therefore, unto the chosen, those whose spirit persuades them to live the higher laws of God, herein are the Twelve Commandments of Elohim, given that the Children of Light might have fruitful and expansive relationships with God, with themselves, and with their brothers and sisters of light upon the world.

20 And these are the words that God speaks unto you who read these words, saying, "We are the Elohim, the Father, the Mother, and the Son, the Lord God Almighty, and by the power of our word, all that exists has been manifested.

21 Unto all who will receive it, we call you out of the world of darkness and give unto you a marvelous light.

22 And they who keep these commandments shall be blessed upon the earth and know us in their hearts and minds and moving upon their spirit."

1 Thank Elohim for all of your blessings from the depths of your heart and, with purity of purpose, ask for your righteous needs, with humility and integrity, and they shall be manifested unto you within the purposes of God.

2 You shall neither worship, nor pray to, nor venerate, false gods or graven images, or men or governments or kings, or spirits or angels, or anything or anyone that is, except Elohim.

3 You shall not curse or swear at all, or use the name of Elohim in vain, in any form, but cultivate a sweet disposition, wherein a curse is alien to your spirit.

4 Remember the Sabbath day, to keep it holy. Six days you may labor and do all of your work, but the seventh day is the day of Elohim. On that day, you shall not work, but gather together with the Children of Light that you might edify and uplift one another, and renew your covenants, and share knowledge of Elohim and of the paths of Celestine Light. Let this also be a day for the family to come together and commune with one another with full attention, to increase their bonds of fellowship and love. Let this also be a day to visit the temples of God: the mountains, the sea, the desert, the forests, and all the wonders Elohim has created for you; that you might reflect upon your journey, strengthen your family, and draw closer to the Celestine Light. And let this be a day of study and of prayer, of reflection and contemplation, of covenants, repentance, and recommitment, and of all wholesome things of rest and renewal, which uplift you and bring you closer to God and to your family.

5 You are a temple of God. Do not defile your temple inside or outside, but keep yourself clean and pure that the Celestine Light of Elohim may illuminate you.

6 You are an emissary of Elohim; strive to always be a worthy representative of the divine that others will see your good light and glorify God. Be humble in heart and rich in spirit. Do good deeds and be a peacemaker. Despise hypocrisy and a double tongue. Do not exalt yourself but give praise to others. Find the blessings in the trials that come upon you. Be slow to anger and quick to forgive. Be not joined with the haughty or arrogant, but befriend the righteous and the lowly. Judge not others and be tempered and balanced in your thoughts and actions. Do not raise your voice in unrighteous anger or instigate violence of word or deed. In all things, do unto others as you would have them do unto you.

7 You shall not covet, or be avaricious, or steal, or be dishonest, or take any unfair advantage of others; nor gather unto you wealth in the world beyond your needs. Give your excess for the building up of the kingdom of God and the Children of Light and store up for yourself treasures in Heaven, not on earth.

8 You shall not commit fornication, or adultery, or in any way be a corrupter of youth.

9 Love your neighbors and your brothers and sisters of light, even in all of their faults, even as Elohim loves you despite your weaknesses. Do generous and thoughtful things for your fellow travelers on the journey of life, as you would have them do for you. Do not bear false witness against them, or slander them, or gossip about them with others. If you have a grievance, go and speak in peace and kindness with them, not anger.

10 Honor your father and your mother as they have honored you with their time and sacrifice and nurturing. Love them all of their days, and when they are old, care for them as they have cared for you.

11 You shall not maim or murder, wherein you shall not grievously injure or take the life of anyone, save it be in defense of mortal attack upon you or your family or your home. Nor shall you kill to eat as food any animal, or bird, or creature of the sea that is of warm blood or nurtures its young, save it be in times of famine or pestilence, when food is not found in the garden and the storeroom is empty. Nor shall you join yourself to armies that bring war to other lands, but only to defend against a destroyer upon your land, and then only after every way of honorable peace has failed. And if it be that you must take a life for any of these causes, you shall make your heart right again with God with fasting and prayer and have a spirit of love and peace before you enter again into the house of God.

12 Be a good and faithful steward of the earth and with all of the creatures thereof. This beautiful world Elohim has given unto you that you might find all you have need of. Take the precious gift you have been given, protect it, magnify it, and pass on a greater gift to your posterity."

CHAPTER 37

Mystery of Moses

Yeshua reveals to the Egyptian merchant, Babuaten, that the brother of the pharaoh Akhenaten was the man the Hebrews know as Moses. Their father was the Egyptian pharaoh, Amenhotep III, and their mother was Queen Tiy, whose mother was a Nubian princess and whose father was a Hebrew. Their youngest brother was who we know today as "King Tut." Yeshua then tells the true story of Moses.

Nine moons had passed since the departure of Lazarus and Yochanan, and Yeshua and Miriam continued to live in the house Babuaten had offered them with their children. And they taught their children from an early age in the ways of God that as it was said by Solomon, "When they were old, they would not depart from them." They also taught them of the many good qualities of the lands of which they knew, including languages and history and cultures.

2 From time to time, Yeshua journeyed to the market to sell his creations to the merchants, but he did not sell directly to the people as he did not wish to spend so much time away from his wife and children.

3 And Yeshua and Miriam and the children did many things together and waxed strong as a family.

4 From time to time, Yeshua and Miriam and the children visited the home of Babuaten, and they were always greeted with great respect and gratitude. And Yeshua and Babuaten had many long discussions, concerning the ways of God, and thus, it was that Yeshua came to reveal a great secret that Elohim the Father had told unto him.

5 This came about when Babuaten said, "Yeshua, when you first came to my house, you invoked the name of Aten. It is no secret among my friends that I revered the ancient pharaoh Akhenaten and believed in the one god, Aten of the sun, which he proclaimed, and turned the soles of my shoes upon the multitude gods of Egypt.

6 "Yet when my daughter was healed, it was because my heart was softened to accept a greater truth and a greater god. I was moved by your words about the one true God, and I perceived that Aten was the glory of one sun, but Elohim was the glory of all the heavens.

7 "Now I realize that perhaps after all, Aten is just a false god.

8 My heart is therefore open, but my mind is still ignorant. I do not fully comprehend your words, and I am still somewhat vexed in my thoughts that the blood of Egypt runs in the veins of both Hebrews and Egyptians as you said. If you would be so kind, enlighten me."

9 Yeshua looked deeply into the eyes of Babuaten, for he was moved by the depth of his thoughts.

10 Many others were also present, including Miriam and the wife of Babuaten as well as his older sons and a priest of Ra and two wealthy merchants who were friends of Babuaten. By now, all of the friends and family of Babuaten knew of the miraculous healing, which Yeshua had done, and most were followers of the religion of Aten, but they were also open to hear the words, which Yeshua would speak of the Almighty God that had wrought the miracle.

11 And Yeshua said unto them, "My friends, listen closely, for upon the foundations of this truth is a path to everlasting brotherhood between the Children of Israel and the Children of Egypt, if they will receive it.

12 You know somewhat of the history of the pharaoh Akhenaten and now you shall know more; for this has my Father in Heaven revealed to me: The man you know as the pharaoh Akhenaten was the brother of the man the Children of Israel know as Moses, the lawgiver.

13 The brothers were neither Egyptian nor Israelite, but both and more, for they and their elder brother and a younger brother, which came much later, were the sons of Amenhotep III, an Egyptian pharaoh of pure blood, and Queen Tiy, whose mother was a Nubian princess and whose father was Yosef, who spoke for a pharaoh, and he was a mighty Hebrew through the loins of Yakov."

14 There was a great amazement among the Egyptians at the words of Yeshua, for they shook the world which they all thought they knew.

15 And Yeshua said, "And often the queen dwelt in the land of Goshen among the Hebrews, in the palace of Zarw, and it is here that Moses was born as royalty of Egypt.

16 Just before his birth, his eldest brother was slain by Amun priests. His mother and father knew not the cause of the disappearance of their older son, but they were suspicious of the priests and feared for the lives of their newborn and of his brother.

17 In truth, many of the priests continued to be angry because of Queen Tiy, the chief wife of the pharaoh, feeling she polluted his thoughts with the beliefs of the Nubians and the Hebrews.

18 The pharaoh and his queen determined they must take action to protect the royal lineage. Therefore, in the darkness of the night, Queen Tiy had her infant taken by boat beyond the walls of Zarw and given into the safekeeping of her family dwelling in the land of Goshen.

19 When it became known that the infant was missing, the priests sent forth spies among the people of Egypt, trying to determine what had happened to the newborn son of Queen Tiy, for they desired to kill him rather than chance that a kingdom of Egypt might someday be founded upon the son of a Nubian Hebrew.

20 But they found him not, for the child was kept safely hidden among the Hebrews for several years and was never permitted to enter into any of the major cities of Egypt.

21 When he was of an age to begin his education, he was sent to Heliopolis to live and train in secret with members of the queen's family.

22 During this time, his brother Amenophis would sometimes visit his relatives at Goshen and then secretly be sent to Heliopolis to receive training with his younger brother.

23 During these infrequent visits, Amenophis was quickened by the concept of the one God taught by his Hebrew relatives and his younger brother. But rather than accept the truth of Elohim the one Almighty God in fullness and purity, he was moved in his thoughts to adorn the one true God with aspects of Egyptian religious beliefs and ritual.

24 Thus, he fashioned a god to his liking that was neither Hebrew nor Egyptian, but his.

25 When he was of age, he appeared in Memphis, taking the name of his father, Amenhotep, and he gained the right to ascend to the throne when he married his half sister Nefertiti.

26 He was then named co-regent by his father Amenhotep III and became known as Amenhotep IV.

27 And the wicked priests of Amun were exceedingly angry at the pharaoh Amenhotep III, because he had made his half-breed son co-regent.

28 And that which they most feared soon came to pass, for not long after his appointment, Amenhotep IV began to erect temples to the God of his creation, whom he called Aten of the

sun.

29 Though Aten was entirely created from the mind of Amenhotep IV, there still remained some of the foundations of truth, for among the secret rites of the followers of Aten, it was made known that the sun was merely a point of light in the crown of the God of all the earth and all the stars in the sky. And this was never said to be Aten, but was left for each believer to ascertain its meaning. Is it not even so today?"

30 Babuaten and his brethren nodded their heads in agreement, perplexed that Yeshua could know the inner secrets of their religion. But still they did not understand that which he was plainly saying. And one of the men with Babuaten said, "What has this to do with the god of the Hebrews?"

31 And Yeshua said, "Verily, I say unto you even as the pharaoh Akhenaten was the brother of the man known as Moses by the Hebrews, so has your worship of Aten laid the foundation in your heart and mind to find and know the one true God of all the suns and stars and earths. This Almighty Lord is Elohim, the God of the Hebrews. Verily, this is the very god which the pharaoh Akhenaten learned of among his mother's people when he was young."

32 Then one of the visitors of Babuaten objected to the words of Yeshua and said unto him, "You are sticking a dagger in our hearts to say that Aten is not the true god we believe and that Akhenaten was not the greatest of all pharaohs and a man of inspired faith as we believe."

33 And Yeshua answered unto them, "Though Akhenaten erred in substance, he was blessed for bringing his followers closer to the truth than any in Egypt had ever been. His heart was filled with righteousness for his family and his followers and his sincere belief in Aten. In his mind were many truths, and he vowed to always walk the path of light, regardless of the consequences.

34 Because of his example and the good that he taught, those who followed him became better than they were, which thing is always pleasing unto God.

35 But great unrest was caused by the actions of Akhenaten, and exceedingly wroth were the priests of Amun. Therefore, his mother asked him to relocate to a place dedicated to no other gods where he might build his temples as he desired.

36 Thus, it was that he came unto a land dedicated to no other gods and built a large new city with great monuments of stone to mark its boundaries. To this place, his followers came to have fulfillment to worship as they would.

37 And many Hebrews came to live in the city built by Akhenaten, for within it, they were given the peace and freedom to worship in the ways of their fathers under the protection of Akhenaten.

38 Upon the death of his father, Akhenaten became the ruler of all Egypt, and he forbid the worship of any god but Aten, except for the Hebrews, who were allowed to continue in their ways, worshiping the one god as they desired.

39 He commanded his soldiers to close the temples to all other gods of Egypt and to remove their names from the buildings and to put the priests of the false gods into the street and to confiscate their estates.

40 With these commands, anger grew among the soldiers, for many worshipped the old gods and paid homage at the temples; and it came to pass that the generals rose up against Akhenaten and forced him into exile in the Sinai along with his followers who would not repudiate Aten, and a relative was given to rule in his stead.

41 And it came to pass that Moses, the younger brother of Akhenaten, who had remained in obscurity, living in contentment among the Hebrews, came to him in the desert.

42 For many days, the two brothers spoke, for Akhenaten was stricken with grief for having lost his kingdom so soon after losing his wives Nefertiti and Kaya and others of his family to a plague.

43 He gave Moses his royal scepter and told him to go and be pharaoh of Egypt as it was his right, but Moses refused to do this.

44 And Akhenaten became sorrowful unto despair, and soon after, he died.

45 His body was returned to the city which he built, but thereafter in Egypt, it was punishable by death to mention the name of Akhenaten in the lands of the pharaoh and his city of the sun was let to fall to ruin and his name was wiped from the monuments throughout the land of Egypt.

46 When the priests of the old Egyptian religions came to power once more, they heard rumors of a forgotten brother of Akhenaten and sought to find him. But God warned Moses and he departed deep into the Sinai, and the Egyptians searched no more for him for a time, thinking he was only a myth or, if a real man, one of no consequence.

47 But many of the Hebrews found him in the Sinai as did many of the Egyptians who still worshipped Aten.

48 But the followers of Moses in Egypt desired to have the priests and generals continue to think of him as a myth of a wishful people and, therefore, only spoke of him in secret by saying MS, which was to mean, the rightful son or heir.

49 There was another brother, the youngest yet, who had also been born to Queen Tiy. A couple of years after the death of Akhenaten, the priests of Egypt put him on the throne for he was only a young boy whom they could control, and thus Egypt returned completely to the ways of old.

50 But he grew into a young man with thoughts of his own, and their control lessened. And it came to pass that he was poisoned in the dark of the night, not to death, but to sickness. And his leg was broken while he was in delirium to hasten his death by what would seem to be natural causes.

51 And then, because they believed in the one true God, the Hebrews that remained in Egypt began to be greatly persecuted.

52 After a time, this came unto the ears of Moses, who had dwelt for almost forty years with his followers in the Sinai. And Moses felt compelled by God to do what he could to save his Hebrew kinsfolk from the persecutions of the Egyptians.

53 The reign of two pharaohs had passed since the death of his younger brother who had been given the throne two years after the death of Akhenaten, and Moses decided that he must leave the wilderness and claim the throne of Egypt to save the Hebrews.

54 As he walked back into Egypt, word was quickly carried across the land that the true successor to Akhenaten and a son of Amenhotep III was coming to claim the throne. And many vowed to find and kill him, but many others came unto him, both Hebrews and Egyptians, to be one with him.

55 Then he came unto the palace of General Pa-Rameses in Zarw, even as he was preparing to assume the throne, and Moses revealed himself to be the brother of Akhenaten and the son of Amenhotep and Tiy. Moses carried the royal scepter of power, which had been given unto him by Akhenaten. And there was much confusion among the priests and wise men as to who should be pharaoh.

56 Therefore, a great meeting was called to determine whether Moses or Pa-Rameses should claim the throne of Egypt. And Moses showed the priests and wise men his royal scepter and revealed to them secret rituals which only the Pharaoh and high priest could know, which Akhenaten had told unto him in the Sinai. And they were convinced and prostrated themselves before him and acknowledged that only he could be the rightful pharaoh.

57 But the soldiers of Egypt answered only to Pa-Rameses and with their power, they put Moses out, and Pa-Rameses took the throne of Egypt and called himself Rameses I.

58 Then there was no place in Egypt for Moses and his followers, and they began to be persecuted greatly. Therefore, Moses sought to depart the boundaries of Egypt, but Rameses would not permit him or those who followed him to leave, for he wanted them to remain under his subjugation.

59 Moses pleaded to Elohim in prayer to deliver his people from the persecutions of Rameses. And Elohim heard the voice of Moses and loved Moses for his goodness.

60 And it came to pass that seven dreadful plagues fell upon the land of Egypt. And each was foretold by Moses to Rameses, and before each, he asked Rameses to allow those who wished to follow him to peacefully depart from Egypt. And each time, Rameses refused.

61 Upon the last, the son of Rameses perished even as Moses had foretold, and at last, the pharaoh Rameses bowed down to the power of the one true God and let Moses depart with his followers, both the Hebrews and the Egyptians.

62 Then Moses led the people across the shore of the desert sea and across the swamps, north of the sea, so the chariots of the pharaoh could not easily follow. Upon the low tide, the sea suddenly retreated farther from the shore than any could remember as the people of Moses finished passing across it.

63 But when Moses and his followers had been gone from the sight of Rameses, the pharaoh conceived a great anger at Moses for the dreadful plagues that had befallen Egypt and for the death of his son.

64 In his anger, he called forth the armies of Egypt to pursue the Israelites and Egyptians who followed Moses and to slay them, every one.

65 Even as the last of the people of Moses came to the far shore of the sea, the army of the pharaoh was fast behind them, crossing near the sandy edge of the receded sea that they might gain ground on those who had crossed when the sea was higher.

66 But the wisdom of Moses and the power of God was manifested. When the mounted army of the pharaoh was racing upon the smooth sand, the wheels of their chariots slowed and wallowed in it. And while they were thus mired the waters of the sea came quickly upon them in a great wave and swallowed them all.

67 But Moses knew that pharaoh would come again to attack the Children of Light. One of his leaders, an Egyptian named Hamadi, counseled that they should hasten to Gaza to conquer and fortify it, that they might have a city to defend when the armies of pharaoh came upon them.

68 But God spoke into the ear of Moses and told him that they must hasten south into the Sinai. When Moses revealed the counsel of Elohim, the Egyptians were not desirous to flee into the wilderness, nor did they see how the food of the wilderness could support such a large number of people. And many of the Hebrews agreed with the Egyptians.

69 Therefore, they divided into two groups with the Children of Israel and some Egyptians taking a trail into the south of the Sinai, and the greater number of Egyptians and some Hebrews following the road to Gaza.

70 But before the Egyptians and Hebrews who marched to Gaza could take the city, a son of Rameses led an army of Egypt against them at many places on the road to Gaza, and they were utterly destroyed.

71 Moses and the Children of Israel and those Egyptians who came with them wandered many years in the wilderness of the Sinai, and Moses communed with God in the great emptiness.

72 And it was in the Sinai that God gave Moses the Twelve Commandments to Happiness and Exaltation inscribed on stone by the finger of God, but the Children of Israel were not worthy of such a gift, for they had become idolatrous and adulterous and cared not what they ate or what they drank.

73 Therefore, Moses broke the commandments upon the ground, and they became as dust. And the wicked people, who remembered not the God who had delivered them from pharaoh, created Ten Commandments that were easier to live, whereby they could find peace amongst them.

74 And the Twelve Commandments whereby they could know God, and find the God within themselves, were taken from the earth, nor will they be given again until a more righteous generation shall come forth in the last epoch.

75 Verily, the words I have given unto you are for a great cause that you might come to desire to know the one true God, the magnificent God of all light, and know that we are brothers in spirit and blood, and never should the Children of Israel and the children of Egypt be enemies,

for there is more that unites us than divides us.
76 Now I declare unto you with the power of God that is in me that the light you have known in the beliefs you have held is but a glimmer of the brilliance that waits for you.
77 It is only as far as your knees to the ground, in humble supplication with a sincere desire to know the truth, a mind open to discover it, and a heart willing to accept it.
78 If you shall ask of Elohim to know if my words are true, then the spirit of Elohim will enter your heart and fill you with a marvelous expansion of light such as you have never known, and in that, you will have a firm knowledge of truth and open your life to receive cherished blessings that endure beyond the span of days."

CHAPTER 38

Sojourn with the Nubians

Yeshua, Miriam, and their children travel to the community of Kush, along the Nile, to live among the Nubians for some seasons. Yeshua and Miriam teach them about Elohim, the one true God, and many abandon the beliefs of the Egyptians. Yeshua has a keen interest in all things, and one day, he goes with a group of Nubians to watch how they fish and gather food. A youth foolishly gathers some crocodile eggs and is attacked and maimed by the crocodile that was guarding the nest. Yeshua calmly approaches the crocodile and soothes it, allowing everyone to escape carrying Suhen, who is near death, with them. Yeshua then miraculously heals Suhen, and great is the wonder among the Nubians.

And it came to pass that from time to time, Yeshua and Miriam and their children left their home at Memphis to journey up the Nile and into the desert and wilderness beyond the Nile, sometimes for many moons, to commune with God and to learn of other people and cultures.

2 On these journeys, Yeshua always sought out the priests and leaders of the area to speak with. And some turned him away in scorn, but others taught him of their beliefs in openness.

3 He forgave those who scorned him, but they received no blessing. But those who welcomed him, he blessed with a greater understanding of truth and sometimes with small miracles.

4 It was perilous for one small family to travel alone. And many were the times when bandits thought to attack and rob or enslave them. But always the hand of God was upon them and protected them, and never did any evil befall them.

5 In his travels into the wilderness, Yeshua came to know the animals that roamed the earth as friends. And he loved them as great as he loved the little children, for they were innocent and pure in his eyes. And he learned to speak to them in their minds and touch their hearts with his.

6 And many were the soldiers or robbers or slavers who thought to do harm to Yeshua and his family, only to flee in terror when the crocodile rose from the banks of the Nile to defend him, or the Lion bounded into their midst, or the eagle dropped from the sky upon them. For wherever he walked, the animals who were his friends looked upon him with gladness and greeted him and protected him and his family.

7 As Yeshua went among the towns and villages of the Nubians of Kush, near the first cataract of the Nile, his heart was glad for their simple ways and the honesty of their feelings, as there was no guile in them.

8 And it came to pass that Yeshua and Miriam and the children lived among the Nubians of the first cataract for some seasons and learned of their culture and the ways of their beliefs. And they spoke often with their matriarchs and their elders.

9 Yeshua and Miriam taught the Nubians the ways of Elohim, the one true God. And many Nubians began to follow the ways of Elohim and abandoned the gods of the Egyptians and of the sun and of the Moon and of the stars, for Yeshua and Miriam taught them that Elohim was the God of all that is and even the very light of the sun and the stars came forth from Elohim.

10 As Yeshua had taught Babuaten the true history of the pharaoh Akhenaten in like manner he taught the Nubians how the grandmother of the pharaoh Akhenaten was a Nubian and how his younger brother lived among the Hebrews in Goshen and came to be known as Moses and led the followers of the one true God to a land of promise.

11 And it came to pass that Yeshua was continually curious about the ways of the Nubians and one day asked to go with a group of men in small boats on the Nile to catch fish and gather water plants for food.

12 Thus, it was that Yeshua left in the company of eight Nubians and came to the banks of the Nile, where they launched themselves into the river in three boats.

13 Two of the boats spent the morning fishing, both by spear and net, and also harvested fish in large traps set in the river shoals and by basket dangled from the boat. The third boat, in which Yeshua rode, used the trunks of young trees cut with several curled roots at one end as rakes to pull up edible plants from the bottom of the river shoals.

14 Yeshua had a keen interest in everything that he saw and engaged the two Nubians in his boat with many questions.

15 At noonday, the three boats pulled up on shore in a tall grassy area underneath a large palm tree to have a meal. Some of the men had brought food with them, and others began preparing some of the fish and plants they had gathered during the morning.

16 The youngest among them was a youth of about sixteen years by the name of Suhen, and he went off some distance from the shore, it was assumed, to attend to private matters. But he quickly returned with great excitement, holding some large eggs and saying, "Look, look, I have found a crocodile nest full of eggs; come quick and let us harvest them before the mother returns."

17 Yeshua made to caution them to say that it was not wise or respectful to steal the unhatched young from a mother's nest, but as a group, they were so excited about the find that they had all run into the grass to raid the nest before he could say a word.

18 He followed slowly after them, pondering what lesson he could teach them. Suddenly, there was a most awful scream of terror and then the cries of many men. Yeshua rushed forward to find that the mother crocodile had returned, and she was larger by thrice than the largest man.

19 With movements of amazing speed that would not be thought possible from such a short-legged and heavy creature, she attacked all around her as she defended her nest.

20 The Nubians tried to mount a defense with their spears, but none could find the mark upon the swift moving crocodile. She knocked several to the ground with powerful sweeps of her thick tail, and the young man who had first discovered the nest had already been caught in her powerful jaws and lay limp on the ground, bleeding and severely mauled.

21 Then into the chaos and fear walked Yeshua, as placid as a summer morning. And he called upon the Nubians to move back into the tall grass and to stand perfectly still.

22 The crocodile saw him as he moved toward her and rushed forward to rend him, but Yeshua stood calmly and opened his arms wide, with his palms facing forward and held at the height of his waist. With a lurch, the crocodile stopped still in its attack, but continued to swing its tail back and forth ominously. Then its tail came to rest, and it began to move its body up and down on its short legs.

23 After a few minutes, the crocodile settled down upon its belly and lay still, and Yeshua came up to it and put his hand upon its head. And the crocodile opened wide its mouth, showing its many large teeth, sharp like daggers. But it did not bite Yeshua.

24 He called then the men to come and take the wounded youth and return to the boats. In haste, they did as he bid, and all left save one named Takka, who remained standing still in the

grass. And he saw Yeshua sit down beside the large head of the crocodile and put his arm around its neck.

25 And thus Yeshua remained for several minutes, communing with the most feared creature of Egypt and giving his peace unto her, and then he and Takka returned to the men who were waiting for him at the boats; and they had feared that perhaps the two had been eaten by the crocodile.

26 Suhen, the young man that had been mauled, was near death and bleeding from many wounds. Yeshua came up to him and, kneeling beside him, began to move his hands all across his body but without touching him. Then he placed his hands upon his head and said, "Father, forgive this man, his youthful carelessness and thoughtlessness. If it be your will, I ask you to heal his body and restore his health."

27 Upon his words, the eyes of Suhen opened, and he called to his friends.

28 Then Yeshua called upon the men to quickly gather mud and to thickly cover his body with it insomuch that he could not even move. And they did as he bid.

29 Four men then carried him and lowered him into a boat, and then they all cast off their boats into the river and hurried to return to their community.

30 As they traveled, the clay began to dry upon the body of Suhen in the hot sun, and Yeshua bade the Nubians to let it remain upon him as they returned in the boats to their village.

31 Upon their return, there was great commotion in the town as word of what had happened was quickly passed from one to another.

32 Yeshua instructed that Suhen remain in the mud for three days, with new mud placed on him whenever the dried fell off, and to be given only a tea made from particular plants which he showed to them. After three days, all the mud was removed, and his wounds were completely healed. Seeing this miracle, one such as they had never supposed possible, the Nubians praised God for the wonder and looked to Yeshua in awe.

27 A house built with love cannot fall, even though a foe may come and throw down every stone, for the house of love is not within the walls of stone, but within the hearts of those who love; and even when parted, the house of love is not broken, and its power is undimmed; therefore, great things are yet to be, and it will find itself again.

28 But a house without love is forever destroyed from within; and when its walls fall, it is a blessing, for it is an end to the misery.

29 Verily, I say unto you, while the house without love stands, it is a curse upon all who dwell therein, for where the family should be growing like the good tree with proper amounts of sun and water and nourishment, instead it is withering like the plant springing up in the desert only to slowly die without water under the endless heat.

30 Now it has been your custom for the rich among you to take many wives and to have children of them, and this is counted as something worthy of the rich but not of the poor.

31 And it has been the man who chooses his wives, without regard for love, but only for what value they can bring to his house of which he is the master.

32 Thus are the wives little more than the beasts of the field that are bought at a price and bred.

33 In truth, the custom of marrying many women to one man has brought many ills upon your homes, not because of the custom, which is blessed of God if fulfilled according to his word, but because of how the custom has been carried out, which has not been in the ways of God.

34 Therefore, hear my words, which God has spoken unto me, whereby you might know how to more fully live that which you practice; that it might be a blessing upon you and not a curse.

35 Verily, I say unto you that in any form of marriage, it is pleasing unto God that there is first love between a man and a woman; that the fruit of their loins will grow up with love; that they may become balanced Children of Light; that the Celestine Light of God may shine forth from them and do good in the world.

36 In a plural marriage blessed by God, all wives must be equal, and the husband is not the master, but the servant, who heads the family in righteousness as God has decreed, but acquiesces to his wives in all things whatsoever they desire of him, concerning the home or the fulfillment of relationships.

37 And I say unto you that among the Children of Light, the man may not choose his wife, except his first, who has also chosen him, for it is not the man who will live the most with his wives, for he will be often gone on the business of men, but it is the wives who must live one with another.

38 For the wives are married to each other as surely as the man is married to each of them. In this, you should understand that a plural marriage is not one man married separately and individually to more than one woman, but one man and multiple women united together in a single marriage, one to all.

39 Therefore, let no man take another wife, save it be that his first wife and later his other wives have chosen a new wife for him, whom they are of one accord should be joined unto their family, for they do love her and desire her to be among them, and she does love and desire to be among them.

40 Only then may the man seek to know closely the woman whom his other wives have chosen, and then he should speak deeply with her on numerous occasions to discover if a love for her can also dwell within his heart and she to see if a love for him can also dwell in hers; and if it is so, then they may marry.

41 And a family of multiple wives so given is meant by God to be a blessing, whereby men and women can expand their lights and increase their capacities for love and goodness and become even more as God is.

42 Therefore, let no man or woman enter into a marriage of multiple wives save they are humble and worthy souls who are honest and virtuous Children of Light that walk uprightly before God and have proven by their lives that they walk a path of righteousness.

43 For this cause, the marriage of one goodly man to one or two or three goodly wives is pleasing unto God if lived in righteousness and is often necessary for the glory of the Children of Light, for since the beginning of time, there have been more righteous and virtuous women than men. Therefore, if all virtuous women are to have children from worthy fathers and mates that inspire and encourage them to expand their light, there must needs be families of multiple wives.

44 And it will ever be so, for it is the nature of men that they are more easily drawn into the ways of evil and are not worthy of the women who would have them, even as it is the blessed nature of women that they are more desirable of the ways of God and must look long and far to find a man worthy of their love and devotion.

45 And for the righteous Children of Light to have the greatest opportunity to expand their own light, they must be in close daily relationships with others whose lights shine bright, for their lights magnify each other.

46 Verily, this opportunity is greatly present within the walls of a family with a righteous husband and virtuous wives, where all have chosen each other for the light that they bring, and all practice virtues taught by God that their house may be a house of love and harmony and growth and expansion, beyond which they could otherwise gain.

47 But among those who are not virtuous and do not obey the teachings of God, this holy union should not be sanctioned, for among the lustful or among those who would practice it unrighteously, polygamy is condemned; verily, among the unworthy, it is a sin and an abomination before God.

48 Nor should any of fertile age enter into this covenant of marriage unless it gives them greater security and time for the desires of their life, as well as greater love.

49 And I say unto you that in any marriage, God commands that man and woman not create life until they have the ability to provide for the temporal and spiritual needs of their children, without squalor or charity.

50 And how shall you know this? Verily, I say unto you: A home of worthy parents gives health and happiness to the children, good food in their bellies each day, teaches them well in the knowledge of men and to walk uprightly before God.

51 So too does a home of worthy parents provide adequately for their children from their livelihood, and not from charity, beyond support of the loving circle of their greater family when in unusual need.

52 Verily, to bear and raise children is among the greatest joys of life and the first commandment of God to the children of men. Therefore, may all desire and make efforts to be worthy in every way of this great calling.

53 Again, I say unto you: Among those worthy Children of Light, who have chosen to be joined to each other in plural marriage, let the husband and all of the wives and all of the children live together in one house with private rooms for each wife or adjacent groups of houses.

54 Verily, they are one family, not many, and for this cause, their goals and desires and their habits of living must be harmonious, and their love for one another be deep and true. And without this order of living, many blessings of the marriage of melding are lost.

55 For this cause, let no man have a wife and children that dwell in a community be removed from his other wives and children, for if they cannot be one family with love and common purpose, they are not prepared to enter into the melded marriage that has great rewards, but also requires greater compassion and unity and selflessness.

56 "For most, it is better that there is only one wife and one husband, that all of their love and care may be focused and undivided on each other and their children, as is their need.

57 And this is not dishonor, nor is it based upon lack of wealth or righteousness, for a relationship of two is sufficient unto itself, with all the blessings of Heaven given if they obey the teachings of God.

58 Verily, God does not bless plural marriage with any greater blessings because of the form of marriage than that of one man and one woman. But a union of many can demand less of the

time of each person, and in spiritual ways, it may give more opportunities for those that choose it to grow and expand from the challenges it offers.

59 And I say unto you, let no couple of fertile age seek to expand their marriage to include more wives until they have proven faithful and nurturing in a union of two.

60 Verily, let it be only when they have mastered love and devotion and respect to each other for at least five years and proven to expand the others light and shown diligence and devotion as parents.

61 For I say unto you, as great are the efforts needed to be a worthy mate to one other, greater still are the needs for a union of three or more that all may be loved and nurtured and grow into the light that is their birthright.

62 Therefore, plural marriage is only for those who have great capacities to love, who are comfortable with themselves, who are self-assured and know their own worth, who are not selfish or self-centered, and who thrive more in community than in solitude.

63 And let no man take more than three wives unless it is under special circumstances and approved by the community leaders. For within this number, it is easy to have love and be one as a family, if that is the goal of all who have by their own desire entered into it.

64 But with more than three wives and their children, it becomes a greater challenge, for the love and the time that needs to be given are divided among too many.

65 Therefore, with the second wife as with the first, prove the union of three by five years of growth and harmony before a third wife is considered.

66 And let no man take as a wife one who is still a girl and cannot yet know her own mind or heart, but only a woman, fully blossomed and acknowledged by all as an adult, free to make her own decisions without coercion.

67 And let no woman marry a man unless she knows his heart and mind and finds it in harmony with hers and that a love for him flows through her.

68 And let no man marry the daughter of any of his wives.

69 And let no man take a wife of fertile age if he is not young enough to expect to live to be a grandfather to the children of their union.

70 And let no man take a wife who is not at least seven years older than his oldest child.

71 And let no woman enter into a marriage of multiple wives unless she feels as strongly for the other wives as she does for the man.

72 And let no marriage with multiple wives be dissolved except for the case of adultery or abuse, and then it is the responsibility of the wife's parents' family to care for her; but the children should continue to be cared for and joined to the family they have been a part of and their mother allowed to remain involved in their lives.

73 And if a man who is married to one woman dies and she has children, and if she desires, let the kinsmen of the deceased who are married, speak with his wife, and let her choose from among them whom she can love and whose wives she can love and whom she will marry, and then is it his responsibility to marry her and care for her and her children, that the children may continue to have a man of their blood to be a father unto them and receive the full inheritance of their family.

74 But when a man dies who has two or more wives and they have children and financial wherewithal, let them remain married unto themselves as wives and know no man, but let them be kept under the protection of the house of a kinsmen of their husband and be of good service to that house, that their children may continue to have a man of their blood to be a father unto them and from their mothers receive the full inheritance that their birth father would have given them.

75 And if a man dies who is married to one or more women and any among them have no children, let those without children seek to find love and a new marriage from among whom they will.

76 And let no man so blessed as to have multiple wives ever be unfaithful to them. And if a

man is so foolish, let his wives decide his punishment both public and private, but not before the children, even until he has proved his humility and contriteness and restored the trust that was lost.

77 And some among you may say that this is too insulting to the man, but I say unto you that it is vital for the continued health of the family.

78 Verily, the light of the family is greater than the dignity of the man and that which is sown in unfaithfulness reaps a whirlwind, which can only be tamed with a contrite heart and humble service.

79 Verily, I say unto you: If you follow these sayings, you shall become a mighty people, and the God of the heavens and the earth shall smile upon you and bless you with great blessings, even more than you can hold.

80 If virtue and righteousness before God are the foundations, then a family of plural marriage has many rewards.

81 For families thus joined will be able to divide the many tasks among the many members, thus will all have more time unto themselves and greater opportunity to expand their light.

82 And wives who come after the first will know with more certainty the life they are entering, for they will have the opportunity to have seen the worthiness of the man and see the fruits that have already blossomed.

83 And wives who came before the others will have no concern about the continued love and faithfulness of their husband even beyond their childbearing years. For why would he be tempted outside his home to risk all that he has, when the daughters of light who come after were given unto him by those that preceded?

84 And the wicked deceits that are so prevalent in the world find no place in the sanctity of a righteous house of multiple wives.

85 For those sins are only in the world, where a man lusts and cleaves unto a woman who is not his wife and thus destroys his family and all trust.

86 And it is only in the world where man's adulterous misuses of the sacred power of creation leaves children without a father to survive as they will.

87 And only in the world does a man shamefully use a woman as a mistress, giving neither her, nor their children, legal rights or recourse.

88 But in the righteous home of plural marriage all wives and children are given their full inheritance and blessed with all the protections of the law.

89 And the wives of one man are always there for each other, and their hearts are not led astray to bring dishonor upon their house; verily, they do not experience the longings of loneliness when their husband is away, for their sisters are ever with them.

90 And think not that a marriage of multiple wives is only to have a multitude of children in a home of light. It is also given to a man and women beyond the years of bearing children to unite together for love and greater growth and light.

91 And within the family of multiple wives, the goodly talents of each may be of benefit to one another, and by their forged efforts, they increase the wealth and security of the family.

92 But I say unto you that plural marriage is reserved only for the righteous and only for those who feel they can grow and expand more in that covenant than in the covenant of one man and one woman.

93 And only a stalwart and dependable man should enter into a family with multiple wives, one who will love all his wives and their children with overflowing zeal and outward demonstration and take responsibility for their spiritual and temporal well-being.

94 For such men are not inclined to sow their seed beyond their wives, and they bring no children into the world that have not a loving father and loving mothers and sisters and brothers to help them expand their light.

95 Nor can a man who is joined to multiple wives ever falsely seduce another woman, for all know that his covenant to his wives only permits his attentions to those whom his wives have

chosen.

96 And a family of multiple wives increases the worth of every other woman, for when one man has many wives, the value of those who are still unmarried are like precious pearls, for they have become rarer and thereby even more desired by men seeking wives."

97 And then it was that Yeshua gave a solution to the problem that vexed the prince of Nubia.

98 And Yeshua said unto him, "Unto you, because of the purpose of uniting the people of the first cataract with the people of the third through this marriage, if your Council of Elders approves, and you vow to be a righteous husband with attentiveness and forbearance, it will be sanctioned by God for you to take a fifth wife, but this only if she loves you and that you love her and only if your other wives also love her and desire her to be numbered among your family.

99 And a marriage based upon the godly principles I have spoken shall not falter, and it will provide you strong sons and daughters that will honor you and be lights to their family and to all the people of the first and third cataracts and even to the lands beyond. Is this not a goal worthy of your efforts?"

100 The prince was amazed by the words Yeshua had spoken and all the people as well.

101 And the prince said unto him, "Never have the words of man ever touched my heart as the words which you have spoken have touched mine.

102 Were our people to do as you say, it would change our traditions. We already honor women who have power and position, but you would have us give honor to all virtuous women, even unto the right to choose their husband's wives. This is the strangest of ideas, but my heart tells me it is true and will bring great things to our people. Therefore, I will do as you have said, but I know not how to do it."

103 Yeshua embraced the prince, which also was not custom, but the prince returned his embrace. And Yeshua said unto him, "Already by your actions, I know you have risen greatly in the esteem of Qalta. Perhaps, your family can remain for a moon that she and your wives may get to know one another. And if their lights are harmonious, then perhaps they will be desirous for you to seek her out to see whether your lights also shine brighter when together.

104 And if it is so, then you can know of certainty that your union will be blessed and the light of your family expanded."

105 And so it was that the prince and his wives did as Yeshua directed, and upon the new moon, the prince married Qalta before her family and Yeshua and Miriam. And in the name of the Holy Father and Mother and Son, Yeshua blessed the union.

106 And upon the new day, the prince and his family departed south to the land of the third cataract, and Yeshua and Miriam and their children began the journey back to Memphis.

107 And great were the tears of many of the Nubians as they departed, but Yeshua promised that to all who were faithful to Elohim, his words and his spirit would always be with them and the blessings of Heaven would pour out upon them.

CHAPTER 41

Miriam's Query

Miriam questions Yeshua about polygamy, seeking further understanding. Yeshua speaks of future events of which Miriam has not yet come to terms with, but Yeshua imparts some words of wisdom to give her some solace. Yeshua teaches Miriam to whistle as a means to bring joy and happiness.

As Yeshua and Miriam journeyed back to Memphis, Miriam desired to know more concerning the things that Yeshua had said to the prince, and she told him, "My beloved, my love for you runs through everything I am. I cannot conceive how it could be that I could ever love another woman enough that I would desire to share you with her, yet I long to be a goodly wife and I ever strive to be a faithful daughter of light. I am torn and seek your wisdom.

2 Yeshua stopped walking and took Miriam into his arms. He sat down upon a rock with Miriam nestled beside him, and while the children played, he spoke thus to Miriam, "You are the light, Miriam, that lifts me every morning when I wake and gives me joy every night as I feel you next to me and hear your sweet voice as the last sounds before I sleep.

3 Know that you fulfill me in every way, and I expand each day because the brightness of your light is upon me. With you, my cup overflows and never would I need or seek another, for in you, my joy is full. And if ever such a thing were to come to pass, it would be because of your desire for it to be so.

4 If that moment were ever to come, you would know it without doubt and would be greatly desirous of it. If you never know such a thing without doubt or great desire, it is because you need it not.

5 In the kingdom of Heaven, there are far more who will never walk that path than there are those who will, and yet their light is as bright as any of the stars of Heaven.

6 In our lives, we have always fulfilled one another. Countless times have we prayed together and felt the power of our Father and the Mother touch our spirits and had their words written upon our hearts. You are a part of me, you know me as no other can, and you know the true depth of my calling in life as much as I do; therefore, you know that the time soon comes when I must give myself fully to the world and who then will comfort you?

7 Our days of bliss and endless time together are even now drawing to a close, for we must return soon to the land of Palestine, and among the Children of Israel, I must be about my Heavenly Father's business.

8 You cannot find that which you do not seek. But if the time comes that your heart has a place of emptiness, know the sign of the time and know that it calls for more light, not from a greater source or to replace the light that is there, but from another lamp to add to the light of our house and to increase the glory of your life."

9 And Miriam wept upon Yeshua and said unto him, "Never will I need or desire more than you, my Lord, and why must Elohim ask the hard things of us that are to be?"
10 Yeshua lightly touched her cheek as he looked into her eyes and answered, "When great blessings are given, great responsibilities follow, for God gives us blessings that they may be magnified and returned with love to our brothers and sisters of the world, with the purity of our faith and by the deeds of our life; for thus do we grow and expand our lights and prove our faithfulness to our Celestine Father and Mother and show that we desire to be like them.
11 Miriam, the day will come when everyone will look to you to know the deepest secrets of my life and teachings, and in the times of persecution, many would flee, except the pillar of your faith and majesty holds fast to give them courage.
12 We are now but two, but soon there will be many disciples, and I will not long be among them; therefore, you must be prepared to speak the truth of my words and life, for there will be some that would lead my sheep astray, and there must needs be one shepherd who knows me more than all others, who can always guide my sheep to safe pastures where the grass is green and sweet.
13 That which I must bear is great, but that which you must bear after me is also great, for many will despise you and mock you and believe not that which you say or deny your right to say it because you are a woman, even some of my most faithful disciples.
14 In those moments, have faith, my beloved wife, and know that my spirit is with you, always and forever, and that our Father and Mother will never ask more of you than they have given you the strength to endure and the ability to fulfill.
15 And it would be good if you were not alone in the times to come; if you did not have to bear the inflictions of men without the solace and companionship of those who love you and who you love; that they may share your burdens and give you comfort and joy.
16 Therefore, open your heart, for it has a greater capacity to love and be loved than you have yet discovered. And with an open heart, your eyes may see that which they have not seen, and your heart may desire that which it has not desired.
17 And verily, the day will come when your light will become greater than the brightness of the sun, until the earth can no more hold you upon it."
18 Miriam's eyes began to water, and she replied with a small tremble in her voice, "I know I should have joy for the many blessings which we have and for the great callings Elohim has given to us, but when I think of the things to be, I am still frightened and unsure."
19 Yeshua nodded in understanding, saying, "When I was a boy, you know that a man from afar land named Anish came to the house of my parents and taught me many things. Today, we say to one another 'Namaste' as Anish gave us this salutation, meaning the spirit of God inside me greets the spirit of God inside you.
20 Anish also showed me how to play music with my mouth and how it brings the light of the sun into the heart even on a day of rain and how it turns sadness to happiness and trembling into confidence."
21 Miriam laughed and said, "You mean like when you whistle to make the sound to call dogs?"
22 Yeshua laughed too and answered, "Yes, it is so, Miriam, but with beats and rhythm like a drum and a flute."
23 Then Yeshua demonstrated to Miriam the musical whistling Anish had shown him, and they learned to blow music from their mouths together, and it gave them joy.

CHAPTER 42

Path of Three

Yeshua and Miriam prepare to return to Palestine, but before they leave, Yeshua meets with some Egyptian priests to speak about the one true God. He tells them about a secret path and draws out an intricate pattern of a labyrinth and maze that they should construct. This he calls the "Path of Three." It represents the three stages of the infinite paths of existence, and the three aspects of God with no limit to the inspiration and knowledge one can attain when walking the path. He leaves them to ponder the words he has spoken and to construct the labyrinth and maze until he returns the next day to share more of the mysteries of God.

Upon returning to Memphis, Yeshua and Miriam and the children gathered all of their belongings and placed them upon the backs of three donkeys, for Yeshua had told them that they must soon return to Palestine.

2 For this cause, they went into Memphis to visit the market so that Yeshua might sell to a merchant who desired his wares, sixteen finely carved chests, which he had finished while in Nubia. And they were inlaid in beautiful patterns with shell and many colors of rare woods.

3 The merchant was happy to see Yeshua again and asked him, "Where have you been, good carpenter? Many have come looking for your fine chests, but my shelves were bare and I knew not what had become of you."

4 And Yeshua said unto him, "These are the last of my chests that shall be sold in Egypt, for we soon shall pass beyond its borders." And upon these words, the merchant was sorrowful and treasured the chests he had obtained all the more.

5 After concluding their business with the merchant, they went shopping throughout the market, and Miriam gathered things she wished to bring with her upon their return to Palestine.

6 When night fell, they dwelt in the house of Babuaten and told him all that had transpired since they had seen him last and of their desire to return to the land of their fathers. And Babuaten said unto them, "While you were among the Nubians, a messenger came from your family in Bethany, but I knew not where to send him, and he returned without giving me the message."

7 Miriam was anxious because of these words, worrying about the content of the message, but Yeshua put her at ease, saying, "Worry not, beloved, for the messenger carried glad tidings, which we shall soon have made known unto us. Now I have yet one thing still I must do to reward righteousness before I leave Memphis, and this shall take two days.

8 I greatly desire for you to accompany me upon the last day, when I make an explanation of the things I will reveal to the priests of the Temple of the Crystals.

9 Therefore, on the second day, have the children remain here while we go to the Egyptians, and that night, we shall return to them and find two messages of joy. Soon thereafter, we will begin our journey back to Palestine."

10 Miriam was most curious as to the cryptic words Yeshua had spoken, and she said unto him, "Dear husband, if you know already these glad tidings, tell them to me that I might not be wondering for two days what they shall be."

11 Yeshua answered, "I know only what I have said, for I have not sought to see deeper into the well. Therefore, we both shall be looking for the second day to discover its rewards."

12 The next morning, Yeshua departed alone, and he went to the temple of the Egyptians, where he had gone with Yochanan and told the temple guard, "Tell the high priest that Yeshua of the crystals desires to speak with him." Soon afterward, the priest named Zebak appeared from within the temple. And he remembered Yeshua from the time of his visit with Yochanan, asking, "Have you returned with more precious stones?"

13 Yeshua answered, saying, "I have no stones, but something of greater worth, for I bring to you, the fullness of the one true God. Whom you worship in ignorance, I have come to declare unto you."

14 It should have been that Zebak was wroth with such blasphemous words from the mouth of a lowly Hebrew, but as he looked upon Yeshua, he saw great innocence and kindness in the depths of his eyes and felt something beyond the dealings of men that spoke to his soul and stirred in his heart, even the very spirit of God.

15 Thus it was that Zebak brought Yeshua into the inner court of the temple and all the priests came to hear the words that he would speak, and one of them asked, "Why do you speak your words to us and not to your own people?"

16 And Yeshua said unto him, "The time soon comes when I will speak to the Children of Israel and to them alone, until the fullness of the Celestine Light of God has been given unto them, as much as they can bear, for that is their reward for the faithfulness of their fathers and thus has my Father commanded. But until that day, I see the light of God in all in whom it dwells, and where I find light, I would give more."

17 Some of the priests were still uncertain as to whether they should give a place for Yeshua's words in their temple, and some murmured against him. But Zebak subdued them, saying, "Let us hear what this man has to say, for he has the light of the sun upon him; in his very face, you can see it. By listening to him, we are not obligated to believe what he has to say, but if we listen not, we may lose a great treasure."

18 And the priests looked at one another with great curiosity, pondering upon the depth of the words that were spoken, and Yeshua said unto them, "For many generations, the priests of this temple have given respect to the pharaoh Akhenaten and worshipped Aten, the one God of whom he taught. And there are many secrets of the most high that you know that are not known by the other priests of Egypt.

19 But I say unto you that there are still many secrets of the one true God that you know not, and if you will harden not your hearts and will hear my words, I will tell you in plainness of the one true God and the path as clear as crystal that leads to glory such as you have never known; and there will be no more secrets among you, for I will give you a foundation to forever gain light beyond your knowing."

20 Hearing this, one of the priests was wroth, saying, "Who are you to tell us such things? For we have devoted our lives to the one God, and it is in Egypt that he was made known unto men, and it is we who are his priests and the protector of his secrets." But the other priests moved for him to be silent and were desirous to hear the words of Yeshua.

21 And Yeshua said unto them, "I am but a carpenter from a land afar, but I know the one true God in every breath I take and every thought I think, and I have been one with God since before the heavens were born.

22 Therefore, if you will humble yourself before God, I will show you a secret path, that you

may discover for yourself the truth and worth of the words I speak to you and, verily, the truth of all the Celestine Light that is inside of you and all that is in the world and beyond."

23 Taking a stick of blackened wood, Yeshua drew out the pattern of a labyrinth and then a maze, most intricate in design, upon the stones of the temple floor. And he said to the priests, "You are much practiced in the use of gems to help you find God within the sun, but I say to you that God must first be in your heart and then will you have the Celestine Light even in the darkness."

24 Then Yeshua showed them the labyrinth and maze, which he had drawn, saying, "Behold the pattern of the Path of Three. Walk upon it and discover all you seek, comprehend all you think you know, and unveil the deepest powers of your eternal soul.

25 The Path of Three has no ending to the knowledge it can give you. Every time you walk its course, you will discover new truths about yourself and greater understandings of God.

26 It represents the three stages of the infinite paths of existence and the three aspects of God. It will give inspiration and understanding to you as great as your desire and effort to know.

27 Each time you walk upon the path with sincere intent, even if you think there can be no more to learn, you will be overflowing in your expansion and, one day, will come to understand that there is always more to know, always more to grow.

28 Look into the path and see your life: youth, parent, and elder.

29 Look into the path and see the three stages of your quest to know God: humility, prayer, and service.

30 Look into the path and see the fullness of the nature of the one true God, who is not one person but three, but the three glorified are one god, for God is the Father, and God is the Mother, and God is the Son; and like unto the sun and the Moon and the stars, each has a light of their own, but they unite to illuminate the heavens above.

31 And there are many more truths revealed within the labyrinth and maze. Therefore, make this image upon the floor of your temple that it may be walked upon as a path. Ponder the things I have said while you place each portion of the path, and I will come again unto you tomorrow to tell you more of the mysteries of God."

32 And Yeshua departed from the temple and returned to the house of Babuaten.

CHAPTER 43

Path to Enlightenment

Yeshua and Miriam arrive at the temple of the Egyptian priests at dawn, and Yeshua is pleased to see that the priests did a good job completing the pattern of the Path of Three upon the floor of the Hall of the sun. He then explains in great detail what it means and what is gained by walking the path. This chapter ends with a spectacular and unforgettable miracle.

And it came to pass that Yeshua and Miriam appeared at the temple the following day upon the dawn of the rising sun, and the priests were all still asleep for they had worked late into the night by torchlight to complete the pattern of the Path of Three upon the floor of the Hall of theSun.

2 But upon hearing of his arrival, they quickly rose and bid him welcome, but were less welcoming to Miriam, and Yeshua said unto them, "That which you learn, she must also learn, nor is there anything I give to any of the children of men that can be kept a secret from her.

3 For it is given to Miriam to know all the revelations of God, that she might be the perfect witness of truth unto the world."

4 He spoke in Egyptian to the priests, but from time to time said again part of his words in Aramaic to Miriam that she might fully understand, as her command of the language of the Egyptians was not perfect.

5 Yeshua was pleased to see what the priests of Egypt had done, for the pattern stretched across the great chamber from wall to wall; and that which he had drawn small, they had drawn large in every detail.

6 Then Yeshua stood at the entrance to the outer labyrinth, and he raised his arms to the right and to the left and said, "The first circle of the labyrinth is only of light, for a babe is born innocent and pure and there is no darkness in them; but even in innocence, choices must be made and consequences do befall; therefore, choose to walk the path of light to the right or to the left and discover what comes unto you.

7 With each step within the Path of Three, ponder upon deep thoughts and seek answers and illumination from your life to your eternity. Learn to see the significance in the subtleties of the path and understand how they show you the answers you seek.

8 See how some places will easily merge to the next progression, while others will require that you turn back nearly upon the way you came. See how some colors stand alone while others merge and form something new.

9 Understand the black path represents evil and the white represents good, and there are many things of significance in their relationship that is revealed on the path.

10 As you return again and again to walk the Path of Three, choose to sometimes walk the

black path that you may learn of the fallacies of evil within the safety and sanctuary of the maze, that evil may have no power over you in the world beyond the temple walls.

11 Upon the same color, you may return back the way you came; even as in life, when comprehending your errors, you may retrace your steps and start anew, having lost your time and sometimes much more, but learning from your experiences; thereby, your future may hold a greater light than your past.

12 Do not think to deviate from the path by cutting across the lines, for as in life, the wisdom is gained in the journey, and if you shorten your journey, you cheat yourself of the treasures of knowledge and light you could have gained. Even as in life there is order in success and chaos in failure, so it is upon the Path of Three.

13 There are times when you may walk alone upon the Path of Three and other times when there will be many other seekers upon the path. There is significance in the times you are alone, the times shared with a few, and the times when many others are with you. How you interact in silence with those you meet is important, as is how you choose to pass or not pass one another.

14 The gray areas represent the vast lands of the lost existing in the world, where both good and evil entice, and man is often lulled into living in the twilight of both good and evil, thinking that because he is not all evil, he must be good.

15 But verily, I say unto you: Only those who valiantly strive to keep the commandments of God are found worthy to dwell in the house of God.

16 The three-colored circles represent the Father, the Mother, and the Son, the three aspects of the one God. As you walk the path again many times, choose to walk it differently on each occasion that you may learn new truths and gain greater understandings."

17 Zebak said unto them, "Let us choose the path to the left for the sun rises in the east and sets in the west."

18 And so it was that Yeshua and the three priests of Egypt took the path of light to the left, and after circling halfway around the outer band, they came to the entry of two paths, one black and the other white, and Yeshua said unto them, "Behold two choices before you, one of light and one of dark, but before you choose, tell me what would have been the consequences had you first gone to the right instead of the left when we began?"

19 One of the priests answered, "We would have returned to the spot from which we started, or coming upon the spot we now stand, but facing the wrong direction, we might pass unknowing by the entry to the path that leads onward."

20 Yeshua complimented him, "You have spoken well, and so it is in life that there are some choices that do not take you down a path of destruction, but neither do they bring you to greater light; they merely keep you in the light you possess.

21 Verily, I say unto you that there will be those who will cling to the light that they have, happy not to be in darkness, but the valiant will take issue with the darkness that they might gain the greater light."

22 Then Yeshua entered the labyrinth along the white path and began to walk into it. And he bid Zebak and two other priests to follow him, and one by one, they came into the Path of Three and Yeshua said unto them, "You enter now into the map of your eternal progression, for the Path of Three shows your past and your present and your future.

23 Upon its steps, you can discern the secrets to everything you have been, everything that you are, and everything that you can be.

24 Within its realm, you can discover yourself as you have never known, and once found, the pure Celestine Light of God can be revealed in ways you could never have known."

25 Once Yeshua had circled the gentle spiral of the labyrinth two more times, he came to the edge of the great gray circle that marked the boundary from the outer labyrinth to the inner maze and he stopped, and turning to the three priests, he asked, "What have been your thoughts as you have circled through the outer labyrinth?"

26 The first priest answered, "I have thought of my life to this point, and with each step upon

the path, moving closer toward the maze, I remember all that I have known and believed, and I ponder if I am doing a good thing to listen to you and follow you upon this path."

27 The second priest answered, "I have thought of how tedious is life that we must continually travel around in circles and everything is the same."

28 Zebak answered, "I have been looking at that which is to come, for the maze ahead is most intricate and I am anxious to know of its meaning."

29 Yeshua elaborated, "Thus, it is that you are beginning to feel the quiet power of the Path of Three and are even now reflecting upon the past, the present, and the future.

30 So it is when you travel your path of eternity in ways that are pleasing unto God, for you are meant to become more than you were born, and only when you comprehend where you came from, accept why you are here, and honorably live your life for the part of eternity it is, can you fulfill the full measure of your creation.

31 And I say unto you, of what good is all that has been unless you have learned from your experiences and they become the foundation to build your life to a greater height and draw closer to God?

32 Tremble not for the adversity that each sunrise can bring, for the path of today is also strewn with blessings big and small, and it is amidst the bad and the good, the sad and the joyful, that you give thanks to God for the smiles of your lives and understand that happiness is all the sweeter for having tasted the bitterness.

33 Amidst the hot winds of life, you see the towers of the city in the distance through the blowing sand, and it is in the lights that await you that you find the strength to press on through the darkness of the night.

34 Verily, the mansions of God wait with burning lamps for all those who keep the commandments and teachings which God has given unto the children of men."

35 Then Yeshua circled his arm, showing the great gray circle upon which lay the inner maze and the spiral path of the labyrinth that had led to it, and he said unto them, "The outer path which circles around itself and leads to the edge of the circle of gray is your life in the world filled with both good and evil, and you must walk through the world and all the confusions therein to find the entrance to the path of God, which leads to eternal life and exaltation.

36 And I say unto you that the spirit of man is a true child of God; therefore, the outer spiral of light draws ever closer to the inner center, even as the hearts of good men and women are ever drawn to the Celestine Light of God, and their eyes remain single to the light and the glory, even when surrounded by the darkness of the world.

37 And in the world, the adversary within and without continually entices the righteous and the unrighteous into darkness.

38 Therefore, with each step upon the outer labyrinth, ponder upon your life in the world and all that has been; that when you reach the inner ring of light, may you be prepared in your heart and mind to leave the world behind and pass through the gray directly upon a path that leads to the God of light."

39 Then Yeshua pointed at the intricate patterns of the inner maze and told them, "Upon the inner maze are three circles of color, which represent the triality contained within the foundation of life and eternity and within man and God.

40 Some will say that it is not triality but duality that is the foundation of all things, even as in the day and the night and good and evil.

41 But I say unto you that duality cannot exist within itself, nor can there be only black and white, for there is also the gray between the black and white, even as there is a dawn and twilight between the day and the night and the many variances of man between he who would be called good and he who would be called evil.

42 Therefore, as you pass upon the outer labyrinth, ponder upon the trialities within mortality and immortality of all that has been in your life and all that will be in your eternity.

43 Ponder deeply upon the meaning of God that you might comprehend that there is one

God, not many, but more to God than just one personage.

44 Look diligently, therefore, to find and understand the triality of all things in your life that have been, your life that is, and your life that may be.

45 See how the three circles intersect, whereby a portion of one is in each of the others, and how at their center they are all one together, even as God is the Father, and the Mother, and the Son; and though each is a distinct individual with their own attributes, they are united and inseparable, and, at their core, a power of infinite oneness and one God.

46 Within each of the intersections of two circles are great lessons for life and eternity if you will ponder upon them.

47 Walking through the maze consider wisely before going back upon forward steps you have taken. If you reverse, you may lose not only the steps you retraced back, but also the additional steps you could have gone forward upon in that time. And all only to retain that which you had already gained and passed beyond. But then there are times when that may be the better choice, and it is for you to learn when and why.

48 Consider wisely why you should not pass back into the outer labyrinth once you have entered the inner maze, even as in life to go back fully into the ways of the world after you have been showered in the Celestine Light of God can make you fade so far into the darkness that the light of truth might become but an ember in your heart. Yet there are times when it may be necessary, and it is for you to learn when and why.

49 Once within the three inner spirals of the maze, stay on the spiral bounds of light within each one and cross not their walls except as the path may lead, for there are lessons to learn at every step.

50 These three spiral mazes are together the inner maze of the Path of Three. They represent the triality of God: the Father, the Mother, and the Son.

51 I remind you that these three are separate and distinct, but also one and undivided; which one represents the Father and which one the Mother and which one the Son depends not upon a constant color and position, but upon which you choose to enter first each time you walk the maze.

52 The path of light within the maze sometimes takes you to the edges of the world, so it is in life that you sometimes come upon that which entices you away from the light and tempts you with the pleasures and ways of the world insomuch that you would forget that you are children of God.

53 Near unto the center, the path takes you also into the sphere of one of the other of the three circles of God, that you may reflect upon the light that is created when they are joined in power and how that can help you in your life.

54 And you will come upon the center of each colored circle, and the path will reverse back upon itself. Take some time at each of these points to give deep contemplation upon the aspect of God you are in before you seek to depart it for another; that by an orderly progression and contemplation, you may gain foundations of great knowledge.

55 And I say again unto you, remain at the heart of each aspect of God with deep meditation upon what you have learned that it may become a part of you before you seek to know more."

56 Then Yeshua led the priests along the spiral path of the first inner circle and said unto them, "As you pass through the first circle that you choose to enter, think of God the Father and of your relationship to him. Ponder upon his goodness and how faithful you have been to his commandments. Feel the power of the male flowing in your spirit and allow the power of the Father to come upon you.

57 When walking the spiral path of this circle, you will touch for some moments within the bounds of the circle of the Mother and should ponder upon the interactions of the male and the female and of all the people, rich and poor, high and low, who come into the circle of your life, seeking the same light that you seek.

58 Consider that though they may be very different than you, how much further you can go

seeking the light united and supportive of one another than either can alone."

59 As they reached the center of the circle of the Father, Yeshua asked one priest to remain there and meditate upon the lessons of the Path of Three to that point.

60 Yeshua beckoned the other two priests to follow him upon the path that led out of the circle of the Father and toward the circle of the Mother, and he said unto them, "When you pass out of the circle of the Father and near again to the twilight of the world, consider all the ways in which the adversary holds sway over the world and entices and lures good souls away from the Celestine Light and precepts of God.

61 And in the depths of your journey near the gray twilight, consider the endless stars of the heavens and the endless lights of God that uplift and love you.

62 Seeing again the glory of the light, reject then the persuasions of the world and allow your understanding and the remembrances in your heart to bring you back into the fullness of the Celestine Light of God that you may have worthy entry into the next circle and the embrace of the family of light."

63 Yeshua and Zebak and the other priest continued along the path out of the circle of the Father and toward the circle of the Mother. And as it passed upon the very center point of the maze, Yeshua remained at that spot.

64 He told the two priests to continue on, and he said unto them, "The Mother is the female that balances the male of the Father, and by the blending of their essences do all things exist and reach their greatest light. Therefore, seek to understand and benefit from the differing aspects of your life and the space that is between, for you are more than a man.

65 Moreover, you must come to understand that even as God is a man and a woman and a son, that inside of you there is a man and a woman and a child, and though one aspect of you may be all the world sees, even as the Father is all of God most people know, your other aspects do not vanish simply because they are ignored; you merely are less than you could be for turning your back upon the fullness God has given unto you.

66 As you travel within the circle of the Mother, consider how you can be more balanced in your life, for God is balanced in the Father and the Mother and the Son; in this, may you discover the importance of this secret of Heaven.

67 In your pondering of balance, remember balance does not always mean equal, but more often the proper amounts, even as a soup may only need a hint of pepper to make a savory blend.

68 Verily, I say unto you: A man or a woman alone is not as balanced as a man and a woman together, and a man and a woman together is not as balanced as a man and a woman and a child, and man and a woman and a child is not as balanced as a man and a woman and a family of children.

69 And the good gained from a family is a treasure that enriches all of life.

70 Therefore, seek these things and great shall be your rewards in Heaven and upon the earth.

71 And I say unto you that even as in the circle of the Father, you will be led from the circle of the Mother back into the gray edges of the world and will have a longer journey to reach the path that leads to the son and will have to travel a great deal more through the world to arrive. Ponder upon why that may be.

72 With every step beside the gray of the world, consider how you can better be in the world but not of it and avoid the snares that await those who watch not to beware of evil and seek not God in all things.

73 Passing along the gray of the world, reflect deeply upon the greatest subversion by which the holiness of God is turned into wickedness in the world, for it is with the sacred urge to procreate, which God has given for purposes of great light, that the demons of evil do ever tempt the children of men to pervert them into a great darkness.

74 So important is mortality that God gave the children of men powerful urges to procreate. And God gave the children of men commandments that they should multiply and replenish the earth, but also that they should not commit fornication or adultery, but cleave only unto they to

whom they are married, and that there should be no divorce among them save it be for adultery or fornication or unrighteous abuse.

75 All these things God did and commanded that there would be pure and worthy tabernacles of flesh, which the spirits made by God the Father and the Mother could reside within without remembrance of their former life, that they might learn and grow from their experiences and gain faith from the union of their heart and mind reaching out to seek the God of light.

76 Therefore, for it to come to pass that the Children of Light born into the world might gain the greatest good, it is of great worth for them to be born into a home of goodly parents, who will teach and raise their children in a like manner.

77 And verily, I say unto you, upon the foundation of the righteous family is the kingdom of God built, both on earth and in Heaven.

78 Therefore, the adversary uses the greatest persuasions to cause the children of men to abuse their sacred urges, which God has given them for great and glorious purposes.

79 Evil laughs and rejoices to see the Children of Light debase themselves, and thus be separated from God and no longer seek or live the light of truth.

80 Like Adam and Eve, who sinned and hid themselves from God, the righteous turn away from the light in their shame until repentance comes into their hearts.

81 And before that day, they justify their wickedness, and in their sin, injure their children. For the parent who cannot stand the light of God will raise their children to not know God or follow the teachings of divine light, and the children then cannot see the light from which they have come.

82 Therefore, when you walk along the precipice, along the edges of the world, contemplate your own weaknesses with the sacred power of creation God has given to you and repent of the transgressions you may have made.

83 Resolve now to never allow evil, within or without, to entice you to misuse your most sacred power. But covenant to reserve it for acts of love and procreation within the holy realm of marriage, as God has ordained."

84 As they walked upon the circle of the Mother, Yeshua pointed to the place where the circle of the Mother met the circle of the Son, and he said unto them, "When you pass through this point, consider your blessings and responsibilities to your closest family, for a parent receives blessings from their heavenly parents equal to their fulfillment of the righteous needs of their children, even as the children receive great blessings from on high when they care for their parents when they are old.

85 And the treasures of life and eternity are many when a family stays united and bonded through the generations."

86 Yeshua then bade another priest to remain in the center of the circle of the Mother and to ponder and meditate upon all he had learned in his journey of the maze.

87 He asked Zebak to travel into the circle of the Son and said unto him, "Know that as you are a good steward of that which God has given unto your charge, abundance is your reward in Heaven, and for proving worthy, you will be entrusted with much more.

88 And I say unto you that faith is the foundation of Heaven and faithfulness the secret to exaltation, even as the Son fulfills the righteous admonishments of his parents by the faith he has in their love and desire for his happiness. And unto him is given glory and power forever.

89 Therefore, within the circle of the Son, ponder upon the blessings which God has given to you, those both big and small, and the things which are asked of you in return.

90 Likewise, consider all that your earthly parents and friends and teachers and others have given to you and that which you do to return and magnify the good they have bestowed upon you.

91 Then consider your children, both those that are and those that may be, and the joys they bring to you and the great responsibility God has entrusted unto you to care for and enlighten the children whose spirits have been sent to you.

92 Consider with great thankfulness the blessing of your wife and ever strive each day to show your affection and appreciation for the light she brings into your life.

93 Consider the community in which you live and all that it provides to you and the responsibility you have to uphold and help your community to prosper.

94 Consider your brothers and sisters of light and remember the golden rule to do unto others as you would have them do unto you."

95 Then Yeshua bade Zebak to remain at the center of the circle of the Son and contemplate all that he had learned.

96 So it was that there was a priest at the center of each of the circles of God, and Yeshua stood at the center of the Path of Three.

97 And all of the priests, both those in the maze and those in the room, as they pondered upon the feelings in their hearts and the opening of their minds, looked together to Yeshua, who stood with his hands clasped and his arms down, looking upward into Heaven.

98 When upon that moment, there was a sharp clap of thunder and the roof of their temple was cracked asunder and dust came down upon them, and a beam of sunlight shone through the crack and, piercing the dust, illuminated the face of Yeshua, and he alone.

99 Yeshua lifted his arms up to the heavens and at that instant, the roof collapsed about them, but the falling stones touched them not and injured none.

100 Through the billowing dust of the fallen stones, the priests looked in awe upon Yeshua and bowed their heads and put their knees to the ground; and Yeshua bid Miriam come to him, and hand in hand, they walked forth from among the rubble, and Yeshua said unto them, "I will always hold a place for you in my heart as you keep the commandments of God and seek to do good in the world; and upon this place, build again the Path of Three and what God has opened up to the light of the sun, leave it to always be so."

101 And Yeshua went out of the temple, and they saw him no more.

CHAPTER 44

Revelations on the Road to Palenstine

Lazarus returns to Egypt after an absence of three years to do some trading and to deliver good news to Yeshua and Miriam. After ten days of trading, he accompanies them on their return trip to Palestine. On their journey back to Palestine, Yeshua and Miriam speak in great depth, and he explains to her that he has finally come to know who he truly is and what he has come to do on earth to fulfill the full measure of his calling.

After departing the temple, Yeshua and Miriam returned to the house of Babuaten, and their children ran out to greet them with warm embraces and kisses, and Dara said unto them, "There is wonderful news; come inside that you may see for yourself."

2 But Uriel could not contain the surprise and exclaimed unto them, "Father, Mother, Uncle Lazarus is here, and he has brought great news and presents!"

3 Yeshua and Miriam followed them laughing into the house and greeted Lazarus, whom they had not seen for more than three years. And Lazarus told them how he had been given greater responsibility in his father's business and was now a merchant of some success and had come to Egypt with spices and nard.

4 After Miriam and the children had given him news of some of the great moments in their lives in Egypt, Lazarus said told them, "Listen, for I have news of abiding joy; for I am now a married man, as is Yochanan. And my joy is full, for I now have a son, and Yochanan is blessed with a daughter."

5 Upon hearing this, Miriam embraced Lazarus with great affection and asked him with a knowing smile, "Who are the lucky women to have such men of God for husbands?"

6 Lazarus smiled broadly and said, "No surprises, you know them both, dear sister; for Yochanan married our sister Martha as I am sure you suspected would occur, and I married Hannah to whom I was betrothed. A messenger was sent to you before the wedding of Yochanan that Yeshua might stand beside him, but the message returned undelivered, for you must have then been among the Nubians as I have heard."

7 Late into the night, Yeshua and Miriam and Lazarus remained awake, sharing with great joy the details of their lives since they had last traveled to Egypt together and reveling in simply being in each other's company again.

8 For ten days, Lazarus remained in Egypt, selling his goods and buying Egyptian papyrus, linen, perfumes, and blue glass to sell in Palestine. He anticipated a great profit and, as he had

promised Yeshua, had dedicated his excess above his needs unto God.

9 On the eleventh day, Lazarus and the family of Yeshua began the journey back to Palestine, in company with a caravan of sixty-two camels and many men.

10 And Yeshua, having lived some years in Egypt, returned now to the land of the Children of Israel to his destiny, once again, as when he was a babe, fulfilling the words of the prophet of Hosea, saying, "Out of Egypt have I called my son."

11 As they journeyed across the barren desert, Miriam and Yeshua spoke to one another in great depth for many hours, and Miriam said unto Yeshua, "We return now to the land of our fathers and to celebrate joyous events in our family; why is it then that I feel a darkness overshadowing the path before us?"

12 Yeshua answered Miriam, with reassurance in his voice, saying, "God has given you the sight to see things that are to be, but they are still far down the path. Therefore, you focus instead on the darkness that looms just ahead. But there is light too Miriam, and it is the great light to come that you must see with your eyes and feel with your heart."

13 Miriam nodded her head in understanding and then spoke with Yeshua about something that had dwelt in her heart for some time, "Remember when we sat at the Wadi under the stars when we first came to Egypt, and you spoke with Lazarus and Kudar-Iluna about who you are and why you are here?" And Yeshua affirmed that he remembered.

14 Then Miriam said unto him, "Yochanan has said that only the Son of God could perform the miracles you have done. Elohim has shown me this in dreams as well. Yet on that day, which now seems so long ago, you were reluctant to say it was so, for you said there was still a mystery you must know.

15 I have sensed that during our time in the desert, when you have communed much with Elohim, that you have found that which you sought. Tell me now, Yeshua, who are you, why are you here, and what will be tomorrow?"

16 Yeshua reached out and held Miriam's hand, saying, "There is more than you know in that question, perhaps even more than you or I wish to know on this day, in the answer."

17 And Miriam said unto him, "But I do want to know, for you are my husband, and I want to know your essence even as you know mine."

18 Yeshua answered quietly, saying, "I am a son of God, even as you are a daughter of God, and even as all who dwell upon the earth are sons and daughters of God in their spirits.

19 I know that we have a Father and a Mother in Heaven who are not two gods, but united in the God of one, the God of Abraham and Moses and all the children of the earth.

20 I speak with them many times in the day, and they with me. I hear their voices, and they hear mine. I am filled with their words, lifted by their spirit, and guided by their wisdom in everything I say and do.

21 In humility, I affirm to you that I am not as other men; I have been chosen and set apart by our heavenly parents for a most high and holy purpose. I am the bridge to eternity. And by the Father and the Mother, I am called Son.

22 But to work as a carpenter, to create beauty from simple wood, to share love with you and our children, to expand my soul by the experiences—good and bad—of life in the flesh, to slowly discover who I am and why I am here, and to fulfill the full measure of the calling my Father in Heaven has given to me, for all these reasons and many more, this life is a treasure.

23 I seek each day to be sufficient unto itself, to live each day in fullness, in ways that are pleasing to my Celestine Father and Mother. Then all that comes to pass is as it should be.

24 Nevertheless, you have sensed true, for during our sojourn in Egypt, my Father in Heaven has shown the path of my earthly life in entirety; I now know all that will come to pass. And very important among the things to come is that you will be beside me through all my days among the children of men.

25 As to my future, where I shall go, whom I shall meet, or what I shall say or do, all is only as our Father and Mother in Heaven desires it to be. He ever whispers in my ear, and she ever

moves my heart.

26 Remember the words we have spoken in times past, how before I was born among the children of men, God gave unto the minds of the Egyptians and the Greeks and other peoples, visions of things that were to come. And they wove these truths among their myriad of false beliefs.

27 This he did that the world might be prepared for the truth when it was among them.

28 So it is that many have believed that a God in Heaven had a son, born of a mortal virgin, who came to earth to benefit the world. Yochanan says that I am the myth made real.

29 I am humbled, Miriam, and though I tremble to know it, to you above all others I cannot deny it, for my Mother and Father in Heaven have told me it is so, but neither will I affirm it before any but you until the day my Father shall first say it unto them."

30 Miriam was greatly humbled and told Yeshua, "Surely you must be the Son come to earth, for you know all things and fulfill the promise that all men would desire to be and do miracles such as never have been known among the Children of Israel."

31 Yeshua answered, "Every birth is a star from Heaven, for all have come to earth from the presence of God, our Father and Mother.

32 And within this life is eternal salvation, through the faith men have, the humility they retain, and the testimony of the life they live.

33 And unto the righteous is given the sacred promise to return in eternal glory, from whence they came.

34 I was born of my mother Miryam, but I know I am not of her. How she came to birth me has always been the cause of much gossip in Nazareth, for it was known that Yosef, her husband, was an upright man of God and knew her not in a carnal way before I was born.

35 Though Miryam was above reproach, there were some who spoke in the darkness that she had conceived before she was married. The weight of this came greater upon her after it was seen that I had blue eyes, while both Miryam and Yosef and all of their kinsfolk had brown eyes. Thus, it was as a mark of shame that I came to be called Yeshua of Nazareth by some instead of Yeshua bar Yosef.

36 That bothered me not at all, nor did Miryam or Yosef care, for when you know who you are and Heavenly Father's purpose for you in life, the idle gossip of the unknowing is as worthless as dust that blows away in the breeze and is forgotten.

37 Think not by all that I have said that I make myself greater than other men, for I have come to serve, not to be served; and there is no miracle I may do that others of faith cannot also do, if they will but desire it with every fiber of their being and call upon Elohim with holiness in their life and a pure and unwavering faith in the certainty of Elohim to work a miracle through them."

38 Listening to her husband, Miriam was filled with the Holy Spirit and saw Yeshua in a new light, and she said unto him, "My Lord, why have you chosen me and what is to become of us?"

39 Yeshua looked into her eyes with deep affection, "Miriam, I chose you before the world was and you chose me, and for that long have I loved you. The path to the highest eternal glory can only be walked by man and woman together, and we chose to take each other on that journey beyond time and beyond the stars.

40 Know that I am here to do the will of our Father and Mother in Heaven. I see what they desire me to see. I do what they desire me to do and live even now as they are pleased that I live.

41 I have been called of God to bring the Celestine Light to the children of the blessed, for they have been chosen among all the people of the earth to first receive the fullness of the light, because of the faithfulness of their fathers.

42 From among them shall come a few choice lamps that shall take the light that I bring and give it unto every nation, kindred, and tongue. It is they who will open their hearts and receive the light more than the Hebrews, for the beliefs and myths of the Gentiles have prepared them more for the truth.

43 And only a handful among the Hebrews will see me for who I am and come unto me, and

the inheritance I brought to them from Heaven shall instead be given unto the Gentiles.

44 Woe unto the Children of Israel; I cry already for their fall. So many will look to me, seeking to see the manifestation of their dreams and will be blind to see the glory of the light beyond their desires. They will seek from me that which I do not bring and will reject that which I do.

45 Except for a precious few, they will turn away from salvation and instead walk away from the illumination of Heaven. They will be left empty, without a home until the day of their redemption, when their children of the last epoch will open their eyes and hearts, embracing the light the parents could not see.

46 The day shall come when by the Romans and the priests, I will spill my blood upon the ground. But do not weep for me on that day, for it is not the end as all others will fear, but is the beginning of the coming of the fullness of the Celestine Light of Elohim, which shall go forth from that spot, on that day in Palestine, into all the world. And it shall be you, Miriam, who shall hold the highest torch."

47 Miriam wept at his words, and Yeshua said unto her, "Fear not, beloved, for the time is not yet, and to die is one of the reasons that I have come to live.

48 Know that no man could take my life save I willingly gave it unto them. And this must be so to fulfill all righteousness and bring to pass the immortality and exaltation of the worthy.

49 I am the last sacrifice. And because of the love of Elohim for the children of men, in me, the debt of the iniquity of man will be paid in full, for all those who believe in me repent of their sins and live the Celestine Light.

50 And they shall inherit glory and happiness such as man cannot imagine in a world without end.

51 Remember now my words, for after that dreadful day, I shall sleep in the earth but three days. Despite the wounds upon my body that you will see, you will hold me again in life and wholeness.

52 For this is the last great cause for which I have been born of woman; that through me, all may have eternal life. And that which they have sowed in life they shall reap in eternity: those that have lived evil to damnation and those that have lived the light to exaltation.

53 But of these things, speak to no one. They are for you alone to know with certainty until the day that the Son rises again.

54 We yet have years to share before those days, but I tell you this day to remember always that you are called to a high and holy calling, and none shall ever know me as you do.

55 After my physical body has again the breath of life, I can tarry for but one or two moons before I must return to my Father and Mother in Heaven. But you must remain for many moons to give courage to the faint of heart and keep the faithful true to my light.

56 Verily, some will rise up, even from among my flock, and will lead many of my sheep into deep pits. Therefore, it must needs be that there is one whom everyone understands knows me as no other, who can speak the words that I spoke and tell of the life that I lived and do the miracles that I did and more, that the way of truth will be made clear for all who have eyes to see and ears to hear.

57 And I say unto you, be not anxious about your life, but trust in God, and you will ever be protected and guided until your calling is done, and we are together again in the glorious Celestine Light of Heaven from everlasting to everlasting."

THE THIRD BOOK OF LIGHT
CALLED
VIVUS

CHAPTER 1

Second Sermon in Bethany

Upon returning to the land of Palestine, Yeshua and his family visit Miriam's family in Bethany. While there, Yeshua is persuaded to give a sermon to the friends and family of Lazarus. He speaks of the pull everyone has between the light of their soul calling them to do right and the weakness of their flesh enticing them to do wrong and surprises everyone by stating that it is Elohim that made man to be at war with himself. He speaks about how repentance washes away the sins of the past and gives the specific steps necessary to accomplish a full repentance. Yeshua is also challenged by a Pharisee and rebukes him strongly and explains why lineage is not a path to Heaven. He ends by reminding his listeners that they are the masters of themselves and their eternity.

And it came to pass that Yeshua and Miriam returned to the land of Palestine and journeyed to Bethany so that they might see again their friends and family that dwelt there.
2 Miriam's family was overcome with joy when she arrived and embraced her and the children with tears of happiness. Her father called for a feast to be held, and from the first moment of their arrival, there was much merriment and celebration.
3 Many people from the town soon came to the house of Miriam's father when they heard that Yeshua of Nazareth had returned. Among some, he was held to be a prophet and among others, a master storyteller. Still others felt he was a rabbi of great knowledge, while more than a few considered him sacrilegious and a blasphemer. But among all, even those who disdained him, there was an anticipation to be able to hear his engaging and intriguing words again.
4 Yochanan and Martha soon joined them, as did Lazarus and Hannah, and the children of several families played together while their parents renewed everlasting bonds of friendship, love, and faith forged in unforgettable mutual experiences.
5. For three days, the welcoming feast continued and crowds gathered each day, hoping to hear Yeshua speak. But each day Lazarus came to them and told them that Yeshua would not speak that day.
6 After seeing the disappointment in the faces of so many people he knew, Lazarus went to Yeshua and beseeched him to say something to the townspeople else they begin to have their good joy of anticipation turn into the anger of frustration.
7 Yeshua explained his reluctance, saying, "Lazarus, my good brother of spirit, I do not wish to make a host of enemies before my time, for it will come soon enough. Though my teachings will bring the elect to God, they will only inflame the pious and anger the unrighteous. That is well and as it should be, but before the persecutions begin, there are still many things I must do and wish to do, in quiet and peace."
8 Upon hearing the words of Yeshua, Lazarus pleaded all the more, saying, "But these are

my friends and the friends of my family, and they are here at our feast, at your feast. It would honor us if you would impart your wisdom among us. I know they will not vilify you even if they disagree with your words. And perhaps there is one among them whose life will be changed, who will find the Celestine Light of Elohim, this day, because of the things you say."

9 Yeshua was greatly moved by the words of Lazarus, and he told him, "God has truly touched your heart, Lazarus, for you have spoken words of might and right. Let us go even now to the courtyard to see if the winnow of my words will uncover the pure grain from the chaff."

10 And it came to pass that Yeshua entered the courtyard of the house of the Father of Lazarus and stood upon the large fountain at the center as a crowd of friends and family and townspeople gathered beneath him.

11 And he said unto them, "Good people of Bethany, I and my family are honored to be among you once more. I am humbled by your desire to hear my words and may each of you find the lamp you need to light the darkness before you.

12 While my family and I traveled in Egypt, we came to know wonderful people of many different nations and races and religions. Despite the differences in their character, they had many good things in common.

13 Whatever the color of their skin, they loved their children. Whether they were Egyptian or Roman or Hebrew, they desired to please the God of their understanding. Whether they were rich or poor, they sought good things for their family. Whether they were city dwellers or desert nomads, they showed us friendship and hospitality.

14 Only among the zealots of every religion did we find harsh judgment and even hatred spit out upon everyone who believed not as they did, sometimes so much so that to take a man's life in the name of their God seemed to them very reasonable.

15 Yet these same men also loved their children and desired good things for their family. When among those who believed as they did, they were honorable and of good character.

16 How then can it be that the precepts of religion or loyalty to tribe or country can cause a man to act in ways that are repugnant to his very soul?

17 Is man's soul at war with itself? Even in your own home, do you find that sometimes you are a dutiful and considerate father and husband or a caring and loving mother and wife, but then at another moment, you say or do things to those whom you love which cause them pain and grief and your own soul, anguish because of that which you have done? Is your soul at war with itself?

18 When you see the clouds begin to gather upon the mountain slope, you know that rains will soon come. But it is not because of the clouds that the rain will fall, but because of the mountain.

19 If the mountain were instead a plain, the clouds would pass on by. But they are blocked in their progress by the wall of the mountain, and the clouds continue to gather and thicken upon the slopes until a storm is brewed.

20 So it is with you. Your immortal soul is a piece of the Celestine Light of Elohim. It is the cloud in its whiteness and purity. For the breath of eternity that you dwell upon this earth, your mortal body is the mountain. And the pure cloud of your soul cannot avoid the impure mountain of your mortal life any more than the clouds of the sky can avoid confronting the mountains of the earth.

21 The war is not within your soul any more than the cloud is at war with itself. It is the encounter with the mountain that causes the storm, even as your own soul is ever at odds with the natural man that is the rawness of the physical.

22 All things have been made by God. Therefore, I declare to you that it is Elohim that has made man to be at war with himself, to be tempted by evil even as he is prompted by the light of God within his own soul to forsake evil and do only good.

23 Verily, this quandary God has given to man that man might overcome himself and discover and follow the Celestine Light of Elohim within his soul.

24 In this, man becomes more than he was, and for this cause has Elohim created all the heavens and the earth and put man upon it, that he might become more than he began.

25 Who then is the adversary? Where is the root of evil that continually torments and tempts man? It is you. Man is his own enemy.

26 To conquer yourself in a far greater measure than you are conquered by yourself is the supreme challenge of life, and only those who succeed will pass the portal of harmonic judgment into eternal glory.

27 Verily, the first door to the first Heaven is only opened by a worthy life. Riches cannot open it, except the richness given in a life of service to others.

28 Living the law and only the law cannot open it, except the law to love God with all of your heart, and if it is so, then your love is shown in the good you do for your mother and your father, your wives and your children, and your fellow men upon the earth.

29 Each day, you must choose who will be your master, the light of your soul or the darkness of your earthly body. Each hour, you must choose to listen to the quiet voice within you, the Celestine Light of Elohim, or give into the temptations of the dark weakness within your body. But remember, nothing is hidden from God.

30 Therefore, choose wisely, for you know not the day or the hour that your life ends and your eternity begins. Whether you rise to eternal glory or fall into the long darkness of desolation depends upon the lamp of brightness or the cold chains of misery you forged for yourself in life, for thus you pass by your resonance through the harmonic portal of judgment into your eternity.

31 Elohim gave you the instrument of your body, but you are the musician that decides the music your life will play.

32 And I say unto you that when you see a man showing goodness and light by his actions, you can know regardless of his color or his tribe or his religion or even his conception of God that he is heeding the promptings of the Celestine Light of Elohim, which resides in his soul, that he is growing closer to Heaven, and that God is well pleased with this man at this moment.

33 Likewise, when you see a man that is acting in darkness, disobeying the commandments of Elohim and disrespecting himself, or his family, or his fellow men, regardless of who he is or what he believes, then you can know with a certainty that this man, at this moment, has forsaken the Celestine Light of Elohim that resides eternally in his soul and has heeded the empty promptings of the lower mortal man that feeds his desires but gives him no succor.

34 Verily, this dance of light and darkness is of greater importance to your eternity than you know, and you dance it every day of your life."

35 Then Obadiah of Bethany rose to speak and said unto Yeshua, "I am a good and pious man. I am faithful to my family and to my God. I am not perfect, but I think all among us will acknowledge that I am a good and godly man. You would make it seem as if I am always at war with myself, and such is not the case."

36 Yeshua smiled warmly and answered, "Your heart is surely good, Obadiah, and your actions speak louder than words that you strive each day to live your life in ways that are pleasing to God. But did you come out of the womb such a good man?"

37 "No, I did not," Obadiah answered, "I have been taught from an early age in the ways I should go and I have strived mightily to follow the good things I have been taught. In my youth I sometimes made foolish choices, but I have learned from my errors, even those I repeated because I did not fully understand them at first."

38 Yeshua smiled and said unto him, "Verily, you are fulfilling the desires of Elohim. It is for this cause, that you might perfect yourself, that God has given unto you and all men and women this life in mortality.

39 That you are a better person in your old age than you were in your youth bears witness that the Celestine Light of your soul has shown through the darkness of your mortality.

40 Yet even today in the wisdom of your years and the fortitude of your experiences, are you not still tempted to sometimes raise your voice in unrighteous anger, to sometimes not say all

that you know if it could be to your advantage, even while it is to another man's disadvantage?"

41 Obadiah wrung his hands as he silently sought to control his displeasure at the words Yeshua had spoken, and he said, "While it may be true that I sometimes think to speak in anger, as I did even now, and sometimes think of an advantage I would gain by my silence that would be lost by my speaking, in my old age, I no longer give into such temptations; I speak only with respect and calm, even if I am in turmoil in my heart. And I speak the truth to my fellow men, even when my silence would not be dishonest."

42 Yeshua smiled again and there was on his face a great contentment, and he said unto Obadiah, "Verily, you are dancing even now, as I have spoken. Thus do all men and women. This is the never-ending dance of perfection. It is the dance of light and darkness. It is your lower mortal man tempting you to darkness, but your higher man heeding your eternal soul calling you to the light that is your birthright.

43 Each day, your lower man invites you to eat what you should not eat, to say what you should not say, and to do what you should not do, all things which lead to an empty cup, no matter how many times you fill it.

44 And every moment, step by step, your higher man, which is the Celestine Light of Elohim in your soul, whispers in your ear, touches your heart, and asks you to turn from darkness and choose the light, to eat what you should eat, to say what you should say, and to do what you should do.

45 The day will come when you will stand before Elohim and be judged by the resonance you have danced in life, with all things revealed, both your virtues and your weaknesses and your sins. And you shall inherit the resonance in eternity that you chose, both openly and in secret, in life.

46 Therefore, let each man and each woman remember that every step you take, every word you speak, and every deed you do is inscribed in either the Book of Light or the Book of Darkness.

47 On the Judgment Day, Elohim will take the pages from the books, and they shall be weighed in the balance to see if you are found wanting."

48 Then rose Saul the Shepherd from among the crowd, and he asked, "What of one such as me? I am ashamed to say I have lived a very ungodly life for most of my years as many amongst us know. I am sorry for so many of the things I have said and done, but I cannot take them back. Now I am an old man, and by your words am I to understand that I am condemned in Heaven while I still yet live in mortality? Is there nothing I can do?"

49 Yeshua was touched by his humbleness of heart, and he said unto him, "Elohim takes deep joy in the repentant sinner, and from a true repentance, you are born again; the record of the Book of Darkness is taken away, never to be seen again for the years that came before, for your resonance has changed, as long as your repentance is true, and you continue to walk in the light, with faith in the love and justice of Elohim, from that day forth.

50 What then is a true repentance that is so great that Elohim would remove the record of your sins in the Book of Darkness? Verily, it is this: that you would feel a sorrow that grieves your heart and brings tears of shame to your eyes, that you would pray to Elohim and confess all of your sins acknowledging your error, promising to sin no more, and humbly asking for forgiveness.

51 Then you must prove the truth of your repentance by seeking out the people you have sinned against, be it small or great, and confess your sins to them or to their posterity if they have passed on and, as much as is possible, make restitution for the darkness you have done.

52 Yet for some things, because of the sin or the circumstances, there can be no direct restitution. For these, you must make amends in the best way that the light of Elohim whispers to your heart is right and just.

53 Repentance is not easy, nor is it done in a day; but it is given to all men and women that once they find again the Celestine Light within their heart, mind, and soul, they may put it in a lamp that will burn from everlasting to everlasting.

54 But I say unto you, do not procrastinate the day of your repentance, for the days of your mortality are numbered, and very small they are. You know not upon which day Elohim will call

for your soul and open the Books of Light and Darkness to weigh your life in the balance to discover the resonance of your soul."

55 Hearing this, Saul the Shepherd fell on his knees upon the ground and, crying out with a loud voice, asked God to forgive him for his sins and promised to live in the light of Elohim from that day forth.

56 Then he arose and immediately went among the crowd and began to confess to them sins he had done to them in the past, to express his deep sorrow for his wrong, and to ask their forgiveness. And many were the embraces of love and friendship that came forth from those to whom he spoke.

57 But some among the people were affronted by the words of Yeshua and thought to themselves that they needed no repentance, for they were descendants of Abraham and Isaac and obeyed all the letters of the laws.

58 And from among them arose Yagur the Pharisee and he said unto Yeshua, "By what authority do you say these things? Which prophets are you quoting that we may know that your words are of true merit?

59 In truth, we know all the prophets and you do not speak their words, but seem to be creating your own. We know the prophets, but we know not you. So by what authority do you speak things that have never before been spoken?"

60 And Yeshua looked down upon Yagur and said unto him, "I speak by the authority of Elohim, and it is from the words of Elohim that I speak. Hear my words, O men of the world, for by them you will be justified, and by them you will be condemned."

61 And many were stunned by the words of Yeshua, for he spoke with power and authority such as they had never before heard.

62 And they turned to whisper to one another, saying, "Surely, this man must be a great prophet, for he speaks with the calmness of still waters, the confidence of a lion, and the power of thunder. He does not quote the prophets that came before, but speaks as if he has been given the words from the very mouth of Elohim."

63 Yagur paled because of the words of Yeshua, but still rose to contend with him again, saying, "The time of the great prophets has passed, and you are blasphemous to speak as you do. You do not speak to uphold the laws that have been given, as a true prophet would, but think to make new laws unto yourself.

64 And more, you speak in ways that are contrary to the law, for you have spoken that even those who are not a part of us, not one of the chosen, can still find equal favor with Elohim, simply because they live a good life.

65 You have spoken of the commandments of Sinai, but then speak as if the law is nothing more than living a life of service. To me, it seems as if you say one thing, then contradict it with the very next breath. And in almost all things you have said, you speak at odds with that which is sacred and holy and has been so from Abraham to our fathers."

66 Yeshua answered him firmly, "Every child born of woman is the chosen of Elohim, for they are all the children of God, and Elohim does not favor one over the other from their birth, any more than you should favor one of your children over another from the time they are born.

67 It has been the custom to favor the firstborn and to give unto them the greatest opportunities and inheritance. Although this may conserve the family's wealth, where is the fairness to the siblings of the first? Are they less deserving simply because they came out of their mother's womb upon a later day?

68 And if the first son should grow into a man of darkness while his brothers and sisters grow into men and women of light, where is the fairness to give all that a family has as an inheritance to the first?

69 Which is more important, preserving the family's wealth even if it is given unto darkness or using the wealth to uplift the righteous and reward those that walk in light?

70 Verily, I say unto you: Elohim does not reward the wicked simply because of their lineage,

and those who say it is so speak as men cloaking their falsehoods in piety to justify themselves
71 Be they king or pauper, the only reward for the wicked in the Kingdom of Heaven is desolation.
72 When a child grows into an age of understanding and accountability, their sins are not overlooked by virtue of their lineage, but only by virtue of contrite repentance.
73 Neither are they rewarded because of their lineage, but only because of sincere acts of devotion and kindness, worthy of praise and great blessings.
74 So it is with the blessings of Elohim upon all men. Each reaps what they sow, not what their fathers sowed, not what the prophets of their faith sowed, but only what they sowed, each and every day of their life.
75 And what think you of the commandments of Sinai? Were they given to be a prison for man or a freedom? I say unto you that Elohim asks nothing of man except to live in ways that would help man to grow into the Celestine Light that Elohim gave to him.
76 So it is with the commandments of Sinai. A man may live them all and follow every letter of the law, but if he does so grudgingly, then in his heart, he obeys none of them, and on the Day of Judgment, he will be weighed in the balance by the sincerity of his heart, not the pretense of his actions.
77 But any man who loves God with the depth of his heart also loves all that lives because Elohim has made it, and this man will live the commandments of Sinai, even if he is from a far land and has never heard of them.
78 Because he loves God, including the light of God that is within him, and respects and cherishes all the life that Elohim has put upon the earth, to live the commandments, even unseen and unknown, is as natural for this man as every breath he takes.
79 And Elohim loves him and favors him, not because of who his father was, nor whether he was the firstborn or the last, nor whether he is a Hebrew or a Gentile, but because of who he has chosen to become inside himself, because of how he has chosen to live both seen and unseen by men, because of the light he gives unto the world.
80 Verily, I say unto you that all who are humble, repent of their sins, and always strive to live in the light shall be blessed with peace in their heart and true friends beyond price.
81 Their faithfulness and goodness in life will open the doors to the glory of Heaven, and in eternity, they shall reap the everlasting harvest of the good seeds they have sown.
82 Before you sleep this night, look upon yourself. Among men, only you know your true heart. But Elohim knows all. Therefore, that which you cannot hide from God, hide no longer from yourself, nor support that which is wrong by contriving to justify how it is right.
83 Vow unto yourself a sacred promise to raise the lamp of the Celestine Light of Elohim that resides in your soul and henceforth always walk with your light held high that darkness can no more dwell within you.
84 You are the master. The light of your soul contends with the temptations of your body. Choose to be the master of your body instead of its slave, and you will find a joy and peace in this world such as you never have imagined and a great reward in Heaven, beyond the descriptions of men, built with every good you have ever sown."
85 Then Yeshua came down from the fountain and walked among them. And many were the men and women who touched him and asked blessings upon him, and many were those whom he touched and blessed with a portion of his light.

CHAPTER 2

Sojourn in the Wilderness

Yeshua and Yochanan journey in the wilderness for many months, away from the clutter of everyday life, to pray to God that they may come to know the fullness of their callings. Lazarus promises to care for their families while they are away. In the fifth month, they fast, drinking only water with honey for thirty days, and are filled with many visions as their connection to Elohim becomes strong and clear. It is after this that they come to fully know the great purposes they came into life to fulfill.

nd it came to pass that Yeshua and Yochanan felt a mighty pulling in their hearts to journey together into the solitude of the wilderness to commune with Elohim, the Father and the Mother.

2 Following the promptings of their hearts, they bid their families farewell, for a time they knew not.

3 Miriam was unhappy that she could not travel with Yeshua, for it was seldom that she had ever been apart from him, but he told her tenderly, "You will be with me in my heart every moment, and when I return, I will share all that I have discovered with you.

4 But you must understand that for this time, this is a journey Yochanan and I must make alone, for it is we who must fulfill the will of the Father and Mother in the days to come and taste the bitter with the sweet.

5 While I am gone, send word to my family in Nazareth that we have returned to the land of Palestine, but that I have gone into the wilderness and will see them again as my Father and Mother in Heaven will it to be so."

6 And it came to pass that Yeshua and Yochanan departed from Bethany and their families, and Lazarus promised that he would watch over and care for the treasures of their hearts while they were away. Though everyone knew they would return, there were still many tears among everyone as they departed.

7 And it came to pass that Yeshua and Yochanan followed the sun, south into the vastness of the Sinai, until they found places of solitude and emptiness where people neither dwelt nor traveled.

8 For food, they ate the grasses, leaves, fruits, and roots of plants, with locusts and wild honey, which they also sought out.

9 Each morning, they arose upon the sunrise and gazed with their open eyes upon the brightness of the sun as it was fully crested above the horizon for the span of twelve deep breaths.

10 With each breath, they drew closer in their heart, mind, and soul to Elohim until the Celestine Light of Elohim filled every fiber of their being so much so that they seemed to radiate light from their heads and the tips of their fingers.

11 Imbued with the spirit of Elohim, they then moved in unison to the Contemplative Movements that Yeshua had practiced from his early manhood so that they might connect with a spiritual heartbeat to all life upon earth.

12 Thus connected to all that is, they remained facing the sun with their closed eyes focused right upon it and prayed together throughout the early hours of the morning, one following the other and then repeating, giving thanks for their families and blessings and seeking to be enlightened and girded for the path before them.

13 They would break the fast in early midday and meditate and pray in private following the meal, until mid-afternoon.

14 On some days, in the early afternoon, they would instead query and teach each other after just a short individual meditation.

15 During the later part of the afternoon, they would walk about the wilderness, gathering food, enjoying each other's company, and being one in spirit with all life.

16 They ate their evening meal before sunset, and as the sun approached the horizon and twilight was imminent, they would once again gaze upon it with their eyes open for twelve deep breaths, to be filled with the Celestine Light of Elohim while they slept through the night.

17 As darkness fell, they most often slept and only occasionally stayed up speaking to one another for some hours into the darkness of the night when it was near the time of the full moon.

18 These things they did for four moons. Upon the fifth moon, they fasted until the next, drinking only honey water, and they were carried away in great visions. Their connection to their earthly bodies became faint even as their connection to Elohim became strong and clear.

19 Thus it was that on the morning of the last day of the fifth moon, as they completed their morning gaze of the sun, Yochanan looked to Yeshua and exclaimed, "Verily, I declare that you are an Elohim, even the Son of Elohim come upon the earth in the flesh, and the Anointed of Israel that has been prophesized. This I have always known in my heart, but now I know it in my soul, for my body is alive with light from within when I think of that great truth."

20 Yeshua bowed his head in silent acknowledgment, then looked up into Yochanan's eyes and affirmed to him, "And you are the prophet Elias come again as was foretold by the prophets, and so grateful am I to our heavenly parents that we can share this life together."

21 Yochanan nodded his head in understanding and agreement. He gazed again at the sun, and then looked again at Yeshua. "In truth, I have had some problem comprehending how you could be part of the Elohim from an immortal realm and still here married to Miriam, with children, covered with dirt, walking in the desert with me, and even now, with blood still healing on your arm from where you were pricked in the thorns yesterday. It all seems so impossible, yet I cannot deny what I know from God to be true."

22 Yeshua answered frankly, "I had many years grappling with the same questions. I have known for some time who I am and why I am here. In the comings and goings of everyday life, it sometimes seemed but a dream, but I knew my time of fulfillment was drawing nigh.

23 It is only here in the desolation and quiet of the wilderness that I have finally come to fully understand why I am in a mortal body and why everything must come to pass exactly as our Father and the Mother have revealed to me."

24 Yochanan nodded in understanding and replied, "I have seen a great vision of what shall come to pass and the voice of the Mother came to me, speaking of all that must be."

25 Yeshua acknowledged, "The same has happened to me."

26 You will die a most ignominious death," Yochanan said with difficulty, caught in his emotions at the thought. "You have not many more years upon this earth."

27 "No more ignominious than yours, my brother, and with more time I think," answered Yeshua. "But more important is how we live in the years that remain to us. For in the good soil of the garden of truth and light that we create, in the days to come, will grow men and women of great power and faith, and through them that which we sow in obscurity shall manifest in grandness, blossoming and growing to fill all the earth, for the Children of Light to discover who

they are and the glory that they can become."

28 Yochanan smiled at Yeshua's words, but he was still troubled and said, "I have seen all you say coming to pass. But I have also seen a quick perversion of our words and teachings insomuch that the flowers and plants that grow in our garden in the days to come are not the same ones we planted.

29 It makes me wonder just a bit, if all we will give, and all our families will lose when we are no more upon the earth is worth the price, or if there is some way we can insure that the purity we teach remains in the garden."

30 Yeshua answered him, saying, "Surely our heavenly parents would ask nothing of us, unless in fulfilling their desires we were furthering their purposes and enlightening men.

31 Be assured, neither our work nor our deaths will be in vain.

32 Certainly, there will quickly be a great falling away from the truth we bring.

33 But that which arises in its place, the artifices of men given in my name, will still nourish many of the flowers of light which we plant, and the great seed of all truth will merely sleep in hidden slumber until I come to awaken it again.

34 In truth, while we live, there will be but few who follow us, for the teachings of the true Celestine Light of Elohim are not in keeping with many of the laws of the world or the ways of the religions of men. They are not the ways of the Hebrews, or those of Judah, or the Romans or Egyptians, or any other peoples upon the earth.

35 Verily, the teachings of the Celestine Light of Elohim are not the Law of Moses for they are above it, even as I have not come to uphold the law, but destroy it and replace it with the purer Law of Celestine Light.

36 For this cause will father turn against mother and children against parents, and there will be much turmoil because of the things which I teach.

37 When we are gone, it will not be many years before those who walked with me and learned the Laws of Celestine Light as they were spoken from my lips will also have passed beyond this physical world. Then it will be that well-meaning men of faith will fall away from the Laws of Light and return to the more-familiar laws they have known before to follow.

38 Then it will be that men of little faith, but much ambition, will usurp the leadership of the remaining Children of Light and bring in all manner of false authority, customs, pomp, and ceremonies, which men so thrive in vanity upon, and the flowers of Celestine Light we planted in the garden shall know many days of darkness, and many shall wither and forget the nature of the true light that was their source.

39 But among the purest of heart, through all the generations of time, the true Celestine Light of Elohim will always abide, and the Holy Spirit of the Mother shall continue to lead them to resonate thoughts and actions, even when they are strange and contrary to the teachings of the laws and religions and customs of the land.

40 Many will be alone, isolated from their friends and family because of their beliefs and some will go to their deaths as blasphemers and heretics. But they will have a peace and light upon them that shines forth even in darkness and the darkness cannot overcome it.

41 I know that the true Celestine Light of Elohim that we bring to the world can never be extinguished. And in a generation far away, there will come hallowed days of promise to herald the renewal of the world.

42 To bring the blessings of these days, our father and mother shall send forth upon the earth some of the choicest spirits of Heaven.

43 To them, the Gospel of Celestine Light shall be given again in fullness upon the earth. And among those who overcome the world, it will burn in their hearts and blossom in splendor in their lives, and they shall do such wonders as men of the world cannot even imagine.

44 For unto these will be given the secrets and the mysteries insomuch that the world can have no power over them, and the powers of Heaven will open for them.

45 And they shall not fall away from the true Celestine Light of Elohim, for it shall be in

them and about them, and they shall be emissaries of the most high and adepts of great power chosen for high and holy purposes to set the world afire with truth and usher in the epoch of renewal.

46 But then as now, there will not be many who follow the way of Celestine Light, for it is and will ever be at odds with the laws of man and religions and cultures, and few will be those with courage and faith, mighty enough to seek it out and live their lives by such a greater light."

47 Yochanan nodded his head in agreement, saying, "That is good. I am happy for our brothers and sisters yet to be born. They will be a blessed generation to be born in that time. But I have seen the vision of all that must come to pass in our lives. Is it now that we must begin?"

48 Yeshua looked at him eye to eye with a slight smile upon his lips and happiness in his voice, saying, "Yes, my brother, it is time for us to begin the great purposes we have come into this mortal life to do.

49 Let us now return to our families. You must then take journey to Gimron and begin to gather disciples, teaching them only repentance and the simple foundations of the way of Celestine Light.

50 As you gain a following, fulfill your promise of youth and take a journey to the outskirts of the greater cities of the land of Palestine and the people of Israel, coming as a whirlwind from the desert.

51 Preach repentance from sins and baptism by immersion as a covenant to a higher path. Prepare the people for the greater light and knowledge that I shall bring.

52 I will return with my family to Nazareth and, from there, begin to discover those who will become my disciples and begin to teach the greater Celestine Light to those few who have ears to hear and a heart open to the fullness of Elohim.

53 You shall grow in fame and followers even as I continue to quietly go about my Father's business unnoticed by most men.

54 Once we part in Bethany, we shall not see each other again for some time. When you have reached the pinnacle of your calling, I shall come to you to be baptized, and you may take that as a sign that you have fulfilled your promise to Elohim and your time upon the earth grows short."

55 "It cannot be," protested Yochanan. "You have no need of baptism. It is a covenant to be born again, pure, with a new faith and a higher commitment. You are the Celestine Light. You do not need the bridge of baptism to travel from the darkness to the light."

56 Yeshua comforted him, saying, "It must be so to fulfill one of my purposes upon the earth. For in my baptism, let there be no doubt among men that all who live upon the earth and would pass to Heaven must pass through this door, in this manner."

57 Despite the words of Yeshua, Yochanan still shook his head and mumbled under his breath at the thought of Yeshua being baptized.

58 Yeshua consoled him, saying, "That will be a fateful day. It will be the time that your ministry has been fulfilled and mine begins in fullness. Thereafter, send your most worthy followers to me when you are no longer allowed to preach, that they may hear my words, and I will give to them some of the mysteries of the Kingdom."

59 Yochanan was still sore troubled and asked Yeshua, "What will become of our wives and families, as our ministries begin and the persecutors become inflamed even unto our deaths?"

60 Yeshua answered, "The ways of our Father and Mother are wonderful indeed as they guide us to the blessings that uphold us. Consider that we are married to two sisters of a family of means, led by a humble and honest patriarch, a loving mother and a devoted and faithful son. Among these most worthy people, we will entrust our families while we minister.

61 Concerning the days to come when we are no more upon the earth, there is something you must know about Miriam. She has a calling decreed by Elohim before the foundations of the world, which is still unknown to her. When it is upon her, she will hold the full power and authority of the Celestine Light, and no force of man or nature will be able to stand against her. Our families, our children, and even a great number of the Children of Light will have a beacon

and a fortress such as no people have ever had."

62 Yochanan raised his eyebrows high in curiosity and said, "What calling can this be? You speak of someone who would seem to be greater than me or even you."

63 "Not greater," Yeshua explained. "I cannot speak more specifically of her calling even to you, my brother, for she must continue to grow into it in innocence with her pure desire for greater light and by her varied experiences. By this, when it comes upon her, she will be surprised and humbled as must needs be. But because of her personality and temperament, her calling will manifest more strongly than it would in others, perhaps even more than it would have in you or I, if her calling had fallen upon one of us instead."

64 Yochanan pursed his lips in some frustration but nodded his head in acceptance of Miriam's secret. Then alone in the emptiness Yeshua and Yochanan stood, holding each other's forearms, looking into one another's eyes, and Yeshua spoke first, saying, "Let us now return to the people of the covenant and give unto them the promise of their fathers."

65 Yochanan gripped Yeshua's forearms tightly and said with deep sincerity in his voice, "To walk with you is the greatest honor I could know. You have my solemn promise that I will be a light that cannot be hidden and will prepare your path well; that those who are humble and courageous will find the greater Celestine Light that you will bring."

66 Yeshua gave Yochanan an embrace and said quietly to him, "I know you will, Elias. I know you will."

CHAPTER 3

Announcement to the Family

Yeshua and Yochanan return from the wilderness and call all of their extended family together to speak about what they must now do. Yeshua proclaims that Miriam will be his one perfect witness to all things.

nd it came to pass that Yeshua and Yochanan returned to Bethany to the house of their wive's father and mother. And they were greeted with much joy by their families upon their return.

2 Shortly after their return, Lazarus came to Yeshua, saying, "My father plans to throw a feast to celebrate your safe return, but being mindful of our talk in the desert, I have told him you may not desire such a thing."

3 Yeshua smiled with contentment and replied, "You know my heart well, Lazarus. Please ask your father if he would donate the money he would have spent on our feast to widows with children at home, where it will be better used." And Lazarus did as Yeshua bid.

4 That night, Yeshua and Yochanan called their extended family in Bethany together, including the uncles and aunts and cousins of their wives, and Yeshua said unto them, "We come from the wilderness entrusted by Elohim to begin in earnest the work we have come to earth to fulfill.

5 From this day forth, we will go among the Children of Israel, preaching repentance and baptism by water and the Holy Spirit of Fire.

6 And the worthy and virtuous shall be given the foundations of life.

7 Many will curse our names, and we shall be reviled and persecuted. But from among the multitudes of the unknowing will come forth those that seek the brightness of the Celestine Light.

8 Those who seek in humility shall be given the greater light. And all who live the Celestine Light shall be given the mysteries of the Kingdom of Heaven."

9 Lazarus stood up and exclaimed, "I am your disciple, Yeshua. I will come with you and aid you in that which you must fulfill."

10 Yeshua gave a warm smile, saying, "Lazarus, it would be an honor to have you by my side, for I know your heart is pure and true. But your calling is greater than to just walk by my side as a disciple. I humbly ask that you watch over my family and that of Yochanan and care for them, for it will not be often that we can return.

11 "In your stewardship, we know they will be well nurtured, and only knowing that can we go forth without conflict in our hearts and do that which we must do."

12 Lazarus bowed his head for a moment as if in disappointment, but then raised it with a slight smile, saying, "I am saddened not to accompany you, Yeshua, but my heart swells with

joy, knowing you love me so greatly that you entrust to my care, your family, even your greatest treasure.

13 I will magnify that which you have given unto me."

14 "Thank you, my brother," Yeshua said softly, as he put his hand upon Lazarus's shoulder.

15 Yochanan came to his opposite side and put a hand on his other shoulder, saying, "Yes, thank you, brother. Knowing that you are here to watch over those I love brings the peace to my heart from which I can preach the words I must, knowing that despite the harsh things that may happen to me, all is well with the treasures of my eternity."

16 Then Miriam came from among the women, and standing beside Yeshua, she looked with uncertainty into his eyes, "Husband, is it your will that I should remain here? Though I would miss our children with pangs of my heart, I have always thought that I would never leave your side when the time came for you to begin the fulfillment of your life. Is that not what we have spoken about for many years?"

17 Turning to hold Miriam's face between his hands, Yeshua kissed her lightly on the lips in front of all the witnesses and said unto her, "Beloved, I am the mountain, and what I have said does not change.

18 Even as I told you on the road from Egypt, you will always be at my side, in the moments of darkness and light, the one person who knows me above all others, that when I am gone from this earth, through you, all the truth of my life and words shall be known without error.

19 You are the one perfect witness whom Elohim has decreed shall see all things."

20 Then turning to the family, Yeshua said, "I say unto you that the day will come when both Yochanan and I are no longer on the earth in the body. And then there will be many who will claim to speak in my name and teach my teachings. And many, even among the righteous and well intended, will speak in error, concerning the things which I said and did.

21 Therefore, in the days that shall come after, remember Miriam and look to her as the pillar of the heavens. There will be some among you, even my greatest disciples, who will expound with mighty spirits upon the things which I taught them. And they shall work miracles and wonders. But only in the steadfastness of Miriam shall all knowledge reside. And the world will never again see another like her.

22 Verily, though the world shall know her not, she is the holy receptacle of truth, and the fullness of the Celestine Light shall flow through her."

23 At this declaration, there was murmuring of discord among the family. There came words of jealousy from the women and words of malcontent from among the men.

24 Yesod, an uncle to Miriam, stood and said to Yeshua, "It is not comprehensible that you would ask your wife, the mother of children still at home, to abandon them. Nor can anyone understand your words elevating her to a position above the men who would follow you.

25 Many of your teachings are good, but some are strange, and this is the most strange of all. I cannot abide it, the law cannot abide it, and I ask that you would reconsider what you have said, lest even those in your family stand against you."

26 In reply, Yeshua stood, facing all the men, and in his height, he looked down upon most. And his words, though spoken softly, resonated like quiet thunder in the room, "You have heard the promise I have given unto Miriam, that she, above all others, is the holy witness of my life and teachings.

27 Even as you have heard me say that I am the mountain, and that which I have said is immovable and unchanging.

28 Therefore, choose as you will, to heed or not to heed my words, even as you may choose to climb the mountain and come to know it, or you may sit idly gazing at it in the distance, always wondering about its nature, and never knowing its blessings."

29 Then Yeshua and Miriam bid good-bye to all who were present and returned to their quarters to be with their children.

30 In careful words and with much love, they explained that their family would journey first

to Nazareth to visit Yeshua's kin and then return to Bethany, where the children would live in the care of their uncle Lazarus while their father and mother did the work of God among the Children of Israel.

31 The children wept a little as they embraced Yeshua and Miriam and one another, and Uriel told his parents, "You have prepared us for some time now that this day would come. Even so, my belly seems to have fallen and my body trembles.

32 But I know Elohim has chosen you for a great calling and also chose us to be your children, and that this too is a great calling. We will be strong, for Heavenly Father and Heavenly Mother will never give us more than we can bear, will they?"

33 Yeshua and Miriam embraced their children in a close family circle and said in unison, "No, children, Heavenly Father and Heavenly Mother will never ask more of us than we can do."

CHAPTER 4

Confrontation in Capharsalama

Yeshua rescues a man named Ephres, who is being beaten by three men who claim they are doing so because they believe he is a homosexual and they are fulfilling the will of God. Yeshua explains the principles of God and how Elohim is more concerned with the virtues of one's character and the faithfulness of their devotion than the choices of their affections. Though there are those who may be scorned by the ignorant, they are loved by God.

And it came to pass that the family of Yochanan remained in Bethany at the house of Martha's parents, under the stewardship of her brother Lazarus, while Yochanan bid them farewell and made a journey to Gimron.

2 And Yeshua and Miriam began a journey with their two children to Nazareth so that they might once again see the family of Yeshua.

3 Their farewells to their family and friends in Bethany were prolonged, causing them to depart late in the morning. A donkey carried their belongings, and they traveled slowly by foot because of the children. After a short first day's journey, they set a camp for the evening, some distance from the road, on the north side of the village of Capharsalama.

4 As Miriam was preparing the evening meal of bread from Bethany and salad from greens they had picked along their route, they saw a man running along the road, being pursued by three other men who caught up with him as they watched and began to beat him with short sticks.

5 "Stay here with the children," Yeshua commanded. Then without another word, he ran toward the altercation.

6 As he came upon the men, they did not even notice him, so intent were they upon beating the hapless fellow on the ground, who was looking up at the stars and calling out in a weak voice, "God is great. Help me, O Lord."

7 Coming beside them unnoticed, Yeshua said in a loud voice of exceeding power, "In the name of Elohim, cease this instant your cowardly deed!"

8 Hearing a voice of thunder coming as seemed to them from the very air around them caused all three of the attackers such fright that they let go of their sticks as if they were hot irons and dropped to the ground trembling in fear.

9 Ignoring them, Yeshua went to assist the man they had been beating. Blood flowed freely from his head and his body, and he moaned softly with his eyes closed. Yeshua knelt beside him and touched his wounded head lightly. Immediately, the bleeding stopped.

10 Yeshua looked up at his attackers, saying, "As his clothes show, this man is poor, so you do not beat him to steal his money. But you have nearly taken his life. For what cause think you to take the authority of God into your hands?"

11 The three men rose up, and seeing Yeshua alone and weaponless, their courage began to return. The largest pointed a finger at the stricken man and said, "He is not from our village, and we have seen that he has unnatural affections for men, which thing we cannot abide.

12 It was only last week that our rabbi exhorted us that it is an abomination for a man to lie with another and such should be put to death. We are devout men, not just in word, but also in deed, and we are here to fulfill the will of God."

13 Yeshua stood up, and in his height, he was taller than the largest of the attackers, and he said unto them, "Has this man sinned against you?" And the three denied that he had. And Yeshua said, "Has he sinned against your family?" And again, they denied that he had. And Yeshua asked once more, "Then how is it that you say he has sinned?"

14 The middle of the three became flustered and, speaking quickly, said, "He was found sleeping in a stable under a cloak with another man. The other ran faster than we could catch, but this one we have. Therefore, leave us be and we will finish what we have begun."

15 "They were naked beneath the cloak?" Yeshua inquired. And the men replied that they had been clothed. "Then how was it that they were showing affection one for another?" Yeshua wondered. But again, the men said they did not see such.

16 "Perhaps, they were merely drawing closer to share warmth on a cold night." Yeshua suggested. "And they are not after all as you assume them to be.

17 As you judge so shall you be judged by Elohim.

18 If you take a life, especially from a false judgment, it is you who will stand condemned before God and pay for your sins, not just with your life, but with your eternity. Are you so sure of your judgment then that you will risk your own eternal reward?"

19 The men looked upon the ground and shuffled about sheepishly, mumbling to one another at the words Yeshua had said and unsure how to answer.

20 Yeshua admonished them, "Return now to your homes and leave this man, for you know neither the will nor the power of Elohim. I will return to Capharsalama in the morning and will speak to your rabbi. Let him know that Yeshua of Nazareth will call upon him after the morning meal."

21 Then the men backed away from Yeshua and, turning about, hurried back to their village to speak of all that had transpired.

22 Yeshua squatted down, and putting his arms beneath the limp body of the man, he easily lifted him and carried him to where Miriam and the children waited.

23 Miriam tended to the man's wounds with water and herbs while Yeshua explained that even though their first day had been a short journey, their second day would be even shorter, as they must return to Capharsalama in the morning so that he might speak to the rabbi.

24 They had no campfire, but there was a bright Moon that night. After the children fell into sleep, Miriam applied fresh crushed herbs to the man's wounds, and Yeshua came to him and touched him lightly at each spot of his injuries, saying, "As you love God, may your wounds so be healed."

25 The man slept soundly through the night and awakened upon the sunrise, startled to see he was still alive, lying with a family about him and his attackers nowhere to be seen. "What miracle has occurred that I am here?" he asked in amazement.

26 Yeshua came to him and, putting his hand upon his shoulder, said, "I am Yeshua of Nazareth and this is my wife Miriam, and our children, Uriel and Dara. Yesterday was not your day to die, and your greatness is still before you."

27 Then Yeshua told him of all that had befallen him from the moment he was hit on the head and fell asleep until the moment he had just now awakened.

28 After listening to Yeshua, the man shook his head dejectedly saying, "I am Ephres, and I have no greatness before me. I have nothing. I am nothing, except miserable. In truth, I am guilty of what my attackers accused me of, so leave me; I am grateful for your help, but now you know the truth, so do not waste your time with one such as me."

29 Despite his words, Yeshua did not move, and he told him, "I have always known the truth. And Elohim is more concerned with the virtues of your character and the faithfulness of your devotion than the choices of your affections. Though you may be scorned by the ignorant, you are loved by God."

30 The words of Yeshua were like the greatest balm of healing to Ephres. A smile of wonder came upon his face, and he glowed with serenity from within his heart. He looked upon Yeshua with awe and told him, "If only all men felt as you do, I could lead a normal life."

31 "There is no other way a man who loves and gives true devotion to Elohim could feel," Yeshua answered. "I am going now to speak with the rabbi and the people of Capharsalama that they may have no confusion on this. If you are well enough, I would like you to come with me and my family."

32 "Of course!" Ephres said in eagerness, standing up quickly, to his own surprise. "You are my savior, and even now go to defend me. I would be less than an ant if I did not stand beside you."

33 After Ephres had eaten a little bread with honey and olive oil, he stood thumping his chest and exclaimed, "I feel like a new man. In truth, I do not even have bruises upon my body. How can this be?"

34 And Yeshua said unto him, "In your darkest hour, you did not call upon men for mercy, but upon God for strength. Even as you have asked, so it has been done, because of your faith."

35 Shortly thereafter, Yeshua, Miriam, their children, and Ephres returned to Capharsalama.

36 As they walked toward the village, they did not have to seek out the rabbi, for their approach had been noted by the villagers and the rabbi and several of the men from the village stood upon the road awaiting them.

37 As they approached, the rabbi raised his hand, saying, "Stop there. You may not enter this village if you walk with this wretch of a man or with a brazen woman who is not covered, for God has said that it is an abomination for a man to lie with another and a shame for a women to be uncovered among men."

38 Despite the bravado of the rabbi and the courage instilled by their numbers, the gathered men still seemed somewhat in awe of Yeshua, for his presence, even without speaking, was powerful and unusual. Because of his height, all upon the road looked up to him, and his hair, though not long, was longer than usually seen among the men of Judea.

39 Because of the influence of the Greeks and Romans, many men his age removed their facial hair, but he wore a full beard, which was a little longer than the current fashion and slightly parted in the middle in a style seldom seen. Lastly, his eyes were a most piercing blue, a rare color in Palestine and unnerving to many who looked upon him.

40 Facing the men, Yeshua held out his arms to his sides, at waist height with his palms forward, saying, "Rabbi, by what law do you bar our passage, condemn this man, and vilify my wife?"

41 And the Rabbi answered, "By the Code of Moses."

42 Taking a moment to look individually at each man in the group, which had a diverse appearance, Yeshua further inquired, "The same code that says that men should not cut their hair or beard?"

43 The rabbi seemed irritated by the question, answering, "There is only one Code of Moses, but there are degrees of graveness; whether one's hair is short or long, whether one has a beard or not, is not comparable with sexual transgressions, particularly the most heinous kind that this man is guilty of."

44 Now Yeshua spoke calmly and quietly, but with great power in his voice, saying, "And I declare unto you that the Code of Moses is only in small part from Moses and more from men who knew not God.

45 And by this, you may know the truth: If a law teaches to honor and respect Elohim and to honor and respect yourself and to honor and respect your fellow brothers and sisters of spirit upon this earth, and to honor and respect all creatures over which you are stewards, then you may

know with a certainty that it is from God.

46 But if it teaches to not honor and respect Elohim, or to not honor and respect yourself, or to not honor and respect your fellow brothers and sisters of spirit, or to not honor and respect life entrusted to your stewardship, then you may know with certainty that it is of man, and any who obey it do so to appease man, not God."

47 The crowd stood unable to move, shocked that any man could say such things. And the rabbi, after his gaping mouth closed, began to sputter in a most angry manner, saying, "This is blasphemy of the highest order. How dare you speak such horrible words? God shall surely strike you where you stand."

48 With a smile, Yeshua looked about him to the sky, as if waiting for a thunderbolt to come from Heaven. And he told them, "If I were speaking that which was not true, then surely I could not stand before you and would suffer the wrath of Heaven. But here I still stand, and I say unto you that the spirit of God is in me, and I speak the truth to you. Therefore, open your ears that you may hear."

49 Now the rabbi was still sorely vexed at the words of Yeshua and was about to respond with a condemnation when Yeshua interjected, saying, "Prove me now, good men of Capharsalama. If I can show you that the Code of Moses is more a code of men than of God, will you then consider that the words which are written concerning women and men may not be after all the truth as you have always been taught?"

50 Hearing this statement from Yeshua, the rabbi practically screamed, "Sacrilege! The Code of Moses was given by the word of God. To say it is not perfect in every way is to say God is not perfect."

51 Yeshua answered, "If all the words which are written came from Elohim through Moses, then you would be correct as would your judgments upon us. But are you so afraid of truth that you will not even allow me to prove to you that the words you hold sacred are often the greatest sacrilege?"

52 "We will not listen to such nonsense," the rabbi proclaimed.

53 But one of the men of the village stepped forward and said, "Let us hear the words of the stranger, for he speaks as one who has authority. If we judge his words to be in error, then we are no worse off and he will be exposed as an affront to God. But if we judge his words to be wise, then we will have gained something of importance on this day."

54 The rabbi glared at the man and began to speak in anger again, but seeing the crowd in agreement with the words of the villager, he acquiesced to Yeshua, "Very well, speak as you will, but know that your very words will be your condemnation."

55 Yeshua looked one by one into the eyes of each man before him and then said unto them, "If the Code of Moses were actually written by Moses as given unto him by Elohim, then it could contain no errors of substance.

56 If it were written only by Moses and no others, there could be no confusion. If it were written by a prophet of God, it would only contain that which leads men to honor and respect God and the creations, which God has made.

57 To prove that some of the laws are of man, I will first show that many of the words written in the books of Moses are from unnamed men other than Moses, for if they fall, so fall the erroneous laws which they contain.

58 Good Rabbi, can you tell me, was Moses a humble man?"

59 And the Rabbi frowned, answering, "The word of God says, the man Moses was very meek, above all the men who were upon the face of the earth."

60 Yeshua inquired further of him, "And in his humility, he wrote these words about himself?"

61 Perhaps, a later writer added that little tribute," the rabbi admitted.

62 And what think you men of Capharsalama?" Yeshua continued. "The Torah also says there arose not a prophet since like unto Moses, whom the Lord knew face-to-face. Did Moses in his humility, write his own eulogy?"

63 And the men of Capharsalama murmured that these were indeed questions.

64 But the rabbi said, "These are trivial things. You speak of nothing of substance."

65 "Then perhaps you will consider the covenant with Abraham significant, as there are different accounts of this blessing from which all the Children of Israel claim their birthright.

66 Or perhaps the name of God, which Moses surely knew, but which is said differently in different parts of the Torah, as is the important account of the revelation at Beth-el to Jacob from which the Children of Israel claim the land of their forefathers.

67 And what of the commandments of Sinai? Are they so complex that Moses must write them twice and differently each time?

68 And what of women? Are they chattel or servants or merely comely beasts to be used as man sees fit? The books of Moses give a record of Lot, a man so righteous that God spared him, but destroyed all the inhabitants of Sodom and Gomorrah.

69 Yet according to the sacred books, just shortly before, Lot offered his two virgin daughters to be raped by an unsavory group of townspeople rather than let them speak to the men who were visiting his house.

70 And what of the recordings of genocide, those places where the books of Moses record God commanding that every man, woman, and child of an enemy should be killed?

71 O men of Capharsalama, consider the feelings in your heart, even as your mind considers my words. Would you give your daughters up to strangers to be raped? Do you think Elohim, the true God of Heaven and earth, would ask you to do such a thing?

72 And if you were in an army that came upon a village of innocent women and children, even babes upon their mother's breast, could you strike them down as they fled or pleaded for mercy and kill them? Do you think that Elohim, the true God of Heaven and earth, would ever ask you to do such a thing?

73 Think not that I speak only of the errors of the books of Moses, for many are the errors of men in the books that came after Moses.

74 Is it not written in the law that you shall not suffer a witch to live? Yet is it not also written that King Saul sought council of the witch of Endor and that she made manifest the dead prophet Samuel, that the king might speak with him when neither God nor the prophets in his Kingdom would? Or has that part been kept from you in the readings of the sacred books?

75 Know you not that if this were so, it would make a witch greater than a prophet of God? Verily, it would make a witch greater than God, for God would not come to Saul in dreams and the prophets of God spoke to him not. Yet it is written that by the power of the witch, Samuel was made manifest, and by the power of the witch, the prophet of God spoke.

76 O men of Capharsalama, these are not the words or actions of Elohim. They are the abominations of men seduced by familiar spirits to write that which is contrary to the very nature of God.

77 Therefore, O men of Capharsalama, consider the words that I have spoken of all these things that are contained within the books of Moses.

78 I say unto you that these writings are the evil desires and commandments of men.

79 They are not possible for a God of infinite love and fairness, and they are not worthy of you."

80 "It is you who speaks sly abominations upon that which is sacred" the rabbi said. "These are weighty matters which confuse those not well versed in the law and cannot be properly addressed by a handful of common men on a village road during the heat of the midday. These are fine points fit only for those trained in the law to comprehend. In any case, the main messages of the law and the sacred books are indisputable, even if there were discrepancies, which I do not say is true."

81 And Yeshua said unto him, "The true words of Elohim are simple and clear to all men and need not the interpretation of priests, for God would ask nothing of man that could not be easily understood by all, lest man error because of misunderstanding and not through willful

disobedience.

82 The true laws of Elohim are meant to be a freedom to man, to establish simple, clear paths of righteousness by which man may prosper when he walks the path.

83 The unrighteous laws of men, both those given by Caesar and those given by priests, are intended to be an enslavement to man, to compel him to give of his time and substance to sustain those in power, to put fear of punishments into his heart, that he can be controlled and will obey dictates of the unrighteous laws which his spirit would otherwise give no concern to or value.

84 Therefore, what man has perverted, let me make clear, and in this listen to the spirit of God that resides within each of you, within every man and woman ever born, for this quiet voice will always testify to you of truth if you will open your heart and mind to receive it."

85 "Of this man," he said pointing to Ephres, "think you that it matters to Elohim to whom he directs the affections of his heart as long as he gives his first devotion to God?

86 And if he gives his first devotion to God, it must follow as night to day that he also does good to all men, for a man devoted to Elohim has only peace and love in his heart.

87 To give sincere devotion to God and to give good in your words and actions to your brothers and sisters of spirit is all that God asks of anyone. Any law that demands other than this speaks not from God, but from man.

88 And think you that it is a shame that my wife is uncovered? Would you also cover the glory of the sun or the Moon or the stars? For they too are God's creations.

89 Woman was made to stand beside man, not behind him; equal to him, not less than him; thus have they been made by Elohim."

90 At this, the rabbi could not contain himself and said, "Numerous are the places in the Law where a woman's place is given. She is clearly under the direction of her husband.

91 And no man of worth wants to see another man lusting after his wife, so it must be that she is well covered when in public. This is just common sense if nothing else."

92 Yeshua took a step toward the rabbi, saying, "Verily, I say unto you any man who would make a woman less than a man, or subject to the will of a man, will find desolation in the world to come.

93 Elohim has made them equal in this life and the life to come. Look you to the books of Moses, which you love, and the story of creation: When Adam and Eve were given the Garden of Eden, God did not give dominion of all the earth only to man, but to both man and woman equally.

94 And thus it is so: Man and woman are equal in the sight of God and whosoever would have dominion over woman in this life acts from an evil heart, and not the true light of God."

95 The mouth of the rabbi gaped again as he prepared to speak, but before he could speak his mind, Yeshua said unto all of the men, "I have said what I have said. I have given you the true Celestine Light of God. How then will you now act? What does your heart feel? What is the truth that whispers in your mind despite all you have been taught before?

96 Here we will leave you, for my family journeys north. But I say unto you that this man, Ephres, is a good and righteous man who is devoted to God and does only good to his fellow man. Will you let him pass your town in peace?"

97 The rabbi blustered, "Nothing you have said has changed anything. Good riddance to you and take that man with you if you do not desire him to meet a worse fate."

98 But the villager who had spoken before stepped forth again, saying, "The rabbi does not speak for all of us. My heart and I think the hearts of some of my friends have been touched by the words you have said. You have given us much to consider.

99 We are not changed from who we were to who you would have us be in these short moments, but we have changed enough to give more thought to the words you have spoken.

100 Therefore, go your way in peace and forgive us the disrespect to your wife. The man Ephres may come in peace to our village. None will harm him."

101 At those words, the rabbi turned in disgust and walked back toward the village.

102 And Yeshua came forward and put his hand upon the shoulder of the villager who had spoken, asking, "What is your name, friend?"

103 "I am called Gimiel," he replied. "I am a simple man with flocks of sheep."

104 Yeshua smiled, saying, "Your humility has not hidden your courage, nor your simpleness the sharpness of your mind. I return to my home in Galilee, and the time will soon come when you shall hear of me again. If you know then what you know not now, come to me, and you shall learn the mysteries of the Kingdom of God."

105 Gimiel bowed his head to Yeshua and said unto him, "Teacher, you have opened our eyes today, but now you depart and we will have no one to give us further knowledge. Lest we soon fall back into our old ways, how then are we to know that which is true from that which is false when we are confronted with a choice?"

106 Yeshua answered, saying, "When you see a fine carpet from the masters of Tarsus, you have no doubt of its authenticity because of the tightness of the weave, the brightness of the colors, the purity of the wool, the subtle highlights of the silk, and the beauty of the design.

107 If a man were to come to you and offer to sell you a carpet he said was from Tarsus, it would take you but a moment of examination to know whether the carpet merchant spoke truth.

108 So it is with the words of God as spoken by prophets and prophetesses through all time and the corruption of the words of men upon the sacred.

109 Like the carpets of Tarsus, the true words of God are built upon a foundation that marks them undeniably as to their source.

110 In this, you have a most easy test. You do not have to get into great theological contemplations, for the ways of God are pure and simple, distinct and easy to know.

111 The commandments of Sinai have been given to you, and they are easy to live. The very first words of God as recorded spoken to Adam and Eve are in innocent purity, as yet undiluted by the machinations of men.

112 Therefore, if the commandments say not to kill, but in other places in the sacred books it records the people of God being commanded to kill every man, woman, and child, is this not a contradiction of the foundation of truth?

113 If Elohim told Adam and Eve that every herb bearing seed, which is upon the face of all the earth, and every tree in which is the fruit of a tree yielding seed would be meat for them, but later the sacred books record God saying to eat the flesh of animals, is this not a contradiction of the foundation of truth, in both the commandments of Sinai and the word of Elohim spoken to Adam and Eve?

114 Do you think that Elohim is a changeable God who gives contradicting commandments or conforms to the desires of men? Verily, I say no! Elohim is the same yesterday, today, and forever.

115 Seek to understand the heart and essence of Elohim, and you will hold the foundation of good by which you may know the truth of all things of light.

116 Here then is the key to understand the foundation of Elohim, whereby you may know the truth of all things of God: Verily, the basis of all goodness and godliness is to love and respect God, the giver of all life and the creator of all things.

117 And to love and respect your neighbors, for every injury to them is an injury to you and every blessing to them is a blessing to you.

118 And to love and respect yourself by treating the body you have been given as a temple and the hours of your life as a stewardship from Elohim.

119 Any law that is contrary to this is a law of man, not God. Any man or rabbi, priest, or Caesar who teaches other than this teaches from a place of darkness, not of light.

120 Therefore, I say unto you, even as you know at a glance a true carpet of Tarsus, know also the truth of Elohim by the firm and simple foundation that has been given.

121 Once you have weighed all things in the balance and the truth you hold does not seem wanting, seek out Elohim in quiet prayer and ask in humility to know of a certainty that which

seems right to your heart and mind is true.
122 If you ask with a sincere heart and a repentant life, you will feel the power of God move within your heart a sureness of thought confirming that which your mind has found."
123 "Surely these are enlightened words," Gimiel said as the others nodded in agreement.
124 Yeshua admonished them, "You now hold the candle of truth. Hold it high that others may see the light."
125 And turning to Ephres, Yeshua said, "Keep your devotion to God and remember my words; your greatness is still before you."
126 Then bidding farewell to all the men, Yeshua and his family turned and continued their journey north.
127 And Ephres and the other men stood upon the road looking after them until they were no more to be seen.

CHAPTER 5

Commitment to the Light

Yeshua and Miriam travel to Nazareth to stay a short time with Yeshua's family, to hear of the events that took place in their lives while they were away, and to share with them the things that they experienced in their travels. Yeshua speaks with his Mother, Miryam, as well as to his brothers and other close kinsfolk about the events of the future that will come to pass. He explains that the time has come that he must begin the fullness of his purpose on the earth and asks for their support.

The remainder of the trip to Nazareth was uneventful. But the arrival of Yeshua and Miriam was an occasion for great celebration among their family and friends.

2 Yeshua's brothers desired to give a feast in honor of his return as was common custom, but Yeshua, knowing of their humble means, told them, "Thank you for your kindness, but a greater honor would be to hear of your lives since we have been gone that we may gain some of the joy that we have missed."

3 In accordance with his wishes, his family gathered around and shared all that had occurred with them in his absence. They spoke late into the night and the following day as well, until Yeshua and Miriam knew so much of what had transpired while they were gone that it seemed in their thoughts, as if they had never departed.

4 During the succeeding days and nights, Yeshua and Miriam also related to their family and friends in Nazareth many of the events that had occurred to them while they were away.

5 On the seventh day after their arrival, Yeshua and Miriam asked to speak in private with Yeshua's earthly mother, Miryam. In accordance with their wishes, they met alone in the house of Yeshua's brother after the midday meal, when the men went back to work and after the wives had departed to the houses of the other brothers.

6 At last, alone and with no others, Miryam came and embraced Yeshua and Miriam, and there were tears in her eyes. "I have missed you so much," she said wiping her eyes with her finger. "Tell me you are here now to stay, and I can grow old with all of my children to nurture me and my grandchildren to uplift me and make me feel young again."

7 Miriam and Yeshua stepped back, and Yeshua held his mother with a hand on each of her shoulders. He bent down and kissed her twice on each cheek, alternating one and then the other, and he said unto her, "I wish I could tell you the sweet words you wish to hear, Mother, but you know it is not my destiny to live and die as a carpenter in the village where I was born."

8 Miryam trembled as she replied, "I know you have a great calling, my son. I have known it from the day when you were conceived as a miracle from God. But Palestine is a small land and Galilee even smaller; can you not find a way to be who you must be and still come home each night to your family?"

9 Yeshua pulled his mother closer, embracing her tightly, "If it were only for the people of Galilee or Palestine that I labored, I would sleep every night within the walls of my home in Nazareth.

10 But I am the Celestine Light of Elohim come to the world, and the foundations I must lay will take me beyond this sanctuary of family and support.

11 I must seek out those who will carry the torch of Elohim once I am gone and teach them in the ways they should go that they might spread the Celestine Light of Heaven to all the world, even though there will be but few who are ready to receive it.

12 So too, I must confront those in power, both those over the flesh and those over the spirit, to declare that which is darkness and give that which is light, that for all time thereafter the spirit of the simple truths of Elohim will permeate the earth and give courage to the true Children of Light, wherever they may be.

13 Thereafter, men will have the spirit of truth to guide them if they seek it, to not be swayed by the craftiness of Caesars and priests who make laws of Elohim unto themselves and take the freedom of men and make them slaves."

14 Miryam was crying openly now. She hit his chest lightly with her hand, "No, Yeshua, no. Do you think the Romans will just let you tell them they are wrong? Do you think the Sadducees will simply ignore you if you speak against them? No, I tell you, no. If you do these things, you will be killed and then where will your family be?"

15 Yeshua led his mother by the hand to a bench, and they both sat upon it. He held both of her hands as he looked into her eyes. His wife Miriam came to stand beside him, with a hand upon his shoulder, and he said unto Miryam, "Mother, there are some things that shall come to pass that you must know. You must be strong for the things which I shall tell you.

16 Know that you shall not be alone for that which shall come to pass. Miriam will be with you, and many others dear to you that you do not even yet know. And Elohim shall ever protect you, comfort you, and provide for you.

17 You have spoken true. I will be killed because of that which I must do. But know that no man could take my life except I willingly gave it and that I will not give it until my work is finished.

18 Know also that my death is not the end, but the beginning, and that I must die that all men and women may have the opportunity to live.

19 My life is like unto the building of a great edifice of the finest stone. Before the construction begins you see only the stones of which the building will be made. You may marvel at the beauty and uniqueness of the stones, but when the building is finished and the last stone is laid, you will no longer think of the stones, for they will have been transformed into something grander, of even greater wonder.

20 That which is laid in mortality shall rise in immortality, far greater and more magnificent.

21 I have come to bring the fullness of the Celestine Light of Elohim to the children of men. But even greater still, I have come to conquer the sting of death, that never more will it be the end of light and the beginning of darkness, but henceforth be the end of darkness and the beginning of light, the end of the finite and the beginning of forever."

22 Miryam was no longer weeping, and she softly patted Yeshua's hand, saying, "I know you have great things to do, son, but what of your family? Do you not also have a responsibility for their welfare? Would God ask such devotion of you that your family would suffer?"

23 "Fear not, Mother," Yeshua replied. "Though there will be trials and tribulations for you and Miriam and our children, as the sun brings the light of life, I promise you the eternal love of Elohim shall always guide and protect the treasures of my heart and provide the means whereby all may live and grow.

24 If it were not so, I would not have been born into the world, for love is the greatest gift of God. And it is because of love that I have desire and commitment for all things.

25 Love is ever faithful; it ever abides. It is only because of love that I can do what I must do.

26 With love, you need have no fear, for you will always have peace within your heart, even when it also aches.

27 It is because of the love of a son for his mother, because of the love of a husband for his wife, because of the love of a father for his children, and because of the love of Elohim for the Children of Light that you may know with a certainty that as great as you know me now in the flesh, you will know me even greater in the spirit.

28 And as great as I watch over and nurture the treasures of my heart in the flesh, I shall watch over and nurture them even more in the spirit.

29 Fear not to have me gone in the flesh, for I will be with you even more in the spirit, far more than you can begin to know on this day."

30 Miryam smiled at her son with contentment. "Your words comfort me, Yeshua, and I know that the power of God is in you. Therefore, there is peace in my heart that what will be is what should be. Call on me for what you will. I will never fail you or your family."

31 Yeshua embraced Miryam again and kissed her softly on her forehead, "Thank you for being the special daughter of God that you are. My cup overflows with the blessings that you bring into my life."

32 Then turning to his wife, he took her hand and put it into the hand of his mother, saying, "May you, the two greatest lights in my heart, ever embrace each other in sisterhood.

33 May you ever be the support, one for the other: the woman who knew me as only a mother could and the woman who knows me as only the most perfect companion of my life and eternity can."

34 The following day, Yeshua went with Miriam to the house of Yakov and called his brothers and other close kinfolk to speak with them about the days to come, and he said unto them, "You are my closest family upon the earth. Although you do not understand my purpose, you know I have been called of God to live a life different from all others.

35 You have been kind through the years to give shelter and support to me and my family when called upon, without thought for your own inconvenience.

36 On the morrow, I begin to fulfill the fullness of my purpose upon the earth. I must step past the boundaries of Nazareth and journey into Galilee and beyond to preach the Celestine Light of Elohim. Miriam must come with me, for she is to be a witness of all things.

37 Can I ask you now, my brothers, to love our children as your own in the days when they are here in Nazareth and we are away? To succor our children when I am not there to provide for their welfare? Will you love them, even as we love them?

38 Can we begin, here in humble Nazareth, to lay a foundation for a Community of Light upon the earth, where all the children are loved and nurtured by all the men and women as if they were their own?"

39 His brothers spoke among themselves briefly about the thing that he was asking, but each had been touched by the spirit of Elohim throughout their life and knew that even as it was given to Yeshua to bring the light, it was given to them to uphold it.

40 Yakov stepped forward, and speaking for his brothers, he laughed heartily and said, "You have been strange since you were young, Yeshua. There were times when we thought we should need to shutter you up until you became right in the head.

41 But you have shown us the error of our thoughts and have proven by your words and deeds to be chosen of God for a mighty purpose.

42 We fear for you, brother, for you give teachings that speak against the laws and traditions of our people and will antagonize the Romans and the Sanhedrin.

43 Were your teachings to come from a lesser man, even one that is our brother, we would leave you to reap the pain your actions will bring.

44 But we have also understood marvelous things from your words: things which we never would have supposed, which have given light and happiness to our lives and the lives of our families.

45 Despite the dangers that heeding your words can bring, you have touched our hearts with your heart and our minds with the sense of your teachings so much so that even now, we can no longer believe many of the things which we believed in the past, for you have given us greater knowledge that resonates in reason, and deeper in our hearts.

46 Verily, in the light and merit of the new, that which is old seems dark and foolish.

47 Therefore, go where you must, be gone as you will, and Miriam too. Your children will be as our children, all of our children; where before they had a father and a mother, now they will have many fathers and mothers; where before they had only each other, now they will have many brothers and sisters."

48 Then everyone came and embraced one another and the love and gratitude that permeated the room from all present was great.

49 That night, Yeshua and Miriam told their children that they would be oftentimes gone, sometimes for long periods of time. They also told them that they would now be a part of every one of their uncle's families and that their cousins would be as brothers and sisters.

50 At first, the children were apprehensive, but after speaking more with their parents, they became calm and began to talk about the benefits they might enjoy with such an arrangement.

51 After the children slept, Miriam lay beside Yeshua and cuddled beneath his arm, speaking quietly, "All has transpired with both our children and your brothers as best as we could have hoped. But I feel negligent to leave without giving them additional support, for we are asking them to feed two more mouths and to teach two more minds."

52 "You are right, Miriam," Yeshua answered. "But we have nothing of value to give to them. I can no longer work in carpentry, for all my time must be given to fulfill the purposes of Elohim and the treasure of the Magi is no more.

53 Let us journey from Nazareth tomorrow. It is my desire to begin to gather disciples unto me, but let us also seek to be guided to a small treasure of the earth that the care of our children not be a burden upon our family."

CHAPTER 6

Covenant of Light

Yochanan begins the fullness of his purpose on earth when he returns to the community of Gimron, where he was raised as a youth, to teach the community members about repentance and baptism. He baptizes twenty-three people, and seven leave to follow him up the Jordan.

As Yeshua began to embark upon the fullness of his purpose, his cousin Yochanan had not been idle.

2 After their departure in Bethany, Yochanan returned to the community at Gimron to seek out those who would listen to his words with an open heart and a mind willing to think beyond the room in which it had always dwelt.

3 Being married now and returning to the community in which he was raised for some years, he was given the right to speak during a gathering of the men for the teaching of righteousness.

4 When his turn came, Yochanan rose up from among them, and standing before the men gathered, he said unto them, "Brethren, most of you have known me since I was a youth, and you know that I am not given to an excess of words or flattery.

5 As you know, I have traveled far in the last years, even to Egypt and the borders therein of that country.

6 I have been amongst not just Hebrews, but also Egyptians, Nubians, Syrians, Greeks, Romans, Persians, and many more people who are different than me, different than you.

7 I have met priests of different religions and men of different beliefs.

8 But the greatest thing I experienced, the greatest that will ever be in all of my life, is to have traveled with Yeshua of Nazareth, who lived among us for a short time in his youth.

9 I have learned of his humility, but have also seen his majesty. I have learned of his commonness, in many ways like any other man, but have also seen in him the light of Elohim such as dwells in no other man, even the light we call Celestine.

10 Through him, I have found myself.

11 I shall not tarry long now among you. I leave within days to begin my life's calling and will journey along the Jordan, teaching repentance and baptism unto all who will hear my words.

12 If I could, I would teach that each one of you and every man in the land should seek out Yeshua of Nazareth and follow him.

13 That day will surely come for some, but it is not yet, and it is not given to me at this time, but to him, to call whom he will to walk with him.

14 I go now to prepare the hearts of the people, to call them to repentance, to teach them the simple truths that are the spark of the greater Celestine Light, which Yeshua shall bring.

15 I go now to baptize the repentant in the river Jordan as a covenant between them and

God that from that day forth; they will leave the darkness behind and walk only in the Celestine Light.

16 And now, O men of Gimron, I begin with you. At this place, on this day, I begin to fulfill my purpose upon the earth.

17 You have isolated yourselves in this spot that you might study the ancient ways and come closer to God. And in many things you found that which you sought.

18 But I say unto you that finding God is far simpler than the complexities of the law and far more difficult than endless days of study.

19 It is closer than the words of the prophets and more distant than the discovery of ancient mysteries.

20 Verily, some may come into a oneness with God in the space of a day, while others will seek for a lifetime and never find that which they seek.

21 I declare unto you that it is not piety and obedience to the law that brings a man or a woman to glory and joy in the life to come and fulfillment in the life you live, but humility with a contrite spirit, honoring the temple of your body, and a willingness to give respect and do good unto all people.

22 It is not seeking to be perfect in the law that brings you to God, but striving to be an emissary of Elohim, with humility, by looking outside of yourself, and doing good unto your fellow men all of your days.

23 What I have learned in my travels among people of many different races and religions is that though they may disagree with my beliefs, though they may not know the truths that I know, though they may not have the Celestine Light that I have, they will respect me and trust me and give honor to God, a place in their hearts when they see the light of God in the life I live.

24 But if I disdained them and gave them no respect, if I looked only unto myself and gave no thought for their life and their problems, then they would not see the Celestine Light of Elohim in me.

25 They would instead see only a crab in its shell, having no interest in them, except to avoid them. And they would in kind have no interest in me except to keep me away. And because of my actions, they may never discover the true Celestine Light of Elohim.

26 If I carry the lamp of God, but they avoid me because of my stoic spirit, how then shall they find it? Wherein shall their curiosity be stirred such that they will seek the source of the light?

27 It is well and good to live here in the peace and solitude to better be able to seek Elohim without the distractions of life in a village or town. But there must be something more beyond just yourselves.

28 Once you have found Elohim in your heart, once you have been strengthened by the wilderness, I say unto you to go forth into the land and share your light with those who do not have it, for they are many. You may always return to the wilderness to renew yourself.

29 Do good in the world, that others may see your good light and desire to seek its source.

30 I know there are many good and honorable men and women who dwell at this place of solitude, and I do not upbraid you for the good that you have, but only ask you to realize that only by sharing the light that you have will you gain more yourself.

31 You cannot be proud, my brethren, you cannot have pride in your heart, but must take joy in humility, for whatever light we have is only that which we have been blessed by Elohim to hold.

32 Every person has sinned and fallen short of the expectations of God. As the years go by, a person's sins are not forgotten by Elohim though the sinner will try to forget.

33 Unrepentant sins, even those you think you have forgotten, stay with you still, slowly pulling you down until one day you may find yourself in a deep pit from which there is no escape and know not how you got there.

34 I do not speak of sins against the law, but only sins against the commandments of Sinai, for

these are the sins of the Holy Scrolls of which God calls man to an accounting and repentance.

35 And the foundation of the commandments of Sinai is to honor Elohim and to treat your fellow men even as you wish to be treated.

36 Look now unto your own life. Do you honor Elohim for all of your many blessings, for your life, your health, your home, your family, your peaceful community?

37 Do you honor Elohim by cherishing the temple of your body, which God has given you?

38 Do you honor Elohim by daily prayer and fasting, at least once each moon?

39 Do you honor Elohim by obeying the commandments of Sinai?

40 I know of one area that every man here is in need of repentance, and understand I speak to you with love, my brothers. You have much light, but you confine yourself to this sanctuary in the wilderness and do not share your light with others in the greater world, who need it so desperately.

41 Put yourself in their place. If you were lost in the world, ignorant of the light of God, and each day must face only the misery of existence and the yoke of the Romans, how dear would it be to you to have someone come into your life and show you a sure path to a greater happiness?

42 Therefore, I call you to repentance that you might be pure in your heart and worthy to make a covenant with Elohim.

43 I challenge you this day to uncover your lamp and henceforth live your life in a greater light.

44 I will remain here but three days more, and then I will journey up the Jordan. I have been gentle with you, for I know you have good hearts, but with the Children of Israel, I shall not be so gentle.

45 I shall call them to repentance and hold nothing back. I shall teach them the simple truths of Elohim, and I will not waver. And those with great sins will be unable to hide, for they will not be able to persuade me or pay me to go away.

46 I will speak with each of you for two more days, for I know some disagree with what I have said and others will want more understanding of that which I have spoken.

47 I ask any who have caught a glimmer of the Celestine Light of Elohim from my words to fast for the next two days, praying often to Elohim. Remember your sins both big and small and confess them to Elohim, asking forgiveness.

48 If you have wronged another person, go to that person and confess that which you have done and make restitution such as you can.

49 If you are humble and honest and hold nothing back, but confess all to God, and tell the truth to all men, then Elohim will forgive you of your sins if you make a covenant to be born anew and from that day forth to live a better life with a greater light.

50 And the spirit of God shall touch your heart, and you will feel the loving forgiveness that is greater than all the feelings of men.

51 If you would do these things, then come to me on the third day, and I will baptize you in the waters of the Jordan, that you may make a covenant with God to be a Child of Light from that day on.

52 As you rise from the water, feel the spirit of Elohim all around you, for at that moment, you will truly be born again.

53 On the fourth day, I shall begin to move north along the Jordan, and I will need those of good heart to follow me and help me teach the people and baptize them of water.

54 For those who follow me, I will teach you of the Celestine Light of Yeshua and the many things I have learned from him so that when you meet him, it will be as if you already know him."

55 And it came to pass that, even as Yochanan had said, on the third day, he baptized twenty-three souls. And on the fourth day, seven of them followed him north along the Jordan.

CHAPTER 7

Yochanan the Baptizer

Yochanan teaches his disciples many of the truths that he has learned from Yeshua, including a full understanding of sin, repentance, and redemption. He and his disciples head north along the Jordan River, stopping near every town and village, preaching repentance and baptism for the humble in spirit and contrite of heart for which he becomes quite renowned. They set up a camp on the shore of the Salt Sea, known today as the Dead Sea, for those who come to be baptized and hear Yochanan preach. Many become new disciples and are sent out to every town to teach. The scribes and the Pharisees, sent by the priests and Levites of Jerusalem, also come to question Yochanan and leave with a self-righteous, condemning attitude.

nd it came to pass that Yochanan and his disciples did not tarry upon the Jordan, but following a tributary to the east running toward Beth Haran, they encamped upon the headwaters in the hills far above the grounds of the palace.

2 They brought few possessions with them, save some camel skins for sleeping at night upon the ground, for Yochanan had told them that they would fast for long times and when they ate, it would be only as God provided in the abundance of the wilderness.

3 And it came to pass that Yochanan and his disciples tarried for one moon in the hills with frequent fasts and many prayers.

4 His disciples learned to find the nests of bees and how to safely extract their sweet honey. They discovered which plants were edible and the myriad of tasty delicacies in the headwaters, including which insects could be eaten for food.

5 Yochanan admonished them that they should not kill animals, unless there was no other choice for food, clothing, or shelter.

6 And though they fasted often, they held their weight the same because of the great nutrition of their food, which Elohim provided in abundance.

7 During their long uninterrupted hours together, Yochanan taught them many of the truths he had learned from Yeshua. Not all he knew, for it was more than they could comprehend at this time, but all of the foundation of the simple truths of salvation.

8 And there grew a great loyalty among his disciples to Yochanan because of the long days and nights they had spent together, sharing in hardships and joys as they learned and grew beyond what they had been.

9 Yochanan's disciples became filled with the new truths they had learned, with a full understanding of sin and repentance and redemption through the Celestine Light of Elohim.

10 Yochanan taught them to disrespect unrighteous authority, both of Caesar and of the

leaders of the Sadducees and Pharisees and the court of the Sanhedrin. He taught that it was the nature of most leaders of institutions, both in government and ecclesiastical authorities, to exercise unrighteous dominion over the lives of men.

11 He taught that only those who brought forth fruits of repentance and thereafter lived in virtue and walked in the light of Elohim, doing good to all men, would be worthy of the positions of power by which they held sway over men.

12 When one moon had passed, they returned to Gimron and each man to his family. And Yochanan returned to Bethany to be with his wife and family for half a moon.

13 Upon the next moon, Yochanan reunited with his disciples in Gimron, and they went forth north along the Jordan, stopping near every town and village, preaching repentance and baptism for the humble in spirit and contrite of heart.

14 The words of Yochanan quickly reverberated across the land, for he was a fiery orator, and many people came from towns and villages far away from the Jordan to hear his words and be baptized into the new covenant that he preached.

15 Coming to the boundary of Samaria, Yochanan turned and began moving south along the Jordan, retracing the path by which he had come.

16 His disciples went forth before him to every town and village, giving the people a portion of his message of the new covenant and causing a great excitement among them.

17 So effective were his disciples at arousing the people that by the time Yochanan again neared the Salt Sea, large multitudes were waiting for his arrival upon the banks of the Jordan.

18 Unto these, he preached a message of repentance, confession, restitution, and forgiveness. And many were the people who repented of their past and took upon them the mantle of the new covenant and were born again of the water.

19 Each moon, Yochanan and his disciples returned to Gimron to be with their families for a few days, and Yochanan's family came to be with him each new moon.

20 Soon his fame spread greatly, and so many people began to follow him to Gimron that the members of the community asked him to no longer come there, for they could have no peace.

21 Yochanan agreed and took his disciples and journeyed to the northeastern shore of the Salt Sea. At the hot springs and baths located there, he made a long-standing camp and baptized and taught those who made the journey to hear him preach.

22 Each new moon, although not everyone, many of the families of his disciples would come to spend a few days with their husbands and fathers, and at this time, they would retreat up into the hills above the hot springs that they could have a few days of solitude with their families, away from the crowds that waited for them below.

23 It was while staying at the hot springs of the northeastern Salt Sea that Yochanan became famous throughout all the Tetrarchy of Herod Antipas. And the crowds of people who came to hear his mighty preaching and be baptized by him never diminished, but only grew.

24 Besides repentance and the new covenant, Yochanan taught that the Kingdom of Heaven was at hand and that though he baptized with water, one was coming after him who would baptize with a fire in the heart.

25 And many were added to be counted among his disciples from those who came to hear him and were baptized.

26 Most did not remain with him, but were sent out into the lands beyond to teach the people in every city and town and village enough of the light that they would desire to journey to the springs to hear the preaching of Yochanan and be baptized.

27 And it came to pass that the scribes and the Pharisees, sent by the priests and Levites of Jerusalem, came to him, trying to snare him in a mistake of the law and said, "Who are you? Are you the Anointed One?"

28 Yochanan was humored by their blatant attempt and confessed, "I am not the Messiah."

29 And they asked him, "Who then? Are you Elias?"

30 He said, "I am who I am."

31 "Are you a prophet?" they persisted.

32 He answered simply, "I am a lowly servant of God."

33 They said to him then, "Do not speak in riddles. Who are you? Let us have an answer for those who sent us. What do you say about yourself?"

34 He replied, "I am the voice of one crying in the wilderness, 'Make straight the way of the Lord,' as the prophet Isaiah said."

35 They were wroth with him and his answers and asked him, "Then why are you baptizing, if you are neither the Messiah, nor Elijah, nor a prophet?"

36 Yochanan proclaimed to them, "I baptize with water for repentance of sins to enter into the new covenant and to prepare the way for one whom you do not know, even he who comes after me, and the thong of his sandal I am not worthy to untie."

37 Then said the Pharisees, "What need have we of your repentance or your baptism? We have Abraham as our father, and we baptize our followers unto ourselves."

38 Then Yochanan towered in righteousness before them, saying, "You brood of vipers! You are warned: bear fruits that befit contrite repentance or flee in vain from the wrath to come!

39 You baptize unto yourselves? I baptize unto Elohim, the Almighty God of Heaven. Of what worth do you think your baptism unto yourselves is to God?

40 Of what value is it to say, 'We have Abraham as our father,' but you have not a true repentance for your iniquities and a humble spirit?

41 For I tell you, God is able from the stones on the ground to raise up children to Abraham, but humility can only come from the truthfulness of your own heart.

42 Repent therefore for the coming of the king is at hand, and even now the axe is laid to the root of the trees, and every tree that does not bear good fruit will be cut down and thrown into the fire."

43 And it came to pass that the scribes and Pharisees turned away from his fearsome countenance and the sting of his words, but the multitudes were amazed and asked him, "What then shall we do?"

44 Yochanan answered them in quietness and humility, "He who has two coats, let him share with him who has none, and he who has food, let him do likewise."

45 Tax collectors also came to be baptized and said to him, "Teacher, what shall we do?" And he said to them, "Collect no more than is appointed you, and if you truly love God, collect only in equality from all, without compulsion.

46 Take not from a man's lands or property and from his coins only by his choice, as payment to Caesar for fair use or purchase."

47 Soldiers also asked him, "And we, what shall we do?" And he said to them, "Rob no one by violence or by false accusation, kill not, save it is to preserve your own life when attacked, and venture not into foreign lands save it is in retaliation for an attack upon your land."

48 Merchants also came to him and said to him, "And what shall we do?" And he said to them, "Be honest in your dealings and never use duplicity."

49 Unto the men he said, "Respect your wives, for they are daughters of God."

50 Unto the women he said, "Honor your husbands, for they are sons of God."

51 To everyone he said, "Treat with kindness and love all children, for they are jewels of God upon the earth that you might always have the light of God before you upon their faces."

52 And the people marveled at the teachings of Yochanan, and they questioned amongst themselves whether perhaps he was the Messiah, even though he had denied it, but Yochanan answered them all, "What I have said, I say again. I baptize you with water for repentance, but he who is mightier than I is coming, and he will baptize you with the Holy Spirit and with fire and light.

53 His winnowing fork is in his hand to clear the threshing floor and to gather the wheat into his granary, but the chaff, he will burn with unquenchable fire."

54 And with many other exhortations, he preached the good news of repentance and

forgiveness and baptism to be prepared for the coming of the Celestine Light of Elohim.

CHAPTER 8

Oneness by the Lake

Yeshua and Miriam travel to Lake Gennesaret (known today as the Sea of Galilee), north of Tiberius, where Yeshua wishes to introduce Miriam to some fishermen. But first, they stay for two days and three nights at the vacation villa of Miriam's family at Magdala so they can have some private time together before Yeshua begins his ministry. It is during this time that Yeshua teaches Miriam many of the secrets of Celestine Light that she did not previously know.

And it came to pass that Yeshua and Miriam left Nazareth and journeyed east toward Lake Gennesaret.

2 As they neared the lake, Yeshua said unto her, "There are some special men I want you to meet who live on the north shore. They are fishermen whom I have known since the days of my youth when I would come here to fast and pray and meditate. I have had long conversations of depth with them and desire to know your perceptions."

3 "If they are fishermen, then I may already know of them," Miriam answered. "Many a moon, I have spent in my family's villa on the shore of Lake Gennesaret, and I know of several of the fishermen who sell to our procurers. What are the names of the men?"

4 "There are two sets of brothers," Yeshua answered. "Cephas and Amram and Ya'akov and Yohhanan."

5 Miriam laughed and answered, "I know Cephas well: big, loud, and always complaining that he does not get paid enough for his fish. He did not come that often to Tiberius to sell his fish, but he is noticeable even if you only see him once.

6 Amram I do not recall by his name, but I will likely recognize him when I see his face if he fishes with Cephas. Ya'akov and Yohhanan are likely the same men that are the sons of Zebedee, who is also a fish procurer, so he knows my father."

7 Yeshua smiled warmly, saying, "I think you know the men, and I tell you that they are more than fishermen. They have deep souls and humble hearts."

8 As they neared the shore, Yeshua desired to sleep away from any settlements, on the hills overlooking the lake, but Miriam demurred, saying, "We know that we are now beginning to walk a road that shall bring great challenges to us. Before the persecutions begin, let us stay at my family's villa, which is so near, that we might have just a few precious days of peace and nights all to ourselves in comfort such as we may never know again."

9 Yeshua embraced Miriam and held her for a long time, saying, "That would be easy to agree to, Miriam, for I love you with all of my heart and desire your happiness. But if I preach that people should live frugally and give their excess to help others in greater need, but then am seen to reside in the vacation house of a rich man, would I not then be a hypocrite and my teachings

unworthy of attention?"

10 Miriam was weeping gently now on Yeshua's shoulder and said in a soft voice, "My Lord, you have stayed in my parents' house in Bethany, and it is far grander than the small villa at the lake. Even as then, you are not staying in a house of your own, but are a guest in the house of another, so there is no hypocrisy.

11 Nevertheless, I know that you have dedicated every one of your remaining days to teaching the Celestine Light and that even the appearance of hypocrisy would take on its substance in the wicked minds of men so that even this innocent but precious wish could be painted with a different face by those opposed to your words."

12 Yeshua wiped the tears from Miriam's eyes, asking, "This is something you truly wish?"

13 Miriam nodded her head in assent, saying, "I do not fear what is to come. I take joy in what you are bringing to the world.

14 But I also know I may never again have time alone with just you and me, without the antagonisms of the world bearing down upon us or others such as your fishermen desiring your time. Can we not stay there at least one night and have this moment just for the two of us?"

15 Yeshua looked at Miriam in tenderness, saying, "Not one night, Miriam, for it would not be enough to fill our cup. You have spoken true. Let us stay three nights that our love will ever be one. We will fast and meditate together. We will greet the sun in the morning and bridge the earth and the heavens.

16 But before I fulfill my vow to teach the Celestine Light all my days yet upon the earth, I will teach you the mysteries that few others in this world will ever know."

17 And it came to pass that late in the afternoon, Yeshua and Miriam came upon the villa, north of Tiberius, and remained there for two days and three nights, spending time with no others, but holding every moment unto themselves.

18 And Yeshua taught Miriam many mysteries of Celestine Light that she knew not, nor did anyone until then. And she discovered the full potential of the powers of light, which she had not previously supposed were possible for any but the Elohim.

19 Those secrets cannot be written or spoken to the world, only given by those who have received them unto those who have proven worthy and unfailing, then called by Elohim to have the greater light.

20 By the last night, and from that time forward, Miriam was more than she had been, for she had a greater light and understanding. Nor could any man reproach her or overcome her, for she had the glory of Elohim in her countenance and the powers of Celestine Light in her words and deeds.

CHAPTER 9

Equality of Women

Yeshua introduces Miriam to the fishermen, Cephas and Amram and Ya'akov and Yohhanan, but the fishermen feel awkward in the company of Miriam, a woman, as it was not common practice for the women to be socially interactive with the men at that time. Yeshua talks about the Communities of Light and explains the importance of the women being equal to men. He then asks Cephas, Amram, Ya'akov, and Yohhanan if they would follow him, but only after pondering upon it for a month, to see if they feel it in their souls.

rising just as the first light cracked the horizon, Yeshua and Miriam had a small meal of fruit and then faced the rising sun together and did the Contemplative Movements, bridging the heavens and the earth.

2 Immediately afterward, making haste, they walked quickly to Tiberius on the road along the lake and boarded a ferry just before it departed for Bethsaida.

3 After arriving at Bethsaida and sharing a small meal of greens and tubers, which they had brought with them, they walked around the town, observing the people while Yeshua continued to elaborate upon some of the things that he had taught her the previous days and nights.

4 Toward late afternoon, the fishing boats began to come into port, and they went down to the shore of the river where the fishing boats landed to wait for the men Yeshua wished to see.

5 Before many minutes had passed, they spied three boats coming toward the shore together and caught the loud voice of Cephas, even from a distance, coming from the lead boat.

6 Two of the boats carried five fishermen, and the third had six. Among the men were all of those whom Yeshua sought. As Cephas and Amram stepped onto the shore, he and Miriam were there to greet them.

7 Cephas looked up in astonishment when he realized it was Yeshua standing before him and exclaimed, "Is it truly you?"

8 Yeshua stepped forward and gave Cephas a big hug, saying, "I told you I would return when it was time to catch the fish of ages. The time draws nigh."

9 Cephas returned a startled look, obviously shaken by that unexpected statement and then ignored it in his response, saying, "I had heard you were in Egypt."

10 "We were," Yeshua answered, "for many moons."

11 Then the others disembarked from the boats, and Yeshua greeted Amram, Ya'akov, and Yohhanan. He was introduced to the other men of the crews as the great teacher from Nazareth they had heard them speak of.

12 Yeshua introduced Miriam, his wife, to Cephas and the others, and there was immediately

some disquiet among the men to have a woman among them, although they were all polite in greeting her.

13 Yeshua and Miriam stood watching while the fishermen unloaded their small catch and secured their boats.

14 Then Yeshua and Miriam and three of the four whom he knew proceeded to the house of Cephas, while Yohhanan went and gathered his wife and children and the wives and children of Ya'akov and brought them to the house of Cephas for a communal meal.

15 The men all sat in the courtyard, and Miriam sat with them. There was an awkward silence, for Yeshua did not speak and the men did not know what to make of Miriam sitting among them.

16 Then Cephas said, "My mother and wife and the wives of my brother and friends are even now preparing the evening meal. Your wife can go through that door to help them."

17 And Yeshua said unto them, "You are right, Miriam should be helping to prepare the meal, but it must needs be that she is also present to hear the words we speak. Therefore, we will both go to help with the food, so she will not miss any of the important things we shall say to one another."

18 With that, Yeshua and Miriam stood up and entered the house, leaving the men to stare at one another in abject confusion.

19 Amram looked perplexed and commented to his friends, "I do not understand why Yeshua is acting so strangely. He would have his wife sit in council with us, and he goes to help the women with their work? Perhaps, he has had an accident and is not right in the head."

20 "That could be an explanation," Cephas agreed.

21 "Unless he is possessed of a devil," Yohhanan conjectured.

22 "He cannot be possessed of a devil," Cephas replied.

23 "And why not?" Ya'akov inquired; "I have known several men possessed of devils, and they do such crazy things."

24 "None of you have spoken with Yeshua as many times as I have," Cephas answered. "He is not like other men, and it is not because he is crazy or possessed of a devil. In truth, he is the most pure, good person I have ever known.

25 Let us not be hasty in our judgment. Although it is a hard thing to have a woman sitting with us, this is probably a way he is teaching us something which has nothing to do with having a woman in our council.

26 Therefore, let us bide our peace and we will learn our lesson. Have faith in Yeshua. I know he will not deceive us or do anything that is not pleasing to God."

27 The women soon brought out the meal, which consisted of sardines and bread with fresh greens from the surrounding hills, and sat it in wooden bowls upon the table.

28 The men gathered to one end of the table and the women to the other. But Miriam came to sit at the right hand of Yeshua, and Yeshua asked for Cephas to sit upon his left.

29 Cephas was affronted to be asked to sit on the left while Miriam sat on the right instead of with the women and said quietly to Yeshua, "I want to understand your actions, Yeshua, but you are bringing insult upon me in my own house, in front of my family and friends.

30 Not only is your wife again among the men instead of the women, but you give her the place of honor at your right hand and ask me to sit on your left, an action which I cannot comprehend even in my most forgiving and tolerant mind."

31 Yeshua reached out and put his hand on the shoulder of Cephas, saying, "Have patience, my friend. I have serious things to say to you concerning this after the meal, and all will be revealed.

32 Know now that there is an important reason that Miriam sits where she does, by my right side, even among the men. Trust me, Cephas. When have I ever given you anything but truth and light?"

33 Cephas nodded his head and sat down to Yeshua's left, saying, "You are truth and light,

Yeshua. Therefore, though I am still disturbed and confused, I will do as you ask and wait for your explanation after the meal."

34 During the meal, Yohhanan asked Yeshua to tell them of some of their adventures in Egypt. And Yeshua obliged him and told of their travels in the caravans and their time with the Nubians and the meetings with the priests of the temple.

35 And he explained the foundations of the Path of Three even as he had to the priests.

36 But of his miracles, he said nothing, for he wanted them to gain a testimony of the Celestine Light with their own eyes and heart.

37 Following the meal, the wife of Cephas beckoned for Miriam to come with the women, but she demurred, and the wife of Cephas gave her a stern and quizzical look and did not understand.

38 Then it was that all of the men and Miriam sat down with Yeshua, and he said unto them, "I know all of you have wondered why it is that Miriam is always with me, even when I sit in council with men. You are not alone in your thoughts, for this has troubled many men from Palestine to Egypt.

39 The laws and traditions of many pious cultures teach that women must be obedient to the commands of their husbands and serve their husbands as they wish.

40 While the men can walk about freely uncovered with the sunshine and fresh air upon their face, women are commanded to remain covered from head to toe, to not be a temptation to the thoughts of men.

41 Even among the Greeks, who many find ungodly in their morals, women, though more exposed in their dress, are still relegated to stand behind and support the men; neither are their thoughts or desires given much consideration in matters of importance.

42 Now here sits Miriam with us, not just to listen but also to give her thoughts. And I will tell you that I value her opinions. Tell me now, my friends, in honesty and openness, what do you think of this?"

43 "I think it is unnatural," answered Amram.

44 "Who will prepare the meals if the women sit with the men?" interjected Yohhanan.

45 Ya'akov was irate and said, "Not only is your wife sitting with us, but she is also uncovered, which as you have said is not in keeping with our laws and traditions.

46 How can men be expected to think clearly if the naked face of a comely woman is sitting right next to them?"

47 Cephas also remained opposed to the presence of Miriam, saying, "What can a woman know that is worth hearing on matters of great importance? Unless she has always been in the presence of men, then the things men speak of will be unknown and incomprehensible to her.

48 And I still wait with patience for an explanation as to why she was given the place at your right hand at the meal that my embarrassment among my friends and family might be abated"

49 Yeshua smiled and was preparing to speak, but Ya'akov still had more to say, adding, "There are many good reasons that women do not associate with men, not just reasons of law, but also of a practical nature.

50 It is indisputable that the principal purpose of women is to bear and care for children, for this is how their bodies have been created, while the bodies of men are not so, but have been created by Elohim to be bigger and stronger, more suited for war and hunting and fishing.

51 The next most important thing is for women to give pleasure to their husbands. Again, they have been uniquely designed for this purpose. I do not have to say more, for we are all married men here.

52 Lastly, women are given to care for their children and the garden and the house they live in, which also includes seeing to the comforts and needs of their husbands who provide all they have by the sweat of their efforts and skill of their abilities.

53 Even as the men are bigger, the women are smaller in stature, so it is easier for them to stoop down to the ground to take care of children and gardens.

54 As they bear the children and are incapable of the strenuous work of men, their duties are logical and reasonable.

55 After all these things, even if it was permitted, they would have no time left in the day to sit in councils with men, and as Cephas has said, even if it were allowed, their minds are not like those of men and the things they would speak of would not be interesting or edifying."

56 Acknowledging the men with a nod of his head, Yeshua said unto them, "Thank you for your honest opinions. I have begun in earnest to fulfill my purpose in life, which is to give the Celestine Light of Elohim that has been hidden, that the Children of Light, both the men and women, may become more than they have been.

57 I am not long for this earth, and there must be others who will carry the lamps of the light that I bring. Many years, I have pondered who these torchbearers should be, and I know that each of you should be among them.

58 But I also know that you are steeped in the laws and traditions of this people. You live in a small house and are in darkness to the world beyond your doorstep.

59 The light that I bring shall be given first to the people of this land, whose fathers found favor with Elohim long ago.

60 But I will need torchbearers who will endure until the end. It will only be to a few of the people of this land that the light will illuminate, for their hearts are hardened, thinking they already have all the light they need. In truth, they have only a candle, when they could have the sun.

61 But there are many lands beyond this small house, and those who would follow me must push open the door and be willing to go forth into the chaos and confusion, into the strangeness and the vastness of all the world, that all who would seek it may find the Celestine Light."

62 "And what of our families?" asked Yohhanan. "Who will care for and protect them if we travel abroad?"

63 Yeshua looked into the distance as if he were seeing a vision, "Those who follow me shall gather their families into Communities of Light here upon the lake, where everyone will be as one family.

64 When a father is away for a time, his brothers in spirit will attend to the needs of his children and the provision of his family, and his sisters in spirit to the comfort of his wives.

65 And more than this, for days of great calamity are coming, and for the people of this land, there shall not be left one stone upon another that is not overturned.

66 Those who stand as lone men defending their home shall perish by the sword, their house laid to ruins, and their wives and children taken into slavery.

67 Nor is there deliverance in armed opposition, for the boot of the Romans shall crush the insects of Palestine under their feet.

68 But the unity of the Community of Light will make great the numbers that are small. With prayer and planning, they shall not be parted, nor taste the bitterness of slavery or death before their time. And Elohim shall send an angel, even the Angel of the Covenant, to watch over them and protect them.

69 Verily, your wives and your children, and the children of your children, shall be more protected and provided for when you serve the Celestine Light of Elohim than if you do not."

70 "You make us seem like important men," Cephas said. "But we are only poor fishermen and know little of the law or the ways of Elohim. Who would listen to anything we have to say?"

71 Yeshua gave a most engaging smile and, with a small laugh, said unto them, "If I sent you to argue the law with the scribes and Pharisees, you would be like babes before wolves, for they have learned the law from early days and would chew you up and spit you out.

72 But I have not come to uphold the law, but to destroy it. I bring a greater light, and those who follow me will know this light more than all others, and none shall be able to stand before them when they speak the truth that I shall give."

73 And Yohhanan inquired again, "But how shall we care for our families if we are going all

over the land with you? You speak of a Community of Light, but such a thing does not exist at this moment. We live in a community now, but if I abandon my family, I cannot expect my friends to take care of them forever.

74 Your words stir my heart, but I cannot see the practicality of following my heart."

75 "The world was not created in a single day," answered Yeshua. "I will still be with you for many moons and seasons upon seasons, and we will make this area of Galilee our home.

76 We shall bring our children from Nazareth to live with us here and begin to build the Community of Light at this most favored spot on the north end of the lake near the river Jordan.

77 While I am with you, our travels need only be limited, mostly in Galilee, for seekers of the Celestine Light will travel from Jerusalem and beyond to find us here.

78 During this time, we will gather the faithful to us as a hen gathers her chicks, and the Community of Light shall wax strong and multiply.

79 When the time comes that my disciples must go forth into the world, their families will be one with the greater Family of Light, more secure and provided for than they ever were before."

80 "Are you asking us to follow you now?" asked Ya'akov.

81 "Not today," answered Yeshua, "I want you to consider well the things we have spoken about and the things we have yet to speak about. But very soon, I will ask."

82 Amram raised his hand to be noticed, "This began as a conversation about women, but we are still ignorant on that accord."

83 "Completely," Miriam agreed.

84 Yeshua quickly spoke again before any of the men could react to Miriam, saying, "No matter how great a man becomes, it is less than he could be with a woman standing beside him in equality, not servitude; giving him wise counsel through her eyes, not being ignored.

85 Verily, the husband who serves his wife with love and respect will be richer by far in the treasures of Heaven than the man who asks his wife to serve and obey him.

86 When respect and service are given with love, they are reciprocated and multiplied, a sure foundation upon which you can always depend.

87 But when respect or service are given out of fear, they are empty and will vanish as an illusion in time of greatest need.

88 Verily, I say unto you: A cornerstone of my tower of light is the equality of the man and the woman in matters of spirit and mind and heart. Only in physical strength is it given to man to be greater than woman, and that, only so he can protect and provide for those that he loves.

89 None may follow me who cannot bear the brightness of this light.

90 And I declare unto you with words of soberness that none who follow me will be greater than Miriam, for unto her is given to know a fullness of the Celestine Light that no other can ever know so full, for she has been with me almost every moment for many years, and all that I have, I have given to her.

91 If I am not present and you wish to know my words or wish to have a clarity of my teachings, it is to Miriam that you must look, for none will ever know me more than she does."

92 Then Cephas said unto him, "Now I understand why Miriam sits at your right hand. Nevertheless, this is a very hard doctrine you teach, and I think you will not find many people who will follow you."

93 Yeshua nodded his head in agreement, "You are correct, Cephas. Many will be called, but very few will be chosen. Now, you are all good men, brothers of my spirit, and I would that you would be kindred of my heart and numbered among the chosen elect of Elohim.

94 What I have said today is only the beginning of the greater Celestine Light I bring. Therefore, consider well if you can abide this light, before you ask for more.

95 Rome may shake the pillars of Jerusalem and tread the armies of their enemies beneath their feet, but my words shall shake the pillars of the world and the gates of Rome shall fall before me.

96 I bid you to sleep now upon that which has been said. In the morning, speak not of this

one to another, but go to the lake and fish as you would always do, pondering upon my words in your heart and mind.

97 Continue thus, meditating with yourself, until the new moon comes; then speak about this again with one another.

98 Miriam and I leave in the morning and will be gone for two to four moons. When we return, I shall call your name.

99 When you hear my voice, see if you do not feel it in your soul.

100 On that day, let your heart and mind answer as one."

CHAPTER 10

Temptations of Yeshua

Yeshua and Miriam travel back to Nazareth to spend some time with their children before heading into the mountains. Yeshua fasts for forty days, drinking only water with a little honey. Both Yeshua and Miriam spend their days in prayer and meditation. After forty days Yeshua finds all the answers he has been seeking, and they prepare to journey to the river Jordan so Yochanan can baptize them. A great whirlwind comes and carries Yeshua onto a mountaintop where he is confronted and tempted by the adversary within but does not allow darkness to take hold. Angels of Light return him to the glade and to Miriam.

And it came to pass that on the following morning after everyone had said goodbye, and the fisherman had taken their boats onto the lake, Yeshua and Miriam began to walk the road to the south along the western shore.

2 Arriving again at the villa of Magdala, they stayed a night and then made haste to Nazareth the following morning that they might see their children again.

3 They remained for eleven days in Nazareth and Yeshua took great pleasure in being with his children, who were excused from many of their normal duties that they might spend as much time as possible with their father and mother.

4 Following the Sabbath, Yeshua and Miriam departed south and avoiding the towns of Samaria they came to the confluence of the river Jordan and the river Jabbok, and followed the Jabbok east into the mountains.

5 They followed a tributary up into the mountains until coming upon a beautiful glade where they prepared to stay for some time, alone and away from all people.

6 In the solitude of the mountains Yeshua fasted for forty days, drinking only water and a little honey. But Miriam did not fast, save it be for a few days at the beginning, but she ate very sparingly and prayed often.

7 Each morning upon arising, they would do the Contemplative Movements together and afterwards pray, facing each other and holding hands, for some time.

8 Afterwards Yeshua would most often go alone atop a hill to pray and meditate, while Miriam remained at the glade, also often in prayer and meditation.

9 Just before dark Yeshua would return and recount to Miriam many of the visions he had, and of the words of his Father and Mother in heaven, which they had spoken to him.

10 After the fortieth day, Yeshua was weak from his fast. He had found the answers to all that he had sought, both within and without, and said unto Miriam, "It is time that we take journey to the Jordan that we might be baptized by Yochanan."

11 And Miriam looked at him questioningly saying, "Why should you need baptism of Yochanan? For he baptizes that men might show they have shed their old skin and will henceforth live a new life pleasing to God. What need have you of this? Your life is already dedicated in purity to the work of Elohim."

12 And Yeshua answered, "I have ascended to a new mountain of light in my fast, worthy of baptism to mark the path now before me.

13 Verily, baptism is an act of commitment to the path of Celestine Light, which all men and women who love the light should embrace, for in it they are born anew and they will know it in their heart.

14 Let me go now into the water and come forth that all who love the light may know without doubt that unless they take a true baptism from their heart, by immersion in the water, they are still in the world and fall short of a sacred covenant with God to be born anew.

15 And after water comes the fire, and only those who have known the water can receive the fire of the Holy Spirit of Elohim to ever be their guide in righteousness.

16 Suddenly a great wind came up and Miriam was afraid, but Yeshua held her and told her to be calm and to wait for him.

17 Then ominous dark clouds came overhead and a mighty whirlwind came down from the sky. Yeshua pushed Miriam to the root of a tree and she watched in fright as a funnel of roiling fury came down and lifted Yeshua up into the clouds and he was gone.

18 And the whirlwind carried him to the top of a nearby mountain and he heard a voice speak to him in his mind saying, "You think you are the only begotten Son of of the Father and Mother in heaven. If that is so then appease your hunger and turn these stones upon the ground into bread,"

19 And Yeshua answered aloud, saying, "Hunger is here today and gone tomorrow, and in the light of forever it is not even a memory; but the word of Elohim is precious and eternal and to that, all who love light will always hold.

20 Verily, the power of Elohim is not given to edify the holder, but to edify others."

21 Then the whirlwind came down again from the cloud and carried Yeshua to the top of the temple, and the voice of the adversary within came again into his head, saying, "Prove to yourself that you are really the only begotten Son of God and cast yourself from the pinnacle, for it is written, 'He shall send angels to protect you, and in their hands they will bear you up, lest at any time you dash your foot against a stone.'"

22 And Yeshua answered aloud, saying, "My Father and Mother in heaven are proven by faith, not tests, and they who would test Elohim have no faith, therefore their test must fail, for they ask not in need and with faith; and only by such is the power of Elohim made manifest."

23 Then the whirlwind came down again from the cloud and carried Yeshua to the top of a high mountain from which he could see the vast waters and the lands far beyond. And the voice of the adversary within came again into his head saying, "If you are the only begotten Son of God, what is man to you that you would be mindful of him?

24 All that you see before you and all the world beyond can be yours. What man could stand before the Son of God? Take what is yours that all men may bow down before you and serve you and obey you."

25 And Yeshua answered aloud, saying, "Leave me! There is no place for evil within me! I have come to serve, not be served. It is only when one is in the service of their brothers and sisters of spirit that one fulfills the greater Celestine Light of Elohim.

26 Only those who walk in darkness seek to be served and serve not others.

27 I am the light and you are the darkness, and the darkness has no place with me. Therefore, I say unto you, be gone, and trouble me no more!"

28 And the darkness left as he commanded, and was no more in his presence ever again.

29 Then came angels of Celestine Light with a warm wind upon their breath. And they lifted and carried him up in the brightness of the sunshine until he came again back to the glade where Miriam awaited.

30 And she rushed to greet him and held him tight. And he told her all that had transpired, and hearing his words she cried.

CHAPTER 11

Baptisms of Yeshua and Miriam

Yeshua and Miriam come to the river Jordan to be baptized by Yochanan the Baptizer, but first Yochanan asks Yeshua to baptize him, which he does. Then Yochanan baptizes Yeshua and when he comes up out of the water, there is a mighty thunder, and into the mind of every person of good spirit comes a voice speaking of Yeshua as the beloved Son. Then comes a white dove that lands upon the shoulder of Yeshua and rubs its face against his before flying off. Yeshua asks Yochanan to baptize Miriam, but she requests that Yeshua do it and he complies.

After the sunrise on the following day, Yeshua and Miriam descended to the Jordan and, coming to the western road, walked southward.

2 Now Yochanan had traveled with some of his disciples north along the Jordan to preach and baptize, and the riverbank was crowded with people who had come to hear him preach, for his disciples had gone before him into the nearby villages and towns, urging the people to come to the river to hear the words of Yochanan the Baptizer. And many people came, for his fame had already begun to spread across the land.

3 Near a ford in the river, northeast of Jericho, Yeshua and Miriam came to the place where Yochanan was preaching and baptizing, and they watched him from afar for a time as he thrust and raised those being baptized into and out of the water with great vigor, saying, "I baptize you with water, but one comes after me who shall baptize you with fire if you are true to the faith of your heart."

4 Then Yeshua and Miriam came to him. Yochanan was overjoyed to see them, so much so that immediately after lifting the person whom he had just immersed out of the water, he came to the shore in great bounds, embracing Yeshua with such enthusiasm that his disciples were disconcerted and amazed.

5 "Yeshua, Miriam, my joy is full today," he exclaimed. "It seems so long since I have seen you. I am honored that you have come to hear me preach and witness the humility of the good people who are baptized this day."

6 Yeshua smiled at him warmly, "Our joy is also full to be with you again, my brother, and we wish to be among the good people who are baptized by you this day."

7 Hearing this, Yochanan protested and forbade him, saying, "It is I who has need to be baptized of you. We spoke about this before, and I still do not understand. Why do you come to me asking this?"

8 Yeshua explained, "I have come into the darkness to show the light.

9 Those of contrite spirit that go into the water rise forth from it in covenant with Elohim, with a greater light, and this edifies our Father and Mother in Heaven, which I do with every breath I take.

10 Therefore, it must be to show all righteousness that I ask you to honor me with this blessing."

11 Yochanan knelt down upon one knee before Yeshua, saying, "I will do that which you ask. It is my greatest honor, but I ask you first to baptize me, for never could I think to baptize you without first being blessed to receive that gift from the Son of Light."

12 Yeshua smiled at Yochanan and nodded his head in affirmation, then waded into the river and Yochanan followed him. And standing in water a little above their waists, Yeshua said unto Yochanan, "With the purity of your heart as the witness of your soul, I immerse you in water that you will come forth with a greater love of God, to ever guide you upon the path of light. By the word of Elohim, so be it." And immediately, he immersed him, and then raised him out of the water.

13 Upon arising, Yochanan embraced Yeshua, and his disciples were confused and astounded, not knowing what to make of all that had so quickly transpired.

14 Miriam stood upon the shore, looking at her husband and brother-in-law savoring their unique bond. Holding her palms together as if in prayer, she touched her forefingers to her lips and gave a great smile of joy for that which she witnessed.

15 Then Yochanan turned and baptized Yeshua, saying, "That all men and women of contrite spirit may know the path to greater light and a new life begins with the water, I immerse in humility he who shall come forth in glory."

16 When Yeshua came up out of the water, there was a mighty thunder from the clear, sunny sky, and it rumbled again and again.

17 And in the mind of every person of good spirit standing upon the shore came a voice, reverberating with the thunder, saying, "This is our beloved Son in whom we are well pleased. Hear him."

18 Then a white dove, a symbol of the Holy Spirit of Elohim, flew from the wilderness and landed upon the shoulder of Yeshua and rubbed its face against his, and then flew off into the brightness of the sun, where none could follow its path.

19 All of the disciples of Yochanan and many of the people upon the shore that had come to hear him preach were amazed at what they had seen and heard, and the awe showed on their wide-eyed faces and open mouths.

20 Then Yeshua embraced Yochanan again, and turning to Miriam, he put out his hand that she would come unto him.

21 Miriam walked into the water and took his hand, and he brought her to Yochanan, saying, "Brother, would you baptize my wife, the greatest treasure of my heart?"

22 "As you wish, Yeshua," Yochanan agreed.

23 But Miriam demurred, saying, "Husband, I love Yochanan, even as you do, but in this sacred ordinance, would you not share it with me?"

24 Now Yeshua was conflicted, for he wanted to fulfill the desires of Miriam's heart, but did not want to undermine the authority of Yochanan in front of his disciples and the people who had gathered to hear him preach.

25 But Yochanan, being guided by the Holy Spirit, turned to the shore and, pointing to Yeshua, said unto his disciples and the people, "Behold Yeshua of Nazareth, the Lamb of Elohim.

26 This is he whom I have said will come after me to baptize with fire.

27 This is he whom I have said that I am unworthy even to unlatch his sandal.

28 This is he who shall pay the greatest price, that all who have a true repentance and faith in him will be freed from the chains of their slavery, for Elohim will remember their sins no more.

29 And now comes his wife Miriam to be baptized. She is the sister of my wife Martha, and even as I did with her, I wish every man could know the joy of baptizing their wife. Therefore, I come out of the water now to watch my brother baptize my sister."

30 Then Yochanan came out of the water and watched with the others as Yeshua baptized Miriam, saying, "With the purity of your heart as the witness of your soul, I immerse you in

water that you will come forth with a greater love of God, to ever guide you upon the path of light. By the word of Elohim, so be it." Straightaway he immersed her, and then raised her out of the water.

31 Miriam came out of the water and her face was aglow with light. And she turned and put her head upon Yeshua's chest and embraced him gently and then lifted her head and kissed him softly on the lips.

32 Seeing the baptism ending with a kiss, some among the onlookers were upset and they departed quickly with angry words.

33 But the pure of heart were touched by the Holy Spirit, and they fell to their knees with bowed heads and hearts filled with thankfulness to have been upon that spot on that day.

CHAPTER 12

Disciples of Yochanan

Yeshua speaks briefly to the disciples of Yochanan after the evening meal.

And it came to pass that Yeshua and Miriam stayed with Yochanan and his disciples that night, and among them was Philip of Bethsaida, who had come to hear the preaching of Yochanan and was baptized by him.

2 Both Yochanan and Philip had spoken to the disciples of Yochanan of their experiences with Yeshua, and some were excited that he was to spend the night with them, but others did not look so favorably upon him, for in their minds he was usurping Yochanan whom they revered.

3 After the people that had come to hear Yochanan preach and to be baptized by him had returned to their towns and villages, Yochanan and his disciples ate the evening meal with Yeshua and Miriam.

4 Miriam was the only woman present, and some of the men objected to this, and others complained that she had not prepared a meal for them.

5 Hearing this, Philip confided to them, "It was the same at the home of my friend in Bethsaida. Truly she is a most strange woman. But she is the wife of the Rabbi Yeshua, and he has told us that women are not to serve men, but to be served by them."

6 Some of the disciples of Yochanan were so angry at the words of Philip that they stood up in disbelief and would have walked away, but Yochanan bade them remain and asked them, "Where do you think to go? Would you leave the light to walk alone, forsaken in the darkness?

7 I tell you in truth that the light of Elohim sits among you, and you know him not.

8 Verily, I say unto you that Yeshua of Nazareth is he whom I have said that I am not worthy to unlatch the strap of his sandal.

9 If you would walk away from him before you have even listened to his words and sought the truth in your own spirit, then your shame is even greater than your ignorance, and you have learned nothing from your time with me."

10 Chastised by his words, the disciples of Yochanan that had stood up to leave sat down again.

11 Yochanan turned to Yeshua and said unto him, "Brother, will you share your light with us this night?"

12 Yeshua nodded his agreement and rose and stood before them, saying, "Verily, among those born of women, none are greater than Yochanan the Baptizer.

13 For those of you fortunate enough to share the cup with him and receive a portion of his light, you are blessed among the children of men, and you shall remember this time dearly, all the days of your life and your children's children shall still speak of it."

14 And knowing the thoughts of those that had been angry, Yeshua said unto them, "Some have thought that I have come to overshadow Yochanan, but I have come to be blessed by him, even as you are.
15 I know him more than any man can know him, for we have shared years in the exclusive company of each other and made great discoveries together.
16 This is his moment; he is doing the work he was called to do before the foundations of the world.
17 Cling to his words, for his teachings will be a part of you, long after his soul has returned to the presence of Elohim.
18 As for me, my teachings taste strange to the children of men fed upon the plate of the law and tradition, for I have not come to serve the meals of the past, but to bring the food of the future.
19 Until you understand the words of Yochanan and live them in your life, you will have no place in your heart for the teachings that I bring.
20 And why do you think that women should serve men? Rather should men serve women, for it is by them that every person comes into the world; and by them that the pure and simple principles of virtue and righteousness are woven into the character of their children, that when they are grown they will walk in the light.
21 What virtuous man would put himself above a woman or above any other man? Verily, I say unto you the first shall be last and the last shall be first. The exalted shall be abased, and the abased shall be exalted.
22 Those that would be called great must feed the least, in both spirit and body, even as Elohim, who is greater than any, freely gives life and love to all that dwell upon the face of the earth.
23 Now, I shall teach you no more, nor answer your questions, for these are the days of Yochanan, until the days of Yochanan are fulfilled. And those who have been pulled by their heart to Yochanan must stand with him until the end, for only those who endure until the end will find the fullness of the light that they seek."
24 Then Yeshua returned to sit by Miriam, and Yochanan said a prayer of thanksgiving and supplication unto Elohim. Without much further conversation, everyone found a spot of comfort for the night and fell asleep, each to their own, beneath the stars.

CHAPTER 13

Kingdom of God

Yeshua and Miriam bid Yochanan and his disciples farewell and Philip asks if he can walk with them and hear more of Yeshua's teachings. Yeshua asks him to ponder a question, and if he answers correctly, then he can learn more; if not, then he must first learn more of the foundation of light from Yochanan. Philip answers correctly, and Yeshua asks him to follow him and promises to teach him the mysteries of God so that he may go forth to teach others.

Upon the sunrise, Yeshua and Miriam rose and asked Yochanan to lead them in the Contemplative Movements, and this he did, teaching the movements and the meaning again to his disciples, for many were lax at exercising and communing with God in what seemed to them a foreign manner.

2 When they were finished, Yeshua and Miriam bid good-bye to Yochanan and his disciples, and without eating a morning meal, as was often their custom, they began a walk to the north.

3 And it came to pass that Philip came after them, and with him came Malachi, who had traveled the previous day from Jericho to hear Yochanan preach.

4 Hearing them approach, Yeshua turned and asked, "What do you seek?"

5 Philip answered, "Rabbi, we are not disciples of Yochanan, but came only to hear him a few days ago for the first time and to be baptized. If we may, we would like to walk with you, for we desire to hear more of your teachings."

6 Yeshua smiled and told him, "Let me see if you are prepared to understand all that I would teach you. At sometime during the day, after you have weighed the merits, tell me if the Kingdom of God dwells within you or without.

7 If you give the correct answer, you will open the door and gain entry to the pinnacle, but if you answer wrong, then you must return to Yochanan and learn more of the foundation before you can climb the tower."

8 Then knowing the aversion of men for a woman to be held equal among them, Yeshua turned to Miriam and asked her, "I desire solitude as we travel, for I have much to contemplate. Would you therefore speak with Philip and Malachi, concerning the Kingdom of God?"

9 Turning to Philip and Malachi, Yeshua said unto them, "I will listen to your conversations as we travel, but desire for you to speak only with Miriam. Anything you would ask of me, ask of her, and anything she would speak to you, it is the same as if I had spoken it unto you."

10 The two men were shocked by the directive of Yeshua, but realizing this was a test of their worthiness, they did not protest, but folded their hands to their chest and bowed their heads in deference to that which he had spoken.

11 And it came to pass that the mother spirit of Elohim came upon Miriam insomuch that

she was enlivened to remember all that she knew, and she engaged Philip and Malachi in a deep discussion that astounded them, for she spoke not only of the law with knowledge, but also of the words of the prophets and the philosophy of the Greeks and the secrets of the hearts of men that women should not know.

12 Many a time, Philip or Malachi thought to make a counterpoint, but before they could form their thoughts into words, Miriam began to answer them.

13 Finally, the frustration of Philip could be bound no more, and he said unto her, "Miriam, my head is overflowing with your words insomuch that it aches. You speak as the most learned rabbi, and I did not even know this was such a large subject. Let us learn no more until we have understood all that has already been spoken."

14 Malachi added, "The words of Philip are true; if all of the teachings of Yeshua are so full, I fear our heads will become so heavy that we will not be able to keep them on our shoulders."

15 Miriam laughed a little and said unto them, "The teachings of Yeshua are like being overwhelmed by a great sandstorm. At first, you may be surprised and confounded, even dim in sight because of the immensity of that which swirls around you, but if you hold fast to your faith and endure through the winds of bewilderment because of that which is new, then the haze and storm will pass, and you will be left in the glorious sunlight of Elohim, with a peace that surpasses all you have known and a warmth sent from God that lifts your heart and fills your soul."

16 Around midday, they stopped and shared a meal, and even then Yeshua did not speak, but seemed distant in his thoughts.

17 But Miriam and Philip and Malachi continued to speak of the Kingdom of God, and Miriam said unto them, "The Kingdom of God begins in your heart, and if it is not there first, then it is impossible for you to ever find it in this life or the next.

18 And were the Kingdom upon the earth but not in your heart, the gates of the Kingdom would be closed to you, not because it was not desired for you to be numbered among those who dwelt there, but because knowing not the Kingdom in your heart, you would not seek it in your life."

19 Upon hearing her explanation, Malachi pursed his lips and asked her, "But if the Kingdom is upon the earth and in it, there is peace and plenty with no tyrants or wars, how could it be that everyone would not desire to belong to such a Kingdom?"

20 Miriam answered, "Those without faith would rather cling to misery than embrace the faith that would bring them joy, because they cringe at the light and find comfort only in the darkness.

21 In truth, would you be happy if you lived in the company of the Roman soldiers and traveled with them as they killed and tortured the innocent, even if you would be given generous food, silver coin, and the spoils of war?"

22 Malachi shook his head, saying, "I would not, for their ways are not my ways and I would always feel like a stranger among them, and their ways would certainly be strange and distasteful to me."

23 "So it would be with the Kingdom of God upon the earth," Miriam explained. "For those of faith who had God in their heart, the Kingdom would be the most joyous place to be, for they would be one in spirit with all others within the Kingdom.

24 But for those who did not have the Kingdom of God in their heart, the ways of the people of the Kingdom of God upon the earth would seem repugnant and disagreeable.

25 Though they would be welcomed with love and abundance, until the spirit of God lived in fullness in their heart, they would turn their back upon the Kingdom and hold its riches of no value."

26 Then Malachi shook his head in disagreement, saying, "The Children of Israel are not seeking a Kingdom of the heart or of the spirit, but a real Kingdom of power ruled by a king who is ruled by God, that we may be free from the bondage of the Romans and any other oppressor.

27 For as in the days of our forefathers, when God is with us, who can withstand us? Tell me plainly, is Yeshua this king or is he a prophet who will reveal the Anointed One to the people? Surely, if ever there was a time that the Kingdom of God was needed on the earth, it is now."

28 "What does your heart tell you?" Miriam asked.

29 Malachi responded, "My heart does not tell me anything. I do not ask my heart such questions. I am looking for what my eyes can see and my hands can touch. You speak of a Kingdom of the heart, but such a Kingdom cannot defeat the Romans."

30 Then Yeshua rose and stood before Malachi and, breaking his silence, said unto him, "Friend, you look for a king anointed by God to overthrow the yoke of the Romans; but verily I say unto you the Kingdom of God begins in the heart, and where dwells two or more hearts united in God, there does the Kingdom begin to manifest upon the earth.

31 By heart upon heart shall Rome fall, and by heart upon heart shall the Kingdom of God rise up and fill the world."

32 And it came to pass that Malachi departed from them, for he knew not his own heart nor in whose presence he stood, and he desired to see the Kingdom of God with his eyes before he found it with his heart; therefore, he was not filled by the words of Miriam or Yeshua.

33 But Philip had listened quietly to all that had transpired, and Yeshua turned to him and asked, "Where is the Kingdom of God, inside or outside?"

34 Philip answered unto him, "The Kingdom is inside me, for I feel the presence of the spirit of God moving my soul; but also, I feel my heart united with yours and Miriam's and a oneness with you that fills me with joy; therefore, the Kingdom must also be outside, for two or more are joined together and upon this road, we walk as one united in spirit and purpose."

35 Yeshua smiled broadly and said unto him, "Blessed are you, Philip, for it is not just by reason that you have understood this, nor only by your heart, but because the spirit of Elohim has come upon you that you know the light.

36 Therefore, I say unto you, come and follow me, and I shall teach you the mysteries of God, that your light may go forth among the children of men, and they will find the Kingdom within and without because you showed them the way."

CHAPTER 14

Disciples from Bethsaida

Cephas, Amram, Ya'akov, Yohhanan, Philip, and Nathanael from Bethsaida all become disciples of Yeshua.

nd it came to pass that Yeshua, Miriam, and Philip walked back into Galilee, and the excitement and joy of Philip grew with each step as he continued to feast upon the words of Yeshua.

2 As they did at every opportunity, Yeshua and Miriam went first to Nazareth so that they might again see their children and the family of Yeshua, and Philip came with them.

3 The family of Yeshua was happy to meet Philip, for they knew his presence meant that Yeshua had begun to publicly allow himself to be recognized as a rabbi.

4 But as Yeshua and Miriam and Philip made ready to depart again for the lake country, Yakov was agitated that Philip walked with Yeshua as his disciple, but his brother had not asked him to come with them.

5 Of all the brothers, Yakov most cherished the teachings of Yeshua, and he desired to be with him in his ministry.

6 Yeshua sensed his brother's feelings and said unto him, "You are a great light upon the land, and your voice shall be heard by all the Children of Israel, who seek the Celestine Light.

7 Where there shall be few who hear my words and hearken to the light, there will be many who hear your words and hearken unto them.

8 I am the light of the world, and you are a great flame of the fire. But your time is not now, while the sun still shines high in the sky, but after it has been buried in darkness, then rises again.

9 Today, you hold the sacred charge to be a steward of our mother and our wives and our children. As you are a good steward over a few, Elohim shall make you a great steward over many, even all of Jerusalem. Let this not be a burden, for the day will soon come when your family shall be one with the Community of Light upon the lake. Then you will be free to follow me."

10 Yakov was humbled and happy at the words of Yeshua, and with new understanding, he bid him God's light until they met again.

11 After saying good-bye again to their children and family with words and warm embraces, Yeshua and Miriam departed again on the road to the east, accompanied by Philip.

12 Because Philip was with them, they did not stop at the villa on the lake at Magdala, but continued on to Capernaum, where Miriam's father owned a small two-room house. They returned to this house often as Yeshua began to teach the Celestine Light of Elohim at Galilee and among the Children of Israel.

13 Leaving Yeshua and Miriam for a short time, Philip returned to his home on the other side

of the river in Bethsaida to let his friends and family know that Yeshua and Miriam had returned and that Yeshua had asked him to become his disciple.

14 Now the brothers, Cephas and Amram, were surprised to learn that Philip was already counted a disciple of Yeshua, for they remembered that Yeshua said he would return and ask them if they were prepared in their hearts to follow him. As Cephas was a local leader of the delta area, they assumed he would be asked before any others.

15 The following day, Philip went to see Yeshua and Miriam at Capernaum, and his friend Nathanael, a merchant, traveled with him. Philip was anxious to introduce him to Yeshua, saying, "He is here, the man of whom Moses and the law and the prophets did write, even Yeshua of Nazareth, the son of Yosef."

16 Nathanael was dubious and said, "A good man I am sure, but can anything great come out of Nazareth? Please do not take offense, but I do not understand how anyone can even stand to live in that place, even though the view is beautiful from the top of the mountain. Surely, if God was going to raise a prophet in our day, he would come from almost anywhere else."

17 But Philip persisted, saying, "We are here now. Let us seek him out, and you can see for yourself. I said he was a prophet, but truly, I feel he is more than that."

18 And it came to pass that they found Yeshua and Miriam conversing beneath a fig tree, and seeing them approach, Yeshua called out to them, saying, "Greetings, Philip and Nathanael."

19 When Nathanael was near, he asked, "How is it that you know my name?"

20 Yeshua answered unto him, saying, "Philip has spoken to us of you as a man without guile. You wear that truth upon your countenance. You could only be he of whom Philip has thus spoken."

21 Nathanael was astounded and said, "Surely, you must be more than a Nazarethian to be able to read such things in the faces of men."

22 Yeshua laughed and said unto him, "Because I said I could see in your face that you are a man without guile, you believe in me? Verily, I say unto you: Hereafter, you shall see greater things than this."

23 Many more things did Yeshua tell Nathanael that astounded him. And from that day forth, Nathanael was counted as a disciple of Yeshua.

24 And it came to pass that Yeshua went with his wife and Philip and Nathanael to Bethsaida that same day, and coming to the shore of the lake, he saw the boats of Cephas and the sons of Zebedee casting nets into the waters of the lake; beckoning them toward shore, he walked into the water to meet their boats.

25 Standing nearly to his waist in the water, he grasped the boat of Cephas on one side, and the boat of the sons of Zebedee on the other, and calling out asked, "Cephas, Amram, Ya'akov, and Yohhanan, can you bear the brightness of the light?"

26 Cephas and Amram and the sons of Zebedee remembered the words of Yeshua from when he had last spoken to them, asking that they ponder upon the teachings he had given them and decide if they could live them in their lives, even though they might be different than the law would dictate and not the same as the traditions to which they were accustomed.

27 They had spoken of these things many days among themselves, and they knew now their true hearts. And Cephas replied, "I will follow you wherever your light leads."

28 Amram bowed his head and said, "I am blessed among men to have a greater light to follow. Though I am only a fisherman with little in my head, my heart yearns for the greater light. I will follow you to learn of it."

29 Yohhanan answered, "You are the light. Your words pierce my heart, and I have awaited your return. I know my family will be cared for as I care for the light."

30 And Ya'akov replied, "Although I still do not understand all that you teach of women, I greatly desire to learn more, and I will follow you and share the light you give to us with others."

31 Then Yeshua bade them to jump into the water beside him, and straightaway, they did, pushing their boats back into the lake; and Cephas turned to the men remaining in the boat and

told them to return to Bethsaida.

32 Zebedee stood in his boat with his servants holding an empty net, and he looked at his sons in disbelief.

33 Yeshua and the four men walked to shore, and Yeshua said unto them, "You have been fishers of the sea, and from the fish, life you have taken. Now I will teach you how to be fishers of men, and to the men, life you shall give."

CHAPTER 15

The Samaritan at Jacob's Well

Miriam, Yeshua, and his disciples depart for Jerusalem as Yeshua wishes to attend the Passover there. To save time, they pass through Samaria rather than detouring around it as was common practice. They stop at the never-failing well, known as "Jacob's Well," where Yeshua asks a Samaritan woman for a drink of water. She is quite surprised to be asked such a thing by a Hebrew, for the Hebrews and Samaritans did not commingle. After a series of questions and answers, which astounds the woman, Miriam encourages her to tell the townspeople what Yeshua has told her and ask them to return to the well to hear him speak. When the townspeople gather, Yeshua makes the well run dry and then creates a great geyser of water that shoots up from the well to show the power of Elohim and to warn them to stop living in enmity with those who should be their brothers and sisters.

And it came to pass that upon the following day, Yeshua and his disciples and Miriam, his wife, departed for Jerusalem, because Yeshua desired to attend the Passover there.

2 As they traveled, Cephas asked him, "How is it that you came to call Philip to be your disciple before you called me? Did I do something to offend you that you would not think to call me first?"

3 Yeshua answered him, "They who are first shall be last, and they who are last shall be first. In my Kingdom, those who serve are the kings, and those who desire to be the kings shall be the servants.

4 It matters not who was called first or who last, for as in the days of Noah, all should be overjoyed simply to be upon the Ark."

5 Because Passover was approaching soon, Yeshua chose a more direct route to Jerusalem that passed through Samaria rather than detouring around it as was the common practice of the Hebrews.

6 They passed close to a town of Samaria called Sychar, near to the parcel of ground that Jacob gave to his son Joseph.

7 The never-failing well of Jacob was there, and Yeshua and everyone with him were glad to stop and rest for they were tired from their journey.

8 There was a woman of Samaria at the well, and for the sake of the Apostles' understanding, Yeshua came to her and asked, "Would you give a drink of water to me?"

9 The woman was startled by his request and asked him, "How is it that you being a Hebrew asks a drink from me; a woman of Samaria? Your kind have no dealings with Samaritans."

10 Yeshua answered and said unto her, "A Hebrew I was born, but that is not who I am. Nor have I come only for the Hebrews, but also for the Samaritans and all the children of the world.

11 Though I bring the light first to the Hebrews because of their fathers, I do not withhold it from others because of theirs.
12 I know your heart, woman of Samaria, and I know it is kind. Look now to your heart, for if you find the spirit of God, you will know who it is that asks a sip of water from you.
13 So also will you know that if you ask of me, you can be given a greater gift, even of living water."
14 The woman of Samaria said unto him, "Sir, you have nothing to draw water with, and the well is deep. I have come here all of my life, and the water is always the same. Where then would you draw water that is different than that which has always been?
15 Living water sounds wonderful, but are you greater than our father Jacob who gave us this well and drank from it himself, and his children and his cattle?"
16 Yeshua answered and said unto her, "Before Jacob was; I was.
17 Whosoever drinks of the water of this well shall thirst again.
18 But whosoever drinks of the water that I shall give shall never thirst again, for they shall drink of living water that springs up into everlasting life."
19 The woman folded her hands together and said unto him, "Sir, please give me some of this water that I may not thirst or have to come again to this well to draw my water."
20 Yeshua said unto her, "Go, call your husband and come here."
21 The woman shrugged, "I have no husband."
22 "You have well said that you have no husband," Yeshua replied, "For you have had five husbands; and the man you live with now is not your husband, so you have spoken true to say you have no husband."
23 The woman was astounded that he knew of her life, and she questioned him, "Sir, I perceive that you are a prophet. Our fathers worshipped on this mountain, but those in Judah say that Jerusalem is the place where men should worship. What do you say?"
24 Yeshua answered her, saying, "Woman, be it on this mountain or at Jerusalem, the hour soon comes when none shall worship at either place, for they will be left desolate.
25 If either place was so holy as the vain do imagine, think you that God would allow its desolation?
26 Verily, I say unto you that you worship the Father whom you know not, even as those in Jerusalem worship the Father whom they know not.
27 But the hour is coming when true believers shall worship Elohim in truth and light. And it is not by the place that they worship that they shall be edified, nor by the manner in which they worship, but by the truth in their heart, the light of their mind, and the deeds of their lives.
28 Verily, Elohim is a Father and a Mother and a Child.
29 The spirit of Elohim is everywhere, even in the heart of those that believe.
30 If you would truly worship God, then you must find the Father and Mother and Son within you.
31 And in spirit and truth must Elohim be worshipped. And by the spirit of Elohim shall the hearts of the faithful be guided in truth and light."
32 Then the woman said to him, "I know the Anointed One is coming. When he comes, he will tell us all things."
33 Yeshua responded to her plainly, saying, "I am he."
34 His disciples marveled that he spoke thus to a woman of Samaria and gave unto her such great pearls of knowledge. Yet not one of them asked, "What are you doing?" or "Why are you speaking thus with her?"
35 Then Miriam came up to the woman of Samaria and told her, "You have found favor of my husband. Go to your town and tell the people what he has spoken to you, that they may come and hear the words of Yeshua as well."
36 Straightaway the woman departed, leaving her bucket at the well, and went and told the people of Sychar how Yeshua had spoken great things to her and how he knew the hidden

secrets of her life.

37 And it came to pass that many of the people of the town came ou
words of Yeshua.

38 Before the people of the town arrived, Cephas asked the discip
Yeshua anything to eat. And Yeshua, hearing his words, said unto them
you know not of."

39 Hearing this, the disciples looked among themselves in confusion
anything to eat. And Yeshua said unto them, "My food is to do the will o
who have sent me. I have come to fill the world, not to be filled by it."

40 The disciples nodded as if in understanding, but Yeshua knew they still did not understand. And he said unto them, "Do you not say, 'Two more hours then our nets will be full?' Did I not say I would make you fishers of men? I tell you, open your eyes and look at the nets! They are full and overflowing. Wherever you cast your nets, the fish await.

41 "Do you not say, 'Four months more and then the harvest?' I tell you, open your eyes and look at the fields! They are ripe for harvest today. Even now, the good reaper draws his wages. Even now, he harvests the crop for eternal life so that the sower and the reaper may be glad together.

42 Thus the saying 'one sows and another reaps' is true, for I send you to reap that which I have sown.

43 Even more, learn from me, that you might come to be both a sower and a reaper, that the fields of Elohim may be planted and harvested in abundance."

44 Turning then to the people of Samaria that had come to the well, Yeshua said unto them, "You revere your holy mountain, even as the Hebrews revere Jerusalem. Certainly, hallowed ground should be revered.

45 Yet you hate them for their belief and they hate you for yours, and I say unto you that you both do err, for the God of your fathers is the same as the God of their fathers, and all the world is a temple of God.

46 Even as a shepherd watches over his flock and goes to them where he is needed, so does the God of your fathers go to his children wherever they may need him.

47 Be it upon this mountain or in Jerusalem or anywhere upon this earth, wherever the virtuous and faithful are, there Elohim is also.

48 Today, this is sacred ground; tomorrow, it can be desolate. Even now Jacob's Well has run dry. What does that mean?"

49 At the startling announcement that the well that never fails had run dry, some who were listening ridiculed Yeshua, but others leaped up with concern and went to the well.

50 A Samaritan threw a small rock down into the well, and then turned to his friends in horror saying, "It is true. The stone hit upon stone at the bottom of the well. There is no water!"

51 At this shocking surprise everyone leaped to their feet in great anger, some screaming at Yeshua, "You have cursed our land."

52 Several men came toward Yeshua menacingly to grab a hold of him, but Yeshua put his hand out toward them and, with a voice of thunder, said, "Stop, cease your foolishness. Even as the power of Elohim can take away the water, so can it be restored."

53 Yeshua stomped his foot solidly once upon the ground, and there was a mighty tremble like an earthquake. Then a rushing sound came from the well, and suddenly, a great geyser of water shot up into the air far over their heads and rained down upon them. And the people marveled, for such a thing had never been known to occur in all the history of Jacob's Well.

54 After a few minutes the geyser ceased and the well became placid again, but the people and his disciples all looked upon Yeshua with amazement and awe, and he said unto them, "You will not see my face again upon this land, but remember the lessons of the water this day.

55 Your people have lived on this land for the passing of many generations. But if you continue to live in enmity with those who should be your brothers, the lines of your blood shall wither and

ntil there are Samaritans no more, even as the well that never fails did run dry.
like the geyser, the power of God manifests where it will to serve the purposes of
, in the time and place that Elohim chooses, not man.
Therefore, do not rest your faith upon a spot of land or a city or the laws handed down by
ur ancestors, for all of these things can be laid waste.
58 But let your faith rest upon the sure principles of Celestine Light that are the true words of
Elohim that speak to your hearts, for they are the same words for every people, be they of Judah
or Samaria or a Gentile from any land.
59 Verily, the words of Elohim that are the same for every people begin with these: Love God
with all of your heart, and love your neighbor as yourself."

CHAPTER 16

Wrath in the Temple

Yeshua goes to the temple in Jerusalem the day before Passover and finds many merchants selling their animals and wares in the temple courtyard. He becomes so enraged at the desecration of a sacred space that he throws their tables with such force that they flip in the air and coins fall like rain from the sky. He explains to his disciples that in most instances, a spirit of peace and empathy can bring resolution, but sometimes there is just cause for righteous anger.

And it came to pass that Yeshua and Miriam and his disciples came into Jerusalem the day before Passover.

2 Straightaway, Yeshua went to the temple, and there he found sellers of sheep and oxen and turtledoves and money changers calling out to him.

3 Miriam looked at Yeshua, and she saw an anger in his eyes such as she had never seen before, save on the day when the robbers of Zin had threatened her and their children.

4 Yeshua turned to his disciples and commanded them, "Remove cords from your clothes and make a scourge of knots and beads." Quickly they did as he directed and, within minutes, handed a scourge of many cords and knots to him.

5 Then Yeshua went amongst the sellers and money changers, swinging the scourge about his head and slapping it onto their tables, right in front of their startled faces, saying in a loud voice, "Depart from the house dedicated to my Father, you workers of inequity." And they all fled in terror at his wrath.

6 He drove their beasts from the temple and overthrew the money changers' tables with great power so much so that they flipped in the air and coins fell like rain from the sky as they were thrown from the tables.

7 His disciples were shocked into startled silence by Yeshua's actions. He was always so calm and peaceful; he so easily diffused contentious situations with his words that they never imagined he could bring forth such anger.

8 Even the temple guards were cowed by his wrath and none made any effort to challenge him.

9 Within a few moments, after all the merchants had left and all the animals were gone, Yeshua returned to his normal calm demeanor and his wife and disciples came to him, and he explained his actions, "In almost all things, a spirit of peace and empathy can resolve even the thorniest problem. But when man dares to defile that which has been dedicated to the sacred, righteous anger is well served."

10 Then came the priests unto him and asked, "You take great authority upon yourself by your actions. Who are you to decide what is right? For the temple is our domain, not yours. Such

usurpation should not go unpunished."
11 Yeshua answered and said unto them, "Destroy this temple, and in three days, I shall raise it up."
12 The priests were incredulous at his audacious statement and said, "Forty and six years it took to build this temple, and you think you could rebuild it in just three days?"
13 Yeshua answered, "If you have ears, hear what I say: When the temple of Elohim is laid desolate, in three days I shall raise it more glorious than before."
14 The priests departed from him, convinced he was mad.
15 But he spoke of the temple of his body, and when he later rose from the dead, his disciples remembered the words he had spoken that day.

CHAPTER 17

Enlightenment of Nicodemus

Yeshua heals many of the sick and maimed who have faith and gratitude but does not heal those who do not. A high-ranking Pharisee named Nicodemus comes to see Yeshua secretly that he might learn some of his teachings. Yeshua teaches him about the light and the darkness and the importance of conquering the adversary within.

And it came to pass that Yeshua and his wife and his disciples departed from the temple and went out into the streets of the city.

2 As they walked among the people of the city, they saw a man sitting on the ground, weaving a basket with his teeth and one hand, for his other arm was greatly deformed.

3 Yeshua came to him and asked what had happened to him, and the man told him his left arm and leg had both been badly cut by a sword when he was a young man, and he had been a cripple ever since, but had learned to weave baskets with his teeth that he might still help support his family.

4 Yeshua asked him plainly, "Are you angry with God because of your infirmity?"

5 "No!" the man cried out. "God has blessed me with my infirmity, for I could have easily been killed and left my family desolate. I am greatly blessed, for I still live, and I still hold my wife and children every day. Surely, God loves me."

6 Yeshua gave a warm and loving smile and said unto him, "You are a faithful father and husband and deserve to be with your family in wholeness for the years that remain to you. You have shown your love for Elohim and your family, and now Elohim returns what you have given."

7 Yeshua reached out and put his hand on top of the man's head, saying, "By the love you have for Elohim, by the love you have for your wife and children, I say unto you, rise up and be made whole."

8 In that very instant, the man's limbs became whole and he rose to his feet, feeling his arm and leg in disbelief. Then he fell to his knees before Yeshua, saying through his tears of joy, "O mighty man of God, thank you for this miracle of miracles."

9 Yeshua pulled him to his feet and embraced him, saying, "The love you have given out has returned to you. Now go to your family." And the man ran with joy through the crowd that had gathered.

10 Then a woman came to him and she had a very thin and pale young girl with her, and she pleaded to him, "Man of God, please heal my daughter. She is infested with worms that eat her from within and crawl out through her skin. I fear she will soon die."

11 Yeshua looked at her and asked, "Do you believe that I can heal your daughter?"

12 And she replied with tears streaming down her cheeks, "Yes, O man of God, I do believe."

13 Yeshua reached out and gently held the girl's hand and, looking into the eyes of the mother, said unto her, "By your faith, so be it."
14 Immediately, color returned to the girl's face, and she embraced her mother.
15 Throughout the day, the injured and the sick and the maimed came to him or were brought to him when they could not come on their own. And those with faith and love and gratitude, he healed, but to those without faith or love or gratitude, he turned his back and healed them not.
16 But many were the people that were healed, and within a single day that which he had done in the temple and the healing of a multitude of people became talked about in excitement in many parts of Jerusalem.
17 As the evening began to fall, Yeshua and Miriam and the disciples went to the outskirts of the city and set up a camp to be in for the Passover, which they did without disturbance from the people of the city.
18 But on the following day, many people from the city came out to the camp to see Yeshua and many came to be healed.
19 That night, a high-ranking Pharisee named Nicodemus came to see Yeshua secretly, for he did not wish to be seen speaking to him in public. But Yeshua called Miriam and his disciples that they might also hear the words he spoke to Nicodemus.
20 And Nicodemus said unto him, "Rabbi, many of my brethren are opposed to you coming to Jerusalem without authority or position and doing such things as you have done, unless God is with you.
21 I am an honest and devout man. I know many things, but I am willing to still learn things I do not know. Therefore, tell me how it is that a man can be sure to attain Heaven in the next life?"
22 Yeshua answered and said unto him, "Verily, verily, I say unto you: Except a man is born again, he cannot inherit the Kingdom of God."
23 Nicodemus was perplexed and asked, "How can a man be born again when he is old? Can he enter a second time into his mother's womb and be born another time?"
24 Yeshua answered, "Marvel not that I say unto you that you must be born again.
25 Elohim is the Father, the Mother, and the Son; therefore, a man must be born three times to enter into the Kingdom of Heaven.
26 After the birth of the flesh, the repentant of heart must be born of the water, cleansed of the dirt of the past, renewed with the spirit of God, sanctified to a new life of purity before God.
27 Then comes the birth of the spirit and the baptism of fire, and except a man is born of flesh and of water and of fire, he cannot enter into the Kingdom of Heaven."
28 Nicodemus was still confused and asked, "How can these things be?"
29 Yeshua answered and said unto him, "Are you not a high teacher of the Children of Israel? How can you not understand these things?
30 The simple truth comes from my lips, but you hear it not. Open your ears, Nicodemus. Even more, open your heart, for I testify of the true Celestine Light of Elohim and only by it will you be illuminated in fullness.
31 If I speak to you of earthly things and you do not believe my words or cannot comprehend my teachings, how will you believe or comprehend when I tell you of heavenly things?
32 How do you think you came to be born from your mother's womb? How do you think to be able to go to Heaven when you do not even know how you came to be upon the earth?
33 Verily, I say unto you, no man has ascended into Heaven, save he who has first come down from Heaven to be upon the earth, even the Son who has come from Heaven and stands before you.
34 And it shall come to pass that as Moses lifted up the serpent in the wilderness, even so, must the Son be lifted up.
35 For Elohim so loves the children of the world that the only begotten Son is given unto them. That whosoever believes in him and lives his words shall not perish, but shall inherit eternal life and exaltation.

36 The Son has not come into the world to condemn the children, but that through him, they might be saved; that through him, they might find the path to greater light, even to the Celestine Light.

37 He that believes in him and does his will is not condemned, but given a greater light because he has believed in the only begotten Son of Elohim.

38 But he that believes not and does not his will condemns himself. By choosing a path of less light, he inherits greater darkness.

39 And this is the condemnation of the world, for the light of Elohim has come upon it, and most will know it not.

40 Those who love light will find joy, but those who love darkness will condemn the light, because their deeds are evil and the light leaves no place for them to hide.

41 Everyone who cleaves to wicked ways hates the light; neither do they come unto it, lest their evil deeds should be reproved.

42 But everyone that lives in truth and virtue, following the teachings of the light, become like the light themselves, and their deeds are pure and wrought by the spirit of God that dwells within them.

43 You are either walking in the light or walking away from it into the darkness.

44 That which you do today reaps serenity or the whirlwind, tomorrow.

45 The darkness does not overcome you quickly, but subtly, like the setting sun; moment by moment, there is less light and more darkness, until you stand enclosed in darkness, unsure how the light was lost and the darkness grew.

46 Thus works the devious and subtle ways of the adversary hiding within all souls, waiting with infinite patience to test the hearts and mettle of men.

47 That you may always be safe from the fiery darts of the adversary, the part of you enticing to darkness; I give you the simple path to righteousness:

48 Always choose right, even when you are tempted to do wrong.

49 Always choose the light, even when no one but you would know that you relinquished to the adversary within and chose darkness.

50 Always choose right, even when all of your friends chose wrong.

51 Always choose the light, even when doing so will cause you to suffer because of the world.

52 Always choose right and the light, Nicodemus, no matter the consequences; then darkness can have no place in you.

53 Be your own master, for if you are not, then the adversary of darkness reigns; and no matter your position in life, you are a slave to your weaknesses; and until you are the master, you will only dimly be able to see the light."

54 Nicodemus was intrigued by the teachings of Yeshua, and he told him, "I desire to choose the light, even as I desire to learn from the only begotten of Elohim. Is he among us? Is it you?"

55 And Yeshua said unto him, "If you truly seek the Celestine Light of Elohim, it will fill all your body with light and the spirit of Elohim will dwell in your heart, and your heart will rejoice and swell with joy when the light is with you.

56 Therefore, look to your heart to reveal the glory your mind does not know."

CHAPTER 18

Baptisms in Bethany

Yeshua baptizes his disciples and gives them the authority to go out and baptize those who have made a full and contrite repentance for the sins of their past; and have committed in their heart and with their words to obey the 12 Commandments of Sinai and to fully live in the light of Elohim. Many others desire to be baptized by Yeshua but he only baptizes Lazarus because he is the only one that is ready at that time. However, the following day Miriam and Yeshua's other disciples baptize many of the people.

Early the following morning, before a crowd came again from Jerusalem, Yeshua and Miriam and the disciples departed for the home of Miriam's parents in nearby Bethany.

2 Lazarus was at home when they arrived and after a meal shared in common by all, Yeshua asked his four friends from Bethsaida to come with him to the large pool in the garden that was fed by a small enclosed stream of water, and he said unto them, "Yesterday I spoke to Nicodemus about being born again of the water and the spirit, and if you would be my disciples you must also be born again of the water and fire.

3 Baptism is a sacred covenant given before witnesses, that you have repented of your old ways of darkness and henceforth you will walk only the greater path of the Celestine Light of Elohim.

4 Cephas stepped immediately into the pool; the water came up to his thighs and he said, "I am ready to be born again Yeshua, baptize me."

5 Then Yeshua stepped into the pool and stood beside Cephas. He turned and spoke to his disciples and the family and friends of Lazarus that had quickly gathered at word of Yeshua's arrival, saying, "Let there be no confusion. Take this covenant with your eyes wide open and your heart full of joy.

6 To be baptized in the water is to renounce and bury the dark ways of your old life, and rise and be born again, dedicated to living in the Celestine Light of Elohim."

7 Yeshua turned and faced Cephas, saying, "Are you at this place in your heart?"

8 Cephas grasped him by both arms and looked into his eyes, saying, "You know my heart; you know that my old life is dust; you know that my only desire is to live and serve in the light of Elohim."

9 Yeshua smiled and said unto him, "Yes Cephas, your heart is true, you are like a rock of abiding faith, and upon such rocks shall the torch of Elohim stand to illuminate the world."

10 Then Yeshua placed the left hand of Cephas on his left forearm, and held the right hand of Cephas in his upturned palm.

11 Yeshua raised his right hand to form a square and said, "With the purity of your heart as the witness of your soul, I immerse you in water that you will come forth with a greater love of God, to ever guide you upon the path of light. By the word of Elohim, so be it," and straight away he immersed him completely under the water, then raised him out of the water.

12 And Cephas came up out of the water all aglow even as Miriam had been when Yeshua baptized her.

13 Cephas stepped out of the pool and embraced his brother and friends, and one by one each of the disciples, except Miriam and Philip who had already been baptized, came into the pool and were baptized in the same manner by Yeshua.

14 Then Yeshua said to his disciples, "As you have seen me do, I charge you to do likewise; and with the authority of Elohim you shall baptize; but only those who have made a full and contrite repentance for the sins of their past; and have committed in their heart and with their words to obey the Twelve Commandments and to fully live in the light of Elohim."

15 Then many of the people that had witnessed the baptisms of the disciples came forward and desired Yeshua to also baptize them, and he said unto them, "The heavens rejoice that you desire to be baptized, but there is only one more among you whose heart is ready today."

16 Yeshua turned to Lazarus and beckoned him into the pool; and Lazarus came and stood beside him.

17 "Why me and no others?" questioned Lazarus.

18 And Yeshua said unto him, "You have been by my side more than any other save Miriam and Yochanan.

19 You have proved by the choices in your life that you follow the Celestine Light and that you have become the light that you have followed."

20 Then Yeshua baptized Lazarus in the same manner as he had done with the disciples.

21 After Lazarus had come out of the water in joy and stepped out of the pool to embrace his family and the disciples, Yeshua turned to the remaining people, who numbered about fifty men and women, and said unto them, "What you have witnessed here today is a sacred ordinance. It is a covenant with Elohim, not taken lightly, to forsake the darkness that is in you, and to hereafter walk only in the pure Celestine Light of Elohim.

22 You can only forsake the darkness with a sincere and contrite repentance for the sins you have done in your life; repentance for the sins you have done in opposition to the commandments of Elohim; repentance for the sins committed against your wife or husband; repentance for the sins against your parents, your brothers, your sisters and your children; repentance for the sins against your neighbors; repentance for the sins against those you work with or sell to or buy from; and repentance for the sins against yourself and the temple of your body.

23 Go now, each to your own home. Ponder upon the words I have said.

24 Pray to Elohim and express your sorrow for the darkness that has been in you and ask God to forgive you.

25 Where you have sinned against others, make it right by word and deed and ask forgiveness from those you have wronged.

26 Seek out Elohim again in prayer and promise to keep the Twelve Commandments of Sinai as my disciples have taught, and to walk only in the Celestine Light all the rest of your days.

27 Those who hear my words and do them, come again to this place on the morrow that you might be born again of the water and embrace the everlasting light that fills you up."

28 Then the people departed, and many went and did as Yeshua bade them do.

29 The next day people began to gather early at the house of the parents of Lazarus, and thirty-eight of the people from the previous day came forth to be baptized.

30 Yeshua baptized none, but asked each of his disciples to baptize some of the people.

31 Lazarus baptized his parents, and Miriam baptized two women and a young man, for Yeshua desired all to understand that the authority rested not only upon the shoulders of men, but upon all who had been called of God.

32 And because those who were baptized had only the love and light of God in their hearts, there was no objection because of Miriam, but only joy; and everyone knew they were witness to something great and marvelous among the Children of Israel.

CHAPTER 19

Testimony of Yochanan

Yeshua gives many sermons during his stay in Jerusalem, many of which were not in keeping with the law or tradition, so he is confronted by priests, Pharisees, and Sadducees. He confounds them all with his answers because he speaks with wisdom and logic and has a supreme understanding of the law and the scriptures of old. Instead of embracing his teachings, they begin to plot against him. Many people come to Yochanan, including his own disciples, to ask him about the teachings of Yeshua. Yochanan testifies that Yeshua is the light of God upon the earth, the Anointed One, and it is of him and the teachings that he brings that he preaches, which include eternal life and exaltation. Yeshua, Miriam, Martha, and Yochanan are all together for the last time.

And it came to pass that Yeshua and Miriam and his five disciples remained in the area of Jerusalem for over a moon.

2 Almost every day, Yeshua would give a short sermon, and each day the disciples would baptize those who had repented of their sins and become pure of heart in the Celestine Light of Elohim.

3 Yeshua gave twenty-two sermons during this visit to Bethany. They are recorded in fullness in the book, "The Sermons of Bethany."

4 At various times, Yeshua was confronted by priests, Pharisees, or Sadducees because of the things that he taught, many of which were not in keeping with the law or tradition. Each had their own complaints against him and his words.

5 Yeshua confounded them all with his answers, and a few came to agree with his teachings. Those that continued to oppose him could answer him not, except with anger and threats, for he spoke with wisdom and logic and a supreme understanding of the law and the scriptures of old.

6 He showed their arguments to be without merit or substance. Yet they preferred to cling to the emptiness they knew rather than embrace the fullness of Celestine Light he offered to them.

7 Even from those early days of his ministry, they began to speak about how they might be rid of him.

8 And it came to pass that word of the teachings and baptisms that Yeshua and his disciples did in Jerusalem came to the ears of Yochanan, who was baptizing in the Jordan near Salim, where there was much water.

9 Many people came to Yochanan from the environs of Jerusalem to ask him about Yeshua.

10 And Yochanan's disciples from Jerusalem came to him, saying, "Rabbi, we have heard your words and partaken of your baptism, but now there is another called Yeshua of Nazareth, whom you baptized and bore witness of, who also preaches mighty words and baptizes with water.

11 Behold, many people are coming to hear his words and take his baptism, and we wonder why if you two are one in spirit, that he preaches apart from you insomuch that people are coming to him instead of you."
12 Yochanan answered and said unto them, "A true son of light can receive nothing, save it has been given to him from Heaven.
13 All that you see in me is only from the Celestine Light that has been given to me, and Yeshua of Nazareth is the light.
14 He is the bridegroom, and the bride has been given to him. I am but the friend of the bridegroom who stands and hears him and rejoices greatly because of the bridegroom's voice.
15 To hear of his great works in Jerusalem fills me with joy, for it means I have faithfully fulfilled my stewardship. It means the time has come for him to increase and for me to decrease, for I have been the lamp that has been filled with oil, but now the lamp is lit and he is the flame which shall illuminate the world.
16 I say unto you, think not that Yeshua comes from Nazareth. I testify to you that he comes from above and is greater than anyone else and above all that exists.
17 Those who are of the earth speak of the things of the earth, for that is what they know. But Yeshua comes from Heaven and speaks of things men know not or are too afraid to understand, and he is above all.
18 He speaks plainly of what he has seen and heard, but few believe or comprehend what he tells them.
19 Those few who hear his words and breathe them in their lives discover the true greatness of Elohim in Heaven, and the true magnificence of God within their heart.
20 Verily, I testify to you that Yeshua of Nazareth has been sent from the bosom of Elohim. He speaks the words of God.
21 The spirit of Elohim is upon him without measure or limit, for he is the Son, and the Father and Mother love the Son and have given him authority over everything.
22 All who believe in the Son of Elohim and keep his teachings shall have eternal life and exaltation in the world to come.
23 But those who walk away from the Celestine Light of Yeshua enter into a darkness that grows ever deeper, even unto eternal darkness instead of eternal light and life.
24 As in Adam all shall die, even so in Yeshua shall all be made alive; but whether alive to eternal darkness which is as death, or alive to eternal light which is life, depends upon the purity of their faith and the diligence of their works.
25 Therefore, choose wisely, for you are choosing a great measure of your eternity.
26 And now the time has come for me to return to my family that they may have some days still to be with me.
27 Remember, therefore, the testimony of my words today, for I declare to you plainly that Yeshua of Nazareth is the Anointed One and far more than that.
28 He is the Son of Elohim come to earth that the humble and virtuous and pure of heart may have the fullness of the Celestine Light of God, a greater light than any man has ever had before."
29 Then Yochanan left the Jordan and returned to Bethany to be with his family, for he knew the days of his life were numbered, and they were not many more. And most of his disciples went with him.
30 Yochanan arrived at Bethany on the same day that Yeshua and Miriam and the five disciples were making preparations to leave for Nazareth.
31 Yeshua had told Miriam and his disciples that they would remain one more day, for his spirit knew that Yochanan was coming. Therefore, they stayed another day, and Yeshua and Yochanan never left the side of one another throughout the day.
32 In the evening, Yeshua and Yochanan went only with their wives up to a hill near the house of the parents of Lazarus, and there they spent the night until sunrise of the next day, praying

and speaking and laughing together and reveling in one another's company.

33 Upon the sunrise, the four of them did the Contemplative Movements in unison and it was a poignant time for each of them, for they knew it would be the last time they would all be together.

34 Returning to the house, they had a light morning meal. Then Yeshua and Miriam departed for Nazareth with his disciples after giving Yochanan and all of his family and the family of Lazarus long and loving embraces.

35 In parting, Yeshua turned to the gathered family and friends and said unto them, "I will again say what I have said before. Of those born of women, there are none greater than Yochanan the Baptizer, whom I am honored to call my brother of spirit and light.

36 No man has been a greater friend to me, nor could another ever be. Cherish every moment you have with him. His words are pure and refreshing like a cold mountain brook, and they are the words Elohim would have him speak; therefore, they will quench the thirst of all true Children of Light."

CHAPTER 20

Imprisonment of Yochanan

Yochanan rebukes Herod Antipas and his new wife Herodias in public for their sin, as it was not acceptable for a man to marry his living brother's former wife. Herodias is furious that Yochanan spoke against her, and she demands that Herod arrest and execute him. Herod has no intention of executing Yochanan because he fears the people's reaction. But to appease his wife and to see if he can convince Yochanan to stop offending the religious order, he orders his arrest. While imprisoned, Herod invites the Sanhedrin to question Yochanan so he can determine what to do with him. After Yochanan speaks against the dictates of the Sanhedrin, he is condemned and imprisoned at the castle of Machaerus, above the Salt Sea.

After Yeshua had departed, Yochanan continued to preach and baptize in the area around Jerusalem and return home every night to be with his family.

2 And it came to pass that Yochanan heard that Herod Antipas the Tetrarch had divorced his wife, daughter of Aretas of Petra, and married his niece Herodias, who had divorced his brother Boethus to marry Antipas; Yochanan reproved Herod Antipas and Herodias in public before many people for their sin, for it was not acceptable that a man should marry his living brother's former wife in this manner.

3 Now Herod was wroth with Yochanan when he heard that he had been rebuked by him, but he deferred to act rashly against him for he knew that Yochanan was highly revered by many of the common people, and fear of revolt was ever upon the mind of Herod.

4 But it was not only for the words spoken against him that Herod was wroth with Yochanan, for Yochanan had also been preaching all manner of new teachings that were contrary to the traditions of the Hebrews; and his words were sowing great discontent among the religious leaders whom Herod depended upon for tactic support.

5 However, Herod's wife Herodias was furious when she heard of the words Yochanan had spoken against her, and she demanded that Herod arrest and execute him.

6 The Tetrarch had no intention of executing Yochanan because of fear of the people, but to appease his wife Herodias and to determine if he could convince Yochanan to stop offending the religious order, he commanded Yochanan to be brought before him to give an account of his words.

7 And it came to pass that Herod's soldiers arrested Yochanan as he was walking with his disciples toward the Jordan, and they brought him to Herod's court.

8 Now Herod was considered a cunning fox and on this day, he gave evidence of why, for rather than interrogate Yochanan himself and perhaps incite the common people by word of this,

he invited leaders of the Sanhedrin to question Yochanan.

9 The court of Herod was a place of finery. Those in attendance wore their best clothes and costly perfumes, and most of the men were clean shaven, with short hair after the manner of the Greeks and Romans.

10 But when Yochanan was brought before the court, he wore clothes crudely made of plant fibers. His dark beard was long, bushy, and uncombed, and his hair that fell to the middle of his back was pulled back and tied in a tail in multiple places with colored ribbons that was not a fashion of the Hebrews. He had a wild look about him that, combined with his stature, was intimidating to many who were present.

11 The first person to speak to him was Shammai of the Sanhedrin, who was known for the strictness of his beliefs and his short temper. Herod had purposefully asked him to be the main interrogator of Yochanan to see if his grating style of questioning and knowledge of the religious laws and traditions would disturb Yochanan into saying things that could be held against him with the people.

12 Shammai immediately got to his points and, staring icily at Yochanan, said, "It has come to our attention that you are teaching that which is contrary to the laws and traditions of our people; that you say that your baptism does away with circumcision; that you insinuate and perhaps even proclaim that some poor bastard child from Nazareth of all places is the Messiah; that you are teaching all manner of strange doctrines that are not in keeping with the laws and traditions that have been followed for generations upon generations. What have you to say about these serious charges?"

13 As he did when he was a youth confronted by high religious authority, Yochanan laughed. It was a long and hearty laugh during which time Shammai became very red in the face because of his insolence.

14 But before Shammai could demand that Herod silence Yochanan, he stopped laughing and answered simply, saying, "I am doing exactly as you have said. I testify that baptism taken with a repentant heart, with a life renewed and committed to the Celestine Light of Elohim, performed by someone with authority to act in God's name, abolishes the ritual of circumcision, which thing does not change a person on the inside, but only on the outside.

15 And I tell you with words of great seriousness that Yeshua of Nazareth has come from Heaven to set men free and bring life everlasting. He is far more than the Messiah you seek. But you will never find his light if you continue to look only in dark houses.

16 As to my doctrines, they are not mine, but those of Elohim; and if they are contrary to the doctrines that you teach, you would be wise to amend yours.

17 So you see I have admitted to all you have accused me of, but in that you should not hold me, but let me go back to my wife and children; for though you are Sanhedrin, this is not a court established to decide matters of religion.

18 This is the court of a small king acting for Rome, and I have done nothing against Rome. Therefore, set me free or face the eternal penalties of your own unrighteousness and unjust ways."

19 As protocol demanded, nobody interrupted Yochanan while he defended himself, but Shammai became so angry at the words of Yochanan that his face became intensely red and his eyes began to bulge.

20 When at last Yochanan spoke his last word, Shammai fairly leaped off the dais and spat his words with great anger into Yochanan's face, rending his clothes as he spoke.

21 "Terrible blasphemer! Your words are poison! Let Herod throw you into prison until we convene a court of the Sanhedrin and put you into a pit where no man can ever again hear your evil words!

22 I had thought before you spoke to question you further, but you are so condemned by the words that you have already spoken that my questions are pointless. You are so obviously opposed to the proper order that even a Roman ignorant of our ways could see it."

23 Then Hillel, the other Sanhedrin, stepped forward and put a kindly hand upon the shoulder

of his associate and spoke to Yochanan in a calm voice, saying, "You have made some grave statements. Surely you know they can bring only misery upon you. But I would like to think that you can see the error of your ways, and if you repudiate your words, I am sure your future would be brighter."

24 Yochanan shook his head in negation, while looking steadfastly into Hillel's eyes, "If I were to repudiate my words or actions I would condemn myself to eternal darkness. Do what you will with me. I have said what I have said and done what I have done, and though I ask to go home to my family, do not fool yourself to think that it is to be silent, to live as a whipped dog with his tail between his legs.

25 Verily, I declare that until my last breath, I will continue to say what I have said and do what I have done, for I speak the truth and I act in the Celestine Light of Elohim. Therefore, what is man to me?"

26 Shammai continued to rend his clothes in anger, but Hillel once again spoke calmly to Yochanan, saying, "I have listened to the fullness of your words, and now I would ask that you would listen to the fullness of mine.

27 I know you believe the words you have said and the things that you teach to the simple people. And if your words are true, then of course, they would be worth dying for. But if you are in error, then to die for your words would be a travesty of your own life, brought about by your own misguided actions.

28 Consider then the points that I will present. In them, perhaps you will discover that your words and teachings cannot be true.

29 As you know, we have had the scriptures, the words of the prophets, passed to man from Elohim to guide us for generations upon generations. Even as far back as Father Abraham Elohim made clear all of the things he wished his people to do.

30 Our ways are ancient; they are the same ways that Elohim gave to Abraham. They are the same ways that were followed by David and Solomon, Moses and Jacob, and all of Elohim's chosen prophets. It is upon this common path that all have gone on to their reward in the hereafter.

31 Let me ask you now, Yochanan. Has the unchanging God of all that is, now decided to change his ways? Has the all-knowing God discovered something he did not know and needed to amend that which he has previously given? Has he created a Celestine Light where none existed before? Is not the very act or teaching of change, of different doctrines, by their own nature evidence of their falsehood?

32 To say that the things you teach and do, which are contrary to the established order, are of God is to say that the Almighty changes his mind. And if Elohim is not unchanging, if he is not the same yesterday, today, and forever, then how could any man have faith in him? How could any man know that what he does today for God would have any merit tomorrow?"

33 Yochanan looked upon Hillel with a smile and said unto him, "I also can see that you believe the words you say. And I appreciate that you have said them with gentleness and tried to sway me with logic not threats. Therefore, I will treat you similarly.

34 You have spoken of the word of Elohim given to Abraham and the prophets who came after Abraham. But why have there been so many prophets? Why did Elohim not just reveal all the truth that man should live by to Abraham and after that there would be no need for God to speak again to a prophet?

35 The scriptures say, surely God will do nothing save he first reveals his secrets to his servants, the prophets. It is plain that there must always be prophets; else it must be that Elohim no longer cares for the worthy people of the world, or there is no longer even one worthy person in the world and Elohim has withdrawn.

36 And why do you think that everything you hold to be a dictate from God actually is what you think because it has always been so from generations to generations? How does that make it true?

37 Verily, I declare unto you Elohim is a God of light, not darkness. Elohim is a God of reason, not illogic. Elohim is a God of love, not fear. Elohim is a God of forgiveness of the humble and repentant, not a God of punishments set in stone.

38 Elohim is a father and a mother taking joy in the virtue of their children of spirit and giving them every word of light to guide their paths to greater knowledge and joy.

39 Elohim is a spiritual brother, an ever-helpful guide to his younger and less-experienced brothers and sisters, helping them each day to live the greater light within them and become more than who they have been.

40 This is the God I declare, and upon these foundations, I weigh truth from falsehood, not upon ancient words written on old skins, practiced by my ancestors whom I know not the men they were.

41 And I would say that the Elohim I declare will resonate in the heart of any man open to the evidence of both his heart and head as to what God must surely be.

42 But the God that you declare, a vengeful and angry God, demanding constant subservience and obedience to tiny points of law that confine one's spirit instead of expanding it, blessing the Children of Israel but ignoring all others; this is a God I know not. Verily, this is not God.

43 Men have taken the true nature of Elohim and perverted it so that God has become their creation, given to control the lives of people and make them subservient and obedient to the rulers of the land and religion.

44 Nevertheless, there is much in the scriptures of our people that is true and good, and this I also declare. But I denounce that which is against the true nature of Elohim, for those are the evil teachings of men given to lead astray the Children of Light.

45 That those false words have been inscribed upon the ancient scrolls of scripture and practiced for generations upon generations does not make them true, but merely evidence of the many sheep that have followed blindly, without thought of their own for all these generations.

46 Elohim is unchanging that is surely true. But the God that I know and the God that you pay devotion to are not the same.

47 I am sorry to say that you worship a divinity you know not, and you obey laws and traditions to suit man, not God.

48 Yes, I am guilty of teaching doctrines different than the laws and traditions of our people, but I am not guilty of teaching doctrines different from the edicts or nature of Elohim; and by that distinction, I am justified in my words and actions."

49 Shammai was beside himself with anger at the words of Yochanan. He paced rapidly to and fro, anxiously awaiting his turn to speak. When at last Yochanan was finished, Shammai said unto him, "Never in all my life have I encountered such blasphemy. It is amazing that the Almighty hasn't simply struck you down with a bolt from Heaven.

50 Who do you think you are? Are you Moses? Are you anyone? No, you are just a poor, unkempt, unknowing piece of dirt who is so ignorant that it is my understanding that your food consists mostly of bugs.

51 That is why all of your followers are poor, lowly people. Nobody of any knowledge or refinement would spare a moment to listen to the rantings of a savage from the wilderness who eats bugs!

52 You call people to come to you in the wilderness; why? Do you think Elohim will come to the barrenness of the wilderness when his magnificent temple is here in Jerusalem? How foolish is that?"

53 Turning to Herod, Shammai said, "Please lock this man in your darkest dungeon until we can convene a court of the Sanhedrin. I tremble to think of the damage he has already done to the minds of the simple people. He cannot be allowed to ever again be free to do more."

54 Herod stroked his bare chin and then directed, "Question him further and then I will decide."

55 Hillel stepped forward again to face Yochanan, "My friend has brought up a very valid

point for you to consider. By whose authority do you baptize? By whose authority do you preach? By whose authority do you teach doctrines contrary to the law and tradition?

56 You are not a priest; you have not attended any of the schools of rabbinical study. Nobody has given you authority to do any of the things you do or say any of the things that you say.

57 You declare things to us, but by what right; by what authority; by what power can you teach us? We are the Sanhedrin; we hold judgment over Israel; we determine what is right and what is wrong. You are an empty wine skin, and you have nothing to give."

58 Turning to Herod, Hillel said, "I agree with my colleague. Put him in prison. We will convene a court to give you all the justification you need to appease the people who follow him."

59 Now Herod had been fascinated by the exchange of words between Yochanan and the Sanhedrin, and he spoke encouragingly to Yochanan, "For a man of no training, you have spoken well, but I fear I must imprison you, for their points seem to hold weight.

60 As this is a religious matter, I will leave it to their courts to decide your fate. But I will give you the opportunity to speak again this day. What have you to say?"

61 Yochanan stood before them all uncowed, and he said unto them, "By whose authority do the Sanhedrin hold judgment over Israel? Where and when did Elohim give that authority to them? You can answer, but you cannot say, for any answer would just be a meaningless justification without merit.

62 But I declare unto you that I do speak for Elohim. My words are not mine, but Elohims. My teachings are not mine, but Elohims."

63 "Are you saying you are a prophet of God?" asked Hillel.

64 Yochanan answered, "I am not a prophet as the prophets of old who heard a voice or saw a vision while they slept and, in the morning, did the best they could to remember their fading dreams of the night.

65 Nor am I an enfeebled old man who hears God and speaks truth, only to be too weak to protest when my teachings are perverted by self-serving priests and scribes, as it has been done oft times with prophets of ancient days.

66 When I tell you I teach the true doctrines of Elohim, it is not from vague dreams but because I know Elohim as one man knows another.

67 Verily, I declare unto you I have walked with Elohim and I have spoken to him face-to-face.

68 I teach what I have been taught by the creator of the light, and if teaching what I teach condemns me, it condemns you far more; for my pain will be brief, but yours shall be for all eternity."

69 Hillel came up to Yochanan, and there was pity in his face. He considered that Yochanan must be insane to say the things he did. And he said quietly to him, "The scriptures say that no man can see God face-to-face."

70 Yochanan answered him, "The scriptures you use are so full of the words of man that anything can be proved from them. You say it is written that no man can see the face of God, and so it is written.

71 But it is also written that Father Jacob spoke to God face-to-face and wrestled with him at Peniel.

72 It is also written that Moses and Aaron and Nadab and Abihu accompanied by seventy Elders of Israel saw God and ate and drank with him. So do not speak to me of what is written, as it is most often used to control the ignorant and trod down the people; not to lift them up. And as you can see, I am not ignorant."

73 Hillel threw up his hands in frustration and said unto Herod, "He is intractable. I implore you. Take him from our sight until we call for him again."

74 Then Herod ordered his soldiers to take Yochanan gagged and covered, so not to be heard or seen by the people, to the castle at Machaerus, above the Salt Sea. And he was taken away that very day.

75 Notwithstanding the fact that he had imprisoned Yochanan and that his wife hated him, Herod was fascinated with him, and while he was imprisoned at Machaerus, he came to visit Yochanan on three occasions to have discourse with him.

76 During these visits, Yochanan beseeched Herod to let his wife and disciples visit him in prison, and Herod's heart was softened toward Yochanan.

77 His disciples, he forbade, but Herod did allow Yochanan's wife Martha to visit him in prison as she desired, and she came to live in the hills near the palace in company with her children and five of Yochanan's disciples and their wives and children.

78 Though Herod had secreted Yochanan away to the castle at Machaerus, by allowing Martha to visit and some disciples to encamp near the palace, it became known among the people that Yochanan was imprisoned at Machaerus.

79 Upon learning this, some people from Jerusalem and Jericho and other towns, never great in numbers, began to come to the springs near Machaerus, and the disciples of Yochanan baptized there and taught the people in the manner that Yochanan had taught them.

CHAPTER 21

Challenges in Nazareth

Yeshua's brother Yakov asks him to give a sermon before he leaves Nazareth. There are those who protest; however, the local rabbi finally agrees. Yeshua tells the men in the synagogue some things that infuriates many who become so angry that they grab him and take him to the brow of a hill where they are about to throw him off when a bright light, brighter than the sun, shines down upon them, and they fall to the ground in terror. Yeshua, Miriam, and his disciples leave for Capernaum, where they are joined by Yeshua's younger brother, Yakov, and Yeshua and Miriam's children.

And it came to pass that Yeshua and Miriam journeyed back to Nazareth with the disciples to visit their children and family for a short time.

2 When they had arrived at the homes of their family, his brother Yakov asked Yeshua to give a sermon before he left, but three elders of the village came to him when they had word of his intent and said he should not speak because many were still angry with him from the last time he had taught them, for he had given them teachings about women that they did not agree with.

3 Miriam was with Yeshua when the elders reproved him, and she was upset by their words and said unto them, "Yeshua last taught the people of Nazareth years ago. Are there still those who after all this time have not comprehended the truth of his words?

4 You have in your midst the light of Elohim upon the earth, and you would turn him away? He has loved you and known you since he was a youth, and you would turn him away? He takes nothing from you and gives everything to you, and you would turn him away?

5 Are your traditions and laws and beliefs such heavy stones around your neck that you cannot make attempt to lift your heads and see a greater light?"

6 The elders scowled as Miriam spoke, and they were angry at her words. One of them raised his voice in anger to Yeshua: "Your wife is a living testament of why we do not want to listen to your words. How dare you allow her to speak to men in such a manner! It is not the place of a woman to reprimand men. This is evidence of the correctness of our position. Surely, your teachings give us great distress."

7 Yeshua reached for a moment to hold Miriam's hand. Then releasing it, he said unto the elders in a calm voice, "When you speak ill of a righteous woman or a child, you offend God. Verily, I say unto you thus you have spoken this day. Lest you die in your sin, make haste to make amends."

8 But they did not make amends. Instead, they turned their backs in unison and walked away from Yeshua and Miriam.

9 "What will happen to them?" Miriam asked.

10 And Yeshua said unto her, "They still have the days they live to see the light of truth and repent of their sins. But they must not procrastinate the day of their repentance, for they know not which sunrise shall be their last.

11 And on the Day of Judgment, all are weighed in the balance by their actions and their words, and each word or action, be it idle or with intent, is either a step forward or backward in their eternal progression.

12 Those that tip to the light shall inherit exaltation, and those that tip to the darkness shall inherit the dreariness they embraced in life. Not by Elohim are they sent to their reward or punishment, but by the resonance of their soul drawn to the destiny they have built for themselves by their thoughts and deeds in life. And so it shall be for a great time."

13 Miriam came to him and embraced him, asking, "Why do people that have known you since you were a boy, who even now are neighbors to your mother and your brothers and your sisters, treat you so disrespectfully? Even if you were still just the simple carpenter of your youth, you should be given more respect than they have shown."

14 Yeshua held her close, saying, "It has always been so since the dawn of time that a prophet has no honor in his own country.

15 Among the people that have known someone as a simple man, it is difficult for them to make the leap and understand that he is more than that. So it is with me and the people of Nazareth."

16 When Yakov heard of the way Yeshua had been treated, he was greatly displeased and he went immediately to the synagogue to speak with the rabbi, and the rabbi agreed to let Yeshua read the scriptures in the synagogue the following day, which was the Sabbath, as this was an accepted custom.

17 When the Sabbath came upon them, Yeshua stood before the men of Nazareth within the synagogue. He was given a scroll containing the words of the prophet Elijah to read. He held the scroll but kept it rolled up and did not read from it, but spoke all the words of the scriptures from memory.

18 Quoting from their scriptures, he said unto them, "The spirit of the Lord is upon me, because he has anointed me to preach good news to the poor. He has sent me to proclaim freedom for the prisoners and recovery of sight for the blind, to release the oppressed, to proclaim the year of the Lord's favor."

19 Then he gave the scroll back to the attendant. The eyes of everyone in the synagogue were fastened on him, and he said unto them, "Today, this scripture is fulfilled in your hearing."

20 There were gasps of astonishment at his words, and many were angry, saying he was being sacrilegious.

21 But others spoke well of him and were amazed at the thought-provoking words that came from his lips. 'Is this not Joseph's son?" they asked, perplexed that he was given a scripture to read that so fulfilled his purpose.

22 Then another observed, "But is he really Joseph's son? Look at his appearance. Could a man who looks like that have had Joseph for a father?"

23 Another man stood and challenged, "If you fulfill the scripture, show us a miracle like those we have heard you have done."

24 Yeshua answered, saying, "Some of you say, 'Physician, heal yourself!'

25 Others have heard of miracles I have done and say, 'Do the same here in your own town.'

26 But it is not the physician that needs healing, but the sick.

27 Nor have I healed anyone. They have healed themselves by their faith. I merely was the river channel through which the healing water of Elohim flowed because of their faith.

28 They believe in me and their belief calls the Celestine Light of Elohim. It flows through me to them and great it is. But where is your faith in me?

29 As I said to my wife, I say unto you: No prophet is accepted in his own town. If it is only

because of miracles you would believe, that is no faith at all.
30 Verily, faith must come before the miracle, not the miracle before the faith.
31 You will hear me no more in Nazareth. I have given you the good light, but too many of you prefer darkness. Let it be as you desire.
32 If there are those among you who can find the faith to see the light, then leave this town and come and join the Community of Light on the north shore of Gennesaret.
33But those who cannot find the faith to see the light, inherit the desolation they sow.
34 You think Elohim must bless you because of who you are, but I say unto you Elohim blesses you not because of who you are, but because of how you are.
35 Therefore, I ask, how is your faith? What are your quiet acts of charity and goodness that show the true light of your heart?
36 I tell you now of a truth that you may find pricks your vanity. There were many widows in Israel in the days of Elijah, when it did not rain for three and a half years, and there was a great famine throughout the land.
37 Yet Elijah helped none of them, not even one, but went instead to a widow in Zarephath in the region of Sidon.
38 And there were many in Israel with leprosy in the time of Elisha the Prophet, yet not one of them were cleansed—only Naaman the Syrian.
39 The blessings and Celestine Light of Elohim are given to the worthy, not the undeserving, regardless of whose children they are. So it was in the days of old; so it is today."
40 Now many of the people of Nazareth in the synagogue, when they heard these words, were filled with wrath.
41 They rose up in anger and drove Yeshua out of Nazareth, notwithstanding the protests of his brothers and disciples and their attempts to protect him.
42 They took Yeshua by his garments to the brow of the hill upon which the town was built, intending to throw him headlong over the cliff.
43 At the very moment, when it seemed he would be plunged to the rocks below, a brilliant light flashed all around them, blindingly brighter than the sun at noonday.
44 They fell to the ground in terror, shielding their eyes from the light, and Yeshua passed through the midst of them and went his way, gathering his brothers and his disciples to him as he passed.
45 Coming to the house of Yakov, he said unto him, "Good brother, thank you for your efforts to protect me from the ignorant. You have known me since your earliest memory. Am I not just the simple carpenter's son to you as I am to them?"
46 Yakov was hurt by Yeshua's words, and he answered, "No, brother, though I call you that I have always known you are much more than a brother. You are a prophet, yes, but I think also much more than that as well.
47 The miracles you can do are wonders. Even nature bows to you.
48 Only a moment ago, the sun came down from the sky and lighted upon your shoulders. What could that possibly be? Something no man has ever seen before. You are connected to God greater than other men. Only by that could you do these things.
49 I believe that if a man would know God, truly know Elohim in his heart, he must follow you, even though your doctrines are strange and difficult sometimes.
50 But as you said, it is not because of miracles, but because of your words and your love that I would follow you."
51 Yeshua gave Yakov a warm embrace and said, "I would be honored if you would follow me, my brother. We are leaving tomorrow for Capernaum. Put your affairs in order and meet us in that vicinity with your family and our children as soon as you can."
52 And it came to pass that Yeshua and Miriam and his disciples departed the following day for Capernaum and Bethsaida upon the coast, in the borders of Zabulon and Nepthalim.
53 Thus, it was fulfilled the words spoken by the prophet Esaias, who said, "In the land of

Zabulon and Nepthalim, on the shores of the sea, beyond Jordan, Galilee of the Gentiles, the people which sat in darkness saw a great light, and to them which dwell in the region under the shadow of death, a wondrous light has sprung up."

54 Shortly after arriving, they were joined by Yakov and his family, as well as their own children.

55 And Yeshua's youngest brother Yudas, who was unmarried, came as well with their mother Miryam.

56 Yeshua's disciples that had traveled with him returned to their families in Bethsaida and related all that had transpired in their travels with Yeshua.

57 From that day forward, they began to meet with all of their families each week to hear Yeshua and Miriam and the other disciples speak when they were home and to share a common meal together.

58 And they began to apportion various tasks that could serve everyone well, and they became very productive, with greater freedom of time for study and prayer and play.

59 Thus began the first Community of Light.

CHAPTER 22

Enduring Blessings

A nobleman asks Yeshua to heal his dying son, which he does after hearing the humble words of wisdom spoken by the nobleman.

A few days later, a nobleman and his retinue who had first sought Yeshua in Nazareth came to Capernaum, seeking Yeshua.

2 When he found him, he besought him, saying, "I have come from Cana to ask you to return with me to heal my son who is very sick, even to the point of death. I was there on the day you married your fair wife, and I drank the fine wine served by your uncle.

3 After you left, his servants told us it had been only water moments before. I know that you can perform miracles such as no other man. Will you please have mercy and come back with me to make my son well?"

4 Yeshua sighed and said to him, "Who will believe without signs and wonders? If I do as you ask, what will you think of me? And if I do not what you ask, what then will you think of me?"

5 The nobleman paused to consider his words well before speaking, and then replied, "I know in my heart that God is with you. Not just from what I witnessed at your marriage, but from all that has been spoken of you in Galilee for some time; not just the wonders you have done, but also the words you have spoken.

6 But words are often fleeting in the minds of men, while wonders are never forgotten. Therefore, if you will come to my home and heal my son, many shall see what I already know: that God dwells with you.

7 But if you will not come to heal my son, though I will have a great sadness, I will know of a surety that it is not by a whim, but by the will of Elohim, that all is as it should be. And even in my sadness, I will be at peace."

8 Yeshua was touched by the words of the nobleman, and he said unto him, "Among the rich, you are rare, for you have a humble heart and a true love for God. Return to your home; your son has been made whole."

9 Then the nobleman knelt down and kissed the feet of Yeshua, washing them with his tears and thanking him with his words.

10 Believing in the words of Yeshua, he had joy in his heart upon every step of his return journey home.

11 As he approached his house, his servants came down the road to meet him, shouting with joy, "Your son lives! Your son lives!"

12 The nobleman was overwhelmed with gratitude and humbled by the blessing God had given him. He asked his servants as to the hour when his son began to get well, and they told

him, "Yesterday at the seventh hour, his fever left him."
13 The father and the servants that had gone with him to Capernaum knew that it was the
same hour in which Yeshua said unto him, "Your son lives."
14 From that day forth, the nobleman's faith in Yeshua waxed great, and from this event, his
entire household, all of his family and all of his servants, also believed.

CHAPTER 23

First Sermon at Gennesaret

A wealthy pious man owning many olive groves challenges Yeshua regarding the temple of God and says that he has been blessed by God with wealth while Yeshua has not because he is poor. From that day on, his olive trees become diseased and nothing he ever plants again on his land ever grows. Yeshua's fame spreads among the people of the delta, and hundreds begin to come to hear him speak. Yeshua gives a sermon on the virtues of the Twelve Commandments and the higher path of Celestine Light, which will overcome any darkness.

nd it came to pass that Yeshua taught his disciples many things during the days that followed and word soon spread in the delta area of his sayings, and many people from the delta region began to come to hear him speak on the day after the Sabbath.

2 But in the three weeks they had been in Capernaum, Yeshua had not visited the synagogue, even on the Sabbath, and for this, some condemned him and spoke ill of him.

3 There was one man from nearby Chorazin who owned many olive groves, and he was very pious; believing God had blessed him with wealth.

4 He came to Yeshua as he was teaching his disciples and many people on a hill near Lake Gennesaret, and he challenged him, saying, "Why do you claim to be teaching the ways of God when you do not even come to the synagogue on the Sabbath?"

5 Yeshua replied boldly, saying, "I am standing upon a temple built by Elohim. What are the works of man to this?"

6 The wealthy man scoffed at the words of Yeshua and said, "That is but a hill of rock, no different than a hundred other hills of rock. Surely the Almighty must be angry that you would claim a hill as sacred and reject the finery of the synagogue, which pays true homage to the all-powerful."

7 Yeshua answered him, saying, "Why is your heart so hardened to the light? Did Elohim not create all the earth?

8 You must understand that Elohim made the earth as a temple for man to live in and prosper and gave man a body most intricate to be cared for and loved, and these are the temples of God.

9 Be good stewards of the temple of your body and the temple of the earth and keep the commandments of Sinai and you will be giving the greatest homage to God that man can give."

10 But again the rich man scoffed at the words of Yeshua, saying, "Those who live as they should are blessed with prosperity, property, and servants, while those who have words without substance are cursed with poverty, no land to call their own and no servants to help with their chores.

11 Look at me and look at you, and it should be obvious to all who God is with and who God is not with. I claim none of my wealth because of my own efforts, but only as blessings from God because of my faithfulness. Do you say that you have been blessed with poverty because of yours?"

12 Yeshua looked up into the sky before answering, then gazed unwaveringly at the rich man and said, "Surely it will be easier for a lion to fly than for a rich man to get into Heaven.

13 If you are so sure that your wealth is a gift of God because of your faithfulness and not because of your prudence as a planter of olives, then by your word, so be it. From this day forth, may your lands be blessed or cursed according to the light of Elohim that truly dwells within your heart."

14 And it came to pass that the man returned to his home and groves of olives in Chorazin, and from that very day, his olive trees became diseased. Though he gave great alms to the synagogue and said long and pious prayers in public, by two moons, all of his trees died, and nothing he ever planted again grew upon his land.

15 When word spread of what had happened to the rich man from Chorazin and the words Yeshua had spoken to him, Yeshua's fame spread among the people of the delta and hundreds began to come to hear him speak.

16 One day as he walked along the shore of the lake, the crowd began to press him into the water and pleaded with him to speak to them his wisdom.

17 He saw two ships anchored nearby in the lake, for the fishermen were ashore repairing their nets.

18 Yeshua waded out to one of the ships, and Cephas, his disciple, followed him, for it was a vessel of his friend. And they entered onto the ship and moved off near the shore into deeper water.

19 Yeshua sat upon the ship's bench, and facing the crowd nearby, he taught them, saying, "The wealthy often spend their lives striving to gain that which can be quickly taken by Caesar or bandits or made empty and worthless by illness.

20 Even if they hold it safe until the end of their days, their wealth cannot be carried with them to the next life, nor will they have one coin in the eternity to come.

21 I say unto you, be wiser than the rich. Let your days be filled enriching your good character by keeping the commandments of Sinai, not just in deed but also with a good spirit and happiness with the simple joys of life.

22 Seek out, good friends, not just with common interests of little worth, but with common characters that seek the greater light of Celestine brilliance, and act selflessly to serve one another and those in need.

23 It is your relationships, one with another, that are a true treasure of this life and eternity.

24 Do not judge others, for every hurtful word or action you mete in judgment against others shall be measured against you by Elohim in the hereafter, and it is only Elohim who sees all and knows all, that can fairly judge anyone for their righteousness and propriety.

25 Do not be afraid of those who are different from you in the way they dress or speak or eat or worship God, for all are the spirit children of Elohim and are your brothers and sisters of spirit.

26 Instead, rejoice in the things you have in common and respect their right to differ from you, as they respect your right to differ from them.

27 In the words that I say, think not that I am condoning any evil act contrary to the commandments of Sinai.

28 I merely implore you to not be as the scribes and Pharisees who strain at gnats and swallow camels.

29 If you have devotion to God, show it by loving the temple of your body which Elohim has given you for your sojourn in life.

30 Praising Elohim in your words and songs brings happiness in Heaven, and when you

honor the temple you have been given, you honor the gift, and in honoring the gift, you honor the giver.

31 But if you honor not the temple of your body with the purity of the things you eat and drink and with the simple yet elegant beauty of your clothes and adornment, then you trample upon the gift of God that you are and dishonor Elohim with your actions far greater than any praises or pious acts may ever overcome.

32 And beware of what evil your eyes behold, for as your eyes see so your life becomes.

33 Look therefore to surround yourself with virtuous friends. Choose to see things that respect, uplift, and edify you and others and turn your back upon that which does not.

34 In the things that you eat, look beyond that which is clean or unclean and choose that which shows respect for life over that which does not.

35 Eat first those things which have been put upon the earth by Elohim to nourish you without taking their life and those plants which will fade after a season.

36 Consider the olive and the fig trees. They give you wonderful substance that comes again and again without harm to the trees of life. And when you eat their fruits, or the birds or animals eat, they help the trees by carrying their seeds to propagate them.

37 Look at the crops of the fields that are here today and wither tomorrow. They also seek only to make again their kind, and as you plant their seeds, you fulfill them even as they fill you.

38 Nor should you neglect the insects that come numberless as the sands of the sea. Most are not sent to consume your crops, but given to feed you in great abundance. Their lives are short that in them yours may be long.

39 In these gifts of God, you find the light of life to live long and in health.

40 "But if you need still more, especially because of famine or drought or cold, gather to you the fish that school, for they have been given in great numbers that in them your years upon the earth may be greatly numbered.

41 In the world, there is much darkness among men in the disrespect they have for life in the food they eat.

42 Show by your example the higher path of life. You can fight against the darkness and thereby make enemies of the men of darkness, or you can bring the Celestine Light and the darkness will depart, for it cannot stand to be in the presence of the light.

43 Darkness cannot bear the Celestine Light, and light can always overcome darkness if it stays connected to the source, which is Elohim.

CHAPTER 24

Sermon on Unorthodox Marriages

Yeshua is invited to read the scriptures at the synagogue in Capernaum, but instead teaches them about acting in the light of Elohim verses following the letter of the law. He speaks about the "Great Commandment" to be good stewards and replenish the earth, which leads him to speaking about homosexuality and how homosexuals can have a relationship sanctified by God as well. He also speaks about the sacred covenant of a righteous marriage. After leaving the synagogue, Yeshua, Miriam, and some of his disciples go to the home of Cephas in Bethsaida and find Cephas' mother sick with a great fever. Yeshua heals her completely, and she immediately gets up to accommodate her guests. Many people arrive at Cephas' home, bringing diseased and possessed people for Yeshua to heal, and he heals those who repent of the sins of their past, but does not heal those who do not.

On the Sabbath of that week, Yeshua went to the synagogue at Capernaum and was given a time to read the scriptures aloud.

2 But he read not a single word from the scrolls. Instead, he taught them with his light, saying, "In the synagogue, much is spoken about the law, much is spoken about keeping the commandments of Sinai, and this is from sincere devotions to Elohim and honest desires to do that which is pleasing to God.

3 But in seeking to be devout, do not be led into the pit of obeying the law but being empty of the spirit and the Celestine Light of Elohim.

4 To obey the law without the spirit is like casting a net for fish on dry land. You are making an effort, but it will gain you only frustration.

5 But the man who casts his net into the lake with vigor, even when done in ignorance as to the proper way to fish or the correct place to cast his net, will still catch fish because of his enthusiasm and effort, even as the man with a true spirit will find the favor of Elohim, while the man who obeys every law without spirit will never know God.

6 So it is in your life. Within the commandments of Sinai are found all the law Elohim asks of you, save the Great Commandment. Live these simple principles with spirit and you will gain the fullest blessings of Elohim, both in this life and the life to come.

7 Know that all other laws are given by men or added to by men, even if they are read from the scrolls in the synagogue.

8 Decide for yourself with the spirit of God as your guide, which laws serve God and help you have the light of Elohim in your heart, and which serve the Caesars, both the grand and the petty, by keeping you passive and controlled like a flock of sheep."

9 Hearing his teachings, many of those present started murmuring, for this was doctrine such

as they had never heard before.

10 But Yeshua continued to instruct them, asking, "Who among you knows the Great Commandment of which I spoke?"

11 Again there was murmuring as they conferred one with another to agree upon the answer to his question. Silias the Elder answered, "It is to marry many wives and bring many children into the world." And there were chuckles and even laughter at his reply.

12 Yeshua said unto them, "You have answered correctly in part, but the response of levity is not in keeping with the weight of this law.

13 Before the commandments of Sinai came the Great Commandment. When this commandment is lived in wholeness and purity, it is a blessing upon the Children of Light. But it is more often lived in perversion, which brings a darkness upon the soul.

14 When the progenitors of man first came upon the earth, Elohim blessed them with the Great Commandment that the righteous might inherit the bounties of earth and Heaven, saying, 'Be fruitful, and multiply; replenish the earth and be good stewards over it.

15 Have sacred dominion over the fish of the sea and over the fowl of the air and over every living thing that moves or grows upon the earth, that in your stewardship, they also might be fruitful and multiply and spread forth over the earth in abundance.'

16 And Elohim said, 'Behold, I have given you every herb bearing seed, which is upon the face of all the earth, and every tree whose seed bears fruit of sweetness or meat, and the milk of the beasts, and the non-fertile eggs of the fowls, and the honey of the bees, and these shall be your food.

17 And to every beast of the earth and to every fowl of the air and to everything that creeps upon the earth, wherein there is life, I have given every green herb from the smallest to the largest, for their meat.'

18 And you will say that these are not the words of the Great Commandment that have been read in the synagogue all of your life, and I say unto you that you have not even lived the portion of the Great Commandment that you have.

19 But now I ask you to be more than you have been and to live the Great Commandment in its fullness that you might receive an inheritance of light in this life and the next.

20 And what is that fullness? Look closely, for there is much given in the first commandment of God for the children of men.

21 Consider what it means for men and women to multiply and replenish the earth.

22 Obviously, a man cannot do it by himself when we speak of children, but only with a woman may he procreate.

23 Does that then mean that a man or a woman with uncommon affections for their own should be scorned and whipped and even put to death as sometimes occurs among the religious zealots?

24 Why do you think those with uncommon affections are the way they are? Did not Elohim make them so? Will you scorn and whip and put Elohim to death?

25 Unless they were irresistibly compelled by their nature from God to be as they are, do you think they would choose to be reviled and beaten throughout their lives?

26 But if they have uncommon affections one for another, how then can they obey the Great Commandment? In truth, they cannot in the way of a man and a woman create children.

27 But there is far more to the great commandment than bringing new children into the world, for what is missed when those with uncommon affections do not have children is more than compensated by the men and women who have a great abundance of children.

28 The central point of the Great Commandment is not merely to have children, but to be good stewards and multiply and replenish the earth and all life therein, in all aspects, of which children are but one.

29 If two people with uncommon affections have love one for another and sanctify it and are faithful to it within the covenant of marriage and are good stewards of the earth, helping to

protect it and all the life therein and helping to increase and magnify it and all life therein, they have fulfilled the Great Commandment far more than the man and the woman who have many children, but are so taxed with so many that they are unable to give them either their time or love or meet their most basic of temporal needs."

30 At this last pronouncement, many stood up, yelling in anger at that which Yeshua taught, and even some of his disciples looked at one another questioningly.

31 Yeshua raised his hands and motioned for everyone to sit down and listen to all he had to say.

32 Then he continued saying, "You see in my words the fulfillment of that which I have said from the beginning. I have not come to uphold the law, but to destroy it, save for the Great Commandment and the true commandments of Sinai, for the laws of Elohim have been perverted by the desires of men.

33 Hear me now. I come not just to destroy, but to bring you a new light far greater than you have known, even the sacred light, Celestine.

34 Before you tear me asunder or turn me over to the persecution of the Romans, hear all that I have to say and weigh my words with the sense of your head and the feeling of your heart.

35 In commanding man to multiply and replenish the earth, Elohim gave men and women a righteous desire for one another and pleasure in fulfilling the desire.

36 But this was countered by the commandments to not commit fornication or adultery. Therefore, only in a bonded relationship, publicly acknowledged in marriage, could a man and woman virtuously fulfill the carnal desire for one another that dwelt within them.

37 Why should men and women not just be like so many of the animals who rut with who they will? The animals' rut, and they are no different after than before. They rut again, and still they change not.

38 Hear me, men and women of Gennesaret. You are spirit sons and daughters of Elohim, of a living Father and Mother in Heaven.

39 Verily, you are here on this earth for more than pleasure and sensual fulfillment. You are here to show God that you can become more than you began and to help others to do likewise.

40 Conquer your lust, keep it virtuous and in your marriage bed where it is sanctified by God.

41 Be a good steward of yourself first, then of the earth and all that is upon it, and Elohim will make you an eternal steward of much more.

42 Unite in the sacred covenant of marriage. Bring forth children, such as you can care for with your time and coin, into the world through love in your marriage bed and teach them by precept and example in the ways of righteousness that they may walk in the light.

43 In this, you are good stewards, helping your children to become more than they began.

44 And you are also a good steward of your own life, for having children helps you to overcome selfishness, one of the most poisonous darts the adversary will embed in your heart and mind.

45 Children teach you patience; they give you a window to see Heaven; they help your weaknesses to become your strengths.

46 For a man to live his life with a woman and a woman with a man, in devotion to one another, and for them to bear and raise children, sacrificing their time and treasure for the well-being of their children, this is a light that overcomes the darkness of selfishness.

47 And once overcome, dealings with all others become more cordial; criminal acts less common and wars less likely.

48 Righteous marriage with children teaches selflessness and compromise by each individual for the happiness of one another and the good of the family, and these lessons carry forth into the wider world of community and nations.

49 Striving to live a righteous marriage with children forges the weaknesses of men and women into their strengths, even as fornication and adultery or a life without marriage and children brings a forgetfulness of the light and opens the transgressor to greater susceptibility to further darkness.

50 These principals of light are so important and needful for expansion of the light within you that the man and woman who are barren should always adopt children who are without parents, so both may be filled with the love and growth that only a parent and child can bring to one another.

51 Consider again now the men who have affections for men and the women who have affections for women.

52 Elohim made them as they are, by their request, before they were born of woman, that they might have the opportunity in life to be sorely tested and grow great in stature as they overcome their challenges, but also that they might more easily embody the balance of male and female that can lead to becoming a living testament of the Celestine Light.

53 Do you think then that Elohim would condemn them for the nature that was given to them and disdain their righteous desire to have greater burdens and greater potential for reward any more than the fish would be condemned for swimming or the bird for flying?

54 But there is a trap laid for them of selfishness, and many are those that are caught by it, for as they are scorned and cast away from those who rebuke them, they may be enticed into their lusts and begin to live for their lust and pleasure and comfort, thus are led step by step down the path to damnation instead of the exaltation they sought.

55 I say unto you, do not, by your actions of condemnation, encourage them down that path.

56 Verily, there are many alternatives within the Great Commandment, and if they accept a stewardship of the earth and the life therein and fulfill it, they have lived the Great Commandment as fully as any husband and wife who cared well for their children.

57 Like with children, fulfilling a stewardship to the earth and all the life therein requires a continued and prolonged sacrifice of your time and your treasure. And in this, you overcome selfishness and become far greater than you were.

58 Therefore, I say clearly unto you: It is not a sin for a man to have affections for a man or a woman for a woman, if it comes not from carnal lust, but from virtuous love, for such was not forbidden by Elohim in the Great Commandment or the commandments of Sinai.

59 But with those who love their own kind, let them lust not after one another into fornication, but remain virtuous and only have intimacy within the bonds of marriage, even as it is for a man and a woman.

60 But there are also differences that must be respected. Where a man may have two or more wives and they may love one another even as they love their husband, let there be no other men but two in a marriage with one another, for beyond this men are given to purely carnal lusts over love.

61 Let all marriages be in public. Let the unmarried keep their chastity before marriage and guard their virtue zealously once married.

62 And I say unto you, let any who would commit fornication before marriage or adultery after marriage suffer the full weight of their transgression before man and God until they have repented and asked forgiveness and made restitution to all they have wronged."

63 Again there arose a great hue and cry and much consternation among the people in the temple at the words of Yeshua, for never had they heard anything similar to what he had said unto them, and it was vastly different from all they had ever been taught.

64 Yet they were astonished at his doctrine and the power of his words, and despite their shock at his teachings, many were not as angry as they supposed they should have been and some found themselves nodding in agreement, for his teachings made sense in their heads and resonated in their hearts.

65 Then a man stood up and yelled, "You are a false teacher! You would undermine the sanctity of our homes and marriages with your words of perversion. Truly, evil must dwell within you to say such things."

66 Yeshua answered him, saying, "It is your actions to put aside and persecute those who are not like you that weakens the fabric of your home and marriage, for cast away and reviled, they

are more likely to be angry and revengeful and fall onto the paths of lust and fornication, as the path of virtue and honor is forbidden by those who condemn them.
67 Let each be as they were created within the boundaries of a righteous marriage, given the opportunity to be good stewards and live lives of virtue and honor, and your home and marriage will be far more protected."
68 Then Yeshua spoke commandingly, pointing into the crowd, "That you may see the truth that I am the light and not be offended by my teachings, but uplifted, bring that man to me."
69 Now the man he spoke of had glared at him in silence through all he had said. But when everyone looked at him because Yeshua pointed to him, his face contorted in rage and he growled like a wild animal.
70 He turned to quickly depart, but Yeshua spoke forcibly to him, saying, "Turn and face the Celestine Light, demon of darkness."
71 The man turned to face Yeshua, drool now coming from his mouth, his face twisted in anger, and his voice garbled and growling, and said, "Let me alone! What have I to do with you, Yeshua of Nazareth? Have you come to destroy me? I know who you are, Holy Son of Elohim. Leave me be!"
72 Yeshua commanded, "Speak no more! Depart this instant! Let the light near every darkness thwart you to ever again dwell in man."
73 The man fell to the floor with a piercing scream and began to thrash about for a few seconds, and then he was still.
74 Slowly, he opened his eyes and, gingerly feeling his body, found that he was unhurt. And his face, which was full of dirt, shone with a countenance of light.
75 All who witnessed it were amazed. And the men and women in the synagogue spoke among themselves, saying, "What power is this? What can this new doctrine be, for with authority and power even the unclean spirits obey him and depart at his command?"
76 As the people departed the synagogue, they separated hurriedly each to their own path, anxious to tell their friends everything they had seen and heard. And Yeshua's fame soon spread throughout all the region of Galilee.
77 After leaving the synagogue, Yeshua and Miriam went with Cephas and Amram to Cephas' home in Bethsaida, and Ya'akov and Yohhanan went with them.
78 Upon arriving, they found that the mother of Cephas was sick with a great fever.
79 Yeshua came and held his hands above her body for a moment, moving them slightly, with his eyes closed as if in silent prayer.
80 Then laying his hands upon her head, he rebuked the fever and took her by the hand, lifting her up from her bed.
81 She arose well and whole with a great smile and words of gratitude and immediately went to the string hanging from the ceiling and brought dates out for them to eat.
82 In the evening, as the sun set, many of the people of the town came to the house of Cephas, for everyone had heard of the earlier events at the synagogue and they desired to see and hear Yeshua.
83 They brought many who were diseased and others who were possessed of devils to Yeshua.
84 And those who were diseased and attested in sincerity to repent of their sins and walk in the light, he healed of many diverse sicknesses.
85 But he rebuked those who would not repent in sincerity, saying, "Only the pure in heart can be healed by the Celestine Light of Elohim.
86 Repent first of your sins that the light may find a place in you. When the light is in your heart, all things are possible."
87 From five men and two women, he cast out demons, but he did not allow the demons to speak, because he did not want them to say who he was as the demon in the synagogue had. The darkness unmistakably knew the light, but the common people were not yet prepared to receive this knowledge.

88 From this day forth, a Community of Light began to form in the region of the three towns
of the delta on Lake Gennesaret.
89 And in the weeks to come, many were baptized by the disciples called by Yeshua, and when
they came out of the water, in their hearts was a light brighter than the sun.

CHAPTER 25

Sermon at Sycthopolis

Yeshua travels throughout Galilee, Syria, and Judea, teaching the Gospel and healing the sick and diseased. Many people come to hear him speak, and he explains in great detail how to pray to our Heavenly Mother and Father and what to pray for. Many are baptized.

During the following months, Yeshua traveled all through Galilee and into Syria and Judea, teaching the Gospel of Celestine Light in the synagogues and in the open-air temples of Elohim.

2 In each town and village, he healed the sick and diseased who were pure in heart and came to him with a contrite spirit.

3 Miriam and his disciples baptized many who had heard his words and felt the spirit of Elohim moving in their hearts, and they rose from the water and were called Children of Light.

4 Those who were baptized showed the truth of their convictions by repenting of their sins and covenanting before man and God to henceforth live in the light.

5 The fame of Yeshua went all throughout Galilee and Syria, and many people with sicknesses and diverse diseases, and torments of the mind and heart, and those possessed with devils and those that had palsy were brought to him; and he healed all of them who were pure in heart.

6 And it came to pass that large crowds began to follow him, and people came from Galilee, from Decapolis and Jerusalem and Judea, and from Perea and lands beyond the Jordan.

7 One morning, while encamped near Sycthopolis, Yeshua arose well before dawn and went out to a solitary place toward the mountain, west of the town, and prayed there.

8 When Miriam and the disciples awoke, the disciples wondered where he was, and Miriam told them and they went to him.

9 When they found him, alone on a hillside, Cephas asked, "A great crowd looks for you this morning. When shall I tell them that you will come?"

10 Yeshua began walking back down the hill as he answered Cephas, saying, "I will come now and speak to those who are here this morning. Then let us go into the next towns that I may preach and you may baptize, for that is why we are here in this moment."

11 Coming down to the people waiting for him on the outskirts of the city, Yeshua said unto them, "When you pray, do not pray to an unseen God without a body or form.

12 Know that you are truly children of a Heavenly Mother and Father, and they are as real and tangible as I am.

13 When you pray to them, do not just let words flow out of your mouth, nor repeat each day the same thing you said the previous day.

14 Speak your prayers aloud when you are in a private place, but only in your thoughts when

you are in public, unless you have been called upon to stand and pray as a representative for your brothers and sisters of spirit for something which you all desire.

15 In all prayers, before you say a word, take a deep breath and slowly let it out, then another and another, until you are in a quiet place of peace in your heart.

16 Then let your spirit expand beyond your body until you feel one with the grass and the waters and the birds and all life around you.

17 Then expand into the sun and the stars and feel the spirit of Elohim moving in your heart and feel oneness with God in all that you are.

18 When you then pray, speak not to the ethers, nor to a rock, or to the wall in your home, but to the spirit of your heavenly parents which dwells within you, which you are one with in your heart.

19 In humility, bow your head, then raise it up with closed eyes to the sun in your prayers, for all light comes from God, both the spiritual and the physical, and when your eyes are upon the light, it is easier to feel the spirit of Elohim moving in your heart and hear the voice of Elohim speaking in your thoughts.

20 Be a thankful son or daughter of God, for you have been given a life on a most blessed world where food grows of its own accord and beauty and life abounds and surrounds you wherever you look.

21 When you are in the sacred place of prayer in your heart, ask of Elohim any selfless and worthy desire, beyond that which you can do for yourself, and the means for it to come to pass shall be given to you.

22 But ask not for worldly things; save it be with selflessness; only for help with your simple needs and for the good of others and the glory of God.

23 Elohim is not like a distant rich relative to be called upon to grant your temporal wishes, but a true parent who teaches you good principles that you may prosper on your own, both spiritually and temporally.

24 Verily, your heavenly parents greatly desire your continual well-being and spiritual fulfillment upon earth and your eternal happiness and progression in Heaven.

25 Know that you have been blessed by your heavenly parents with great gifts when you were born to help you in your journey in life.

26 With your talents and listening to your inner light, you can gain all that you seek in the world that is worthy of a son or daughter of God.

27 Not by wishing it were so, but by using the gifts you have been given with prudence and diligence."

28 Then a man named Zuriel asked, "The previous moon, my fishing boat was overcome by a storm and sank into the sea. Now it is hard for my family, for I cannot earn as much working for another as I can for myself. I have asked God for another boat, but you say I should not pray for such things. How then may I get a new boat, for I cannot pay for one on my own?"

29 Yeshua answered him, "You may certainly ask Elohim to help you acquire another boat as it is not for you alone that you ask, but for the good of your family; and you do not ask for an excess, but merely to fulfill your humble needs.

30 But do not expect a new boat to magically appear the next morning at your door, for Elohim helps you with inspiration and ideas and by guiding the answers, the people, and the situations and materials you need, to help manifest your prayer. Then it is in your hands to use the gifts of Elohim along with your own gifts and talents to help yourself.

31 Have you used your talents and done all that you can do?"

32 Zuriel rubbed his chin as he considered the words of Yeshua and answered, "In truth, I have not. Even as we speak, I have thought of a way I can acquire a boat that I had not considered before and realized that I have spent more time lamenting my misfortune than doing things within my power to remedy it.

33 I will act now in earnestness and call upon God to lend favor to my actions."

34 Yeshua smiled saying, "And so shall your worthy desires and prayers be fulfilled."

35 Then Yeshua continued with his sermon, saying, "Remember, Elohim is the essence of love and light, while the adversary within and the minions of evil spew forth hatred, violence, and darkness.

36 Therefore, let every action of the righteous man or woman always be one of light and life and love, and you shall ever have the spirit of Elohim as your constant companion to lift your spirit and surround you in the light you seek, and the adversary shall have no place within you.

37 With the Celestine Light of Elohim in your heart and guiding your thoughts and actions, you will find contentment in simple things and success in your selfless endeavors, both great and small.

38 If you choose your actions based upon the good that will be gained for others by accomplishing your tasks, you will always find the favor of Elohim to help you in your desires.

39 That is not to say that you cannot also gain, but that he who seeks only for himself has no favor from God and no friends upon the earth, while he who seeks righteous things of which others may also freely benefit shall be blessed by Elohim and honored in sincerity by men."

40 Then Yeshua beckoned for the sick and afflicted to come to him, and the repentant and pure in heart, he healed, every one.

41 When he made ready to depart to another city, the people asked him to stay with them and were greatly desirous that he should not depart from them.

42 But with love, he said unto them, "It must needs be that I also preach across the land that others might see the true Celestine Light of Elohim and repent and be healed both inside and out; that they might be a light of God among men even as the good people of Sycthopolis."

43 And though they were sad at his departure, they understood his words and, with thankfulness, asked that he would return again to them soon.

44 But some could not bear to see him leave, and they followed after him.

45 And the families of Hiram and Abner having heard from his disciples about the new Community of Light at the north end of Lake Gennesaret gathered their families, and carrying their belongings, they moved there straightaway.

CHAPTER 26

First Sermon at Ptolemais

Yeshua sends his disciples into the city of Ptolemais to gather people for a sermon that he will give the following day in the synagogue. Over four hundred people show up, and he teaches them about longevity and the necessary lifestyle to have a long happy life upon the earth, which includes vegetarianism, particularly raw foods, as a means of sustenance. He tells them a wonderful parable about the virtues of good stewardship, explaining that as you are a good steward of your body, the earth, and all that is on it, God will bless you with happiness in this life and fulfillment in eternity.

From Sycthopolis, Yeshua and Miriam and the disciples returned to Nazareth for a night, and then journeyed to Ptolemais on the coast, where Yeshua had gone sometimes during his youth to meditate while looking over the sea and to mingle with the many foreigners in the city.

2 As they traveled, Miriam walked with him, and one time when the others were trailing far behind, she asked, "My Lord, when shall you reveal the greater secrets of the Celestine Light to the disciples you have called to follow you?"

3 Yeshua answered her, saying, "They are still like babes upon their mother's breast. They must continue with milk before they can tolerate the substance of that which is greater. And there are others I must call, and there must be a Quorum of Twelve before I will speak of the fullness of the Celestine Light to them.

4 Many things I shall not tell them until the very last days before I depart from the world. And many things will wait for you to reveal to them once I have returned to my Father and Mother in Heaven."

5 Miriam protested, saying, "My dear husband, you know they only tolerate me because I am your wife. When you are gone, I fear I shall have no standing with them and they will not heed my words, nor do I wish to even be upon the earth if you are not here with me."

6 Yeshua held her hand as they walked and kissed her lightly on the cheek, saying, "Though my body may be gone, my spirit will never leave you, and the substance of my essence will be so strong with you that it will be as if I walk beside you still.

7 It must needs be that you remain for a time after I have returned from whence I came to nurture our children and the flame of Celestine Light, for before a night has passed ere I have left the earth, there will be many who will begin to pervert my teachings.

8 Even among my elect who hold fast to my light, there will be some who will not be able to overcome their own weaknesses and will heed you not.

9 Then will come those who never knew me, but act in my name, calling themselves my

Apostles and bishops. And they will have a fanatic zeal to purge all of your words, even the record of your life from the annals of men.

10 Such as these are not worthy for the higher Celestine Light that you will offer. But those who are worthy, though their numbers will be small, will receive you with love, honor, and humility. And as marvelous as you are, the Miriam they will know then will be far more than the Miriam they know today."

11 That evening they slept outside the walls of the city, and as the sun rose, they entered through the east gate.

12 Yeshua sent his disciples to go into the markets, along the quays and into the streets, proclaiming his coming.

13 The disciples were diligent in their task, and many people came the following day to hear Yeshua speak during their midday break.

14 Many were interested because the disciples told them how Yeshua did not teach the same teachings of old they had heard before, but shared how to have a better life and know God as a friend.

15 And it came to pass that over four hundred people gathered at the synagogue where Yeshua had come, and he blessed them for seeking a greater light and said unto them, "Though you may have a comfortable home and a work that pays you well, if you do not have the spirit of Elohim in your heart, which is evident by your actions of kindness, selflessness, generosity, and love, you have nothing.

16 For the things of this world are here today and gone tomorrow, but the spirit of Elohim abiding in your heart and manifested in your actions gives a comfort in life that all the money of the world cannot buy and a palace in eternity greater than any Caesar can imagine.

17 Though you may think you are young and have good health, if you do not live as God has given for you to live in the food you eat and that which you drink and in the way you love the temple of your body which Elohim has built, then your end is misery in life and wretched remorse for what could have been in the world to come.

18 You have heard it said from the prophets of old that the people of ancient days lived for hundreds of years, even Methuselah, the son of Enoch, who lived for 969 years. How is it then that you know not one person who has reached one hundred years and will count yourself blessed if you live to fifty years?

19 Were the people more righteous than you in the days before? Nay, most were not, for the scriptures are ripe with the accounts of their unrighteousness.

20 But there were some who walked closer to the ways of Elohim, and they reaped many blessings, which included a long and fruitful life.

21 Think not that I speak of the law, for most of the law is of men and I have come to destroy it, not honor it.

22 But if you remember that you are a temple built by Elohim and have been given to live upon a paradise created by Elohim and you honor your temple and partake of your Eden in righteousness and respect, then all that the righteous ancients had shall be yours as well.

23 Your Eden was given to be breathed in purity, and in such your body is renewed by the very air. Therefore, do not breathe the smoke of fires or even a candle lest you destroy the renewal God has blessed you with. And let the barbaric practice of breathing the smoke of herbs to ward off evil spirits have no place in your life or within the walls of your home, for the smoke of anything is death, not life.

24 Elohim has charged you to be a steward over every living thing and over all the earth, all of which are given for your benefit and as you have need.

25 As a good steward, you must respect your charges and never despoil a land no matter how small, without restoring it to its splendor, nor take a life no matter how insignificant, save there is no other way to sustain or protect your own.

26 Therefore, do not kill the animals or the birds to eat their flesh, for they love their life, even

as you love yours.

27 Choose whenever possible to eat only those things of life that Elohim has put in your Eden to give you sustenance without taking life that would have continued for years.

28 Therefore, first eat the fruits of the trees and bushes that give you freely of their pulp that you might spread their seeds and propagate their kind.

29 If you still hunger, eat of the vegetables that give you their fruit and of the plants that wither and die each year and were therefore given to be consumed.

30 But cook them not, for then you have sustenance without life, and each bite brings you closer to your own death. Heat them only enough to enhance the life, not extinguish it.

31 If because of drought or famine or your situation at the time, you cannot be strengthened from plants alone, then eat the lower forms of life: the insects and the schooling fish of the sea.

32 And all others, you should never eat, save it be that there is no other way to save your life at the time.

33 Remember well my words. The more you eat that which still has life and is given freely without fight or resistance, the more you will be renewed to live beyond the years of men in health and wisdom.

34 Use this simple test: If the meal you desire that lives free would try to escape from you and not go meekly and quietly to your plate if it knew your intentions, then it is a life you should spare unless you have no other way to sustain your own.

35 If you domesticate animals to help you with your tasks and treat them with respect as a good steward, Elohim will show you favor. But do not eat for food those creatures which have pleasure in the company of their friends, for they are like you, only in a different kind of body, and eating them would be the same as eating your best friend.

36 Though you might have sustenance in the moment, the despair the animal you slew felt in death taints the meat with a toxin of death that brings you closer to your own grave with each bite.

37 Consider now the sun in the sky that brings you warmth and light each day. This is the very essence of Elohim, and as such its power is greater than you can imagine. It can give you life or death depending upon your wisdom.

38 Each day, you should come into the light of the sun. Let it shine into your closed eyes; feel its warmth upon your bare skin, for this very light of Elohim purifies your body inside and out.

39 But be wise and do not linger too long lest you get burned like the bread left too long in the oven, making that which was good become bad.

40 Consider also the water that you drink. Let it be pure without the waste of people or animals, for your body is an ocean and if you keep your water clear, your ocean will still have life long after your friends who heeded not my words have dried up and blown away with the wind.

41 Nor should water just be to drink but also to keep your body clean, and I speak not just of your hands and feet and mouth. Cleaning only those is like only cleaning the doorways of the synagogue. If you love your temple, clean all of it each day. As you care for your temple, so it shall care for you.

42 Nor should you be slothful in the use of your body. Elohim did not create your temple with all its moving parts for you to lounge around on couches, eating grapes as the Romans do.

43 Each day, consider how you can move all parts of your temples in a myriad of ways. Stretch them, strain them, challenge them, and they will become stronger and bring you health and longevity.

44 Take the path of ease and you will have comfort in the moment, but the total of your moments will be far less upon the world.

45 What of your habits? Have you considered how your traits and the way you treat yourself and others might be a great weight upon the scale of your health, life, and happiness?

46 Your actions begin with your thoughts, and if these are not pure, neither will be the actions that follow.

47 What then is a pure thought? Does that mean you cannot lust for your wife? No, it does not, for lust for your wife with love is of God, but lust for another man's wife is impure and will shorten your days upon the earth and lessen your reward in Heaven, even if you never act upon your thought.

48 If you say a mean and spiteful thing to your brother or sister, it will eat like a sickness in your heart and take away the days of your life. Even if you only think an evil thought of your brother or sister, but say it not, it will still be a sickness inside that consumes you.

49 Therefore, be not easily offended by the actions of others, whether they are your brother or sister, father or mother, children or friends. Be quick to smile and laugh and slow to condemn or judge and your years upon the earth will be greatly multiplied, and each one will be a treasure.

50 If you would have the happiness of a new bride and the age of the ancients, then let your greatest habit be love. Let each thought and breath be an expression of greater love, not just for your family, but for your friends and your acquaintances and even your enemies.

51 For Elohim loves you with a love greater than the sun, despite your weaknesses.

52 Love is the greatest fountain of life you will ever know. Therefore, let it flow from you in abundance by your thoughts and words and actions.

53 And by this, your enemies will become your friends and your friends will honor you, and your family shall cherish you, and your life will be long and full of great joy.

54 And if you love your family and friends, you will be a good steward and serve them and help them in their lives. In this, you also serve yourself, for in every good deed you do, Elohim adds to your days of joy upon the earth.

55 Lastly, remember to have a good balance in your life.

56 Many people and duties call to you and are in need of your time. Give to all with equality, but do not neglect your own needs for contemplation and prayer and rest.

57 Your temple needs proper amounts of good food and water and air and movement. Therefore, take heed to have balance each day in these things.

58 Take heed to consider the merits of all points of view and do not pass judgment upon others simply because they are not like you, for all are children of your Father and Mother in Heaven.

59 Never forget that Elohim has taken a portion of Heaven and put it upon the earth to be your Eden that you might live long upon the land and prosper. And so it shall be if you live your life worthy of the gifts you have been given."

60 Then Yeshua was quiet for a moment so that his words might move within the hearts of the people. And in the eyes of some, a new light dawned, but in others, their countenance was dark for they could not abide the things Yeshua had said, which for them were not as they were inclined to live.

61 Yeshua, perceiving the thoughts of the people, said unto them, "There once was a noble man who owned much land and hired many men.

62 The Lord was a good steward over the lands and people that had been given to his dominion, and he continually looked for ways to reward his faithful workmen and to give them greater responsibilities and stewardship that they might become more than they began.

63 And it came to pass that there was one young man he greatly favored, for he had a willing heart and a quick mind.

64 Therefore, one day the Lord said to his worker, 'Today is the day of your fulfillment. You have worked diligently and faithfully for me, and now I shall make you master of my mill and of the men who work there. It shall all be in your charge.'

65 The man was very grateful for his reward and worked even more diligently than before. He kept the mill clean and organized the work to be more efficient so that soon they were producing more flour than the mill had ever produced before, and the Lord was pleased.

66 Three years passed and the mill continued to prosper under the stewardship of the mill master, but despite his greater wealth, the man seemed to age far more than three years.

67 The Lord was concerned for him, so he went in secret to inquire in his village about the man, for he favored him and worried that he might be in some trouble.

68 In the village, he was told that since he had become master of the mill, the man thought only of his work. He neglected his wife and children. He slept little, and he came home later than all others and drank far too much wine every night.

69 Straightaway the next morning, the Lord called his mill master to him and spoke of the things he had learned. And the mill master answered, 'It is true, my Lord. I have neglected my wife and children, because I have served you first as I knew I must.

70 It is difficult to run a mill well, for there are many things to deal with each day. When I come home, I am tired, and the wine has helped me to sleep quickly so I can be prepared to arise early and serve you again the next day.

71 Please do not be angry with me for I have only wanted to serve you well. I have been saddened to see what has become of my personal life, but I have willingly given up some pleasures that I can have others that more money can buy, that my children can have more than I had as a child.'

72 The Lord, seeing the man's good heart, could not be angry with him, but he said unto him, 'You have served me well, and in that I am pleased. But if in the course of your service you destroy your own life, you will steal from me the many hours of good work I could have otherwise had from you if you had cared as much for yourself and your family as you do for your work.

73 I did not ask you to lose your life because of me, but gave you your reward that you and your family might have a better life.

74 Understand, it is not from money or position that happiness comes, but from being a good steward over all that is in your charge.'

75 The mill master was confused, saying, 'My Lord, you must know that I am a good steward. The mill has never produced as much as it does under my care.'

76 And the Lord answered, 'I speak not of the mill for that is but one board in the wheel of your life. It is of the other boards that I speak and of the hub.

77 Your wife is a part of your wheel of great importance, and you must take the time to love her and be with her.

78 The mill can be destroyed tomorrow and it can be rebuilt, but if you destroy the love of your wife because of your neglect, it will be much more difficult to rebuild that which was lost.

79 Each of your children are also parts of your wheel, and whether they will grow strong and delightful depends upon your presence and love and example of virtue.

80 They are children for only a precious few years. If you do not cherish every moment with them and seek out time to share with them, then the sun will set on your time together and will never rise again, for they will be children no more.

81 And your family and friends are also parts of the vitality of the wheel of your life. If you neglect them and do not listen to their problems and help them in their needs, they will turn away from you, and in your time of need, your wheel will fail for lack of support.

82 Lastly, my good mill master, you are the hub of your wheel. If you drink too much and sleep too little, if you eat poorly and do not take time to reflect and contemplate and commune with God, then your hub will become bound and you will be seized.

83 Your journey will end before its time because you were not a good steward over the things that were actually the most important.

84 If you can be such a wonderful mill master and such a good steward over the things which I have given to you, then can you not be an even greater steward over that which God has given unto you, even your very life and your wife and your children and family and friends?'

85 And the mill master fell to his knees in tears, for the truth of the Lord's words had been like a spear into his heart. And he cried out, 'Lord, forgive me for being a steward more over that which was least and not enough over that which was greater.

86 Give me another chance and I will be the good and faithful steward you have shown me

I should be.'

87 The Lord was well pleased. He raised the mill master from his knees and bid him go home, saying, 'I will see you at the mill tomorrow, but today I think your greater stewardship beckons.'

88 Quickly, the man returned to his wife and children, and there was great joy in their house thereafter.

89 I say unto you, be like the mill master; remember that being a good steward is pleasing to God, but it begins with honoring and caring for the temple of your own body that Elohim has given to you and then by loving your wife and nurturing your children with your time and sincere attention.

90 Verily, it matters not what success you have in the world. If you fail to care for the vessel God has given you, if you fail to give ample love and time to your wife and children, then all else you do is for naught, for your life will be unhappiness and your eternity will be emptiness.

91 But do not despair; for you are children of God, you are Children of Light. Remember who you are, let your heart go to Elohim, and it will always guide you to happiness in this life and fulfillment in eternity."

CHAPTER 27

Second Sermon at Ptolemais

Yeshua gives another sermon in Ptolemais, and over six hundred people show up to hear him speak. He teaches them about the Temple of Forever and how to have a joyful and fulfilling life.

The following day, Yeshua again gave a sermon during the midday rest, and the number of people who came to hear him was greater than the previous day, numbering over six hundred, including men, women, and children.

2 Many people came early and brought food and drink with them so they could listen to his preaching while they ate their midday meal. And numerous small awnings were set up in the crowd to shade the young and old from the sun.

3 Ptolemais was a bustling city with residents and visitors from all parts of the Mediterranean and beyond. Among those who came to hear Yeshua were both the rich and the poor, Hebrews of many persuasions and Gentiles of many lands, including a number of Romans. It was with this varied audience in mind that Yeshua chose the subjects of his sermon.

4 And Yeshua said unto them, "Is Elohim the God of the life to come or the God of the life you live?

5 Truly, Elohim is the God of both. Yet how different is the life you live from the life you expect to live in the hereafter?

6 Your life in mortality is meant to be a challenge that you may grow stronger and of more sure faith. But it is not meant to be misery, for the man who is beat down without end eventually becomes so numb from torment that he stops trying to rise to something better.

7 It is for this cause that those who unnecessarily cause pain and suffering in others, giving pain and suffering instead of compassion, will reap the evil that they sowed, seventy times seventy in the hereafter after they are weighed in the balance and found wanting.

8 So too will the man or woman who gives compassion instead of torment reap their good reward in the hereafter, seventy times seventy after they are weighed in the balance and found to have multiplied their light.

9 Nevertheless, though you may die in a moment, the hereafter seems distant and far away, even but a dream, while your challenges of today are unavoidably before you, both those you inflict upon yourself and those inflicted upon you by others.

10 But you are the master of the Celestine Light that dwells within you. If you choose to embrace the light, there is no darkness deep enough to overcome you.

11 If you choose to let the Celestine Light of Elohim fill your body, no problems in life are great enough to take away the warmth and tranquility you will feel inside.

12 Though you may be poor, you will feel rich.

13 Though you may be persecuted, you will feel peace, without anxiety.
14 Though you may hunger even for food, you will feel filled.
15 Think not that Elohim is the God only of the world to come, for it is Elohim that made the world you now live upon and everything in it, and this for your happiness, joy, and fulfillment.
16 Life becomes sour for many people only because they do not take good actions to make it sweet like honey; therefore, it spoils and becomes unpalatable.
17 Verily, I say unto you that Elohim gave you a world where life abounds that your life might have exceeding joy by being one in spirit with all the life around you.
18 Go and stare for an hour at the sea, listening to the waves lapping on the beach. Rest in your garden for an hour and quietly watch the bees gathering nectar on the flowers or the ants patiently building their nest by removing one small grain of sand at a time.
19 Take time to immerse yourself often, if only for an hour or a day, in the life of the world around you, and you will find the Celestine Light of Elohim comes alive inside of you, and your burdens become lighter and your life becomes brighter.
20 When a man becomes a man, he stops being like a child and he thinks well of himself. But in truth, when a man stops being like a child and takes life too seriously, it becomes drudgery and monotony, and his life goes from the continual pure happiness of a child to the frequent unhappiness of a man.
21 The more years of drudgery and monotony that pass, the more unhappiness builds within the man, until in his old age he becomes as shriveled as a stale dried date, with little of the soft joy remaining from his youth.
22 Does this sound like anyone you know? Perhaps even you? Have you become so caught up in being an adult that you have forgotten how to be a child?
23 Do you play with your own children, sharing in their delight at a new discovery or accomplishment?
24 You may say that you have no time for the foolishness of children. But I say unto you there is little that is as great of importance, for unless a man can easily and often become as a little child, he can in no way enter into the glory of the Kingdom of Heaven.
25 Being as a child does not throw off your responsibilities as an adult. It merely seeks a balance of stewardship to your family and stewardship to yourself of recognizing that there is a time to work and a time to play, and that the time to play, just like the time to work, comes every day, except for the Sabbath.
26 For this cause look often for occasions to celebrate. At the end of each week of work, reward yourself and your family with a special celebration, even if it is only an extra date for a dessert and a quiet hour on the beach with your family.
27 Celebrate the planting even if you are not a farmer, for you still hope for fair weather and a good crop that you may have food on your table.
28 For the same reason, celebrate the harvest; whether the bounty came from the farmers' fields or your own plot of land, it is the blessing of life and the pleasure of good food.
29 Celebrate each full moon, even if your life has been greatly challenged during that moon, for you still live and still enjoy great blessings.
30 If the lamp of Elohim is lit inside of you, then you will always see the blessings that surround you. Your joys will be magnified in your heart, and your sorrows lessened.
31 Celebrate each birthday in your family, even if only with an orange and a day off from work, for each soul of life is a blessing, and each step you walk in life is laying the foundation for your eternity.
32 As you celebrate the lives of your loved ones, your thoughtfulness reminds them of how special they are to you, even as they will remember how wonderful you are to them.
33 As a community, look for occasions to be festive and celebrate things great and small, for sharing and rejoicing together is the glue that binds the stew pot of cultures and people, that is, Ptolemais.

34 Why do you think I speak to you of these things? It is to help you to know that God did not create you to have endless sorrow, but to have endless joy.

35 You were not born to wait for death as a blessing, merely hoping to escape life and pass to an eternal paradise. Verily, God gave you life and gave you this world that you would have joy and make it into a paradise, beginning within the walls of your own home.

36 You may be accustomed to hearing a long list of laws you must obey from your priests, but the only laws I give you today are to acknowledge God in all things and to treat your neighbor in your thoughts, words, and deeds as you would hope to be treated by them.

37 Respect and humility toward God and respect and courtesy to your neighbors are the foundations of peace on earth and everlasting joy in Heaven.

38 But what does that mean to you who live in Ptolemais? Here your neighbor may be a Roman or a Persian or a Syrian or a Greek, all with beliefs and habits different than yours and perhaps even objectionable. Is this a cause to fight with your neighbor or just to disdain them?

39 I say unto you, do not fight them or disdain them, but accept them and respect them if they are of good character."

40 Then Yeshua pointed to a man with a red sash far to his right at the edge of the crowd and another with a brown sash far to his left and beckoned them to stand, and he said, "Though Elohim is the one God of all the earth and every star in the sky, there are many ways to find and know God, even as those who sit to my right see me differently than those who sit to my left; yet both see me.

41 If I were to ask these two men to come to me, they could not walk in each other's footsteps. In truth, they would have to take very different paths. Yet both would have their eyes upon me, both would be seeking me, and in the end, I would embrace them both as they came to me.

42 Therefore, do not look to see if a person is from the same country as you or the same faith to befriend them. But look to their good character and virtue as a sure foundation worthy of friendship.

43 If they are seeking God with virtue and good character, even on a path different than yours, know with certainty that they are loved by Elohim. And if they are loved by Elohim, can you treat them any less?

44 And I say unto you that the day shall come in your lifetime when there shall be contentions among those who live in Ptolemais, and among the narrow-minded, there will be some who will incite violence against those that are not of their tribe or country or faith.

45 On that day, remember my words. If you would show devotion to God, then give only peace and solace and refuge to everyone who has virtue and good character, even as they would return it to you, regardless of the color of their skin, the language they speak, or the path they walk to God.

46 On that day, turn your back upon the instigators of intolerance; support them not. For in the eyes of Elohim, it is far better to give comfort to a man who walks a different path than you, but walks toward God with humility, honesty, and virtue than to stand against such a man and is far worse to stand with the ignorant and intolerant, simply because they are of your faith, or speak your tongue, or are from your tribe.

47 The fact that you listened to the spirit of Elohim that led you here today testifies that you are seeking something greater than you are and are seeking to become more than you have been, not in the ways of the world, but in the ways of God.

48 Remember now my words and the twelve pillars of the Temple of Forever and the capstone over all, which I give to you now in my love for you.

49 The true temple of Elohim is in a circle and no other shape, for only in a circle are all good things included in harmony and unity.

50 Though man may build a likeness to fulfill his needs for sanctuary and communion on earth, the true temple of Elohim is not built by man, but is within man, as he lives in harmony with the spirit of God.

51 Live these pillars; rest your thoughts and your words and your deeds upon them, and they will support you in life against all that the world may bring upon you and lift you to the highest mountain in the eternity to come.

52 These are among the things God does for you, and you should do no less for yourself and your fellow men.

53 When a choice is to be made between conflict and peace . . . choose peace. Be ever willing to find the path of harmony and common ground and ever reluctant to walk down the path of discord and anger because of differences.

54 There are many pious people who consider themselves godly, but do not act in ways that are pleasing to God; who become angry when others do not walk the same path to God that they do. But I say unto you that a faith that is worthy of God is not based only upon what you believe, but even more upon that which you do.

55 Your actions are the gold of your life, which is weighed in the balance of the scale of Judgment of Resonance. And in the world to come, it will not be asked of you what you believed in life, but rather what did you do in life?

56 Therefore, do unto others as you would have them do unto you; for that which you do to others, both the good and the bad, will come back and in an equal way to you from others, both in this life and the next.

57 And when good is done to you, reciprocate it back twofold.

58 But when evil is done to you, find forgiveness in your heart; and unto the repentant, do not hesitate to forgive them in your words and your actions.

59 Laugh and play and listen and watch and wonder; be a child each day, for it is one of the secrets of perpetual joy and communion with God, and for this cause have you been created and given this world; that you might have joy in abundance.

60 Be a good steward of all that is in your care by protecting, increasing, and enhancing all that has been entrusted to you, beginning with your own life, then your family, then your brothers and sisters of light, then your community, then your world and the life of everything therein.

61 Verily, the more you serve others, the greater grows your own spirit and stature.

62 Seek knowledge every day; for ignorance is slavery and knowledge is freedom; and these enliven your soul.

63 Verily, it is easier for a man or a woman with knowledge and freedom to do good in the world than one existing in ignorance and slavery.

64 Embrace love as a star to guide your life, for more miracles are possible with love than any other power save faith. In truth, these two work together, and one without the other is but an empty cup.

65 Love yourself first, in humility and truth, for only then can you give true love to others. Such is the circle of love.

66 Love your wife or husband as you would like them to love you, for when the love within a marriage is returned, it blossoms into a fulfillment and tranquility that is equaled only by the spirit of God flowing in your heart. Such is the circle of love.

67 Love your children as the most precious jewels and show your love by giving them your time each day, which speaks more powerfully of love to them than anything you can say, and it will be returned to you multiplied many times when you are old. Such is the circle of love.

68 Love your brothers and sisters of light and remember you are all part of the family of light; therefore, their concerns are yours, and their joys should be in your heart as well.

69 Care for them in their times of need, even as they will care for you. Such is the circle of love.

70 Love your neighbors, even those who are different from you. Verily, you are all still children of God and brothers and sisters of spirit. An injury to one is an injury to all, and a blessing to one is a blessing to all. Such is the circle of love.

71 Love the animals of the wilderness and the deep waters and the fields, for when you give

love even to those creatures who know you not, you gain a greater capacity to give and receive love from the people in your life that you do know. Such is the circle of love.

72 Love the plants and the mountains and the valleys and the forests and every life and place that is upon the earth, for as you love all that Elohim has made for you, your heart opens to receive all the love that Elohim has for you. Such is the circle of love.

73 In loving all these, your kinsmen and all the world and everything therein, show gratitude to them and to Elohim, for with gratitude, you become worthy to receive all of the miracles Elohim would give to you.

74 Let it be known across the land that love is married to faith. Even in the face of great hardships and grief, do not abandon your faith in the reality and omnipotence of Elohim, for faith is the conduit to powers unseen and the channel through which all miracles flow, both the small and the great.

75 Therefore, waver not in the face of adversity, for only those who do not falter prove their faith is true and thus open the door to all the powers of Heaven.

76 Each day, choose to eat a variety of simple foods that retain life; various fruits and vegetables, sprouted bread, and sometimes a little honey for a treat. Such brings you both pleasure and health.

77 But if you were to eat only one food, such as dates, for every meal, and dates alone, you would soon become sickly and be very unhappy and disagreeable before that occurred from having to eat only dates for every meal.

78 Even as a wise man eats many different foods for happiness and health, so should you embrace balance in all of your thoughts and actions, if you desire to obtain happiness in life and true progression of your soul.

79 Too much of anything, even things which are wonderfully good, entombs a man in a grave he has dug, while moderation leads to a long life full of wonder and contentment.

80 If you nourish only one part of your life, you allow the other parts to recede, and all are needed for the journey.

81 It is fine to be a zealot for a short period of focus to gain a specific desire, but to be continually zealous to the point that reason and harmony hold no sway is to condemn yourself to contentions that trample lives that should instead be uplifted, both yours and those of whom you love.

82 But balance alone can be a false justification to squander the sands of your life, if you do not insure that virtue guides your path.

83 Elohim delights in the virtuous man and woman; virtue is the fruit of the tree of Celestine Light, and the sweetness thereof is made known to all, but tasted and savored only by the worthy.

84 Virtue is gentle and sleeps soundly at night. Virtue is faithful and kind. Virtue has patience and self-mastery. Virtue is peaceful and loving. Virtue is honest and reliable. Virtue is chaste and pure.

85 Find a virtuous man or woman, regardless of their religion or culture, and you will have found a true son or daughter of God.

86 To hold virtue in your life, you must instill it in your heart, so the habit to be virtuous becomes greater than the temptation to be unvirtuous.

87 By this, you conquer yourself; you defeat the adversary within; and in overcoming yourself, you become greater than he who conquers a city.

88 The capstone of the Temple of Forever is a golden sphere that has no beginning or end and endless mysteries to discover hidden within. It is the admonition of Elohim that all who would walk the earth in righteousness would leave a legacy; that they might continue to uplift their brothers and sisters of spirit long after they have been freed from the bonds of mortality.

89 Even as Elohim has left you a legacy of the commandments of Sinai and the Eden of the earth and the true teachings of the prophets, that you might become more than you began.

90 As you see God do, so do you. You cannot give commandments unto men, nor can you

reveal the truths of Heaven to the prophets, but as Elohim created the earth and everything therein, so you can create beauty and wonders which edify your brothers and sisters of spirit long after you have gone to your eternal reward.

91 As worthy, righteous, and virtuous Children of Light, true sons and daughters of God, let it be so."

CHAPTER 28

By their Fruits You Shall Know Them

When questioned by his disciples about the chosen people of God, Yeshua explains that they are not from one tribe or one nation or one religion, but they are those who live the Celestine Light of Elohim, which light is imbued upon all souls from before birth regardless of what they have been taught to believe in life.

And it came to pass that Yeshua, Miriam, and his disciples departed from Ptolemais and walked a path to Bethsaida that traveled east over the ridge of hills.

2 They went out of their way to climb to the summit of a tall hill where they could look down upon Lake Gennesaret. At this place, they had their midday meal, and Philip asked a question to Yeshua that others had also wondered, saying, "Rabbi, we have just savored your words at Ptolemais, but I would ask you a question, not about what you said, but to whom you said it."

3 Yeshua rolled his hand, indicating that Philip should proceed, and Philip asked him, "In the synagogue, we have always been taught that we are the chosen people of God and that all other people are unworthy to have God's favor. Yet in Ptolemais, and also in Samaria, you have given your light and the wisdom of your words, and even mysteries and mighty miracles to those whom we have been told since our youth should be scorned.

4 In Ptolemais, I think there were more Romans, Greeks, Syrians, and other foreigners than there were Hebrews hearing your words. I must confess that I am confused." And all of the disciples nodded their heads in agreement.

5 Yeshua answered them, saying, "I am thankful you have asked me this and were not afraid. And I hope it will always be so, for it is important that you understand the fullness of the Celestine Light.

6 But I have spoken about this already to you; how is it that you have not understood the words I have said?

7 If my own disciples cannot comprehend this most basic truth, how will others see the light?

8 Every person on this world is a spirit son and daughter of our Father and Mother in Heaven, who loved their children and helped them to grow before they were born upon the earth.

9 Therefore, every man and woman is truly a brother and sister of one another.

10 Each is a child of God, so how could it be that Elohim would look upon all of the souls upon the earth and say this small number here alone will we love. Only these few will we bless or acknowledge or give an inheritance in our Kingdom.

11 The ignorant and the prejudice look for ways to puff themselves up by tearing others down. They will say, 'These people are not of our tribes, and they do not live the laws of God. Therefore, their inheritance is desolation and separation.'

12 But I have said unto you that I have come to destroy the laws that mock the true Celestine Light of Elohim, for man has elevated falsehoods to sacredness for his own purposes.

13 I bring the fullness of the Celestine fire, which most will not be able to bear, but that you, my brothers, must not falter in, even though because of it, those whom it scorches will try to bring death and torment to some of you in retaliation.

14 I came first to the Hebrews because in important times past, their fathers were faithful to the simple commandments of Elohim.

15 Elohim the Father made a solemn promise to the faithful Hebrews of ancient days that the fullness of the Celestine Light would be brought first to their descendants.

16 I am the fulfillment of that promise, and when I first spoke of the light, it was to the Hebrews, in the cities and towns of the Hebrews.

17 But I am not the light to the Hebrews alone, but the embodiment of the Celestine Light of Elohim to all the world, and everyone is my brother and sister of spirit.

18 There are some parts of the Celestine Light which the Hebrews know and do well; to them, I teach the parts that they do not know or do well.

19 So too there are parts of the Celestine Light which many Gentiles know and do well; to them, I will also teach the parts they do not know or do well whenever the opportunity comes upon me to share the Celestine Light with them.

20 If man is to become more than he is, if war is to cease and peace is to reign, then man must have respect for others beyond his tribe, beyond his nation, and beyond his practices and traditions and beliefs in God.

21 It is a foolish man of any religion who thinks that Elohim has given hundreds of laws that man must follow to please God.

22 Elohim gives no commandments to the children of men save the Great Commandment and the Twelve Commandments of Sinai, and these not to burden man but to uplift him and help him to become more than he began.

23 All other laws, be they written in the scriptures or not, are given by men to control other men.

24 Now the spirit of the Great Commandment and the commandments of Sinai do not need to be written upon scrolls of scripture to be known, for these principles are a yearning of the soul. They are inscribed upon the heart of every man and woman before they are born into a physical life by Elohim the Mother.

25 Through the teachings of parents and priests and cultures and traditions and actions that are contrary, the fullness of the true commandments may become lost in the hearts and heads of some men and women, and the light all but extinguished because of these things.

26 Yet even when a man commits acts contrary to the Great Commandment and the commandments of Sinai, there will continue to be a still, small voice whispering to him in his head and a feeling in his heart that what he does is contrary to the will of God and contrary to his own happiness and well-being.

27 Only after he has repeated the same error many times will he become deaf to the still, small voice and the flutter in his heart, and hear and feel it no more.

28 Yet even then, in a place inside he keeps imprisoned and never visits, the Celestine Light will whisper reminding him that he does wrong. And sometimes despite all his best efforts to convince himself otherwise, the truth he has hidden from himself will come to torment his consciousness.

29 Now I ask you: Who are the chosen people of God? I tell you plainly. They are not of any one tribe, or any one people, or any one nation, or any one religion.

30 Verily, the chosen people of God are they who keep the spirit of the Great Commandment

and the commandments of Sinai and by this live the essence of the Celestine Light. And the tribe they are from, or the people they are a part of, or the nation they live in, or the religion they believe in, are all nothing of consequence in the eyes of the Elohim.

31 And what is the spirit? What is the essence? Love God, be respectful and a good neighbor to all people, be virtuous and of good character in your words and deeds, be of service to others, and be a good steward over all that you have been given responsibility over, beginning with the temple of your body.

32 How then may you know a Child of Light? You will know them by the fruits of their life. How well do they live the spirit of the few true commandments of God and the essence of the Celestine Light?

33 It does not matter whether they are Hebrew, Roman, Greek, Syrian, or someone from any other tribe or land. If they live the spirit of the true commandments, they are sons and daughters of God, true to the Celestine Light within them.

34 Seek them out and do not turn them away because they are not exactly like you, for these are your true brothers and sisters of the light."

35 As Yeshua took a pause in speaking, Yohhanan asked, "Rabbi, what you say resonates in my heart, but I am still having difficulties in my head. You say that if men hold to the spirit of the true commandments and the essence of the Celestine Light, they will be numbered among the chosen, even if they are Greeks or Romans or other people.

36 But the commandments are very specific, even as the second commandment of Sinai says to only worship Elohim and even condemns veneration of anything except Elohim.

37 I have seen the ways of the Greeks and Romans and some of other people. They do not even know the name of Elohim. Some of them may be virtuous and of good character and good stewards, but they worship a myriad of false gods and venerate many objects and places. How then can they be numbered among the chosen?"

38 And Yeshua answered him, saying, "Men are not held accountable for that which they know not, but only for that which they know. The essence of the Celestine Light and the virtues of the Great Commandment and the commandments of Sinai are etched into the soul of every man and woman born upon the earth. But the beliefs of religion, including the name and substance of God, are taught differently within the family and the tribe.

39 Concerning the nature of God, as the children are taught, so they believe until they are shown the true light. Then the true light kindles a fire in their heart that they did not even know was there.

40 If a man from another land has been taught that God is a big rock that sticks up from the ground and he leads his life in righteousness, with virtue and good character, worshiping the big rock in the faithfulness of his beliefs, he has as much favor with Elohim as the man who knows and faithfully follows the Elohim.

41 It is the virtues and good character that distinguish a Child of Light, and they are not held accountable for the realities of the nature and fullness of God until they have had the opportunity to be taught and understand them fully.

42 It is for this purpose that you have been called to be my disciples. You learn from me now, but the day soon comes when I shall send you out into the world to preach the Gospel I have taught you and bring a portion of the Celestine Light I have given you to those who will rejoice when you come.

43 Many will hate and revile you because of me, but some will open their hearts to you and receive the Celestine Light, which will be much greater and fulfilling than the light they had previously held in their beliefs.

44 The principles of virtue and character that I teach, which is the spirit of the true commandments and the essence of the Celestine Light, will spread forth across the world through you and those who come after you, for the Children of Light wait with a yearning heart for what they know not, until it is upon them, and then great will be their joy.

45 Millennia will pass, and many men will become more wicked than their forefathers; but because of the seeds you plant, some men will become more righteous, preparing the way for the fullness of the Celestine Light of Elohim upon the world and the beginning of the Epoch of Promise.
46 Therefore, when you are sent out into the world to bring souls to the light, remember to find the Children of Light who are waiting for you, not by their tribe or nation or beliefs, but by their fruits.
47 By their fruits, you shall know them."

CHAPTER 29

A Prophet Rises to His Glory

The evil plan of Herodias comes to fruition as she forces her beautiful daughter, Salome, to seductively dance for her stepfather Herod Antipas in return for the head of Yochanan the Baptizer. The spirit of Yeshua comes to Yochanan while he is in prison and shows him exactly what is currently transpiring that will bring about his demise. Just as the guards come to take Yochanan, Yeshua takes his spirit from his body, and he is instantly transported to Heaven, thwarting the guards' attempt to behead him alive.

On the following day, it came to pass that as the afternoon waned and they neared Capernaum, Yeshua suddenly stopped walking, and bowing his head and covering his eyes with his left hand, he began to cry.

2 Miriam and the disciples all went to him with great concern, and Miriam embraced him, saying, "What is it, Yeshua? What has happened that grieves your heart so greatly?"

3 Yeshua kissed her lightly on her forehead, his tears falling onto her, and said, "I grieve to my depths because at this moment, the mold has begun to be carved in the evil mind of Herod's wife Herodias, and on the morrow, Yochanan, my friend of friends and brother of brothers, will pass from this life.

4 And though I know it is as it must be and that we will be together again soon and be brothers forever, I still ache to know his pain and that of Martha and his children and the loss for all the world when he is no more upon the earth.

5 I rejoice for the brightness of the sun to which he goes, but weep also for the world that will be darker without his light."

6 Then pulling Miriam away slightly, he held her with a hand on each of her arms, saying, "We will spend the night tonight at Capernaum, and tomorrow at first light, we will journey to the castle above the springs with the children. Your sister and family will need you."

7 Then turning to his disciples, he said, "Miriam and I must make haste to the south and will be gone for at least a moon on matters of family, for Yochanan, the mighty prophet of Elohim, rises to the heavens tomorrow.

8 Though I know each of you would desire to come with us, please take this time to be with your own wives and children, for once we return, all things will quicken and only then will you realize how precious this time with your loved ones will have been."

9 The disciples nodded solemnly in agreement, and after bidding good-bye to Yeshua and Miriam, each made their way to their own home and families.

10 After coming home to their children and family, Yeshua spoke to Miriam quietly, saying,

"I need to go up into the hills, and I must go alone. Please do not wait up for me, but prepare for our journey tomorrow."

11 Miriam was curious about Yeshua's request, and she asked, "Of course, I will do as you ask, Yeshua, but have you not said that I should witness all things? How can I be a witness if I am not with you?"

12 Yeshua answered her, saying, "I will not be there to witness; I go now to Yochanan, and as I go, you cannot yet follow. But I will return before the daybreak tomorrow."

13 With a nod and a smile of understanding, Miriam embraced her husband and watched him depart for the hills from which they had just descended.

14 As darkness fell, Yeshua sat upon the ground at the top of a bare knoll overlooking the lake with his eyes closed.

15 Nearby, a lion growled quietly, and from the underbrush down the slope, it moved silently toward Yeshua.

16 Only when it was very close did Yeshua open his eyes, and he held out both hands inviting the lion to come to him. It stood and stared at him for many breaths and then came into his arms.

17 Yeshua embraced the head of the large male lion and ran his face through its mane, saying, "Thank you for coming, my friend. Please remain here with my body and watch over it while my spirit goes to my brother."

18 Then Yeshua lay upon the ground, and the lion lay beside him against his body. And unseen to any eyes, Yeshua's spirit rose from his body, and in a heartbeat, he stood before Yochanan.

19 Though Yochanan was in a prison cell in the castle of Herod above the Salt Sea, because of Herod's fascination with him, he was afforded more comforts than was accustomed to prisoners, and his cell had a bench and table and bedding to sleep upon.

20 Yochanan was in prayer upon his knees when the spirit of Yeshua appeared before him, and so real it was that Yochanan shouted with joy and went to embrace Yeshua only to discover it was his spiritual form, without physical substance.

21 Yeshua spoke to him, saying, "Namaste, brother, I have come to be with you in your time of deliverance from your persecutions and your ascension to the Celestine Light of the heavens."

22 Yochanan stared at him somewhat in wonder, saying, "I have longed to see you again, Yeshua, but this is your spirit before me. How is it that your spirit can appear and speak to me while I am still in the flesh? Is this a vision I am being carried away into?"

23 Yeshua answered, saying, "Only the eyes of the most virtuous can see the essence of a holy spirit while they are still in the body. None can claim more virtue than you, my brother."

24 Yochanan was embarrassed and said, "You of all who know me know well enough that though I have virtues, I also have many faults. Am I truly worthy to see your spirit even to the point that we can speak? It would not seem so to me, but as you will, so be it."

25 Yeshua looked into Yochanan's eyes with love and compassion and said, "This is the day you have known would come, when you shall be undone by the spite of a woman. Everything is as it must be, and I could be no other place than with you on this day.

26 Though you leave the earth, the essence of your light will always remain across many religions. Even as you have kindled the Celestine Light in many souls while you have been in the body, so you shall continue to bring forth the light in many more for all time.

27 Whereas both good and bad will be spoken of me, your name and the works you have done will be known only for good among men, save a few, for all time."

28 Yochanan let out a big sigh, saying, "We have known this day would come for some years, and in truth, it is not hard to leave this wicked world except for those I leave behind that I love and will miss greatly.

29 But I know that it will be but a blink of an eye before we are together again forever in paradise. Knowing that is a great comfort that calms the turmoil of parting."

30 Yeshua nodded saying, "You will only be parted in the body, which is not much different

than what has been since you have been preaching and now in prison.

31 But more than when you were in the body, your spirit will be able to commune with the spirits of those you love, and in many ways, you will be closer to them each day than you have ever been able to be during your ministry.

32 As long as their heart still loves you and they think of you in their thoughts, your presence will be felt most profoundly, and they will know you are the Angel of Light, who watches over and counsels them always."

33 "Should I do anything more to prepare for what is to come?" asked Yochanan.

34 "You have been prepared since our last days together in the wilderness. But let us now look upon that which is even now transpiring so you will know with a certainty who is at fault and who is not."

35 Then the spirit of Yeshua waved his hand and the stone wall became as if a large portal into another room, and in the room, they saw the fate of Yochanan come to pass.

36 As they looked into the room, they saw Herodias, the wife of Herod Antipas, speaking harshly to her daughter Salome, who was fair and lithesome, saying, "You will do what I require, daughter, or I shall see you married off to a loathsome man to live in wretchedness and squalor all of your pitiful days!"

37 Salome prostrated herself at her mother's feet, pleading, "Please, mother, do not make me do this horrid thing. I do not wish to dance for Herod. I am not a harem slave. It is not proper for a man other than the one I love to see me displayed in such a manner."

38 Herodias kicked her daughter away from her, and she lay sprawled on the floor, looking up at her mother and searching her eyes.

39 "You will do more than dance, daughter. You will dance seductively. I will instruct the servants to keep Herod well supplied with potent wine before you dance, and foolish as he is under the wine, you will be able to elicit promises from him with each sway of hip and, if necessary, shed of clothing.

40 "No, mother! No!" Salome pleaded. "You will make me into a whore. Why O why? What have I ever done to you to make you hate me so?"

41 Herodias answered, "I do not hate you at all, as long as you do as I desire; I merely want revenge on the baptizer, and Herod turns a deaf ear to me on this because he fears a revolt by the commoners if he puts the baptizer to death.

42 But with your beauty and sexuality on display and Herod's head fogged by wine, you will be able to get him to give you the head of the baptizer on a platter!

43 He will not want to do it, but it is his birthday and there will be many nobles in attendance. If you get him to make an open promise to you in front of the nobles, he will not be able to withdraw his promise when you ask for the head of the baptizer."

44 At the words of Herodias, Salome let out a terrible shriek of agony, weeping, and said, "Please, do not tell me to do this. I will be cursed forever if it is because of me the baptizer is killed! Your feud has nothing to do with me. Please leave me be, please. I beg you."

45 Herodias strode up to Salome, and pulling her to her feet by her hair, she slapped her twice across the face and then pushed her again to the floor, saying, "You will do as I command, you insolent wretch! Everything you have is because of me, and you cannot even begin to imagine how horrible your life will be if you do not exactly fulfill my desires."

46 Salome lay in a heap, crying, while Herodias continued to speak vilely to her, saying, "If you so love the baptizer, whom you have never even met, more than me, your own mother, then consider your punishment if you refuse to do as I command. I will disown you. You will be dressed in rags and locked in the dungeon for six moons with only bread and water for food and whatever bugs and rats you can catch.

47 When you come out, you will serve as a whore for Herod's soldiers for another six moons. After that, I shall find a most loathsome man to give you to, but I'm sure he will not want to marry such refuse, so you shall be a slave till your last breath.

48 Or you can choose to continue to live a life of ease and privilege, to marry a nobleman within the same six moons, and to always have the finest clothes and food and servants at your call.

49 Your fate is in your hands and yours alone. Decide now!"

50 Salome pulled herself up to her knees, and exhaling a deep breath, she said unto her mother, "May God forgive me, for I will never forgive myself. I will do as you demand. Too meek am I to withstand the tortures you present today even though I know my actions will inherit many more torments in the world to come."

51 Then the scene faded and the wall became a wall again, and Yeshua asked, "What do you think of what you have just seen, my brother?"

52 Yochanan was obviously disturbed, and he answered, "Whatever happens, please do not take vengeance on that girl. It is obvious she is being forced down a path her own good virtue would never choose.

53 But as for her mother, how can someone so callously discard the lives of others, both her daughter's and mine? Is she possessed of a devil?"

54 Yeshua answered, "It is the way of many people in power, that they are possessed by a devil of their own creation inside of them inciting unrighteous dominion over others, but it is only their own darkness, which they have embraced instead of their own light.

55 Verily, that which they have given in darkness in life shall be meted out in darkness to them in the next life."

56 "What will become of them still in this life? Will the people rise up in revolt as Herod has feared?" Yochanan inquired.

57 "No, they will not," Yeshua answered. "At least not because of taking your head. But Herod will not keep his Kingdom in a way that is pleasing to Rome, and he and Herodias shall be exiled into the wilderness of the Western Empire and shall die in obscurity and poverty."

58 "And what of Salome?" Yochanan asked. "Surely she deserves more happiness than she has received in the house of her mother."

59 "Salome shall repent of her weakness, and it shall become her strength. And she will find the light, Yochanan. She shall become one of us."

60 "That makes my heart glad," Yochanan replied. "And now I have another important question for you, Yeshua, which is what shall become of my family when I am gone?

61 I know that by the law, we are not brothers of blood, but I wish for you to marry Martha, that she will be within the Community of Light and have the continual friendship of her sister Miriam in this time and in the coming years."

62 Yeshua nodded in understanding, saying, "You know it would never be a marriage consummated with intimacy, but you are wise to suggest it, as my own time in this world is also short, and it would be a way to ensure our wives could remain with each other, without a husband, in the Community of Light, and also continue to receive support from their family and Lazarus."

63 For the next several hours, Yeshua and Yochanan continued to talk, reminiscing about times past and speaking with excitement about times to come, both in the world and in Heaven.

64 Meanwhile, the evil designs of Herodias were coming to pass even as she desired.

65 As Herod's birthday party progressed, Herodias made sure the servants kept him liberally supplied with wine, and she had asked many of the nobles to toast him often so that he always had reason to drink again from the cup.

66 Now Herod Antipas had often lusted after his stepdaughter Salome, the daughter of Herodias, but she, knowing his lecherous designs, had always managed to stay far away from him and see him but seldom and then always in the company of others.

67 But on this his birthday, because of the threats of her mother, she came to him in his court dressed provocatively and asked him if he would like her to dance for his birthday.

68 Hardly believing his good fortune, Herod readily agreed, and Salome began to dance a

seductive and beautiful dance to simple music, even though her heart ached beyond measure to do so.

69 Herod was spellbound watching her. His mouth gaped open, and even a little drool escaped and ran down his chin.

70 Suddenly, Salome stopped dancing and came up to Herod, asking, "Did you like my dance, Herod?"

71 Herod replied, "It was entrancing, please do continue."

72 Salome looked apprehensively to her mother and then said to Herod, "What will you give me, Herod Antipas, if I dance more for you?"

73 Herod and all the nobles laughed at the boldness of the girl, and Herod asked, "What is the worth of a dance that stirs the loins of men from a daughter of nobility like you? Make your dance even more seductive. Make us want to take you on the floor, and I will give you anything you ask that is in my power to give."

74 Then Salome danced as she had been taught to dance for the husband she hoped to have someday—slow and sensuous, tantalizing, showing parts of forbidden flesh and then covering it again as quickly as it had been shown.

75 When she was done, there was great applause and many men ready to seek her in marriage.

76 Then she approached Herod and asked, "I am ready for my reward now, Uncle."

77 Herod was somewhat giddy, thinking she would ask for some trinket such as girls desire, and he looked forward to giving it to her in front of all the nobles and said, "Ask your desire, beautiful one, I am here to fulfill it as I promised."

78 Salome tried to ask the terrible thing her mother had demanded, but when she made attempt to speak, her voice became mute. Though she moved her lips, no words came out.

79 Her mother Herodias commanded a servant to bring her a cup of water, and after drinking it, Salome was sad to see she was able to speak, and she bowed her head and asked in a quiet voice, "Bring me the head of Yochanan the Baptizer."

80 Hearing her words, Herod was shocked out of his drunkenness! "What did you ask?" he inquired, hoping to hear something different than he had heard.

81 Salome looked nervously at her mother and then back again to Herod, repeating in a louder voice so all nearby could hear, "Bring me the head of Yochanan the Baptizer."

82 Herod looked over at Herodias, and knowing how much she hated the baptizer, he suspected she must be behind her daughter's request.

83 He did not wish to kill Yochanan, for he admired his boldness and feared a revolt from the people.

84 Nevertheless, he could not easily back away from his promise given in front of so many nobles and wealthy citizens. Therefore, worrying less about the commoners and more about his peers, he ordered his soldiers to go to the prison and immediately bring him the head of Yochanan on a platter.

85 Now all that had transpired had been watched in the portal in the wall by Yeshua and Yochanan, even as they had watched Herodias force her daughter to carry out her evil desires.

86 Yochanan was therefore prepared as the soldiers approached and was even a bit jovial, saying, "Perhaps, this would be a good time for a heavenly vanishing."

87 Both Yeshua and Yochanan laughed, and as the door to the prison opened, Yeshua said to Yochanan in seriousness, "My spirit will always be with you, my brother, even as yours will be with your family and friends. Come with me now, for you need not suffer the pangs of death."

88 Yochanan gave a great smile, understanding the words of Yeshua, and the soldiers entered, having heard his laughter, asking, "What are you laughing at, idiot? This is the day of your destruction."

89 Yochanan looked at them and smiled, saying, "You are so wrong, friend. This is the day of my eternal life."

90 Then Yochanan's earthly body fell to the floor and breathed its last breath. And Yeshua

reached forth his hand and grasped the hand of the spirit of Yochanan and led him into the Celestine Lights of Heaven.

CHAPTER 30

The Nature of Eternity

Yeshua is asked by the father of Martha to speak at the funeral of Yochanan, and he speaks at great length about the nature of Eternity and what can be expected when one passes from mortal life.

As the sun rose the next morning, the spirit of Yeshua returned to his body. The lion remained nestled against his side as he opened his eyes and arose, saying in his mind and heart as well as his words, "Thank you, faithful friend. May you live long and always be cautious of men who would hurt you."

2 The lion looked up into his eyes for a moment, unblinking, then turned and quickly disappeared in silence into the underbrush.

3 Absorbed in his thoughts, Yeshua descended back to his house and family. As he neared his home, he began to whistle, which was a very uncommon thing for a man to do, but something Yeshua did often.

4 Hearing his approaching whistle, Miriam stepped out to greet him with a smile on her face, saying, "Yeshua, my love, it is good to hear you whistle, for I know then that you are happy inside. Do you have good news for us of Yochanan?"

5 Yeshua came and embraced her and held her tightly for a moment in silence, and then the children came out to greet him and he opened his arms to them.

6 Turning to Miriam, he answered forthrightly, "Though you may be saddened, know that I bring you good tidings. With contempt for a light greater than he could know, Herod thought to behead Yochanan in ignominy, but was left in fear of the power of Elohim when the jailers told him that Yochanan laughed at them and died, robbing Herod of his victory."

7 Miriam swallowed deeply and a tear formed in her eye, and she asked, "Yochanan is gone then?"

8 Yeshua smiled again and said, "He has returned from whence he came, having left a light upon the world that will never be extinguished."

9 "I am happy for Yochanan," Miriam said. "He lives now in light and glory; but what of my sister and their children? I feel their pain already. Let us make haste to go to them."

10 And it came to pass that Yeshua and Miriam and their children made a quick journey to Bethany. Though Yochanan's family had been near the castle of Herod by the Salt Sea, they had returned quickly to the house of the parents of Martha and Miriam in Bethany upon word of Yochanan's death; and this Yeshua knew.

11 The body of Yochanan had been given to his disciples by the soldiers of Herod, and at the direction of his wife Martha, they had treated it with herbs and spices after the manner of the Egyptians as Yochanan had taught them and followed behind Martha, bringing the body of

Yochanan to the house of her parents for a funeral and burial.

12 Thus it was that the body of Yochanan arrived on the same day as Yeshua and his family, and with it came many people, for the word of his death had spread quickly and he was much beloved of the common people.

13 Even many people from Gimron, who seldom left their isolated community, followed after the body of Yochanan.

14 As Yeshua and Miriam arrived, Lazarus was waiting at the gate for them, and all the family came out to greet and comfort one another with tears and hugs and soft words of love.

15 And it came to pass on the following day that the body of Yochanan was wrapped in a simple knotted, white linen shroud and buried in a tomb owned by Martha's father in a hillside northwest of Bethany.

16 Over one thousand people followed the funeral procession and watched in silence as Yochanan's body was interred and the tomb was sealed.

17 Then the father of Martha spoke to the people assembled at the foot of the tomb, saying that Yochanan was a good man who walked with God. And he thanked them for coming to give him their respect.

18 As he sat down, he asked Yeshua to speak also to the people. And Yeshua rose up, and standing in front of the tomb, he said unto them, "It is good to grieve, to cry, and to acknowledge the empty place in your life when one you love is no longer there to hold you and make you laugh and comfort you just by their physical presence.

19 But in your grief, know this with certainty: As surely as the sun rises in the sky, so too rise the souls of all who have died to their reward in an eternity that never ends.

20 Those you love wait for you still, and the virtuous need not fear separation, for mortality is but a heartbeat, and in eternity, they shall not be parted.

21 As in Adam, save for a precious few, all will die a physical death. The spirit essence will rise to the realms Elohim created for eternity. And because of the love of Elohim, everyone shall live again in the spirit.

22 But unto the virtuous and righteous, it is given not only to live again in the spirit, but for your immortal soul to become one with a glorified new physical body, made whole and perfect by Elohim, for your life eternal.

23 Your future began with your past, for your existence is an eternal walk that never ends.

24 Before you were born of woman, your spirit was created by Elohim, and before it was born upon the earth, the spirit of all things lived in a spiritual realm called Koropean.

25 And to the Koropean, the realm of spirit, all things of spirit born into a physical existence shall someday return, even the birds in the air, the fish in the sea, and every blade of grass beneath your feet.

26 So vast it is in expanse that the earthly mind of man cannot even begin to comprehend the magnitude and diversity of the Koropean.

27 Verily, there is nothing that lives or that has lived or that will ever live upon the earth whose spirit was not first created by the Elohim and then existed in the Koropean. Nor is there anything or anyone that has ever lived that shall not return to that realm.

28 But everything that has a spirit does not also have a soul, for only the children of men and women, whose spirits were all birthed in a sacred union of love by your Father and Mother in Heaven, have been given a soul; and more precious than all the treasure of earth, it is.

29 For a soul created in the celestial union of love, it is given an ember of divinity that ever calls the soul to a greater light called Celestine, that it might ever be moved to return to the blessed Kingdom from which it came, expanded in stature from its humble beginnings.

30 When the soul comes to earth and it is born of woman into a body of flesh and bones, it dwells in the body of a man or a woman and is thrust into a physical world of darkness and light.

31 Mortality is the crucible, the refiner's fire, and the soul within the body ever beckons to the light, even while the physical man or woman in the body is ever seduced to darkness by the

temptations of the world and the pleasures of the body.

32 Therefore, man has been given the years of his life to feel the warmth of his soul calling him out of darkness and back to the Celestine Light that is his home.

33 Throughout the days of his mortal life, the warmth of the ember of divinity ever burns quietly within the heart of man: that he may always know good from evil and right from wrong; that on the day of the Judgment of Resonance, he may be weighed in the balance by his own choices and not be able to say, 'I did not know.'

34 Therefore, take heed, for you know not which breath upon the earth shall be your last, whether your life will end when you are young or when you are old.

35 I say unto you, do not ignore the warm and gentle calling of the divine ember of light burning in your bosom. It is calling you from your mundane life to the glory that you can be.

36 Think not to say, 'Today I will eat, drink and be merry, for I still have my old age to become virtuous,' for though you may be young, these may be the last days of your old age.

37 When your physical body is laid in the grave, your soul held within your spirit rises immediately to the first Judgment of Resonance, at the place of transition in the Koropean realm.

38 For a moment, whatever you believed the afterlife to be will seem to be as it is, but then at the direction of Elohim, the angels of Heaven will come and the illusion will vanish like a mirage on the desert, and the reality of eternity will become apparent.

39 The angels of Elohim shall look with you at the life you have lived in mortality and the virtue you had or had not.

40 Every iota shall not be reviewed; not the rivulets, only the rivers.

41 Then you shall be inexorably drawn to the place of your resonance within the Koropean: the virtuous to a place of warmth and light and the unvirtuous to a place of bitter cold and darkness; the greater the virtue, the brighter the light; the less the virtue, the deeper the darkness.

42 It matters not whether you are of Judah or Samaria or Rome, whether you are a man or a woman, whether you were rich or poor, whether you lived free or as a slave.

43 Each shall be judged, not by what they believed or who they were, but by what they did and even by what they thought but did not do.

44 Did you live a life of virtue? Did you uphold the Great Commandment and the commandments of Sinai as the ember of God within you ever beckoned and guided you to do?

45 Your spirit shall again have a form of a physical man or woman without the substance, and your soul will dwell within it.

46 Those in the Celestine Light will be among their friends and family who also had virtue, and they shall have joy together and delight in new knowledge and opportunities.

47 Those that are in darkness shall be among others in the darkness, but none that they know or love or miss or take pleasure to be around.

48 Misery and loneliness shall be the lot of those in the darkness. Their only hope will not be for new knowledge and opportunity like those in the light, but simply to regain that which was lost by their foolishness.

49 Though beset by the pain of their own mistakes, those in the darkness will still have a promise. From the lonely place of cold and dreariness where they dwell in misery, far and away, they will see a distant lamp shining from the realm of warmth and happiness, illuminating the path they can still walk to come back into the light, with faith and repentance, and sorrow and confession and restitution and good works.

50 For each moment, whether one is in the darkness or in the light, every spirit will continue to make choices that can show virtue or vice. As they act upon their choices, they will move either into a greater light or into a deeper darkness.

51 Then at an hour you know not, nor expect, will come a final Judgment of Resonance upon your soul.

52 Verily, all men and women who have ever lived shall stand someday before the Elohim to be weighed in the balance and judged, not only of their life in mortality, but also their life before

mortality and after it.
53 And all the angels of Heaven shall stand as witnesses on the day of your final judgment.
54 So shall every person whose life was ever touched for good or evil, by those being weighed, also stand as witnesses to see the life before them, with nothing hidden.
55 Nor shall anything that was done, not be seen, for at the final judgment, every iota shall be judged. Of your thoughts and of your actions, both good and bad, from your entire mortal life, nothing shall be hidden.
56 With every good and virtuous deed you ever thought or did, light will flow to and be added to the essence of your soul.
57 And with every evil or loathsome thing you ever thought or did, light will flow out of and be taken away from the essence of your soul.
58 When all has been seen, your soul will be weighed in the balance, and those who lived selfishly, without virtue and kindness and gratitude and stewardship, shall be found wanting.
59 The virtuous will be pulled by resonance of their own light into warmth and greater light, and they shall be given a new and perfected, immortal physical body and live near the presence of Elohim in the Celestine Realm. They shall be given great blessings and new stewardships worthy of their light.
60 But those lacking virtue shall be pulled by their own dark resonance into a bitter cold and deeper darkness, where there shall be weeping and wailing and gnashing of teeth and an endless torment upon the soul for the warmth and light that could have been.
61 But remember, even this is not the end, but only the beginning. The love and forgiveness of the Father and Mother is boundless, and even those in outer darkness can still reach the Celestine Light and savor the warmth and the love of paradise among their family and friends and gain new knowledge and be given a greater stewardship.
62 Even in outer darkness, they will have the choice to do good or do evil, and when the good weighs more than the evil, they will draw light to their soul.
63 After millennia, if they continue to seek the light and do good, their balance shall be with the light, and they will inherit the just reward they deserve after overcoming the suffering and punishments they inflicted upon themselves.
64 Knowing this—that for lack of virtue in mortality your soul could be in torment for millennia—may each of you choose the light each day.
65 There is still another path in the afterlife, one bestowed upon few, and that is to return again to mortality. This was the path that had been given to Yochanan by Elohim.
66 For Yochanan is a choice soul who has faithfully served Elohim from before the creation of the world. Your ancestors knew him as Elijah the Prophet, and so great was his vision and power to sway the hearts of men that after he had died in the flesh and had risen to his glory, he was asked by Elohim to come again into the flesh, that the world might hear his voice once more; that he might prepare the world for the greater light to come.
67 Thus was the scripture fulfilled saying, 'Behold, I send my messenger before thy face, who shall prepare the way before you.'
68 Therefore, when you remember Yochanan, his laugh, his honesty and frankness, his simple words of power, and his example of a life of virtue and righteousness, remember that you had a true prophet of the most high walking among you.
69 You had a man who had been born twice of woman, walking among you.
70 My hope for each of you is that you will remember this glorious son of God and live your life as he showed us how to live: full of spirit and love and unwavering virtue and faith.
71 And for those of his family, know that he waits for you even now and that mortality is but a heartbeat of eternity. I admonish you to live in virtue, doing good upon the earth, fulfilling your stewardships, and surely, you will be together again and for all eternity to come."
72 Then Yeshua slapped his hands together and proclaimed, "Now, let us rejoice! Play glad music, prepare a feast, talk with one another, and remember Yochanan. Celebrate and thank this wonderful man of God who served you all of his days!"

CHAPTER 31

Second Marriage of Martha of Bethany

By the request of Yochanan and Miriam, and with the agreement of Martha, Yeshua and Miriam marry Martha, who becomes Yeshua's second wife and Miriam's as well in keeping with the teachings of Celestine Light, but they do so with the understanding that the marriage will never be consummated between Martha and Yeshua because she is the eternal mate of Yochanan. The marriage is primarily for the companionship of Miriam and Martha, as well as for the comfort and protection of Martha and her children in the days to come.

And it came to pass that Yeshua and Miriam lingered in Bethany, and Yeshua was weighed heavy by the thought of his promise to Yochanan, concerning his wife Martha, for he understood that to marry her, as was Yochanan's wish, would cause contentions with many people, not only the priests, but even among his friends and followers, for a marriage to two sisters at the same time was not permitted among the Children of Israel.

2 One day as he was sitting atop a small hill meditating upon this vexing situation, Miriam came to him, asking, "Husband, you have been often alone since Yochanan's funeral. As your witness in all things, I wish that you would share with me what it is that you have been in such deep thought about."

3 Yeshua touched her face as he loved to do and, looking into her eyes, said, "I have been thinking much about you my love and the days that are coming and much about the family of Yochanan."

4 Miriam smiled mischievously, saying, "I have been thinking also of the family of Yochanan, and I have come to speak to you about it."

5 Yeshua raised his eyebrows in interest, and Miriam continued, "When we returned from Egypt, we spoke about the day when I might want to have another wife in our family.

6 At the time, the thought seemed repugnant to me. But in the days since Yochanan's death, I have thought much of my sister Martha and her children and also of the knowledge that you will be gone from this earth in the days to come and that I will be left alone with our children.

7 It seems most reasonable that I should ask you now to marry Martha, that she can be a wife with me, for we have loved each other since we were children, and when you have left the earth, no greater helpmate could I have than my sister.

8 Though she could remain in Bethany with my parents, I feel she would benefit immensely more if she could be with me during these times of trial and I with her; as will all of our children;

that we would all benefit from being a family together at the Community of Light."

9 Yeshua gave a big smile of appreciation at the wonder of his wife, and he said unto her, "You are a light beyond the angels of Heaven. It is upon this very thing that I have been pondering, for I gave a promise to Yochanan that I would take Martha as a wife and care for her and their children, but I have been vexed, for to fulfill all righteousness it is only by your desire and initiative that such a thing could be."

10 Miriam leaned toward him and kissed him on the lips, saying, "It is by my desire and initiative, dear husband, and you show how great your love for me is by marrying my sister."

11 Yeshua spoke again to her plainly, saying, "As you desire so shall it be, if it is also the desire of Martha."

12 "It is," replied Miriam, "We have already spoken about it."

13 "You must know that I told Yochanan that I could not consummate a marriage to Martha," Yeshua cautioned, expecting Miriam's agreement.

14 But instead Miriam frowned, saying, "I understand the proprieties of the law and that this marriage will cause great opposition among some. But what do I care about the evil thoughts of wicked men or the weight of law without the light of Elohim or compassion or love?

15 I know that you made such a promise from your honor and purity, thinking you would be honoring both me and Yochanan by giving such word.

16 And perhaps that is how it will be. But do not on my account close the door to a fullness of relationship, for I will ever be with you, and because you will honor and respect your wives, nothing would occur without the consent and desire of all.

17 Perhaps in your intention to honor and not offend, you would end up causing great offense, for Martha might lose her esteem, thinking you did not desire her in fullness.

18 Even though she would understand the wisdom and reason of our marriage for greater comfort and bond of family, she is also young and may not wish to no longer know the righteous pleasures of the flesh and hence become an elderly woman before her time.

19 I do not ask you to say yea or nay today, but speak to Yochanan about it in the heavens beyond and know that it is my wish that you remain open to fulfilling your full obligations of a husband, as both my sister and I may desire."

20 Yeshua never took his eyes from the eyes of Miriam and said unto her, "Never has a man had a wife such as I have in you. For your words, I am grateful, but you must understand that Martha is Yochanan's wife for all eternity, not just for this life as men suppose.

21 I can marry her for convenience and security and for the happiness of both of you. But I can never have more than chaste brotherly love and affection for her.

22 Because her marriage in eternity is still in force, to be with her in any other way would be adultery."

23 Then Miriam bowed her head in sorrow, saying, "Forgive me, my Lord. I knew this was true, but in my desire for my sister's happiness, I forgot this most important of laws that is not of man, but from Elohim. I am ashamed for what I have said."

24 Yeshua touched her face again, saying, "Be not ashamed of love, nor of your righteous desire for the happiness of those that you love.

25 Know that though I will never touch your sister in intimate ways, nor will any other man, she will not be unfulfilled or an old woman before her time."

26 Miriam nodded slowly, understanding the meaning of his words, and she was happy.

27 Upon returning, they went immediately and spoke with Martha. Miriam explained all that she and Yeshua had spoken of and agreed upon, and Martha fell to her knees before Yeshua, saying, "My Lord, it is my honor to become your wife. In your face and your words, I see my Yochanan, and I know this does not displease you. Living with you and my sister in holy marriage will seem almost as if Yochanan still walks beside me."

28 Yeshua lifted her to her feet, holding her two hands, and said unto her, "Though you have yet many years upon the earth, never forget that Yochanan looks upon you every moment and

that you shall be with him again for time and all eternity.

29 For the years I have left upon the earth, it is my honor to embrace you into my family and deliver you to the comfort of your sister, who loves you with a pure love."

30 Then Yeshua and Miriam and Martha went to tell the sisters' parents and family of their intention to be married, and as they had feared, except for Lazarus, great was the discord at their announcement.

31 The father of the sisters came to Yeshua, saying, "How can I condone this? You know it is not permitted by the law to marry two sisters."

32 Yeshua answered him, saying, "In the beginning, it was not so. I care not for the laws of men, though they pretend to be of God. Nor would I do anything that was not pleasing to my Father and Mother in Heaven."

33 But the father of Miriam and Martha was not consoled by the words of Yeshua, and he left immediately in distress to go and speak with the Levites.

34 Shortly thereafter, he returned and two Levites came with him, and they were very agitated because of what he had told them.

35 Approaching Yeshua, one said unto him, "We have been told that you think to marry a second daughter of Abara of Bethany. Such a thing is strictly forbidden in the law. Besides the shame it would bring upon this esteemed house, the consequences could be very grave for you."

36 Yeshua answered unto them, "If man's laws are in opposition to God's laws, to obey one is to disobey the other and to find favor of one but wrath of the other. Whom do you think I choose to obey and find favor with, man or my Father in Heaven?"

37 The Levites eyes widened in disbelief at Yeshua's words, and the other Levite said unto him, "It has been said by the people that you are a learned rabbi. Therefore, how can you be so ignorant of the law?"

38 Yeshua answered unto them, "You charge like lions for the kill, understanding not the nature of your prey. Verily, it would be easier for a lion to eat a millstone than for you to move me today.

39 The law you call upon condemns not the marriage of a man and two sisters, but that a man should not cleave unto two sisters.

40 I declare to you and all the world that I shall not cleave unto Martha of Bethany, but shall always hold her apart as the wife of my brother who has died in the flesh.

41 But it is not because of your law that I make this declaration, but because of the love of my brother and his wife.

42 Verily, I declare unto you: Your law is not a law of God, but a mockery of God issued by the vanity of men.

43 "Did not the tribes of Israel spring from the loins of Jacob? And did Jacob not marry the sisters Leah and Rachael, the daughters of Laban, and even cleave unto them both and this in righteousness, and from this sprang many of the tribes of Israel, including the Levites, from whence come you?

44 Do you think Elohim is a changing God? That the laws of Heaven given to men would change with a new generation; that good would become evil and evil good?

45 I declare unto you: No! Elohim is the same, yesterday, today, and forever! God does not give the commandments of Sinai to one generation, saying to not covet or steal and then to a later generation, saying that it is now good to covet and steal.

46 Neither does Elohim rejoice in the marriage of two sisters to Jacob, blessing them with the fruitfulness from whence sprang most of the Hebrews who walk the land of Palestine today and then make a new and opposite law, saying it is forbidden to marry two sisters.

47 Only men could think up such contradictory doctrines, for Elohim is like a rod of iron, constant and firm, unmoving and unyielding in the foundations of light. In no other way could man depend upon God.

48 Verily. I declare unto you: You insult and mock Elohim with your petty laws. Therefore, get

away from my sight and do not return until you bear the fruits of repentance!"
49 The Levites hurried away from his mighty countenance and the force of his words, and all the family and their friends that had been watching were once again in awe of Yeshua.
50 Abara came to him contritely and said, "You have opened up my eyes, and my ears have heard different things than I had thought. Forgive me for my weakness. I would be honored to give Martha to you in marriage."
51 And it came to pass that Yeshua and Miriam and Martha were married one to another after the manner that Yeshua taught, and Abara threw a great feast that lasted for three days.
52 Though there were some in Bethany who still spoke ill of the marriage, and harsh words of it were carried to the priests of Jerusalem, among Yeshua and Miriam and Martha and their children and kinsfolk, there was a deep sense of unity and happiness.

CHAPTER 32

Challenges of the Children of Light

Yeshua explains to his disciples the difference between the laws of Heaven and the laws of the natural world. He tells them that he will teach them the secrets of Heaven, which will be known by no others and by which all things are possible.

And it came to pass that on the first day of the feast, the disciples of Yeshua arrived from Lake Gennesaret, and they were sore distressed upon learning that Yeshua had taken Martha as a wife and that they had not been invited to attend the wedding.

2 But Yeshua, knowing their thoughts, came to them, saying, "My brothers of light, do not despair that you were not present for our marriage. Know that my days upon the earth are numbered and they are not many. Therefore, each one is precious, and we could not wait for your arrival, for already the days following the feast and all the days to come have been assigned for greater tasks and of those things, you are very much a part."

3 Upon hearing his words, his disciples were mollified and apologized to Yeshua for their weakness of understanding.

4 Without speaking of it again, Yeshua bade them to enjoy the first day of the feast and then meet with him in council upon the sunrise at the hill near the house of Martha's father.

5 The following day, the five disciples that had come from Lake Gennesaret came at daybreak to the top of the hill, along with Lazarus, the brother of Miriam and Martha, and found Yeshua and Miriam already there, kneeling in prayer facing one another, with hands held and heads touching.

6 The disciples of Gennesaret and Lazarus stood aside quietly with their heads bowed, honoring the sacredness of the prayer until they were finished, and then they approached.

7 Yeshua and Miriam rose to meet them, and Yeshua embraced each one with various greetings, while Miriam put her hands together upon her chest and, holding their eyes, bowed her head slightly toward each as they came before her, calling them by name and greeting them with "Namaste."

8 Yeshua bade them all to sit upon the ground in a circle with Miriam at his right hand, and he said unto them, "You think that your lives have changed since you became my disciples, but the change has been only like the Jordan after a small rain. Like the river that swelled for a time with new water, you have grown with new knowledge.

9 But your lives have been affected only a bit. In the coming days, if you will follow me, you must be prepared to have them affected greatly.

10 I will tell you now of some of the things that shall come to pass in the lives of those who walk with me and are my disciples. You will sacrifice much, and I will understand if the burden

is too great and you desire simply to return to the life you have always lived.

11 You know I teach the true Celestine Light of Heaven and that it is oftentimes at odds with the laws of men and the falsehoods taught by men in the name of God. Because of this, as word of my teachings spread, the opposition against me, from Caesar and Herod and the Sanhedrin, shall grow.

12 I shall be opposed openly and in secret even unto my death, and those that follow me shall be cast into the same storm, and many will suffer similar woes.

13 Even should you live to old age, you will be away from your wives and children many more days than you are with them.

14 You will find no reward of money, and though you will always have enough to eat, you will never grow fat from having too much.

15 Many of you shall be arrested and thrown into prison, and some shall be persecuted unto death at the hands of those angry at you for preaching my words, unless you gain the full knowledge and power of Celestine Adepts.

16 Despite the dedication of your life to preaching the Celestine Light of Elohim, you will find precious few who will heed your words and will be saddened by the many who will pervert them for their own ends.

17 After all you have sacrificed to bring forth the Celestine Light, you will see false churches spring up in my name that teach not my teachings, and they shall draw many to them, for their path is easy.

18 In the generations to come, these churches shall grow mighty and wealthy. They shall have a form of godliness, but will be empty of the true spirit of Elohim and barren of the fullness of truth.

19 Of the things that you shall teach, the very words and truth you heard from my lips, you will find few who will listen and embrace the light for fear of what others will think of them or the persecutions they might invite or from their own weakness to give up the comfort of the sandals they have always worn.

20 The few Children of Light that gather in my name, faithfully living my truth that you have shared, shall not have temples of gold and precious gems, but will be thankful just to have a roof over their heads.

21 Knowing all this, what do you say?"

22 Amram raised his right index finger and said, "First, know that I will follow you through any storm and count the endurance of any pain as evidence to Elohim of my faithfulness to the true light.

23 But I would like to understand why it is that Elohim would allow all the things you have said will befall us to come to pass? Why would Elohim allow the true Celestine Light to be perverted by men and your faithful disciples to be persecuted even to death?

24 How can it be that those who would follow the Celestine Light of Elohim would only have the means to worship in simplicity, while those who teach a perversion of your words would find prosperity and be able to build grand temples in which to worship Elohim?

25 I am just a simple fisherman and know my understanding is slow, but it would seem to me that everything would be the opposite of this; that God would reward those who are faithful to the Celestine Light and make difficult the paths of those who teach perversions."

26 Yeshua smiled at the words of Amram and said unto him, "Your questions show a depth of understanding greater than you give yourself in your humility, and it is important that you comprehend the answers.

27 Know that there are laws of Heaven, and there are laws of earth. I speak not of laws made by men, but of immutable laws of existence.

28 There is the law of the sun. If you go outside on a cloudless day, you will see the sun in the sky and feel its warmth upon your shoulder. If you are righteous, you will see and feel the sun, and if you are wicked, you will see and feel the sun.

29 To see the light and feel the warmth of the sun is a law of earth that comes to all and makes no qualms about who it rewards with its light and warmth. Regardless of who you are, if you stand outside at midday beneath a cloudless sky, you will receive the reward of the light and warmth of the sun.

30 So too, there is the law of the storm. When the clouds darken and the wind blows and the rain comes in torrents, you know that if you choose to be outside, uncovered, you will quickly become wet and uncomfortable. It does not matter whether you are rich or poor, wicked or righteous, if you stand outside, uncovered in a storm, you will suffer the consequences.

31 So too, there are several laws pertaining to fire. If you build it correctly and strike a good flint, you will create a fire. If you do not get too close, it will warm you on a cold night, but if you step into it, you will get burned. Whether you are rich or poor, wicked or righteous, the laws of the fire treat all men equally, except for Celestine Adepts that have mastered control of the natural world.

32 I have spoken to you only about laws of the natural world, which are easy for all men to understand. But there are many other laws that are more subtle, and the consequences from obeying or disobeying these laws can be far greater.

33 I speak of the laws of interaction from one person to another, from a man to a man, and a man to a woman, and a woman to a woman, and a parent to a child, and a child to a child.

34 And I speak also of the laws of blessing and consequence, some of which are easy to know and others which require insight and understanding.

35 If you needed to dig a well and you and your brothers applied yourselves with diligence throughout the day, at the end of the day, you would have dug deep enough to be blessed and rewarded for your efforts with cold, clear water.

36 But if you desired a well and were slothful, working for a short while, then taking a long break, working a bit more, then taking a longer break, as nightfall descended, the consequence of your lack of diligence would only be a small dry hole.

37 These are the blessings and consequences of obeying or disobeying the law of diligence.

38 Remember, the laws of life have no favorites among men. Without passion, they reward only those who follow the path they dictate.

39 If wicked brothers apply the law of diligence to dig a well, they will be rewarded for their efforts with the water they seek.

40 Even as the righteous brothers, if they are slothful, will suffer the consequence of their disobedience of this law.

41 Therefore, when you ask how it is that those who teach the false truth might have prosperity, while those who teach the true Celestine Light may not, understand that it is not by their worthiness that they manifest their situations, but by their understanding and obedience to immutable laws of Heaven and earth.

42 Those who love ease and comfort and power heed the call of priests of falsehood because they have itching ears, seeking those who will tell them what they wish to hear, and so they hear, 'Pay generous alms, say your prayers, and listen to the scriptures on the Sabbath, and all is well every other day of your life.'

43 These doctrines are delightful to those who love the ways of the world, for then they suppose to themselves that they can forget about Elohim and the ways of God and do as they will except on the Sabbath.

44 Therefore, each of the other days, they devote to acquiring the spoils of the world, and in the ways of the world, they become great.

45 But the Children of Light understand that the path of Elohim is a way of life each and every day, not just on the Sabbath, and that the steps they take each day bring them abiding joy, not just in this world, but also in the world to come.

46 While the foolish and worldly are spending their days making money and immersing themselves in the pleasures of the world, the Children of Light are investing their days playing

with their children, loving and comforting one another in word and deed, helping the poor, giving their time to serve Elohim, honoring the temples of their bodies, helping their community, and building qualities of good character and all manner of virtue in their hearts and the actions of their lives.

47 That which you pursue with focus, you are likely to obtain.

48 Those who love the ways of the world obtain the fruits of the world because that is what they seek, while giving just a passing nod to the ways of God.

49 Those who love the ways of Elohim obtain the fruits of God because that is what they seek, while giving just a passing nod to the ways of the world.

50 Therefore, each gains that which they seek and lacks that which they acknowledge only sufficiently to appease the necessities.

51 Understand too that there are laws of wickedness as well as laws of righteousness, for if a robber accosts a lone traveler and holds a dagger to his throat, demanding his coins, he has a great certainty from his past experience that the man so attacked will yield up his coins. He has employed the law of intimidation, a wicked law, but a law nonetheless.

52 But for every law, there is an opposite law that will oppose it and overcome it, if applied sufficiently.

53 In the days to come, you will be learning much about these many laws and how to utilize them and how to counter evil when it is cast upon you. Therefore, take heed to be astute students, for your very lives and livelihood will be at stake in the future.

54 When a false priesthood teaches a path of ease and the true priesthood teaches a more difficult way, which do you think more people will embrace?

55 If a false priesthood says, 'Sacrifice a lamb or two turtledoves and all will be well between you and God regardless of how you live or what you eat or drink or take to befuddle your mind,' but the true priesthood says, 'Honor the temple of your body, eat only living foods that grow upon the earth, drink only pure drinks, and take nothing that befuddles your mind,' which priesthood will draw more followers?

56 If a false priesthood says, 'Pay great alms that we may build a temple of gold and your sins will be forgotten,' but the true priesthood says, 'Only a sincere and contrite repentance and restitution will wash away the sins of men,' which priesthood will draw more followers?

57 If a false priesthood says, 'Become rich, live in a grand manor, but give generously to the church, and you will be loved of God,' but the true priesthood says, 'Live in simplicity and give your excess to the poor;' which priesthood will draw more followers?

58 If the false priesthood says, 'Give your intimate affections to whoever you desire, just continue to show your devotion to the church with your alms, and all will be well between you and God,' but the true priesthood says, 'Honor the sacredness of intimacy only within the union of marriage,' which priesthood will draw more followers?

59 If the false priesthood says, 'Only men may hold the priesthood or speak in council,' but the true priesthood says, 'Men and women are equal before God,' which priesthood will draw more followers?

60 If the false priesthood says, 'Men who lay with men and women who lay with women must be shunned and even stoned,' but the true priesthood says, 'The choice of intimate relationship is not important as long as it is a union in marriage and virtue,' which priesthood will draw more followers?

61 If the false priesthood in collusion with Caesar says, 'Obey the laws of the land, and you shall find peace and security and be in God's favor,' but the true priesthood says, 'Obey not the laws of men that are in opposition to the teachings of Heaven, even if it brings the wrath of Caesar upon you,' which priesthood will draw more followers?

62 If the false priesthood says, 'Believe only in Yeshua of Nazareth and by this alone, you shall go to Heaven for all your sins will be forgiven,' but the true priesthood says, 'Believe in the teachings of Yeshua of Nazareth and demonstrate the truth of your belief by doing good works,

having virtue and good character, and obeying the Great Commandment and the commandments of Sinai,' which priesthood will draw more followers?

63 If the false priesthood says, 'Whatever sins you do, just give alms and confess them to a priest and they will be forgiven,' but the true priesthood says, 'Repentance comes only after remorse, confession, restitution, forsaking of the sin, and humbly asking Elohim and those that have been wronged for forgiveness,' which priesthood will draw more followers?

64 Verily I say unto you: Straight and narrow is the way that leads to the Celestine Kingdom of Elohim, and very few will be those who are willing to walk the virtuous path that leads to physical resurrection and immortal exaltation.

65 But wide and easy is the path upon the earth that leads to misery and separation of the body and the soul in the worlds to come, and many are those that shall go that way.

66 Therefore, understand that the false priesthood uses laws of persuasion that allow men to imagine that they can be wicked and still be welcomed into Heaven.

67 But no unclean thing can enter into the presence of Elohim in the Celestine Kingdom on high. And those who live their lives in wickedness, thinking they will inherit glory, have deluded themselves into eternal misery.

68 The seeds you plant in life blossom in eternity. That which you sow, so shall you reap.

69 In the days to come, there will be many who will profess to follow me, but only a few who will live their lives as I have shown and taught them to live, that they may become more than they are.

70 When those who have been faithful to the Celestine Light knock upon my door in the world to come, I shall welcome them to their glory, even those who professed me not in life but nevertheless lived my teachings by the light of God that was within their heart.

71 But those who professed me, even loudly from the rooftops, but did not do the things which I taught, will not see me or my Kingdom.

72 Be mindful of the things I have revealed to you this day. As we go into the world to preach the Gospel of Celestine Light, remember that many will come to it, some because of the miracles, some because of rebellion against Caesar, some because of the welcome of the community, some because their noble soul pulls them toward the light.

73 But when those who seek only miracles find none forthcoming when they desire, they shall fall away.

74 When those who seek only rebellion find we are not trying to overthrow the government, they will fall away.

75 When those who seek only the embrace of community but find they must give as well as receive, they shall fall away.

76 When those who are pulled to a brighter light are unwilling to hold it because it requires them to change too much, they will fall away.

77 In the end, the refiner's fire will take away the dross, leaving only the pure in heart.

78 Look diligently therefore for those precious few of pure light. Among the crowds, look for those whose countenance shines above all others, for the Celestine Light will shine in the face of all true Children of Light, even those who have never heard of me or my teachings.

79 Teach to them what I have taught to you by my words and deeds.

80 Know that there shall be great grief upon the people of this land in the next generations. The people think they suffer now under the yoke of the Romans, but their suffering shall be greater in the days to come.

81 We are making a Community of Light at the delta of Gennesaret, but know it will be abandoned in the days to come and not one stone will be left upon another that is not overturned.

82 The faithful shall scatter across the world, a few here, a dozen there, another beyond. So shall the seeds of the Celestine Light of Elohim, which you will plant, settle upon many lands until the time of their maturation comes and the flowers of truth and light planted in the dust of yesterday's bones blossom in fullness and glory.

83 Therefore, do not concern yourselves with riches or grand temples or gathering great numbers of believers. Instead, concern yourself with finding and teaching the chosen few who are true, royal Children of Light.

84 Know that Elohim will give a great blessing to all those of noble heart that you find and cherish. The resonance of truth will pass through their loins from one generation until the next.

85 In the Epoch of Promise, when the fullness of the Celestine Light shall be given again among men, the descendants of the chosen shall feel the resonance that burned in the hearts of their ancestors. And the seeds sown by their progenitors shall grow and bear fruit within their hearts."

86 Then Cephas asked of Yeshua, "You are here and have the power of Heaven upon you. We are few in numbers, but mighty in our faith and our willingness to spread the Celestine Light you give us. How is it that we can fail to establish a torch of truth that is never extinguished? Why must we suffer so and why must the Children of Light be scattered? I still do not fully understand why that which is false would be allowed by Elohim to rise, while that which is true would be allowed to vanish from the sight of men."

87 Yeshua answered, "Though I walk among you, I do not compel you or anyone to follow me. Those who walk my path despite the challenges do so because they desire to feel the love and Celestine power of God, burning in their bosom greater than they desire a life of conformity and ease or enticing words of emptiness.

88 Nor should you think that suffering must be your lot. Among the Children of Light, let there always be love and support for one another, and may the sweetness of this comfort and the sure knowledge of your eternity ever shield you from the pain and inflictions of the world.

89 Nor is the scattering of the Children of Light in the days to come a curse, but a blessing, for it is in distant lands and upon distant shores that they will find sanctuary and a peace they could never know in the lands of Rome.

90 Nor should you wish to give more command upon the affairs of men to Elohim than Elohim would take. For each man and woman to grow beyond their birth, they must be free to choose their course in life; they must be free to make mistakes and amends.

91 Even though they may be slaves, bound to a master who controls their days, their eternal fate is still in their own hands by the choices of virtue and character they make every day.

92 There was a sower that sowed his seeds, and some fell upon the road and was walked upon and eaten by birds; some fell upon rock, and as soon as it sprouted, it withered away because it could find no moisture; some fell among thorns, and the thorns grew up with it, cutting it off from the light of life; some fell in a marsh and sprouted but could find no soil of substance and also perished; but some fell upon a cultivated field of fertile ground and sprang up and bore fruit that fed the cultivators and all whom they called family.

93 You are the sowers, and so it shall be with the seeds of Celestine Light which you sow.

94 Some will be sown in the byways of the world; it will be crushed and taken away by those who will pervert it, that they might teach their version of truth without the fullness of light in evidence for men to compare.

95 Some of your seeds will fall upon people who are like the rocky ground; they are closed tightly like a clam and are afraid to even consider any light other than the little candle they have.

96 Some of your seeds will be cast among thorns; they will begin to sprout in the hearts of those who want to know and believe, but will wither when they are shunned by their friends and family and will fall away in their desire to please others instead of God.

97 Some will be sown in the swamp of zealots, who, lacking a foundation of balance, will grow furiously for a time only to fall away when their narrow-minded zeal finds no support among the Children of Light.

98 But take heart, some of your seeds will be sown among those who will live and support one another in Communities of Light. As long as true believers gather to the fertile field of community and live the light they have been given in fullness, they will always grow and prosper.

99 If they do not choose to live it in fullness and their community falters, it is by their own choices and actions; and Elohim would have it be no other way, for only by allowing each person to make their own choices can each person be given an eternal reward according to their faithfulness and their deeds.

100 Never forget that many are called, but few are chosen. Nor is it Elohim who chooses, but each of those that have been called choose whether they will heed the call and walk in the Celestine Light that their heart tells them is true, or follow the enticing words of conformity and ease spoken to them in the world.

101 Therefore, I say unto you: follow me, do as I do, speak as I speak, live as I live. Let those who would inherit the blessings of the Children of Light in this world and the next do likewise, and Heaven shall pour forth blessings upon you greater than you can imagine.

102 You shall become Celestine Adepts and have the power to control your destiny. You will be given the secrets of Heaven by which all things are possible; such secrets as shall be known to no others of this generation. The challenges of these early days are your growing pains. And it is not until you are fully grown that all things will be understood in fullness."

CHAPTER 33

Sermon in Capharsalama

Yeshua and Miriam return to Capharsalama with Yeshua's disciples. At the request of Gimiel, Yeshua gives a sermon that over two hundred people attend. As it takes place during the time of the midday meal, some people bring food, but most do not, so Yeshua asks those who have food to please give it to his disciples so they can distribute it to everyone present. The amount they gather only fills four small baskets, but after Yeshua blesses the food, there is a never-ending supply coming out of the baskets and there is enough to abundantly feed everyone in the crowd. Yeshua speaks about "obeying the law" and the "fear of God" verses the "love of God," as well as which laws are the creations of man in the name of God and which are actually of God.

And it came to pass that early in the morning, after they had broken their evening fast and communed with the earth through the Contemplative Movements, Miriam and Yeshua, accompanied by his disciples, began the journey to return to the Community of Light at the Delta of Gennesaret.

2 Martha did not journey with them but remained behind to spend more time with her parents. She made plans to bring all of their children in a fortnight, in company with Lazarus when he made his monthly trip to Tiberias to meet with the manager of the family fish business on the lake.

3 And it came to pass that Yeshua and his followers came upon the town of Capharsalama as they traveled north on the road. Seeing it in the distance, Yeshua bade everyone to stop their journey for a moment, and they listened intently as he shared the events that had occurred on the road north of the town when he and Miriam had journeyed through there previously.

4 While he was speaking to his disciples, a citizen of Capharsalama passed them on the road as he was returning to town. He was one of the men that had previously confronted Yeshua. He recognized him immediately and, without a greeting, hurried into town to alert the citizens that Yeshua had returned.

5 Seeing the startled recognition on the man's face and his haste to arrive at the town, Cephas conjectured, "From the rudeness of that fellow, who gave not even the slightest greeting, I'd say the way is even now being prepared for a less-than-friendly welcome."

6 The other disciples nodded in assent, but Yeshua merely smiled knowing the true intent of the citizen of Capharsalama.

7 Nor did they have to wait long to discover that intent, for within minutes, a group of at least three dozen men issued forth from the town and came down the road toward them with obvious intent.

8 "We are outnumbered and virtually weaponless," Amram said. Looking to Yeshua, he asked, "How shall we protect ourselves if they attack us?"

9 But Yeshua was as calm as a summer morning and said unto him, "Fear not, they mean us no harm."

10 Despite his words, the disciples were tensed for a confrontation. But as Yeshua had assured them, when the men were near, one of them opened his arms to embrace Yeshua, who returned his welcome, saying, "It is good to see you again, Gimiel. I can see from your countenance that the Celestine Light of Elohim has grown in your heart since we last met."

11 Gimiel nodded enthusiastically and said, "So it has, good Rabbi, and also among many of the others that have come out to greet you."

12 Yeshua gave his great warm smile and said unto him, "It gladdens my heart to know that the few seeds I planted when last I was here have taken root and grown."

13 Then looking at the faces of the men of Capharsalama, he inquired, "But where is Ephres? I would have hoped to see him again as well."

14 Gimiel looked down at the dirt for a moment and said, "I know not where he has gone, good Yeshua. Many of us followed your admonition and welcomed him or at least did not malign him. But some others who did not hear you speak in person still treated him with disdain and continued to threaten his life. He remained but a few days in Capharsalama after you left, and I know not what became of him."

15 "And your kind-hearted rabbi?" Yeshua inquired.

16 "He remains still in Capharsalama," answered Gimiel. "But I doubt he will show his face while you are in town, as you embarrassed him greatly when you were last here, showing by your teachings, words, and wit upon whom the light of Elohim truly dwelt."

17 And it came to pass that Yeshua and the disciples mingled and spoke with the men from Capharsalama for some time, standing on the road outside of town. They introduced themselves and told of their families and their experiences with Yeshua.

18 Gimiel asked Yeshua, "Would you bless us with a sermon while you are here? For we may never again have you among us."

19 "Of course, Gimiel," Yeshua answered. "Let us pass through the town and you can gather those who would desire to hear my words. On the small hill north of town, I will speak at the midday."

20 And it came to pass that upon the midday, Yeshua and his disciples sat atop the small hill and a crowd of over two hundred men, women, and children came to hear him speak. The men sat to one side and the women and children to another, as was the way of the people of Capharsalama.

21 Some had brought food with them to eat their midday meal while listening to his words, but most had not, and seeing this, Yeshua asked that those who had brought food would bring it to his disciples so that they might share it and distribute it to all.

22 Those with food came up to the hill and gave the disciples the fish, bread, vegetables, and cheese that they had brought, and it filled four small baskets.

23 Looking at the small amount of food and the large number of people, Yohhanan commented to no one in particular, "There will only be enough for each person to have maybe one or two bites."

24 Then Yeshua came and blessed the food, saying, "Our Father and Mother in Heaven, we are grateful for this bounty and the good earth, which has borne it. We ask your blessings upon it, that it will come forth in abundance and deliciousness, that all might be filled and nourished."

25 He beckoned for the disciples to bring some large empty baskets, and taking a loaf of bread from one of the small baskets, he began to break it into large chunks and place them inside the larger basket. Soon the larger basket was filled, and he bade some of the men from Capharsalama to distribute it to the people.

26 Likewise, using two hands, he scooped several of the small fish from the smaller basket and

placed them into the larger basket and continued to do this until the larger basket was filled to a weight that two men could carry and then bade some men from Capharsalama to make sure each person had enough for their satisfaction and to return for more if they were lacking.

27 In like manner were the vegetables and cheese distributed. And the disciples were astounded by the miracle they were witnessing as the four small baskets never diminished the food they held, even though the items from them filled several larger baskets.

28 Even among the people of Capharsalama, it became evident that there was far more food remaining after they had all eaten their fill than had been present before the first bite had been taken. And seeing this, they spoke in quiet wonder to one another and gave great attention to Yeshua as he began to speak.

29 And Yeshua said unto them, "My brothers and sisters of Capharsalama, when I was last here, I heard much about the law and what the law as recorded in the scrolls of the prophets say about the things you can and cannot do in your life. These laws are said to be from Elohim; therefore, who cannot obey them without condemnation? The penalty for disobedience, for even small things, is severe. And for greater things, death awaits.

30 Knowing a sword hangs ever over your head lest you take too many steps on the Sabbath or eat or touch something that is unclean, or (pointing to the crowd) sit men with women, does the fear of the law and the punishments therein not weigh upon you and cause you to act or not act from fear, rather than love of God?

31 I speak now as I spoke before when I came upon your town. Because I see you are very devout in keeping the law, I will speak more upon it because of my love for you.

32 Only man can craft a god that must be obeyed because of fear not love. Only man can create a god who demands actions which are contrary to common sense and God's own interest.

33 Every person upon the earth lives today because Elohim made alive their first ancestors in the Garden of Eden. Just as your children are a part of you, so every person who has ever walked the earth from the descendants of the garden has a spark of God within them.

34 Every man from every country is your brother, and every woman from every country is your sister.

35 I say unto you with words of soberness that every man and woman upon the earth is a child of God.

36 Would you kill your own children because they disobeyed you in some slight thing or even in some great thing? How about your neighbor's children? How about the children of the Egyptians or the Romans?

37 I hope you would not. Do you think that Elohim, a God that is real and living, and not a contrived creation of men, would demand some of the children upon the earth to kill others or would give favor to some over others, when all are children of Elohim?

38 Would a God that created all people as equal sons and daughters demand that some be sacrificed at the altar, slaughtered in war, or given as plunder to be raped and enslaved?

39 Could you separate your children and say, 'These will find my favor, but these are to be raped, enslaved, and killed as needs be?"

40 Do you truly believe that a true and living God, creator of all that is, father and mother of all the children of men, would ever treat their children so blessed with love in creation to such a despicable and ignominious end?

41 You have heard it said that it is easier for Heaven and earth to pass away than for the smallest of the laws to pass away. But I say unto you it is easier for a lamb to get into Heaven than for a man who obeys a law that is contrary to the very essence of Elohim.

42 Elohim is love.

43 Elohim is inspiration.

44 Elohim is fair and just.

45 Elohim is compassionate and understanding.

46 Elohim loves virtue in whomever it is found and gives no preference to one child over

another for any other reason.

47 Elohim cherishes the life of all things that have been created and blesses the man that honors and protects life.

48 But men who take life without necessity for food or in self-defense bring a curse upon themselves, not from Elohim, but from their own soul, for their inner guilt cries out for the sin they have done against God.

49 Consider how you would be if you were the perfect father or the perfect mother to your children; as you would so be, even so is Elohim many times more to each of you, the children of God.

50 Nor would true laws of the true God demand the beauty of the body to be hidden. What would be the point to create the most magnificent work of art that is, the human body, only to hide it forever under great coverings of clothing?

51 If the body is not hidden but seen, there is greater incentive to honor it and honor the creator by keeping it fit and trim. But if it is forever hidden under flowing and voluminous clothing, with only the eyes and the feet to be seen, then it can be allowed to get fat and sagging, for who will know or see it to condemn the poor steward?

52 And why do you think men and women lust for one another? Is it evil as many would have you believe? Consider that it is a desire Elohim instilled in every person. How then can a gift of God be evil?

53 Is it simply to insure the race of men perpetuates as others proclaim? If that were so, then you would cease to have desires of that kind once you were beyond the age of fertility, for there would be no need for such desires. But any of you who have passed that age know of a certainty that the desire remains.

54 Verily, I declare unto you that you desire one another and can give physical pleasure to one another because that is a gift from Elohim that you might always have a source of joy and pleasure, even if you do not have a single coin or a roof over your head or food to eat; and not just any joy or pleasure, but one that fills you with a glow that lasts and a happiness that does not diminish with the waning day.

55 But in this joy, procreation does bear weight, for within the true laws of Elohim, the Great Commandment says to multiply and fill the earth and the commandments of Sinai say to not fornicate or commit adultery.

56 Therefore, it is only in righteousness that men and women may quench the fires of their lust, only within the halo of a marriage, given before witnesses, with commitment for life.

57 Elohim gave the commandments; Elohim gave the desire that stirs the loins; and these two were given that they might be fulfilled in each other, even as the man and woman are fulfilled in one another.

58 Marriage then becomes the only resolution that honors God and fulfills the desires that stir the loins.

59 It is for children that all of this is so, that they might be born into homes of balance and light and have the best chance to grow into balance and light in their lives.

60 And it is for the parents that they might overcome their weaknesses and selfishness and make their weaknesses their strengths.

61 But never forget this total pleasure has been given to you by Elohim to enjoy, and enjoy often for all of your life.

62 Remember, the time to procreate is but a few hours in your lives; all the other days Elohim has given this great gift of pleasure and comfort and love, that you might have joy and fulfillment that is above the cares of the world."

63 Bending his left arm and holding his chin with his hand, Yeshua looked toward the heavens and asked aloud, "Let us consider what other laws of the prophets can be revealed as merely the foolishness of men who would be kings over their brethren.

64 Certainly, circumcision must fall into this pit. Consider that if circumcision was necessary

or important, the sons of men would be born from the womb already circumcised.

65 Who is man to cut up a child made in the image of God so that the child is no longer in the image of God? Why would Elohim create a child one way only to ask the child to be disfigured by men once he was born?

66 They say it is to distinguish the sons of Israel from the Gentiles and to show obedience to God, but I say unto you if that were important, the sons of Israel would have been born circumcised.

67 Verily, Elohim would ask men to cut off their own finger to show obedience before they would ask them to cut an innocent and defenseless child.

68 In my condemnation of the law, know that I do not condemn all of it for there are some parts that are reasonable and just, but they are few and the unreasonable and unjust are many.

69 Therefore, I will teach you some of the signs by which you can judge a law of Elohim from a law of men in the scrolls of the prophets.

70 If obedience to a law gives Celestine Light to your life and only light and causes the light within you to shine and to always shine, then it is of Elohim and you should give it a place in your heart and life.

71 Respect those laws which have eternal significance and bring Celestine Light to you. Cherish those laws and live them as your life.

72 Do not listen to the interpretations of men, concerning the law and the prophets, for many are the laws of man that have been said to be the laws of God but have no value in the world to come or value in the world in which you now live.

73 Verily, if it is of God, it will have eternal significance and will bring Celestine Light into your life, and if it is of man, it will have no consideration or merit for your entry into glory in Heaven and, instead, will often be onerous and not of light.

74 The ways of Elohim are simple to live and easy to understand, not convoluted and ritualistic like the ways of men and the religions of men.

75 The laws of men have no meaning in the world to come, but the laws of Elohim involve the purity of your heart and your good works in this life, and those jewels of character have great weight on the day of eternal judgment.

76 If a law is of man, it will give power to men to judge the spiritual correctness of other men, and God has not given to men to judge the spiritual worth of souls or to take life or abase the spirit of the children of God upon the earth.

77 Nevertheless, there are some things in the traditions and the law of the prophets that are true and worthy, given for your benefit and edification; and these are easy to recognize, for they have significance both in this world and the world to come.

78 Verily, if that which is given or expected expands your spirit, or is for your health or for the strength of your family, or for building your good character, or for helping your relationships to be deeper and more fulfilling, or to increase your knowledge, and does not demean you or take away your spirit or constrain your finite time upon the earth or hurt others and keeps balance in your life and promotes harmony and peace in your heart and among all men and women, then you may know that it is good and of God."

79 Then Yeshua stopped speaking, and gathering his wife and his disciples, he bade the people of Capharsalama farewell, for he desired still to travel far upon this day.

80 Gimiel came to him as he prepared to leave and said, "Good Yeshua, once again my heart has been moved by the wisdom and sense of your words. May I follow you and become one of your disciples?"

81 Pointing to some of his friends, he said, "Not just me, but several of my friends would also be honored if we could walk with you wherever you go and hear more of your divine wisdom."

82 Yeshua grasped his right forearm in a way that Gimiel also grasped his, and holding him thus, he said unto him, "My friend, you are welcome among us and any that would come as well.

83 But already I have taken my brothers here (pointing to his disciples) from their wives and

families. If you would truly help build the Kingdom of God, come with your wives and children to the delta of Lake Gennesaret, where you will find a Community of Light, wherein dwells my family and the families of all of my disciples, and where I most often reside.

84 We are in need of stout men, devout women, and happy children to build up this community of God. Will you accept this important calling?"

85 Gimiel bowed his head, saying, "I cannot express the joy my heart feels. Nothing has ever felt so right. I know this is where I belong and where my family should be."

86 And it came to pass that as Yeshua continued northward on his journey home with Miriam and his disciples from the delta, they were joined by Gimiel and his wife and children and three of his friends and their wives and children.

87 And great was the joy in Capernaum and Bethsaida upon the return of Yeshua and Miriam and the disciples to their wives and children and the joy upon meeting the people of Capharsalama who had come to join the Family of Light.

CHAPTER 34

From This Day the Light Goes Forth

After returning to the Community of Light at Lake Gennesaret, Yeshua asks Cephas to form and administer the community. When Cephas chooses only men to be on the council, Yeshua speaks to him about the merits of balance in all things and overcoming the incorrect teachings and prejudices he has previously known.

nd it came to pass that Yeshua, Miriam, and the disciples that came with them arrived at the delta of Gennesaret, and for some days, each stayed mostly with their families, taking care of family business.

2 After the first day and night of visiting with the members of the community, Yeshua and Miriam retired to their house to fast and pray and did not join the community for meals for three days.

3 The Community of Light at the delta was growing with new members, in addition to the several families that already resided there. Before going into seclusion to fast and pray, Yeshua asked Cephas to form and administer the community, to call others to be a council, and to help all the men to be immediately employed in fruitful labor that benefited both their families and the community.

4 Now Cephas pondered greatly upon the men he should call to be a Council of Elders to help him plan for the activities and policies of the community.

5 Thinking only in his mind and without prayer, he concluded that he would need to ask all of the disciples that Yeshua had asked to specifically follow him so he would not offend anyone's sensibilities.

6 As most of the disciples would often be away from the community, traveling with Yeshua, he considered who among the new men he should also call upon. Unable to come to a conclusion, on the fourth day after their return, he went to visit Yeshua at his house in Capernaum to get his advice, for Yeshua said he would be in seclusion for three days only.

7 Yeshua questioned him, asking, "How many men do you think to call for the Council of Elders?"

8 And Cephas answered him, saying, "I thought twelve would be the best. It is a sacred number, sufficient to get a variety of advice, but not too large to become undermined by an overabundance of opinions."

9 Yeshua nodded and asked, "How many men, including those of both strength and vigor and the old and weak, who are not among those I have called to walk with me in my journeys, do you

count among the Children of Light in the community?"

10 Cephas pondered this for a moment and then answered, "Including those who have just come from Capharsalama and Gurion and his eldest son who came with their families from Ptolemais while we were in Bethany and those who already lived here at the north end of the lake, we have eighteen men firmly committed to the community, plus those you have called as disciples."

11 "That is a small number to choose twelve from without offending the six who were not chosen," Yeshua replied.

12 Cephas raised his eyebrows and nodded in agreement, but added, "I only thought to call eleven as I would be the twelfth. But even then, you are correct that the other seven might take offense.

13 Perhaps, my err is that twelve is too many and that a smaller number such as six or even two others besides myself would be better."

14 "Did you pray to Elohim to seek guidance before you decided upon the number twelve?" Yeshua asked.

15 Cephas answered, "I prayed about how many the council should be, but I neglected to ask for guidance about who should be numbered in the council, assuming this would be easy for me to know of my own accord."

16 "Then it must be that eleven is the right number for the council with you as the twelfth, even as the light has been revealed to you in your thoughts by Elohim," affirmed Yeshua. "But now you must pray more earnestly and discover who should be numbered among the eleven."

17 Cephas nodded in agreement and prepared to depart that he might find a quiet place to pray for guidance, but Yeshua reached out and grasped his arm, saying, "One more thing, my brother, before you ask of Elohim, you must be open to receiving the answer, and you are not quite in that place of wholeness."

18 Cephas looked with wide-eyed surprise at Yeshua, saying, "What could I have done to be unworthy of an answer? I promise you that I strive mightily each day to live up to the Celestine Light and do not feel unworthy to seek Elohim in prayer in any way."

19 Yeshua smiled and answered him, saying, "My brother, I did not say or mean to imply that you are unworthy, for surely you are a pillar of the light.

20 Nor is anyone ever unworthy to seek the comfort and guidance of their Father and Mother in Heaven in prayer.

21 Many pray in all sincerity, humility, and worthiness, but cannot receive the counsel they seek because in their pride or prejudice or cultural or religious upbringing, they are incapable of accepting the answer.

22 It is of this that I spoke. Your Heavenly Father and Heavenly Mother will answer your prayers and give you the guidance and inspiration you seek; yet your cup will not be full, for it has a mouth that is too narrow and cannot gather all the wisdom poured into it. Therefore, most will be spilled upon the ground and lost to your understanding."

23 "I do not comprehend why," Cephas stammered. "You know my heart is in a good place, and my eyes seek only the light. If there is something in my character or customs that blocks me from the fullness of the Celestine Light, please reveal it to me that I might unblock this dam."

24 Yeshua answered plainly, saying, "You have only chosen men for your council, yet women outnumber men in our community, and every decision made for the community affects them as much as the men. Where the men are often away because of work, the women are always here.

25 Exclude the women from the council and you deny yourself the wisdom of those who see all things from a different perspective.

26 Exclude the women and you also exclude those who are present almost every hour of every day and thus better prepared to understand the dynamics and immediate needs of the community.

27 A good council will have both men and women and be stronger because of it. From the

men, there will be an understanding of the currents of the outside world.

28 From the women, there will be an understanding of the currents of the Community of Light.

29 From the men will come strength and wariness and protection.

30 From the women will come compassion and welcome and action without rashness.

31 Each is a branch of the tree of light. For the tree to grow large, the needs of all the branches must be considered and the gifts of all branches must be accepted.

32 Cut away more than half the branches of a tree and the tree will soon die or only live as a scrub of what it could have been. But nourish all the branches and the leaves and the roots and the shoots and the buds, and the tree shall grow magnificent beyond comprehension.

33 So it is with men and women and all things within the Community of Light.

34 I know your heart and your head, Cephas. Both desire that which is right, but both are swayed by the customs and teachings you have grown up with, concerning the proper place and duties of women.

35 If you truly follow me, you must overcome that which you have lived all of your life and live the teachings that I have given you in fullness.

36 Only then will the mouth of your cup be wide enough to receive all of the wisdom and blessings your Heavenly Father and Mother pour upon you every day."

37 Cephas listened very intently to the words of Yeshua, but squirmed a little uncomfortably in his skin as he began to answer him, saying, "This is a hard thing you speak, Yeshua, for women are . . . they are . . . it is hard for me to say what they are.

38 You know I have a love for my wife. I do not treat her as my property as is my right by law, and as many men do their wives, but show her respect and consider her happiness and not only how she can please me.

39 But her thoughts are very simple. She only knows how to clean and cook and garden and take care of the children. Her emotions come upon her easily, sometimes in a most unbecoming manner, and I know the wives of many men are far worse than her.

40 In honesty, I do not see how women could be of any help in a community council. Let them do the things that they do, but how could they give any useful advice outside of the tiny world they live within? And how they decide to cook or clean or take care of the children is of no consequence to the community as a whole."

41 Yeshua looked to his wife, who had been listening in silence as he spoke to Cephas, and asked, "Miriam, how would you answer Cephas?"

42 And Miriam said unto him, "Good Cephas, I too know your heart and your head, and I admire you for both. But your understanding of women is like an empty chest. It has nothing at all inside of it. But that can be a good thing if you are willing to listen and learn, for there is much space to fill it with scrolls of knowledge."

43 Before she could continue, Cephas interrupted, saying, "Wait, Miriam, I do not speak of you when I speak of women, for you are like unto a man in your knowledge and experiences in the world.

44 I know you have the greatest favor of Yeshua, and I would not hesitate to ask you to be on the council. But surely there is not another woman like you in the entire world, and in any case, like the other disciples, you travel with Yeshua.

45 The rest of the sisters of the community are lights to us all, but would it not be a mockery of wisdom to ask them to sit in council with men?

46 And even if I could persuade my head to abandon the law and all I have understood my entire life, could we expect the same to occur with all of the other men of the community?"

47 Miriam scoffed, "What part of me do you find is like a man? Is it my long hair which I do not hide, for many men also have long hair?"

48 "No, it is not your hair, Miriam. As I said, it is your understanding of the dealings of men and the places you have been, even to Egypt, and the knowledge you hold from being with

Yeshua these many years.
49 "When I first met you, I did not understand why Yeshua allowed you such freedom, but having come to know you more, I understand you are like a brother to us. But in that you are surely unique.
50 And even understanding all that I have said, it is still difficult to accept all that is given to you by Yeshua. For in the end, you are still just a woman. And in the eyes of the law and of men, you should not be allowed to be the way that you are allowed to be. I do not mean to offend, only to speak in honesty.
51 For me, it is enough that Yeshua has said this is the way it should be. If there is rebellion inside of me, it comes from the adversary, not from the light of Elohim, and I will steadfastly follow the light of Elohim wherever it leads, and heed not the darts of the adversary within.
52 But even as you know more than other women, so too have I been blessed to understand more than most men, because of my longer association with Yeshua and my dealings with men in the world.
53 Therefore, I can bring myself to accept and live this higher truth: that some women can be considered equal to men in a few select areas; even that some women might be capable of serving on a community counsel.
54 But let us be honest, not just with one another but about this situation. Though I might accept for some women to be elevated thus, do you believe that except for you, the other men in the community would accept it?"
55 Miriam let out a deep breath before speaking and then said unto him, "I believe that the other men in this community are more uplifted in their understanding than you credit them.
56 Consider that every man in the Community of Light is here by their own choice.
57 And why are they here? Because they have heard the teachings of Yeshua and some have seen his miracles, and they want to follow him and be a part of that which he establishes.
58 Yeshua has made no secret that he has come to upturn the laws and traditions and much more than that as well. Surely, there can be no man in our community without that most basic understanding, for almost everything Yeshua does and says is contrary to the law and tradition.
59 Therefore, I think if you, as the disciple he has chosen to lead our community, as a lifelong resident and leader of Bethsaida, and as a fisherman of three boats, speak to our community as one, both the men and the women, and speak the words you have heard from Yeshua and give an account of his teachings about women, there will be no dissension.
60 Surprise perhaps, some confusion perhaps, but no dissension. For every man here is a son of Elohim, a Son of Light. Even as every woman here is a daughter of Elohim, a daughter of light.
61 When they see or hear the light, it will dance in their hearts, no matter how different it may be from all they have known.
62 Though they may not understand the fullness of the Celestine Light at that moment, they will have a deep desire to learn and understand it, no matter how simple their life has been.
63 I know that is true, Cephas. I am not so different than other women, even as you are not so different than your brothers of light in our community.
64 Speak and they will listen. Testify of the truth and they will believe. Live the Celestine Light and they will live it also."
65 Cephas was humbled by Miriam's words and said, "Thank you, Miriam. You have opened my eyes and heart greater than they were before, and I will ponder and pray about the words you have spoken. But even now there is a greater peace in my heart about this."
66 Looking then to Yeshua, he asked, "Miriam is correct to say that all will follow that which you say to do, even if it is contrary to what they have known.
67 I did not mean to make this such a large issue, only to seek advice. Perhaps, you can give us a sermon about this on the Sabbath and then the path will be laid for all to understand that which would seem to many to be contrary to the laws of nature."

68 Rather than answer him, Yeshua looked from his eyes into Miriam's and gestured for her to answer for him. And she said unto Cephas, "Another reason we are blessed above all the generations of the world to have Yeshua among us is that we can have a testimony of him from what we have seen and what we have heard, and because of this, we can be special witnesses to the world of the Celestine Light he has brought.

69 On a dark and dreary day, not far away, Yeshua will part from us and rise to the Heaven from whence he came to dwell again with our Celestine Father and Mother.

70 He walks among us and gives us the Celestine Light of Heaven that we might teach the light to others. Once he is gone from this world, it will only be by the words we speak and write, and the things which we do, that the people of the world will learn of the brilliance of the Celestine Light he brought. Even then, it will only be held by a few.

71 I speak to you now because he desires me to grow in my confidence and stature while he is still here to teach and nurture me. It is the same for you, brother Cephas. The day will soon come when you must stand alone and lead the Children of Light on the paths that Yeshua has blazed.

72 The day has not yet come when you must stand alone, but the day has come when both of us must not be afraid to stand.

73 And for this cause, Yeshua desires me to speak to you rather than speaking himself, even as he desires you to speak to our community about the council and women and the true Celestine Light of Elohim."

74 And it came to pass that two days after the Sabbath, Martha came to the community with her children and the children of Yeshua and Miriam in the company of her brother Lazarus, and there was great joy in their family with the reunion and among all the people of the community, especially with Miryam, the grandmother of the children of Yeshua and Miriam.

75 And it came to pass that on the next Sabbath, Cephas spoke to the community, to the men on the right and the women on the left.

76 He had contemplated and prayed about the Council of Elders and the words of Yeshua and Miriam, and in his heart, there was now a great understanding.

77 Because of this, he had the Celestine Light of Elohim upon him, and his countenance exuded the light. It seemed to radiate from his very pores.

78 He spoke with a great and majestic voice that pierced the hearts of all that heard his words. And even as Miriam had predicted, although he spoke contrary to all they had assumed and believed about women, there was a resonance in their hearts and no dissension among them.

79 As he concluded his talk, Cephas called the men and women he had chosen by the guidance of prayer and contemplation, to be the eleven who would be the Council of Elders for the Community of Light.

80 And numbered among them was Martha of Bethany, the wife of Yochanan the Baptizer and second wife of Yeshua, and Miryam of Nazareth, the mother of Yeshua, and Shabala, the wife of Cephas.

81 And among the men was Gimiel of Capharsalama.

82 Then Yeshua rose among them and said unto them, "My brothers and sisters of light, remember this day; remember this place. Tell it to your children, that they may tell it to their children and they to theirs, unto every generation.

83 For on this day, at this place, with this action, you have witnessed the beginning of the expansion of the Celestine Light of Elohim upon the earth.

84 And the light shall expand throughout all the world and to generations unborn, even all the generations of man, by the words and deeds of those who know and love the light.

85 Though the light will be fought, though it will be resisted, though men will try to pervert it and change it to their desires, it will never be stopped, and from this day, the world will begin to change.

86 Never forget you were here at the beginning, on the very first day. On this day, I call each of you to a high and holy calling. You are special witnesses called of Elohim to hold the Celestine

Light to cherish the light and bring the light unto the world. So let it be."

CHAPTER 35

Many Miracles at Gennesaret

Many people come to Gennesaret hoping for Yeshua to heal them of sickness, disease, and injuries. He sends his disciples out to see who is worthy to be healed and who is not. Simon the leper is one found worthy and Yeshua heals him first. Yeshua's fame spreads and more crowds of people arrive to be healed. Yeshua speaks to the crowd from a boat on the waterfront about being healed, and in order for that to happen, they must forsake their evil ways and repent of their sins. Those pure in heart, he invites to enter the water and come to him and they will be made whole by their faith, but cautions those of impure heart to not enter the water because it will be their death. Many are baptized that day and healed of all manner of afflictions, but one man is not.

And it came to pass that during the following days, many people came to visit the community of Gennesaret to see and speak with Yeshua, and many came, hoping he would heal them of all manner of infirmaries, diseases, and injuries, as it had been spoken about in Galilee and Judea that he had done.

2 But though he wandered freely through the community and ate meals each day with the members, he met in depth only with his disciples and continued to teach them of the Celestine Light of Elohim and the things to come.

3 Some of his disciples wondered why he would not speak with the infirmed and the scholars and scribes that had come to see him, and he answered, "The mason must lay the foundation of bricks before the building can be built, and the building must be built before it can give shelter to many people.

4 But the days of the mason are numbered upon the earth, and if he is distracted from his task, the foundation will not be laid ere he must depart.

5 Then the many that would have had shelter and comfort will be alone in the cold and dreary world because the time of the mason was robbed to help a few at the expense of the many.

6 Nor is it given to me to prepare the people of the world for the Celestine Light, for you have seen the light and hold it in your hearts. Therefore, it is given to you to bring the Celestine Light to the people and then bring those who love the light and have repented of their sins to me.

7 For only those who have repented and hold the Celestine Light in their heart are worthy of me. Only those have a resonance that turns my face to them."

8 The disciples understood his words and that very day went among the visitors to Gennesaret and spoke to them to see who it was that came to contend, and who it was that came in selfishness to find favor of Yeshua and who it was that had come in humility seeking to be healed or to grow within themselves because they loved the light and had come seeking that which called to them.

9 Among those that they found bathed in humility and sincerity was a man known only as Simon the leper. His lot was misery, and even the disciples spoke to him with some revulsion and from a distance.

10 Nevertheless, when Yeshua met with his disciples that night, he inquired if they had found any of the visitors of pure heart. Cephas replied they had found several including a man who stank very badly, whom none could approach too near, called Simon the leper.

11 The following day, after the community meal to which uninvited visitors were not permitted to attend, Yeshua walked with Miriam and his other disciples, and they came upon Simon the leper sitting upon the ground and seeing them approach, he knelt upon his knees, saying, "O Yeshua of Nazareth, blessed be your father and mother that you stand before me. I know you are blessed above all men and that the power of God is upon you. Though I am but an unworthy clod of dirt, I beseech you to make me clean, for I know without doubt that you need only say it will be so, and so it will be."

12 Yeshua stood before him and asked, "If you were not a leper who would you be?"

13 Simon answered him with a crack in his voice, saying, "I would be a faithful husband to my wife who has not seen me now for almost two years because of my affliction. And I would be a loving father to my children who think that I am dead. And I would be a hard-working man that I might support my family. And I would repay my brother who has supported my family in my absence twofold. And if God so wills, I would bring my family here that I might labor in your community and repay in some small measure the gift I ask of you."

14 Yeshua put forth his hand and touched him upon his forehead, saying, "You have answered well Simon, and I perceive that your heart is pure and your words are true. Therefore, by your faith, be clean."

15 Immediately, his leprosy began to vanish and great scabs fell off his body and onto the ground, even from within his wrappings. As they fell upon the ground, they turned immediately into dust and were no more. And all who were present marveled greatly and with wonder at what they had seen and at the new Simon who stood before them, for he was glowing in his appearance and the air around him smelled like a fresh spring day.

16 Yeshua told him, "Go and show yourself to your wife and children that they might know of a surety that the one they love has returned. Then come with your family to Gennesaret, and you will be welcomed and can be baptized. But speak not of what has happened except to the pure in heart who are open to the Celestine Light that I bring, even as you have been."

17 Then Amram came forward, and taking the robe off his back, he handed it to Simon and said, "I will return to my home for another. You are a new man; bury the rags of your past in the ground and remember your ordeals no more, for now you are one of the Family of Light."

18 Simon put on Amram's robe with the joy of a child, and after bidding good-bye to Yeshua and Miriam and each disciple one by one, he hurried on the road to Jericho so that he might find again his family that had been lost.

19 When he came to his wife and revealed himself, she fainted straightaway upon seeing him. But once she revived, her joy was full, and upon hearing of the miracle of his healing by Yeshua, she went out of the house and began to joyously proclaim to everyone what she saw: "My husband, who was as dead, is now alive again! Yeshua of Nazareth has healed him in an instant! Do you hear? He was afflicted with leprosy, and now he is whole! From the moment Yeshua touched him, he was made whole! Praise to God in the highest!"

20 Now Simon, remembering the admonition of Yeshua to not speak of his healing to any but the pure in heart, tried to dissuade his wife from publicly proclaiming the miracle, but so great was her joy that she could not be persuaded.

21 Because of the proclamation of Simon's wife, many came to see for themselves the miracle man. Before he had been afflicted, Simon had been a prosperous merchant of dates and owned a large grove down by the river with his brother; therefore, he was well known among the people of Jericho.

22 Many knew he had disappeared after being sorely afflicted with leprosy and now to see him whole and to hear the story of his miraculous healing amazed them all.

23 Word of the miracle performed by Yeshua of Nazareth soon spread across the land far beyond Jericho. It was matched with stories heard by others of additional miracles Yeshua had performed. In a very short time, his fame grew, and many more people with afflictions began to journey to Gennesaret to be healed by his touch.

24 In a matter of days, the crowds coming into the area around Gennesaret began to swell even greater in number. Yeshua asked his disciples to go each day and preach to them the principles of the true Celestine Light of Elohim and to note those with whom it resonated.

25 Then taking only Miriam with him, he departed into the wilderness to the east of the community, and they remained there for several days, communing with the Father and Mother and with each other.

26 The day following the Sabbath, Yeshua and Miriam came down from the wilderness into the town of Hippos on the east shore of the lake, and being recognized by no one there, they returned quietly by boat to Bethsaida.

27 But no sooner had they set foot upon the shore than the news quickly spread that Yeshua had returned, and people began coming toward him hurriedly from several directions, many crying out, "Heal me," while scribes beset him with doctrinal questions without any respect.

28 Most of his disciples were out upon the lake, fishing, and it was Gimiel of Capharsalama, who seeing Yeshua, waded through the crowd to stand before him and clear a path so that he and Miriam might return to their home in Capernaum.

29 As they walked along the road to Capernaum followed by the crowd who still called out to him, they came upon a man with palsy being pulled on a litter by his wife, and as he approached, she fell to her knees and said, "Praise God in the highest; good Yeshua of Nazareth, I plead with you to heal my husband, for our children starve since he can walk no more or use one of his arms."

30 Yeshua stopped before them, and all the crowd stopped with him in expectant silence, sensing a miracle was about to be.

31 Looking at the woman, Yeshua asked, "Are you and your husband one with Elohim in your thoughts and desires and actions?"

32 The woman answered humbly, "We have always strived to do right, but in truth, we have done much wrong, and it is our children that suffer the most because of our inequities. Many say it is because of evil my husband has done that he has been cursed to walk no more or even barely move. I know we are unworthy to ask to be healed, but our life is almost death and we knew not where else to turn."

33 Then Yeshua asked, "If your husband were healed by the power of God, what would you do?"

34 The woman answered him, saying, "We would give thanks beyond words in our very heart and body, and my husband would go before the priests and make an offering and show himself to them that they might see God's miracle.

35 But more than this, we would turn our backs upon our iniquities, which are greater afflictions than the palsy. We would seek you out, not to heal our bodies, but to heal our souls."

36 Yeshua nodded in appreciation of her words and asked, "If your husband is not healed, what then will you say and do?"

37 The woman answered him again, saying, "We will surely be very sad. No one could be aught else if their hope is so lost. But it will not change our determination to live a better life than we have, to be more worthy of life itself, however limited it might be. If my husband must remain as he is, despite standing before you, then surely it is God's will. And if it is God's will, it must be for our good, and we will strive to appreciate and understand the good God gives to us."

38 Then Yeshua came up to the woman and held her by each shoulder. And looking into her eyes, he said unto her, "Your honesty and humility are deeper than the pools of the Jordan."

39 Then turning to her husband on the litter, he said unto him, "Brother, be of good cheer, your sins are forgiven you."

40 There were in the crowd that witnessed this event certain scribes that had been sent to discover the evil that might be in him. And hearing Yeshua's words, they spoke among themselves, saying, "This man commits blasphemy, for who but God can forgive sins?"

41 Yeshua, knowing their thoughts, said, "Why do you think evil in your hearts?

42 Which is easier to say, 'Your sins are forgiven you' or to say, 'Arise and walk?'

43 But that you may know that this son of man is more than that and has the power and authority on earth to forgive sins, watch now that you may testify of the truth that condemns you."

44 Then looking to the man upon the litter, Yeshua said unto him, "Man of misery, by your repentance, you are forgiven, and by your faith, you are made whole. I say unto you: arise, take up your bed, and walk. Go now to your house and your children."

45 Immediately, the man stood up and then fell to his knees before Yeshua in thankfulness. Then he and his wife departed in unabashed joy for their home.

46 The scribes were aghast at what they had seen and heard, but the multitude saw it and marveled and glorified God, who had given such power to be upon the earth.

47 At last, Yeshua and Miriam reached their home, and Martha and the children were there to greet them. Gimiel had called out to other men of the community as they traveled so that there were four who stood before the entrance to the house once Yeshua and Miriam were inside to bar the multitude from pressing too close.

48 And after a time, being assured by Gimiel that Yeshua was not coming out, the crowd dispersed. Some left altogether to return to their towns, but many others merely removed to their camps or accommodations to await Yeshua's reappearance.

49 The following day, before the sun arose, Yeshua and Miriam slipped out of their house unseen except for their faithful friends who had remained on guard before the door. Going down to the lake shore, they met Cephas in one of his boats along with three of Yeshua's disciples, and boarding, they pushed out into deep water just off the shore.

50 As daylight came upon the land, one of the multitudes that waited to see Yeshua spied him on the boat, sitting off the shore, and quickly, the crowd formed upon the beach nearest to the boat as it lay at anchor, broadside to the beach.

51 Then Yeshua stood up in the center of the boat on the side, facing the beach, and spoke to them, saying, "Many of you have come to be healed of your afflictions, but like the woman whose husband had palsy yesterday, you must first be healed of the affliction of your sins in your life before you can be healed of the afflictions that beset your body.

52 Know this, I heal you not, but it is you who heal yourself; for your true affliction is not on the outside but on the inside, and you are the only physician that has the cure.

53 Some may say that their malady is on the inside, and it is something tangible and physical like a broken bone or worms that devour them, but it is not of the physical that I speak when I speak of the inside, but of the disease of your sins, which eats at the essence of your soul with more finality than worms will ever consume your body.

54 Your sins are like a millstone that weighs you down and prevents you from rising to the light. If you do not free yourself from their weight, they will crush you and drown you, making your life unfulfilled and destroying your eternity that could be.

55 I call upon you this day to forsake your evil ways and commit to walk henceforth only in the simple and true Celestine Light of Elohim, which you can learn from the mouths of my disciples.

56 I call upon you to shed your old skin and become a new and better person.

57 I call upon you to forsake your friends who have enticed you to do evil and make new friends who will entice you to do good.

58 I call upon you to publicly proclaim that you are forsaking the darkness of old and

embracing the Celestine Light that dawns in the new day, in your new life, and to seal that promise with the covenant of baptism this very day by the hands and authority of my disciples.

59 Any of you who are ill and afflicted and are ready to be born again, who are ashamed of your sins and ready to live in the brightness of the Celestine Light, I invite you now to enter into the waters of Gennesaret and come to me. By my word, I declare if you are pure in your heart in your intentions, you shall be made whole.

60 But do not enter the water if you are not pure in your heart in your intentions, for the very water that gives life to the pure will be death to the impure.

61 If you are not numbered among the pure, turn your backs and leave this place; there is nothing here for you. Return to your towns and homes and come back to Gennesaret once you have healed yourself of your sins and are ready to be born again into the light."

62 Despite his words, no one left, but many people who were afflicted of all manner of disease began to enter the water and walk toward him.

63 There was another man who also had the palsy, and his relatives held up his litter and waded out into the lake toward the boat where Yeshua stood with open arms.

64 As they neared the deep water and could walk no further, Yeshua bade them to throw the man from his litter into the lake.

65 The relatives all looked at one another uncertain of whether they should follow the words of Yeshua, but the man on the litter raised his voice and beseeched them to throw him into the lake as Yeshua had bidden.

66 Heeding his request, they threw him into the deep water beyond them, and he immediately sunk beneath the surface. But then in the next moment, he bobbed up and began to float toward the boat flailing his arms.

67 Soon, he was at the gunnel and was pulled up into the boat where he stood beside Yeshua, beaming in happiness and waving to his friends and family on the shore and standing in the lake.

68 Many other people with both minor and serious afflictions were also shouting for joy as they stood in the water, finding themselves free of their disease, both on the outside and the inside.

69 There was still another man stricken with palsy, a rich man who had been brought upon a litter by his servants, and he commanded them to bring him into the lake as they had seen the first man stricken with palsy be cured.

70 But his head man hesitated and said, "Forgive me, Master, to speak out without your command. I think only of your welfare. You have done many things God would not countenance to acquire your wealth. Have you repented as this rabbi has said must needs be, else you shall perish in the water?"

71 The rich man scoffed at him, saying, "You know people have been hurt sometimes by my actions, but that is the nature of business. I am sure God understands, for I have given many alms to the temple. Now get me into the water this instant while the power of the miracle is still there. Only good happened to the first man, and you have not seen anyone in the water suffer ill effects, so it is safe to say the rabbi's warning was just so much pomp to create the right mood."

72 Even as the servants entered the water, bearing the rich man on the litter, the head man still spoke with caution to him, saying, "You do not even believe the teachings of this rabbi. He has said you must repent and have faith, and he teaches many things contrary to the law which you obey. Perhaps, it would be better to wait until another day and reflect more on the things he has said."

73 "You fool!" The rich man said, raising his voice. "It is no wonder you are a servant, and I am the master; you can't think any better than an ass. Now throw me into the deep water as you saw the other man thrown."

74 Abiding by his command, the servants threw him into the deep water of the lake. Like the first man with palsy, he quickly sank beneath the surface. But unlike the first man, he did not reappear, for he was weighted down by his unrepented sins and lack of true faith, and the lake

became his grave.

75 Seeing this, the servants were terrified, thinking they would be blamed for their master's death, they came back to the shore, shaking in fear.

76 But once back on shore, they were approached by a well-known doctor of the law who had come to question Yeshua. He had the scribe who attended him write a note to which he gave his seal, saying he had witnessed their master command them to throw him into the lake because he thought he would be healed by Yeshua of Nazareth.

77 He absolved the servants of guilt in their master's death upon the promise that they would testify against Yeshua as culpable, should they be called upon before the Sanhedrin.

78 Despite the death of the rich man and the sinister actions of the doctor of law, the mood among most of the people was jubilant, with the happiest being those in the water that had been healed, with a digression in happiness obvious as the people stood further away from the shore of the lake.

79 The people standing most distant were those who felt Yeshua was speaking to them when he said that those who were not pure in their hearts and intentions should return to their homes. They did not share in the joy of those closer to the lake, but neither had they been able to pull themselves away. They were fascinated by the possibilities, but unwilling to embrace the purity Yeshua had asked of them.

80 After all the worthy who had desired to be healed had come forth, the boat came in closer to shore and the disciples went into the water and waded toward the shore until they were waist deep.

81 Then Yeshua called forth unto the multitude, saying, "All who have forsaken their wickedness and waywardness from the simple teachings of the commandments of Sinai and the Great Commandment and, in humility, seek to be born again into the greater Celestine Light of Elohim, come forth now to one of my disciples and be baptized that you may begin from this moment forth to be filled with the spirit of Elohim and ever guided on the paths of greater light and joy."

82 The people came forth, and the disciples baptized them one by one, and forty-two people were baptized that day in Lake Gennesaret.

83 By the following day, the multitude had dispersed, and everyone had returned to their towns and homes. But during the coming weeks, another ten families moved to the Community of Light at Lake Gennesaret from among those that had been present on the day of the healings in the lake.

CHAPTER 36

Callings of the Children of Light

Yeshua speaks to the Children of Light about the many religious sects that will spring up in his name once he has departed from the earth, but warns that none will contain the wholeness of his teachings. Only the Children of Light will know and live the true Celestine Light of Elohim, for they are "in the world but not of it" as they do not allow the world to hold sway over their lives. He explains to the Children of Light what it means to be a Child of Light and the gifts bestowed upon all of them by Heavenly Father and Heavenly Mother.

nd it came to pass that on the following day, Yeshua called a meeting of his disciples and the Council of Eleven whom Cephas had called to lead the Community of Light, and they met in privacy up on a hill beyond the community.

2 Everyone wondered what it was that Yeshua had called them for, and they spoke about it in hushed voices with one another before he walked among them, for he had been up beyond, in the wilderness, meditating.

3 Yeshua called upon Martha to say a short prayer to begin the meeting; then he said unto them, "My brothers and sisters of light, thank you for gathering here today. I must speak to you of the coming days and how our community must be and become.

4 I will be with you but for a short time longer. Understand that no man could take my life save I willed it to be so, and I so do will it that you might see with your own eyes that you are far more than this frail, mortal body.

5 For as my mortal body passes, my eternal soul still lives. As my eternal soul lives, so it shall become one with an immortal body, as physical and tangible as the man before you, but glorified and perfected that it will never die.

6 As you see me do, so shall each of you do.

7 You are sons and daughters of God, and I am merely your elder brother upon the earth to show you the way to your greatness and the inheritance of all that our Father and Mother in Heaven wait to pour upon their good and faithful children.

8 We live in a world of turmoil, and many good people look to a God of their conception to help them to cope with the burdens of life upon their shoulders.

9 In the days to come, there shall be many sects that shall spring up in my name, not just in Palestine, but across the world. They will have a likeness of godliness, but it will be wrapped around their previous upbringing and beliefs about the nature of God.

10 There will come a great and powerful church from Rome that will trample under foot all of the other sects that follow after me. With pomp and ritual and the authority of the emperor, they shall hold sway over the world in my name, but I will know them not.

11 The generation after I have returned to our Father and Mother, Rome shall destroy much of the land of Palestine. Even the temple at Jerusalem shall be laid to ruins.

12 The teachings that I give to you have never been meant for all the people of the world, for most in the world cannot accept truths that are so different from what they have known; and even if they could accept them, they are not sufficient masters of themselves to live them.

13 That is why they are of the world, and you are not, because you both know the truth, and you live it.

14 When I have returned to our Father and Mother in the Celestine Lights, you must go out into the world to teach the precepts and understandings I have given you, for though there are not many, scattered far and wide are your fellow brothers and sisters of the light, and you must find them.

15 Know that you will be reviled and ridiculed by the people of the world, and by many of the sects who desire to teach a form of my teachings without the substance.

16 Some of you will be put to death, unless you heed the warning of Elohim and flee ere your persecutors arrive or have become Adepts of the Celestine Light and need fear no men. But some of you will not flee. And most of you will not have taken the time to become the Adepts you need to be.

17 But when choice is to be made in your life, I would rather you become an Adept than not or rather you flee than perish. Think not that there is any less honor in avoiding death in my name than there is in accepting it, for Elohim would not have warned you, save it be that it would be better for you to live rather than die; for in life there is still much good you can do.

18 When I am no longer among you, continue to live in this community and call those of true Celestine Light to come and live here with you.

19 Let the disciples I have called and any they shall call be emissaries of the Celestine Light and go forth into the world and find those who wait for you.

20 When you find them, and remember they shall be few in number, ask them to journey here to become one with the Community of Light.

21 Do not draw attention to yourselves or concentrate only in one town, for then you will be seen as a threat by the Romans. See that the community is spread all along the north shore of the lake. Let the members of our Family of Light live in Bethsaida, Capernaum, Chorazin, and Gennesaret.

22 Know that even as you seek out your other brothers and sisters of the light in the world, that the sects I have spoken of shall grow larger than you by far and all in my name or a perversion of it.

23 Even as they create stories of my life and teachings that are not true, they shall deny the accounts of my life and words that you teach which are true.

24 Do not fight against them in any way. Let your countenance always be one of peace toward them. Even in their perversion of the truth, they are bringing more light to their followers than they had before. In this, I am grateful and so should you be.

25 And any true son or daughter of the greater Celestine Light will be drawn to you when they hear the words you say, despite all the obstacles that may be before them.

26 I shall be calling twelve to be my special witnesses. They will walk with me wherever I go until the day that I walk upon the earth no more.

27 Because there will be many false teachings in the world, always cherish the words of the twelve I have called, for they will not speak of things they have heard about me, but of things they have seen with their own eyes and heard with their own ears.

28 Know that if there be any who would say something about me that is contrary to the word of one of my special witnesses, you may always know with assurance that the word of the witness is true.

29 In the mouth of two or more witnesses attesting in agreement to that which they have seen and heard shall all be established.

30 To that, there is but one exception. Miriam is the special witness of the special witnesses. Only she has been present since the beginning to see all things or hear them from my lips. She is the sacred scroll of my life and teachings. Cherish her and protect her, even as she shall cherish you and protect you.

31 Beyond this, there is nothing. Though many will go forth into the world in my name and will convert many people to a semblance of the Celestine Light that I brought, if they do not teach the same precepts and understandings of my special witnesses who received their knowledge from me, then they teach a doctrine of their own imagination.

32 Think not that the Community of Light shall ever be large or prominent in the world. How could that be? You are not of the world.

33 In this world, there are people of all races, cultures, and positions of prominence, from the emperor who is Caesar to the lowliest slave. In this cornucopia of people, you exist. Some of you are of one color or shade and some of another. Some of you have been affluent, and some have lived in simplicity.

34 In the world, those things all have significance, but among you, they mean nothing. Never forget—you are in the world, but you must not be of it.

35 You might say that you are just a simple fisherman who has lived on this lake all of your life or a simple woman who has been just a wife and mother. But I say unto you that you are far more.

36 You are in the world, but you are not of it. The world looks at you, but they do not see you for whom or what you are. Even many of you look at one another and do not comprehend who it is that you gaze upon.

37 "When I say that you are sons and daughters of God, do you think I am just using a figure of speech? I am not just using a figure of speech. You are as much a son or daughter of Elohim as I am.

38 The souls of all the people of the world were created by our Heavenly Father and Mother; therefore, all are literally sons and daughters of God. But with you, there is far more than just that.

39 Before you came down into the body your soul now wears, you lived in the Celestine Lights. Much the same as this life, you could choose right or wrong, and you did some good things, as well as some things in need of repentance. The same is true for all people.

40 What separates the Children of Light from all others is that you were exceedingly good in your prelife in the Celestine Realm, and you received a greater reward in this life than all others, even as those who are exceedingly virtuous in this life shall be rewarded greater than the less virtuous, in the next life.

41 Some of you will say that you have had nothing but misery and challenge in this life, so how could it be that you have been rewarded greater than others?

42 But you are thinking of the rewards of the world when you say that, and it is not with the treasures of the world that your Heavenly Father and Mother reward you.

43 Your challenges in mortality are merely opportunities to build your eternal character and become greater than you are and to forge eternal relationships based upon the essence of your character and not upon your worldly ways or possessions.

44 Therefore, give thanks and pray for greater strength and understanding, not for your burdens to be taken from you. By this, you may become greater than your challenges and overcome them and become still greater in the essence of your eternal soul.

45 How is it then that you have been made greater in this life by the goodness of your souls in your preexistence?

46 Listen closely now, for I will reveal a great secret unto you: The greatest souls of the preexistent Celestine Realm were given a portion of the essence of Elohim to abide within their mortal bodies.

47 Therefore, while all souls are sons and daughters of Elohim, all souls were not created equally. A very few, and you are numbered among them, were given a portion of the physical

light of Elohim to reside within them in mortality. This is your reward for a life in the premortal realms that was well lived.

48 With the Celestine Light of Elohim that within you physically dwells, you can do marvelous wonders when you become Adepts of the Celestine Light. Verily, there is nothing that you have seen me do that you cannot also do and even more than this, if you have enough knowledge, confidence in yourself, and faith in Elohim.

49 If you say, with confidence born from knowledge and faith, to that tree, 'Uproot and be thrown upon the mountain,' it shall be done. If you say unto the mountain, 'Take up and be cast into the sea,' it shall be done, by the power of Elohim that is alive within you.

50 The Greeks will tell you that there are laws of nature to which all things must abide, such as if you throw a rock up in the air, it will fall to the ground. But I say unto you that there is much more to the laws of nature given by Elohim than the Greeks can ever know."

51 Then taking up a fist-size rock, Yeshua threw it up into the sky. Everyone watched as it reached its apex and began to fall again to the earth. But when it was at the height of their heads, it just stopped and remained standing still in the air, neither rising nor falling.

52 Then the rock rose slowly until it was about the height of two men above the ground and then remained motionless.

53 Yeshua taught them, "To each of you and all the true Children of Light is given the power to know the thoughts of men and have influence upon them, to know the thoughts of one another without speaking, to heal your body and the bodies of others of all manner of infirmities, to call upon the sun or the storms, to see events of the future that will unfold, to have slight control of time and the ability to change the essence of one thing to another.

54 And like this rock or the tree cast upon the mountain or the mountain upon the sea, it has been given to Adepts of the Celestine Light to have the power to make rise that which the world would say cannot rise and to make fall that which the world would say cannot fall.

55 All these powers and more I have not spoken of sleep inside of you, waiting to be awakened by your confidence and faith. Are there any of you who have that confidence and faith today?"

56 Notwithstanding their amazement at the rock that hung still suspended in the air, most everyone nodded their heads affirmatively, and Cephas said, "I know my faith in Elohim is like a mountain. Of my confidence, I am not so sure, for though I believe if you say we can do these things, then surely we can do them, convincing myself that I actually can is another net of fish."

57 Yeshua pointed at the rock above and said unto him, "The test is easy, brother Cephas. Fetch that rock from the sky however you can by the powers manifested by your confidence and faith."

58 The eyes of Cephas became very large as he contemplated the challenge before him, but he went into intense concentration and tried to will the rock back to earth but it would not move. He excused his lack of success, saying, "It is by your power that it remains where it is, and surely I cannot be greater than you, no matter the strength of my confidence or faith."

59 Yeshua answered him, saying, "By my power it floats in the sky, but as soon as any one of you manifests the barest power to move it, so it shall be moved as you will."

60 Once again, Cephas concentrated upon moving the stone to the ground, but once more, he was disappointed.

61 Others came forward and made a similar attempt, until five had tried and failed.

62 Then Miriam stepped forward and bowed her head to Yeshua, saying, "I will fetch the stone, my Lord, that my brothers and sisters may know with assurance that the powers we have been given are as you have said, that their confidence and faith may be emboldened by what they see me do, even as I have been emboldened by the many miracles I have seen you do."

63 With that, she made as if to step upon an invisible step, and in a heartbeat, her body rose off the ground until she hovered before the stone and gently grasping it in her hand, she descended slowly and gracefully back to the earth, until standing beside Yeshua, she opened her hand and presented the stone to him.

64 There were gasps of overwhelming surprise and awe, for this was an ability of the Celestine Light; more than any had ever seen. Yeshua explained, "Marvel not at this, for you can do likewise, if along with your faith your confidence is borne from a foundation of knowledge of the mysteries of Celestine Light, as it is for Miriam.

65 To hold a stone floating in the air or to rise above the walls of the prisons that would hold you, or walk across the lake that would impede you, are merely manifestations of one of the abilities Elohim gave each of the Children of Light to be used with prudence and thankfulness by those who grow in knowledge of the secrets of Celestine Light and become Adepts of the highest.

66 Now I reveal these things to you that you will open your thoughts to the magnificence that you can become, for only by thinking of yourself in greater terms than you have can you begin to become greater than you have been.

67 And more than this, I have asked you to go into the world and find the other Children of Light, but how will you know them? You will meet many good and honest people of many different faiths and beliefs. In the years to come, many will say they follow me.

68 Look to discover those who are pure in heart, who are virtuous in their life, who honor the temple of their body and have one of the sacred abilities I spoke of, or who have them not but are drawn to discover and know of them.

69 By this means, you can begin to winnow the wheat from the chaff, for the false doctors of religion and philosophy will flee with condemnation from things they can never have or understand.

70 But the true Children of Light in their virtue and goodness will be drawn to the Celestine Light, even as one lodestone is irresistibly attracted to another.

71 Beware of those who would seek these powers for dark purposes. These gifts of Elohim are only to be used in righteousness, virtue, and selflessness.

72 If any would seek to know of or use these powers for unrighteous, unvirtuous, or selfish purposes, then you may know with assurance that they are not Children of Light.

73 Nor ever think to yourselves to use your special gifts for any purpose other than one that is righteous, virtuous, and unselfish. For that which you might so unworthily gain in this life will be taken from you sevenfold in the next life.

74 Nor should you ever use your special gifts except in secrecy and privacy, or within the sanctity of a quorum of the Children of Light, or in defense of the Children of Light. Other than that, let the people of the world remain blind and in ignorance to things beyond their understanding or appreciation.

75 There may also come a time when you will seek to use your special gifts for noble and righteous purposes, only to find they will not manifest. Know that there will be times when Elohim, who knows all that is, may deem it better for the situation to remain as it is than for you to change it by use of your special gifts.

76 Perhaps one day as night is falling, you are late for an important gathering that will begin on the other side of the lake at sunrise. You think to yourself to walk across the lake at night when no one can see you, only to find that when you step on the water you sink into it.

77 In times like this, know that Elohim is watching over you and that there is more importance in your staying the night on this side of the lake or taking a ferry in the morning than there is for you to make the journey at night, by foot, across the lake.

78 In the days to come, there will also be Children of Light who are seduced by the world and become Children of Darkness; it was even so in the premortal realms.

79 Because their special gifts are a physical part of them given by Elohim as a birthright and magnified by the knowledge and experience they have gained, they remain even when they turn from the light, but only in a weak semblance of their potential, for they cannot be fully empowered without virtue and faith in Elohim.

80 Nevertheless, such wayward children can cause harm in the world with gifts that were

intended only to bring great good.

81 Therefore, whenever you encounter a Child of Light that has become a Child of Darkness, first go to them and try to turn them back into the light.

82 If they will not turn back to the light, let three of you go into a place of privacy and form the Circle of Three and, by the power of three, remove the special gifts of Elohim from their body and the knowledge from their mind, that they may manifest the powers of Elohim no more.

83 Now why is it that I have told you all of these things at this time? And why only to each of you and not all of the members of the Community of Light?

84 Some of you are my special witnesses and must know all things, and all of you are leaders of the community which shall continue to grow and prosper.

85 It is my desire that you remember the words I have spoken and the things you have seen this day. You hold a sacred responsibility as leaders of the community. You must be able to utilize your special gifts in times of need, such as when a member is sick, or when a storm threatens, or when the Romans would come to take that which is not theirs to take.

86 In the coming days, you shall make this north end of Lake Gennesaret like a garden, but know that it will soon have to be left behind, for the Children of Light must soon leave this place.

87 Among the tribe of Judah in the land of Palestine, there are many who think the end of the world is coming soon. The end of their little world as they have known it is coming, but the larger world that holds the children of men will continue, and the suffering they will know here will not even be heard as a rumor in many a far place.

88 Even as you strive to make this a garden, you also need to be preparing for the days to come when you will be here no more.

89 This community is the egg that must be nurtured with great care, for it will bring forth the radiant birds of Celestine Light that will illuminate the world.

90 When the ways of the world come upon you and surround you, know that your time of departure draws nigh. When the wind brings word of the movement of the Romans toward the communities of Gennesaret, know it is time to go. Teach this to your brothers and sisters in the community and to your children, that all will be prepared.

91 Cherish this time of community for such a family will not come again for millennia.

92 While you are here, grow in the Celestine Light of Elohim, edify one another, increase in the ability to use your gifts, and ever seek out other Children of Light in lands near and far, baptize them, and send them to the communities at Gennesaret, that they may learn and grow further among their own kind.

93 From the travels abroad of those called to be Apostles and Seventies, you should establish places of refuge, not for the entire community, but for a family here and another there.

94 Once the time of departure has come, leave quickly to the many places you have pre-appointed, some to Egypt, some to Syria, some to Greece, some to Rome, some to the land of the Gauls, some to the land of Anish, some to islands in the seas, some to the lands of the Nubians, and some to the lands beyond these.

95 Were you to remain as one community in Palestine, you would soon be beset by those who would destroy that which is different than they are, and instead of a life of peace, you would have a life of confrontation.

96 It will be hard to separate from those who are like you and go into unknown places, but it is only by this that the true Celestine Light of Elohim will spread across the world, unseen by the eyes of the men of the world, but found by other Children of Light wherever they may be. And I give my promise to this generation that the faithful Children of Light though scattered shall be reunited.

97 But make good use of the time of dispersion to plant the seeds of Celestine Light among many peoples. From the seeds may plants of beauty grow and prosper that from generation to generation there will be a light here and a light there and another there, all across the world of darkness.

98 As the great religions grow in power and breadth, let the true Celestine Light of Elohim remain hidden, kept in sacredness by those who are called to it in ways the world could never understand.

99 Every year as time goes on, Heavenly Father and Mother will send down to earth a greater number of their more righteous and virtuous children, and they shall teach their children the ways of Celestine Light and they will teach theirs, even as each of you shall teach the ways of light to your children.

100 While the people of the world grow in numbers and the churches of the world wax great, the Children of Light shall remain hidden until one hundred generations have passed, when there shall be enough of them upon the world that by their united powers, they can change the world from darkness to light.

101 Upon that day, the fullness of the Celestine Light will be brought again upon all the earth, that the Children of Light may know it in fullness and inherit their destiny."

CHAPTER 37

The Gifts of Elohim

Yeshua further expounds upon the gifts of the Children of Light: when to use them and when not to use them. He also explains the five points of the star of light by which all miracles occur.

The following day, after completing the Contemplative Movements at sunrise, Yeshua departed with Miriam and his disciples on the road to Tiberias.

2 While walking, Yohhanan asked, "Concerning the special gifts we have been given as Children of Light, I am still uncertain of how or when to manifest my gifts."

3 Yeshua answered him, saying, "Your gifts are to be used only in selflessness for the glory of God and only before the eyes of true believers, when there is a true need. If a man who is committed to the Celestine Light asks you to show him the special gifts of God it is rumored that you have, show them not, not in the least degree, for there is no purpose in this except fostering pride in you and false faith in him.

4 If an unbeliever says that if you will but show him a miracle he will believe, turn your back and walk away from him, for faith built on miracles is like a house built upon sand that will fall at the first great storm.

5 The majesty of Elohim is not a circus, and those who ask first for a sign have not yet found Elohim in their heart, and it is only those who have first found Elohim in their heart that should ever be privileged to witness the powers of the Celestine Light upon the earth; but even then, only when there is a need."

6 Cephas interjected, saying, "But you have healed those with great infirmities before the eyes of many nonbelievers, even the Sadducees and Pharisees."

7 Yeshua answered him, saying, "I desired the enemies of righteousness to know me, and thus it must be that all is fulfilled as it should be. But you will have enough challenges without drawing undue attention to yourself with miracles given before the Ganish.

8 To help you prosper in the days to come, I have shown miracles to many people. This is necessary, for many are called but few are chosen, and there must be many who see but do not believe, to find the precious few who see and do believe.

9 Miracles were necessary through me that the word of it would spread quickly across the land near and far that the true Children of Light would hear of it and come unto me. Among those, the spirit of Elohim moves in their heart, and they will follow me and come to you.

10 The Celestine Light that emanates from me is meant for but a short time upon the earth, and the greater glory is in my leaving, when my light shall shine even brighter through the lives of those who love me and keep my teachings.

11 Know that your light is meant to be longer upon the earth, that you may seek out other

Children of Light and help them to find the true path. But this, do quietly, out of the sight of men of the world, or seen, but thought to be of no consequence.

12 Verily, it is better to be thought mad than to be proved true to the eyes of the unbelieving Ganish. For an unbeliever who witnesses a miracle with his own eyes will be an unbeliever still, and instead of simply dismissing you as mad or a charlatan and letting you go your way in peace, he will now fear you and seek to control and confine you because of his fear.

13 If the Romans call you before them and threaten you with death lest you show them your powers of the Celestine Light, show not the gifts that they can see while they look upon you, but when they look away, do as you must to be free.

14 If you have ears to hear, listen well. One of the most powerful of all gifts is not to walk upon the water or to raise a stone into the air or command a flame to appear, for these visible powers are all things that the magicians of Egypt can also do.

15 Your great power as a Child of Light is to exert the Celestine essence of Elohim that is within you, to protect yourself and your loved ones, to heal the sick by imparting to them a portion of the essence of Heaven and of your own vitality, and to influence and change the thoughts of men, and in this, you can begin to change the world.

16 Though you desire that all men would come to love and live the Celestine Light of Elohim, it is not possible, except for those who are first prepared and desire in their heart to bury the sins of their past and live the higher light as a way of life.

17 Therefore, though it is never righteous to compel a man to God, it is righteous to expand and project the Celestine essence of Elohim that is within you so that the man is touched by your words in the deepest part of his heart.

18 Then it must be on his own that he wrestles with himself to discover whether he can live what his heart knows is true.

19 But to any who would compel you to do that which is evil, or impede your freedom to worship Elohim and live in the ways of Celestine Light, or imprison you unrighteously, you are justified in projecting the power of Elohim upon them, that they would desire and act to change the wrong they have done unto you.

20 When you exert the Celestine essence of Elohim within you, the minds of men can be led to paths they would not have chosen, and this is justified if it is for righteousness sake.

21 Thus, when you are imprisoned by your persecutors, you are justified to exert the Celestine power of Elohim within you that your guards will desire to set you free and remember the circumstances not at all.

22 But think well before you act, and pray to Elohim for guidance, for the better path might be to remain in prison if that is where you can do a greater good.

23 For in all things, as special emissaries of Elohim, you will be led upon paths and to places where it is important for you to be, both for your growth and for the purposes of Elohim that you may know not.

24 So too will you meet people, even adversaries, whom it is important that you should meet.

25 Though it may at first be a mystery to you, never forget who you are and why you are here upon the earth.

26 Look therefore with wonder upon the places and people that come into your life, however simple or even undesirable they may seem, seek with humble prayer to ever understand the purposes of your life, and the places you end up being, and the people whom you meet."

27 Then Ya'akov asked, "How is it that we can manifest our own gifts? What exactly do we need to do or learn? Since the miracles we witnessed yesterday, even Miriam flying like a bird, I have tried to lift just a single grain of sand, but though I can blow it away with my breath or wipe it away with my hand, by no other means can I get it to move."

28 Yeshua answered him, saying, "What purpose of Elohim would be served by you moving a grain of sand? If you were to move it without purpose, you would soon be doing it often and would become proud and vain because of your ability, because it was serving you but not serving

Elohim.

29 It is possible for you to move a grain of sand or a rock even without a righteous purpose, and if you continued to practice, you would succeed because it is a gift given to you as a birthright by Elohim.

30 If you use your gift for things that are trivial, you will not be able to manifest it for things that are great, for that which becomes common is not valued. But if you have learned the Celestine secret of moving both sand and mountains, then your practice would be with the purpose to perfect your gift. Therefore, the first essential is to gain the secret knowledge necessary to accomplish the miracle.

31 There are five points to the star of Celestine Light by which all miracles occur, and only with confidence, humility, faith, awe, and love can the great miracles be accomplished. And before confidence comes, you must have knowledge."

32 "If I cannot practice my gifts on small things such as moving a grain of sand, then how will I ever know that I have any gifts? Ya'akov asked. "And how will I discover other Children of Light out in the world if our gifts must be kept in secret?"

33 Yeshua answered him, saying, "You may use your gifts often and with power for the purposes of Elohim. You should practice your gifts by embodying the five-pointed star of Celestine Light and prove to yourself that you are a vessel for the miracles of Heaven by using your gifts for selfless and righteous purposes.

34 Simply remember the five-pointed star as you seek to become proficient in the use of your gifts. The stronger each of the five points is, the greater will your gifts be able to manifest.

35 Once you embody the five points, practice on as many grains of sand as you desire until you have perfected your gift. But know that even if you never move a grain of sand, you should still be supremely confident that you do have special gifts, for I have told you that you do.

36 You must not be puffed up with pride because of your gifts, but humbled by the honor that Elohim has bestowed upon you.

37 And how do you relate to Elohim, the unseen God? Do you know Elohim the Father and Mother, even as you know me? Is your faith great enough that though not seeing, you still know the living God and feel the spirit of the living God moving in your heart? Is your faith great enough that though not hearing, the voice of Elohim still speaks as a still, small voice silently in your head, imparting wisdom you did not know, ever showing you the way to go?

38 The greater your faith, the greater your power.

39 It is for this cause that you neither see nor hear Elohim while you sojourn in mortality, except as the warm feeling that overwhelms your heart or as the still, small voice in your head that tells you the truth you did not know or in your dreams that seem so real.

40 If you could see and hear God as men see and hear one another, what would be the need of faith?

41 Give thanks for your blindness and deafness, for it is through them that you learn to listen with the part of you that is of God and learn to hear your Father and Mother in Heaven when they give inspiration to your head, seek you in dreams, or touch your heart and move you to good actions.

42 Because of your deafness and blindness, you can build the faith that moves mountains.

43 Let confidence, humility, and faith lead to awe and wonder in the majesty of all Elohim has created and the power of God that has been given to you to come forth as the lightning of the storm and the balm that calms the storm and heals all wounds.

44 Lastly, draw upon your love. If faith is the power of your gifts, love is the activator.

45 You must have a love that burns as a passion that can never be dimmed in your heart, for without it, confidence, humility, awe, and faith are for naught.

46 Whatever gift you desire to manifest, you must first focus on a love that will activate the gift.

47 If you are in prison for the sake of Elohim and desire to be free, think of the love you have

for God. Become one with the passion of pure love that it may activate your commands.

48 If you are asked to heal a young girl, think of your own daughter or son and how much you love them. Feel the passion of your love for them, then lay your hands upon the infirmed and, with your gifts, empowered by your confidence, humility, awe, faith, and love, heal them!

49 Concerning finding the other Children of Light in the world, you will seldom see them manifesting their gifts, for most will not know yet that they have them, and those who know will likely hide them for their own safety lest they be thought a witch and stoned.

50 But when you preach, you will speak of the gifts given to the Children of Light. There will be those that hear you and know that they have the gifts, and they will be righteous and virtuous and honor the temple of their body, and they will come to you as the spirit of Elohim moves them to be among their own kind.

51 And there will be those who hear you and know not that they have the gifts, but they will find themselves drawn and fascinated to learn of them. Those that are also drawn to live in righteousness and virtue and honor their bodies as temples are surely Children of Light.

52 But those who are drawn to learn of the special gifts of Elohim but do not desire to live in righteousness and virtue, honoring the temples of their bodies, are not called to be Children of Light at that time, and they should be taught no more of the special gifts of Elohim.

53 But some of those have just lost their way and are too weak to be masters of themselves.

54 Therefore, do not turn away sincere seekers of truth, even those who are not strong enough to be their own masters.

55 Instead, show them a path where they can become the master of themselves, where they can throw off the old and love to live in the new. Then let them wrestle with themselves to see which will be the victor.

56 When the master of self has won, and they are ready to be born again, lead them to the gate that they may enter and discover how much greater light fulfills than darkness.

57 And all who walk through the gate of virtue shall become Children of Light and inherit all that Elohim has to give to the worthy and the righteous."

CHAPTER 38

The Calling of Mattayah

Yeshua speaks to Mattayah, a tax collector, who invites him to his house to share the midday meal so that he can learn more of his teachings. Yeshua is condemned by the Pharisees for eating with Publicans and speaking to those known to be liars, thieves, and adulterers. Yeshua asks Mattayah to be one of his disciples and Mattayah accepts.

And it came to pass that Yeshua journeyed into Tiberias accompanied by Miriam and his disciples.

2 Near midday, as Yeshua was walking through the town, he saw a man named Mattayah sitting at the Custom House, and he went up to speak with him, saying, "I know there is light in your heart. Therefore, why do you labor in the darkness for Caesar?"

3 Mattayah was startled by the question of Yeshua and disquieted to be seen in the company of the notorious Galilean and his disciples, for Yeshua's fame had spread throughout Galilee, and he said unto him, "I am just a simple man, working as best I can to feed my family. I know Publicans are not well thought of, but I do my best to treat all men fairly."

4 Yeshua answered him, saying, "Is it fair to take the coins earned by a man's diligent toil and labor and give them to Caesar, who labored not for them, to live in luxury, gluttony, debauchery, and idleness?"

5 Mattayah put his finger to his mouth and, speaking in a whispered voice, bade Yeshua, "Do not speak thus, good man, for I have seen zealots imprisoned and crucified for less."

6 Yeshua responded firmly, "You have called me a good man, but if good men stand idly by while evil is rendered and speak not against it or do not take actions to thwart it, then they are as guilty as they who committed the evil."

7 Mattayah shook his head in disagreement, saying, "Taxes are not matters of choice. Paying what is due is not like standing idle while a man is murdered before your eyes. Therefore, it is not just to call this an evil.

8 To not pay is to die at worst or bring great misery to your house at best and all for something that cannot be changed by the common man.

9 Whether taxes are just or unjust is not even a question to consider, because they are as they are, and to speak against them is fruitless. They are a compulsion that brings severe penalties for any who would try to escape them or entice others to avoid them. How then could obeying a compulsion be evil?

10 I am warning you in the strongest terms to stick with preaching religion and not to meddle with the affairs of the government."

11 "Are you afraid then to talk with me?" Yeshua asked.

12 "Not at all," Mattayah answered. "It is you, being a man of faith, who has people that follow you and look up to you that should be afraid to be seen speaking to me, a Publican. I do not think my company will be good for your reputation."

13 Yeshua turned and opened his arm pointing at Miriam and his disciples, saying, "This is my beloved wife Miriam, and these are my brothers and disciples: Cephas, Yakov, Amram, Ya'akov, Yohhanan and Philip. It is important that they do see me speaking with you; that they may know with a surety that it is not among those who have found the light that they will do their greatest work, but among those that still are in the darkness.

14 Mattayah looked surprised at Yeshua's answer, and he said unto him, "If you have neither fear of persecution from the Romans nor being reviled by your followers, then accept my invitation to share the midday meal, for I desire to hear more of your teachings that I might better understand the mystery that you are."

15 And it came to pass that as Yeshua sat at the midday meal with Mattayah, other Publicans came also to eat and he was sitting among several. And there sat others at the Custom House, also eating their midday meal, who were known to be liars, thieves, and adulterers.

16 When the Pharisees saw him eating and speaking freely with such people, they beckoned to his disciples to meet them outside of the Custom House, and they asked them, "Why does your master eat and drink and speak with Publicans and sinners?"

17 But Yeshua heard their words, and standing to address them, he spoke loudly so they and everyone else could hear, "They that are whole and well have no need of a physician, but only those who are sick.

18 Go and learn the meaning of that, and Elohim will show you mercy.

19 Be warned that murderous sacrifices will not bring you to the reward you seek, nor make you the man you think you are.

20 Only having a love for Elohim that causes you to live as God lives and a love for others that is not constrained by prejudice and class can mark you as a man of God and a worthy Child of Light.

21 Know that I am here to bring the Celestine Light of Elohim to everyone and have come to call those who are lost out of darkness, just as much as to call those who have always walked a good path into the greater Celestine Light.

22 When a man who has lived in a darkened pit repents and pulls himself up from the depths of darkness into the light, it is a greater journey than when the virtuous repent and become more virtuous, and the Celestine Light thus gained by the greater journey brings also a greater bliss."

23 The Pharisees scoffed at him and departed, deriding Yeshua for his words, and he admonished his disciples, saying, "Remember to teach by both precept and example. Nor ever forget that every person upon the earth was born as a son or daughter of God, even the Pharisees and the Publicans.

24 Though many have lost their way and sinned greatly, all save those who have murdered or fought with vile against Elohim can come again into the light from whence they came with a sincere and just repentance."

25 Then turning to Mattayah, he said, "Mattayah, son of Cleopas, you are as you have said, a man of fairness, as you have been given to understand what is fair. But I call you now to a high and holy calling. Repent of your sins this day and follow me. I will give you a greater light, even the greatest light that men may have, and by this, you will see all the world through new eyes, and the man you truly are will breathe the first breath of life."

26 And Mattayah, to his own surprise, was moved to tears, as his heart was overcome with a peace and joy he had never known. He fell to his knees and kissed the feet of Yeshua, saying, "I feel a power moving over me such as I have never imagined, and it can only be the power of the Almighty God.

27 My very flesh tingles and is alive such as it has never been. I know not what will become of me and my family, but never have I known as surely what I know now. Yeshua of Nazareth, lead me where you will and I will follow."

CHAPTER 39

Standing for the Truth

Mattayah throws a big feast and invites his friends and fellow Publicans to announce that he is now a follower of Yeshua and is resigning his duties as a Publican. He gives a moving testimony of his conversion. Outside his house, the Pharisees, as well as some of Yochanan's disciples, question Yeshua as to why he is feasting on a day that should be set aside for fasting according to "the law." Yeshua explains the true value of fasting and when it is appropriate to fast.

The following day while Mattayah was at his large house, preparing to begin journeying with Yeshua in his travels, Yeshua, Miriam, and the disciples came to him, as Yeshua had promised they would meet him again at midday.

2 In anticipation of his coming, Mattayah prepared a feast and invited his friends and fellow Publicans, so when Yeshua arrived, there was already a crowd of people present and many were already eating and drinking.

3 The disciples of Yeshua were somewhat reluctant to go into the house of Mattayah, for Publicans were considered unclean in their culture and to even enter the house would be to become unclean.

4 Cephas broached the subject with Yeshua, saying, "I feel uncomfortable to enter this house. Look at the people who go there. They are not of the light but of darkness. They eat and drink, and certainly much worse as well, and continually do evil to their fellow men by exercising unrighteous dominion. How can this be a place for us? Surely you do not wish Miriam to be seen in the company of such people."

5 "You speak truth, Cephas," Yeshua answered. "But if those who are in the dark never are shown the light, how then will they ever know it? By entering into Mattayah's house, we are not condoning corrupt and evil choices that have been made by those within. And we are having an opportunity to show them by our example a better way. An opportunity we would not likely incur in our accustomed travels.

6 Yet you must never forget that all men and women were created as sons and daughters of God, and there is redemption and forgiveness for all who would repent of their evil and turn to the light.

7 Thus has it been for Mattayah, and thus it can be for others as well, but only if those who have the light first reveal it unto those who do not.

8 Once the light has been shown, those who walk in darkness no longer can say, 'I knew of no other way.'

9 Never hesitate to show the Celestine Light of Elohim, even to the most corrupted, for there always remains an ember of Heaven in the heart of every man and woman, and if encouraged

and shown the way, it can be fanned into a flame of virtue and righteousness.

10 But woe to those who see the light and still mock it and turn their backs upon it. They will have no excuse when the Judgment of Resonance is upon them.

11 When they cry out in agony in the life to come, it will be from within the prison they built for themselves.

12 Those who choose to follow darkness, even when a torch is held high lighting a better path, choose not in ignorance, but in knowledge, and therefore close the door to their prison with their own hand."

13 Cephas nodded in understanding as Yeshua, Miriam, and the disciples entered into the house of Mattayah and were quickly amongst a throng of Publicans, overlords, and harlots.

14 Yeshua went straightaway to Mattayah and said unto him, "It is good that you have called those who have known you to be here today, that they might see a man they have never seen. Show them by your words and your deeds the man of light that you have become."

15 Mattayah answered him, saying, "But how will I know this new man? I just met him yesterday and still have much to learn of his ways."

16 Yeshua smiled at his answer and told him, "The man you are seeking to know has been with you for every breath of life, merely hidden away by the worldly man that had prevailed.

17 Listen now to the still, small voice of the Celestine Mother, who has ever whispered to your heart that you would know right from wrong.

18 Listen to the voice you have always heard. Only now, heed the gentle promptings of your heart and the sure knowledge of your head, for they will ever guide you to say and do that which is right."

19 And it came to pass that Mattayah did as Yeshua bade, and he listened to the still, small voice of Celestine Light inside his heart and head.

20 And he called out to his friends and associates, and they all turned to hear him and he said unto them, "This is a farewell feast, and I thank you all for coming. In the coming days, my family and I shall be moving to Capernaum to live in the communities of the Celestines, which have been established on the north end of the lake."

21 Upon hearing these words, many of the people who were present laughed heartily, for they thought he was jesting. And one of the Publicans said unto him, "We have heard of that community and trust me, Mattayah, they would not let you through the gate, nor would you want to go, for they do not eat meat; you can do nothing of pleasure there; they follow a crazy prophet named Yeshua; and it is rumored they are zealots who have a special hatred for Publicans."

22 Mattayah laughed with them and said, "You are right, Helias, the Mattayah you knew would never desire to go to the place you have described. But the Mattayah you knew disappeared yesterday. More than that, the Mattayah you knew died yesterday by his own hand and desire.

23 The person you see standing before you now may look the same on the outside, but on the inside, he has become a different man."

24 Then pointing to Yeshua, who was leaning with his back against a column, with Miriam standing beside him, he said, "And that crazy Yeshua you spoke of? There he stands. Behold the light of the world!"

25 Helias looked to Yeshua at whom Mattayah pointed and laughed again, saying, "That fellow? Surely you are jesting. He is dressed in the simple clothes of a worker of the land. You expect me to believe that you, who have so much, are going to walk away from all of this and follow after this man who obviously has so little?"

26 Mattayah held up his hand and, in a most serious voice, said unto him, "Stop, Helias. Cease to speak in disrespect to Yeshua. There is more to a man than the clothes he wears. And there is a depth to this man that will pierce you to your soul.

27 I have said that he is the light of the world, and I know this as certainly as I know the sun will rise tomorrow, though it was just yesterday that I met him.

28 For the essence of Yeshua flows out from him and fills the heart of any who in sincerity

seeks a greater light, even as I sought and I found.

29 Life is more than eating and drinking and making merry, and then tomorrow we die. For in death we do not die, and in life we have not truly lived.

30 Though many have hated me because I am a Publican, you know that I am also an honest man.

31 There is much I still must learn myself about the ways of light, but there is also much I have always known, but had forgotten, that now has again come upon me.

32 Therefore, know that I speak the truth when I admonish you to listen and hear the words of Yeshua of Nazareth and his disciples who are among us. Open your hearts and your thoughts to a light greater than you have lived, and you may find like I have, that a warmth fills your heart more sweet than any you have ever known, and a peace comes upon you which no travail of the world will ever overcome.

33 You whom I have called my friends, hear now the greatest admonition of friendship I can give, do not in ignorance close your hearts to Yeshua, but hear his words and the words of his disciples, and see if they do not touch your heart with a beam of light that calls out to the nobility of greatness that still beats within you."

34 And it came to pass that many in the crowd who were at the feast were touched by the words of Mattayah and the change they had seen come upon him in just a day.

35 And the disciples of Yeshua mingled among them and engaged them in conversation. And to those who would listen in sincerity, they taught the foundations of the Celestine Light of Yeshua. And the feast of Mattayah lasted into the night as the conversations continued in earnestness and few wanted to leave.

36 And it came to pass that three of the disciples of Yochanan came to the house of Mattayah, and they encountered four Pharisees standing without, looking in, and making critical comments among themselves as to the things they witnessed and imagined were going on inside the house.

37 The disciples of Yochanan came up to the Pharisees who were discussing fasting, for the day upon which those in the house of Mattayah were feasting was a day that had been set aside among the Pharisees and the Hebrews for fasting. And the disciples of Yochanan also were fasting on this day.

38 Standing together, the disciples of Yochanan engaged the Pharisees in conversation, concerning fasting, and Hosea, one of the disciples said, "I do not understand how Yeshua, whom Yochanan loved, can so blatantly disregard that today is a day to fast."

39 "That is the least of it!" cried one of the Pharisees. "He is not only feasting on a day he should be fasting, but he is cavorting with all manner of sinners. By his very actions, he is repudiating his own claim to be a man of God."

40 Hosea was not so quick to judge. He said, "We should go and ask him about this, for Yochanan would not have loved him had he not been worthy. Therefore, let us go and find an explanation for such outrageous behavior."

41 The Pharisees demurred, saying, "We will not cross the threshold of a house so unclean lest we be tarnished. Perhaps, he could be enticed to come out here that we might question him."

42 In the house of Mattayah, Miriam pulled lightly on the robe of Yeshua to get his attention and whispered, "I have heard the words that the Pharisees and the disciples of Yochanan speak without understanding in the street beyond the house. Without hearing a voice, I have heard them. Let us go out to them now, that you may speak with them, for they are afraid to enter into the house of Mattayah, but I know the followers of Yochanan are good and upright men."

43 Yeshua smiled and put his arm around Miriam, and speaking softly into her ear, he said unto her, "It is with joy that I see you use your gifts, from rising to grasp the stone in the air to hearing the voices beyond your ears. Remember to help the others to discover and use their gifts as well."

44 Then Yeshua beckoned to Cephas and Amram to come with them, and the four of them went out to the street and walked up to the group of seven men talking amongst themselves.

45 Seeing them coming, the circle of men parted, forming a half circle that they might all face Yeshua. Spreading his arms at waist level, with palms facing toward them, he said unto them, "He whom you seek is before you."

46 They looked about themselves nervously, for his appearance and words were unexpected. Then Hosea said unto him, "Today is a day of fasting among all who are devout. How is it that we fast and the Pharisees fast, but you and your disciples not only do not fast, but insult the sanctity of this day by feasting?"

47 Yeshua answered him, saying, "Those who fast each week on Mondays because it is said to be the day that Moses went up to the mountain and then again on Thursdays because that is said to be the day he came down from the mountain and then again nearly every tenth day for some other purpose to supposedly please God, know not the God whose favor they seek.

48 Elohim is a God of people and of love, not of continually repeated ritualistic laws, the obeying of which becomes more important than the lives of the children of God.

49 According to the Scroll of Fasts, a widow who recently lost her husband may not mourn on a day of fasting. What God worthy to be honored as such would be so callous as to tell a widow she could not mourn her lost husband, but instead that fasting again, and again, and again, was more important?

50 Men have told you that this is what you must do to please God, but instead of listening to traditions and the laws of men and priests, listen to your heart, because it is in your heart that the true words of God are spoken and where you will find the Celestine Light of Elohim that surpasses all the laws of men."

51 One of the Pharisees stepped forward, saying, "You speak only of fasting as if that is all that we do, but it is merely one of the three holies required to prove true devotion. These are not our laws, but laws that have been handed down from God through the prophets from generation to generation. If you are saying things that are contrary, it is you who is going against the will of God.

52 Fasting alone is for naught. It must be combined with prayer and the giving of alms to show God true devotion. By fasting regularly, we not only remember the great teachings of Moses, but we also show God that we are willing to punish ourselves in mortification for our sins.

53 By our prayers we show that we know our forgiveness and reward can only come from God.

54 By giving alms, we show that we earn coin only for God, not for ourselves, and show our compassion for the poor, even as we pray that Elohim will have compassion upon us."

55 "You hypocrites!" Yeshua said unto them with a raised voice. "You fast and pray and give alms twice each week and almost every tenth day to show Elohim your contriteness for your sins, but if you had truly repented of your sins, you would do them no more!

56 Woe unto those who think they can sin and do penance with a fast and a prayer and a handful of alms, then sin again the following days, only to once again find forgiveness by a repeated fast and prayer and gift of alms.

57 Think you that the favor of Elohim can be bought with a fast and a prayer and a handful of alms?

58 You Pharisees, in your false piety, give trespass offering every day for sins of which you are ignorant. Think you that Elohim cares so much about your imperfections that things so trivial that you cannot even remember them are going to draw the wrath of God?

59 Elohim forgives the sinner who repents of their sins and sins no more, but does not forgive the sinner who sins and thinks by simply following the rituals of the law that they can be cleansed.

60 You are not perfect, and Elohim looks with a forgiving eye upon those who in their weakness do small sins, but each day strives to be better.

61 But for those who commit grievous sins, who steal, and fornicate, and commit adultery,

and murder, and exercise unrighteous dominion over others, their forgiveness comes only with a true repentance and a forsaking of the sin.

62 If you truly repented, you would sin no more; therefore, if you fast to cleanse your sins, why then would it need to be done twice a week?

63 Verily, fasting is important at the time of repentance to help you to find the place of humility and sorrow that brings about a true repentance.

64 But the man who fasts twice a week either obeys the law like a sheep and knows not the God he proclaims or is a hypocrite who never repents and therefore always feels a need to fast, having never abandoned his sins.

65 Other than in pursuit of true repentance, a fast should only be used on rare and special times in a man's life when he seeks to spiritually rise to a higher understanding of Elohim and the Celestine ways of God.

66 Or for health, once a month to cleanse the body and mind of accumulated sludge, a fast is useful, but should not be required. Let each help themselves as they will.

67 For these reasons, neither I nor my disciples, nor the Children of Light, fast on this day or on any of the days prescribed by the law.

68 We fast when it has true meaning and brings about a true transformation of the body and soul, not merely because it is one of many ritualistic days set aside to fast."

69 The Pharisees were angry at the words of Yeshua, but they knew not how to reply to him, and they stormed off, muttering to themselves. But the disciples of Yochanan remained, for they had been touched by his words. And Hosea asked, "Good teacher, how is it that Yochanan taught us to fast often, but you do not?"

70 Yeshua answered him, saying, "That you were disciples of Yochanan speaks already of your devotion to God. It was given to you to learn more of the mysteries of Elohim because of your worthiness, and for this cause fasting can be of benefit. Therefore, Yochanan encouraged you to fast often to aid you in your quests.

71 But search your memories and you will discover that in his encouragement, he never admonished you to fast as the Pharisees fast or to fast on a frequently repeated schedule, for then the very purpose of fasting is lost in repetition.

72 Yochanan is my brother of spirit more than any other man. I speak the very words he would speak, so you know that I speak true. Therefore, you know that Yochanan would never teach that frequently repeated ritual would draw one closer to God.

73 Only with a heart that beats as one with the Celestine spirit of Elohim may man become more than man and become a Child of Light."

CHAPTER 40

The Old and the New

When Yeshua is questioned by the disciples of Yochanan as to why so many of the old ways and customs must change, he explains the significance of the new.

And it came to pass that the disciples of Yochanan came to understand and believe in the teachings of Yeshua as they continued to speak with Cephas and Amram, and on the following day, they agreed to gather their families and accompany Mattayah and his wife and children to Capernaum to become a part of the Family of Light.

2 But among the guests who had known Mattayah and came to his feast, none came unto the light at that time or desired to learn more of the teachings of Yeshua.

3 Before they departed, Hosea, who was the eldest among the three disciples of Yochanan, sought further enlightenment from Yeshua, saying, "Good teacher, everything you speak of and that we have heard from your disciples seems so new and different from all that our people have lived for generations upon generations. Perhaps we have strayed some, but is it really necessary to change so many traditions and introduce so many new doctrines and do away with so much of the old?"

4 Yeshua answered him, saying, "If you have new fermenting wine, do you put it into old bottles or new?"

5 "New," Hosea answered.

6 "And why is that?" Yeshua asked.

7 Hosea gazed at him for a moment with a somewhat-curious look and then answered, "If you put new fermenting wine into an old wine skin, it will swell and burst the bottle and all the wine will be lost."

8 And so it is with the Celestine Light of Elohim, which I bring," Yeshua said unto him. "It cannot be merged with the ways of old, for they cannot bear its light, and in bursting both the new and the old, the good that had been gained would be lost.

9 For this cause, I have said that I have not come to uphold the law, but to destroy it. In that, the scribes and Pharisees and Sadducees fear, thinking I am trying to rip asunder that which they hold dear.

10 But the ways of old will remain, for it is better that men have some truth to live by than none at all.

11 Only a precious few will be able to understand and embrace the greater Celestine Light that I bring, and not all of them will bear it when they first learn of the new covenant I have brought.

12 Some will have to chew upon it, and ponder it, and pray about it, and speak with others to

hear of the good and the bad that they might comment, even as few men having drunk old wine will straightaway desire new wine, for they will say to themselves that the old is better.

13 And it is only after they have been convinced by their pondering and praying that they will consider that perhaps this new wine is from a grape that has never been and is delicious beyond all that is aged.

14 Therefore, because I love the precious few who will dare to drink the new wine, I do not remake the old, but give them the new in all of its glory.

15 Seeking to repair the old would be to invite misery upon all, even as no man sews a piece of new cloth onto an old garment; else, the new piece that filled it up will take away from the old and the rent is made worse.

16 Most people are like the wheels of a cart in a rut worn deep; they are comfortable in their rut even if it does not bring them to the most wonderful places, and they would protest in anger and violence should someone try to move the cart.

17 But those who are Children of Light do not feel comfort in the rut, but imprisoned. When they see the new path I make before them, they see freedom, and a new cord pulls upon their heart, calling them home to a Celestine glory beyond."

18 And it came to pass that at the request of Yeshua, Mattayah took his family to Capernaum, and Philip the disciple went with them that he might introduce them to the members of the community and to help them get settled.

19 And the three disciples of Yochanan and their families also came with them.

20 Before they left, Philip inquired of Yeshua as to what was to be done with the Passover that was coming in the next days, for Yeshua and most of the disciples would be away from their families if they did not return to the Communities of Light on Lake Gennesaret.

21 Calling all of the disciples to him, including Miriam and Mattayah and the disciples of Yochanan, Yeshua answered Philip, saying, "If there are those among the Communities of Light that wish to keep the Passover, then let them keep it as they will.

22 But you are no longer that people, nor are any who come among us from whatever tribe or race or religion, who they once were.

23 You have been given the greater Celestine Light of Elohim and that which is old has been laid in the grave.

24 Though the time has already passed this spring, henceforth let the Children of Light celebrate the seasons of the earth, which Elohim has given for the joy and abundance of man.[a]

25 Let there be celebrations on the day of greatest light and the day of longest night and upon the days twice each year, when the day and the night are equal.

26 Let the spring celebrate renewal.

27 Let the summer celebrate life.

28 Let the fall celebrate abundance.

29 Let the winter celebrate the light of Elohim, which pierces the darkest night.

30 Let these be special times of the year when you fast and pray as you deem best and make special efforts to touch the light of Elohim in your heart and soul and become greater than you are.

31 Do not become as the people of the world who have holidays or special religious requirements many days in each month.

32 These four times of celebration are sufficient for the Children of Light and will have more significance in your lives if they are not cluttered among numerous celebrations.

33 Make these days and the days leading up to them very special, and they shall carry you to higher and higher heights every year of your life upon the earth."

(a) Celestines celebrate four seasonal holidays during the times of the year Yeshua specified. These are:

Spring Equinox: Excelsior: Celebration of Renewal
Summer Solstice: Vitalta: Celebration of Life
Fall Equinox: Majakpler: Celebration of Abundance
Winter Solstice: Luminaire: Celebration of Light

CHAPTER 41

Passover at Jerusalem

Yeshua heals an infirmed man on the Sabbath but is condemned by the Pharisees for breaking the Sabbath and commanding another to do likewise. After speaking with Yeshua, they seek to find ways to have him killed.

nd it came to pass that Yeshua, Miriam, and the remaining disciples that were with them went into Jerusalem during the time of Passover, but they did not celebrate it as did the tribes of Judah, the Levi, and the other Children of Israel.

2 Now there was in Jerusalem, by the sheep market, a pool, which was called Bethesda in Hebrew.

3 In and around this pool lay a great multitude of the blind and the withered, waiting for the waters of the pool to move in sudden waves.

4 For it was believed that from time to time, an angel would come down and blow upon the water, stirring the waves in only a place, and whosoever should get into the water and get to that place first would be healed of their infirmity.

5 A certain man was there, named Gesari, who had been weakened and enfeebled for thirty-eight years. Each day of his later life, he had pulled himself from his sleeping space to the edge of the pool, hoping that someday, he would be the one to reach the waters stirred by the angel and be healed of his infirmity.

6 When Yeshua came upon the Bethesda pool, he saw Gesari and knew that he had been infirmed for most of his life, and walking up to him, he asked, "Do you desire to be made whole?"

7 Gesari looked up with hope alive in his eyes and said, "Sir, I desire it so greatly that I have crawled on my elbows to this spot every day for more years than I can remember. But I have no servant or friend to put me in the water when it is stirred, so always there is someone else who steps in before me and is healed while I remain as I am."

8 Yeshua looked upon him and asked, "Are all who step first into the water after it has been stirred healed?"

9 Gesari shook his head and answered, "No, only a few, but even knowing a healing only happens for some, I still have faith God will bless me if I can just show him I am faithful enough to make it into the water before all others."

10 Yeshua continued to question him, asking, "Why do you think some are healed and some are not?"

11 Gesari answered him, saying, "It is by the grace of God that an angel comes to stir the water, but God does not reward the wicked. Therefore, only the righteous are healed."

12 "Why then do the unrighteous go into the water, if only the righteous are healed?" Yeshua

asked.

13 "Because they do not believe it is an angel that stirs the water, but magic they know not," Gesari answered. "Therefore, they enter in ignorance and take the place of those like me who live in righteousness and could truly be healed in the waters."

14 "And how is it you are righteous?" Yeshua inquired.

15 "In my heart, I love God," Gesari answered. "Many have said that God has cursed me and wonder why I do not revile him. But I know that I have become as I am that I might grow stronger in my faith. God rewards those who endure, and I shall never deny him or turn my back upon him.

16 Though I am crippled, I have learned many things over the years from lying here each day and observing the people and the way they are, things I never would have learned if I had not become as I am.

17 Therefore, I still thank God each day for all the things he has allowed me to learn because of my infirmity."

18 Hearing this, Yeshua had a tear that fell from his eye and ran down his cheek, and turning to Miriam and his disciples, he said, "In this man, see the faith of ages."

19 Then turning to the man, he asked, "Do you know who I am?"

20 Gesari shook his head, saying, "No, kind sir, I am afraid I know you not. But I perceive that you are a teacher or a preacher, for you dress well, but simply, and there are several in your party, and they watch and listen to you with great attention."

21 Then Yeshua said unto him, "I am Yeshua of Nazareth. I am the Alpha and the Omega, and I say unto you now, good brother of light, Rise up; take your bed and walk. Remain righteous in your words and deeds, lest a worse thing befall you."

22 Immediately, the man stood up and was made whole. Throwing his hands up into the air, he shouted with joy, and then fell at the feet of Yeshua, kissing them and giving thanks. Standing up sprightly, he grabbed his bed, picked it up, and walked away to go to his family to show them the miracle that had been wrought.

23 Though there were many other of the infirmed lying about the Bethesda pool, none asked Yeshua to heal them, and they turned their faces from him, for it was perceived that he had broken the Sabbath.

24 As he was walking away from the pool of Bethesda, Gesari encountered three Pharisees, and seeing him whole, they confronted him, asking, "How is it that we saw you yesterday and you were enfeebled and infirmed as you have always been, and now you are a new man made whole? Cursed man, you reward the miracle God has wrought by breaking the Sabbath and carrying your bed?"

25 Gesari protested their accusations, saying, "For thirty-eight long years, I have been infirmed. But on this day, I have been made whole. A man came up to me and told me to stand and pick up my bed and walk, and I knew in my heart that as he commanded so it would be. So I stood and picked up my bed and walked as he bade me do."

26 "Who is this great Sabbath breaker?" the Pharisees inquired.

27 Gesari pointed back toward the Bethesda pool, where Yeshua remained with his disciples, and he said, "It was that tall man there, Yeshua of Nazareth, whom the others gather around. But I assure you he is a man of God."

28 "How can you, an ungrateful Sabbath breaker, recognize a man of God?" the Pharisees taunted.

29 And they approached Yeshua and asked, "Was it you that healed a man on the Sabbath and then commanded him to break the Sabbath by carrying his bed?"

30 Yeshua, knowing the time had come to reveal himself to his adversaries, answered them, saying, "My Father in Heaven does good works upon this day, and as I have seen my Father do, so do I likewise. And a man who carries a bed on the Sabbath, not for work, but in celebration of a miracle of God, is honoring Elohim and the Sabbath."

31 The Pharisees were beside themselves in anger, for not only had he broken the Sabbath and taught others to do the same, but he had also called God his Father, making himself equal with God. And in unison, they cried out, "Blasphemer!"

32 But Yeshua answered and said unto them, "Verily, I say unto you: The Son can do nothing of himself, but only what he has seen the Father first do. And whatsoever the Father does, these things also shall the Son do likewise.

33 For the Father loves the Son and shows him all the things which he does, and he will show him greater works than what has happened here today.

34 Verily, you shall yet see the Son do mighty works for which even you will marvel.

35 For as the Father rises up the dead and quickens them back to life, so the Son will quicken whom he will.

36 And the Father shall judge no man, but the fate of a man's eternity shall be judged by the Son, for the Father has committed all judgment unto him.

37 This, that all men might honor the Son, even as they honor the Father.

38 He that honors not the Son, honors not the Father who has sent him.

39 Verily, verily, I say unto you he that lives according to my words and the example of my life, believes on he who sent me and shall inherit everlasting life. They shall never come into the throes of condemnation and shall pass in peace and bliss from death back into life.

40 Verily, I say unto you: The hour is coming when the dead shall hear the voice of the Son of God, and they that hear and follow that which they hear shall live.

41 For as the Father is a life unto himself, so is the Son a life unto himself. They are not one, but two, but the two are one in purpose.

42 "Nor is there a Father without a Mother, for then how could there be a Son?

43 And the Father and the Mother have given the Son authority to execute all the judgments of Heaven, for he is the Son of the Elohim.

44 Marvel not at this, for the hour is coming in which all that are in the graves shall hear my voice, and they shall come forth: they that have done good unto the resurrection of life and exaltation and they who have done evil unto the resurrection of torment and damnation.

45 I can of my own self do nothing. As I see and hear, I judge, and my judgment is just, because I seek not my own will or glory, but the will and glory of my Father and Mother who have sent me.

46 If I alone bear witness of myself, my witness is not true.

47 But you know the other who has borne witness of me; even Yochanan the Baptizer and all who love God know that witness is true.

48 You went unto Yochanan and heard his words and his testimony of me, for he bore witness of the truth he knew more than any man.

49 But I need not be upheld by the testimony of any man, for the very spirit of God testifies of me in the heart of any true seeker of the light.

50 But I speak to you of Yochanan, that you might remember the man and his testimony and turn your heart from cold to warm, that you might yet be saved.

51 There is a greater witness in the world of the Son than that of Yochanan, and that is the works which the Father has given me to finish, the same works which I now do. And greater things shall you yet see and hear of, bearing witness of me, and know that the Elohim have sent me.

52 The Father himself has borne witness of me by the power of Heaven which I hold. And the voice of the Mother ever speaks my name into the ears of those who would hear.

53 But you have never seen his shape or heard her voice, for Elohim cannot dwell in unclean vessels.

54 You have not had his words abide in you and have not felt her spirit stirring your soul. Therefore, he whom the Elohim have sent, you believe not.

55 Search the scriptures, for in them, you imagine you have eternal life, and in them, you will

find testimony of me.
56 But even knowing the truth, like a fire burning inside that you cannot deny, you still, in
your stubbornness and devotion to the law and tradition, will not come unto me that you might
have life.
57 But I do not expect to receive honor from the men of the world, for how can they honor
he whom they do not know.
58 But it is by your choice that you know me not, nor desire to learn of me and the Celestine
Light I have brought. Therefore, I know that you do not have the love or light of God within you.
59 I have come in my Father's name, and you receive me not. Yet if another Pharisee were to
come in his own name and do the things that I do, you would receive him and honor him.
60 How can you seek the honor of one another and not seek the honor that comes only from
God?
61 Do you think that it will be me who accuses you to the Father? It will not be me, but
Moses whom you revere. He will accuse, and I shall judge you and weigh your soul in the balance
by the resonance in your heart, which will be testified to by the actions of your life and the words
you have spoken.
62 But Moses will first judge you as hypocrites, for you say you believe Moses and believe the
words he wrote, but you do not believe, for he wrote of me.
63 And if you believe not the words of Moses, whom you revere, how then shall you believe
my words?"
64 The Pharisees were beside themselves with anger but could find no words to respond to
him. Angrily, they stormed away and returned to their conclaves in Jerusalem to spread ill words
about Yeshua of Nazareth.
65 From that day forth, they sought to find ways in which they might have him killed, for
not only had he broken the Sabbath and commanded others to do likewise and said that God
was his Father, but he had also said that there was a Mother in Heaven, even as many among the
Gentiles and pagans believed.

CHAPTER 42

By Their Love You Will Know Them

Yeshua is once again condemned by the Pharisees for breaking the Sabbath when his disciples eat some ears of corn while walking through a cornfield. Yeshua heals a man of a withered hand while teaching at the synagogue, which further angers the Pharisees for once again breaking the law of the Sabbath, and they plot anew in ways to have him destroyed.

During the following Sabbath Yeshua, Miriam and his disciples walked through a cornfield, and his disciples who were hungry began to pluck some ears of corn and eat them.

2 Seeing this, Yeshua reminded them to leave a coin for the farmer in payment for that which they had eaten, for they had taken without asking.

3 But when the Pharisees saw it, they chastised him, "Behold, your disciples have done that which is not lawful to do on the Sabbath day."

4 Yeshua answered them, saying, "Have you not read what David did, in the days of Abiathar the high priest, when he and those who were with him were hungry; how they entered into the house of God and ate the shewbread, which was not lawful for them to eat, neither for those who were with him, but only for the priests?

5 Or have you not read in the law that if a priest who is serving in the temple violates the Sabbath, they are blameless?

6 Think you that David or the priests are greater than the Lord of the Sabbath?

7 Verily, if you understood the meaning of the words of Elohim, that I desire mercy, not sacrifice, you would not have condemned these innocent men.

8 The Sabbath was made for man, not man for the Sabbath.

9 If you have ears to hear and eyes to see, use them, for I say unto you that in this place is one greater than the priest, even one greater than the temple, even the Lord of the Sabbath."

10 From the cornfield, Yeshua went straightaway to the synagogue to teach, and the Pharisees followed to see if they could catch him in more acts of breaking the laws of the Sabbath.

11 Yeshua walked among the people in the synagogue, and they parted like the sea before Moses to let him pass, for word that he was coming had preceded his steps.

12 Standing before them, Yeshua said unto them, "You have heard it said that a pious man prays many times a day and gives alms to the temple or synagogue. But I say unto you, of what good to the God of Heaven are alms given to priests or prayers said upon prayers, simply for the sake of praying?

13 If you would give alms, give them until you feel their loss in your own comfort.

14 Give some to support the synagogue and temple but not all, for Elohim would see you make your own good choices.

15 Give a tenth of your excess to the synagogue and temple to support your spiritual community, but then give what remains of your excess to the poor or to your temporal community.

16 Not in random should you give or to the man who says he will distribute your money for you. Give directly to the poor or your community in ways unseen, that you may see the benefit of your alms in the lives of those in need, but that they will not see their benefactor.

17 By this means, you will see with your own eyes that your money has been well-given. Because they will not see their benefactor and only God will see, you will grow in your character, having given for love and not for the acclaim of men.

18 And of what purpose or benefit to either you or Elohim is the endless repetition of the same prayers? Do you think that by praying the same repetitions again and again, you are proving your devotion to God?

19 Nay, you are only proving your slavish acceptance to the dictates of foolishness given by priests that neither brings you closer to God, or God closer to you, and demonstrates a lack of spiritual depth that you do not speak words from your own heart.

20 If you truly wish to be closer to God and to show your devotion, then do so by your good deeds of love and selflessness. Treat others as you hope Elohim will treat you. And when you pray, pray without repetition, but with a connection of love to God as the words flow from the depths of your heart, whatever they may be.

21 If you truly want to hear and feel Elohim in your life, then pray in sincerity and humility and speak with God, not in repetition, but as one friend would speak to another, for the righteous and virtuous have no greater friend than Elohim."

22 There was a man present by the name of Yoab who had been born with a withered hand that hung limply upon his arm. Notwithstanding his infirmity, Yoab was a good man. His countenance was pleasant, and with a smile on his face, he always sought ways to help his brethren and those in need, even as Yeshua had spoken of.

23 After he was finished speaking, Yeshua began to walk out of the synagogue, and he passed next to Yoab. Seeing his withered hand, he said unto him, "Though your hand is withered, your heart is full of love."

24 Yoab nodded his head slowly in silence and then said unto him, "I love every day of life, for it is another day that I can do good in the world. I stopped thinking of my withered hand long ago; else, it would have stopped me from being who I prefer to be.

25 Who can fathom the ways of God? I am as I was created. Perhaps, if I was not born as I was, I would have taken a different path in life, not so fruitful."

26 Now the Pharisees had been watching and listening as Yeshua spoke to Yoab, and sensing that they might trap him into again breaking the Sabbath, and this before many witnesses, they questioned him, asking, "Is it lawful to heal on the Sabbath?"

27 Yeshua answered, saying, "What man among you having many sheep shall see one fall down a pit on the Sabbath and not lay a hold of him and pull him out?

28 How much greater is man than a sheep? Wherefore, I will ask you, is it lawful to do good on the Sabbath or is it better to let evil have its way? Is it lawful to save a life or is it better to let it perish?"

29 And the Pharisees looked at him in silence, not knowing how to answer.

30 Then Yeshua looked around him to see that all eyes were upon him. Then to Yoab, he said, "Stretch forth your hand."

31 Yoab stretched forth his withered hand, and Yeshua held it clasped in both of his hands and said unto him, "Let your hand be as the hand of the man would be if it was in your power to help him."

32 And opening his hands, Yeshua released the hand of Yoab, and it was whole and healthy, and all who saw it marveled.

33 But the Pharisees were filled with madness, and leaving the synagogue in anger, they plotted anew what they might do to Yeshua and how they could bring about his destruction.

34 After they had departed, Yeshua told the people gathered in the synagogue, "Today you have witnessed the power of Elohim, and it did not come from endless prayers of repetition or from the giving of alms that vanish where you know not.
35 It came from love and virtue and righteousness. If you desire the blessings of Heaven, love one another. And let your good deeds done in secret testify of your love.
36 By this means, may you separate the wheat from the chaff and know the people of God from the pretenders; by their love, you shall know them. And from love comes all virtue, righteousness, and good deeds."

CHAPTER 43

Calling of the Twelve Apostles

Yeshua calls to four men in a crowd of people that have never met him in person, to follow him. They join Miriam and his disciples and together hike into the hills to the west. Yeshua calls each of those with him to a high and holy calling as Apostles—special witnesses who will testify of his life and teachings, to act in his name, and be empowered to do all manner of miracles. Those he calls and ordains as Apostles are his wife, Miriam of Magdala, whom he proclaims "Apostle of his Apostles," Cephas of Bethsaida, Yakov of Nazareth—brother of Yeshua—Amram of Bethsaida, Ya'akov of Bethsaida, Yohhanan of Bethsaida, Philip bar Talmai of Bethsaida, Mattayah of Tiberias—son of Cleopas—Shim'on the Zealot, Yuda son of Cleophas, Yuda Toma of Ptolemais—known as Toma—and Yudas Iscariot of Jerusalem.

And it came to pass that Yeshua and Miriam and the other disciples returned to the Communities of Light at Lake Gennesaret.

2 A multitude of people followed them from Judea and Idumaea, bringing with them their infirmed and diseased, calling out periodically for Yeshua to heal them.

3 As they passed through Galilee, the residents drew notice, and word that Yeshua the healer was present spread quickly insomuch that the multitude increased.

4 As they approached the first community, on the northwestern shore of the lake, they spied another large group of strangers waiting beside the road, and coming upon them, they found citizens of Ptolemais and Tyre and Sidon, who, also having heard of the miracles of Yeshua, had come to see him for themselves and to have their relatives healed.

5 As he passed through the throng along the road, many reached out to touch him, hoping to be healed, and it was with great effort that the disciples formed a protective circle around Yeshua and Miriam to prevent them from being crushed by the crowd.

6 Passing through Gennesaret and by Chorazin, Yeshua, Miriam, and the disciples continued on to Capernaum, where they had hoped to part ways, each to their own homes and families, and wait until the following day for Yeshua to speak to the crowd.

7 But the multitude was persistent in their desires for Yeshua to come among them insomuch that they would not leave and began to clamor in their voices for him to come to them.

8 Scarcely had Yeshua and Miriam come near their house, than another group of travelers came upon them from the road to the east, coming from beyond the Jordan.

9 Seeing that something must be done and could not be delayed, Yeshua had Cephas tell the multitude to let Yeshua pass to the lake and then he would speak to them.

10 Yeshua asked Cephas to have a boat ready by the shore to carry away him and Miriam if

the teaming throng pressed too much upon them.
11 Thus it came to pass that Yeshua stood on the shore of the lake with the multitude before him and the lake and a waiting boat behind him, and he said unto them, "I know that you have come to be healed of your infirmities and diseases as you have heard it said that I can do.
12 But I tell you in soberness that I do nothing of my own, but only the will of they who sent me, my Celestine Father and Mother in Heaven.
13 You seek to touch me and be healed, but the power to heal does not emanate from me, but from you.
14 I am merely the water that sprouts the seed of virtue that must first be inside of you.
15 All the water in the world will not sprout a seed that is not there, for my water is holy and it only helps grow a seed which is planted in righteousness and virtue.
16 But do not despair, for I know that many of you have come from far away, and your travel need not be in vain.
17 If you came this day without a seed of righteousness and virtue inside of you, it is in your power to plant one even now.
18 If evil has dwelt in your life where righteousness and virtue should have been, purge it from you now this very moment.
19 In all humility and sincerity, confess your sins to those you have wronged and covenant to them and to God that you shall do them no more.
20 If they are not with you, then confess to someone who knows and cares for you, and if they are not here, then to the stranger beside you.
21 Repentance is a process, and this will begin to lift the weight of your yoke of darkness and help you on the path to a new life.
22 Only by this will the water I give quench your thirst and sprout your seeds and bring you that which you desire.
23 Make camp for the night, and I will come among you again tomorrow. Those who are pure in their heart will get their reward and their past of darkness will be as if it never was."
24 The multitude was quieted by his words and many were humbled, and they threatened no more to press him into the sea in their exuberance.
25 Then he looked into the crowd and announced, "Among you are four men that have never met me, but who know me in their hearts as if they always have. You, of whom I speak, know who you are, and I say unto you: come into the lake and be baptized and then follow me." Upon his command, four men came forth from the crowd with great suddenness as if they were being pushed by an unseen hand, and after giving their names, Cephas and three other disciples baptized them straightaway.
26 Immediately thereafter, Yeshua set forth through the crowd, which parted to let him pass, and Miriam and his disciples came with him, and they were followed by the four men from the multitude.
27 Yeshua walked in silence, holding Miriam's hand, and they passed beyond the borders of Chorazin and into the hills to the west.
28 Arriving upon a knoll, Yeshua sat down, and Miriam was beside him on his right hand. His disciples and the four other men sat down below him in a semicircle facing him, and he said unto them, "Some of you have known me since my youth. Others have only recently heard my words. But all of you are called to a high and holy calling because of your worthiness, both in this life and the life that was before this life.
29 The time has come for you to begin to fulfill your destiny.
30 By this, I do not say that you have an irrevocable compulsion or requirement to fulfill your calling, for your choices in life are always your own.
31 Though you are loved greatly by Elohim, you are never compelled upon a path, merely foreordained and predestined as your reward for lives well kept.
32 But in the end, every day, the choice to do or do not is still yours, because foreordination

is justified only upon continued worthiness and predestination only upon continued desire to remain upon the path.

33 Some of you have been my disciples and the others desire to be so. On this day, at this spot, I call all of you to accept a higher and holier calling. I ask you to be my Apostles, my special witnesses, who, along with Miriam, shall testify of my life and teachings.

34 To you, I give all authority to act in my name, and by acting in my name, you act in the name and on behalf of the Elohim.

35 To you, I empower to do all manner of miracles, even as you see me do. And there is nothing that you see me do that you cannot also do, if you remain worthy; your faith is strong enough, and you learn the secrets of Celestine Light and become true Adepts of the light.

36 Let those who are new among us learn from those who have been with me for a longer time, that all might know the truth of my life and teachings without dilution or change, such as will quickly come among the people once I have returned from whence I came.

37 Once I am no more upon the earth, in all things when there is confusion or a dispute, it is only to Miriam that you can turn for resolution, for she knows every minute of my life and all of my heart. If she speaks of my will, it is as if I had spoken it, for in truth, if she speaks it, I have.

38 But the days will come when Miriam is also no longer among you. In those days, let your decisions be in a quorum and let there be unanimity, for if you are truly being guided by the spirit of Elohim, you will all be guided to the same conclusion and understanding.

39 Now turn to one another and let every man embrace every other man as a brother."

40 The Apostles did as Yeshua bade, and each embraced one another. And in their embrace, there was kindled a divine feeling of brotherhood, different from anything they had ever felt, and it set chill bumps upon them all.

41 Then turning to Miriam, he asked her to kneel before him, and laying his hands upon her head, he said, "Miriam, Child of Light, Daughter of Elohim, beloved of my heart above all others, with the authority of Elohim and by the power of my word, I do ordain you to be my living testament, my Apostle to my Apostles, and the spiritual head of the Quorum of the Twelve while you remain upon the earth.

42 You are granted all the rights, privileges, power, and authority to perform on earth whatever you shall deem necessary in wisdom, virtue, and righteousness for the Celestine Light of Elohim."

43 Miriam then rose, and holding her hands in a prayer position upon her chest, she bowed her head and backed away from Yeshua that another might come forward.

44 Yeshua called Cephas next. Cephas came and knelt down before him, and Yeshua laid his hands upon his head and said unto him, "Cephas, you are the rock of the Celestine Light of Elohim upon the earth, and upon this rock shall the Children of Light always find inspiration to hold fast against the world. With the authority of Elohim and by the power of my word, I do ordain you to be my Apostle and call you to be the organizational head of the Quorum of the Twelve while you remain upon the earth.

45 You are granted all the rights, privileges, power, and authority to perform on earth whatever you shall deem necessary in wisdom, virtue, and righteousness for the Celestine Light of Elohim."

46 Then Cephas rose and holding his hands in a prayer position upon his chest, he bowed his head and backed away from Yeshua that another might come forward.

47 And one by one, each of the Apostles came forward and knelt before Yeshua and were ordained to their Apostleship and given special rights and authority.

48 And these are those who were called and ordained as Apostles and special witnesses to the life and teachings of Yeshua on that day:

49 **Miriam** of Magdala—wife of Yeshua, **Cephas** of Bethsaida, **Yakov** of Nazareth—brother of Yeshua, **Amram** of Bethsaida, **Ya'akov** of Bethsaida, **Yohhanan** of Bethsaida, **Philip** bar Talmai of Bethsaida, **Mattayah** of Tiberias—son of Cleopas, **Shim'on** the Zealot, **Yuda** son of Cleophas, **Yuda** Toma—of Ptolemais—known as Toma, and **Yudas Iscariot** of Jerusalem.

50 Afterward, Yeshua spoke further, saying, "While I remain upon the earth, follow me. Walk

with me on my walks through Galilee and Judea and beyond. Let your brothers and sisters of the community care for your families that you can be with me and be a living testament to my life and works.

51 I know that this is a sacrifice I ask, but I will soon be gone and your families will still be with you. Our time together is precious but short, and it is in the sacrifices we make for one another that the friendships of ages are formed.

52 "After I have returned to the Celestine Lights, go forth two by two to preach my gospel, that those who are dead in spirit might be baptized and born again into the wonder of the Celestine Light. Heal the sick who have repented and have virtue and cast out devils from those possessed, that they might make their way into the light unhindered by the encumbrances of confusion.

53 Take nothing for your journeys, except a simple wooden staff. Carry no bread or bag or money in your tunic. Wear quality but simple clothes, adorned in Celestine ways, and sandals upon your feet, for you will be walking far.

54 Go first into all the towns of Galilee, then into Judea, then into Syria, then into Greece and Rome and Egypt, and all the lands beyond.

55 You will inspire many, and they will form churches, and choose leaders and practice a semblance of my teachings that you have given them.

56 But because of the desire of men to have power over other men, the churches built by men will be ruled by the laws of men, not Elohim, and many of their doctrines will be of man, designed to suppress and control their believers rather than free and uplift them.

57 Nevertheless, do not lament this, for those who are drawn to these churches shall still find more light than they had before, if they seek it.

58 If at some point they should find the true Celestine Light of Elohim inside of them, it will call them to their greatness, and they shall find the children of the Family of Light, wherever you may be.

59 In your travels both near and far, when you discover a true Child of Light, it shall be a rare day and cause for great joy. You shall know them by the resonance of your hearts and spirits.

60 On these days, once they have been baptized and become one with you, have them come to the Communities of Light on Lake Gennesaret and their families with them.

61 As I have said, the day will come when you must abandon the communities on Gennesaret, but until that day bring the Children of Light to it.

62 When Miriam has joined me in the eternal life to come, there shall be none who shall or could take her place, for only she has known me so well. Thereafter, let a quorum seek Elohim in prayer and find unanimous agreement upon all things of common spiritual guidance.

63 When Cephas has joined me in the eternal life to come, let the most senior of you who were my original Apostles take his mantle as leader of the Children of Light, with the unanimous support of the remaining quorum, after a confirmation of prayer.

64 When one of you passes from this life, let those remaining form a quorum and, with a confirmation of prayer, unanimously choose another from among the Children of Light to replace he who has passed.

65 In your choice, consider well women who are worthy and capable, for though men are more often in situations allowing them to travel and preach, it pleases Elohim when sisters of power are not overlooked, but called upon that the Children of Light may benefit from their light.

66 And upon all that you shall call, lay your hands and confer the same powers and authority I have given to you.

67 Finally, the day shall come when the last of you, my original twelve, will no longer be upon the earth. After that day, when there is no longer an original Apostle upon the earth who can speak as an authoritative witness to my life and teachings, let there be no new Apostles until the restoration of all things that shall come in the Epic of Promise to generations unborn.

68 After that day, when there are no more Apostles upon the earth, the Children of Light shall be scattered across the earth, and let each group decide in ways that are best for them and their circumstances, how they shall be led and edify one another.

69 That all might be led by the same light, I charge each of you to write down an account of my teachings and my life such as you know and have been uplifted by. If you are not accomplished in writing, take an honest and worthy scribe to write your words.

70 Do not neglect this important charge, for it is through the chain of the written, as well as the oral words, that the principles of Celestine Light shall continue to edify the Children of Light, generations after generations, after all of us have passed into the eternal life to come.

71 In the days to come, watch me well and listen closely to my words. You shall see me do miracles, but nothing that you cannot also do. Therefore, observe how I speak and the motions I make with my hands and my eyes.

72 Faith powers everything, but if you do not understand how a miracle was done, ask me or Miriam or one of your brethren, until you are sure of the means by which it was accomplished, that you might do likewise, with faith.

73 Beyond the miracles that are seen by the people, there are many other powers, even secret powers, which I desire you to have that you might be a shield to the Children of Light, a source of testament to the faithful, and empowered to walk as a mystery among the children of men.

74 Therefore, watch, listen, and learn, for I shall make you men such as no men have ever been."

CHAPTER 44

Salome

Salome comes to the home of Yeshua, Miriam, and Martha with a great weight of sorrow upon her shoulders as she confesses that she was the cause of Yochanan's death. Yeshua explains the circumstances of the situation to Miriam and Martha, and they welcome her into their home.

nd it came to pass that Yeshua and Miriam and the other Apostles came down from the hill and returned as evening was falling to their homes. They walked through the midst of many people encamped, but were not put upon by them.

2 Yeshua and Miriam approached their home with contentment, looking forward to seeing their children again and Martha, and they spoke in amazement to one another that they had been within sight of their house for a day and were just now making their way to it, for it had been an event-filled day.

3 As they came near the door, they heard Martha speaking with another woman, and Miriam, not recognizing the voice, asked, "I wonder who that is speaking with Martha."

4 Yeshua answered her with a big smile upon his face, "It is the one you have waited for."

5 Before Miriam could ask who that might be, they were at the door and over the threshold.

6 Seeing them, there were cries of joy from Martha and the children, and Yeshua and Miriam were swamped by the many embraces of their family.

7 Through the tangle of arms and heads, Miriam spied an unknown young woman standing against the wall with her head down, so she could not see her face. And looking to Martha who was still embracing her, she asked, "Who is the young woman among us?"

8 Martha pulled away from Miriam, and going over to the young woman, she reached out for her hand and then pulled her toward Miriam and Yeshua. Still the woman would not look up, so they could not see her face. But Miriam noticed that she was dressed in the finest clothes, such as only a noble woman could afford.

9 "Yeshua, Miriam," Martha began, "before I introduce you to this lady, I need to tell you that I have welcomed her into our home. She has a great weight upon her heart, greater than any I have ever known someone to have.

10 I have told her that in her sincere sorrow it should be lifted, but she will not let the weight depart. I hope your words will have more effect than mine; otherwise, I fear she will be crushed by the weight of her sorrow."

11 Then turning to the lady, she said, "Please lift your face and look upon my Lord Yeshua and my sister Miriam. Have no fear; if I have shown you only friendship, they will show you no less."

12 The woman seemed to bring her head up a fraction, but then she broke down into uncontrollable crying and fell into a heap upon the floor. The children of Yeshua and Miriam

and Martha stood around, looking at her uncomfortably, while the adults looked to one another silently seeking a consensus upon how to act.

13 Then Martha gathered the children into their common bedroom, and Yeshua and Miriam knelt one on each side of the woman, each with a hand laid lightly upon her back. And Miriam said unto her, "Milady, do not sorrow so. Speak to us, and let us comfort you."

14 But the woman continued to cry and remain in a heap upon the floor until Martha returned and also knelt beside her, saying, "Come, come, you spoke not ten words to me for hours because you wanted to wait for Yeshua. Well, now he is here; please speak.

15 I have pity for your sorrow for things unknown, but the children are becoming frightened, and nothing is accomplished by having us merely watch you cry. We can help, but you must let us."

16 At the words of Martha, the woman looked up. Even though her face was swollen and red from crying, they saw that she was beautiful. She looked Martha steadfastly in the eye and said in a wavering voice, "I am a murderer. I killed your husband."

17 With that confession, she stopped crying and simply fainted upon the floor.

18 Martha and Miriam looked with confusion at one another and then looked to Yeshua questioningly. He explained, "This is Salome, daughter of Herodias, stepdaughter of Herod. Herod had granted her one request, and her mother compelled her to demand the head of Yochanan, who was in prison. Though it was not her will, it is her enduring sorrow."

19 Martha and Miriam looked to one another and then, still kneeling, embraced each other. Martha took a deep breath, and then exhaling told Miriam, "If Yeshua says that it was not her will, and even still she has such great sorrow for her complicity, I bear her no malice."

20 Miriam nodded her head and said unto Martha, "The beauty of her soul emanates even in the disarray of her body. It is unconditional love that will heal her heart and none more so than from you, the wife of the man whose death she grieves."

21 Then Yeshua reached forward and held the hand of Salome as she lay upon the floor, and he said unto her, "Wake, child, and be at peace."

22 In that instant, she awoke, and still holding her hand, he lifted her up and they all rose with her, until they were all standing side by side, with Yeshua on her right, Martha on her left, and Miriam straight in front of her.

23 Then without a word, the four of them reached out and put their arms around those beside them, and they pulled close into a circle of one embrace, and Yeshua asked Salome, "What do you feel?"

24 She answered him softly, saying, "Love, love such as I have never before felt. Love such as I had never imagined could exist. It fills me. I feel as if I am lifted upon a warm breeze, touching the clouds.

25 But how can this be? How can you touch me, let alone embrace me? You should revile and hate me, for it is only because of me that a great man who was your kin is dead.

26 I have come here not to seek forgiveness, for I know that is not possible, but to ask that I might be the servant of your house for the rest of my life, to make an insufficient, but small amend for the evil I have done."

27 "We are all servants of Elohim," Miriam said looking into her deep brown eyes. "But beyond that, we hold no servants, nor compel any, for we are all brothers and sisters of the light, and though called to different callings, we are all equal in the sight of our Father and Mother in Heaven and judged not by our station in life, but by the Celestine Light of our soul and the evidence of the light in our lives."

28 "How wicked must be my soul then that I could have done such a terrible thing?" Salome protested.

29 Martha gave her a small rub with her hand upon the small of her back and said unto her, "Yeshua has said that you were merely the tool of your mother, and therefore, it is she who has been wicked and must make account before God for the death of my Yochanan."

30 "But, my Lord, you were not there," Salome said softly. "In my weakness, I did do evil, and I must make amends."

31 Yeshua turned so he could look into her eyes and said unto her, "But I was there, Salome. I stood in prison with Yochanan, and together, we watched as your mother compelled you to demand his head from Herod.

32 Though we were unseen to you, Yochanan and I watched as you valiantly tried to defer that which your mother compelled you to do.

33 Even when at last she broke your will, the deed you have sorrowed for all of these days never happened. The moment before the executioner came forward, I held the soul of Yochanan close to me, and before the axe fell upon his neck, his mortal body was already lifeless upon the ground.

34 Even as all mortal bodies shall die, so shall all souls continue on: the righteous to the resurrection of glory. And so has the eternal and glorious soul of Yochanan risen to his glory. He lives still today and shall forevermore.

35 His widow does not grieve, because she knows it is only for a breath of eternity that they have been separated, and together they shall be again.

36 I promise you he looks down upon you even now from the Celestine Realms and has only love for you, even as we do."

37 "You do not hate me?" Salome asked incredulously.

38 In unison, Yeshua, Miriam, and Martha shook their heads and silently affirmed that they did not hate her.

39 Salome spoke to them with quiet astonishment, "Instead, you give me love, such as I have never felt or imagined? What manner of man and women are you? For this is not how people are."

40 Miriam again looked into her eyes with great compassion and, holding her gaze, said unto her, "We are Celestines. We are Children of Light. We are the son and daughters of Elohim, even as you are. We are not as the people of the world, because we are not of this world. We are among them, but they know us not. Only another who is one, as you are, can know the Children of Light."

41 "This is a great deal for me to grasp," Salome said with a sigh of happiness. "I came here feeling on the edge of death, and now I feel more alive than I have ever felt."

42 Then Yeshua spoke unto her, saying, "We must decide now how to care for you and where you shall go . . ."

43 Before he could finish his words, Salome interrupted, saying, "I desire to go no place other than here. Despite your kind words and love, I feel I still have amends to make and desire still to serve your house."

44 "But you are Herod's stepdaughter," Martha pointed out. "Besides the fact that you cannot stay with us as a single woman and that we also have no room in our small house for another, you bring danger to us, for the king shall certainly come looking for you and bring trouble upon us were he to find you here."

45 "I will sleep outside in a shed, on some hay," Salome answered. "And neither Herod nor my mother will come for me, for I am dead to them. I spoke ill to them and very severely. I told them I was coming here to be your servant. At first, Herod thought I was merely trying to connive something from him; then he was incensed.

46 But at the last, it was my mother who threw me into the street, calling me the most vile names, with only these clothes upon my back. She said henceforth I was dead to them.

47 She grabbed Terah, one of her slave girls, and her parting words to me were that Terah was no more, for she was now Salome, and if ever they saw my face again, it would be that I was Terah.

48 Trust me, they will not come looking for me, and it will be as they said. There is surely another Salome now in the palace, even the slave girl Terah, and I am not even a memory."

49 "It is astounding the depths of evil that those of the dark can fall to," Miriam commented. "Certainly, we must find a place for you."

50 Again Salome objected, saying, "This is the place for me; I desire no other. Please do not send me away. I meant the words I spoke. I know I cannot live under your roof, for it would be against the law, but it is with gladness that I will make my bed upon the straw under the stars."

51 Miriam laughed, saying, "The law does not have the same meaning in this house as you have been accustomed to. We will not board you as an animal outside, but in truth, there is not room enough inside."

52 Miriam looked questioningly in silence to Yeshua, seeking his thoughts, and he said unto them, "This week, we will have the men of the community build another room where Salome may stay, and we will welcome her into our home as a friend.

53 Let her serve as she desires. She may travel with us on our journeys or remain and help Martha with the children or choose other tasks that she feels called to.

54 Let her learn of our ways and we of hers, for she has wisdom beyond her years and training such as few women will ever know, having been a daughter of the palace.

55 Let her walk and listen and see and breathe the Communities of Light that she will know her home and her home will know her."

56 Salome could scarcely contain her joy, and she bowed to Yeshua, saying, "Thank you, my Lord. I will do all of those things which you have said and serve in every other way I am able.

57 But most of all, if I may, I desire to walk with you, even as we have heard in the palace that Miriam is said to go all places with you. I desire to learn of your teachings until every word is etched into my heart and flows into the world with every word I speak."

58 Yeshua brought them all together again, holding hands in a circle, and looking upon Salome, he said unto her, "As you have desired, so it shall be."

CHAPTER 45

Sermon on the Mount

Yeshua delivers his most famous sermon to thousands of people on a big hill northwest of Chorazin. He speaks with authority and wisdom as he covers many topics, and his poetic and profound words amaze the people.

The following day, at sunrise, Salome first learned the Contemplative Movements as she stood barefoot upon the ground outside of the house of Yeshua, following the movements she watched Yeshua, Miriam, Martha, and the children doing and listening as Yeshua explained the significance of each movement while he was doing them.

2 Miriam gave her some of her garments to wear, and they put away Salome's expensive bejeweled clothes from the palace so that undue attention would not be drawn to her.

3 Later, Yeshua told the Apostles who she was, but asked them not to reveal her true identity to others for a time.

4 From that day forth, she remained with Yeshua, Miriam, and Martha, and if there were any who condemned them, it was only in their thoughts, for none spoke ill of the arrangement.

5 Within a week, a small room had been added to Yeshua's house by three men from the community so Salome could have a place of privacy of her own as he had promised.

6 Soon after daybreak, multitudes of people began to gather at Yeshua's house from every direction.

7 The eleven Apostles came with their families within two hours of first light, as Yeshua had asked them to do the previous day.

8 Some people called out from the crowd for Yeshua to heal them or to heal one of their relatives that were with them, but he moved about as if he had not heard them.

9 Once Cephas arrived, he spoke to the multitude and asked them to have patience and promised that Yeshua would speak to them soon. And they were calmed by his words insomuch that no longer did any call out to Yeshua to be healed.

10 On the third hour of light, Yeshua, Miriam, and the Apostles commenced a walk toward the hills to the west and all of the people, including Salome and Martha and the children, followed them.

11 The day was beautiful, warm, and sunny, and there was almost a festive atmosphere as people spoke with smiles and cordiality as they followed Yeshua up into the hills.

12 Northwest of Chorazin, about the distance to Capernaum, was a large hillock, and upon this hill, Yeshua and the Apostles settled at the top and the multitude sat down on the ground below him, spreading their linens and setting up their sun tarps. Many of the children played at the base of the hill while their parents sat up higher to hear the words of Yeshua.

13 Spreading and raising both hands high into the air, Yeshua said unto them, "On this beautiful day, with the sun's light and warmth upon you, and the blue sky above you, and the green hills beyond, and the magnificent expanse of lake below, and the songs of birds upon the air, give thanks to Elohim for the glorious world that was made for you to live upon.
14 And I say unto you: Blessed are those who are humble in spirit, for humility opens the gate of Heaven.
15 Blessed are the challenged; those who long to live in the Celestine Light, but are faced with many impediments which block the path to the light. Elohim shall give them comfort.
16 Blessed are the calm; those who are not overcome by their own desires or the chaos around them, but trust in God. They shall have peace in their hearts in the world and inherit the earth to come.
17 Blessed are they who hunger and thirst after righteousness. They hearken to the still, small voice and, with desire and action, seek to fulfill the will of God. They shall be filled overflowing with the Celestine Light that they seek.
18 Blessed are the merciful, who see in the misfortune of others their own life that could be and help others as they would wish to be helped, not just with alms, but also by giving of themselves and their time. They shall be blessed with the mercy of the Almighty.
19 Blessed are the pure in heart; those who are upright and sincere, honest in every thought and activity. They will have the Holy Spirit abiding always with them, and they shall see God with a special witness.
20 Blessed are the peacemakers, both among nations and among neighbors, those who have a peaceful mind and a harmonious heart to resolve the disputes of men. They shall be the treasurers of Elohim, guiding divine peace from the heavens to light the lives of men upon the earth. And they shall be called the Children of God.
21 Blessed are those who are persecuted for righteousness sake; they that live the highest light despite the condemnation of the world. They shall rise a step in Heaven for every lash they take upon the world, and the Kingdom of Heaven shall be theirs.
22 Blessed are you, when you resist evil, and men revile you and persecute you by word and deed and say all manner of evil against you falsely, for my sake.
23 Rejoice and be exceedingly glad, for great is your reward in Heaven, and thus did they persecute the prophets which were before you.
24 You are the salt of the earth, but take heed not to lose your savor or be contaminated by the impure; else with what will the food find its flavor? It would thenceforth be good for nothing, but to be cast out and trodden under the feet of men.
25 You are the Celestine Light of the world. In the example of your life, how you eat and speak and dress and live, you should be as a city upon a hill that cannot be hidden.
26 For you do not light a candle and then hide it under a basket, but put it on a tall candlestick that it can give light to all who are in the house.
27 The world is your house. Therefore, do not hide the Celestine Light of Elohim that burns within you, but hold it high that all the world might be illuminated by your light.
28 Let your light so shine before the world that those who condemn you will know in their hearts that they condemn a Child of God and that those who are lost Children of Elohim will see your light and find their way home.
29 Think not that I have come to uphold the law and the prophets, for I have not come to uphold any but those of truth and to fulfill the promise of Elohim given to men and destroy those that are not.
30 And there is far more to be trampled underfoot than to be upheld, for the teachings of God have been taken and the teachings of man have been given.
31 I am he who is the builder, and I have come to tear down the feeble works of man and to restore the mighty temple of God.
32 Some of you here are of the world, but conquer yourself and you can be numbered among

the Children of Light.

33 Some of you here are Children of Light that have been lost in the world, and now you have found the source of the light, but cannot see how to reconcile the life you have lived with the life you know you should live.

34 Choose that which has eternal significance and you shall have joy, both in this life and the life to come.

35 Some of you here are Children of Light who have committed in your heart and shown by your deeds that you are Children of Light indeed.

36 Unto you, I say that your righteousness must exceed the righteousness of the scribes and Pharisees, for much has been given to you and much is expected.

37 You know that it is the law that you shall not murder, and whosoever murders another shall be judged in both this life and the next.

38 But I say unto you that there are far more ways to murder than killing the body, and all are accountable to God and should be accountable to the laws of men.

39 Therefore, let whoever has a raging anger against another, be it a man or a woman or an animal, be liable to judgment on the earth, even as they shall be in Heaven.

40 For a raging anger is a murderous anger. It is an anger that misses the final blow of murder only because of fear of the consequences.

41 Therefore, I say unto you that a man who has barely controlled anger without a righteous cause and injures a man or a woman or an animal, either in their body or their spirit, must be judged the same as the man who attempted murder and failed.

42 Knowing this, let peace and calm always flow in the heart and mind and thoughts and words of the Children of Light, save in defense against that which is unrighteous.

43 When you speak, speak with respect to all men, and to all women, and to all who work for you, and to all animals. Though you may command them to do this or to do that, do it only with kindness in your words and respect in your thoughts and actions, except for those who do not reciprocate the respect which you give.

44 And if a Child of Light should curse another person without cause or spit Raca unto another, giving contempt without cause, let him come before the council and be held accountable for his actions.

45 Let the Children of Light always be the embodiment of the Celestine Light, especially among one another, especially among husbands and wives and their children.

46 If you have a disagreement with someone, speak of it together and come to a solution with words and reason and respect and love.

47 Do not sulk in silence, for that is only fuel for the fire and shows a disrespect, not just for others, but for yourself and for Elohim.

48 Almost as bad as anger is to treat another, especially a husband, wife, or child, as if they are an idiot and that their thoughts and opinions are not even of worth to listen to with intent to hear.

49 To not listen with respect to the thoughts and opinions of your husband, wife, or children, or brothers and sisters of light, even when you are in disagreement or even when they are simple in their method of explanation, is a grievous sin in the eyes of Elohim, needing not only repentance before God, but restitution to those you have wronged by your words and actions.

50 When you are wrong, admit your wrong with humility and ask the forgiveness of both God and the person you have wronged. And prove your sincerity by restitution to the person you have wronged.

51 Do not think you can alleviate your sin by making an offering before the altar of God and then go your way. First, you must be reconciled with whoever you have wronged, and only then will Elohim recognize your gift before the altar.

52 Do not be hardheaded and unreasonable when you are in the hands of your adversaries, nor docile like a sheep, allowing others to do with you as they will. Endeavor to give them

no cause to do worse to you while you are in their hands, but neither stand idle in defense of righteousness and fairness.

53 Keep your peace until you can stand before the fair and impartial to present the facts. If no fair and impartial are to be found, call upon Elohim to deliver you.

54 You know that by the laws of God and men, it is said that you shall not commit adultery.

55 But I say unto you that whosoever looks upon a married woman or man with lust in their thoughts has already committed adultery in their heart.

56 You see my wife Miriam, beautiful, with her face uncovered, and it is not a sin to look upon her. Nor is it a sin to look upon her and admire her beauty, for she is a creation of Elohim, and you honor Elohim by admiring the creations of Elohim. It would be no different if she were standing here before you naked in all of her splendor.

57 Yet the man who looks upon her with lust, who thinks impure thoughts of her, but does not act upon his thoughts by either word or deed for fear of the consequences, has nevertheless already committed adultery in his heart.

58 This silent adultery may not be punished by man, for it is kept hidden and unknown from men. But it is known to Elohim and shall be punished by God, both in this life and the next.

59 Therefore, if you are weak to lust, you must separate yourself from the temptation, lest you are burned by the fire you start.

60 If your eyes cause you to sin, cover your eyes that you will not see the temptation, for it is better that you are blind to temptation than your whole body and soul is cast into the rubbish dump.

61 Verily, your eyes are the windows of your soul, and what your eyes see, your body becomes. Therefore, let your eyes be focused only upon righteousness, that your whole life may be full of light.

62 And if your right hand is causing you to sin, tie it to your side, lest it lead your whole body away from the light; so demeaned of value that it must be cast into the garbage pile of Ge Hinnom and burned in the fire.

63 Now lust is the greatest temptation of the adversary within: lust for a woman or man, lust for power, lust of gluttony, lust for money. All things of lust lead man to commit acts for which the eternal consequences are far more painful and enduring than the pleasure of the fleeting fulfillment, which is here today and gone tomorrow.

64 Of these, lust for a woman, be she married or not, often clouds the better judgment of man, more so than all other types of lust. Therefore, against this lust must you ever guard.

65 To prevent this lust, by law and tradition, women cover themselves from head to toe in uncomfortable garments that men cannot look upon them and lust.

66 Yet it is not the woman who is sinning, but the man. Therefore, it should not be the woman who must be covered in uncomfortable coverings, but the man.

67 Let the woman dress in comfort and freedom. And if a man finds that seeing the bare skin of a woman causes him to lust, then let the man hide himself away in his house or cover his eyes with a hood or coverings so that he is nearly blind. The woman should not have to suffer because of the sin of the man.

68 That the fires of lust may be righteously quenched, all men and women should also be wed, and this they should do while they are young, shortly after their eighteenth celebration of birth, that the natural lust which Elohim gave to men and women for pleasure and procreation can be satisfied righteously within the bonds of marriage.

69 For the man or woman who is receiving pleasure and fulfillment within their marriage will not give into temptation to look elsewhere.

70 It has always been so, since the beginning of time, that there are more righteous women of light than there are men of light.

71 This will not be changed by all the proselytizing and preaching that you may do, for Elohim has always sent down into the bodies of women, the greater portion of the virtuous and

faithful spirits of Heaven.

72 Therefore, let some among the righteous men of the Children of Light take another wife, one chosen with love by the wife they have, that all righteous women will have the opportunity to be married to virtuous men in this life.

73 And a plural marriage is not just a man to another woman, but also the new wife to the wife that stands already with the man, and among them there shall be no secrets.

74 Nor is it meant for women to be always with child, for how then are they to have a life beyond caring for children? And this is easier to accomplish in righteousness in a house with multiple wives.

75 Verily, the spirits of Heaven wait with joy to come down into a body upon the earth, that they might further grow and expand their light by their choices and experiences.

76 But use alternatives in your intimacy to insure you do not bring children into the world until you are prepared to nurture their hearts, bodies, minds, and spirits, for all who are married will be held accountable, not only for choosing in selfishness to not have children, but also for choosing to have children when they were not prepared to care for them in all ways to encourage their growth, expansion, and happiness.

77 It has been the law that whosoever desires to put away his wife shall give her a certificate of divorce.

78 But I say unto you that wives may put away their husbands as well for just cause and demand lifelong support.

79 But neither the husband nor the wife shall put away the other, save it be for just cause, which is fornication or adultery, or violent or continual torment of the spirit, mind, or body.

80 And whosoever marries someone who has been divorced for fornication or adultery commits adultery by their marriage, save there has first been a true and contrite repentance, including restitution that has washed away the sin of the sinner.

81 Again, you know that the laws of old say that you shall make an oath to God before men to prove the seriousness of your intent.

82 But I say unto you: take no oaths to God before men to demonstrate your veracity or intent, but to men only say yes or no.

83 Let any oaths to Elohim only be for the purposes of Elohim, not for the purposes of man, and these only in private or within a close circle of your brothers and sisters of light.

84 You know that the laws of old say that there should be an eye for an eye and a tooth for a tooth. Yet have you ever known of a judge to demand an eye for an eye or a tooth for a tooth? No, not in all the history has it been so.

85 The meaning of this law then is that when an injury has been given by one to another, that the compensation to the injured must be equal to the injury suffered. No more or no less. And this is a true law of Elohim.

86 But not for all injuries does this apply, but only for those which cause a man grievous or irreparable harm to his life or income.

87 When grievances are more petty than grievous, let them be settled one man to another, one brother to another, one sister to another.

88 When petty disagreements and grievances cannot be settled brother to brother, then let there be a mediation of the family.

89 If the family decides the outcome, but one brother cannot abide the decision, let there be a mediation of those with that responsibility in the Family of Light, and after hearing the facts and circumstances, let their decision be final.

90 Avoid the courts of law except for the most grave matters; those that are so grievous or have caused such irreparable harm that they cannot be reconciled by your family or the Family of Light.

91 Other than this, courts of law will inflict both the petitioner and the defendant with a poison to both their spirit and their life, from which they will not easily recover.

92 There are times when you will be burdened by the unreasonable actions or requirements of others. When these are in opposition to righteousness or of great seriousness, you should oppose them.

93 But often, they are merely an irritation, the acts of bullies and people in power. In such cases, it is better to affect indifference and even go beyond what is demanded, for then you take away their sport and they become bored and let you be.

94 Therefore, if a Roman comes and compels you to carry their pack for a mile, offer to carry it for two.

95 If a man slaps you in the face without cause, turn your other cheek to him as well, provided you or your family or the Family of Light are not threatened with real harm.

96 But if your family or the Family of Light is threatened, or your own life or safety, do as you must to defend yourself, but in that, do nothing that will make the matter worse.

97 If a man asks your help, turn him not away. And if a brother or sister asks to borrow that which you own, let them have it as long you are not in need of it at that time and think not for its return until they either bring it back to you as a good steward should or you have need of it again.

98 You have heard in the laws of old that it is said to love your neighbors and to hate your enemies.

99 But I say unto you, hate not your enemies; love them as misguided children of God. Ask for blessings upon those that curse you that they might find the errors of their ways and do good deeds even for those that hate you, that their hate might be turned into admiration and respect.

100 Pray for those who spitefully use you or persecute you, that you might always be an example of the higher path walked by the Children of Light, who show by their lives that they are true sons and daughters of God.

101 Remember Elohim loves all the children of men and makes the sun to shine and the rain to fall for the blessing and benefit of everyone, both the good and the evil, the just and the unjust. Can you do any less than your Mother and Father in Heaven?

102 For if you only have love for those who love you, what could be your reward? For even the Publicans do the same.

103 And if you give greetings only to your brothers and sisters of light and ignore the wayward in the world, how are you any different than the Publicans or Pharisees, for do they not do the same?

104 Therefore, strive each day to be better in every way than the day before and strive each day to live your life in ways that are loving and virtuous and just, even as Elohim is loving and virtuous and just with you, even in your imperfections.

105 Take heed that when you give alms, you do not do it before men to be seen. Do not sound a trumpet for the poor to gather and know that it is you who is their benefactor.

106 But when you give alms, do it in secret, that only those overseeing the largesse's may know from whence it came, and even then, if you give in anonymity, it is more pleasing unto God. And that which you do in secret shall be rewarded openly to you by Elohim.

107 When you give alms, do so without consideration for how much you are giving, except to be sure that it is not too little. Other than that, do not let your right hand, which gives alms, know how much your left hand took from your purse.

108 And when you pray, do not be as the hypocrites who love to pray long and tedious prayers, standing in the synagogues and on the corners of the streets so they may be seen by men. Verily, they shall have their reward, and it will not be what they think it will be.

109 But when you pray, go into a closet or a room where you are alone and shut the door that you can have privacy and pray to Elohim in secret as a friend speaks to a friend, and Elohim, who remains hidden from the eyes of men and is your truest friend, shall answer you openly.

110 When you are asked to publicly pray as a representative of your brothers and sisters, do so only in humility, with gratitude for the honor you have been given, and speak only with words that truly express the feelings, desires, and beliefs of those who have called you to represent them

before Elohim.

111 When you pray, except in prayers of sacred ritual, do not use vain repetitions as the heathen do, for they think that they shall be better heard by God for their many repetitions, but in fact, God hears them not, for their repetition shows that they pray only with their words and not with their hearts.

112 Verily, I declare to you: Elohim does not listen to the words of men said in prayers, except prayers that are said with feeling from the heart and with sincere love of God. To prayers other than this, God is deaf.

113 Understand that Elohim knows everything you are in need of before you ever ask. But by asking with passion and feeling from your heart and with sincere love for God, you demonstrate that you actually value that for which you ask.

114 When men sin against you and do not repent and confess to you and make restitution to you, you have no obligation to them.

115 But when men sin against you and are truly sorrowful for their action and offer a sincere repentance and honest restitution to you, then you must forgive them in full and remember their sins no more, even as Elohim forgives you in full and remembers your sins no more when you have given a sincere, full, and contrite repentance.

116 When you fast, do not be like the hypocrites who wear a sad countenance and stumble along that men may know they are fasting. Verily I say unto you they shall have their reward, and it will not be what they think it will be.

117 But when you fast, make yourself clean and tidy, wear nice garments, have a smile on your face and warmth in your countenance that men may not even guess that you are fasting, unless they are fasting with you. And Elohim, who is in secret, shall reward you openly.

118 Lay not up for yourselves treasures upon the earth, where moth and rust decay and where thieves break through the gate and steal.

119 But lay up for yourselves treasures in Heaven, such as acts of kindness and love, of honesty and fidelity, and of goodwill and good stewardship, for these are the treasures which neither moths nor rust, or any of the plagues of men, can decay or corrupt. These are the treasures which thieves cannot break in and steal.

120 These are the treasures of enduring value, which mark you as a man among men in life and a prince among princes in the world to come.

121 The love of money and power are the Gods of the world and if you pursue and lust after either, let it be a warning that you have strayed from the path of Celestine Light.

122 For you cannot serve two masters; you cannot serve money or power and Elohim; either you will hate one and love the other or favor one and deny the other or hold to one and despise the other.

123 You cannot be a Child of Light and also love and avidly pursue money or power, for they are oil and water to one another and cannot mix, and only one can be first in your priorities.

124 But what shall become of you if you do not pursue money? Fear not; do what you love, and trust in God. Verily, I say unto you: do not be anxious about what you shall eat or what you shall drink or how you shall clothe yourself.

125 Be content with less, not working endlessly for more, for life is more than food and drink and the clothes you wear. It is more than the house you live in or the men that you command.

126 Life is meant to be lived in tranquility and joy, and these come from contentment with less, not always seeking more of the things of the world.

127 Fulfillment and happiness come from quiet days with your wife or husband, playing with your children, listening to the concerns of your brothers and sisters of light, being of service to your community, being a good steward of the land and to all the creatures of the earth.

128 If you have all the treasures of the earth, but you have not these things, you are most destitute among men and a pauper in the world to come.

129 Behold the fowls of the air; they neither sow nor reap, nor gather into homes, yet Elohim

feeds and cares for them. If Elohim so loves the birds of the air and cares for their needs, how much more are you loved and cared for?

130 Why do you worry about tomorrow? Sufficient is the day for itself. Which of you by worrying or planning for a tomorrow that may never come can add one day to his life?

131 Verily, in worrying and working for the tomorrow that may never come, you sacrifice the day that is in your hand.

132 In that sacrifice, you lose more than a day; you lose the moments with those you love that never were and prevent the moments that would have been from ever becoming.

133 And why do you worry about the clothes you wear? Consider the lilies of the fields, how they grow; they toil not, neither do they spin.

134 Yet I say unto you even King Solomon in all his glory was not arrayed like one of these.

135 Wherefore, if God so adorns the flowers of the field, which are here today, but wither tomorrow, and are cast into the oven, shall not Elohim so clothe you, O you children of little faith?

136 Therefore, take no thought, saying, 'what shall we eat or what shall we drink, or where shall we live, or how shall we be clothed?'

137 After all these things, those who are lost seek and sacrifice their lives for emptiness.

138 But Elohim knows you have need of all of these things, and if you do not pursue them foremost in your thoughts and actions, but instead store up for yourselves treasures in Heaven, then all these things shall come to you as you have need.

139 Like the birds of the air and the flowers of the fields, look to the earth to provide your needs, from the food you eat to the clothes you wear, to the homes you live in, to the money you need to buy little pleasures.

140 The earth has been given to you that you may have all of these things and have them in abundance, if you have faith; seek that which you desire to find, do not expect it to simply fall out of the sky, and remain balanced in your life between your needs and your desires.

141 Therefore, do not live today for tomorrow, but live today for today. The days to come will have their own challenges. When living a life of peace, joy, and true fulfillment, sufficient is each day for the challenges therein.

142 Do not condemn others for their lifestyles and choices that are different from yours and do not despise those who do not believe as you do or hold the same things of value.

143 The more you judge others, the more they will reciprocate and judge you. And with the disdain that you show, so shall you be disdained.

144 Be careful not to speak with critical words or critical inflection in your voice to members of your family or your brothers and sisters of light, if they have not asked for your critical opinion.

145 Every fault you see in them, you likely have even greater in yourself, and only because of that can you recognize it in others.

146 Therefore, rather than criticize your brothers or sisters by word or even inflection or even by what you may think is a friendly suggestion, seek first to improve yourself and wait for them to seek out your opinion if they desire it.

147 When your brother or sister is ready for help, they will ask for your opinion or advice; therefore, a suggestion unasked for, that does not seek to improve without judgment, but first belittles by word or inflection, are words that should never be spoken.

148 When you desire to praise another, shout it from the hilltop, but when you think to criticize another, chew upon your tongue.

149 Give not that which is holy to the dogs; neither cast your pearls before swine, lest they trample them under their feet and turn again and rend you.

150 Each day, there are only so many hours, and in your life, only so many days. Therefore, every day is precious and should not be squandered, trying to help those who do not desire your help or teach those who do not desire to be taught or uplift those who prefer to stay in the pit.

151 Be of good service, but only to those who value the time you give, only to those who seek

the help you offer, only to those who desire to hear the good news you speak, and only to those who wish to be tomorrow more than they are today, not in the ways of the world, but in the ways of the Celestine Light.

152 Ask with faith, with selflessness, for anything of righteousness that is a need of in your life, and it shall be given to you. Seek with faith for anything of merit, and you shall find it. Knock with faith upon any door where you need to enter, and it shall open unto you.

153 For every person of virtue, who asks with faith, with selflessness, shall receive, and every person of virtue who seeks with faith shall find and every person of virtue who knocks with faith will find all doors open unto them.

154 Which one of you, if your son asked for a loaf of bread, would instead give him a stone?

155 Or if he asked for a fish, would instead give him a snake?

156 If you who are with faults still know how to give good gifts to your children, how much more shall our Father and Mother in Heaven, who are without fault, give good things to the Children of Light that ask of them?

157 Therefore, all the good things whatsoever that you wish men would do for you, do you even so for them; verily, this is the fruit of the law and the prophets.

158 I have spoken often of the Children of Light, and many here have wondered who they are and if they are one.

159 Verily, the Children of Light care not for the ways of the world, but are enraptured with the ways of Celestine Light and the Community and Family of Light. They walk a different path than the path of the world, a path that leads them to peace and fulfillment and community in this life and overwhelming joy, exaltation and expansion in the life to come.

160 A Child of Light comes not by birth or by decree, but by choice and the conviction to follow the precepts of Celestine Light they know to be true, because both their heart and their mind say it is so, and their prayers confirm it.

161 Many are called to be Children of Light, but few are chosen because only those who tend the orchard are allowed to harvest the fruit.

162 Many have not been called, but are still chosen because having seen the Celestine Light, they make the choice to abandon the darkness and live the light. Like a wayward son, they are welcomed into the arms of Elohim.

163 If you would be a Child of Light, enter in at the strait gate, for wide is the gate and broad is the way that leads to destruction; and many are those that go that way.

164 But strait is the gate, and narrow is the way, which leads to life in the Celestine Light, and few are those that find it.

165 Beware of false prophets, for there shall be many that shall spread like a plague upon the land. They will come to you in sheep's clothing, but inwardly, they are ravenous wolves.

166 Everyone who preaches in my name is not of me, but only those who live the teachings of Celestine Light that I have given.

167 Words are like dust; alone they are worthless. It is only when someone speaks the teachings I have taught and their words are proven with actions of love, and service, and humility, and virtue, and respect, and stewardship that you may begin to accept that they are from me and true emissaries of the Celestine Light.

168 It is not by miracles that you will know them, but by knowledge that works miracles.

169 It is not by wealth that you will know them, but by austerity, that they give their excess above their needs to the poor.

170 It is not by having many men to command that you will know them, but by seeing them toiling by the sweat of their brow in common with their brothers and sisters of the community.

171 It is not by power that you will know them, but by a tenderness and stewardship for all life.

172 It is not by great oratory that you shall know them, but by the teachings of the Celestine Light they demonstrate with the example of their kind and virtuous life.

173 It is not by the deference that men give them that you shall know them, but by the respect and attentiveness they give to others, especially those of little means or position.

174 Therefore, though false prophets shall abound, there is no need for you to be led astray. Look to the things which I have given, by which you may separate the false prophet from the true. Then go in private and ask God to confirm the conclusions of your mind and the feelings of your heart.

175 Simply remember that you will know them by their fruits and that the life they live is a greater witness of their veracity than any of the words they speak.

176 Remember, you shall know them by their fruits. Do men gather grapes from the thorn bushes or figs from the thistles?

177 Every good tree brings forth good fruit, in harmony with the teachings of Celestine Light I have given and the life I have shown to you. But a corrupt tree brings forth fruit that does not come from the vineyard and orchard of Elohim, and it is fit only to be discarded upon the ground to rot.

178 Now some will say that they receive a little good fruit from the teachings of a false prophet, and therefore, they just ignore the words which have no harmony in their heart and lift themselves up with the words that do.

179 But I say unto you that every good tree brings forth only good fruit. There is not a good tree that has one branch that bears sweet fruit and an adjacent branch that bears rotten fruit. And when fruit is gathered into a basket one bad fruit will spoil the basket, even as a single bad influence can decay that which would otherwise have remained good.

180 A truly good tree cannot bring forth evil fruit; neither can a tree corrupted bring forth good fruit that is not already tainted with its demise.

181 Every tree that does not bring forth good fruit must be hewn down and cast into the fire, lest it taint the purity of that which is good.

182 Wherefore, remember this test of a prophet and of a Child of Light: By their fruits of their life, you shall know them.

183 But do not think that a Child of Light or even a prophet or an Apostle will never have fault or err in their personal choices or that a leader of the Communities of Light will never sin and be in need of repentance. If they were already perfect, they would be translated in the blink of an eye and be no more upon the earth.

184 But in the life they live, you see them live as I have shown you and taught you to live. Not as the world lives, but only as the Children of Light live.

185 Nor should you think that everyone that calls out to God or praises Elohim or who claims to be acting in the name of God will actually ever enter into the Kingdom of Heaven, but only those who live the life and truly do the will of my Father and Mother in Heaven.

186 Many will say to me on that day, 'Lord, Lord, have we not prophesied in your name? Have we not cast out devils in your name and in your name done many wonderful works?'

187 Then I will profess to them, 'I never knew you; you spoke in assuming words, but you never prophesied for me; you cast out devils, but they only laughed, for you had no authority; you have done many good works in my name, but with vanity for your glory, not in humility for mine. Depart from me you that work iniquity.'

188 Therefore, whosoever hears my words and lives them, I will liken to a wise man who built his house upon a rock.

189 And the rain descended, and the floods came, and the winds blew, and his house did not fall, for it was founded upon a rock.

190 And everyone who hears my words and lives them not shall be likened unto the foolish man who built his house upon the sand.

191 And the rain descended, and the floods came, and the winds blew and beat upon his house, and it fell, and great was the fall of it."

192 And it came to pass that when Yeshua ceased to speak, the people were astonished at

what they had heard him say, for he spoke doctrines that put down things they had believed and presented doctrines they had never heard.

193 But he spoke teachings that made sense and resonated in their hearts. He spoke as one with authority, not as one of the scribes. An aura of divinity spread over them, emanating from him insomuch that his words pierced them that they had tingles throughout their body. And though many might choose to not heed the words they had heard, none could doubt the veracity of what he had spoken.

CHAPTER 46

Miracles and Suffering

After a break for lunch, Yeshua continues his sermon and speaks about why God allows suffering in the world. He announces that after he is through speaking, he, Miriam, and Cephas will walk through the crowd and people who wish to be healed may touch any one of the three, and through their own worthiness and faith, they will be healed. Many are healed and some are not, but almost all see and feel things that they have never even imagined.

While Yeshua had been speaking, his Apostles had been sitting in a semicircle directly below him and the multitude sitting beyond them. But in the place closest to him sat four women, and the order in which they sat was meaningful.

2 Facing Yeshua, his wife Miriam sat on the left, which was Yeshua's right hand and the place of honor reserved always for her; beside her was Salome; Martha was next; and Miryam, his mother, beside her.

3 Throughout his discourse, the women held hands or linked arms or leaned against the woman beside them. This was common practice among Miriam, Martha, and Miryam, but Salome had purposely been included with them and, by Martha's request, sat between her and Miriam, that she would have no doubt that they accepted her as one of their family and held no animosities for her part in the death of Yochanan.

4 After Yeshua had stepped down to go to the company of his family, Cephas stood up on the pinnacle and announced to the multitude in a loud voice, "We have been blessed by the teachings of Yeshua, Son of Light; surely, none have heard his words this day and not been pierced by their significance and inspired by their promise.

5 Yeshua has told me that he desires to still speak more this day, but first, as it is already well into the afternoon, let us all break for a meal. But please remain where you sit, and once Yeshua has finished eating, he will speak to us again."

6 Then after asking for silence and saying a short prayer of thanksgiving and blessing for the food they would all eat, Cephas stepped down and went to his family.

7 The people did as Cephas bade. As most had traveled from other areas and encamped around the Communities of Light, they had ample food with them, and those that had none found the strangers around them happily shared whatever they had.

8 When Yeshua was ready to ascend again the pinnacle, he informed Cephas, who went up to the pinnacle and announced to the multitude that Yeshua would now to speak to them again.

9 Once again, Cephas offered a prayer for the multitude, asking, "Elohim, God of the earth and all that is, thank you for this opportunity we have to hear the words of Yeshua, your Son of Light. Let our hearts be open to receive the Celestine Light that he brings and our heads be clear

to understand his words. So let it be."

10 Then Cephas stepped down from the pinnacle and Yeshua stepped up. Looking over the multitude, he said unto them, "I know many of you have come to Capernaum to see me because you have heard it said that I have healed people in miraculous ways, and you hope that I will heal you or a member of your family.

11 When I come down from the mount, I will walk among you, and you may reach out and lightly touch my garment, and those who are prepared shall be healed.

12 That you may know that it is not through me alone that the Celestine power of Elohim comes to heal, but through any of the Children of Light who have been given that authority; my wife Miriam, who is one of my Apostles, and Cephas, another, will also walk among you.

13 If you are ready to be healed, you have repented of your weaknesses and stand upright before men and God. If this be so, then simply touch our garments as we pass by and ask aloud with your words for Elohim to heal you. We are bridges of the Celestine Light, and if you are prepared in your heart, it will be as you desire and you shall be made whole."

14 At this revelation, the Apostles were surprised, all save Miriam and Cephas, for Yeshua had not spoken of this to any of them or taught them how they could be channels of the Celestine power of Elohim as he was.

15 Then Yeshua preached to the multitude, saying, "This will be an afternoon of miracles, but it will also be an afternoon of disappointment. Many will seek to be healed, but only some will obtain that which they seek.

16 How can that be? Why would some be healed, but others not? Is it the fault of the healer? Are they not true channels of the Celestine Light of Elohim? Nay, that cannot be so, for there are some that will be healed, even of very great diseases and infirmities.

17 Have you ever wondered why Elohim even allows suffering and disease and infirmities at all?

18 Have you not seen at times when the pain of suffering is so great or the agony from the loss of a loved one; that a person will cry out in despair to God, asking why?

19 If there truly is a benevolent God in Heaven, a mother and father who love their children beyond measure, how could this God of all that is, with the power to make or destroy the earth and all the heavens above with a single command, allow such misery and suffering and pain to their children who walk the earth?

20 You would be less than honest with yourself if you did not admit that at times, such questions have passed through your thoughts.

21 Today you will have the answer to those questions. You may not like the answers. You may not accept the answers. But you will know the answers.

22 I tell you these things with the hope that in understanding the truth, even if at first you may not accept its reality, that you will accept it enough that it will begin to alter your habits and choices and will make a beneficial difference in your life.

23 It is taught by the priests and leaders of the faiths of this land that God is an omnipresent, omnipotent, presence. God is referred to in our times in the masculine structure of speech, but only as a form of speech, and is not thought of as actually having a form of a man.

24 But in ancient times, God was not so considered. In ancient times, God was spoken of in the plural and in both the masculine and the feminine.

25 When next you are in the synagogue and they are reading from the scripture scrolls, ask them to read of the creation of the world.

26 In truth, much has been removed from the sacred scrolls that were originally written, and more has been removed than remains.

27 Why was much that was written removed? Because the scrolls as they were originally given by Elohim to the prophets were given from Elohim and the true understanding and implications of that are at odds with the teachings that men desire to hear.

28 The very nature of the name Elohim, by which God chose to be known to man, is plural

in its composition. More importantly, it embodies both the masculine and feminine. Even in what remains of the tattered scriptures read in the synagogues, this name of God is used over two thousand times.

29 But it is almost always used in contradiction upon itself, and this was not done by they who originally wrote the scrolls, but by the scribes and priests who came after them and desired a different God, for it is employed as a singular and masculine title, but it is in fact, not only plural, but both male and female, even as the true God of Heaven is.

30 I speak now from the same scrolls that still are read in the synagogues, and God said, 'Let *us* make man in *our* likeness and let them have dominion . . . '

31 And again, 'Behold the man has become as one of *us* . . . '

32 And again, 'Let *us* go down, and there confound their language, that they may not understand one another's speech.'

33 In these words, you see mankind was made in the image not of God, but Gods. They were made male and female in physical appearance like the physical appearance of God, one a male, one a female; a father and a mother, a part of the Elohim whom you worship.

34 Elohim is not a faceless aeon without substance or form as is taught today. Even the very text of the scrolls read in the synagogues record Moses speaking to Elohim, face-to-face. That there is no doubt that the scroll records an actual event and not a metaphor, the scripture concludes, as one man speaks to another.

35 Understand that Elohim is not a faceless aeon of the male persuasion. Nor is Elohim only one aeon as you have been led to believe, but many.

36 But the Elohim that is the creator of this world are three: the Father, the Mother, and the Son, who is your brother, for the eternal soul of each of you is a creation of our Father and Mother in Heaven.

37 And more than this, an Elohim is also what each one of you can become someday as you learn and grow from your experiences and choices and become perfect.

38 And it is for this cause—to learn and grow and become more perfect—that you should be striving for every minute of your physical life upon the earth.

39 And it is for this cause—that you might learn and grow by your experiences and choices—that suffering is allowed to exist in your life and the life of every person, some to a very great degree.

40 There is no greater desire of your Father and Mother in Heaven than you should return to them in glory, and they wait with love to embrace you and welcome you home.

41 But you cannot return to a realm of perfection ruled by the Elohim, unless you are first more perfect.

42 You do not need to be perfect as the Elohim are, for you continue to expand for all eternity and you have forever to improve upon your perfection.

43 But you must grow beyond the bonds of the ways of the world; you must grow into the ways of the Elohim; and in that, you become greater than you are, greater than you began, and with a harmony that can live in the presence of the Elohim.

44 When you seek to understand the nature of Elohim and try to comprehend why suffering exists and why bad things happen, even to the most wonderful and righteous people, remember how you help your own children to become more than babes, in the same manner your Father and Mother in Heaven seek to help all of their children upon the earth.

45 You let your children experience their life. You teach them right from wrong, what can hurt them and what is good for them. You admonish them to be of good character and virtue.

46 They journey through life, and they never forget the teachings you gave to them, both by word and by example.

47 But until your teachings are confirmed by their own experiences and observations, they do not shape them into more than they were.

48 By the teachings of your words and the examples of your lives, you lay the foundation for

the building upon which your children construct their lives.

49 But the building is not built until they can prove by their own experiences and observations that the foundation is true.

50 By this, they learn and they grow. Sometimes, they make mistakes, and even those confirm the foundation you built and help them to become more the next day than they were the day before, if they so choose.

51 And I say unto you that every day of life is a school, no matter your age, and each day, there are many tests; and each choice you make, be it big or small, is one.

52 Sometimes people, even well-intentioned and righteous people, make the wrong choices. They learn from the pain and the error of their ways. When the choice comes again, they hopefully choose wiser.

53 It is better to experience a little pain and suffering for your short time in mortality to help you to walk a better path than to not have that incentive to walk in righteousness and condemn yourself by your poor choices to far greater pain and suffering for days without end in the life to come.

54 It is by this means—to experience the bad and the good, to make choices, both right and wrong, to have the opportunity each day to become better than you were the day before—that your sojourn in mortality is fulfilled, and you may pass beyond the shining gate and into the realm of the Elohim forevermore.

55 "Consider this now—when a man is born crippled, it is asked who sinned, he, or his parents, that he was thus born.

56 I say unto you that neither the man nor his parents sinned, for Elohim is a God of love and would never punish a newborn with any punishment, for any cause.

57 I know it is not taught thus among many, but when you consider the nature of Elohim, consider your own nature as parents. Let your heart feel how you would feel. Let your mind think how you would think.

58 Would you who love your children cripple them at birth to be punished for your sins, instead of you?

59 Nay, you who love your children, yet are mortal and imperfect, would beg Elohim to put an infirmity upon you, rather than see your child suffer. Do you think that your Father and Mother in Heaven, being immortal and perfect, could act any less loving or caring for their children of spirit?

60 How then is it that a man is born crippled? Or another suffers from disease when he is a man? Or another, a lover of peace, is murdered at the hands of bandits? Or why is one man healed by a spiritual blessing, but another remains as he is?

61 One answer to all of these questions returns to the journey of mortality and what it is that each of you desired to gain in your sojourn upon the earth, as you contemplated the journey, before you were ever conceived in your mother's womb.

62 Verily, verily, I say unto you: Before you were born of woman, you were born of spirit, and before you lived upon the earth, you lived in spirit beyond the earth.

63 You came down into mortality that you could experience things that only a physical and mortal body can experience, and this that you might learn from your experiences; that you might become an eternal soul of greater wisdom, of more love, and fuller empathy and sympathy for your brothers and sisters of life and eternity.

64 That you might become more like the Elohim.

65 Therefore, when you see a man born crippled, do not imagine who sinned that he was thus born; do not scorn or pity him. Instead, honor him, for he has shown uncommon love for himself and his family and an intrepid courage and devotion of desire to grow into a magnificent Son of Elohim by being thus born.

66 Having lived within the challenges, he will gain empathy and sympathy for the plights of others such as no one who has not lived thus can ever gain.

67 Having lived within the challenges, he will learn to cherish love, both that which he receives from others and that which he can give to them; and this in ways such as no one who has not lived thus can ever gain.

68 Having lived within the challenges, he will see all the world with different eyes and learn to appreciate the beauty and wonder of many common things, in ways such as no one who has not lived thus can ever gain.

69 Having lived within the challenges, he will afford his closest family and friends an opportunity to also learn empathy, and sympathy, and love, and stewardship to a greater degree than they otherwise would have been able, had he not been born thus and lived among them.

70 Therefore, when a person is born crippled, but still capable, this is someone who chose to be born thus, before they were ever birthed, that both they and their family and friends might have greater opportunities in their sojourn in mortality to become more than they began.

71 Sometimes an affliction will strike a man in the prime of his life, for no apparent cause of his own. But like the man born crippled, this can sometimes be a choice made before he was ever born into the world or a choice made by his higher spirit later in his life to help him or those in his life to learn greater empathy, sympathy, faith, and love.

72 But there is also a second aeon that may overshadow the man who becomes afflicted later in life, and it is this aeon that is usually the cause.

73 Like the man who was born crippled, it is often the case that the man who acquires a disease or infirmity also made the choice to do so. But unlike the man born crippled, he may not have made the choice by action, but by inaction or incorrect action.

74 There are certain laws of health by which you would be wise to abide. These are not necessarily laws written on the sacred scrolls, but they are taught and known to the Children of Light.

75 Living the true laws of health and vitality produce superior wellness. More pointed, not living the laws of health, whether by choice or ignorance, bring about greater disease and afflictions.

76 This body you wear is mortal. It is subject not only to death, but to all manner of diseases, infirmities, and imperfections. That is how it was created by Elohim that through your mortality, you would be given the opportunity to make wise choices.

77 As you are a good steward of the temple of your body, that habit becomes a part of who you are, and you become a better steward of other things given to your care such as your children, your animals, your crops, and your community.

78 As you prove yourself with lesser things, Elohim will give you greater things, both in this life and the next.

79 Elohim rewards the good steward, but has an empty cup for the poor steward, save they recognize the error of their ways, repent, and commit to living a greater light.

80 Therefore, when you find yourself sick and afflicted, do not curse what has happened to you, but give thanks that through your infirmity you are reminded that you are the master of yourself and can make changes in your lifestyle that will improve the state of your wellness in the times to come.

81 If you do not learn the lesson of your poor health, even as you recover, you are doomed to fall to another infirmity soon again.

82 Therefore, this day, as I walk among you as a bridge of light between man and God, to bring the healing Celestine Light of Elohim upon you, reach out and touch my garment if you will; if you have the faith; if you have the desire; if you are dedicated to living the greater light called Celestine.

83 Consider the man who took off his garments and labored in a loin cloth for all of the day under the hot sun, because he was uncomfortable and sweating wearing his clothes.

84 At the end of the day, his body badly burned, he sought to be healed. He reached out to touch the light, but it did not come upon him and he was not healed, for it had been by his choice

that he had forsaken his clothing that protected him from the sun, and he had not learned from his error, and upon another day, the same thing he would do.

85 Then there was the man who was imprisoned by the Romans and forced to work all day in the hot sun in just his loin cloth. He too was badly burned; he too desired to be healed by the light; but when he reached out with faith and hope to touch the light, his body was restored as it had been, because the cause of his suffering had not been by his choice, and in his desire to be healed, he held humility and faith and love and desired to be a better man in his heart.

86 As I walk among you today, ask yourself which man are you: the wise man who seeks to ever act in wiser ways or the foolish man who seeks always immediate comfort and pleasure and considers not the painful consequences that shall fall upon him on the morrow."

87 Then Yeshua stepped down into the crowd, and he beckoned Miriam and Cephas to also come down into the multitude. And the three of them walked out in different directions that they might go among all of the people.

88 As they passed through the multitude, nearly everyone present reached out a hand to touch them, not just those who were noticeably infirmed or afflicted.

89 The old and the young, the Hebrew and the Gentile, the Egyptian and the Roman, all reached forth their hands and let them linger on their garments, with softness and respect, as they moved slowly among them.

90 And of miracles, there were many. Men on litters stood up and walked. People with sundry pains from sources they knew not suddenly had none. Men, women, and children who had been blind for years or since birth at once saw the wonder of the world, and they fell to their knees and praised Elohim.

91 Many who had no noticeable affliction still were changed, and you could see it in their countenance, which as they touched Yeshua or Miriam or Cephas went from an expectant, hopeful smile to rapture and joy and tears.

92 Though some were not healed, as Yeshua had said would be so, upon the joyous faces of the thousands of people in the crowd, it could not be doubted that almost all had seen and felt a light such as they had never imagined, even the Celestine Light, and they would return to their homes with a warmth in their hearts that before had never been.

CHAPTER 47

Setting Apart the Apostles

Yeshua ordains and sets apart each of his Apostles for the specific tasks for which they will have responsibility. He then begins to teach them the mysteries of Heaven and how to be masters of all the energies of Heaven and earth, which must be kept secret from the world but given to any of the Children of Light, who are prepared to receive them.

fter coming down from the mountain, Yeshua asked his Apostles to meet with him at his home that he might further instruct them. Miriam, his mother, Martha, Salome, and his children and the children of Martha and Yochanan were also present.

2 Martha brought out a basket of figs and another of dates, and the children were given the dates and sent to play in another room while the Apostles met, but the women who were not Apostles also stayed in attendance.

3 Before he spoke, Yeshua looked out upon the faces of everyone, and sensing a discord in some of them, he asked, "Yohhanan, something troubles you, and I know it is not you alone. Please speak freely."

4 Yohhanan answered him forthrightly, saying, "Thank you, Yeshua. I am moved by more than one emotion and thought. I was lifted to the highest mountain by your words today, and the miracles I witnessed and the lives I saw changed.

5 But I was also left to wonder, not in selfishness or pride, but just seeking understanding, why Cephas and Miriam were called upon to be bridges for the Celestine Light of Elohim, but the rest of us were not called or instructed on how this is accomplished.

6 And I wonder about the presence of Salome, not among the Communities of Light, for certainly she is welcome, and not even in your home, as unusual arrangement as it is.

7 But here among us, your chosen twelve, as we meet in private as a quorum, why is there any stranger who is not intimate family or of our quorum among us?"

8 Yeshua nodded in understanding and said unto him, "Your questions are well placed, Yohhanan. All of you, my chosen twelve, shall do great works among the people of this land and some of you among people of lands far and away. Nevertheless, there are important reasons that today occurred as it did, and I would ask Cephas to answer your question further."

9 Seeming somewhat surprised, Cephas looked first to Yeshua, then to his brethren, and said unto them, "We are all apprentices to the master, no different than the boy who learns to fashion jewelry after years of watching and learning from the great goldsmith.

10 So shall we learn to create jewels of light, by watching and receiving instruction from the Son of Light.

11 Some of us, such as Miriam and me to a lesser extent, but still more than any of you,

have had the honor of sharing many days with Yeshua, of hearing his teachings and seeing the miracles of Elohim flow through him.

12 We are still apprentices, but each somewhat further along the path because of our greater time of instruction. We were not put above you, I think, but merely given the opportunity to use the greater knowledge we had gained from the good fortune of having had more time with Yeshua."

13 Shrugging his shoulders, Cephas concluded, "That is all I have to say."

14 Yeshua thanked him and then, speaking to his Apostles, said, "It is even as Cephas has spoken. Not through lack of desire, nor from lack of faith, but only from lack of knowledge of that which was required did I not call upon you?

15 Miracles can happen from faith alone. But there are also specific things that you can do, both inside and outside, that can expand the miracle or focus the miracle or even manifest the miracle.

16 It is only now that you are assembled as twelve that I can begin to teach these things to you, because it is only now that your life is fully dedicated to learning and understanding the mysteries of the Celestine Light that come from Elohim.

17 Miriam has been with me from the beginning, from before the world ever was. All the mysteries of Heaven are known to her as she remembers from experiences in both this life and the one that came before in the realm of Celestine Lights.

18 Cephas I have known since my youth. Though I have also known others of you since then, it is Cephas with whom I have spent much time with over the years. In our youths, we would sometimes set upon the lake shore after the evening meal, when I would come to visit the lake, and speak for many hours under the stars about the ways of Elohim and of men.

19 You still have many things to learn and not from me alone, but also from Miriam and Cephas and from one another.

20 The time will soon come when you are called upon to fulfill the full measure of your creation. Therefore, seek out the mysteries of Celestine Light every day, and soon you will hold the powers of Heaven in your hands.

21 Concerning the presence of Salome among us, it would have been an insult to ask her, whose home this is, to go and stand outside while we speak, even more so as the children were allowed to remain.

22 More than this, there is nothing I will teach you that Salome or any other Child of Light cannot also know. There are many mysteries of heaven which the people of the world shall never be given to know. But no secrets will be kept secret from the Children of Light once they are prepared to receive them.

23 Yeshua opened his palm toward Miriam, "Now Miriam has more to say concerning this."

24 Miriam nodded toward Yeshua and stepped forward and spoke to the Apostles, "It is a wonder to behold the ways of Elohim, none more so than concerning Salome.

25 As you know, she has just come among us, and yet my heart confirms and my spirit testifies that I have known her from before this world ever was, even as I have known Yeshua and Martha and mother Miryam and each of you.

26 Therefore, she is not a stranger, but an honored friend and member of my family, and I am overjoyed that she has returned to us, as is my sister Martha and mother Miryam.

27 When you look upon her, please do not see a stranger, nor see she who once was the stepdaughter of Herod. When you look upon her, see me and Martha and mother Miryam, for she is a part of us and we of her.

28 The people of the world could never understand this: how someone you just met could be treated as if she had lived within your heart and home all of your life. But in truth, we have lived with her for longer than life and shall continue to live with her and love her beyond life; therefore, she is not a stranger; she is dearest family. She knows it and we know it, and now you know it, so let there be only peace in your heart concerning this forever more."

29 Each of the Apostles was touched by the words of Miriam and thereafter treated Salome as a dear sister.

30 Yeshua began to speak to them again, saying, "It is time that as a Quorum of Twelve, you are more organized, for Elohim is a God of order not chaos, and with order, time slows and much is accomplished.

31 I have already spoken to you about the respective positions of Miriam and Cephas among you. Now it is time for Cephas to call two to stand by him as his closest counselors.

32 Even as Miriam may speak for me when I am no longer among you, even so shall it be understood that the counselors of Cephas may speak for Cephas, with his authority, when he is not present."

33 Then turning to Cephas, Yeshua asked, "Whom do you call, Cephas?"

34 Cephas looked into the eyes of the Apostles and then upon the eyes of two and said, "I call upon your brother Yakov and my brother Yohhanan to stand with me as my counselors"

35 "So be it," Yeshua said with approval.

36 Then Yeshua asked Cephas to lay his hands upon the heads of his counselors and ordain them to that calling, giving them the right to know all he knew and the authority to act in his stead, and this he did.

37 Addressing again the Apostles, Yeshua said unto them, "Now we must call upon one person to be responsible for the treasury of the Communities of Light, and he must call upon two counselors to assist him and to act in his stead when he is not present.

38 For this important task, I call Mattayah, for he has had much experience with gold and silver and the payment of money for debts."

39 "Then turning to Mattayah, who bowed his head toward him, Yeshua asked, "Whom do you call to be your counselors, Mattayah?"

40 Mattayah stroked his beard for a moment in thought, then said unto them, "I ask Yudas Iscariot and Philip of Bethsaida to help me with this sacred trust, for they have traveled some and learned things that will be of value in the stewardship of the coin of the communities."

41 "So shall it be," approved Yeshua. "As the treasure of the communities supports both the community and our sacred purposes on earth, tomorrow seek out two additional counselors from among the community members to also assist you in this important task."

42 Mattayah bowed his head again slightly toward Yeshua, saying, "As you will."

43 Then Yeshua called Mattayah to come forward, and Mattayah kneeled before him and Yeshua laid his hands upon his head and ordained him to his calling, giving him the authority.

44 Once ordained and set apart, Mattayah called his two counselors before him and ordained them, even as Yeshua had done unto him.

45 Turning now to the remaining Apostles, Yeshua called Shim'on the Zealot and ordained and set him apart to be the eyes and ears of the community in the world apart so that they might always be forewarned of the threats of men and prepared to preserve themselves.

46 Turning to Toma, he laid his hands upon his head and ordained and set him apart to be his scribe and the scribe of the Apostles and to make a record of events that transpired and the teachings that were taught. And Toma was instructed to call two counselors from among the community to assist him with this effort.

47 Then he called upon Ya'akov, son of Cleophas, and laid his hands upon his head and ordained and set him apart to be the Apostle responsible for learning and teaching the secrets of the earth, the plants, the minerals, and the animals and how these can be used for healing and aids in manifesting other sacred powers.

48 Then he called upon Yuda, son of Cleophas, and laid his hands upon his head and ordained and set him apart to be the Apostle with special responsibility to find and teach the Children of Light among the youth of the world.

49 Lastly, he called upon Amram and laid his hands upon his head and ordained and set him apart to be the Apostle of music and to learn and teach others how to use music to accomplish

miracles, great and small.
50 Then turning to all of them, he said unto them, "Now begins your training in earnest to be Apostles and bridges of the Celestine Light from Elohim to man.
51 From this day forth, not only shall you learn by observation, but I will teach you day by day all the mysteries of Celestine Light and how to be masters of all the aeons of Heaven and earth.
52 And this we will begin tonight, in this place, that you may know how to coalesce the aeon of Elohim that it can flow through you and bring about wonders both small and great, such as the world has never known."
53 But of these secrets, the world is to be kept in total darkness. Therefore, they cannot be written here, but are revealed only to the Children of Light, as they are prepared to receive the greater light Celestine.

CHAPTER 48

Builder of Eternity

A Roman centurion chief officer named Valerius, with faith, asks Yeshua to heal his servant, and he is healed that very hour. Yeshua speaks to the crowd that remains about the consequences of their actions; the good will draw light to their soul and the bad will draw darkness, and reminds them that it is never too late to turn from darkness to the light for you never know when your last day upon the earth will be so do not delay, as your eternity awaits you—the good to the good, the bad to the bad.

After spending the night in his home with his family, Yeshua arose on the following morning to see that many of the people from the multitude of the previous day were still encamped around Capernaum and the Communities of Light.

2 Within two hours of daylight, Cephas and some of the Apostles arrived by boat, and Yeshua told them that he would preach briefly to the crowd once more and desired to do so from their boat on the lake as he had done previously so that everyone might see and hear him easily.

3 Walking the short distance from his house to the lake shore, Yeshua was approached by the Roman centurion Valerius, who was a chief officer of the Galilee area and lived in a large villa overlooking the lake between Gennesaret and Tiberias.

4 He was well known among the people living on Lake Gennesaret, for his generosity of purse and benign treatment of the people. He had given a goodly sum of money to help build the synagogue at Capernaum.

5 Valerius came to Yeshua, beseeching him, saying, "Man of mystery, I know not who you really are, but that great powers work through you; this I know.

6 Despite your words, which can inflame minds, I have commanded my men that none should harm you or your people or interfere in your movements.

7 I pray you will hear me now and give favor in return for the favor I have given to you. I have a cherished servant, a kind and gentle man, who is even now lying on a bed in my home, wracked with pain and suffering from palsy. I ask you with deep sincerity and good will if you would consider healing this fine man."

8 Yeshua answered him, saying, "When I have finished speaking to the people at the lake, I shall come to your home and heal him."

9 But Valerius protested, saying, "I am not worthy that you should come into my house and be under my roof, for I do not live as you teach, though I have studied your teachings, and they have led me to much thought and contemplation.

10 But we have still some things in common. Like you, I am a man of authority. I command men to go here or go there, and it is done; or to do this or do that, and it is so.

11 Therefore, do not soil yourself at my home, but merely speak the words as you will, and I

know without doubt that my servant, who faithfully lives as you teach, shall be healed."

12 Yeshua marveled when he heard the words of Valerius, and turning to his Apostles, he said, "Verily, I say unto you: Seldom have I found such great faith among all the people whom Elohim has blessed in this land.

13 In this, you see the future coming to pass, for when those who are given the birthright cast it upon the ground; it shall be picked up and cherished by those to whom it had not been given.

14 And I say unto you that many shall come from the east and the west and the north and the south, saying, 'We shall sit with Abraham and Isaac and Jacob, in the Kingdom of Heaven, for it is our birthright.'

15 But on that day, they shall be cast into outer darkness where there shall be weeping and wailing and gnashing of teeth, for what has been abandoned cannot be inherited, even as the future is written by the present."

16 Then turning to the centurion, Yeshua said unto him, "You are a good man, but there is a great man inside of you desiring to come out. Listen to your heart, and it will tell you things your mind does not know.

17 Go now your way as you will. As you have believed and had faith, so it has been done for you." And the servant of Valerius was healed that very hour.

18 Shortly thereafter, Yeshua was in the boat with Cephas and Yohhanan while his family and the other Apostles sat or stood along the shoreline with the gathering crowd of people.

19 About the third hour after sunrise, Yeshua began to speak to the multitude, saying, "Some of you have been away from your homes for many days now, and it is time for you to return.

20 Will you be the same person when you return as you were when you left or will you be different?

21 My teachings are like seeds sown upon good soil. Each of you is the good soil. You would not have come here and remained here for these days if your hearts were not beating to my words and your eyes not seeking a greater light.

22 But when you return to your home, you become the gardener of your life, which is your greatest stewardship. For my seeds to grow and fill you with light, you must wisely cultivate the garden of your life.

23 You are also the steward of many more things, including your relationships, which can span eternity. But unless you first are a good steward of your own life, unless you first cultivate and blossom the garden that bears your name, a good steward of anything else, you can never be.

24 What do you hope for in the days to come? What do you work and strive for? Are you caught in a rut upon the road of life? Do you see tomorrow as only another day of the same challenges and maybe more or as a new dawn, rising upon a new and better life?

25 To know the answer, you merely need to look at your life. If you return home and nothing is different with the way you think and speak and act, if your weaknesses are still your weaknesses and the friends who would lead you to temptation still beckon, then you remain upon the road you have always traveled. Today will be as yesterday and tomorrow as today.

26 But new seeds have been planted in your heart. They will grow into marvelous flowers of the sun if you will but cultivate and nourish them.

27 And how is this done? How do you cultivate the flowers of Celestine Light planted in your heart? With love and humility, with repentance and restitution, with respect and honesty, with service and prayer, with a life renewed as the old garden is turned under that the new garden may blossom.

28 Therefore, do not just hear my words and nod your heads in agreement, but hear my words and do them."

29 Then a man stepped to the lake shore from the crowd, and he was a zealot who had been standing with the Apostle Shim'on. And raising his voice, he spoke out to Yeshua, saying, "You speak of being a steward over your own life and that is all well and good, but how can a man who is a slave be the steward over his own life or even a man who is not a slave, but under more subtle

bondage as a citizen of a Kingdom ruled by a tyrant king?"

30 Yeshua answered him, saying, "Thank you for your question, Garz-el. You have well introduced that which I desired to speak upon."

31 The man was startled to hear Yeshua call him by name, and in surprise, he asked, "How did you know my name? We have never met or spoken."

32 Yeshua answered him, saying, "A shepherd knows his sheep, even as the sheep know their shepherd. When a new sheep joins the flock, he does not need to be shown to the shepherd to be known by him, any more than the shepherd needs to be introduced to the sheep to be able to single him out from among the flock.

33 Even a slave can be a steward over themselves. The master may dictate where the slave must go and what he must do, what he must wear, and what he must eat and drink. But the master cannot dictate what the slave will think, nor hear his prayers to Elohim, or know the true desires of his heart.

34 In all things, Elohim expects the best you have to offer of yourself, but does not expect more than you can give, even as the slave who is a good steward over his thoughts and prayers and desires, but is not held accountable for the food or drink he is compelled to consume by his master or the clothes he must wear or the things he must do.

35 And woe unto the master who compels his slave to do evil or to the officer of the army who compels his soldiers to initiate attacks against the peaceful instead of only protections and defense against the marauders, or to the rulers of Kingdoms who compel the innocent to evil, who would otherwise be pure.

36 For them, it would almost be better that they had never been born, for when one man forces another to sin, where to object would be death or great penalty, that man takes upon him the sins of they who were compelled, and the penalties in the hereafter shall be multiplied seventy times upon that man.

37 And though a man of darkness may compel one of light to commit evil and may escape a penalty in this life, know that it is only for a breath of eternity, and in the hereafter all shall be held accountable for the actions of their lives for much longer than a breath.

38 In the hereafter, each person's light and darkness shall be weighed in the balance, and they who are found wanting shall be cast out into outer darkness, into the place of torment which they created in life, and are pulled to in the life to come by their own resonance.

39 And in that prison of their making, there shall be great weeping and wailing and gnashing of teeth, until they have paid the utmost and redeemed themselves.

40 In outer darkness, the evil will burn; every part of them inside and out shall feel as if fire is eating at them, but they will never be consumed; always burning, but never scorched, in the flames, but without light, but also in utter cold, in impenetrable darkness and loneliness without solace.

41 And it is not by Elohim that their torment comes, but only by their own hand by the resonance they created by their thoughts and actions in their previous life.

42 Before the world ever was, Elohim laid out the plan by which all things would be, not just in this life, but also in the life to come.

43 And to all the thoughts of man, there would be an accounting. And to all the actions of man, there would be an accounting. And the accounting is written upon the resonance of your soul.

44 Good thoughts and deeds are credited with light upon your soul. Wicked thoughts and deeds bring darkness to your soul.

45 Once your last breath in mortality is taken, your soul will rise at once to a place of judgment, or so it is thought. But in reality, this is but a house of measures.

46 Your soul is put into a balance, and the light and the darkness which you put into it in mortality are weighed one against the other until your place of resonance is determined.

47 And there you are sent, not by force or decree, but by the inexorable pull of your own soul

toward its resonance, the dark to the darkness and the light to the light.

48 The difference is in this life; you may sin and not only feel no pain or consequences from your actions, but might even feel pleasure in your sin. But in the eternity to come, you cannot escape the consequences of your darkness.

49 If your balance is found wanting, you will be pulled by the resonance you created in life, into the outer darkness.

50 The greater your darkness in life, the deeper into outer darkness you will be drawn; and the deeper into outer darkness you fall, the greater the pain that never ends will wrack you and torment you, and the fire that burns but never consumes will torture you.

51 Knowing this, a man should consider well before he compels another to sin, for the darkness of the sin is multiplied seventy times upon the head of the man who compels or seduces another to do evil.

52 How much greater then will be the weight of the darkness of his soul when it is weighed in the balance?

53 But even as the soul of a man can be drawn into outer darkness in eternity because of his sins in this life, so can the soul of a man be drawn into greater light, even into the presence of the Elohim, by the weight of the light in his soul from the good thoughts and deeds of his sojourn in mortality.

54 The same man who owns a slave and has compelled him to do evil can free his slave and ask forgiveness of his slave by word and make restitution by deed. In this, great light comes into his soul and puts away the darkness.

55 The same commander who ordered his men to attack a city whose people had not attacked them could, when given the choice again, refuse to so act. In the future, helping to build instead of destroy, he could bring light to his soul instead of darkness.

56 The same king who ruled his people unjustly and compelled them to act against their light could repent and ask forgiveness of his people and then prove the value of his words by his good deeds; thus where before his soul drew darkness unto it, now it would draw light.

57 It is never too late to turn from darkness to the light. But you know not which day and hour your soul shall be called from this life to make an accounting for eternity. Therefore, do not procrastinate or delay to think, act, and live in the Celestine Light.

58 Your eternity awaits you, and whether you live in a world of light and joy and abundance or a world of darkness and cold and hunger depends entirely upon the choices you make every moment of every day, for you are the architect and builder of your forever."

CHAPTER 49

Destiny Fulfilled

Yeshua goes alone into the hills to pray, and while he is away, Miriam and Martha speak to one another about Salome. After confirming what they feel in their hearts and what they know in their minds, they ask Salome to join them in marriage with Yeshua so they can all be married to one another, and she agrees. When he returns, they tell Yeshua, and he is happy for their happiness and abides by their choice.

fter Yeshua finished speaking, he and his family returned to their home. Most of the Apostles remained with the multitude by the lake and spoke with them further, with individuals and in small groups.

2 After the midday meal, most of the people who were not from the communities around the north end of the lake departed for their home villages and towns in good spirits, uplifted by everything they had seen and heard.

3 Yeshua and his family shared a midday meal, and then Yeshua told them he was going alone into the hills and would return the following morning. Miriam prepared to come with him, but he asked her to remain this once.

4 Perplexed, she nevertheless did as he bade, and after embraces and kisses to his family, he set off.

5 Rising into the mountains, he came eventually upon a glade and here knelt down and began to pray to his Father and Mother in Heaven. During all the remaining hours of light, he prayed, about every subject imaginable, the small and the great, the present and the future.

6 As nightfall came upon him, he moved to sit in a crouch in a bent tree trunk, and leaning back against the trunk and looking up at the light of the Moon and the stars in the heavens, he resumed his prayers. And it wasn't until well into the night that he ceased to pray and fell asleep.

7 Now the manner of his prayer was most interesting, for he spoke as if in a conversation and obviously heard the answers to his questions spoken conversationally, for he would often ask a question, then after a silent pause, nod his head and say, "I understand" or "I agree" or "As you will, so it shall be."

8 While Yeshua was up upon the mountain, momentous events were beginning to unfold back at his home, as Miriam and Martha spoke with one another, while Salome played with the children.

9 "How do you feel about Salome?" Miriam asked of Martha.

10 "It is the very same thing I was about to ask you," Martha answered. "In truth, I have pinched myself several times since she arrived, for it seems so unlikely that I can have such affection for her.

11 It is as if she has always been one of our sisters, as if she grew up in our house and shared our parents. Yet the life she has lived is so different than the ones you and I have lived, it is difficult to understand how I can feel as close to her as I do."

12 Miriam nodded in agreement, saying, "Yeshua once told me that I would meet a woman whose heart would beat as one with mine.

13 Though it would seem to others as if I have known Salome but a few days, in truth, I have known her beyond time, and she is the woman he spoke of."

14 "What does that mean, beyond time?" Martha wondered.

15 Miriam reached out both of her hands and held her sister's, saying, "Oh Martha, someday you will have the veil lifted from your eyes and memory, and you will see not only the heavens that await, but also the glory that you have lived before you ever set foot upon this earth."

16 "You can see the heavens that await?" Martha whispered quietly. "And the life we lived before we lived? Show me how to do this wonder, Miriam."

17 Miriam shook her head and smiled a little smile, saying, "I remember all that has been before I came from the womb, and I see all that will be ere mortality is no more; but how I remember or how I see cannot be taught.

18 It is not something that can be learned, but something that must be acquired, the greatest treasure of Heaven or earth, and its name is faith.

19 Until one's faith is perfect, the veil cannot be lifted to the past or the future. The past forgotten and the future longed for are necessary to develop faith, and only once one's faith is perfect can the veil be lifted."

20 "What is it to have perfect faith then?" Martha asked.

21 Miriam answered her, saying, "Perfect faith is to know that any righteous, unselfish thing you ask of Elohim shall be done; that any command you give to men or demons or mountains in the name of Elohim, in virtue, shall be done as you have commanded; to know it with every fiber of your being; and to know it without doubt.

22 Perfect faith is to know that the will of Elohim is your will, and this by your free choice and desire, not by fear or because of pleasant association with your friends or family, but because the Celestine Light burns bright in your heart and illuminates the path before you with a torch that cannot be dimmed.

23 Perfect faith is to hear the voice of Elohim in the wind moving through the trees; in the songs of the birds and the music of the crickets; in the rush of the river or the tinkle of the creek.

24 Perfect faith is to feel the embrace of Elohim in the arms of all whom you love in the deepest part of your heart. I feel the embrace of our Heavenly Father and Mother when I hold you or our children or Yeshua.

25 And yes, I feel Elohim when I embrace Salome, and by this among all else, I know she is meant to be more than she is among us."

26 "What is there left for her to be, more than she is, dwelling under our roof and sharing our meals?" Martha wondered.

27 Miriam looked at her sister with a great seriousness and said unto her, "She must become a wife to truly be one of us."

28 Martha's eyebrows arched high, showing Miriam's statement came as a surprise to her. She said, "On the one hand what you say seems preposterous, for we have just met her. On the other, it is as you have said, we have known her beyond time, and I too have felt a strength of love for her that is surprising. Have you spoken to Yeshua about this?"

29 "Not a word," Miriam answered. "But there are no secrets from Yeshua. He knows what has been upon my heart these last days. That is why he went up into the hills alone, I am sure, that we might have time to talk with one another about this."

30 "What will Yeshua say?" asked Martha.

31 "Yeshua will abide by whatever we decide, for it can be no other way with the husband when there are wives more than one, even when the husband is Yeshua.

32 Perhaps even more particularly, because the husband is Yeshua, the example must be set for all of the other Children of Light.

33 You know my heart, Martha. I desire this to be so, but only if you also desire it, not because of me, but because of your own heart."

34 Martha gave a small laugh and said unto Miriam, "There will not be much difference than the way things already are. She will still sleep under our roof and eat our food, teach us the ways of the nobles, and play with the children.

35 I would welcome her as a wife. I do not think I feel for her as you do, but as I said, it is as if she is a sister I have always known."

36 Looking at her with soft love, Miriam spoke lovingly to Martha, saying, "There would actually be many differences, dear sister. Foremost, her bond to us would be legally joined so that when Yeshua has left this world, the three of us would remain inseparable, along with our children.

37 And among the Children of Light, the marriage of a man and women is not as the marriages of the Hebrews or the people of Palestine, where one man has many wives, living separately and distinctly.

38 Among the Children of Light, those who are married in plurality are one family, married one to another.

39 In your case, Yeshua is a brother, merely holding the title of husband, as the guardian of your eternal covenant to Yochanan, and I am your sister by birth.

40 But in my case, we would be married one to another, Yeshua, Salome, and I, as would you, Salome, and I. If the world and the Sadducees did not already have enough cause to persecute Yeshua, this will give them more. Even among our own people, those who are new to our ways may not understand."

41 Martha laughed heartily at the last statement of Miriam, saying, "When have we ever made a decision based upon what the Sadducees or the world thought?

42 As for the Children of Light, they love Yeshua and you with a pure love. When you explain what it is we do, I know all will stand with us with blessings."

43 Having come to common agreement, the sisters then approached Salome after the children had been sent to play on their own outside. The three women sat down upon the ground, facing one another, and Miriam and Martha each took a hand of Salome's and rested it in theirs, and Miriam said unto her, "Salome, in just a few days, you have become like one of our family, and it seems to us as if you have always been with us. How do you feel?"

44 Salome's face lit up with joy, "I have never even imagined such happiness could be possible. In my life, I have never aspired to have what I now feel in my heart since I have been with you, in your home, because I never comprehended that such a feeling could exist.

45 If I were to die today, I would die as the happiest woman on earth, for I have tasted unconditional love and it has changed me.

46 In the community, there is much talk about the Celestine Light. Until I feasted upon the love and acceptance I have been given in your home, I would not have been able to understand what was meant by the Celestine Light. But now that I know, now that you have shared, it is a part of me; it fills me and uplifts me and leaves no place for darkness in my life."

47 "How do you feel about Yeshua and who do you think he is?" Miriam asked.

48 "I am not sure how I am allowed to feel about Yeshua," Salome replied. "He is like no man I have ever known or seen before. I know he is a prophet of Elohim, but also far more than this, for no prophet has ever done the things that he can do.

49 I feel a love for him that is similar to the love I feel for you, so I am somewhat confused by it, and I do not want to give you cause to worry, for my love is pure.

50 I am honored to be allowed to be in your home as one of your family and do not know what would become of me if you were to send me away.

51 I have a thirst for the things Yeshua can teach me, but also I love spending every moment

here with the two most amazing women I have ever known."

52 "Miriam hesitated but a moment, then asked, "Would you like to legally become part of our family?"

53 Salome seemed shocked and even hurt by Miriam's question, and she answered, "Thank you for asking, Miriam, but it would make me sad to do that. You mean as a wife of Yeshua, for that is the only way I could legally be a part of your family, but I think that would push me away from you, whom I desire to be closest to. Do not think ill of me, but my heart is very drawn to you, Miriam, in ways I do not even understand.

54 If I became a wife of Yeshua, I would be given a separate house, and though we would often still be close, it would not be as it is now where I am always with you.

55 No, as I said when I first arrived, I would rather be a servant in your home than to be cast away from you. I know it would be a great honor and I should be happy, and I ask your forgiveness for declining. I do not see happiness greater than the happiness I have right now coming from it."

56 Miriam smiled, and patting Salome's hand that she held with her other hand, she answered her, saying, "You misunderstand, dearest Salome. When a man marries more than one wife among the Children of Light, the wives are also married one to another, and they live as one family, under one roof, not in separate dwellings.

57 Though you have been among us but days, we know you, and you have already been a part of our family, before any of us were ever born into this world.

58 It seems like a lifetime ago that Yeshua and I were returning from a long stay in Egypt. As we were walking along the road to Palestine, Yeshua told me that the day would come when I would meet a woman whose heart would beat as one with mine, even as mine did with his.

59 I told him then that such a thing was not possible for me, and all the time since then, I have never had a reason to doubt my words, until I met you. Then my world changed, for even on that very first day, I knew that Yeshua's words had been fulfilled.

60 I need not ask how you feel, for my heart would not feel thus toward you unless yours also felt thus toward me.

61 You know Martha has a special arrangement in her marriage to Yeshua, but such an arrangement would not exist between we three women, as we do not encroach upon the sanctity of the marriage of Yochanan and Martha."

62 At the words of Miriam, Salome put both hands to her face in disbelief, and tears came pouring from her eyes. Then she threw herself upon Martha and Miriam, pulling them together in one embrace, and she kissed each of them lightly upon their foreheads, "Thank you, dearest sisters. I thought my joy was full. Little did I realize my cup was just beginning to be filled.

63 I am speechless. I am overwhelmed. I am in love. And I say *yes*."

64 As sunset neared, Yeshua returned from the mountain and was greeted by the simultaneous embraces of all three women and kisses on his cheeks above his beard as he came through the doorway and by his children and the children of Martha, who embraced him on his legs.

65 Miriam smiled at him coyly and asked, "Dear husband, do I need to tell you anything about what has transpired while you have been away, or is it all known to you already?"

66 Yeshua smiled broadly and answered with great happiness in his voice, "I know you have found that which you said you would never seek or discover, and in this, you may know that destiny finds you, even when you seek it not.

67 I know that you have been given a balm that will calm your heart and clear your head, even in the most difficult days to come.

68 You have found one of the great stars that has been missing from your Heaven, and her name is Salome. Knowing your happiness and the happiness of Martha and Salome, my joy is also full."

69 Martha clapped her hands together in excitement and said, "Let us begin immediately to plan the wedding."

70 But Yeshua held up his hand and said unto them, "We do not have as much time as you would probably prefer to prepare, nor should we make this wedding into a great affair, but let us keep it in some simplicity.

71 Tomorrow is the Sabbath, and we will marry on the third day after. The community will wish to have a celebration feast, but let us limit that to the wedding day, plus three.

72 On the day after the following Sabbath, Miriam, Salome, and I will leave along with all of my Apostles and some of their wives, on an extended trip through Galilee.

73 I trust that in that time and even under those circumstances, the three of you along with your friends, can plan a wedding we will all remember."

74 In unison, all of the women said, "Yes," and then began to speak with enthusiasm to one another while Yeshua went in and played with the children who had been waiting for him."

CHAPTER 50

Eternal Love

Martha announces to the members of the community that she, Miriam, and Salome have committed their hearts and lives to one another and would like to take their vows of marriage to one another and to Yeshua before their friends and family. Yeshua explains to the community that with love and within family, the greatest work for Elohim can be accomplished, and emphasizes that this is an essential part of the Plan of Eternal Progression.

he next day, on the Sabbath, the Children of Light, both the old and the young, from all of the Communities of Light along Lake Gennesaret, met together at Capernaum for edification, one with another, as was the custom on that day.

2 Martha had made it known when she first married Yeshua and Miriam that unlike her sister Miriam, she did not desire to travel Galilee and beyond, following Yeshua in his journeys, and preferred to remain at home in the community, taking care of their home and the children and helping to build the Communities of Light.

3 Abiding by her wishes and happy to have such a pillar of strength remaining always in the community, Cephas called and set her apart shortly after her arrival to be numbered among the Council of Eleven.

4 The Council of Eleven had also been given the responsibility of overseeing the weekly Sabbath meeting, as most, if not all of the Apostles, could be expected to be away with Yeshua at any time.

5 Thus it was on this Sabbath that following community announcements and task and event scheduling conducted by Gimiel, Martha rose to speak to the congregation of the Children of Light. And she said unto them, "Brothers and sisters of Light, as always, I am humbled to have the opportunity to speak with you, even more so on this day, for I have momentous and joyous news.

6 As you know, most recently, a dear friend, Salome, has come to live in our home. I know many of you must have wondered about the circumstances of her arrival and how it is that she dwells with us in our home."

7 Then motioning to Miriam and Salome, she beckoned for them to join her on the rise, and they came up and stood with her, one on either side, with their arms interlocked behind Martha's back.

8 Martha continued saying, "Miriam is my sister by birth. We were fortunate to have had the same wonderful parents and to have grown up in this life together.

9 As Yeshua has taught us, like many of you with your families, Miriam and I know we have been sisters for much longer than these few years upon the earth. In truth, we have been best

friends for time beyond time, before we ever came upon this place of mortality. I know this deeply in my heart.

10 Then upon this earth came Salome into our lives. From the moment we first met her, there was a feeling in our hearts for one another that transcended this world. We each knew, before words had ever been spoken of it one to another, that though we had not known each other before in this life, we had been inseparable for time beyond time in the life that came before. This too, I know deeply in my heart.

11 That is why we never could have abided for Salome to dwell anywhere but under our roof once she came among the Children of Light, for though the world counted her not among our family, our hearts shouted that she was a part of us that could not be separated.

12 Yesterday, for the first time, the three of us spoke with each other about the feelings in our hearts for one another, as powerful as any feelings could be. Hearing in the words of each other, the truths our hearts already knew, we understood without doubt or hesitation that we must henceforth be always as one.

13 In our home, in embrace of each other, we committed our hearts and our lives to one another.

14 When Yeshua returned later in the day, we told him of our decision, and he blessed it and abides with it in joy.

15 Now we would like to make our commitment to one another and to Yeshua formal, and three days hence, we shall take our vows of marriage with Salome before you who are our dearest friends and spiritual brothers and sisters."

16 Martha became quiet and nodded her head toward the Children of Light of the communities indicating she had finished speaking. For a moment, there was utter silence as those gathered considered the words that Martha had just spoken. Then like a wave building to crescendo, everyone began to clap their hands together and whistle and stomp their feet upon the ground in approval, until the very earth seemed to shake and the air was alive with sound.

17 Martha, Miriam and Salome were very grateful to see and hear the unconditional support of their friends. Tears of happiness fell down each of their cheeks as they reveled in the enthusiasm of their friends and they looked at one another with wide smiles of joy and love.

18 Shortly afterward, Yeshua came up to the rise and spoke to the Children of Light, saying, "Words cannot express the happiness I feel because of the joy of these women whom I love and am honored and blessed to call my wives.

19 You look to me to guide and teach you in the ways of the Celestine Light of Elohim, and that is one of my great purposes upon the earth in mortality. But even as you, I experience light every day, and I learn and am uplifted by the light that comes upon me.

20 Each of you brings light into my life. Witnessing your victories each day over the adversary within; seeing your own growth in the Celestine Light, how each day you strive and most often succeed at becoming better than you were; seeing how you teach your children with love and tenderness and by honest example—these things and so many more uplift and inspire my spirit every day.

21 But it is within the walls of our own home, within the embrace of our own wives and children or husbands as it may be, that we truly glorify one another and help our dearest loved ones to transcend the bonds of mortality in spirit, even while we are still in this physical life.

22 So it is with my wives and children.

23 To marry with love, to have children, and to share an unbreakable bond and devotion to one another—this is a great part of the Plan of Eternal Progression that Elohim laid out before the world ever was.

24 It is with your family that you are called to do your greatest work for Elohim. Though you may be a busy man of commerce or called to be an Apostle and carry great demands upon your time or called to be a missionary far from your family for a time, you must never neglect your family.

25 Your family, and love itself, is like the most delicate and beautiful of flowers. It requires constant devotion and attention to thrive, and when it thrives, it brings you a joy and fulfillment as great as anything you will ever experience.
26 Do you desire to truly know Elohim? Do you wish to feel the endless and boundless love that your Father and Mother in Heaven have for you? Then embrace the companions of love with whom you journey through eternity, not just in passing, but hold them tight, listen to their breathing, and feel their heart beat against yours. Smell the sweetness of their hair and feel the softness of their skin.
27 Drop down all of your walls and merge your aeons as one. Savor the feeling of oneness that washes over you and through you, in you, and around you.
28 From the depths of your heart speak to them of your love; tell them in softness and with your aeon alive with light that you love them with every fiber of your being, with every part of your body, mind, and spirit.
29 Now go and embrace your children one by one. Give them the fullness of your unconditional love. Let there be no doubt by your words and aura that you are their rock upon whom they may always depend, the bright fire upon whom they may always count upon to guide them to safe harbors.
30 As you hold your children in your arms, feel their love emanating unto you, a love so pure, without judgment, seeking only the same love in return.
31 In the arms of your dearest families, in their words of love spoken softly, in their praises given often, in their harsh words or voice never heard, is a taste of Heaven on earth.
32 Therefore, partake of the love of your family and partake often. As you partake, so should you give.
33 As you hold and cherish those whom you love, think of how greatly your Heavenly Father and Mother love and cherish you. By this, you will come to experience and feel their infinite love in every part of you, more surely than by any other thing you can do."

CHAPTER 51

The Powers of Lanaka

Yeshua continues his talk to the members of the community and speaks about the aeons (energies) of the universe that can be controlled and used for things that would seem like miracles to those that do not have the same understanding. He also speaks about the energy centers of the body and specifically what their names are, what powers they hold, and how to unleash them, as well as the eighth energy center that is formed when all seven are in harmony.

Yeshua continued to speak unto the Children of Light, saying, "My Apostles shall be leaving soon on a journey with me through Galilee. Before we depart, I desire to speak to you as my brothers and sisters of the Celestine Light and to impart to you teachings beyond which I give to the world, that you might be more surely guided and grow in your lives while we are away.

2 Consider Aeon. What is it? Where is it? How is it?

3 Aeon is from Elohim. It is everywhere. It is in everything, including you, and it takes many forms.

4 Aeon is energy like a fire, power like a wave of the ocean, and a force unknown like a lodestone.

5 All people are affected and influenced by the aeons that surround them, both those that touch them from other people and those that touch them from beyond.

6 The people of the world understand that they are affected by mysterious aeons, but to them, the cause is unknown. Among the Children of Light, let those mysterious aeons be known and understood that they may be called upon as needed.

7 You can enliven the aeons that are a part of you, and you can create and control aeons beyond you. Even as you make a recipe for the food you prepare and gather all of the ingredients, so too can you call aeons from beyond the oceans of the sky to accomplish what you will; so too can you create a shield that will repel aeons that have come upon you undesired and unbidden.

8 Not with the natural man of the world are these things possible, but only with the Children of Light who live in virtue and righteousness.

9 You have within your body seven abodes of aeon. Each creates an independent fire, but each is also affected by the others. When one is perturbed, all become out of sorts.

10 As Children of Light, it behooves you to always be striving for balance in your life. As you reach for this worthy goal, it is wise to consider the state of your seven abodes of aeon. Are you continually nurturing and caring for each aeon in ways that makes the whole of your being vibrant and full of light?

11 I am going to explain to you now about the seven abodes of aeon in your body and the

eighth that is formed when all seven are in health and harmony with one another.

12 The name for each one was not chosen at random, but is an essential name, for the sound of it spoken embodies the essence of the aeon and induces it to become more active within you.

13 Merely speaking the name of the aeon attunes your spirit and body to that abode of power.

14 Some of the sounds may not be familiar to you because of your native tongue. Therefore, let all learn together some of the melodies of Heaven.

15 Your seven personal aeons of power, including the eighth when it is formed, are called the Lanaka.

16 The sacred sounds of your aeons of power, beginning at the top and following to the bottom, are Xe (zēē), Ka (käh), Qo (kwōh), Ja (jäh), Za (zāy), Wz (wĭz), and Vm (Vĭm).

17 The aeons of power align vertically, and there is a powerful relationship between all of them, as well as groups of them.

18 When all of these are in harmony and unison, they create an eighth aeon of power, the sound of Oo (oo), which appears not in one place, but everywhere in you and outside of you. Your aeon of Oo radiates from the core of your soul. It fills you and everyone and everything around you that it reaches with the essence of your desire.

19 Understanding the Lanaka within you is essential to your ability to channel the aeons of Heaven. It is not enough to merely learn of these seats of power and how to enliven them. You must also learn how they relate one to another and how to attune and harmonize groups together for specific purposes.

20 You will first begin to learn how to do this with methods that take thought and time and action. But as you become accomplished and the master of your Lanaka, you will be able to call upon your seats of power and marshal them, with but a moment of thought.

21 I will teach you some of this today, and my Apostles to whom I shall teach a fullness will share the greater knowledge with you in days to come.

22 The first aeon is called the Xe (zēē). It is located in a space outside of your body and slightly above your head. This is the seat of power for your spiritual gifts. This is your straight channel to Elohim.

23 Enliven your Xe by picturing in your thoughts and feeling with your senses the space just above your head.

24 Take a full breath and slowly exhale. Near the bottom of your breath, begin to spin the aeon of your Xe round and round in various directions until you find the direction that is most comfortable for you.

25 Breathe in and out again and spin your Xe once more, but now spin it faster and push it outward. Repeat this as many times as you desire. By this simple exercise, you highly activate your Xe and prepare it to serve you.

26 But the Xe does not function alone. When you desire to call upon your sacred powers to heal another or yourself or to command nature as you need to fulfill the will of Elohim or any other thing that is good and virtuous, selfless and noble, you must form a harmony and unison of movement with the Xe, the Ka, and the Ja.

27 A supporting harmony is necessary from all of your other aeons of power, but it is these three which become the active force, empowered by your faith to fulfill your desires.

28 Below the Xe, residing within your head, is your aeon of Ka (käh). This is the abode of your thoughts, and your thoughts can be projected with both subtle and great physical power.

29 Each moment, both while you are awake and while you are asleep, your Ka is forever active. Though it may rest, it never sleeps.

30 One of your great reasons for being born into mortality was to give you the opportunity under the challenging circumstances of the physical life, to more fully enliven your Ka.

31 Each day, in your normal activities, conversations, and thoughts, you call upon only the tiniest piece of the aeon of power, that is, your Ka.

32 Imagine the many baskets of grapes that go into the vat to make a large jug of wine. If the

full jug is the power of your Ka that can be, then a single cluster of grapes from among the many in the baskets is all of your Ka that is empowered by your typical daily activities.
33 In the Celestine Kingdom of Elohim, no one is given more responsibility than they have knowledge to carry out that with which they are charged.
34 Therefore, whosoever is of virtue and faith and gains greater knowledge and ability to call upon the power of their Ka in mortality shall have so much more opportunity in the world to come.
35 Though mortality is but a few breaths of your eternal life, they are very significant breaths. In the fire of the furnace of mortal life, you must begin to think very clearly and well or you will be consumed by the fire.
36 The challenges of the fires of mortality give you the opportunity to enliven a greater portion of the power of your Ka. If you take advantage of the fires and use them as a tool instead of a threat, the power and ability of your Ka will increase.
37 Activate your Ka and all of your other seats of power in the same manner that you did your Xe.
38 At least once each day, preferably soon after you arise and before you begin calling upon your Ka for understandings and decisions, you should, one by one, rapidly spin each of your aeons of power; that you may be fully enlivened and prepared for the day to come.
39 Likewise, each night, before you enter your dreams, it is beneficial that you should enliven all of your abodes of aeon in the same manner.
40 When you do this, continually say aloud the name of the aeon which you are empowering while exhaling a single breath.
41 Below your Ka, residing within your throat, is your Qo (kwōh). This is the seat of power for your confidence and ability to express your thoughts and desires.
42 In essence, your Qo is your faith in yourself. It partners with any and every other aeon of power as needed, and no other aeon of power can fully achieve its glory without the unwavering support and harmony of the Qo.
43 Below your Qo, residing in the area where you feel the beat of your heart, is your Ja (jäh), the seat of power for your emotions.
44 The Ka and the Ja—what you think and what you feel—are the two most important aeons of power. But to be magnified to their greatest potential, they must be in harmony with one another and called upon in equality.
45 The natural man calls upon the aeon of his Ka when he thinks he needs it and calls upon the aeon of his Ja when he feels he needs it.
46 To the natural man, the Ka and Ja are more often opponents rather than friends, and many people guide their lives by their preference for one, while ignoring the other.
47 In truth, one without the other is like a mallet without a chisel. Certainly, you can do some things with either alone, but together you can build something of greatness.
48 So it is with your Ka and Ja. They have very similar sounds, the only two aeons within you that do, a testament indeed that they were designed by Elohim to be used together in harmony.
49 You should train yourself to never rely just on one or the other, but whenever one is called upon, let it always call its opposite twin that they might merge in a harmony of truth, light, and power.
50 Whenever a choice is to be made, ask your Ja how it feels and ask the Ka what it thinks and allow them to be equal partners in the choice to be made.
51 I would speak now of the harmony of three. Three is an even more empowering number, a very strong union capable of great power, as you see in the Father, the Mother, and the Son that are the Elohim of this world and the heavens above.
52 Do you want your Xe to manifest the powers of Celestine Light unto you? First empower and spin your Ka and then your Ja, and then your Ka and your Ja in perfect harmony and unison.
53 Then enliven and spin your Xe. Once it is moving with excitement, marry it in harmony to

the movements of the Ka and the Ja, so the three move as one, even as the three who are Elohim act as one in all things of consequence.
54 When the Xe and the Ka and the Ja are enlivened and move together in unison as one, your aeon of Aura, the field of force that emanates from all that you are, expands outward in power and reach.
55 When the Xe and the Ka and the Ja are enlivened and move together in unison as one, your divine soul begins to sing in resonance with the aeon of Elohim, which fills all things.
56 In resonance and harmony, you will become one with the energies and powers of Heaven, and your faith will be whole.
57 With the essence of faith filling your Xe, Ka, and Ja, you will no longer be as a mortal upon the earth for that moment in time, but one with the Elohim, and all things shall be possible unto you, and the power that is faith shall be upon you and in you.
58 It is in this state that you can most clearly communicate through prayer with the Elohim and most profoundly feel and understand the promptings and guidance of the Holy Spirit of Elohim as the Mother sends it forth upon you.
59 Below your Ja is your aeon of Zā (zāy). This is the seat from which you may call forth the memories of all that has come before this life.
60 The memory of every moment you lived in Xeon before your mortal life is accessible through your Zā when it is helpful for you to remember and if you have learned how to channel it through your Xe, and see it in your Ka, and feel again the emotions that coursed through your Ja.
61 For some of you, there is more than Xeon to remember, for some of you have lived in mortality before the life that is upon you today. Memories of the lives before this life can also be called forth by the power of the Zā.
62 These memories do not reside within the Zā, but are inscribed by Elohim in the heavens and called forth by those who understand the mysteries through the aeon of the Zā.
63 In the days of the first men upon the earth in mortality, the usual life span of each man and woman was about three hundred years. Many lived to five or six hundred years and some such as Methuselah even beyond that time.
64 Thus each person had many years to learn the lessons of mortality and become fully prepared to live in immortality.
65 But the earth changed, as did the people upon the face of the land. The foods they ate and drank become corrupted and full of death, and death and disease came into their bodies and upon the face of the land.
66 As these things came to pass, the span of the life of man began to shrink; until today, a man has only a small part of the years that his ancestors had to learn the lessons of mortality and become prepared for immortality.
67 Even so, most people still learn and demonstrate enough in the short years of a single mortality to be drawn by the resonance of their soul into the heavenly light or pulled to the cold and dark, in the life to come.
68 Verily, for most, one life in mortality is enough, providing sufficient time that by the choices in life the individual can be drawn by their resonance to the light or the dark in the hereafter, as they will.
69 But there are many, including those who die as children, that in their short mortal life of less than one generation, were not afforded sufficient time to learn the lessons of mortality and be given fair opportunity to become the resonance of light or darkness that will call to them in the life to come.
70 For these, after they have died, they must return again to another life into mortality that they may be afforded the time and experiences necessary to learn the lessons of mortality and fully form their resonance of light or darkness.
71 Only by this can they be drawn to their true place of resonance in the world to come.

72 Therefore, understand the words which I speak. Most come into mortality but once. But there are others who will come twice and still others three times, and rarely more, until they have had the opportunity to participate in all of the essential experiences of mortality, involving family, friends, and the challenges of life, which prove their allegiance to either the light or the dark.

73 Those of you that have experienced more than one mortality cannot freely remember your lives of the past any more than you can remember your preexistent life in Xeon.

74 If you could fully remember your life in Xeon in the presence of Elohim, how would you develop faith? For faith is needed for belief in things you cannot see or have not proof of, not for things you can see and know.

75 With the tiny bit that man utilizes the power of his Ka, it would become overwhelmed if all the memories of Xeon and previous mortalities were flooded upon it.

76 It is for this cause that you have your Zā. Through the empowerment of your Zā, you can call forth into your Ka selected memories of your preexistent life in Xeon and any other lives you had in mortality.

77 You can only call forth past experiences you have had that directly aid you in making choices and decisions in the life you now live.

78 Perhaps in a former life, you found a special spot upon the lake where the fish always clustered. One day, you truly had a great need to catch fish, perhaps to feed your hungry family or to pay a debt. On that day, you could empower your Zā, which would then channel the memory of your former mortality to your Ka, that you might be fulfilled in your need.

79 Perhaps in a former life you learned the secrets of the power of command. Now in this life you begin to study it again. If you studied just as a man, you would need to learn every step once more. But if you empowered your Zā, you could channel the memories of what you already had learned in a previous life, so you would not need to waste time relearning it all over again in this life.

80 Without accomplishing this, to remember what had already been learned that is of significance, those who return to mortality squander their precious opportunity.

81 Not that the memories will necessarily come instantly in whole into your Ka, but because of your past understanding and affinity, knowledge from your past lives will flow into you quickly and easily, like honey on a hot day into the bee man's pot, as you command your Lanaka to make it so.

82 And how may you know if this is your first life or another opportunity in mortality? Very simply, if you seek the past with the secrets of the Children of Light, but do not find it, then you know this is your first mortality and there are no memories of past mortalities to find.

83 This will be the case for most of you and most of the people of earth. If it is, rejoice, for in this, your first mortality, you may yet learn all you need and therefore progress much quicker than those who must return again to learn and experience what they did not in their first mortality.

84 In addition to that which I have already revealed, I will teach my Apostles all of the secrets for empowering the Zā, and they shall teach them to you.

85 Once you have learned these techniques, you may delve into your prelife in Xeon or your past mortalities as you need the knowledge in this mortality.

86 On very rare occasions, Elohim will ask one of the pillars of Heaven to return to earth for another mortality, not to learn more or experience more, for they were already a pillar of Heaven, but to fulfill a specific mission for Elohim. Such was the life of Yochanan the Baptizer, who was the prophet Elias come again at the behest of Elohim.

87 Your Zā is also the portal to your primordial fears. Certain fears encompass all people. Because most of your ancestors for generations upon generations had cause for fear concerning certain things, the aeons of those fears become an active part of the Zā of all children born upon the earth.

88 Therefore, a child does not have to learn to be cautious of heights, for they have a primordial

fear that is continually being channeled through their Zā, unbidden and unrelenting.

89 Even as someone may benefit by recalling the memories of their former lives through their Zā, so every individual upon the earth benefits from the collective knowledge of all who have proceeded them and shared powerful, similar experiences.

90 Below your Zā is your aeon of Wz (whĭz). This seat of power pertains to all things having to do with your physical body: your health, your vitality, your strength.

91 When you are confronted with a person who is physically diseased or ill, before you seek to channel the aeons to heal them or help them heal themselves, you must look upon the center of their Wz and then at the aeon, emanating to all parts of their body to determine the path and seat of their malady.

92 Only then will you know which energies of Elohim to call upon and where and how to direct them to effect the healing you desire.

93 It is exceptionally important that you do everything within your capabilities and opportunities to maintain the temple of your body, which is reflected in your Wz, in the greatest of health, for all the aeons of your Lanaka are hindered by the weaknesses of the Wz.

94 It is possible, with great intent and focus, for someone that has been crippled to nevertheless empower the other aeons of the Lanaka, for though a part of them may be dead, the other parts are still very much alive.

95 But for someone that is infirmed or enfeebled because of sickness and afflictions of the body, the weakness of their Wz overshadows all of their other aeons of power, and they must first refresh and renew the strength of their Wz before they will be able to know the fullness of their gifts.

96 Below the Wz is the aeon of Vm (vĭm). This is the seat of your creativity and all things sexual, as well as a source of great activation and magnification of all the seats of power above it.

97 Verily, the Vm is the most misunderstood and neglected of aeons.

98 The priests of the world teach the suppression of the Vm and insult Elohim the creator by teaching suppression of the Vm in the name of Elohim.

99 The Vm is the anchor, a foundation for all the aeons seated above it. When the Vm is suppressed, all the other aeons of power within a body are muted and cannot fulfill the full measure of their potential.

100 It is Elohim that created man and woman. It is Elohim who gave them lust one for another. It is Elohim that gave them the ability to experience great pleasure when they activate, stimulate, and spin their aeon of Vm, both in works of creation and in sexual activities.

101 If Elohim gave all of these things to men and women, who are the priests of the world that would take them away? Who are the teachers of falsehoods that call good evil and evil good?

102 But do not mistake my words. There should only be chastity before marriage and only fidelity after.

103 Men and women should not partake of the sacred, even to taste, without a loving and faithful commitment of marriage for life or eternity as they desire. To do so is a vile abomination in the eyes of Elohim and a sin that is only washed clean by a deep and profound repentance.

104 In the Vm, you are given an extraordinary and sacred gift: a small but delicious taste of what it is to be an Elohim.

105 You are not as the animals, but like a god enabled to make marvelous creations, from a tapestry to a boat, to a child, and to experience sublime joy in the process of the creation.

106 Elohim has given you this wondrous gift of creation, but also told you that in the aspect of sexual relations; to have none with another, save with those to whom you have given an abiding commitment and bond through the covenant of marriage.

107 By this, the gift of Elohim is honored, not desecrated, and men and women are uplifted, not degraded.

108 By this, the sacred remains sacred, strengthening the bonds and contentment of those who have pledged themselves to one another. When the sacred remains sacred, you can experience a

depth of love and fulfillment unknown to those who have trampled upon sacredness.

109 By this, children are more likely to be raised by parents who will love them and teach them balance and respect, righteousness, and love of the light. When they are grown, they will make better choices and find greater fulfillment in all aspects of their lives.

110 By this, each individual may grow and expand far beyond the possibilities of the misguided who partake of the sacred without commitment to the holy, for the virtuous learn the divine lights of fidelity, compromise, interdependence, and selflessness, which fills their hearts with joy and fulfills their lives, love, family, and dreams.

111 Therefore, in sexual relations, expand your Vm and expand it often, with creativity and diversity and nothing held back. But only within the sanctity of marriage to those to whom you have committed faithfulness and fidelity.

112 The ways of the world teach that wives must obey and serve their husbands, but the ways of Celestine Light teach that in life, husbands and wives should serve and consider one another.

113 And in their relations of intimacy, let the man find pleasure in serving the woman and the woman find pleasure in being served.

114 When the weaker serves the stronger, both are brought down to places of greater darkness. But when the stronger serves the weaker, both are raised up to places of greater light.

115 Nor should you feel ashamed or hesitant to spin the sexual aspect of the aeon of your Vm in solitude, both before and during marriage. It is an aeon of great desire. It calls to you often that you might become more than you are by helping to enliven all of your other aeons of power.

116 But spin it with virtue, without thought of any to whom you are not married, save those who are merely imaginations of your Ka, and then only in ways of respect, not degradation, for this is an essential of an intimacy of virtue and true love.

117 Verily, upon the foundation of the aeon of the Vm, all other seats of your power rest. As your Vm expands, so too do all your other seats of power enlarge.

118 Of all the aeons of power, the Vm is the most easy to spin and enlarge. It is like the flint that easily sparks the fire.

119 As it spins, it resonates with its opposite—the Xe. Thus, the Xe also becomes more activated and more capable of channeling the powers of Elohim through you.

120 As both the Xe and the Vm harmonize, they spin together and cause a deep resonance within the five aeons that are framed between them, and all seven aeons expand and become full of light, filling your very body with strength and clarity, enabling you to see what you did not see, to feel what you could not feel, to know what you did not know, and to do what you could not do, because you become more than you were.

121 Now I give a challenge unto the men of the Communities of Light. Verily, the women are more virtuous than you. They could look upon a naked man other than their husband, and they would not lust after him. But how many of you would look upon a naked woman other than your wife and not lust after her?

122 Among the world, in the land of Palestine, women are forced to be covered from head to foot in formless fabric, that the men will not be tempted by the barest of skin that they might show.

123 The men who are Children of Light must be greater than the men who are of the world.

124 Through prayer and fasting, you must overcome yourself. You must become your own master and rule over every part of the mortal house of your soul.

125 Elohim did not make the beauty of the bodies of men and women to be hidden beneath volumes of shapeless clothes.

126 The sisters of light must not be required to be bound by the wickedness of the world, but must be free within the Communities of Light to uncover their head and their face and any other part of their body that they desire even unto nakedness, without worry of stirring the lusts of the brothers of light who are not their husbands.

127 Therefore, let this be so in the places of the community that are set in privacy from the

eyes of the world.

128 And if any brother looks upon a sister with even the slightest of lust, let him cover his eyes and walk about as a blind man until he can look upon her only with pure and virtuous thoughts.

129 And if he still is at war with himself, let him go into his house and remain there with prayer and fasting until he has overcome his adversary within.

130 Each day, you should enliven and expand your abodes of power that they may become as useful to you as they were intended when Elohim gave you your gifts.

131 When you enliven your abodes of power one after the other to begin or end your day, or even in the middle of the day if you are tired, there is an order that you would do well to follow, as the former is a spark for the latter.

132 First, enliven your Ka, followed or quickly accompanied by your Vm, followed by your Ja, followed by your Qo, followed by your Xe, followed by your Zā, followed by your Wz.

133 Once you have more fully enlivened each of your primary abodes of aeon, unify and amplify them as one with your Oo. Finally, after taking a deep breath in, slowly exhale. As you near the bottom of your exhale, spin your aeon of Aura as one energy throughout your body, faster and faster, until you can feel it alive inside of you.

134 At the bottom of your next breath, speed your aeon of Aura still faster and expand it outward still further.

135 Do this for as many times as you desire, each time speeding the spin and expanding your aeon of Aura outward.

136 This exercise builds the divine powers inside of you, prepares you to more easily use them for good, and stores reservoirs of power in your soul that will abide in peace, awaiting for your call in time of need or desire.

137 Verily, I promise unto you: I shall teach my Apostles all of the secrets of the seven aeons of power that reside within you. And with the worthy and virtuous, they shall share all that I have spoken and shown to them, and nothing shall be impossible to the worthy Children of Light.

138 In this, you will no more be as the people of the world, but will know the secrets of your own creation and how to unleash the powers that reside within you, which Elohim has reserved for the righteous Children of Light.

139 You will need no more worry about the powers of the world; for you will be above them and greater than they are or ever could be."

CHAPTER 52

In the World but Not of It

As a continuation of his talk to the community members, Yeshua speaks about the importance of self-sufficiency and not being dependent upon, or in debt to, the things of the world. He encourages them to make all the things they need for food, clothing, and shelter, within the community and to do so with great creativity. He also speaks about making good choices for health and longevity.

eshua continued to speak to the brothers and sisters of the Communities of Light, saying, "I exhort you now, my brothers and sisters of light, to always set yourselves apart from and above the world.

2 As you grow in numbers and talents of the members of the communities, seek to become self-sufficient in your most basic needs, that though you may know of the world, you will not be dependent upon it, or in debt to it, or under threat of the vacillations and pettiness of its leaders.

3 Be always proficient in the making of homes and boats and all things such as you have need of in your daily lives.

4 Let each brother who has a skill teach it to many other brothers of the community, and let each sister who has a skill teach it to many other sisters of the community.

5 There will always be both necessities and gifts that you will purchase from the merchants of the world, but as much as it is possible with your numbers and talents, provide for yourselves the things in which you are in need.

6 Strive with diligence to have bounty and excess far beyond your needs, that you may store some for days of famine and pestilence that will surely come.

7 It will be well with you if all of the things which you eat and drink come from your own hands, from fruits and vegetables you have planted, harvested, and collected wild from the bounty of the earth, from fish you have caught and sea plants you have gathered, from honey you have fetched from the bees, and from all manner of foods you have prepared from the things you have brought unto you.

8 Food, shelter, clothing, and a means to earn a livelihood—in these things, let the Communities of Light become as self-sufficient as your numbers and talents and resources will allow.

9 The greater your self-sufficiency, the more you will be above the world and beyond the reach of its poisons, with the opportunity every day to live a life of happiness, joy, and fulfillment.

10 But the less self-sufficient you are, the more you will be within the grasp of the evil and people of the world insomuch that your life will often be darkened by the clouds of the world, the storms thereof which only bring pain, suffering, broken lives, and lost dreams.

11 The things you eat and drink must be of great importance to you. As you grow as a Child of Light, you learn which foods and drinks benefit your body and which do not.

12 As many of the foods and drinks of the world bring darkness into your body instead of light, it is far better if all of your food and drink comes only from those things which you have grown, caught, gathered, and prepared yourself.

13 Let the wine you drink also only be from your vineyards and orchards, from fruits you have grown and harvested and made into wine.

14 Let not your wine be defiled with excessive spirits that befuddle the head, but let it be like Tiyrosh of the pure fruits—sweet to the taste, slight of spirits, invigorating to the body, and calming to the restlessness of man.

15 Let Celestine wine be of two types—that of normal consumption which is like sweet water and should contain not more than three parts per hundred of the spirits to help preserve its freshness and purity, and that of celebrations and holidays which may contain up to five parts per hundred but is limited to one cup each day of the holiday or celebration, and then shared only within the privacy of your homes among friends and family in a salutation of inspiration.

16 And make no excuses for a second cup or a large cup that is in reality more than one. For that is the way of the world where one cup leads to another until drunkenness and defiling of the temple occurs. But be Celestines as you have been called—honoring your temples and master of yourselves.

17 Of the wines of the world, drink not at all, save in a most dire need, and then only Tiyrosh and never Shekar or any other type of strong drink on any occasion.

18 Only with the wine you make with your own hands, grown from grapes in your own vineyards, and fruits in your own orchards, can you depend on to be pure and of light, free from the poisons and errors that men of the world might put upon that which they make, be it intentionally or unintentionally.

19 Let this be an endeavor of the Communities of Light that Celestine wine shall become known among the world for its purity and deliciousness insomuch that even Caesar and the priests shall come unto you for an elixir of heaven.

20 Listen now, brothers and sisters, for I have another thing of great importance to share with you. Even now as you build the Communities of Light around Lake Gennesaret, you must begin preparing for the days when you shall depart from this land, never to return.

21 For there shall come great tribulations upon all the land of Palestine because of the Romans, and when those days come, the Children of Light must be no more in this place.

22 Therefore, begin preparing for your departure, not to one place alone, but to a few places upon the world where you can take root in peace upon the land and let your light shine forth upon it, until the days when the pull of the world can no longer hold the righteous and virtuous, and they shall be changed in the twinkling of an eye from mortality to immortality and rise to meet me in the sky.

23 Some will go into the sanctuary of the mountains, and others shall be children of the sea. Still others will dwell at the very heart of the world and be unseen.

24 While you are still nurtured in the communities of Gennesaret, become learned in skills that will serve you well, both in the community and upon the far places of the world. By this, even when you are living among the Ganish, you will be respected for your abilities, virtue, and character.

25 With the gifts given to you as Children of Light by Elohim, while you are still upon the earth in mortality, you are called to be stewards of the land and all the creatures therein and healers of both animals and people, both among the Children of Light and among those of the world who are lost, but still of virtue and righteousness, looking for a greater light to guide their lives.

26 When you depart the communities of Lake Gennesaret, see that you remember and continue to live the principles of life you have learned here, that your light will kindle the fire of truth in others to whom it shall touch, until the day comes when you are called together again to travel home to the greatest light and to your reward as faithful Children of Elohim.

27 Whether you become part of those who form a Community of Light on an isle of the sea, or in a land afar, or in the heart of the lands of the Ganish, see that you keep alive all of the things I have taught you, especially about your gifts and callings and the exclusivity of your food and drink from that of the world and the importance of self-reliance and self-sufficiency, leaning only upon your fellow brothers and sisters of light, and not upon the world.

28 Teach these precepts to your children and admonish them to teach them to their children and on unto the last generation for those who remain behind by their choice, when most will depart to their glory. By seeing these precepts lived, it shall be a way by which one Child of Light shall recognize another when they first encounter one another in lands far away.

29 For in the days to come, new Children of Light shall come down to the earth from the Celestine Light, sprinkled like celestial rain upon the earth, born into families of many cultures, races, and religions. Many will never have seen another Child of Light before they meet you or those who remain behind to hold the light.

30 Regardless of the color of their skin or their culture or class or the religion they may profess, by the light of their life you shall know them, and by the wonder of your light, which will resonate in their heart, they shall recognize you.

31 And there are those who become Children of Light as they live their lives and make good choices despite the darkness that may surround them.

32 They too will shine in a way unlike all others around them, and you may know them by their light, and they will know you by yours.

33 Let them gather unto you that they may leave the dreariness and darkness and discover the Family of Light and be one with the light that their brilliance may come forth.

34 For whether a Child of Light came from Heaven and held true to their essence despite the adversity of the world or came upon the earth without light, surrounded by darkness, but by choices of virtue and nobility became a Child of Light, in the eyes of Elohim, they are one and the same.

35 I would speak to you now somewhat of miracles and healing.

36 When those who only see with the eyes of the world see a miracle, it seems like magic to them because they do not understand the well from which it issues.

37 When the blind see, or the lame walk, or the storm is stilled, or the food is multiplied, or any other miracle that you may see or do is accomplished, it is not by some magic power, as it would seem to the eyes of the world, but by an understanding and adherence to immutable laws of Elohim that permeate all of nature, even the very air we breathe.

38 A person of the world, even one without education, thinks that they understand the law of the attraction of the earth that if something is dropped, be it a stone or a beam, it falls to the ground.

39 But they do not understand, nor can they learn in any school, that there is also the law of the attraction of the sky, whereby the stone upon the ground may fly up into the air. Someday, men will learn of this law, but it is given to the Children of Light today to understand every natural law by which Elohim governs all things.

40 Therefore, when you command a stone to rise off the ground and fly through the air, it will seem as if you are endowed with magical powers to the people of the world, but in truth, you are merely Children of Light, utilizing laws of Elohim, unknown to the world, but known to you, because to the faithful, Elohim shares all the secrets of Heaven.

41 As Children of Light, you are blessed to learn the secrets and mysteries of Heaven. Anything you have seen or heard that I have done, you also can do, and much more than that, as you learn and understand the laws of all creation, given by Elohim.

42 The mystery of all things I shall teach to my Apostles, and they shall teach to the faithful, one step at a time. Do not seek to learn of the greater powers until you have mastered the lesser, for it is by mastery of the lesser that the great powers can be manifested.

43 Now I would speak to you concerning health and longevity and healing of the sick and

afflicted, for unless you have an understanding of these things, you will always be blocked in your understanding of greater things.

44 In all things, you reap what you sow, and concerning how long you shall live or how robust your health shall be while you live, these things are like the miracles I spoke of; they are governed in many ways by immutable laws laid down upon all creation by Elohim. They who know the laws sow in understanding and reap accordingly, and great is the harvest.

45 Now it is taught in the synagogues and in many of the religions of the world that the days of man are numbered by Elohim, but this is not so. The end is written not in the stars, but in daily choices people make for life or death. The number is known to Elohim, but set by the choices made by man.

46 Though death can come suddenly and unexpectedly by accident or war, it most often comes in a thousand bites of poison that slowly sap the health and life of even the man of strongest vigor.

47 Now Elohim sees the number of days of man upon the earth, not because they were numbered by Elohim, but because they have been numbered by man by his choices of health and vigor, and seeing this, Elohim knows when the end shall come upon the man.

48 But the ways of man can change, and in saying this, know that I include women and children too. If a man continues upon the path of health he walks, be it good or bad, Elohim knows when his end shall come upon him.

49 But when the man changes a bad habit for a good, a poor choice for a better, the days he has numbered upon the earth increase, and Elohim then sees the days to come that were not there before.

50 It is given unto you to understand how to utilize faith and call upon the powers of Heaven for healing the sick and afflicted, but I exhort you to be prudent in the use of this gift of knowledge, ability, and faith.

51 All the people of the world and many of the Children of Light are afflicted with diverse afflictions and diseases that cause them pain and suffering and shorten their life. Should you spend your days healing all of these people?

52 Better it would be to spend your days teaching them the ways of health and longevity as revealed by Elohim unto the faithful that by better choices, many of the people could heal themselves.

53 And what shall you do when a man who is afflicted comes to you begging for a healing, and your heart beats in sympathy with his because of his pain? Or the man who is dying and offers to give you his fortune if you will just give him more days upon the earth? Or when one such as this is, a friend or a member of your family whom you love greatly?

54 Verily, I say unto you: It is your obligation as a son or daughter of light and love to use the knowledge and powers that have been given to you to heal all those who are ready to be healed, who call upon you and Elohim, be they a Child of Light or a confused wanderer in the world.

55 But for those not ready to be healed, even among the Children of Light, you have no obligation, nor should you heal them, even from compassion, save it be for a greater glory of Elohim.

56 Who then is ready to be healed? Always those who are of good heart and character and have proven by their actions a commitment to live the greater laws of health and vigor and longevity as given by Elohim, also those who strive to live in the light and whose affliction was not caused by their choices, but simply by adversity.

57 This may sound to be without compassion, but it is truly said with the greatest of love and desire to see all be in health and wellness.

58 Your greater task is not to heal the afflicted, but to teach the afflicted better ways to live, that their afflictions will be no more.

59 When a man does not love himself enough to treat his body like a temple, as Elohim has asked, he dishonors both himself and Elohim.

60 To heal the afflicted of pain and suffering caused by their own choices before they have shown a commitment to the higher path of health is to squander your time and talents upon something you will not change except for a moment in time.

61 For a time, the afflicted will be healed by your blessing and the healing may even be momentous. But unless the person was changed in their heart to a higher path of health before you healed them, they will continue on the path that led to their infirmity, and their end will still be a destruction of their temple, despite all that you did.

62 Consider the fisherman who, thinking himself cunning, sought to slip among the crocodiles of the river Nile to catch a great fish, but instead was caught in the jaws of many teeth. Staggering back to safety, he sought a Child of Light to restore his arm torn asunder.

63 Once healed, he thought to himself still of the great fish and, vowing to be even more cunning, sought it once more among the crocodiles, and this time, lost not just his arm, but his life.

64 Of what good then was the healing upon his arm if in his heart he had not changed? Without first a change of heart, the healing is not esteemed, Elohim is not glorified, and the man's fate is not averted, merely delayed.

65 Therefore, even if it is your own wife or husband upon the sickbed, let the sickness run its course, unless they have shown by word and deed and the truth of the vision of their aura that they are committed to the higher course of health as given by Elohim, and if that is so, heal them quickly.

66 If it is not, love them, teach them, and help them to be stronger in their will than they have been. But do not heal them until they have proven commitment to the path that will banish sickness and afflictions that come only because of their own slackness in obedience to the laws of health as given by Elohim.

67 With children who are afflicted, use your wisdom and give your love. Because of their youth, they may not yet fully understand the consequences of their actions and may become sick or afflicted in ignorance.

68 Therefore, where their life is not in danger from their sickness, let it be upon them just a bit so they learn the pain of poor choices, then heal them quickly that they learn the power of Elohim through the hands of the righteous, endowed with the knowledge of the workings of all things.

69 And what are the laws of life and health you must teach? To keep the Twelve Commandments of Sinai, to breathe good air and drink good water that is clear and flowing and abounding in life.

70 To eat the foods you have been taught to eat is of the greatest of importance to your health and longevity, as are the habits of cleanliness that you keep.

71 In that regard do not keep domestic animals in your home and let the place of sleep, even for pets, be beyond the threshold, except for those that are tiny, and leave no fur or waste amidst the places you dwell.

72 Wash your body often with herbs of cleansing and your hands more so, even every time you touch anything unclean and always before you prepare or eat your food.

73 You need to be outside often with vigorous movements of your body, sweating sometimes and drinking in sunshine over every part of your bare skin.

74 Therefore, if you are a Child of Light, do not be ashamed of your nakedness, for thus were you made by Elohim that you might be blessed by the healing light of the sun and invigorated by the depth of its warmth. But suffer not those who lust upon those so revealed to see their glory. And if the lustful cannot repent and overcome themselves, suffer them not to remain among you.

75 Among all the creatures that roam the land, it is man whom Elohim has blessed with a scarcity of hair that their bare skin might more readily absorb the healing light and warmth of the sun than any other of Elohim's creations. For this cause, nudity in the sun for a short time each day should be common and encouraged among the Children of Light.

76 But you must be ever vigilant in both yourself and others of lust outside of the sacredness

of marriage. If anyone sees another in nakedness to whom they are not married, of whom they have thoughts of lust, let them not be in their presence. If this requires separation of the sexes when naked, and by sexual inclination, so must it be, but only if you cannot look upon one another simply with admiration and without lust.

77 For your thoughts are the foundations of your actions. When your thoughts are pure, so shall your life be in virtue. But if your thoughts are impure, so shall your actions become defiling.

78 And for health and longevity, your thoughts are also of great importance. Good humor and good thoughts birth long life, while a sour disposition brings about an early death and much misery along the way.

79 Cultivate a love for one another that is deep and abiding insomuch that even beyond the family under your roof, you have a love that is felt in your heart for each of your brothers and sisters of light in the community so much so that whatsoever they should ask of you that is righteous and within your power to grant, you will give it to them with joy and gratitude to be able to help someone you love.

80 And in that channel, find service to one another and to your community. Even as you love one another, love your community, for it is a part of you and you are a part of it.

81 Any good thing therefore that you can do in the service of your brothers and sisters of light or your community is pleasing unto Elohim, warming to your heart, and enlarging upon your soul.

82 Remember to be balanced in all things and gracious, not judgmental in your toleration of the weaknesses of others. Seek first to perfect the temple of your own life before you judge others about theirs.

83 With balance and nonjudgment, see that you also have no grudges or grievances among you, for such become the wedge that splits the rock.

84 If one of you find a wedge coming between you and another member of the community, first go to them and seek a resolution of peace and with love.

85 If you cannot find this harmony, then go together to the patriarch or matriarch and seek their wisdom.

86 If you still cannot find harmony one with another, go to the Council of Eleven and seek their advice.

87 If you still cannot find harmony, let the council pass a binding judgment to settle the matter and let they who were at odds with one another find a place of peace and love and harmony with the judgment of the council.

88 If one or both cannot find such a place in their hearts, that their disagreement can be forgiven and forgotten, let them leave the community; else, they become the wedge that splits the rock.

89 Understand that all of these things of which I have spoken concerning health and longevity and peace and love and harmony are not commandments but admonishments.

90 You will not be punished by Elohim if you do them not, but will only be punishing yourself with greater sickness and afflictions and life and community challenges when you do them not.

91 Now I would speak to you of joy and revelry, for there should be much of it in the Communities of Light. Let music by instruments and songs ring forth in the communities from many places, from the women in the kitchen to the man upon the sea; let there be songs and whistling and humming and rhythm and harmony of voice with others.

92 Let everyone learn to play an instrument even if only to beat a stick upon a pot. And let music be heard often in the communities, both when alone and with many.

93 Now Elohim is the great creator of all that is, and wondrous are the beautiful creations of Elohim. But you are children of Elohim, and the ability to create works of beauty and wonder also resides within each of you.

94 Therefore, let everything in the community be done with beauty and creativity so that it is pleasing to the eye as well as of function. When you cast a pot, do not simply make a pot, but

give it symmetry and adorn it with patterns and designs.

95 When you make a simple gate, do not merely make it with branches laid side by side, but weave them into a pattern of beauty and wonder.

96 When you make a boat to catch the fishes of the sea, do not merely make a boat like all the other fishermen, but create designs upon it, not necessarily with function, but some simply for beauty and artistry.

97 When you lay your food upon the table, do not simply heap it into a bowl, but present it like a flower with patterns and colors that are pleasing to the eye.

98 When you build your house, do not build it plain or exactly like your neighbor, but let it be an expression of you and show creativity in design and color, with artistic accents abounding.

99 When you seek to give a gift to your husband or wife or child, do not simply buy a piece of cloth or a hook for fish or give them an extra bowl of dates, but create something by your own hands with love and artistry, be it functional or just for beauty, that they may have a piece of you with them every time they use it or gaze upon it.

100 Verily, you are the chosen children of Elohim. You are blessed to learn of and know all the mysteries of Heaven: to be able to live in the world but not be of it; to have joy, prosperity, peace, health, and long life, such as the world cannot even imagine.

101 Therefore, remember always who you are, be worthy of yourself and of the great blessings Elohim has given unto you. Live always in the light. Be ever the noble princes and princesses of Heaven; it is your blessing to become as you fulfill the full measure of your creation."

CHAPTER 53

The Destiny of Miriam

Yeshua reveals to Miriam the fullness of her destiny and the powers that she must wield in order to fulfill all that will be asked of her. He teaches her secret knowledge of the Elohim that no one else knows or will ever know. She is then imbued with the power of the Elohim as three blinding bolts of lightning shoot out of the sky and land upon her and Yeshua as they stand upon a mountaintop.

And it came to pass that early on the following day, Yeshua departed with Miriam and his other Apostles. And Salome and three wives of the Apostles came with them.

2 Rather than follow the roads into the towns of Galilee, the group immediately struck out toward the high mountains northwest of Capernaum and by early afternoon, they had reached a broad meadow below a prominent peak, and at this place, Yeshua asked his Apostles to remain along with their wives and Salome, while he and Miriam climbed up to the peak.

3 Cephas questioned him, asking, "Why must we remain behind? Surely, we are as interested in the goings on upon the mountaintop as Miriam."

4 Yeshua consoled him, saying, "We shall be gone until the evening, Cephas, and where we go, we must go alone. Please do not take offense that it is only Miriam that must come with me this day upon the mountain.

5 As I go alone with her today that she might see the fullness of her destiny, so too will I go with each of you at some point in our travels to reveal to you the greatness that you are.

6 We are living a great drama written by Elohim before the world was, and each of you has a part to play that can be accomplished by no other, and this I shall reveal to you in your time.

7 Today is the day for Miriam to discover her destiny, and it is she who must be first, not because she is above you, but because of the nature of her calling by Elohim and the time she will need to nurture the full potential of her power.

8 You have heard me say that I will not be long among you, but do not fear that I will leave you alone to the wolves; Miriam who was with me before the world was, who has walked with me every day of the fulfillment of my destiny upon this land, and who knows me as no other can shall remain with you for a time.

9 The power of Elohim shall be upon her. She shall be a tower of refuge for the Children of Light, with walls of protection that cannot be breached by all the armies of the world.

10 But she must still become more than she is, even as each of you must for the destiny that calls to you. Like the young bird that needs to grow stronger and learn to fly, she must more fully learn who she is and of what she is capable and then gain faith and confidence in her ability to fulfill her destiny.

11 The steps she begins to climb today, each of you will also begin to ascend on the day that I

call to you, but not to the place that she goes, but to a mountain that bears your name alone the stairway of your destiny will lead."

12 Cephas nodded his head in understanding as did all of the other Apostles. So it was that Yeshua and Miriam departed from among them and went up onto the mountain.

13 When they arrived at the top it was a beautiful, warm, and sunny day, with only the slightest of breezes. And Yeshua reached forth and touched Miriam lightly upon her cheek and asked, "Miriam, my love, are you ready to begin to more fully become who you were called to be before the world was?"

14 Miriam reached out her hand and touched his cheek lightly as he did to her and said unto him, "Our Father and Mother have shown to me much that shall come to pass while I yet walk the earth, dear one, but not everything. Though some of it seems but a dream, I am ready to receive all that you have to give at this time that I might accomplish all they would have me do and return to them as a worthy daughter."

15 Then they commenced to speak of the days to come and of the powers that Miriam must call unto her that she could become a tower and shield of Elohim for the Children of Light.

16 For several hours, Yeshua imparted unto her secret knowledge of the Elohim, such things that cannot ever be written; nor were they ever known upon the world, even to the Apostles, but only by the Father and the Mother and Yeshua and Miriam. And even this was merely the beginning of all Miriam needed to learn to fulfill the full measure of her destiny.

17 When at last Yeshua was finished speaking, darkness had begun to descend upon the land. Miriam held his hands and said unto him, "I am so humbled, my husband, by that which you have blessed me with, even some of the greatest secrets of the Elohim.

18 Though my mind says I am a foolish girl to imagine that I could ever manifest the great powers you have spoken of, my love for you is pure and my faith in you is absolute. Therefore, if you tell me I can do these things, surely I know that I can do them."

19 Yeshua answered her, saying, "You still have much to learn and some time still to practice that which you have already learned, using the methods I have given unto you to call upon the powers of the Celestine Light. But practice in secret. Even to my Apostles, never reveal your powers, save it be at the very moment they are needed for the protection or edification of the Children of Light.

20 And when you manifest the great powers of the Celestine Light, see that you follow afterward with a sleep and a forgetting upon all who witnessed that which you did, save for the Apostles whom I have called and the highest of Adepts within the Celestine Light.

21 Let there be no others to bear witness of the miracles you shall call forth, lest they forget about the Elohim they cannot see and begin to venerate and worship you whom they can."

22 Miriam nodded in assent, saying, "I understand, my beloved. Whenever I call upon the great powers of Heaven, the effects shall be evident, but the source shall be unknown among men."

23 From that day forth, Miriam began to practice in secret the greater powers of the Celestine Light that Yeshua had given to her openly, and she quickly became an Adept among Adepts.

24 Then Yeshua stood up behind her and laid his hands upon her head and called her and set her apart to her destiny, saying, "Miriam of my heart, I call forth the aeon of Elohim to come upon you in fullness as you have capacity to receive it. Let every power and aeon of the Celestine Realm that you need at this time flow into you and imbue you with its light.

25 You are called to fulfill your destiny in mortal flesh given to you at the foot of our Father and Mother before the creation of the world. And this until the time of your mortality is fulfilled, and you are called to your greater calling that still awaits.

26 Unto the Children of Light, you shall be a tower of strength and a shield of protection against all the fiery arrows that might come upon them. As you continue to grow in knowledge and ability and into the fullness of your destiny, nothing shall be impossible to you as long as your love for me is eternal and your faith in the power of Elohim is perfect, even unto the filling

of your soul. This I seal upon you in the name of the Elohim and by the authority given unto me. So be it!"

27 "So be it!" echoed Miriam.

28 Then Yeshua and Miriam stood facing each other, and holding hands, they stretched out their arms and lifted their hands up to the level of their heads. Looking steadfastly into each other's eyes, Yeshua instructed, "Reach out to the heavens, Miriam; let the power of the Celestine Light come into you; call for it; beckon it; open yourself without doubt; and let it be one with your soul."

29 Miriam turned her head sharply upward toward the night sky, and still holding onto Yeshua's hands, she cried out with a loud voice, "Father, Mother, I am here; your will be done."

30 In the distance, a great rumbling of thunder commenced and rolled quickly toward the mountaintop upon which they stood. So great was its sound that the very earth began to shake, and at the base of the mountain, the Apostles looked at one another questioningly and some with apprehension.

31 Then with a loud crack of thunder that caused all those at the base of the mountain to fall to their knees upon the ground, a mighty bolt of lightning shot forth out of the sky and, with a blinding explosion of light, landed upon Yeshua and Miriam.

32 For a moment, the entire mountaintop was brighter than at noonday. Three times the thunder roared and three times the lightning struck the mountaintop so squarely upon Yeshua and Miriam that they disappeared completely in the light.

33 Then the rumbling of the thunder faded, and the lightning was no more. But Yeshua and Miriam were still standing, illuminated in the moonlight, their skin aglow, holding hands and gazing into one another's eyes, united in ways that perhaps no other two people ever could be.

34 They remained like that, standing, holding hands, and staring with gentle intensity at one another for many minutes. Then in a quiet voice, Yeshua said, "In me, the world sees miracles of renewal, and they question if what they see is of God. In you, they shall see miracles of power, and they shall not doubt the source from which it comes."

35 At last, they came down from the mountain and returned to their friends. But they spoke not a word about what had occurred upon the mountain. And though everyone wished to know, none dared ask them.

CHAPTER 54

The Youthfulness of Age

After the evening meal, Yeshua invites his Apostles to ask him any question they wish, and Yuda asks about Enoch and if it is also their destiny to translate to Heaven without tasting death. Yeshua speaks about the trials and tribulations of life and how they should help you to grow so that you leave life greater than you began and that taking care of your body is of utmost importance, more so than living a perfect life.

That night, they encamped in a meadow high on the mountain, looking down upon a vast expanse of valley below them.

2 After the evening meal of small fish and wild greens they had gathered on their walk up the mountain, they sat in a circle to hear the words of Yeshua. Miriam sat at his right hand, and Salome sat next to her, holding her arm and resting her head upon her shoulder. Cephas was to Yeshua's left, and the other Apostles and their wives sat wherever they desired to complete the circle.

3 Yeshua invited them to ask any question they desired, and Yuda, son of Cleophas, was first to speak, asking, "It is said that Enoch and all the people of his city never tasted death, but changed in a moment from mortality to immortality. Is this also the destiny for us that serve Elohim with all our life?"

4 Yeshua answered him, saying, "If you become so enraptured and harmonious with the Celestine Light of Elohim that you are perfected beyond the world and are unaffected by the mortal world around you, then you will be translated in the blink of an eye from mortality to immortality, for this world will no longer be able to keep you upon it, because your resonance has exceeded its capacity to hold you.

5 There have been some through the generations that have found this path, but I tell you in truth, it is nothing to aspire to.

6 If Elohim had wanted your mortal bodies to go from mortality to immortality without tasting death, that is the way you would have been created or the promise you would have been given to worthy Children of Light. Though it would seem to be a sweet reward for the pure and virtuous, in truth it only makes their path longer.

7 Never forget that one of the reasons you are here in this mortal world of strife, pain, and turmoil is to learn from your experiences, both the bitter and the sweet. If you never tasted the bitter, you would not fully appreciate the delight of the sweet.

8 If you never had to test yourself against the physical challenges of work and life, you would not become strong and healthy, but would become a husk without muscle or strength.

9 If you never had to speak with others and learn to sometimes have a game of wit and words,

you would never become a leader, but live and die as you began.

10 If you never had occasion to fall ill or see your body begin to age, you would have far less motivation to eat a proper diet, have good hygiene, or do all the other things I have taught you to have health and vitality.

11 To first live a full life and then to lay the mortal shell down for its final rest, be it in peace or with pain, is an important step on the path of eternal progression. And whether it is with peace or pain is most often in your hands.

12 Most people are not afraid of growing old or infirmed. They are afraid of what comes after that.

13 Many do not have an unwavering faith in the life to come. They are afraid that when they die that will be the end of their existence. And fearing this, they cling in desperation to every last breath and wish to extend their mortality to the utmost, even when it is in a painful and degraded state.

14 Others have a faith in the hereafter, but still fear death, knowing they will have to make an accounting for the poor life they have led and fearing the place of cold and darkness they intuitively feel must be their destination. Though enfeebled and infirmed, they hold with intensity to every breath of mortality, apprehensive that the next life will be even less kind to them.

15 But the Children of Light should have a different understanding about life and death and the door to immortality that opens at the very moment of your last breath.

16 If you did not have challenges in life of all kinds-physical, mental, spiritual, and emotional-you would leave mortality no greater than you came into it. You would be like the stunted tree standing alone on the plain, always receiving water and sun but never growing tall and mighty among its kind because it lacked the challenge of competing for water in sun among its brethren in the forest.

17 In trees and man, it is not good nourishment alone that builds greatness, but also learning to deal with adversity and growing stronger and taller because of it.

18 This does not mean you should not always be striving for a life of peace and harmony, for you should be. But know that despite all you can do, there will be times when adversity still comes knocking at your door, and you will be tried by the fires of mortality.

19 At those times, do not pray for Elohim to take your trials away, but for Elohim to bolster your fortitude and help you know and do the things you must to overcome your challenges, that your soul will grow and expand from your experiences. For this is one of your great purposes upon the earth.

20 But then comes the day when mortality slips away, and your spirit and soul rise in freedom into immortality.

21 This is not the end, but a new beginning. For those who endeavored to walk mortality with love, honesty, and respect, the immortality that greets them is more glorious than you can possibly imagine.

22 What I wish you to clearly understand is that aging and leaving the shell of mortality is a helpful part of your eternal progression. Experiencing that, allows you to, all the more, cherish and appreciate the immortality that follows.

23 Those who never taste death in mortality, who simply lay the body upon the ground and rise with their spirit and soul to the fullness of the Celestine Light, are blessed greatly for the personage of light they have become that enabled them to transcend the body.

24 But they are also lacking in understanding from experiences, of the frailties and limitations of mortality. These are things they must then learn by proxy and indirect experience over a far longer time in the world to come.

25 It is like a carpenter who learned by experience how to inlay wood for a perfect fit. When he sees the work of another, with a fine and perfect inlay, he admires it greatly and appreciates the skill and expertise of his fellow craftsman. If the other craftsman were to have a challenge, the first would have complete understanding and sympathy, for they had walked the same path

and shared the same challenges.

26 But were an observer to come that had never learned to inlay wood, that had never experienced the frustration of time gone to naught when the tiny sliver of inlay breaks, he would not be able to have the same empathy as a fellow carpenter who had walked the same path.

27 At least not at first. Over time, if the man without experience was open to the heart of the carpenter, he would learn to understand and empathize with his challenges.

28 So it is in the life to come and with those who die in mortality and those who transcend.

29 What do you think life in the world to come is like? Do you think you are just going to be sitting around on the clouds, playing music and singing praises to Elohim?

30 Not on any day; though you will find a complete peace and relaxation such as you have never known, it is also an eternity of great activity and accomplishment, where your eternal progression does not end, but increases.

31 In mortality, it is those who either have false piety or simply little understanding of the nature of God, that are given to excessive praise to Elohim. As in mortality, your praises to Elohim in the world to come are heard more by the things that you do than in the things that you say.

32 And in the Celestine Realms, you do a great deal. Elohim is the architect; you are the builders. Where in mortality you may have built a house or brought a garden to bloom every season; in immortality, you will build paths that lead to the Celestine Light for your brothers and sisters still in mortality and plant gardens that bloom, not just with flowers, but with entire new earths.

33 And much more than that you will do in the Celestine Realms. And it will be all the easier and more effective from the moment you arrive, because of your experiences, including growing old and the frailties of mortality."

34 Everyone was silent for a few moments after Yeshua was finished speaking as they contemplated that which he had spoken. Then Salome asked, "My Lord of Light, I am young, so it is difficult to imagine being old, and having seen a little of the suffering that some have in their last years, I cannot say I look forward to such an end to mortality. Is there not a way that we can avoid the slow degeneration of the body and still learn the lessons we must?"

35 Yeshua smiled broadly upon hearing her question, and he answered her, saying, "Sweet Salome, it is my hope that you and all the Children of Light will have health and a maturity of youth until your very last day.

36 If one seeks to never die a mortal death, but to be translated to Heaven, they need only live a perfect life of love and virtue, with good service among their brothers and sisters of light. That is a path many good Children of Light will walk, but almost none will reach the pinnacle, for it is distant and high.

37 But though that pinnacle will be beyond reach for almost all, think not that you must then be like the people of the world who gather unto themselves new infirmities with every passing year and pass away withered into a shell of their former glory.

38 You are Children of Light, and your life and your departure from mortality should not be like those of the people of the world.

39 It has been given unto you to know every good food that enlivens and renews the body, and every good herb to heal and invigorate.

40 The Celestine powers of Heaven are within your worthy souls, and by your faith and love, all selfless acts of virtue can come to pass.

41 Unto you, it has been revealed the secrets of youth and vitality, and if you follow all that you have been given, you will be young in body, heart, mind, and spirit until the very last breath of your mortality.

42 You will still age, for there is eternal benefit in that experience, but even in your last days, you should retain a countenance, vigor, and happiness of youth that belies your years.

43 Live as you have been taught to live, and most often infirmities shall pass you by and

sickness will have no power over you.

44 When either comes calling upon you and catch you unaware, make them but passing unwanted visitors, for you have the power of Heaven within you and the secret knowledge I have given you of water and plants and herbs and rocks of the earth to banish all infirmities and illnesses of the world.

45 Even without the Celestine powers of Heaven, there is no sickness upon the earth that Elohim has not also given man a cure in water, plants, herbs and rocks, good diet, sunshine, and good spirit.

46 Among the Children of Light, all these things are known. Therefore, if you wish to be given the glory of the Celestine Realms in the life to come, love one another, love Elohim, and fulfill your potential in the Terrestrial Realm where you now live.

47 In this, you honor Elohim: to be a good steward of the temple of your body and prove by the love and honor of your temple, and your willpower to resist temptations that would degenerate and defile your temple, that you are faithful sons and daughters of God, Celestine Lights of fire, worthy to enter into your glory in the Celestine Realms of Elohim.

CHAPTER 55

Miracles of Body and Mind

Yeshua brings a young man back to life whose body is being carried in a funeral procession to be buried. Word about the miracle quickly circulates, and many people crowd around Yeshua and his Apostles but he disappears. Miriam tells the Apostles that he teleported to a nearby mountain and waits for them, which he communicated to her telepathically. When they reach Yeshua, he and Miriam teach the Apostles and Salome how to communicate telepathically.

And it came to pass that Yeshua and his Apostles journeyed throughout Galilee for a time, and Yeshua did many miracles, but not as many as people desired, for he only healed those who had a humble and repentant heart.

2 In every town and village, Yeshua preached the Celestine Light of Elohim, but few there were who listened to his words with real intent, because he admonished them to live a lifestyle to which they were not accustomed and put the responsibility for their lives and their eternities solely upon their own choices, which was a most disagreeable doctrine for many.

3 And it came to pass that Yeshua and his Apostles entered into the city called Nain.

4 As they came near to the gate of the city, behold, there was a dead man being carried out on a bier, followed by a woman wailing in deepest grief. And much of the city followed her, for she was a widow and mourned the death of her only son, who had been much admired by many.

5 When Yeshua saw her, he was so touched in his heart by the depth of her love and loss that he had compassion and came up to her and said unto her, "Weep not, for your son has only fallen into a deep sleep and needs but to be awakened."

6 At his words, the woman paused in her wailing, even though she continued to weep softly. For though she knew her son was dead, she still clung with a mother's love to the hope in the words of Yeshua.

7 But many of the men of the town who followed behind her and those who carried the bier were very angry at Yeshua, a stranger, for interfering in the funeral and giving the widow false hope, and they prepared to come upon him and cast him away from the gates of the city.

8 But ere they could lay their hands upon him, he came up to the bier, parting through those that held it, and using the palm of his right hand, he strongly struck the chest of the dead man, commanding, "Arise!"

9 With this astounding affront, the men who had come to lay their hands upon him stopped in their tracks, shocked at his audacity and irreverence for the dead.

10 Ere they came out of their shock enough to attack Yeshua, the young man in the bier called out in a loud voice, "Mother!" And he who had been dead sat up, and seeing his mother, he cried out, "I am your son."

11 The young man slid off the bier and stood up, and his mother came to him and embraced him with torrents of tears, but now they were tears of joy.

12 Then there came a fear upon those who were present, and their eyes were wide with amazement and their mouths open in disbelief. With one accord, they fell to their knees and glorified Elohim. Many were heard to speak in awe of the great prophet that walked among them. Others gave thanks that Elohim had not forgotten his people.

13 And the word of what Yeshua did that day quickly spread forth all across Galilee and Samaria and Judea and beyond, for it was as great a miracle as any could imagine.

14 So thick then was the enthusiastic crowd that pressed upon Yeshua after he returned the deceased young man to life that it was all the Apostles could do to stay close to him and keep him from being trampled.

15 While he was thus surrounded by the multitude from Nain, he suddenly vanished and was no longer among them. The people, seeing he was gone, looked all about them to discover where he had slipped off to, but none could find him, not even his Apostles.

16 Shortly afterward, not discovering Yeshua anywhere and seeing his own Apostles at a loss to his whereabouts, the people of Nain dispersed and returned to their homes.

17 After they had departed, the Apostles spoke anxiously among themselves, for in actuality, none knew what had become of Yeshua.

18 Then Miriam came among them and said calmly, "He is not here, but upon the mountain to the east of the city. Follow me, for he waits for us there."

19 As they walked toward the mountain, Cephas came to Miriam and asked, "Miriam, how is it that you know where Yeshua went to, but that no other saw him slip away from the multitude? Did he speak to you and no other heard or give you a sign?"

20 The other Apostles had been listening, and they leaned in to hear Miriam's reply. "No, Cephas," Miriam answered. "He did not speak to me or give me a sign. For a moment, I was as baffled as you as to where he had gone."

21 Cephas looked perplexed, but inquired in earnestness, "How is it then that you know he is on the mountain, and how is it that he could be one moment in the city and the next moment upon the mountain?"

22 "Oh, Cephas," she exclaimed, "Surely you know by now that nothing is impossible to Yeshua. To be one moment in the city and the next on the mountain is as simple as breathing to him, for all he needs do is think it, and so it is.

23 As for how I know where he is, he speaks to me in my head with words of silence that only I can hear."

24 Cephas was intrigued by this and inquired, "Is it because you are husband and wife that this is possible? For never have I heard his voice in my mind or heard of any others who have."

25 The other Apostles overhearing the conversation spoke quickly among themselves, and each affirmed that they had never heard Yeshua speak to them silently in their head.

26 Miriam answered him, saying, "We have spent much time together, and our essence is in peaceful and familiar harmony one with another. It was years ago that I first heard his voice in my mind, and now it is often that we speak this way to one another, he to me and me to him.

27 We have spoken of this gift, and Yeshua has said that the ability to speak to one another in silence, with words in the head that no others can hear, is not unique to us, but is a gift of Celestine Light to all the Children of Light who love one another with a pure love, especially among husbands and wives.

28 The day will come when Yeshua no longer walks among us. He will always be in our hearts, but never forget he will also still live in the Celestine Realms, watching over us. And for those who love him with a pure love, his words will come clearly into their heads, and you and the other Children of Light will be able to converse with him as easily as you do with one another so much so that it will seem as if he is still among us."

29 Cephas and the Apostles were amazed at the words of Miriam, and Yohhanan asked,

"How is it that Yeshua has never told us of this gift before?"

30 And Miriam replied to him, "We all learn a great deal of wonderful things from Yeshua each day. But for all things, there is a time and a season. Until this day, it was not the time for you to know of this power of the Celestine Light because you were not yet prepared by your knowledge and experiences to receive it.

31 But now that it is revealed, it is the time, for you have prepared yourself in the lesser things and are now ready to receive a greater thing."

32 Later, they came upon Yeshua praying on the mountain, and they spoke to him in excitement to discover how they might speak in their minds with him as he and Miriam did.

33 For the remainder of the day therefore, he taught them how to listen in their minds and how to project their thoughts and focus them upon just one person or more than one if desired.

34 Though none of the Apostles succeeded at hearing him or each other, they continued to practice with enthusiasm that day and the next and many that followed, until this was a gift they all were able to use, with varying degrees of success.

35 And Miriam taught the gift to Salome, and she alone mastered it that first day and thereafter could always speak in privacy with Miriam and Yeshua, even when surrounded by many people.

36 Later, when Yeshua and the Apostles returned to the Communities of Light, the Apostles began to teach the secrets of the silent talk as it came to be known to all the Children of Light when they were ready to receive it.

CHAPTER 56

He Who Is Last Shall Be First

Yeshua explains to his Apostles that he has come to teach those who are humble of heart with an openness of mind, for the high and mighty will be blind to the truth, even if it stands right before them.

The following day, Yeshua and the Apostles journeyed to Nazareth and met with Yeshua's family for the midday meal.

2 All through the morning while they were walking toward Nazareth, the Apostles continued to speak to each other with excitement about the special gifts and techniques they had learned yesterday from Yeshua and Miriam and to practice the silent talk with one another.

3 While walking, the Apostle Toma approached Yeshua and asked him, "Lord of Light, as you can see, we are all overjoyed and overwhelmed to learn of the mysterious Celestine powers you have shown to us, but in truth, some of us feel unworthy, for who are we but common people, lacking in knowledge, poor in wealth, and naive in the ways of the great people and things of the world."

4 Yeshua answered him, saying, "I thank our Father and Mother in Heaven because they have hidden the Celestine mysteries from the great and powerful and commanded me to give them to the lowly and meek.

5 Good brother Toma, the powers of Celestine Light that I bring to you are only given to those who are babes, willing to learn, and humble of heart that they can feel the Holy Spirit sent by the Mother in their hearts.

6 To the high and the mighty, the mysteries I share with you will continue to be mysteries, even were I to tell them the secrets, for those who think too highly of themselves have no place in their heart to honor something greater, with the humility and openness needed to see the truth.

7 Celestine gifts that a man is not open in humility and gratitude to understanding, he cannot see, even if he holds them in his hand.

8 To you, I could show a crystal of power, and you would be amazed and able to call upon the Celestine powers of Heaven and earth that could flow through it. But the high and mighty man would see only a rock and would not even lower himself to acknowledge it could be a tool of power. Therefore, for him, it will forever only be a rock.

9 By their own actions, men mete judgment upon themselves, whatsoever it shall be, and he who is first shall be last, and he who is last shall be first.

10 Verily, I have not come for the high and mighty. They cannot see me for who I am, for they are too proud of whom they think they are. I have come unto you my humble brethren and unto all who labor and are heavy laden with the challenges of life.

11 Those who hear my words and plant my teachings in their hearts will grow a Celestine

garden of great delight, and unto them, I will bring peace and hope and reveal the secrets of Heaven."

CHAPTER 57

Sins Forgiven

Yeshua, Miriam, Salome, and his Apostles along with their wives, are invited to the home of a Pharisee named Abracomas for dinner. But when they arrive he does not have room inside the house for the women so he intends to put them outside on the patio but Miriam alters the architecture of his home so everyone can hear the words of Yeshua together. A woman, known to be a sinner also comes to the home, but before she can be turned away by the servants of Abracomas Yeshua asks her to come in. Through the pain of her tears she withdraws an alabaster box and anoints Yeshua's feet with oil of Spikenard. He forgives her sins but the Pharisees are aghast that he would be so bold because only Elohim can forgive sins.

s evening came nigh, five Pharisees came up to Yeshua as he was walking with Miriam and some of his Apostles and invited him to eat with them at the house of Abracomas, who was chief among them.

2 Yeshua thanked them and said he would come if there was a place at the table for all of his Apostles. And they assured him there would be a place for them.

3 Then Miriam whispered in his ear, and Yeshua said unto them, "My wife, being also one of my Apostles, does not desire to dine as a woman alone in a room full of men and asks that our wife Salome and the wives of some of my Apostles who are also with us might also come to your table."

4 The Pharisees were aghast at this request and knew not how to answer, for Abracomas had explicitly commanded them to bring Yeshua for the evening meal so that he might observe and question him. But he would think they had been bewitched were they to invite women into the councils of men.

5 Nevertheless, despite their uncertainty and trepidation, they invited Yeshua to bring whomsoever he would.

6 And it came to pass that Yeshua went unto the house of Abracomas, and Miriam and Salome and all of his Apostles and their wives came with him.

7 Now Abracomas was a shrewd man, and having been told by the Pharisees who had invited Yeshua that he would be coming with an entourage of both men and women, Abracomas commanded his fellow Pharisees to also bring their wives that it would seem that a social gathering of mixed persuasion had been his intent from the start.

8 Nevertheless, he had no intention of allowing men and women to mingle, and besides, his house was too small for so many. Therefore, he had an area set up outside on the rear courtyard for the women so they could share gossip and things of children and food while the men dined

and conversed on the law inside.

9 But when Yeshua came to his house and after they had met and saw what he had arranged, he said unto him, "You have invited me to sup with you and I have come, but you have made to segregate the men from the women and this I cannot countenance, for among the Children of Light, women are not considered less than men."

10 Abracomas flashed an angry look at Yeshua, but quickly it was replaced with a feigned smile and a soothing reply: "Oh, I have heard that your wife is one of your scribes. A strange thing for a woman, but I understand if you desire her presence to record your words."

11 Yeshua replied to him, saying, "She is much more than a scribe, Abracomas. If you desire to know of me, you would do well to first learn of her and of my other Apostles and of all the Children of Light, for in them, you see me. The least of them can show you more of the Celestine Light of Elohim in one day of their life than you will learn in a lifetime of studying the law.

12 I did not come to sup just for idle chatter, and if things of importance are to be spoken of, it should be arranged that everyone can hear and question."

13 Still trying to project a veneer of the cordial host, Abracomas answered, "Alas, Rabbi, as you can see, my house is too small for everyone who has come. Surely, it is but an inconvenience for the women to sit and sup outside after they have served the men, and their husbands can tell them later of things that were spoken of that might be understandable and of interest to them."

14 Abracomas turned his palms up, saying, "It is unfortunate, but as I said, if the women are included, my house becomes too small for us to eat with pleasure and comfort."

15 Yeshua looked at him with an air of noble mischievousness, saying, "Perhaps, if we could include the outside in the inside, there would be room for everyone."

16 Abracomas shrugged once again, smiling in smugness, and said, "That would be a good solution if my house had no walls."

17 "Surely it would be," Yeshua answered. Then calling to Miriam, he said unto her, "My beloved, would you be so kind to go and look at the wall of the house that stands between the patio garden and the main room? Perchance it was made weakly and is in danger of falling. If so, the outside might become the inside."

18 Abracomas bellowed a hearty laugh, saying, "Come now, you go too far in your jest. Do you expect me to believe that your wife has the skills of an architect or builder and can assess the strength of my home? I assure you it was built stoutly, and were the earth to shake beneath it, my walls would stand.

19 "My wife has many skills," Yeshua replied. "Let her assess the wall."

20 As Yeshua and Abracomas were speaking, Miriam moved over to the wall that Yeshua had indicated, and turning to him, she asked, "Yeshua, is this the wall you were speaking of?"

21 "The very one," he replied.

22 Despite his protestations, Abracomas kept his eye on Miriam as she stood next to the wall examining it, as did the other Pharisees. The Apostles watched also, suspecting more was occurring silently between Yeshua and Miriam than Abracomas and the Pharisees were aware.

23 Then Miriam reached out a single finger toward the wall of brick and said, "As you have spoken, so it is, Yeshua. This very wall is exceptionally fragile. Why a strong gust of wind would surely topple it . . ."

24 "This is absolutely ludicrous!" Abracomas yelled. "Are you people possessed of devils that you have no sense for even the most obvious things! I tell you a thousand winds have blown against that wall and not even a grain of sand has moved."

25 Then Miriam looked directly into the eyes of Abracomas and said, ". . . or a finger," and ever so lightly touched her finger against the wall.

26 At the very moment the tip of her finger touched the wall of brick, there was a loud and frightening rumble as if the thunder of the sky was in the room, and in a sudden movement, the wall was torn asunder and fell in a heap of broken bricks and dust outside upon the ground.

27 A large circular hole leading to the outside courtyard remained, about the height of a tall

man, and in its center stood Miriam, as calm as if she had just awakened on a pleasant summer morning.

28 When the wall collapsed, there were shrieks of fright and surprise from both men and women, and in amazement, everyone looked at Miriam as she calmly wiped dust from the collapsed wall off her clothes. And Salome quickly came to her and helped her sweep off the dust that was upon her.

29 Regaining his senses, Abracomas bellowed, "What just happened here!"

30 And Yeshua answered him, saying, "Let your eyes that have seen and your ears that have heard testify to you of what your mind did not know and your prejudice could not conceive.

31 The emptiness of your wall will be there for you tomorrow to repair in greater strength than it had been, but tonight, the inside is now the outside that all who are gathered might be one.

32 Even as you will build your new wall stronger than the old, let all who witness this night forge new bonds of faith and greater understandings about the true Celestine nature of man to woman and woman to man.

33 For there is nothing given by Elohim unto men that is not also given unto women. But there is within the lives of most women more evidence of what has been given by God than there is in the lives of most men. Therefore, it is the women who can more often manifest the greater powers of the Celestine Light of Elohim."

34 And it came to pass that everyone did sit down to sup, and though most of the wives were still out in the courtyard, they could now clearly hear and see everything going on within the house through the large hole in the wall.

35 Not many minutes had passed from the moment they had eaten the first food, when they were interrupted by a commotion at the entry to the house. Rising from his couch, Abracomas bellowed to his servant at the door, "What is it now that disturbs me and my guests?"

36 The servant came into the great room and said unto him, "Sir, there is a woman at the door who demands to see your guest. She is familiar with many men and is not the sort of woman that should be in your presence, certainly not within your home. I have forbidden her to enter, but she will not leave the gate."

37 Abracomas opened his eyes wide and exclaimed, "Can I have no peace from women this night? We are here to discuss important matters of the law not entertain harlots. Be gone with her one way or the other."

38 But before the servant could move, Yeshua spoke, saying, "Let her enter, for she has come for me."

39 Now Abracomas was most dumbfounded by Yeshua's words. And while his servant looked to Abracomas for instructions, Yeshua spoke to him saying, "You desired to speak of the law. Let this woman enter, and the law of Elohim shall speak to you."

40 Mystified by Yeshua's words, but nevertheless intrigued, Abracomas bade his servant to admit the woman at the gate.

41 In a moment, she came into the room, covered in clothing that only her eyes and her hands could be seen. She carried an expensive alabaster box in her hands and came immediately up to Yeshua and knelt at his feet.

42 Uncovering her head, she revealed herself not comely, but with graying hair and a lined face that had seen much torment in life.

43 Looking up upon Yeshua's face, she burst into a torrent of tears that flowed freely, falling upon his feet. And thus she cried for a few minutes without anyone saying a word.

44 Then her tears began to ebb, and she pulled her long hair forth from within her clothing and began to wipe her wet tears from Yeshua's feet with her hair. And she bent low and kissed his feet as she wiped them.

45 And still not a word was spoken by anyone watching.

46 She opened the alabaster box and from it withdrew an ointment of Spikenard, which was

a very expensive perfume and, removing his sandals, anointed his feet with it, even every part.

47 Abracomas, seeing this, exclaimed to Yeshua, "This woman is a sinner, which if you are a prophet as many proclaim, you should know. How can you allow yourself to be touched so intimately by her hands and hair?"

48 Yeshua answered him, saying, "Abracomas, the law of Elohim is being fulfilled before your eyes. Do you not recognize it?"

49 Abracomas shook his head in silence and bewilderment, indicating he did not understand the meaning of Yeshua's words.

50 "Would you like to understand that which is now a cloud?" Yeshua inquired of Abracomas. And he nodded his head in silence that he would.

51 There was a certain creditor who had two debtors. The one owed him five hundred silver coins and the other fifty.

52 When both were unable to pay him even a single copper, they begged his forgiveness and he forgave them both, with their promise that they would not err again. Tell me therefore, which of them will love him the most?"

53 Abracomas answered, "I suppose that the one who he forgave the most." And Yeshua said unto him, "You have rightly judged."

54 Then he looked at the woman, and putting his hand upon her head, he turned again to Abracomas and said, "See this woman? I entered into your house and you gave me no water for my feet, but she has washed my feet with her tears and wiped them with the hair of her head.

55 You gave me no kiss of greeting, but since the time she has come, this woman has not ceased to kiss my feet.

56 You did not anoint my head with oil, but this woman has anointed my feet with nard.

57 Wherefore, she has shown by her heart and her actions the purity of the light that now guides her life. Wherefore, I tell you that her sins, which are many, are forgiven, for she has much love for the Celestine Light of Elohim.

58 And for those to whom little is forgiven, it is because they have little love for the Celestine Light of Elohim and know not the Son of Light in their heart."

59 Reaching down, he lightly touched the old woman's chin that she would look up at him. And looking into her eyes alone, he said to her, "Your sins are forgiven. Your faith has saved you. Go in peace for your past is forgotten. Sin no more and become the daughter of light who dwells yet inside of you."

60 Then crying once again, but now with tears of joy, she kissed his feet once more and got up quickly and left the house. Miriam and Salome excused themselves and followed after her.

61 Seeing and hearing all that transpired, the Pharisees spoke among themselves in amazement and consternation, saying, "Who is this Rabbi or even a prophet as some have said who would dare tell someone that their sins were forgiven? For only Elohim can forgive sins."

62 But among the Apostles of Yeshua, there grew an even greater love and devotion for he whom they knew to be the Lord of Light.

CHAPTER 58

Confrontation on the River Qishon

Yeshua and his Apostles travel west along the River Qishon so Yeshua can preach, but they cannot find even one person who will listen to him. As they continue along the river, they stop so the women can bathe, but when the women are alone, they are attacked by some drunken men. Miriam takes aggressive actions to protect her sisters of Light, particularly Salome, which causes unforeseen consequences.

Yeshua and those who followed him on his journey through Galilee stayed in Nazareth through the Sabbath, visiting with Yeshua's family and continuing to have talks with Abracomas and the Pharisees.

2 The Pharisees never came to believe the things that Yeshua taught, but they came to fear him for the authority with which he spoke and his knowledge of the law which could not be confounded and of the things they had seen which they could neither understand or explain.

3 On the day following the Sabbath, Yeshua and everyone who walked with him on this journey left Nazareth and departed for Gabae, a town west of Nazareth.

4 Seven of the Apostles including Cephas departed at first light in the morning so they could arrive a few hours ahead of Yeshua and have time to motivate the people of Gabae and nearby Besara to come and hear the teachings of Yeshua, who was soon arriving.

5 But when Yeshua came in the early afternoon, they met him on the road, ashamed that they had not been able to find even one person who desired to come and hear him preach the Gospel of Celestine Light.

6 Cephas was particularly distraught and told Yeshua, "We spoke to groups of many, and with one accord, they turned their backs on us. We testified of your miracles and healings, but even the sick among them gave us no heed. I feel unworthy to be your Apostle when in the course of a morning, I cannot even find one person to come and hear your teachings."

7 Yeshua answered him, saying, "You can bring succor to the man withering from famine, but you cannot force him to eat. I know you have spoken well to the people of Gabae and Besara with love and enthusiasm from your heart.

8 If they will hearken not to your words enough to even take a small look at the light, they shall inherit the pain of their folly, both in this life and the life to come, save they repent and seek the light they now disdain."

9 Cephas nodded in silent agreement and then went to find his wife among the group that had come with Yeshua.

10 Then Shim'on the Zealot came to Yeshua and he was angry that the people of Gabae and Besara had rejected Yeshua to the point that they would not even listen to his words, and he protested, saying, "This is surely a wicked people to give you the soles of their feet before they

have even seen you or heard your words. I will pray that Elohim puts a curse upon them and this land that it will ever be a misery unto them and all the generations that come after them."

11 But Yeshua forbade him, saying, "In this life and the next, every person draws to them their own resonance and is blessed or cursed, not by Elohim, but by reaping what they have sown.

12 Nor would it be just to punish the land for the sins of the people or to cause generations unborn to pay a price for the sins of their forefathers, for they are born in innocence and did not commit the sin.

13 We will pass by the towns of Gabae and Besara, even as we have passed by other towns when there is not one soul within them who will hearken to the Celestine Light.

14 But do not condemn the towns or the land or even the people and return to each another day, for as time and seasons change, so change the fortunes of people's lives and the inclinations of their hearts. The person that would listen not today may drink of the Celestine Light of Elohim in the future as a man parched from thirst."

15 And it came to pass that Yeshua and his followers continued west along the river, for they desired to visit the great sea.

16 As they passed by a gentle curve in the river, there was a large, calm pool near a shallow ford, and seeing this, the women desired to stop that they might bathe in the clear water of the river.

17 The men agreed and remained up on the road while the women descended into the river basin that they might bathe.

18 Walking into the water fully clothed, they splashed it on their faces and lifted their garments to wash their bare skin beneath. And they frolicked and played, splashing water on one another.

19 While they were in the water, seven men appeared on the opposite riverbank and called out to the women with obscene words and immediately began to wade into the water toward them, spreading out as if to encircle them.

20 Salome cried out to the women, saying, "These men are drunk. We must flee now!" Immediately, the other women began moving as quickly as they could through the heavy, impeding water to the nearer bank, all except Miriam, who stood calmly in the middle of the river, facing the drunken men who were moving rapidly toward her, some walking in water waist deep.

21 Looking up the embankment to the road where their husbands were, Salome shouted out, "Yeshua, Cephas! Come now to us, for we are attacked."

22 Hearing her cry, the men moved at once to descend to the river and protect the women, but standing upon the road's edge, looking down upon the scene before them, Yeshua held out his arms and bade them to stop for a moment, saying, "It is in times of greatest challenge that the true person of light and power can emerge from within the shell in which they are usually held by everyday life. Let us watch for a moment to see if Miriam discovers who she really is."

23 Looking at the crazed men rushing toward her, Miriam muttered to herself, "These men are more than drunk. They are possessed by devils to act as they do."

24 Seizing upon that realization, she said in a loud voice, "In the name of Elohim, I command the devils within you to depart!" Her forceful words were heard by all, even by the men up on the road.

25 But the possessed men approaching her only laughed, and now they were almost upon her.

26 Salome turned when she heard Miriam's voice, and seeing the demented men coming upon her from three directions, Salome quickly moved back to help defend the one she loved.

27 Miriam did not see Salome turn to come back toward her. Even as the attackers were almost upon her, she stood somewhat dazed and bewildered, not understanding why the devils had not departed when she had so commanded in the name of Elohim.

28 She was awakened from her momentarily disconnected thought by a scream from Salome as she was grabbed by two of the men as she was almost to Miriam.

29 Miriam turned quickly and her eyes were wide and her brows creased with anger. Without

uttering a word, she forcefully threw her right hand forward with her palm slightly raised and fingers widely spread pointing at the men holding Salome. Immediately, they released her and fell into the water, screaming in pain and agony and holding both hands to their eyes.

30 Still in a fury, still speaking no words, Miriam turned toward the remaining five men and in quick succession, with forceful movements of both her right and left hands held in the same manner, she called up the power of Celestine Light within her soul with her righteous anger. The attackers were hurled violently out of the water and flung far across the river, landing with bone-crushing impact on rocks and trees.

31 Standing on the road looking down onto the river, the men gazed in amazement at what they had just seen, and even having seen it, they could scarcely believe that which their eyes testified of.

32 The women in the river huddled together, uncomprehending of what they had just witnessed and unsure if they should be grateful to Miriam or fear her.

33 Salome came to Miriam in a rush, and they embraced one another and did not let go. Even as Yeshua and the men came down to the river and went to their wives, Salome and Miriam still embraced and remained holding one another until Yeshua came upon them.

34 As he approached his wives, Yeshua passed the two men who had tried to take Salome. They still thrashed in the water screaming in pain, and where their eyes had been, there was now only cauterized flesh.

35 Coming upon his wives, Yeshua looked Miriam in the eyes and lightly touched her cheek, saying, "All is well, my love. You are not as other women, and you have always known that. We will speak more in a moment, but know that I love you. Be not afraid or ashamed of what you have done here today. All things were as they needed to be."

36 Going up to the first man, Yeshua held him by his right arm, and holding his right hand over the man's eyes, he said unto him, "Evil spirit, you are cast beyond outer darkness." As he spoke those words, the man screamed one last time very loudly, then collapsed into Yeshua's arms.

37 Yeshua removed his hand from the man's eyes and everyone marveled, for his eyes were restored as they had been, except for some scarring, which remained around the edges.

38 Philip came up and took the man's limp body from Yeshua and moved toward the riverbank with his charge while Yeshua went to the other man in the river who had lost his sight. Upon him, he also cast out a devil and returned his sight, and he released him to Yohhanan to bring to the riverbank.

39 Several of the Apostles crossed the river to check on the men Miriam had tossed like so many rag dolls across the water and onto the rocks and trees. Toma called to his friends in the river that the man he was near on the rocks was dead. Yudas Iscariot checking on another of the marauders shouted that he had also perished. The other three attackers were alive but severely injured.

40 Hearing this, Miriam turned her head into Yeshua's shoulder and began to weep. She moaned, "What have I done, my Lord? I did not mean to kill them or even to hurt them, merely to push them away and keep them at bay until you arrived with the men. Why could I not cast out their devils? What is this darkness that has come upon me?"

41 Yeshua held her close and comforted her, saying, "Miriam, your motives were only from the purest love to protect Salome and your sisters whom you love. Though the power you manifested wrecked havoc reminiscent of darkness; in you, that power came only from the purest Celestine Light of your soul.

42 In time, you will learn to find a place of calm inside of you, which cannot be shaken by any storm. Then the Celestine Light of your soul will come forth as you desire, in greatness or subtleness, but on this day, the storm shook you, and the light rushed forth barely contained, acting in might before your head had time to calm your heart.

43 But do not lament the fate of these men. Because of their drunkenness, they received evil

spirits and would have done terrible things, even murder, to you and your sisters had you fallen into their hands.

44 Darkness such as this, driven into sudden violence and maim, is only countered by a power of greater force to subdue it.

45 In most things, love and light will rule the day, and few can fight against it. But know too that there are times and situations when even the hand of Elohim goes forth with a mighty sickle to hew down the wicked, for it is only that type of power that they fear and only that which can bring them to a place where they can feel and understand the love and the light that can follow."

46 Then taking Miriam's hand in his, he beckoned her, saying, "Come let us pass over to the other side of the river that we can attend to those who have fallen."

47 Crossing the water, waist deep for Yeshua and chest deep for both Miriam and Salome, they came to the other side of the river.

48 Yeshua went straightaway to the men who were injured, and casting the devils out of them, he touched them and healed them, but not completely; nor had he for the men that had lost their eyes, for each was left with scars and diminished physical abilities than they had previously.

49 Seeing this, Cephas was most curious, as were the other Apostles and questioned Yeshua as to why he only restored the men to a part of what they had been.

50 Yeshua answered him, saying, "Even without devils, these men do not follow the light; they do not have repentance in their hearts for the evil they have wrought. Let them therefore carry a painful memory of this day, that perhaps in the future, having considered for many days the cause of their pain, they might yet repent and seek the light."

51 Hearing this, Yuda son of Cleophas asked, "Wise Yeshua, I know you understand the hearts of men, even if they sleep. If these men had hearts full of repentance, what then would be their fate?"

52 Yeshua answered him, saying, "If they had a place in their heart for remorse for this and all their other wickedness, if they desired to make a full and honest restitution for their evil acts, they would have been made whole on this day."

53 Then Yakov, the brother of Yeshua from Nazareth, called out, "What are we to do with these two who are dead?"

54 And Yeshua answered him, saying, "Let them lie where they are for their friends to attend."

55 At his words, some were surprised for he had healed the others, and they knew he had raised the dead on more than one occasion; therefore, Cephas questioned him as to why he would not restore the spirits of these who had died from the actions of Miriam.

56 Yeshua answered him, saying, "To return a life is a great gift, one that requires a passion to see them live again and a willingness to part with much of your own life essence for a time, that the dead may be revitalized.

57 These were evil men before they ever drank or had a devil. They died with rape and murder upon their minds and have paid the price for their folly and foolish choices.

58 I love the men they could have been, but have no passion to see the men they would still be, return to life. Nor am I willing to part with my essence for such as these."

59 Yeshua turned to return across the river, but Miriam tugged on his arm and said unto him, "My Lord, I have a passion to see these men live again and am willing to part with some of my essence for a time that it might be so. Is it possible that I might be a bridge between Heaven and earth to bring the aeon of Elohim that these men might live again?"

60 Yeshua held her gaze for a moment, then answered slowly and quietly, "Yes, Miriam, it is possible. All that you have seen me do, any Child of Light may also do with knowledge, none more so than you, if you have faith, love, and passion, and do all things as you must.

61 But knowing the evil hearts of these men, why would you desire them to return to a life of further evil, where they will still do evil to others, likely even rape and murder even as they tried to do to you and your sisters? For they are unrepentant in their hearts."

62 Miriam answered him softly, saying, "I grieve for having been the cause of their death, even

though they might have been the cause of mine and my sisters had I not acted. Nevertheless, I know that they must also have wives and children that will miss them if they never return. Please tell me what I must do that they might live again."

63 Yeshua pondered his wife and her motives for a moment before he answered, and then he said unto her, "You must love them with as great a love as you have for me, or for Salome, or for Martha, or for our children.

64 You must have faith in yourself and your ability to do this, and in my word telling you that you can, and in the power of Elohim through the Celestine Light, by which the river of life flows.

65 You must have a passion to see them live again, a passion as strong as you would manifest were one of our children to die before their time.

66 Lastly, you must merge your aeon with theirs, which even in death still resides with them for a time. You must join your aura to the parts of them that are broken, and from those, parts of you must let flow as much of your own life essence as is necessary for them to be healed on the inside and the outside and be made whole."

67 Hearing his words, Miriam was crestfallen, and she said unto him, "O my Lord, your words hurt my heart, for though I desire these men to live again, I know I do not have within me all that you say I must.

68 I cannot love them like I love you or Salome or Martha or our children.

69 Though I would gladly give them a portion of my life essence and have faith in all that you said I must, I cannot find within me a passion as great as I have for our own children."

70 Once again, she wept and Yeshua and Salome comforted her, and Yeshua said unto her, "Miriam, sweet Miriam, as I said before, be not afraid or ashamed of what you have done here today. All things were as they needed to be.

71 Sometimes the lessons of mortality are painful, even for you, even for me. But the future will be brighter, and you will become more glorious because of the lessons you have learned here today."

CHAPTER 59

Belief and Faith

Yeshua speaks to his Apostles about the difference between belief, faith, and sure knowledge, which are the foundations for wielding the powers of Celestine Light. When questioned about obtaining faith, particularly faith in herself to the point of performing what most people would consider astounding acts, Miriam explains the process of her progression and how she gained the belief and faith in herself that enables her to do the things that she does.

Leaving the men restored to care for themselves and their fallen friends, Yeshua and all who were with him renewed their journey to the sea.

2 As they walked along the path, many questions came to the anxious minds of the Apostles concerning all they had just witnessed, but Yeshua deferred their inquiries and promised he would speak in detail of everything that had transpired once they reached the great sea.

3 While they traveled, he never left the side of Miriam and spoke to her often in a quiet voice that none could hear, save Salome, who walked on the other side of Miriam.

4 They came at last, on the same day, to the mouth of the river where it met the sea. They passed a Roman outpost near the mouth of the river, but the soldiers did not stop them or bother them. Having seen Miriam look upon the post with intensity as they approached it and speak some words upon it, Salome knew why.

5 Arriving to the water, Yeshua bade them all to bathe, first in the salt water and then in the fresh water of the river.

6 He asked them to separate into two groups, the women to the right and the men to the left, and to enter the sea naked so that their bodies might be fully cleansed and feel the freedom and joy in both the air and the water upon the nude bodies of their birth that Elohim had given to them.

7 He further told them to bring their clothes into the water and to move them vigorously in the salt water so that they too might be cleansed.

8 Having only recently been attacked by men, some of the women were hesitant to go naked so close to the Roman outpost, but Miriam reassured them, "Fear not, sisters, the Romans will not come near us, for we are beyond their sight and forgotten in their minds. But if you need a balm upon your hearts, enter into the water fully clothed and once you are covered by the sea, remove your clothes that you may feel the exhilaration of your nakedness in the water."

9 The women smiled, trusting the wisdom of Miriam, and only Salome understood the fullness of Miriam's words.

10 Unlike most of the people of their time, being almost fully immersed in the water of the sea or the river was not strange or unnatural to the Children of Light of the Communities of

Light, for Yeshua had taught them from the beginning to be at home in and upon the water and to bathe often, both their bodies and their clothes.

11 Some of them had even learned to swim with simple strokes and a few like Philip, with excellence, much to the amazement of everyone.

12 And it came to pass that they frolicked and played in the water, even Yeshua. And with some hilarity and to everyone's amusement, Philip endeavored to teach some of the others to swim.

13 "But if I release my feet from the bottom I will sink like a rock!" protested Cephas.

14 "Just try it, Cephas," Philip encouraged. "Stand here, where the water is only chest deep and lay your body out upon the water and just begin to kick your feet and put your hands in the prayer position and then push them out and away as I have shown you."

15 "I tell you without the support of my feet upon the bottom, my body will not float like a log, but sink like a rock," Cephas reiterated.

16 "Just try it, Cephas," Philip asked again. "You see me swim; you see others float; are you not a man like us? Plus, you are a fisherman. How can you be a fisherman and not know how to swim?"

17 "Humph! And what do you know?" Cephas retorted amicably. "I am a fisherman because I have a boat and have no need to swim because my boat floats. Nor do I need to be in water above my head to catch the fish because my nets bring them to me. When I do have occasion to be in the water, my feet touch the bottom. And if the bottom is too far for my feet to touch, then I am in my boat."

18 Everyone laughed at Cephas' explanation and encouraged him and assured him that he could swim if he followed Philip's instructions. "All right," Cephas grumbled, "I will try." With that, he launched himself forward with a mighty splash and began to kick his feet and move his hands as Philip had demonstrated.

19 With everyone laughing uproariously at his attempt, he disappeared completely below the surface even as he continued to thrash his arms and legs trying to swim. He quickly shot up out of the water, standing again with his feet on the bottom and sputtering and spitting water out of his mouth. Cephas looked at everyone laughing at him and, somewhat chagrined, laughed with them, "Let me see each of you try this silly feat, that I might also laugh at you. And am I not a prophet? Did I not say I would sink, not float?"

20 His words, said in jest, brought even more laughter, and his attempted swim seemed to lighten everyone's mood from the sadness they had felt since leaving the scene of the attack on the River Qishon.

21 After everyone had finished playing and washing in the Salt Sea and then rinsed in the river, they prepared a light evening meal, and when all were full and feeling better from their activities, Yeshua at last invited them to gather together, as darkness fell, to speak of the shocking event that had occurred earlier in the day.

22 And he said unto them, "My brothers and sisters, you have witnessed today events that have singed your spirit, even as your body is in pain when it comes too close to a hot fire. I know you have many questions, so ask what you will and I will answer that you might come to a fullness of peace and understanding."

23 It was Mattayah who asked the first question, saying, "Wise Yeshua, there are so many questions I have; scarcely do I know where to begin. My first concern is for the death of the two men. Their friends will have a tale to tell. What it will be I cannot imagine, but the end result I fear will be that the Romans will come upon us for judgment in their deaths.

24 After that, I need to understand what my eyes saw occur at the hand of Miriam. I have not traveled with you long, so perhaps her astounding feats are common place. But extraordinary, even unbelievable they were to me. I know it must be by the power of the Celestine Light of Elohim, but I ask you to explain how this power was manifested by a mortal, even a woman."

25 Yeshua answered him, saying, "They will tell their tale, even greater than it was, to justify

their own wounds and their two friends that are dead. But who will believe them? Surely not the Romans who scarcely leave their own fortifications beyond the cities, unless an enemy they recognize, with swords and shields, is marching upon them.

26 But those who wield the powers of Celestine Light as a sword and shield are nothing more to the Romans than the wind, so invisible they see no threat, until the day comes that they too feel its power."

27 Then you have come to lead us against the Romans?" Shim'on the Zealot interrupted hopefully. "And you will teach us to do what Miriam did?"

28 Yeshua shook his head and smiled like a father who continues trying to teach a child the same lesson and finds humor that the child still does not understand. "No, Shim'on, I am not the looked-for Messiah of the Children of Israel coming to free them from the bondage of the Romans. Nor will I teach you any disruptive physical power you can use for anything against them or anyone else, save in defense of your life and those whom you love.

29 Nor did I teach Miriam the ability to do what she did. But I have said unto all of you that if you have the faith as small as a mustard seed, you can say to a mountain to 'take up and be cast into the sea' and it shall be done as you command. But as you have learned, faith is the power, but to activate the power, you must also have knowledge, love, and passion at the very least.

30 If so little faith, knowledge, love, and passion can cast a great mountain into the sea, how much easier is it to throw men across a river?"

31 "I despair!" lamented Amram. "How can we be your Apostles when such feats, minuscule as you say they are, seem so impossible to us? I have seen many of your miracles and witnessed Miriam do things no mortal should be able to do. I understand all of this is by the power of the Celestine Light of Elohim, which flows through those of faith. But my faith must be smaller than a speck of dust, for verily the only way I could move even a speck of dust, is to blow upon it."

32 Upon hearing Amram, all the other Apostles nodded their heads in agreement with the words he had spoken.

33 Yeshua explained, "There is more than one thing to consider, concerning these things. Therefore, let us look at each.

34 "Oftentimes, faith and belief are used as twin words, but they are in fact very different aeons. Belief can exist without faith, but faith cannot exist without belief.

35 Sureness of belief is the foundation upon which well-founded faith must be placed. But faith is often placed without a foundation of sureness of belief, and such faith is a house that tumbles to the ground from its own poor construction.

36 When a mason takes an apprentice and he studies diligently with the master for a year, will he understand the fullness and be able to create the magnificence of the apprentice who has studied with the master for several years and become a master himself?

37 So it is with Miriam. She has been with me for more years upon the earth than any of you will ever be able, and before we came out of the womb, we were together for a great time in the Celestine Realms.

38 Because she has seen many miracles, she believes in miracles she has not seen that are of similar aeon.

39 Because she has a sureness of belief in what she has seen, she also has gained faith in miracles she has not seen that are of different aeon, and this is the essence of faith.

40 Understand, belief is simply confidence in the outcome of something unseen, based upon the outcome of something similar that had been seen. But faith is confidence in the outcome of something dissimilar to anything that has been seen. Once you have seen it and know it, repeating the same action is no longer done with either belief or faith, but sure knowledge of truth that was attained from first having belief and then faith.

41 These then are the steps of faith necessary to wield the greater powers of Celestine Light. First to think that something can be done; then to believe it can be done, based upon having witnessed something similar; then to gain faith that something dissimilar can also be

accomplished by the same power; and having seen this, to then have both your heart and your mind affirm with a sure knowledge of truth that you can call upon the Celestine Light for any righteous purpose and it shall be done.

42 A man came to a carpenter and desired to have a table built. Upon arriving at his shop, he found there were no tables, but only chairs. Not seeing a table, nor having visited this carpenter before, he did not have a sure knowledge that he could build the fine table he desired.

43 But looking at the chairs, he admired the craftsmanship and the scrollwork. Seeing this, he gained a sureness of belief that the carpenter could also build a table equally as fine.

44 Therefore, sureness of belief is the substance of something hoped for, built on the evidence of something seen.

45 If I go to heal a man who has a withered arm, you may never have seen me do this, but you have seen me restore a man's sight or remove palsy from another; therefore, you have a sureness of belief that I can also heal a man's withered arm. But this is belief, not faith, because it is based upon something similar you have already seen.

46 But if I were to tell you that at my command, the sun shall stop in the sky, you would need faith to accept that, because nothing I have ever shown you would give you a sureness of belief that I could do this, for stopping the sun in the sky is an entirely different aeon from healing a withered arm and is an aeon you have not seen me wield.

47 Then, were you to have faith that I could stop the sun at my command, you would need to discover if it was true faith, wavering faith, or misplaced faith.

48 Now if the man desiring a fine table was directed by neighbors to a man addled in the head, who knew neither his name or where he was or what was his foot and what was his hand, as the man to build his table, it would be an act of faith for him to employ him, for he had no evidence of things seen to believe the man could build a table.

49 And it would be an act of foolish and misplaced faith that would bring him only sadness and disappointment, for it was faith placed without the evidence of a sureness of belief, and such faith is most often doomed to bring an unpleasant and painful end to he who gave it with poor judgment.

50 Now if this same man desiring a table, had known the man addled in the head years before and had known him to be a competent carpenter, he would have a foundation of a sureness of belief in the man's past abilities to give to a faith that the man could again recall his skills and build him a fine table.

51 But because of the addled man's recent behavior, he could not be certain in his heart that he would be able to build a quality table for him. He would need to have faith in him based upon his past experience, but it would be a faith easily shaken if the man did not quickly regain his senses and commence building an excellent table. Therefore, he had wavering faith, which sometimes fulfills and sometimes disappoints.

52 Even as many of you have a wavering faith in yourselves. You have seen me do great miracles, and now you have faith in other miracles I can do, and some of you have gone beyond faith and have a sure knowledge of truth in some things.

53 To do miracles yourself, you have some faith, because I have told you that you can do it and you have faith in me, but your faith is of the wavering kind, for though you believe in me, you do not believe as much in yourself.

54 Until you believe as much in yourself as you believe in me, you will never be able to do the things you have seen me or Miriam do.

55 Think it is possible, Gain a sureness of Belief, Have Faith that is Unshakable, Gain a Sure Knowledge of Truth. These are the four steps you must climb to wield the fullness of any power of Celestine Light and to realize the fullness of the gifts that have been given to you.

56 If at any point you are faltering, step back to the last step upon which you were firm and seek to begin again your quest from that point with renewed confidence and new perspectives."

57 Everyone nodded as Yeshua finished speaking, but most still had uncomprehending looks

upon their faces. And Amram asked further, "I understand some of what you have said, but in truth, some is still muddled in my mind. Perhaps, I am becoming addled like the man in your story."

58 At his words, everyone laughed, and then he continued, asking, "Can you tell us exactly how Miriam gained her ability to do what we have seen her do, how exactly she did it, and how may we gain a fullness of our gifts and connection to the Celestine Light that she has evidenced?"

59 Yeshua considered his question and answered by deferring to Miriam who was sitting next to him, "Let Miriam answer, for having lived that which you seek, there is no one better to light the path for others to follow."

60 Miriam looked at Yeshua and smiled, then turned to face the circle of her brothers and sisters and said unto them, "Yeshua spoke of the apprentice becoming the master, and I know to some it would seem that is what I have done, but in truth, I know the powers of Celestine Light that have flowed through me are a mere trickle of the powers that reside in Yeshua and abide for us until we are ready to receive them.

61 From the moment Yeshua and I were first married, he began teaching me by both precept and example how to understand, call, and control the powers of Celestine Light.

62 He taught me how to recognize them and know which to call upon for the task at hand and how best to command them to obtain a fullness of the desired results.

63 Nor are we alone, for there are many angels in Heaven, each given stewardship over specific aeons of power. After my years with Yeshua, I know them all by name and when I speak first to our Father and Mother in Heaven, I always follow by calling upon the angelic steward of the aeon I need.

64 At least, that is the way I normally call upon the powers of Heaven. That is what I did on the day I rose above the ground to fetch the stone Yeshua held in the air.

65 But what you saw upon the river was something different, a more direct path to the powers of Celestine Light than I ever knew. I had no time to pray or to call upon angels, but only to react to what was occurring. I felt the power well up from inside me, focused by my righteous and passionate anger when I saw my Salome threatened. I reacted without thought other than to protect her quickly and surely.

66 I cannot really say why it happened that men lost their eyes and others flew across the river, save it be that Elohim sent the powers of Heaven through me that were needed, and this because my faith is true and unwavering. I did not ask or call for either of these things to occur.

67 Know surely what I mean by that, my brothers and sisters. I could be scourged by the Romans until the blood ran from my body. I could be told my suffering would end if I would just deny Yeshua, but never would I do it, not in my heart or with my words.

68 Even though the last drop of blood would drip and my life would cease, I would never deny Elohim, and will always be true to the Celestine Light, for it is better to die in the light than to live in the embrace of the darkness.

69 Because this is the depth of my faith, I know I will never face that which I have described, for Elohim will always send the powers of Heaven to protect me, even in ways I did not expect or call upon.

70 When the men lost their eyes, my thought was not for them to lose their eyes. As I said, I had within me a righteous and passionate anger, and without thinking, I threw my boiling anger at them, sending Celestine Light from my core focused through my open hand. That their eyes were lost was the manifestation of the power, not the intent.

71 But the motion with my arm thrust and my palm held so, with fingers outstretched, is something Yeshua taught me when we were in Egypt with the Nubians, as the best way to physically propel the invisible forces of Celestine Light that can flow from Heaven through us or come up from the reservoir that is within us.

72 Understanding this way to physically focus and send forth the powers of Celestine Light, that is what I did, with an instinctual intention to push the men in the river away from me and

Salome. But such was my anger that instead of merely being pushed a little away and held at bay, they were sent flying high in the air and far and away.

73 Again, that was not my intention, and the deaths of the men was not something I foresaw, but merely the consequences of the power of Celestine Light sent forth with a greater anger and passion than I have ever before had and my own inexperience understanding how to control the power. I did not know, desire, or imagine that the results would be such as they became.

74 I am truly sorry for their deaths, and I must ask forgiveness from each of you for wielding such mighty powers with recklessness. Please do not fear me. I am still just Miriam.

75 I promise you that never again will the powers of Celestine Light flow through me uncontrolled, but only as I desire and direct and always in righteousness for the good of the Children of Light."

76 As she stopped speaking, there was complete silence in the circle. No one spoke even a whisper, but all looked at Miriam.

77 Then Philip said the words that must have been on the minds of all, "Miriam, thank you for sharing your heart with us. But know surely, never in our eyes will you ever be just Miriam, unless it is that just Miriam is the state of blessedness we all aspire to."

78 Everyone nodded in agreement with the words of Philip. Then Yudas Iscariot asked, "Miriam, please continue to enlighten us as to how you have come to the place where you have the ability to call upon these great powers of both Heaven and from inside your soul essence."

79 Miriam answered, saying, "Everything I have learned from Yeshua would fill many books, but it would all mean nothing and would be of no more worth than the dust on my clothes to me, if it were not for the two most important lessons Yeshua taught me, lessons everyone must learn before they can have success with any of the powers of Celestine Light.

80 The first is you must have an unwavering faith in the Elohim and a full understanding of their nature, for how can you have faith in them if you do not know them in both your heart and your mind? Without that knowledge, you do not have a clear focus upon which to direct your faith.

81 Elohim is not one individual, but three individuals, and you must know that Elohim is a title for who they are—not Elohim, but the Elohim, our God, three who are separate, but act in all things of the spirit as one.

82 They are the Father, the Mother, and the Son, even he whom we are blessed to have among us now.

83 Yet even Yeshua at this moment resides in a mortal body. He does great miracles, but his body still bleeds and he shall still taste death, although he could choose not to. Knowing this, can you believe that he is one of the Elohim? Do you have faith that he is?

84 Perhaps that is a faith too easy to come by, for we are in his presence, and even if we witnessed not a single miracle, we feel the power of his aura, which overwhelms us such as the aura of no person ever has or can. In his presence, our soul testifies that he is of the Elohim and that he is very different from us.

85 But what of Heavenly Father and Heavenly Mother whom we hear Yeshua testify of, whom we pray to and hear answers in our hearts and minds, but neither see nor touch?

86 Can we have as great a testimony of faith in them whom we neither see nor touch as we have in Yeshua whom we can both see and touch?

87 This was the first important lesson Yeshua taught me: to pray often to Elohim, to speak to them in earnest conversation, even if it seemed at first that I was just talking to the soundless wall of my house or the unhearing rock outside.

88 To not say prayers of repetition, but to speak as I would to my dearest friends.

89 I began to pray every free moment when I was not in conversation with someone else. And my prayers became like deep conversations with my parents or my closest friends. Even when I was working at mundane tasks, I would be speaking to our Father and Mother in Heaven, just as if they were my earthly parents sitting beside me.

90 I did not speak in hallowed ways, but about everything in my life, as I would to my best friend. I talked about great things like my spiritual desires and mundane things like how I disliked washing clothes as often as Yeshua likes us to wash them.

91 I spoke to them first about my joys, such as when our children were born, healthy and strong. And I cried to them when my heart ached, such as when our brother Yochanan the Baptizer was beheaded by Herod.

92 On any given day, I spoke to our Father and Mother more than I spoke to all other people put together.

93 Though I never saw them as I see you, I came to see them standing before me in visions during the day. And during the night, I was often with them in my dreams.

94 Though I never heard them speak as I hear you speak, I heard their voices in my mind. Though I never felt their embrace as I feel Yeshua's, I felt their love and comfort just as warmly in my heart when I needed solace.

95 Over time, I came to have a faith and to cherish my Heavenly Father and Mother whom I could not see with my physical eyes, but could testify with a real faith that could not be shaken that they live and love me and await for me to come back into their arms.

96 Some will think that having faith in Heavenly Father and Mother is easier for us than it will be for those who come after us, for we have Yeshua among us, and our belief in him is sure. Therefore, it is easier to leap into a faith in Heavenly Father and Mother.

97 While this is true, there is a testimony of belief and faith that is greater than actually seeing, touching, and hearing Yeshua, and that is the witness of the Holy Spirit of Elohim, a part of their actual living essence, which is sent by our Mother in Heaven to those who believe and seek the Celestine Light.

98 Each of you that have been called to be Apostles has felt the burning in your bosom that is the testimony of the Holy Spirit that cannot be denied. Upon that foundation, you must now build.

99 The second step Yeshua taught me was that I must have a faith in myself as great as my faith in Heavenly Father and Mother and in him.

100 This was a more difficult challenge for me. Even so, I realized it was much less for me than it was for many others, especially most women who are subjugated to men in our society and have little sense of self-worth.

101 How did I gain faith in myself? Step by step. My faith in myself did not come in a day. Once again, it began with Yeshua. I accepted that this most wonderful man loved me and put me on a pedestal by his words and actions.

102 If he whom I admired above all others held me in such high regard, should I not also hold myself?

103 Understanding this gave me a shield that protected me from those who would put me down upon the ground. Especially when a man would act in ways condescending, I would remind myself that Yeshua whom I respected and admired above all others held me in great esteem. Therefore, what are the petty words or actions of a lesser man to me?

104 I came to a point that the words and actions of men or women that would demean me or try to control me or tell me I must act in a certain way as they decreed had no effect upon me.

105 Yeshua has praised the goodness of the Children of Light. Yeshua has affirmed the equality of men and women. Yeshua has assured each of us that we have only begun to call out the greatness that resides within us.

106 If Yeshua thus has faith in us, can we have any less belief or less faith in ourselves; else, we dishonor Yeshua?

107 Girded now with a sure knowledge of Yeshua's faith in me, I could only mirror that faith in myself; else, I would be denying Yeshua.

108 It is the same for others in our lives whom we love and admire. If your husband or wife has faith in you and your abilities and you respect and honor them, you must then also have faith

in yourself; else, you dishonor them.

109 Think about it; if Yeshua, or your husband, or your wife, or your father or mother or brother or sister or best friend comes to you and assures you that you can do something you doubt you can do, you must either then believe in yourself and have faith that you can do what you have never done, or you are dishonoring those who love you, who have said you can do it.

110 For if you say you do not believe you can do it, it is the same as calling those who love you a liar, for they have assured you that you can do it.

111 From the day I understood that, I believed in myself. Once I believed in myself, I began to exercise my belief with greater confidence in the things I did and the words I said. This in turn began to produce fruits that were evidence that my belief in myself was true. Then I gained faith, followed by a sure knowledge in my ability to manifest the powers of Celestine Light.

112 Once I held a sure knowledge, I was able to make leaps of faith, such as on the day I retrieved the stone in the air. That was nothing I had ever done, but I had blossomed within myself enough to have an unshakable faith that if I acted in unselfishness for the glory of Elohim, nothing was impossible.

113 And so it is with each of you. The path to faith in Elohim and faith in yourself is the same one I have traveled.

114 I know you have faith in Yeshua. Now have faith in my words as your sister who loves you, for I testify to you that you are worthy, you are capable, and the powers of Celestine Light can flow in you and through you as quickly and fully as you in humbleness accept your greatness and open the gate of the aqueduct through which flow the powers of Heaven unto you, filling you to the brim."

115 Then the Apostle Toma questioned her, asking, "From your words, it is obvious that it is important to have the encouragement and support of those whom you love and are in contact with every day.

116 How can one gain a faith in self, when instead of supporting and encouraging you, your family and friends speak to you poorly and in ways that undermine your confidence? For surely this is more the case than one of support, especially among women."

117 As Yeshua had turned to Miriam to answer the question of Amram, she now looked to him to answer the question of Toma, and he explained, "Encouragement and support are so important for self-esteem that to be in a home without these is to be in a pit that is continually dug deeper every time you begin to climb out.

118 Among the Children of Light, let it always be taught to praise one another with love and sweet words and to bite your tongue ere you say an unkind word or even speak in an unkind tone.

119 And if a Child of Light continually speaks in ways that take away the self-esteem and self-confidence of another and, despite repentance, continues to sin in this way, it would be better for them to leave the community rather than remain and continue to poison the well of hopes and dreams.

120 And know this, when someone by their words stands as an obstacle to the growth and fullness of another, it is no different than if they locked them away in a prison, and the sin is just as great in the eyes of the Elohim.

121 Either by actions or with words, if you dam the progression of another, you damn your own even more. But when you encourage and support the progression of others and call them to their greatness, you also grow and become more than you were."

122 Then Cephas asked, "What shall we do if the person who is thus damning another with words that take away their self-esteem and confidence is their husband or wife to whom they are wed at least for this life and perhaps even for eternity?"

123 Yeshua answered him, saying, "If the precepts we speak of are taught and taught often in the Communities of Light from the time of childhood until the time of the old and wise, they will be lived, for that will be the example that will be seen and emulated.

124 Among new converts, who are not yet steeped in our ways, there may occasionally be

challenges in the way they speak to their husband or wife, and these should be addressed with love.

125 First, it must not be a secret within the home, but a sin that is confessed with remorse and dedication to change from criticism to praise.

126 If the sinner does not confess to priesthood authorities, let they who are oppressed speak of their oppression to those in authority that the healing may begin.

127 In either circumstance, let the healing begin with love. Reaffirm the teachings of Celestine Light in this regard and with love censor and support those who have sinned to repent and walk in a new light. Encourage them, love them, and in all ways show them the goodness and kindness you desire them to show to their husband or wife.

128 If someone has walked far enough and high enough on the path of Celestine Light that they have become a Child of Light by baptism and have come to live among their brothers and sisters in the Communities of Light, this and any other issue that may arise should be able to be willingly solved with a sincere repentance and loving and supportive brothers and sisters illuminating the better path."

129 With those words, Yeshua invited everyone to lie down to sleep for the night, with the promise that the lesson would continue the following day.

130 Yeshua asked the wife of Amram to say a group prayer for them, which she did, and everyone then embraced one another and said their parting words for the evening.

131 Upon the following day, they went once again to the seashore, and Yeshua invited Cephas to give them a demonstration of his swimming prowess. Cephas waved at him sheepishly and said, "Can the same jest continue two days in a row? I am still the same rock I was yesterday. Is everyone in need of a hearty laugh to begin the day?"

132 Yeshua answered him, saying, "Yes, Cephas, you are still a rock, but not the same one that you were yesterday, because now you are a rock that can swim."

133 Cephas looked at him with a pained look on his face and said unto him, "I wish it were so. Is it a miracle you then are going to bring that I will float instead of sink?"

134 "Remember our lesson from last night," Yeshua replied. Then looking at everyone else gathered on the beach, Yeshua asked, "Who believes that Cephas can swim?"

135 At first no one raised their hand, but Yeshua quickly did and Miriam followed and soon everyone had their hands raised. Then Yeshua turned to Cephas and said unto him, "All of us, your brothers and sisters, believe you can swim; some even have faith that you can swim. Therefore, being mindful of our lesson last night, I ask you now, brother Cephas, will you swim for us?"

136 Cephas looked around at his friends and then only at Yeshua, and he said unto him, "Yes, I will!" And he turned immediately and, shedding his clothes and sandals, began walking into the water.

137 Philip hurried after him and caught his arm, saying, "Good, brother Cephas, all you need to do is to keep the same vigor of yesterday, but remember to balance your movements."

138 "What do you mean?" Cephas inquired.

139 "Move your hands in unison from the prayer position, extended before you, to a sweep like an oar on either side. Just as you row a boat with the oars in unison, so you must row the boat of your body in unison with the oars of your arms."

140 The eyes of Cephas opened wide as he now understood the instructions of Philip, and plunging in the water, he immediately began to swim. He swam far out into the sea, until at last he returned when everyone began to call to him.

141 He came upon the shore elated, saying, "Did you see! I swam like a fish!"

142 Yeshua embraced Cephas with an arm around his shoulder and assured everyone, "And so may all of you accomplish great things, when you believe in yourself as much as others believe in you.

143 This then is the beginning of the path to holding the powers of Celestine Light in your

hands: ***think it, believe it, have faith, and do it.***"

CHAPTER 60

Miracles of Knowledge

Yeshua speaks about the importance of gaining knowledge, which is one of the principle reasons we came into a life of mortality.

And it came to pass that Yeshua and those who walked with him journeyed north toward Tyre.

2 As they traveled, they stopped at towns along the way, but at no place were they welcomed except at Ptolemais, where there remained some who remembered Yeshua fondly from his previous visit.

3 But even among these, there were none that desired to follow him, for they considered that their life was good enough as it was, and the way of life that Yeshua taught was more difficult.

4 Experiencing the rejection of the people in town after town and the reluctance, even of those in Ptolemais who welcomed Yeshua to live his teachings, Toma asked him, "Is there not some miracle you can do to arouse these people from their apathy? If they will not take action other than nodding their head, even to you, how will we ever cause them to move beyond the meager comfort they cling to?

5 In truth, why do we even bother to travel all these days? Would it not be better to remain among our family and friends and those who have accepted to follow the Celestine Light in our communities?"

6 Yeshua answered him, saying, "Have you swallowed a bitter herb this morning, Toma, to make you all grumbly?"

7 "Nay, good Yeshua," Toma answered. "It is merely my frustration. I worry about my family and friends when we are away. And to stop in these towns oftentimes seems pointless for the people are deaf and blind.

8 To hear your words each day is a treasure, but we could hear them as easily and in more comfort with our families at any of the communities of Gennesaret.

9 Please do not misunderstand. If you desire us to go from city to city and have the gates shut upon us, so be it. I will follow you even when I do not understand.

10 But it would give my heart more peace if I could comprehend somewhat more about why we travel abroad and why you simply do not cause a mountain to fall into the sea to awaken these people out of their sleep, that they will listen and heed your words."

11 Yeshua answered him, saying, "When you physically lift a boulder from the ground and walk with it even a small distance, you must focus your strength and continue to exert it until the task is done. The effort, however small, takes some of your vitality.

12 Were you to thus move several boulders, enough of your vitality would be taken that

you would need to rest for a time and renew yourself before resuming your tasks. So it is with miracles big and small."

13 Many of the others had been listening as Yeshua answered Toma, and now he beckoned them all to come closer that they might hear the rest of his answer.

14 "Many things are called miracles simply because of ignorance. If you know how to make fire and another does not know how, then when you make fire, it will seem as a miracle to them because they cannot fathom how it occurred.

15 These are simply miracles of greater knowledge, and I exhort you to gain greater knowledge at every opportunity for it will free you from the chains of life by which you would otherwise be bound.

16 A true miracle occurs not from employing secret knowledge of the fundamentals of nature, but when you give up some of your own life essence, such as when you heal someone by calling forth your love and passion within the arms of faith. Though at the time you will feel only peace, afterward you will feel the loss of essence you have given.

17 Other miracles come from Elohim and the power of Celestine Light that Elohim has given to the worthy, to flow through you. You are the bridge between Heaven and earth.

18 Your earthly body cannot long endure such powerful aeons, and it will be both energized and exhausted by the flow of power. This is the type of miracle that moves mountains, for the mortal body does not have such power on its own.

19 When a great healing is to be done, such as to give sight to the blind, hearing to the deaf, walking to the paralytic, you must give of your essence with love, passion, and faith and also call upon the greater powers of Celestine Light to flow through you.

20 So you see, Toma, though it takes only a small amount of pure faith bundled with love and passion and a call upon the powers of Celestine Light to move a mountain into the sea, doing so also takes some of the essence of the worker of the miracle for a time.

21 Therefore miracles, other than miracles merely of greater knowledge, should only be given to the worthy or in defense of life and never simply as a show of power or divinity.

22 In truth, even if I were to stand at the gates of the city and call a mountain to fall at my feet, almost all witnesses would still deny the source of that which their eyes had seen, for to admit the truth would compel them to accept changes in their lives they do not desire.

23 It is not outward miracles that bring people to the light, but inward. Only someone who is seeking a greater light will find it. Most are not seeking. They may be in misery or luxury, but in either, they are more comfortable than in change.

24 Only when a person accepts in their heart that their life is more than a few decades of toil in mortality and honestly desires to learn of the eternity to come and the truth of God, can a miracle of truth and light begin to expand within their heart.

25 Someone may be awed by a miracle for a day or even a week. Maybe it will even hold them in its spell for a month or a year. But unless they were seeking to find and live a greater light, they will soon cease to give credence to the miracle. Rather, they will accept every other explanation given by the ignorant, that they may be justified to continue to live their life outside the light.

26 We go from city to city, town to town, preaching the Celestine Light, for the few who seek it and are willing to walk down the path it illuminates.

27 But we go as much for ourselves as for others. As we journey together, we teach one another by our words and our actions and the experiences we share, which are different and more challenging than the experiences we have amongst our friends and families in the Communities of Light.

28 By this, we grow and become more than we were. As we bring the Celestine Light to the world, we draw greater light to ourselves, even if all the doors of the world are closed to us."

29 "That is a wonderful explanation you have spoken," exclaimed Mattayah. "But what of our own lives? Can we use the powers of Celestine Light to enrich our lives? Not with worldly things, but with boons such as long life and health, peace from the Romans, and bounty in our

lands?"

30 Yeshua answered him, saying, "As I said before, there are miracles of knowledge, and to gain greater knowledge is one of the principle reasons you come into a life of mortality.

31 Elohim has put upon the earth all of the plants and herbs, minerals, and animals needed to benefit man in every way. But to know which plant is food and which is poison and that which is poison but also medicine when used in small amounts, these are among the things you must invest your life in learning.

32 When you heal a man of an infirmity using an herb, it is no less a miracle than if you had given of your essence or called upon the powers of Elohim. Knowledge is as much a part of Celestine Light as a miracle given from your essence.

33 And for the person healed, it may be a greater miracle to use the herbs than to give of your essence, for most infirmities come from poor choices of food and wrong habits in life.

34 If you take away a man's infirmity by giving of your essence, but he does not change his diet or his habits, his sickness will return or its cousin, but where will you be to heal him again?

35 Hopefully, not at his side, for if he was healed by love and faith, but loved himself so little that he returned to his weakness, then he is not deserving to be healed again by a Child of Light until his heart changes to a sincere love of Elohim and of himself.

36 But if you had previously given him herbs to counter his sickness and showed him that which you gave, when you are gone, he can continue to treat himself, even if he is too weak of spirit to change his habits that brought the infirmity.

37 So it is with your own lives. Seek to gain all that you have asked: longevity, health, peace, and bounty of your lands by gaining greater knowledge of the things you seek and then employing your knowledge wisely, for this is one of the principal reasons you are in mortality.

38 You can ask Elohim in prayer to bless you with all of the things you have asked: health, longevity, peace and bounty, and much more than this. But know that Elohim will not answer you with a miraculous wave that immediately brings about the things you seek and desire, for how would you grow by that?

39 In truth, if you went up to a man and asked him to give you ten gold coins and he immediately complied, you would have little respect for the man, and the value of the gold to you would only be in proportion to your effort required to obtain it.

40 But if you had to labor by the sweat of your brow for a year to obtain the same gold coins, they would have great value to you because you would have exchanged a year of your life for them in toil.

41 Therefore, when you ask Elohim to bless you with the things you have spoken of, do not look for an immediate effect without effort, for that would be contrary to the very purpose for which you are here upon the earth.

42 Rather, look for a door to open to knowledge that you can gain and employ that which will bring the blessings you seek, for it is that door that Elohim will open for you in answer to your prayer.

43 By knowledge, you may gain all of the things which you have spoken of as you exercise the will to live that which you know.

44 Let knowledge be the miracle that brings health, longevity, peace, and prosperity, living the word of Elohim that blesses your soul and loving of one another that enriches your lives."

CHAPTER 61

Miracles at the Ladder of Tyre

Marit, the wife of the Apostle Ya'akov, falls from a cliff high above a treacherous area of the sea, and Ya'akov leaps off headfirst after her. Instead of falling to their deaths, Yeshua uses his aura to land them all safely upon a large rock jutting up from the sea. After healing Marit and Ya'akov of their injuries, he teaches them how to expand and spin their auras to connect to the Celestine Realms. Together, they calm the sea and buoyed up by their auras, they walk across the water to safety upon the shore.

And it came to pass that Yeshua and those who traveled with him continued on their journey to Tyre.

2 After passing through the coastal town of Achzib and again finding not one person interested in speaking with them other than for commerce, they continued along the coast until they came to the steep and treacherous trail along high bluffs jutting out into the sea, known as the Ladder of Tyre.

3 Following the trail and climbing the rough-hewn steps cut into portions of the south side of the headlands were tiring for everyone, especially for some of the women, with the strong wind that was blowing off the sea.

4 While negotiating a particularly narrow passage, barely the width of a thin person, where the sea cape rose vertically on the inland side and the cliff fell away vertically on the seaside for over two hundred feet, Marit, the wife of Ya'akov, son of Cleophas, slipped and fell off the precipice with a heartrending scream of terror.

5 Ya'akov had been holding her hand, helping her to pass the narrow trail, and no sooner had she slipped from his grasp and cart-wheeled off the edge of the cliff than he leaped off headfirst after her, calling out her name.

6 The events occurred so rapidly that other than those who were nearest and witnessed it, no one knew the tragedy that had transpired.

7 As there were few places on the trail that one person could pass another, it was by yells passed down the line that everyone came to understand what had occurred.

8 "Quickly go back the way we have come that we can reach the shore and rescue them!" Cephas commanded to everyone below him on the south side of the cape.

9 "They must have already perished," mourned Amram who was standing beside Cephas. "If the fall did not kill them, being tossed by the waves onto the many rocks at the bottom surely did. And if by a miracle they survived the fall and the rocks, they will surely drown before we can arrive, for the waves below are huge and merciless."

10 "Be quiet and move quickly" was all Cephas said in response, and everyone did as he bid and rapidly, but cautiously descended back down the trail.

11 They soon came to a place where they could see the coastline to the north where Marit and Ya'akov had fallen, but the sea crashed against the cliff face and there was no beach or sanctuary from the pounding waves, nor any sign of the couple.

12 Suddenly, Mattayah let out a shriek, crying, "Yeshua is not with us! He also must have fallen off the cliff!"

13 This declaration was more than many could bear. Many of the women began to howl in grief, and many of the men held their heads between their hands overcome with the thought.

14 Then in a calm but strong voice, Miriam said unto them, "Fear not, brothers and sisters. Yeshua has not perished, nor have Marit or Ya'akov, although I think they are injured. Yeshua is with them even now upon the sea. They have ascended upon a rock above the waves and wait for us to rescue them."

15 Everyone looked at Miriam, almost dumbfounded. "How do you know this, Miriam?" asked Cephas. "Did you see Yeshua also fall off the cliff and can you see them even now down the coast where no other eyes of ours can?"

16 "All of you, must have more faith," Miriam upbraided them. "You are not the ordinary men you seem to keep trying to convince yourselves that you are, nor is Yeshua as any other man.

17 We are all upon this earth for the high and holy purposes of Elohim, and until those purposes have been fulfilled or unless we become unworthy, you must know with certainty that the hand of Elohim will ever protect us.

18 I cannot see Yeshua or the others with my physical eyes, but I see them with my spiritual eyes and I know that they live. Nor did I see Yeshua leap, fall, or jump off the cliff. One moment he was beside me, and the next moment he was not.

19 But as surely as I know you are alive and here before me, I know they are all alive and waiting for us as I have said.

20 Go now back to Achzib and gather men, boats, ropes, whatever you need to rescue our loved ones. You know me. You know I am not given to idle words. If I have said that it is so, so it is."

21 Miriam spoke with firm conviction, and both with hope and faith, five of the Apostles ran back toward Achzib to mount a rescue, while the others remained and tried to find a way that they could approach closer to the point below the cliff where Marit and Ya'akov had fallen.

22 Within two hours, the Apostles returned from Achzib, and with them came ten men from the town, carrying ropes.

23 Himaschel was chief among them, and he quickly took charge, ordering the men to a place above the sea where he knew they could access the area the travelers were said to have fallen. Driving stakes into cracks in the rocks, they tied ropes to the stakes, and Himaschel and another man descended.

24 Cephas insisted upon following them, and he overheard one man speak to Himaschel, saying, "Let us be careful that we too are not injured. The waves are very treacherous today. This is really a fool's errand, for nobody could have survived the fall. In all the history of this country, nobody ever has and nobody ever will. We will be lucky to even find the bodies."

25 "I agree," Himaschel responded. "But these are the people of the strange religion that just came through our town. We have seen their ilk before, and in their fervency of belief, they will not accept the death of their friends until they see it with their own eyes."

26 Cephas began to respond to what he had heard, but then closed his mouth and kept his silence.

27 After the three of them had passed below the edge of the cliff, they were followed one after another by all the other men who had come from the town, as well as many of the Apostles. As Yovan, another of the townsmen, explained, they must form a human chain along the cliff face that the bodies could be passed along the bluff until they reached the inclined area where they

descended and could be passed up.

28 But Yohhanan, who walked beside him, took great exception to the words of Yovan and said unto him, "We are not going to recover the dead but to rescue the living."

29 Yovan shook his head with an all-knowing smile and said unto Yohhanan, "I understand these were your friends and I am sorry if I offended you, but the truth is still the truth no matter how much we might wish it to be otherwise. And the truth is that no one could survive a fall from these cliffs."

30 "Where Yeshua is, there is always hope. More so, his wife Miriam has said that they live. And that is the truth you shall see. So let us make haste as they must be getting assaulted by the waves."

31 Yovan simply shrugged, and they continued working their way down to the base of the cliff.

32 Suddenly, a cry of exclamation was heard from Himaschel, who was at the head of the rescue party and furthest along the cliff. He had just rounded a large rock giving him an unimpeded view of the place Yeshua, Marit, and Ya'akov had fallen. "They live! I see them upon a rock, and they are moving!"

33 This good news was quickly passed up the line with shouts of joy by all of the Children of Light as they received it and looks of disbelief and incredulity by all of the townsmen.

34 Yovan shook his head and muttered to himself, "It is impossible."

35 Yohhanan, overhearing him, assured him, "Nothing is impossible when Yeshua is with you."

36 As the nearest men, including Cephas, worked their way along the narrow shoreline at the base of the cliffs, they came to the spot nearest to the rock that the three who had fallen lay and sat upon. It was barely high enough to be above the waves sweeping in from the sea, and even so, those upon it were sopping wet, sprayed by the crash of every wave upon their tenuous place of refuge.

37 Cephas came up to Himaschel and asked, "How do we now gather them from the rock in the sea to our arms upon the shore?"

38 Himaschel answered him, saying, "It will be a challenge. I am not sure how they came to be so far from the shore. They should have fallen close to the base of the cliff. But they are where they are, and it is beyond the reach of our ropes even if a man had the strength to throw a rope that far.

39 Nor can men reach them by boat from the sea, for their boat would be capsized by the waves or dashed upon the rocks. Nor can others swim from the shore to their rock, for the water is deep and the waves would throw them about like flotsam."

40 Cephas tried yelling to his friends on the rock that they were perplexed at how to reach them, but they could not hear his words over the crash of the waves and movement of the sea.

41 Ya'akov was sitting and held Marit's head upon his lap as she lay prone with her eyes closed and her breathing shallow. She was bleeding from her head, and Ya'akov had broken his left arm and held it limply at his side.

42 Then Yeshua stood, and he was uninjured. He looked all about him, first toward the men on the shore and then turning he gazed out into the sea. Looking down at Ya'akov and Marit, he reviewed their situation, "Our friends will not be able to gather us to them, for we are beyond their reach. Today is a test of your faith Ya'akov, for only calling upon the powers of the Celestine Light of Elohim will we be saved. How is your faith?"

43 Ya'akov smiled and, looking up at Yeshua, said unto him, "We were falling to our deaths, and then we were caught up in a great gust of wind and landed upon this tiny refuge, broken but still alive. My faith was great before, but it is certain that it is even greater now. What must I do?"

44 "I cannot explain it all at this moment," Yeshua began. "But the wind that carried us to our refuge issued forth from me. Raising that wind and landing us softly upon this, the only rock near the shore large enough to hold us, has taken a large part of my essence. It will return, but for

the moment I am weak and with the tide rising, we do not have the luxury of waiting.

45 But the same power of Elohim that is in me is within all who believe in the true Celestine Light. It is in you too, Ya'akov; and in Marit.

46 I wish to use another portion of my soul essence to heal you and Marit now, but then I will be further weakened for a time.

47 After you are healed, if we join together in faith, we can still the sea and walk upon it as dry ground that we may reach the shore in safety. Do you have so great a faith as that, Ya'akov?"

48 "Truly, Yeshua, I know you never speak ought but the truth. If you say the sea will calm and we may walk upon it as dry land, I know without doubt that it is so."

49 "Very well," Yeshua replied. And without another word, he put his right hand upon the head of Marit, and breathing a deep sigh, he gave her of his essence. In that very moment, she awakened refreshed. And looking about her in amazement, she asked, "What has happened?"

50 Ya'akov kissed her softly on her head and said unto her, "In a moment, my precious wife, I will tell you a little, and when we reach shore safely and are again with our friends, I will tell you everything."

51 Then he nodded at Yeshua and Yeshua came to him and touching him on his broken arm, he gave him of his essence, and immediately his arm was made whole.

52 Ya'akov briefly then explained to Marit that which Yeshua had spoken to him and her faith was as full as his and she was anxious to begin.

53 Yeshua bid them rise and stand, facing one another. He then asked them to reach their arms to the right and to the left and to hold the person on each side about their waist and then to bring their heads forward that all touched upon their foreheads.

54 The men on shore saw this and were amazed to see all three not only alive but capable of standing, and Himaschel turned to Cephas and declared, "God must surely be with your friends, and it is right that even now they must be praying to him."

55 Cephas nodded in agreement but turning to Toma who was next to him, asked, "Is it in prayer that they stand or something more?" Toma shook his head, unknowing.

56 Back upon the rock, Yeshua spoke to Ya'akov and Marit, saying, "As we stand, we three are united as one, and the power of three thus united is very great.

57 Let us now unite our soul essences that they are three in harmony that move as one.

58 Let us now swirl our one soul essence in a great vortex beginning in the space between our bodies and rising above us into the heavens, expanding as it goes ever higher.

59 We are three confined for a time in frail mortal bodies, but through this vortex, we are one with all the great Celestine powers of Heaven. Feel and know these powers even now, for you are connected through the vortex from the highest Heaven to your very soul.

60 Know that connected to Celestine Realms through the vortex, we could call upon the angels of Heaven to lift us from this rock and carry us to safe ground, but what growth to us would that be?

61 Verily, our Father and Mother in Heaven are most pleased when we discover and use the gifts they have given us. Therefore, let us use them now.

62 United three as one, let us now swirl the vortex faster than the greatest storm, that it may build in its power, amplifying the Celestine Light to our own great potential." And as Yeshua bid, so they did.

63 "Now together as one, let us command the sea to be calm. Say again after me in unison, 'In the name of Elohim, we command the sea before us to be calmed.'" And as Yeshua bid, so they did.

64 No sooner had the words, spoken as one, left their lips than the last wave crashed against their rock refuge, and then all was quiet except for a gentle movement of the sea.

65 Upon the shore, the men of Achzib exclaimed in wonder as the sea suddenly stilled. And Himaschel explained to Cephas. "The ways of the sea are strange, one moment ferocious and the next falling into a sleep. But this bodes well for your friends, for now with a calm sea, we may

certainly find a way to bring them to safety."

66 While Himaschel was speaking, Cephas had not been looking at him but at his friends upon the rock, and seeing them now move toward its edge, he knew that the sea had calmed not by chance and that a greater miracle of Elohim was about to take place, and he told Himaschel, "A rescue is no longer needed." And pointing to his friends, he declared, "Behold, they come to us!"

67 Even as he spoke, the three upon the rock came to its edge insomuch that the water of the sea covered the toes of their feet, and Yeshua said unto them, "The same power of Celestine Light that landed us safely upon this rock can bring us even now safely to our friends across the water.

68 The weight of your body can be lifted by the strength of your aura, which is the manifestation of the essence of your body, mind, and spirit.

69 Let us stay linked arm in arm, walking as one across the water, each upheld by the strength of the other.

70 The vortex to the Celestine Lights of Heaven has renewed all of our strengths. Now our return to our family waits only for our faith in Elohim and in ourselves to manifest a power given to all but known by only a precious few, even the limitless power of Celestine Light.

71 My brother and sister, are you ready to expand the light of your essence until your aura is flying away and you are as light as a feather upon the sea?"

72 Both Marit and Ya'akov nodded in agreement, and Marit asked, "Will we fly like birds, Yeshua?"

73 Yeshua smiled as he looked into her eyes and said, "Not like birds, Marit, more like logs upon the water but incapable of sinking into it. This is all we need, and we should not call upon more than we need, lest we lose that which would have been better to keep for another day."

74 Then without further ado, linking arms with Yeshua in the middle, they stepped upon the water and they did not sink. Only their feet were covered up to their ankles. Without hesitation, they began walking toward their friends upon the shore.

75 Seeing this, all the men of Achzib exclaimed in amazement, and even among the Apostles, there was wonder. And most of those who had been traveling with Yeshua had come near enough so that they could see the miracle of their friends walking upon the sea.

76 But even as they witnessed the miracle, the men of Achzib recovered from their initial astonishment and began to deny what they were seeing, even as it was occurring, as one said to another, "It would seem that they are walking on the water, but remember there are ridges of rock just below the surface. It is surely one of those that they walk upon."

77 The other men of Achzib nodded in agreement, and even as Yeshua, Ya'akov, and Marit were almost upon them, Himaschel told Cephas, "Your friends are certainly the luckiest people in the land; not only to somehow safely survive a fall of great height onto unforgiving rocks, but to not be drowned in the sea and then to be uninjured and then to find an underwater ridge to return to shore. Surely the luckiest three people I have ever seen."

78 Cephas answered him, saying, "Good Himaschel, you yourself have agreed with your friends that surviving such a fall in this place is impossible, let alone surviving uninjured. Therefore, admit the truth your heart proclaims that you are witness not to luck, but to a great miracle of God that can be explained no other way."

79 Himaschel shook his head negatively in response. "No, it is just great luck, and no more. Were it to be more, my life would be turned upside down, and I like my life just as it is."

80 Then before another word could be spoken, Yeshua, Ya'akov, and Marit walked ashore and into the waiting embraces of their friends and family.

CHAPTER 62

Lessons at the Beach

Yeshua, Miriam, Salome, and the Apostles and their wives take a break from their traveling and spend a day relaxing and playing on the beach. After the midday meal, Yeshua speaks about the lessons of mortality and growing from one's experiences, which is evidenced by the demonstration of character. He also speaks about the power of prayer, what to pray for and what not to pray for. Yeshua emphasizes the importance of knowledge and continual learning and how members of the Community of Light should have varied expertises that collectively make one community with great knowledge and abilities. He details the importance of living on the sea for health and longevity. He concludes by teaching them the Celestine Light techniques needed to call forth the energies required to do as he did when saving Ya'akov and Marit after they fell off the cliff.

And it came to pass that Yeshua and those who traveled with him continued on their journey to the city of Tyre.

2 After they descended down the north side of the Ladder of Tyre, Marit and Ya'akov came to Yeshua as he was walking with Miriam and Salome, and Ya'akov said unto him, "Marit and I wanted to thank you again for saving us from certain doom."

3 Yeshua smiled and answered him, saying, "As Miriam has told me she reminded everyone, you still have much work to do for Elohim before you can go off to paradise."

4 Ya'akov let out a deep sigh and responded, "Still it was an amazing joy to still be alive. One moment, the few seconds I thought would be my last, I was reaching as I plummeted down to touch Marit's hand that we might die together, for I could not bear to be without her, and she was looking up reaching for me even as she fell.

5 The next moment I was somehow alive, next to Marit, looking up at the imposing white cliffs and at you, being where you couldn't have been, but you were.

6 No matter how or why, I, we, can never thank you enough for saving us."

7 Yeshua put an arm around Ya'akov's shoulder and pulled him toward him in the friendly manner of men and answered, "You are welcome. But the how and the why are important, so let us discuss that with the others when we stop for the midday meal."

8 "As you wish, Yeshua," Ya'akov answered, and he turned to move back with Marit to the group that followed so Yeshua could again be alone with Miriam and Salome as he walked. Marit came first to Yeshua and grasping his hand, she kissed it reverently and said, "I too must give you my deepest thanks, Yeshua. I was so foolish to not be careful walking along the precipice. And in my foolishness, both my husband and I would have lost our lives save for you.

9 Nothing I can say or do will ever adequately show the gratitude in my heart, but call upon

me as you need for the work of Elohim and I will be there before the dawn. You turned my darkness into light, even as you do in so many ways for each of us every day. Thank you, Yeshua, Lord of Light, thank you."

10 Yeshua kissed Marit's hand even as she had kissed his and said, "In the days to come, you will have much to do for the work of Elohim, Marit. But each day, simply continue to be the light of sweetness and kindness that you always have been, and you will be serving Elohim well. The example of your life is as great as any other thing you can say or do."

11 Marit bowed her head to Yeshua and said thank-you once more; then she and Ya'akov stepped back to be with the others who walked in a group behind Yeshua.

12 They came at last to a beautiful sandy beach, and as far as they could see in any direction, there were no other people. Salome ran onto the beach and, throwing off her sandals, went onto the sand and twirled around with her arms extended, exclaiming, "It is as if we are the only people in all the world, and such a beautiful world it is!"

13 The others soon followed and, casting off their sandals, began to revel in the feeling of the warm sand and water upon their feet as they walked on the beach and in the small surf.

14 Miriam came up behind Salome. Leaning over her shoulder she kissed her mischievously on the cheek and pointed down the beach. "Alas, we are not all alone. Look further down the beach and you can see a Roman villa and beyond that the island of Tyre."

15 Salome turned, and holding both of Miriam's hands, she looked at her playfully and said, "I like my illusion just fine as it is, dear Miriam. So let us leave the cities and the Romans for another day and today stay in my illusion."

16 As they spoke, all of the others had also begun to relax and even play on the beach, and Yeshua seeing this gave a great smile of joy. Raising his voice just a little, he said unto them, "Though we have barely traveled today, this is a very good place. Therefore, after you have frolicked for a while, let us make camp and spend both the day and the night here. Tomorrow, we shall come upon Tyre, and for all the peace and serenity here, there are great challenges of spirit in that city. Therefore, store up good spirit from the earth and the sea, and your love one for another today that the reservoir will uphold you tomorrow."

17 And it came to pass that with Yeshua's encouragement and participation, everyone reveled in the sun and the sea and the sand, playing with one another like the children they once were but had long forgotten.

18 Casting a net they had brought with them, some of the fishermen quickly caught many small fish, and everyone ate a fine midday meal accompanied with vegetables they harvested from both the land and the sea.

19 When they were finished eating, they sat on the beach and Yeshua spoke to them, saying, "Please remember this day and the feeling you have had upon this beach. The cares and challenges and strifes of the world have been forgotten for this moment in time.

20 Released from your many responsibilities and worries, you have been able to give your adult a rest and let your child out to play.

21 There is no one here to bother or persecute you or demand payment or labor, and that is a very good feeling, is it not?

22 You have only the clothes on your back, but want for nothing including food as a sumptuous meal provided by Elohim that was easy to catch and harvest.

23 The air is warm, the friendly company outstanding, and it is easy in this place to realize how little is really needed to find contentment.

24 I say again, remember the feeling of this place each of the days to come in your life. Use it as motivation to remove yourselves from the ways of the world and seek out and live the simple life of contentment you feel today.

25 Because of who you are, you will still need to venture into the world from time to time for the purposes of Elohim. But seek to build communities that are alive with the carefree serenity that you feel today. You do not have to go to Heaven to find it, for you can create it and live it

even upon this world.

26 earth is still an Eden for those who see it and desire it to be so.

27 But the pure carefree joy and vibrant energy you feel on this beach cannot be found away from the warm sea. The sea warmed by the sun is a great reservoir of good aeon. And where the land meets the sea, the energy is released for the benefit of the Children of the earth.

28 I tell you these things that you may plan for your future. In Palestine, we are in the cauldron and the land of Palestine shall only become hotter upon the cauldron in the days to come.

29 As I have spoken before, the time will soon come when you must abandon the communities you have built and travel to lands beyond the reach of Rome or under the fist of tyrants.

30 It will ever be so that people fight over desolate pieces of land while staying away from the sea of bounty, which they fear.

31 You must not fear the sea. The Children of Light are meant to be children of the sea as well as the earth. Upon the sea, the Children of Light would do well to live or to return to often.

32 We will come tomorrow upon the ancient island city of Tyre. Consider it well. Though Alexander of Macedonia destroyed the city, it had remained virtually impregnable for thousands of years before his day.

33 As an island upon a sea of bounty, protected by its natural virtues and the fortifications of its citizens, it grew to great opulence and decadence. When you see it, do not dwell upon what it once was or is today, but envision what it could have been if it had been a city of light instead of darkness.

34 Appreciate the harmony of an island in the sea as a place where the Children of Light can have the best of both the land and the sea, while also being apart and protected from many of the perils of the world.

35 This is what you should seek in the Communities of Light to come as you are given the light by Elohim to find and create them.

36 The sea is much more than water and fish. It is life. It is the renewal of the life of the mortal tabernacle wherein dwells your spirit and soul.

37 Do you remember why you are in these frail bodies? Why do you not simply go from spirit to eternal life in an immortal body? Why bother with this life of mortality at all? Especially considering the terrible pain and trauma it is for many people?"

38 Cephas answered, "As you have told us, Yeshua, we are here to learn and grow from our experiences and our relationships and to build faith in Elohim and ourselves as we contend with the challenges of mortal life."

39 Yeshua nodded his head in agreement and told them, "Teach that and you will be teaching the Celestine Light, but know that there is still more light than this. What is the purpose of contending with the challenges of life: to learn and grow?

40 To learn is easy to understand: If you touch a hot fire, you are burned and you learn from that lesson not to touch a hot fire again. But how did you grow from that experience?

41 If you have learned the lesson of not touching the hot fire and one day have a man about your fire who has never understood that lesson and reaches for the fire, what do you do before his hand is singed?"

42 Yuda answered, "Let him burn his hand a little so he too can learn and remember the lesson from his own experience and be sure to never do it again."

43 Yeshua laughed hearing this and said, "Yes, you could do that, and in truth, lessons learned from experience are the ones best remembered. But in the goodness of your light, what would be another alternative?"

44 Yuda responded, saying, "I could warn him of the consequences because I have already tasted those consequences, admittedly when I was a little child, so I don't know where this man has been sheltered all of his life. But being hardheaded as most men are, he probably would not listen or believe until he had been scorched himself."

45 Yeshua nodded in agreement, saying, "It is as you say. But the difference is when you gave

warning, you shared from what you had learned in life and sought to prevent the pain of another person. In doing this, you demonstrated character, and it is character that is the fruit of your experiences and the evidence of your growth.

46 Know then that mortality is more than just a place to learn and grow and develop faith. It is the place where you demonstrate by your character your worthiness to exaltation in the eternity to come.

47 You have heard me say that faith without works is like a cart without wheels. By this, I do not mean works such as the Pharisees do, meaningless actions simply because they believe those actions please God and show their devotion.

48 Rather, works are simply the character by which you live your life. Your character, good or bad, dictates your actions, your responses, and your interaction with others.

49 These are the works Elohim looks upon, and these are the works by which you are judged, not how you cut or style your hair, nor how you wear your clothes, nor how many steps you take on the Sabbath.

50 How you treat your fellow men and women, even when there is no one to see, and how you choose to do right even when there would be no one to see you do wrong and how you are not apathetic, but are ever seeking for ways to improve your world and help the lives of your family, friends, and fellow travelers in mortality.

51 This then is the answer to how you grow. You grow by continually adding to the depth and quality of your character, and this is the path with faith and love to the Celestine Lights of Heaven."

52 Yeshua was silent for a moment to allow his words to reach into the hearts of those who listened to him.

53 After a time, when no one spoke, he continued saying, "Each day, mortality puts a weight of challenges upon every person. Some are small like the advent of a slight illness that comes for a day or two and then is gone.

54 Others are great, such as an infirmity that strikes, causing ever-increasing pain every day of life thereafter.

55 Relationships that are not harmonious can cause an anguish to the heart greater than the pain of any affliction of the body.

56 There are also those who suffer in slavery and then there are those who are called free but suffer as slaves to their weaknesses. They ever give in to their lusts to be fulfilled for a moment, but emptier and emptier in their spirit day by day.

57 There are challenges to put a roof over the head of your family and food upon the table, to raise your children well, and to overcome the grief that is felt when someone you love passes beyond mortality.

58 Day by day, in ways both small and great, you are tested by life, and it seems natural to call upon Elohim to help you, to ease your suffering or make the road before you easier.

59 But if life's challenges are the furnace in which you learn and grow from your mortal experiences and through which your character is forged and these are the measures by which your exaltation in eternity is judged, is it really in your best interest to have Elohim intervene on your behalf?

60 Nay, it is not.

61 There are many faiths and religions that are believed and followed among the people living upon this great Salt Sea. Some worship the earth, some a plethora of gods. All pray to the gods of their belief for their deliverance, for victory over their enemies, to be healed of their infirmities, to find wealth and many more things in their personal lives.

62 And to all these requests to receive a blessing, how does Elohim respond? In most instances, not at all. Though the matter may be life or death for the person saying the prayer, even a Child of Light, it is better in most instances for them to experience what they will and make the choices they will to deal with it, rather than have an intervention in their lives by Elohim."

63 Again Yeshua stopped speaking to let his words settle into the hearts and minds of those who listened, and there was immediately much talking one with another about the words he had just spoken.

64 Yudas Iscariot raised his hand to catch attention and said, "Yeshua, I understand that those who pray to false gods would have nothing but emptiness for an answer, but is this also true for the Children of Light? Wherein is our faith placed if it is not with the conviction that by living in the Celestine Light, we are answered and upheld by the greater light of Elohim in our hours of need?"

65 Yeshua answered him, saying, "Elohim does hear and answer your prayers, but not every prayer you utter, only those given to make you greater than you were, not less.

66 But most of the prayers given by men to any God are given to make them less not more, and the true light of Heaven, even our Mother and Father, love their children too much to give them less instead of more.

67 Therefore, Elohim hears all prayers, but answers few, because the supplicants are asking for the wrong things.

68 Do not ask to be healed of your sickness. Ask to be guided to the knowledge to heal yourself. You truly can heal yourself of illnesses with proper knowledge. But you must be girded up to have the willpower to take the necessary actions to accomplish your healing, beginning with acquiring the knowledge in times before it is needed.

69 Verily, when it comes to health and sickness, Elohim has put upon the earth every herb, mineral, and substance necessary to cure any illness that will ever afflict man when coupled with correct diet and right living.

70 As we walk and heal others I teach you the secret powers of stones, herbs, sounds, colors and of your own aura. Remember these lessons well and continue to expand your knowledge and experience even when I am no more among you.

71 Seek therefore in prayer to be guided to greater knowledge and to better remember the things that you learn. Seek to be strong, not weak, and to live in ways that promote health, instead of destroying it.

72 Nor ask to be delivered from your enemies, but ask to be given the strength of arm or quickness of mind to be able to save yourself. Even better, ask to be guided by the Holy Spirit to paths and places where enemies will not be encountered or to learn to expand your aura of harmony whereby enemies may become friends.

73 In your prayers, therefore, do not seek solutions to your problems from Elohim, but seek from Elohim enhancement of your own knowledge and abilities that you might find a good solution for your own challenges, be they small or great.

74 Even in that, do not seek to instantly know of that which a moment ago you were ignorant. Rather, seek to be led to opportunities to learn, to find time to learn, to find a means to learn, and to remember what you learn.

75 Seek to become more by becoming greater than you were, rather than less by doing nothing for yourself and only asking Elohim to take away your challenges.

76 Give thanks for your challenges, for they are the seeds of your greatness and glory."

77 Yet still there is a time for prayers to Elohim asking for direct intercession and that is after you have done everything within your own power, knowledge and abilities, as have your friends, family and brothers and sisters of light.

78 Only then, after everything you could do has been done in faith and love and knowledge, should you ask Elohim in prayer to directly intercede with a miracle. And you have the sacred promise of Elohim to answer all such prayers that have been offered with faith, humility and love.

79 The people of the world worship a myriad of false gods. But in each instance they pray to their god expecting their god to do everything for them. Do not be like these people of the world who worship gods of their imaginations that they know not, for this is an expectation that

cannot and should not be met even by Elohim the one true creator of all that is.

80 You are literally the children of Elohim the Father and Elohim the Mother. Your relationship to Elohim can best be understood and felt in your heart and mind if you compare it to your relationship with your own children, or your relationship with your parents when you were a child.

81 You hope for the best for your children, even as your Father and Mother in the Celestine realms hope for the best for you.

82 You teach your children the good morals that you live to guide them in their life. But you do not force your children to obey them once they are of age. So has your Celestine Father and Mother given you the good morals which you live and teach, but without compulsion to live them.

83 You teach your children all they need to know to make their own way in the world, even as your Celestine Father and Mother teach you all you need to understand and master the mysteries and secrets of Celestine Light, by which you can yourself do great miracles, rather than call upon Elohim to do them for you.

84 And you take joy when you see your children overcome challenges and make their way in the world with happiness and success, even as your heavenly Father and Mother have joy in watching you grow and expand your light as you overcome the challenges before you.

85 But should your children, though well armed with knowledge and abilities, encounter a challenge they cannot meet, and in their need come to you in supplication, you will not turn a deaf ear, but in your enduring love, will do all you can do to help them.

86 So it is with our Father and Mother in the Celestine Kingdom, who take joy in watching you grow in faith and power. But when you have done all you can do in a worthy endeavor and have still fallen short, they are compelled by an even greater measure of love to answer your prayers for assistance."

87 Once again, Yeshua stopped speaking and waited for someone to seek greater knowledge about that which he had revealed.

88 Then Toma spoke, asking, "Good teacher, our lives are short, and there is so much to learn. If we are not to pray to Elohim for quick deliverance but to seek respite in knowledge, how will we ever gain all the knowledge we need in an entire lifetime, much less for those who are still young and have not had as many years of opportunity to learn?"

89 Yeshua answered him, saying, "One person alone seeking knowledge would be like one bee alone trying to gather all the honey for the hive. But you are not one but many, and the many should be as one.

90 The knowledge of one does not need to be the knowledge of everyone. In some things, your knowledge will be the same as the knowledge of your brothers and sisters, but let each choose a few areas of immersion that they may learn and excel greater than most of their brothers and sisters in those things.

91 Then let the Children of Light be as one body, that all challenges may be met by one among them who has the knowledge.

92 Part of character is learning to live and work harmoniously within your Family of Light that as a body of one all challenges will be met.

93 Therefore let some become adept in the ways of planting and the harvest and others in the ways of fishing and the sea. Let some learn the deepest secrets of the healing arts and others the hidden mysteries of the power of aura and spirit.

94 Let some become readers of the scriptures and others historians of the people. Let some become teachers and others learn to lead and administer.

95 Let some become artists and others craftsmen; some inquirers of science and others philosophers and lovers of languages.

96 Let none be above any other, but all equal before Elohim and one another in their efforts to become the best they can in the areas they serve.

97 And may all serve one another not for personal glory, but for the good of the Family of Light and the glory of Elohim.

98 But also seek to be well-rounded and ever questing for knowledge in many areas. Though you may become an expert in one thing, ever seek to become more adept in many others as well and even an expert in more than one, even many more.

99 Never forget why you are here, and learning is among the greatest of reasons. You learn greatly from your experiences, but should learn no less every day from your studies and observations.

100 Nor forget that whatsoever you gain in mortality in knowledge, character, and faith will bring you ever higher in the world to come. Your knowledge, character, and faith along with your relationships of love are the treasures that rise with you.

101 Again I return to the sea, to the warm sea that comes ashore gently on sandy beaches and is a delight to the senses to feel upon the body, whether just the toes or swimming naked and free.

102 Children of Light should be lovers of the warm sea, for it is a great and marvelous source of health and longevity.

103 Gaining knowledge does take more than a lifetime, and with the sea, you can give yourself more time, for it will renew the very life essence of your body and prolong your life and health far beyond the years accustomed to men and women in this time."

104 With these words, everyone seemed to listen more acutely, and Marit asked, "How then shall we use the sea to receive a reward of health and longevity?"

105 Yeshua answered, saying, "If you desire to add years to your life that you may have more time to learn and serve and prepare your character for the world to come, swim naked each day in the living, warm, salt sea for one hour. That, along with the proper diet, good amounts of pure fresh water to drink, and the other good habits of health I have taught you, will find sickness banished from your life and your years of opportunity upon the earth greatly extended in number."

106 "But what if we do not know how to swim?" Shim'on asked, lifting up his hands questioningly.

107 Hearing his query, everyone laughed, and Yeshua answered him, saying, "Then that should be the first thing you learn in your lifetime of seeking knowledge."

108 After everyone finished laughing, again, Yeshua spoke to them in earnestness about how it was that he had saved Ya'akov and Marit. He taught them the techniques of Celestine Light needed to call forth this ability and how great faith and love would magnify it.

109 And he cautioned them to never use this gift except within the Family of Light and then only in dire need and not for a trifle, for it was a secret not to be seen in the world. Therefore, it cannot be written in any book, but must remain a mystery to the world and only told by the words of one Child of Light to another, as they are prepared to receive greater knowledge and light.

CHAPTER 63

Gifts of the Earth

When Talitha, the wife of the Apostle Toma, becomes ill, Yeshua takes the opportunity to teach everyone how to determine the source of her illness, as well as the herb that will heal her, and emphasizes once again the importance of knowledge.

The following morning, they continued their journey toward Tyre. As they walked, Talitha, the wife of the Apostle Toma, complained of pain in her stomach.

2 Toma immediately desired to heal her by giving of his essence, but Yeshua asked him to refrain for the time and continue walking for a few minutes.

3 As they walked on the land near the beach, they came to a place where Yeshua bade them stop. And turning to face them all, he said unto them, "Both small and great miracles of healing can be done by giving of your essence to the person needing to be healed. But this should be the last choice, not the first.

4 In all things, seek to do that which brings the greatest growth to both you and those around you.

5 To heal someone by giving of your essence requires pure love and faith, both on the part of the healer and the person being healed.

6 When a healing is thus done, the love and faith is confirmed and thereby magnified. And that is the entirety and completion of the growth, save for future actions that may come because of the faith and love that was magnified.

7 But there are most often other means to heal besides giving of your essence. And when the affliction may be small, such as a stomach ache rather than great, such as paralysis, then it behooves you as sons and daughters of Elohim, our Father and Mother, to gain and utilize your knowledge before your essence.

8 Gaining knowledge, and regularly using the knowledge gained, is as important as gaining faith. And in both this life and the next, the rewards for those who gain and use both knowledge and faith are great.

9 When someone comes to you with a sickness or affliction, you must first determine whether they are truly desiring to be healed. Many people complain mightily about their afflictions, but when offered the cure, they are unwilling to take it when it involves a change in their habits, which things they love more than they hate their affliction.

10 If you have felt their spirit and know that they truly wish to be healed, even if it means a change in their habits, you must then ascertain what is the true cause of their affliction, and that is where we are now with Talitha.

11 We know she is a good and pure woman of faith, truly undesiring of her affliction and

willing to do whatever is necessary to alleviate it.
12 So let us consider what could be the cause of her pain." Then turning to Talitha, he asked, "How long has this pain been upon you?"
13 Just since this morning," she replied.
14 Looking then at his friends, Yeshua asked, "From the things you already know and that I have taught you, what are some of the likely causes of her pain?"
15 Marit answered quickly, saying, "She could be pregnant as this could be the nausea of the morning, heralding the birth to come."
16 "No, I do not think it is that," Talitha interjected, "As it is more pain than nausea."
17 "It could just be an upset stomach from the berries we ate this morning," suggested Yudas Iscariot.
18 "Or from drinking impure water," added Salome.
19 "It could also be the warning of something more serious," Cephas added somberly.
20 Yeshua clapped his hands once, and smiling at his friends, he said unto them, "Excellent! These are all well-thought possibilities. With those in mind, let us now look with insight upon Talitha's aura."
21 So saying, Yeshua came beside Talitha and passed his left hand several times over her stomach without touching her and a few times further up even to her head and then said unto her, "With your permission, Talitha, may all of our family with us this day come and do as I have done?"
22 "Of course, Yeshua," she answered.
23 With her permission, Yeshua bade them to each come and move their left hand over Talitha as they had seen him do, and they each came forth. He instructed them, saying, "After you have first used your thoughts and observations to determine the possible causes and have looked for evidence in her pallor and her eyes and her tongue and her nails, and whether she is hot or cold, dry or sweating, you now must see or feel her aura, that you can know the seriousness of the symptoms and how deep and far they spread into her body.
24 I have taught each of you to see the sparkling jewels of light the body emanates, showing the state of all things both spiritual and physical. Now learn to feel this energy as well, for to feel is a more sure knowledge than to see.
25 Pass your left hand over her stomach; close, but not touching her; feel how the energy thickens and grows warm as you are over her stomach; how your hand tingles a little.
26 Now move over other parts of her body and see how the energy thins and cools and no longer tingles. This is showing you that her problem is only in her stomach and that other parts of her body are neither affecting nor affected.
27 Return once again to her stomach and hold your hand still and close. You can feel the beat of your own heart in your hand; now feel the pulse of her heart in her aura.
28 Close your eyes and lose yourself from all things around you and be one with Talitha's aura. Do you feel another aura beating, or only yours and hers? Answer me only after everyone has felt Talitha's aura."
29 One by one, they all came and did as Yeshua bade and then answered his last question with unanimity, saying they had only felt the beat of their heart and Talitha's.
30 "Therefore, you know she is not pregnant," Yeshua expounded.
31 "Did you sense a spreading beyond her stomach of the affliction?" he asked.
32 Again, they answered with unanimity that they had not.
33 "Then it is likely that it is as Yudas has said that her stomach rebels against that which she has recently eaten.
34 Within our sight is a quick cure for stomach ailments. Who among you knows already of this?"
35 Several among them raised their hands in answer to his question, and Yeshua pointed to his brother Yakov to answer the question. And Yakov said unto them, "It is the scrub you stand

beside." Pointing at a sage-like plant near Yeshua, he continued, "Maramiyya is the cure, even as it is also for problems of breathing and women's afflictions and depression or nervousness."

36 "Yes, it is as Yakov has said and as many of you already knew," Yeshua responded. "Merely chewing on the leaves or drinking a tea will alleviate all the symptoms of Talitha. And not eating those berries again in such a number as she did this morning will prevent the affliction from ever returning.

37 Therefore, though you have been given great power to heal by giving of your essence, I beseech you to diligently teach one another of the many miracles of the earth our Father and Mother have given to you and use the gifts of the earth for all of which they have been provided before you think to give of your essence.

38 And know that all my days left among you, I will impart knowledge to you like a spring that ever flows that you may become bounteous fountains of life and Celestine Light.

39 Therefore, hold your essence unto yourself until the moment when it is truly needed. Upon that time, with faith and love, release the light, and nothing will be impossible to you."

CHAPTER 64

The Healing of Tyre

Yeshua brings his Apostles and wives to the city of Tyre and tells them the details of the horrific attack and destruction by Alexander of Macedonia. Because the destruction was so horrendous, there is a great darkness that permeates the land, which overshadows the people who reside there. To assist the innocents, Yeshua teaches his Apostles and their wives how, as Children of Light, to expand their Celestine Light to overcome the darkness and bring light back to the land and its people.

And it came to pass that Yeshua and those who walked with him came upon the environs of Tyre and stood at the base of the thin bridge of land that led to the prominent point on the sea where the remnants of the ancient Phoenician city remained.

2 Having come through the new city, which stood upon the mainland, they prepared to proceed down the land bridge to the island of the old city, but the women began to speak excitedly among themselves and to Miriam, who at last came to Yeshua to speak their desires for all of them, "Beloved, I know you have great things to reveal to us at the spot of the old city on the island. But my sisters and I want to insure that you have allotted time for us to shop here in the new city upon the mainland, for it is not often we have occasion to visit Tyre, and though it is rare, there are still places we may find the purple dye which we all cherish."

3 Upon hearing the request of Miriam, Yeshua nodded affirmatively with a little laugh, "Life is meant to have fun as well as to accomplish serious and great works. Be assured that we will all return to enjoy the shops of new Tyre and purchase the little things that bring large happinesses."

4 Hearing his words, Miriam gave him an embrace and a thank-you kiss on the cheek, and Salome, who had stood beside her as she spoke, kissed him also on his other cheek.

5 Commencing down the bridge of land, Yeshua spoke to them as they walked, saying, "This bridge connecting the mainland to old Tyre was built by the army of Alexander of Macedonia when he conquered Tyre a little over three hundred years ago.

6 You have probably thought we have come to Tyre to preach as we have in other places, but that is not why we are here. If good citizens in small towns and hamlets will not listen to my words, even less would the citizens of Tyre, for they are today as they have ever been, a riotous people not inclined to the purities of spiritual life.

7 That you may fully understand why we are here, I am going to tell you the history of Tyre when it was conquered by Alexander of Macedonia. I wish I did not need to tell this story, for it is bloody and despicable, showing the greatest darkness of the children of men. But only by understanding the fullness of the darkness will you be able to bring the healing Celestine Light to this land, for which cause I have brought you here this day; because when you have an understanding of the depths of the darkness, your desire to change it to the light surges forth

with greater passion.

8 Before Alexander, old Tyre was a gem of the world, as far as cities can be thought of in that way. It certainly was a city wealthy beyond the dreams of other cities, for it is situated in the heart of the trading routes, with fine harbors, and, until Alexander, was nearly impregnable.

9 During the times of King David and King Solomon, Hiram, king of Tyre, supplied the cedar wood and many other exquisite and rare building materials for the temple and the houses of the kings and sent many carpenters, masons, and builders to Israel, for their skill was greater than any in the land.

10 The Tyrians were perhaps the world's best traders. They were masters of the sea and traveled to lands further than any others. So had they also come, for their ancestors came into the Great Sea we are upon, far to the west, from sparkling cities on an even greater sea beyond the Portal of Ba'al, as it is called by the Tyrians, in years lost to antiquity, before the days of the pharaohs of Egypt.

11 Most of the gold that adorned the temple of Solomon was only acquired because Hiram, the king of Tyre, lent Solomon some of his navigators to guide them to foreign lands that they might obtain the metal.

12 When Alexander came to Tyre, he sought to gain entrance under the guise of paying tribute with a personal sacrifice at the temple of Heracles. As he had been conquering one nearby city after another, the Tyrians rightly did not believe his motives and denied him entry into the city.

13 It had been Alexander's intention to take Tyre, but with the insult given, he became obsessed with revenge for the indignity of refusal put upon him by the Tyrians. He determined not only to take the city but to make them suffer greatly for trying to humiliate him.

14 Until that time, Tyre had never been taken by a hostile army though it had sometimes paid tribute to invading kings such as Nebuchadnezzar, who laid siege to it for thirteen years, but never entered the island city.

15 The land we now walk upon was first laid down by the slaves of the army of Alexander.

16 After his refusal of entry, he quickly attacked the mainland city and laid it to waste. There were hundreds of buildings made from stone, and none were spared. Each was torn asunder and, along with many great trees, was used to build this land bridge to the island upon the backs of over ten thousand slaves, most from the conquered city of the mainland.

17 The Tyrians were caught by surprise by Alexander's action in building the bridge of land. This was a strategy which they had never considered plausible as their island stood far off shore with deep and swift waters in between.

18 But to their astonishment the bridge grew, and after several months had reached almost to the island, despite their continual attacks on the builders with archers, catapults, and slingers from their ships, even though many of those killed were their own countrymen, forced into slavery. But many of the soldiers of Alexander were also killed.

19 Then a ferocious storm came and much of the bridge, the parts made from trees and sand, washed away. The Tyrians exalted, assuming Alexander would give up after such devastation, even as all other would-be conquerors had before him.

20 But the anger still burned in Alexander's heart and he had no intention of going away. He called upon his allies in nearby cities and a fleet of ships descended upon Tyre neutralizing their supremacy at sea and preventing them from further meaningful attacks upon the construction crew and soldiers of Macedonia.

21 The slaves then resumed their work upon the bridge of land and as it neared the island the Tyrians became desperate. They sent divers beneath the water to attach hooks to the logs and repeatedly pulled apart that which was built near the city.

22 But the soldiers of Alexander eventually killed all the divers and were soon within a stone's throw of the island.

23 Now the king of Tyre sent out men in the night to kidnap officers of Alexander's army. With

stealth and cunning, night after night, they made raids into Alexander's camps and successfully took many men, even though some of them were also killed.

24 The day following each successful raid, the soldiers and officers of Alexander's army would be taken to the top of the high city wall where they could be seen by all the Macedonians below.

25 While the soldiers of Alexander watched, their friends and officers would be stabbed repeatedly and their bodies would be weighted with stones and thrown to rot in the sea, unable to be recovered by the Macedonians for proper funerals.

26 This action was meant to cause fear in the hearts of the Macedonians, but it instead enraged them and they redoubled their efforts to complete the bridge and attack the city.

27 Before the land bridge was complete, Alexander began to pummel the city with great stones thrown by mighty catapults and these stones caused immense destruction, not only of the great walls about the city, but also among the people and buildings within.

28 The fateful day came when the bridge of land was completed and the walls of Tyre irreparably breached.

29 Before the attack upon the city commenced, many thousands of Tyrian slaves that were still alive from the mainland city were brought close to the walls of the island city, just beyond the reach of the archers.

30 Even as the Tyrians had forced the Macedonians to watch as they murdered their soldiers and officers and threw them off the walls of the city, so the Macedonians now put one out of every three male Tyrian slaves from the mainland to the sword before the eyes of their friends and family within the island city. And their bodies were thrown into the water and many floated like a flotilla of logs upon the restless sea.

31 Then poured the army of Alexander through the breach in the wall and into the doomed city of Tyre.

32 Before I continue, let us say a prayer that despite the darkness you will hear next, you will still be filled with the sweetness of the light.

33 It is better in the course of your lives if you avoid darkness, to see it or even to hear of it, like the greatest of plagues, for it can injure your spirit.

34 But for the reason we have come to Tyre, you must understand what has happened here. But if there are any who are faint of heart, or cannot bear the darkness, even if only in words, and wish to wait here while others choose to continue to old Tyre, there will be no shame, only understanding and love."

35 At his words, Marit said, "I wish to remain, Yeshua, for the things you have already said have burned terrible pictures in my mind and I feel very nauseous inside."

36 Upon hearing Marit's words, all of the other women save Miriam also voiced their desire to remain and hear no more, as did Yudas Iscariot and Philip.

37 But Miriam upbraided them, saying, "Sisters and brothers, be of stout heart and take courage from Elohim. Facing words of terror and places of darkness are aeons we can feel in our hearts, but they do not touch us. And surely this is less than the evils that shall confront us physically in the days to come.

38 We must take courage today and increase our light rather than shy away from darkness we should confront, ere it defeats us simply by fear.

39 If Yeshua says that you can stay and that is well, then so be it. But I ask you to consider what great light you shall not be a witness to if you do not continue with us, for surely Yeshua has not brought us all the way here just to hear horror stories and look at old ruins."

40 Hearing Miriam's words, they were emboldened and bolstered in their hearts and everyone agreed to continue on to the island.

41 Yeshua then called upon Miriam to say a prayer for all of them, and she prayed, saying, "Our Father and Mother in the Celestial Heaven above; please send your Celestine Light unto us. Though we hear of the darkness of days gone by and walk upon a land that flowed with blood; let there only be sweet light in our spirits. Uphold us and lift us up. Send your angels to be with

us, and your Celestine Light to be upon us in every way. Help us to call the part of you that is in each of us, to be within every part of us, guiding us, loving us, and protecting us from being overcome by the darkness. May we ever be the light that makes the darkness pale. In your name, we humbly ask. So be it."

42 Following Miriam's prayer, Yeshua and the others walked on, and Yeshua continued to unfold the events of the destruction of Tyre.

43 "As they had done to the mainland city, the Macedonians tore asunder every building and laid waste to everything within the city. A large number of women and girls and some boys that were not killed or did not take their own lives were raped repeatedly over several days. And every woman and child that remained alive was taken into slavery.

44 Alexander gave orders that no wounded man was to be killed but held for execution. Accordingly, over five thousand men were captured and executed, in many cases while their wives and children were forced to watch.

45 As great a darkness had been upon Tyre during the siege and battle, the greatest darkness was yet to come, for Alexander did not quickly put his prisoners to the sword as he had done to the slaves earlier, but chose to make their end as painful and horrifying as possible.

46 Those who were gravely wounded and would not be able to realize their suffering were beheaded and their heads impaled upon poles throughout the ruins of the city.

47 Those who were not so gravely injured but still wounded and would soon die were burned alive.

48 And those poor souls who were uninjured or only lightly wounded were crucified, but seldom in the usual manner. Many were crucified upside down, and many with wooden stakes impaled inside of them. And all only after they had been scourged and large patches of their skin burned with torches.

49 When the army of Alexander departed, they took down every stone and burned every piece of wood so that nothing remained of the ancient city. No man who defended the city was left alive. Over three thousand men who were not soldiers and twelve thousand women and children were taken from the city into slavery along with those who had not been killed from the mainland."

50 As he finished speaking, they walked in silence the remaining distance to the old city contemplating the history of the fall of Tyre which Yeshua had told them, until they came to the gates that had been built for the new city in the years that followed.

51 Entering into the city that had been built upon the ashes of the former, they passed through narrow streets until they came to a hill upon which stood a temple. Stopping before it, Yeshua spoke again to them, saying, "You see a new temple built in recent years before you. It stands upon the spot where the temple of Heracles stood that Alexander had desired to go to make a sacrifice, but destroyed when he took the city.

52 The ancient stone temple had changed gods it was dedicated to over time, but had been upon this spot for over two thousand years. Because this was the instigation of Alexander's wrath, it is the center for the negative aeon that still hangs about Tyre like the darkness of death that it is.

53 Yesterday, I spoke to you about the importance of using knowledge before choosing to give of your essence, and to wait for something of great importance, wherein knowledge alone would be insufficient, to give of your essence and use your gifts.

54 Now is the time of great importance. In the world, you will encounter other places of darkness like Tyre. Oftentimes, the darkness comes from great battles that were fought on that spot where many men died.

55 Other times, it may be a small area wherein a terrible atrocity occurred. Wherever you shall find pools of darkness, be they small or great, I charge you to give of your essence and call upon the powers of Heaven to seed that place once again with light. This is one of your greatest responsibilities as my Apostles.

56 These areas of pain and misery form vortexes of darkness, and they continue to grow and expand. They poison the surrounding area around them and continue to be the cause of further suffering among the people of the land, year upon year, even as the old city of Tyre has been now for over three hundred years.

57 In these places, people who are continually overshadowed by a cloud of darkness become darker within themselves, and thievery, murder, and all manner of atrocities abound.

58 Because these places continue to expand their darkness, much of the world would someday fall into darkness and evil if it was not countered by light. To prevent this, you shall now learn one of the great purposes of the Children of Light, and especially you whom I have called to be my Apostles.

59 This you shall teach from generation to generation that the Children of Light might always be the hope of the world that knows them not.

60 This task—to seek out vortexes of darkness and counter them and subdue them with your light and the Celestine Light that comes from Elohim—this is one of your most important tasks to fulfill for Elohim while you are in mortality.

61 Gaining knowledge, adding to your character, growing in the understanding of the teachings of Elohim, raising your children well, being of service to others, and gathering and loving one another as brothers and sisters in communities—these are all wonderful and worthy endeavors, but they are pursued as much for your benefit as for others.

62 But in countering vortexes of darkness, you are directly serving God, and helping to preserve the Eden of earth that Elohim has given to the children of men that they may become more than they are.

63 Let us go now into the temple, which is the center of the dark vortex, and I will further instruct you there."

64 As Yeshua bid, they followed him up the steps of the temple but were prevented from entering by two guards at the entrance. Yeshua asked to speak with the high priest, and one of the guards left and went into the temple to seek out someone in authority.

65 When he returned, he was accompanied by a tall, richly adorned man with black hair wearing a headdress. The guard pointed out Yeshua, and the man walked over to him and said, "I am Ashtzaph, a priest of this temple. Are you pilgrims come to worship Ba'al Sur, Lord of Tyre?"

66 Salome couldn't help herself and let out an audible laugh at his words even as she covered her mouth with both of her hands.

67 Ashtzaph scowled at her even as Yeshua cracked a subtle smile. Looking again at Yeshua, Ashtzaph said, "You look like Hebrew peasants by the way you are dressed, so you must be looking for work. Well, we have none, so be gone; your feet are despoiling the temple steps."

68 Yeshua looked him in the eye with the loving but piercing gaze that seemed to mesmerize people and told him, "If we may move aside I would speak to you in private, and I assure you it will be worth a few moments of your time."

69 "Unlikely, as you are already wasting my valuable time." The priest sighed with exasperation. But he walked quickly over behind a pillar, and motioning for Yeshua to follow, he commanded, "Say your words quickly for I am a busy man."

70 "We need your temple for an hour."

71 "What?" Ashtzaph asked with incredulity.

72 Yeshua repeated, "We need your temple for an hour, exclusively. No other people should be inside at the time."

73 "Are you mad!" Ashtzaph said raising his voice. "I should have you arrested for sacrilege upon the gods. We would not turn the temple over to a visiting king, much less a Hebrew peasant!" He then turned on his heel and began walking quickly back into the temple, yelling at the guards as he left, "Throw these scoundrels off the temple steps and do not even speak to them for they are dirt!"

74 But as he entered again into the temple, he suddenly screamed a horrifying scream of

terror. Ignoring the Hebrews, the guards ran into the temple to see the cause of the commotion. In moments, they came running out followed by Ashtzaph.

75 "What was that all about?" Cephas wondered aloud as the men sped past him and down the street.

76 "Snakes," Miriam, who was standing near him, replied, "in fact, a great many angry cobras; all over the temple floor."

77 "Cobras!" Cephas shouted in surprise. Did you see some? Do you see cobras? If there are cobras, we should head in the same direction as the priest."

78 Miriam gave a little laugh. "There are no snakes, Cephas. It is only something Yeshua made them see. I think we should go quickly now into the temple before they return with more men to fight the cobras that are not there."

79 Stepping quickly, they all followed Yeshua into the temple, but scarcely had they passed the threshold than they were confronted by a beautiful young woman clothed in brilliant Tyrian purple robes that flowed lightly all around her in layers. A gold chain encircled her waist, and her long black hair flowed from her golden headdress down to the small of her back. "Who among you cast the spell of snakes?" she asked.

80 "It was not a spell," Yeshua answered.

81 "But there are no snakes," she replied, "only illusion."

82 "More than illusion," Yeshua responded. "The power of suggestion upon minds that are weak is very powerful. In their heads it was a reality. Had they been bitten, they would have died.

83 "But you do not see the snakes, only the floor. And for this, you must be more than they are."

84 She held herself up a little straighter and replied, "I am Elissa, high priestess of the temple, and you are walking upon holy ground."

85 Before Yeshua could reply, Miriam stepped in front of him and said unto Elissa, "I am Miriam, wife of Yeshua of Nazareth who stands before you. If this ground is holy, it is only because Yeshua now stands upon it."

86 "The Galilean prophet?" Elissa asked.

87 "Some have called him by that title," Miriam replied. "How is it that you know of him, for this is the first we have visited Tyre."

88 "Pilgrims come from many lands, and there is little of significance that occurs within the realm of Rome that I am unaware of," she answered. "I have heard of his miracles and now understand more how it is that the men thought they saw snakes."

89 "Are there others still within the temple?" Cephas interjected.

90 She looked at him somewhat disdainfully. "There were others," she answered, "but they all fled when they saw the cobras on every floor of the temple. I alone remain, but the others will soon return and likely, there will be soldiers with them."

91 She looked again at Yeshua. "Why are you here?" she asked pointedly.

92 He answered her, saying, "We have come to cleanse your temple and this land of a great darkness. If you remain while the others have departed, it can only be because you are in harmony with the Celestine Light, even though you preside over darkness."

93 For a moment, with a scowl upon her beautiful face, Elissa seemed to contemplate an angry answer to Yeshua, but then her face softened and she smiled, "I do not preside. I am only the figurehead, the token virgin priestess. I have witnessed many vile abominations within these walls, but I do not partake of them, nor bless them, only endure the knowledge that they occur and there is nothing I can do to change that fact."

94 Now Yeshua spoke, saying, "You are truly a Child of Light, Elissa, cast among the darkness. We are not your enemies, but your friends, even your true brothers and sisters, with a love for you that is pure. Even now, you know in your heart that my words are true."

95 She smiled and shook her head affirmatively at the same time, saying, "I do feel a sweet harmony in your presence, and I feel no threat from any of you. And I do feel your love, which

in truth, I cannot understand, for we are strangers.

96 You have not answered my question, but do what you have come to do and I will not oppose you."

97 Elissa's eyes opened in surprise as Yeshua boldly took her hand, which was never touched by priests or supplicants, and said unto her, "If you remain, you must be a part of what we are here to do, for there can be no spectators, only all united together as one. Come with us."

98 She looked at him with wonder, as if trying to fathom who she was beholding, and answered him, saying, "Lead, and I will follow."

99 Yeshua released her hand, and motioning to the others to proceed, they walked toward the center of the temple.

100 There was a room at the center just large enough for them to all fit in with an altar off to one side and a beautiful motif on the floor in various-colored tiles.

101 Yeshua bade them to form a circle in the room so that every woman had a man on either side of them, and he asked Elissa to stand between Cephas and his brother Yakov of Nazareth.

102 Looking to Cephas, he asked, "Brother Cephas, would you please hand out to each person the tools I asked you to bring?"

103 Nodding in acknowledgment, Cephas took a plain wooden box out from within his personal backsack. Opening it, he removed a linen wrap and, unraveling it, revealed many long, clear quartz crystal wands.

104 Cephas cupped the linen with the wands close to him and then went around the circle, handing one to each person including Yeshua. When he returned to his spot in the circle, he held the last one. Had Elissa not joined them, they would have had one extra.

105 Now Yeshua spoke to them, saying, "You hold in your hand, not solid water, but a common rock of the earth, in a most uncommon form, grown into the shape that you see it by the very intention of Elohim, within the bowels of the earth.

106 "These wands, though extraordinary, have no power of their own, but are useful tools to help you focus and magnify the Celestine Light that flows in you, to call to you the greater forces beyond and to impede and counter dark forces that may oppose you such as this terrible vortex of darkness we stand within even now."

107 At his words, everyone looked around trying to see what it was he was speaking about and each cast glances at their wand, for never had they seen anything like it, and Cephas had not even hinted that he carried them.

108 Yeshua spoke again, saying, "We are here to subdue the darkness and bring the Celestine Light that this city and the lands nearby may no longer have a shadow of death hanging over them.

109 What I teach you today, you must teach to all other Children of Light wherever you find them, even as we have included Elissa with us this day. It matters not whether they are a part of our community or even associated with us.

110 If you find them to be Children of Light in their hearts and the actions of their lives, share with them this knowledge as they are prepared to receive it, that they too may be a force for light against the darkness.

111 We are standing within a dreadful vortex of darkness that has grown larger and larger, year by year, since the time of Alexander of Macedonia. It has brought a curse upon this city and land insomuch that it deadens the love and light and hope of the people. It grips their hearts with passionless disregard for life or virtue.

112 The distance of this island city to the mainland doubled is how large a bite of the land this vortex now consumes.

113 Let us begin by getting to know this monster. It is a ferocious whirlwind twirling rapidly, counter to the path of the sun. We will subdue it by creating a more powerful opposing vortex of Celestine Light twirling in harmony with the sun.

114 There will be some among you who can see the aeon of this vortex of evil with their

spiritual eyes. Others will be able to sense it and feel its putrid breath with their aura. A few may be able to both see and feel it, and some will be able to neither see it nor feel it at this time. Wherever you find yourself in your senses, you are all essential to our success.

115 Close your eyes now and heighten your other senses. Hear the breathing of the person next to you and feel the warmth of their body.

116 Now become aware of your personal aura, your sacred aeon. Feel it inside of you and surrounding you. Feel its movement through you and around you.

117 Now become aware of the aura of the people on either side of you. Feel their aeon and let your aeon beat in one resonance and harmony with theirs.

118 Now let the circle become united, one aura melded in harmony to the next and that melded in harmony to the one beside it and so on, until all within this circle are of one harmony of Celestine Light.

119 Now that we are one light, we cannot be overcome by the darkness. Therefore, open your spiritual eyes and the fullness of your aura that you might see and feel the presence of the heartless monster whose maul we stand within. And speak out what it is you see or see not, feel or feel not."

120 As Yeshua directed, they all opened their spiritual eyes, and for some, this meant their physical eyes were open, while others kept their eyelids shut but reached out with eyes unseen to see that which physical eyes could not see.

121 And each of them opened the shields of their aura that they could feel the well of darkness they stood within.

122 Cephas was the first to speak. "I see it!" he proclaimed. "It is like the darkest cloud of the most terrible storm, circling us as fast as a whirlwind, but there is no wind," he expressed in amazement.

123 "I see it too," exclaimed Philip, "but it is translucent, not black. I can barely make it out. It is like a mirage."

124 "I neither see nor feel anything," Mattayah said with a tinge of disappointment.

125 "I cannot see it," said Yohhanan, "but opening my senses, I can feel a malevolent presence moving all around me, while I stand in a circle of golden protection."

126 One by one, they all reported that which they saw and felt or did not see or feel.

127 And there were only four besides Yeshua who both saw and felt the whirlwind of darkness, and they were Miriam, Salome, Marit, and Elissa.

128 But on this day, there was no hurt pride by the men that some of the women saw or felt what they did not, especially considering that other than Miriam, none were even Apostles. For on this day, at this moment, everyone was of one light and one heart and one thought.

129 Yeshua spoke once again, saying, "In your lives, you will encounter vortexes of darkness of many sizes and power. Some will be smaller than a wisp of smoke from a camp fire. Others will be like this one: monsters upon the land.

130 How large and powerful they are depends upon how dark was the deed that created them and how many years they have had to grow.

131 Small vortexes, you can deal with individually, depending upon your natural ability and training. Larger ones require more Children of Light to be united in a circle of light.

132 Within that circle, there will be some who are Adepts and others who are Neophytes, and this too must be taken into account, for three Adepts could subdue a vortex of the same size and power that would require one hundred Neophytes.

133 But one Adept alone could only subdue a vortex of the same size and power that seven to nine Neophytes could subdue. Therefore, understand there is much greater power in two untied than there is in one and more still in three or twelve or more. Your individual power and intention is magnified many times by the number of you that stand shoulder to shoulder united as one.

134 Even as you, my twelve Apostles, shall one day all be Adepts. And on that day, the power

of you twelve as one shall exceed that of many thousands of novices. Therefore, take heed of my words and study and practice faithfully the secrets of Celestine Light that I share with you, that you can wield it with effectiveness in the name of Elohim.

135 Now let us tame this beast. Each of you, take your left hand and place it on the right shoulder or waist of the person to your left. In this manner, we are all connected physically as well as aurically.

136 Hold forth your wands with your right hand, pointing them just above our heads toward the center of our circle.

137 Repeat now this prayer after me." And they repeated each few words immediately after he spoke them, saying, "In the name of Elohim, we call upon the Celestine Light of Heaven to flow to us and through us, to magnify us, that we might be one with the aeon of Elohim, that we might serve our brothers and sisters and banish this darkness and free the land to live again in light. So be it!"

138 As they spoke their last word, there was a brilliant beam of light that came forth from each of their wands, and colliding in the center of the circle, it produced a radiant flash of light that expanded quickly beyond the circle and past the confines of the room.

139 Yeshua continued to lead them, saying, "Now hold your wands pointing not to the center, but up and to the left, angled up above the head of the person to your left.

140 Call forth your essence from within you. At the bottom of each breath, focus your essence to flow through and up your right arm, into your hand. Swirl it then for a moment, building its power still greater until your body can no more contain it, and it bursts forth from the tip of your wand.

141 Let the power continue to flow through you and up your arm and out of your wand. Do not allow yourself to become weakened by loss of your essence, but open yourself to receive the limitless Celestine Light of Heaven and send it out through your wand.

142 We have formed our own vortex of Celestine Light, and it swirls now in the heart of the vortex of darkness." And within the circle swirled the most amazing rainbow vortex made of innumerable scintillating points of light.

143 Yeshua continued, "Keeping your wands pointing up, in unison so that everyone's is pointing to the same degree, begin to physically swirl your wands in unison all around the circle as I do, passing over the head of each person in the circle including yourself.

144 Let us continue this movement, increasing our speed with each revolution around the circle. Call up from within and out from the heavens for pure Celestine Light to flow to you and through you, and out your wand in unison with our brothers and sisters of the sacred circle." And the beautiful rainbow vortex expanded as they moved their wands faster and faster with each revolution around the circle.

145 Almost complete, my brothers and sisters," Yeshua said supportively. "With one last intensity, send now a final burst of light out into this scarred land with a shout of Elqeris!" As Yeshua directed, so did they do.

146 When it was done, most of them fell to the ground in exhaustion, for even with the aeon they had drawn from Heaven, they had still given up much of their essence.

147 Cephas, Miriam, Yohhanan, and Yakov remained standing along with Yeshua, and he bid them to quickly go to their brothers and sisters and give them some of their essence that they might be revived, for Ashtzaph was returning in moments with soldiers.

148 They did as Yeshua bid, and as a group, they were departing the temple just as Ashtzaph arrived with the other priests and soldiers. Ashtzaph ordered the soldiers to arrest the Hebrews because they had violated the temple.

149 But Elissa made her way to the front of the confrontation and forbade the soldiers saying, "Cease! You will not arrest these good people. They have been in audience with me, and as high priestess, it is my prerogative to give audiences to whom I will."

150 Ashtzaph was grinding his teeth in frustration. It was he who ran the affairs of the

temple, but by their own rules of faith, the high priestess was the direct representative of the God and could grant audiences to whomever she desired.

151 "What of the snakes, highest one?" he said through a forced smile. "The soldiers must enter the sanctuary to rid us of the vipers."

152 "The snakes are no more," Elissa said dismissively.

153 "No more?" stuttered Ashtzaph. "But how can that be? There were hundreds of them."

154 Elissa stood straight and tall and stared at Ashtzaph until he looked down, saying, "You do forget yourself, Ashtzaph, and that it is the high priestess of Ba'al who tells you that the snakes are no more."

155 Looking very confused and flustered, Ashtzaph nodded his head, saying "Of course, it is as you say." Then turning to the soldiers, he bid them return to their barracks and assured them that all was well.

156 After the soldiers had departed and Ashtzaph and the priests had entered the temple, Elissa remained to say some words of parting to Yeshua. She looked at him crestfallen and said, "Having tasted the sweetest of fruit, how can I ever go back to eating dirt?"

157 Before he could answer, Talitha interjected, saying, "Come with us, Elissa. You are one of the Children of Light."

158 But Elissa shook her head sadly, saying, "Would that I could, for my heart longs to be with you and aches already at the thought of being apart from you. But I am chained to this temple until the day I die, which is only a few more years, for high priestesses are not allowed to live past thirty, but are given in sacrifice on the high holy day to Ba'al.

159 While I live in the temple, I am treated like royalty, but were I to voluntarily take a step onto the ground away from the temple, I would cease to be high priestess and would be given in sacrifice on the very next holiday."

160 Well, that makes it easy," said Philip who was standing near. "We will just come back and kidnap you. If we wait for a moon or so, your disappearance will not be associated with us, and if by some chance we are caught, you will not be sacrificed because you did not leave voluntarily."

161 "Thank you, noble Philip," she whispered. "But were I to taste freedom among the light and then be caught and returned to slavery in the darkness, I fear I would so despair that I would welcome death. And even if it did not come then, I have only a few years remaining as high priestess."

162 Yeshua comforted her, "Fear not, good sister of the light. We will not abandon you to live among the darkness or die before your time. Even as Philip has said, we will return for you, but perhaps not so overtly as a kidnapping.

163 You are blessed with the Holy Spirit of Elohim to be ever with you and comfort you until the day we shall return for you. Therefore, be of good cheer. I will come to you in your dreams and make all known to you that needs to be known to bring you safely among us."

164 "Thank you" was all she said, and then she slipped quickly back into the temple lest she draw too much attention by lingering with the Hebrews.

165 As they turned to depart, Cephas looked at Yeshua and said unto him, "This has been an event-filled day. I think we shall have much to talk about this evening."

166 "Yes," Yeshua agreed, "more than you know."

CHAPTER 65

Escape from Tyre

Yeshua creates a grand illusion to aid in the escape of the high priestess Elissa from the city of Tyre.

That night, as he promised, Yeshua came to Elissa in a dream when she first fell asleep, and again just before she awoke, and revealed to her all that he would do to affect her escape from the Temple of Ba'al at Tyre and all that she must do to insure success.

2 Before he came to Elissa in her dream, Yeshua taught his Apostles the mysteries of the gifts of spirit that he would use to aid in her escape that they might understand how to expand their own abilities to use the gifts they had been given by Elohim.

3 He spoke to them, saying, "A centurion thinks his greatest strength is in his sword arm. A farmer thinks his greatest strength is in the size of his fields, a shepherd in the size of his flocks. Ask a man of any profession what his greatest strength is and you will receive many answers, but seldom the correct one, for it is a mystery to the people of the world, save those few who have a harmony with the Celestine Light.

4 I declare unto you that the greatest strength of a Child of Light is not something they can do with the strength of their arm or measure by their labor but is their faith in themselves and Elohim, empowering the gifts of spirit which in them dwell.

5 Among the greatest of the gifts of the spirit when in confrontation with men of the world is the power of illusion, which is easily projected by your thoughts and aura upon the impressionable thoughts of the weak minded and those with little light. Such as these have no defense against that which they do not know, for how may a city be defended when its citizens do not realize they are under attack?

6 By using your gifts of the spirit, you may accomplish great ends without violence and with a finality that battles never bring. Thus it will be upon the morrow."

7 Then Yeshua spoke in detail to his Apostles about the secrets of projecting illusion through the aura and how illusion accomplishes most when married with reality, but the details of how Elissa would escape, he did not reveal, instead told them they would understand everything the next day.

8 He admonished them strictly that they were never to use such gifts for anything other than a noble and virtuous cause in which Elohim would delight.

9 The following day, many pilgrims came into the Temple of Ba'al for the sunrise ceremony, which was presided over in silence by Elissa the High Priestess, who sat upon a small, intricately carved throne of stone with ribbons of gold woven through its many lattices, while the male priests of the temple spoke with the pilgrims, directing them in their devotions.

10 After the ceremony concluded, the pilgrims departed. They would return again four more

times during the day to pay tribute to Ba'al and receive blessings from the priests.

11 Once the pilgrims had vacated the temple, Elissa retired to her quarters and sat on a large purple cushion while two of her handmaidens removed her elaborate gold and feather headdress and combed her luxurious black hair.

12 During this time, Yeshua and those who were with him remained in their simple camp beyond the southern edge of the mainland city of Tyre.

13 After Yeshua explained to his Apostles the gifts, but not the details of that which he would do the night before, they sat now in a circle along with their wives and watched Yeshua as he stood in the center with his eyes closed and his arms crossed over his chest so they could see how he accomplished that which he had spoken about.

14 They were startled when suddenly, without a sound, he threw his arms up and out toward the heavens and opened his eyes wide. But looking into the sky beyond, he seemed to be unaware that anyone else was even present.

15 At this exact time, Elissa rose from the cushion and walked out to her balcony, overlooking the city. Her handmaidens followed and remained a respectful distance at the balcony threshold lest she call or have need of anything.

16 Suddenly, there was a great and dreadful shadow over the sun. Looking up into the sky to see the cause of the darkening of the sun, the handmaidens screamed in terror at the sight of an enormous white bird descending upon Elissa. Its plumage was streaked with iridescent gold, and its tail was bright red. It looked like an eagle, with mighty talons and a ferocious hooked beak, but with a wingspan many times larger than that of any eagle known to man.

17 The terrified handmaidens fled in panic to the inner sanctuary of the temple, screaming for help with all their voice.

18 Hearing their cries, the priests of the temple quickly entered the chambers of the high priestess only to exclaim in astonishment and fear as they looked onto the balcony and saw the high priestess encircled by the mighty talons of an enormous bird and lifted off the balcony up into the sky.

19 The bravest among them crept cautiously to the balcony and saw the giant bird still carrying the helpless high priestess as it flapped its great wings and rose higher and higher into the sky.

20 Ashtzaph, the priest of administration, ran into the room, bellowing, "What is happening?" Not seeing Elissa, he swore an oath and yelled, "Where is the high priestess?"

21 A priest who had remained in the room and not ventured onto the balcony pointed to it and said, "A great eagle, larger than any ever seen, has taken her and flown off into the sky."

22 Ashtzaph hurried to the balcony and followed with his eyes the pointing fingers of the priests with their arms raised toward the sky. With a shock of disbelief, he saw the great white bird with the vivid red tail and the slumped body of the high priestess in its massive talons.

23 The other priests looked to him in confusion, and one asked with fear in his voice, "What have we done to incur the wrath of Ba'al that our high priestess has thus been taken by a bird of myth?"

24 That was no myth," another exclaimed. He touched the railing of the balcony, and holding his fingers up for the others to see, he exclaimed, "Here is the blood of the high priestess upon the railing, testifying that we have not seen a myth but a fearful manifestation of the anger of Ba'al. We must go immediately and make great sacrifices upon the altar, lest Tyre suffers an even more terrible fate."

25 Ashtzaph scowled as he watched the giant bird as it became smaller and smaller in the distance until it could be seen no more. "Search everywhere in the temple for the high priestess," he commanded. "Perhaps that was not her, but one of her handmaidens."

26 "But it was her handmaidens who called to us," protested one of the priests.

27 "That may be," Ashtzaph admitted. "But let us not give up our high priestess so easily unless we are sure she is truly no more."

28 And it came to pass that they did as Ashtzaph bid and searched every cranny of the temple

and brought before him Elissa's two handmaidens. And the handmaidens recounted to him every detail of what had transpired from the moment they had entered the chambers with the high priestess until the moment she had been seized by the giant bird from the sky.

29 At last, Ashtzaph could no longer deny the facts before him, and turning to one of the priests, he commented, "First a thousand snakes and now a giant bird that magically appears and just as quickly disappears. These are truly bad omens."

30 Then he commanded another priest, saying, "Bring the daughter of Zatel to me. We must immediately begin the initiation of a new high priestess before Ba'al sends even more frightful terrors upon us."

31 And thus did Elissa of Tyre pass from the thoughts and memory of the priests of the Temple of Ba'al.

32 Back at the camp of the Apostles, Yeshua had soon lowered his arms and remained in somewhat of a trance for several minutes while the bird had come upon and taken Elissa. But once it had vanished from sight, he opened his eyes and, after taking a deep breath, spoke to his friends, saying, "It is done."

33 "What has been done?" asked Cephas.

34 "The priests have witnessed Elissa being carried off by a great bird," Yeshua responded. They will not look for her, for in their minds she is no more."

35 "A great bird?" Cephas spoke quietly with a bit of confusion and uncertainty.

36 "Remember our lesson of last night," Miriam admonished him.

37 "An illusion?" Cephas asked.

38 "Yes," Miriam affirmed. "An illusion; it was the same as with the snakes in the temple, but grander."

39 "You saw it?" Philip inquired.

40 Miriam nodded, saying, "I am blessed to see what Yeshua sees when I have intention."

41 "But how can an illusion carry off a woman who is real?" Cephas wondered.

42 "It cannot," Miriam acknowledged.

43 "In my simple mind, I am confused," Cephas admitted. Then turning to Yeshua, he asked, "Did you not say a great bird had come and taken Elissa away? How can an illusion do such a thing?"

44 Yeshua walked over to him and put his arm around his shoulder, saying, "Good brother Cephas, I said that the priests saw this event occur, but as no such great birds exist in our day, what they witnessed and believe with all fervency in their hearts was only that which I created in their thoughts to see, even as I taught you last night how to use the power of this gift of spirit."

45 "Then what of Elissa?" inquired Toma. "If she was not really captured and taken away by a great bird, how is it that she will be able to escape from the temple?"

46 Yeshua answered him, saying, "Let us prepare our camp for quick departure, and when we are ready to leave, the answer will come upon us."

47 Following Yeshua's cryptic reply, they broke camp for their return journey to the communities of Gennesaret, and just as the last item was secured, they were approached by a small old man, bent over, walking with a cane and wearing the cowled robe of a devotee of Ba'al.

48 Everyone turned to face the man, and as he came up to them, he threw off his hood and they were astonished to see the smiling womanly face of Elissa, high priestess of the Temple of Ba'al.

49 Miriam came to her immediately and embraced her, saying, "Welcome to the Family of Light, Elissa, daughter of the light."

50 Then each person, beginning with the women and ending with Yeshua, came and introduced themselves and gave an embrace of welcome to Elissa, and she told them, "If I were to die today, I would have a peace and joy and wonder such as I have never imagined, for I have felt more love already in your welcomes than I have ever known in all my life. Thank you for taking me, a stranger, to be among you, just by what you see in my heart."

51 Marit was standing beside Elissa, and with an excitement she no longer could contain, she said, "Tell us now before we burst with curiosity; how did you escape from the temple?"
52 Before she could answer, Cephas admonished, "Let her tell her story while we travel and let us make haste and depart, for there may still be those who look for her."
53 Agreeing that this was prudent, they all turned south and began the trip back to Galilee. But rather than travel due south as they had come, Yeshua bade them to bear to the southeast toward the mountains, saying, "The priest Ashtzaph still suspects something is amiss and contemplates a wider search. Therefore, let us lose ourselves from eyes that may seek us in the forests above, and this will also be a more direct route home."
54 Cephas nodded in agreement, and thus they traveled, passing over the mountains of Lebanon to return back to the Communities of Light.
55 As they traveled, they stopped periodically, and Elissa related the details of her escape from the Temple of Ba'al at Tyre, saying, "As he had promised, Yeshua, blessed he be, came to me in a dream moments after I had fallen asleep.
56 We stood in conversation as if I were awake, and so real it was that even in my dream I had to continue to remind myself that I was asleep.
57 Yeshua showed me what it was that everyone else would see the next day, even a great white bird with a red tail, swooping down from the sky and carrying me off.
58 Yeshua said all this would be an illusion, but to be believed, it must be supported with things that were real.
59 Therefore, I was to gather some lamb's blood from a temple sacrifice and thin it with a tiny amount of water; then pour it on the balcony railing just before I left that those who saw the illusion would think it was my blood.
60 Also he told me before I departed to leave my headdress on the table beside my favorite purple sitting pillow, and this I did.
61 In the morning, as there is most mornings, a group of pilgrims had come for morning devotions. I usually preside in silence over the ceremonies from a small throne at the end of the room.
62 On this day, I was not sitting upon the throne, but hiding in my chambers waiting for the pilgrims to depart. My two handmaidens had moments before walked with an illusion of me created by Yeshua to the room of ceremony to stand in waiting should I need anything while presiding over the morning devotional.
63 They and everyone else in the temple saw me sitting upon the throne, but there was truly nothing there except an image planted in their minds by Yeshua.
64 When the pilgrims departed, I was dressed as they were and simply followed after them, making to be as if I were an old man. They did not know that I was not just another pilgrim from a group other than theirs, and the temple priests merely assumed I was what I appeared to be, an elderly pilgrim attached to the group that was departing.
65 Assuming that everything continued in reality as it did in my dream, after the morning devotion, my two handmaidens returned to my chambers with me, although by this time I was already on the streets of Tyre and making haste for the gate.
66 To give me time to escape ere the gates of the city were sealed, they thought to be brushing my hair for some time as I sat upon my pillow.
67 They even imagined that they had removed my headdress and sat it upon the table, when in fact I had left it there to be discovered to give physical evidence to the illusion and the story they would tell the priests about what had transpired.
68 Shortly after I had departed from the city and was about halfway down the isthmus, Yeshua had told me in my dream that the illusion would be no more. Since that time, I have continued to look over my shoulder with trepidation, expecting any moment to be put upon by soldiers or priests, but none have come after me.
69 And that is really all there is to my story," she concluded.

70 "All there is?" Talitha exclaimed. "Why that is such a wonderful and inspiring story! How blessed we are to be able to walk with Yeshua and be witnesses to such marvelous events, even as men have never known!"

71 Hearing her words, but also knowing somewhat of the challenges to come and how little time Yeshua would still be among them, Miriam said unto her, "More blessed than you know, my sister, more blessed than you know."

72 And Yeshua, speaking to everyone, said unto them, "In the escape of Elissa, you have witnessed a powerful gift of the Celestine Light, which also resides in all of you. Contemplate it well, for the days will come when being able to call forth this gift will be as valuable to your life and the lives of the Children of Light as it was for Elissa on this day."

CHAPTER 66

Bringing the Light

Upon his return to the Communities of Light, Yeshua speaks to the Children of Light about the vortexes of darkness in the world. He tells them that as Children of Light, they should seek out the vortexes and subdue them, bringing light instead of darkness and providing everyone that resides in the vicinity greater opportunities to become the light they are capable of becoming, and create the eternity of their hopes and dreams.

And it came to pass that they returned to their families in the Communities of Light on Lake Gennesaret and told them everything that had transpired on their journey to Tyre. Only of Elissa's true identity they made no mention, for Yeshua had asked them to keep their silence in this, and she was accepted in the communities as simply a new sister of light, as it was not unusual for new members to be added to the communities when Yeshua returned from a journey.

2 When the Children of Light next met to edify one another, Yeshua spoke to them, saying, "We journeyed to Tyre not to preach, but to conquer darkness. By diminishing the darkness, we gave the people of Tyre a greater chance to find and embrace a greater portion of the light while they are in mortality.

3 To diminish darkness and bring more light to the world is one of your great purposes in life as Children of Light.

4 Do not suppose that you just happened to be in harmony with the fullness of the Celestine Light when it first came upon you. Verily, you were exceptional before this world was and held in esteem by Elohim. When the Celestine Light came upon you in this life, you felt a resonance with your true identity that your heart could not deny.

5 Every person born into mortality is given this life to create their eternity, and by the choices they make while upon the earth, so shall their eternity become.

6 But for you, choice souls who are Children of Light, more is asked of you by Elohim, even that you would give a special lifelong service to all those who dwell now upon the earth, that they might have a greater opportunity to walk the path of light rather than darkness and inherit eternal glory rather than despair.

7 Evil and heartless actions create an oppressive darkness that remains long after the perpetrators have departed. The greater the evil, the more the darkness encompasses.

8 So pervading and heavy may the aeon of darkness become that even good people become burdened by its weight upon their hearts and minds. Coupled with the vexing challenges of life, they may fall into despondency and depression, and good may turn to evil simply out of hopelessness and despair.

9 Thus it has been in Tyre since the time of Alexander of Macedonia, and so it is in many other places, both great and small, because of evil acts committed in those places.

10 Even as evil creates darkness and weighs and oppresses, enticing men to the part of them that is darkness, so good creates light which frees and uplifts and calls men to the greater part of them that longs for the Celestine Light.

11 This then is the special calling that Elohim has given to every Child of Light: to do good in the world, to create light which abides and uplifts upon the land, and, more than this, to find darkness wherever it abides and spread such a brilliance of light upon it that it becomes but a shadow, no longer having influence upon the hearts of the people of that land or place.

12 Consider a boy who had been raised among a family and a people that had fallen into darkness. Each day, all that he saw was mostly of darkness and evil and only occasionally some small act of kindness and light.

13 Then there was another boy that had the opposite circumstances. He was raised among a family and a people that loved and promoted all things of light, and everything he witnessed each day in the words and actions of those around him were of kindness, forgiveness, love, and light and only occasionally of pettiness and darkness.

14 Which of these two boys would most likely grow to become a man of light? Of course, it would be the second. Though he could still fall into darkness, even as the first could still find and choose the light, the second because of the light he was raised in would have the greater opportunity.

15 Verily, I say unto you: It behooves you as Children of Light to seek out the vortexes of darkness upon the world and bring the Celestine Light to subdue them, that the world may grow in light not darkness and that all upon it may have greater opportunities to become the good they are capable of becoming and create the eternity of their hopes and dreams.

16 Go about your daily lives overcoming and growing each day in your personal challenges. But do not neglect or forget this special calling from Elohim given to all Children of Light, to be accomplished as they have the knowledge and ability to fulfill it and led always by one or more Adepts.

17 There are two ways whereby united in purpose, you may subdue the darkness and encourage the light. The first begins in your communities where you should not suffer people or things that oppress, degrade, or take advantage of the weak to be among you. Nor should you suffer the unrepentant to remain among you or those who create a continual disharmony in the community by their words or actions.

18 Know that the natural man is the adversary within and an enemy of the Celestine Light. This is why your greatest growth comes from conquering yourself.

19 In the world, the natural man is continually enticed by greed and lust and power. Oftentimes, so great are the enticements and so continual and pervasive that even the best of men in a moment of weakness submits to the abased desires of their adversary within.

20 Therefore, in the Communities of Light, see that those things that promote the light are encouraged, while those that promote the darkness or needlessly tempt the adversary within are forbidden.

21 If a brother or sister wishes to partake of the sins of the world such as gambling, or unrighteous sexual gratification, or taking drink or herbs that addle the mind, or eating to gluttony, or exercising unrighteous dominion over others, let them leave the community and go and live in the world they wish to be like, until they have repented and are ready to live again among the Children of Light, in the ways of Celestine Light.

22 Sufficient are the challenges of each day even in a virtuous life to overcome the adversary within. Additional and unnecessary temptations should not be tolerated or appeased, for they have no place in your life, in your family, or in the Community of Light.

23 The second is in the larger world, where you must seek out vortexes of darkness such as the one that was upon Tyre and, united in desire, focus, love, and faith, subdue it with the powers

revealed to the Children of Light.

24 That you will understand how this is accomplished, my Apostles will go among you now and in the coming days and weeks and months and teach you the secrets and mysteries that I have taught to them that you may be able to wield this sacred power.

25 In the days to come, you will be scattered upon the earth: some here and others there. No longer will you be a community of one as you are now in the towns upon the north shore of Gennesaret, until the time of the gathering when your time on earth is fulfilled. And this needs be that your light may touch the lives of many in the world and not just a few.

26 In the years to come, there will arise churches and religions built upon vestiges of my teachings, and they will do both good and evil in the world. Do not associate with them, for they shall have a form of the light, but not the substance.

27 Seek only to find and discover other Children of Light and gather them to you, in whatever your circumstances are, and teach them the secrets of the Kingdom.

28 Think not that you must build great temples to Elohim, for the only temple Elohim cares to see you build is the temple of your body and the simple sanctuaries you build to gather together to edify and instruct one another with words and music and light."

29 Even as Yeshua spoke it, so was it done. The Apostles went forth that very day among the Children of Light and began to teach them the secrets and mysteries of the power that Yeshua had shown unto them in Tyre.

30 And from that day forth, as they became accomplished and capable, Children of Light went forth upon the world in groups of two or more, and most often three, subduing the darkness and bringing the brilliance of the Celestine Light.

CHAPTER 67

Greater Gifts Come Forth

Yeshua teaches his Apostles how to unite and swirl their auras, enabling them, with faith bound with love, to literally rise above the clouds where he instructs them more on the mysteries of Elohim and the secrets of calling upon and using their gifts.

Yeshua remained a few weeks at his home in Capernaum, enjoying his family and meeting with his Apostles every day to further instruct them in the mysteries of Elohim and the specific ways whereby they could call upon their gifts.

2 On the day following the Sabbath, he asked them to all meet him an hour before the rising of the sun, and they came to his house as he bade.

3 Gathering them into a circle outside as he had done in Tyre, with Miriam on his right and Cephas on his left, and no others but Apostles present, he had them stand close and drape their arms across the back or waist of those on either side.

4 Then he instructed them further in the mysteries, saying unto them, "One of your gifts as Children of Light is to be able to float upon the air, even as a log floats upon the water, even as a bird soars on the breaths of hot air high into the sky.

5 To accomplish this gift, you must have complete faith in Elohim and faith in yourself as a son or daughter of Elohim. And when you are joined together in a circle as we are, you must also be bound with a true love for one another with no animosities open or hidden.

6 When you have complete faith, you have no doubt. Therefore, if there are any among you who do not have complete faith this day in either Elohim or themselves, let them step out of the circle at this time lest all be put in peril. Likewise, if any of you have issue with anyone else in this circle and do not at this moment hold a pure love for them, please step out of the circle." But none stepped out.

7 Yeshua smiled when everyone remained and told them, "I am honored to call you my brothers and to have you for my wife," he said, leaning down to give Miriam a kiss on her forehead as she looked up at him.

8 Many of you remember the day Miriam rose a little above the ground to fetch the rock that was suspended in the air above," Yeshua began.

9 That which we shall do today is no different than her feat then, save your faith must be even greater than hers was upon that day. But this is easy, for united together, your faith will be greater than the faith of one and even far greater than the faith of twelve.

10 Remember, faith is literally a tangible power, and the power of Celestine Light is multiplied, not added upon itself, with each person that is united as one within a group with purpose; even more so when it is you, my Apostles unto whom great gifts have been given.

11 "Know that it is you that shall do this, not me, for it is you that must learn to use your gifts. I am merely here to help you discover them.

12 "First, reach out with your aura and feel the aura of each and every other person in the circle. You must all be in harmony and have only pure love for one another. There can be no malice, no unforgiven grievances amongst you."

13 At this, each looked at one another and affirmed their brotherly love and that they held no grudges or grievances.

14 Yeshua continued their instruction, saying, "Because pure love is essential to the success of this gift, it is a power that can only be manifested by Children of Light, for those of the darkness do not have pure love for one another and harbor many grievances, jealousies, and hidden agendas.

15 Though it is still dark as night, above us is a dense cloud and when the people awake, they will not find the blue sky they are accustomed to seeing most days, for it will be overcast and raining upon the land today.

16 But above the clouds, the sun remains, and it is there that we rise to greet the sun. Therefore, impress that destination upon yourself. Focus upon it and leave all other thoughts behind, save rising through the clouds in the sky to the sun above.

17 Now to rise as one, all of our auras must be as one. Therefore, with your eyes closed, use your aura to feel the aura of the person on either side of you and harmonize and merge together until you are as one, then the person beyond them in the same manner, until all in the circle are in a harmony of one."

18 They did as Yeshua bade. When he knew that they had accomplished what he had asked, he instructed them further, "We are one. Begin to swirl our aura through our bodies in the circle. Keep it close and build its power by swirling it faster and faster in the direction of the sun as it travels across the sky."

19 Then he said three sacred words that cannot be written, but only passed by the words of one Adept to another, and he told them to say these words over and over while using their aura to sense the weight of their bodies lightening and focusing with their Xe and Ka, willing themselves up into the sky.

20 As they spoke the sacred words and did as he bade, they rose off the ground about the height of a man and as thirteen bodies holding onto one another in a circle, the circle began to spin slowly. And thus they rose up into the darkness.

21 As they rose, the sky began to lighten, and when they passed through them, the clouds were visible as a fog, although unseen to them for all still remained with their eyes closed.

22 At last, they burst through the top of the clouds and came to a stop seeming to be standing upon the clouds, and Yeshua bade them to open their eyes.

23 As they did so, there were cries of wonder from almost every mouth, for they beheld a sight none had ever imagined, even a gorgeous sun rising over a sea of clouds upon which they stood as firmly as upon the ground, though the clouds were but a dense mist.

24 There upon the cloud, in the light of the sun, high above the Communities of Light on Lake Gennesaret, Yeshua taught them more of the mysteries of Elohim and the secrets of calling upon and using their gifts.

25 But these things cannot be written, only passed by word of mouth from one Adept to another. Thus commanded Yeshua to his Apostles, and so it is.

CHAPTER 68

A Peculiar People

Yeshua teaches the Children of Light how to use many powerful herbs and minerals for healing and making potions. He also explains the consequences and benefits of how we dress, how we adorn ourselves, how long we wear our hair, and whether or not men have beards.

nd it came to pass that Yeshua remained among the Communities of Light for one moon and taught both his Apostles and all the Children of Light in the use of herbs and minerals.

2 He explained the properties of 111 herbs and minerals and specifically how to use them with prudence for the healing of the body, to make potions, and for many other purposes.

4 Many of the Children of Light were quite surprised to learn that plants and rocks that they walked by every day could be used as such powerful tools of light, when applied with understanding.

5 But amongst the 111 herbs and minerals, which Yeshua taught to them that day, there were many that were rare and not to be found in the land of Galilee.

6 To procure these uncommon plants and minerals, Yeshua charged Gurion of Ptolemais and Gimiel of Capharsalama to journey together to the north and south, and east and west, to obtain the items of which he taught that could not be found in Galilee or even Palestine.

7 They were each given three gold coins and twenty of silver from the treasury of the communities to fulfill their callings and set out to do as Yeshua bid once he was finished with his teaching to the Children of Light. (Though they returned from time to time to the Communities of Light, ten moons passed before they had procured all that Yeshua had asked them to find.)

8 Yeshua further instructed the Children of Light, concerning their dress and adornment, saying, "You have heard me say that it does not matter to Elohim how you choose to dress or adorn yourself or grow or cut your hair, save you do so with cleanliness and dignity, as is fitting of a temple of Elohim that you are.

9 But you have also heard me say that it is both the inside and the outside of the cup that matters and not just one or the other. And though your choice of adornment is of no consequence to Elohim, it is of greater consequence to you than you have imagined.

10 In the world, there are people who think that only the outside is important. They imagine that rich clothes make them like kings or that a beardless face shows that they are still young.

11 Then there are those who do not care for the outside, and they often look and smell like a dung heap. They think only the deeper inner things of the spirit are important, so they disdain taking time to maintain the outside in cleanliness or beauty.

12 But I say unto you unequivocally that a path that looks only at the outside or only at the

inside is a path of little understanding in the Celestine Light. Verily, it is only a path that strives for the purity and cleanliness of both the inside and the outside that finds the greatest light.

13 Therefore, take care to not be enticed by either a greater love for the inside or the outside, but to maintain both in a harmonious balance, for together they are your temple.

14 When looking to the inside, see that you do not become overly pious. Do not think that in your devotions you are above another, but judge none and seek only to improve yourself. Others will emulate your example if they find it worthy.

15 But when looking to the things of the outside, there are many more traps of which you must beware, for more than the inside, the outside calls to your vanities and entices you into the ways of the world.

16 Not long ago, it was the fashion for both men and women to grease their hair and body with perfumed oil. Those who followed this fashion proclaimed the joy of covering the stink of their unwashed body by a perfume that attested to their personality and with heavy oil that gave them a gloss of sensuality and the slipperiness of a wet frog.

17 And true enough, some women of Palestine would pass by veiled and covered from head to foot but of who it was that passed there was no doubt, for the heaviness of their distinctive perfume proclaimed them.

18 The people of the world are like a flock of sheep who blindly follow the leader wherever they go. Therefore, when one who is admired or of elevated rank in society begins to apply perfumes and gloss themselves with oil, the rest of the sheep think that they must emulate this fashion that they too may be considered in a similar light of admiration.

19 What of you, Children of Light? You are a divine priesthood, a peculiar people, a chosen generation, for you have a fullness of the Celestine Light of Elohim. Are you in the world but not of it, or have you followed after the fashions and styles of the world?

20 Lest anyone is tempted to dress and adorn themselves in the ways of the world, let them ask themselves this question: Who am I trying to impress?

21 For to dress and adorn as the world dresses and adorns in the passing moment of current fashion can only be meant to impress people of the world, as this has not been asked of you by Elohim.

22 Then how is it that you can impress Elohim in the way that you dress and adorn yourself? Simply by honoring the creation and magnifying it.

23 Consider that Elohim has already dressed and adorned you with the color of your skin, eyes, and hair, and the shape of your face and body.

24 For most men, you have been given that as you mature, hair begins to grow on your face and for both men and women that the hair on your head does not cease to grow at any age, but does turn silver for many as the years pass.

25 Therefore, consider that, for both men and women, your hair is one of the greatest adornments given to you by Elohim and a true reflection of your outward beauty if you care for that which you have been given.

26 Does that mean that every man and woman should just let their hair grow unabated and unattended? Nay, it does not. To show love and honor for the outside of your temple, you must keep it clean and be creative with styles and adornment of both your hair and your beard, in ways of respect, even as a gardener weeds his garden and arranges it to best showcase the beauty of the flowers and herbs.

27 Some of you have adopted the styles of the Romans and Greeks wherein men remove the hair from their face, with the pain of such action to ever remind them that they are taking away that which Elohim has given.

28 Likewise, some cut the hair of their head very short, even to the point of bareness such as with slaves, for thus do some of the Romans, and it is the fashion, is it not?

29 And the fashion today among Roman and Greek women is to remove all hair from the face and body except a shoulder crop on the head and then to draw on fake eyebrows to replace the

real ones that were ripped out. Even many men are emulating this torturous style that requires plucking, burning, and caustic herbs.

30 I am not here to reproach you. In truth, it is important for you to be pleased with your own appearance, and what you choose to do with your body hair is of little consequence to me or our Mother and Father in Heaven.

31 Keep it or remove it as it makes you happy, as its main purpose is to alert you when bugs alight on your skin and to hold your scent. But the hair of your head and beard is another matter.

32 If you remove your beard or cut off the hair of your head or if a woman shortens her hair substantially so it no longer falls at least below the blades of her shoulders, consider why you are making that choice and if in doing so you are showing the greatest honor to your creator and to the most glorious temple you have been given.

33 If you are not doing it because it is the current fashion and are not doing it out of disrespect to Elohim, who created you and gave you hair that desires to grow long, but only because that choice of appearance makes you most humbly proud of who you are as a son or daughter of God, then Elohim will not look upon you with disfavor and neither should anyone else.

34 I just ask for you to consider thoughtfully and prayerfully how you choose to create your appearance and how you adorn your body, and in this, I would give you some thoughts to ponder upon.

35 Let us first consider the hair of your head. If never cut, for many it would be down below their waist and even to their knees before they died. So there is practicality in trimming it from time to time. But how much is a goodly amount and how much is excessive to the point that perhaps you are dishonoring Elohim the creator or injuring yourself in ways that you are unaware?

36 I tell you with words of soberness that there is far more to this than the honoring of the creator.

37 Remember the story of mighty Samson and how it was his hair that gave him strength? The Roman men cut their hair very short, and they think it makes them more fearsome and less like women who tend to have longer hair, but verily, I say unto you it is the opposite of what they suppose.

38 Your hair is your crown; even for those men who may lose some of their hair as they age. Elohim would not have created you with endlessly growing hair unless there was a very important reason for it. And that reason is that your hair is a special reservoir of your Celestine power and mystical gifts as Children of Light.

39 It is for this cause that women, more than men, more often exhibit the special gifts of the Children of Light, for it is they who tend to allow their hair to grow long and by that hold much power unto them, waiting to be called upon in time of need.

40 Though men and women, who are Children of Light, may be of equal faith and love, the women will more often be able to manifest their mystical gifts because their long unblemished hair helps them to call upon their greatest potential and succeed where men fail.

41 Of this, you have a great testimony in my wife Miriam. Many of you have witnessed, and others have heard of her great feats utilizing the sacred power of Celestine Light. Many assume it is because she has been so long with me, and there is truth in this. But no less is it because like Samson, she has never cut her hair, save to trim the ends. Nor has she ever poisoned it with caustic dyes or dyes of incongruent color or with suffocating or perfumed oils. And like Samson, her lustrous hair is a reservoir of power that has served her well.

42 Nevertheless, it is among men, few though they are, that more often the greatest power in the gifts of the Children of Light can be seen, for they have the advantage of being able to grow hair not only from their head, but also from their face, perhaps a compensation for the hair they often lose on their head as they age.

43 Let us now consider the coverings of poison that have been in fashion to put upon the hair. Of what use is a torch if it is covered? And of what use is a reservoir of power, even long hair, if

it is suffocated beneath a heavy perfumed oil or altered from its natural color with an indigo or henna dye, changing it from the perfect form and color Elohim created just for you to maximize your ability to harmonize with your essence and call up the power of Celestine Light?

44 Yet in the world both men and women cut their hair. Men remove the hair from their face; both use dyes to change their natural color or cover their hairs of silver and heavy oils to gloss them. Why? All this in the pursuit of false youthfulness that is more truly realized by good food and a brisk and physical life.

45 And why does a man or woman that is married, as all are at a youthful age, have the need to look younger than they are? Will their husband or wife love them any less because they look their age? Are they afraid that their mate will look for someone younger if they do not look younger themselves? Or are they playing with fire and with adulterous thoughts trying to catch the attention of someone who is not their husband or wife?

46 Even as Elohim created man and woman with hair that always grows, so too were they made that in their latter years for many, their hair may become tinged with silver and even all white. Again, other than from a vain desire to appear younger than their true years, why would a man or woman seek to counter that which Elohim has given to mark the span of years and maintain a harmony with your knowledge and experiences?

47 Please understand clearly that retaining your natural hair color at every age supports the harmony of your essence and facilitates the calling forth of your Celestine powers.

48 Only when your hair color results from disease or poor health is this not true. Then it is another issue that must be first addressed, not with dyes, but with healing and wholeness.

49 In truth, most people who become silver-haired do so years prematurely because of their incorrect diet. Instead of eating foods filled with life, they eat foods full of death. Because of this, their hair turns silver before its time, and they die many years before their time.

50 If without vanity and with harmony, you simply do not desire silver hair, then eat the herbs and foods I have told you, and for most, your hair will retain its natural color until the day you die and return to its former glory if the silver has already appeared.

51 But for some, even with all this, silver hair will still arrive. If it does, realize it offers you greater power if you embrace it because it is has been given to you by Elohim to most purely harmonize with your essence.

52 If your diet does not maintain the color of your hair of youth and for your self-esteem you still cringe to see the silver, then cover it only with gentle natural herbs and only in your natural color; else, you create a significant disharmony in your aura that cannot be overcome in ways other than returning your hair to its natural color.

53 "I have spoken at length about hair, which to many would seem a trivial subject, inconsequential to spirituality. But among you, the Children of Light, I hope you now understand that the condition of the hair of your head is of great consequence, for it is one of your most important reservoirs of power and you will never be able to become master Adepts of all the secrets of Celestine Light that could be yours if you cut and treat your hair and beards as poorly as do the people of the world.

54 How is it that hair is such a reservoir? Verily, it is the record keeper of the aeon of every experience of your life. Your hair grows about the width of a fingernail each moon, more if it is very healthy from a good diet and not being attacked with heavy oils and caustic dyes.

55 That fingernail of growth has aurically stored all of the experiences, both good and bad, that you have had during that moon. Those experiences remain an energy within you, no less powerful than when you experienced them.

56 Your mind may remember the events, but your hair remembers the energy, if it has not been poisoned by heavy perfumed oils or caustic or incongruent dyes.

57 Whether your experiences were good or bad is irrelevant once you understand the secrets of how to use the aeon stored in your hair and harness it to help empower your special gifts.

58 Even anger has a beneficial power if it is righteous, and even that which hurt you in the

past can be called upon and aided by the energy stored in your hair, to help you in the present.

59 There are several things which contribute to your ability to use your gifts. Chief among these are faith and love, but also important are knowledge, courage, self-confidence, tools that magnify and focus, and a reservoir of power in your temple to call upon. A wise Child of Light will seek after all of these things.

60 Now I would also speak to you somewhat about your adornment and dress. Be not gaudy such as harlots of the world, but neither absent of adornment such as the zealots.

61 Would you build a temple to Elohim out of stone and then put no further adornments upon it to beautify it and make it special and unique? No, instead you would build it of the finest stone and then enhance its appearance with gold and gems and fine woods and carvings placed with elegance and dignity.

62 All throughout the temple you built to Elohim, you would inscribe the sacred symbols of power, unknown to the world but given to the Children of Light.

63 As you would do this for a temple of stone built to Elohim, should you do any less with the temple that you are, which Elohim has created for your glory and exaltation? In no way should you appear like the people of the world in your clothing and adornment. I tell you plainly that you should not look like them. Again, I speak not of gaudiness or extravagance or garishness, but of color, quality, uniqueness, and style.

64 Adorn yourselves not with copper or silver, for their usefulness in calling the Celestine Light is not so great, but only with gold, even if it is only threads woven into your garments, for this is the metal through which the powers of the Celestine Light easily flow.

65 In the stones that you choose to wear in your rings and pendants and other adornments, abandon the glass trinkets of the world and choose only those stones of power which I have taught you, that you may always have near-at-hand tools to aid you in the use of your special gifts of the Celestine Light.

66 If you fashion jewelry of gold, let it contain some of the secret symbols of power. Others may be intrigued by them, but only a true Child of Light steeped in knowledge will know their meaning and how to use them.

67 In your clothing, please do not wear drab colors like the people of the world, for the colors of their clothes are a reflection of their conformity to the fashion of the day or to the poor state of their spirit.

68 Rather, choose to wear bright and cheerful colors, even if only accents upon a predominance of white, that you will draw to you aeons of the same. In this, be not gaudy, for you are not court entertainers, but in all things show the class of Celestines, for more noble than kings and queens you are."

69 Then Yeshua began to teach the Children of Light many of the secrets of which he had spoken that they knew not, including further enlightenment upon sacred symbols, and how to use tools of focus and gold and gemstones and the formulas for many healing elixirs and potions of power.

70 These things cannot be written, but only spoken of in secret among the Children of Light, for Yeshua commanded those of the light not to cast their pearls before swine or reveal the sacred mysteries of Elohim to the world, which could comprehend their divine purposes not at all.

71 As he has spoken, so shall it forever be.

CHAPTER 69

Secrets of Magic Revealed

Yeshua teaches the Children of Light some of the secrets to calling forth their "gifts," particularly levitating objects by utilizing unknown natural laws created by Elohim. He also explains some of the secrets to making instant fire and how Moses turned his staff into a snake, which are things that an unbeliever might think of as magic, but to the Children of Light, they are merely employing the gifts bestowed upon them by Elohim through the understanding of how to utilize natural laws.

And it came to pass that on the following Sabbath, all of the Children of Light of the communities of Gennesaret came to Capernaum to hear the further instructions and teachings of Yeshua. And he brought them down to the lake, and standing with his back to the water and they upon the shore, he spoke to them saying:

2 "Each one of you is a worker of miracles, for as Children of Light, it is your blessing to be able to call upon the greater Celestine Light of Elohim as you have needs, whatever those may be, provided you are seeking only that which is righteous and needful and not for riches or acclaim of the world.

3 Yet you could live your entire life and never be the conduit through which a miracle flows, unless you understand the principles upon which the powers of Celestine Light bring wonder upon the earth."

4 Then reaching down, he grabbed a fist-size stone and threw it high over his head and above the lake. Turning toward the lake and extending his arm, he pointed his right forefinger at the stone just as it reached its apex and commanded, "Kel Arz!" and the rock remained suspended in the air.

5 Then turning to look over his left shoulder at the Children of Light, he said unto them, "You see a rock that does not fall, and because every rock you have ever seen thrown into the air always falls, you think that you now see a miracle or magic.

6 But verily, I say unto you: There are no miracles or magic, events the ignorant call what they do not understand, which seem to violate all that they hold as natural and normal.

7 In truth, every miracle from a healing to a rock floating in air is but the manifestation of a natural law created by Elohim that is unknown to the world, but given to be known and understood by Children of Light of uprightness and virtue."

8 Then he quickly sliced his arm through the air, and bringing his hand to his side, he turned again to face the Children of Light, even as the rock plummeted and fell into the lake behind him with a loud splash.

9 Then he continued to instruct them, saying, "The rock remained suspended in the air, not because Elohim made a great miracle, but because I understand all of the natural laws created by

the Elohim and called upon those I needed to cause this rock not to fall.

10 And what are these natural laws to be known by the Children of Light but mysteries to the world? They begin with faith and love. These two essences, which you cannot hold in your hand, are some of the essential attributes needed to affect the physical world, including suspending rocks in the air.

11 This is incomprehensible to the people of the world. They understand how one physical action can create another, such as when you hit a tree sufficient times with an axe, it is felled. But it would seem the greatest mystery of magic were the same tree to be felled without anything physically touching it, but merely by the unseen powers of faith, love, passion, and focus, harmonized with the knowledge of how to use the unseen aeons of Celestine Light.

12 Understand that it is by absolute faith in our Mother and Father in Heaven, whom we cannot see, that we can call the unseen forces of the Celestine Light to manifest that which is seen.

13 It is because of my love for you and desire to see you grow in the Celestine Light that the aeons activated by my faith come to me when I bid them.

14 I pointed my finger at the rock just as it reached its apex, when it was neither propelled to continue rising higher, nor compelled to descend rapidly downward into the lake. This was the easiest moment to have effect upon it.

15 With my eyes steadfastly upon the stone high in the air, I extended my arm and pointed my finger at it that the energies of Heaven flowing through me would be exactly focused and could have a most sure effect.

16 Understand then that undiluted and undistracted focus upon your desire is also imperative to your success. But no less than this is, you must also have a passion to see your desire accomplished.

17 By extending your arm and your finger, you are channeling all of the necessary aeons through a long conduit and the single small point of your fingertip. As the powers of Celestine Light swirl inside of you and then travel through your arm, they compress and increase their strength.

18 As the aeon shoots from your fingertip, it is both highly focused and of greater power because of the focus through a narrow channel. This effect can be even further enhanced by holding another object that is both long and slender, coming to a point, and intrinsically holding Celestine aeons, such as a crystal, a spiral shell, or a specifically fashioned wand of wood and gems."

19 Yeshua then beckoned a young man of about fourteen years to come to him, and a youth of humble and noble visage stepped forward from among the Children of Light.

20 "You are the son of Daoud and Thara, who recently came to us from the wilderness beyond Bahr Lut?"

21 The young man nodded his head affirmatively and said, "Yes, most revered teacher and light of lights. I am Galal. My father saw a vision in the night as he slept, and so real it was he thought he was awake.

22 He saw these communities upon the lake and saw you clearly although he had never in life even heard your name.

23 He saw a pillar of light pierce dark clouds in the sky and fall upon you as you walked in these communities, and a voice came upon his mind, saying, 'Behold the light of the world.' The very next day, our family departed from our brethren and have lived now among you for these past two moons."

24 "And we are happy that you are among us," Yeshua said unto him. "Truly, you and your parents and your brothers and sisters are Children of Light and one with us. What the world would separate, Elohim has brought together."

25 Yeshua looked upon him squarely and asked, "Before you came among us, you were raised to believe in a God that is different than we know. For Elohim of the Children of Light is different than the imagined God of the Hebrews or the Egyptians or any other that men do

worship and venerate.

26 "Having lived among us now for a short time and having learned somewhat of our ways, have you through your prayers and in your heart and mind come to a greater understanding?"

27 Galal nodded affirmatively and said unto Yeshua, "I have a witness in my heart and head that cannot be denied, nor would I dare even on pain of death. My witness is that I have a divine Father and Mother in Heaven and that I am their son of spirit.

28 So too have I a noble brother of spirit, who is their son of the flesh. And he ever watches over me as an elder brother should. And through them, we call the Elohim, by our efforts and virtue, all good things come and all things are possible."

29 Yeshua looked upon the Children of Light before him and said unto them, "Verily, no greater testimony of the Celestine Light could be given than this. Galal may be young in years, but his soul resonates with the wisdom of Heaven."

30 Then Yeshua bent down and whispered into Galal's ear, saying, "Do as I shall direct, hold your faith true and unwavering, and do not be weakened in your conviction or focus if you do not succeed on your first attempt, for he who perseveres with faith, focus, passion, and love shall succeed."

31 Then rising, he again addressed the Children of Light, saying, "I have explained to you how to hold a stone in the air. Size is important, and the larger or heavier an object is, the greater aeon is required to hold it or move it.

32 The words you heard me command, "Kel Arz!" are not found among the languages of men, but are words of power from the Celestine language of the Elohim. Spoken by unbelievers, they are merely empty words, but spoken by a Child of Light, for a purpose of righteousness, with faith, love, passion, and focus, they call upon a great aeon of the heavens, which overcomes the lesser aeon by which all things fall to earth."

33 Turning to Galal, he reached down and picked up a stone, and instructed, "As you saw me do, so do you now."

34 Galal's eyes went wide in astonishment, but quickly became peaceful and resolute as he took the stone from Yeshua and turned to face the lake. For a moment, he remained silent with his head bowed in contemplation and perhaps a silent prayer.

35 Then he threw the stone high into the air, and as it reached its apex, he extended his arm and, pointing his finger, yelled out, "Kel Arz!" However, the rock did not hesitate or remain in the air, but ignoring his words and intent, it fell quickly back into the lake with a high splash.

36 Galal looked back to Yeshua with some embarrassment upon his face, but Yeshua smiled at him and patted him on the back, assuring him that he did well.

37 He then reached upon the ground and picked up a fairly straight stick about the length of his arm and snapped a third of it off including the unbroken tip and handed it to Galal, saying, "Hold this stick in your right hand and point it instead of your finger. And remember to have a passion for your desire." Then he threw another stone into the sky, and once more Galal waited until it was at its apex then extended his arm and pointing at the rock with the stick he held, he commanded, "Kel Arz!"

38 For the barest moment, it seemed that the rock lingered for an extra heartbeat at its apex; then it too fell into the lake.

39 Galal looked back to Yeshua, and Yeshua took the stick from his hand. Then reaching inside his clothing, he pulled out another stick about the same length as the first, only this one was perfectly straight and tapered to a distinct but rounded point with a delicate spiral pattern finely cut into it, beginning at its base and rising to its tip. Its wood was very dark and unfamiliar to Galal as he took it and rolled it in his hands after Yeshua handed to him.

40 Without further instructions or words, Yeshua reached down and picked up another stone and threw it high into the air above the lake.

41 Once more, Galal waited until the rock reached its apex, then extending his arm and pointing the fine spiraled stick, he commanded, "Kel Arz!" and this time, the rock remained

undeniably suspended in the air.

42 As it did, there was an audible gasp from those who were watching and Galal moved his eyes for a moment to look at the crowd, and when he did, the rock immediately fell into the lake.

43 Again Yeshua smiled at him but did not speak. But he did hold out his hand by way of asking for Galal to return the spiral stick to him. But in its stead, he took out another item from within his clothing and handed it to Galal.

44 This new item was also a like a stick, but one such as neither Galal nor any but the Apostles had ever seen, for it was heavy and made of clear crystal, having also been finely worked with a spiral pattern. On its base was a rounded cap of deep-blue Lapis spider, webbed with golden lines and held to the crystal wand by a band of gold.

45 Turning to the Children of Light, Yeshua said unto them, "When you have learned to harness all of the aeons Elohim has blessed the Children of Light to know, you will have no need for sticks or wands of crystal to aid you in accomplishing that which you desire.

46 But until that day, there are tools upon the earth that can magnify your abilities because they readily call to them the aeons you seek and further amplify the power of Celestine Light that flows through you.

47 You have seen what was manifested by the finger of Galal and when he held a simple stick and then a wand of wood fashioned to serve the Children of Light. Now he holds a wand of crystal put upon the earth by Elohim and spiral cut and inlaid with gold and Lapiz by my own hands. It resonates with the powers of Heaven and beckons still greater aeons to aid young Galal in his quest. See now the final difference."

48 Once more he threw a stone into the air, and once more Galal thrust his arm upward and pointed the crystal wand at the rock as it reached its apex, commanding in a loud voice, "Kel Arz!" This time, the stone remained in the sky and did not fall back to earth.

49 As Galal continued to focus his eyes and thoughts upon the stone, Yeshua spoke to him, saying, "You now are one with the stone. It is merely an extension of you. Like your own hand, it moves where you guide it and will it to move. Therefore, continuing to point the wand of crystal and keeping your focus, move the stone some distance to the right."

50 As Yeshua bid so Galal did, and there were more gasps from the spectators as the stone moved the length of a fishing boat to the right.

51 "Now make the stone begin to dance," Yeshua bade. "Move it up and down and all around."

52 Again, as Yeshua bade so Galal did, and the stone moved through the air following exactly as he moved his arm in a figure-eight pattern. Then he brought the stone down to a point that it nearly touched the water, and he held it there.

53 Yeshua put his right hand upon his head, saying, "Well done, good brother of light. You may release the stone now." As he spoke, Galal quickly pulled the wand away from the lake and handed it to Yeshua, and the stone quietly dropped into the water.

54 Galal returned to his parents and family who embraced him, and Yeshua returned the crystal wand to the folds of his clothing and continued his discourse and instructions, saying, "To hold and move objects that otherwise could not rise or move without a visible physical action upon them is only one of many gifts that are given to the Children of Light.

55 But you must not use any of these gifts before unbelievers, for they will accuse you of magic and to them it is, and such is incomprehensible to their minds and forbidden by their beliefs. Therefore, you would bring not only unwanted attention, but even persecution.

56 Nor show these gifts to Neophytes who are not yet one with you, for they might not remain with you and should not be given secrets they could misuse or reveal to the world.

57 Nor even among yourselves should you manifest these gifts except in time of true need or within your quorum while teaching or practicing, and never simply to show another that which you can do, for to do otherwise calls forth pride, which is a destroyer of gifts of the Celestine Light.

58 Today only, I show some of these gifts unto you that you may begin to comprehend and

know of a surety that which the world cannot understand.

59 My Apostles shall further instruct you in the days to come, as I have instructed them. Let each of you learn and understand the principles of the natural laws of Elohim by which all these things can be, and then go alone into the mountains or within the sanctuary of your home or in solitude upon a boat on the lake or within your Q-roms, and practice that which you have learned until you have with certainty mastered the unknown natural laws of Elohim that they will stand ready to do your bidding in time of need.

60 Then grasping a stout and sinewy tree branch that was before him on the ground, Yeshua demonstrated further, "You have heard of how Moses in pharaohs' court turned his staff into a serpent. Behold!" Suddenly, the branch began to twitch and then it became a dark, thickly bodied snake, which Yeshua held behind its head even as it wrapped its coils around his arm.

61 Again there were many gasps of shock and fright from those who watched, for they were gathered very close to Yeshua, and he said unto them, "Fear not, good brothers and sisters, for this is not a snake, but only an illusion."

62 As he said that, Yudas Iscariot reached forth his hand and touched the snake and exclaimed, "But it moves beneath my hand. I can feel its strength, and its skin is like a serpent, not the bark of a tree branch."

63 Yeshua shook his arm, and once more he held a lifeless tree branch and he said unto them, "Nevertheless, as real as it seemed, it was but an illusion, but one created not by tricks but by calling upon natural laws of Elohim. Truly, this can be one of your greatest gifts if used only in righteousness and time of true need."

64 Then before he spoke another word, holding the branch up in his left hand, he waved his right hand over it, and immediately, it burst into leaping flames.

65 And Yudas Iscariot asked, "I feel the heat, yet is this also only an illusion?"

66 Yeshua answered him, saying, "No, Yudas, this is no illusion, and creating fire at your command is one of the more powerful gifts given to the Children of Light." And saying that, he flipped the branch over his head, and it tumbled in the air until it landed with a hiss in the lake where the flames were quickly extinguished.

67 Yeshua explained several other natural laws of Elohim to them that day and manifested their effects, so they would understand. And he commanded them that they should speak to no one not numbered among the Children of Light of the things they had witnessed.

68 He admonished them to listen to his Apostles and heed their teaching as if it were from him, promising he would give the Apostles understanding of all mysteries that they could share with all the Children of Light as they were worthy and prepared to receive the greater knowledge.

69 And he spoke to them once more, saying, "Today, you have seen some of the more spectacular gifts of the Children of Light, but do not forget that in your day-to-day lives, the teachings I gave to you about the miracles that come from herbs and minerals are of greater worth, for these are the skills you can use openly every day to heal the sick, uplift your spirits, prosper the land, and help create Eden wherever you are.

70 Nor ever forget that your 'gifts' are not special powers that people of the world do not have, but secret knowledge they do not have, which allows you to call and use natural laws they cannot comprehend or call upon, because they are called forth by knowledge, faith, love, and passion for the Celestine Light and the good it can manifest, all things which they have not.

71 Be not prideful or boasting, but in humility and gratitude, make your way upon the earth, bringing the Celestine Light and making the world a better place for all people."

CHAPTER 70

Conversion of Adronicus and Yunia

Yeshua, Miriam, and the Apostles visit the unusual city of Hyppos, where they meet a woman named Yunia and her husband Adronicus who are amazed by their encounter, and lead them on a tour of the city. As dinner guests of Yunia and Adronicus, when asked by another guest about dreams, Yeshua explains how to understand and interpret them. On the following day, Yeshua casts out a horde of demons from a man, saving his life. Afterward, Yeshua tells Yunia and Adronicus to put their affairs in order so they can join them in the Communities of Light on the north end of the lake.

nd it came to pass that Yeshua and his Apostles departed in the early morning from the Communities of Light and were ferried in three fishing boats to Hyppos on the eastern shore of Lake Gennesaret.

2 As they sailed upon the lake toward Hyppos, it reared up majestically before them on a tall flat-topped mountain that stood apart from all other mountains, and thus it was easily seen from a great distance away in any direction.

3 Pointing up to Hyppos, Yeshua spoke to Miriam, Cephas, Yakov, and Yohhanan, who were with him, saying, "Behold the city upon the mountain that cannot be hidden. Let it be always in your memory, and may you ever strive to be like an unforgettable city upon a mountain that cannot be hidden.

4 But more than this, let your light so shine that men see the temple that you are, by day and by night, that they may come to wonder, and then to seek, and then to know the Elohim in Heaven, who have made the temple."

5 Arriving at the port of Hyppos on the shore of the lake, Yeshua and the twelve Apostles disembarked and immediately set forth upon the steep switchback road up the mountain and arrived by midday at the Western gate of the main city. After being stopped and questioned briefly by the ten Roman soldiers that guarded the western entrance, they were waved on and they passed through the walls and tower of the gate without incident.

6 As they walked toward the center of the city, the Apostles took notice of all the Greeks and Romans and whispered among themselves how most of the citizens of Hyppos seemed to regard them with some disdain.

7 And they marveled that a city so close to their own communities could be so different in the designs of the buildings and the dress and customs of the people, for though many of them had lived their entire lives just a few hours away, none had ever visited Hyppos before.

8 As they came upon building after building, many times they could not fathom the purpose of them. They were baffled and perplexed and began to joke with one another as they speculated

upon the purposes of various buildings that they passed.

9 As they entered the central market area, the men looked about them in astonishment at the women of Hyppos. Not only were there as many of them as men upon the streets, but almost none were covered, and some seemed barely dressed at all.

10 Though Miriam, who was with them, and the other sisters of light of the communities seldom covered their heads, in the other cities and villages of Palestine a women uncovered was seldom seen, much less uninhibited exposure of bare arms, neckline, and lower legs as was displayed by many of the women of Hyppos.

11 Yeshua, seeing their astonishment, admonished them, saying, "Remember that it is Elohim that made the naked body in which your spirit dwells and man that made the clothes which drape upon it. Therefore, put not the restrictions or condemnations of men upon the creations of Elohim.

12 Respectfully admiring the beautiful creations of Elohim, be it a plant, a butterfly, or a woman, is not a sin and gives honor to the creator. But to lust after a woman that is not your wife, particularly if she is the wife of another, is a grievous sin and a weakness of character that would be unworthy of the great men that you are."

13 Seeing them looking in wonder at the sights of Hyppos, a comely young woman richly adorned in colorful clothing and much jewelry, who was passing by accompanied by a man, looked to her companion and, laughing, exclaimed in Greek, "The barbarians have arrived!"

14 Those walking with Yeshua who clearly understood Greek, were taken aback by this sudden statement from a stranger, much less a woman, for such a thing would be unheard-of in Palestine. And seeing that shock was holding their tongues, she spoke to them again, saying, "By your gawking and your clothes, you announce that you are the uncouth from the unknown. What purpose could you possibly have in the market of Hyppos?"

15 Most of the Apostles understood just enough Greek for basic commerce and looked to Yeshua, Miriam, Mattayah, and Yudas Iscariot to translate the full meaning of the woman's words. Yudas made to step forward to answer the lady, but Miriam held up her hand as he came forward, signaling for him to stop, and she went forward instead.

16 Walking right up to stand before the woman, she asked her in Greek, "Whence comes the red sky, when the sun rises or when it sets?"

17 The woman showed surprise that Miriam asked her this simple and elementary question that seemed to have no relevance to anything, and she answered her, saying, "It can be either, neither, or both. It depends upon the day. Is this a barbarian riddle?"

18 Having seen the things Miriam could do when she was righteously angry; some of the Apostles began to look to one another and to Yeshua in uneasiness at this budding confrontation.

19 But Yeshua did not intervene, and Miriam spoke again to the woman in a quiet and calm voice, saying, "If you would see a sun that is ever rising and never sets, with the glory of the flaming horizon ever upon the sky, follow these barbarians wherever they go in Hyppos, and you will see wonders such as you have never imagined and come to understand that the greatest treasures are sometimes found in the simplest of containers."

20 The woman stammered as she tried to answer Miriam, for more than her words, she was humbled by her aura, which flowed over her and through her, and she answered with politeness, saying, "Who are you dear lady; and why is one such as you keeping company with men such as these?"

21 Yeshua came up behind Miriam and put his hands upon her shoulders, and Miriam answered the woman with a fullness of love, saying, "I am Miriam of Magdala, wife of Yeshua of Nazareth, who stands with me." Then sweeping her arm toward the other Apostles she said, "And these are my brothers of light, good men all, the best you will ever find. We follow and learn from Yeshua, things no men or women know. Come with us this day and you too will see a light you have never before seen or imagined."

22 The woman looked to her companion questioningly. Her mouth was open in silent

astonishment, and she answered slowly, saying, "I am Yunia, and this is my husband Andronicus. Never would I imagine going with men such as these, but we seek to know the truth of all things and that which I feel in my heart is something I have never before felt so much so that it overrides what might be the better judgment of my head.

23 I feel in my heart like I have just entered a beautiful and spacious temple and that all I have ever known was merely the narrow and dark corridor leading to this great room of light.

24 Therefore, if my husband agrees, we will follow you in your wanderings through Hyppos that our curiosity might be satisfied, and we may yet see and learn some things of which we are ignorant and discover the source of the new beating in my heart."

25 Andronicus nodded his head and said, "My wife speaks my own words. I too have felt a strangeness in my heart, standing with you and listening to the words of this mysterious lady." He said pointing subtly at Miriam, "Lead on therefore and we will follow and see what manner of people you are."

26 Upon this agreement, Yudas Iscariot and Mattayah turned to the other Apostles and explained in detail everything that had transpired in Greek between Miriam and Yunia.

27 When everyone understood all that had come to pass, Yeshua invited Adronicus and Yunia to lead them on a tour of the city, and Yunia walked beside Miriam and Adronicus beside Yeshua, explaining the sights.

28 Mattayah and Yudas Iscariot walked directly behind them that they could turn and tell the other Apostles the details of what they heard, spoken in Greek. As they walked, Yuda tapped Adronicus on the shoulder and inquired where they found water atop a mountain sufficient for a city of so many people.

29 Adronicus answered, "We have great cisterns that catch the rain, and that is our only source and the single thing that limits the growth of our city. As you can see, this is a wealthy city for we are renowned traders and many are the people that desire to live here.

30 But because of the scarcity of water, only those born into Hyppos can remain upon the mountain to live, except for rare exceptions. All others that desire to rub shoulders with us must dwell in the lower village upon the lake and truly that is nothing more than a dung heap."

31 After they had toured the city, observing the temples, the forum, the massive walls of the Eastern Gate with its formidable round tower, and the plaza with its expertly worked paving stones, Adronicus turned to Yeshua and inquired, "Why is it that you have come to Hyppos? We have shown much to you, but you have yet to show anything to us. Are your wife's moving words empty after all?"

32 Yeshua answered him, saying, "We have come for you Adronicus, and your wife Yunia, for your future is greater than Hyppos. But there are still some things you must see and hear before you will know the truth of my words. Therefore, invite us to dine with you and sleep in your house tonight, and more shall be revealed to you."

33 Adronicus was surprised at the boldness of Yeshua to invite himself and all his followers to dine and sleep at his home, but this boldness only whetted his curiosity greater. He wondered what sort of man this could be, and he agreed and suggested they head to his house immediately that the servants could begin preparing the meal.

34 Shortly thereafter, they arrived at the spacious house of Adronicus, which commanded a spectacular view overlooking Lake Gennesaret. Yunia instructed the servants to prepare an evening meal for at least thirty people, and they hurried to accommodate her wishes in the few hours remaining before the allotted time.

35 Adronicus called aside one of the servants and gave him instructions to go to the homes of several of his friends and invite them and their wives to share their evening meal and to hear the Hebrew prophet Yeshua of Galilee, whom they had heard spoken of.

36 And it came to pass that the meal was served three hours later, and seven of the friends of Adronicus were present with their wives.

37 After the last course was served, Yeshua rose to address them about the importance of good

character. But scarcely had he begun to speak when one of Adronicus' friends, who had drunk too much wine, rose up and said, "Do not lecture us with things we already know better than you, for we are Greeks and Romans and learn such things when we are youths from teachings of the greatest philosophers.

38 We have heard that you are a sorcerer, and that is what we have come to see. So do not talk to us, but entertain us." And though some of the guests present protested his impolite words, more nodded their assent and encouraged Yeshua to show them some magic.

39 Yeshua answered, saying, "You have been misinformed. I have no magic, only the light of God. And such light is not for the haughty, but for the humble." And with those words, Yeshua sat down.

40 "Oh, come now," exclaimed another of the guests. "He did not mean to offend you. Surely there is something you can show us. It is because you are here that we have come tonight at the invitation of Adronicus."

41 "What about dreams?" interjected another. "Can you interpret dreams? Because I had quite a nightmare last night." And at his words, there was much laughter.

42 Yeshua rose again after his question and said unto him, "I will speak to you about dreams, not for you alone, but for the edification of my Apostles.

43 Describe if you will what you remember of your dream."

44 The man did as Yeshua bade and related the details of his dream. "I saw a great army invading; I know not where. But I found myself completely naked, holding only a knife, as a horde of soldiers descended upon me. I awoke just as they were all attacking me so I know not how the dream ends, but I fear the worst, for what can one naked man with a knife do against many soldiers with swords and javelins?"

45 This statement was again greeted with much laughter, but Yeshua answered serenely, saying, "To interpret a dream, you must decide what type of dream it is, and there are five possibilities:

46 Your most common dreams are simply your spirit of the night, taking events of your last days and recreating the themes with real or fictional characters in scenes that may or may not exist in reality. And you may or may not be one of the characters in the dream.

47 These dreams may be a continuation of thoughts you were pondering just before passing into sleep or completely unrelated to your thoughts during the day. Either way, they are often useful to help you understand problems that may be vexing you from perspectives you may not have considered during the times you were awake.

48 Therefore, do not dismiss these dreams as mere fanciful wanderings of your night spirit, but seek to remember them and consider how their lessons can apply to your current life challenges.

49 If your dream is of this type, you will seldom awaken from it at the end of the dream.

50 The other four types of dreams are dreams of fear, dreams of hope, dreams of lust, and visions of prophecy or revelation.

51 The dream of being naked and almost defenseless while being attacked by overwhelming numbers is a dream of fear."

52 Yeshua looked at the man that had spoken of his dream, and he said unto him, "In your daily life, you may be fearful of being exposed for something you have hidden from others and, once exposed, attacked and perhaps even killed because of what was revealed, with little to save you from your fate.

53 Even if such a thing is unlikely to happen, your guilt from your transgression causes you to fear just retribution, and this can be manifested in dreams such as you have described."

54 The other men at the table looked at their friend now with suspicion, and he leaped up proclaiming wildly, "It was just a silly dream! Why are you all looking at me like that?" Then grabbing his wife by the hand, he pulled her to her feet, snapping angrily, "Come we are leaving, this is nonsense!" And quickly, they strode across the room and departed from the house.

55 Yeshua continued to speak, saying, "Then there are dreams of hope. They often relate to your daily life. For instance, if you are a fisherman, you may see yourself catching a net full of fish,

more than it can hold.

56 If you are a bachelor seeking a wife, you may see several beautiful women desiring your favor. If that scene becomes sexual, it transitions into a dream of lust.

57 Dreams of hope can also be fanciful. You may see yourself flying in the air like a bird or discovering a treasure chest of gold.

58 Dreams of fear and hope do often have a common ending. When they are powerful, they will cause you to awaken from your sleep.

59 If you have had a dream of fear, you will awaken with a dread in the pit of your stomach and a heart that is beating rapidly.

60 If it is a dream of hope, you will awaken with a feeling of euphoria in your heart and a joy that fills every part of you.

61 Like the dreams of fear, dreams of hope often relate to your daily life, but more often in a less-direct way than dreams of fear.

62 If you have just asked the woman of your heart's desire to marry you, and all is well, you may dream that night of flying like a bird, for in truth, your spirit is soaring with happiness.

63 On the other hand, you may dream of women without love, but only with lust, or women may have lustful dreams of men or even of another woman or a man of another man. Lustful dreams imagine acts that your awake self likely would find repugnant and would never contemplate, much less consummate.

64 If you were to imagine these thoughts in your awakened state, especially of people of flesh and not imagination, other than your husband or wife, your sin of thought would be almost as grievous as the act.

65 "But at night, while you sleep, or in the morning when you are half awake and half asleep, or in the night as you drift into slumber, lustful dreams are not a sin if they are of imaginary people, but a benign means Elohim has given you to harmlessly expunge the natural urges that build up during the day, that they will not prompt you while awake to commit acts which you and others would forever regret.

66 Visions of prophecy are rare and do not come to ordinary men or women, for they are sent by Elohim to warn those who walk the pleasing paths of Elohim of things to come. But they can come to Children of Light wherever they are found without regard for race, sex, religious beliefs, or social standing.

67 If you live your life with honesty and honor, show kindness and respect to others, and treat your body like a temple of God, you can receive dreams of prophecy and revelation concerning that over which you have been given responsibility.

68 A true vision of prophecy will come more than one night while you sleep. They will be very memorable, vivid, and detailed, and you will almost always awaken directly after the vision.

69 Unlike dreams of hope and fear, you will feel neither dreadful nor euphoric, but will simply understand in calmness.

70 Most importantly, a true vision of prophecy will repeat more than once and sometimes often, even nightly, if it is showing you an event that is to occur very soon.

71 Successive visions of the prophecy will always show again that which you have already seen, but they may also add additional details with each reoccurrence.

72 Understanding your visions of prophecy correctly is of great importance, and it is sometimes prudent to seek out the advice of a knowledgeable Child of Light to correctly interpret that which you have seen, for sometimes the vision shows an actual event as it shall occur and other times, it shows representations of reality, such as a lion representing a king, or a soaring eagle representing victory.

73 Understand foremost that your prophetic visions will only involve your sphere of responsibility. If you receive a vision of something beyond your responsibility, it only pertains to how that vision will affect your sphere of responsibility.

74 Even as Noah saw great destruction coming upon the world, but did not try to save it,

but only used his vision to prepare to save the worthy Children of Light he could reach and the animals that came to him, as he was commanded by Elohim.

75 Therefore, if you are a parent, you may receive a vision of prophecy or dream of revelation regarding your children.

76 If you are the owner of a trading caravan, you may receive a vision of prophecy or dream of revelation about your business.

77 If you are the leader of a community, you may receive a prophecy or revelation concerning the community.

78 If you are the leader of a congregation of worshipers, you may receive a prophecy or revelation concerning your flock.

79 If you are an Apostle, you will receive prophecies and revelations about the specific responsibilities of your calling, but never for all of the Communities of Light unless all the other Apostles received the same vision of prophecy or revelation.

80 If you are the prophet of Elohim, you will receive visions of prophecy and revelation concerning not only all of the Children of Light, but all the world as well.

81 Beyond this, there is no constant meaning in the images you see in dreams, but each must be understood and interpreted according to the life and challenges of each person and the type of dream or vision that was seen."

82 Once more Yeshua sat down, and shortly afterward, the guests began to get up and depart, saying good-bye at the threshold to Adronicus and Yunia while expressing disappointment that they had not witnessed any magic and had to endure a boring and useless talk, as if a Hebrew peasant could teach them anything.

83 Later that night, after everyone had found a place to sleep, Adronicus and Yunia lay beside each other and Adronicus told her, "I fear we will be the butt of endless and hurtful jests from now on, for without exception our friends think we are mad to have invited them to dine with these people, much less allow them to sleep in our home."

84 Yunia put her hand upon his face and kissed him lightly, saying, "They are strange and simple and certainly have not yet lived up to our expectations. But my heart still feels buoyant when I think of them, and yours?"

85 "It is the same," replied Adronicus nodding. "My head says I have been a fool, and my friends will surely affirm it. But my heart still has the most peculiar feeling within it, and I still desire to understand from whence it comes."

86 Yunia agreed, saying, "They have said that they are departing for their homes upon the lake tomorrow. Let us continue to walk with them and listen to what they have to say until they depart, in hopes that we will yet see or hear something to justify the rash curiosity of our hearts."

87 Upon the sunrise, before they broke the evening fast, Yeshua invited Adronicus and Yunia to join them in the courtyard overlooking the lake while they participated together in the Contemplative Movements and the Lanaka amidst the breathtaking, beautiful view from their home.

88 Both Adronicus and Yunia deferred to participate and asked to observe only. Yeshua courteously agreed, but asked Miriam to sit with them and quietly explain all that they witnessed.

89 Adronicus and Yunia sat next to one another on a stone bench, and Miriam directly behind them leaning close to their ears so she could whisper without distracting the Apostles, who seemed to be more enlivened from the Lanaka and more connected to all that is, with the Contemplative Movements than usual because of the expansive view before them.

90 When it came time for the Apostles and Yeshua to reach out and touch the auras of those around them, Miriam whispered to Adronicus and Yunia to pay close attention to what they next felt.

91 As the wave of twelve auras simultaneously flowed over and upon them, they were startled and amazed and looked to one another with wide-eyed wonder. "Did you feel that?" exclaimed Adronicus.

92 Yunia nodded, saying, "Like a hot fire, but ever so peaceful and soothing, filling every part of my being."

93 After that, they watched the remainder of the Contemplative Movements with rapt attention and wonder.

94 When Yeshua and the Apostles were finished, Yeshua came over to Adronicus and Yunia and told them, "The light of your hearts is beginning to resonate, filling all of your being with light. And so shall it ever build until the darkness around you can no longer overcome the Celestine Light within you."

95 After the morning meal, Yeshua told Adronicus and Yunia that it was time for them to depart as they had arranged with the fishing boats to be picked up at noon.

96 Adronicus and Yunia accompanied Yeshua, Miriam, and the Apostles down the mountain to the port to await the boats that would return them to the communities at the north end of the lake.

97 While they were waiting, they noticed a man running along the shore, screaming obscenities and kicking and pushing over people in his path.

98 At the far end of the port, a group of six Roman soldiers noticed the commotion and hurried in the direction of the disturbance.

99 Adronicus, seeing this, leaned over toward Yeshua and said, "You best ask your wife to turn toward the lake and perhaps even to walk out on the quay, for I think we will soon see a terrible scene.

100 "This man has been crazy beyond belief, more so every day, since his wife and two children drowned when his fishing boat capsized in a storm. The soldiers have tolerated him for weeks, but now that he is attacking other people, I fear his end will be swift and bloody."

101 "We must insure that this is not so," Yeshua replied with conviction. Immediately, he set forth rapidly toward the madman with Adronicus, Yunia, and Miriam and all the Apostles following him.

102 Arriving quickly next to the man, with minutes still before the soldiers would be upon the scene, Yeshua held up his right hand and called out to the madman, "Cease this moment. Bind this man of sorrow no more!"

103 At his command, the man let out a bloodcurdling and anguished scream, holding both hands to his head and pulling on his hair. He looked at Yeshua and tried to speak but only gargled unintelligible words came out.

104 Yeshua looked at him steadfastly and commanded, "Depart now! Depart from this man. Depart from this place, ere you shall become even less than you are, even nothing."

105 Then the man spoke, his face contorted with effort to bring forth the words, and he said, "Spare us, Son of God. We beg thee, cast us not into outer darkness, but send us to any body, even a pig or a worm or a bug, anything but the cold and the darkness."

106 Yeshua crossed his arms in front of him and drew them rapidly across one another, saying, "You chose your fate before this world was. Begone spawn of darkness!"

107 Then the man let out a gasp and fell to the ground unconscious, even as there was a loud clap like thunder that rent the air above their heads, causing everyone to look fearfully up into the clear sky.

108 Immediately afterward, the man awoke asking, "Where am I? What has happened?" And his friends, those who had been his friends before he had become crazy, came to him now with joy to see he was again in his right mind.

109 By the time the Roman soldiers arrived, the man had been taken away and hidden with his friends, and they were left to wonder what had occurred.

110 Adronicus and Yunia looked at Yeshua with awe and reverence, and Adronicus marveled, "I have seen more than I imagined seeing, and felt more than I imagined feeling, though I understand not all that which I have seen and felt.

111 Nevertheless, a man without a mind reasons once more, and the same man about to die

still lives; and it was by your words that this was so.

112 And from within that man came, I know not what, but as you commanded, so it abided, even as it was gone against its wishes, calling you the Son of God.

113 I stand in awe, in wonder, and ask in humbleness, 'Who are you?'"

114 Yeshua answered him, saying, "I am who I am, and in your heart, you already know the answer to your question, and upon what path your destiny spreads before you.

115 Therefore, put your affairs in order and join us in the communities at the north end of the lake, for the greatest days of your life are yet to be."

116 Yunia came up to Yeshua, and kneeling on one knee before him, she kissed his hand, saying, "Forgive me for the harsh words I said against you and your friends when first we met. Never again will I pass judgment upon someone because of their appearance, and ever will I look to find the true person that dwells within.

117 I feel I have learned more in a day than I have in my whole life, not in knowledge, but in understanding the roots of all knowledge and the purpose of all life. Thank you for coming to Hyppos and into our lives. I know they shall never be the same and am exhilarated to contemplate what is to come."

118 Yeshua pulled Yunia up and embraced her and then held out his arm to also embrace Adronicus.

119 When they released one another, Miriam came and embraced Yunia, and from that day forth, they were numbered among the Children of Light and great were the deeds they would do in the days to come.

120 At noon, the three fishing boats arrived and Yeshua, Miriam, and the Apostles boarded them and waved good-bye to Adronicus and Yunia, who remained on the quay, watching the boats shrink into the distance until they could be seen no more. And they held each other and shed a few tears. But they were tears of joy.

CHAPTER 71

Astonishing Powers of Heaven Revealed

Yeshua is confronted and challenged by the Sanhedrin at the baths of Tiberius. Between Yeshua and Miriam, eight amazing powers of Heaven are righteously exercised.

And it came to pass that Yeshua and the Apostles returned to the Communities of Light and spent the remaining days of the week with their families.

2 Following the Sabbath, many of the Children of Light of all four communities, including children, made their monthly visit to the hot springs at Tiberias. Yeshua had encouraged them to frequently soak in the natural hot waters and vapors that issued from the depths of the ground as a way to aid their health and longevity, energize their auric centers, and to be in greater harmony with the living aeon of earth.

3 When they arrived, there was a greater commotion about the town than was customary. Salome was somewhat worried, for there were many soldiers of Herod Antipas present and she feared being recognized.

4 It was only in recent years that Herod had taken what had been the village of Chamath and renamed it Tiberias after the emperor, and since that time, he had declared it to be his new co-capital. Since that declaration, his court and soldiers had been ever more present.

5 Also since the creation of Tiberias as the co-capital of Herod, the court of the Lesser Sanhedrin in Tiberias, with its beautiful lake and comforting hot springs, was considered by the judges of the Sanhedrin to be the choicest of locations and received frequent visits from members of the Greater Sanhedrin in Jerusalem.

6 Thus it was on this day that while over sixty of the Children of Light came to the springs to soak and meditate, six soldiers of Herod barred their way and ordered them to depart immediately as judges of the Greater Sanhedrin of Jerusalem had just arrived in Tiberias and were coming to the springs within the hour to bathe in privacy.

7 Without thought of protest or complaint, almost everyone nodded their heads and made to comply, as no one desired unwanted attention from either Herod's soldiers or the Sanhedrin.

8 But Miriam, who was standing with Yeshua, Salome, Martha, Miryam, and their children, was incensed, for they had barely arrived after a long walk on a hot day. Turning to Yeshua, she asked, "Must we always be meek as sheep, beloved?"

9 He answered her, saying, "Today is as good a day as any to begin our inevitable confrontations with the Sanhedrin. If it is in your power to make it so without harm to any of the Children of Light, let it be so Miriam."

10 With Yeshua's approval, Miriam looked steadfastly upon the soldiers of Herod and pulled from beneath her garment the rainbow crystal that hung from a chain on her neck.

11 She removed the chain from her neck, and holding the crystal and chain in her right hand, she stepped in front of the soldiers, and pointing the point of the crystal at them, she moved it in three circuits in a wide figure-eight motion, while quietly speaking words that none could hear.

12 "What is that you are doing, witch?" shouted one of the soldiers. "Stop this instant if you value your life."

13 But she did not stop, and the man who spoke and another made to take a step toward her but stopped in mid-stride as she transferred the crystal to her left hand in a very fluid movement, and held up her right hand as she had on the river Qishon, with the palm upward and her fingers splayed, and said, "Ollinaris," in a firm but quiet voice.

14 Suddenly, all of the soldiers seemed to fall into a stupor. They gazed ahead but did not see. That lasted but a few seconds, and then the soldier that had confronted Miriam looked at her and said amiably, "You may pass, and we shall protect your privacy."

15 Thus did all of the Children of Light who were present pass by the soldiers of Herod and into the baths of Tiberius. Many looked at the soldiers with incredulity as they passed, wondering what had occurred, for few had seen what Miriam had done. But the soldiers regarded them not at all and stared straight ahead as they passed by.

16 As they were assured of privacy, something they had never been assured of on any of their previous visits, most removed their clothes, both men and women as well as children, and enjoyed the hot waters of the earth in nakedness to better commune with the earth. And there was no lust among them.

17 After they had been in the hot waters for a little over an hour, they heard a commotion beyond the wall and discerned that the Sanhedrin judges had arrived and were angrily demanding entrance while Herod's soldiers steadfastly denied them.

18 Hearing this, Yeshua spoke to Miriam, saying, "Let us go, along with the Apostles, and speak with the Sanhedrin. I am sure we can engage them for quite some time, while our families and the rest of the Children of Light continue to enjoy themselves in the hot waters until they are content.

19 Gather the Apostles and follow me out to confront the Sanhedrin. Tell Salome and Martha to instruct the Children of Light to quietly depart the baths through the lake gate once they have finished their soaking, meditations, prayers, and contemplations."

20 "So shall it be, beloved," she affirmed.

21 Then Yeshua came up out of the waters, dressed himself, and went through the gate onto the street where over thirty Sanhedrin were seeking entrance into the baths through the gate guarded by Herod's soldiers.

22 At once, seeing Yeshua emerge from the baths, one of the Sanhedrin in the forefront of the crowd yelled at the soldiers, "Who is this riffraff that comes from the baths, while you keep the judges of Israel waiting like beggars on the street?"

23 The soldiers looked to one another in confusion, seemingly unsure how to answer. But before they could speak, Yeshua stepped before the Sanhedrin and said unto them, "I am Yeshua of Nazareth."

24 Upon hearing his name, the judges suddenly looked up at him with alertness, and another stepped forward from behind the fore and asked, "The Galilean prophet?"

25 Yeshua looked at him and nodded, saying, "I have been called that by some."

26 "The very same man who has said he has come to destroy the law?" shouted another Sanhedrin from the crowd.

27 "I have come to destroy the laws of men that pervert the light of Elohim, and by this, I uphold the true laws of God. It is only foolish men, full of their pride and awash in their ignorance, who try to destroy the laws of God, for that which had no creation can have no destruction. And that which is immutable is immovable and unchanging." As he spoke, Miriam

came through the door and stood beside him, and she was soon followed by the other eleven Apostles.

28 Seeing a large crowd gathering, a contingent of twelve Roman soldiers moved closer to observe from a street corner, as did many people from the town.

29 "Nonsense!" shouted another of the Sanhedrin, "You are no prophet!" "What scriptures foretell your coming?" yelled another. "We already have all the law, so why then do we need a new prophet?" added a third. "What schools did you study at? What great teacher gave you knowledge of the law?" demanded a fourth. "I have heard he is nothing but a cheap magician," added a fifth.

30 Yeshua raised his hand and they became silent waiting for him to speak, and he said unto them, "I am, who I am, and those who know the Celestine Light of Elohim know me, even as those who wander in darkness cannot see me, and someday shall fall off a cliff into an eternal abyss unless they find the torch of Elohim to light their path."

31 Yeshua looked at one of the Sanhedrin standing in the center of the group. His dress was embroidered with gold, and the others deferred to him in their looks and words. "I have told you who I am. Return the courtesy if you will."

32 "Ha!" exclaimed the man. "If you were a prophet, you would not need to ask, for Elohim would tell you who I am. By your very question, you expose yourself as a fraud."

33 Yeshua smiled in tolerance and said unto him, "Being in purest harmony with Elohim, who you are is not a mystery to me, Abraham ben Obias, vice-chief justice of the Greater Sanhedrin. I was merely giving you the courtesy of introducing yourself in a manner of your pleasure, and if this is it, then I must thank you for doing so in a way that verified my oneness with Elohim."

34 The eyes of the vice-chief justice momentarily flared up in anger, but he quickly regained his composure and politely spoke to Yeshua, saying, "Deluded man, while not knowing who I am would be a sure sign that you are not a prophet of Elohim, knowing who I am is not an indication that you are, as I have some notoriety and am well known among many of the Children of Israel.

35 In truth, I do not have time to quibble with a destitute man from Nazareth. Move aside now and let us pass and no harm shall come to you for your insolence."

36 Yeshua merely crossed his arms and smiled mischievously.

37 Abraham ben Obias looked at him in his disobedience with incredulity, saying, "Are you lacking in wits? I gave you a chance to go about your way in peace, but now you draw my wrath, which is as the wrath of God, for we are his judges."

38 Ignoring Herod's soldiers and pointing to two of the Sanhedrin guards that had accompanied them on their trip from Jerusalem, he ordered, "Remove that man and clear a path for us to enter."

39 The two guards immediately moved to comply with his command. Each came up on one side of Yeshua, and grabbing him on his forearms and under his arm pits, they attempted to lift him and carry him bodily away. But try as they might, they could not move him from the spot upon which he stood.

40 "Oh, this is ridiculous," exclaimed the vice-chief justice. He called forth two more guards and ordered, "Assist them."

41 The two new guards each went on one knee and, reaching down and holding onto Yeshua's legs, attempted to lift his feet off the ground, while the earlier two guards continued to struggle to lift him by his arms; but still, they could move Yeshua, not at all.

42 Yeshua looked again at Abraham ben Obias and, smiling, said unto him, "Four or forty or four hundred, I shall not move until I decide to move, for I am one with the earth, even as I am one with Elohim, and the earth shall not move for you, Abraham ben Obias."

43 Suddenly, though Yeshua still did not move or utter a word, all four guards yelled in pain and let go of him as they fell back onto the ground.

44 The vice-chief justice moved to the front of the Sanhedrin, and looking down at the guards upon the ground, he asked, "What is wrong with you? Why are you moaning upon the ground

as if you have just been wounded? This man has not even moved a finger, so why are you acting as if you have just been bested in battle?"

45 All four of the guards began to answer in the same manner saying, "We have been burned by a fire with great pain. Suddenly, to have our hands upon him was the same as grabbing a red hot iron out of the forge fire."

46 "Let me see your hands," demanded Abraham, and the guards turned up their palms to show him.

47 The vice-chief justice reached out and took hold of one of the guard's hands, saying, "There are no burns on your hands. This is all just a trick. Was it not said that this man is a magician?"

48 Yeshua shook his head as he looked at Abraham and, pointing to a large flat rock beside the road, said unto him, "Truly, the proud will never find the path to Heaven, for only the humble can see it. But the high and mighty shall be given in justice even as they have dealt. If you would see what awaits such as those, turn over that rock and behold that which can be no trick, even the end that awaits those who see but are blind and hear but are deaf."

49 "I will not obey your commands, false prophet of Galilee," attested Abraham. "And I am sure I shall see you next at the court of the Sanhedrin, for if ever there was a blasphemer, it is you."

50 Despite his refusal to do as Yeshua bid, others of the Sanhedrin began to murmur among themselves and beseeched the vice-chief justice to look beneath the rock, for what could there be beneath it but dirt and proof therein that this was a false prophet.

51 Their words made sense to the vice-chief justice, and he caught the eye of three of the bigger guards and nodded his head toward the rock. They went over to it and struggled together to turn it over, for it was a large rock used to mark a corner of the road.

52 No sooner had they rolled it over than they stepped back in horror, for a gaping black hole of the diameter of a small well was revealed in the ground, and a frightening howl of wind was issuing from the hole, sounding like the mournful wails of a many men in agony.

53 A mighty suction of air began to build coming from the shrieking hole, and a whirlwind of dust quickly formed above it. The robes of everyone nearby began to flutter and then stand on end as they were sucked toward the abyss.

54 Smaller rocks upon the ground, the size of fruits large and small, began to slide and roll toward the hole, moving faster the closer they were to the blackness until they were sucked over the edge and down into the depths. And never was there heard the sound of splashing water or impact upon ground, and fear came upon those present as they perceived this was a bottomless pit.

55 The Sanhedrin and all other onlookers except Yeshua and the Apostles backed rapidly away from the hole and away from its sucking grasp. But many were the loose items of man and nature that were sucked into the hole never to be seen again.

56 Yeshua and the Apostles remained where they were near the gate to the baths. They stood serenely, in an invisible bubble of protection, and their robes fluttered not at all, nor their hair, for in that spot alone, there was no wind or suction.

57 Then Yeshua looked to Philip, the slightest physically of all the Apostles, save Miriam, and directed him, "Return the rock to the hole. Let the disbelievers see the power of the Celestine Light of Elohim that flows through the Children of Light."

58 Philip did as Yeshua bade, walking several steps over to where the rock lay next to the howling hole. And it had no power over him. Nor did his hair or clothes even flutter from the wind. Reaching down, he squatted and grasped the rock with two hands and then stood up and easily flipped it back to cover the screeching hole, silencing the sucking wind. And the utter quiet of the awestruck crowd was palatable.

59 The vice-chief justice took a moment to compose himself and then approached Yeshua closely and said, "I might have judged you prematurely. You are either a prophet of God or one of the greatest magicians that has ever been upon the land. If you are a magician, that is likely all

that you know, but if you are a prophet, you will know all that we know of the law and be able to teach us things we know not.

60 I still want my bath, but in the interest of fairness, I will hear your teachings for a few minutes and determine which you are. Therefore, teach us, if you can, that which makes us better understand the law."

61 Yeshua nodded silently, and then answered, saying, "There are laws of men and laws of God. The difference is, the laws of Elohim are few and simple, given to inspire, uplift, and guide all people on paths leading to greatness and glory. But the laws of men are numerous, complex and onerous, most often given to subdue the spirit of man and cause him to conform to the will of the lawmakers.

62 All of the laws of men are not evil; some are beneficial to both the individual and to the community.

63 But you cannot judge obedience to the laws of God justly because you are also the arbiters of the laws created by men, and the two often seek different ends though both are found in the Torah and proclaimed as the will of Elohim.

64 Think not that Elohim has anointed you or any men to create laws in the name of Elohim, saying that men must do this or do that because doing so is obeying the will of God.

65 The will of Elohim is that men and women would know with an unquenchable fire in their hearts that they are children of God and that they would prosper upon the earth and return to Heaven as greater Children of Light than they departed.

66 For this cause only, that the eternal exaltation of the Children of Light might come to pass, Elohim gave the Great Commandment and the Twelve Commandments of Sinai. What more is necessary to have harmony in the relationship of man and Elohim? Live these simple laws and you will grow in spirit, closer to God and more beloved by your fellow sojourners in mortality."

67 The vice-chief justice of the Sanhedrin stood looking at Yeshua. He cocked his head as if waiting to hear more, but Yeshua just looked at him.

68 "That is all?" Abraham ben Obias stammered incredulously. "That is your all-knowing answer to my question? Surely you have more to say. This is a rare opportunity for a common man to be able to speak directly to me and my brethren. Are you going to squander it?

69 You have not spoken to us of a single law other than the most basic and do not even seem to know that there are Ten Commandments of Sinai, not twelve. We consider six hundred twenty four major laws contained in the scriptures upon which all edicts are based. These are the commandments of God through his prophet.

70 Nor is there or can there be distinction between a religious law and a civil law, for all laws governing both life and religion are from God. Nor do we make laws; we merely interpret those given by God through the prophet to guide our lives.

71 It sounds as if you are proclaiming all of the Torah invalid except for the commandments of Sinai, which you cannot even count, so you must not actually know. Surely, you cannot have grown up in this country and be so simple of mind.

72 You have certainly shown yourself to be a great magician and worthy to be tried for sorcery and blasphemy. But your knowledge of the laws of Elohim is embarrassingly lacking. Young boys know more than you. Now step aside before I have you arrested."

73 "I have answered you fully," Yeshua replied. "But only the humble hear and understand my words." Without another word, Yeshua turned and walked away from the vice-chief justice and toward the wooden gate that was the entrance to the baths. Seeing him approach, the guards of Herod stepped aside.

74 As Yeshua departed in silence, Abraham ben Obias turned to his fellow Sanhedrin and gloated, "Certainly, put that simpleton in his place." A hearty round of laughter came from the Sanhedrin in agreement.

75 As Yeshua turned toward the door, he called out to Miriam in his mind, beckoning her to come with him to the entry gate and explained to her his intention as they took the few steps.

76 Without drawing notice, the milling Apostles blocked the view of Yeshua and Miriam, who had disappeared behind them, from everyone on the street.

77 Coming to the gate, Yeshua put his right hand upon it and Miriam her left, and they looked at each other with subtle, knowing smiles and together said in quiet voices, "Elxpedia." After only a few seconds, they removed their hands and walked away with the Apostles, accompanied by taunts from some in the crowd.

78 As they were still laughing and commenting about the encounter with Yeshua, it was a few minutes before the Sanhedrin approached the gate to enter the baths. When they did, they discovered it would not open.

79 The vice-chief justice looked at the guards of Herod and commanded them to open the gate, but even with the two pounding against it with their shoulders and all their weight, it would not budge.

80 "What can possibly be the problem with a simple gate?" demanded Abraham ben Obias.

81 The guards could not answer, for the gate had no locking mechanism and only hung loosely in the portal, although it seemed to have swollen until it occupied all of the space with no light escaping around the edges from the side beyond.

82 Seeing the continued commotion, the Roman soldiers, who had been observing the events from the far street corner, came up to the gate to discover what was causing the continuing disturbance. But they too could not open the gate.

83 The commander gave an order to one of the soldiers, and he departed, but soon returned with an axe and commenced to take mighty swings into the wooden door.

84 Meanwhile, Yeshua and the Apostles had met up with the last of the Children of Light who had departed from the baths, and Salome was among them.

85 She came up and embraced Miriam and said unto her, "We stayed longer than most of the others, for when you did not return, they began to worry and departed with all the children by the lake gate. I was worried for you also, as we could hear the voices of angry men, and we saw the funnel cloud of dust and heard the dreadful screaming of we know not what."

86 Miriam walked with her, holding her hand, and told her all that had transpired with Yeshua, and the Sanhedrin and Salome was astounded. "And what of the gate?" she asked. "How did you stop it from opening? And why did Yeshua ask you to come with him?"

87 Miriam answered her with a wry smile, saying, "We merely rejoined in life that which Heavenly Father and Heavenly Mother had created, but man had torn asunder. Where boards had been, a tree became.

88 Yeshua could have accomplished it alone, but in his love asked me to help; and in truth, the spark of life most easily comes with the union of male and female."

89 Back at the gate, the Roman soldiers had taken huge chunks out of the wood with the axe so much so that the head of the axe now disappeared beneath the wood with every chop. Yet still the gate did not open, and the commander looked to Herod's soldiers and demanded, "How thick is this infernal gate? I passed through it just yesterday and remember it as nothing more than rough hewn boards."

90 "And so it was," answered one of Herod's guards. "I know not what has become of it, save the Galilean prophet touched it just before he departed, along with a woman."

91 "Look!" exclaimed one of the Sanhedrin, pointing to the door. "It lives!"

92 Everyone looked to where he was pointing, and there was a sprout of green leaves coming out of the wooden gate. More were quickly noticed shooting out of the wood in several places.

93 "This is impossible!" exclaimed the commander of the Romans, and he ordered his men to dig down into the ground beneath the gate.

94 "The gate continues beneath the ground!" shouted one of the digging soldiers. "By Jupiter! This is a tree, and these are its roots!"

95 Seeing what his eyes could scarcely believe, Abraham ben Obias looked with some apprehension in the direction Yeshua had departed, and one of his fellow judges standing beside

him asked, "What manner of man can turn a gate of boards into a living tree? Is not life the domain of God? Surely, magic like this has never been seen in Israel."

96 Abraham continued to look with vacant puzzlement out into the distance and answered almost in a whisper, "Surely not."

CHAPTER 72

Yeshua Explains the Celestine Powers

Yeshua explains the eight heavenly powers he and Miriam used when confronted by the Sanhedrin to the Children of Light so that they can understand the foundations by which each unique gift of power is called upon and employed.

The day following their arrival back at their homes in the four communities on the lake, almost every member from each of the communities came to the house of Yeshua, for everyone, both those that had gone to Tiberius and those that had remained at home, desired to hear the details of what had transpired at the baths the previous day.

2 Yeshua, Miriam, Martha, and Salome remained outside their house and greeted each person as they arrived with hugs of brotherly and sisterly affection.

3 Among those gathered, there were some murmurings of fear, for though the powers Yeshua had shown were awe inspiring, it also seemed to some that in a single day, he had made himself an adversary, if not an enemy, of the Sanhedrin, Herod Antipas, and the Romans.

4 Knowing this caused apprehension and anxiety among some of the Children of Light who noted that on the same short road they had taken to and from Tiberius, the soldiers of Herod or the Romans could quickly come and arrest them.

5 But Yeshua, knowing their thoughts, said unto them, "Brothers and sisters of light, you have come to gain greater insights into the events of yesterday, and I shall give you that which you are prepared to receive.

6 First, becalm your anxious hearts and know that neither the soldiers of Herod nor the Romans, nor the guards of the Sanhedrin, will come upon us this day or in the days near to come.

7 There will come a time in the not-too-distant future when because of the threats and actions of our adversaries of the world, you will need to leave the communities on Lake Gennesaret, never to return; but that time is not now, and you shall be given ample days to prepare for the departure.

8 As you desire, I will share with you some understanding, concerning the powers of Celestine Light that were revealed this day. A fuller understanding will be given to you by my Apostles in the days to come, as you are prepared to receive it.

9 Marvel not at these things, for nothing is impossible to the Children of Light if they have virtue, faith, love, focus, knowledge, and a passion for that which they desire to occur.

10 But to fully understand the mysteries of the Celestine Realms of Elohim, you must be willing to live your life even as the Elohim live theirs, as is revealed in completeness to the

Adepts. And then you must have patience and perseverance, for knowledge is gained during decades of study, and the ability to use the knowledge, only with diligent and faithful practice.

11 Because the treasures of sacred ability come at the price of years of life and adherence to a path of virtue and righteousness, few are those who will walk the path, though the gate is open for any to enter.

12 You are not esteemed any less by Elohim if you choose to not walk this path. For of no less worth is the man who is simply a loving and faithful husband and father, providing for his family, and a conscientious and contributing member of the community or the woman who is a loving and devoted wife and mother, beloved by her brothers and sisters within the community for all the light that she radiates by her words and deeds.

13 But for those who are called by the majesty of their inner light, there is much to learn.

14 That you may have a fuller understanding of the events of heavenly power yesterday, I will share with you their foundations.

15 While we were in Tiberius in confrontation with the Sanhedrin, eight powers of the Celestine Light of Elohim were called upon. These are aeons that flow freely but without form. They only come into focus when a Child of Light calls to them, becomes one with them, and focuses them.

16 The first and second came when Miriam used a powerful tool of focus, along with a specific prayer and movement, finalized by uttering a sacred word of power to mesmerize and then compel the soldiers of Herod to do as she commanded.

17 The third was when I knew the name of the Sanhedrin vice-chief justice. But this is a simple thing, which many of you have already learned.

18 The fourth was when the guards of the Sanhedrin tried to remove me, but could not as I had become one with the earth. Understand that your body is a great storehouse of aeon. It resonates with all life and with the earth, for it is of the earth that it is made and to the earth that it shall return.

19 If you walk the path of Celestine Light, you will learn how to focus your aura to attune and resonate with any living thing or any part of the earth so much so that you will become like the most powerful lodestone and can call any object to your hand, repel it away, or, as was the case in Tiberius, become immovably one with the earth or any part of it.

20 The fifth was when the guards felt burned as if in a fire from touching me. This was accomplished by combining two gifts of power. I raised the temperature of my skin by commanding it to be so, and my body obeyed my command, not to a heat as hot as a fire, in fact, just a bit hotter than normal. But like Miriam with her compulsion, in the minds of the guards, I was as hot as a steaming red iron out of the forge fire.

21 The sixth was the opening of the hole to outer darkness, a place of sadness where dwell the unrighteous, a place not within the earth or upon the earth, but a place beyond the stars.

22 These portals and others to diverse destinations appear in various places from time to time, usually never for more than a few hours or even minutes. But they can also be summoned and appear upon the command of an Adept of the Children of Light, and thus it was yesterday in Tiberias.

23 The seventh was when Philip lifted the great stone and covered the passage to outer darkness, the same stone that it had taken three large men to roll over. Though Philip is strong, it was not his muscles that accomplished this, but calling upon his gifts of power to coalesce the aeons and become one with the rock so much so that it became as if it were a part of his body, and rolling it over was no more difficult than standing up.

24 The eighth was when Miriam and I brought life back into the plain boards of the simple gate at the street entrance to the baths of Tiberius. This was a challenging use of sacred power and is most easily and quickly accomplished with a male and female energy, the left hand of one and the right hand of the other, lying on opposite ends of the object to be resurrected and renewed.

25 The essences of both must be sent into the object until the energies of the male and female merge and then swirl in unity through each other and the object. A Celestine word of power is also said, which calls upon the greater powers of Elohim, the original giver of the life, and if Elohim is in harmony with your action, life will flow again.

26 Though I have done these things openly, you must do them only in secret, save for the direst of circumstances when you may use them openly, but only so much as is necessary.

27 For if the Caesars of the world, both the petty and the mighty, knew of the true powers of the Children of Light, they would try to use you for evil purposes and persecute your families and your brothers and sisters in the community to achieve their desires.

28 It is not meant for us to be at war with the world, but to be unseen and unnoticed as much as is possible with our peculiar ways and colorful dress—in the world but not of it—to use the blessings of the gifts of Elohim to be of service to our families and brothers and sisters of light and to benefit and bless the world at large, but only in secret benevolence.

29 But it must needs be that I walk a different path. So it is that in me, the powers of Celestine Light must be seen that the word of it shall endure through the history of man, ever calling the Children of Light of each succeeding generation to the fullness of Elohim and the fulfillment of their truth."

30 Then Yeshua ended his words with the Children of Light, and Cephas stood before them and admonished them to return to their homes and their work and promised them that the Apostles would teach the mysteries to them in the days to come as they were prepared to receive the knowledge.

31 After everyone except the Apostles had departed, they went to the lake shore and into three boats. When they were far off shore and alone, they tied the three boats together, and Yeshua revealed the deepest secrets of all the powers of Celestine Light they had seen that day. But these things cannot be written, but only spoken among the Children of Light who are prepared to receive the knowledge.

32 When he had completed revealing the mysteries of the powers of Elohim they had witnessed in Tiberius, Yeshua spoke again to them, saying, "The time has come when we must increase the Communities of Light with more of your brothers and sisters who are still lost in the world.

33 There are many in particular that must come to this place, even from cities in distant lands, that they may have the opportunity to fulfill their destiny and grow into the person they were called to become before the world was.

34 I am going to teach you now how to enter the dreams of people while they sleep, and each of you will be given three people as your stewardship. You will enter their dreams each night and appear as yourself and explain who they are: a Child of Light, a son or daughter of God.

35 Show them this place and this people; relate to them all the things you have both seen and heard since you have been with me.

36 Their dreams will be so vivid they will not seem as dreams. It will be as if you stood in person before them, showing them the path to the light.

37 Invite them to leave their homes and come here with their families to be among their brothers and sisters of light, even though for many that will be a great sacrifice.

38 Some will see the light and heed the call, and others will see the light but heed it not.

39 When any of your three have either turned away from the light or heeded it and begun their journey to us, I will give you another to take their place. And so shall it continue until I am no longer among you in the flesh."

40 At his last words, Philip seemed distraught and asked him, "Why must you leave us? I have heard you speak of this before, and each time it causes me a pain in my heart."

41 Yeshua answered him, saying, "We are each here upon the earth to be of service to our brothers and sisters, our fellow travelers of eternity. You have your calling, and I have mine, two parts contributing to the same grand design.

42 I have come to bring the Celestine Light. You have come to expand the light.
43 I have come to save the people that will be saved by giving them a path of redemption and exaltation. You have come to help them on their way and save the world upon which all live from sinking into a final darkness. For if the world is in darkness, so too are the people of the world.
44 I have come to show life eternal and bring exaltation and glory to the worthy. You have come to teach life eternal, to find the worthy, and bring hope to the hopeless.
45 My time to depart this world is not yet, for I still have much to teach you. But when you have a firm foundation, the world must be given to rest upon your shoulders. And for this, you cannot remain in my shadow, lest your own light would never be seen."

CHAPTER 73

A Question of Nudity

Cephas speaks on behalf of himself and the other male Apostles to Yeshua about the uncomfortable feelings that they had when nude in mixed company at the baths of Tiberius. Yeshua responds by speaking about making one's weaknesses their strengths and expounds upon the virtues of a strong and passionate marital bond and the service the men must give to their wives to make it so.

And it came to pass that on the following day, Yeshua met with Miriam and his other Apostles in the mountains west of Capernaum and taught them further concerning the mysteries of Elohim.

2 When he had finished speaking, Cephas spoke to him, saying, "Yeshua, as you know our minds, I have no doubt that you know there is something that has been troubling me and my brethren since our time in the baths of Tiberius."

3 "I know," Yeshua affirmed. "But I have been waiting for you to broach the subject; that you might grow in the understanding of both your strengths and weaknesses."

4 Cephas looked at Miriam and said unto her, "Forgive me, Miriam, for discussing this in front of you as it is a subject of men. But as an Apostle, you are like unto a man in the things you have heard and seen. Therefore, I know that Yeshua would not put you out of the conversation, nor will I ask such a thing. Nevertheless, do not take offense at the subject."

5 Miriam gave a slight smile and said unto him, "Fear not, Cephas, I am not a delicate flower, and I will not wilt under the heat of your conversation with Yeshua, even if it is a conversation for men."

6 Being assured of this, Cephas continued speaking his thoughts to Yeshua and, waving his arm to include all of the other male Apostles, said, "Our visit to the baths of Tiberius the other day left all of us very uncomfortable, and it was not from your confrontation with the Sanhedrin, but from our time in the baths.

7 In the past when the community has gone to the baths, we have allowed the women, girls, and young children to go in for a time, if they were to go in nakedness, and when they had departed, the men went in and took their turn.

8 But this last time, you had everyone go into the baths together in nakedness. You must know this was a very difficult thing for us to see women other than our wives naked in such close proximity. This problem was made greater by having so many people at once in the baths, which forced us to be closer to everyone than we were comfortable or accustomed to.

9 I have spoken with all of my brethren here, and to a man they attest that they had no lust for any of the naked women milling about them, but this was not easy. In fact, it was a very difficult thing and took so much of our willpower that we did not enjoy the baths at all, for we were

constantly averting our eyes and working mightily to avert our thoughts.
10 Normally, soaking in the baths is a most blissful experience, where thoughts of the world and the challenges of life vanish for a few hours, and there is a serenity and peace and oneness experienced with the spirit within.
11 This last time was a far different experience, where we had to fight with ourselves instead of communing with ourselves.
12 If we, your Apostles, had so much difficulty, we must consider that the other men of the community had even greater challenges.
13 You have told us that we should be able to have no lust or impure thoughts, even when a naked woman is before us. But to a man, we are sad to say, that we have not reached that pinnacle of virtue, save it is with such focus and willpower that other thoughts are barely possible.
14 You have said that we should be able to look upon a naked woman as a beautiful work of art by Elohim, the master artist, as is man. In truth, when we were in Hyppos, we saw statues and frescoes of naked women, and no effort was needed to keep impure thoughts at bay. But the naked body of a living woman of flesh is entirely different!
15 Forgive me for speaking so much on this subject and being so weak that this is even something of which we must speak. Our humble request is simply that our future visits to the baths can once again be segregated, that the baths may again be one of the great pleasures of life instead of one so full of trepidation and challenge that we simply desire to remain at home."
16 Yeshua stroked his beard for a moment as he contemplated the words of Cephas. Then he said unto him, "Brother Cephas, know that you will never be tested beyond your power to overcome and that all temptation is to help you become stronger.
17 The weak man gives into his lusts, be it for food or idleness or sexual thoughts or proclivities. But the strong man grows mightier by each test of his strength, until the day when that which used to be a test is a test no more, nor even a temptation, for he has overcome himself and his weaknesses become his strengths.
18 Single young men should not be in the close presence of any young woman, save both are fully clothed, for it is too much to ask a young man to hold back the tide of his thoughts when faced with such a powerful temptation as a naked young woman, and that is why no young men were present with us in the baths at Tiberius as I had asked them all to remain in the communities.
19 But for a man who is married and lives and loves the laws of Elohim, there should be no temptation seeing the nakedness of a woman not his wife, especially if she is a sister of light and is not enticing him in any way by her words or actions. Even if that were the case, any sage or Adept of the Celestine Light should be stronger than the adversary—the natural man within.
20 If you are married and fulfilling your duties to serve your wives and give their bodies intimate pleasures, you should be so complete and fulfilled yourself that there is no temptation or test in seeing a woman who is not your wife in nakedness.
21 If this is not true, then it is not your willpower that must be improved, but your attention to the righteous fires of love and lust that should be burning at home.
22 Nevertheless, impure thoughts or unrighteous lust for someone other than your wife is like a poison that can destroy not only you, but also others whose lives you touch.
23 For this cause, until you and your brethren and the other brothers of light in the community can be masters of yourself in this, we shall return to segregation in the baths. And while the Children of Light remain in community in the land of Palestine so shall it stay, until the men of the community can overcome themselves insomuch that virtue of thought prevails without the need for constant willpower and personal surveillance as you have indicated was the case at Tiberius.
24 But the time will come when you are far from this land and in a place where the Community of Light shall stand apart as a world of its own.
25 When you see the dawn of that day, surely it is time to begin to live a higher law of

righteousness, step by step, until soon, other than the single young men, the entire community could go about in nakedness, and there would be no impure thoughts or lust for any to whom you are not married.

26 And even among the single young men, impure thoughts can be overcome if the desire to be in harmony with the Celestine Light of Elohim is strong enough.

27 Much grief is left behind, and many fine qualities emerge, when a young man and a young woman marry shortly after their eighteenth year, as is the custom among most of the diverse peoples living in the land of Palestine.

28 The blessings of this are evident in lasting marriages of love, where righteous lust is satisfied at home with the beloved; where affections do not wander; where children grow up balanced, comforted in their hearts, and delightful in their dispositions.

29 But there are some, such as the Didorites, that disdain marriage and simply choose to take mates and live together for such time as it pleases them.

30 The results of this are equally evident: In the years of early adulthood, lust for others besides their companion is rampant, fornication and adultery are common, relationships seldom last even until the oldest child is of age, and growing up without an example of committed love produces young men who live for lust and are incapable of a deep and abiding love.

31 In years of later adulthood, the passions of lust fade, even into nothingness, leaving those who built their lives upon nothing, with an emptiness that cannot be filled.

32 Verily, I declare unto you, as in all things, you reap what you sow, and those that sow iniquity shall reap the whirlwind. Before the last Child of Light leaves this land, the Didorites shall be no more. Their days are already numbered.

33 They shall be consumed unto death by the fires created from their lusts. That which gave them pleasure shall give them pain, which pain shall increase day by day until many will take their own lives rather than suffer another day.

34 Those who take not their life, but endure the pain hoping for relief from sources unknown, merely prolong the inevitable, and their end shall be all the worse, until the Didorites are no more.

35 So shall misery and unhappiness, and often disease and early death, fall upon all who seek to gratify their carnal lusts without a bond of love and a commitment of fidelity in marriage. And those who live long in the years shall most often find only a great loneliness at the end of their sojourn in life.

36 But even for the lost, there is always redemption if they will repent in fullness and sincerity and choose to live in the light. But let them not procrastinate their day of repentance, for they know not when their last breath shall be, even this day.

37 I tell you these things that you might learn the wisdom that comes from the Celestine Light, that you might understand that impure thoughts and unrighteous lust are most easily conquered by an early marriage, founded on love, where lust is given fulfillment within the marriage, and the man seeks the pleasure of his wife or wives, first and foremost.

38 You have told me this day that in the baths at Tiberius, you had challenges controlling your thoughts for women other than your wife. And I say unto you that if this is so, you must each look to your own marriage, for if you are serving your wife and seeking her loving and lustful pleasure each day, first and foremost, your own lusts will be more than satiated, and being brothers of light, you will then find the nakedness of other women not a temptation at all. Such a thing will not even occur in your thoughts.

39 We speak often of being in the world but not of it, and that which we speak of today is of great measure your fulfillment of that admonition.

40 It is my honor to know each of you. It is my honor to be with you each day. I am uplifted by the strength of your characters, even to speak today of this rather than let it linger and fester in the shadows of your thoughts.

41 You are far-greater men than you allow yourselves to acknowledge. Yet even in your

greatness, you are still as babes compared to the men you will yet become.
42 But if you are to become those men, you must tend to the fires of love and lust within the walls of your own home. Upon this firm foundation, you will have a serenity the world cannot know and a shield through which the darts of temptation cannot penetrate."

CHAPTER 74

The Importance of Dreams

Yeshua speaks about the importance of dreams and how to attain the proper dream state, explaining that it is through our dreams that we commune most directly with Elohim.

The following day, Yeshua asked his Apostles to again meet with him on the hills nearby to the west of Capernaum, and there he taught them once more.

2 After a prayer said by Yudas Iscariot, Yeshua greeted his Apostles by asking, "How were your dreams last night?"

3 "I cannot remember my dreams," answered Toma.

4 "I dreamed of my former life causing people misery by collecting taxes," Mattayah answered solemnly. "I felt guilty even in my dream, but could not change the story that was unfolding."

5 "For me," said Cephas, "I dreamt of catching so many fish that our boat burst apart and sank, returning to port, and we ended up losing everything, both the fish and the boat."

6 "My dream made me apprehensive," stated Yudas Iscariot; "especially as I have seen this same dream before. I saw all of us standing with Yeshua at the edge of an enormous cliff; so big it was that the bottom could not be seen. Yeshua was asking for a volunteer to leap off into the abyss, and none of us seemed so inclined."

7 "I also cannot remember my dreams, except on rare occasions, and remember nothing from last night," said Yohhanan. "And with dreams like Cephas' and Yudas', it is probably for the best."

8 "Nor can I remember mine," added Shim'on, "except for vague feelings and wisps of memories that I cannot bring into fullness."

9 "I was exploring a city in a far-off land," answered Philip. "The people were darker skinned, and some of the buildings were wondrous in design. It was a fulfilling dream because I was able to change what I saw. It was as if part of my awake awareness was inside my dream. For instance, I would come to a fork in the road, and instead of merely watching which road I took in the dream, a part of my waking self was able to help make the decision to go to the right. The dream seemed very real. I do not have dreams like this often, but I take great joy in them when I do."

10 "My dream was of our brothers and sisters in the community," offered Yeshua's brother Yakov. "But there was something different about the community and the people that I cannot remember now that I am awake."

11 "An old man with a long white beard and a goat came to me in my dream," said Yuda, son of Cleophas.

12 "And . . . what?" asked his brother Ya'akov.

13 Yuda shrugged and answered, saying, "And I know not what. That is all I remember."

14 "Well, I am not much better," Ya'akov said consolingly. "There were three maidens in my dream, and my wife was not one of them. They were beckoning me. But to what they were beckoning me, I either did not discover or cannot remember."

15 "I saw great battles, and many people slain," stated Amram sadly. "I saw blood and slaughter all around me. I spoke to those fighting; trying to get them to stop, but it was as if they could not hear me."

16 All of the Apostles had spoken now of their dreams, save for Miriam, and Cephas looked at her and prompted her, asking, "What of your dreams, Miriam? Are they much different than the dreams of men?"

17 Miriam sighed and answered, saying, "Sometimes, my dreams are very different than those of men. Sometimes, they are simply things of a woman's world that men know little of. But I also see things such as all of you have spoken about. And also strange things that none of you have spoken of.

18 Last night, I saw something like the flood of Noah. The rain came day upon day, and the waters rose. We along with our brothers and sisters of the communities and all the people of Palestine were each day moving to higher ground, climbing higher upon the mountains to avoid the rising waters. I went to the top of the tallest mountain and called to our Father and Mother in Heaven for help. A voice came from the clouds, the sweet voice of our Mother, and she said to build boats and leave the world."

19 "What do you understand by that dream?" asked Philip. "How can you leave the world?"

20 "I know not," answered Miriam. "But I suspect that it is a warning of calamities to come and a means of salvation, which I do not yet comprehend."

21 Yeshua nodded his head in approval and said unto them, "We have spoken before about the importance of dreams, and last night, there was a diverse variety among you.

22 Yet it would seem that none of you have fully understood the essential nature and opportunity that dreams present to you each night, nor the potential for harm, and it is for this cause that I speak to you again.

23 Dreams serve many purposes, but there are only a few that I wish to emphasize today.

24 The world in which man dwells and the world in which the Elohim dwell are like the land and the sea from the perspective of a tortoise.

25 The tortoise is a creature of the land. He can look upon the sea, but he cannot go there lest he would perish, even as man can look to our Father and Mother in the heavens but cannot go there to be with them while they are still in the flesh.

26 But it is possible for the tortoise to go to the edge of the sea and walk into it for just a bit so that its feet still firmly touch the land beneath, while its body is immersed in the waters of the sea. Thus it is at one moment, both on the land and in the sea.

27 So it is with your dreams. It is a hallowed time when you remain still in the flesh, but can also touch a part of Heaven and commune directly with our Father and Mother and the angels of Heaven.

28 For those like each of you, who seek the purity of the Celestine Light, this is something you are already doing each and every time you sleep, even though you may remember it not.

29 Dream time is a time when a part of your spirit is freed from the bonds of your body and this world and can visit and commune with all other worlds, and other spirits wherever they may be, as well as travel and explore the world in which you live in ways your physical body never can.

30 But this is also a time of great vulnerability for the unprepared. For even as a part of your spirit can commune directly with the Celestine Realm while you sleep, so too can your spirit visit other worlds while you dream and interact with the spirits of those dwelling there.

31 But even as your spirit of the night can travel far and wide to places beyond the understanding of your day spirit, so too can spirits of those from other worlds and from living people in this world also come to you in your dreams while you sleep and interact with and influence the part of your spirit that remains grounded in this world, even those that would lead you to darkness

and away from the Celestine Light.

32 Therefore, it is greatly important that you set your intentions before you pass into sleep and not just thoughtlessly fall into your dreams.

33 In your nightly prayer with our Father and Mother in Heaven, ask to be shielded from all evil while you sleep and be led only upon dream paths that will uplift and inspire you and reveal greater light and understanding. Ask no less for the night than you do for the hours when you are awake.

34 Thus, you will be protected from that which would do you harm and open to receive a fullness of Celestine Light from Heaven, both that which you ask for and that which is brought to you as a gift.

35 When you seek an answer to a question, small or great, concerning matters either temporal or spiritual, ask in your nightly prayers to be shown the solution in your dreams, and so it shall be given unto you.

36 Even if you do not recall your dreams, a part of your spirit of the day will remember the essence of what your spirit of the night learned and will be pulled into a resonance with it while you are awake.

37 But for the Children of Light, it is very beneficial if their spirit of the day remembers the travels of their spirit of the night.

38 This is even more important for you, my Apostles, as your dreams are the time when you can touch the realms of Celestine Light and receive pure answers for your questions, learn more of your gifts and powers, and gain divine inspiration for your family and your personal growth.

39 Most importantly, it is a time to receive heavenly messengers, to hear the guidance of Elohim and see great visions of things that are to come that you might be prepared to prosper and not perish.

40 Your dream time, when your spirit of the night visits the Celestine Realms, is also your divine school of knowledge where you may learn and practice the mysteries of all things.

41 Each day, I teach you how to use your gifts and develop them into powers that can benefit the Children of Light and the world. But your learning needs not end with our times together, for each moment that you sleep, you can receive further instruction from the angels on high in your dreams.

42 In your travels of the night, you can observe others using their gifts that you might be more prepared to use yours. And you can practice using your powers in places where a mistake causes no pain or damage, but merely becomes an opportunity to learn how to become successful.

43 All of this and much more is available to you as you remember more and more of your dreams. For this cause, I am going to give to you the formulas for three potions which should be taken just before retiring to sleep in the night to help the spirit of the day to remember the dreams of the night.

44 These can cause no harm, only good. No greater insight or memory is gained by taking greater amounts, so do not overindulge lest you overexcite your body and lose the good you could have gained.

45 The first is to be given only to those who are new to the Communities of Light and are not yet fully versed and in harmony with the ways of the light. This potion will allow them to recall much more of their dreams than they have in the past and accelerate their learning and harmony.

46 The second is to be given only to the sages among the Children of Light. It will allow them to clearly remember essential parts of their dreams with an immediate understanding upon awakening of the meaning of their travels of the night.

47 The third is only to be taken by Adepts, for it will bring everything of the other two potions, plus, will bring their night spirit quickly and directly to the Celestine Realms from which they will be given prophecies, secrets, and mysteries to protect and bless the Children of Light and the world upon which you live.

48 Now if your spirit of the day were always in total recall of the adventures of your spirit

of the night, you would become very haggard in appearance, because the time you most easily remember dreams is the time when you are not yet into a deep sleep or are just awakening out of one.

49 Therefore, it would only be by failing to have a sound sleep that you would be able to remember everything you dreamed in the night. While remembering essential parts of your dreams is important, so is a long and sound sleep that your body will wake refreshed and with renewed vigor for the day that dawns.

50 For this cause, when you seek something of great importance, a prophecy or clear guidance, do not seek it in the night, but take your potion and sleep for two hours during the day while the sun is still in the sky. By resting in this manner at a time you are normally active, you will usually not fall into as deep of a sleep as you do in the long and accustomed hours of the night.

51 By sleeping lightly at this time, you will remember much more, even all of your dreams, especially if you set that as your intention before you nap.

52 Lastly, I would encourage you to share dreams you feel are important with one another, not in passing conversation, but after a joint prayer of intention to clearly understand the meaning of the dream.

53 This is most important if you feel you have received a prophecy or direction from Elohim for something greater than your own life, for others, be they a wife or a community, should not be asked to follow blindly, but only after they have prayerfully considered the matter and come to the same conclusion."

54 When Yeshua was finished speaking, he gave his Apostles the formulas for the dream potions and admonished them to commit them to memory.

55 Then one by one, he gave each of the Apostles an interpretation of the dreams they had received the previous night. And this he did even for those who could not remember that which they had dreamed.

56 When he was finished, he spoke once more of the importance of dreams, saying, "As Children of Light and Apostles, you know you have been given great gifts that can blossom into mighty powers. But these powers are to be kept hidden unto you and are only for the Children of Light.

57 Verily, save for the healing of the sick, the people of the world are not prepared for that which has been given to you and would be more apt to be burned by the fire rather than benefited were they to see it."

58 Yeshua smiled and gave a chuckle, adding, "And fearful of the unknown and unexplainable, they might wish to burn you in the fire if they were to witness even a small part of the gifts you have been given.

59 So it is even with your dreams. These are not things to share with the people of the world, save for prophecies Elohim gives unto the twelve to be spoken by them.

60 Your dreams are for you and your stewardships. They are not something the people of the world can comprehend, and to speak of them among them would be foolishly casting your pearls before those who understood not their value.

61 Even among the Children of Light, in both gifts and dreams, let them show themselves capable of holding the lesser gifts before you reveal unto them the greater gifts.

62 But teach the importance of dreams as a foundation of all gifts, both the small and the great, for it is through dreams that man communes most directly with God, and by this means, the small may become great."

CHAPTER 75

Unrighteous Taxation

Yeshua speaks to the Children of Light about taxation, explaining that the ways of the world are not the ways of God. He clarifies when taxes are righteous and when they are not and does the same thing for moneylending and credit.

Confrontation with the Pharisees and Herodians about Taxes

Following the Sabbath that week, a contingent of Pharisees and Herodians came to Capernaum and sought out Yeshua that they might question him, concerning the law, but he was with his family and refused to take the time to see them.

2 The Pharisees were somewhat incensed at what they perceived to be an affront by Yeshua, for they had journeyed from Jerusalem. They tried to come to him when he was sitting with his family and friends by the lake, but they were blocked in their approach by Cephas and Yohhanan and politely asked to return the following day.

3 The next day when the Pharisees and the Herodians approached Yeshua's house, they saw all the Apostles gathered there and a Roman tax collector just storming away in anger. He turned as he parted and yelled at Yeshua, "This was your last opportunity! Rome will not suffer your refusal with impunity; the price you will pay for your folly will be more dear than what you were asked to pay today!"

4 Seeing this, the Pharisees counseled among themselves how they might ensnare Yeshua in his words, and they sent their disciples to question him along with the Herodians.

5 They crafted a trap for him, asking, "Rabbi, we know that you are true and teach the way of Elohim in truth and that you bow before no man of authority, for you regard only the man, not his position.

6 Tell us, therefore, what do you think? Is it lawful to give tribute to Caesar or not?"

7 But Yeshua perceived the wicked intentions of the Pharisees and the servile desires of the Herodians and said unto them, "Why do you attempt to thwart me, you hypocrites?"

8 Beckoning unto them, he said, "Show me the tribute money." And they brought unto him a small coin.

9 And he said unto them, "Whose is this image and superscription?"

10 They said unto him, "Caesar's." Then Yeshua said unto them, "Render therefore unto Caesar the things which are Caesar's and unto God the things that are God's."

11 When they heard these words, they were confounded. And they left him and went their way when they saw that he was not going to speak to them further.

Yeshua Speaks about Overcoming Sexual Lust and Unrighteous Desires for Money and

Power

12 Then Yeshua turned to his disciples and said, "The Pharisees squander their lives pondering upon emptiness, but I ask you to understand the fullness of my words. Therefore, what is Caesar's? What is worthy of tribute?"

13 And a lively contention of opinion arose among the Apostles, with the Zealots saying nothing was Caesar's, because all the land had been seized by force of arms.

14 Others argued that for all the evil the Romans brought upon the people, they also provided works of engineering, defense against invading armies, coin and peace for commerce, and enforcement of civil order, all for which taxes were necessary.

15 To this, Shim'on the Zealot replied, "When the land is ruled by a king of our people, ruling in righteousness before God, such tribute is worthy of the sacrifice, but every coin that goes today to Caesar is merely used to forge another link in our chain of slavery to a foreign master."

16 Then Yeshua raised his hand slightly, and all became quiet, waiting to hear his words. And he said unto them, "Children of Light, you each have caught a sunbeam of truth, but your lights have been shaded by the ways of the world.

17 The ways of God are not the ways of men and never will they be. But the Children of Light must stand firm upon the truth and should live by the teachings of Elohim, even when an ungodly world teaches otherwise.

18 Thus, it is given to you to comprehend the justness and fullness of God that your lives may be fulfilled; that you will shine in the darkness and all the world may see the Celestine Light of truth.

19 If it then be that those of the world who see your light choose to live in darkness, they cannot say on the Day of the Judgment of Resonance that they never saw the path of truth and light.

20 Verily, I say unto you that unrighteous lusts of the flesh and the wicked desire and use of money and power are the three greatest tools of darkness against the children of men.

21 With your sins, be not fooled, nor try to lay blame upon something or someone apart from yourself.

22 There is a shadow of darkness in all men, and even the righteous can be lured away from the light by the persuasive calls of lust, money, and power.

23 Therefore, be vigilant and alert to your own weaknesses, for from the poison of these three great temptations do lives and Kingdoms fall.

24 Concerning lust, each man is the master of himself. Despite all that may be around him, enticing him to sin, in the moment of decision, it is the man who chooses between sin or virtue, the man who chooses to follow the darkness inside him or the light, and the man who will reap that which he has sowed, be it good or bad.

25 With money, the darkness that dwells in all men ever entices them to be selfish and gluttonous to gather more than they need for simple comfort, to build spacious homes and palaces far in excess of their necessity, to eat and drink more than they should with great dishonoring to the temple of their body.

26 Power over others is the most insidious of the three evils in man. If you are in a position of authority, whether it is over your children, your workers, or the citizens of a land you rule, you are meant to be a steward to watch over and protect them, to help them have peace and joy and growth in their lives.

27 To betray this trust with unrighteous dominion is to give in to a great darkness because you are hurting others even more than yourself.

28 But the unrighteous ever seek to be the masters of other men, and whosoever uses coin or debt or taxes or a position of authority to enslave or grievously burden others becomes consumed by darkness.

29 Though coins of gold and silver are a great corrupter of men, they taint kings and the governments of men with a foul stench even more.

30 Succumbed to the darkness within them, rulers unworthy of fidelity are intoxicated by the pleasure of spending the hard-toiled coins of others.

31 It will ever be the dismal lot of the virtuous to be downtrodden by unrighteous kings and rulers unless they stand side by side, unmoving in their light, despite the consequences.

32 And it is only this, an army without swords, of righteous men standing united in the light, willing to follow diverse nonviolent paths in protest that cause the Caesars to fear.

A Child of Light is Always a Child of Light Even When Living in the World

33 "Verily, the Romans are content when the followers of various religions keep separate the practices of their faith and the actions of their life in the world.

34 As long as you act the same as those who have no light while you are interacting in the world, they care not what the Children of Light practice in the privacy of their religion. In this, they see no threat.

35 But for those of true faith, there can be no separation between their way of life in private and that in public.

36 Verily, you cannot be both a man or woman of God and a man or woman of the world, for the ways of the world are darkness and the ways of faith are light.

37 You may live in the world, but you do not have to live like it, nor should you if you are a Child of Light.

38 Even as you are in the world but not of it, so be one in the Celestine Light of Elohim despite all the world may do.

39 Desire and commit unfailing fidelity and support to one another, for a house divided cannot stand.

40 Though you are not many, you are one in the Celestine Light of Elohim. And that is a very great and powerful unity.

41 When one is hurt, all are hurt. When one has joy, all have joy, for you are the Family of Love and Light.

42 Know your convictions well. Ask the Holy Spirit of Elohim to sear your heart with the light of truth that can never be denied or abandoned.

43 For each day is a new dawn and brings new challenges and temptations.

44 Each day, you must choose again whether to walk in the light or be lured into the shadows.

45 As you must choose, please choose the Celestine Light, for in it, there are wonderful joys, both in this life and the next, while darkness brings only never-ending despair.

Life is Meant to Be a Joy, not a Hardship

46 "Verily, I say unto you: Elohim is the God of the living, not of the dead; therefore, know with a certainty that if man does not live by the principles Elohim has given to live in the life, then he will never find enduring happiness while he lives and will be dead to God in the world to come.

47 But Elohim is not a hard taskmaster and gives no commandments to the children of men, save that their lives in the flesh may have greater fulfillment and that they may be better prepared to inherit glory in the world to come as worthy spirit children of God.

48 I say unto you plainly that life is not meant to be a great hardship, but the rulers and taskmasters of men often make it so, with unnecessary wars, unjust laws and unrighteous taxation.

49 Your life is meant to be a joy, a piece of Heaven on earth, no matter the size of your abode or the weight of the coins in your purse.

50 The principles and teachings of Celestine Light were not given simply to help a person be worthy for the world to come, but also as a code to live by, to enrich your life that you may have joy and fulfillment in every moment that you live in the flesh.

51 Were it not for the sins of men and the evils of those who would rule over them, man would have great joy and satisfaction every day.

52 Elohim has put everything upon the earth that man needs to find contentment and

fulfillment, and it is only because of a man's own sins and the wickedness of those who rule that the children of men often live in misery and tribulation instead of joy.

Children of Light Must Stand for That Which is Right

53 "Therefore, I say unto you: let the Children of Light be beacons of hope in the world of despair. Do not bow to the Romans or to the ways of the world of darkness.

54 Live your lives true to the teachings of Celestine Light; live united in your truth, despite the adversity and scorn the world may bring upon you.

55 Living in the Celestine Light of Elohim, you have a gentle peace and fulfillment in your heart that those of the world can never know.

56 In your stance for that which is just and right, you give courage to the fearful and hope to the hopeless.

57 Standing for light, uncowed before the darkness, you open the hearts of those that seek the light, and by the Celestine Light of your life, they will find it.

58 In you, others will see the unwavering Celestine Light of Elohim; the light that allows you to be in the world but not of it; the light that is more powerful than all the compulsions of men and kings.

59 And upon the day that you return from whence you came, our Father and Mother in Heaven will say, 'Well done, good and faithful sons and daughters, enter now into your glory and inherit your Kingdom.'

60 But you should not have to wait for the world to come to have peace and joy and expansion in your life.

61 Therefore, I say unto the Caesars of the world, both the petty and the mighty, those that exercise unrighteous dominion over they for whom they should be faithful stewards: beware.

62 Separate not the sons and daughters of God from their lives of light; else, Elohim will separate your soul from the wonders of Heaven.

63 And even as the chaff is winnowed from the wheat, so your eternity will blow away in a hot and scorching wind.

64 Children of Light, remember who you are. Though you may be treated unjustly by others, remember to always treat those you deal with by choice, with fairness and honesty.

The Just Use of Moneylending

65 "Consider the moneylender. You have heard it said by some that it is just for a lender to charge interest every moon for his service as incentive and reward for his risk.

66 Verily, I say unto you that a fair exchange is due to the lender. But he should not charge interest every moon in the fortunes of his fellow men; else, he is stealing from his brothers and intruding upon the sanctity of their lives.

67 In fairness and light, a fee may be charged when money is first lent, varying based upon the amount that was given. But let it not be in excess of 3 percent of all that was lent.

68 If you seek a moneylender, you are obligated to him for up to 3 percent in total as a fee, for that is a fair and just exchange; but beyond that, you are being robbed and have no obligation to aid a thief in his theft.

69 Therefore, do not barter with the darkness, lest you be overcome by it and consumed."

70 Then Mattayah, who had been a Publican, asked, "Lord of Light, if it is right for a merchant to buy an item for one shekel and sell it for two to the man who willingly buys it, why would it not be acceptable for the lender to loan a shekel for the price of another, or even for only a tenth, to a man who willingly accepts the bargain?"

71 Yeshua answered him, saying, "Gold and silver were given by Elohim for the benefit of all men. In their rarity, they are precious.

72 In the goods of the market, a man has a choice to buy or not to buy. If he does not wish to pay the price of the merchant's dates, he can grow his own or seek out a better bargain with a different merchant.

73 But gold and silver he cannot grow, neither can he make it from the dirt of the ground. Therefore, the moneylender has an advantage over the man that no common merchant can ever have.

74 Where much has been given by Elohim, much is expected in stewardship. The righteous moneylender must therefore be a better steward than the merchant and a more faithful friend to his brothers.

75 Nor should the moneylender be excluded from making greater profit, provided it is done in partnership with the man who seeks assistance.

76 If the moneylender gives only money, he cares not whether the borrower succeeds or fails, for he has been paid in either instance.

77 But if he desires greater profit, let him take greater risk and become a partner with the borrower in the venture to whatever degree they agree upon.

78 Thus then they succeed or fail together. And the moneylender will only invest in that which he strongly feels will succeed, thereby acting as the wise brother to stay the hand of the man who might otherwise risk money foolishly.

Yeshua Speaks about Righteous and Unrighteous Taxation

79 "Regarding taxes, as a man of God, you cannot say that you will not pay tribute to Caesar because the Romans are not the rulers of your choice.

80 If that were so, no king, even one from your own tribe, could ever have sufficient fidelity to support the needs of the Kingdom, for there will always be many standing in opposition with grievances real and perceived.

81 But does that mean that you must simply give whatever tribute it is that the Romans demand? Nay, it absolutely does not.

82 To pay an unjust tax is to demean yourself before the unworthy and to become a slave to that which is unrighteous.

83 If Caesar builds a road and charges a toll to use the road, it is righteous and right for you to pay the tax when you use the road, for it is of benefit to you, and you can choose to not pay it by traveling a different way.

84 If Caesar decrees a tax upon all cloth sold or jugs of wine or jars of dates to help support the government, you can deny this tribute by making your own wine, weaving your own fabrics, and growing your own dates.

85 Therefore, these are not unjust taxes, for when you pay it, you have given your coin with a good heart of your own free will for something you choose to use rather than invest the effort to create your own or use an alternative.

86 But I say unto you that any tax upon the coin or land or property held by a man is among the most evil of darkness.

87 Children of Light that pay such a tax, even under coercion, bare their heart to a poisoned dagger that will prod them ever further into the dark ways of the world and away from the Celestine Light of Elohim.

88 When you give into darkness, you abandon the defense of light, and once abandoned, it becomes easier to do so again and again, until those who once were light become the darkness they once fought.

89 But you are not accountable when that which you gave in light is used for darkness, unless you knew it would be used for evil.

90 When the Publican says one man must pay more than another because of his greater wealth or property, the door is open to all manner of evil and corruption. No longer is a man his own master, but the slave to they who intrude upon his privacy and dictate what must be given from his purse and lands and property.

91 Deceit and lies and much worse spring from this well of evil.

92 Verily, Elohim does not grant any Caesar, great or small, be they governor or priest, the

right to take from a man's purse or lands or crops or flocks or property by compulsion.

93 These are unholy acts against the sanctity of man and the very purpose of the Celestine Light of Elohim to help the Children of Light grow, expand, and have joy, because they take away the privacy and peace of the home and heart, which should be parts of Heaven on earth inviolate, and steal the fruits of the labor of man.

94 Taxes by compulsion upon a man's wealth of coins, lands, or property rob him of the hours, days, and years of his life he has exchanged to acquire them and give those fruits to others, most often they who robbed the fruit and their supplicants, those miscreants who earned wealth not by the sweat of their brow and the keenness of their knowledge, but only by the unrighteous use of their positions of power to steal from those who did.

95 If Caesar decrees that all men must pay ten percent of their coins or property or land or flocks as tribute, that is no different than telling a man he must spend one day out of every ten in prison. Because to earn his coin, property, land, and flocks, he traded hours of his life. He lost hours of his life, which can never be given back to him. Therefore, to take those things is to take away those hours of his life when he is given nothing in return.

96 Taxes by compulsion upon a man's wealth of coins, lands, or property makes him fearful and resentful of the rulers that should be frugal and wise stewards over the peace and welfare of his country, not intruders into the privacy and sanctity of his home and affairs.

97 Intrusion into the sanctity of the family and privacy of a man and the forced removal of his wealth by those who rule invite even honest and righteous men to do evil to avoid evil.

98 Be not deceived. The Children of Light who meekly give tribute to Caesar when their privacy is invaded and their wealth demanded are supporting darkness instead of light and are not worthy of me.

99 Only to Elohim should a man tithe 10 percent of his annual increase, and this by choice and love for God, not by compulsion or fear of punishment.

100 Increase is not a measure of a man's wealth, but the amount that year that he gained above his basic needs to care for his family.

101 Therefore, I say unto you: be not in doubt. If a Publican violates your privacy and tells you that you must pay to Caesar the amount he demands, he is a minion of darkness.

102 Hold your light high and give nothing to darkness of your own free will.

103 Be you rich or poor, do not give to Caesar that which you labored for, trading precious hours of your life because of love for your family and dignity for yourself, simply because Caesar so decrees.

104 But neither deny paying any taxes at all, for regardless of which Caesar rules, you live in a community that is part of a still-larger community bound with common bonds.

105 As part of a larger whole, benefiting from common association, you owe it to your neighbors to contribute to society in ways that benefit everyone.

106 But let those ways be by your choice, not by theft of the privacy of your home and the sanctity of your property or by any form of coercion or compulsion by Caesar or his Publicans.

107 If you let Caesar steal your wealth by compulsion, be it small or great, Caesar will think that he is the master and you are but a servant. A righteous king is a steward who governs with the consent of the governed to not rise up in rebellion, by providing a just government; else, even the dictator is overthrown.

108 But if Caesar considers you to be a slave, you are without merit. Your treasure will be taken by force in any amount Caesar desires and will surely be perverted for purposes you know not and would not support.

109 And once perverted, it will surely continue to be used not for the good of the governed, but to enrich the unrighteous and the thieves and for purposes in complete opposition to the teachings of the Celestine Light of Elohim.

110 Therefore, do not let the coin earned by your worthy desires for good be given under coercion or compulsion to enrich the Caesars, big or small. Do not allow the coins you sacrificed

hours of your life to obtain to be taken from benefit to your wife and your children, to instead build palaces for Caesars and soften the lives of their slothful supplicants. Do not acquiesce to government theft that leaves you with less that they may have more.

111 That which is taken by Caesar in unrighteousness will surely be used for unrighteous purposes.

112 The fruits of your labor, they will give to the wicked and lazy who whisper vanities unto them. They will stab you with your own dagger; they will use your money for great evils that you would countenance not at all.

113 Verily, if you pay the Publican under coercion or compulsion from the fruits of your labors, you are helping to build the Kingdom of darkness, not the Kingdom of Celestine Light.

Taxes That Are Just

114 "Nevertheless, if there are to be communities of men, there must always be taxes to support those things which are for the common good of all.

115 But let these be just taxes, not given to excess beyond the need, not given to enrich the few upon the backs of the many, or forcing a man to contribute to something which his faith denies and decries.

116 For this cause, only taxes upon use or consumption of items not your own can be justified before God. In this way, each person is free to choose whether to pay the tax or not, by choosing to consume or not.

117 If Caesar wants more tribute, he may tax greater the items of luxury that only those who have more wealth can afford. But even in this, only by their choice to buy that which is so taxed, not by compulsion.

118 And it is righteous that Caesar should tax, even great taxes, upon vanities such as expensive wines and carpets and spices and resins and gems, for these are luxuries that no man needs, but only desires. They are beyond the means of the poor who are therefore not taxed, and if a rich man does not wish to pay the tax, he merely does not buy the goods.

119 As only goods of luxury are taxed greatly, the greater share of money for the king comes from those with the greatest wealth, but this is by their choice, which is pleasing unto God, and not by compulsion, which is pleasing only unto despots and devils."

Importance of Standing Up for Truth and Righteousness

120 Then spoke Abraham of Arimathea, one who had followed to hear him speak, saying, "It is a good thing that you say, Rabbi, and would that it was so that all men and kings would act this way. But I fear that if I refused the tax collectors when they demanded the fruits of my toil, then they would instead take the blood of my body."

121 Yeshua answered him, "Fear not those that can harm your body, only those that can injure your spirit.

122 It is better to stand for right than to cower in wrong, and evil is defeated not by acquiescence, but by action founded upon conviction and anchored in faith.

Willingness to Move to another Country for Freedom and Justice

123 "Verily, Rome is not all the world. If your burden is too great in this country to bear and the price you would pay for defiance too severe, then denounce the land of your birth and ask Elohim to guide you to a land of greater succor that knows not the yoke of Caesars who tax the people with unrighteousness.

124 For Elohim hears the prayers of the virtuous and will ever bless the worthy who seek the help of Heaven.

125 Verily, if must needs be, it is better to take your family and live in a tent in the wilderness than to live in a city in a land where you must exist under the yoke of unrighteous taxation or compulsion.

126 And atop the mountains of the wilderness and the heights of the islands of the sea, the

Children of Light will always find refuge from the world, protection from Caesar, and abundance from God.

127 Open your ears and hear my words. Let them settle in your heart, never to be forgotten. What I speak of is no small matter, but of great importance to your spiritual well-being in this life and the next.

Make Peace and Pay Righteous Taxes

128 "Be wise, not foolish, in your dealings with Caesar.

129 Remember the olive branch of peace. Speak with the Publicans if they will listen with an open heart.

130 Let it be known that you are not opposed to taxes, even great taxes upon the goods that you might buy, but only upon intrusion into the sanctity and privacy of your home and personal life and taxes upon your coins or land or property by coercion or compulsion.

Stand Strong and Together for Light and Right When Persecuted

131 "But do not fight Caesar to the death in rebellion of compulsive taxes, for where would your family be then?

132 But neither simply give in to the unrighteous demands of Caesar and the Publicans. Be willing to suffer pain and even imprisonment for the Celestine Light of Elohim in your life.

133 Stand ever together with your brothers in the light, for you are the Family of Light.

134 If one is persecuted, let all others help him freely as they can, both openly and in secret. If one is imprisoned, let the others care for his family.

135 Refuse to turn back upon that which you know to be right.

Refuge in a Land Far Away

136 "If after all you can do, Caesar continues to intrude into your privacy and steal from your coins, your flocks, your lands or property or punish you for not obeying his dictates, then you must leave the land of your birth and seek one where you can live in the Celestine Light of Elohim that you have been given.

137 Be that land a foreign one with customs strange or a Community of Light atop a mountain tall or a distant isle in the sea, it is better to live righteously, in the Celestine Light, apart from all you have known than under the evil cloak of darkness worn by the unrighteous.

138 Know this with all of your heart and mind: If you walk in the Celestine Light, Elohim will always walk with you."

CHAPTER 76

Circles of Power

Yeshua meets with the Children of Light from the four communities on Lake Gennesaret and first explains that no one should be their lord or master, but they should be their own master and lord. He follows this with some prophecies concerning the Children of Light in the years directly after the time of his pending departure. He says that what he has established among them is not a religion but a sacred society. He then speaks about the three Circles of Power, the Katah of three, the Shanar of six, and the Q or Q-rom of twelve and how they are to be utilized, including the circumstances surrounding them.

And it came to pass that on the Sabbath of that week, Yeshua called all of the Children of Light from the four communities on Lake Gennesaret to meet together near Capernaum.

2 And as he had done in the past, he stood in a boat just a few paces offshore to address the crowd, and many were the people present, for the community had been growing with new members in recent months, and there were also curious nonmembers in the crowd as there always were whenever Yeshua spoke in public. Even so, he spoke only to the Children of Light.

3 "My dear brothers and sisters of light," he began, "the time comes soon when I will no longer be among you as we are today, and I wish to prepare you for the days to come that you may prosper in your spirits and your families and your communities."

4 Upon hearing that he would soon be departing, many cries of disbelief went up from the crowd, and many voices were heard to say, "No, Master, do not go" and "Stay with us, dear Lord."

5 Hearing this, Yeshua rebuked them with love, saying, "I am not your Lord, neither am I your master. I am your brother, and you are my brothers and my sisters. Call no man Lord or master, be they a noble, a great teacher, or even a king.

6 For you are your Lord and you are your master, and only if you esteem yourself not at all is there a place in your life for anyone else to be your Lord or master.

7 And if you esteem yourself not at all, then you need to get on your knees and pray mightily to our Father and Mother in Heaven from whence you have come, until you feel their love in your heart, even more than you feel the bonds of your earthly parents.

8 For you are children of spirit of our Heavenly Father and Mother. Your physical body has come from your earthly parents, and it shall someday turn to dust. But your spirit was born from our Father and Mother in Heaven, even as mine was, and it shall never taste death, but live forever.

9 Children of Light, Children of God, know who you are, and with humility and understanding, esteem yourself greater than any lord or master!

10 Verily, I say unto you: If you see me high upon a mountain, remember that I have called

you my brother and I have called you my sister. If I esteem you so greatly that I would call you my brothers and sisters, can you esteem yourselves any less?

11 If you would prove to Elohim that you are Children of Light worthy of all that has been given to you, then begin by loving and honoring yourself and treating everyone with respect that reciprocate the honor. And debase yourselves to none, for you are Children of Light, children of the divine Father and the Mother, and there can be no greater glory than that.

12 The time has come that the Children of Light must begin to blossom into their true flowers, such flowers as have never been seen upon the earth.

13 I will still remain among you for some time and shall be teaching my Apostles many more of the secrets and mysteries of the Elohim. Both while I remain and after I have departed, they shall teach to you that which I taught them, as you are worthy and prepared to receive the knowledge.

14 That the days of your greater enlightenment will more quickly be upon you, hear now some of the important foundations of the greater Celestine Light.

15 In the years to come, the Communities of Light will be no more upon Lake Gennesaret.

16 The Children of Light from these communities shall separate into smaller groups and shall travel and settle in diverse places, in foreign lands, for a time.

17 Then once again, most of you shall be reunited as one body and, from that moment, know a glory and wonder such as you never have imagined.

18 After I have departed, many religions will grow up upon the world based upon a select few of my teachings, sprinkled liberally with the teachings and desires of men. In generations to come, one of these religions shall be great upon all the world, and many will follow after it.

19 You will see its early form and its cousins in many of the lands you shall travel to, but do not associate yourself with any of them. Neither support them nor fight against them. You are to be in the world but not of it. Like all the religions that came before and all that shall come after they are of the world—creations of men, therefore, not in harmony with who you are.

20 Know that I have established a sacred society among you. Call it a religion if it brings you comfort, but it is not mere beliefs and traditions that you hold, but a way of life and a wondrous path to eternity.

21 The number three is its foundation, for this is the number of the trinity of Elohim: the Father, the Mother, and the Son.

22 Three is also the smallest number in which you may gather to amplify your gifts substantially and cast forth your power for the good of the Children of Light and the world.

23 Three doubles to six, and this is the smallest number that the Children of Light may gather together to act with authority in the name of Elohim and call upon the higher powers of the Celestine Light.

24 But when using your gifts, power is never added, but always multiplied at least. Therefore, the power of six in relation to three is not doubled, but sextupled or more.

25 Six doubles into twelve and this is an important foundation of the Family of Light. Even as there are twelve Apostles to guide you with all the light of Heaven given unto them, so should you gather into small groups beginning with three and growing to twelve that you might edify and support one another and call upon the greater Celestine powers as one multiplied as many.

26 Choose three and six and twelve who are most compatible and harmonious with your own spirit and thoughts that your power may be more magnified and your gifts more revealed.

27 Let this be your family within the Family of Light. Form a great bond between you that will allow you to act with power far beyond your numbers.

28 And call a group of three a Katah, and a group of six a Shanar, and a group of twelve a Q or Q-rom.

29 Therefore, a Shanar is composed of six individuals who are not part of a Katah or from two Katahs. A Q is formed from two Shanars or four Katahs.

30 Let each meet in times when all the aeons of the Celestine Realm flow most freely upon

the earth. Let the Katahs meet together often when the sun is at its zenith to plan and carry out good in the world and benefit to their lives and the lives of the Family of Light.

31 And let the Shanars do likewise weekly and the Q upon the evening of the rising full moon, or the rising or setting sun, or the sun at its zenith, or in all cases, more often, in a time that is appropriate, if the circumstances before you call for it.

32 To bring about the greatest magnification of your gifts, a Katah should be either all male or all female, or both male and female when composed of three Children of Light that are joined together in marriage to one another.

33 A Shanar may be a mixture of both male and female, but only if it is composed of married groups of equality, either three of two or two of three. Otherwise, it also must be either male or female.

34 A Q may be either all male or all female or a combination of both. If it has both male and female members, then it must be composed only of equal married groups: either six of two, four of three, three of four, or two of six. Four of three is inherently a very powerful combination.

35 Any Child of Light of age, holding the priesthood, may belong to a Katah, Shanar, or Q. But only those living in virtue should participate in the Circles of Power, lest the power of the circle be diminished or even disrupted.

36 Verily, if a Circle of Power is to do the good and bring forth the beneficial aeons that are called upon with faith and love, it is necessary for the circle to be accurately cast, built from the foundation of virtue, and purified of evil.

37 If a member of the circle is not pure, the circle cannot be pure, nor bring forth the good desired.

38 Therefore, let those in need of greater virtue first repent before Elohim and those of the circle, before they enter into that sacred space.

40 Nor forget that greater power is also manifested even when only two are joined in harmony for common purpose or when four or five, seven, eight, nine, ten, or eleven are united. But it is the three, six, and twelve that are the most powerful alignments.

41 It is also a goodly thing from time to time to join one or more Q-roms together into larger Circles of Power to affect a great good or conquer a great evil or to join as a congregation of several Q-roms.

42 Now it may have come to the attention of some of you men that by and large, women tend to be able to exhibit a greater range and potency of their gifts and powers of Celestine Light than men, and you may have wondered why this is so.

43 Elohim created men stronger of body and muscle than women, and it is to their physical strength that men by choice first look.

44 Women lacking the physical strength of men more readily turn to the alternatives of their divine gifts of Celestine Light and more easily understand and utilize them.

45 Also, as I have spoken of before, long, healthy hair is a great storehouse of power, and almost without exception, all of our women have long, healthy hair.

46 However, many men keep their hair shorter, and some have either no beard or a closely cropped beard. Even I do not let my beard or my hair grow endlessly. Therefore, because of this, it is a greater challenge for most men to call upon and activate the greater powers of Celestine Light.

47 Whenever a Shanar or Q consists of both men and women, let an Adept always lead. And the leader of a Shanar or Q should be known as the Xeja, for only those who connect both their heart and their divine self can truly know the powers of Celestine Light. If an Adept is not a part of the group, let a Sage lead.

48 But remembering these differences between men and women, let the leader in all things concerning the use of gifts of Celestine Light be a woman whenever there are both men and women of the same priesthood within the group.

49 Even if there is a man in the group of a higher order within that priesthood, let it still be

the woman of the lower order within that priesthood, who is the leader of the Shanar or Q, if she is within one degree of the man, with the most senior man assisting her and taking responsibility for the management of all things other than the use of the gifts of power.

50 But if there is only one Adept in a Shanar or Q and it is a man or if the separation between the senior man from the senior woman is greater than one degree, then the man must be the Xeja because of his greater experience and knowledge, with the most senior female priesthood bearer of the same order standing to assist.

51 Remember these things and do them, and your Shanars and Q-roms will be guided down the paths that shall most greatly benefit the manifestation of the gifts of all the members.

52 In the Katah let none be the leader, but all be equal in authority.

53 Let what transpires within your circles be kept as sacred secrets beyond the circles, excepting among husbands and wives, among whom there should be no secrets. But beyond your sacred circles, your enemies are more numerous than you know, both in the world and beyond it, including both the intentional and the misguided.

54 Beyond the Family of Light, our ways cannot be understood, and men fear what they do not understand. Therefore, let none outside the circle see or hear what transpires within the circle. Give them no knowledge and they will have nothing to fear.

55 Therefore, let no one become a member of a Katah, Shanar, or Q that has not first taken a vow of secrecy, not only to keep the mysteries of the circle and the Children of Light from the people of the world, but even under torture to not reveal the secrets or other members of the Family of Light to those who would do us harm.

56 And let no Child of Light who has taken the vow of secrecy ever reveal their gifts or powers to the people of the world, those we call Ganish, for profit or pride or under coercion, lest they bring the Curse of the Vow upon themselves and their life becomes unbearable.

57 Please understand, my dear brothers and sisters, this is not a curse from Elohim or any of the Children of Light. Even as you are drawn to your reward in the life to come by your own resonance, so the Curse of the Vow picks away from inside of you, created by your own revulsion and guilt if you break the vow.

58 Even though you might feel you have no guilt or sorrow and care not for breaking the vow, your spirit forever remains true to the Celestine Light and will call justice upon you despite your denials.

59 Let disputes within the Katahs be settled by speaking to one another with love, respect, and understanding of different points of view.

60 Let disputes within a Shanar or Q be settled likewise and if an amicable resolution is not forthcoming, let the Xeja decide and all abide by that decision with honor and love in their heart or depart forever from that circle.

61 For there can be no divisive forces within the circle if the good you would do is to be done.

62 Let no one join to more than one Katah, Shanar, or Q at one time. If you for any reason must leave a Katah, Shanar, or Q or seek to join with another, seek first the permission of all within the circle of which you are already a part, with the Xeja being the final voice of decision.

63 Each of you will find prayers and spells and potions and all manner and means of exerting your gifts, both individually and within your circles, and some of these will be very potent.

64 Let the greatest of these within a Q be recorded for all within the circle to learn from, but encode it within a crystal after the manner of the Savasi that the eyes of the Ganish can never see it.

65 Make efforts each day to commit all things concerning gifts and the manifestations of powers and formulas and all secret things of the Children of Light to memory; that the secrets may never fall into the hands of the unbelievers.

66 And if it would seem that a written record was in danger of falling into the hands of the Ganish, let that record be first destroyed. But to prevent this as a possibility, it is always best, when something must be written, for it to be encoded within a crystal in the ways of the Savasi.

67 The time will come when some of you will be captured by the Ganish and brought before the unjust justice and commanded to reveal the secrets of the Children of Light.

68 If you are among these, answer naught, nor reveal anything of the secrets of the Children of Light, but keep your faith in Elohim.

69 Connect with your brothers and sisters with your minds as my Apostles shall teach all of you to do, and by that means, with faith in Elohim, plan and execute an escape from the hands of the Ganish. Know that in this situation, using all powers of the Celestine Light known to you are permissible to counter those that oppose you, except the taking of life, unless it is to prevent your own from being taken.

70 Always remember you are the lights of the world, but the world cannot comprehend your light. Therefore, spend your days doing good, even being in service to the world that can comprehend you not, but do so as the hidden Children of God. Let the world see your good and glorify Elohim, but let them not see in you what they cannot understand.

71 Do not boast or threaten or wish ill upon anyone. You have been given much, and where much is given, great things are expected.

72 Though you may be mighty, that should never be shown to the people of the world except to save your life or protect your family or brothers and sisters. Even then, let the manifestation of your gifts of Celestine Light not be understood by the Ganish to be connected to you if at all possible.

73 Let the world see the great things that come from your actions, but never see that the actions came from you.

74 Nor may you accept payment for the good that you do with your gifts in the world, whether as an individual or a circle or a community, it is the same.

75 You may teach the Ganish who wish to learn, some of the simple foundations of the gifts that even they possess or knowledge of healing or art, and for this, you may ask payment, as a teacher is worthy of their time and knowledge.

76 But when you do good in the world or among your brothers and sisters of light, neither seek nor accept payment. But reciprocation of energy in the form of a good deed done for you is acceptable and desirable as it allows those that have benefited from your actions to grow even more by giving thanks in reciprocation.

77 Now there is one use of your gifts which you can freely exercise, for it cannot be discovered by the Ganish, and that is to influence their minds to favor those causes which you desire. But your causes can only be righteous, and none may be harmed by the outcome.

78 Therefore, if you need a piece of land and are offering a fair price, it is permissible to say a prayer and cast a spell to motivate the land owner to sell to you that which you desire, if doing so will harm neither him nor anyone else. But that qualifier must be specifically included in the words of your spell.

79 Or if you are fishing, it is permissible to say a prayer or cast a spell that your net may be filled with fish as long as you are not calling them out of the net of your neighbor.

80 And in this manner, you may use this gift to your benefit in all things, used with honor and harm to none.

81 You sit empowered with great gifts of Celestine Light. You meet together often in Katahs and Shanars and Q-roms. Now what is it you are to do?

82 Each time you meet, consider what good you can do with your gifts of power that is within your capabilities and brings a greater light.

83 Consider these as worthy of your blessings: yourself, your circle, your families, your community, your world, and all the people and animals therein, for Elohim has given unto the Children of Light to be the good stewards over all.

84 Be ever mindful of identifying and subduing vortexes of the darkness, as this is a single action that benefits many.

85 It is also given unto you to see and feel the presence of the myriad of entities of darkness

that the Ganish cannot see or feel. When these are encountered, banish them to outer darkness and heal the void and the wounds from where they had been.

86 When you see great injustice in the world among the Ganish, do not turn away, for you are still a part of them even if they are not a part of you.

87 Therefore, use your gifts to subdue the evil that lurks in men and bring out the good; that they might become more harmonious and forgiving with their fellow men and treat one another and the earth and all its inhabitants with greater respect.

88 Among almost all people, the goodness of Elohim, their creator, permeates their soul. However, because of cruel circumstances and the great challenges of mortality, their inner light may be hidden beneath a surface that seems dark and foreboding.

89 But love and light and a little help from your circle may be all they need to bring forth their greater light. See this then as another good you can do.

90 And if they cannot be helped, if their darkness has become too deep, you may use your gifts to lessen the harm they can do to others in the days that remain to them.

91 It is also given to you to understand all things regarding the healing of the body from infirmities and sicknesses small and great. Lovingly heal the people of the world through herbs and potions and techniques of renewal and life.

92 Unto those who have a great light, you may bless with a healing using your gifts of spirit to call upon the aeons of Heaven, if the situation is such that your herbs, potions, and knowledge of healthy life would not avail.

93 This is your cause upon the earth: to harm none and do good to many.

94 Though you may be hidden from the world, through your good actions, your Celestine Light shines ever brighter upon them. And when you are in the service of this world, you are in the service of Elohim."

CHAPTER 77

The Power of Sound

Yeshua speaks to the Children of Light from the four communities of Lake Gennesaret at Capernaum about the power of rhythmic sound when performed individually or in groups in harmonious patterns with focus, passion, and intention.

The following Sabbath, Yeshua once again gathered the Children of Light from the four communities together on the shore of Lake Gennesaret at Capernaum.

2 And he spoke unto them, saying, "Today, I will give you pearls of great price, concerning the power of sounds and more.

3 These sounds include the sounds of the earth and the animals of the earth, but more importantly, intentional sounds that you make, especially when gathered together in a Katah, a Shanar, or a Q and focused upon a purpose.

4 The spoken voice alone can become a magnification of your inner or group power. All that is required is passion and unwavering focus upon that of which you speak.

5 This activates and expands your aura which calls in still greater powers from beyond to aid you in empowering the words that you speak.

6 Beyond the spoken word, there are chants, of both the individual and a group, where the same word or words are repeated rhythmically, with each repetition acting as a lodestone to call in greater aeon from beyond to combine with your aura and be sent forth with greater power.

7 In a like manner, the singing of songs or whistling or humming can invoke greater powers to swirl upon you or the group that blends their sounds melodiously.

8 In this, harmony and resonance of the voices combined are vital, as disharmony or discordant sounds will usher in energies of darkness rather than Celestine Light.

9 The same is true for instruments of music. The sounds they make should bring a peace and uplifting of the spirit if they are intended to magnify the Celestine Light.

10 Therefore, with either your instruments or your voice, create harmonious melodies that stir the soul.

11 And create with intention. Have a purpose in your song or music beyond simply soothing sounds to be enjoyed.

12 Each of the seven aeons of the body resonate to certain sounds and music, and when they are in resonance, they heal and strengthen and expand.

13 Because rhythm and repetition are used to magnify specific aeons, drumming is very powerful in calling in and enlarging the desired energies, especially the drums of deep sound—not tinkling, and drums that beat in harmony with many others, with increasing and decreasing tempos as is appropriate.

14 Let drumming begin with the beat of the heart and increase in tempo and complexity. But harmony and unison are essential, and only those who can beat as one, even with complex rhythms, should drum together.

15 Lastly, once entranced into a focus of mind, heart, and harmonic aura, by the rhythmic sounds, if you are moved to dance, not aimlessly, but in unison and harmony with others—naturally, without thought to the union—you greatly amplify the aeons of that which you are seeking to accomplish. But if your dance is not in harmony with the others, you sever the link to the greater powers.

16 These things, I shall teach to my Apostles by word and example, and they shall teach them to you in like manner. In this, even in your idle hours or those at work, you will find greater power from a simple whistle or song or humming of melodies.

17 And when you join in your Katahs and Shanars and Q's, your powers will be greatly magnified and your goals more quickly and easily accomplished.

18 In all these forms of sound used to call upon and magnify powers, practice both alone and in groups that you might become more perfect, before you begin in earnest to use sound for a greater good, for disharmony of sound or movement prevents the energy from building.

19 Therefore, only those who have proven the ability to be in harmony in sound and movement should join together in a circle, using sound or movement to magnify the power of Celestine Light. Else, the power of the circle is diminished rather than enhanced.

20 Let those who are still challenged to find harmony of sound or movement with others watch only, humming quietly to themselves in harmony, that they may begin to feel the oneness and unity in their heart and aura, until the day that they are prepared to become one in the circle, without thought, guided true, simply by the rhythm of their heart and spirit.

21 Each of these skills can be added one upon another to bring still greater power. Therefore, drumming and dancing together are more powerful than either alone, even as drumming and dancing and singing or chanting are more powerful still.

22 Once you have built the power of sound and raised it to a crescendo in volume, beat and complexity, stop it in an instant, in unison, to release the power for your desired goal.

23 In this, it is best to find a single simple word that sums up your purpose, to shout out in unison as the sound ends abruptly. This is the surest way to send forth your desire with the greatest and most focused power.

24 If you are playing musical instruments, it is best to begin with a single instrument such as the beat of a drum. To this, add another instrument in perfect harmony. Once the two have become one, add a third, and once the three have become one, add a fourth. In this way, you weave a spell of magnificent power.

25 Nor does the weaving of spells of sound need be limited to musical instruments. When the second is added to the first, perhaps it is not an instrument but a voice in song or voices singing or whistling in harmony and adding to the melody.

26 Raising your vocal tones up the musical scale is another way to magnify the powers you are calling upon. This should be led by the person with the best voice and most perfect tone that the others can most harmoniously follow and again should be ended suddenly with a unified shout of a single simple word to send forth your intention.

27 You are Children of Light, which implies that your very soul essence embraces the essence of rhythmic sound and music and song and movement, for these are among the foundations of the powers of Celestine Light that can be manifested by the Children of Light, especially when they are gathered together for common purpose.

28 Therefore, take time to practice that you may become proficient; that in your proficiency you will be able to join with your brothers and sisters of light and become a sound that touches souls, that carries upon the wind and is felt around the world."

CHAPTER 78

The Power of Colors

Yeshua speaks to the Children of Light about the significance and power of colors used in healing and all manner of health of the body, with the greatest power of colors being the sun, a direct conduit to Elohim.

The following Sabbath, Yeshua once again asked all of the Children of Light from the four communities to meet together on the shore of Lake Gennesaret at Capernaum so that he might speak to them from a boat floating a few feet from shore, held in place with a line from the bow to land and an anchor cast off the stern.

2 Many visitors were also present from cities near and far, including Pharisees and a number of people with afflictions that had come to be healed.

3 Standing high on the prow of the boat, with Cephas offsetting his weight by sitting in the stern, Yeshua spoke to the Children of Light, saying, "You are called the Children of Light because you have chosen to walk in the path the Father and Mother have given for the exaltation of their children.

4 You have chosen not to take the easy road of the world, but have risen to the challenge of the higher road of Elohim that you might reap the greater rewards, both in this world and the next.

5 Unto you is given greater knowledge that you might manifest greater manifestations of the Celestine Light with the gifts of God that have been given unto you.

6 Today, I shall reveal to you some of the secrets of colors and how to call upon and use the powers of colors to manifest wonderful things, both great and small."

7 What about the Pharisees who are here?" yelled out someone from the crowd. "Do we want them to know the secrets of our gifts?"

8 Yeshua answered, saying, "Today, I speak of foundations it would be helpful for everyone to understand, even Pharisees. But even this will be more than they can do. Even if a man knows the winding secret path up the mountain to the treasure room, if he does not have the inner strength to make the climb, no matter how much he desires, the treasure will never be his.

9 Verily, the greater treasures of Elohim can only be found by those who seek the true Celestine Light and live it in their lives.

10 The lost will remain lost, until they repent and humbly seek to live in the fullness of the light.

11 Until the blind hold up the torch of truth in all its brilliance, naught but the beginning of the path up the mountain can be seen through a fog, and the way to the pinnacle will forever be beyond their sight.

12 You have heard me say to cast not your pearls before swine when you are among them, for

they will not value the sacred and will trample it underfoot. But these today are just a pearl or two, not a great strand. It is all right for the Pharisees to hear of them, for they will no more be able to do them than a swine that can do nothing but wallow in the mud.

13 But do not turn your face in disregard to them, but be friendly and courteous to all who reciprocate.

14 Even among your enemies, you might sometimes find a friend who, when hearing and seeing that which they have never before imagined, might find a new and beautiful music playing in their soul, which cannot be denied, even until they desire to become one with you in the Celestine Light.

15 As to color, it is much more than you see with your eyes and what you do see is not what it is.

16 The colors that you see—white, black, blue, red, green, yellow, and all the colors that your eyes behold—are simply signposts guiding you to doors which open upon different aeons of power. Understand the signposts and you will know which door to open in your hour of need.

17 It is not here that you will learn the specifics of each color of power, but I shall teach them to my Apostles, and they shall teach them to the Children of Light in small groups within your weekly meetings in the School of Mysteries.

18 What I wish to share with you today are some examples of how you can utilize the powers behind the doors of color.

19 Colors can be used to move emotions and desires in any direction you wish, both your emotions and desires and those of others. The movement remains a subtle but powerful force in place as long as the color remains present with an undeniable presence.

20 This may not seem like a great power, but it can be if you understand the fullness of how it can be used."

21 Then Yeshua walked to the back of the boat and facing the lake, he waved his hand over the water and suddenly, it was alive with the glint of silver sparkles shimmering on its surface.

22 The crowd pushed to the edge of the lake in wonder as they saw the surface of the water behind the boat turn into a million sparkling silvery jewels.

23 In less than a minute, many fish came up from the bottom of the sea, both small and large, and started to thrash about near the surface of the water with some leaping above it.

24 Before five minutes had passed, the surface of the lake behind the boat was alive with hundreds of large fish and thousands of smaller ones, all thrashing and leaping in an excited frenzy. Over a dozen of the large fish leaped right into the boat of Cephas.

25 Then Yeshua waved his hand once more over the water. Immediately, the sparkling silvery color disappeared. In a short moment, the fish ceased to move about the surface, and within another few minutes, they had all vanished.

26 Yeshua looked back toward the crowd and smiled. Many of them had walked into the lake to get a closer view, and several were chest deep in the lake, holding onto the gunwales of the boat. There were many fishermen among them, and one and all, they were wide-eyed in wonder at what they had just witnessed.

27 "Praise Elohim!" shouted one of the fishermen holding onto the boat.

28 "We will never need nets again!" exclaimed another.

29 "We will become the wealthiest, most successful fishermen in all of Galilee!" added a third.

30 "In all the world!" proclaimed a fourth.

31 Hearing this, Cephas moved forward in the boat with some anger showing on his face, and after receiving Yeshua's permission to speak, he said unto them, "Foolish men, think you that we can abuse the gifts of Elohim for our personal gain? If you thus called the fish, there would soon be no fish left in the sea, and then what of your livelihood? What of your stewardship?"

32 Cephas was about to say more, but Yeshua put his hand upon his shoulder and moved in front of him to speak to the crowd once again. And he said unto them, "You imagine that using your gifts could make you wealthy, but that is not why they were given to you, and should

attempt be made to so use them, they would be as empty in you as they are in the Pharisees.

33 The gifts of the divine Mother and Father to their Children of Light are intended to serve the purposes of Elohim. Attempt to use them for any other purpose and you will see them no better than you can your hand before your face on a dark and starless night.

34 I showed this to you, not to give you an easier way to catch fish, but to demonstrate the power of color to you, that you might understand the great good you can do amongst yourselves and in the world by calling upon the aeons of color."

35 "It is just as well," replied one of the fishermen still holding onto the gunwale of the boat. "Surely, none of us could make this miracle anyway. It is a miracle of Yeshua, he who is chosen of God. So why do we speak as if this is something we could also do?"

36 Yeshua looked down upon the man who had spoken and said unto him, "Good brother Amos, kindly come up into the boat." And reaching down, Yeshua grasped his right forearm to the right forearm of Amos and easily lifted him over the gunwale and into the boat to the great surprise of Amos.

37 Yeshua put his arm over the shoulder of Amos and turned again to the crowd, saying, "It was my intention to speak today of colors, but I see there is a more important lesson that is begging to be learned.

38 Please know, my dear brothers and sisters, that my time is precious, and if I am with you today or any day, it is because that is the most valuable investment of my time and yours. I am not given to idle chatter, nor do I seek fame or adulation.

39 If I am here before you, showing the gifts of Heaven to you and teaching you of them, it is not so you can be in awe of that which I can do, but that you can understand the greatness of that which you can do.

40 I am going to tell brother Amos now the secret of making the sparkling silver color upon the lake. It is very simple, and as long as you are virtuous in your life, have a worthy need, and sufficient faith, any of you can also do it."

41 Then Yeshua whispered into the ear of Amos, who nodded his head repeatedly as he listened to the instructions of Yeshua, the smile on his face growing larger with every nod.

42 After a few minutes, Yeshua finished instructing Amos, and Amos walked to the stern of the boat, facing the lake as Yeshua had, while Yeshua and Cephas remained amidships.

43 Standing on the stern, Amos looked back at Yeshua, and Yeshua nodded his head to indicate that he should continue.

44 Amos closed his eyes and stood silently for a few minutes in contemplation and prayer. Then opening his eyes, he waved his hand across the water as Yeshua had done, and a tiny circle of silver about the width of the boat immediately appeared off the stern.

45 As had happened before, fish soon were drawn up from the deep to the circle, but only a few dozen, for the sparkling silver circle of Amos was much smaller than the circle of Yeshua had been.

46 Nevertheless, one large fish leapt out of the water right at Amos, and he quickly tried to grab it from the air. But the fish was very slippery, and losing his footing as he leaned out from the boat to grab the fish, Amos fell overboard into the lake with a great splash.

47 As he popped to the surface, Yeshua, Cephas, and everyone on the beach, even the Pharisees, were laughing heartily in bemusement at his folly.

48 Amos waved sheepishly to the crowd as he began swimming toward shore, and he was helped out of the water by two of his friends, who still laughing were patting him on the back and congratulating him.

49 After everyone had quieted down, Cephas returned to sit at the stern, and Yeshua returned to stand at the prow and address the multitude again. And he said unto them, "It is good that we all laughed today and laughed with gusto, not at brother Amos, but at the entertainment he so spontaneously provided.

50 Laughter returns to our lesson of the previous week, concerning sound; and it is one of the

most powerful sounds you can ever utter.

51 Therefore, never allow yourself to become as a sour fruit, but laugh easily, and when warranted like today, laugh with gusto.

52 Know that with every laugh you give forth to the world, the aeons of health add length to your life, even as the aeons of happiness adds serenity that ever overcomes the little pricks of life.

53 Now there is more to color than calling fish. Colors have a marvelous ability to help in healing. Many of you have seen me heal the afflicted, and many afflicted have come here today to be healed.

54 Many, especially those who are not numbered among the Children of Light, wonder how these miracles are accomplished, and I will tell you in part.

55 Again, there is nothing that you see me do that any Child of Light cannot also do with the correct knowledge, virtue, worthy need, love, passion, and faith.

56 Before any healing takes place, specific aeons relating to the opposite of the sickness, must be called in.

57 Some of these may be in the form of herbs or potions of herbs. Others may utilize aeons of heat or water or sound.

58 At last, the healer must be a bridge for the aeons of the Celestine Realm to cross the heavens and flow into the person who is afflicted.

59 But before any of these, the very first aeon that must be called upon is the aeon of color, specifically, the color that carries the opposite energy of the sickness or affliction. As the color envelopes the afflicted, it begins immediately to weaken the affliction and give strength to they who have been laid low.

60 Therefore, look upon the aura of the afflicted. What is the predominant color? Once that is known, simply bring in the opposite color. Put it around them and in them, both physically and energetically, and it will be a toxin to the affliction, weakening it and preparing the sickness for purging with the greater powers to come.

61 So too can color soften the heart of the angry or anger the heart of the soft.

62 Color can also open the mind to great thoughts or inspire the heart to noble deeds or fidelity.

63 As you learn more about the powers of colors from my Apostles, please take to heart and into your life all that you learn.

64 I strongly encourage you to wear brighter, more colorful clothing, and refrain from the drab colors so commonly worn among the people of Palestine. This can be bright sashes or simple accents of colors upon your clothes and need not be your entire garment. But even in this, avoid the drab and dreary garment with firm conviction.

65 If you desire melancholy in your life, wear the drab and dingy colors, and they will assuredly overcome you with the thoughts and feelings for which they were created.

66 If you desire to just be one of the masses, wear all white or all black, and you will become the blandness you desire.

67 But if you desire to be alive with life and connected to Elohim in your heart and mind, then add color to the white, along the trim, in the sash and woven in patterns through the material. And learn to gather the gifts of the earth that you may make dyes without cost and color even greater swaths of the clothes that you wear with brightness and life, even until the entire garment radiates colors seldom seen among the people of the land.

68 Nor neglect color in your home. Color your walls with colorants and art and light your rooms with beautiful flowers.

69 But not with random impulse should you add color to your clothes and your home and your life, but only with knowledge and wisdom and intention, that the colors you surround yourself with will be harmonious, and with purpose and intention, add to the quality and joy of your life.

70 After we each go our way today, contemplate my words and the colors in your life. Reflect

upon the colors that bring you happiness and determine to surround yourself more with them.

71 In the weeks that come, you shall learn much more of the specific powers of colors in the School of Mysteries from my Apostles. Remember your lessons well, for Elohim has given unto you the power to both see and feel colors and to utilize them for marvelous wonders.

72 Now I shall tell you of one of the greatest powers of color. One that you can use even today, without any practice, and even if you are a Pharisee! This is the power of the light of the sun, which falls each day upon everyone.

73 Within the light of the sun are all the colors of the rainbow and many more. Like the variety of foods that you eat, the properly balanced colors of sunlight in adequate amounts are essential for your well-being, health, and longevity.

74 You were created by Elohim as beings of light. The sun was put in the sky by the divine Father and Mother to feed their children, just as surely as the plants were put in the ground and the fish in the sea to provide sustenance for you.

75 The sunlight that falls so generously upon you is free. Because the king cannot tax it, and you do not have to plant it or harvest it, and the rich man cannot hoard it or charge for it, it is most often taken for granted. But I tell you a secret: The sun is one of the greatest, most precious treasures of Elohim to the children of men.

76 Whether you are out in the sun or inside a dark building is seldom considered. Whether you rise from the darkness late in the day or early in the morning is not thought to be of consequence.

77 But I say unto you that the consequence is significant. Every moment of sunlight that shines about you in moderation is a moment that you add to the length of your days upon the earth and insure the health of your body as it passes through the days of your life.

78 Therefore, if you desire all good things in your life—happiness, health, longevity, and success in your endeavors—do not remain awake by torchlight into the late hours of the night as the Romans so often do, but retire early enough to sleep that you can rise near to the time of the sun and feed yourself the marvelous free nourishment of sunlight in all its array of colors, for the maximum hours each and every day.[a]

79 The light of the sun is a great conduit to Elohim; it comes from Elohim. Even on a cloudy day, the light of the sun pierces the clouds and comes to you, feeding you, nourishing your body and soul, even as Elohim is always with you if you open your heart fully and let the love of the Mother and Father in.

80 Verily, if you wish to become the fullness of your destiny, you must embrace the fullness of the sun and of light, for you are Children of Light, and light is the food of the gods which feeds you and ever beckons you to your greatness."

a Yeshua was speaking to people in the mid-latitudes. Obviously, if someone lives in the near-polar latitudes, they will not stay awake in the sun for the long days of their summers. And during the long nights of their winters, they will have no choice but to remain awake for some hours by artificial light.

CHAPTER 79

The Power of Stones

Yeshua speaks to the Children of Light about the power of stones and how to utilize their special attributes based upon faith.

nd it came to pass that on the following Sabbath, Yeshua once again met with the Children of Light from the four communities on Lake Gennesaret by speaking to them from the boat of Cephas as they sat and stood listening to him on the shore.

2 Looking at them, he asked everyone to pick up a nearby stone and hold it in their hand. Some reached for stones the size of a chicken egg, and others for small pebbles they could rub in their fingers.

3 Yeshua said unto them, "How often do you trod upon the ground and pass by stones big and small and think nothing of them? Yet to every stone, there is one or more special attributes given by Elohim imbued by the forces of its creation.

4 When you were conceived in your mother's womb, the moment of creation and the gestation of pregnancy had some bearing on the person you became. What your mother ate while you were in the womb, what stresses were upon her from life, and whether you were conceived in love or only in lust, all exerted forces that contributed more than you imagine to the person you are today, both your personal challenges and your virtues.

5 So it is with all of creation, even with the stones under your feet.

6 Whether a man grows to become a mighty man or a weak and sickly man begins in his mother's womb. There is much more to it than that, but that is the beginning. So too, whether a rock becomes just a hard piece of dirt or a stone with amazing properties depends upon its conception and gestation within the womb of the Mother earth.

7 Most stones and the elements in the stones have far more uses than you understand, even as clay, which can be used not only to make vessels of pottery, but also to heal wounds and stings, and certain varieties that are even taken into your mouth and stomach to counteract poisons and other noxious upsets.

8 Know with certainty that there is no stone, no element, no type of soil, put upon this earth, save it was put by Elohim for the benefit of man. But the benefits of most are far more than you have ever known.

9 Some elements have powers that stand alone, even as sulfur by itself can be used to heal many diseases of the skin, speed the healing of wounds, and kill vermin that may infest the body. Besides the healing benefit of the hot water, it is because of the sulfur in the water, along with various salts, that the mineral spring baths are so therapeutic.

10 Other minerals are given more to be used as tools, even as obsidian makes the finest

instruments of surgery, or Kazza is used to filter impurities.[a]

11 These are the uses you can easily see and understand with your eyes and senses. But there are many uses of elements and stones that you cannot easily see or understand with your senses, and it is of these that I speak.

12 Some years ago, my brother Yochanan the Baptizer journeyed in Egypt with me and my family. On one occasion, he sold some rock crystals to priests of a certain temple. These were crystals he had discovered in a small hole in the ground during his journeys in the wilderness as a youth.

13 Now the priests of the temple were most delighted to receive these particular crystals, and they paid Yochanan a goodly sum for them.

14 It was not for adornment that they paid such a price, but because they understood how to use the powers of these particular rock crystals, and they had singular faith to invoke the powers. Verily, there is power within some crystals, and though unseen, it can sometimes be powerfully felt.

15 More often, crystals of various minerals are merely another tool. They can be used to focus your own energy or other aeons you are calling upon, to very specific points, for healing or other purposes.

16 Whether a stone or a crystal has power unto itself or is only waiting to be used as a tool depends upon its birth and gestation, even as who you became depended in some part upon yours.

17 Some rocks and crystals are birthed deep within the Mother earth. Others are deposited over time at the bottom of the seas. Still others are birthed from cataclysms.

18 Where a stone is birthed and gestated will have bearing upon whether it can be used solely in a physical way that is easily seen with your eyes or can be used in a greater way that affects the auras and energies of the people and things it is directed upon.

19 Those stones that will have unseen power, both in themselves and as tools, are those that were birthed deep within the earth and have either clarity or profound color and usually a greater hardness than most other stones.

20 That is not to say that other stones not birthed deep in the earth cannot also have unseen powers or be utilized as tools to focus unseen aeons. But as a simple measure, those stones with the most clarity or vividness of color or unusual color or rainbow effect and with the greatest hardness, coming from the deepest womb of the earth, are going to be the greatest gemstones of unseen power.

21 Once you hold a stone of power in your hand or wear it in a ring on your finger or a pendant about your neck, how does the aeon come forth?

22 It is not enough to merely hold the stone. You must also hold faith in Elohim, faith in yourself, and have a harmony and oneness with the earth from which the stone came forth.

23 So while anyone may use a stone for its physical properties, only a person of deep faith can call upon the unseen powers of Celestine Light within the special stones of the earth.

24 Let me demonstrate the meaning of my words. I would like to ask my wife Miriam to step forward upon the beach to the edge of the water so that all can see her and also call upon the Pharisees present to send a representative to stand beside her."

25 As Yeshua spoke, Miriam stood up from where she had been sitting at the front of the crowd with their children and Salome and Martha and walked a few steps to the edge of the beach.

26 Off to the side of the crowd stood a group of six Pharisees who had come, as the Pharisees often did, to listen to Yeshua speak.

27 Hearing Yeshua's bidding, they conversed quickly among themselves and most were against participating in his demonstration, thinking it would be a trap to embarrass them. But Zophas, one of the Pharisees, told his brethren, "I will go forth, for I have some knowledge of the tricks of magic, and in this, perhaps it will be the blasphemer Yeshua who is embarrassed in front of all

of his followers and exposed for the charlatan that he is."

28 So saying, Zophas came and stood a pace away beside Miriam. Yeshua reached back and taking a stone that Cephas handed to him, he tossed it ashore, and Zophas caught it in his hand.

29 Yeshua said unto him, "Good Zophas, thank you for coming again to hear my words today. I know little by little, as you see and hear, that the true Celestine Light of Elohim has been touching your heart."

30 "Humph!" grumbled Zophas in response.

31 Speaking to the multitude, Yeshua elaborated, saying, "Zophas holds a piece of lodestone in his hands from Greece. Some of you may think this rock has magic of its own because objects made of iron are attracted to it with an invisible force. But this is not magic, merely the way it has been created to form in its gestation by Elohim."

32 Speaking again to Zophas, Yeshua said, "Zophas, would you hold the lodestone above your head along with a piece of iron so everyone can see how the iron is attracted to and held by the lodestone?"

33 Zophas thought for a moment, then removed his sandal, which had an iron decoration, and held it above his head. Bringing his other hand holding the lodestone toward it, he attached it to the piece of iron, then let go of it so everyone could see how it held fast to the iron on the sandal.

34 "This power of the lodestone will work with any person and with any object made of iron," Yeshua explained. "It could do the same for Miriam as it did for Zophas or any of you.

35 But there is another invisible power in this unusual stone that also has to do with attraction and repulsion, not of iron, but of people, but it will not work for anyone as it does with the iron, but only with someone of faith."

36 Yeshua asked Zophas to hand the lodestone to Miriam, which he did. Then speaking to Miriam, he asked, "Daughter of light, would you please invoke the power of repulsion in the stone?"

37 Miriam nodded her head, and after bowing it for a moment of silence, she lifted up her head and turned to the multitude with a subtle smile upon her beautiful face.

38 Speaking again to Zophas, Yeshua said unto him, "Zophas, attempt now if you will to touch the garment of Miriam."

39 But Zophas protested, saying, "It is not proper for me to touch another man's wife or even her garment. I will not do it."

40 "Very well," Yeshua responded. "Then touch her not, but simply move your hand toward her as if you were going to touch her."

41 Zophas considered Yeshua's request for a moment and then nodded his head in assent and lifted his arm and moved his hand toward Miriam's shoulder, but did not touch it.

42 He then lowered his arm and took a step back, and Yeshua asked him, "What did you feel?"

43 And Zophas replied, "I felt nothing, except perhaps my imagination running around trying to deduce what hoax you are trying to perpetrate."

44 "So the effect is too subtle for you then?" Yeshua inquired of Zophas.

45 "Subtle is defining this charade with greater certainty than warranted. The slight breeze off the lake is felt, but nothing from your wife or her stone," Zophas replied.

46 "Why do you continue to try to delude these simple people?" Zophas inquired accusingly. "You are leading them astray and away from the teachings of the prophets to their destruction before God."

47 Yeshua did not answer him, but instead spoke again to Miriam, saying, "Perhaps, you should further invoke the power of the stone."

48 Miriam spoke no words in reply, but once again bowed her head for a moment and then looked up smiling and turned to look right into the eyes of Zophas, which was most disconcerting for him, for never did women look into the eyes of men that were not of their family.

49 Yeshua spoke again to Zophas, saying, "If you will, reach once again as if to touch the

shoulder of Miriam."

50 But Zophas crossed his arms across his chest, and taking another step away from Miriam, he said, "I shall not. This is nonsense."

51 Yeshua then spoke again to Miriam, saying, "If Zophas will not come to you, perhaps it is appropriate to go instead to Zophas."

52 Miriam's smile widened ever so slightly, and nodding her head in agreement, she took a step toward Zophas. When she did, he put his arms down and showed surprise on his face. As she began to take another step, he looked visibly nervous, and as her reaching foot planted upon the ground and she began to walk upright before him, he fell violently backward upon his posterior, as if he had been hit by a mighty blow.

53 He rapidly stood up brushing the dirt off his clothes and retreated back toward his fellow Pharisees.

54 "It certainly appeared as if you felt something that time," Yeshua said to Zophas.

55 "I cannot deny it," Zophas responded. "I felt suddenly sick to my stomach and as if I was a lodestone being repelled by another. It was very strange, but proves nothing, for your wife is spoken of in Galilee as a witch. Surely, the power was not in the stone, but in her mischief or yours."

56 "You speak words of truth, Zophas," Yeshua answered. "Though you understand them not, the power was not in the stone, but in the faith of Miriam. With faith, the secret powers of the stones can come forth, but without it, they are simply stones, the same in one person's hand as another's."

57 Then Yeshua once more addressed the multitude, saying, "Children of Light, when you meet this week in your Q's, my Apostles shall go among you and begin to teach you the many uses of stones and how to call upon their secret powers that the world will never know.

58 Until then, begin to look at every stone, no matter how simple or plain it may seem with new insight and understanding.

59 Verily, there are no simple or plain stones, for every grain of sand upon the earth has been put here by Elohim for the benefit of man.

60 The men of the world know how to use the minerals of the land to build and fabricate and dye and in some things heal. But it is given only to you, the Children of Light, to understand and be able to call upon the greater powers of the stones and elements and crystals, both as conduits of power and of the aeon contained within some, waiting for those of true faith to call them out.

61 I say again, look anew at every stone you see and remember the other lessons we have recently shared on sound and color, for the colors of each stone are important and define part of their power, even as each stone has a sound that conveys additional secrets and mysteries to those of faith who understand them and call upon them."

62 Later in the day, Yeshua went upon the lake in three boats with his Apostles, away from the eyes of unbelievers and taught them many wonderful things concerning stones and elements and crystals and the wonders that can come from them and through them when empowered by the faith of a Child of Light.

63 These secrets are taught to this day within the School of Mysteries and practiced in sacred circles of the Katah, Shanar, and Q-roms of the Children of Light.

a Kazza was the word they used for diatomaceous earth.

CHAPTER 80

The Power of Herbs

Yeshua speaks to the Children of Light about the beneficial properties of herbs.

It came to pass that on the following Sabbath, Yeshua once more spoke from the boat of Cephas to the Children of Light and others who had gathered along the shore of Lake Gennesaret.

2 And he said unto them, "Good brothers and sisters of light and seekers of the Celestine Light who have also come and are among you, in recent weeks, I have spoken to you about the powers of sound and color and stones. Today, I wish to speak to you about the powers of herbs.

3 Elohim has put all things upon the earth that are needed for your well-being and health, and plants and herbs are special storehouses of both and much more.

4 They can be used for healing and other uses, both great and small, and every Child of Light should become as familiar in their use as the physicians of the kings and as adept in their special properties as the priests of the Egyptian temples.

5 I charge you to regularly teach the uses of herbs and plants whenever you meet together in your accustomed meetings, that all may be knowledgeable in this storehouse of treasure.

6 There is almost no effect you cannot manifest with the proper use of herbs and plants. You can make a man appear dead or raise one almost dead from sickness back into life.

7 You can make potions that nourish your crops while stunting the weeds and others that entice the butterflies and bees, but discourage the insects that would devour your fields.

8 There are herbs to make your mind alert and others to fill your body with unbounded energy, while still others will sooth you into a deep and peaceful slumber.

9 There are herbs to dampen pain and others that feel like fire yet cause no harm.

10 For every malady, there is an herb or potion of herbs, and for every need of mind or body, Elohim has provided plants and herbs to be of benefit to man.

11 Now you may say, 'We will heal with faith and the powers of the spirit and call upon the aeons of angels and Heaven, so what need have we of herbs?'

12 But I say unto you that when you heal by faith, you have only begun the healing, and what the powers of the spirit have begun are often best completed with the powers of herbs."

13 Looking out into the multitude, Yeshua pointed at a man on a litter that was set upon the ground, having been carried there from another city by his four sons hoping that Yeshua would heal him of his infirmity of the lungs.

14 Yeshua said unto the man, "Simon of Bersabe, come to the shore." After so saying, Yeshua stepped out of the boat and waded to the shore to meet him.

15 Simon's sons quickly lifted him up on the litter and moved him to the shore all the while

asking one another how it was that Yeshua knew their father's name and where he was from.
16 Yeshua knowing their thoughts and words with one another greeted them when they met upon the beach and said unto them, "Marvel not at this that I would know your father and the place he calls home, for what shepherd does not know each of his sheep and wither they go and bed down for the night?"
17 Coming to Simon, Yeshua held his hand and said unto him, "Last year, before you became ill, you helped to dig a well for your neighbor, and after the water had come in, you also left his wife with a gold coin from among the few you had saved for your sons. Why did you do this?"
18 Simon was astounded that Yeshua should know this and his sons also, for though they had helped their father dig the well, they had not known he had given the wife one of his few gold coins.
19 Simon nodded his head in affirmation and said unto Yeshua through a cough, "How you know this is a mystery. Surely Elohim whispered it in your ear. And it is true. I did as you have said, for my neighbor was in need. He was my friend Gastal, who had some months before been injured in a fall and had been unable to work much to help his wife and three children. I was one of many who helped dig the well. I gave the coin in secret, knowing it would help my friend's family. I gave it to his wife because I knew my friend would not have accepted it."
20 "But when your friend recovered and was able to work again, you never asked him to repay the gold you had given to his family," Yeshua stated knowingly.
21 Simon's eyes opened wide with surprise that Yeshua was aware even of this, and he said to him, "Surely, you are of God to know these things." Simon proclaimed as he coughed severely once more, "So too, you must know that I would never ask a friend to return money given in time of need, for in such times, it is not a loan but a gift. Once it left my hand, I thought of it no more and would be offended if my friend tried to return it to me on another day."
22 Yeshua smiled broadly at Simon and said unto him, "Blessed are you, Simon of Bersabe. Inside you dwells the true Celestine Light of Elohim."
23 Then taking him by the hand, Yeshua pulled Simon to his feet and said unto him, "By the power of the Celestine Light of Elohim that is within your good heart, you are made whole this day."
24 Upon hearing his words, Simon took in a great breath, and breathing it out, he exclaimed, "My infirmity is gone. My breath is full and without cough!" Taking Yeshua's hand in both of his, he bowed his head and touched his forehead to Yeshua's hand, saying, "Blessed are you, Yeshua of Nazareth. Thank you for this wonderful blessing."
25 Then Yeshua put his arm over the shoulder of Simon, and facing the multitude, he said unto them, "Simon has been healed this day, but the cause of his illness remains, for the powders of the flowers and trees that grow all about his home are a poison to him, and this poison has begun to affect him more with each passing year.
26 So he will return home and be well for a time, but within two years, his infirmity will return and once again worsen with each passing year, unless he follows this healing of spirit with daily consumption of the antidote for the poison, which is the pollen of bees mixed with a tea of Suman.
27 So it is with many of the sicknesses and infirmities you would heal by calling upon the Celestine Light. The healing is complete for a time, but the problem will return if the cause remains. But with the use of herbs, the cause too may be overcome when it is something of the physical realm.
28 Each day, if you will drink teas from the herbs you are given to understand in your Q-roms, you will live far beyond the normal years of man and live in health and vigor all of your days. Is something so simple and easy not worthy of the effort for a reward so great?"

CHAPTER 81

The Power of the Aura

Yeshua speaks to the Children of Light for what is thought to be the last time before his crucifixion. He teaches them about the power of the aura and promises that he will always be with them as long as they hold true to the Celestine Light of Elohim.

Several Sabbaths passed before Yeshua again spoke to the Children of Light of the communities on Lake Gennesaret. Instead, each day, he spoke in private with his twelve Apostles, instructing them in the higher mysteries of the Celestine Light and how they should act and what they should do when he was no longer among them.

2 With Miriam, he spoke more than with any of the others. When the other Apostles had not yet arrived at his house in the morning, he would walk outside, speaking in private with her. And when the other Apostles had departed after the day's lessons, he and Miriam would once again walk along the lake or up into the hills, speaking earnestly with one another.

3 And it came to pass that on the seventh Sabbath after Yeshua had last spoken to the Children of Light, he gathered them once more very early on a beautiful, clear morning to speak to them from the boat of Cephas as they were assembled in comfort along the shore of the lake.

4 Because it had been many weeks since Yeshua had last spoken, there were no Pharisees present, and few visitors sitting among the Children of Light.

5 The scene was truly awe inspiring as the sun rose behind and slightly to the side of Yeshua as he stood on the prow of the boat, and he seemed to glow from the intensity of the sun's light.

6 Yeshua raised both of his arms perpendicular to the sides of his body with his palms facing the multitude, and he said unto them, "Brothers and sisters of Light, it is so wonderful to be among you! Good day to you on this glorious morning!"

7 "Good day, Yeshua!" they all shouted as one.

8 Still holding his arms outstretched to his sides, Yeshua spoke to them, saying, "The light of the sun is behind me, illuminating me, even till your eyes cannot stand to behold the light.

9 But the light of the sun is also within me as it is also within you. Come to know the light of the sun that is within you, your soul's essence, even the very light of Elohim, and there will be nothing that is impossible to you.

10 The physical light of the sun is a healing balm from Elohim that can cure illnesses of the mind and spirit, as well as the body.

11 But though the sun lights and warms all the world, the Celestine Light within you is no less spectacular when called upon with knowledge and faith.

12 The light within, your aura, is the very essence of your soul and a literal part of the Elohim. With it, you can be one in mind and spirit with all living things surrounding you, from the grass

beneath your feet to the birds in the air and your friends or adversaries that may be gathered round.

13 In your Q-roms in the coming weeks, my Apostles shall teach you how to both see and feel the aura of your soul that emanates and radiates from your body.

14 Even as the light of the sun emanates and radiates to fill all the earth, so the aura of your soul emanates and radiates from you to fill the void beyond as far and as powerfully as you have the knowledge and faith to make it so.

15 In your imaginations, hold your arms outstretched from your sides as I have been and see yourself surrounded by a transparent sphere, an arm's length from your body. This is the normal extension of the aura of your soul from your body.

16 Come closer than this to another person and your auras will interact. Even if the person is a stranger and speaks to you not at all, you will perceive much about them through the interaction of the lights of your souls.

17 If this person were then to speak, you can know if what he speaks is true or false. For regardless of his words, his aura cannot lie. If you then learn to be sensitive and aware of that which you feel when the light of your soul is touched by another, you will never be able to be deceived again by the words of men.

18 When you call upon Elohim and the powers of the Celestine Light and the assistance of the angels of stewardship to heal someone of their illness or disease, you know it is by knowledge, love, passion, and faith that it is so.

19 But by what means do these great powers that you have called flow to and through you? Why do the angels of stewardship respond to your call? Why do the Celestine powers of Heaven come when you beckon? Why does Elohim hear you among the cacophony of the innumerable?

20 It is through the aura of your soul essence that all is accomplished.

21 Just as the light of your soul intersects the light of the soul of another person when you stand near them, so does it intersect the light of the soul of the angels of stewardship and of Elohim and the powers of the Celestine Realms.

22 When you have great emotion and passion about anything, it awakens your aura, empowering and expanding it.

23 Add to this righteousness of pursuit, conviction of purpose, knowledge of method, and faith unwavering, and your aura can expand so greatly as to fill all the world, even as does the sun in the sky.

24 Thus expanded, the light of your soul becomes a beacon that cannot be hidden. It is seen by all the hosts of Heaven and felt by all the powers therein. And all the powers of Heaven shall come as you ask to fulfill the righteous purposes for which you have called upon them.

25 But knowing this is not enough to accomplish it. You must teach one another and share your experiences and listen to the teachings of the Apostles at length in your Qs, that you may come to an understanding of the feelings that come upon you, filling every fiber of your being with a tingle of awe, as you light the fire of your soul and expand it outward for good and glorious purposes."

26 Then Yeshua paused, and from the words he next spoke, we must conclude that he was considering that this would be the last time that he would speak to the Children of Light assembled together.

27 When after a couple of minutes of silence he spoke again, he wiped a tear from his eye and said unto them, "brothers and sisters, let me say what an honor it has been to be numbered among you. You are truly the brightest lights of Heaven come down to earth to illuminate the world.

28 Thanks to your efforts of spreading the good, sweet teachings of Celestine Light among your friends and families scattered abroad. I have had the great pleasure of watching our number grow from a mere handful to over two hundred today, plus many delightful children.

29 The day soon comes when you shall see me no more in the flesh. But know that I will

always be with you in the spirit, and as you continue to live your lives in righteousness, you will always be my family.

30 My mother and brothers are here among you, but you too are my mothers and my brothers and my fathers and my sisters.

31 And I shall always be your elder brother, watching over you, ever prompting you to live with virtue and to do good.

32 The days to come will bring you both sadness and joy, but let there not be apprehension among you, for the Celestine Light of Elohim is ever in your heart; it is ever a part of you, and there is nothing upon the earth that is greater than that.

33 When I have departed from this earth, you will know that the time of fulfillment of all that has been prophesied has come.

34 This is a time above all others when you must carefully heed the guidance of the Apostles and use your gifts of Celestine Light with prudence and forethought as you have been taught.

35 Cephas shall lead you. Listen well to the councils and directions he gives, for through him, Elohim shall speak to guide and protect the Children of Light.

36 Like the angels of Heaven, each Apostle has been given a stewardship. Listen well to their councils within their stewardship, for when they speak and act within those realms, it is as if Elohim were speaking and acting, for they act in the name and with the authority of Elohim.

37 In your darkest hours, when all may seem lost, hold fast to your faith in the truth and the Celestine Light and pray and manifest miracles within your Circles of Power.

38 Even so, when darkness still descends upon the Children of Light, fear neither man nor demon, nor the legions of Caesar, for you are the blessed ones of this generation, and unto you has been given the Angel of the Covenant, against whom neither man nor demon, nor the legions of Caesar can prevail.

39 It is Miriam of whom I speak, my virtuous wife, the love of my youth, the heartbeat of my eternity. In her will be vested all the knowledge I have brought upon the earth, and in her resides the greatest faith of all the ages, by which the very earth will tremble.

40 Where much is given, much is required, and where the tests are greatest, there stand the mightiest.

41 There are those who hear my voice today who shall no longer be among us ere the new moon rises, for they came for peace not turmoil, for ease not challenge, and knowing not the fullness of the Celestine Light, they still fear the power of the darkness.

42 So must each of you choose to return again to the world, even though I tell you that you will not find solace there or seek to know the Celestine Light even greater than you now do, that within its glow, you will find passage through the darkness.

43 You have heard it said by some to resist not evil, but I say unto you that evil is like the most noxious weed, and if not resisted, it will spread forth until it chokes all life from the land.

44 Turning your backs upon evil will not make it go away, simply because you no longer see it. It will merely grow in power without opposition, until the light becomes darkness, and you will no longer be able to avoid seeing it.

45 Therefore, let it be others who run and hide from evil, but not the Children of Light.

46 Let it be others that appease evil, hoping it will seek no more, but not the Children of Light, who know that evils' hunger is never filled.

47 You are the Children of Light. You are the guardians of the world. You are the bulwark that stands between the sanctity of the earth and all living things upon it and the darkness that would overcome it if unchallenged.

48 Therefore, ever seek out the vortexes of darkness and encircle them with light until they are purged and the land can breathe again.

49 When evil rears its ugly head, be it from the actions of men or demons, even if it molests you not but seeks another, remember that you are lights to all the world, not just to yourselves. And if you are worthy of me, you will always seek to overcome the darkness wherever it descends

and replace it with light.

50 Remember, you are not alone. I am always with you, and our Father and Mother in the Celestine Realms hear your righteous prayers and answer them.

51 So too have you one another, not simply as friends, but bonded in love as Children of Light. You are many, but you are one, and in that one, you are much more than many.

52 And you have the Apostles, my brethren one and all. They will never betray you; they will never abandon you. They are as stalwart as the mountains of Lebanon.

53 And you have Miriam. And in her, you have more than you can imagine.

54 Therefore, make peace with yourself, pray and meditate, and pray some more. Decide if your path returns to the uncertain peace of the world or remains with the certain upheaval that shall come upon the Children of Light.

55 But know this: Those that endure to the end, with faith unwavering and joy and good spirit remaining, shall inherit a marvelous wonder in this life and the next, more fulfilling than words can say or dreams can dream.

56 I go now to have some time with my family and then with my Apostles. Soon, I shall journey once more throughout Galilee and Judea that all that was prophesied might be fulfilled.

57 Those who love the light, follow me on my journeys, and we shall be one."

58 While Yeshua was speaking, many people among the multitude began to weep, and when he was finished, some began to cry openly and loudly, and many were heard to exclaim, "Please stay with us!"

59 Hearing this, Yeshua spoke to them once again, saying, "Listen well to the words I speak and feel them in the depths of your heart: I will always be with you. As long as you hold fast to my light, I shall never be apart from you.

60 Wherever you are, I will be there beside you and inside you, with a spirit that is more real to you than the flesh and bones you see before you now.

61 When you are with your family and children, I will be among you.

62 When you are taken ill, I will be there to help bring you back to health.

63 When you suffer a loss and your heart grieves, I will be there to comfort you.

64 When you are challenged by life, I will be there to gird you and strengthen you that you may overcome all things.

65 When you seek to grow and expand your light, I will be there to inspire you and uplift you on golden wings to the greatness you can become.

66 Verily, verily, I covenant unto you, as surely as the sun rises, my love for you will never falter, my faith in you will never diminish, and my promises to you shall forever remain true.

67 I go now, not to leave you, but to bring to pass your eternal life and to prepare a place for you in my Father and Mother's Kingdom that we might always be together.

68 Therefore, rejoice! This is not a time of sadness, but of joy. This is the time when the prophesies are fulfilled, when death shall be overcome, and the fire of Elohim is forever lit in the hearts of the children of men."

CHAPTER 82

Preparations for a New Beginning

With the time for his departure nearing, Yeshua teaches Miriam additional essentials about the mysteries and powers of Celestine Light. At Miriam's request, he also explains why he must die the ignoble death that he does. Yeshua talks to his Apostles about his crucifixion and resurrection and why things will be as they are. He also tells them about Miriam's transition to the Angel of the Covenant and endows each of them with new gifts of power with special blessings for specific callings that are unique to each. He lastly gives each a rare and beautiful gemstone of power to aid them in their missions.

During the next moon, Yeshua spent almost all of his time with his family. He held no public meetings and met with his Apostles and went among the gathered Children of Light only on the Sabbath.

2 Many hours each day he would walk alone with Miriam, teaching her the deeper mysteries of Celestine Light, and on several occasions they spent the night alone in the hills above Capernaum and sometimes two or three.

3 As the time of the new moon began, Yeshua spoke to Miriam upon the mountain, saying, "Your knowledge is now vast. No other person on earth shall ever know all that you know about the mysteries and powers of Celestine Light. This knowledge is entrusted to you as the Angel of the Covenant that you may ever be the shield of protection to the Children of Light and the well of knowledge for all who seek it in humility and the selflessness of service."

4 Miriam put her arms around Yeshua's waist and looked up into his eyes with love and said unto him tenderly, "Beloved, I am thankful beyond words for all that you have taught me every day we have been together. And I will serve as Elohim desires.

5 I have listened dutifully, almost without speaking, for this moon as you have blessed me with knowledge beyond even that of the greatest prophets.

6 As we prepare to go down now, that you may speak with the Apostles and begin your fateful steps toward Jerusalem, I must ask of you a few questions. Hard they may seem in nature, but it is not with criticism that I ask them, but merely seeking a complete clarity of understanding that I may better serve our divine Father and Mother as you have shown unto me.

7 I know you are aware of my questions before they ever are uttered from my lips and that you can answer my unspoken questions in words in my mind, but please allow me to say them lest I grow atrophied in voice from my prolonged silence."

8 Yeshua was quiet then and spoke not a word but merely smiled in understanding at Miriam and nodded for her to continue.

9 Still holding him gently about his waist and looking up into his eyes, Miriam began, "Everything you have shown unto me that I must do I understand. And I shall faithfully fulfill all things as you have asked, as our Father and Mother give me strength.

10 It is concerning the things that you shall do that I do not fully understand, and I desire most ardently to have my understanding complete before you do these things, lest I not be able to endure with the fortitude you ask of me."

11 Yeshua nodded again for her to continue.

12 Miriam nodded and said, "You have said that soon you will allow yourself to be crucified and then resurrect and return to us for a time before you ascend forever more up into the higher realms of Celestine Light.

13 I understand the purpose for which you shall die and return to life, that the resurrection shall begin for all people, not just the select; that those spirits who have languished long in prison and paradise will finally be able to come forth into the fullness of resurrection to reap their reward or punishment as they merit.

14 I understand that you who are most pure and need not suffer at all in repentance will suffer in solitude the sins of the world the night before the journey to the cross begins; that all who repent of their darkness and live the Celestine Light you have brought into the world will not have to fully pay the penalty of their own sins, because you, their elder brother who loves them beyond measure, will have suffered in their place.

15 These are most noble and virtuous sacrifices you make for wanderers in darkness that know you not and who almost without exception reject you when you are revealed to them. Those who actually find and live the Celestine Light with a resonance in their soul are few indeed, so your suffering for the untold multitude seems to me, your loving wife, to be more than is needed.

16 Yet even with this, I do understand in my head why it is you must do that which you shall do. It is just my heart that does protest.

17 What I cannot yet comprehend is why it is that to do it, you must be crucified and why it must be so soon upon us.

18 Can you not prove the resurrection of eternal life by something as simple as leaping off a high cliff and restoring your shattered dead body and broken bones for all to see?

19 Why must you choose so ignoble a death as crucifixion? You are the only begotten son of our Father and Mother. You are a part of the Elohim and Lord over all the earth. Why will you allow common lowly men to lay hands upon you and humiliate you and scorn you and laugh at your suffering?

20 And even to accept this horrible way to die, why must it be so soon, before our children are even grown? Could you not wait just a few more years that we may have you with us just a little time longer, that you can see our son married and give our daughter's hand?

21 Please do not think me selfish in asking these things. Merely am I a wife who loves her husband beyond words to say and would see him walk his path only in the nobility that is his birthright and continue with his family in the flesh until our children stand on their own.

22 I do not ask for you to not walk upon your path. I know you must, and my love and unfailing support is ever with you. Merely, I wish to fully understand the manner in which you have chosen to walk the end on this earth and the timing you have chosen to finish your journey in mortality."

23 Yeshua cupped his hands around Miriam's head and ran his fingers through the soft hair near her neck. He kissed her gently on the lips and put his arms around her and held her close, saying, "Blessed are you, Miriam, and blessed am I to have you as my wife. Though by my word worlds begin, only our Father and Mother could have created a marvel such as you.

24 Know that I will never leave you or our children, and I will be there each and every important moment in their lives in a way that is as real and tangible as I stand before you now and not merely in the spirit as the Apostles shall see me.

25 After I have ascended to Heaven, no others upon the earth shall see me in the perfection of

resurrection, save you and the children of our union, you at all times when you so desire, for you will be the Angel of the Covenant. With our children, whenever a time of significance is upon their lives and they so desire, I will manifest myself unto them.

26 On those days, when our son is married and our daughter's hand is to be given, I shall be there as you see me now and hear my voice. As so shall you see and hear, and so shall they see and hear, but no others except you."

27 Upon hearing his words, Miriam was joyous, and she embraced him with exuberance. She said, "My heart is calmed with the balm of your words, and my happiness knows no bounds. Can you now so fully assuage my concerns about your chosen path to part mortality?"

28 Yeshua looked at Miriam and lifted his eyebrows hopefully even as he shook his head slightly in negation, and he said unto her, "The words you have spoken about crucifixion are true, but it is because they are true—that this is a most vicious and cruel way to take the life of a man—that it must be the way mine is taken.

29 And more than this, they shall break my bones, rip my flesh, and run a spear through my side and into my heart. By this, which all the people of Jerusalem shall see, there will be no doubt that my mortal life has truly perished.

30 But pity me not for the suffering you think you shall see. As you said, my suffering shall be in the long night before the journey to the cross begins. During the spectacle to the cross and upon it, rest assured, I will feel no pain, nor be broken by the cruel words and actions of men, no matter the ravages you shall witness put upon my body.

31 After three days in the earth you must come for me. I will wait for the presence of your exquisite love, which even death cannot stand against. Then shall I appear again before my Apostles and many people of the city. And they shall feel the prints of the nails in my hands and my feet, the scourges on my flesh, and the wound in my side, and they shall know that it is me and that mortal death is not the end, but the beginning of life eternal."

32 Miriam nodded her head in understanding, but still questioned him further, saying, "Yet will not people say that 'This is Yeshua, a man known for great miracles,' and not understand that the resurrection will be also for them and all others?"

33 He nodded his head and explained, "If I alone were to return in the glory of perfection, so might they doubt. But on the day that I rise, so shall many of the virtuous who have lain long in the grave also rise and go about the city for a day. And one other special resurrection shall occur that day.

34 And it will come to pass by the word of the Father and Mother, and by that which men have seen with their own eyes, that the understanding that life is eternal will be forever seared into the memory of man, beginning at this place.

35 From one generation to the next, across all religions and cultures, will wash the innate comprehension that mortal life is not the end, but the beginning of a greater eternity.

36 This divine understanding will take many forms even as it now does among many: some will believe in a Heaven of spirits, others of a continual reincarnation of the soul. Still others will believe in a paradise where they who were servants shall become kings, and others shall say to men that there is nothing beyond this life, even while the divine Celestine Light of their soul makes hollow the false conviction of their words.

37 This undeniable whisper of eternal life will not be limited to the understanding of a few, but undeniably written upon the souls of every person. In many and diverse ways, the truth of eternal life shall encompass the earth and the soul of everyone therein and every person to be born in every generation to come.

38 And for every generation to come, this unfathomable understanding shall be the impetus to humble the proud and turn men from the darkness to the light, in hopes that their eternity might be greater than their mortality.

39 Because all things must be weighed in the balance and tallied for their worth, I shall suffer some of their sins that they shall not suffer them all and shall give a sacred portion of the

Celestine Light of my soul to take away a great part of the darkness from the souls of those who repent and live in my light, that they might have the purity needed on their day of judgment to enter into Celestial glory.

40 And it shall come to pass that those that repent of their darkness and live in my light shall inherit the eternal life of Celestial glory their soul forever whispered in sure knowledge upon their heart and mind."

41 Now Miriam buried her head upon his chest and cried many tears. When she had composed herself somewhat, she spoke softly unto him, saying, "Thank you, my dear Yeshua. Thank you."

42 With Miriam's head still upon his chest, Yeshua held her with one arm around her waist and stroked her long hair with the other and said unto her, "When the time of your angelic calling is upon you in fullness, you shall have all the powers of Heaven except the creation of life vested within you.

43 Considering all that you could do and the fiery temperament you have sometimes shown, you must make a promise to me."

44 "Anything," she answered softly.

45 "Promise me you will never take the life of any man, woman, or child," Yeshua asked.

46 Miriam replied with conviction, saying, "Beloved, I promise you that when I am filled with the fullness of my calling and the powers of Heaven given unto me to fulfill it, I will never intentionally take the life of any man, woman, child, or creature upon the earth."

47 Yeshua nodded in silence, and still stroking Miriam's hair, he said unto her, "That is well, my love, but you must promise that you shall never take a life, even unintentionally. For with such great power comes even greater responsibility."

48 Miriam looked up at him then, saying, "I would promise that if I could, but as you say, my temperament is sometimes fiery, and as happened that day on the River Qishon, the unintentional consequences of my righteous passion are not always favoring of life for the wicked."

49 Yeshua looked in her eyes and gently upbraided her, saying, "On that day on the River Qishon, you were merely Miriam, righteously angry and overly passionate because of a threat to one that you loved.

50 But soon you will be more than Miriam, the woman. You shall be an exalted representative of our divine Father and Mother. And except for life protecting self-defense, which you shall never be in need of, they grant the right to take the life of man unto none and expect those whom they have called to high and holy callings to serve them even unto perfection."

51 Miriam nodded her head in understanding and said unto him, "Your words are so true. I am humbled by their calling and shall trust their never-failing light to ever guide me on the paths of righteousness and perfection within the responsibilities they have blessed upon me."

52 And it came to pass that on the following Sabbath, after the sunrise meeting of the Children of Light, Yeshua called his Apostles to come into the mountains with him and Miriam for three days and three nights.

53 After spending the night with their families, all of the Apostles met at sunrise the next day at the house of Yeshua and went with him and Miriam up into the mountains.

54 Though Salome asked to also go with them that she might be with Miriam, none, save Miriam and the other eleven Apostles, were allowed to go up onto the mountain with Yeshua.

55 During their time upon the mountain, Yeshua told them again of the things that would shortly come to pass, including his crucifixion and resurrection and why this needed to be, even as he had told Miriam. But most of the Apostles, other than Yudas Iscariot, Mathew, and Philip, had difficulty understanding the depth of the words he spoke.

56 Seeing their confusion, Yeshua said unto them, "Marvel not at this that I should resurrect from the dead and come again among you, even as you too shall resurrect and come again among your friends and loved ones in the Celestine Realms.

57 If the divine Father and Mother can breathe the breath of life into all men and creatures, think you not that they can just as easily give life back to those who have died and decree that

the life given once more shall now be given unto perfection and perish never again?"

58 Yeshua also spoke somewhat concerning the mysteries of Celestine Light and the powers therein that he had shared with Miriam. But only a portion of the secrets that he shared with Miriam did he share with the Apostles. In truth, only Miriam with her many years of experience and instruction by Yeshua could comprehend the vastness of all he could teach.

59 One by one, Yeshua called forth the Apostles and laid his hands upon their heads and gave unto each of them a specific calling to fulfill from that day forth until their last day in mortality.

60 He also gave unto each Apostle specific blessings, each according to their need and calling, and unto each, he bestowed new gifts of power that they might better serve the Children of Light and support one another.

61 Lastly, unto each, he gave a gemstone, beautiful and rare. To each was given a different stone. Unto Miriam who came to him last, he gave the largest and most beautiful of all. And they marveled at the gems and spoke quietly among themselves momentarily, wondering where he could have obtained such expensive stones.

62 And he said unto them, "Each of you have been given a gemstone of power that is in harmony with your soul essence. As your heart beats and the Celestine Light of your soul expands upon a foundation of sure faith, love, and knowledge, your gemstone will come alive and draw to you the powers of Celestine Light from near and far to aid you in your righteous purposes.

63 Others may think that they have gemstones like unto yours, and they will say unto men, 'See, I have the same gem as the Apostles of Yeshua, and I am as great as they,' but it will be a foolish man who speaks these words, for their stones will be dead, nothing but pretty baubles for their vanity.

64 Verily, only a gemstone given by those in authority and attuned to a single virtuous soul can be used to call upon and command the powers of Celestine Light and then only with faith, love, and knowledge to fulfill a righteous purpose that serves Elohim.

65 As I have given unto you, so may you give in like manner unto other Children of Light that are worthy and prepared to receive such a gift."

66 Yeshua then bade the Apostles to sit down. Some sat upon the ground, others upon logs, and some on rocks. And Yeshua sat before them upon a log and spoke unto them again, saying, "After I have ascended into Heaven, Miriam will no longer be numbered among you as an Apostle, for she has been called to serve you as the Angel of the Covenant, known as Shalanawyn, after my ascension and then for eleven years upon the earth after I have departed.

67 When this comes to pass, you must quickly choose another to take her place as an Apostle among you that you will continue to be a Q-rom of twelve. And this should be with the spirit of Elohim upon you. Therefore, your choice for a successor should be of one accord."

68 Now Yeshua said this in a quiet and simple manner as if Miriam becoming an angel was not something unusual. But one and all the Apostles looked at each other without comprehension, shaking their heads in confusion.

69 Cephas spoke for all of them, asking Yeshua, "What do you mean Miriam has been called to be the Angel of the Covenant? Who of us save your mother has ever even seen an angel? And then only in a vision while she slept. How can a mortal be an angel and how can an angel stand among us as an ordinary person?"

70 Hearing the questions of Cephas, which he had spoken with great seriousness and surprise, Yeshua laughed in a good-natured manner and said unto him, "As you all well know, even now, there is hardly anything ordinary about Miriam.

71 Consider that I am among you and have been since I was born of woman. If this can be so, then surely an angel may also be among you."

72 "But angels are not mortal," Shim'on stated, seeking clarity.

73 "Nor shall Miriam be mortal when the time of her calling is upon her," responded Yeshua.

74 Miriam, who was kneeling beside Yeshua, bowed her head deeply at his words, while the eyes of each of the Apostles opened wider in incredulity.

75 "She shall die and return, even as you shall then?" questioned Yohhanan.

76 "No," answered Yeshua. "She shall never feel death's sting, but shall be changed in the twinkling of an eye from mortality to immortality, yet have the special ability given only to angels, to be immortal yet able to remain in the mortal realms."

77 "This is more than my simple head can understand," mumbled Yakov, the brother of Yeshua. "If she does not die and return, but simply remains, how will we ever accept her as anyone other than the Miriam we have always known?

78 And seeing her as she has always been, what will be different that we should think of her as an angel? And for what purpose would you anoint her such? And how are we expected to treat her when that time comes?

79 She can already do things we cannot. Why is more required of her? Why not give more gifts to us who are also faithful and true? I am sure that each of us, one and all, will volunteer to become angels."

80 Yeshua spoke now in seriousness as he answered the questions of his brother, and he said unto him, "Her calling is not from me, but from our divine Mother and Father, who have always entrusted the Angel of the Covenant to uphold their promises to the Children of Light.

81 He who now serves as the Angel of the Covenant will soon rise to a new glory and the angelic mantle shall be given to Miriam that she who knows you best, and all the Children of Light so well may serve you to the fullest as no other can.

82 When that day comes, you will understand without doubt that it is upon you, for Miriam will come with a different aura and appear in ways distinct and different than she now does.

83 But see that you speak to no one about her angelic nature. Never call her by the title of her divine calling, Shalanawyn, save you are in certain privacy or far from her and in great need of the messenger Elohim has given unto you that you might surely fulfill your destinies. Even then, call not upon Shalanawyn, but upon Elohim to send Shalanawyn unto you.

84 Let all others, including the Children of Light, know her only as the Miriam they always have, lest they call upon her for blessings reserved only for the Elohim to give."

85 Philip next began to ask a question, but Yeshua cut him off, saying, "There is no need to speak more of this. You know that which shall come to pass. It is better that your questions are not answered with more words today, which can still be without comprehension, but instead, by that which you shall witness in the days to come, which shall be with an understanding that cannot be denied."

86 "This is somewhat depressing," mumbled Yuda the son of Cleophas to everyone, but to no one in particular. "As I ponder all the things, we have learned today about what will come to pass in the days near to come, and all we have previously learned concerning these days to be, it honestly seems far more dismal a future than should be put upon the Children of Light.

87 Yeshua is going to leave us, and Miriam is going to become even stranger than she already is." Looking quickly to Miriam, he added, "Please take no offense, Miriam, for in truth, you are peculiar and not as other women."

88 He then continued saying, "We will be persecuted and have to abandon our homes and communities. Some of us may be killed, and life will surely be unpleasant, perhaps even miserable for everyone.

89 While few people will listen and follow the true Celestine Light of Elohim that we teach, many will come to follow a perversion of the light taught by others. Meanwhile, our numbers will dwindle when the times become too difficult for some.

90 Our prayers of salvation to Elohim to lift us up from the trials will go unanswered, so we can instead learn to rely on the gifts of the spirit within us. If we are not successful in manifesting the gifts we have been given, then the painful, perhaps fatal, consequences are upon us.

91 I do not mean to sound disrespectful to the divine Father and Mother, to Yeshua, Miriam, or any of you my brethren; but if this seems almost overwhelming to me, a man that has been called an Apostle and given secret knowledge. How will the Children of Light not so aware as I

am be able to keep the faith?

92 There, I think I have spoken all of my thoughts," he concluded. Looking around at the others, he asked, "Did I forget anything?"

93 "More of us will probably be killed than you allotted," Cephas replied with straight-faced humor.

94 "Very funny, Cephas!" laughed Yuda, and everyone laughed with him.

95 Now all eyes looked to Yeshua to hear the answer he would give to Yuda.

96 "All you have spoken is true, Yuda," Yeshua began. "But it does not have to be true.

97 Within each of you is a piece of divinity, a piece of our divine Father and Mother who created your soul and breathed the breath of life into your body. This spark can help you live in a different world, even while you still walk in this one, if you connect to your divinity with absolute faith.

98 Even among you, my closest friends and Apostles, it is easier to get caught up in the ways of the world and the reality that has been accepted by all the people of the world than it is to have absolute faith in something quite different.

99 You have witnessed as have many others that if a man is shot through the heart with an arrow, he quickly dies.

100 The man so shot also believes he must die if he is shot through the heart, and so he does.

101 Someday, perhaps some of you shall be shot through the heart with an arrow or run through with a spear or felled with the lead of a sling or worse.

102 Upon that day, where will your absolute faith be? Will you believe that you shall die? If so, surely you shall.

103 Will you have absolute faith that if some of your brethren come quickly to give you a blessing that you will live? If so, that will be.

104 But can you believe in yourself? That you are in fact a divine child of spirit of our Heavenly Father and Mother and that there is nothing impossible to you if you connect in total faith to your divinity.

105 Can you have unwavering faith that the sliver of divinity in your soul is enough to conquer death, to forget the structures of belief created by the world and instead embrace a oneness with our divine Father and Mother through whom all things are possible? If so, like Miriam, never will you taste death's sting.

106 Finding that state of understanding and faith is to conquer the mountain of your purpose in life. It is the greatest choice of all, but few will find the faith to go there and must therefore suffer the blessings or consequences of the reality in which they have the greatest belief.

107 Understand too that Elohim has put a special blessing upon you and all of the Children of Light of the communities of Gennesaret. You will always be challenged in diverse ways, that you may grow and become more than you are by overcoming your challenges, even as Yuda said.

108 But you will never need to suffer as greatly as the world will wish." He then reached down and touched the head of Miriam, who still knelt beside him. "In me, you have heard the gentle voice of the Celestine Light and seen the love that may heal all afflictions.

109 You are a chosen people reserved in Heaven to come forth at this time for great purposes of Elohim. Think you that you would be abandoned to muddle through the world as unprotected babes?

110 Even as I came to be the voice and the love of the Celestine Light and to bring eternal life to man, when I am upon this earth no more, you will have a shield greater than me in Miriam.

111 Because I am the creator and love all my creations, only my gentle heart goes unto them. Though the wicked grieve me greatly, I wait for the Day of the Judgment of Resonance for them to be called by their own soul to the house of their compatibility, be it darkness or light, bliss or despair.

112 Miriam has no such onus and a far more fiery temperament as well. When she is filled with her calling, the powers of Elohim will be upon her that she may faithfully serve our divine

Father and Mother.

113 And they have asked that to serve them, she serve you and the Children of Light: not to take life, for that is forbidden to her, but to do all else to insure that the covenants the divine Father and Mother have made to the Children of Light are fulfilled.

114 I am the voice and the light. She shall be the whirlwind and the majesty of Elohim made manifest.

115 And you, each of my dear friends, have no less a destiny. As you gain greater knowledge and faith, even as has Miriam who has walked each day with me for fifteen years, so shall you be called to your glory in the service of Elohim.

116 So shall every Child of Light who endures until the end, with head unbowed to man and faith in Elohim unshaken and true."

CHAPTER 83

Yeshua Walks on the Sea

During a full moon preceding the trip to Jerusalem, Cephas and a group of fishermen went out on the lake to catch fish to provide the community members who are staying behind with a good supply. A sudden storm comes upon them, and as they pray for deliverance, Yeshua comes to them, walking upon the sea. Cephas falls into the water and Yeshua pulls him up, so he is standing on top of the water.

And it came to pass that preparations were made by Yeshua and his family, and the Apostles and their families, and many of the Children of Light of the communities to embark upon an extended journey with Yeshua to Jerusalem.

2 Miriam and Martha spoke happily together about seeing their family in Bethany again and affording their children the opportunity to mingle with their many cousins.

3 Only Salome seemed sad at the thought of returning to Jerusalem. Miriam, seeing her sitting forlornly, leaned over and embraced her and said, "Little sister of the great light, why are you hiding your glory today?"

4 Salome reached up and held onto Miriam's forearm and smiling meekly said unto her, "You and Martha seem so happy to be returning to be among your family in Bethany, and I am happy for you, but it also reminds me of how alone I am.

5 "I love my life here with you, but I think it will be difficult to see the palaces of Jerusalem and not be sad for some of the things I have lost."

6 Miriam nodded in understanding and said, "In your thoughts, remember that you only lost those who did not love you, while gaining many who will love you beyond time.

7 You lost the life of a puppet who could make no choice of her own of consequence and gained a life of self-worth where every day, every choice in your life is yours and yours alone.

8 You lost a life surrounded by those in darkness and gained a life surrounded by those in light, even to becoming a wife of the Lord of Light himself.

9 Of course, you lost the excitement of court with lofty visitors from afar and elaborate entertainments and foods, but you have gained a life of greater worth, in a community of loving light, which grows each day with honest, humble, and interesting people from distant places that can become true friends.

10 And though there may be some things here that are less exciting than the courts of Jerusalem, where else besides this place with your family of light will you regularly see mighty miracles beyond the understanding of the people of the world?"

11 Miriam cupped her hand around the back of Salome's neck, and kneeling down beside her, she said, "There is no joy Martha or I will share with our family in Bethany that shall not also be your joy. You are a part of us, yesterday, today, and forever. When you are tinged by sadness, reach

out and feel the beat of my heart and the joy I know, and you shall also know it, for we are one."
12 Salome laid her head upon Miriam's shoulder and simply said, "Thank you."

Walking on Water in a Storm at Sea

13 There was a full moon the few days preceding the departure for Jerusalem and for three nights, Cephas, Yohhanan, Amram, and Yakov went fishing on the lake in two boats along with four crewmen from the communities on each boat to catch a good supply of fish for those in the communities that would remain behind.
14 On the third night, a sudden storm came upon them, and they lost all bearings of the land and stars. They lashed their boats together so they would not be separated in the dark ferocity of the storm and as one prayed to Elohim for deliverance.
15 And it came to pass that Yeshua heard their pleas, and he came to them, walking on the water, which was becalmed before him, even while the storm continued to rage all around.
16 Seeing him coming through the waves and mists and darkness, their joy was full, and they called out to him and beckoned him to hurry.
17 Coming up next to the boat, he stood upon the surface of the water and said unto them, "You are certainly most diligent fishermen to come out even in the darkness of the night to provide for your brothers and sisters. I thought you were in need, but it seems that all is well."
18 "No! Everything is not well!" Cephas shouted above the whistling wind. "Our boats are full of fish and awash with water so much so that we must either throw our fish overboard or sink. We had even begun to do it as you appeared. Therefore, rebuke this storm if you will, lest we lose all the good we have gained for our communities."
19 As he spoke, the boats slid down into a large wave trough, and as they came up, a great wave burst through the prows and over the boats, drenching everyone in a heavy wall of water. Even Yeshua, still standing beside the boat on the water, was covered and soaked by the huge wave, but he seemed not to mind.
20 "It is you who should rebuke the wave, Cephas," answered Yeshua. "You and your brethren, for I will not long be among you, but storms of all types you will still continually have to contend with."
21 "We have tried," Cephas yelled above the howl of the wind. Before he could say more, another big wave crashed over them, and he was thrown out of the boat and into the sea because his attention had been diverted as he spoke to Yeshua.
22 He surfaced nearby and Yeshua calmly walked over to him and reaching down into the water, he grabbed him by his forearm and pulled him upright so that Cephas also now also stood upon the water and did not sink.
23 "How marvelous!" Cephas exclaimed. "Would that I could do this on my own," he said wistfully.
24 "No man can walk upon the water on his own, Cephas," Yeshua answered, "only a man who walks with Elohim. But you are certainly a man of the Celestine Light. Therefore, as you ask and have faith and love and a passion to do this, expand your strong aura, so shall it be." And with those words, he let go of Cephas' hand.
25 For a moment, Cephas stood upon the water on his own, and the joy on his face was like a child in wonder when he realized that he was standing upon the water, even though Yeshua touched him not.
26 He turned to look at his brethren in the boat, but no sooner had he begun to say, "Look at me," than he began to sink because of his pride, whereas his humility would have upheld him.
27 Quickly, he was awash to his waist again in the angry sea, and Yeshua once more reached over to rescue him and pulled him up onto the surface. Together, they then stepped over to Cephas' boat and entered into it.
28 Yeshua held up his arms and, looking to the sky and the sea shouted, "Cease!" and immediately, the storm ended and the waters of the sea quickly calmed.

29 One of the crew members who was a fairly new member of the Communities of Light looked at Yeshua with awe and said, "Who is our Yeshua that even the wind and the sea obey him?"

30 Cephas, standing beside him and hearing his question, answered with reverence in his voice, "He is the wind and the sea."

31 Three days later, and two days after the Sabbath, all the Children of Light from the four communities gathered near Yeshua's house in Capernaum at sunrise, as he prepared to depart on his journey to Jerusalem.

32 There were many who had packed to accompany him. And a large number of those were bringing all of their children.

33 There were also many new faces in the multitude as the Communities of Light had continued to grow rapidly in the last year as Children of Light from lands near and far had heard the small voice inside and followed its light to this place.

34 Yeshua then went out among the multitude and touched and spoke to each one of them, especially to every child. And there was not even one whom he did not touch or speak to.

35 When he was finished, he began to walk on the road leading south toward Tiberias, with Miriam on his right, holding his hand, and Salome on her right, holding her other hand. Martha and all of their children and Yeshua's mother Miryam followed closely behind, and then came the Apostles and their families and then many of the Children of Light and their families.

CHAPTER 84

Last Tour of the Holy Land

Yeshua's last tour of Galilee and Judea covers a lot of ground. He does many miraculous healings and has serious encounters with the Greater Sanhedrin, Pharisees, and Sadducees. He speaks in parables to fulfill ancient prophecies and for those who have ears to hear and eyes to see.

Final Tour of Galilee

During the following weeks, Yeshua went from town to town in Galilee and did many miracles of healing and cast out many demons. As on previous tours to spread the light of Elohim, the Apostles would precede him to each town to alert the people of his coming. This time, they made sure everyone knew that this would be the last time that Yeshua would ever come among them.

2 As Yeshua's fame had spread—that all illnesses and maladies vanished at his touch—the crowds had grown larger in every new city and town for his reputation as a miracle worker had grown greatly since his first preaching in Galilee, and even people who had disdained to pay him any attention before came out to see him now.

3 After a morning of healing the infirmed and diseased, Yeshua indicated to the people that he intended to proceeded south through Samaria and into Judea. As he entered the border area of Samaria, many of the Galileans that had been following him from town to town fell away and returned to their homes or took another route into Judea rather than pass through the lands of the despised Samaritans.

4 Seeking a reprieve from the crush of people, after the midday meal Yeshua quietly slipped away, taking only Miriam, Salome, Amram, Judah the younger and Mattayah with him. He asked his other Apostles to remain with the multitude and the many Children of Light that had come from the communities and rendezvous with them for the evening meal at a location previously chosen for that night by Cephas.

5 His opposition had also increased in step with his growing fame and the Pharisees, scribes, Sadducees, and lower Sanhedrin all came to hear him speak and to see his miracles in every town in which he stopped. Each for their own reasons opposed him and sought to prevent his ministry and miracles.

6 But in this, they were greatly frustrated, for none could contend with his reasoning or knowledge of the law, nor refute his miracles. Much of his doctrine they argued to be false, but the people heeded not their arguments for the miracles of Yeshua were a more powerful persuader.

Cast the First Stone

7 In yet one more attempt to discredit Yeshua in the eyes of the common people to prove that he disobeyed well known and widely accepted laws, the Pharisees found him with his small entourage resting under a tree in a plaza and brought a woman accused of adultery before him. A crowd of perhaps forty men followed them.

8 The woman was cloaked completely in black, including a hood covering her head with only a woven mesh for her to see out of and breathe near her eyes and nose. She was whimpering in fear as she was thrust prone onto the ground at Yeshua's feet.

9 "Rabbi, this woman has been charged with adultery," one of the Pharisees spat out in contempt, looking at Yeshua. "Two honorable men have born witness against her and the man with whom she committed her sin has also confessed. They are standing there among these good men of Israel," he said, pointing into the crowd.

10 The Pharisee turned and looked out upon the gathered men declaring, "By the laws of God she must be punished with stoning. If God wills it, she will die. If not, so be it. We are merely the hands of God to execute his will."

11 Speaking to the crowd, the Pharisee called out, "Who here will cast a stone and be a servant of the Almighty?" As if they had never heard a word of the teachings of Yeshua there was a chorus of 'ayes' and many men, including her accusers hastily searched the surrounding ground and picked up rocks, some of them larger than a fist.

12 The Pharisee looked at Yeshua smugly, saying, "Rabbi, it is you who should give the command for her to be stoned. By this we will all know that in truth you uphold and support the laws of Israel and God."

13 Seeing this spectacle, the ordeal of the woman, the willingness of the mob to so easily be swayed to violence, and the Pharisees rude and despicable behavior, Miriam began to step forward to confront them with righteous anger and perhaps more, but Yeshua grasped her garment and held her back.

14 Holding her hand he stepped with her in front of the woman upon the ground, standing between the accused woman and the Pharisees and the crowd of men.

15 Yeshua shook his head and said unto them, "How easily you forget all that you have heard me teach as I have traveled through your towns. Do you think that my miracles come from God but not my teachings? I ask you in the name of Elohim, the god of fairness, why is the woman put to death while the man who sinned with her is merely given a few lashes and then given a stone with which to injure her grievously?

16 Was it the woman who lusted for the man and convinced him to commit adultery, or the man who lusted for the woman and convinced her? All of you men already know the answer in your heart, for it is in men that lust leads to stupidity and sweet words of false love to entice women of virtue into abasement."

17 Looking then at the Pharisees, Yeshua scolded them, saying, "Woe unto you Pharisees for trying to spring a trap of the law upon me. Have you not already heard me say that I have not come to support the law that is unjust, but to overthrow it and crush it beneath my feet?"

18 Turning again to the gathered men, Yeshua said unto them, "Are you the just judging the unjust, or are you the unjust seeking to condemn another when your own house is a cesspool? Alright brave men of Israel. You seek the justice of your law by your own hands? Then let he who is without sin among you be the only ones to cast a stone, else you are the unrighteous judging the unrighteous, and where is the justice in that?"

19 Hearing his words a few men dropped their stones, but most held onto them with lethal intent and it was plain that for most of the men, his words had fallen on deaf ears, for from among the crowd came shouts of, "Death to the adulteress!" "Serve God!" "Uphold the laws of Israel!"

20 Yeshua breathed a deep sigh of disappointment and spoke to Miriam in his mind, saying, "These men are blind to the truth, let them be blind for a short time to life and perhaps then they

will give it greater value. I leave it to you Miriam to protect this woman and teach these men of the Celestine Light in a way that they will never desire to repeat this event. Use the gifts you have been given, in the fullness you have learned so well."

21 "As you wish my Lord," she acknowledged in their unspoken communication. "Very happily it shall be."

22 Even in that short silent exchange between Yeshua and Miriam, a group of over a dozen men with one or more stones in their hands had formed a half circle close about Yeshua, Miriam and the woman in black, who was now sitting upon the ground, still whimpering in fear. The Pharisees had faded back behind the men intent upon stoning the woman, and a larger group of onlookers had gathered behind the original group of men waiting to see what would transpire.

23 Miriam stepped away from Yeshua and took a step forward toward the threatening men. Yeshua stood immediately beside the woman in black. Salome and his three Apostles stood a pace or so behind her.

24 "Good men of Israel. Drop your stones and move away, before you reap in pain what you sow in foolishness," Miriam commanded. "You will not stone this woman today or any other. You are merely being used by the Pharisees. They think you are ignorant louts that they can manipulate to hurt Yeshua of Nazareth. Are you going to prove them right or show them you are men touched by the light?"

25 "Ha!" Exclaimed one of the Pharisees standing behind the men holding stones. "Does the scandalously uncovered wife of the Rabbi now speak for her husband, because her husband listens more to his brazen, disobedient wife than to God?

26 What more proof of blasphemy than this—that any woman, let alone one so shamelessly unclothed, would be so insolent to command men, and her husband, the good Rabbi, would simply stand idly by and not rebuke her?"

27 There were many grumblings of agreement in the crowd at the words of the Pharisee, both among the men with stones and in the multitude that stood back observing the events.

28 Hearing this, Yeshua spoke to the Pharisee, saying, "Rather than rebuke my wife, I am the one that has always asked her to dress more in the manner of the Greeks, to not hide the beauty that Elohim created.

29 It is I who has also asked her to speak. The blasphemy against Elohim is not in a woman showing her beauty, or speaking, or commanding men, but in your laws which condemn such. Until you realize your women are your equals, not your property; your co-creators in both this life and the next; you will never know God or taste the fruits of the life to come."

30 "Stone her!" Yelled out someone from the crowd. "Stone her!" More voices repeated.

31 "Move aside Rabbi," ordered the Pharisee. "And your wife and disciples as well. This crowd has heard your words and they have heard mine. They have seen your actions and judged them to not be in keeping with the teachings of God. You are not judged to be stoned this day, but this woman is, and her time has come to receive the wrath of God for her iniquity. Stand aside at this moment lest you and your wives and disciples all suffer her fate by proximity."

32 But among the Celestines—Yeshua, Miriam, Salome and the three Apostles, not one moved or spoke in response to the admonition of the Pharisee. They all stood resolute, courageously facing the ring of the men with stones.

33 "Stone her!" Someone yelled once again. At this latest call the men holding the rocks quickly raised up their arms to cast their stones, even as more men in the crowd behind picked up stones from the ground so they too could participate in the judgment.

34 Miriam's eyes narrowed as she saw the men raising their arms with lethal intent. As their arms whipped forward slinging their missiles she uttered a single Celestine word of power, "Lakadonz!" As the word left her lips the hurtling rocks instantly disintegrated into sand in midair and fell harmlessly to the ground.

35 Immediately after uttering the word of power, in a rapid sweeping motion, Miriam put her hands in the prayer position across her chest, then quickly raised them both high opening her

palms and spreading out her fingers. At her beckoning, the fallen sand from the former stones was joined by a rapidly forming whirlwind of sand and dust from the ground.

36 So thick was the swirling mass that the entire multitude quickly disappeared behind the funnel cloud. In its calm core the woman in black stood up in amazement looking at the wall of fury just beyond her touch, while in the peaceful center she remained with Yeshua, Miriam, Salome and the three Apostles.

37 After just a minute or two the whirlwind settled and vanished. A haze of dust remained hanging in the air. Many of the crowd had hurriedly dispersed to escape the biting sand and dust, but many still remained including the Pharisees and each of the would-be assailants. But every man who had held a stone now held their eyes moaning in misery and stumbling and falling in blindness.

38 One by one friends and family of the stricken men came to them and led them away. The Pharisees also gathered together disheveled and confused and departed without saying another word.

39 When all of her adversaries were gone Yeshua turned to the woman in black, saying, "Where are your accusers who would condemn you?"

40 The woman shrugged and answered meekly, "I know not sir, they are not here."

41 "Nor are there any here who would condemn or judge you," Yeshua assured her.

42 "You save the unworthy good sir," the woman said, bowing her head deeply with a deep sigh and a burst of crying. "I am guilty of that of which I have been accused. I hate myself for what I have done, but it does not change that which has transpired."

43 Yeshua put his hand gently on the top of her head, "But your true and remorseful repentance has changed you. And it has changed your present and your future as you continue to walk in the light from this day forth.

44 Because of your repentance, the Elohim do not condemn you for your sin, nor even remember it any more. I know the depth of your sorrow for all that has transpired. Go your way and sin no more. Prove yourself worthy of the life you have been given again this day. Live it in the light that all who truly know you will praise you and your virtues."

45 The woman then departed, thanking Yeshua and Miriam profusely, and two of the Apostles went with her to see her safely to her home. Watching them leave Salome put her hand gently upon Miriam's shoulder and asked, "What of the men who became blind in the sandstorm? Will their sight return?"

46 "Yes," Miriam assured her. "Yeshua only meant for them to have a lesson equal to their folly. It is important when true justice issues from the light of Elohim, that it is in actuality just and fair. Neither too harsh nor too lenient from the punishment that is warranted."

Miracle Soup

47 As evening was coming upon them Yeshua, Miriam, Salome and the three Apostles, rejoined the other Apostles and a still large following of people, including many of the Children of Light from the communities on Lake Gennesaret.

48 Many people took care of their own food as they followed Yeshua on his journeys, having brought it with them, purchased it, or foraged it along the way. Nevertheless, Yeshua instructed the Apostles to create a warm soup each night, which they prepared in a large clay pot over a small fire and distributed it along with a little coarse bread to everyone who sought food.

49 The soup was nicknamed "miracle soup," because it consisted of everything they could find each day, from greens along the trails and roads to bugs of many types, occasional raw fish, a copious base of water, and liberal seasoning with wild spices.

50 Whenever the pot was half empty, they would fill it again with water, throw in anything else edible that might have shown up, and continue dispensing until everyone had been satisfied.

51 Yeshua had charged the Apostles in particular to be responsible for the miracle soup, both to show that in the Kingdom of Light, it is an honor for even the greatest to be of service to

the lowest and also to give them practice using their gifts to insure the miracle soup always was sufficient for the needs.

52 "This is very good soup!" exclaimed one man who had just begun to follow Yeshua since the last town. "What is in it?" he asked Yudas Iscariot, who had served him.

53 "Things that are good for you," replied Yudas.

54 "What kind of things?" the man persisted.

55 "Things that taste better when they remain a mystery," answered Yudas dryly.

56 "Oh, those type of things," the man muttered less enthusiastically.

57 "Yes, those type of things," Yudas agreed, stifling a chuckle.

58 The man walked away, and Toma, who was also serving people, gave Yudas a nudge in the side with his elbow as he chuckled over the exchange.

59 Yudas looked at him and feigned innocence, saying, "What else could I say? I spoke tactfully, but also truthfully."

60 They looked at each other and both laughed a little and Toma said unto him. "Nothing is wrong with what you said, nothing at all. It was just funny."

61 Now Ligia, the wife of Yudas, had been standing nearby with their two children, speaking to another woman, and seeing her husband and Toma talking jovially over the soup, she called to Yudas, saying, "Be sure to save some of the mystery for me, Yudas."

62 "I am still trying to unravel the mystery that you are," Yudas replied with a smile. "Perhaps, it would be unwise to let you eat something that might make you more mysterious. You are already a Greek. Who knows what might happen to you if mystery was added upon mystery?"

63 "I would probably be changed into an Apostle, the most mysterious of all God's creatures!" Ligia laughed in reply. And Yudas and Toma laughed with her.

Healings in Northern Judea

64 Following the Sabbath, Yeshua entered into Judea and performed many miracles in the northern towns during the next three weeks. The paralytic walked again, the lepers were cleansed, the blind saw, the dumb spoke, the sick and the ill were made well, and many demons were cast out of those whom they had tormented.

65 The opponents of Yeshua continued to fume as his fame grew day by day, and there seemed to be nothing they could say or do to thwart his sway over the people.

66 The Romans were also growing increasingly uneasy with the large and sometimes-boisterous crowds that were following Yeshua, and they kept an ever-vigilant eye upon his activities, with increasing numbers of soldiers shadowing his movements.

Arrival at Bethany

67 Two days before the Sabbath of the new moon, Yeshua and his family arrived in Bethany at the childhood home of Miriam and Martha.

68 They were greeted with much enthusiasm and affection by their brother Lazarus and all the members of their family and extended family.

69 The father of Miriam, Martha, and Lazarus loved to put on feasts and desired to immediately commence a five-day feast, but Yeshua forbade him saying, "Good patriarch of the house of those that I love, Miriam and I must depart on the morrow, for the field is ready to harvest. But would you do me the great kindness of keeping my mother and Martha and all the children of our family while Miriam and I journey through Judea?"

70 "Keep them!" cried the father of Lazarus indignantly. "I should be affronted if they did not stay."

71 And it came to pass that after Miriam and Yeshua departed the following day, the father of Lazarus still threw a feast in celebration of his children and grandchildren whom he and his wife saw too seldom.

72 But Lazarus and his wife departed with Yeshua and Miriam and the Apostles, for having been much apart, Lazarus longed to spend every moment with them.

Confrontation at the Home of the Chief Judge

73 And it came to pass that Yeshua came unto Jerusalem and was met at the gate by emissaries of the Great Sanhedrin, who bade him come with them to see Chief Judge Caiaphas at his home.

74 Among the Apostles, there was some trepidation, for to be summoned to appear before the judges could not bode well. But they could see that Yeshua seemed happy at the prospect, so decided they should be as well.

75 When they came near to the house, the women were told to remain behind at a small outbuilding, as only the Apostles could pass with Yeshua into the premises of Caiaphas's home.

76 But Yeshua said unto them, "Where I go, Miriam goes, or I go not."

77 The emissaries did not balk at the words of Yeshua, but immediately one said unto him, "But of course, we did not mean your wife, whom we know to be one of your closest disciples. For her, an exception has been granted."

78 Yeshua then followed the emissary leading the way into the courtyard, and Miriam came after him and the Apostles.

79 But then a cry went up from the other emissary, saying, "Wait! There are twelve men here; with his wife, that is thirteen. We were told only to admit twelve disciples."

80 The first emissary looked back and, counting the men and Miriam, saw that there was indeed thirteen, and he said unto Yeshua. "Why do you try to deceive us? Do you think us fools that we cannot count to twelve?"

81 Yeshua answered them, "Count as you choose. These are the hearts that beat as one with mine. Pass us all or not one shall pass, but decide now, lest I conclude you are wasting my time."

82 "How dare you speak so insolently concerning a command to appear before the Chief Judge Caiaphas," exclaimed one of the emissaries. "It is not for you to choose, but for him. Now follow me quickly, lest you draw the wrath of Caiaphas even greater than you already have."

83 So saying, he turned on his heel and headed again into the courtyard. "I suppose that is his I-feel-very-important way of saying we can all come," Lazarus chuckled quietly. Yeshua smiled and nodded his head in silent agreement.

84 Upon entering the main courtyard, Yeshua looked to see a little over a dozen of the Greater Sanhedrin sitting about the courtyard and these were almost all Sadducees, and the Chief Judge Caiaphas sat on a raised dais at the end of the courtyard.

85 Walking directly to him, Yeshua said unto him, "You have brought the light; do you now have torches to illuminate the darkness?"

86 "Please do not insult me by speaking to me in riddles or meaningless parables," Caiaphas replied stonily.

87 This is an informal meeting to ascertain if you are a threat to the way of life of the chosen people of Elohim. Are you a threat, Yeshua of Nazareth? Someone we should fear and put away in prison or just a misguided but harmless healer to ignore?"

88 Yeshua answered him, saying, "I am your greatest fear and your greatest hope. Which is more important to you?"

89 Obviously irritated at Yeshua's answer, Caiaphas replied, "Were you never taught to speak as a normal person and with respect? A simple yes or no will suffice for most questions, and those requiring more than one word answers should use words that clarify the answer, not make it more confused. And do not respond to my queries with questions, lest you draw my ire thinking you are insolent."

90 "If you never allow questions, then you must have already concluded the answers," Yeshua responded. "If that is so, then it would be better to have trained monkeys appear before you rather than men, for they will always give you what you seek."

91 "Humph!" Caiaphas grunted. "From what I hear, you are a poor man of little means, the questionable son of an equally poor carpenter from the dilapidated town of Nazareth."

92 "Because I have heard that you have some healing abilities, I have invited you to my home to learn more; yet you speak to me without respect or fear of which you should have both in

ample quantities.

93 Does it make you feel important to thus speak to your betters, Yeshua of Nazareth? Are you trying to impress the motley lot that follows you? I wonder how impressed they will be to see you thrown in prison for your blasphemes? What do you think?"

94 "I know that men will be uplifted or condemned on the Day of Judgment by every idle word they have spoken," Yeshua answered.

95 "I am the light that others follow, and my path is true and straight. If my words or tone offends, consider why and reflect that even the life-giving sun will burn your skin like a fire if you do not act with prudence in its presence."

96 "Are you speaking again in riddles as I have forbidden you to do?" exclaimed Caiaphas. "You would do well to remember that I am the chief judge and by my command all things can occur, both the pleasant and the unpleasant in your life. I am not trying to be your enemy, but you seem intent on making me so."

97 Yeshua looked at him and smiled mischievously and said unto him, "Caiaphas, you are an important man in Judea, but Judea is not all of Rome and Rome is not all of the world; and in the world beyond Palestine and Judea, the earth does not tremble at your name."

98 Pointing to the sun, Yeshua said, "Can you in all your power stop the sun?"

99 "Of course not!" protested Caiaphas. "Only Elohim can stop the sun as the scriptures record he did in the days of Joshua."

100 Without saying another word, Yeshua walked over to a small tree, and snapping off a branch, he went to a spot of dirt nearby. Placing the broken stick vertically into the ground, he marked the spot where the shadow of the stick fell upon the ground.

101 Turning to Caiaphas, he said unto him, "That you will have no excuse on the Day of Judgment, let there be no doubt to whom you speak. Until I decree it, the sun shall not move again from its spot in the sky."

102 This proclamation brought about a chorus of derisive laughter from the gathered Sanhedrin, and Caiaphas, laughing too, said unto Yeshua, "If nothing else, you are a bold rascal. But I think you shall soon be shown to be a false prophet by your own overreaching bravado, so we will wait for an hour to see you undone by your words.

103 In the meantime, this is not a court, but simply an informal gathering of learned men. Perhaps, you would be so kind to clarify some of your doctrines for us while we wait for the sun to move?"

104 Yeshua lifted his eyebrows and turned his palms up toward Caiaphas, indicating that he should continue with his questions.

105 "It has come to my attention," Caiaphas began, "that according to the Pharisees who were witnesses, on at least one occasion, you and your Apostles plucked and ate some corn from a field on the Sabbath. How can you justify breaking the Sabbath in this way?"

106 Yeshua answered him, saying, "Your question is trivial, but the answer can have substance. Therefore, I will answer. Haven't you read what David did when he and his companions were hungry? They entered the house of God and ate the consecrated bread, which was not lawful for them to do, but only for the priests.

107 And haven't you read in the law that on the Sabbath, the priests in the temple desecrate the day and yet are innocent? Does that not seem strange to you that the priests who are supposed to be servants of God can make themselves above the laws of God? Or perhaps they are only men making laws unto themselves in the name of God?

108 But I tell you that one greater than the temple is here. And if it is permissible for priests who serve Elohim to eat that which is forbidden, how much more shall the Lord of the Sabbath have mercy on those who hunger?"

109 At Yeshua's answer, Caiaphas looked slyly over at his fellow Sanhedrin to make sure they had all heard his blasphemy.

110 Then continuing with his questions, he said, "I have heard that you are a great healer, and

that is to be commended if you are in fact healing by the power of Elohim. But I have heard it said that you do much of your healing on the Sabbath, which is forbidden by the law. It would seem then that your healing comes from a place of darkness, not light as you profess."

111 "You err in your understanding of the law, Caiaphas," Yeshua responded. "If ever there was a day to do good, it is on the Sabbath. If any of you has a sheep and it falls into a pit on the Sabbath, will you not take hold of it and lift it out? How much more valuable is a man than a sheep! Therefore it is lawful to do good on the Sabbath."

112 Caiaphas rubbed his beard as he contemplated Yeshua's answer, then said unto him, "I have also heard that you cast out many demons, so many in fact that I had no idea there was such a multitude of them in Judea and Galilee.

113 It seems most strange to me that in all my life, I have only on four occasions ever met a man with a demon, yet you seem to find them every day and everywhere you go.

114 "Some have said this is because you are in fact a minion of Beelzebub, the prince of demons, and so see your demonic friends on every corner and simply make a meaningless show of casting them out."

115 "Oh foolish men," Yeshua answered. "Every Kingdom divided against itself will be ruined, and every city or household divided against itself will not stand.

116 If Satan drives out Satan, he is divided against himself. How then can his Kingdom stand?

117 If I drive out demons by the power of Beelzebub, how would that be helping the darkness? But if I drive out demons by the Spirit of God and men who have been enslaved are now free, then the Kingdom of God has come upon you.

118 Have you never watched the farmers grow the good fruit? If a tree is good, its fruit will be good, but if a tree is bad, its fruit will be bad. A tree is recognized by its fruit, be it good or bad, and so am I and so are all of you.

119 Are you bringing forth good fruit or are you a brood of vipers poisoning the people? How can evil say anything is good? For out of the truth of the heart, the mouth speaks. Therefore, the good man continually brings good things out of the light stored up in him, and the evil man continually brings forth evil things out of the darkness stored up in him."

120 "You are not helping your cause by insulting us," Caiaphas replied with a scowl. "But I still have one question if you are brave enough to answer."

121 "If you are brave enough to question," Yeshua answered.

122 "It has been reported," Caiaphas began, "that you preach that Elohim is not one God but many, such as the heathen religions do, even to the point of claiming a mother figure in your array of gods as equal to Elohim.

123 Of course, admitting this will condemn you, but you seem oblivious to the pit you are digging, so what have you to say about your plurality of gods, including female gods?"

124 Yeshua answered him quickly, saying, "Choose your words with care, Caiaphas, for by your words, you will be justified and by your words you will be condemned. I tell you solemnly, every sin and blasphemy can be forgiven with repentance, but blasphemy against the Holy Mother will not be forgiven, but must suffer the cold, dark resonance.

125 Anyone who speaks a word against me or my Apostles or Elohim the Father can be forgiven with repentance. But anyone with malicious intent, who speaks against the Holy Mother, will not be forgiven, either in this age or in the age to come. Their road back to the light will be cold, dark, and lonely, if ever they find it."

126 Then another of the Sanhedrin spoke up, saying, "You have said many things that condemn you should we hold a court against you, and you obviously cannot be a true prophet for you disobey the law at every opportunity and teach others to do likewise. But if you would have our mercy, show us a miraculous sign that you are more than just a charlatan or a man demented, lest we conclude that you must be removed for the safety of the Children of Israel."

127 Yeshua answered him, saying, "When evening comes, you say, 'It will be fair weather, for

the sky is red,' and in the morning, 'Today it will be stormy, for the sky is red and overcast.' You know how to interpret the appearance of the sky, but you cannot interpret the signs of the times.

128 It is a wicked and adulterous generation that asks for a miraculous sign! But you will know a great blessing has dawned when you shall witness the sign of the prophet Jonah.

129 "As Jonah was three days and three nights in the belly of a huge fish, so the son of light will be three days and three nights in the heart of the earth; but only three.

130 Verily, unless you repent, the men of Nineveh will stand up at the judgment of this assembly and condemn it, for they repented at the preaching of Jonah, and now one greater than Jonah is here.

131 So shall the queen of the South rise at the judgment of this assembly lest you repent and condemn it, for she came from the ends of the earth to listen to Solomon's wisdom, and now one greater than Solomon is here."

132 "I have heard enough!" shouted Caiaphas. Then pointing at Yeshua, he commanded, "Leave my house, you pollute it! But do not leave Jerusalem, for I will see you again soon, and if you try to hide, it will be the worse for you."

133 "Fear not, foolish man, the sun will not be hidden, but brighter than on any day."

134 With those words Yeshua, Miriam, and the Apostles turned and departed from the house of Caiaphas.

135 After they had left, the Sanhedrin spoke of him derisively among themselves, mocking him and the things he had said.

136 Sometime later, one of them noticed the stick Yeshua had stuck in the ground to cast a shadow from the sun. He walked over to it, proclaiming, "Look, here is the stick the charlatan would have us believe would mark his stopping of the sun. See how the shadow has . . ."

137 When he looked closer, he saw that the shadow had not moved, and with a tremble in his voice, he called the other Sanhedrin to come and look. One by one, they all came over and stood looking at the shadow of the stick, which had not moved one iota past the mark Yeshua had made in the dirt, then lifted their gaze to glance, uncomprehending at the bright sun in the sky.

138 "What can this mean?" asked one of the Sanhedrin.

139 Almost in unison, they glanced up quickly at the sun. "Could it actually have stopped?" asked another.

140 "Of course not!" exclaimed Caiaphas. Walking over to the stick, he grabbed it and pulled it out of the ground. "It was just a simple magician's trick," he stated. "Nor was he here hardly long enough for the shadow to move!" But even as he spoke, the stick he was holding in his hand disintegrated into gray ash and blew away in a fine powder upon the wind.

141 The Sanhedrin looked at one another in bewilderment, and Caiaphas said unto them. "This Yeshua of Nazareth is a dangerous man, the likes such as we have not seen before. The sooner we remove him from the presence of the people, the safer all of Israel shall be."

142 And the rest of the Sanhedrin nodded their heads in agreement.

143 Despite the warning of Caiaphas for Yeshua to remain in Jerusalem, he and Miriam returned with the Apostles to the house of Miriam's parents in the evening so they could be with their children.

Conversation with the Zealots

144 The following day, Yeshua, Miriam, and the Apostles, accompanied by Salome, returned to Jerusalem where Yeshua once again began healing many people of all manner of infirmities and quickly drawing large crowds unto him.

145 While he was healing a paralytic man, two zealots came up to the Apostle Shim'on and confided in him, "Your teacher is a mighty man of stature, words, and deeds. It is said by many of our friends that he is the Messiah that has been prophesied and has come to Jerusalem to lead us in a revolt against the Romans. We have come to ascertain the truth of this, and to enter the secret army, we have heard, he is gathering. And we can bring many others with us."

146 Hearing the words of the two men, Shim'on was cautious, for they could be spies as easily as zealots. He said, "Yeshua comes with a sword of truth to slice away the darkness that has covered the eyes of men, but you are mistaken to think he is here to lead a revolt against the Romans."

147 "And so you must say," replied one of the zealots cunningly. "We understand. But tell us where we can meet privately to plan, for we have many mighty men who have waited only for God to send us a leader, and seeing his strong stature and his miracles and hearing his words against taxes and oppression, few doubt that it is Yeshua whom God has called."

148 "That is not why he is here," protested Shim'on.

149 "What has happened to you?" demanded one of the zealots. "Are you not Shim'on the Fierce? Your reputation as a zealot has gone before you, but today you sound like a sheep afraid of his own shadow.

150 "Look around at this crowd," he said pointing at the multitude. "Half the people here are zealots like us, looking to Yeshua and seeing the salvation we have been waiting for. Surely this is a day given by God, and we shall heed the call to deliver our people.

151 Do not waste time with petty diversions of words. Let the master know we are here and ready to fight."

152 Shim'on shook his head and said unto them, "I am Shim'on once known as the Fierce, but Yeshua has changed my heart to a peace my life has never known. He is here for your salvation and mine, but it is a salvation of the soul, not of the sword."

153 "We shall see," one of the zealots replied. "Let him know we are here, amassing even now in Jerusalem, waiting his initiative. There will never be another time as ripe as this one. Make sure he knows." With those words, the two men disappeared back into the crowd.

154 Shim'on went immediately to tell Yeshua of his encounter, and when he had an opening, he pulled him aside to relate his conversation with the zealots.

155 Yeshua, already knowing of their conversation, stopped him before he could speak, saying, "You spoke well to your two visitors, Shim'on, although they seemed to be deficient in hearing, for they did not comprehend your words."

156 "I tried to explain that you are not here to lead an army of revolt," Shim'on began. "But having once been a zealot, I can say that other alternatives are not much considered, so they did not believe me when I refuted their desires."

157 "Worry not about this," Yeshua consoled Shim'on. "The zealots have a more important part to play than they realize in the days to come."

158 "I do not understand," Shim'on said with bewilderment.

159 "You soon will," Yeshua reassured him. "When you encounter the zealots again, tell them you have spoken to me and reaffirm that I will not be leading or participating in their revolt."

Parable of the Sower

160 That same day, Yeshua stood outside the temple and preached in parables to the large crowd that had come to see him.

161 And he said unto them, "A farmer went out to sow his seed. As he was scattering the seed, some fell along the path, and the birds came and ate it up.

162 Some fell on rocky places, where it did not have much soil. It sprang up quickly, because the soil was shallow. But when the sun came up, the plants were scorched, and they withered because they had no root.

163 Other seed fell among thorns, which grew up and choked the plants. Still other seed fell on good soil, where it produced a crop—a hundred, sixty, or thirty times what was sown. He who has ears, let him hear."

Parable of the Weeds

164 Yeshua told them another parable, saying, "The Kingdom of Heaven is like a man who sowed good seed in his field. But while everyone was sleeping, his enemy came and sowed weeds

among the wheat and went away. When the wheat sprouted and formed heads, then the weeds also appeared.

165 The owner's servants came to him and said, 'Sir, didn't you sow good seed in your field? Where then did the weeds come from?'

166 "An enemy did this,' he replied.

167 The servants asked him, 'Do you want us to go and pull them up?'

168 'No,' he answered, 'because while you are pulling the weeds, you may uproot the wheat with them. Let both grow together until the harvest. At that time, I will tell the harvesters: First collect the weeds and tie them in bundles to be burned, then gather the wheat and bring it into my barn.'"

Parable of the Tiny Unknown Seed

169 Then he told them another parable: "The Kingdom of Heaven is like a small unknown seed, which a man took and planted in his field because it appeared unique and curious.

170 Though it was tiny, when it grew, it became a tree, so vast that the birds of the air came and perched in its branches and built nests and thrived."

Parable of the Yeast

171 He told them still another parable: "The Kingdom of Heaven is also like yeast that a woman took and mixed into a large amount of flour until it worked all through the dough."

172 Yeshua spoke all these things to the crowd in parables, and he did not say anything to them without using a parable.

173 So it was fulfilled that which was spoken through the prophet: "I will open my mouth in parables. I will utter things hidden since the creation of the world."

174 For a moment, Yeshua stopped speaking and told the multitude to remain while he rested a moment. Then the Apostles came to him and asked, "Why do you speak to the people in parables?"

175 Yeshua replied, "The knowledge of the secrets of the Kingdom of Heaven have been given to you, but not to them, because you have seen the light and embraced it into your heart, but they have seen the light yet kept their hearts closed.

176 Whoever has been a good steward of his life will be given more, and he will have an abundance. Whoever has not been a good steward, even what he has will be taken from him.

177 This is why I speak to them in parables. Though seeing, they do not see; though hearing, they do not hear or understand. In them is fulfilled the prophecy of Isaiah: 'You will be ever hearing but never understanding; you will be ever seeing but never perceiving.

178 For the hearts of these people have become calloused; they hardly hear with their ears, and they have closed their eyes.'

179 Otherwise, they might see with their eyes, hear with their ears, understand with their hearts, and turn to the Celestine Light, and then I would heal more than the infirmities of their body. I would enliven their spirit with the light that is never extinguished.

180 But blessed are your eyes because they see and your ears because they hear. Many prophets and righteous men longed to see what you have seen, but did not see it, and to hear what you have heard, but did not hear it.

181 Listen now to what the parable of the sower means: When anyone hears the message about the Kingdom and does not understand it, the adversary within comes and snatches away what was sown in his heart. This is the seed sown along the path.

182 The one who received the seed that fell on rocky places is the man who hears the word and at once receives it with joy. But since he has no root, he lasts only a short time. When trouble or persecution comes because of the word, the adversary within steals his courage, and he quickly falls away.

183 The one who received the seed that fell among the thorns is the man who hears the word, but the adversary within allows the worries of this life and the deceitfulness of wealth to choke

it, making it unfruitful.

184 But the one who received the seed that fell on good soil is the man who hears the word and understands it. He overcomes the adversary within and produces a crop, yielding a hundred, sixty, or thirty times what was sown."

185 "Can you also explain the parable of the weeds?" asked Salome.

186 Yeshua nodded in affirmation and said unto them, "The one who sowed the good seed is the Son of Light.

187 The field is the world, and the good seed stands for the sons and daughters of the Kingdom.

188 The weeds are the people of the world who sin without repentance and restitution and the enemy who sows them is Lucifer, who ever works to bring out the worst in all people and stir the adversary within.

189 The harvest is the end of the mortal life, and the harvesters are angels.

190 As the weeds are pulled up and burned in the fire, so it will be at the end of the mortal life of they who acquiesced to the adversary within and sowed darkness instead of light.

191 The Son of Light shall send out his angels, and they will weed out his Kingdom of everything that invites and entices to sin, and all the weak of will who have given into the adversary within and given excuse to evil rather than sincere repentance and restitution.

192 The wages of unrepentant sin are torment of the soul, because those of darkness cannot bear the brightness of the light, but they shall still long forlornly for the light they cannot bear.

193 The angels will release them to be drawn by their own resonance into the fiery furnace, fueled by their own despair for what might have been. There they shall remain, wallowing in the torment of their own creation, within the darkness they can scarcely bear, until they become greater than their adversary within and return to the glory of the light through repentance and restitution.

194 The wheat are the righteous, those that have endeavored continually to do good and sincerely and fully repented when they have done wrong, and they will shine like the sun with me in the Kingdom of Heaven, forever."

Parable of the Hidden Treasure

195 Then Yeshua spoke again to the multitude in parables, saying, "The Kingdom of Heaven is like a treasure hidden in a field. When a man found it, in his joy, he went and sold all he had and bought that field."

Parable of the Pearl of Great Value

196 "Again, the Kingdom of Heaven is like a merchant looking for fine pearls. When he found one of great value, he went away and sold everything he had and bought it, for its worth exceeded all else."

Parable of the Fish in the Net

197 "Once again, the Kingdom of Heaven is like a net that was let down into the lake and caught all kinds of fish. When it was full, the fishermen pulled it up on the shore. Then they sat down and collected the good fish in baskets, but threw the bad away.

198 This is how it will be at the end of mortality. The angels will come and separate the wicked from the righteous and release the wicked to be drawn into the fiery furnace by their disharmonious resonance. And there shall be much weeping and wailing and gnashing of teeth.

199 In the world of the darkness and fire, the wicked will see what could have so easily been in the world of the light. But even seeing, even knowing and understanding how simple it would be to change, most will still be unwilling to walk the path of repentance and turn torment into joy because of the restitution they would have to make.

200 Have you understood all these things?" Yeshua asked. "Yes," they replied.

201 May your affirmation lead you to greater light," Yeshua encouraged. "Therefore, every teacher of the law who has been instructed about the true Celestine Light of the Kingdom of

Heaven is like the owner of a house, who brings out of his storeroom new treasures, as well as old."

Unwashed Hands

202 Then some Pharisees and teachers of the law came to Yeshua and asked, "Why do your Apostles break the tradition of the elders? They don't wash their hands before they eat!"

203 Yeshua replied with a laugh, "Can you not think of something new to ask? Only when you are near do they not wash their hands, for I have asked them not to do so whenever they see you, to refute your traditions.

204 A greater question is why do you break the command of Elohim for the sake of your tradition? For in the commandments of Sinai, Elohim said, 'Honor your father and mother.' But you say that it is acceptable if a man says to his father or mother, 'Whatever help you might otherwise have received from me, I cannot give, for it is a gift devoted to God.'

205 Thus you nullify the word of God for the sake of your tradition. You hypocrites! Isaiah was right when he prophesied about you: 'These people honor me with their lips, but their hearts are far from me. They worship me in vain, and their teachings are but rules taught by men.'"

206 Yeshua called the crowd to him and said, "Listen and understand. What goes into a man's mouth does not make him unclean, unhealthy perhaps, but not unclean. But what comes out of his mouth; that is what makes him unclean before Elohim."

207 Then the Apostles came to him, and Cephas said, "You are making more enemies every day. You know that the Pharisees were greatly offended when they heard what you said?"

208 Yeshua answered him, saying, "Every plant that does not grow under the light of our Heavenly Mother and Father will be pulled up by the roots.

209 Do not concern yourselves with them or those who follow them; they are blind guides. If a blind man leads a blind man, both will fall into a pit."

210 Yohhanan then asked, "Will you also explain the last parable to us."

211 Yeshua replied, "Lest I begin to think you are dull or not listening closely yourself, why don't you tell us what it means, for I will not long be with you to answer such questions."

212 Yohhanan stammered a little as he was put on the spot and tried to answer, but then he found his voice and replied, "Whatever enters the mouth goes into the stomach and then out of the body. So though it may be unhealthy and make a man sick if he does not eat with prudence, it is not unclean.

213 "But the things that come out of the mouth, the words a man speaks, these come from his heart, and these are the things that make a man unclean if they are contrary to the Celestine Light of Elohim.

214 For out of the heart can come evil thoughts, murder, adultery, sexual immorality, theft, false testimony, slander, and many more things of darkness.

215 Certainly, these are what make a man unclean, but eating with unwashed hands, though not wise, does not make him unclean."

216 "Well spoken!" Yeshua exclaimed. "Now all of you, remember to ponder upon my words often that you may understand them fully. Be at peace in your heart and in love with the light, and surely the Holy Spirit of Elohim will ever enlighten you to the greater truths."

Parable of the Two Sons

217 Turning again to the multitude that had gathered to hear him speak, Yeshua noticed that more Sadducees and Pharisees had appeared among the crowd near him.

218 And he spoke to them again in parables, saying, "What do you think? There was a man who had two sons. He went to the first and said, 'Son, go and work today in the vineyard.'

219 'I will not,' he answered, but later he changed his mind and went.

220 Then the father went to the other son and said the same thing. He answered, 'I will, sir,' but he did not go."

221 Addressing the Sadducees and Pharisees directly, Yeshua asked, "Which of the two did

what his father wanted?"

222 "The first," they answered. And Yeshua replied to them, "And you are like unto the second. Verily, the tax collectors and the prostitutes will enter the Kingdom of Heaven ahead of you, for they have seen the error of their ways and have been humbled unto repentance. But you, seeing the error of your sins, remain haughty and full of words that justify, but empty of deeds that testify.

223 Remember my brother Yochanan? He came to you to show you the way of righteousness, and you did not believe him, but the tax collectors and the prostitutes did. And even after you saw this and heard the purity of the light as it was spoken from his lips, you did not repent and believe him. What is this sand you stand upon?

Parable of the Unworthy Tenants

224 "Listen to another parable: There was a landowner who planted a vineyard. He put a wall around it, dug a winepress in it, and built a watchtower. Then he rented the vineyard to some farmers and went away on a journey.

225 When the harvest time approached, he sent his servants to the tenants to collect his fruit.

226 The tenants seized his servants; they beat one, killed another, and stoned a third.

227 Then he sent other servants to them, more than the first time, and the tenants treated them the same way.

228 Last of all, he sent his son to them. They will respect my son, he thought.

229 But when the tenants saw the son, they said to each other, 'This is the heir. Come, let's kill him and take his inheritance.'

230 So they took him and threw him out of the vineyard and killed him.

231 Therefore, when the owner of the vineyard comes, what will he do to those tenants?"

232 He will bring those wretches to a wretched end," they replied, "And he will rent the vineyard to other tenants, who will give him his share of the crop at harvest time."

233 Yeshua said to them, "Have you never read in the scriptures: 'The stone the builders rejected has become the capstone; the Lord has done this, and it is marvelous in our eyes?'

234 Therefore, I tell you that like the evil tenants, you have failed in your stewardship, and the Kingdom of God will be taken away from you and given to a people who will produce its fruit.

235 Like Belshazzar, you have been weighed in the balance and found wanting, and your Kingdom shall be given to another. He who falls on this stone will be broken to pieces, and he on whom it falls will be crushed."

236 When the chief priests and the Pharisees heard the parables of Yeshua, they were greatly offended, for it was obvious to everyone that in many of his stories, he was talking about them. They looked then for a way to arrest him, but they were afraid of the crowd because the people held that he was a prophet and a healer sent by God.

Parable of the Wedding Banquet

237 Yeshua spoke to the religious leaders and the multitude again in parables, saying: "The Kingdom of Heaven is like a king who prepared a wedding banquet for his son.

238 He sent his servants to those who had been invited to the banquet to tell them to come, but they refused to come.

239 Then he sent some more servants and said, 'Tell those who have been invited that I have prepared my dinner, every type of delicacy imaginable, and everything is ready. Come to the wedding banquet.'

240 But the invitees paid no attention and went off—one to his field, another to his business. The rest seized his servants, mistreated them, and killed some of them. The king was enraged. He sent his army and destroyed those murderers and burned their city.

241 Then he said to his servants, 'The wedding banquet is ready, but those I invited did not deserve to come. Go to the street corners and invite to the banquet anyone you find. But tell them to come prepared for the occasion and to give the honor that is due.'

242 So the servants went out into the streets and gathered all the people they could find, both the good and bad who said they would come prepared and willing to give the honor that was due, and the wedding hall was filled with guests.

243 But when the king came in to see the guests, he noticed a man there who was not wearing wedding clothes. 'Friend,' he said, 'You disrespect me and the honor I have given you. Why are you here without wedding clothes?' The man was speechless to have been caught unprepared, for he had thought to partake of the banquet without needing to pay tribute to the king.

244 Then the king told the attendants, 'Tie him hand and foot, and throw him outside, into the darkness, where there will be weeping and wailing and gnashing of teeth for what has been lost and could have been.'

245 Verily, many are invited to partake of the Celestine Light, but few are worthy to be chosen."

Parable of the Ten Virgins

246 And he spoke another parable unto them, saying, "The Kingdom of Heaven will be like ten virgins who took their lamps and went out to meet the bridegroom.

247 Five of them were foolish, and five were wise. The foolish ones took their lamps but did not take any oil with them. The wise, however, took oil in jars along with their lamps. The bridegroom was a long time in coming, and they all became drowsy and fell asleep.

248 At midnight, the cry rang out: 'Here's the bridegroom! Come out to meet him!'

249 Then all the virgins woke up and trimmed their lamps. The foolish ones said to the wise, 'Give us some of your oil; our lamps are going out.'

250 'No,' they replied, 'we have prepared ourselves to be ready for the bridegroom, and we do not have enough oil for both us and you. You must go instead to those who sell oil and buy some for yourselves.'

251 But while they were on their way to buy the oil, the bridegroom arrived. The virgins who were ready went in with him to the wedding banquet. And the door was shut.

252 Later the others also came. 'Sir! Sir!' they said. 'Open the door for us!'

253 But he replied, 'Your lamps were needed at the beginning, and now there is no place for you.'

254 Therefore, be prepared. Live your life each day in ways that are worthy of the Celestine Light within you and the eternal reward that awaits the valiant because you do not know the day or the hour when your soul shall be called to come before Elohim to be weighed in the balance."

Parable of the Talents Multiplied

255 "Again, I urge you not to neglect the stewardship of your life. It is like a man going on a journey who called his servants and entrusted his property to them. To one, he gave five talents of money, to another two talents, and to another one talent, each according to his ability. Then he went on his journey.

256 The man who had received the five talents went at once and put his money to work and gained five more. So also, the one with the two talents gained two more. But the man who had received the one talent went off, dug a hole in the ground, and hid his master's money.

257 After a long time, the master of those servants returned and settled accounts with them. The man who had received the five talents brought the other five. 'Master,' he said, 'you entrusted me with five talents. See, I have gained five more.'

258 His master replied, 'Well done, good and faithful servant! You have been faithful with a few things; I will put you in charge of many things. Come and share your master's happiness!'

259 The man with the two talents also came. 'Master,' he said, 'you entrusted me with two talents. See, I have gained two more.'

260 His master replied, 'Well done, good and faithful servant! You have been faithful with a few things; I will put you in charge of many things. Come and share your master's happiness!'

261 Then the man who had received the one talent came. 'Master,' he said, 'I knew that you

are a hard man, harvesting where you have not sown and gathering where you have not scattered seed. So I was afraid and went out and hid your talent in the ground. See, here is what belongs to you.'

262 His master replied, 'You wicked, lazy servant! So you knew that I harvest where I have not sown and gather where I have not scattered seed? Well then, you should have put my money on deposit with the bankers so that when I returned, I would have at least received it back with some interest.'

263 'Take the talent from him and give it to the one who has the ten talents,' he ordered.

264 'For everyone who multiplies will be given more, and he will have an abundance. But whoever does not multiply, even what he has will be taken from him.

265 'And throw that worthless servant outside, into the darkness, where there will be weeping and wailing and gnashing of teeth for what might have been.'"

Parable of Helping a Stranger

266 "When the Son of Light reigns in his majesty, and all the angels with him, he will sit on his throne in heavenly glory. All the nations will be gathered before him, and he will separate the people one from another as a shepherd separates the sheep from the goats. He will put the sheep on his right and the goats on his left.

267 Then the king will say to those on his right, 'Come, you who are blessed by my Father and Mother; take your inheritance, the Kingdom prepared for you since the creation of the world.

268 'For I was hungry, and you gave me something to eat; I was thirsty, and you gave me something to drink; I was a stranger, and you invited me in; I needed clothes, and you clothed me; I was sick, and you looked after me; I was in prison, and you came to visit me.'

269 Then the righteous will answer him, 'Lord, when did we see you hungry and feed you or thirsty and give you something to drink? When did we see you a stranger and invite you in; or needing clothes and clothe you? When did we see you sick or in prison and go to visit you?'

270 The king will reply, 'Verily, whatever you did for one of the least of these brothers or sisters of mine, you did for me.'

271 Then he will say to those on his left, 'Depart from me, you who were selfish, into the tormenting fire prepared for the unworthy. For I was hungry and you gave me nothing to eat, I was thirsty and you gave me nothing to drink, I was a stranger and you did not invite me in, I needed clothes and you did not clothe me, I was sick and in prison and you did not look after me.'

272 They also will answer, 'Lord, when did we see you hungry or thirsty or a stranger or needing clothes or sick or in prison and did not help you?'

273 He will reply, 'Verily, whatever you did not do for one of the least of these my brothers and sisters, you did not do for me.'

274 Then they will go away to the torment they have earned by their selfishness, but the righteous will enter into eternal life and glory because of their selfless love."

275 Then Yeshua was finished speaking, and he departed again to Bethany to be with his children for the evening.

CHAPTER 85

Resurrection of Lazarus

Yeshua allows his essence to flow to anyone who merely touches him to be healed, even the unworthy. He explains to his Apostles how a healing cannot remain for those who do not embrace the Celestine Light within them. Yeshua, Miriam, Salome, and the Apostles travel to a mountaintop where Yeshua undergoes transfiguration and communes with the hosts of Heaven, including Heavenly Father and Mother, during which time the Apostles including Miriam and Salome are able to see and hear all that takes place. While Yeshua is away, Lazarus is bitten by a viper and dies. When he returns, he raises him from the dead.

nd it came to pass that Yeshua remained in Bethany with his family for several days and returned to Jerusalem the day after the next Sabbath with Miriam, Salome, and all of his Apostles.

2 Many of the Children of Light who had come with him from the communities on Lake Gennesaret continued to follow him from place to place, even when he took up residence for some days at the house of the father of Lazarus. And they continued to walk with him as he returned again from Bethany to Jerusalem.

3 Lazarus, however, did not accompany Yeshua this time as he had business he needed to attend to in Bethany. Martha also remained in Bethany with all of the children as this was her joy.

4 Once again, Yeshua was beset by the ill and the maimed and those with all manner of afflictions begging him to heal them.

5 So great did the throng of people seeking to be healed grow that Yeshua allowed his essence to flow to any who merely touched his garment, and for a time all who touched him, even the unworthy, were healed.

6 When noontime came, Yeshua retreated with his Apostles and Miriam and Salome into the walled garden of a man named Lartus, who had invited him to take the noon meal in the privacy of his garden, away from the multitude.

7 Yeshua invited Lartus to sit with him and his wives and Apostles, and Lartus was humbled and thanked him with great sincerity.

Healing Those Who Do Not Seek to Live the Celestine Light Does Not Last

8 As they were all eating the noonday meal, Mattayah asked Yeshua, "Why is it that you healed all people this day without regard for their worthiness, while in the past you have only healed those who have sincerely repented and committed to follow the light?"

9 Yeshua answered him, "It is for you and your brethren that I have done this, that the people

will more readily listen to you when I am gone.

10 But in truth, it is still only the righteous and those that are worthy by their sincere repentance for whom the healing shall remain.

11 If you heal a man by giving of your soul essence with love who is unrepentant and not committed to following the Celestine Light, that healing will remain only until your essence dissipates from his aura, which will occur within days for many, weeks for most, but months for some.

12 During the time while your essence of love remains with him, he will remain whole, and should he repent and seek the Celestine Light during that time, his healing will remain and not leave him.

13 But if he returns to the ways of darkness, it will drive your essence of love out of him all the sooner, and he will succumb again to that which ailed him."

14 "But will that not lead some to call you a false prophet?" asked Toma, "If they are healed but their wellness does not remain?"

15 "Most will remember the love and light that came upon them when they were healed," Yeshua explained. "When they return to illness, many will understand that it is because they are still living in darkness and that which afflicted them previously still remains to afflict them again. That realization will, for a few, be the motivation to again seek out the Celestine Light and love that made them whole."

Why Yeshua Antagonizes the Religious Leaders

16 Then Cephas questioned Yeshua, asking, "It seems you are purposely antagonizing the religious leaders by your confrontations with them and surely no good will come of this, especially when we are here in Jerusalem in the mouth of the lions. Are we to all be caught up like lambs taken to the slaughter in the tempest you are stirring?"

17 Yeshua answered him, saying, "The priests and scribes, Pharisees and Sadducees, and most of all, the Sanhedrin have been taking unrighteous advantage of their positions for many years to the detriment of the people they are meant to serve.

18 They have become confused and think it is they who are the masters and the people who are supposed to serve them.

19 I confront them to tear them down before the eyes of the people that they may be exposed for the jackals that they are, that in this, the common man will be shaken from the traditions that benefit only those of higher station and awakened to the greater light that will bring ample blessings upon them, even the holy Celestine Light that you shall bring to them.

20 Never forget I have not come to bring peace in the land at this time but strife, as the old does battle with the new. I have cast a blazing fire upon the earth, and I remain only long enough to see that it is well stoked, that it will become a wildfire that shall light the world.

21 The zealots think that I have come to bring war upon the Romans. Other men think I have come to bring peace upon the world. Neither knows me or why I am here.

22 The Romans will destroy themselves in time, and men are freed not by overthrowing their governors, but by overthrowing the adversary of darkness within themselves.

23 Verily, it is not peace that I have brought, except the beautiful peace in the hearts of those who discover the Celestine Light of Elohim.

24 But in that discovery, they will become at odds with their friends and family, even to the point of the sword and war. For there will be five brothers in a household, and two shall see the new light that has dawned and follow it. But the other three will fight against them, even to the death, for turning away from the traditions and the laws.

25 Hear and understand the words I am saying that you will not be caught unaware when the tempest strikes.

26 Recognize what is happening, the things that are in your sight even today, and then all that has been unfathomable shall become plain to you, and there is nothing that is now hidden that

shall not be revealed to your understanding.

27 Beware of the religious leaders of all shades. They come in sheep's clothing but inside are ravenous wolves.

28 If they ask you, 'Where did Yeshua come from if not from Nazareth?' tell them, 'Like us, he came from the light.'

29 If they ask if you are the light, tell them you are Children of Light; that you are in it and it is in you.

30 Bring forth the Celestine Light that is within you, and it will save you from any darkness. But if you do not bring forth the light that is within you, then you have no more promise than the man who has no light."

31 Then Lartus, who had been listening off to the side, stepped forward and raised his hand, seeking permission to speak. Yeshua nodded to him indicating he should pose his question. And Lartus said unto Yeshua, "I am a wealthy man as you can see by my house and garden.

32 I have heard you speak and seen your miracles on five different occasions and know you to be a man of God like no other, even though it is a strange doctrine you preach.

33 I wish to do good in the world but in ways that will be pleasing to God. What can I do?"

34 Yeshua answered him, saying, "Find people that you do not know who are worthy of the gift and in need and give them money sufficient to help them to help themselves.

35 Charge no interest and do not ask to receive your money back on any day.

36 And go also to people that you know who are worthy and in need of the gift and give them money sufficient to help them to help themselves, but do it in such a way that they know not from whence their benefit has come.

37 Again, charge no interest and never ask or expect a return of your money, for it is a gift of light, not a debt.

38 The more money you give away, the more your Celestine Light shall grow inside of you. And if you shall give away all you have to help those in need, great shall be your joy in both this world and the eternity to come."

39 "Thank you," Lartus said in humility. "I will go and do as you have said. Already I feel a lightness and a joy just thinking about it!"

40 "That is good, Lartus," Yeshua answered. "Today, you have truly embarked upon the path of exaltation in your eternal life, and it is each day henceforth that you will reap the blessings if you continue with that which you have begun.

41 Understand that exaltation does not wait for mortal death, but begins the moment you let the Celestine Light of Elohim swell inside of you and burst out.

42 Exaltation is a life of passion, enthusiasm, and full use of all of your strengths, resources, intelligence, and gifts.

43 Exaltation is much more than living forever; it is living in fullness, passion, excitement, and curiosity, every day of both mortality and immortality.

44 As you live in the Celestine Light, you open the door to eternal life's exaltation. And the great powers that have lain dormant inside of you awaken from their deep slumber beginning a miracle that will transform your life.

45 It is not anything outside of you that will transform your life, but the kindling of the Celestine Light of Elohim that is inside of you. Now that the fire has started, fan the flames and the miracles will happen."

46 After the noon meal, Yeshua once again went back to the multitude and preached to them and healed them.

47 And a man came to him with a young teenage boy who was slobbering at the mouth and shaking his head violently and uttering sounds like an animal.

48 The boy's father said to Yeshua, "I beg you to heal my son. He used to be a delightful boy, but a terrible sickness came over him a little over a year ago, and now he growls like an animal and has little control of his body. Often he must be rescued after he falls into the fire or the water.

49 I brought him to your disciples, those who are with you now, when they came to Jericho to tell of your coming, but they could not heal him, and when you arrived, I was tending to my son and could not come.

50 He means the world to me and my wife, for he is our only son. I know you can heal him even though your disciples could not, for I have heard of many miracles you have done greater than this."

51 Yeshua put his hand on the man's shoulder and said unto him, "Love as deep as yours is a call that must be answered. Your son is not sick but has been possessed by a demon of darkness who has been condemned to never have a body, so it covets those that do.

52 Its presence has disrupted the life flow of your son's body so that it can no longer function as it should. But these pools of darkness are easily dealt with, for they cannot endure the light."

53 So saying, Yeshua reached over and put his right hand on top of the boy's head and said in a voice of power, "Be gone!"

54 In that instant, the boy fell to the ground, crying out in a loud voice. Within a few seconds, he opened his eyes, and seeing his father bending over him, he reached out and touched his face and whispered, "Father, thank you."

55 The father and son embraced, and through his tears of joy the father told his son, "Thank the Almighty God and Yeshua, his prophet of light."

56 Then the Apostles Yuda and Ya'akov, the sons of Cleophas, came close to Yeshua and said unto him, "We are the two disciples the man spoke of that tried to heal his son in Jericho but could not. We thought he was ill from a disease and did not suspect he was being made sick by a demon of darkness that had come upon him.

57 How are we to know the difference? And even without knowing, we gave our essence together upon the lad and called for more from heaven as well, but he was not healed and the demon remained.

58 Why were we inadequate to the task even though we were sincere in our attempts to bring greater Celestine Light into the boy?"

59 Yeshua answered them, saying, "Your desire was strong, but your faith in your authority and ability to bring Celestine Light to the boy was weak.

60 "And knowing whether you are dealing with a demon or a sickness or both is very important, as the way you command the Celestine Light to come will need to vary depending upon which confronts you.

61 Lift up your faith, my brethren! All things shall be made known to you before I depart this world insomuch that your faith will grow, and you will not doubt your ability or authority to call the Celestine Light or discern and dispel the darkness."

62 Later that day, Yeshua brought his Apostles to a steep ridge on a mountain northwest of Jerusalem, and they climbed the ridge to the top of the mountain.

63 The multitudes and those who plotted against Yeshua all fell back as he and Miriam, Salome, and the other Apostles began ascending the steep ridge, and by the time the summit was reached, none from the crowd remained.

64 Yeshua called everyone to come and sit with him, and he said unto them, "I ask you all to remain here until I return."

65 Everyone looked at one another in confusion at his words, and he answered the questions on their faces, saying, "I am going to leave the earth for a time to commune in the Celestine Realms with my Father and Mother and brother Yochanan, as well as some of the other great lights of Heaven.

66 You will still see me as if through a fog and those with whom I speak, but it will not be me, for I will not be here."

67 "How long shall you be gone, my love?" asked Miriam.

68 "Five passages of the sun," Yeshua replied.

69 "That is a long time!" exclaimed Cephas. "What are we supposed to do for these days, just

sit and wait? And what shall we do for food as we brought none with us."

70 Yeshua smiled and answered him, saying, "You will find this to be one of the most sacred moments of your lives. To you, it will seem as if I am sitting near you, and you will be able to hear everything I say and everything said by those to whom I speak.

71 Marvelous will be the mysteries and secrets you shall learn if you are humble and listen carefully, and think not of the things of the world, such as eating."

73 "Then we should fast for five days?" asked Toma.

74 "Yes," Yeshua affirmed. "If you wish to see heaven while you still live on earth and hear the wisdom of the wisest in the Celestine Realms."

75 Everyone nodded their heads in agreement at the words of Yeshua.

76 Then Yeshua posed a question to them, asking, "Who do people say I am?"

77 "That depends upon which people you are speaking about," offered Yudas Iscariot. "If you are speaking of the scribes, priests, Pharisees, Sadducees, or Sanhedrin, I think they have all made it clear that they consider you a troublemaker at best and a blasphemer of the highest order at worst, deserving of death."

78 "But if you are speaking of the common people," interjected Philip, "some say you are Yochanan the Baptizer; others say Elijah; and still others, Jeremiah or one of the prophets."

79 "But what about all of you who follow me and know me so well?" Yeshua asked. "Who do you say I am?"

80 Cephas answered with authority, saying, "You are the Son of Light, the Son of the living God."

81 "Yes!" cried out several of the Apostles in unison.

82 "The Son of Light!" proclaimed Mattayah.

83 "The King of kings!" exclaimed Amram.

84 "The heavenly template of a father, a husband, a brother, and a teacher," added Miriam.

85 Yeshua bowed his head in thanks to those who were with him and said unto them, "Blessed are all of you, for this was not revealed to you by man, but by the Holy Spirit of our Mother in Heaven.

86 And I tell you this: that upon the rock of the testimony of the Holy Spirit of Elohim shall the Celestine Light grow upon the earth as the Children of Light scattered across the world hear the still, small voice within and heed the call.

87 And those so touched by the Holy Spirit shall become the pillars of Heaven and earth and neither demons nor the pains of man, nor the hordes of the realm of everlasting darkness will overcome them.

88 When I return after the sun has passed five times, I will give you the keys of the Kingdom of Heaven and whatever you bind on earth will be bound in Heaven and whatever you lose on earth will be lost in Heaven, for you are the leaders of the Children of Light and one in spirit with the Elohim."

89 That night they all slept on the mountain, and the following day at noon Yeshua embraced Miriam and kissed her on the lips and Salome on the forehead, then embraced each of his other Apostles.

90 Standing alone on the apex of the hill, Yeshua was suddenly enveloped in a blinding white light that made the illumination of the noonday sun seem dark.

91 The flash of light lasted but a second and afterward all those remaining on the hill looked at the spot Yeshua had been, but he was gone, and only the rocks and dirt and plants of the mountain remained where he had been.

92 Just as suddenly about an hour later, a strange cloud descended over the top of the mountain, covering only the very top and not even reaching to where the Apostles had withdrawn to sit a short distance away.

93 "Look!" exclaimed Mattayah pointing at the cloud, for it had begun to become less dense and a light had begun to emanate from it filling its space.

94 "There's Yeshua!" Salome said with excitement, pointing at a personage in the cloud.

95 "And there's Yochanan the Baptizer, Martha's husband," Miriam sighed with joy. "It is so wonderful to see him so full of life."

96 "Yeshua," Cephas called out.

97 "Cephas," Miriam chastised. "He told us we would be able to see him only, not speak with him."

98 "Yes, I know," Cephas agreed, "But the mirage seems so real it is hard to believe he is not actually standing there. My mouth simply reacted before I remembered his words."

99 Then they saw Yeshua simultaneously embrace a radiant man and resplendent woman, both of statuesque beauty and form, and they held the embrace for well over a minute.

100 "Is that who I think it is?" asked Cephas to no one in particular.

101 "It is our Heavenly Father and Mother," Miriam affirmed with reverence. "We are on hallowed ground."

102 All the remaining hours of daylight, each of those blessed to witness the transfiguration of Yeshua moved hardly at all, but sat in rapt attention at the perimeter of the cloud, watching and listening to all that transpired.

103 Periodically, someone would enter into the cloud and begin to speak with Yeshua, but those watching did not hear their name spoken and knew not whom they were.

104 The first three times an unknown personage came into the cloud, one or another of the Apostles would ask Miriam who it was, and each time she would tell them she knew not.

105 When the fourth unknown personage came into the cloud, Cephas asked Miriam who it was, and once again she answered that she did not know.

106 "But you are the Angel of the Covenant," Cephas objected. "You should know these things."

107 "I am not yet the Angel of the Covenant," Miriam replied with slight agitation. "Nor do I know if when that day comes I will suddenly be filled with all knowledge on the hosts of Heaven. So please, let us not speak now among ourselves, lest we miss some of the sacred words that are being spoken within the cloud."

108 Cephas nodded his head in agreement, and they both looked and listened again with great attention to Yeshua in the cloud.

109 Yeshua continued to converse with many exalted personages within the cloud until the sun fell below the horizon. Upon that very moment, the cloud disappeared, and Miriam, Salome, and the Apostles were left alone upon the mountain.

110 For a long moment, no one spoke or moved, for they were still spellbound by all they had witnessed.

111 "That was an amazing experience," Yohhanan said with reverence at last to everyone.

112 "I feel so humbled to have witnessed this," Yudas Iscariot said, wiping a tear from his eye.

113 "It is one more testimony we have been given that Yeshua is the Son of Light," Cephas said with authority. "We are blessed with special testimonies of the divinity of Yeshua because of the things we have seen and heard on this day and many other days before this day that no others have ever seen or heard.

114 Remember this, my brothers and sisters: From everyone to whom much has been given, much will need to be reciprocated, and from those to whom much has been entrusted that have proven to be good stewards, even more will be asked.

115 We have seen and heard the divine in ways such as no others. Because of our blessings, we are called as special witnesses, that in us the life and teachings of Yeshua will not die, but must go forth unto all the earth."

116 The following day, the moment the sun dawned over the horizon, Yeshua appeared again in the cloud in the light, and it settled to the ground atop the mountain. Several of the great personages of the Celestine Realms appeared with him as the hours passed, and it seemed as though they were just standing on the ground a few feet away in earnest conversation.

117 About two hours past noon, Miriam's sister Martha and several of the Children of Light that had remained at the base of the mountain came up hurriedly to the Apostles.

118 For a few moments, they stood in awe, looking at Yeshua and other divine beings inside the cloud with him, all of whom shone with a brilliant light.

119 But Martha soon broke from her fascination and ran up to Miriam with tears in her eyes, saying, "Miriam, Yeshua must come quickly, for Lazarus was bitten by a viper while he reached for a jug of water on the ground.

120 I left him hours ago in terrible agony. He sometimes screamed in pain and other times whimpered like a child, but then he ceased to move and barely still breathed.

121 I came at once as fast as possible that Yeshua could come and heal him before it is too late and he dies."

122 Miriam held her sister closely and said unto her, "Yeshua is not here."

123 "But he is right there!" Martha said in a raised voice, pointing at Yeshua in the cloud. "But a few paces away speaking with that man."

124 "That is not him," Miriam explained. "It is only a mirage showing us what is transpiring far from here in the Celestine Realms."

125 "I do not understand," Martha moaned. "Yeshua is not far away; he is right there. If you will not go to him, I will."

126 Breaking away from Miriam, Martha ran into the cloud, but coming to Yeshua, he answered her not when she spoke to him. And when she reached to touch him, her hand passed through him.

127 Then Miriam was beside her, slipping her arm through Martha's and pulling her gently back out of the cloud, saying, "I told you Yeshua is not here. You are only seeing a living image of him, though he seems as full of substance as me.

128 Nor would it matter if he were here," she said softly. "It is too late for our brother, I am so sad to say. When you went into the cloud, I sent my spirit out to our home in Bethany, and Lazarus has died. They are already beginning preparations for his burial."

129 "No!" wailed Martha. "Call Yeshua back. He raised a priest from the dead when he was just a boy. Surely he will do no less for Lazarus, who is like a brother to him."

130 "All right, Martha," Miriam agreed. "I will call Yeshua, but he may not come. What he is doing now is of transcendental importance to him and us and truly everyone in the world who will ever see the Celestine Light.

131 He may not come back before the time he has allotted to accomplish his task, just for one man, even if that man is Lazarus."

132 So saying, Miriam stepped back into the cloud and opened her arms with her palms up and looked up into the sky, saying, "Hear the humble words of my mouth and feel the emotions welling in my heart, divine Son of Elohim."

133 Then a blinding white light emanated from Miriam even as it had from Yeshua, and when the light subsided after a few seconds, everyone looked into the cloud to see Miriam standing and speaking with Yeshua.

134 But none could hear the words Yeshua and Miriam were speaking to one another.

135 After a few minutes, Miriam walked out of the cloud, and immediately, it vanished behind her and there was once again only the mountaintop.

136 She stood again before Martha, Salome, the Apostles, and the Children of Light, and they all looked at her in awe and knew not what to make of her.

137 Seeing the spellbound looks upon everyone's faces, Miriam told them, "Do not look at me as if I am a spirit or some divine being from on high. I am just Miriam, and I did not travel to the Celestine Realms, where no purely mortal person can be.

138 Yeshua heeded my call and came to me in a place between this world and the realm of heaven. Even then it was not him, but a mirage like unto the one we have been watching in the cloud. We could speak, but I could not touch him."

139 "But what of Lazarus?" asked Martha with impatience.

140 Miriam shook her head, saying, "Yeshua said to wrap the body of Lazarus in many layers of burial linens impregnated with crushed thyme and to bury him in a tomb of air, not earth, before his body begins to stink. He will come to him when he has finished that which he has begun."

141 "How long will that be?" Martha asked tremulously.

142 "Yeshua said he would be gone for the passage of five suns, and only one has passed thus far," Miriam answered.

143 "Four more days!" shouted Martha. Even prepared for burial, his body will have already begun to decay in four more days!"

144 Miriam came to Martha and held her face gently between her hands and said unto her, "You must have faith, dear sister, that all will be well. Yeshua is the Son of Light from whom all life has flowed and can flow again if he so wills it; even the dead who have been buried in the ground for some days; even those whose bare bones have lain decaying for years in the earth.

145 But you must also have faith that the will of Elohim will be done, and in that, it may be that Yeshua may not bring Lazarus back from the dead, for he did not say that he would. He only said that he would come to him.

146 Lazarus has already done much good in this world, more than many other men combined. Perhaps, he has been called home to a greater stewardship in the Celestine Realms. Unless there is a great purpose that serves Elohim, he will not come back to this life."

147 Martha gently hit Miriam's shoulders with her closed fists, and then buried her head on her shoulder, crying. "Of course, there is a great purpose in having our brother back. He takes great care of his family and honors our elderly mother and father by taking care of them as well.

148 He runs our family businesses and employs many men who then provide for their families because of the work that Lazarus gives them.

149 He teaches the Celestine Light of Yeshua to many people, both in Bethany and on his travels, and many souls have found the light because of the spark that Lazarus gave them, including some that have come to live in our communities on Lake Gennesaret.

150 I have lost my husband Yochanan; Yeshua is going soon as a lamb to the slaughter; our parents are elderly and enfeebled and will soon die. I cannot also lose my brother who does so much for so many. Oh, Miriam, it is just more than I can bear."

151 Miriam held Martha close to her and said, "I will return to Bethany with you at once, dear sister. All will be well no matter the course of events. Remember who you are and who Yochanan and Lazarus and Yeshua are.

152 Remember that this life is but a few blinks of your eyes in eternity and that the righteous that pass mortality before you wait with love faithful and true to unite with you again forever."

153 Then Miriam, Martha, and Salome departed from the mountain, along with all the Children of Light that had come up with Martha, and they returned to Bethany.

154 After they were gone from sight, down the mountain, Yohhanan spoke to Cephas, saying, "How unusual that this momentous time on the mountain is the one time that Miriam is not here to be the witness for all that Yeshua says and does."

155 "They have a link with one another that we will never know," Cephas answered longingly. "Even when she is not here, I do not doubt that there is still nothing that transpires with Yeshua that she is unaware of."

156 "Truly?" asked Yohhanan.

157 "Truly," replied Cephas.

158 Shortly after Miriam's party had disappeared from view, down the mountain, the cloud with Yeshua illuminated within reappeared upon the mountaintop, and once again the Apostles gathered round to watch and listen with rapt attention.

159 And so it continued throughout the remaining hours of daylight that day and for the three days that followed. And marvelous beyond description were the mysteries of the Celestine

Light seen and heard by the Apostles those days.

160 On the morning of the sixth day, as the Apostles awakened at dawn, Yeshua stood among them in the flesh. And he said unto them, "Unto you has been given a glimpse of Heaven and the secrets of mysteries never known among men. Now you are prepared to fulfill the full measure of your stewardships."

161 Then Yeshua and the Apostles descended down the mountain to return to Bethany. And none remained at the bottom of the mountain to greet them or travel with them.

162 Toma came up to Yeshua and told him he feared for him returning to the heart of Judea, where the religious leaders had made it so plain that they were plotting to destroy him.

163 Yeshua put his hand on Toma's shoulder and said unto him with some exasperation, "Remember all the secrets you learned upon the mountain.

164 Fear not, my good brother. Every step I take is foreordained, and nothing will happen to me except by my word that it is time for it to be so.

165 Never doubt or fear; hold fast to the Celestine Light of Elohim that expands within you, and it will ever guide you and uplift you and help you to understand things that are still mysteries to you.

166 If you remain committed to walk by the light, you will never stumble, but woe unto the man who digresses and walks into the darkness, for he will surely stumble because his light has been covered, and he may never find the light again."

167 "What will you do when we reach Bethany?" asked Mattayah. "Lazarus has been dead now for some days and is surely buried and decays, sealed inside a tomb. Will his spirit come into another that through another he may live again?

168 "Where do you come up with such ideas, Mattayah?" Yeshua replied once more in exasperation. "Have you been with me so long and seen so much, yet still understand so little?"

169 And Mattayah was downcast and hung his head because of the words Yeshua had said unto him.

170 Seeing this, Yeshua went over to him and walked beside him with his hand upon his shoulder, saying, "Forgive me, Mattayah, I spoke to you with a harshness that belies the love I have for you and the gratefulness I feel because you are numbered among us."

171 Then speaking to all of the Apostles, Yeshua said unto them, "We have come together for great and glorious purposes of Elohim that transcend the transitory purposes of man.

172 Remember all that you have seen and heard while you have walked with me these many days.

173 Remember the miracles you have all done because of the power of the Celestine Light of Elohim that has flowed through you.

174 Yet each of you was raised without the knowledge of the mysteries of Elohim that you now have.

175 Each of you were raised and lived surrounded by certain beliefs and customs that were the creations of men, yet because of the years, they became a part of you.

176 Now has come the time when you must forever cast off the old that has chained you to a ship without a sail or a rudder or an oar and embark upon the ship of God whose sails are full, whose rudder is sure, and whose oars dip deep.

177 You are my special witnesses, and you above all others must live the Celestine Light in its fullness and allow none of the darkness or false teachings or customs of the past to intrude.

178 By your examples, so shall others become."

179 After a time, Yeshua and the Apostles approached Bethany.

180 As they came near to the house of Lazarus, there were many people milling about, for Lazarus and his father were well-known and respected merchants and there were as many people who had come from Jerusalem to pay their respects as there were from Bethany.

181 When word reached the house of Lazarus that Yeshua had come, Miriam and Martha were inside and Martha hurried out to meet him, but Miriam remained behind, for she was

holding and comforting the children.

182 When Martha saw Yeshua, she moved quickly to him and embraced him tightly and said unto him, "My Lord, if you had been here, my brother would not have died."

183 Yeshua stroked her covered head lightly and said unto her, "Your brother will rise again."

184 Remembering that Miriam had said Yeshua might not resurrect Lazarus, Martha answered. "I know he will in the resurrection of the righteous on the last day."

185 Yeshua put his hand gently behind her head and looked deeply into her eyes and said, "I am the resurrection and the life. Do you believe this?"

186 "No, my Lord," she told him, "I more than believe. I know. I know that you are the Son of Light, the Son of the divine Father and Mother, who has come into the world, and by your word all things can be."

187 Yeshua put his arm around her waist, and together Martha and Yeshua came up to the house of Lazarus, where his widow and family stayed grieving.

188 Seeing Yeshua and Martha entering the house, Miriam excused herself from the children and went to her husband and sister and embraced them. And Salome was with her, and she came to be embraced with them as well.

189 Well over three hundred people were still congregated outside. Among them were many Children of Light from the communities, most of the extended family of Lazarus, and people from Bethany and Jerusalem and many other towns that had known him well as he had traded with them for many years.

190 "Take me to the tomb," Yeshua commanded.

191 "Come with me, my Lord," Miriam answered taking his hand. Followed by Martha, Salome, and all the family of Lazarus, she led him through the people gathered outside and to the tomb.

192 The tomb was a cave cut into rock and set in a depression of the ground. Yeshua came and looked down upon it from the ledge above, and tears came into his eyes.

193 "Look, he is weeping," exclaimed someone in the crowd.

194 "I heard Lazarus was like a brother to him," chimed another.

195 "How he must have loved him," added a third.

196 Pointing to the large round stone that had been used to seal the tomb, Yeshua commanded, "Roll away the stone."

197 Immediately, four of his Apostles descended down into the depression of the tombs and went to the stone sealing the tomb of Lazarus and began to roll it open.

198 "No!" cried someone in the crowd. "He has been dead for days; the body will have a bad odor.

199 "Who cares about the odor?" demanded another. "It is a supreme sacrilege to defile a grave."

200 Hearing them, Amram leaned toward them and told them, "Quiet, you men of ignorance, and you shall see a miracle such as no men have ever seen."

201 "Bah!" exclaimed the one pointing to Yeshua. "It is said he has given sight back to the blind and hearing back to the deaf. Yet he could not heal his own friend before he died?"

202 "Only so something greater could come forth today," Amram replied. "So keep your tongues still and you will be able to tell your grandchildren you were here on this day and a witness to the mighty miracle of God that transpired."

203 Then Yeshua clasped his hands and holding them down, he bowed his head and prayed aloud, saying, "Father and Mother in the realms of Celestine Light beyond the dreams of men, hear me. I know that Lazarus is even now in the Celestine Lights that one so worthy as he deserves.

204 But that men may know the power of Elohim, unite with me that we may be three of one thought, three of one heart, three of one purpose for that which you know I desire."

205 One of the men near Amram turned and hurriedly departed saying, "I cannot bear to

stand here another moment and listen to this false prophet praying to false gods."

206 Yeshua looked up into the heavens and his countenance beamed with radiance, and he said, "Thank you, my Mother and Father; I know you hear me always and are with me in all I desire.

207 But as you know, it is for the people standing here that they may know that I am from you, that I have asked this."

208 The four Apostles had finished rolling away the stone of the tomb, and now Yeshua turned to them and said, "Remove the body of Lazarus from the tomb and bring it out into the sunlight."

209 They did as Yeshua commanded and brought the body of Lazarus out into the middle of the depression of tombs and laid the body, which was very stiff and rigid onto the ground.

210 Then Yeshua, who was still standing some distance away at the top of the ledge, cried out in a loud voice, saying, "Lazarus, arise and come forth!"

211 Suddenly, there were gasps of fear from many in the crowd as the body of Lazarus wrapped in several layers of burial linens began to move.

212 The Apostles standing nearby lifted the wrapped corpse, which was now moving with life to its feet.

213 "Remove the grave linens from him." Yeshua commanded. Four Apostles immediately set to the task, and the corpse of Lazarus wrapped inside the linens began to help them.

214 The gasps of fear from moments earlier were soon replaced with gasps of wonder and awe as the last of the grave linens were removed from Lazarus, and he stood there before them alive and whole!

215 Many were the people that fell to their knees and began to offer prayers unto Elohim because of the astonishing miracle they had just witnessed.

216 Lazarus and the four Apostles ascended the stairs out of the pit, and Lazarus came to Yeshua and stood before him, looking steadfastly into his eyes and said, "I was in a place more glorious than I could dream, and I felt a peace and tranquility such as I never could imagine.

217 But then I heard your voice calling me back into this world of strife and challenge, and not even for a moment did I hesitate to come to your call. For what greater fulfillment can there be than to heed the call and fulfill the stewardship given by the Lord of Light?"

218 Yeshua and Lazarus embraced tightly and most of the people who had witnessed the miracle stomped their feet upon the ground in joyous approval of all they had witnessed, for this truly was a miracle of the ages.

CHAPTER 86

The Conspiracy of the Sanhedrin

The Sanhedrin begin their conspiracy tactics. However Joseph of Aramathea rebukes his fellow Sanhedrin.

After Yeshua resurrected Lazarus from the dead, his fame spread even more throughout Judea and Galilee.

2 Hearing of this mighty miracle, the Sanhedrin, being mostly Sadducees, gathered together with the Pharisees to discuss again what they should do regarding Yeshua.

3 "This is an untenable situation," spoke one. "We must make a decision quickly as to how we are going to react to this Yeshua of Nazareth. Do we honor him as so many people now do because of his numerous and great miracles? Or do we declare him a fraud, a blasphemer, a false prophet, and seek to have him killed?"

4 "I for one do not think we can leave him to continue as he has." interjected another. "Lest all the Children of Israel soon believe that he is an emissary of God, and we draw the fury of the Romans upon our special positions and our nation."

5 "Of course, he cannot be allowed to live." The high priest Caiaphas stated emphatically.

6 "I have spoken to my *father Hanana* and he said that tomorrow is not too soon for this blasphemer to disappear from the earth.[a]

7 Yeshua of Nazareth is a blasphemer; he is a false prophet; he is a false Messiah; and even now the zealots are preparing to follow him into a revolution that cannot succeed.

8 If we do not soon find a way to see him gone for good, then it is we and our people that shall suffer and be torn asunder because of the wrath of the Romans.

9 I know a few of you have sympathies for him, but it is better that one man should die than a whole nation be upturned and destroyed."

10 "But how shall we accomplish it?" asked one of the Pharisees. "Only the Romans are allowed to put people to death. They will not care about our religious issues, and how can we prove the seditious affairs to them?"

11 "It will not be difficult," offered one of the Sadducees. "He is frequently surrounded by people known to be zealots among our people.

12 Deliver Yeshua as a prisoner to the Romans along with some other zealots, with the promise to the zealots that we will ask Pilate to let them go with only a little of the lash if they will testify against Yeshua."

13 "But they are zealots!" exclaimed one of the Sanhedrin. "They will not bear witness against their leader, even if it means their death."

14 "They only wish he was their leader," interjected another Sanhedrin. "In fact, our spies have

told us that Yeshua has rebuffed their overtures."

15 "Quiet!" Caiaphas ordered. "Do not complicate a simple matter with useless speculation.

16 We will have another meeting with Yeshua. All of the Greater Sanhedrin should be present. It is merely a formality. We already have decided that he is a blasphemer. His followers think of him as God come to earth, so he also induces sacrilege. For the sake of our religion, which we are sworn to uphold, he must die.

17 But as was said, death comes only at the hands of the Romans. Bring witnesses to them that he has been called the king of our people and others to testify that the zealots see him as the Messiah come to trample upon Rome.

18 Remember we have our positions only because the Romans have appointed the highest among us. The governor trusts us because he knows we are in his power, and without him, we are on the street like beggars.

19 If we assure him that this man Yeshua is a destroyer of our religion and plots to overthrow Rome in Judea, he will heed our advice and put him to death before the new moon. I know with a certainty this is true."

20 Most of those present nodded their heads in agreement with the words of Caiaphas, and from that moment on, they began to counsel together to quickly find a way to put Yeshua to death.

21 But before they could depart their separate ways, Joseph of Aramathea spoke, saying, "Can I believe what my ears are hearing? How can you so easily dismiss Yeshua of Nazareth and plot to send him to his death?

22 Who in the annals of our people has ever done the many miracles we know he has done?

23 More than this, in our presence, he stopped the sun! He stopped the sun, my brethren. Who but God can stop the sun? Nor would God stop the sun upon the word of anyone but his highest and greatest prophet.

24 If he came among us without evidence of his authority, saying the things he has, he would be the sinner you have called him to be. But he has come among us with power such as we have never seen, the likes of which has seldom been recorded in the scriptures.

25 Just this last week, he raised from the dead a man that had been decaying in the tomb for days and restored him to life with a fullness and health of the body. Think of that, my brethren. Let it sift deep into your heart and mind.

26 Who has there ever been in Israel that can bring the dead back to life? And it is rumored that this man was not the first. Only the greatest prophet of God could do this.

27 And knowing that he has raised a man from the dead, what hope do you have to kill him? If he can bring another back, do you think that he will simply lay quietly in the grave?

28 Or will he return to take vengeance on all those who saw not his pure light and sought to stymie his calling from the Almighty to do good in the world?

29 Consider these things with honest deliberation, my brethren, for the actions you have committed to will, I believe, come back to destroy you."

30 "How can you be one of us, Joseph, and say such misguided, terrible things?" asked Caiaphas. "We are only doing our duty to uphold the law. This is our calling, and we are faithful to our people. It is you who should consider your errant words before they condemn you as surely as the man you have just defended."

31 Then the meeting of the Sanhedrin and the Pharisees was over, and each went his way. But Joseph of Arimathea did not return to his home; he instead went to seek out Yeshua that he might warn him of the plot of the Sanhedrin and the Pharisees.

a Former high priest."

CHAPTER 87

Eternal Principles of Truth and Light

Yeshua spends his last night with his children and explains that he will always be with them. He has his Apostles rent a large room from a Persian man so they can meet in safety and privacy. Yeshua speaks with each of his Apostles individually, counseling them and thanking them for their good service to Elohim. Out of envy, the Apostles ask Yeshua who will be the greatest in Heaven. Yeshua explains that there are good traditions in other religions as they contain universal and eternal principals of truth and light. He also explains the significance of the Feast of Unleavened Bread. Yeshua makes a special request of Yudas Iscariot.

Yeshua's Last Night with His Children

That day, Yeshua was very solemn in his demeanor and spoke little to his Apostles.

2 The previous night, he had spent alone with his children and the children of Yochanan and Martha and their mothers and told them frankly, but also with gentleness and love, what was going to happen to him and what their future would be.

3 His son and daughter and the children of Martha as well all cried at his words, and his son and daughter held him tightly as if to prevent him from ever leaving. He kissed them and held them tight, "Fear not, beautiful Celestine Lights of Heaven. I will return after three days and remain with you for another forty more.

4 Then I will be gone from the sight of others, but you will always be able to see me and hear me. In your times of need, just call my name and I will come to your side in an instant, even as I am right this moment.

5 You will not grow up alone, but will always have me and your mother to comfort and guide you, your aunts and uncles and cousins to enliven your lives, and all the other Children of Light that are one with us, to enrich all your days.

6 This life is but a blink in eternity, not more than a sneeze. We will be together forever in eternity so surely you can't miss me so much during the short moment of a sneeze?"

7 With those words, he pretended to sneeze, and Yeshua turned their tears into laughter. He slept that night with all of them in his arms and lying upon his legs and body.

Acquiring the House of the Persian for the Feast

8 At sunrise following the Passover, Yeshua departed for Jerusalem with Miriam and the rest of his Apostles. Salome desired to come also, but he gave her an embrace and a kiss on the

forehead and asked that she would remain in Bethany to comfort the children for two days and then come to a house that she would be led to by a dove. She replied with a slight tinge of disappointment, "As you wish, my Lord."

9 As they approached the gates of Jerusalem, Yeshua asked Toma and Yudas Iscariot to go into the city and told them that they would soon meet a man wearing an unusual conical cap encircled by bands of colored cloth, carrying a pail of water.

10 They were to approach him and ask to rent his room for the Feast of Unleavened Bread celebration and then follow him to it and pay him for its use. When they arrived, Yeshua and the other Apostles would be waiting for them.

11 Toma and Yudas did as Yeshua directed and soon found the man with the unusual hat. He was a Persian, and Yudas spoke to him in Greek. Hearing their request, the man asked, "How did you know that I have a room large enough for your number?"

12 Yudas answered, saying, "Our teacher, Yeshua of Nazareth, knew of you and sent us to you."

13 The man replied, "I have heard of this teacher, but I know him not. How is it he knows of me? I am a Persian and not well liked by anyone in this town, be they Jew or Roman or Greek. So how is it your teacher knows of me?"

14 Yudas answered him humbly, saying, "He is the Lord of Light, and though Persian you may be, in you he surely saw a worthy soul and knew that in your house, he would have peace and safety."

15 "I should like to meet this man who can see inside me before he has met me," answered the Persian.

16 So saying, the Persian led them to a house on a hill just outside the city gates.

17 As they approached, they saw Yeshua and the Apostles waiting for them, and seeing their approach, Yeshua walked up to the Persian and greeted him, saying, "Teiuxra, I am Yeshua. Thank you for the use of your room. Will you ensure that we will not be disturbed during our stay, save for a woman named Salome who will shortly arrive?"

18 Teiuxra's eyes opened in surprise, and he answered Yeshua, saying, "Unless the Romans come knocking on your door, whom I cannot deny, I can ensure you that you will not be disturbed. But how is it that you know not just of my house, but even the name given by my family, which name I have never used living in this land?"

19 Yeshua replied pointing at his Apostles, "When next you see any of these men after a week has passed, ask them what became of me, and your heart will tell you how I know who you have been, who you are, and who you will become."

20 Then Yeshua and Miriam and the rest of the Apostles went up into the upper room and shut the door.

21 The room was spacious and had a large table and several benches.

22 Yeshua asked Yudas Iscariot and Philip to go out and return soon with food for the evening and the morning, including unleavened bread and unfermented wine.

Yeshua Speaks Individually with Each Apostle

23 While they were gone, Yeshua spent time speaking with the other Apostles individually, counseling them and thanking them for their good service to Elohim and the Celestine Light of truth.

24 When Yudas and Philip returned, Yeshua spoke privately with each of them as well, first with Philip and then with Yudas.

25 Yeshua spent more time with Yudas than he had with any of his other Apostles and Yudas' face paled and he seemed disconcerted as Yeshua was speaking to him.

Who Will Be Greatest in Heaven?

26 Seeing all the time that Yeshua was speaking with Yudas, some of the other Apostles felt pangs of envy and reasoned quietly among themselves that they had been Yeshua's disciples longer than Yudas and wondered why Yeshua was speaking more with him than he had with

them.

27 When Yeshua was finished speaking with Yudas and came back to the group of Apostles on the other side of the room, Cephas asked Yeshua, "Who among us will be greatest in the Kingdom of Heaven?"

28 Yeshua smiled at them and asked, "I see eleven men, but who is the most humble as a child?" And his words caused some chuckling among them.

29 Then Yeshua said unto them, "Each of you has been given a sacred responsibility and called to fulfill the full measure of your greatness.

30 Your life is a stewardship of the gifts and callings that have been given to you.

31 You are not in a competition with your brethren for whom will be greatest. Truly, everyone can become equally as great in the Kingdom of Heaven by righteous living and tending to their earthly stewardship and expanding upon it.

32 Magnify your stewardship, and it shall magnify you.

33 Humble yourselves as little children and fulfill your stewardships to their fullest extents, and you shall inherit an eternal glory and joy worthy of your efforts.

34 Let you who are the greatest live righteously and forever give humble service to those who are the least among the Children of Light and the yearning people of the world, not simply giving to them, but helping them to become more than they are. Do this and the fruits of your labors and the sweetness of your spirit shall bring you a just and beautiful reward beyond your comprehension.

35 But be not confused; the heavenly realms of the Celestine Kingdom are certainly a blissful reward for your faithfulness in mortality. However, your arrival in the wondrous light is not the end of your journey, but just the beginning.

36 Beyond the chronicles of time and for all eternity, you will forever have the opportunity to expand and grow, and limitless are your possibilities and potential.

37 The question should not be, 'Who will be greatest in the Kingdom of heaven?' Your life is your Kingdom, and a wiser query would be to ask yourself, 'How can I be a better king of my Kingdom today?'

38 As you are a superior king in the realm of your life, you are a better servant of Elohim. And the Celestine world that you shall gain in glory, because you have fulfilled and expanded your stewardship, is greater by far than this one that you see or any that you can imagine."

Emulating Good Traditions of Other Religions

39 Then Toma posed another question to Yeshua, asking, "You have brought a new and greater light into the world and taught us many new doctrines, which we alone practice in the world.

40 You have called us Celestines, followers of the true Celestine Light of Elohim. Yet as is evidenced with our preparation for the Feast of the Unleavened Bread, we still adhere to many of the traditions of the Children of Israel. Why is this so?"

41 Yeshua answered him, saying, "Just because all the light has been given unto you does not mean it is substantially lacking in the beliefs of others or that you alone possess all the ways to express it.

42 In truth, the other religions of the world have prepared the way for the fullness of the Celestine Light that has come upon you.

43 Many religions, even among those with practices strange to your understanding, contain a great deal of light in the universal and eternal principals of goodness that they teach. That is why they produce believers who are good and honorable people, no less worthy to be called Children of Light than you are.

44 If you desire the Celestine Light you shall build to become the lantern to the world that it should, then do not disdain the traditions of other religions, for many are founded upon sound principles of the Celestine Light of Elohim, and you would be wise to emulate some of their foundations of them as your own, because of the principles of light that they teach through their

traditions.

True Meaning of the Feast of Unleavened Bread

45 "Consider the Feast of Unleavened Bread that follows the Passover celebrated by the Children of Israel.

46 This feast is meant to celebrate freedom from the bondage of slavery to others and the slavery of each person to their own sins and weaknesses.

47 But more than this, this celebration should be a poignant reminder that personal weaknesses not conquered and vanquished will return again and again to extract another pound of flesh from the unrepentant sinner.

48 He who does not overcome the darkness within himself is doomed to see it overshadow him again and again, controlling his life and dictating his choices and actions, even as the Children of Israel remained in bondage for four hundred and thirty years.[a]

49 In this festival practiced by only eating unleavened bread for seven days, there is an inspired purpose and lesson for any person of any faith open to the light.

50 Let those who partake of unleavened bread do so with a contrite heart and gain a greater understanding that sin is like leavening, for it puffs up and expands in a person or a church or a society, even as leavening puffs bread, until the person or the church or the society is full of sin.

51 From this festival, come to understand that if sin is not resisted inside you or your church or your society, then like the leavened bread it will continue to puff up until it overwhelms and you or your church or your society are full of sin and consumed even unto destruction.

52 Bondage and slavery to the sin is a greater bondage than any ever put upon the Children of Israel by the pharaohs or a master who takes everything, even down unto your life.

53 Therefore, be wise in your stewardship and joyfully study the traditions of all religions that help teach and understand good principles of light.

54 Do not be hesitant to embrace and adapt in your own manner the good things that others may teach and their celebrations and traditions, if they help you to more easily understand and live the truths that you know.

55 In the battle against the adversary within, you face your greatest foe, and you need to rejoice and embrace every ally you have that helps you not to become a slave to your weaknesses.

56 Even small weaknesses today, if not opposed, can grow to become great sins tomorrow, sins that destroy not only the sinner, but his family and even his nation.

57 Of the sins that lead you down into the darkness, lust is the most dangerous. Do not allow yourself to be led into darkness by lust for anything, be it idleness, food, money, sexual immorality, authority over others, or any other unrighteous desire.

58 Even one step on the road of lust and the gratification of unrighteous desires leads to another, even as every step into the Celestine Light and the joyous living of righteous principles leads to more.

59 You are never simply standing between the light and the darkness, but always moving toward one or the other. Therefore, be ever aware of where the path of your thoughts and actions are leading you and choose the light.

60 Be masters of yourselves and teach that principle to the Children of Light, for if you are not the master of your lusts and weaknesses, then you are a slave to them."

61 Later, as they ate, Yeshua spoke to them again, saying, "Soon the days shall bring anguish to your hearts because of that which you see done to my body.

62 But you need not be so anguished, if you remember that there is more to life than mortality and more to me than the physical body that you see and touch, even as there is more to you.

63 The days to come are of great importance in the lives of all mankind; those that live; those that have ever lived; and those that are yet unborn and shall come upon the earth in future generations."

The Turmoil and Calling of Yudas Iscariot

64 Speaking now in greater detail, Yeshua said unto them, "Some of you have wondered why I spoke in private with Yudas Iscariot more than any of you. It is because I have asked him to lead the Sanhedrin to me that I might be taken to judgment and turned over to the Romans to be crucified. Such a thing none of you could do, but Yudas can because of his former life before he became one with us."

65 "What!" shouted Cephas leaping up from where he was sitting. "Of course, none of us could turn you over to be killed, and neither should it be possible for Yudas if he is truly a follower of the Celestine Light." And Yudas hung his head deeply at the words of Cephas.

66 "But I have asked it of him," Yeshua responded. "If he is truly a follower of the Celestine Light, he will do as I have asked, even though it may tremble his soul. And more than this have I asked of him.

67 Nor can you speak against he who would give me up to the Sanhedrin, Cephas, for on that fateful day, you shall deny me three times, ere three cocks' crow."

68 Though you have spoken it, I will not let that be so, for my faithfulness to you cannot be moved," Cephas answered soberly. "Sooner would I give up my own life than deny the light that you are."

69 "We will all be faithful to you until the end, no matter where and what that end may be," Yohhanan affirmed to Yeshua. "But tell us now, if you will, what else it is you have asked of Yudas?"

70 "I have asked him to willingly go as a lamb to the slaughter, even as I will, and to die and be resurrected to life, even as I will, that the people who will come to see the light will know that the resurrection is not for me alone, but for all people.

71 Whereas your names will be given glory in the annuals of men, the name of Yudas Iscariot shall be falsely reviled by the ignorant from our day until the end of the final dispensation of earth before it is reborn.

72 There are some, such as the Sadducees, who believe there is no resurrection of the dead, and others such as the Habidites, who think the resurrection is only for a chosen few.

73 When I rise, so shall Yudas and some of the saints who have lain long in the grave and a few who have not been so saintly. And they shall return for a day to walk among those in mortality, save for Yudas, who shall return to be numbered among you again for a time.[b]

74 By this, it will be understood, even if not accepted, that the resurrection is not for me alone, but comes to all, both the saint and the sinner, for the path of progression is eternal, not just for a chosen few, but for everyone."

75 "I do not understand?" stammered Mattayah "If you desire to be tried by the Sanhedrin, why do you ask all these convolutions of Yudas? Why not simply present yourself to them and say, 'Here I am.'

76 Nor have you said how Yudas will die. Can he not just jump into the sea or off a cliff? Why does his death need be tied to yours? If he dies or resurrects the same day or the next moon, what is the difference?"

77 Yeshua answered him, saying, "Were I to go to the Sanhedrin, I would be in a position of power, coming to them rather than being apprehended by them, and they would be afraid to judge me because of the many people who follow me.

78 If Yudas brings them to me in secret, they will take me to their judgment in secret, and few will there be outside of their circle that know of it. Then they will be able to pass their judgment without fear of the people.

79 As to his death, I have left that to Yudas to decide, but it is upon each of you to bear witness of it, even unto his burial. It is not his death that is so important, but his rebirth into life.

80 His death shall come close to mine that his resurrection shall also. The two events will be as one in the eyes of those who truly seek the light. For the enlightened, this will be another testimony of that eternal principal.

81 To bring about the resurrection of all people and provide a path of redemption for those who repent of their sins and follow the Celestine Light, have I come into the world, and now all things will come to pass to fulfill that purpose."

82 Then Yudas Iscariot, still appearing somewhat shaken, spoke, saying, "My brethren, know that this is a difficult thing for me to do. Knowing that any of you would also lay down your lives for the Celestine Light of Yeshua girds me up to have the courage to lay down mine.

83 But I fear for my family—my wife and children—for it is only for one year that I can remain with them in mortality before Yeshua has said the growing light of my resurrected body will no longer be able to be held within the bonds of this dark mortal world.

84 He has shown me how I will be reviled by the ignorant for a crime I have been asked by the Lord of Light to do, even though the thought of it shakes me to the morrow of my bones.

85 I beg of you, my brethren, to care for my family. They will hear so many falsehoods about me all of their lives. Please bear witness to them of the truth after I am gone, that they will never doubt that I was faithful until the end to Yeshua."

86 So saying, Yudas put his head in his hands and burst out in a torrent of tears, and for many minutes, everyone remained quiet, bearing the pain in their own hearts that his sobbing brought upon them. And many of the others began to cry with him.

87 Then Miriam went over to him and knelt down beside him and put her arm around his shoulder and said unto him, "Yudas, weep not anymore. You have cleansed your feelings. Now open your heart to ours and know that each and every one of us knows that you are a true and faithful servant of Elohim.

88 Though the world may forget, we will not forget, nor will the true Children of Light who follow Yeshua and obey his teachings.

89 Nor will we ever let your wife or children forget the magnificent man of light that is their husband and father.

90 You and your family are a precious part of our greater Family of Light. You are today, and you always will be."

91 At the words of Miriam, Yudas ceased weeping and looked up at her and gave her a feeble smile of thanks, even as the other Apostles all spoke to him their own words of encouragement and came to him and put their hands upon his shoulders and head.

a In Egypt

b A Note on Time: Occasionally, the terminology "a time" is used ambiguously to indicate an unspecified number of days that can be either few or many. In this context with Yudas, and in most instances, "a time" is one biblical year. A biblical year can be either 360 days or 390 days, with the long year having a thirteenth month and falling on the Sabbath year (every seventh year) and Jubilee year (every fiftieth year). Every ten Jubilee years equal five hundred years, and every twenty Jubilee years equal a millennium.

During a Sabbath year, Israelites rested for a year from their labors, even as they did each week on the Sabbath and did not even plant crops, but had faith that their storehouses of food would see them through the year.

The Jubilee year was considered the great year of pardon and forgiveness, not just for the Children of Israel, but applicable to "all inhabitants of the land" (Lev. 25:10). During this year, all debts were forgiven, slaves were emancipated, prisoners were freed, and leased land was returned to its owners, maintaining hereditary ownership of all land.

CHAPTER 88

The Last Supper

Yeshua has his last supper with his Apostles at which time he institutes the sacrament. Yeshua washes each of his Apostles' feet as he explains "no master is greater than his servant." The nature of Elohim is explained as well as the promise and fullness of the Holy Spirit. Yeshua explains that people of the world will persecute the Children of Light. Yeshua asks Salome to sing for them with her beautiful, angelic voice.

Institution of the Sacrament

hat evening they supped together at the table and Yeshua broke the bread and blessed it, then gave a piece to each of them, saying, "As you eat this bread, remember my physical body, which has labored tirelessly for your good. In that memory, be inspired to do no less in your labors for the good of your brothers and sisters in the light.

2 When I am no more upon this earth, let the Children of Light meet together each week and pass the bread among them that they might eat it in remembrance of the life I have lived for them and covenant in their hearts to follow my example and uplift and do much good for one another."

3 Then Yeshua took the wine and poured it into a cup and gave thanks to the divine Father and Mother for the fertile earth upon which the grapes grew and the farmers that tended and harvested them into fullness.

4 And he blessed it and said unto them, "Take this cup and pour the wine among you, each into your own cup, and drink it in remembrance of my blood which shall be shed for you.

5 Not upon the cross at Calvary, where mortality simply shall breathe its last breath, but upon the tree at Gethsemane, where the torment of all wickedness shall be suffered, that those who repent of their sins and live the Celestine Light might be freed from the full anguish they would otherwise be called to bear.

6 With every small sip of the wine, contemplate this sacred sacrifice and commit to live your life worthy of the holy gift you are given.

7 Let this become a ritual with the Children of Light when they meet together each week to edify one another and grow in the light: that they would be pure of heart, holding malice toward none of their brothers or sisters, and eat of the bread and drink of the wine in remembrance of me and, in this, renew their covenants with Elohim and to one another."

Yeshua Washes the Apostles' Feet

8 When the supper was finished, Yeshua went over to the wash basin, and removing all of his

clothes, he washed himself, and then emptied the basin.

9 Girding himself with only a loin cloth, he took the basin and poured clean water into it, then went over to Miriam, and removing her sandals from her feet, he washed them.

10 No one spoke as he washed Miriam's feet, and the other Apostles knew not what to make of it.

11 When he was finished, Yeshua went to Cephas and knelt down before him and took his foot to remove his sandal, but Cephas withdrew his foot from Yeshua's hand and forbid him to wash his feet, saying, "It cannot be, Yeshua. I cannot allow you to wash my feet. It is I who am your disciple and should be the one that washes your feet."

12 Yeshua answered him, saying, "You have heard me say that the greatest among you must serve the least if you are to come unto the heavenly Kingdom of Celestine Light, and so I come to wash your feet that you may know my love for you is simple and pure and in my service to you I have happiness.

13 Do not deny me this, Cephas, for if you do not allow me to wash your feet, you have understood nothing that I have taught you and must part from among us even this moment."

14 Cephas was startled by Yeshua's words and the seriousness with which he gave them and quickly agreed to his request, "Well, then, please wash not just my feet, but also my head and hands as well!"

15 In a more jovial tone, Yeshua replied, "You can bathe yourself, good Cephas. I am satisfied with the honor of washing your feet." At his words, there was light laughter among them, notwithstanding the sacredness of the moment.

16 Then Yeshua went one by one to all of the other Apostles, washing their feet.

17 When he had finished washing their feet, he put on his clothes and asked them, "Do you understand what I have done for you?

18 You call me your teacher and the Lord of Light and rightly so, for that is what I am.

19 Now that you have seen that I, your teacher, whom you have called the Lord of Light, have washed your feet, see that you also wash one another's feet, especially in moments of great sacredness or importance.

20 As I have done for you, so should you do for one another; that humility may ever be one of your greatest strengths, a strength that bonds you together in the Celestine Light of Elohim.

21 Verily, no master is greater than his servant, nor is a messenger less than the one who sent him.

22 For the greatness of each person is testified to every day, not by their station in life or their knowledge or wealth or fame, but by the simple purity of their heart and the honest, humble light shining in their life as they seek to do good.

23 Now that you understand these things, you will be blessed if you do them.

24 Remember as you go forth in the world to love one another. As I have loved you, so you must love one another.

25 By this, all men will know that you and all of the Children of Light are my disciples, if you love one another with a pure and humble love.

26 And in this, you will have a sanctuary of peace beyond the comprehension of the world, one that will support you and uphold you, even in your darkest hours.

Apostles' Missions beyond Palestine

27 "Now in the past, when you have gone into towns before me, I have asked you to go without bags or staff or money and even without sandals if you had none. In this, did you lack anything?"

28 And the Apostles answered him that they lacked nothing.

29 "But now when I am gone, you will be traveling two by two or three by three to lands near and far, and I say unto you that he who has bags or a staff or money, let him take them, for as you have, so will you find a need to fill—equal to that which you have, both for yourselves and the

Children of Light whom you shall meet.

Methods of Self-defense

30 "And in the past, most of you have gone without staffs, feeling safe near your home in the land of your people. But now, you shall travel beyond the places that you know and the protection of the Roman peace, and for some who are not yet adept in the use of their spiritual gifts, a stout staff will be a welcome companion.

31 If you cultivate harmony in your soul, though all the world may be your enemy, in it you will find mostly friends. And a peaceful and loving spirit will insure your safety more than all else you can do in most circumstances. Therefore, most often, you should first endure much in peace before you respond in opposition.

32 But sometimes, violence will come suddenly upon you and often by those who know not your sweet spirit and care naught for your peaceful ways.

33 Elohim does not ask you to go as sheep meekly to the slaughter, for you can do far more good every day that you live.

34 If unopposed, those who would prey on the meek are emboldened to prey on others, but those who are opposed with greater strength will prey on the helpless no more.

35 Therefore, when despite your loving spirit and peaceful ways, the minions of darkness would still rape your wife, steal your goods, compel you into slavery, or commit any other grievous sin against you, do not hesitate to oppose them justly and in more than equal measure by whatever means you are capable.

36 But if it is your life or the life of your family or your brothers and sisters of light that they seek to take, then you are justified to mete out to them that which they sought to deliver upon you by whatever means you are capable.

37 For this cause, you should daily cultivate your gifts of the Celestine Light that can stand with hidden power in opposition to the unrighteous.

38 If you have attained a level of competence, always use your abilities within the Celestine Light rather than traditional means of physical defense, because by this you can preserve your life without taking the life of another.

39 But if you do not yet have faith in your gifts of power, do not simply stand idly by praying for deliverance when you are attacked by those who would take all that you have, even your life and the lives of those that you love.

40 But take a sword or staff to hand, call upon Elohim for strength, and be not hesitant to protect your life or the lives of those that you love from the minions of darkness who would take them or enslave them.

41 Yet if you will heed the inner voice of your secret guardian, seldom will be the times when you are in danger. As you travel, listen to the voice of the spirit of the divine Mother ever warning you and directing you to protected places.

42 Avoid trouble whenever you can, even if it means a delay in your journey or an arrival at a different destination. Though it may be a different location than you had planned, it will be the right place for you to be to serve Elohim and fulfill your goals.

43 Trust the still, small voice of the Holy Spirit to guide you, and you will always be delivered into safety, even when at times it may seem that all is lost.

44 When trouble does come upon you, your powers of the Celestine Light will protect you if you have faith in yourself and are in harmony with the light. But if you do not have faith in your gifts of spirit, trust the strength in your arm, the quickness of your mind, and the courage in your heart.

45 Do not be troubled about this, for though you desire only to live in peace and harmony, the spirits of the men of the world are moved by darkness, and there is no peace in their hearts, save the peace in which they perceive advantage over others.

46 Trust in your divine Father, trust in your divine Mother, trust in me, and trust also in

yourself in the gifts and abilities you have been given, and all will be well.

Relationship and Nature of the Elohim Explained

47 "Nor tremble because I will no longer walk among you or think that I shall not come back for you. When I am gone, the Holy Spirit shall fill your heart in a joyous and splendid way that shall make you closer to the Elohim than you have ever been, even more than now when you sit in my presence.

48 As I have labored tirelessly for you upon the earth, so shall I labor in heavenly realms of the Celestine Light. In my Father's house are many lands of beauty and wonder and, upon them, many mansions of splendor. I am going there to prepare a place for you.

49 And if I go to prepare a place for you, it is because I will come back for you and take you to be with me, that you also may be where I am.

50 You know the way to the place where I am going. Hold fast to the straight and narrow path and soon we shall be together again in paradise."

51 But hearing his words, Toma was confused and said unto him, "Lord of Light, we know you are going to the Celestine Realms, and we know that it is a paradise beyond description. But we have only seen it from the pictures your words have described, and in truth, we know it not. Therefore, how can we know the way to come there?"

52 Yeshua answered him, saying, "I am the way and the truth and the life. No one comes to heavenly glory except through me, by living the Celestine Light that I have brought.

53 If you know me and follow the example I have given and live the teachings I have taught, you are on the path that leads to eternal glory."

54 Then Philip asked him, "Yeshua, can you show us the divine Father and the divine Mother or tell us what they look like and how they speak and what they do? This would mean so much to us"

55 Yeshua answered him, saying, "Philip, I love you greatly, but have you been with me so long and yet still you do not fully know me even at this, the last hour?

56 How can you ask for me to show you the divine Father or the divine Mother or ask how they speak or what they do?

57 Verily, if you know me, you know them, for I am in them and they live in me. The words that I speak are not my words, but their words. And the things that I do are not my acts, but their acts.

58 Know with a sureness the truth when I say that I am in my Father and Mother and they are in me.

59 As you see me, so you see them. As you hear me, so you hear them. More than this will be a discovery unique to each person, as will be the Father and Mother they both see and hear.

60 For those who have not this testimony, let them believe in Elohim through the miracles you have seen me do, which great things could only have come from the love of the divine Father and the Mother.

61 But listen well to my words, for verily, I say unto you that any of you that have faith in me without wavering and ask what you will of our divine Mother and Father, in my name, you will be able to do all the miracles I have done and ever greater than these.

62 Because I am going to the Celestine Realms to again be in the presence of my Mother and Father and be one with them in the Celestine Light, joined in one place, and I will be your advocate.

63 Therefore, whatsoever righteous thing you ask of them in prayer, in my name, that is of the light, I shall ask them to fulfill. And because I will be your advocate, that which you asked shall be fulfilled.

64 And in this shall men come to know me through you, and knowing me, they will come to know the Celestine Light and glory of my Mother and Father in Heaven.

Promise of the Fullness of the Holy Spirit

65 "Now you have heard me speak of the Holy Spirit. Listen now as I tell you more of the secrets that the world will never understand.

66 Since I have been among you, if you had a question, you would come to me in person and ask it, and in person I would answer.

67 So too, you have seen the miracles I have done and can bear witness with the words of your mouths to that which your eyes have actually seen and your ears have actually heard.

68 But when I am gone to the Celestine Realms, another comforter will come upon you in fullness, even the Holy Spirit, who shall touch your soul with a sure knowledge of the Celestine Light beyond the comprehension of the flesh.

69 This is the united spirit of the trinity of Elohim given unto the Children of Light, but it comes to you through the essence of the divine Mother. She will bring to you a testimony of the light that is even greater than the flesh you have felt or the miracles you have both seen and heard.

70 From time to time, you have felt the spirit of the divine Mother move within you, and you know that it brings a feeling of joy, peace, and contentment not of this world.

71 So too have you been in times of need, and the Holy Spirit came and comforted you.

72 While I have been among you, the occasional touch of the spirit of her essence from the heart and oneness of the Elohim was sufficient for your needs.

73 But now that I will no longer to be with you in the flesh, it must needs be that you and all the Children of Light who have found the path are given the greater comforter of the Holy Spirit.

74 The people of the world will never believe in the Holy Spirit of the divine Mother, for they cannot see her or feel her within their bosom.

75 But you shall know her, and all the Children of Light who walk the path shall know her. For after the baptism of water will come the baptism of fire, even the baptism of the Holy Spirit, when the oneness of the Elohim shall come over you and you will know that which the eyes cannot see and the ears cannot hear.

76 A knowledge you cannot touch or give to others, yet so complete that it shall fill every fiber of your being.

77 And once so filled, you will never again be empty; once so found, you will never again be lost; once so empowered, you will never again be powerless, as long as you stay true to the path of Celestine Light.

78 More than this, know that the testimony that comes from the Holy Spirit will be greater than the testimony you have gained from all that you have seen and all that you have heard.

79 For the things which you have seen and heard were given to the understanding of your mind and your heart. But when you are filled, each moment with the bliss of the Holy Spirit, your soul is enraptured beyond the understanding of your heart or your mind.

80 You have heard me say that I am going to die and resurrect and ascend into Heaven, but that I will come back to you.

81 Know that it is through the Holy Spirit of Elohim, which comes by the Mother, that this will be so. For I am in her and she is in me, and she will teach you all things you have need of and remind you of everything I have ever spoken to you or revealed unto you.

82 Through the Holy Spirit, I shall come again unto you and we shall never be parted, for the union of spirit is greater than my presence in flesh."

83 Then Yeshua paused for a moment and looked at each of his Apostles one after another as if waiting for them to ask a question. But they all seemed too amazed by everything he had spoken and remained quiet, waiting for him to speak again.

The Vine and Branches

84 "I am the vine of truth and light; you are the branches; and my Father and Mother in

heaven are the gardeners. Remain in me, and I will remain in you. And if I am in you, so shall the light be also.

85 But the gardeners shall cut off every branch that bears no fruit, while every branch that does bear fruit, they will prune so that it will be even more fruitful.

86 Remember that no branch can bear fruit by itself; it must remain on the vine. Neither can you bear the delicious fruit of the true Celestine Light of Elohim unless you remain true to me in the light.

87 If a man remains in me, he will live the principles and teachings of the Celestine Light and bear much fruit. But apart from the light, nothing can grow.

88 There are many in the world that walk in the Celestine Light that will never know my name in this life. But they are still a part of my vine because they live within the light that I am.

89 But you have been nurtured and given so much more, for you are a branch that knows the vine that gives it life.

90 If you remain in me and my words remain in you and you live the Celestine Light that fills you, ask whatever you wish of the divine Mother and Father, in my name, that is of the light, and it will be given to you.

91 This is the joy of my Father and Mother, that you would bear much fruit, living the Celestine Light and teaching others to do the same by both precept and example.

92 As my Father and Mother love me, so have I loved you. Now remain in my love.

93 If you live the Celestine Light I have brought, you will always feel my love, just as I have lived the Celestine Light of the Elohim as it was revealed to me by my Father and Mother and have always felt their love.

94 I have told you this so that my joy may be in you and that your joy may be complete in me.

95 Seldom have I ever given a command unto you, preferring to teach you as I have asked you to teach, by precept and example.

96 But now I give a command unto you, and my command is this: Love each other as I have loved you.

97 And greater love has no one than this: that he would lay aside his own life to help those whom he loves.

98 Everything that I learned from my Father and Mother that you can use and benefit from, I have made known to you. Now has come the time to marry experience with all that you know.

99 You did not choose me, but I chose you and appointed you to go and bear fruit that will last.

100 Live fully with love and joy in the Celestine Light; bear fruit to be savored and our divine Father and Mother will give you whatever you ask in my name.

101 Remember my command: Love each other."

People of the World Will Persecute the Children of Light

102 After washing, everyone retired for the night on mats on the floor. The following day, Yeshua spoke to them again, saying, "If the people of the world despise you and persecute you, keep in mind that many hated me and fought against me first.

103 If you were like the people of the world, if you dressed like them and ate like them and acted and spoke like them, they would love you as their own.

104 But you are not of this world. You are Children of Light who have come from a realm of greater glory and have remembered who you are. And I have chosen you out of the world and given you secret knowledge and shown you your gifts.

105 That is why the world will disparage and persecute you, because you are not like them and care not for the things that they cherish. And you hold secrets and gifts, which they will never know.

106 Remember the words I spoke to you: No master is greater than his servant. If they persecuted me, surely they will persecute you also.

107 They will treat you this way because of me and the teachings I have brought; for they do not know the divine ones who sent me, and they are afraid of that which they do not know or understand.

108 In this place, the Sanhedrin are the most guilty, but you will encounter the persecutors in diverse places beyond your communities.

109 If I had not come and spoken to the Sanhedrin and shown many miracles to them, they would not be as guilty. Now, however, they have no excuse for their ignorance or actions.

110 They have heard the truth and seen the miracles, and yet they hate me. They say that I am a blasphemer and that they are defending the one God. But I say unto you that he who hates me, hates the loving Mother and Father who sent me.

111 For my divine Mother and Father have so loved the children of men that they have sent me to come to them, that all those who repent and live in the Celestine Light might be freed from the long suffering of sin to which their resonance would otherwise call them.

112 The people of the world will hear the voices of their priests for that is all that they know or want to know. And they will put you out of their synagogues and towns and lands, for that is what their priests will tell them to do.

113 And the time will come when anyone who thinks to kill you will think he is offering a service to God. Therefore, beware and seek out quiet places away from the world where the communities of the Children of Light can live in peace and harmony.

114 The people of the world will do such things because they have not known the Father, the Mother, or me.

115 If you are the light, you are not like them. Your very existence—the way you eat, dress, speak, and act—so different from their ways, refutes their darkness, even if you do not speak a word to them.

116 In the muddle of the darkness they think to destroy you, the living evidence of the light, thinking that to do so will make them no longer seem to be in the darkness.

117 I have told you this so that when the time comes that you are persecuted, you will remember that I warned you and be prepared.

118 I did not tell you this at first because I was with you. But when I am gone, you will have the greater presence of the Holy Spirit to guide you and the Angel of the Covenant to protect you from the onslaughts of those in darkness."

Grief Will Turn to Joy

119 After this talk, everyone took a break and several of the Apostles went for walks to contemplate all that they had heard. When they returned, Yeshua spoke again unto them, saying, "I have heard you talking with one another as you have walked about.

120 Most of you seem very sad in your thoughts and in your hearts because of the short time of anguish that will soon be upon me and because of the persecution I have spoken about that will come.

121 This is not something to grieve about, for the travails of the mortal body are here today and gone tomorrow. Instead, rejoice in the eternal principles of repentance, righteousness, and resurrection that are being firmly established.

122 And how can you worry about persecution when you have the love of all of your brothers and sisters, the haven of your communities, the guidance of the Holy Spirit, and the protection of the Angel of the Covenant—the servant of the Elohim?

123 Yes, you will grieve for a little time in the coming days. But your grief will turn to joy.

124 A woman giving birth to a child has pain because her time has come, but when her baby is born, her anguish is forgotten and replaced with joy that lasts beyond time, because of her precious child born into the world.

125 So it is with you. A time of grief will soon be upon you, but I will see you again soon and you will rejoice, and no one will ever take away your joy.

126 I have told you these things, not to make you afraid, but that you will know to ever seek me out with your words and in your heart so that in me, you will always have peace through the love and comfort of the Holy Spirit.

127 In this world, you will have some trouble. But take heart! I am in you and you are in me, and I have overcome the world."

128 Yeshua paused again in his speaking, and Miriam stood up saying, "Salome comes." And she went downstairs to meet her so that Teiuxra the Persian would allow her to pass.

129 When Salome entered the room where the other Apostles were with Yeshua, some immediately began to grumble among themselves because of her presence.

130 Yeshua, hearing their words, asked, "Why do I hear words of disharmony because of the presence of Salome?"

131 Cephas answered for the Apostles, saying, "We wonder why she who is not one of the twelve you have called is among us at this most sacred time of our unity.

132 And we wonder why, if she is here, that our wives cannot also be here to keep us company and hear your words."

133 Looking about, Yeshua answered with some humor, saying, "It is unlikely that we would all fit in this room, Cephas. And if we did, surely the floor would collapse from all of our weight."

134 The Apostles, including Cephas, laughed at Yeshua's words, and he continued his reply in seriousness, saying, "Salome is soon to lose the life she has known with both me and Miriam, at least in the way she has known it.

135 She has brought great happiness to our family, and we wanted to give to her just a few more days of the Yeshua and Miriam she has known before all is changed.

136 And you must know that the relationship she has with me and Miriam has brought her closer to the Celestine Light than the wife of any other can be.

137 Though she is not one of the twelve by calling, she has mastered the gifts of the Adept. And verily, I say unto you, the day shall soon come when you will owe your success and freedom to her mastery of the powers of Celestine Light.

138 Lastly, I have asked her to be with us and share one of her most special gifts. Please accept her in perfect harmony. This I ask."

139 Cephas and all of the Apostles looked down at the words of Yeshua and were humbled because of the thoughts they had to exclude Salome. After a moment, they all welcomed her with sincerity to be among them, and she thanked them with kind words and grace.

Yeshua Prays for Himself

140 "I would like to pray now, my brethren," Yeshua said. "And I would ask that all of you would join me in a Circle of Power that you might feel the depth of my soul."

141 Upon Yeshua's request, everyone stood, and Miriam, Salome, and all of the Apostles gathered into Circles of Power. After a short prayer led by Cephas, they quickly began to swirl a vortex of energy between them.

142 When the vortex became a peaceful light, Yeshua prayed, saying, "My divine Mother and Father, the time has come. Glorify your Son, that your Son may glorify you.

143 You have granted me authority over all people that I might give eternal life to all and eternal exaltation and glory to those who repent of their sins and live the Celestine Light of Elohim I have brought to the world.

144 I have brought the fullness of your light to the earth and have almost completed the work you gave me to do.

145 Now, precious Mother and Father, prepare to receive me into your presence with the glory and joy I had with you before the world began.

Yeshua Prays for His Apostles

146 "I have revealed you and your secrets to those in this room whom you blessed that we might be one in spirit and purpose, even as I am one in spirit and purpose with you.

147 Now they know that though I am one with you, it is still your words that I follow, even as they are one with me and it is now my words that they follow.

148 For I gave them all of the teachings you gave to me, and they accepted them into their hearts and they live them in their lives.

149 They know without doubt that I came from you, and they believe with all of their heart, mind, and spirit that you have sent me.

150 I pray now to you for them. I am not praying for the world, but for these most precious spirits within this room, the kindred spirits of my spirit that you have blessed me to have in my life and eternity.

151 All I have is yours, and all you have is mine. And glory has come and will come to me because of them.

152 I will remain in the world but for a few moments longer, but they are still in the world for some time. I am coming home to you with joy, and I ask that you will protect them and send your angels to watch over them, even the Angel of the Covenant.

153 Let them become as one. Let all things they ask of light be done by the power of my name—the sacred name you gave me in the Celestine Light—that they may be one as we are one.

154 I am coming to you now, but I say these things while I am still with them in the world so that they may know the depths of my love for them and have the full measure of my joy within them.

155 I have given them your word, and the world has hated them for it and shall hate them even more in the days to come, for they are not of the world any more than I am of the world.

156 My prayer is not that you take them out of the world, but that you will inspire them to always remain true to the Celestine Light. Give them the strength and resolve to always put down the adversary within and the means to always overcome all adversaries outside of them.

157 They are not of the world, even as I am not of it. Your word is the truth and the light. Sanctify them by the majesty of the Celestine Light.

158 As you sent me into the world, so shall I send them into the world. Watch over them, I pray, even as you have watched over me and never faltered.

Yeshua Prays for All Children of Light

159 "My prayer is not for them alone; I pray also for the Children of Light wandering in the darkness upon the world, that they will come to believe in me and know the fullness of the Celestine Light through the message of my Apostles and others that they shall call with authority to bring the light to the world.

160 I pray that all who find and live the fullness of the Celestine Light will become one in heart, mind, and spirit and become true brothers and sisters of the light, just as you, my beloved Mother and Father, are in me and I am in you.

161 May all those who seek the Celestine Light find it, and all those who live it gather together as Children of Light that they may edify one another.

162 May the Children of Light be brought to complete unity and abundance of all good things, even to the amazement of the world, that the people of the world will know that the Children of Light are blessed of God and that you love them even as you love me.

163 Divine Mother and Father, I want those who find the Celestine Light and live it, to be with me where I am, and to share in my joy and the glory you have given me.

164 As you have loved me before the creation of the world, so I have loved them. I know you too love them as parents, but they are my brothers and sisters and very precious to my heart.

165 I pray your love will shower upon all who wander in darkness that they will see the light and heed it and that those who have found it will take great joy in sharing it, that the Celestine glory shall be filled overflowing with the righteous."

Salome Sings

166 The following day while everyone was still gathered together in the upper room, Yeshua asked Salome to share her special gift and sing a song.

167 She had a moment of hesitation, for though she had sung at Herod's court, she had never sung to any of the Children of Light, except for the family of Yeshua to which she belonged.

168 But she obliged Yeshua happily, saying, "My Lord, thank you for allowing me to honor you with the music, which Elohim has so blessed to flow within me. Surely it is for this at least that you have asked me to be here among you. Would a song of the Persians be all right to sing?"

169 Yeshua nodded his head affirmatively, sweeping his arm around the room and saying, "If it uplifts our spirits and unites our hearts, let it be from any land, and we will be one with it."

170 Now all of the Apostles looked at Salome with curiosity, for none had ever heard her sing before. But as she began to sing, their eyes widened in amazement, and it seemed from their looks of awe that none had ever heard a sound so sweet.

171 Salome began to dance gently and modestly in harmony with her song. There was no need for musical instruments to accompany her singing, for her voice was as melodious and enchanting as any musical instrument could ever be.

172 She sang clearly, in her soft and angelic voice, with great variation in the pitch and punctuated by occasional thrills of her tongue. Culminating her song, she threw her head and arms up as she sang the last note, and dropped down onto her knees with her head bowed to the floor before Yeshua.

173 After a few moments of stunned silence, Yudas Iscariot, who knew some Persian, whispered, "This was a song of a hero who died to save his friends."

174 After he spoke, the silence lingered for a moment. Then beginning with one and then another, everyone stomped their feet in awestruck appreciation and began to compliment Salome. Miriam came to her and gave her a warm embrace and whispered something in Salome's ear that made her smile as she lifted her up to stand before Yeshua.

175 Yeshua complimented her, "Salome, you have always been a beautiful woman of great light. But when you sing, you bring out and expand the light inside everyone who is fortunate enough to be touched by your voice. I hope from this day forth, you will sing often for the edification of the Children of Light."

176 Her face beamed with happiness. "I will, my Lord. Surely if you wish it, I shall do it with great gladness."

CHAPTER 89

The Garden of Gethsemane

Yudas Iscariot says farewell to everyone and departs for his special mission given by Yeshua. The remaining Apostles, Yeshua, Miriam, and Salome go to the Garden of Gethsemane on the Mount of Olives. Yeshua and Miriam ascend to a place between Heaven and earth, where she takes on the mantle of the Angel of the Covenant. Yeshua and Miriam enter the Garden of Gethsemane, where Yeshua suffers the full weight of the sins of all the people of all worlds. So great is his suffering that he bleeds from every pore.

At the end of the feast days, Yeshua had Miriam, Salome, and all of the Apostles join him in a circle at the center of the room, and Yeshua said unto them, "This will be my last day with you before I return from the light of my divine Mother and Father.

2 "Yudas Iscariot will leave us as we depart this place to fulfill that which I have asked him to do. To others, it will seem that he betrays me, but let it be known to you and the Children of Light that he has honored me by obeying my wishes."

3 Each and every one of the Apostles including Miriam and Salome all spoke a few words of gratitude to Yudas Iscariot and promised they would remember why he did what he was about to do, although none, save Miriam, knew exactly what that was to be.

4 Then Yudas made to depart, and turning one last time to look at his friends, he said unto them, "As Yeshua has said and Salome sung for us, greater love has no man than this, that he would lay down his life for his friends. I know each of you would do no less, and please know that I have been so greatly honored and humbled to be numbered among you." Then he went out the door and closed it behind him, and he was gone.

5 Following the departure of Yudas Iscariot, Yeshua, Miriam, Salome, and the remaining Apostles left the building where they had been cloistered for the feast and walked to the Mount of Olives, where Yeshua led them to a secluded garden area, absent of any other people, called the Garden of Gethsemane.

6 Together, they gathered in a circle upon their knees and prayed to the divine Mother and Father, first Yeshua and then each of the others in turn.

The Angel of the Covenant

7 When they were finished, Yeshua took Miriam's hand and led her to the center of the circle. He spoke quietly to her in her mind so no others could hear, "It is now time to fulfill your greater calling, my love. Are you prepared to become that which you were foreordained to before the world was?"

8 "Yes, my Lord," Miriam affirmed. "I am ready to serve the Elohim with humility and clarity

as I have been called and foreordained before the world was."

9 Yeshua smiled at her, and she smiled back. They were facing each other and holding one another's hands, and Yeshua leaned forward and kissed Miriam lightly on the lips.

10 Then they both closed their eyes and tilted their heads up toward the clear sky. Suddenly, great puff balls of white clouds began to gather until the sky was soon thick with billowy white clouds hanging low toward the ground.

11 As Yeshua and Miriam continued to hold hands with their eyes closed and their heads tilted toward the heavens, a dense white pillar of cloud came swirling down from the mass of clouds above and completely engulfed them.

12 It was but a moment upon the ground, and then it quickly withdrew and rose back into the sky, becoming one again with the great body of clouds. And when it had cleared, the Apostles and Salome saw that Yeshua and Miriam were no more among them, but had disappeared with the pillar of cloud up into the sky.

13 Yeshua and Miriam came to stand atop the highest cloud. In the distance and from all directions, there was the approaching sound of trumpets, and then suddenly, many heavenly beings encircled them.

14 And Miriam asked Yeshua, "Who are these hosts of Heaven?"

15 Yeshua answered, saying, "They are some of my Father and Mother's angels who have come to witness the moment when you will be numbered among them."

16 "Truly?" Miriam said somewhat in awe. "Even now, when there is so much upon your shoulders and weighing upon your heart, you do me this honor? But if it is to be now, I know of a certainty that it is the time that best serves Elohim, and I am most humbled."

17 "Yes, Miriam," Yeshua replied. "Now is the time that you are called to fulfill the greatness of your promise."

18 Then a man with brown hair and a flowing beard, dressed in white robes with shimmering gold and colored threads and a large purple sash around his waist, stepped forward, and Yeshua put his hand upon his shoulder and introduced him to Miriam, saying, "This is Halakata. He is currently the Angel of the Covenant and will remain so in fullness while you learn the secrets of your calling."

19 Miriam nodded her head toward Halakata and said unto him, "It is an honor to meet you, Halakata. How long have you been the Angel of the Covenant? And pardon my ignorance but I thought the Angel of the Covenant was called Shalanawyn."

20 "I have no idea how long I have been in this office," answered Halakata. "I know exactly when I am supposed to be any place in the Celestine Realms or upon any earth in the heavens, but know not how that relates to the time as you keep it upon the world you have called home. As to my name, Halakata is for male holders of the angelic office of the Covenant and Shalanawyn for the females. As your angelic name for the office implies, you will bring different energies to your calling."

21 "He has served faithfully and well for a very long time," Yeshua assured Miriam; "and this on many earths. Now he has progressed in the expansion of his Celestine Light beyond the office of the Angel of the Covenant and has been called to something greater.

22 All of this is as my divine Father and Mother have decreed it should be, even down unto the very minute and hour of the time that only the Elohim know.

23 Now it is upon you, Miriam, to receive the mantle of the Angel of the Covenant and to fulfill that calling upon this earth and all others in the heavens, but upon this one in particular for the next eleven years. Do you accept this high and holy calling?"

24 You know that I do, my Lord," she answered with conviction.

25 Yeshua nodded his head in acknowledgment, and then said unto her, "In the name and by the power of Elohim, so let it be!"

26 A blinding white light immediately emanated from the body of Miriam and filled all the sky as far as the eye could see. Just as suddenly as it came upon her, it was gone, and she

stood before Yeshua and Halakata and all the angels who bore witness, no longer as Miriam of Magdala, but as the Angel of the Covenant, emissary of the Elohim, and protector of the Children of Light.

27 As the mantle of her angelic office settled upon her, Miriam's hair became as white as the light had shone in brilliance from her soul.

28 When Yeshua and Miriam returned quietly to the garden, most of the Apostles were napping. Salome saw them first as they walked from behind a tree, and she ran over to Miriam and embraced her with incredulity, saying, "Miriam, what has happened to you? Where did you vanish to? Why is your hair all white?"

29 "Calm down, Salome," Miriam requested in a loving voice. As she spoke, all of the Apostles came and gathered around them. "All is well," she said quietly. "Yeshua brought me to a place between earth and Heaven to fulfill my promise to Elohim."

30 She reached up and pulled some of her long hair in front of her so she could see it. She let the white strands fall a few at a time through her fingers and looked at them quizzically.

31 I'm not sure why my hair turned white, as I am not any older, and the one whose office I am assuming had a full head of brown hair." Saying this, she looked to Yeshua for an explanation, but he merely smiled at her in response.

32 "So it is done then?" asked Cephas. "Are you now the angel that Yeshua spoke of?"

33 "Somewhat, Cephas," Yeshua answered. "She is now the Angel of the Covenant, but the previous Angel of the Covenant will remain, still carrying the greater load and helping to guide her in her new calling, until her time in the flesh upon this earth is complete."

34 "But I am still the woman you have known in most ways that you can see, other than my hair," Miriam replied.

35 "Then pardon me for asking," Toma interjected, "but if you are still the same, standing here among us, how are you an angel?"

36 "In ways you shall discover when the time is appropriate, Toma. And the first of those times will soon be upon you," answered Yeshua.

No Greater Love Has Anyone Than This

37 Yeshua took a deep breath and let it slowly exhale. Then he spoke with great seriousness to Salome and his Apostles, "My time has come to fulfill much that I have come here to do. Miriam and I shall withdraw together further into the garden, a stone's cast away. Please keep watch upon the gate and insure that we are not disturbed."

38 The Apostles affirmed that they would watch the gate, and Miriam and Yeshua withdrew to a secluded part of the garden.

39 Standing next to a tree with a low-lying swayed trunk, Yeshua disrobed except for his loin cloth and laid his robes upon the ground, a short distance away from the tree.

40 He asked Miriam to kneel upon the far side of the tree trunk, and he knelt on the near side. They reached across the trunk and held hands and bowed their heads.

41 Then Yeshua prayed, saying, "Father and Mother, hear my words. At last, the time has come to fulfill all that you have asked me to come here to do, for your children of spirit upon this world and for your children of spirit upon all other worlds.

42 This I gladly do, for they are all my brothers and sisters and I love them.

43 I know that it is your desire that all of your children would return home to you in glory. But also I know that no unworthy soul can enter into your presence, for they cannot endure the brightness of your Celestine Light, unless their own resonance is in harmony and their own light shines in ways greater than the mortal world.

44 But all of my brothers and sisters upon this earth and upon all others have sinned and fallen far short of your glory.

45 Even my brethren, my Apostles who wait at the gate, have lived in the world and in many ways have been a part of it. They seek so much to do good and to please you. They have repented

of their sins, but there is still darkness even in them.

46 You have decreed that there is no darkness, only diminished light, and that no one whose light has diminished can enter into your presence until they have become purified in fullness of the Celestine Light.

47 I am your firstborn of spirit and only begotten son in the flesh. I am in you, and you are in me in all things; therefore, I am pure and I am in fullness of the Celestine Light.

48 Because of the love you have both given me and the knowledge you have guided me to and the example you have shown me and the wisdom you have taught me, my Celestine Light is great.

49 I come to you in purity and love and ask that you will let me bear the pains of torment of every soul, upon every world for the darkness that they carry in their soul.

50 Not just the souls who live today upon worlds innumerable, but also all the souls who have ever dwelt upon a physical world in the flesh and all the souls that have not yet come down onto a physical world, but shall come down someday.

51 Let me give some of my Celestine Light to them, to suffer the pains they would otherwise need to suffer as they sought to purge the darkness and become purer in the light that they might be worthy to be in your presence.

52 I tremble at the magnitude of that which I have asked. If there was a way that this cup of misery could pass from me, I would be tempted to take it. But I know there is no other way, and my love for my brothers and sisters of spirit is too great to let any of them perish or suffer needlessly, when I could save them.

53 Therefore, let the weight of the sins of the world and the weight of the sins of all worlds come upon me. Let me feel the torment that all people would suffer without a portion of my Celestine Light to be given for them.

54 I pray that you will grant that hereafter, any who repent of their sins and do them no more and live joyously and fully in the Celestine Light will not have to suffer at the last day on the Judgment of Resonance for the darkness that might still be in them. Let the inadequacies of their resonance be filled with my Celestine Light, even until they are worthy to come into your presence."

55 So saying, Yeshua cried out with a loud voice of agony. Miriam held tightly to his hands and called out to him, but he did not answer her.

56 For three hours, he remained kneeling at the tree, holding Miriam's hands, sobbing, and frequently crying out in pain and torment.

57 He began to sweat profusely. So great was his anguish that soon his sweat turned into drops of blood that ran down and covered his naked skin until he was red with blood.

58 As the third hour ended, he let out a great sigh and laid his head upon the tree, and still holding Miriam's hands, he fell asleep.

59 Before the next hour, he awakened, and going over to a basin at a nearby flow of water, he and Miriam washed the dried blood off his body.

60 Putting on his garments once again, he nodded silently to Miriam, and together, they returned to the place where the Apostles and Salome waited for them.

CHAPTER 90

The Trials of Yeshua

Yudas Iscariot meets with the Sanhedrin to inform them of Yeshua's whereabouts. They question him as to his motives and then send guards to arrest Yeshua in the Garden of Gethsemane. In his fervent desire to protect Yeshua, Cephas swings his sword and cuts the ear off one of the guards. Yeshua fully restores the man's ear and asks him to repent of his sins and heretofore live his life worthy of the Celestine Light that has been given to him. Yeshua is condemned by the Sanhedrin and held in a wine cellar where Miriam appears to him, and upon her request, he gives a full explanation of why he did what he did in the Garden of Gethsemane. Yeshua is handed over to the Roman governor of Palestine, Pontius Pilate, for final judgment. In a self-righteous rage, Pilate denounces Yeshua and sentences him to fifty lashes after which time he will carry his own cross to the spot where he will be crucified, naked.

Yudas Iscariot Comes before the Sanhedrin

During the time that Yeshua was in the Garden of Gethsemane, Yudas Iscariot went to the Sanhedrin who were meeting at the palace of Caiaphas, as Yeshua had secretly instructed him.

2 When it was recognized who he was—one of the principal disciples of Yeshua of Nazareth—he was brought before Caiaphas, who asked his father-in-law Annas, the former chief judge, to question Yudas.

3 Though Annas had officially retired and used his influence with the Roman governor Pontius Pilate to see his son-in-law Caiaphas made chief judge in his stead, he still held great influence over the Sanhedrin.

4 As evening fell, Yudas was brought into a chamber with only a short roof around its perimeter, where Annas and Caiaphas sat on small high-backed seats surrounded by more than a dozen of the Greater Sanhedrin standing behind them. Servants went around the room, lighting torches on the walls and on posts in the ground of the courtyard.

5 Yudas began to speak, but Annas held up his hand and demanded, "Silence! I will let you know when you may speak."

6 Then Annas looked at Yudas as a predator contemplates its prey. He studied him in silence for several minutes until the quiet became uncomfortable for many in the room, and they began to shuffle their feet and sigh.

7 "Why are you here, follower of the blasphemer?" Annas asked at last.

8 "I . . . ," Yudas stammered. He closed his eyes and taking a deep breath and exhaling, he

continued saying, "I have come to lead you to a place where Yeshua is sleeping this night. He is away from the crowds of people and alone with only his Apostles.
9 From Yeshua's previous encounters with the Sanhedrin and particularly Caiaphas, I have sensed that the Sanhedrin would appreciate the opportunity to bring Yeshua before them in secrecy, to question him without fear of the wrath of the people who hold him in great esteem."
10 "Very thoughtful of you," Annas said with slight sarcasm. "But why would you, one of the blasphemer's principal followers, betray him in this manner? It would seem that this must be more of a trap for us than it is for him."
11 "I assure you it is not," Yudas affirmed. "What could he do to you? He is but a poor man from Galilee, and you are the chief judges of the Greater Sanhedrin."
12 "Why are you doing this then?" asked Annas.
13 "It is something I must do to serve God," answered Yudas.
14 "Betrayal is a terrible stigma from which you will never be washed, even though in your mind your motivations may be noble and serving of God," Annas replied.
15 "I know," Yudas said quietly as he hung his head and looked at the ground.
16 "It is not often that we encounter someone so devoted to God that they would willingly sacrifice their reputation and maybe even their life if their former associates seek vengeance," Annas ventured.
17 "You do understand that if we judge him to be guilty of blasphemy or sacrilege, we may be compelled to seek his death?"
18 Yudas, with his head still hanging toward the ground, nodded in silent affirmation.
19 "Even so, I am not sure I believe you or your simple reason for why you would do this," continued Annas. "And that makes me suspect your motives."
20 Caiaphas then leaned over toward his father-in-law and whispered something in his ear.
21 Annas perked up upon hearing the words of Caiaphas and immediately looked to Yudas and asked, "You are named Yudas Iscariot?"
22 "That is one form of my name," Yudas answered.
23 "Then you are not only a Zealot, but also a Sicarii?" Annas asked. "That would explain a great deal. So you are a zealot among the Zealots."
24 "That part of my past is known to but a few. I doubt you deduced it from the Greek version of my name in which my past is hidden. Instead, your spies must be commendably good," Yudas replied.
25 "Yes, they are," Annas affirmed. "Of course, you looked to this man Yeshua to be the Messiah, and now you are wallowing in disappointment, as are all the Zealots, when you find he has no intention of leading you in a revolt against the Romans."
26 "It is true," Yudas answered. "I have seen him as the Messiah. But I know he is not going to lead even a small uprising against the Romans, let alone overthrow their rule."
27 "Why come to us?" asked Caiaphas. "You are a Sicarii; why not just slip your blade into him while he sleeps and then your disappointment is ended, as is his life, without risking political or religious turmoil?"
28 Yudas shook his head with vigor, saying, "No, not in any circumstance could I take his life or any man's except in defense of my own. I come before you because I know I must. But I love him still."
29 "What a pot of puke!" yelled Caiaphas. "We should judge you for being king of the liars. You come to betray your leader, but you say you still have great affection for him. You claim you are a Sicarii, but also that you would only kill a man in self-defense. You contradict your own statements and must consider us idiots if you think we would believe a word of it."
30 Then looking to his father in law, Caiaphas said, "We should not listen further to this Yudas, but put him away where no one will ever hear of him again. He lies like a serpent and undoubtedly desires to lead us into a trap of some type to embarrass the Sanhedrin in front of the people.

31 Let us be the masters of our own destiny and wait for Yeshua of Nazareth to return to Jerusalem, then follow him and take him while he sleeps and bring him before us to make an account and receive judgment."

32 At the words of Caiaphas, many of the Sanhedrin standing behind him voiced their approval, and Annas nodded his head in agreement, saying, "You speak with wise words, my son. Let us not go off upon unknown paths, but wait with patience for a time and place of our choosing."

33 Yudas was now in a quandary. He had been given a mission to bring the Sanhedrin to Yeshua, but now it seemed all he had accomplished was to be sent to a Roman prison himself.

34 Thinking quickly, he said, "Most learned judges, I have more to say that bears weight upon this matter and would ask that you withhold your judgment until you have heard all of the facts."

35 Caiaphas rolled his hand in a forward motion, indicating that Yudas should continue speaking.

36 Yudas said unto them, "I have no desire to be sent to prison. Nor would my wife or children appreciate it. I have not come here to deceive you, but have spoken only the truth.

37 Yeshua of Nazareth is alone with his Apostles and two wives at this time.

38 I was a Sicarii but not a typical one. I honored the commandments of Sinai, therefore could not take a life except in defense of my own. I was known to sometimes provoke situations with my adversaries in which I needed to defend myself, but that was unusual.

39 More often, I did not find it necessary to kill. In truth, if the dagger is used as a tool of persuasion rather than one of final judgment, it is far more effective. If you kill a man, little is accomplished, but if you put fear in his heart that he could die at any time from unknown assailants, he becomes a reliable source of influence and treasure.

40 That is my past, not my present. If you so easily recognized my past in the name I took during those times, I think it is time that I change my name again.

41 I am a loyal follower of Yeshua of Nazareth and now, and more than ever, keep the commandments of Sinai and the teachings of Yeshua that life is precious.

42 It is you that have accused me of being here to betray Yeshua. The opposite is true. I am here because he asked me to come to you and invite you to come and take him.

43 I think he is testing you to see if you have the gumption to dare lay hands upon him, even when there are none of the people present to witness if you fail.

44 You had him standing before you in recent days, and yet he walked away of his own will. Personally, I am convinced that without his agreement, you could never take him, try him, judge him, or do anything to him.

45 Your actions now bear witness to this very fact. You are so afraid of him that you have become impotent and cannot even move from your chairs toward him.

46 Nor have you cause to hold me or see me sent to a Roman prison, for I have done nothing but speak the truth to you. Why should I suffer because you are too afraid to act when the opportunity is given to you to defend what you believe?"

47 "You dare speak to us in this insolent manner?" demanded Caiaphas.

48 "If you are unaccustomed to hearing the truth, then surely you had better stay far away from Yeshua of Nazareth," Yudas replied.

49 Caiaphas was about to reply, but Annas cut him off with a gesture, then looked to Yudas and said, "You are sly, Yudas Iscariot, and think to goad us by using our own pride against us. I see what you are doing, but I am nevertheless affected by your words.

50 We will send a contingent of guards to follow you to the place where you say Yeshua of Nazareth is almost alone. They may not be familiar with his appearance; therefore, you will go to him directly and kiss him on the cheek so the guards are sure of who to take.

51 If everything is as you have said and we take him prisoner, you shall be rewarded with thirty pieces of silver. But if everything is not exactly as you have said, then it is you that our guards shall return to us and you who will never see the light of day again."

52 "Agreed," Yudas replied. Shortly afterward, about two dozen Sanhedrin guards armed with short swords and staves were assembled and followed Yudas out onto the street, their torches flickering in the darkness of the night.

Arrest of Yeshua in the Garden of Gethsemane

53 The Apostles had been both sitting and standing as they listened to Yeshua sharing with them the great importance of what had transpired at the Garden of Gethsemane.

54 Yeshua stopped speaking when they all saw the approaching lights of many torches and heard a number of people coming toward the garden. Soon they saw Yudas Iscariot come through the gate at the head of a group of armed guards from the Sanhedrin.

55 Immediately, Cephas spoke with urgency to Yeshua, saying, "Flee out the back gate; we will hold them until you are away."

56 But Yeshua did not move and instead remained standing serenely as a summer's morning, looking at Yudas and the men approaching. He calmly told Cephas, "Fear not, my brother. This is as I told you it would be. Be strong in your spirit."

57 "I cannot," Cephas replied with anguish. "I cannot see you taken to be tortured and killed like a common thief. There must be another way."

58 "This is the way I have chosen," Yeshua answered. "Please honor me by honoring my choice. And worry not for the pains of mortality. The soul is not the body, and neither these men nor the Sanhedrin nor the Romans can do aught to my eternal soul."

59 Yudas approached Yeshua with his head bowed and lifted it only enough to give him a kiss on the cheek.

60 Yeshua put both of his hands upon the head of Yudas and said unto him, "Well done, good and faithful brother."

61 At his words, Yudas fell to his knees and held his hands to his face as he wept.

62 Seeing the kiss of Yudas upon the cheek of Yeshua, which had been the agreed-upon sign of recognition, the guards quickly approached him.

63 Before they could lay their hands upon him, Cephas drew a short sword, and leaping forward, he slashed at the head of one of the guards, missing his head but cutting off his left ear, which fell to the ground.

64 The stricken man cried out in pain and fell to his knees, holding the bleeding hole where his ear had been.

65 The remaining guards hesitated in surprise, for they had not come expecting a fight. In the moments of their hesitation, Yeshua stepped forward and reached down to grasp the guard's severed ear off the ground.

66 He turned to the guard who looked up at him without fear and even with wonder. Yeshua stepped close to him, and holding the severed ear to the spot from whence it had come and calling the man by name, he said unto him, "Malchus, remember the good that has been done for you this day. Repent of your sins and live your life worthy of the Celestine Light that has been given to you."

67 As he stepped back, there were several gasps from the other guards as they saw that the man's ear had been fully restored to his head.

68 Turning then to Cephas, Yeshua told him, "Dear brother, let that be the last time you ever use your sword against a man.

69 Swords and weapons of violence are only for those who have not found the powers of Celestine Light within them.

70 And many who take up the sword for defense shall instead die by it. But those who defend with the gifts of Celestine Light shall prevail, for the weapons of men cannot do battle with the powers of Heaven.

71 You are my Apostle, and you must call forth the greater man of spirit within you that you can become more than you have been and be worthy of all that has been given to you."

72 Cephas nodded his head in understanding, and looking intently into Yeshua's eyes, he dropped his sword to the grounds and answered humbly, saying, "I will."

73 Yeshua turned now to the remaining guards and said unto them, "I am Yeshua of Nazareth whom you seek. I will come with you in peace, and you need not fear me or any of those with me."

74 So saying, Yeshua walked purposefully into the darkness of the night toward the gate of the garden through which the guards had come, followed closely by Miriam and Salome.

75 The guards and the Apostles stood still for a moment slightly dumbstruck by Yeshua's actions, and then looking at one another in some amazement, they all followed after them.

Final Appearance of Yeshua before the Sanhedrin

76 The guards came up and surrounded Yeshua, pushing Miriam and Salome behind them as they walked, and once again, they brought Yeshua to the palace of Caiaphas.

77 Yeshua was quickly led into the courtyard room where Caiaphas, Annas, and many of the Greater Sanhedrin awaited him. His Apostles and Salome were made to wait outside the inner walls with the servants, where they could hear those speaking but not see them. However, at Yeshua's request, Miriam was allowed to enter and stand in the shadows, watching and listening.

78 A scribe announced those who were present, and afterward, Caiaphas spoke to Yeshua, saying, "We have brought you here in secret to question you in great seriousness without the threat of interference from the multitudes who seem to love you. We only seek fairness and further clarification of the things you have said and done."

79 "Let us not dance around the truth, Caiaphas," Yeshua replied. "Everyone, including me, knows that you have brought me here in hopes of finding evidence of the blasphemy you have already concluded I spread. So ask your questions and find the truth."

80 "Very well," Caiaphas replied sourly. "By what means do you accomplish your miracles?"

81 "Do you mean miracles you or your priests have witnessed, such as when the sun stood still the last time I was here, or miracles such as the hole of Hades that opened in the ground at Tiberius or the gate at that place which became a living tree?"

82 "Bah," muttered Caiaphas. "Those were merely peculiar manifestations of nature that you tried to make us believe you had caused. Man can control nature a little, but not command it."

83 "But all things that have been created belong to Elohim and ever follow the commands of their creator," answered Yeshua.

84 Caiaphas was surprised by Yeshua's answer and told him, "By your own words, you condemn yourself. Are you saying that you are God the creator? Or that Elohim does as you bid? Make a lightning bolt come from Heaven and strike this spot as we speak, and I will believe you. But I have no worries, for you are just a man who either thinks he is God or one that has assumed the mantle of a prophet without authority."

85 There was silence for a moment; then Caiaphas looked to the sky and spoke again, saying, "No lightning bolt, hence you are but a man and not even a prophet; a very clever man, but just a man."

86 "What of that follower of yours that reportedly came back from the dead?" asked Annas. "I suppose he faked his death by taking some poisonous herbs? How did you accomplish it?"

87 "Not by elements of darkness," answered Yeshua. "But by the light of faith was this done."

88 "He must be tested further," demanded Annas. "Put a cloth over his face and then one of you go and smite him. Let us see if he can tell who does the deed."

89 Following the command of Annas, a thick cloth sack was placed over Yeshua's head, and two Sanhedrin and one Pharisee stepped forward and smote him with force on his face, knocking him backward with their blows.

90 Afterward, the assailants stepped back into the group of priests and the sack was removed from Yeshua's head.

91 "Tell us now who it was that smote you," demanded Annas. "If you are a prophet, this

should not even be a challenge, but if you are merely a deluded man, how will you know?"

92 Yeshua just stood looking at Annas and answered him not.

93 "Is anyone surprised?" Annas asked.

94 "Let the witnesses come forward," Caiaphas ordered. "As the scriptures demand, all shall be verified in the mouth of two or more witnesses."

95 Three different men stepped forward: one Pharisee, one Sadducee, and one temple priest. Each bore witness against Yeshua, giving evidence of his blasphemy.

96 "I saw him cast out the sellers and moneychangers from the temple and call it 'his father's house,'" said the temple priest sarcastically.

97 "I saw him heal a man on the Sabbath," accused the Pharisee. "And he justified himself as if he was above the law."

98 "I heard him say that if the temple of God was destroyed, he would build it again in three days," stated the Sadducee.

99 At the account of the Sadducee, there were murmurs and even some chuckles from those gathered, but Caiaphas was angry and mocked Yeshua, saying, "Have you anything to answer to these witnesses, oh, powerful one?"

100 Yeshua answered him, saying, "All they have said is true. I have healed those in need on the Sabbath; I did chase the dispensers of darkness from a place that is dedicated to the light of my Father; and if the temple of God is destroyed, even rent to the last piece and burned in the fire, I will build it again in wholeness in three days."

101 "Certainly, there can be no doubt this man is a blasphemer," Annas stated matter-of-factly. "He is probably also a lunatic, but he cannot be excused because of that affliction. The question now is what shall we do with him?"

102 "Death by stoning is appropriate!" shouted one of the Sanhedrin.

103 "Yes, it is appropriate," agreed Caiaphas. "But even though Pilate would probably not mind if we took this matter into our own hands despite the decrees of Rome, it would be best if we are not associated with this man's death, for he is still held in high esteem by many of the people."

104 "The timing is perfect to send him now to Pilate," Annas proclaimed. With the holiday, there are a great many more people in Jerusalem, and the Romans are already uneasy because of the risk of insurrection. Particularly during this celebration, which gives thanks for liberation from the oppression of the Egyptians, while we now grate under the command of the Romans.

105 This blasphemer is also a Galilean, which province has always caused Rome the most trouble, and they look to see more trouble coming from there.

106 We have not even spoken of the fact that many people, especially the Zealots from Galilee, look at him as the Messiah, even the king of Israel appointed by God, specifically come to liberate them from the Romans. I am sure Pilate will be interested in that morsel."

107 "No trial before the entire body of the Greater Sanhedrin?" Yeshua asked Annas and Caiaphas. "The twenty that are here tonight are as one against me, but many who are not here that are numbered among you would stand with me. How can you pass a judgment of death without all of the judges?"

108 "We cannot," Caiaphas admitted; "nor are we. As concerned citizens in high positions, with responsibilities upon us to do what we can to insure the safety of our people, we have identified you as a dangerous rabble-rouser and rebellious leader of the Zealots.

109 Although we also know you are a blasphemer, no trial before the entire body of Greater Sanhedrin is necessary, because as responsible leaders of our people, we are merely going to give you to the governor, along with the evidence we have gathered of your danger to Rome, and let him do away with you.

110 Bind him and throw him under guard into the wine cellar until the morning," ordered Caiaphas to the four guards standing nearby. "Then round up his close followers and bring them here that we may find the Zealots among them and send them also to Pilate."

111 One of the guards leaned toward Caiaphas and reminded him that all of Yeshua's principal followers had come with him and even now were just beyond the inner wall.

112 "Well, get them quickly before they flee!" Caiaphas bellowed. "And get his wife as well standing there in the shadows," he said pointing at Miriam. But when the two guards who were very near her pivoted to grab her, she was gone, and they looked at one another in bewilderment.

113 Nor could they capture Salome or any of the Apostles, for immediately upon hearing the order of Caiaphas, they fled quickly into the darkness, despite the efforts of several servants who had been standing with them listening to the proceedings that tried to detain them.

Yeshua Explains the Significance of His Suffering in the Garden

114 Yeshua had been sitting in the darkness of the wine cellar for about an hour when a bright light lit up the room, and when it dimmed slightly, Miriam stood before him and went to him. And the light that came with her remained.

115 They held each other for a few moments in a loving embrace, and Yeshua assured Miriam he was fine. Then she asked him with words in her mind, "Beloved, besides coming to be with you to comfort you, I came seeking greater understanding about what transpired in the Garden of Gethsemane, beyond what you were explaining to the Apostles."

116 Speaking also to her in her mind, Yeshua answered, saying, "You want to know why I suffered rather than just letting men suffer their own punishments in full for the choices they make."

117 "Of course, my Lord, you know my thoughts before I think them," Miriam answered. "And I do seek greater clarification. You suffered more than it seemed possible that the physical body of man could endure, even one that contains your power.

118 I understand that carrying the weight of the sins of others would certainly bring about such suffering. But I do not fully understand why you needed to do this, and I know that it is important that I do understand very clearly.

119 Each man and woman make their own choices of whether to live in the Celestine Light or live in the darkness every day, even in the small things they say or do and of course also in their larger acts of nobility or debasement.

120 Why did you desire to take some of their suffering away? Should not each person be fully liable for their own poor choices, even as they are fully rewarded for their good ones?

121 If there is a penalty to be paid in suffering in remorse or even agony of sadness for some time, should not the person who made the choice of darkness be the one who suffers?

122 If restitution is needed, if light must be made to counterbalance the darkness that was sowed so a man may be worthy to enter into Heaven, should it not be the man who sowed the darkness that is required to create the light that washes it away?"

123 Yeshua looked deeply into Miriam's eyes and gently ran his finger along her hairline. Continuing to project the thoughts of his mind, he answered her, saying, "I suffered, not so men will not have to suffer, for all will still pay a price for the darkness they have not washed clean with repentance.

124 And those sins that have not been washed clean with repentance are many, for even the most virtuous person, even you, my love, have some darkness in their past that was never fully washed clean with the Celestine Light of a full repentance and restitution.

125 For many are the sins of commission and omission that are forgotten by man, but all are remembered by Elohim.

126 And many are the moments of darkness in a person's life that simply cannot be repented of in fullness.

127 With repentance, 'I'm sorry' is not enough. There must also be restitution, a restoring of that which was taken. But sometimes that which was taken cannot be restored.

128 Such as the evil man who steals from another, not his goods, which can be returned, but his good name by spreading slanderous rumors in secret whisperings to those he knows not.

129 The rumors will spread like a plague, and there is nothing the evil man can do to undo the darkness he has sown. Though he may cry in remorse for the dark deed he has done and beg God and the good man he has wronged for forgiveness, he can never make a full restitution, for the words of falsehood he cast are beyond his power to call back and will continue to injure the good man all of his life.

130 So too, everyone is guilty of sometimes casting a little unrepented darkness with less-than-loving words, less-than-honest replies, less than a full day's work for a full day's wages, less-than-complete compassion, less-than-gentle patience with children, and many more little moments of darkness.

131 Even good and noble Children of Light seldom think of repentance when they do these things, yet their actions were of darkness, not of the light, and repentance is needed for the small sins even as it is for large ones.

132 In a lifetime, all of these little moments of darkness that have been forgotten add up to an oppressing weight, even upon the most wonderful Children of Light.

133 So too do the moments of darkness that cannot be fully repented of continue to weigh down the soul of man as the years pass by.

134 Then comes the spirit and souls of men to the gates of the Celestine Realm of Light when they die. And many will come knowing they have been good and honorable in life and expecting to pass on to a greater light as their reward.

135 But the highest realms of the Celestine Kingdom are realms of light in which no darkness can dwell. It can still remain on the inside as it must for balance, but must be completely overcome on the outside. Even the most virtuous man or woman, even you, my pure Miriam, fall short of that glory.

136 I suffered and offered some of my Celestine Light to help bridge the gap between man and Elohim so that I could be with you, my true love, for time and all eternity in the highest Kingdom of Celestine glory and beyond that into the Kingdom of the Elohim.

137 I suffered and offered some of my Celestine Light to help bridge the gap between man and Elohim so that all men and women, my brothers and sisters of spirit, who diligently, humbly, and sincerely endeavor to live the teachings I have brought, will be able to obtain the reward they seek.

138 I am an Elohim. But like all men, I am also a spirit son of my divine parents and, by that, a true brother of all mankind. Because of this, I am a part of both and the bridge of Celestine Light between man and God.

139 No one comes to the highest Kingdom of glory, save they come by living my words and following my light.

140 To all who live the good light, be they Children of Israel, Romans, Greeks, Persians, or Pagans, they shall find salvation in me, for I gave it to them with my blood and light, on my knees in love for them, in the Garden of Gethsemane."

The Meeting of Caiaphas and Pilate

141 And it came to pass that in the morning, Yeshua was bound and brought to the Roman prison and Caiaphas, the chief judge of the Sanhedrin, met with Pontius Pilate, the Roman governor of Palestine to inform him of the danger to Rome presented by Yeshua of Nazareth.

142 Pilate was keenly interested in the words of Caiaphas but doubted that Yeshua was a threat, so he answered him dismissively, "I am surprised you have brought this man to prison. I have received reports of him in recent times, and it is said he does many miracles. I have not heard it said that he promotes insurrection. In fact, my spies told me he rebuffed the Zealots.

143 "He is one of your people, and he seems to be popular with many. Why bother to send him to a Roman prison? If you have differences with him, can't you deal with them yourself?"

144 Caiaphas answered Pilate, saying, "He may have favor with the simple and ignorant who are fooled by his tricks and illusions, but the Sanhedrin are not fooled.

145 But many of the common people have been deceived, even to abandoning our faith and following after the new faith he teaches, for he is charismatic and a magician that knows no peer.

146 Rome should fear as well, for he teaches that he has come not to uphold the law, but to overthrow it. And he means not just our religious law, but also the laws of Rome.

147 Surely you are aware that along the north shore of Lake Gennesaret, his followers have built communities, and even now they almost outnumber the native populations of the four towns located there.

148 Galilee has always been the greatest source of insurrection against Rome in all of Palestine. Now comes this man, Yeshua of Galilee, who preaches disobedience to the laws and who has steadily been gathering his followers on Lake Gennesaret. Soon, he will have enough men to lead an army against you.

149 Spies may or may not discover truth, but with this man they are not needed, for his own followers openly have told us that among the Zealots, he is seen as a promised savior and the rightful king of the land sent by God."

150 "Very well," Pilate responded with disinterest. "I thought you had something important to tell me. You have made a small case for him to be in prison, so we shall keep him there for a few days, at least until your festival is over and all these additional people are out of the city.

151 But as for insurrection, the army of Rome has little to fear from the stone throwing and inept swordplay of farmers and tradesmen, let alone magicians and preachers."

152 Caiaphas seemed surprised by Pilates' answer, and he said, "If you feel that way, esteemed Governor, then I have not presented the facts to you sufficiently.

153 While it is true that this man is not a soldier, nor are any of his followers as far as I know, his power is not in his sword, but in his words, which stir the hearts of men to take actions they would not otherwise take, even actions against the power of Rome.

154 Do not underestimate this power. It is as great as any army, for men convinced they are acting under the direction of God's chosen leader will make up in fearlessness and willingness to fight to the death what they lack in actual experience of fighting and war."

155 "That is true," Pilate answered as he rubbed his chin in contemplation. "I have seen men under the sway of passionate belief, and they can act like rabid dogs with ferocious fury and tenacious desire to kill with no regard for their own life at all.

156 Still, it seems that he is causing more problems for you than he is for Rome. But I will have this man Yeshua brought before me, and I will question him myself just to satisfy my curiosity as to why you are in such a lather over him.

157 If there is any insurrection in him at all, I will send him to the cross. That is the quickest way to end any threat. If not, I will send him back to you, and you will have to deal with him as you will.

158 If he is fomenting rebellion, you will see that any followers he might have will vanish once they see their leader crucified to death like any common thief. If he is a leader of the Zealots and irritates me when I speak with him, I'll see him crucified upside down."

159 Caiaphas nodded his head solemnly as if he was sad that the fate of Yeshua had to come to death, and he said, "Life is precious, and you know how we feel about the cruelty of crucifixion. But sometimes for the good of many, some things of revulsion must be tolerated.

160 But there are other things you must be aware of with this man. As I told you, he is a great magician, if nothing else. In recent days, he fooled many people, including some of my own Sanhedrin, into believing that he had raised a man from the dead.

161 Of course, no magician operates alone, and surely he has many accomplices that are participants in his acts of trickery.

162 Because it is believed that he raised a dead man from the grave, it is likely that his followers will try to rob his body from the grave, that then one of them can claim that he is Yeshua resurrected from the dead and perpetuate the falsehoods this man taught.

163 Considering this, if you crucify him, as I am sure you will, you would be wise to guard

the grave site so his followers cannot steal the body and then claim he has risen from the grave."

164 "This man is becoming a great deal of trouble," asserted Pilate. "But if you truly fear this nonsense, I will see soldiers at the grave until the body rots. Or better yet, I will leave his body on the cross in public view until the birds have picked its bones, and then there will be no talk of rising from the dead."

Yeshua before Pilate

165 And it came to pass that Yeshua was brought before Pilate, and Pilate questioned him saying, "I have heard it said that you are called the rightful king of the land. Do you consider yourself to be this?"

166 Yeshua answered him, saying, "If I was given a crown and Rome and all of the people said, 'Let him be king,' I would hand back the crown to he who gave it and walk away, for I have come to serve, not to be served."

167 "Some would say that being a good king is a very great service," Pilate pointed out. "I know being a governor is taxing on patience and civility, and sometimes decisions that carry a heavy burden must be made for the good of the people. Is that not service?"

168 Yeshua answered, saying, "Service is thinking of others and acting for their interests without taking gain for yourself.

169 Service is not forcing your will upon others or only assisting your friends or tribe, but instead acting unconditionally to help anyone in need who calls upon you with a humble heart and a worthy desire.

170 Service is not being pampered while those you rule live in squalor.

171 It is not eating in such excess that what you discarded as scrapes from your table is more than many people will eat that day.

172 It is not living in a great house of many empty rooms while many have but a single room with a leaking roof over their head.

173 Service is not capriciously taking the lives of those who disagree with you or torturing them into despair or taking the lands and the vineyards of those in disfavor or even holding such authority and threat over them.

174 Service is the blessed path to Heaven, but few will be the wealthy or rulers of men who find it. They who hoard excess unto themselves or squander it on riotous living during their brief mortal life pay for their pleasures, not with their gold, but with their eternity.

175 Among men, the rulers, leaders, and rich men most often have the least understanding of the truths of eternal significance, and that which they despised in life shall be their undoing in eternity. For in the Kingdom of Heaven he who has been least on earth shall be greatest, and he who has been greatest shall be least."

176 Pilate gave Yeshua a mocking little bow with his head and a small rolling wave of his hand and said, "That was quite a little speech. All wrong, but it sounded good. I've a mind to send you to Rome, in chains of course, but you would be entertaining: a simple carpenter, proclaimed a king, who speaks with the glib tongue of a Roman senator.

177 But what of your magic? I've heard you are a magician without peer. If you can really do some of the miracles men have said of you, as well as speak like a Greek philosopher, I really must send you to Rome."

178 Yeshua looked deeply into the eyes of Pilate. There was no anger upon his face, only a look of great seriousness belying Pilate's lightness of speech, and he said unto him, "The Son of Light walks the path decreed by the Elohim and not by the vain desires of the sons of men. Upon this land was this body born, and upon this land shall it die, in the time and place and manner that I choose."

179 Hearing these words from Yeshua, Pilate's face contorted in rage, and suddenly, he lashed out and smote Yeshua with great force upon his face, knocking him to the ground. Three of his personal guards quickly came up with drawn short swords, their sharp points touching Yeshua

on his body and throat as he lay upon the ground.

180 Pilate shouted at Yeshua in a loud voice, saying, "Let me put you in your place, beggar from Galilee! You will decide nothing! It is upon my command whether you are a slave or free. It is upon my command whether you remain here or go to Rome. It is upon my command whether you live or die."

181 Yeshua pulled himself up onto one elbow, and before the soldier could react, with his other hand, he grabbed the sharp two-edged sword that was pointed at his heart and quickly swept the pointed tip across his exposed forearm.

182 When he released the sword from his grasp, blood flowed freely from his hand and from the self-inflicted wound upon his arm.

183 Yeshua stood up, and Pilate bade the guards to allow it. Blood still flowed from his hand and arm, dripping into a small pool on the floor. He held out his bleeding hand and arm toward Pilate and said unto him, "I fulfill the will of the Elohim, and the vain desires of men are as dust to me."

184 Then through the openings to the building, a strong wind blew in and one of the soldiers pointed at Yeshua's outstretched arms and cried in fear, "Look, look at his wounds; they are healing before our eyes!"

185 It was as he spoke, and even as Pilate and the three soldiers watched in amazement, the blood flowing from the wound on Yeshua's hand and the other on his arm ceased to flow, and the skin sealed up and became normal and healthy. And the pool of blood upon the ground dried in a few seconds into a pile of dust and blew away in the wind that came through the building.

186 Yeshua had been looking steadfastly into the eyes of Pilate as these moments passed, and once again he said unto him, "I fulfill the will of Elohim, and the vain desires of men are as dust to me."

187 Pilate, seeing the look of awe and fear upon the faces of his guards and catching his own voice, said to them, "Gird yourselves up men; this charlatan is nothing more than a magician. This is Yeshua of Nazareth. Have you not heard him spoken about in Jerusalem?"

188 "Yes, I have," said one of the men, relaxing at Pilate's reassurance. And the other two nodded in agreement.

189 "It is said he does many miracles," added another; "even among the Romans that come to him."

190 Pilate spoke with scorn, saying, "They are merely tricks and illusion; only miracles to the simple and the ignorant."

191 Turning again to Yeshua, Pilate spoke to him with hardness in his voice: "I thought perhaps the fear the Sanhedrin have of you was misplaced and their warnings about you exaggerated, but now I see they spoke wisely. You are indeed a danger to Rome.

192 My duty is clear. Rome will never see your face, and upon this land you shall die, even as you have said. But it will not be by the choice of you or your God, but by me as guardian of the rule of Rome.

193 That was the last trick you shall ever perform, so at least it was a good one. Tell me how you did it and reveal yourself to be a fraud, and I will show you mercy and send you away to the mines to work until you die. And who knows how long that might be?

194 Say one word in disagreement to me and you shall die soon, but slowly, as your life ebbs away hanging on a cross of crucifixion."

195 Yeshua answered him, saying, "Crucify me and you shall see a far greater miracle than you have seen today. Or repent of your wickedness and humble yourself before Elohim and you shall yet find a glory you have never imagined."

196 "Enough!" cried Pilate. "You are the most audacious scoundrel I have ever had the displeasure of speaking to. I cannot suffer to hear any more of your words. And it is your words that have condemned you, not mine."

197 Then turning to his guards, Pilate commanded, "Take him to be crucified on the morrow.

Crucify him naked that he might remember that he is nothing. Give him fifty lashes with a leaded scourge before he departs for the hill that he may see that his blood spills and his flesh rips out just like any other man's. And have him carry his own cross that he might be reminded with every step of the weight and consequences of his own foolishness."

198 Then the guards bound Yeshua's arms and hands tightly behind his back and put a rope around his neck and pulled him by it and led him away as Pilate commanded.

199 As he was passing from the room, Pilate called after him, saying, "Where is your great magic now? Where is your god?"

200 Yeshua turned his face back toward Pilate and answered, saying, "Where it has always been, inside of me. And inside of everyone who believes in me. It is a light that has no beginning and can have no end, a light that shall ever grow, and all the power of Rome and all the kings of earth cannot extinguish it."

CHAPTER 91

Crucifixion and Resurrection

Miriam, Salome, Martha, Miryam, and all of the Apostles except Yudas Iscariot witness the scourging of Yeshua, along with many other people that had gathered. The Apostles begin to lose faith, and in despair, Cephas denies three times that he even knows Yeshua as was foretold by Yeshua. Yeshua is made to carry his own cross, but when he falters, the Roman guards accost a Cyrenian and force him to carry the cross for Yeshua. Yeshua is crucified and dies in the ninth hour after he speaks to Heavenly Mother and Father. Joseph of Aramathea asks Pilate if Yeshua can be buried in his sepulcher. Caiaphas asks Pilate if the tomb can be sealed and guarded. Yudas Iscariot dies a peaceful death beneath the water in company of the Angel of the Covenant, but out of ignorance, once recovered, many revile his body and hang it from a tree. On the morning of the third day, Miriam removes the heavy mortared stone of the tomb of Yeshua, much to the dismay of the Roman guards who run away in fear, and finds Yeshua resurrected before her, but she cannot touch him until his resurrection is perfected by Heavenly Mother and Father. Miriam tells the Apostles of Yeshua's resurrection, but they doubt her. Yeshua returns to meet with his Apostles where they feel his wounds and attest to his resurrection. Yudas Iscariot also returns from the dead.

The Scourging of Yeshua

And it came to pass that the following day shortly after dawn, Yeshua was brought to the place of scourging.

2 At first light, while still with the Roman guards in the prison, he was stripped as had been ordered by Pilate and then draped with an old ragged purple robe. A hard, dry reed was put in his right hand, and a crown of long thorns was pushed onto his head by one of the Romans, causing him to bleed thin rivulets of blood down his face.

3 And they all mocked him, saying, "Hail to the king of Israel." And they spit on him and took the reed from his hand and hit him about his head and face with it. Once again, the Romans put a rope tightly around Yeshua's neck and pulled him to the public scourging ground with violent yanks that often brought him to his knees, which were soon bloody and raw.

4 At the place of scourging, the soldiers removed the ragged robe and brought Yeshua naked to face a thick post. His arms were pulled forward to encircle it and his wrists tied together on the other side. Then two men stood on opposite sides and took turns lashing Yeshua with rawhide whips of many tails, one using his left hand to swing the lash, the other his right. The tails had double-spiked iron and lead weights on each end that bit into Yeshua's flesh, ripping

out pieces as he was flailed.
5 Many people gathered to watch Yeshua's scourging, and among them standing as near to
him as was possible was Miriam, Salome, Martha, and his mother Miryam.
6 With each lash upon Yeshua's body—some on his back, others upon his legs and arms—
Salome, Martha, and Miryam let out their own cries of anguish and a flood of tears.
7 But his wife Miriam had a piercing and resolute look upon her face and cried not at all, nor
did she exclaim, and Miryam his mother upbraided her saying, "How can you watch my son and
your husband tortured so terribly and shed not a tear?"
8 Miriam his wife answered her, saying, "I am one with your son, Mother Miryam, in ways
you cannot even imagine. What he feels, I feel. I am not writhing in pain, so I know that neither
is he, though the destruction we are witnessing to his beautiful body saddens me greatly."
9 Miryam his mother was astounded at the words of her daughter-in-law and exclaimed,
"How can you say he feels no pain; how could he not?" Pointing at Yeshua, she said, "His body
is covered in blood. His flesh comes out in pieces from the lash. He moves to escape the lash
that he knows is coming. He shudders and gasps with every blow. I understand you not at all,
Miriam."
10 Miriam of Magdala stood closely next to Miryam of Nazareth, holding onto her arms,
and looking deeply into her eyes, she spoke softly unto her, saying, "It is Yeshua you need to
understand, Mother, not me. Though he came from your womb, he is an Elohim and not of you.
Though he is in the form of a man, he is greater than the form.
11 He does feel some pain, but not as great as his wounds proclaim; his body bleeds and is
tortured and will die, but only because he has said it will be so, to prove the resurrection that all
mankind may know the path to glory.
12 Have faith in my words, Mother, despite what your eyes may see. And know that I speak
to you not only as your daughter of marriage and twin star of Yeshua, but as given to me to speak
by the Elohim as the Angel of the Covenant."
13 Miryam of Nazareth nodded her head in silence and smiled weakly at her daughter-in-
law, saying, "There is still much that I do not comprehend, but I have felt the truth of your heart
and surely it has been a balm to mine." Then she reached out and gently held Miriam's hand,
saying, "Thank you, daughter."
14 All of the Apostles except for Yudas Iscariot had also gathered at the scourging ground
to witness the lashing of Yeshua, and not having heard the words of his wife Miriam, they were
shuddering in inner pain with every lash they saw Yeshua take, and for many, despite all the
miracles they had witnessed in the times they had been with Yeshua, their faith began to ebb.
15 Cephas was standing apart from his fellow Apostles. He no longer could bear to watch the
whipping of his beloved teacher and friend. He held his head in his hand, covering his face and
exhaling in deep sighs. A woman standing next to him called to him, saying, "Man, I saw you
with him when he was in Jerusalem preaching. I am sorry for you and your friend."
16 Cephas looked up at her with apprehension and replied, "No, you are mistaken. I know
him not." And he quickly turned and walked away from her.
17 As he was walking through the gathered crowd, a Greek grabbed his arm and said to him,
"You are one of his students. What do you think of this?"
18 Cephas pulled his arm away angrily and answered, "You have me confused with someone
else. I do not know that man."
19 Cephas hurried now to depart from the scourging grounds, and as he was at the gate,
another woman accosted him and said, "They are killing Yeshua of Nazareth. You are one of his
stalwarts. Why do you flee?"
20 And Cephas cursed at her and hurried through the gate, yelling at her as he left, "I do not
know that man on the post. Leave me be!"
21 Immediately, a cock crowed nearby, then another, then a third. And Cephas remembered
the words of Yeshua that he would deny him three times before the cock crowed, and he was

ashamed to the depths of despair at what he had done. He fell to his knees upon the road, bent his head to the ground, holding it in his hands, and began crying with great gasps of remorse and rivers of tears.

22 As the final lashes were slashed across Yeshua's back, his eyes held the eyes of his wife Miriam, and they spoke to one another in their minds. But the words they said are for them alone and cannot be recorded.

23 After the last lash ripped across Yeshua's bare back, he was given a soiled, putrid-smelling loin cloth to wear.

The Crucifixion of Yeshua

24 Yeshua was led out of the scourging place and brought to a large cross made from a thick tree lying beside the road. The Romans placed it over his shoulder and prodded him with the tips of their short swords and whacked his wounds with the broad blades to get him moving toward the Place of the Skulls to be crucified.

25 But before he had taken many steps, he faltered from the weight and fell to his knees. After he had done the same twice more, one of the Romans accosted a Cyrenian and forced him to carry the cross for Yeshua.

26 The Cyrenian was named Shimon, of the tribe of Judah, and was the father of two sons, Alexander and Rufus, who followed after him as he carried the cross.

27 As the sons spoke with people in the crowd, they were astonished to learn that the man going to crucifixion was none other than Yeshua of Nazareth of whom they had heard wondrous stories of in Cyrenaica and had just now arrived in Jerusalem with their father to see if the stories were true.

28 Seeing Yeshua being taken to be crucified, they were confused and knew not what to make of it, as were many others who followed after him having witnessed his miracles, and did not understand how he could now be so beaten down and taken away to die by the Romans.

29 The sound of wailing from many, many women in the crowd was an unnerving noise all about. When the Romans stopped the procession for a moment and ordered the women to be quiet, Yeshua turned to the multitude and said, "Daughters of Jerusalem, weep not for me, but weep for yourselves and for your children.

30 For behold, the days are soon coming in which they shall say, 'Blessed are the barren and the wombs that never bear and the paps that never gave suck.'

31 Then shall they say unto the mountains and the hills, 'Hide us and cover us.'

32 For if the Romans do this that you see in times of green, oh, what shall they do to the children of Jerusalem in times of dry?"

33 When Yeshua reached the Place of the Skulls, the cross was laid upon the ground and Yeshua was laid naked on top of it. Large nails were pounded through his wrists and hands and feet, and the cross was lifted up by the Roman soldiers and raised upright as the base was placed in a deep hole that had been prepared for it. Two thieves were also crucified with him, one to each side.

34 The soldiers then sat down at the base of the hill and gambled for Yeshua's clothing and possessions, which they had brought with them. They nailed a crude sign upon the cross in Latin, Greek, and Hebrew, saying, "Yeshua of Nazareth, king of the Israel."

35 Then a Sadducee came up and stood before Yeshua, and shaking his head, he turned to the multitude and said, "He saved others, but he cannot save himself. If he is truly God's messenger, let him come down now from the cross, whole as he has made others whole, and we will believe.

36 He proclaims God; let God deliver him now, if he will have him, for he claimed he is the Son of God." Then he pointed at Yeshua and said, "You see, nothing happens. He dies on the cross the same way as the common thieves beside him. Your faith has been misplaced."

37 Then a Pharisee came also before the crowd and, pointing at Yeshua, said, "He said the temple could be destroyed and he would rebuild it in three days all by himself. But look at him.

He is helpless, powerless. He is nothing but empty words and promises."

38 As the time passed, the soldiers continually came up to Yeshua and taunted him and reviled him, hitting his legs with their hands and wagging their heads, and mocked him, saying, "You said the temple could be destroyed and you would build it again in three days? But you cannot even save yourself?"

39 Another said, "You are the Son of God? Let us tremble in fear. But wait, first come down from that cross, oh, Son of God, and show us who you are. Reveal your dreadful power. Show us why we should be afraid." And the soldiers pretended to be afraid, then laughed and derided Yeshua when nothing happened.

40 Through all of this, Yeshua never looked at the soldiers or the priests or anyone in the crowd, save for his wife Miriam, who stood directly before him. And from her, he seldom took his eyes.

41 Once more, three soldiers took turns coming up and hitting him on his legs, and when the last had passed, Yeshua looked upward toward the sky and said, "Forgive them, Father and Mother, for they know not what they do."

42 Then looking down upon the four most important women in his life, Miriam, Salome, Martha, and his mother Miryam, he said to his mother, "See my wife Miriam, your daughter. Hold fast to her."

43 And to Miriam his wife, he spoke, saying, "See my mother Miryam, your mother too. Protect her."

44 Then to Salome, he spoke and said, "Remain by the side of Miriam through all things, and everything in your life shall be fulfilled to the fullest."

45 Then to Martha, he spoke, saying, "Raise up good children and they shall walk great paths of Celestine Light. You have much life still to live, but know that your beloved waits for you in eternity."

46 The day had been clear and sunny when Yeshua was led to the Place of the Skulls, but as the fourth hour began, the sky became very black with thick and ominous clouds.

47 One of the Roman soldiers soaked a sponge with vinegar and impaling it on a long reed, he raised it to Yeshua's lips offering it to him, but he did not partake of it.

48 By the end of the fourth hour of Yeshua's crucifixion, the sky had become blacker with thicker storm clouds than anyone could remember, and many in the crowd spoke with some trepidation about the uncommon blackness of the sky.

49 In the ninth hour, to insure the men were not still dying on the cross when the Sabbath arrived, some priests came to the Romans and asked them to hasten the death of Yeshua and the two thieves.

50 In keeping with their wishes, the soldiers went and broke the legs of both thieves but when they came to Yeshua he commanded them in a strong voice, saying, "Hold." They were perplexed that he could speak with such vigor to them after all he had been subjected to, and they held off breaking his legs.

51 Then Yeshua looked once more to Miriam and said in a clear voice, "In the days of darkness, uphold the Celestine Light. I am always with you, always and forever."

52 Then he lifted up his head once more toward the heavens and said in a loud voice heard by many, "Father and Mother, I am the good son. I have done as you have willed. My spirit now comes home." After he said that, his head tilted down onto his shoulder as he gave a last exhale of breath, and then his spirit was gone and his body died.

53 "Is he dead?" asked one of the Romans to the other soldiers.

54 "Too quick," another stated. Then he took a spear and stabbed it through Yeshua's side and into his heart, saying, "But he's dead now."

55 But he suddenly stepped back in fear as he pointed at the wound in Yeshua's side. And many were frightened to see not only blood, but also a clear liquid like water dripping out and running down his body.

56 A minute or so passed after the departure of the spirit of Yeshua, when suddenly there was a blinding flash of lightning in the clouds and a mighty roar of thunder. Then the ground began to shake in an earthquake, and many people throughout Jerusalem lost their balance and fell to the ground.

57 In the temple, Miriam went as the Angel of the Covenant, unseen by the eyes of men, and rent the Veil in two from top to bottom and cast it to the floor that the priests would know the wrongness of what they had done and spoken against Yeshua.

58 At the Place of the Skulls, standing beneath the cross, the Roman centurion who had led the soldiers looked about and saw the crescendo of sky and the earth upon Yeshua's death, and he said to his fellows, "Perhaps, we laughed and mocked to our own peril, and this really was the Son of God."

Joseph of Arimathea Asks to Bury Yeshua

59 Shortly after the body of Yeshua died upon the cross, Joseph of Arimathea, a good and just man of the Sanhedrin and a secret follower of Yeshua, asked at the gate of the governor's villa to speak immediately to Pilate.

60 Because Joseph was a well-known and respected leader of the city, Pilate consented to see him. And Joseph asked him forthrightly, "Good Governor, grant me the liberty to take the body of Yeshua of Nazareth and lay it in a sepulcher I had hewn into solid stone, thinking to use it myself someday.

61 I fear for villains to desecrate the body of Yeshua if it is left to a common burial. He was a good man and deserves better than that."

62 Pilate contemplated Joseph for a moment and then asked, "Why would you give a rich man's grave to a poor man? Just bury him deep beneath a stone, and nobody will bother the body."

63 Then a thought seemed to spring into Pilate's head, and he exclaimed, "You are a Sanhedrin. It was the lot of you that brought this Galilean to my attention in the first place. Why would you honor him now in burial?"

64 Joseph bowed his head in thought, let out a deep sigh, and answered Pilate, saying, "Not all of the Greater Sanhedrin were opposed to Yeshua of Nazareth and what he taught and did.

65 In truth, like me, many, if not the majority, found enlightenment in his teachings, which helped us to become more than we were—kinder, thoughtful, humble, and helpful.

66 So too were we astounded by his miracles which brought us to praise God and know with certainty that there is more to life than existence and that man is but an embryo of what he can become.

67 He lifted us in spirit to places we had never been and brought a peace into our hearts that stills all turmoil.

68 His success and teachings threatened the hierarchy of our religion, even as he was crucified because you felt that he was a threat to Rome. But he is dead now and a threat to none anymore. Therefore, I beseech you to give me his body that he might find in death a peace and protection from those who understood him not at all in life."

69 "Fine; take the body!" Pilate exclaimed with some irritation as he turned quickly on his heel and strode away, ending the meeting. "See that it is arranged," he ordered the centurion who stood in the entry as he passed through.

The Burial of Yeshua

70 And it came to pass that Joseph of Arimathea took the body of Yeshua and laid it on a raised stone slab in the spacious tomb he had cut into solid rock. And in the manner of the tribe of Judah, Miriam, Martha, Salome, and Miryam the mother of Yeshua came into the tomb, with Nicodemus of Bethsaida.

71 They washed and straightened the body of Yeshua, then took strips of clean linen about the width of a forearm and tightly wrapped the body from the armpits to the ankles.

72 Upon each layer of linen, they liberally smeared a heavy coating of a gummy mixture made from about one hundred pounds of myrrh, aloe, and other aromatic spices.

73 Layer upon layer, the body of Yeshua was wrapped until it had the almost-rounded appearance of a cocoon.

74 Yeshua's face and hair were then anointed with oil of nard, and a small separate linen napkin was placed over it. Lastly, his body was lifted and placed on a large linen that then folded back over and covered him on the top as well as the bottom.

75 Then a large, circular, solid stone was rolled down in a groove and set into place completely sealing the tomb. The stone was as tall and thick as a man, and standing at the bottom of a downhill slope, only several strong men could ever move it again.

76 The following day, Caiaphas, the chief judge of the Sanhedrin, came to Pilate. "I understand one of our own has buried the body of the deceiver in his tomb."

77 "Yes," Pilate replied casually. "He asked permission, and I could see no reason to deny him. Nor do I care to be bothered anymore about this Galilean. So if you are here to talk about him, it is best you leave."

78 "Favor me but one more thing," Caiaphas pleaded. "As I told you previously, it has been said by some that when the deceiver said he would rebuild the temple in three days, he was secretly telling his followers that he would rise from the dead after three days.

79 I fear that his followers might come in the night and steal away the body that they can proclaim to the people that he has risen, for the tomb will be empty. A myth perpetuated about the deceiver would be worse than having him still alive and inspire the Zealots to actions they might not otherwise take.

80 Therefore, I beseech you to seal the tomb with mortar and place a strong guard about it, at least until the three days have passed."

81 "Very well," Pilate replied with exasperation. "Now never, never speak to me of this man again, unless you see him come back from the dead, walking in the street, leading an army of rebels."

82 Then Pilate turned to his centurion and ordered, "See that the tomb of this Galilean is sealed and guarded by a Contubernium until the fifth day of the week has passed. And see that nobody comes near the tomb until after the fifth day."

83 "As you command, so shall it be done," replied the centurion, and he turned and departed from the room to obey the orders of Pilate.

84 And the eight soldiers of the Contubernium went to the sepulcher that held the body of Yeshua, and they made their camp nearby, then sealed the entry stone with mortar and placed two guards to stand before it.

The Death of Yudas Iscariot

85 Now it came to pass on the same day that the body of Yeshua died that Yudas Iscariot sat alone in a field, contemplating the dreadful thing that Yeshua had asked him to do. And Miriam came to him, asking, "Yudas, why do you still remain among the living?"

86 Yudas turned to her with a dour look, saying, "Yes, it is nice to see you too, Miriam."

87 "Pardon me for being so abrupt, Yudas," Miriam answered contritely. "I honor you for the courage you have and your devotion to Yeshua to do all that he has asked. But the day is ending, and it is to this day that you made your promise to Yeshua."

88 Yudas sighed and replied, "Yes, it is easy to be courageous when we are speaking about doing something. Then I was filled with humble pride that Yeshua had called upon me. But now when what was spoken of must be done, my courage is gone.

89 My faith in the resurrection of promise given by Yeshua remains. My spirit is willing, but the man of this world whose body I am in is weak and afraid to do what I promised to do."

90 "I can help you, Yudas," Miriam said gently offering him her hand.

91 Yudas held her hand and looked at her, and a countenance of peace came over his face. He

said, "I would like that, Miriam. I would like that very much."

92 Then Miriam took him in an instant to the Gihon spring, and they appeared below the water and she was with him. He looked at her serenely with perfect faith and breathed in the water and died in peace.

93 Shortly thereafter, some people of Jerusalem came to the spring to fetch water and saw his body and retrieved it from the water. One of them, a disciple of Yeshua named Nemiah, exclaimed, "I know this man. He is Yudas Iscariot; he whom the priests have been telling everyone betrayed Yeshua of Nazareth, who was crucified."

94 Others were there who were also disciples of Yeshua, and they knew not that Yudas was said to have betrayed him. But hearing of it and seeing the body, one of them proclaimed, "He has killed himself in sorrow at his treachery."

95 Another added, "Death by drowning is too good and easy for such a scoundrel. Let us take him to a tree and hang his body that it can be eaten by the vultures as befits a traitor."

96 So saying, three men pulled the body of Yudas out of the building of the spring and tied a rope to his feet and dragged his body along the rocky ground until they found a suitable tree, and then they took the rope off his feet and hung him by his neck from the tree and departed.

97 There hung the body of Yudas for some hours while daylight remained. Many people who were followers of Yeshua came to see it and revile it, for the word had quickly spread that it was he whom the priests had said betrayed Yeshua, leading to his crucifixion

98 And they hit and poked the body of Yudas with sticks, and the rope on his neck broke and his body fell to the ground, splitting open on a rock. And the people spit upon it and threw rocks upon it until it could no longer be recognized as a man.

99 As evening was falling, the wife of Yudas Iscariot heard of the fate of her husband and came with the Apostles, and they took his battered body and buried it.

100 And Cephas rebuked those who were present that had come to revile and desecrate the body of Yudas and said unto them, "Who has told you that this man, who was one of us, betrayed the Lord of Light? Whatever you have heard, it is not true.

101 He was called to a high and holy calling by the Lord of Light himself and breathed every breath to do as Yeshua desired, as do we all.

102 He did nothing, save that which the Lord of Light asked of him. Therefore, put away your sticks and stones and seek to repent of the evil you have done unto him and his family, for he was an honorable man."

103 Thereafter, because of the words of Cephas and the other Apostles in days that followed, some of the people came to understand the righteousness of Yudas Iscariot, but most continued to believe the worst and continued to speak of Yudas in unkind ways. And these erroneous assumptions continued to be encouraged by the religious hierarchy as a way to further destroy the people's faith in the teachings of Yeshua.

Miriam Opens the Sepulcher

104 After three days, following the changing of the guard when four soldiers were present, Miriam came to the sepulcher of Yeshua. She walked down to the base of the stone that sealed the entry and put her hand upon it.

105 Seeing her, one of the Romans exclaimed, "Begone, woman! No one is allowed to come near the tomb."

106 And Miriam replied to them, saying, "I am the wife of the great one inside, and I have come to see him as he asked me to come upon the morning of this day."

107 One of the soldiers pointed to the tomb and said, "Are you blind? The tomb is sealed. And were it not sealed, it would need four or more strong men to move the stone up the hill. Now begone, lest you incur our wrath."

108 "Perhaps, it is you who should begone," answered Miriam with words both quiet and sure, "before you incur my wrath."

109 Seeing she would not move, one of the soldiers called to his fellows back at camp, and the four other soldiers of the Contubernium also came to stand at the tomb and confront Miriam.

110 The Roman soldiers did not seem to want to hurt her and tried to reason with her; one of them said, "Come back in a couple of days and we will be gone, and you can pay your respects before the tomb. But our orders are clear, and you cannot be here now. We do not wish to harm you, a grieving widow as you are, but if you do not leave, we will be forced to remove you."

111 "But I have not come to pay my respects," Miriam replied. "I have come to see my husband. For today he who was dead is alive."

112 Some of the soldiers laughed at her words, and one of them told her, "It is for that cause that we are here and the tomb has been sealed, for it was rumored that those who followed him thought to make it appear as if he had come back from the dead. That is not going to happen, woman, so leave!"

113 "I think not," Miriam responded. "Leave me be or stay and you shall see that he has risen as he said he would."

114 "I have had enough of this nonsense," exclaimed one of the soldiers, and he made to grab Miriam and haul her away. But no sooner did he reach out to grasp her than, before he could lay his hand upon her, he fell to the ground with an exclamation of pain, holding his one hand in the other. And the hand that he held was bright red as if it had just been withdrawn from a hot fire.

115 "By Jupiter!" exclaimed the soldier on the ground. "That woman is a witch! I did not even touch her, and my hand burns in pain."

116 Hearing his words and seeing him upon the ground, the other soldiers quickly drew their short swords and encircled Miriam as she stood before the tomb, her hand still resting upon the great stone laid before the entry.

117 One of the soldiers spoke to Miriam, saying, "We tried to be nice to you widow, but now you have forced us to arrest you. Come with us now peacefully and we will not hurt you."

118 "No, I think not," Miriam answered again. "I have come to open the tomb as my husband bade me to do. And so must I do."

119 "Foolish woman," spat one of the soldiers. "You are drawing our ire. Come with us now and it will go better for you. The tomb is sealed. And were it not, ten women could not move the stone, and we certainly are not going to do it for you."

120 "I have not asked you to move the stone," Miriam replied. "I can do it myself."

121 Then Miriam reached up as high as she could with one hand to touch the top of the great stone along its edge where it met the mortar. With seemingly little effort, she pulled it forward, and there was the sound of crumbling as the mortar sealing the stone gave way.

122 As the heavily sealed stone tilted forward toward the soldiers, she gave it a push, and they stepped back to protect themselves from its fall and watched in astonishment as it toppled with a loud thud that shook the earth and laid flat upon the ground at their feet.

The Resurrection of Yeshua

123 Uncomprehending what they had just seen, the soldiers fled from the tomb, and Miriam walked alone into the sepulcher.

124 Upon the stone table were the linens that they had wrapped Yeshua in. She came to the table and touched them and held them in her hand, and as she did, she heard his voice calling to her and turned to see him standing beside her.

125 She stepped forward to embrace him, but he forbade her, saying, "Touch me not, beloved, for I have not yet ascended to our Mother and Father in the Celestine Realm, and to them I must first appear that my resurrection may be perfected before my body may be touched. But give me the kiss in spirit that was promised."

126 "The Celestine Realms are far, beyond the stars," Miriam responded, even as she kissed him with her spirit. "How will you go to our Mother and Father and return again in time that I may see you again before I too pass from this world?"

127 "Fear not," Yeshua answered. "To the resurrected, even beyond the stars is but a thought away. I shall go there and return to you in glory before the next day comes.

128 Until I come again, go and speak to Cephas and my other Apostles. Tell them of all that you have seen and heard."

129 Miriam bowed her head and said, "As you will, my Lord, so shall it be." And when she looked up, Yeshua was gone.

The Soldier's Tale

130 While Miriam was going to announce the resurrection of Yeshua to the Apostles, the soldiers that had been on watch at the tomb came into the city and related to their superiors all that they had seen and heard.

131 A runner was sent to the temple to demand the immediate presence of priests, and when a priest and three Sanhedrin, who were all Sadducees, had arrived, the Roman centurion in charge of the tomb watch led the party back to the sepulcher.

132 They all entered and saw the burial linens upon the table caked with spices and the napkin that had been upon the face of Yeshua and the shroud that had covered his body, and they knew not what to make of it.

133 The centurion questioned the men of the watch, saying, "Tell me now in truth, how was the guardian stone felled upon the ground? What has happened to the body that was here?"

134 The leader of the watch answered him, saying, "As we told you, a woman came to the tomb claiming to be the widow of the man inside. She said she had come to see him. We forbade her and went to arrest her when she reached up with one hand and pulled the guardian stone forward so that it fell upon the ground, even as you now see it lying."

135 "That is impossible," the Centurion proclaimed. "It would take at least two men and a lever to topple the stone. No woman could do it alone with her hand. Have you men been drinking?"

136 "No, Centurion," replied the chief of the watch. "I assure you that we had been here faithfully fulfilling our duty as soldiers of Rome."

137 "Perhaps, there were others of his followers hidden above the tomb," suggested one of the Sanhedrin. "And they secretly inserted a pry bar from above making it seem as if the woman felled the stone."

138 "No!" the chief of the watch announced firmly. "There were no others, only the woman."

139 "I have heard it said that the wife of the man who was in the tomb is a witch," offered one of the other soldiers of the watch as an explanation. "Perhaps, it is by magic that the stone was felled, and the body disappeared."

140 "Unlikely," interjected another of the Sanhedrin. "It is certain that more of his followers were present and opened the tomb and took the body. You were deceived by their trickery; that is all."

141 "No," replied the chief of the guard. "We were here, all eight of us. You were not. We know what we saw.

142 As for the body, where it went, we cannot say, for so startled were we by the woman toppling the guardian stone that we came at once to the centurion. It is our shame, for we should have left some on guard, and surely we will be punished for our dereliction."

143 The centurion nodded his head in agreement, saying, "When the governor hears of this, it will go hard for you; that is certain."

144 One of the Sanhedrin stepped forward and put his hand on the arm of the centurion, saying, "Let this not get to the governor's ear or to any of our people, at least nothing about the widow and the fallen guardian stone or the missing body. Let it be as if your tongues have been cut out about this, and we shall reward you handsomely."

145 Speaking to the soldiers of the watch, the Sanhedrin said, "We are certain that despite what you think you saw, that something else entirely occurred, and we do not want false rumors

circulating among our people.

146 Obviously, a woman cannot topple the guardian stone of a sepulcher, no more than a body can disappear from one without thieves coming in the night to take it.

147 Surely that is exactly what happened. The man in the tomb said he would come back in three days. But as the dead cannot rise, some of his followers must have come and taken the body in the night, and you were fooled by the woman toppling the stone. There can be no other reasonable explanation. Would you not agree?"

148 The leader of the watch shook his head negatively, saying, "I am sorry, but I do not agree. I know what I saw, what we saw, and it was not as you say."

149 "Do you look forward to your punishment for failing to stay at your watch?" asked the Sadducee.

150 "Of course not," replied the chief of the watch. "But we are Roman soldiers, and will take our due."

151 "Or," began the Sadducee, "you could take three month's wages, each man, and a year for the centurion, to relate the events as we have deduced them: that there was no woman and that a group of his followers came in the night while you slept and toppled the stone and stole the body before you could stop them."

152 The soldiers looked at one another, weighing the Sadducee's offer. "We will still be punished for letting the thieves steal the body," the leader of the watch stated. "But the money will help ease the pain. So perhaps what occurred is as you say."

153 "I do not want their money," one of the soldiers announced angrily. "We will be punished whether we tell the truth or a lie, and I would rather speak true than false."

154 "We have the ear of the governor," offered one of the Sanhedrin. "If you all, every man, will tell only what we have said and nothing more, we will speak with the governor on your behalf. If he still punishes you, we will double everything that we pay to each man."

155 Hearing this, all the men nodded in agreement, and thus was the story put forth among the Children of Israel about how the body of Yeshua disappeared from the tomb.

Miriam Announces Yeshua's Resurrection to the Apostles

156 During the time that the soldiers and the Sanhedrin were at the sepulcher, Miriam sought out the Apostles as Yeshua had bade her, and she found them gathered in a house on the outskirts of Jerusalem.

157 She went among them and told them that Yeshua had risen as he had promised, and she related how the tomb was empty and the linens they had wrapped him in had been opened asunder, and that the napkin they had put over his face lay even now upon the stone table of the sepulcher along with the covering shroud.

158 She also related to them how she had seen him and spoken with him and that he had promised to soon be among them, but many of the Apostles seemed to doubt her.

159 "Oh, that it could be true," sighed Philip. "But you said you did not touch him, so perhaps you only imagined he was there. Maybe it was in a dream of desire that you saw the tomb was open." And several of the other Apostles nodded in agreement with his words.

160 Miriam looked at them with a startled expression and said, "What men of faith are you? Did I imagine that the sepulcher is opened and Yeshua's body is gone? It is a simple thing for you to go and see.

161 Yeshua told you that he would rise and return on the third day, and you doubt that it has come to pass?

162 I have testified to you that I opened the tomb and spoke to him and he promised to return to you. Knowing this, you question whether I have told you the truth?

163 Perhaps you who doubt should return to your homes and let Yeshua come and call new Apostles who will have the faith needed to move the mountains that must be moved."

164 "I believe you, Miriam," Cephas assured her.

165 "As do I," added Yohhanan.

166 The other Apostles were chastised and contrite, and all nodded and voiced their assurances as well, even Philip.

167 "Still, let us go now to the tomb," added Cephas; "that our eyes may also be witnesses of the miracle."

168 And they went to the tomb, all save Toma and Mattayah, who had gone into Jerusalem, and they entered the sepulcher and saw that it was empty.

169 They took the linens with which Yeshua had been wrapped and the napkin that had been upon his face and the shroud that had covered his body, and they returned to the house where they had been, giving praise and thanks unto the Father and the Mother for the resurrection they knew had occurred.

170 The next morning as they were gathered together for the morning meal, and Miriam and Salome with them, Yeshua appeared in the midst of them and said unto them, "Peace be unto you." The Apostles were startled by his appearance, for the door was shut and several fell to their knees, giving thanks unto Elohim when they saw him.

171 Yeshua called them to him and opened his robe and said unto them, "Come, feel the scars of the nails in my wrists, my hands, and my feet and the wound in my side, that you may testify to the world that I am Yeshua of Nazareth that was crucified and now has risen to be among you again, not as a spirit, but with a body of flesh and bone."

172 And they came forth one by one and touched the scars on his wrists, hands, and feet and in his side and embraced him.

173 Then Yeshua sat down at the table and supped with them on boiled fish and fresh greens.

174 He spoke to them, saying, "Blessed are you, for now you have seen everything, and you believe. But even more blessed are those who shall come after you and not having seen will believe.

175 And it is by the testimony of the Holy Spirit of Elohim that they shall believe. Such a testimony is greater than the witness of the eyes and the hearing of the ears, for it is a touching of the soul of man to the soul of God."

176 Yeshua got up from the table and walked over to a corner of the room and said unto them, "Come now to me and receive the Holy Spirit in fullness, all save Miriam in whom the Holy Spirit already in fullness dwells."

177 And they came forth one by one and knelt down before Yeshua, and he laid his hands upon their head and said unto them, "In the name of the Father and Mother, I call upon the Holy Spirit to come into you in fullness. You have been touched by their love in the past; now be overcome by it even to the depth of your soul, that no more can you doubt, for the testimony of the Holy Spirit will burn like a fire within you that you cannot deny. So be it!"

178 As each came forth and knelt before Yeshua and had his hands upon their head and received the Holy Spirit of Elohim into their soul in fullness, a look of rapture came upon their faces, and for a moment, it seemed as if they were no longer of this world, but of one far grander and glorious.

179 Shortly after the Apostles and Salome had received the Holy Spirit, there came a knock at the door.

180 Philip answered and fell back into the room with an exclamation of surprise. Three men entered. One was Toma, another was Mattayah, and the third was Yudas Iscariot, who though he smelled terrible, with clothes all torn asunder, was in fact alive and whole before them.

181 Immediately, Toma and Mattayah went to Yeshua and fell to one knee and bowed their heads before him. And Toma kissed his feet, saying, "Blessed be, it is you, Yeshua! All is as you said it would be.

182 "As you commanded, we went in secret after the third day of his death to the place where Yudas was buried and waited for the sign that you said would come.

183 For several hours, we waited when suddenly the ground erupted forth into the sky and

fell in pieces all about us. And rising from the hole was the same Yudas Iscariot that we had buried in several pieces three days before."

184 Then Yudas made to come forth but stopped and spoke from across the room to Yeshua, saying, "Lord of Light, I was dead, and now I am alive. I was torn asunder, and now I am whole; praise be to Elohim from whom all things, even life after death, can be.

185 Forgive me that I come not closer to you; though I am now alive again and my body whole, I know that I stink greatly from lying in the ground, and I pray you will allow me first to clean myself and change my clothes and apply oils that I may greet you in sweetness, rather than putridness."

186 "Of course, Yudas," Yeshua replied. "We have much to discuss, you and I, and your brother Apostles. But first clean yourself, for you are a new man in many ways.

187 Go then to your wife and children that they may grieve no more and know with a certainty that you live again. Show yourself to no one else. Then come again to us at this place on the morrow."

188 Yudas bowed to Yeshua with his head and a slight bend of his body and said, "Thank you, Lord of Light, thank you; thank you for everything." Then he backed out of the door and closed it behind him.

189 "An amazing miracle," Cephas exclaimed in awe. "Yeshua and Yudas return to us again. I am at a loss for further words."

190 "Not a miracle," Yeshua announced. "You merely see in the flesh the resurrection given by the Elohim to all people: some to resurrect to greater light and others to greater darkness, by the purity or impurity of their soul.

191 Verily, the righteous live each day with happiness, knowing something greater awaits in a life to come that will never end.

192 But the wicked fear death, for they know in their deepest heart that they will be held accountable for their wickedness, and the darkness of judgment that awaits chills their soul."

193 Miriam came to Yeshua and held him close to her and Salome held close to Miriam, and Miriam looked to him, saying, "Beloved, let us move outside to a place of fresher air and leave open the door that this place may also be refreshed before we meet here again."

194 Yeshua smiled at her, knowing she was referring to the odor left by Yudas Iscariot, and nodded his head in agreement. And with eagerness, everyone in the room quickly went outside.

195 Together, Yeshua, Miriam, Salome, and the Apostles walked out into the country toward the Jordan, and Yeshua began to tell them marvelous things about themselves, who they truly were, who they had been, and who they would become if they stayed faithful to what they knew to be true.

196 With each step, as their eyes beheld the living, resurrected Lord of Light and his words fell upon their ears and into their hearts, they walked out of the shadows of the past and into the glorious light of their destiny to fulfill.

CHAPTER 92

Illumination by the Jordan

Yeshua teaches his Apostles including Yudas Iscariot, along with Salome, more of the mysteries of Celestine Light. He also teaches them how to be one with the Elohim, how to create a "Circle of Light," and the benefits of having commandments. He speaks about the Benjamite named Saul, who will change his name to Paul, whom they will meet, and what will transpire.

And it came to pass that Yeshua remained upon the earth for forty days after his resurrection.

2 The first six days following his return, he went in secret to the house of Lazarus in Bethany with Miriam, Salome, and Martha and spent much time with all of their children.

3 Yeshua instructed the Apostles to also go and be with their families for six days. And so they all did.

Teachings in the Wilderness of Jordan

4 On the morning of the seventh day, Yeshua, Miriam, Salome, and all of the Apostles, including Yudas Iscariot, departed from Bethany and went into the wilderness near the Jordan River, and Yeshua began to teach them more of the mysteries of Celestine Light and the powers given unto them as Apostles and Children of Light.

5 They remained encamped near the Jordan for several days. Each day during the late afternoon Yeshua would answer questions that were asked, and many mysteries were revealed by his answers, most of which cannot be written and recorded, but only spoken of within the Sacred Circles of the Children of Light.

6 The first day together in the wilderness, everyone was caught up in the excitement of all of the marvels they were learning from Yeshua and they did not want the day to end so much so that they pleaded with him to keep teaching them well into the night by the light of the Moon and stars, and he did as they asked.

7 When he was finished speaking in the late hours of the night, Yeshua departed from them all and promised he would return again in the morning.

8 When the morning arrived, the Apostles were still in the throngs of fatigue. The sun was already rising in the sky when Miriam came to where the men were sleeping to wake them, "Rouse yourselves brothers; you must be alert, for the Lord of Light comes even now."

9 Suddenly there was a bright light upon the ground, and Yeshua stood before them. Miriam came to him, and he held her and kissed her tenderly.

10 Then came Salome, and she fell to her knees and made to kiss his feet, but he raised her up and held her with Miriam and kissed her lightly on the lips.

11 Yeshua spoke to everyone present, saying, "I will not linger long upon the earth, but ere I go for the last time, I shall teach you in the coming days the fullest mysteries of the Kingdom of Heaven and the Celestine Light, which comes from it.

12 You shall learn that which you have never known or imagined. And with the knowledge I give, you will hold some of the power of the Elohim and will be able to do all manner of wonders, as long as you remain humble, and worthy stewards of the Celestine Light you are given.

13 Many of the things I shall reveal to you are the means to change that which is seen into something that is not seen, to affect and alter the minds of men and matter, to cause the properties of one substance to change into another, and to travel in spirit anywhere in this world and beyond at the speed of thought to witness any event or to discover any secret of men.

14 Some of the things you shall learn can only be accomplished by worthy Children of Light having great experience and understanding of the foundations of Celestine Light that uphold all things which exist.

15 Others can be mastered even by the Ganish, simply by following the steps that open the secret doors to the unseen powers of Celestine Light that uphold the world that the world knows not.

16 Because these are merely steps taken in an exact manner to produce a result, they can be done by anyone who follows the steps, even the unworthy. Therefore, you must guard the secrets of the steps zealously, lest they become known to the unworthy who would call forth the hidden currents of power for unrighteous purposes.

17 Therefore, I give you a sacred trust: keep the secrets of that which I reveal only in your heads. Never let them be recorded upon a scroll that the unworthy could unveil and read.

18 With some secrets I teach, there is power simply in the form to call in the force, and this by anyone that follows the form, both the worthy and the unworthy, the righteous and the unrighteous.

19 And it shall come to pass that a handful of the secrets of the forms shall escape into the world, for the virtuous do not always remain so, and some shall stumble by the wayside.

20 Then shall there also be times when you will be seen by the Ganish calling upon the powers of Celestine Light and doing things which in the minds of men cannot be done.

21 In their observation there will be a remembrance of the form, even unto the words you said and the substances you mixed and the movements you made.

22 And so shall they emulate. A few will succeed in calling in some of the powers that can be called in by the forms of simplicity, even as priests, witches, and sorcerers have been able to do since the days when they saw the first Children of Light using the powers of Heaven upon the earth.

23 Thus it shall come to pass that some of the forms and a small part of the power shall come to be known and used by witches, sorcerers, and priests seeking to wield a power they know not, some for purposes of good and some for evil.

24 A little healing they will do, but to them, it will seem great. Small miracles they will accomplish, and though feeble, they shall acclaim them from the mountaintops.

25 But worry not at all for this. The true power of Celestine Light, even to say unto a mountain to take up and be cast into the sea, or unto the paralytic to rise up and walk or to the storm to come or go, they will be incapable of accomplishing.

26 Though they may know some of the forms that call in the power, they can never possess the Celestine Light of Elohim that is the activating force behind the greatest powers.

27 Only a worthy Child of Light can be one in completeness with the Celestine Light. And only by being one with the power of the light can it be called forth in its fullness and majesty.

28 Therefore, always remember: There is far greater effect when the form is wielded by the righteous and virtuous, and greater still when it is manifested by those who are Children of Light that have been set apart and ordained by Elohim to be stewards of the Celestine Light, even as each of you has been, my brothers and sisters.

29 And it is not because of the witches and priests that you must never write the secrets of the inner sanctum, for they too will keep the secrets that they know, but to protect this knowledge from ever being possessed by the Caesars or the foolish.

30 With the Caesars, it is better to rot in prison and even to pass in silence from this life than to reveal that which I shall give to you. For even with a feather of the knowledge of the simplest forms, twisted for evil, they could do great harm upon the land and to the people.

31 Know that you are the stewards, not just of your families and not just of the Family of Light, but of all the earth. It is given to you to protect the land and the great waters upon the vastness and to serve all the inhabitants thereof, both man and beast, even as I have served you.

32 Let your light shine among the children of men that they will open their hearts to the Celestine Light of Elohim that they may become more than they have been, even unto inheriting the glory of the Kingdom to come.

33 When I have passed beyond this earth, you are ordained to be the bearers of the secrets that I shall give to you.

34 You may share these secrets in fullness only to the worthy who are also baptized Children of Light, who love their bodies as temples inside and out, who have a firm foundation of understanding and proven ability with knowledge already received to warrant new and greater knowledge to be given, who live and cherish the Great Commandment and the Twelve Commandments of Sinai and have been faithful stewards of all that has been given unto them.

Healing the Worthy in Need

35 "You may also use the secret knowledge of Celestines to help any in the world who ask for your help with selflessness and love, in humility, and with sincere repentance of their sins, for all are spirit children of the Father and the Mother and deserving of the blessings of the Celestine Light when they are in harmony with it.

36 As they are prepared to receive the light, so shall it come into them through your hand and a miracle in the eyes of men shall be born.

37 I give you the power to heal both the small and the great, and nothing shall be impossible to you if it is within the will of Elohim to restore the human body to its health and wholeness, if you remain pure and humble and are blessing a Child of Light committed to living as a temple.

38 When those who are not numbered among you seek you out for a blessing, the power of Celestine Light will flow through you in balance and equality to their faith, purity of heart, repentance of sins, and love for their temple and their fellow brothers and sisters of Elohim upon the earth.

39 Those who have not faith to believe in things unseen and unknown or who are not pure in heart but think selfishly and deviously, or who have not repented of their sins or love not their bodies but destroy their temple with the things they put inside or outside, or care not for the lives of their fellow brothers and sisters of the spirit children of Elohim upon the earth—these have no promise, and they cannot benefit from a blessing.

40 Not because you do not have the power, but because healing is a circle of light. It is only when the circle completes that the healing occurs.

41 You call in the great power of Celestine Light and send it unto those to be healed. In a Child of Light, it is received; it heals, and it is sent back out to you with love and gratitude.

42 But a person of the world cannot send back the light, because they do not really believe in it.

43 They cannot send back the light because their character is flawed, and they do not seek to make the effort to live upon the mountain of higher ideals given to man, but seek instead the easy way, wallowing in the swamp of that which is nothing.

44 They cannot send back the light because they have not repented of their sins, and when the healing light encounters unrepented sins it fades away, for the Celestine Light knows where it is not wanted.

45 They cannot send back the light because they do not treat their bodies as temples inside and out, and the light will not dwell in polluted waters.

46 They cannot send back the light because they are selfish and make no effort to serve and help their fellow brothers and sisters upon the earth.

47 You are merely the riverbed of the stream that is the Celestine Light of Elohim. The light rushes forth to heal the pure and the less pure and the impure.

48 As each person is open to the Celestine Light and have lived it in their lives, so each shall receive the portion that they can hold—the pure of heart and life made whole, and the less pure made less whole, and the impure not changed.

49 Ponder upon my words for in them are life eternal and dominion over disease and death before its time.

How to Be One with the Elohim

50 "When you are alone, you are a single lamp of the Celestine Light of Elohim, but far from alone, for Elohim—the Father, the Mother, and the Son—are with you. You will forever have their Holy Spirit to guide and direct your paths as long as you live the light.

51 When you are in solitude, call upon the Father and the Mother in my name with focused thought, a clear intent, and a heart that reaches beyond the world, and you will be one with the Elohim, with the Celestine Light, to accomplish the purposes you seek.

52 When you are gathered together, two or more reaching out to the Elohim, you must be of one heart and mind as you call upon the Celestine Light and the power it brings. Focus your thoughts and let your hearts reach out until they touch the heart of Elohim and you are one with the light."

53 Toma asked, "Great Lord of Light, how may we do this wonder that you describe? How do we focus our thoughts and reach our heart beyond the world until it is one with Elohim and the light?"

54 Yeshua answered, saying, "You are in the world, but you should not be like it. If a man lives in the ways of the world, how would he know how to be one with God?

55 But it has been given to you to know the ways of the Elohim. You hold in your hearts and live in your lives the Great Commandment and the Twelve Commandments of Sinai.

56 You honor and respect your bodies as temples made by the Elohim and eat, sleep, and work in ways that enhance the vitality of your temple.

57 You are continuously on a quest to gain more knowledge of the ways of the Celestine Light, and as your knowledge grows so you are prepared to speak with intelligence to the Elohim about the mysteries of the Kingdom.

58 As you live the way the Elohim live, your spirit is able to pass through the gate of Celestine Light and be in their presence, even as you are worthy vessels to have the Holy Spirit of Elohim upon you that they can come and be in your presence.

59 By this, the table has been set and the meal prepared, and now the Elohim will come and sup at your table.

60 In humble prayer, invite them to come to you and be one with you, and the Holy Spirit will fill your heart and speak in your mind, and you will for a moment transcend the bonds of earth and be one with the Celestine Light of Elohim in fullness.

61 Herein is the true power that is greater than the form. This is the power of the snake of Moses to eat the snakes of the priests of pharaoh.

62 This is the power that the sons and daughters of Light used to lift the stones of the great pyramids of Egypt for the pharaohs, allowing their community to live in peace and prosperity in the land of the Egyptians and not in subjugation as were the Hebrews and other peoples.

63 This is the power that even if they knew, a witch, a sorcerer, a priest, or a Caesar could never use, for they are unworthy vessels, and the Celestine Light of Elohim cannot dwell within them, nor the fullness of its power."

Cephas Reminisces

64 Then Cephas, who had been sitting, stood up saying, "Good Yeshua, what a marvel this is that each day we still have so much to learn from you!

65 What a wonderful journey you have taken us on! I recall when you used to come to the lake when you were still a young man, and it is overwhelming to remember all that has happened in our lives since then, all we have learned, all we have seen, and the promise of all that is to come.

66 Now you have shared still greater knowledge with us, when already I thought my cup was full and overflowing.

67 I myself am so different now than those long-ago days at the lake that it sometimes seems as if I am visitor from another land as I pass through this place I have lived near all of my life.

68 I know what the Savasi must have felt like when they first returned to this world and began to live among the people of the land: in some ways just like them, but in others so very different.

69 Forgive me if I ramble. The understanding of the enormity of everything that you are and everything we are because of you has just now come upon me like the eyes of a traveler being opened for onto the most amazing vista.

70 I think for the first time, I have truly comprehended all that has transpired in our lives and all that is yet to be." And tears began to well up in his eyes.

71 But he continued speaking through his tears, saying, "Thank you for the honor of being called an Apostle of your light. Thank you for being my guide upon this journey and finding and bringing out the Child of Light that was inside of me; that the gruff fisherman that was on the outside never would have recognized if it were not for you.

72 I am overwhelmed and humbled to the depths of my soul." Then he could speak no more through his tears, and he sat down upon a rock and smiled at those around him, laughing a little at his own emotions.

73 Yeshua came over to Cephas and, offering him his hand, pulled him up and embraced him, saying, "You are welcome, good brother. You are welcome. I have always been honored to call you a friend and a brother, and I always will be.

The Workings of a Circle of Light

74 "But this was not what you actually stood up to say, was it?"

75 Cephas shook his head and answered, "No, I had a question about that which you had just taught us, but the spirit of my soul came over me and the words I spoke came out unbidden from the depths of my heart."

76 Then Cephas put a hand on each of Yeshua's shoulders and laughed lightly as he looked at him, saying, "You see, even those words I just said—very flowery they were—nothing at all like how a normal man should speak and certainly not how I used to speak before I was changed by you."

77 Yeshua laughed back good-naturedly, but then said with calm serenity, "It was not me, Cephas, save perhaps as a catalyst. You simply heard and heeded the call of the greater Cephas beckoning you to become the fullness of the man you can be, even as all men and women are called by the inner voice of their soul to become more than they are, not in the ways of the world, but in the ways of the Celestine Light."

78 Cephas nodded his head in agreement and Yeshua asked him to present the question he had begun to ask, and Cephas did, saying, "You spoke of the circle of light necessary to effect a healing, but how is the circle completed when we call upon the Celestine Light to affect things that are not people, such as moving a mountain?"

79 "All things that exist," began Yeshua, "are creations of the Elohim.

80 Unto man, and others like unto man in intelligence and experience, has been given the opportunity to freely make choices of light or darkness in every aspect of their lives, beginning with their thoughts.

81 This that they might begin to walk the path that leads to the realm of the Elohim, which

realm is far greater than the Celestine Realm of which you have learned so much and aspire even now to gain.

82 Understand that even that may be, for some, just a way point in their eternal progression.

83 For the Celestine Realm, though it is grander than your imagination can conceive, is merely a small part of the greater, more-glorious realm of the Elohim that awaits the most faithful.

84 For where you now are, how you now are, even the Father and Mother once were, and where they now are, how they now are, you may someday become as you continue through this life and time untold that follows to be one with the Celestine Light.

85 When you are one with the light, you are no longer of this world, though your feet may still tread upon it.

86 That is why you feel somewhat disconnected from the world already Cephas. Even in the land and among the people you have known all of your life, as I'm sure all of your brethren do as well." Hearing his words the other Apostles all nodded in agreement.

87 Then Yeshua added a caution, saying, "But while you still live upon this world, never become so much in the next that you forget that it has been given to you to be the faithful stewards of the world upon which you live, to guard it and protect it, and all of the creatures and life therein that are in need of your guardianship and protection.

88 For all of these, all life upon the earth other than man, are pure in the Celestine Light of their creation. They are innocent of sin, save those that have been corrupted by man, but even then the sin is upon the corrupters, not upon the corrupted.

89 Because the land and the sea and the sky and all creatures therein are innocent and pure in the light, when you call upon the Celestine Light to affect them, the circle is immediately completed as the light runs through them, changes them as you have commanded, and returns to you.

90 The light is of Elohim, and so are all things. And save for man who has been given knowledge of good and evil, the Celestine Light sent out shall always return to the sender, for therein lies its resonance and abode."

Why We Have Commandments

91 Then Yeshua posed a question to the Apostles, asking, "Why do you think your place in the next life depends so much upon your faithfulness in this life to the principles and precepts I have taught?

92 Why did the Elohim bother to give man the Twelve Commandments of Sinai or any of the higher precepts? Man is surely of sound-enough mind and reason to have thought of these principles himself as a way to live in harmony with his fellow man and progress in his life.

93 So why did the Elohim command some things and why have many others been taught to you by me with precept and example many times, in multiple ways, but not by commandment?"

94 Yohhanan lifted his hand, signaling he wished to answer the question, and Yeshua nodded affirmatively for him to proceed. And Yohhanan answered, saying, "When we hear words of wisdom, such as those from the Greek philosophers, we ponder upon them and reason them out in our mind. We only adopt them in our lives if they seem practical and do not require too much effort for the promised reward.

95 But when we hear or see the same principle given by the Father and Mother or shown or taught to us by you, there is something more that occurs after the pondering and reasoning.

96 With the Greek philosophers, we may understand the truth of a teaching and the wisdom of adopting it in our lives. But as it is just the teaching of a man, we are likely only inclined to act upon it if it does not require too much effort, and the reward is quick to come.

97 Then something similar is taught to us by the Elohim in the words of the old prophets or in the things we see you do or hear you teach. Though there is always a promise of benefit in this life for living the teachings, the greater reward is saved for the eternal life to come, in a world we

cannot see, and with faith alone must accept to be real and waiting for the valiant.

98 This then is why I think the Elohim have given us the Twelve Commandments and taught us to follow other higher laws of righteousness that we will do so in faith, with faith abiding and growing inside us.

99 Obeying the commandments and following the precepts make us better people—better husbands and fathers and sons. But so would following the teachings of the philosophers.

100 But building faith is something far greater, for you have taught us that faith is a power, like a fire, and by it all things were created and by it come all miracles. By it, we have command of the Celestine Light.

101 By following the good words of wise men, we can become good men ourselves, but by living in fullness the commandments and teachings of the Elohim can we become men of faith, in whom the Elohim can trust and in whom the power of the Celestine Light can come and abide, in this life and the next.

102 As to why some are commandments and others only admonitions—surely all are of equal worth in our lives, but the handful of commandments have weight beyond their numbers when we are weighed in the balance at the Judgment of Resonance as all the admonitions are truly encompassed within the commandments."

103 As Yohhanan finished speaking, Yeshua walked over to him, and placing a hand on either side of his head, he kissed him lightly on the top of his head, saying, "Truly, Yohhanan, the Holy Spirit has come upon you. You are ready now to bring the Celestine Light to the world, for in you it abides and from you it comes forth."

Concerning Paul

104 Yeshua then addressed something completely different, saying, "As I have spoken about before to you, in the days soon to come, a religion shall build up upon the earth from fragments of my teachings, and it shall cover the world in generations to come.

105 But it will to the greatest extent be based upon the teachings of a Benjamite named Saul. A learned man who shall at first persecute the Children of Light and anyone who follows even a part of my teachings.

106 Then shall come his day of remorse and repentance and thereafter, he shall be known as Paul, and he shall dedicate his life to building a church throughout the lands of the Romans and Greeks based upon the part of my teachings that appeal to him.

107 He will convert many Gentiles to his church after the name the Greeks call me—Iesous. And he shall call himself my Apostle.

108 But Paul will not be an Apostle such as you are, one who has traveled with me day to day and heard and seen the wonders of Heaven.

109 Nor will he be called by me and set apart and ordained to be my Apostle on earth, to speak and act in my name, or given the great secrets of the Celestine Light, which have been given to you.

110 Nor shall you give these things to Paul or ordain him to be an Apostle or teach him the ways of the Adepts, for he will continually be opposed to the fullness of the Celestine Light and therefore never worthy to receive its greatest secrets and powers.

111 Some of his teachings will be from the teachings of old that are in opposition to that which I have taught, and you will have cause to be angry with him and to cast him out from among you.

112 But this I would ask, my brethren. Love him, even as I have loved you. Teach him what he is ready to learn and be not angry with him for that which he is not ready, for every person should be given the light only as they are capable of receiving it in good stewardship.

113 Though he will teach some things that are false and omit others that are true and important, the portion of my light that he shall bring upon the world will still be great in many ways, one that shall uplift those that follow it and bring them closer to Elohim in a greater

measure than they had been before the teachings of Paul came to them.

114 And that which he shall teach, in my Greek name, shall spread across all of the world and touch the lives of many people, causing many to forsake their sins of the past and live their lives closer to the Celestine Light of Elohim.

115 While that which you teach shall only be for the elect, and they shall not long remain upon the earth, save those who shall remain behind as earth stewards.

116 Verily, the people of the world are not yet ready for the immensity of the Celestine Light you shall bring, and they will be blinded by its brightness until the generation of promise comes forth."

117 "What shall we do with this Paul when he comes?" asked Cephas. "Shall we invite him into our communities? And how shall we teach him all that he should know if he is going to preach even a small part of the Celestine Light you have given us and yet will be opposed to some of the foundations of our understanding?"

118 Yeshua smiled and answered, saying, "You will be like two hawks fighting whenever in each other's presence, unless you both remember to love one another even as I have loved you.

119 Do not condemn him for his weaknesses or the fallacy of his doctrines. Do not find reasons to be angry with him.

120 Correct him as you can with gentleness; help him see as much of the Celestine Light as he can receive by your teachings and the examples of your lives.

121 See the good in him; see the light; see his devotion to service and his eloquent uplifting of his fellow men.

122 When he has received all the Celestine Light from you that he will accept, send him to the Gentiles where he will find fertile ground.

123 Then when you see the children of Paul in churches, springing up across the land, wearing my Greek masquerade of a name; be not offended by them, for they are humble, sincere seekers of the light, even as you are.

124 In truth, Paul will be doing you a favor by bringing his followers closer to the Celestine Light than they previously were and more receptive to the resonance of the greater light that you can bring to those who are ready to receive it.

125 Because of the light Paul first brings, some who become children of Paul shall later become Children of the true Celestine Light and receive it in fullness and be numbered among you."

Finding the Children of Light

126 Another day, Yeshua spoke to Miriam, Salome, and the Apostles further, saying, "You will face many adversities in the days to come. So great will some be that you will begin to wonder if I have thrown you as lambs to the lions.

127 In those times, remember the essence of your calling. Do not put more upon yourself than needs be.

128 All that is asked of you, concerning the lives of men and women of the world, can be said by this: help them to remember who they are and help them understand how to live in harmony with the Celestine Light of Elohim that they might inherit the fullness of their birthright from their Father and Mother in Heaven and a joy inside that surpasses all the world has to offer.

129 Remember that every person ever born upon the earth was born in innocence. They came from the Celestine Light, and at the moment of their birth, all are pure Children of Light.

130 But as they gain years, they are molded by the light or darkness that surrounds them. Most that are surrounded by good parents, friends, and teachers who walk in the light become as the light that surrounds them.

131 But those that have darkness around them most often become as the darkness. They are molded by the wicked examples they see and hear as they grow into men and women.

132 The Celestine Light they had at birth grows dim, sometimes until it can no longer be

perceived.

133 But know this: the Celestine Light of Elohim still remains at the core of all but the most wicked. They are not unredeemable, merely lost. To show them by precept and example the way back to the light is a stewardship I have given unto you.

134 Even when the Celestine Light is but a faint glimmer within them, it still calls them to be greater than they are; to do good and live with virtue and honor, even when their life may be just the opposite of that ideal.

135 And always will they know in their heart that they are fighting against themselves when they do evil.

136 It is unto the lost souls that I send you as a sacred stewardship that they may be lost no more.

137 Show them by the example of your life how to live in the Celestine Light and the benefits of health, happiness, and love that abide with you every day because of the light that you embrace.

138 Let them know that the joy of the light is not just for you, but that they too were born Children of Light and can find again that happiness that was lost.

139 Teach them with your words that they can know the paths they must walk to find the Celestine Light again in their lives.

140 When they are ready to be born again, to cast off their old dry skin and take upon them the beauty of the light, then let them repent and be baptized and show their commitment to living the Celestine Light they love.

141 Unto the baptized Children of Light, you are charged to teach the mysteries and the secrets of power I have given to you, as they are prepared and capable of holding them and fulfilling them in stewardship.

142 This then is the essence of your stewardship among the children of men in this life and the next, and all other things that I have asked you to do are a part of this."

143 Many more things Yeshua spoke to them on that day, but these are things that cannot be written but only spoken among the Children of Light.

Light and Darkness

144 On another day, Yeshua elaborated upon good and evil and the light and the darkness that he often referred to, saying, "Because the Children of Light within the communities live in the fullness of the Celestine Light, they will make enemies of both those that live in darkness and even among many of those who live in a part of the light.

145 Those that live in the darkness will hate you because you oppose them.

146 Those that live in a partial light will resent you and despise you because you remind them that they are slaves to their weaknesses, instead of masters over them.

147 Though you will live apart from them, you will still encounter them, and in their own guilt, they will desire to control you and dictate the things in your private and community lives that you can and cannot do.

148 They shall try to force you by law or violence to be like them or be no more, that none would remain whose lives would remind them of the error of their own.

149 They will desire to absorb you into a community of common darkness, where all walk the same wrong path, that they may no longer remember or consider that there was any other choice.

150 With no other choice, they can justify themselves as being just like everyone else. And if that is how everyone is, how could it be wrong?

151 Take heed that you are not caught unaware. At times, the attacks upon your way of life may be strong and blatant.

152 But at other times, they will be subtle and insidious, so slowly eating away at your light that you do not even realize it is diminishing, until you find yourself in a place of great darkness without understanding how you arrived there.

153 But light has nothing to fear from darkness. It is only darkness that needs fear the light.

154 In a battle of good and evil, light will win simply by increasing the light.
155 Darkness is nothing of itself. It has no power; it has no form or substance. Darkness is merely the dimness of light or the void left when light is no longer present.
156 You can bring a light into a dark room, but you can only make a room dark by taking away the light.
157 Darkness can only exist in the absence of light. It can only increase if light diminishes; it can only spread forth across the land if the light capitulates and only win if the light abdicates.
158 But light increases with faith and desire, holding fast to that which you know to be true, and magnifies when it abides in Communities of Light.
159 No darkness, no matter how gloomy or pervasive, can withstand the Celestine Light intent upon overcoming it.
160 Therefore, remember these things and never fear the darkness or the evil intentions of men upon you, for you are the light, and the Celestine Light shall always have the power to overcome the darkness."

CHAPTER 93

Harmony and Resonance

Yeshua teaches his Apostles and Salome about the difference between harmony and resonance, as it relates to worlds within worlds or worlds that share the same space but have a different resonance.

Difference between Harmony and Resonance

eshua continued, "To understand the fullness of creation, you must comprehend the organization of creation that the Elohim established in which all things exist as they have been designed.

2 This world upon which you live as vast as it may seem, is only one of innumerable earths that to you are like stars in the heavens. But know this: Beyond the stars that you can see are earths greater in number than the sands of the sea.

3 All of these earths are a part of the same Kingdom of Salanha as the world upon which you live, and beyond the comprehension of man is this breadth of this Kingdom.

4 If you had a ship that could sail to the stars, you could go to other earths and walk upon them and speak with the people who live upon them, even as some of them have come here in ancient days and will come again to speak with your posterity during the Generation of Promise.

5 However, the countless earths and the innumerable people therein are not the end of creation, but only the beginning."

6 Yeshua then asked everyone to harmonize their voices and sing a common shepherd's song of a few verses together, which they did.

7 He then asked them to face another person with mouths close but not touching and sing the single sound of "O" into the others mouth, and they each did.

8 When they were all finished, he asked them, "What was different between the song sung and the single sound?"

9 "We sounded a little uneven when we sang together," Philip answered. "But when we sang the single sound into each other's mouths, we soon had nearly perfect harmony, and the very air seemed to physically vibrate."

10 "That and we had to smell each other's bad breath!" chortled Amram, breaking the seriousness of the moment and causing everyone to laugh.

11 Yeshua laughed too and said unto them, "I am glad to see that you all have learned well the lesson of laughter, even amidst that which is serious. May it help you to live long with health and joy.

12 Now I asked you to do these two things to help you understand the difference between harmony and resonance.

13 You had somewhat of a harmony when you sang the song. If you practiced together, you

would have more harmony and become pleasing to listen to as your voices of varying pitch and ability blended together to make a common sound.

14 But when you sang the single sound directly to another, you became more than harmony, which is the blending of different energies meshing well together. You became in perfect resonance; you became identical energies recognizing each other and expanding their power from close harmonic association. With harmony and resonance together, each became far more powerful than either could have alone.

15 When this occurred, the air between you vibrated; your mouths vibrated. If you were sensitive to the sensation, then you noticed that your entire body physically and noticeably vibrated as well. This is an effect of resonance."

16 Then Yeshua asked them to all come to him, and he handed each one a small, flat, clear crystal, with many naturally faceted faces and said, "Hold this crystal tightly in your hand and separate at least two paces away from one another."

17 When everyone had received their stone, he asked, "What do you feel?"

18 They all looked at one another and shook their heads. Toma answered for all of them, saying, "I do not think any of us feel anything." Everyone nodded their heads in agreement.

19 "Please keep these crystals all of your lives," Yeshua implored. "Do not misplace them or lose them for they would be very difficult for you to replace," he admonished. "They are both a gift to you and a stewardship.

20 As you know, when the Savasi departed from the earth for the last time, they left behind the vast repository of knowledge known as the Great Library on the isles of the Guache. There are also six branches of this library at various places around the world, and you each have been given an activator crystal to one of the ancient libraries.

21 To protect them from discovery or damage, each library is underground and exists on a different resonance, both from one another and from the general physical world of this earth.

22 Still close enough in resonance that they can remain in this physical world, but sufficiently different that they are hidden and invisible to the people of this world.

23 Entry into one of the libraries can only be gained by touching an activator crystal with a matching resonance to the portal of the library. This will create a harmonic resonance between the holder of the crystal and the library.

24 There are fourteen of you and two activator stones among you for each library. Mingle now close to one another, keeping the crystal tightly held in your hand. When you are next to the other person with a resonant crystal, tell us what you experience."

25 They did as Yeshua directed, and soon they were all talking with excitement. "It tingles when I stand next to Mattayah," Cephas exclaimed.

26 "When I am next to Shim'on, it feels like a small bug is trapped in my hand, trying to escape," said Yohhanan.

27 "Mine grows hot in my hand when I am next to Miriam," Salome marveled.

28 And so everyone began to exclaim as they came close to the person that held a resonating crystal in their hands.

29 "This then is resonance," Yeshua explained. "When two things in the same resonance come together, they reveal themselves to one another. But when two with a different resonance come together, they remain hidden from one another. Understand this principle and you will understand the rest of what I have to tell you, concerning the seven Kingdoms.

The Seven Kingdoms of Existence

30 "Consider all that you see on this world; all that you can see in the sky at night; and all the other earths that you know exist because I have told you that it is so—all of this merely comprises one of the seven Kingdoms that exist within the same harmony but with different resonances, even as the seven libraries of the ancients here on your earth exist in the same harmony but with different resonances.[a]

31 The earths and stars that are in similar resonances can be seen, but those in the other Kingdoms are a discordant resonance and they cannot be perceived by men from this earth, which dwells in a different resonance.

32 The other six Kingdoms are invisible to the men who live in this resonance, and they ever shall be. But they are just as real as this world you call home and exist within the same harmony, within the same limitless space, but in a different time with a different resonance.

33 This Kingdom, the one in which you live a physical life of mortality and in which all of the other earths of this resonance reside near visible stars in the heavens is in the middle of the seven Kingdoms in resonance. It is the Kingdom called Salanha.

34 Three Kingdoms resonate above the earths, suns, moons, and stars of the Salanha Kingdom, and three Kingdoms resonate below it.

35 Above the Kingdom Salanha are the Koropean, the Celestine, and the Elohim Kingdoms. They are like the glory of the stars, the Moon, and the sun.

36 Below the Salanha Kingdom of the earths are the Qaorroz, the Scarnz, and the Datarz Kingdoms. These are like the ignominy of the wilderness, the swamps, and the abyss.

37 Those that live in the higher Kingdoms above the Salanha can see and hear the public occurrences that transpire in the lower Kingdoms, for the resonance of the lower was once the resonance of those that now exist in the higher, and they can see and hear that which is known to them once they have progressed to a higher resonance beyond the one you live within.

38 But except for the Elohim and angels of Elohim who are their messengers, no one from the higher Kingdoms can physically exist again in a lower Kingdom. The resonance of the lesser Kingdoms would bring destruction upon their physical bodies of greater light and higher resonance.

39 Although the appearance of those that rise to a higher Kingdom often remains much the same, their bodies transform into a more-purified form when they leave the lower Kingdom behind, and they no longer can physically tolerate the lower resonance.

40 But the higher Kingdoms above the Salanha are unseen and unheard by those who dwell in the Salanha and lower Kingdoms. Both the harmony and resonance of the higher Kingdoms differ too greatly from that of the lesser Kingdoms to blend in the least bit, and their synchronicity of time is different.

41 Now I wish you to consider a pot sitting on one end of a table and another sitting at the other end. The table is the harmony. The pots are in resonance, or so it would seem. But there is more here to see.

42 Think of one pot as this world you live upon and another pot as another earth that is one of the small stars in the heavens. They are in different places, but still on the same table, still in the same Kingdom. They are visible to each other if only as tiny lights in the sky if they are close enough, even as you can see a ship on the horizon once it comes near.

43 But what if there were other pots hidden inside each of the visible pots on the table? And what if the hidden pots were only visible while men were asleep?

44 Pots inside of the pots occupying the same places on the table, that is, the harmony, but of this, men are unaware of even if they look inside the pot on the table because the inner pot is clear like water—a different resonance, darkening and becoming visible only when men are asleep—a different time.

45 So it is upon this world you call home and the Kingdom in which it dwells. For every earth that exists in this Kingdom, there are six Kingdoms of different resonances that men of this world cannot see.

46 Like the pot within the pot, the six other Kingdoms are here as well in the harmony, that is, the immensity of the heavens and the earths. But they cannot be seen by the men from this world in the Salanha Kingdom, for they exist in a space between a space, a time between a time. They are in a similar harmony but in a completely different resonance of space and time.

47 But you are not as other men and women. You are Celestine Adepts called, set apart, and

ordained to serve the purposes of Elohim.

48 From this earth upon which you live, utilizing your gifts, you can not only view the lower Kingdoms, but can also travel to them without harm.

49 But you must also beware; for a short time and with great harm, some of the creatures from the lower Kingdoms can sometimes come here to your world as well; and that, we must explore, for some of the creatures are fearsome indeed."

50 Everyone's eyes opened large as they listened with both amazement and some apprehension to the description given by Yeshua.

51 With a nervous laugh, Mattayah tried to lighten the mood, saying, "The creatures in those lower Kingdoms must be very small indeed if they fit in a space between a space!" And everyone laughed with him including Yeshua.

52 "And the people there are like specks of dust!" added Toma, laughing even harder, as did all the others.

53 When everyone's laughter subsided, Yeshua continued saying, "So it would seem from my simple description. But remember, the higher Kingdoms also exist in a space between a space, in a different resonance and synchronicity of time. When you arrive there on your paths of eternal progression, I assure you that you will not be specks of dust.

54 That you may better understand that of which I speak, tomorrow I shall begin to take you to some of the innumerable worlds of the lower Kingdoms that you can witness with your own eyes and ears the space between the space and the time between time.

55 Some of the shadow worlds are very much like this one and the people as well, made similar to the image of Elohim, but not fully of your physical attributes and likeness.

56 Others are very different and the creatures upon them also. And of these, you must be most wary."

57 But how will you take us there, Yeshua? asked his brother Yakov. "We do not have ships that sail in the sky."

58 "The worlds of the sky are far away, Yakov," Yeshua answered. "But the lower shadow Kingdoms are like the pot within the pot—they are very close, even as close as walking from one room into another."

a Yeshua's explanation in this section may be somewhat obtuse to modern readers, and the subject itself is somewhat difficult to grasp, so here is further explanation with a couple of examples.

Harmony is used to define a common setting and parameters of perception. So everything that exists on the earth is in a common harmony with all other things that exist on the earth. Because they coexist in a common setting and can be perceived with one or more of the five senses, they share a harmony. On a larger scale, everything that exists in our solar system or universe in the same harmony can be perceived with one or more of the five senses, because they share a common harmony. Things in harmony share a common stage and may in fact be very different from one another.

Resonance is a measure of compatibility. Some things are quite close in resonance and have the potential for greater compatibility while other things are quite far apart and clearly incompatible.

Example 1: *A man and an elephant share the same harmony. They coexist on the same planet, nurtured by the foods and air and water they obtain from this planet. They can perceive each other with their physical senses. However, they have very different resonances. They have no affinity for one another and for the most part are mysteries to each other.*

Example 2: *You can have your hearing tested with a machine that makes tiny noises in your ears that have different tones and amplitude. At some point as the technician runs the machine up and down the tonal scale, you will no longer be able to hear the sound that is being made. The sound is still ringing in your ear, but you cannot hear it. Because the sound is still being made in your ear on your earth, it is in the same harmony and you were initially able to hear it. But as its resonance changed sufficiently, it literally disappeared from your perception even though it was still there.*

Yeshua gives the example of the seven libraries of the ancients in verse 30. These are real, physical places on this earth that were purposely put into a very different resonance to protect them from unwanted visitors. They exist in this harmony, the world we live upon, but they have never been discovered by archaeologists. Why? Because of their starkly different resonance. Like the hearing machine making the sound that cannot be heard even though it is being played, though the libraries physically exist on this earth, they cannot be seen because their resonance is too out of sync with our ability to perceive them.

CHAPTER 94

Portal Between Worlds

Yeshua teaches his Apostles and Salome about the portals that enter into the worlds of different resonances and the purpose for them.

Explanation of the Lower Kingdoms

The following day, Yeshua took them to a spot where the river cascaded in a small waterfall into a circular pool cut into the rock by years of erosion.

2 Yeshua pointed to the pool, saying, "Stare at the space in the air immediately above this pool. Do you notice anything unusual?"

3 They all stared where he indicated, and Cephas said, "I see a vortex of energy, a distortion of the air like heat waves upon the hot desert sands, like the vortexes you have taught us to look for since our trip to Tyre."

4 "Very good, Cephas," Yeshua commended. "But there is still more here to see."

5 "I see something more," Salome said somewhat timidly as if it were not her place to speak.

6 "What do you see?" asked Yeshua.

7 Salome pointed to the far bank of the river and said, "Over there, near the water's edge. Look through the vortex in the middle of the river over to the far side, and there is a strange blue light that is spinning."

8 Everyone looked to where she was pointing, and many quickly exclaimed in wonder at what they saw.

9 "Who has ever seen a color blue such as that?" wondered Toma.

10 "It is more than a color," Philip said in awe. "It is as if it is alive."

11 "How could we have not seen it before?" wondered Yudas Iscariot. "It is more brilliant in hue than anything I have ever seen, with an entrancing spiral movement that seems to beckon us."

12 "Everyone look to me for a moment," Yeshua requested, and everyone turned their heads to him to comply.

13 He held their gaze for just a few seconds, and then invited them to turn again and look at the shimmering blue spiral.

14 As they turned, they all exclaimed once more, but this time with dismay in their voices.

15 "But it is gone!" cried Yohhanan.

16 "Can anyone see it still?" asked Shim'on. Everyone shook their head negatively in response.

17 Shim'on turned to Salome and asked, "How about you, Salome? You were the first to see it. Can you see it still?" But Salome said that she too could no longer see the blue spiral light either.

18 Then all eyes turned to Yeshua, and he explained, "What you saw was a gateway to one of

the worlds of the lower Kingdoms.

19 Natural portals such as this are very rare. But when they are found, they will always be immediately adjacent to an energy vortex or even within them.

20 That the vortex may be positive or negative is not relevant to the gateway's presence.

21 Today, I will teach you how to create these portals so you can travel to the lower worlds of the shadow Kingdoms and also how to block the gateways for a time when necessary so that no living thing from them can travel here to your earth. And it is for that cause that you will most likely ever act.

22 The gateways always remain in place, but the door itself is seldom opened by its natural cycle.

23 To command its opening when not at a time of its natural cycle requires a secret Celestine word of power, which is . . . (not written). Do not reveal this word to any but the highest Adepts, even upon threat of death, lest dreadful things may be unleashed upon your unsuspecting and unprepared world by those who understand not what they do.

24 The gateway you saw emerged during its natural cycle, which, in the case of this one, is to appear for thirty seconds, once every day, one hundred and fifteen minutes after the sun has risen in this place.

25 Other portals may remain open for a minute or two longer and some for seconds less during their natural cycles, and some may remain open for much longer.

26 While this gateway opens each day, others may only open once every fifty years or even one hundred or one thousand years.

27 The longer time between openings, the longer the portal will remain open, with one of a thousand years remaining open for many moons on its natural cycle.

28 However, all gateways, opening on their natural cycle or by your command, can be held open for any period of time by your focus. As Celestine Light Adepts, as long as your eyes remain fixed upon them, they will remain visible to your sight, even if the time is long past for them to vanish.

29 But the time of the shadow worlds is not in harmony or synchronicity with the time of the earth upon which you live, save for the interior of the tunnel gateways, which bridge both worlds. Because of this, neither is the coming of their day or night or the length therein the same as the one you know.

30 The moment you look away, even if only for a blink, time moves in both worlds, but not the same, and the portal will close if its time is past. This is what happened with this gateway when I asked you to look to me."

31 Yuda raised his hand as Yeshua finished speaking and asked, "This is all most interesting, Lord of Light, but what has it to do with our stewardships here on this earth with the people of this world?"

32 Yeshua answered, saying, "There are dangers in the shadow worlds of the lower Kingdoms, threats to the people and creatures of this world that are unlike anything seen here.

33 Though you cannot travel from this Kingdom to one that is higher, those creatures of the lower Kingdoms can travel here. From time to time, some of the more dangerous ones are drawn through the gateways. Though their time in this world is short, they can wreck much havoc and misery on man and beast during those few minutes or hours.

34 Other times, people or creatures of a higher order from the lower Kingdoms are drawn through the portals. They can exist for an even shorter time in this world than the lesser creatures before they are pulled back into their own, but can still do much mischief while they are here.

35 So too can people and beasts from this world be drawn unsuspectingly through an open gateway into one of the shadows if they are caught in a gateway when it opens.

36 Some will perish over there and return to this world only as a corpse. Those that return alive are most often so disturbed by what they experienced that they return as empty shells of their former selves."

37 Salome raised her hand, and when Yeshua spoke her name in acknowledgment, she questioned him, "Why did our heavenly parents create such dreadful places?"

38 Yeshua answered her, saying, "Know that there is nothing created by the Elohim that is not for the good of man and for the good of all the creatures that have been created throughout the heavens, though how that is so may sometimes seem difficult to grasp without a full knowledge.

39 That you may understand, I will tell you that all things including the Elohim must have exposure to a mixture of light and dark and other energies that are part of the light and dark, to thrive, not an equal balance, but a mixture.

40 It is easy for a man to be virtuous when he is surrounded only by virtue. But what kind of strength does that give to his character and his soul?

41 Far greater is the man who remains virtuous even when tempted, for in overcoming the temptation, he adds to the strength of his character and the energy of his soul.

42 But a preponderance of temptation will break the will of many virtuous men. Therefore, there is a balance that must be found, enough opposition to build strength, but not so much as to overwhelm the foundation of virtue.

43 The tree that never has to struggle to reach through the canopy to find its share of light and stretch its roots into the earth to find sufficient water and nourishment never reaches the fullness of its possibilities, but remains forever just another average tree among many.

44 Understand then that challenges make you stronger if you do not shirk or run away from them.

45 And more than this, they are necessary for your growth. They provide the nutrients to your life to help you reach your fullest potential even as the earth provides the nutrients for the tree that struggles through the hard clay and sends its roots deep into the fertile ground.

46 A tree that stands out alone in an open valley, always receiving abundant rain, sunshine, and only gentle breezes, planted in fertile soil that is easy to till, may be fruitful, but it will never become a giant among trees for it lacks the opposition necessary to push itself to become greater than it is.

47 When the Elohim created all the earths that exist, we did not make them all the same; not only are the climates and sizes different, but so is the light and the air and the quality of the water.

48 Beyond these physical attributes, the very energy of one earth is exceedingly different from the energy of another.

49 Each and every world within each of the seven Kingdoms has been given life that is compatible with its environment.

50 But each and every world, if left only within its own environment, would soon cease to be a source of life for its inhabitants.

51 A room must have windows and doors that fresh air may come in; else, it will stagnate. So too must each world have breaths of fresh air to enliven them; else, they will also stagnate and become inhospitable to the life they nurture.

52 This is the primary purpose of the gateways between the earths of the Salanha Kingdom and the shadow worlds of the lower Kingdoms: to reinvigorate each world with a portion of the energy from other worlds that are very different.

53 This is why all of the gateways have been set to open at the time given by the Elohim, and this for time without end.

54 So too do the worlds of the Salanha Kingdom receive fresh breezes of greater light from gateways to the Koropean, Celestine, and Elohim Kingdoms. But to these Kingdoms, you may only pass as your whole soul becomes in their resonance on your path of eternal progression.

55 Understand that all life upon the earths of the Salanha Kingdom, and all upon the worlds of the lower Kingdoms and all life upon those of the higher Kingdoms are connected and in some ways dependent upon the energies that each receives from the other Kingdoms.

56 Without this exchange of energy, all things would stagnate and their eternal progression

would end.
57 In the past, I have charged you with the stewardship to keep the vortexes of positive and
negative energy in balance wherever you go.
58 And to build up the Communities of Light as safe havens of virtue for the Children of
Light and as beacons of the light to all the world.
59 And I have charged you with going forth into the world and finding other Children of
Light and to enlighten and bless them and to bring them into the fold with you, that they may
be baptized and numbered among you.
60 Now I give one more charge unto you: to become aware of the gateways to the lower
Kingdoms and to watch over them all across your world. I shall teach you how you can accomplish
this charge.
61 And it shall be your responsibility to see that no Ganish ever gains a knowledge of how
to open a gateway.
62 And if one does gain this knowledge and begins to open gateways at times other than
those given by Elohim or to seek out the dangers therein, it is your duty to place a spell of
forgetfulness upon them that they can remember the gateways no more.
63 When, from time to time, people or creatures from the worlds of the lower Kingdoms
intrude onto your earth, it is your responsibility, not to close the portal, for it is necessary for
the free flow of energy between worlds, but to send them back to their world and cast a net of
disresonance across the opening that unwanted visitors can no longer pass through until the time
of the net is over."

CHAPTER 95

Explanation of Entities

Yeshua takes Miriam, Salome, and the Apostles to the darkest of the underworlds, the Kingdom of Datarz, to experience what it is like and see what exists there. He also explains the purpose of such a place with beings of little substance.

Fifteen Walk Across the Water

When Yeshua finished speaking, there was silence among everyone for several seconds as they contemplated all he had said to them. Then Cephas asked, "When do we go?" Yeshua answered, "Now."

2 Yeshua approached the edge of the riverbank and asked everyone to form a line along the bank side by side, linking arms and holding hands. Yeshua was in the middle, Miriam was on his right, Salome on his left, and the Apostles split on either side of them.

3 "Are you Celestines, followers of the full Celestine Light of Elohim?" Yeshua asked in a loud voice.

4 And in an equally loud voice, everyone in the line shouted, "Yes!"

5 "Are you good stewards of the earth and all life therein?" Yeshua asked anew.

6 Once more, everyone shouted, "Yes," in affirmation.

7 "Are you masters of the Celestine Light that all things are possible to you with faith?" Yeshua asked them.

8 Without hesitation, they all shouted, "Yes," once more.

9 "Then walk with me now in the fullness of faith, Adepts of the Celestine Light. Walk across the river that we may enter into the gateway," Yeshua bade. And with that, he stepped forward, and Miriam, Salome, and all of the Apostles stepped forward with him in perfect faith.

10 Yeshua's foot touched the water but did not sink into it. As each of the others stepped upon the water immediately after him, they did not sink either, and as one, they strode across the river, walking in a line arm in arm and hand in hand, until they reached the far bank and scrambled up onto it.

11 Upon the far bank, the Apostles looked at one another with smiles of accomplishment, proud and humbled by that which they had just done.

The Kingdom of Datarz

12 Not far from the riverbank, Yeshua took a stick and drew a diagram in the dirt at their feet and told them, "To pass through the gateway into the shadow earth at a time other than its usual and accustomed opening, you must draw this diagram vertically in the air at the place of the gateway, with a consecrated wooden wand or rainbow crystal, as if you were drawing on a

door of wood at the entrance to a building."

13 Yeshua spoke again a Celestine word of power unto them and cautioned, "I command you once again to never reveal this word or the diagram that I shall now show unto you to any, save those who are the highest Adepts among the Celestine Children of Light.

14 After you have drawn the diagram, speak the word of power I have given you, and the gateway shall be revealed and open to you. It is that simple, at least if you also have all the other qualities of a higher Adept of the Celestine Light.

15 When I am not with you, never pass through the gateway without a consecrated rainbow crystal to amplify the Celestine Light of Elohim upon you, lest harm come upon you while you are in one of the worlds of the lower Kingdoms.

16 A consecrated rainbow crystal coupled with your great faith will always allow you to return to your earth at the instant you merely think for it to be so. There is nothing else you need do if you have correctly imbued the sacred object with the Celestine Light of Elohim and a connection to this earth as you have been taught."

17 Then Yeshua turned to Salome and said, "It is fitting that the one among you who could first see the gateway should be the one who opens the door."

18 Yeshua looked to Miriam, who was standing beside him, and asked, "May Salome use your consecrated crystal to open the gateway?"

19 "Of course, my Lord," Miriam answered. She reached inside her garments and lifted a gold chain from around her neck. Dangling from it was a clear crystal about the size of her index finger that radiated the colors of the rainbow.

20 She handed the crystal to Salome, who turned to Yeshua, waiting for his instructions.

21 "Curl the golden chain in the palm of your hand and hold the point of the crystal parallel to the ground, pointing away from you," he instructed.

22 He continued, "Turn slowly now in a circle with the thought in your mind to discover the location of the nearest gateway."

23 Salome did as Yeshua told her, and as she was almost at the point of completing a circle, she suddenly lurched forward as if an invisible person had grabbed her by her outstretched arm and pulled her toward them.

24 "Oh my!" She exclaimed. "I am being physically and strongly pulled forward. I must indeed resist if I am to remain rooted and not step forward."

25 "Consecrated wands of wood and rainbow crystals act as tools of resonance when you have imbued them with the energy you seek," Yeshua explained. "As you are all Celestine Adepts, you can do this with simply a thought.

26 Once imbued with righteous purpose, they sing in harmony with that which you seek. When you are far from it, they will merely whisper and the pull of direction will be ever so slight.

27 But when you are upon the item, place, or person that you seek, the pull will be so strong that you will have no doubt that you have arrived.

28 Step forward into that which pulls you until something changes," Yeshua instructed Salome.

29 She did as he bade and moved forward four steps with her arm outstretched, pointing the crystal before her. Suddenly, she stopped and, turning to Yeshua, said, "I am no longer being pulled. The crystal is radiating heat, but no longer is an invisible hand pulling me forward."

30 "You are no longer being pulled because you have arrived at your destination, Yeshua affirmed.

31 Now take the tip of the crystal and draw the diagram I have shown you, in the same size that I drew, vertically in the air before you. When you are finished, say the Celestine word of power that I gave to you. In a whisper or a roar, it is the same, as long as you speak the word aloud."

32 Once more, Salome did as Yeshua bade her, and as soon as she spoke the word of power, the shimmering blue spiral gateway opened directly in front of her, taller by a head than she and

the width of her arms if they were extended to either side.

33 Miriam came to Yeshua on his right side and slipped her arm through his and held close to him. Yeshua stepped forward, and Salome came to his other side and also put her arm through his and held close to him.

34 Together, they stepped forward into the turning blue spiral light and disappeared.

35 As they vanished into the blue light, the Apostles all looked at one another with both amazement and some looks of concern.

36 Then Philip came up to the gateway and pointed at it, saying, "Look, you can see them vaguely as if they are standing in a fog at the end of a long tunnel."

37 Everyone came and pressed close to the portal where Philip had indicated, and they could faintly see Yeshua, Miriam, and Salome through the gateway as if they were barely seeing someone deep underwater.

38 "Come, brothers!" Cephas encouraged. "What are we waiting for? Let us quickly go and join Yeshua before he is off on a great adventure without us!" So saying, Cephas stepped through the gateway and was quickly followed enthusiastically by all of the other Apostles.

39 When they arrived on the other side of the gateway, their enthusiasm was quickly dampened by the dark and foreboding world in which they found themselves.

40 Yeshua, Miriam, and Salome stood facing them as they came through the portal. As the last Apostle came through, they all looked around in silence at the strange world to which they had come.

41 In mere moments, they were all shivering and holding their arms across their chests or rubbing their hands together in a feeble attempt to stay warm. "This is the coldest place I have ever been," Philip said through chattering teeth.

42 "I thought it was night when we first stepped into this world," Shim'on said as he covered his face with his hands and then pointed with one at the sky, saying, "But there is the puny sun, I think, low on the horizon and barely seen through the thick, dark clouds that lay even upon the ground."

43 Miriam turned to Salome and asked for the crystal on the gold chain she had given to her to open the portal.

44 When she had it in hand, she pointed the crystal toward the ground, and then drew her outstretched arm in an arch over the grouped Apostles, ending the arch on the far side of the ground from where she had begun, then spoke a single Celestine word of power, "Saxteris."

45 Immediately, a bubble of warm light was created surrounding the Apostles and Yeshua, and Miriam and Salome stepped into it with them.

46 "What wonder is this? asked Toma as he stood with open arms and palms up, basking in the new found warmth of their sanctuary from the cold.

47 "Can you teach me to do that, Miriam?" asked Yohhanan with childlike enthusiasm. "Or is it something only you can do because of your calling as an angel?"

48 This is a blessing given to any virtuous Child of Light to do as they are prepared in heart and mind, certainly any that are Adepts," she answered calmly. "I can teach you the method, Yohhanan, but only the faith of a child, singular focus, and the harmony of oneness will manifest it for you."

49 "Perhaps, we can leave that lesson for another day," Yeshua interrupted. "There is much to accomplish and learn that already is lined up before us like the fishing boats coming into the dock at the end of the day to unload their catch.

50 Before the evening falls completely, all essential tasks must be accomplished on this world."

51 "Of course, Yeshua," Yohhanan and Miriam demurred with bowed heads.

52 "Tell us then, Lord of Light, what is this place?" asked Cephas. "And why is it so cold and dark?"

53 "Nor can we see anything but gray and black rocks," added Amram. "Not a creature is to be heard or seen nor even a tree or a bush or a blade of grass. What manner of dreary place is this?"

54 Suddenly, a black shadow shot out of the darkness beyond and would have come upon them, but it was held back as if by an invisible wall, for it could not pass into the protection of light that they stood within.

55 Everyone except Yeshua and Miriam jumped back in fright when the shadow glob came out of the darkness. As they realized it could not pass through their protective bubble of light, they looked at it in fascination as it spread itself outward in a chaotic fashion just beyond the invisible surface of the bubble.

56 In seconds, it was joined by another shadow blob and then another, and in less than a minute, the entire bubble of light was covered just beyond its invisible surface with slithering, dark amoeba-like shadows.

57 "This is a world of unclean and unformed spirits that abides within the Kingdom of Datarz. These formless creatures are called Raval," Yeshua explained. "They have existence, but without shape or form and barely a substance.

58 "There is no life of any type on this particular world except for them, and they are not life as you have known it."

59 "What do they eat?" asked Yakov of Bethsaida innocently.

60 Yeshua answered, saying, "They eat nothing, for they have no bodies to build or mouths to put food into. They get the little sustenance they need to maintain their existence by absorbing light. That is why they have swarmed upon our little bubble. I am sure they are enjoying quite a feast."

61 The Apostles were mostly aghast at Yeshua's description, many with raised eyebrows and sour faces.

62 Yeshua continued his explanation, saying, "I have spoken to you before about the need for balance in all things. I am a spirit child of our Father and Mother in the Celestine Kingdom, even as are all of you. We are eternal spirits of light."

63 He hesitated for a moment, then continued saying, "These primitive, dark spirit forms you see now before you were also created by our Celestine Father and Mother, but devolved from the love and light in which they were created into spirit beings of bare existence.

64 They have no thoughts, no emotions, no relationships, no needs other than an innate attraction to be drawn to and cling to light. It feeds them, but they have no way to even know that.

65 The danger arises when these dark, broken spirits escape into your world when a gateway is open, drawn there by the great light that comes through the portal. They are the most common visitor to your world from the worlds in the lower Kingdoms.

66 When something of greater substance from one of the shadow worlds comes onto your earth, it cannot long remain, for its energy is too different and its resonance pulls it back through the portal returning it to the world from whence it came.

67 But the simpler and more primitive a creature is, like these Raval, the longer they can remain on a world in the Kingdom of Salanha before it is pulled back through the portal.

68 If it can move fast enough, it can pass beyond the influence of the gateway and not be pulled back at all. For creatures of more substance, this is a death sentence, for they cannot remain long upon the earths of Salanha before their very different resonance destroys them and they become as dust.

69 So it would be for anything from your earth that would come to one of these worlds of the lower Kingdoms and remained for other than a short time, save for you who are Celestine Adepts.

70 But the dark spirits of this world are so simple in their nature that they can exist in your world for many moons and even years if they find a good source of light.

71 When I say good, I do not mean bright. The full brightness of your sun would destroy them in moments.

72 They seek the dark places where the lowest of men congregate to do their dirty deeds and

partake of forbidden vices, places where the light is dim enough to feed upon but not so bright to harm them.

73 But they bring with them a pall of darkness that covers the spirits of the men in those places and attaches to them and hides underneath their clothing when they are in the sun, continually agitating their emotions and thoughts and bringing out a greater evil within them that might have otherwise lain dormant.

74 For this reason, you must be especially vigilant of gateways that open to this particular type of shadow world. Wherever you discover them, if a great number of Raval are passing through, cover the gateway with an aura net of disresonance by which these dark spirits will be repelled for the duration of the spell.

75 But let that duration not be for more than twelve moons, for the Raval are a part of the flow of energy between worlds, which energy must not long be impeded, lest your earth begin to stagnate.

76 When you discover people and places already infested with these spirits, do not destroy the Raval, for they are not intentionally creating harm. Instead, open a momentary gateway at that spot, then command them off their hosts and out of their dark corners and send them back to their world."

Why Dark Spirits Exist

77 Yuda son of Cleophas raised his hand. "Yes, Yuda, speak," Yeshua said.

78 "Forgive me, Lord of Light. I do not mean to ask an impertinent question, but why did the Father and the Mother create such spirits? If our heavenly parents are beings of light, as I know they are, what was their purpose in creating spirits of darkness?"

79 Yeshua smiled broadly, "I know you are my Apostles indeed when you ask such excellent questions." Yuda smiled back at him, letting out a sigh of relief at his words of praise."

80 Yeshua continued saying, "We spoke about the need for balance and the need for opposite energies to have some points where they mix. Thus all are stimulated toward maximum growth and expansion in both the physical and the spiritual."

81 You must couple this understanding with your comprehension of the full nature of the eternal progression of souls and the progress of the spirit children of the Father and Mother since the days of their creation.

82 The greatest purpose of the Father and the Mother, the source of the creation of everything, is no different than the cherished purpose of each of you that are fathers and mothers: to see your children grow in the Celestine Light and reach the magnificence of their potential.

83 To do this, you teach your children in the good ways they should go but do not force them to go that way as they mature, for a child forced is unlikely to remain upon the path once the force is removed.

84 Nor would they learn the value of the good path of Celestine Light if they had no comprehension of the darkness by which to compare.

85 Thus it is that in the beginning, the Father and the Mother created the spirits of all living things and made worlds of innumerable resonances in different harmonies for them to be drawn to, each according to the light that they could hold.

86 And they created all the worlds, both the light and those of less light and the bright and the shadows, that their children could come down to a world that resonated with them and learn from their experiences the value of the light and desire from their own will to cleave unto it."

CHAPTER 96

Rebellion and Fall of Lucifer

Yeshua explains in detail Lucifer's confrontation with Heavenly Mother and Heavenly Father and what resulted from his rage.

Lucifer's Confrontation with Elohim

And Yeshua continued, "As you know, though it seems incomprehensible to you because of the Celestine Light of Elohim in your hearts, many of the spirit children in the land of Xeon, in the Kingdom of Koropean, rebelled against our Father and Mother, who told them they were free to choose their path each day and for eternity.

2 Our spirit brother Lucifer desired to compel everyone in both spirit and flesh to know only good to insure that all would come to the Celestine Realms once they had transited a physical life. But not for the benefit of others did he propose this, but to gather glory for himself.

3 But I was there, and I told Lucifer that those who would return, having never been allowed to make mistakes and given the choice of light over dark, sometimes choosing wrong and then repenting, would be no further progressed in their souls than they were before they were born into the physical.

4 And that it was for this cause that the spirit children of the Father and the Mother would be given mortal bodies of flesh; that they would be free to choose their path and progress and learn from their experiences, to taste sin and overcome it, to gain faith and become more than they were in Xeon.

5 Nor would they ever be alone in emptiness, for always they would recognize the Celestine Light and always would it call to them in their hearts and always would the foundational commandments of the Elohim be inscribed upon their souls, that they would forever be inclined to walk the path of light.

6 And great was the anger of Lucifer to have his plan of salvation rejected. He told me, 'If you and the Father and the Mother will not agree to that which I have decreed shall be, then I shall gather the hosts of Xeon and come upon you and banish you from the Koropean Kingdom and forever block the way back that those from the Kingdom of the Elohim can never return here again.'

7 And so he tried, and he persuaded many with his words to believe as he did, and many were those who followed him until a great war of pain and anger was building in the Koropean realms, between those who followed Lucifer and those who remained true and faithful to the Elohim.

8 But our Father and Mother told those who loved them to cease to argue and contest, and they allowed Lucifer and his horde to come to the gate of the sacred sanctuary where the Elohim dwelt when in the realm of Koropean.

9 And it came to pass that the horde of unclean spirits poured over the land up to the very gates of the sanctuary where the Father and Mother sat awaiting them.

10 But great was their surprise when they came before our Mother and Father with all of their might and rage and demanded they depart from the Koropean realms, and the Father and Mother merely looked at each other with love and smiled with sad humor.

11 Then our Father stood up in all of his majesty and our Mother stood beside him in all of her magnificence, and they faced Lucifer and the evil horde of Xeon.

12 And our Father said unto them, 'All of our children have been given the freedom to choose their path that they might eternally progress and become more than they are. You who say you want to be forced forever upon the path of light, do you not recognize that even now you have chosen the path of darkness and upon that path you shall become less than you are?'

13 And our Mother said, 'We have created worlds of less light than the ones you have known, less than the ones for which you were intended to dwell upon in wonderful physical bodies.

14 Now you have a different harmony calling to you, one you have chosen. A harmony of the other darker worlds, and to those, you must now go, not because we command it, but because you can no more resist it, for it is the place that calls to your soul. It is your resonance.'

15 Lucifer screamed with anger at the words of our Father and Mother and incited his horde into a frenzy so much so that the Koropean realm shook with the crescendo of their angry voices.

16 And he spat out his words with hatred, saying, 'It is the two of you and your firstborn son who will leave this place now and return to the realm of the Elohim. You are not wanted or welcome here any longer, nor are your words or your teachings or your pious commandments.

17 You are but three and we are many. Together, our power, my power, is greater than yours, so depart now and never return!'

18 Then our Mother took three steps forward toward Lucifer, who stood not far from her, and he stepped back a step as she came up to him.

19 She looked into his eyes without speaking, and he held her gaze. She shook her head slightly and said firmly, 'No, Lucifer, your power is not greater. Nor is the combined power of all those who follow you. Nor do you even have an inkling of the immensity of power of the Celestine Light of the Elohim.'

20 As she spoke, every soul in all the realms heard her voice. And she said, 'By our love, you were created as were the misguided souls that follow you. And by our love, all the heavens and all the earths were created and all things that exist, even this immensity of the Koropean realm you call home and seek to bar us the creators from. Where is your power, Lucifer? What speck of dust have you created?

21 Do not doubt that by our word all things could also be destroyed, in the blink of an eye, even you. But we love you, even in our sadness at this what you have done. And we would not and could not destroy that which we love.

22 It is only because of our love and by our command to the Celestine Light that you remain here now in our presence that you may gain a full understanding of the magnitude of your sins.

23 It is you, Lucifer, and all those who have followed you that shall now depart from the Koropean realms, for your resonance has changed and there is no longer a place here for you.

24 But we leave you with our eternal promise: that even for you there is a way back into the Celestine Light.'

25 Once again Lucifer threw a fit of rage, but this time the horde that had followed him remained silent, for they were cowed by the brilliance of the light that emanated from the Father and the Mother and the words of truth our Mother had spoken. A fear came over them for that which they had done.

26 Our Father came and stood beside our Mother and said unto Lucifer, 'You have lost the Celestine Light that you had when we created you, that was freely given to you with love. You have tainted your soul with a great darkness, as have all those who followed you, and darkness cannot abide the light. It is time for you to go now to the worlds we have prepared for those who

choose paths of darkness.'

27 'I will not go!' Lucifer screamed in anger. 'It is you who must leave this instant!'

28 'Or what, Lucifer?' asked the Father. 'You only have power in your own imagination and among the beguiled souls who have believed in you. Over those who follow the Celestine Light, you have no power, nor could you ever have. You stand now before the Lords of the Celestine Light, only because we have granted it to be so.'

29 Then our Mother spoke again saying, 'And we grant it no more, Lucifer. We now release the hold upon the Celestine Light that has allowed you to stand in our presence. Begone now to the worlds of darkness that beckon to you.'

30 A brilliant light began to emanate from our Mother and Father. It was white but tinged with rainbow colors throughout, scintillating like a million tiny jewels. It spread forth over Lucifer and over the entire horde that had followed him until it was so bright that nothing but the light could be seen.

31 Then in a last burst of brilliance it was gone and with it Lucifer and all that had followed him down the dark path.

Eternal Progression from the Lower Kingdoms

32 "Some were pulled to one shadow world and some to another, each according to the amount of Celestine Light that remained in their soul.

33 Unto this world in the Datarz Kingdom were called some of those of the greatest darkness, who devolved from the spirit children of substance and awareness that they were and became these unaware blobs of darkness you see now."

34 "Can they ever become more than this? wondered Ya'akov, son of Cleophas.

35 "Yes," Yeshua answered. "All things are given the opportunity to have eternal progression, each in the manner that has been given for it.

36 About every thousand years as time is kept on this earth, the Raval are restored to the land of Xeon by our Mother and Father to the spirit bodies that they had before they were compelled by their darkness to their world of darkness. They remain for a time in their former form in a segregated part of Xeon.

37 They have no memories of their time as Raval, but they know what happened to them. They have full memories of all that occurred during their rebellion, and they can see all that has transpired since they were banished from the light by their darkness. And they can see those who did not rebel both in the Koropean and Salanha Kingdoms and all they have become and how far they have progressed since that time.

38 Each cycle that they are again in the form of a spirit child of our Father and Mother, they remember all of the previous times this has occurred.

39 During the time when they are again in a spirit form of substance, heart, and mind, they have the opportunity to sincerely repent of their past sins and make amends.

40 If they repent with sufficient humility and restitution to change the harmony of their soul and the balance of light and darkness therein, they will never again devolve into a Raval.

41 Instead, they will be drawn to one of the other shadow worlds, perhaps in the Scarnz or Qaorroz Kingdoms, far less than the earth you call home, but a place of much greater light and substance than this world we are now visiting.

42 Now I think you have learned all you need to know about this place, so let us return again to your earth."

43 Yeshua asked Miriam to give her crystal to anyone she chose that they could open the portal. She handed it gently to Cephas, who was standing near her.

44 Yeshua pointed to the spot where they had come through, saying, "Draw the diagram in the air as you saw Salome do and say the Celestine word of power that I gave to you."

45 Cephas did as Yeshua bade, and the shimmering blue gateway immediately opened before them, spinning in a slow spiral.

46 Cephas turned back to look at Yeshua and he nodded for him to proceed, so he stepped through the portal and was followed by all of the Apostles, Salome, Miriam, and, lastly, Yeshua.

CHAPTER 97

The Sixth Kingdom

Yeshua takes Miriam, Salome, and the Apostles to the junction of the river Jordan and the river Jabbok, where a gateway exists to another world. Once they learn to see it, they wait until it has enlarged enough for them to step through to the "Sixth Kingdom," known as Scarnz, or as we might call it today the "sixth dimension." They have some very interesting adventures during their several-day stay, but upon their return, they find out that they've only been gone mere hours and they realize they've become "Timewalkers."

Upon returning to their earth, Yeshua, Miriam, Salome, and the Apostles remained for a night and a day, speaking further about their visit to the strange Seventh Kingdom.

2 When they next ventured beyond their camp, Yeshua led them on a long walk north to the point where the river Jordan met the river Jabbok. There they camped for the night.

3 As the darkness began to settle, Yeshua gestured toward the rivers and said, "The point where two rivers join will frequently have a vortex, and sometimes a gateway to another world will also be present. So it is with the confluence of these two rivers.

4 As the darkness comes upon the land, look steadily at the point where the two rivers join. There is a gateway there to a world in the space between the space that is open even now, though none of you have seen it."

5 "What must we do to see it?" wondered Philip. "Is there some prayer we can say or spell we can cast upon it?"

6 "Of course, you could do either or both," Yeshua answered. "And surely it would then manifest to your eyes.

7 But I wish you to learn to see things with your eyes that you have never before seen because you have never trained your eyes how to look.

8 You need to be able to see these gateways, not only after a prayer or a spell or other special actions and words, but simply by glancing upon them or even feeling their presence. Else, you will be squandering your time finding them and not enough being good stewards over them.

9 To see the portals with merely a glance, you must train your eyes to see differently than you have all of your lives. You must focus not upon the spot where the gateway stands, but through that spot and to the place beyond the gateway.

10 If you are focused upon the spot, as your eyes naturally will, you will never be able to see the portal with a simple glance, but only with eyes that have been altered by Elohim through your prayers, spells, or words of power.

11 This gateway has been open for over an hour and will remain open through the night until

the sun rises tomorrow. I have asked you to discover it now as the time of dusk is often the time they are most easily seen.

12 Remember to look at the spot of land where the rivers join, but focus your eyes on the space beyond it."

13 Everyone did as Yeshua directed, but none could see the gateway. Salome seemed somewhat vexed as she asked Yeshua, "Why can I not see this one? The other came easily to my eyes. Is there something different about this gateway?"

14 "Yes Salome, there is," Yeshua replied.

15 He did not elaborate further, and after a minute or so, Toma asked, "What should we be looking for, Yeshua? What is different about this one?"

16 Yeshua answered, saying, "Let us see who best remembers the description I have already given for the portals, for in that description is the answer you seek, and I shall not give it again."

17 "A puzzle!" Mattayah declared with enthusiasm.

18 Miriam shook her head and told him, "No, he is merely testing us to see how well we have listened to that which he has already given to us."

19 "Indeed," Yeshua agreed upon hearing Miriam's words. "I will happily give all the knowledge of the Elohim unto you, my faithful friends. But you can only receive the new when you have first proven to understand the old, for it is upon the old that the new is built."

20 "Is it smaller or larger?" asked Yudas Iscariot. "Is that why we cannot see it because we are only looking for something similar to that which we have previously seen?"

21 Yeshua smiled with happiness at his answer and nodded his head affirmatively. Seeing this, everyone began to look anew for a gateway of less or greater size than the one that they had already passed through.

22 In moments, Shim'on shouted and pointed at the ground near the confluence of the two rivers, saying, "There it is! It is very small, barely seen above the ground. And it is not round like the other, but more like a thin-angled bar of moving color."

23 His announcement was quickly followed by a chorus of "I see it too."

24 Everyone walked over to where they saw the gateway near the bank of the river. As they came upon it, they saw that it was actually a round spinning spiral of unearthly blue light, the same as the other had been but much smaller.

25 However, it was not standing vertically as the previous gateway had been, but was lying at an angle close to the ground, which is why it had seemed bar-shaped from the position they had been viewing it from at a distance. And it was only about the size of a man's head.

26 "How strange this portal is!" Salome declared as they all looked upon it.

27 "How shall we pass through such an opening?" wondered Yohhanan, scratching his head. "I certainly will not fit, and Cephas could hardly reach one of his big arms through." And everyone laughed at his words.

28 Toma looked to Yeshua and asked, "Is this perhaps just a portal to stick our heads through and see the other world but not pass completely into it?"

29 "Or maybe we can do something to make the opening larger," ventured Amram.

30 "Thank you, Toma and Amram, for your excellent thoughts," Yeshua complemented. "Indeed, you could just stick your head through, and so too could you make the opening larger if you desired.

31 But the opening will not remain this size through the night. At times, it will be much smaller and at other times, it will be substantially larger. Its size fluctuates with the amount of energy that is exchanging through it between your earth and the shadow earth on the other side of the gateway.

32 If we are patient, we can pass through this one when it enlarges. Though we could pass through immediately with a word of power, it is better for your education that you wait for this one to grow that you may gain a better understanding of the cycles of energy that flow between worlds."

33 Following Yeshua's directions, they waited by the portal as night fell over the land and for another couple of hours.

34 They watched the gateway as it continually grew and shrank in size several times in a single minute as if it was breathing. At other times, the portal would hold its size for several minutes.

35 "Do they all act as this one, expanding and contracting?" inquired Mattayah.

36 "Yes," Yeshua replied. "The energies that flow through, and in all the worlds and the spaces between them, are never still. They are always moving like invisible rivers, revitalizing all life.

37 However, the smaller gateways such as this one will have more frequent movements, while the larger ones will have less.

38 As you stand beside this one, feel the pressure of the energy that flows through it and the sensation upon your aura.

39 Attune yourself to that energy and become one with it so much so that in the future, you will be able to feel the presence of a gateway before your eyes ever see it."

40 As Yeshua bade, so they all did. When he was satisfied that they each had become familiar with the unique sensations of a gateway, he grasped Miriam's hand and she Salome's, and he led them through when the portal next enlarged. And the Apostles quickly followed after them.

41 After passing through, everyone had a smile on their face. "This is an improvement," Philip commented with satisfaction as they all looked around at the land before them. The sun was radiant in a clear blue sky and green plants and short thorny trees grew sparsely about. In the distance down the hill upon which they stood, they spied a river snaking through the bottom of the valley.

42 "How strange we departed in the night and have arrived in the day!" Salome commented.

43 Yeshua nodded affirmatively and said, "The shadow earths do not have days and nights as the earth you call home. They exist in the same space but in a different time, so your night may be their day."

44 "But I thought they were in a space between a space where we live?" Cephas said with some confusion.

45 "Yes, Cephas, they are," Yeshua affirmed. "But within that space is infinity, and time without end or beginning, and all creation can fit within it.

46 Upon the innumerable earths, both the seen and the unseen, there is all time and no time."

47 Seeing their confused looks, Yeshua elaborated, saying, "Time is something beyond your ability to understand today. But greater understanding will come to you as you become more practiced in your gifts and more diligent in your stewardships."

48 "What about Miriam?" asked Salome. "When she was called to be the Angel of the Covenant, was she not given all knowledge?"

49 Miriam stifled a laugh at Salome's words and said unto her, "I confess that I had somewhat of that expectation soon after I was called, but have learned that even angels only acquire more knowledge as they gain it from seeking, not because it is simply given to them.

50 "Since the time of my calling, my mind has been quickened and understands many things that were like a haze to it before. But it is not as if I have suddenly been filled with knowledge; only that things I have barely understood before have become clear because my comprehension comes quicker.

51 I have been gifted by the Elohim with greater powers of Celestine Light and the knowledge to use them that I may begin to fulfill my calling, but beyond that, only with a clarity of thought that allows me to grasp and learn all things much quicker than before. I still must seek out the knowledge. It does not just fall into my head.

52 Though Yeshua told me in years past about these shadow earths, I am learning the details about them now from my experiences with them, even as you are.

53 And please, you must all understand I am not yet truly the Angel of the Covenant, but merely the designated angel in training. He who I am replacing still remains in the fullness of the stewardship. And so he shall remain until I have fulfilled my apprenticeship.

54 Once Yeshua ascends from this earth, I will remain for eleven years in my physical body, which has been changed so it is no longer quite like yours, but neither is it yet fully Celestine. During this time, I can travel freely between Kingdoms, learning both from my experiences and from the tutelage of Yeshua and the current Angel of the Covenant."

55 "Marvelous are the ways of the Elohim," Yohhanan said reverently upon hearing Miriam's explanation, and the other Apostles voiced their agreement.

56 Yeshua smiled as he often did when he saw those whom he taught with special teachings grasp important principles. Then he lifted his arm toward a path and beckoned, "Shall we explore this world?"

57 They had not traveled far before everyone began to sweat profusely from the heat and loosen up their garments in feeble attempts to get cooler. "What a contrast!" Yudas Iscariot exhaled. "The last place was so cold I realized that I did not know what cold really was until I experienced that world, and now I am beginning to think the same thing about this world and heat."

58 Yuda the Younger looked to Miriam hopefully, "That bubble of light was very nice in the other world. Can you perhaps make a bubble of coolness over us in this place of unforgiving heat? At first, I thought it looked like parts of Palestine, but now I hope there is no place like this on our earth."

59 Before she could answer, Yeshua interjected, saying, "You will become accustomed to the heat soon enough and will have a more authentic understanding of this world if you experience it as it is for those who dwell here."

60 "Who does dwell here?" Toma asked with a slight wavering trepidation in his voice.

61 Yeshua walking at the head of the group smiled mischievously, unseen to any but Miriam, and answered, "Creatures more frightful than the last you encountered."

62 "Truly?" asked Philip with concern.

63 "Truly," Yeshua affirmed. "But there are also some more benign creatures as well."

64 Miriam looked at Yeshua quizzically and asked him silently in his mind, "Why are you scaring them, yet you seem to be amused?"

65 "I am sadly amused," Yeshua answered in her mind. "That after all these days with me, witnessing all they have seen and experiencing all they have, that they could still have fears and not know with resolute conviction that they are greater than any creature they could encounter.

66 They have been given so much yet at times still seem no different than men of the world. I see the greatness inside of them, but only they can bring it out."

67 "Have patience, my love," Miriam replied. "You have chosen them, knowing of the men inside the men; knowing too that their faith in you is only exceeded by your faith in them.

68 You are perhaps impatient to see them in their glory before you depart from this earth. Perhaps it will be so, perhaps not. But you know that in the end, they will all become the fullness of the men you knew them to be on the day that you called them to follow you."

69 Yeshua turned to look at Miriam and, still speaking to her in her mind, answered, "You are my greatest treasure, Miriam. I shall savor every minute of this life and eternity, watching the Apostles progress into their greatness and Salome into hers and our children into theirs. But most of all, Miriam, you into yours."

70 Miriam looked lovingly into Yeshua's eyes and silently whispered to his mind, "Thank you. I am blessed by your love."

71 They walked on for about an hour and saw several indiscernible creatures skirt cautiously near them, but never close enough to actually clearly see their appearance.

72 As they rounded a large boulder, they came upon a natural cistern worn into the rock. Yeshua pointed to shady spots under some short trees, saying, "Let us sit here and wait. Soon we shall see some of the creatures of this world coming to the water."

73 And so they waited. At first, some of the Apostles began to speak among themselves but Yeshua asked them to remain silent so the creatures would approach the water.

74 After a few minutes, they heard some snorting and saw a short six-legged, bristle-haired animal about half the size of a man, with a huge head and a mouth full of two rows of long, sharp-pointed teeth, come up to the water and drink. Everyone's eyes were wide with amazement, looking at the strangest creature they had ever seen.

75 Suddenly it lifted its wide, squat nose and sniffed the air. Spying them across the small rock cistern, it sprang instantly into motion, its six legs moving furiously, and in seconds it was upon them. It had just begun to leap forward toward Philip, who was falling back from his seat with his hands and arms held up in front of him for protection, when Miriam quickly waved her hand at the creature and it immediately fell fast asleep right in its midair lunge and dropped with a thud between Philip's outstretched legs.

76 Philip scrambled up and exclaimed, "I hope there are none worse than that here!"

77 And Yeshua answered, "Some far worse, but also some much more pleasant."

78 Philip, still somewhat shaken by the encounter, looked to Miriam and stammered, "That sleeping spell is so useful . . . Can you please teach me . . . ? Oh, and thank you . . . How did you do that so quick? Oh, . . . I think I need to sit down." And so he did, but several steps away from the sleeping creature which everyone else gathered around to examine.

79 "What is it?" inquired Shim'on.

80 "It is a Deldarq," Yeshua informed them. "This world is inhabited by over three hundred different types of creatures. Some are much more primitive than this one and others more advanced. The Deldarq are about in the middle.

81 In the cycle of repentance and rebirth, those spirits that are drawn here to inhabit the bodies of these creatures return many millennia to this Kingdom in many types of bodies, until their souls have repented sufficiently that they are called to higher life forms in the Kingdom above this one in resonance."

82 "Are all the creatures here as ferocious as this one? asked Yohhanan. "A Deldarq may be smaller, but I would fear for the lion of our earth against one of these."

83 "All are not outwardly as fierce," Yeshua answered. "But all live only by killing and consuming others. Some are just more subtle about it.

84 When creatures from this earth escape through an open gateway onto your earth, they cannot survive more than a few hours, nor venture far from the pull of the portal, and most will be drawn back into their world before they perish. But in that short span and space that they are free, they can kill many, both man and beast that fall into their grasp."

85 Why do the Elohim allow such catastrophes of life?" wondered Yeshua's brother Yakov. "And why not simply create the portals with nets already across them that allow the energy to flow between worlds, but not the creatures. Why do they allow innocent men and beasts of our earth to be slain by these monsters when they could so easily prevent it?"

86 Yeshua was silent for a moment before he answered Yakov's question, and he exhaled deeply before he said, "You are correct, Yakov. The Elohim could have created the gateways so only energy could pass through, but the creatures in the shadow earths would be condemned to a far-longer repentance.

87 Realize first that most of the creatures on these worlds of the lower Kingdoms are not devolved spirit children. They are just innocent creatures having spirits but without souls. Each progresses in their own way, life after life, and someday will have spiritually evolved to the point that they gain a soul. Some choose to never gain a soul or another life, but are happy to remain in their current form in spirit after their physical life. This is nothing like the path of eternal progression that has been given to the children of men or to those creatures of the lower Kingdoms that had once been spirit children of our Heavenly Father and Mother.

88 As I spoke to you earlier, at various lengths of time depending upon the amount of Celestine Light in their souls, the creatures of the lower Kingdoms that are devolved from spirit children are returned in full spirit form to the Koropean and have the opportunity to show fruits of repentance during that time.

89 Unless they have repented sufficiently to resonate with a higher Kingdom, they will return again to the one from whence they came. If they have gained a measure of repentance, they will return there as a higher creature.

90 But it is not only at the time that their spirit is restored in fullness that they can repent. Every day of their lives on the shadow earth, the opportunity is also given to them.

91 As they gain more light, they return to the shadow earths with a stronger instinct of right and wrong.

92 As they progress to creatures of higher and higher resonance, the small part of the light within them becomes fuller and their desire to cleave to the light stronger and their understanding that they need to forsake the darkness more clear.

93 So it is that some that have always killed wantonly kill with less relish and then with none and then even with sadness, often more than the men of earth, most who still kill animals and birds of warm blood for food, when simple plants and the fruits of the animals and the earth would give them superior food without killing.

94 In time, it comes to pass that many of the creatures of the lower Kingdoms will fight against the desire to pass through a portal where mischief awaits and will turn away from them, even when their friends beckon them to accompany them. On that day, they are done with the creature they have been. They will soon die and be reborn as a creature of a higher order. Until someday, step by step, they have the opportunity to regain the fullness of all that they had lost.

95 Therefore, if the passage between worlds was permanently netted, forbidding them passage to your earth, they would be denied their greatest opportunity in this world to show evidence that they have repented and become more than they were.

96 On your earth, you have been given stewardship to put nets of power across the portals. Your nets at first will be very feeble and will not stop many on this side from passing through if that is their desire.

97 As you gain experience, your nets will become stronger, but they will only last for hours, then maybe a day or two.

98 As you become stronger in the ability to use the Celestine Light, your nets will also become stronger and will last for several days, which will be long enough to guard most portals until they close.

99 If you practiced and focused enough, in time you could put a net across the portal that would keep out creatures from the other world for many years. But your time on earth is limited, and I hope you will invest it in greater things than the long-term netting of portals. And in no case should you net a portal for more than twelve moons.

100 You protect the people of your earth by your efforts, casting nets when those efforts are necessary, and by so doing, you gain knowledge, wisdom, and ability to use the gifts you have been given. But value your time in a physical body as a precious gift and invest it wisely for the greatest good.

101 Thus have Adepts among the Children of Light been called upon since the days of Adam and will continue to be until the end of days. When the Adepts are few, the angels of Elohim become the temporary stewards of the portals. But it is a calling truly given for Adepts of the Celestine Light, still progressing through mortality.

102 By calling upon all higher Adepts to place nets over the portals when necessary, the Adepts are given an important opportunity to grow in their gifts and demonstrate their good stewardship.

103 By most often leaving the gateways open for the denizens of these worlds to pass through if they choose, the principle of freewill is maintained, and it is upon this principle that repentance and eternal progression are founded.

104 Because of Adepts and angels throughout time, the actual incidences of maim and death that have come across the gateways into your world have always been very slight.

105 When death or maim does occur, the lives lost will be given again in a new birth upon

this earth that they may fulfill the full measure of their creation.

106 Thus, Elohim has hindered the eternal progression of none and kept open the door to eternal progression for all."

107 As they continued to walk, Toma posed a question to Yeshua, saying, "I understand how some of the creatures of these worlds were drawn here by their loss of Celestine Light from the day of the rebellion in the Celestine Realms. But why did they become such low and fearsome creatures? Why did they not remain as men in appearance, just cast away to inhospitable worlds as punishment?"

108 Yeshua answered, saying, "Men and women are created in the image of Elohim the Father and Elohim the Mother. A certain level of Celestine Light must abide within one's soul essence to enable them to maintain a physical form after the image of our Heavenly Mother and Father.

109 In their rebellion against the very order of eternal progression given by Elohim the Father and Elohim the Mother before time began, those so misguided lost a very great quantity of Celestine Light from their soul essence, a punishment they enacted upon themselves by their actions. So great was their loss that they became much less than they were, only that which their feeble light could manifest, even creatures such as these."

110 Further along their journey, they came upon another good-size natural cistern of water within a rock shaded by a cliff ringed by some short, sweet-smelling, flowering trees.

111 The water was clear and had a freshness about it, enticing the Apostles who had become parched in the blistering hot sun to go to it to drink. Shim'on the Zealot was the first to kneel down beside the pool. He dipped his hands into the water, pushing aside a small amount of bright green algae that was near the surface to reach into the cool water beneath to drink. Philip and Yohhanan also knelt down similarly and prepared to drink from the pool.

112 As Shim'on brought his cupped hands full of water toward his mouth, a large amount of the green algae still clung to his hands. In disgust, he shook it off as did Yohhanan and Philip, who were encountering the same difficulty as they tried to drink.

113 Dipping his cupped hands again into the pool, Shim'on brought them once more toward his mouth but found his lower arms entangled in a still-larger mass of the stringy algae. "This is ridiculous!" he exclaimed. "Not only is it unbearably hot on this world, but you have to work far too strenuously to get a simple drink of water."

114 "How deep is the pool?" asked Yakov, who was standing behind those kneeling at the water's edge. "Perhaps, after drinking, we can all jump in and cool ourselves."

115 "That is disgusting," Salome retorted. "If we bathe in pools from which we drink, they will no longer be fit to drink."

116 "I do not think we will be able to drink or bathe in this one," Philip said dejectedly pointing at the pool's surface. "Look at all the algae that has risen. It covers the pool now, and it is no longer so inviting."

117 Before he could say more, there was an explosion of water, and the three men at the pool were suddenly showered and covered with thick, green algae so much so that it knocked them all into the pool as they had been bending over precariously, trying to dip a drink with their hands.

118 At first, the three Apostles in the pool were laughing at their misfortune, but soon their laughter subsided as they struggled to pull themselves out of the water and back onto the rock.

119 "Come, give us a hand," Yohhanan called to his brethren. "This algae is heavy as mud, and it is more than we can do to lift ourselves out of the water as we are covered in it."

120 The other Apostles went to the edge of the pool, and reaching out to grasp the hands of their brethren, they pulled with all their might but could not extract them from the pool.

121 The heads of the three men in the water began to go under as they struggled to stay afloat. "I think you better hurry and help us," Philip bade his friends. "There is no bottom upon which we can stand and the algae is entangled in our arms and legs and its weight is pulling us under."

122 "Use your gifts," Yeshua implored the men in the pool.

123 "What gifts?" Philip asked.

124 "Whichever you choose to use from among the many that have been given to you," Yeshua answered simply.

125 The three men in the water did as Yeshua bade, and each commenced actions which they thought would help. Shim'on called out to Elohim for help. Philip formed an incantation, commanding the water and algae to free him. Yohhanan thrashed around violently, trying to rip the algae off his body with his strength and escape from the water.

126 But their efforts were to no avail, nor were their friends able to pull them free, and in moments of one another, they disappeared beneath the surface of the water and did not come up again.

127 Miriam let out a big sigh of exasperation and taking a few steps to the water's edge, she waved her hand over the surface and within seconds all three men popped up to the surface gasping for breath, and their friends were able to pull them free of the pool for the algae was no longer upon them.

128 After a few minutes when the Apostles that had almost drowned had recovered their breath, they thanked Miriam, for they had been told by the others that she had freed them, and then they asked Yeshua why they had been unable to free themselves.

129 "The reason is different for each of you," Yeshua explained. "Yohhanan tried to use brute strength, but as strong as he is, his strength alone could not free him. Shim'on called out to Elohim for help, but Elohim helps not those who can help themselves, save it serves the purposes of Elohim. Philip quickly said an incantation, which would have succeeded if he had practiced it previously and had been able to say it well, with confidence and faith."

130 "I never doubted all would be well," Philip assured everyone, and Shim'on and Yohhanan nodded in agreement. "But I am most curious about that algae. It seemed almost as if it were making a purposeful effort to drown us."

131 "It was," Yeshua stated to everyone's surprise. "Remember I told you that everything on this world lives by killing something else, but that some are more subtle about it? That algae is called Rhall, and it is not an algae at all, but an animal that lives by catching hapless victims like you just seeking a drink of cool water.

132 You would do well to remember the Rhall, for there are many harmful people and situations on your earth that like the Rhall seduce unwary victims with facades of normalcy or enticements of seemingly harmless pleasure. Like with the Rhall, those who succumb do not realize the danger until it is too late to extract themselves.

133 When you return to your earth to lead the Children of Light and seek out the others in the world, tell them the story of this day and your encounter with the Rhall, asking them to be ever vigilant for the Rhall that exist on your earth. Though the appearance may differ, the allure of seduction and end of destruction are the same."

134 "I have a further question," Shim'on ventured. And Yeshua bade him to ask.

135 "I called upon Elohim for deliverance from my predicament, but I was not saved from the Rhall. I understand that the Elohim wish us to grow and expand by learning from our experiences, both the good and the bad. Therefore, though we may call upon them for help, it will not necessarily be forthcoming if it would be more beneficial for our growth to solve the problem completely on our own. The exception being when helping us also serves the purpose of the Elohim.

136 Now you have called me to be an Apostle to spread your true light, to find and teach the Children of Light, and to be a good steward over the portals between worlds and negative vortexes. Many more things you have asked of me and your other Apostles, which we happily give all of our days to fulfill with no earthly reward, in fact, at a substantial cost of lost income and precious time with our families.

137 This being so, that I have sacrificed much and dedicated my life to the service of Elohim, how could it be that they would not intercede to save me? Would not saving me so that my life did not end in that pool before I have had a chance to fulfill the fullness of my calling certainly

qualify as contributing to the desires and goals of the Elohim?"

138 "Yes, it does," Yeshua assured Shim'on. "But even as it is beyond your comprehension today to fully understand the intricacies of time, even more beyond your understanding is the fullness of the Elohim.

139 But know this: Though the moments of your life are not predestined, they are known to the Elohim before they occur. Again, this is not because of predestination, but because of time. Even as the seven Kingdoms exist in the same space, but at different times, so the Elohim are in the past, the present, and the future. Not that they were in the past and are in the present and will be in the future, but that they are in all three times even now as we speak, even in the future that is yet to be.

140 Nor is the future yet to be, already written, and multiple are the ways the events may unfold. In your case, Shim'on, of course our Heavenly Father and Mother desire you to live and fulfill your calling. They knew that in every possible future, you would survive your encounter in this pool with the Rhall without their intervention. Therefore, they did not intervene.

141 In the two most likely futures, you would either save yourself or be saved by Miriam, and so it came to pass. Now the question is what have you learned from this experience?"

142 Shim'on looked at Yeshua with great sincerity in his eyes and said, "I have come to understand that I had better learn to use my gifts because Miriam will not always be around to help me."

143 At his words, everyone burst out in laughter, even Yeshua, but he then admonished Shim'on, saying, "Yes, you better master your gifts, Shim'on." And turning to the others, he added, "As should you all; else, the day will come when one or more of you shall perish unnecessarily. I hope it does not take such a tragedy to motivate you to take the time and effort to become the Master Adepts you have been called to be."

144 Though they had been laughing moments before, Yeshua's words were very sobering, for the Apostles had not considered that there could be circumstances where they would be allowed to die before they had completed all they were upon earth to do and that even in this, the grander purposes of Elohim would be being fulfilled.

145 They camped for the night, and everyone was rather quiet and contemplative before they retired for sleep.

146 The following day, Yeshua continued to lead them on a tour of the shadow world and the creatures upon it. Though they encountered many strange beasts and flora such as they had never imagined in brilliant hues of purple, orange, and red, they had no more encounters with dangerous animals.

147 On their third day, Yeshua told them they would soon be returning to their earth. No sooner had he spoken than they spied a group of six very hairy manlike creatures, each carrying a heavy club and moving rapidly in their direction. "What shall we do about these?" Cephas wondered aloud.

148 "Merely remain still and observe them as they approach us," Yeshua admonished.

149 As the manlike creatures came ever closer, Mattayah whispered, "Are they blind? They act as if they don't even see us, yet I can already smell them, an awful stench like rotting carcasses."

150 "They cannot see us," Yeshua revealed. "I have lifted us to a higher resonance for the moment to avoid potential conflicts. Just watch and listen."

151 As the manlike creatures came upon Yeshua and his group, they stepped aside so the creatures could pass by. In passing, they almost brushed the Apostles who along with the women were all holding their noses and breaths, trying to avoid breathing the foul odor that wafted from the creatures.

152 Suddenly, as a group, the six creatures all stopped and began to sniff the air. They began to speak rapidly to one another and look around in all directions. But their words were completely unintelligible, sounding only like gibberish.

153 "Oh, I cannot take the smell! Salome exclaimed. "Rather than remain with them standing

next to us, let us move upwind quickly, lest we succumb to the odor and faint."

154 Everyone murmured in agreement, but the manlike creatures had heard her voice and now they were frantically searching for the source of both the sound and the scent they had evidently also perceived.

155 Then the air was split by a terrifying, high-pitched scream of an animal, and in a blur, the manlike creatures disappeared in frenzied fright around a large boulder some distance away.

156 When after a few minutes they did not reappear, nor did the animal come upon them that had rent the air with its primordial call, the Apostles and the women let out a collective sigh of relief and turned to Yeshua for answers.

157 Seeing the looks of shock on their faces, Yeshua could not help but laugh, saying, "I told you they could not see us, why did you fear?"

158 Perhaps, it was because they could hear us and smell us and looked for us and carried big clubs," ventured Amram.

159 "Or perhaps," stuttered Philip, "it was because as scary as those creatures were, they were gravely alarmed by the scream of a still more frightening beast that we could not see. And if hearing it motivated them into instant flight, we had to worry at least a little about ourselves and perhaps should still be worrying, for we know not yet where this monster lurks."

160 "If I may add," Cephas interjected, "I should like to know why, if they could not see us, they could still hear and smell us?"

161 "Very well," Yeshua responded. "I shall answer your questions. First, you should know that there is no other more fearsome creature near us. I made the sound of the large beast that hunts the man-creatures and projected it with my aura to frighten them away before they had any type of encounter with us.

162 As for their perceptions of our presence, the sense of sight is a most complicated part of the physical body and requires many physical aspects to be working well for someone to actually see out of their eyes. It is easy to conceal your presence from someone's sight merely by slightly altering your resonance, which removes some of the accustomed clues to your presence.

163 But the senses of hearing and smell are far more simple. They require less abilities of the physical body to perceive and are therefore more difficult to conceal by the small resonance change we did.

164 Even on your earth, when creatures from the shadow worlds enter, they will often be heard and smelled, but not seen. Their resonance is different enough that the lower senses can perceive them, but not the higher more complex.

165 This is why it is so important for you to become sensitive to what you feel with your aura because with this, you can sense far more energies than your eyes can see or your ears can hear or your nose can smell or your mouth can taste or your skin can feel.

166 In time, with experience, you will be able to identify nearly everything, both from your world and others, merely by how its aura feels as it comes in contact with yours.

167 Truly, your aura is the sum of your being. It embodies every iota of your body and every iota of your spirit. It is connected to all existence from the most inconsequential bug to the essence of the Celestine Light of Elohim.

168 A worthy pursuit of all Children of Light is to know yourself so fully that your aura is your best friend, for in this, you will be in harmony with all creation. Then to strive to be so perfected in your body, mind, and spirit that you can be in resonance with all things as you desire, even as are the Elohim.

169 In this life, you will never achieve that level of perfection, but by striving for it, with focus and faith, but without fanaticism, you will still gain more than you can imagine, and amazing will be the wonders that shall be yours. You will truly be in the world but not of it."

170 Yeshua, Miriam, Salome, and the Apostles remained upon the shadow earth for two more days, encountering more strange and peculiar creatures and being taught the intricacies of the power of the aura by Yeshua.

171 But the teachings revealed by Yeshua, concerning the aura, cannot be written; else, the secrets might become known to the people of the world. The mysteries can only be revealed to the Children of Light as they are prepared to receive them.

172 The following day, after a good night's sleep on the shadow world, Yeshua asked Toma to open a portal back to Bethany for them, and following the instructions Yeshua had previously given them, Toma inscribed the Celestine symbol in the air and spoke the word of power and the gateway opened before them and they all passed through.

173 They appeared in the courtyard of the home of Lazarus, who encountered them a few minutes after they had arrived and exclaimed in astonishment, "Why have you returned so quickly? Have you changed your plans and decided to remain with us longer or did you forget something?"

174 Cephas looked at Lazarus quizzically as did the others, and he replied, "I understand not the meaning of your jest."

175 Now it was Lazarus who looked at Cephas perplexed. He said, "What do you mean, brother Cephas? I made no jest. I merely asked why you have returned so soon after you departed. I am happy you are here again. I was just surprised to see you come back so quickly."

176 Many of the Apostles looked at one another with complete bewilderment written upon their faces, and Mattayah spoke to Lazarus, saying, "Your words are confusing, brother. You speak as if we have been gone but hours, when we have been away for many days."

177 Now it was Lazarus whose face expressed surprise, and he replied, "Why do you say that? Have you eaten a noxious herb that has affected your minds? It was but a couple of hours ago that you departed."

178 Lazarus pointed to a servant at the basin outside of the courtyard and said, "Look there at Bibi. She was washing clothes in the basin when you left, and she is still tending to the same clothes as they dry on the line."

179 As it dawned upon the Apostles that something peculiar had occurred, they looked to Yeshua for answers, and perceiving their thoughts, he said unto them, "We have walked in the space between the spaces where time is not set by the sun that is in this sky.

180 For those Adepts who walk in the Kingdoms of different resonances, time is not at all, save that which they want it to be.

181 I have shown this unto you, and now it is given to you to teach the highest of the Adepts among the Children of Light how to be Timewalkers, even as you have become."

182 Turning to Lazarus, Yeshua put his hand upon his shoulder and said unto the Apostles, "Here is the first of your new students. Let he who has tasted death be the first from beyond the Apostles to truly learn and understand that life never ends, for time has neither a beginning nor an end, and death is just the passage to a new resonance in the timelessness and continuity of infinity and eternity."

CHAPTER 98

The Fifth Kingdom

Yeshua takes Miriam, Salome, the Apostles, and Lazarus to another strange world. This one is in Qaorroz, the Fifth Kingdom of resonance. Accompanied by Lazarus, they enter through a portal in the courtyard of the home of Miriam's parents. Once there, they have some interesting experiences with beings called Hebs, who are very different in appearance from an Alamar and very scientifically advanced.

eshua, Miriam, Salome, and the Apostles remained only a single night in Bethany, but it was a joyous time of reunion with Martha and the children who had all not expected to see everyone again so soon and Yeshua, not ever again in the flesh.

The Lanaka

2 That night, Yeshua asked everyone at the house to group into threes and to separate into different rooms or outside into different areas and share the Lanaka together.

3 When they were all finished, he asked them to now group together with six or seven in a group and do the Lanaka once more.

4 After they had all completed the Lanaka a second time, he asked everyone to group together in a Circle of Power in the central courtyard outside and share the Lanaka once again.

5 When they were finished, everyone quietly began to look at one another and acknowledged with soft-spoken words the humbling power of what they had just experienced.

6 And Yeshua said unto them, "With this, you have felt the outpouring of the spirit of Elohim that fills your being and radiates out from your aura with the Lanaka, some of you for the first time.

7 You have seen how when more Children of Light are added to the circle the strength you feel is multiplied many times more than the numbers that have been added.

8 From the sacred Circles of Power, the essence of the Lanaka and many other wonderful blessings of the Celestine Light can be manifested.

9 I show this to you now that you will all remember this when I am no more among you in the flesh, both the adults and the children. Remember then to share the Lanaka often among yourselves, whenever two or more Children of Light are gathered together with love and one intent."

Lazarus Seeks Permission to Accompany

10 The following morning, everyone rose at first light before the sun came above the horizon. After breakfast, Yeshua asked his wives and Apostles to gather inside the garden courtyard, for it

was surrounded by the house on one side and walls on the other three, giving it complete privacy from curious eyes.

11 Lazarus came out into the courtyard with them, and when Yeshua told everyone that they would depart for the Fifth Kingdom from this spot, Lazarus asked if he might go with them.

12 Yeshua put his hand upon the shoulder of Lazarus and smiled gently with love and said unto him, "Alas, my good brother Lazarus, it cannot be. Where we go, even my Apostles will scarcely be able to bear the strangeness, and they have seen and experienced many unusual things as they have traveled with me."

13 Lazarus's face was crestfallen, and he implored Yeshua to let him come with them, saying, "Surely if my sister and Salome can bear the shocks, then so can I, a man who has faced brigands on the Caravan trails and experienced a slow, painful death. What could be worse than death?"

14 And Miriam overhearing his words came over and putting her arm through Yeshua's said unto him, "My brother has been so faithful and true. Please grant him permission that he may come and see the wonders of the places to which you take us. Surely, no harm will come to him, for you will be there, and I will stay near to him."

15 Lazarus thanked his sister, but was piqued with some surprise and said, "I am grateful for your support, Miriam, but surely you will not need to be near to me for my sake. I am a man and can take care of myself, and you and Salome too, if needs be. If there will be danger, it is all the more reason I should accompany you. I will bring my sword."

16 All of the Apostles were standing near enough to hear the conversation, and there was laughter from several of them upon hearing the declaration of Lazarus. Cephas came up to him and said, "Your sister is not quite the sister you remember, dear brother. I think she will fear no place, nor man or beast, and I would happily have her with me anywhere I might go that I would fear. And best leave your sword here if you come. Wherever we are going, I am sure it would not be of much use."

17 Lazarus looked at Cephas perplexed and replied, "Yes, there can be no doubt Miriam is remarkable among women, but let us not forget she is still a woman, and it is we men whom Elohim has endowed with strength that we might be a protector of women and children. And for this, swords can be useful."

18 Amram spoke then to Lazarus, saying, "We have been humbled by all we have learned as we have accompanied Yeshua and Miriam, chief among the humbling being that beyond strength of arm or mind, there is something greater, and that something, Miriam has in abundance."

19 "What something? Lazarus asked with rising curiosity.

20 Yeshua smiled as he listened to the verbal exchanges, and his heart softened insomuch that he decided to allow Lazarus to come with them to the Fifth Kingdom. "Though you do not yet understand, you may accompany us, as long as you promise to remain by your sister's side, and this, I assure you, is for your protection, not hers. And leave your sword here, for where we go—Cephas is correct—it will not help you."

21 Lazarus gave a little laugh, and with a big smile, he replied, "Thank you, Yeshua. In deepest sincerity, this means so much to me. Although I think you and the brethren are still playing a little game with me and Miriam. But I will do as you ask and see what comes."

22 Yeshua smiled back at him, saying, "So you shall, brother. Let me know if you have any surprises." And Lazarus nodded to him affirmatively.

Yuda the Younger Opens the Portal

23 Yeshua then walked over to one of the high courtyard walls and asked for a volunteer to open a gateway there to the Fifth Kingdom. Yuda the Younger stepped forward and hesitantly raised his hand, saying, "Good Yeshua, if I may be so bold, might I attempt to open the portal?"

24 Yeshua smiled with happiness to see Yuda the Younger, who had some timidity, ask to open the gateway, and he said unto him, "That would be excellent, Yuda. And you will not be needing Miriam's crystal, will you?"

25 Yuda answered with some surprise and a smile of appreciation, "Oh, you have seen me as I have whittled my wand?"

26 "What my physical eyes see not, my spiritual eyes behold," Yeshua replied.

27 Then Yuda stepped toward the wall and pulled a straight wand of wood from his sleeve where he had made a pouch to hold it. But as he stepped toward the wall with his wand raised, he was intercepted by some of his brethren who grasped his arm that they could examine more closely the wand he had produced.

28 Philip in particular was very excited, and he asked Yuda if he could look closely at his wand before he used it.

29 Yuda nodded his head and handed his wand to Philip, and he noted the very fine workmanship that Yuda had wrought upon the wood. It was made of an exceedingly hard wood, yet nevertheless, had a deeply carved spiral groove going from its base to its tip. "When did you make this?" Philip inquired.

30 "Last night while everyone slept," Yuda answered. "I took the wood from a fallen piece of the peculiar flowering tree standing near the spring that wanted to eat you at the last Kingdom. It called to me in spirit. I carved a spiral into it last night by the light of the full moon, for Yeshua has said that a spiral enhances the flow of the powers of Celestine Light upon which we call."

31 "It is impressive," Philip commended him. Then handing the wand back to Yuda, he admonished, "Please, without delay, let us see the power of Celestine Light you can call forth and focus with such a tool."

32 Yuda smiled with almost childlike enthusiasm. After looking to Yeshua and getting a nod of approval, he went over to the wall, and using the tip of his wand, he drew the Celestine diagram to open the portal and uttered the Celestine word of power. Immediately, the shimmering, unearthly blue spiral light appeared, and the portal opened before them in the wall the height and breadth of a man. The wall became opaquely translucent at that spot, and though it could dimly be seen, there was a land that was far different than the land that was usually on the other side of the wall.

33 "Marvelous!" Yeshua exclaimed. "Well done, Yuda." Yuda beamed with Yeshua's compliment.

34 Yeshua, Miriam, and Salome then walked to the entry of the portal, and Lazarus came with them that he might remain by his sister's side as he had promised Yeshua.

35 Before passing through, Yeshua turned to the brethren and said unto them, "The world we now travel to is in the Fifth Kingdom. Upon this world are beings that are greater than you in all things, except the spiritual and the powers of Celestine Light that are your gifts. Do not be awed or cowed by the strangeness of these people or the grandeur of their cities, for compared to the glories of the Celestial Kingdom that await you, we travel to a city of bare branches and camel hair."

36 "It will be like a trip to Egypt," Lazarus exclaimed with anticipation in his voice; "hopefully without the flies, heat, and bandits."

37 "Much more than that, brother," Miriam replied; "and much quicker too."

The Power of Both Belief and Non-belief

38 Yeshua moved his arm forward with an open hand toward the portal, saying, "Lazarus, why don't you pass through first and we will all follow? Just step into the blue light."

39 Now that the opportunity he had so sought was before him, Lazarus hesitated, saying, "Stepping into the light, I will truly be taken to another land? I will not just be hitting my head against the hard wall to everyone's humor?"

40 "Perhaps, you will hit your head, Lazarus," Yeshua answered. "If that is what you expect. The gateway is open, and even those who have no faith in what lies on the other side can pass through, as long as they do not disbelieve. Yet disbelief or absence of faith can make it impassable.

41 If you believe nothing, then you affect nothing. But if you believe something, either in this gateway to another world beyond the blue light or not, your belief or lack of belief will manifest

unto you.

42 If you simply walk through the blue light without thinking there is a passageway behind it or fearing there is a wall, neither believing nor disbelieving, you will pass through with ease. It will be the same as one who has faith in the existence of the portal.

43 But if you doubt its existence or believe there is only a stone wall behind the blue light, then surely you will end up sitting on the ground with a headache from hitting the wall and look around to find all of us gone, for we will have passed through while you were rubbing your aching head."

44 Lazarus looked at Yeshua with devotion, saying, "You have told me there is a portal to a new land, beyond the blue light. Therefore, I have not faith, but a sure knowledge that it is so! Stand aside now, for here comes Lazarus!" And without looking back, he leaped in one bound into the spinning blue light and disappeared. All the others rapidly followed after him.

First Impressions of the Fifth Kingdom

45 "Amazing!" Lazarus exclaimed as he stepped out of the gateway into the Fifth Kingdom. "To take a single step, as simple as passing into another room . . . but it is not another room to which we have come . . . but another land . . . one such as I have never seen or imagined," he said in awe as he looked around at the strangely hued and shaped vegetation.

46 The Apostles soon followed and also stood looking all about at the astounding world upon which they had arrived.

47 "Look in the sky!" Yuda the Younger said incredulously, pointing upward. "There are two suns!"

48 "And look at that forest in the distance!" Shim'on said, pointing in wonder. "The trees rise to impossible heights. Even from as far away as we stand, those trees are surely ten times taller than any trees we have ever seen."

49 "Those are not trees," Yeshua interjected calmly. "Those are tall buildings in a city greater by far than Rome."

50 "Buildings?" queried Yudas Iscariot. "How can buildings possibly be so tall and thin and not fall down?"

51 "We must consider that it is possible," Cephas proffered. "We are looking at the city. And there are great trees, like the Cedar forests of Lebanon, that are tall and thin, and they do not fall down. Therefore, perhaps the men of this land can likewise make buildings of great height and thinness that somehow also do not fall down."

52 Yeshua spoke quickly after Cephas, saying, "Concerning the men of this world, you should be aware that there are no men here such as you. You have never seen their likeness. But they have seen Alamar-like creatures that look somewhat like you, and they are mortal enemies. Therefore, do not expect a warm greeting when they first come upon our party."

Apostles Left on Their Own to Call Forth Their Gifts

53 "Do you think they will attack us or merely be offended by our presence?" Philip wondered; "for we have no weapons to defend ourselves. You even told Lazarus not to bring his sword."

54 Yeshua turned and looked at Philip with some sadness, saying, "What need would you have of weapons, Philip, even if an army attacked? Have you not the authority of Elohim upon you? Have you not received gifts of Celestine Light that can see you through the greatest darkness and overcome the mightiest foe?"

55 "Yes, of course," Philip stammered. "We all have our gifts and our faith in Elohim. But in truth, it is not faith in Elohim I lack, but faith in myself and in the current usefulness of my gifts of Celestine Light, which I am only beginning to understand and have virtually no experience at using or even a sure knowledge of how to use them.

56 "It is as if a man who had never seen a sling is given one and told to defend himself as an enemy is preparing to charge him. Perhaps he will intuitively figure out how to use it, or perhaps he will wonder how a skinny piece of cloth and string could possibly be used for a weapon and

will be slain while he is trying to understand it.

57 I am ashamed to say that is how I feel about my gifts of Celestine Light. I am honored beyond measure to have been deemed worthy to receive them. But I am woefully unaware of how to use them."

58 Hearing his confession of ineptitude, most of the other Apostles spoke up in agreement, saying they too lacked faith in their capability to employ the sacred gifts they had been given.

59 "To master your gifts of Celestine Light and gain an unshakeable faith in yourself is why we have come to this particular world in the Fifth Kingdom today," Yeshua explained. "You will encounter people and their creations, such as you have never imagined. They will consider you an enemy and seek to have power over you. You will need to rely upon your gifts to save yourselves."

60 Yeshua pointed to a nearby hill. "Miriam and I shall move to that hill along with Lazarus to observe you, but we will not interfere to aid you overtly. However, we shall give you counsel in your minds as you receive the challenges of a civilization unlike any upon the earth you call home. As you move to different places, we will continue to move with you, staying back far enough to not be physically involved in your affairs."

61 "No, no, no; please no," Toma protested. "You cannot leave us alone to fend for ourselves against an enemy we know not, with no weapons save our gifts, which none of us have shown any significant ability to use.

62 We are like the ignorant man with the sling in the example Philip told. Please forgive me for so saying Yeshua, but it seems unreasonable to expect this much of us when we are still just infants in our abilities."

63 Yeshua answered, saying, "As I have said before, where much has been given, much is expected. You have received great gifts of Celestine Light that you may accomplish great things. When you have a light, you do not hide it under a basket, and you are the lights of the world.

64 Tomorrow is the day that the weak will become strong and the ignorant enlightened. But today is the day that the strong recognize their strength. Today is the day that you discover who you really are."

65 Cephas took a step forward, and holding his hands spread in front of him, he lifted them up and down, saying, "We have all been practicing, a little here and a little there with our gifts." Then he cupped his hands closely together with his palms up, saying, "But it is only this little bit that we have actually mastered.

66 I think I am further along than most, but even so, I would still prefer a sharp sword or a stout staff to defend myself against attackers until you have taught us more in the ways to call forth our gifts of Celestine Light with power and focused direction and we have had more time to practice using what knowledge we gain."

67 Yeshua smiled slightly as he answered Cephas, saying, "Swords may help you against brigands on your earth, but here, they would be as useless against your foes as throwing an ant at an armored Roman soldier. Only your gifts will save you."

68 Then looking around at all of them, he elaborated, saying, "There are some things that need to be taught, such as Celestine words of power that call in certain specific forces of the Celestine Light, but these things you have already learned in our days together.

69 What remains is simply the need for total faith in Elohim, in yourself, and in the gifts that you know you have; that and a love for your brethren and a passion to succeed using your gifts. Remember, even if they have yet to be seen, I have told you that you have these gifts; therefore, you know that it is so.

70 You have heard me teach often that with faith, nothing is impossible to you. If you believe in me, you must also believe in yourselves; else, you deny your belief in me.

71 Now, before the first citizens of this world come upon you, prepare yourselves. Find a stick of wood that you can quickly fashion into a wand to more surely focus your gifts or dedicate a rock crystal or a spiral shell that you carry to serve the same purpose, if you have not already done so.

72 Give thanks for your callings and offer a prayer to Elohim to be able to call forth your gifts.
73 When the time comes upon you to resist the people of this world, remember that all life is precious, for everyone is on a path of eternal progression, and it is wrong to end someone's progression in the physical life unless there is no other way to save your own or that of your friends. And with your gifts of Celestine Light, there will always be another way if you are calling upon them in their fullness.

74 And how is it that you should call upon them? Do now as I say: Focus your energy this moment into your core. Pull in your aura and concentrate it near your Ja. Feel it inside of you. Swirl it around faster and faster and feel it swirling inside of you.

75 Use your Ka to direct your auric energy to swirl here and there, within you.

76 Command yourself to feel it, swirling through your abdomen, then down your arms, and shooting out your fingertips, then swirling again in your abdomen, then shooting out of your eyes, then your feet.

77 Call upon Elohim and the energies of Celestine Light, which permeates all things, to come into you and strengthen you and augment and increase the power of your own aura so much so that your body lightens and feels as if it is beginning to float off the ground. And so it can if you call forth your gifts in fullness."

78 The Apostles did as Yeshua bade, each in their own way: some with eyes closed, some with eyes open, some standing, some on their knees, praying, some looking upward into the heavens, as they called upon the powers of Elohim to imbue them.

79 While they were thus engaged, Yeshua, Miriam, and Lazarus began to walk away toward the nearby hill where Yeshua had said they would go. Salome had not been doing any of the things Yeshua had directed, and seeing Miriam departing, she called out to her and ran up to be with her, saying, "Why do you leave me here alone with the men?"

80 Miriam embraced her with great affection and, kissing her forehead softly, said unto her, "It is also your destiny, dearest flower, to blossom into your fullest splendor. This place is a garden in which you will come forth in your glory."

81 "But I am not an Apostle," Salome protested. "I have not been given the multitude of special gifts they have because of their calling. What shall become of me?"

82 Miriam took a step back, still holding onto each of Salome's hands. She smiled at her lovingly and said, "The men need their special callings as Apostles to more easily bring forth their gifts, but you need no such calling, for you are a virtuous woman who loves and is loved, whose eye is single to the light of Elohim. Therefore, the Celestine Light is one with you, in ways the men can scarcely comprehend, for they know not the Celestine love that you know.

83 You are a daughter of God who knows who you are, and all the powers of the Celestine Light in all the heavens upon the numberless worlds of creation are waiting to come to you as you call upon them.

84 The men will struggle. They will succeed, but it will be a great effort for many of them. But for you, dearest Salome, to call forth any gift of Elohim that is given for mortal men and women to have is as easy as breathing. Whatsoever you can conceive, you can manifest, even if you do not yet know the structure, as long as you keep love at your core and fear not."

85 A wide smile of happiness spread across Salome's face, and she stepped forward and lightly kissed Miriam on the lips and gazed for a moment with deep love into her eyes, saying, "Thank you, my precious Miriam." Then she turned and ran back toward the men and, looking into the heavens, began to call upon the powers of God.

86 After about ten minutes, everyone seemed to walk with a more upright stance and confidence as they had been filled by the Celestine Light of Elohim, which they had sought.

87 They spread out a little then as some sought sticks, which they could fashion into wands. Salome and some of the others brought out rock crystals or spiral shells, which they had been carrying in their garments, most no larger than the length of a hand and some barely as long as a finger.

88 Each person performed a quick bonding ritual with their wands of wood or crystal or shell, and then Yeshua spoke to them in their minds, saying, "Begin to now explore this world. As you walk, continue to call in more Celestine Light from the heavens. Continue to keep your aura very close to you and feel your own energy swirling inside of you."

89 Yeshua, Miriam, and Lazarus walked up on a sloping ridge of short, red grass that stretched out a great distance, forming the side of a narrow valley, and followed the Apostles and Salome at a distance as they walked about in the valley below.

Attack of the Silver Orbs

90 After about an hour, Cephas, who was leading the Apostles, pointed into the sky toward the city, saying, "Look! Rapidly approaching are some type of birds."

91 They all looked at the sky toward the city and saw the seven small dots grow larger as they approached, until they could discern that they were not birds, but small spheres about four times the size of a man's head. Nothing protruded from them, and they were entirely made of a brilliant, silvery substance, which reflected the light of the two suns in bright glares.

92 The seven orbs were quickly upon them, encircling them, in complete silence. Two suddenly broke away and zoomed over to hover above Yeshua, Miriam, and Lazarus.

93 The Apostles gazed at the silver orbs in awe. Mattayah blinked his eyes and held both hands to his face in bewilderment, asking, "How are they staying up in the air without wings?"

94 The other Apostles looked equally perplexed, and all began to utter similar questions among themselves. Some looked back toward the hill where Yeshua, Miriam, and Lazarus were standing in the distance, but they received no sign from them.

95 Suddenly, all of the Apostles, Salome, and Lazarus, standing beside Yeshua and Miriam, became rigidly straight, with their arms flattened against their sides. The Apostles and Salome then turned and faced the city and began to walk and totter with what seemed to be great reluctance toward it.

96 Lazarus, however, seemed not at all reluctant, and immediately after standing rigidly and facing the city, he sauntered down the slope off the ridge and began walking in easy steps toward it.

97 Only Yeshua and Miriam seemed unaffected, and the Apostles and Salome were crying out to them in their minds: "Help us! Help us, Lord of Light!"

98 "Our bodies are not our own," Cephas called out to Yeshua in his mind. "We are possessed of demons and are being compelled against our will. Help us!"

99 Miriam heard the voice of Salome calling to her in her mind and pleading, "Miriam, please help me! My body moves even though I command it to stay. I try to resist, and there is terrible pain through all of my body. It is unbearable! Please help me!"

100 Hearing Salome in agony, Miriam looked to Yeshua, but knowing her thoughts to rescue Salome, he shook his head and said unto her in her mind, "We must love them enough to let them fight their own fight and find themselves and their own power."

101 "But this is so strange to them, my Lord," Miriam spoke aloud to him. "Their senses and their minds are overwhelmed so much so they cannot even line up their thoughts to consider how to use their gifts to resist. Most of them are so confused they cannot even speak to us in their minds."

102 Yeshua nodded in agreement and answered, "Nevertheless, we must give them time to discover themselves. They will be in pain, but will not be killed, even if they resist."

103 He then pointed to Lazarus walking away and said, "But see to the safety of your brother, for he has not been given the gifts of the Apostles and goes happily as a lamb to the slaughter without understanding the consequences or means to prevent them."

104 Miriam nodded her head in agreement and forcefully thrust each hand skyward with fingers splayed, each pointing toward one of the orbs hovering over them. She closed her eyes and uttered a single Celestine word of power, and immediately both orbs dropped to the ground

with clanging metallic thunks and rolled down the slope to come to rest at its base.

105 Lazarus immediately stopped walking and stood shaking his head for a few moments and turned to look back up at Yeshua and Miriam atop the ridge and then looked at the group of Apostles to his right who seemed to be walking with great stiffness toward the city.

106 Turning once more toward Yeshua and Miriam, he saw her beckoning for him to return to the ridge, and he complied and walked toward the slope.

107 As he came upon one of the fallen orbs lying on the ground, he reached out and touched it with his finger. Immediately, he let out a loud shriek and fell to the ground as if dead and did not move again.

108 Seeing this, Miriam ran down the slope to him, and kneeling down, she reached with her left hand and cupped his head raising it slightly off the ground. Then she put the palm of her right hand upon his forehead and within a few seconds, his eyes opened and he looked at her groggily and said. "Have I died and been resurrected again?" he asked innocently.

109 "Nearly," Miriam replied. "Now come back to the height with us and do not touch any more things of this world that you know not."

110 Lazarus stood up feebly as Miriam took his hand, helping him, and assured her, "That is sage advice, my sister. Be certain that I shall follow it henceforth."

111 Upon arriving atop the ridge, Lazarus looked back in confusion at the Apostles and Salome. Some of them were walking stiffly toward the city but seemed to be resisting their own body and trying not to walk. Yudas Iscariot was prone on his belly, being dragged backward toward the city by some unseen force while clawing madly at the ground trying to hold himself in place. Then Yohhanan was also facedown on the ground, being pulled by an invisible force toward the city, then Amram, and then in quick succession Shim'on, Mattayah, and Yuda.

112 Salome was standing with her fists clenched while her clothing was nearly being pulled off her body by what seemed to be a great wind. Yet there was no sound or other visible sign of wind; nor did any of the Apostles seem to be affected by a similar phenomenon.

113 Cephas and Philip were both yelling at the orbs in the sky, but they did not respond to them.

114 "What is happening?" Lazarus asked Yeshua and Miriam with some fear tinged in his voice. But Miriam shushed him, saying, "Please do not speak as we must concentrate so we can talk with our brethren in their minds as they fight with the orbs."

115 Ignoring her, Lazarus spoke anyway, saying, "Fight with the orbs? What do you mean? The orbs are not fighting with them; they are just sitting there peacefully in the sky."

116 Rather than answer him, without looking back or taking her eyes off the Apostles and Salome, Miriam cast her hand back toward Lazarus, opening her fingers wide. Immediately, he was struck dumb. Nor could he move his feet from the ground where he was standing.

117 He called out in protest to Miriam in his mind, as he knew that she and Yeshua communicated that way between themselves and the Apostles, but she did not answer him.

118 The Apostles meanwhile were obviously fighting mightily against some unseen physical force apparently emanating from the orbs, according to the words of Miriam.

119 Among the Apostles, there was a great deal of chaos in their actions: Some were praying, some were trying to cast spells, some with their words, and others with the aid of their wands or crystals, but in every case to no avail, as they all were losing ground and being pulled against their will toward the city.

120 "We must unite!" Salome yelled loudly above the din.

121 "She is right!" Cephas shouted above the chaotic sounds of struggle, hoping the others could hear. "Alone, we are losing this battle!"

122 "But how?" Philip, who was standing nearby, yelled. "We are all doing different things, fighting different orbs. I'm not even sure many of the others can hear you as they have been dragged too far away already."

123 Then Cephas heard Yeshua speaking in his mind, saying, "Speak to them with your

thoughts. They all can hear you, no matter how far they may be from you. You can do it, Cephas."

124 And Miriam spoke to Salome in her mind, saying, "You are stronger than the men Salome in the power of the Celestine Light. Go now to Cephas. Ignore the pain and will yourself to do it. Touch his gateways and with love give of your essence to him to strengthen him. Give freely, as much as he needs. Do it now."

125 Hearing the words of Miriam, Salome turned with eyes fiercely intent upon Cephas standing about five paces away and, with steely resolve, resisted the force pulling her toward the city and began to walk toward him, her face a grimace of pain as she fought to pull away from the nerve-wrenching compulsion.

126 "Salome is coming to you," Yeshua told Cephas in his mind. "She will touch you and impart her soul essence to you. Share her strength and reach out then in your mind and command your brethren, as I know you can, to be one, for when you are one, there is nothing that can stand against you."

127 Salome's last steps to Cephas were a mighty struggle, like trying to walk through thick mud while being pricked by a thousand dagger points. Seeing her great effort to reach him, Cephas willed himself to take a step toward her. She stretched out to reach him and fell to her knees, but grasped his hands in hers, intertwining their fingers as she fell, uniting their Alpha/Omega gateways.

128 Immediately, Cephas' countenance changed as Salome's soul essence poured into him, empowering him beyond his own capabilities.

129 Imbued with her essence, he called out to his brethren with confidence, speaking to them in their minds as one, saying, "Each of you, ignore all the other orbs, no matter how great the pain or what is happening to you. Look at the orb closest to me, almost over the head of Philip. In whatever way you can, focus on this orb and command it to be cast dead upon the ground."

130 Barely had the words left the mind of Cephas and entered the minds of the others than they did as he bid. Turning from their private struggles with the various orbs, they all looked at the orb nearest Cephas, and using their various gifts, and each in a different manner, they focused and called upon the powers within themselves and the powers of Elohim through the Celestine Light. As one, they commanded the orb to fall to the ground dead, and so it did, almost hitting Philip as it fell.

131 Salome still held fast to Cephas as he clasped her hands in his, but now she stood facing him, and Cephas commanded his brethren once again, saying, "Now the same to the next nearest orb, that is, near Mattayah." Once again the Apostles turned to focus on the orb Cephas has singled out, and once again in seconds it fell to the ground dead.

132 And so they continued one orb after another until all of them had fallen to the ground and moved no more, and only then was their pain and compulsion gone.

133 Still holding her hands intertwined in his, Cephas looked at Salome and, with great gratitude, said, "Thank you sister. I know you gave that which is most precious, and I and all my brethren are most grateful."

134 Salome smiled weakly at him and sighed deeply; "For a good cause, brother. And I know that which I gave shall come again, even more so, because I gave with unselfishness and love for you, my brethren."

135 Cephas smiled at her and nodded warmly. Then turning to the scattered Apostles, he called them to him, even as Yeshua, Miriam, and Lazarus began to make their way down the ridge to also be with them.

Taking Life Unnecessarily

136 When everyone had gathered together, Yeshua commended them for their efforts, saying, "Well done, my good friends and brothers. Here you faced a challenge unlike anything on your world, beyond your imaginations to conceive, and uniting together, you were still able to overcome the great unknown. Remember the lesson from this encounter well, for you will have

more opportunities in the years ahead to employ its principles."

137 "But what is it we did?" asked Toma. "We commanded things, we know not, to die, without even knowing how it is that such things perish."

138 "In that, you did both good and bad," Yeshua replied. "The good is that using your faith, you were able to affect something with your gifts that you had absolutely no comprehension of. Despite your ignorance of the orb and what its strengths and weaknesses might be, nevertheless, your will was accomplished upon it.

139 But you erred in willing it to perish. For in your lack of knowledge of this world, you may have been killing one of the beings that reside here.

140 The orbs caused you great pain. They compelled you against your will. But never did they give an indication that they intended to kill you or even maim you. Therefore, in your defense, you overreacted. Using your gifts of Celestine Light, you called upon the orbs to die, and so it seems they did. But you must consider that these orbs may be the life of this earth in this Kingdom."

141 "Seriously?" asked Yeshua's brother Yakov. "You are implying that these shiny balls could be some form of life, like an animal?"

142 "Because you do not know what they are, that possibility cannot be discounted," Yeshua responded. "If they are not life, then what do you think they are, Yakov? Or any of you?" he inquired.

143 Considering Yeshua's question, the other Ya'akov reached forth to touch the nearest orb in curiosity, but Lazarus quickly grabbed his arm and pulled him back, saying, "Do not touch it, Ya'akov. I did so earlier, and I assure you that you will not enjoy the experience."

144 Yeshua turned to Miriam and directed her, saying, "Please put each of the orbs to sleep that the brethren may touch them without pain."

145 Miriam then went forth and quickly touched each of the orbs, then returned to Yeshua's side.

The Hebs and the Broz

146 Yeshua again addressed the Apostles, saying, "You may now freely touch the orbs. They will not harm you as they did Lazarus when he touched one on the ground. I will tell you that they are not life, but creations of the people who live here. But be gentle with them, for they contain a surprise within that must not be damaged."

147 "A surprise?" mused Amram. "Perhaps some food, for I am hungry after all of this unfamiliar Xe and Ka exertion."

148 "We shall see," Yeshua replied pointing toward the orb lying on the ground nearest Amram. "Let us open one that you may discover its contents."

149 Amram went over and hefted the orb, saying, "It is very light. I do not think there is any food inside of it."

150 He shook it gently, observing, "I do not hear anything rattling around inside. Nor can I see any way to get into it other than punching a hole with something sharp, for there are no seams."

151 He knocked on it with his knuckles producing a faint empty echo. "I think it is hollow, but we will have to make a hole in it to see inside."

152 "I think not," Yeshua responded. "There is a way in, but Miriam will need to open it. Surely, each of you could accomplish it, but until you see her do it, you would spend too long of a time trying to fathom it and we have much still to do."

153 Hearing Yeshua's words, Miriam went over to the orb next to Amram. She placed a hand on opposite sides of the orb, then said the Celestine word of power, "Ezavant," and immediately a seam appeared around the circumference of the orb and one half of it slid back inside the other half, revealing a small unmoving figure, dressed in resplendent clothing and accouterments, reclining on its back in a tiny chair.

154 "What in the world is that?" Mattayah exclaimed, hitting his face lightly with his hand.

155 “Is it some type of animal?” wondered Toma.

156 “Not an animal,” Cephas declared. “It is some type of thing like one of us, except, very small.”

157 “It is not at all like us,” Yakov refuted. “Look at the proportions. Besides being no bigger than two rats end to end, its head is disproportionately too large for its very, very long and slender body. The girth of our bodies is much bigger than the girth of our heads, where its head is greater in girth than its body. And it has almost no neck. It has no hair whatsoever, and it is entirely green. Have you ever seen a green person?”

158 Philip stuck his head quite close so he could see the creature more clearly. “I think it has three eyes as well,” he announced. “I cannot be sure, for the slits are tiny like the creature. Nor do I see a mouth or ears of any type. No, other than two arms, five—excuse me—six fingers, and two legs, this creature does not resemble anything close to a human.”

159 Salome put her hand on Yeshua’s arm, asking, “Are there creatures like this inside all of the orbs?”

160 “Yes,” Yeshua answered. “The orbs are merely the ships. These beings are the masters.”

161 “Ships that fly, mastered by peculiar creatures the size of rats, without mouths or ears? This is certainly the strangest of worlds,” mumbled Yohhanan. “I wonder how it is that they eat or speak” he muttered to himself.

162 While everyone else spent several minutes gathered around the orb, looking at the creature within, Miriam went quietly to all of the other orbs and opened them up. Gently extracting the small limp pilots, she returned to the group, cradling all of them in her arms. She laid them down gently in the soft burgundy grass beneath her feet and took out the pilot from the orb the others had been observing and laid it alongside those on the grass.

163 Yeshua gestured toward the unmoving pilots laid out on the grass, saying, “Now you see the wrong that might have been done. In your efforts to extract yourself from the grip of the orbs, which as far as you knew might themselves have been alive, you certainly killed the pilots, by your commands for the orbs to die.

164 As I have taught you, it is permissible to take a life, if there is no other way to save your own or protect your family. But there was nothing to indicate that the orbs were trying to kill you, only compel you. Therefore, the force you meted out was in excess of what should have been and the consequences unfortunate and, in other circumstances, forgivable only after a long and fruitful repentance.”

165 Hearing this, the Apostles wailed in grief, some holding their hands over their face in shame. And Cephas spoke for all of them, stammering, “Forgive us, Lord of Light . . . we did not think that the orbs could be life or that there could be life within them . . . and I was the one who directed my brethren into sin, so let the consequences fall only upon me.”

166 Philip raised his arm slightly to draw attention and added meekly, “Even if we had imagined such possibilities, we were blessed simply to see our gifts of the Celestine Light called forth with focus successfully. But to have more control of the power, to be able to say, ‘This much to disable, but not so much as to kill,’ is beyond our understanding and abilities at this time. Please forgive us and tell us how we might make amends and create a worthy repentance.”

167 Yeshua answered, saying, “Learn from your mistakes. Practice more and learn to control the power of your gifts that you have discovered this day. Covenant to use them only for the light and only in ways that honor and respect all life and all will be well, for the error that was done this day can still be undone.

168 This world is called Ferrtho, by these beings, which are Hebs. They are one of three different types of very intelligent beings that inhabit this world in the Fifth Kingdom, which is only one of countless worlds in the vastness of the Kingdom filled with innumerable creatures, greater than the sands of the sea.

169 Though the Hebs are very small in relation to you, they are so far advanced in their civilization and knowledge of science that you would seem barely above the animals to them.

170 In fact, there also lives upon this world another intelligent life that the Hebs do consider animals. They are similar in appearance to you, but the males are covered in thick body hair, and both the males and females are shorter of stature and more squat. They call themselves Broz, and they are similar to those that lived upon your earth many thousands of years ago.

171 They are still in the age of stone, whereas the Hebs fly in the sky in orbs without wings and build great cities whose towers reach far into the sky and many other marvels that would be incomprehensible to you.

172 As I said when we first arrived, these two species are mortal enemies. The Broz, being so much larger than the Hebs, try and sometimes succeed at overrunning outlying parts of Heb cities.

173 The Hebs would prefer to just be left alone, but are vigilant in defense, even to the point of sending hunting parties out to seek out and engage the Broz.

174 They thought you were Broz. If they had captured you, they would not have killed you. They simply destroy the reproductive ability of any captured Broz, hoping to diminish their numbers and thus diminish the threat."

175 "Why?" wondered Amram. "What is the point of the Broz causing such trouble? Why attack a city of the Hebs? If they take it, it might be grand and reach into the sky, but the rooms would be far too small for the Broz to stick more than a hand into, and the civilization beyond their understanding to take advantage of, so why waste resources and probably lives, attacking a city from which nothing can be gained except stirring up the wrath of the Hebs to their own misfortune?"

176 "Sadly," Yeshua answered, "the Hebs are the favorite food of the Broz."

177 "The Broz eat the Hebs?" Salome exclaimed incredulously.

178 "Yes, Salome," Yeshua acknowledged; "The Broz eat the Hebs."

179 "But the Hebs do not kill the Broz?" Philip said in astonishment. "If they are continually attacked, it would seem that their castration tactic is insufficient to counter the threat."

180 "When their cities are attacked, they do kill the attackers when they can, and they are justified before Elohim, for they act in defense of themselves and their families," Yeshua answered. "But it is not such any easy task when the attackers are five times larger and attack in hordes with nets and clubs from many directions at once."

The Hebs Return to Life

181 Then Yeshua looked at the deceased Hebs lying on the ground side by side and turned to his Apostles and Salome, saying, "As it is you who killed the Hebs, it is only fitting that you should also restore their lives."

182 "But how?" wondered Shim'on. "I thought only you could bring the dead back to life."

183 "I will help you," Yeshua replied. "But you must give them your love from the depths of your Ja and bless them with a portion of your soul essence, even as Salome did for Cephas, when you were being attacked.

184 Only when you love them enough and freely give of your most precious soul treasure, will they return to the living. I will only give them the final breath of life. Everything else, even if they live again or not, is up to you and your love and unselfishness."

185 Then he turned to Salome, and putting his hand on her shoulder, he said unto her, "As you gave so much of your essence just moments ago, I do not ask for you to give another portion again so soon, and excuse you from this."

186 "Thank you, my Lord," Salome replied reverently. "But I plead to be able to join in the circle of love with my brethren, the Apostles. I was as much a part of the demise of the little ones as they were, perhaps even more so. I do not mind giving up more of my essence of Celestine Light for the little ones to live again and am honored and humbled beyond words to have the opportunity to undo the mistake that was done."

187 Yeshua gave a warm and loving smile at Salome and bent over and kissed her on her

forehead, saying, "You are a treasure, Salome."

188 He then bade Salome and the Apostles to join in Circles of Power and Love surrounding the Hebs and to reach deep into their hearts and call forth all of their love and send it unconditionally to the Hebs, to put aside all thoughts of anger or upset, to be at peace with themselves and the world upon which they stood and with the Hebs, and to have no malice toward them, but only love.

189 He then called upon them to immerse the Hebs in an auric light of soft purple changing to deep green called forth from the very core of their soul essence. And though physical eyes could not discern it, the spiritual eyes of one and all soon saw a translucent purple light stretch out from the bodies of Salome and the Apostles, forming an oblong, waving mass that settled over the Hebs and then began to spin faster and faster until it was but a blur that changed to deep green as it swirled.

190 Then Yeshua cast forth his hand toward the spinning green mass of light, and it was suddenly filled with many tendrils of bright white lightning, which exploded and turned into sparkling rain falling down upon the Hebs.

191 Then the hazy green mass slowed its spin, turning again to purple light, then stopped altogether, and in another moment, it dissipated and was gone.

192 At that moment, the Hebs all opened their eyes. Looking up, they saw all of the giants looking down upon them and hastily got to their feet and tried to flee.

The Hebs Meet the Children of Light

193 But Miriam spoke a word of power as she waved her hand at them, and like Lazarus had been earlier, they suddenly found that their feet were stuck to the ground and could not be moved.

194 And all who were with Yeshua soon heard the Hebs speaking to one another in their minds. And every word the Hebs said, in their fear, disbelief, and curiosity about the giants, each of the Apostles, and Salome was understood as if they were speaking in the language they were most familiar with—some Aramaic, some Greek, and some Hebrew.

195 And they heard Yeshua speaking to the Hebs in their minds, saying, "Have no fear, my friends. We are not Broz. Nor are we your enemies. We come in the light of peace from a world far from this one."

196 "Impossible!" Everyone heard one of the Hebs shout in their minds. "No creature but Hebs can speak in their minds. Beware my comrades. This is some type of trap!"

197 Though no one else seemed to have a clue as to which Heb had been speaking, Miriam knelt down in front of one of them, and smiling mischievously, she shook her head a little and reached forth and touched the Heb lightly on his chest.

198 Then everyone heard her say to him, "Not so, my friend, for all of us hear the words you speak in your mind. I speak to you now, because I know it was you who just spoke."

199 "Impossible!" the Heb exclaimed again.

200 "They are very strange-looking Broz," everyone heard another of the Hebs comment. "Look at their nice clothing. Far more than a Broz could ever conceive or create."

201 "That is because we are not Broz," Miriam spoke again. "We are Alamars, and we come from a world in another time and place."

202 She looked directly at the Heb in front of her, who with spindly arms crossed seemed to still be in denial that any creature other than Hebs could mind speak. "I caused your feet to be stuck to the ground," Miriam confessed. "If you promise not to run or to try to hurt us, I will release all of you, with the promise that none of us will do anything to hurt you in any way as long as you reciprocate the courtesy and kindness."

203 The Hebs spoke quickly among themselves in their minds; then the one before Miriam said, "Agreed. Release us, giant." And with a wave of her hand, she did, and they stepped free of the bonds that had held them.

204 Another of the Hebs boldly walked over to Miriam and spoke to her in her mind, which all heard, saying, "How did you accomplish this feat of holding our feet to the ground? And by what technology did you render us unconscious and bring our ships to the ground?"

205 Hearing his questions, the Apostles realized that they did not understand that they had actually been dead and returned to life, and apparently Miriam did not plan on enlightening them, for she answered simply, saying, "There is much about your civilization that is beyond our ken to understand. In a like manner, the means by which we accomplished that which we did is beyond your ability to fathom, for it has nothing to do with science, but only with that which is spiritual, and of this you have no foundation to comprehend the edifice."

206 Another Heb came up to Miriam and spoke to her in her mind, saying, "You say you are from another world. That is remarkable. We have studied the other worlds through our sky glasses, but never did we suppose that any life existed upon them. We thought ours was the only place in the cosmos fortunate enough to have life."

207 Miriam nodded her head with understanding, saying, "Yes, from what my husband Yeshua tells me, that is a common misconception on many worlds."

208 "Many worlds?" asked another Heb incredulously. How many other worlds have life on them?"

209 Yeshua spoke to them then in their minds, saying, "You know the beach of sand beyond the far side of your city?" "Yes," many Hebs said at once. "If you were to take all of the grains of sand upon that beach and multiply them enough to fill your entire world, you still would not have even begun to count the worlds of life that exist, which the Elohim have created," said Yeshua.

210 "That is too many," another Heb commented. "There are not that many worlds in the cosmos."

211 "The Elohim?" They heard another Heb speak. "If you are Alamars, who are the Elohim?"

212 "The Elohim . . ." answered Philip also kneeling down to be closer to the Hebs, "are the creators of all life. They are the creators of us. And they are the creators of you and the Broz and every speck of life upon this world and every other."

213 "You have strange and primitive notions," said another Heb. "Life creates itself or in some cases is created in our laboratories. But no creature from another world created life here!"

Yeshua the Elohim

214 Hearing this, Yeshua walked over to a mottled red and green plant with many spike-like leaves and a tall central shoot that was just preparing to release seeds. He plucked one of the seeds and knelt down in front of the Heb, asking, "What is this?"

215 "That is the seed of a Gerbob," one of the Hebs answered.

216 "And how long is its germination from planting to maturity?" Yeshua inquired.

217 "One hundred and eighty sleep cycles are required before a gerbob bears its fruit," answered one of the Heb.

218 Yeshua used his index finger to punch a hole in the sandy soil, then dropped the seed into the hole and covered it. Then looking at each of the Hebs, one after another in their tiny eyes, he quietly announced, "I am an Elohim." Then he waved his hand over the spot where he had planted the seed and stood up.

219 Within moments, a tender shoot pushed through the ground and rapidly grew upward. Within ten breaths, it shot forth spiky leaves. Within another five breaths, the tall central shoot had grown up. Within another five, it flowered. Within another five, it fruited, and in the time it took Yeshua to step over to it, the fruit ripened and he plucked one off and sat it down upon the ground in front of the astonished Hebs, saying, "There is more to know than that which you know, and if you would become more than you are, you should listen now to what we have to share with you."

220 There was dumbfounded silence for a moment, and then one of the Hebs answered Yeshua, saying, "You are certainly more than we have conceived any other being could be. If you

will teach us of your ways, we will listen."

The Children of Light Minister to the Hebs

221 And it came to pass that Yeshua, Miriam, Salome, Lazarus, and all of the Apostles walked forth to the city of the Hebs, many of them carrying the Hebs upon their shoulders.

222As they approached the city, the Hebs that were with them communicated with those in the city, telling them of all that had transpired, and hundreds of thousands of Hebs came out to greet the giants from another world who could render them unconscious in their ships and stick their feet to the ground and fruit a Gerbob seed in just a handful of breaths.

223 And the visitors from earth stayed with the Hebs for many, many days, teaching them the story of the Elohim and the creation of all the worlds and the principles of light.

Who are the Hebs?

224 And it came to pass that Yeshua announced one day that the time for his group to depart would soon be upon them, and before they left, he had a great secret to share with them.

225 And it came to pass that all the Hebs everywhere stopped whatever they were doing and listened in their minds to that which Yeshua spoke. And he told them that though they were beautiful as Hebs, that they too once were Alamars in the Kingdom of spirits.

226 He shared with them the events of the rebellion in the heavenly realms led by Lucifer and how their spirits had been among those who did not follow Lucifer, but neither did they support Heavenly Father and Heavenly Mother, but instead stood aside waiting to see who would emerge the victor.

227 Because of this, they lost a great deal of the Celestine Light of their soul essence so much so that they no longer could maintain the appearance of an Alamar, which is made in the image of the Elohim. And thus it is that they were born as Hebs, having two eyes, two arms, and two legs, even as the Alamars and the Elohim, but in so many other ways appearing and acting very differently.

228 Yeshua explained that every creation of life was on a path of eternal progression, and that progression was achieved not by gaining wealth, physical beauty, or strength, but by humbly accepting one's imperfections, repenting of actions not of the light, and striving to henceforth live in the light and gain greater knowledge, faith, and love.

229 He encouraged them by saying they were already very far along the path and that is why they came into this life as Hebs, and not as Broz or even as a Gerbob plant.

230 He admonished them to commit to living the Celestine Light that they might greatly add to their soul essence: that in their next physical life they might come forth once again as Alamars made in the image of the Elohim.

231 And many more things did Yeshua speak to the Hebs that day, even as he had taught the people of Palestine for many years.

Conversions and Baptisms of the Hebs

232 As he came to the end of his sayings, he spoke to the Hebs of baptism as the threshold that must be crossed to leave your old life behind and embark upon a new life in the Celestine Light.

233 During the next ten sleep cycles, the Apostles, Miriam, Salome, and Lazarus baptized hundreds of Hebs and gave them authority to baptize others in the name of Yeshua, and this they immediately did in great numbers.

234 And it came to pass that when the time came for Yeshua, Miriam, Salome, Lazarus, and the Apostles to depart, over fifty thousand Hebs had repented of their sins and been baptized with a commitment to henceforth live in the Celestine Light.

235 And Yeshua promised he would come again to them soon to teach them more of the principles of Celestine Light so that they might become more than they had been.

236 Then the Children of Light from earth returned through a portal to the world from

which they came, and other than Yeshua, they never saw any of the Hebs again, but neither did any of them ever forget the profound experiences they had among them.

CHAPTER 99

Pathway to Exaltation

Yeshua gives one last talk to all the Children of Light around the world, not with his voice, but with his mind, speaking his words in their minds, even to those who have never even seen him or heard of him, but have lived good lives worthy to be called Children of Light. He calls for a gathering to the Communities of Light on Lake Gennesaret and speaks about the Six-pointed Star of Longevity, including how to live one thousand years upon the earth. He gives prophecies of the coming days and speaks of the Generation of Promise that shall come.

And it came to pass that Yeshua, Miriam, Salome, and the Apostles returned to the house of the family of Lazarus in Bethany through the same portal they had traveled through to the world of Ferrtho in the Fourth Kingdom.

2 As had happened previously, it seemed to the other family members in Bethany that only mere hours had passed, while to those returning it seemed certain they had been gone many days.

3 Everyone returning from the Fifth Kingdom rested for a day and a night, and the following day Yeshua made an important announcement to his Apostles, saying, "I desire to speak one more time to the Children of Light to help them on their journeys of discovery and personal growth before I leave this world to not return again, save by the spirit within, for their spirits call out to me, and I must give them one more solace."

4 Yeshua sensed that many of his Apostles were saddened contemplating his departure, and he told them, "Do not be sorrowful that the time has come for me to leave this physical world that we have shared. Know that as I leave, you will be propelled into the fullness of your callings, into the majesty of your potential, and I hope that you will take joy in this.

5 Prepare yourselves now for something you have not experienced in such magnitude, which we shall embark upon after the noonday. Children of Light in every land shall hear my voice speaking to them in their minds, such a thing as most have never conceived. And those who are ready to be numbered among you will heed my words and gather unto you."

6 Later that day, after the noonday meal, Yeshua went with his Apostles, wives, children, and the family of Lazarus to a grove of trees on a nearby hill. A crude bench with the sun shining down upon it had been made out of a long, flat stone set upon two squat stones on either end, and upon this Yeshua sat while everyone else gathered around him, some sitting on the ground and others with their backs against trees.

7 Yeshua closed his eyes, and tilting his head up toward the sun, he held his lower arms up and level, with palms open and facing up. After but a few seconds, his resonant voice came into the minds of all of those sitting near him, even members of the family of Lazarus and many of the

children who had never before heard the voice of someone speaking in their mind.

8 And not just those present heard his voice, but every Child of Light in the communities upon Lake Gennesaret also heard his voice at the same instant speaking to them in their minds regardless of what they were doing.

9 And more than this as well, for every Child of Light upon the earth heard the voice of Yeshua speaking to them in their minds at that very moment, causing great consternation among many. For in far-off lands, many people, though Children of Light in the actions of their lives, had never heard of Yeshua, nor ever imagined a sane man could hear voices in their minds.

10 Yeshua spoke to them all in one voice saying, "Fear not, my brothers and sisters of light. I am Yeshua, your elder brother who has come to earth to illuminate the path of eternity for you.

11 Many of you have never seen my face or heard my voice or even my name spoken upon the lips of men, but you know me in your heart, for we were together before this world was.

12 And I know you, for you are a Child of Light, my brothers and sisters of spirit. It matters not the color of your skin, whether you are male or female, young or old, rich or poor, or the religion you profess. By the good actions of your life, you have been numbered among the Children of Light, and I now call you to come and embrace your true family and the path of greater glory and fulfillment.

13 You live in a world of challenge and much darkness, but that does not mean your life must be an endless challenge or continually dimmed by the darkness of the people and places that surround you.

14 Even if you are a slave, chained to a dais, you can change your thoughts and take yourself in your heart and mind to a place within your essence where resides the spirit of Elohim, and there you will find peace and an abundance of Celestine Light that cannot be taken or dimmed by the world.

15 For those who have their freedom, your thoughts may be just the beginning of the light you can bathe yourselves in, for your feet can walk and carry you elsewhere to a place where the Celestine Light that comes from God never dims, even to the Communities of Light where you can bask each day in the uplifting spirits, words, and actions of your brothers and sisters of light.

16 This is my call now to every Child of Light upon the earth, wherever you may be: come to the Communities of Light upon Lake Gennesaret in the land of Palestine.

17 Come to the place where your brothers and sisters dwell.

18 Come to the place where the Celestine Light of divinity glows on every face and the darkness of the world can find no place to cast its shadow.

19 Come to the place where harmony reins, where your belly will be full and your life will be fuller.

20 Come to the place of Celestine Light where you will become more than you are and more than you imagined you could be.

21 Where the divine fills your heart and mind, guiding the lives of everyone to greater happiness, health, knowledge, longevity, and spiritual fulfillment.

22 Come to the place where you will be given secret knowledge and the mysteries of all things shall be revealed; that with this knowledge you may go forth in the world but not of it; in it but no longer fearful of it; in it but greater than it.

23 Come to the place of Celestine Light where you will learn the secrets of longevity, where the life of a Child of Light may exceed those of the children of the world tenfold, as does the knowledge in their minds and the empathy and love in their hearts.

24 I would speak to you now more about longevity, for this is a desirable pursuit, for with greater years you can do greater good.

25 People of the world pursue longevity too, but it is something they will never hold, for they seek only to extend the life of the physical body and longevity can only be obtained by also nourishing the soul.

26 How then is the soul nourished, my brothers and sisters, you who are the Children of

Light?
27 It begins with community. Not a community of neighbors and even friends, but a Community of Celestine Light, where all are family, and the love and concern for your neighbor is as great as for your own children.
28 Community then is the foundation of longevity, not the individual or the individual's actions or choices, no matter how good they may be.
29 Good actions of health and diet may add some years to the life of man, but they will not double or triple his lifespan, save he does them nourished in the bosom of the Family of Light.
30 Therefore, I say unto you: put your affairs in order and come now to live among your brothers and sisters in the Communities of Celestine Light upon Lake Gennesaret in the land called Palestine. Though you may not know them, they wait for you, to welcome you home.
31 Fear not the cost, nor the Romans, nor the Greeks or the Persians or the Egyptians or any other people upon the earth, for the hand of God shall be upon all who make the journey and none shall forbid your passage or slow your way, and whatever money you have shall be sufficient.
32 When you have arrived, you will begin to change. The darkness of the world will fall away, and health and knowledge and joy shall begin to come unto you in abundance.
33 And to all who live in the Communities of Light, both those already there and those still to come, I say unto you: live long, be one, seek out the Celestine Light in all things.
34 There is so much for you to learn and experience that you could never do it in the one short lifetime of the people of the world. Nor would it benefit you to come back in another lifetime, having forgotten everything you learned in the previous and needing to start all over again from the beginning.
35 It is only by living a life two or three or four or even ten times longer than the people of the world, that you can learn all that you need to learn and experience all that you need to experience, to become all that you have the potential to become and do all the good in the world you are capable of doing.
36 Upon the foundation of life within the Community of Light, you can now add the other ingredients of the master recipe of longevity.
37 Consider not just the physical body when you think of longevity, for those who do are doomed to die before they ever taste of the longevity they seek.
38 Your body is the vessel for your eternal soul, your eternal spirit that cannot be neglected. It is only when these two are nourished equally, within the Community of Celestine Light, that the fullness of longevity can be manifested.

Six-pointed Star of Longevity

39 "The six-pointed star of longevity is this: life in a Community of Celestine Light, physical vibrancy, continual mental expansion, service and empathy to others, spiritual nourishment, and discovering and using the powers of your Xe.
40 There is more to fulfilling each of these than you might imagine. For with each, you must look to perfecting yourselves, to becoming more like the Elohim, to consider how it is you can fulfill the highest potential of the energy, not wallow in the lowest.

Point One: Community of Light

41 "The simplest would seem to be to live in the Community of Celestine Light; but living there is not the same as being alive there, and being alive is what you must be: alive in the fullness of the teachings of Elohim, lived faithfully in your life; alive by being a very active and contributing member of the community, not a hermit in your house; alive by relishing and loving the Family of Light to which you are a part.

Point Two: Physical Vibrancy

42 "So physical vibrancy would seem to be straightforward, for the teachings of diet and healthy lifestyle have been given to you in detail. But physical vibrancy is more than diet and

exercise. It is so much a fulfillment of the word vibrant.

43 Are you sweet of disposition? Do you judge none, including yourself? Do you speak ill words of none and gossip not at all about others? When you speak to friends and family, is it only in praise and never with an uninvited or subtle criticism? Do you laugh easily and smile often? Do you whistle and sing happy tunes, even while you work? Do you make your home a piece of Heaven by the ambience you create and the example you set by the things you say and do?

44 And the physical aspect of longevity is still much more than this. Your Vm plays a vital role in the physical aspect of your longevity. It should be activated daily throughout your life, even when you are alone, but not in the crude and debasing ways of the world, nor is a culmination necessary or even any connection to things sexual, for there is much more to the energy of the Vm than that. And with this, you learn one of the secrets within the secrets of longevity.

45 The essence of your Vm is a very sacred power, even the power to create life, but includes other wonderful creations as well. It is castrated when it is used in worldly ways only for physical pleasure or sullied by debasing language or illicit thoughts.

46 Nevertheless, within the sanctity of your marriage, you have great latitude with respect to how you give and receive pleasure through your Vms. All is well if what you do strengthens your bonds together. But be certain that it does. And understand clearly that physically pleasuring your Vms in the debased ways of the world will not add to the length of your days, but doing so with love within your marriage will.

47 To achieve physical vibrancy and longevity when physically stimulating your Vms, you must do so within the realm of sacredness and only within the bonds of marriage publicly proclaimed. Seek to become blissfully lost in the wonder of Celestine Love, without crude words or disrespectful actions, but focusing only on one another and pleasure mutually given and received.

48 It matters not the composition of your marriage to other Children of Light, be it one man and one woman or two women or two men or a mixture of a man and women, or a woman and men. What is important is the depth of your love evidenced by the steadfastness of your commitment and the exclusivity and sacredness of your unions.

49 But let none among you be fornicators or adulterers, for this is the spirit of darkness and the world.

50 And may all among you be open and accepting of the vows of fidelity and commitment given in marriage by any of your brothers and sisters of the Celestine Light, in whatever arrangement of love among one another that they choose.

51 Beyond that, remember the secret within the secret.

Point Three: Expansion of the Mind

52 "What then of the aspect of the mind? Is it just ever pursuing greater knowledge? A worthy endeavor to be sure, one that all Children of Light should seek every year of their life. But there is much more to this aspect.

53 What is it you are learning? Is it about the latest fashions in the cities or learning how to create the clothes? Is it watching the street dancers or learning the dance? Is it marveling at great art or practicing to become a great artist? You can do the former as long as you also choose to do some of the latter that expands your creativity. But the former without the latter contributes naught to your longevity.

54 Nor is learning only concerned with matters in the Ka. For the Ka and the Ja are intimately connected. What affects one profoundly affects the other.

55 Therefore take heed about what your eyes see and what your ears hear.

56 Seek things that uplift and inspire rather than belittle and disparage.

57 Seek things that warm your heart and calm your mind, not things that cause fear or anxiety.

58 Seek association with situations, places, and people that make you want to become more than you are, not encourage you to be less.

59 Seek out that which is light and calls you to your greatness. And turn away from everyone and everything that does not.

Point Four: Service to Others

60 "And what does it mean to serve others? It is not just giving alms for the poor or to support the community or worthy institutions.

61 Money is but a token that is both helpful and appreciated, but true service requires your participation.

62 So true this is—that you can consider the wages from a day's work donated to a worthy cause of less value than one hour of your time given in sweetness to the same cause.

63 True service is when one who is stronger, be it physically, mentally, financially, emotionally, or spiritually, comes to one who is weaker, in humility, and serves them to their happiness with respect and kindness.

64 This is the service a man gives to his wife, when he seeks her joy before his and does as she asks in giving intimate pleasures.

65 This is the service a mother gives to her children when she counsels and cajoles rather than commands and does not force her will upon them.

66 This is the service those of greater means give to those of lesser when they rise with the first sun to work side by side and help them build a house, rather than donate alms in a minute and have the matter forgotten.

67 This is the service of the ruler who listens to the will of the people rather than imposing his own will upon them, even when he disagrees with that which the people call to be done.

68 These are the services and others like unto them that build Communities of Celestine Light, instead of just communities of friends, acquaintances, and coworkers.

Point Five: Spiritual Nourishment

69 "In the world, among the Ganish of all persuasions, it is thought that to be nourished spiritually is to learn more of their faith and to live it more faithfully. Alone, this is just partial nourishment, like unto the mother who feeds her children in the morning but not in the afternoon or evening.

70 Like service to others, spiritual nourishment in fullness is more than you.

71 To be filled, you must commune with others of your faith. You must share your experiences and knowledge with those who have less experience and knowledge and avidly seek out and learn from those who have more.

72 Therefore, know with certainty that spiritual nourishment is much more than what you learn that is written on a scroll, even much more than my words set down by a scribe.

73 Spiritual nourishment is an unquenchable thirst and curiosity about what you do not know, fulfilled as much by what you learn from others and what you teach to others as by what you learn from reading the words written on a scroll.

74 Remember, all points of the six-sided star, concerning seeking the higher path when a choice is before you, not the lower.

Point Six: Discovering the Powers of Your Xe

75 "Your time upon this earth is very finite. You know not when the last day shall be. Perhaps even now you will breathe your last breath in the physical life. Therefore, do not squander time, which is a commodity more precious than gold or jewels.

76 More than this, live your life to increase its length, rather than abuse your life, shortening its days.

77 Many religions teach that your days are numbered before you ever are born. But I say unto you: this is not true.

78 Based upon how you live, the Elohim know the exact day you shall leave the physical life. But you are the master of you, and that day is not written in stone.

79 If you choose to live differently, to live better, healthier, smarter, more in balance with the aeon of life, more in harmony with the Celestine spirit of the Elohim, then you lengthen your days upon the earth.

80 Elohim still knows the very day that shall be your last in the physical life, but your actions have moved the day and it is not the same day that it was. And you can continue to move it, adding more and more years to do good, even until you have lived for one thousand years upon the earth.

81 But remember, remember, that even as good actions move the day further away in time, so do bad actions bring it closer.

82 All the things I have spoken about contribute to the lengthening of your days. But there is one more thing, often forgotten or unknown by many, that has as vital a role as any other, and that is discovering and using the powers of your Xe.

83 The physical men and women that you see all around you, probably even in yourself or your beloved, are not the men and women that can be.

84 You were endowed with gifts of Celestine Light before you were born into this life: the power to hear when others have not spoken, the power to travel from one place to another without traveling, the power to levitate objects and yourself, the power to make fire by calling the aeon and focusing it in your hands, and many, many other powers of Celestine Light have you been gifted with.

85 Until you discover these gifts and can use them, you are but a cripple. Until you can discover these gifts and use them, your life will come and go just like any other person upon this world, for until you discover and use these gifts, you are still like the people of this world and are bound by their beliefs of mortality.

86 But to discover the secrets of these gifts is not something that can be done in solitude. Nor for many can it be done in days or months or years.

87 Knowing the secrets of your Xe and how to use them releases the aeons of Celestine Light upon you, and this shall add as many days to your physical life as all the other things you can do.

88 Each day, there are hours to sleep and eat and work and a precious few remaining for you to choose to do with them as you wish.

89 If you choose to spend them rather than invest them, to squander them on mindless entertainment or time lost doing nothing, then nothing is what you shall inherit, both in this life and the life to come.

90 Your time is precious, more than gold or jewels. Invest it in becoming more than you are in every way and your investment shall reward you in every way as your years upon the earth lengthen.

91 While king after king after king passes away and their Kingdoms too, you shall remain. And more good shall be done upon the earth than if you had returned for one hundred lifetimes.

Mind the Bridge upon Which You Stand

92 "Please consider that each of you stand on a bridge that leads to other Children of Light.

93 On one side of the bridge are the Children of Light who have more knowledge and experience than you. These are your mentors and teachers to help you grow and expand in the Celestine Light of the Elohim.

94 Look to them often that you may gain a greater understanding of all things. Observe what they do and how they do it, how they pray, how they work, how they call and use their Celestine gifts of power, and how they speak and treat others, both Children of Light and the Ganish.

95 Do not hesitate to inquire of them when you seek an understanding of all things Celestine. Of course, they will help you, for you are all here to serve one another with love.

96 On the other side of the bridge are the Children of Light who have less knowledge and experience than you. You are the one who stands at the other end of their bridge as their mentor and teacher.

97 Even as you look to those with greater knowledge and experience, so those at the other end of your bridge look to you to help them gain a greater understanding of the Celestine Light.

98 Know that this is a sacred duty to which you are called all of your life: to faithfully be an example of the Celestine Light to all those who see your life and to share your knowledge and experiences with all Children of Light who ask of you or to whom you are called to teach.

99 Therefore, always remember that you are on a bridge crossing the great chasm of the world. To the right, anchoring that side, are those that teach you by precept and example. To the left, anchoring that side, are those that you teach by precept and example.

100 Both sides are needed to safely anchor the bridge to insure it does not give way and fall into the chasm of the world. Therefore, gratefully seek out your mentors and teachers and, with humility, be willing to be a mentor and teacher to those who look to you for greater understanding and knowledge.

The Foundations of the Community of Light

101 "How are the communities of Celestine Light different than any other community upon the earth?

102 They are different because they are not just a grouping of like-minded people, but the unity of a Family of Light, where the love for everyone is as family, not just friends.

103 They are different because they are in the world, but not of it, and in their cloistered locations, not even in it very much.

104 They are different because the members live according to the health and diet teachings of Celestine Light, resulting in fulfilling lives of joy and happiness, with little sickness or disease and with years upon the earth far in excess of the people of the world.

105 They are different because everyone is a servant to all others, and none is a master to any.

106 They are different because they are neither patriarchal in nature, nor matriarchal, but are led in the temporal by the elders, both men and women, with the most knowledge, experience, and abilities of all things temporal and in the spiritual by the Apostles, both men and women, called because of their knowledge, experience, and abilities in the gifts, powers, and responsibilities of the Celestine Light.

107 They are different because that which is considered magic, fantasy, and impossible among the people of the world is normal and common among the Children of Light.

108 They are different because in a world where most people live in poverty, the Children of Light create self-sufficient abundance.

109 They are different because they are filled with hope not despair, with faith not doubt, with love not hate, with smiles not frowns, with easy forgiveness not quick judgment, with working together not at odds, with self-confidence not self-pity, with unity not divisiveness, with acceptance of differences not prejudice, with words of praise not criticisms, with purpose not aimlessness.

Prophecy of the Days to Come

110 "Now I would give you some last words, my brothers and sisters of this generation. I have spoken many things to the Children of Light over the years I have walked in the flesh upon this earth. Some of you have been with me for many of those years, while others are hearing my voice now for the very first time.

111 My words have been written for the Children of Light. They are for you who hear my voice as I speak to you now.

112 I will give no more new to you, for all you need to gain exaltation and eternal life I have already spoken. Now it is you who must take it upon yourselves to know and live that which I have spoken.

113 And those that know and live my words shall be no more of this earth, even though their feet may still tread upon it. For those who know and live my words shall be more than men and more than women. They shall be Celestines, who, staying steadfast in the light, shall someday

become Adepts against whom the fiery darts of the adversary within have no persuasion, the forces of the world be they army or king, have no power, and to whom the body is the servant not the master.

114 But your time on the earth is short. You are few, and the Ganish are many. Gather now to one another at Lake Gennesaret and live together and prosper as long as the world will let you.

115 Grow and expand yourself in the ways of the Celestine Light of Elohim. Learn the secrets I have given unto my Apostles to teach unto you. Become Adepts of the Celestine Light, each and every one of you, that the people of the world may have no power over you, for you will be one with the Celestine Light and the Celestine Light shall be one with you.

116 When the world hates you, and they shall, when they seek to destroy you, and they shall, defend yourselves and your families when you must by whatever means you have, but seek not confrontation.

117 Be willing to burn your homes and farms and boats and depart from the land, if it will save the spilling of blood, either yours or the Ganish's who persecute you.

118 But do not surrender to them or put yourselves willingly into their hands, save you are an Adept over which they can have no real power, only imagined. And great shall be their surprise when that misconception is revealed.

119 Those of you who are just beginning to walk the path of Celestine Light seek the protection of the Adepts. When the peace and bliss of your communities is broken by the jealous people of the world who think to take that which they have not earned, leave them stubble and ash and withdraw from the land to the sanctuary that shall be revealed by the Elohim to my Apostles.

120 And it shall be that you shall continue to grow in the Celestine Light. Under the trials and tribulations, you shall become more than you were until the earth can no longer hold you in its thickness, for you will be of the light.

121 On that day, this generation shall rise up without tasting death, even as the people of Enoch, and I shall meet you in the sky and show you the way to the heavenly glory that awaits the faithful Children of Light, even you, my dear brothers and sisters.

122 When you are no more upon the earth, the fullness of Celestine Light shall be taken from it for two thousand years, save from those who remain as earth Stewards, and the Ganish shall wander in the darkness they created.

123 But each new generation born upon the earth shall have more souls who humbly and sincerely seek the light that is not there in the world, but flourishes in their hearts and manifests in their lives.

The Generation of Promise

124 "Therefore, the Celestine Light shall grow again upon the earth, generation upon generation, until two thousand years have passed. Then there shall be sufficient light upon the earth that once again the Celestine Light shall be reborn, and upon this day begins a new era as the Generation of Promise is also born.

125 Unto the Generation of Promise will be given all that has been given to you, for on that day, there will be more Children of Light upon the earth than there are people in all the world today.

126 They shall hunger for the light, and it shall be given to them in fullness, and Adepts of knowledge and power shall walk the world once more to protect it from those that still remain in darkness.

127 Were the Adepts not to come, it would be the end of the world, for the leaders of great countries and those not so great will have the power to destroy all life, and this they will do, save the Adepts of Celestine Light join as one with the other Children of Light to stop the travesty.

128 For when the power of the light unites as one, the darkness has no place to be. Darkness of itself is nothing, but the absence of the light. When the light asserts its place in brilliance, the darkness is no more.

Final Words

129 "And of all the words I have said to you, my brothers and sisters, these I say to you last: Love one another, even as I have loved you. In this is all the power of creation, all the power of the Elohim, and all the potential of the Celestine Light that is within you, waiting to shine unto the world."

CHAPTER 100

The End of the Beginning

Yeshua calls forth the stalwarts of Celestine Light, including those who appear from faraway places, to carry the light forward. He councils them briefly, reminding them of that which is most important. He says his final words to his children, and then Miriam leads everyone in creating the greatest Circle of Light ever to exist on earth, which causes everyone to levitate to a place between Heaven and earth where angels from Heaven, including Yochanan, meet them for a short time. Yeshua kisses Miriam one last time and exits in magnificence.

And it came to pass that after Yeshua had finished speaking in the minds of the Children of Light in every corner of the world, he went to Miriam and embraced her and did not let go.

2 Then he beckoned Salome to come to him, and the three of them embraced in silence with their foreheads all touching.

3 After a couple of minutes, he bade his children and Martha to join them, and they all came and held each other closely in a Circle of Power for a few minutes of silence.

4 Then he looked up once more to his Apostles and Lazarus and bade them to join in the circle, and they immediately joined into it.

5 After a few more minutes of silence sharing in the love and energy of all those in the circle, Yeshua looked up once more and bade everyone else present, including all of the children, to join in the circle facing one another so that all might be one in love, faith, and spirit. And everyone did as Yeshua bade and joined into the circle and held one another in power and love.

6 When everyone was together, Yeshua spoke to them aloud, saying, "Some of you were with me at Tyre when we formed a circle of great power. So it will be again today.

7 But that which you shall make today will be the greatest Circles of Power that has ever swirled upon the earth. And it shall be you who shall call it, you who shall wield its power, and I will remain this one last time, only to be a guide and remind you of the sacred words of power.

8 If you have a wand of wood or spiral shell or crystal, grasp it now in your right hand." At his command, all of the Apostles, Miriam, and Salome withdrew wands from their garments.

9 Yeshua then spoke to all of the children present, saying, "Children, go now to the center of the circle and carefully dig in the ground. Soon you will come upon a treasure, not of gold, but something more precious. Each of you, take one of the treasures for yourself and then go about the circle and give one to any person who does not already have a wand."

10 At his direction, more than a dozen children scampered into the center of the circle and began digging in the loose, sandy soil. Soon many high-note tinkling sounds were heard, the

unmistakable distinct audio cue of crystals of power touching one another.

11 The children looked with wide-eyed wonder at the clear, six-sided wands that were as long as their forearms and brilliantly reflecting the sunlight. But remembering their instructions they quickly got up and began passing out the long, tapered crystals to anyone in the circle that did not already have a wand of shell or wood or crystal in their hand. Many unused crystal wands remained lying in the hole in the ground.

12 When the children all had rejoined the circle with their crystal wands in hand, Yeshua spoke again to everyone, saying, "Close your eyes now so you are not distracted by anything around you. Remember friends and strangers you have encountered in your life that were Children of Light, even those who may not have known they were, but whose lives of goodness, love, and stewardship left no doubt.

13 Remember your wives and children who may not be here now and how much you love them and wish they were here in spirit and so shall they be.

14 Those of you who have walked with me upon the earth as I have shared the teachings of the Elohim, remember the special people whom we have encountered over the years. See them clearly in your mind, hear their voice, and look into their eyes.

15 Now each person, man, woman, and child, holding your wand in your right hand, point it toward the center of the circle and place your left hand on the shoulder or around the waist of the person to your left. In this, stand closely together with each of the people beside you so that your shoulders or sides are also touching.

16 You that are many are now becoming one in the light, and the light shall be in you and outside of you, all around you, and multiplied many, many times more than your numbers.

17 Reflect upon your love for the person to your right and to your left and for all the other brothers and sisters of the Celestine Light that are one in this circle with you.

18 Remember your faith. Feel it welling up deep inside of you, a force that cannot be slowed or stopped, for it is of God; it is of Elohim; you are of Elohim; you are the sons and daughters of God. And to you, nothing is impossible.

19 Now swirl the energy of your aura; swirl it faster and faster. At the bottom of every breath, before you inhale again, swirl your aura until you feel it inside of you at the core of your being, even your very soul essence.

20 Now unify your breathing. Listen to the breath of the person to your right and to your left and be one with it. When they breathe in, you breathe in. When they breathe out, you breathe out.

21 When you are at the bottom of your breath, do not breathe in again for several seconds as you spin your aura into your core and feel it radiating its power inside of you.

22 Breathe in now in unison; as you breath out in unison, swirling your aura deeply inside at the bottom, forcefully say the Celestine word of power, 'Yizataz!'

23 And so they all did: the men, the women, and the children. Immediately after they forcefully spoke Yizataz in unison, Yeshua quickly spoke another sacred word of power; then another was spoken by Miriam and then another by Cephas. Then marvelous things began to occur.

24 A dense mist surrounded all the Children of Light. Where they stood was clear, but beyond them was only impenetrable mist.

25 Their own spirits spoke to them, giving them knowledge they had never learned; even so they all knew that the mist was a veil of illusion that none from the outside world would see anything at all upon the hill upon which they stood, except that which had always been there.

26 Then there was a sudden burst of yellow light in the middle of the circle that caused everyone to close their eyes for a moment because of the brightness. When they opened them again, they were astounded to see several people standing before them that had not been there a moment ago.

27 After a few seconds, many of those in the circle began to discern who it was that had appeared, and then their amazement was even greater.

28 For standing all around them, both inside the circle and outside of it, were many of the Children of Light Yeshua had met in his travels over the many years.

29 Tall above all others was the former warrior bandit Kudar-Iluna. Yeshua's mother Miryam was also there and Babuaten the Egyptian and Ephres whom Yeshua had saved from death in Capharsalama, as well as Gimiel were also there.

30 And from his youth, there stood Dryhus the repentant and Anish of Bharat.

31 And from his days in Jerusalem, there were Valerius the Roman centurion and Nicodemus the Pharisee.

32 And the converts from Hippos—Yunia and Adronicus—stood together in the center of the circle.

33 And Elissa the High Priestess of the temple in Tyre was also numbered among those who had miraculously appeared.

34 Before anyone began to speak and break the focus of the circle, Yeshua spoke to everyone in their minds, saying, "Welcome to our brothers and sisters of light that have come among us. Be not startled by your appearance at this place for you were drawn here, not in the spirit, but in your physical body, called by the power of the Celestine Light in this circle, because your spirits are in perfect harmony and resonance with the spirit of light that shines here upon us and within us.

35 Please, do not speak, but take a crystal wand from the center and join us in the circle. Allow your spirit to know all it needs to know." And so they all did, quietly merging into the Celestine Circle of Power.

36 As the last of the newcomers blended into the circle, everyone within it felt an overpowering stirring in the core of their aura, and Yeshua said unto them in their minds, "In this circle are the leaders of Celestine Light, when I am no longer among you. Some may have more visible callings, some may have the ability to manifest greater gifts, but all who stand here have a faith that is unbreakable. You are the stalwarts, the candles that burn everlasting and cannot be extinguished.

37 In the days to come, when the world shall seek to destroy the Celestine Light and those of weaker faith may fear and falter, it is you, my brothers and sisters, even you my youngest ones, that I trust to be the light that uplifts and gives courage to the weak; who lead by example; who speak words of praise and confidence, not negativity or fear.

38 Never forget that each of you is here today not simply because I called you to be or willed you to be; you are here because this is your resonance, and when the portal was opened, your body came to the place of its greatest resonance, here among your closest, brothers and sisters of light.

39 Look now at one another, at every person within this circle, for each of you are part of one another in very deep ways and must think of yourselves as one from this day forward.

40 But see that you have not pride, but humility. Yours is an open group that in the future shall be joined by many others of the Children of Light who grow into your resonance.

41 Now the time has at last come for me to part from you in the physical, and none but my wives and children shall ever see me in this physical form again until we meet again in the Celestine Realms.

42 Be faithful to what you know to be true and live it in your lives. You are my teachings. In the perfection of your lives, the other Children of Light will learn more about the Celestine Light of Elohim than if they read or heard every word I have ever spoken.

43 Therefore, if you would honor me, live the teachings I have given unto you.

44 And of all the things I have taught you, there are a precious few which I desire to remind you of again that you might faithfully do them and by your example help others to do them as well.

45 Remember to not judge your brothers and sisters unless they are creating disharmony within the community by actions that are not in harmony with the Celestine Light. And then, see that none of you or any Child of Light places a judgment against them in your heart or mind, but let them come before the Council of Elders or before a quorum of the Apostles, as is

appropriate, and be judged in that manner after evidence has been presented and the accused has had ample opportunity to present a rebuttal and defense.

46 And let there be no judgment, save it is a unanimous one. For if those judging do not have unanimity, then the Celestine Light of Elohim has not been with them.

47 I have told you that it matters not what you wear for clothing, because it is the actions of your life that are important, not the style or color of your clothing.

48 But you who are the stalwarts should choose to dress and adorn yourself with the vibrant and precious colors, styles, symbols, and gemstones that enhance your gifts and should not be concerned with how odd you may appear in contrast with the latest fashions. And when the other Children of Light see these things in you and the good that they bring, they too will desire them.

49 I know that hair continues to be a divisive issue with many of the Children of Light and even among some of you. It matters not what length of hair a Child of Light has, be they a man or a woman, or whether a man has a long beard, short beard, or no beard. All can still be worthy and lovely Children of Light and greatly loved and productive members of the community.

50 But for those who desire to someday become Adepts in the powers of the Celestine Light, the length of hair and beard does matter, for hair is a storehouse of the fruits of every event in your life, both in your day and your night while you sleep. When you seek to use your Celestine gifts of power, your hair is as great a tool as any you shall ever wield.

51 But it must not simply be long hair, but long hair of health and luster, healthy because the body within is also healthy.

52 Nor should it be dyed, except with herbs that nourish such as sage, and then only to enhance your natural color and appearance not your vanity.

53 Therefore, let all women who would be Adepts grow their hair long. And let all men who would be Adepts do likewise, even if it is only from the side for those whose top is barren. But let it never hang scraggly. Let it be combed at the least and made beautiful, with ties and jewels and enhancements of gold threads as you resonate.

54 Concerning beards, the brothers have an advantage in this as women cannot grow beards. But let the sisters not take affront, for Elohim gave men the ability to grow beards only so they might have an extra tool to help call out their Celestine gifts, as Elohim has already endowed women with so much greater ability to call forth their gifts than men because of their weaker physical stature.

55 Not every man can grow a beard of substance, and no beard is better than a scraggly one or a partial one cut into the latest fashion, for these cannot make a good path of power any more than can a head that has been shorn of hair.

56 Nor is it necessary for a brother Adept to have a beard any more than it is necessary for him or any of the sisters to have a wand. If you can manifest your Celestine gifts without either of these or long hair, so be it. But if you cannot, you must consider the tools you can add to help you in your quest.

57 I have given you three additional tools to help you discover the glory of your true self and ask that you, the stalwarts, remember to do the Lanaka each day and to expand into the world with your light through the Contemplative Movements at least once each week and to walk the Path of Three at least once each moon.

58 And if you would please the Elohim and grow greatly in your own power and faith, remember to fulfill your stewardship to overcome the negative vortexes that weigh upon the land and to be watchful over the portals to the shadow Kingdoms, protecting your world from theirs and theirs from yours.

59 In your leadership to the Children of Light, give nothing to them by way of commandment, save the Twelve Commandments of Sinai and the Great Commandment. In all else, lead by example and allow each to emulate you if they choose or walk a different path if that is their preference.

60 If they want to grow in their knowledge and powers, they will attune themselves to the best path by their own choice and without compulsion.

61 Concerning the Great Commandment, to multiply and replenish the earth, remember to teach that this concerns all living things, not only children born of women. If someone chooses instead to be a good steward over the trees of the forest, the birds of the sky, or the fish of the sea, helping them to multiply and replenish, it is the same.

62 But to ignore this commandment and to live only for self-indulgence, without faithfulness to the Great Commandment, is a terrible act of selfishness and affront to Elohim who made men and women for a grander purpose and gave them greater capacities that they could fulfill the full measure of their creation."

63 Then Yeshua called out to Miriam and his children and asked them to come to him. When they came, he knelt down and held his two children in his arms while Miriam put her arm across his shoulder. Looking up into their eyes, he said unto them, "Lights of my heart, I have taken such joy in watching you grow. I am leaving this earth we call home now and going to the house of my parents, which is in the place of everlasting lights beyond the edge of the sky.

64 But know that I am not leaving you, and I shall continue to watch you grow and have happiness unbound because of you, each and every day.

65 Remember that which I told you before. Henceforth, in this life, all others shall know me only in spirit, but for you, I will always appear when you call to me."

66 Both children held him even more tightly at his words and began to stifle whimpers and tears. And he said unto them, "Cry not, great lights of the earth. This is not a day of sadness but one of joy, for in it is fulfilled promises made by the Elohim to the children of man since the dawn of creation.

67 Go now to be among your brothers and sisters of light. Teach them by the good examples of your lives what it means to be Children of Light and sons and daughters of God, for thus they all are. More so than they even know."

68 Then he kissed them on each cheek, holding his cheek against theirs, then lightly on the lips, looking into each one's eyes, saying, "I love you." Then hugging them once more together, he stood up and bade them to return into the circle.

69 Now Miriam alone remained beside him. He put his arm over her shoulder, and she put one arm around his waist and held her other hand upon his chest and looked up upon his face.

70 Yeshua smiled at Miriam, a soft smile of deep love and contentment, and said unto her, "You know this is the end of the beginning?"

71 She nodded her head silently and then replied in a soft voice, "Yes, my Lord, the third step of the twelve you have said must transpire before man and earth are transformed into the crystal resonance of Celestine Light and the earth rises to its glory."

72 Yeshua nodded his head in acknowledgment, saying, "Now you begin the fourth step, my beloved Miriam. And it is the middle steps that you begin that will be the greatest challenges.

73 Remember who you are and that all things are possible to you; nevertheless, you must let the Apostles and Salome grow into their own lights by their own efforts and not do for them what they can do for themselves, even when it causes them pain and failure in the attempt. For those are the stepping stones of tomorrow's joys and successes.

74 Take the life of no man or beast, save one that will demand it of you, for with your gifts and powers there is always another way.

75 Be assured, I will be with you in your thoughts with my words in your head every moment you speak to me.

76 I will not set foot upon this earth again in the flesh, but will meet you in the everlasting lights each lunar cycle upon the night of the full moon, that we may renew our love in the bonds of warm embrace. And I will come in a semblance of the flesh for our children when they need me.

77 Now I must go, Miriam. My time on earth is over. Yours is just beginning.

78 Know that I love you with a depth and a breadth that is beyond the understanding of men."

79 Miriam looked at Yeshua with loving adoration, saying, "And so do I love you, my beloved Yeshua, always and forever, beyond time, for everlasting and everlasting."

80 Yeshua bent down and kissed Miriam fully on the lips, and it was a long and lingering kiss, bringing tears to the eyes of almost everyone who was watching from the circle surrounding them.

81 Looking up but still clinging closely to Miriam, and she to him, Yeshua spoke to everyone in the circle, saying, "Know that I love each one of you so very much. You are the brightest lights upon the earth of this generation.

82 In the times to come, you will see great challenges. Know that these are given that you who are great might grow from the challenges and become even greater. They are some of your most wonderful blessings, if you remember who you are and to act accordingly. Then shall your challenges become your strengths and your joys."

83 Then Yeshua beckoned Salome and she came to him and he and Miriam held her closely, holding her hands and kissing her on her cheeks. And Yeshua said unto her, "Your heart is one with Miriam, and I am glad. She has great power now, but her heart still needs soothing and affection from one who loves her in sacred ways.

84 Your gifts and powers are also great, Salome, far more than you imagine. Go with Miriam for three years. She will cultivate the garden of your magnificence. Then seek to merge your light with a new star and cherish the new light that will be born."

85 Salome looked at Yeshua with some dismay, pleading, "I will stay with Miriam always, my Lord. She is as one with me and I could not seek another star, for what star could be brighter than she or you?"

86 Yeshua kissed Salome on her forehead and said, "Years ago, I told Miriam that one day, she would meet another whose light would resonate so strongly with her that it could not be denied. She doubted it could ever be, but here you stand one with us today, the living testimony that it could.

87 It is the same for you, dear Salome. I ask nothing of you except to feel the resonance of your heart and listen to the harmony of your mind, each and every day, and then all will always be well."

88 "I will do that, my Lord," Salome agreed. "But my resonance and my harmony will always be with Miriam."

89 Yeshua nodded at her, and then kissed her once more gently on the lips, saying "I love you, Salome." Then sent her back to the circle once more, where she went and stood next to Kudar-Iluna, as if his great bulk might repel any other lights that might try to enter her heart other than Miriam.

90 Looking once more into Miriam's eyes, Yeshua said unto her. "Your time has begun, my beloved. Command the Circle of Power."

91 Miriam kissed him one more time briefly, whispering "I love you," as she looked into his eyes. Continuing to hold her left arm about his waist, she turned to face the circle, saying, "Hold forth your wands, each and every one."

92 At her command, all wands were drawn, some of wood, some of shell, and some of crystal.

93 Then, still holding onto Yeshua by his waist with her left hand, she drew her wand with her right and spun both of them around so they could pass in front of everyone in the circle.

94 "Look up into the heavens and point your wands skyward," she directed. And every wand quickly pointed to the sky.

95 Then she pointed her wand straight up and said unto them, "Unite your auras as one. This is the Great Circle of Celestine Light.

96 Send the aura that is one into the earth and call forth its power.

97 Send the aura that is one into the heavens and call forth their power.

98 Now as one, let us say the sacred word of Celestine summoning." With all wands raised to the sky, they spoke aloud, as one voice, the sacred Celestine word of summoning that cannot be written.

99 As the word escaped their lips for a third time, brilliant beams of light shot forth from the tip of each wand, uniting as one and shooting straight up into the sky until it could be seen no more.

100 Then there was a tremendous rumbling upon the earth and in the sky above like thunder from a thousand storms.

101 Still looking upward into the sky, they saw a sight such as no men had ever before seen. Though it was bright day, the sky was suddenly filled with brilliantly blazing shooting stars in a rainbow of hues, converging from points across the heavens into a single nexus of blazing white light far above them.

102 Miriam spoke to them again, saying, "Swirl the energy of the circle from east to west. Expand the light to fill the circle. Fill your aura with the light. Be one with the light."

103 They did as she directed, and the circle was soon filled with a spinning vortex of white light that engulfed everyone. But each person, even the children, faithfully held their wands to the sky and kept their focus upon the light above.

104 Suddenly, everyone's feet lifted off the ground, and as a group, the circle of Yeshua's closest disciples began to rise up into the sky. But so intent was everyone in the circle upon their tasks that it seemed that not even one had noticed that their feet no longer stood upon the ground.

105 Higher and higher the Great Circle of Celestine Light rose up toward the convergence of the multicolored shooting stars, until suddenly they were among them, and Miriam said, "Lower your wands and see where it is that you are and who it is that you are among."

106 In awe, everyone lowered their wands to their sides and looked around them in wonder. Blazing like pillars of golden light stood hundreds of angels in a circle all around them.

107 And one called out, saying, "Martha." Martha of Bethany looked to see her husband Yochanan, and she broke from the circle and ran to him with her children and he to them, and they embraced with rivers of tears flowing. And only here, in the sacred space between Heaven and earth, could this be done.

108 Seeing Yochanan, Salome fell to her knees upon the empty sky, silent tears running down her fair face as she recalled that which she had done to Yochanan, taking him from his wife and children and causing him to be on the earth no more.

109 Seeing her grief, Yochanan and Martha walked over to her and pulled her up to them. Salome was crying in gentle sobs saying over and over again, "I am sorry. I am so sorry."

110 Martha and Yochanan comforted her, and Yochanan put his arm around her lithe form, saying, "Wipe your tears, Salome. You repented of this long ago. It is forgotten by Elohim. It is forgotten by me and Martha. And now you too must let it go."

111 Yochanan gave a great comforting laugh and said unto her, "Anyway we are family now. You are my . . . well I'm not exactly sure. But I know you are family. And I love you even as Martha loves you and has loved you all these years."

112 Salome smiled demurely wiping her tears away and laughed a little and all was well.

113 Then other figures came out from the ranks of the angels. They were not in glorified bodies as was Yochanan, but were astral spirits of the wives and husbands and children of all the people who were in the Great Celestine Circle of Light.

114 Unlike Yochanan, because they were just spirits, they could not touch and hold their loved ones, but their forms were clear and sharp. They were present in their spirits as Yeshua had promised, and this gave great comfort to everyone, to have their family with them at this most special time in their lives.

115 But Yochanan's time with Martha was brief. With a tender kiss, he whispered into her ear words that only she could hear and then returned to the ranks of the angels encircling Yeshua and all who had come from earth.

116 Then Yeshua spoke again, and all eyes were upon him. And he said unto them, "Remember who you are and to live your truth, no matter the opinions of the world.

117 Grieve not this day, for nothing is lost and much is gained. Live by the spirit of the Celestine Light of Elohim, and your next eleven years shall be as rewarding and glorious as all you have shared with me."

118 Yeshua kissed Miriam one more time upon her lips, then stepped behind her with his hands upon her shoulders, and they spun in the air completely around the circle so that all could see them. And he said unto them, "And I leave you with my greatest treasure; may she also become yours."

119 Then the angels held onto the waists of each of the angels beside them, and their great outer circle began to spin and emanate a bright golden light.

120 Yeshua and Miriam continued to turn slowly in the circle so all could see them, the third of three rings. And Yeshua spoke one last time to them, saying, "You are the lights of the world. Go forth and shine in your glory. Fear not, for always I am with you. Always I will love you."

121 As he spoke his last words, the circle of angels was spinning so rapidly that it was just a brilliant golden blur of light.

122 All eyes remained fixed upon Yeshua and Miriam. As they spun slowly in the middle, they turned to face each other. They embraced in a deep kiss, which was immediately overwhelmed by a blinding white light so intense that none could continue to look upon it, and everyone's hands and arms momentarily went up to shield their eyes from the brightness.

123 Then the light was gone, and there was a great silence in the void. Slowly, everyone lowered their hands and arms that had been shielding their faces from the blinding light. Looking to the center of the circle, they saw that Yeshua was gone and all of the angels too.

124 Only Miriam remained, standing alone in the center of the circle. Her face looked straight upward into the heavens. Only she had the eyes to see the pure light of God. And it lay upon her still glowing and gently undulating. Every inch of her body was radiating a soft ethereal white light.

125 In the hearts of everyone, there was an overwhelming feeling of the sweetest love, a Celestine Love, a love such as had never been imagined or experienced. It flowed through them and enveloped them and filled them with bliss.

126 Holding one another once again in the Great Circle of Celestine Light, they gazed at their friends and loved ones with smiles of joy writ upon every face, both young and old, and tears of heavenly happiness flowing down every cheek.

127 Salome broke from the circle and went to stand with Miriam, putting her arm around her waist, and looked up with her into the vastness of the dark blue heavens above.

128 "Do you see him still?" she wondered. Miriam nodded as she continued to gaze upward. "I see everything, Salome. I see everything. And it is more beautiful, amazing, and glorious than I ever imagined."

The final word of chapter one hundred of Vivus, concluding the Oracles of Celestine Light, was revelated and written on July 29, 2009

NOTES

Made in United States
North Haven, CT
11 February 2023

32440889R00450